THE LAW RELAT
DOMESTIC BANKING

AUSTRALIA

LBC Information Services—Sydney

CANADA and the USA

Carswell—Toronto

NEW ZEALAND

Brooker's—Auckland

SINGAPORE and MALAYSIA

Sweet & Maxwell Asia
Singapore and Kuala Lumpur

THE LAW RELATING TO DOMESTIC BANKING

Second Edition

JOAN WADSLEY
Solicitor; Lecturer in Law, University of Bristol

GRAHAM PENN
Partner, Sidley & Austin; Visiting Professor, University College, University of London

LONDON
SWEET & MAXWELL
2000

First Edition 1987
Second Edition 2000
Reprinted 2002

Published in 2000 by
Sweet & Maxwell Limited of
100 Avenue Road, Swiss Cottage,
London NW3 3PF
Phototypeset by LBJ Typesetting Ltd of Kingsclere
Printed in England by
MPG Books Ltd.

No natural forests were destroyed to make this product; only farmed timber was used and replanted

A CIP catalogue record for this book is available from the British Library

ISBN 0421 413808

PREFACE

The thirteen years since this book was first published have seen remarkable changes, both in banking practice and in the law applicable to that practice. For this reason, it was decided that the book needed a fresh start, and the opportunity was taken to change the style slightly. The first edition, a leader in its field, established itself as a guide to practitioners of banking law and to bankers, as well as students. The new edition has also been written with practitioners in mind, and it is hoped that it will continue to be useful for students taking the examinations of the Chartered Institute of Bankers, but one of the primary objectives is to provide a text for the growing number of postgraduate and undergraduate students of banking law. Banking is not so much a coherent field of law in itself, but depends on the application of the general law in the particular context of banking practice. This means it is important to have regard to the level of the reader's knowledge of general law in setting the level of discussion. We have tried to set out the law, particularly in considering the banker-customer relationship, in a way that would be comprehensible for postgraduate and undergraduate students of law as well as experienced practitioners.

Since banking law covers such a wide range of specialised and general fields of law the changes which needed to be reflected in the new edition of the book were substantial. Not surprisingly, therefore, much of the book has been rewritten and it has been substantially re-organised in order to make it more comprehensible to postgraduate and undergraduate students.

One of the most significant areas of change has been that of banking regulation, which has also developed into a topic of academic study in its own right, particularly at postgraduate level. Consequently, Chapter 1 has been completely rewritten and expanded to take account of the radical change made in supervision of banks by the Financial Services and Markets Act 2000 (which received the Royal Assent shortly after delivery of the final proofs!), and the Bank of England Act 1998. Important developments have also taken place in the practice of banking supervision as a consequence of high profile bank failures like BCCI and Barings and the supervisory rules that have been implemented by the European Union—many of which have their origin in documents produced by the Committee on Banking Regulations and Supervisory Practices more commonly known as the Basle Committee.

The changes in the law governing the banker-customer relationship have also been striking. Technological developments have revolutionised banking practice and its effect is now very apparent in the law. The section dealing with payment introduces some of the problems and describes the methods used, including electronic funds transfer. Old methods like negotiable instruments and cheques are contained in separate chapters and a chapter on the law dealing with the newer methods, including plastic cards and electronic banking has been added.

Considerations of space, as well as organisation, meant that some topics, such as those on partnership, agency and company customers, no longer justified separate chapters, and have been shortened and collected into other places, including another new chapter, on accounts. This chapter also includes discussions of joint accounts and local authorities' accounts—an area which has given rise to radical changes in the law by providing the source of much of the dynamic law of restitution. Restitution as it relates to banking, and the law of constructive trust have been retained in separate chapters, but have required substantial rewriting to attempt to reflect the updating and rationalisation of the law by academics and the courts. Even the areas which are most basic to the law have undergone fundamental changes; standard banking contracts, for example, have had to be rewritten because of the effect of the Regulations on Unfair Terms in Consumer Contracts 1999.

Graham Penn, who was responsible for so much of the first edition, has revised the material on banking regulation. We were very fortunate in persuading Neil Levy, an expert banking practitioner, to undertake the revision of the chapter on the complex and central topics of the banker's lien, appropriation and right of combination. Joan Wadsley is responsible for revising the remainder—the law of banker and customer and the sections dealing with payment, security and insolvency.

The authors of the first edition made the point that it is impossible to write a book of this sort without being heavily indebted to the learning of others. It has certainly proved to be so in writing the second edition. Many of our colleagues have provided their expert and generous assistance but we would like to thank Denise Brett, Nigel Furey, Jonathan Hill, Andrew Marsh, Helen Norman, John Parkinson and Keith Stanton, in particular for their help in reading huge amounts of text and making comments, suggestions and corrections. The errors that remain are entirely due to our own failings, not to any lack of effort or expertise on their part. We must also acknowledge our debt to Sweet and Maxwell, who have been most patient and helpful during the many vicissitudes in producing this edition.

Joan Wadsley
University of Bristol
Bristol

Graham Penn
1 Threadneedle Street
London

Preface to First Edition

The idea for a two volume work in banking law, the first of which deals with domestic banking law and the second dealing with international banking law, arose out of a series of meetings between Graham Penn and Don Fiddes, a former Director of Studies at the Chartered Institute of Bankers, who were both concerned about the absence of an up-to-date text which covered the entire spectrum of banking law. It soon became clear that such a project would require the specialist knowledge of more than one individual, hence Tony Shea and Anu Arora were invited to "join the team" of authors.

This new work was originally conceived as being intended for degree and post-graduate students and for practitioners who regularly find themselves engaged in this complex area of law. The emphasis in both volumes is directed firmly towards the law in practice, and it is hoped that those who concern themselves with banking law, in its broadest sense, will find some of the answers to the often difficult questions which arise. Where the material fails to provide an answer we hope it will at least lead to other sources, and thus assist in solving practical banking law problems, hence the heavy referencing which is to be found throughout both volumes.

The original conception became slightly altered during production in order that the two volumes would cover the Chartered Institute of Bankers' examinations in both Law Relating to Banking and Practice and law of International Banking. This slight change in emphasis has led to the omission of some material but the addition of other new chapters, namely, the sizeable chapters on Securities and Insolvency, and the expansion of the original material dealing with Agency, Partnerships and Corporate Customers.

Anybody who writes a book of this sort could not possibly start without the benefit of the learning of others. We have relied heavily upon a number of articles (many of which are acknowledged in the footnotes), and upon the publications listed in the Table of Abbreviations. Special mention must be made, however, of Philip Wood's excellent book, *Law and Practice of International Finance* and of the *Encyclopaedia of Banking Law* which provides the most comprehensive coverage of English Banking Law presently available.

In addition to published material we have placed considerable reliance on the knowledge and practical expertise of many lawyers and bankers, who have made helpful suggestions during the preparation of this work. Unfortunately, the individuals themselves are too numerous to mention. The authors would, however, wish to acknowledge the very considerable assistance given by the following people:

David Lewis of the Reserved bank of Australia (Volume 1, Chapter 1 on the Regulation of Banks); Maurice Allen of Clifford Chance (Volume 2, Chapter 8 on Transferability of Loans and Loan Participations); Stephen Edlmann of Linklaters and Paines (Volume 2, Chapter 10 on Notes and Commercial Paper); Armel Cates, Robert Palache and Phillip Palmer of Clifford Chance (Volume 2, Chapter 11 on Swaps and Related Instruments); Andrew McKnight of Cameron Markby (Volume 2, Chapter 16 on Legal Opinions). These experts are not, of course, responsible for any errors or omissions, which remain those of the authors alone.

The authors would also like to express their indebtedness to National Westminster Bank PLC for permission to reproduce their standard form documentation in Volume 2, Chapter 12 and for supplying copies.

The law is stated as at May 31, 1987.

London
May 31, 1987

G. A. Penn
A. M. Shea
A. Arora

Table of Abbreviations

Statutes

BBEA 1879	Bankers' Books Evidence Act 1879
BA 1979	Banking Act 1979
BA 1987	Banking Act 1987
BEA 1998	Bank of England Act 1998
BOEA 1882	Bill of Exchange Act 1882
BSA 1878	Bill of Sales Acts 1878
CA 1948	Companies Act 1948
CA 1985	Companies Act 1985
CA 1989	Companies Act 1989
CCA 1974	Consumer Credit Act 1974
CJA 1987	Criminal Justice Act 1987
CJA 1988	Criminal Justice Act 1988
CJA 1993	Criminal Justice Act 1993
DPA 1998	Data Protection Act 1998
FSA 1986	Financial Services Act 1986
IA 1986	Insolvency Act 1986
LRA 1925	Land Registration Act 1925
LPA 1925	Law of Property Act 1925
LPMPA 1989	Law of Property (Miscellaneous Provisions) Act 1989
LA 1980	Limitation Act 1980
PA 1890	Partnership Act 1890
PACE 1984	Police and Criminal Evidence Act 1984
TA 1968	Theft Act 1968
TrA 1925	Trustee Act 1925
TLATA 1996	Trusts of Land and Appointment of Trustees Act 1996
UCTA 1977	Unfair Contract Terms Act 1977

Statutory Instruments

IR 1986	Insolvency Rules 1986
MLR 1993	Money Laundering Regulations 1993
UTCCR 1994	Unfair Terms in Consumer Contracts Regulations 1994
UTCCR 1999	Unfair Terms in Consumer Contracts Regulations 1999

CONTENTS

Table of Cases

Arab Bank Ltd v. Barclays Bank (Dominion, Colonial and Overseas) [1954] A.C. 495; [1954] 2 W.L.R. 1022, HL 3–005, 6–019
Arab Bank plc v. Mercantile Holdings Ltd [1994] Ch. 71; [1994] 2 W.L.R. 307, ChD 21–071
Arab Bank v. Ross [1952] 2 Q.B. 216, CA 6–026, 13–060
Arab Monetary Fund v. Hashim (No. 5) [1992] 2 All E.R. 911, ChD 4–014
Arbuckle v. Taylor (1815) 3 Dow. 160 8–043
Arbuthnot Leasing International Ltd v. Havelet Leasing Ltd; *sub nom.* ALI Finance Ltd v. Havelet Leasing Ltd [1992] 1 W.L.R. 455; [1991] 1 All E.R. 591; [1990] B.C.L.C. 802, ChD 24–107, 24–124
Ardern v. Bank of New South Wales [1956] V.L.R. 569 8–017
Argo Caribbean Group Ltd v. Lewis [1976] 2 Lloyd's Rep. 286, CA 18–006
Armagh Shoes, Re [1984] B.C.L.C. 405 19–021
Armour v. Thyssen Edelstahlwerke AG [1991] 2 A.C. 339, HL 20–001, 20–013
Arnold (RM) & Co., Re [1984] C.I.L.L. 119 ; [1984] B.C.L.C. 535 19–047
Arnott v. Hayes (1887) 36 Ch.D. 731 4–011
Arrows Ltd (No. 4), Re; *sub nom.* Hamilton v. Naviede and Director of the Serious Fraud Office; Adviser (188), Re; Trachtenberg, ex p. [1995] 2 A.C. 75, HL... 4–031, 4–035
Ascherson v. Tredegar Dry Dock & Wharf Co. Ltd [1909] 2 Ch. 401, ChD 18–036
Aschkenasy v. Midland Bank Ltd (1934) 50 T.L.R. 209 2–037
Ashburn Anstalt v. Arnold (WJ) & Co. (No. 1) [1989] Ch. 1, CA 21–113, 21–118
Ashbury Railway Carriage and Iron Co. Ltd v. Riche (1875) L.R. 7 H.L.653, HL.... 7–011
Ashley Guarantee (Formerly Gulf Guarantee Bank) v. Zacaria [1993] 1 W.L.R. 62, CA 18–051
Ashley v. Ashley (1829) 3 Sim. 149 22–006
Associated Japanese Bank (International) Ltd v. Credit du Nord SA [1989] 1 W.L.R. 255, QBD 3–036, 18–023
Atlantic Computer Systems plc (No. 1), Re [1992] Ch. 505; [1991] B.C.L.C. 606, CA 19–008, 19–021, 19–024, 19–026, 21–064, 24–016, 24–025, 24–026
Atlantic Medical Ltd, Re [1993] B.C.L.C. 386; [1992] B.C.C. 653 ... 19–008, 19–021, 19–024
Att.-Gen. v. De Winton [1906] 2 Ch. 106, ChD 9–034
Att.-Gen. of Hong Kong v. Reid [1994] 1 A.C. 324, PC 9–007
Attwood v. Griffin (1826) 2 Ry.& Mood 425 13–035
Auchteroni & Co. v. Midland Bank Ltd [1928] 2 K.B. 294 14–030
Australia & New Zealand Bank Ltd v. Ateliers de Construction Electriques de Charleroi [1967] 1 A.C. 86; [1966] 2 W.L.R. 1216, PC 7–005
Automatic Bottle Makers Ltd, Re [1926] Ch. 412 19–054
Aveling Barford Ltd, Re [1989] 1 W.L.R. 360; [1989] B.C.L.C. 122, ChD 24–060
Avon C.C. v. Howlett [1983] 1 W.L.R. 605; [1983] 1 All E.R. 1073, CA 7–020, 10–013, 10–034, 10–038
Avon Finance Co. Ltd v. Bridger [1985] 2 All E.R. 281, CA 3–050, 3–052
Awilco of Oslo A/S v. Fulvia Spa di Navigazione of Cagliari; *Chikuma, The* [1981] 1 W.L.R. 314, HL 12–006, 12–031, 12–034
Axa Equity & Law Life Assurance Society plc v. National Westminster Bank [1998] C.L.C. 1177, CA 4–012
Ayala Holdings Ltd, Re [1993] B.C.L.C. 256 19–049

B & C Holding, Re; *See* British & Commonwealth Holdings Plc (Joint Administrators) v. Spicer & Oppenheim
Babanaft International Co. SA v. Bassatne [1990] Ch. 13, CA 4–024, 4–025
Bache & Co. (London) Ltd v. Banque Vernes et Commerciale de Paris SA [1973] 2 Lloyd's Rep. 437, CA 18–018
Backhouse v. Charlton (1878) 8 Ch. D. 444 8–044
Baden v. Societe General Pour Favoriser le Developpement du Commerce et de l'Industrie en France SA [1993] 1 W.L.R. 509; [1992] 4 All E.R. 161, ChD ... 9–013, 9–014, 9–018, 9–020, 9–022, 9–034, 9–035
Bailey v. Bodenham (1864) 16 C.B.(N.S.) 288 14–039
Baines v. National Provincial Bank Ltd (1927) 96 L.J.K.B. 801 .... 6–021, 6–022, 14–030
Baker v. Australia and New Zealand Bank Ltd [1958] N.Z.L.R. 907 6–015

Table of Statutes

Table of Statutory Instruments

Table of European Directives

1977 Dir. 77/780 [1977] O.J. L322/30 ... 1–006, 1–011, 1–018, 1–021
1985 Dir. 85/577 [1985] O.J. L372/31 18–003
1987 Dir. 87/102 [1987] O.J. L42/48 15–028
Art. 11 15–041
1989 Dir. 89/299 [1989] O.J.124/16 1–021, 1–074, 1–115
Dir. 89/646 [1989] O.J. L386/1..... 1–021, 1–128, 1–129, 1–130, 2–023, 2–033
Dir. 89/647 [1989] O.J. L386/14 ... 1–021, 1–023, 1–101, 1–123
1990 Dir. 90/88 [1990] O.J. L61/14 15–028
1991 Dir. 91/308 [1991] O.J. L166/77......... 4–036, 14–062
1992 Dir. 92/30 [1992] O.J. L110/52 .... 1–022, 1–136
Dir. 92/121 [1992] O.J. L29/1 ..... 1–022, 1–116, 1–117, 1–119, 1–138
1993 Dir. 93/6 [1993] O.J. L141/1.. 1–023, 1–024, 1–083, 1–084, 1–085, 1–087, 1–089, 1–091, 1–116, 1–117, 1–120
Annex III 1–081
Dir. 93/13 [1993] O.J. L95/29.. 3–031, 5–083, 18–003
1994 Dir. 94/19 [1994] O.J. L135/5 .. 1–023
1995 Dir. 95/26 [1995] O.J. L168/7 1–058, 1–062, 1–125
Dir. 95/46 [1995] O.J. L281/31................ 4–071
1996 Dir. 96/61 [1996] O.J. L257/26.............. 21–005
1997 Dir. 97/5 [1997] O.J. L43/25—
Art. 8 12–025
1998 Dir. 98/26 [1998] O.J. L166/45.............. 12–044
Dir. 98/31 [1998] O.J. L204/13 ... 1–024, 1–081, 1–089, 1–092

Table of International Treaties & Conventions

1930 Geneva Convention providing a Uniform Law for Bills of Exchange and promissory Notes
Art. 30 13–049
1950 European Convention for the Protection of Human Rights and Fundamental Freedoms (November 4).. 2–021
Art. 6(1) 4–031
1957 The Treaty of Rome Establishing the European Economic Community (March 25) 298 U.N.T.S. 11—
Art. 48 21–160
Art. 52 1–018
Art. 59 1–018
Art. 60 1–018
Art. 85 .... 19–022, 21–052
Art. 86 19–022
1968 Brussels Convention on Jurisdiction and the Enforcement of judgements in Civil and Commercial Matters (September 27) [1978] O.J. L304/1 /77.......... 4–024
Art. 16(1) 15–044
1970 Hague Convention on Taking of Evidence Abroad in Civil or Commercial Matters (Hague) (March 18) 4–023
1988 Lugano Convention (September 16) [1988] O.J. L319/9................. 4–024
Vienna Convention (UN Convention against Illicit Traffic in Narcotic Drugs and Psychotropic Substances)................ 4–036

Section I

BANK REGULATION

Chapter 1

Banking Regulation in the United Kingdom

In wild periods of alarm, one failure makes many and the best way to prevent the derivative failures is to arrest the primary failure which causes them.

Walter Bagehot (1873)[1]

Introduction

The continuing validity of Bagehot's aphorism has long provided the rationale for prudential supervision of banks and other financial institutions. However, only comparatively recently have attempts been made to place prudential supervision of banks in the United Kingdom upon a formal footing. The law pertaining to the supervision of banks and other financial intermediaries has recently grown into a discipline worthy of study in its own right. Not only does banking supervision encompass numerous facets of the law of banker and customer, but it transgresses regularly into the fields of public law, securities regulation and, more generally, financial economics. **1–001**

It is now generally accepted that a mechanism for ensuring adherence to appropriate prudential standards is a necessary component of a developed banking sector.[2] Not only do banks play a key role in distributing financial resources to the rest of the economy, but in doing so they act as repositories for the public's savings. Their stability is a matter of considerable political concern; yet banks are particularly susceptible to instability and collapse. The nature of some of their business necessitates relatively high financial gearing and involves extensive maturity transformation. There is invariably an element of risk in the business they undertake. This rather fragile scheme depends on the continuing confidence of depositors and investors in banks. When confidence deserts a financial intermediary, disaster is almost inevitable and the effect can be highly contagious throughout a financial system. The vulnerability of banks to sudden demand for withdrawals of deposits increases the likelihood that such withdrawals will take place. In the event of a disturbance in confidence, depositors will

---

[1] *Lombard Street: A Description of the Money Market* (1873) p. 51.

[2] See however the comments of Brian Quinn, formerly Executive Director of the Bank of England in *Bank Regulation and Supervision in the 1990s* (Norton ed., 1991) p. 2.

be alert to the need to withdraw their funds ahead of a "run" on deposits. The danger is that pessimistic prophesies can be self-fulfilling; they need not be well founded. This loaded situation is exacerbated by inadequate supply of information to depositors and market analysts which might enable them to make a reliable assessment of a bank's investment portfolio.

1–002 The imposition of a regime of prudential supervision aims to foster an environment of bank safety and soundness and thus to dispel those errant fears that may overcome depositors. This is done by establishing procedures to ensure that risk is properly recognised and measured and that the institutions concerned have adequate capital in place to support the level of business they undertake and risks which they run. It is also necessary to ensure that financial institutions maintain adequate liquidity to meet prospective net cash requirements. Further, many prudential regimes put in place a safety net by way of deposit insurance or a lender of last resort facility in order to bolster depositor confidence. Nevertheless, the task of bank supervisors is becoming increasingly complex. The latter part of the twentieth century has seen a dramatic boom in competitive banking activity. Financial institutions have expanded and diversified. At the same time, traditional banking markets have been invaded by other financial intermediaries. There has been a sharp acceleration in the pace of innovation which has led to a fundamental change in the nature of business entered into by banks. Banks now offer a plethora of financial products and services ranging from those traditionally offered by retail banks to securities business which was, until fairly recently, undertaken by non-bank regulated institutions. Banking has also become a global business and its global nature has focussed attention on the growing interdependence of national banking systems, while at the same time highlighting the inadequacies of international or cross-border banking supervision.

1–003 The stimulus for financial innovation in an increasingly competitive and global market is strong and although many of the recent developments have vastly improved the efficiency and profitability of financial markets, they have also been accompanied by an increasing incidence of instability and risk, exposing the inherent vulnerability of banking institutions.

The dramatic changes in the banking environment has also forced changes to the supervisory techniques customarily employed by central banks. Traditionally conservative, players in the financial and banking markets are now much less averse to risk taking. The information in which they deal is highly complex and increasingly difficult to assess against general predetermined standards. Moreover, it can move rapidly through the market. Prudential supervision is itself becoming as risky as the business it seeks to oversee. The suddenness of the demise of Barings in February 1995 and the proceedings brought against the Bank of England following the collapse of the Bank of Credit and Commerce International (BCCI)[3] and Johnson Matthey plc[4] testify to that risk.

However, in promoting the need for prudential safeguards, a bank supervisor cannot be oblivious to the need to foster a competitive banking environment. Indeed, until very recently considerable efforts were made to avoid detailed rules and regulations in the United Kingdom banking sector and as recently as 1991 Brian Quinn, an executive director of the Bank of England at the time, made the following observations: **1–004**

> "There is little doubt that the growing internationalisation of the business currently being done in London is creating a steady source of pressure on the Bank of England's customary way of determining supervisory policies. At first blush this seems somewhat odd since London's pre-eminence as a financial centre owes a good deal to the absence of detailed rules and regulations; and current preoccupations notwithstanding, it is the Bank of England's intention that this will continue to be the case. As a digression, it is interesting to report the different perceptions to which the Bank of England's approach to supervision give rise. Some overseas supervisors consider that the absence of a detailed body of legal requirements is clear evidence of laxity in the United Kingdom's prudential arrangements and is driven by the need to preserve London's position; whilst those of us in the United Kingdom see it as a welcome and, indeed, quite necessary, freedom from rigidity."[5]

In the same paper Mr Quinn also recognised that the Bank of England was increasingly making explict:

> "its supervisory policy in respect of new services, products and transactions and the United Kingdom's increasing involvement in the European community during the 1980s and 90s also circumscribed the discretion left to member states and the supervision with banks although the changes were not introduced in the United Kingdom without the Bank of England first seeking to persuade others as to the merits of a non rule-based system."[6]

Some of the most important developments at the European Union level are considered later in this Chapter.

---

[3] See *Three Rivers District Council and others v. Governor and Company of the Bank of England (No. 3)* [2000] 2 W.L.R. 15, HL and *Three Rivers v. Bank of England (No. 1)* [1996] Q.B. 292, CA.

[4] See *Johnson Matthey plc v. Arthur Young and the Governor of the Bank of England* [1989] 2 All E.R. 105.

[5] *Bank Regulation and Supervision in the 1990s*, p. 2.

[6] *ibid.*, p. 4.

1–005 The move towards a more formal statutory based supervisory regime has continued under reforms proposed by the present government and it is that government's view that once the Financial Services and Markets Bill becomes law[7] it will, when taken together with the Bank of England Act 1998 (BEA 1998) put the United Kingdom "in the forefront of regulation, and ensure the [banking] industry is ready to meet the needs of the 21st century". In order to more fully appreciate the significance of the reforms currently being introduced it is necessary to have some appreciation of the historical development of the supervisory regime in the United Kingdom and the traditional philosophy which underpinned that regime.

Historical Development of Banking Supervision in the United Kingdom

Prior to 1979

1–006 Until the passing of the Banking Act 1979 (BA 1979) there was no formal legal framework to banking regulation in the United Kingdom. An institution was free to establish itself as a deposit-taker without any requirement to be authorised for that purpose by any regulatory body, and without being subject to formal regulatory restrictions in the way it carried on that business.[8]

The reason that this state of affairs continued until 1979, well after a formal regulatory system had been put in place in the USA and elsewhere in Europe,[9] can be found largely in the particular historical role of the Bank of England and perhaps also in the English tendency to favour pragmatic rather than conceptually tidy ways of dealing with practical issues.[10]

1–007 The Bank of England was established in 1694, as a private company, to raise a large loan for the government. From the outset its role as government financier, and the size of its balance sheet, gave it a powerful role in the English financial system. Government's continuing need for further finance in the eighteenth and nineteenth centuries gave the Bank of England considerable leverage with government, which it was able to use to obtain legislation cementing its commercial position at the expense of its

---

[7] At the time of writing it is expected that the Bill will receive Royal Assent around Easter 2000. The most important changes likely to be introduced by the Bill are described later in this chapter. For an excellent overview see Gleeson, *Financial Services Regulation: The New Regime* (1999).

[8] The Money-lenders Acts 1900 and 1927 established a registration requirement for money lenders, but "bankers" (a very loosely defined term) were exempt.

[9] At the time of the adoption of the First Banking Directive in 1977 (Directive 77/780 [1977] O.J. L322/30) the U.K. and the Netherlands were the only member states which did not have a legal requirement for banks to be authorised.

[10] See J. Norton, "The Bank of England's Lament: The Struggle to Maintain the Traditional, Practices of 'moral suasion'" in J. Norton (ed.), *Bank Regulation and Supervision in the 1990's*; K. McGuire, "Emergent Trends in Bank Supervision in the United Kingdom" (1993) 56 M.R.L. 669; C. Hadjiemmanuil, *Banking Regulation and the Bank of England* (1996).

competitors. A notable example of this process was the granting to the Bank of England in 1844 of an effective monopoly in issuing bank notes.

It was clearly in the Bank of England's interests as a major participant in the money markets, with corresponding credit exposures, for there to be order and stability in the banking sector. Increasingly, the centrality of the Bank of England in the financial system, its financial muscle and prestige, gave it, in practice, considerable ability to impose its will. In particular it became commercially important to banks for bills of exchange bearing their name to be eligible for discount at the Bank of England. This gave the Bank of England an ability to control the structure of the money markets, and also meant that the Bank of England's judgment as to an institution's quality could have major implications for that bank's ability to do business.[11] By these and similar means there evolved, by the latter part of the nineteenth century, the embryo of a *de facto* system of banking regulation based on the commercial power of the Bank of England.

In time, the Bank of England's position as a monetary authority, and as **1–008** government banker and intermediary between government and the banking system proper, and the special privileges it enjoyed, came to be seen as also carrying with it various responsibilities of a public character. A feeling that the Bank of England ought to act as "lender of last resort"[12] was a part of this, and indeed the Bank of England has played a central role in dealing with bank crises over the years, the most recent public example being the collapse of Barings in 1995.

The huge financing requirements of the government arising from the First World War led rapidly to the loss of the Bank of England's independence in monetary matters, and the continuing private status of the Bank of England became increasingly difficult to reconcile with its public role. However, the financial crisis between the wars did not have the same catastrophic effect on United Kingdom banking as it had for example in the USA, and no great need was felt for an overhaul of the regulatory system.

At the end of the Second World War the incoming Labour government **1–009** implemented its manifesto pledge to nationalise the Bank of England with the passing of the Bank of England Act 1946. Nationalisation was implemented by the transfer of the Bank of England's stock to the Treasury, but as regards operational measures the Bank of England remained largely independent of government.

The manifesto had also promised the regulation of commercial banking for the purpose of ensuring it met the financing needs of industry. This promise is behind section 4(3) of the Bank of England Act 1946 (which has

[11] The origins of the Bank of England's regulatory role in its own credit exposures to the banks, and in its dealings in the bill market in particular, can be seen in the fact that until 1970 it was the Discount Office of the Bank of England which was responsible for the collection of supervisory information from the banking sector.

[12] See, *e.g.* Walter Bagehot, *Lombard Street: A Description of the Money Market* (1873).

never been repealed), which may be seen as marking the first symbolic step towards the formalisation of the Bank of England's regulatory role. This section gives the Bank of England authority, if it thinks fit in the public interest, to "request information from and make recommendations to bankers" and, "if so authorised by the Treasury", to issue "directions to any banker for the purpose of securing that effect is given to any such request or recommendation". Section 4(3) in fact has never become operational, as its effectiveness is contingent on secondary legislation to define the expression "banker" and no such legislation has ever been made. The informal, non-statutory nature of the Bank of England's regulatory role therefore remained unaffected.

1–010 The leverage of the Bank of England in its dealings with the banking sector increased further with its role in enforcing exchange and credit controls in the post-war period. However, strains in the system were certainly being felt by the 1960s with the growth in the number of banks active in the United Kingdom and in the number of people involved in directing the affairs of banks. Even so, no great need to formalise the Bank of England's authority or to change the content of its supervisory approach was felt necessary until the secondary banking crisis which broke on December 19, 1973.[13]

The secondary banking crisis was precipitated by so-called "fringe banks" which had been borrowing short and lending long without sufficient regard for their liquidity over time. In addition, many had become over-committed to a property market which had turned against them and for these institutions, insolvency also threatened. The result was a liquidity crisis which threatened to escalate to other parts of the banking system. A more major crisis was only avoided by the launch of a "lifeboat" on December 21, 1973 by the Bank of England and the large clearing banks to bridge the liquidity gap.[14] The crisis brought home the systemic risks which can result from the failure of even relatively small institutions, some of which up to this point had largely escaped the Bank of England's supervision altogether. It also showed that many of the Bank of England's supervisory techniques were in need of improvement and required a much greater commitment of resources.

1–011 In the years immediately following the secondary banking crisis the Bank of England moved to strengthen its supervisory capability, both by extend-

[13] There had been a move to formalise the regulatory system in the 1950s, caused largely by a substantial increase in the number of small deposit-takers. The Bank itself produced a draft bill for this purpose in 1956, but it was never enacted. For an excellent account of the secondary banking crisis see Reid, *The Secondary Banking Crisis 1973–1975*.

[14] The large clearing banks agreed to support the "lifeboat" plan on the mistaken assumption that the so-called "fringe banks" were facing a liquidity crisis because of a temporary loss of public confidence in such banks, which were otherwise solvent and potentially viable. See *The secondary banking crisis and the Bank of England's support operations* (1978) 18 B.E. Q.B. 230.

ing the range of institutions falling within its oversight and by the imposition of new substantive requirements on supervised institutions. These included for the first time a general obligation to submit financial returns for prudential supervision purposes, and the publication of a more formalised approach to assessing the capital and liquidity adequacy of supervised institutions.

Notwithstanding these measures, the tide was turning in favour of a formal statutory regulatory regime and the First Banking Directive,[15] issued in 1977 as the first of a series of directives designed to harmonise the laws of EEC states relating to credit institutions, necessitated legislation by the end of 1979. The result was the Banking Act 1979.[16]

The Banking Act 1979

There were two main limbs to the BA 1979: the introduction of a **1–012**
statutory requirement for institutions to be authorised by the Bank of England in order to be entitled to take deposits, and the establishment of a deposit protection scheme. In addition the BA 1979 provided for the regulation of the issue, form and content of advertisements for deposits, and for controls over the use of banking names and descriptions.

The BA 1979 made no attempt to provide an all-embracing definition of a bank or banking business. Rather, the need for authorisation was founded simply on the business of taking deposits. However, the BA 1979 recognised different types of deposit-taking institutions by distinguishing between "banks" and "licensed deposit takers". This distinction was based principally upon the range of services being offered by an institution, with only those institutions providing traditional "banking" services being entitled to call themselves banks. The distinction reflected a complex hierarchy of deposit-taking institutions which had been recognised for various statutory purposes prior to the BA 1979, and also the sense that use of the title "bank" carried with it in the mind of the public a status which was not appropriate to more narrowly focused institutions.

The Bank of England's supervisory style and philosophy were not **1–013**
seriously undermined by the BA 1979. Indeed, the BA 1979 can be seen in large part as expanding and legitimising its regulatory role. A large measure of discretion was reserved to the Bank of England within certain very broadly stated parameters. In practice the Bank of England's approach to supervision of banks continued very much as before.

The introduction of the deposit protection scheme was a genuinely new development. The scheme involved the establishment of a deposit protec-

---

[15] The First Council Directive (of December 12, 1977) on the coordination of laws, regulations and administrative provisions relating to the taking up and pursuit of the business of credit institutions (Directive 77/780 [1977] O.J. L322/30).

[16] For an excellent account of the Banking Act 1979 see Morrison, Tillett and Welch, *Banking Act* (1980).

tion fund, funded by a levy on the banks themselves. Depositors of a failed institution were entitled to claim back 75 per cent of their "protected deposits" from this fund.

As the secondary banking crisis in 1973 precipitated the BA 1979, so it was another banking collapse that brought home the inadequacies of the BA 1979 and precipitated its replacement with the Banking Act 1987 (BA 1987).[17] Johnson Matthey Bankers Limited was a "recognised bank" under the BA 1979 and was an important participant in the gold bullion market. In late 1984 it became apparent to the Bank of England that Johnson Matthey was in serious difficulties. The Bank of England took the decision to lead a rescue by acquiring the company, providing a limited guarantee of its liabilities and exerting pressure on the large commercial banks to provide further guarantees.

1–014 Johnson Matthey's difficulties had been brought about principally by a small number of large exposures to customers. The Bank of England had largely been kept in ignorance of these by late reporting by Johnson Matthey. However, it was apparent that the Bank of England's supervision had been more relaxed than it would have been had Johnson Matthey been merely a licensed deposit-taker rather than a recognised bank. Other issues brought out by this episode included the desirability of the Bank of England having a closer relationship with banks' auditors, and the recognition that supervision of a bank which forms part of a wider group must make some attempt to assess the risks to the bank arising from the position of the group as a whole. The committee charged with investigating the causes and lessons of the affair recommended that these lessons be implemented in a new Banking Act.

The Banking Act 1987

1–015 The principal innovations of the BA 1987, all of which owe their origins to the Johnson Matthey episode, were as follows. The distinction between recognised banks and licensed deposit-takers was abolished. The Bank of England's regulatory powers were increased with the formalisation of its ability to object to bank take-overs and changes of control. New reporting requirements were introduced for large exposures. The Bank of England's ability to obtain information was enhanced in various ways, including importantly by releasing banks' auditors from their duty of confidentiality to their clients where necessary to facilitate the free flow of regulatory information to the Bank of England. The BA 1987 also established the Board of Banking Supervision, principally as a consultative body but to some extent also as a body to which the Bank of England would be accountable in its banking regulatory functions.

[17] For a detailed account of the BA 1987 see Penn, *Banking Supervision* (1989).

The Bank of England Act 1998 and the Financial Services and Markets Bill

The BEA 1998 came into force on June 1, 1998. It has two main elements: establishing the operational responsibility and independence of the Bank of England in monetary policy, with the aim of implementing the government's inflation target; and transferring responsibility for banking regulation from the Bank of England to the Financial Services Authority (FSA). Although it has lost its regulatory functions, the Bank of England does retain a general responsibility for the overall stability of the financial system as a whole. **1–016**

The transfer of the Bank of England's regulatory functions to the FSA is part of a wider move to concentrate the regulation of the whole financial sector in the FSA as the sole regulatory body in this area. In addition to banking regulatory functions, the FSA has already taken over (from the Bank of England) the regulation of the money markets, and (from the Securities and Investments Board[18]) high level responsibility for the regulation of investment business and investment markets. This concentration will be completed when the Financial Services and Markets Bill becomes law—expected during the course of 2000. At that point the FSA will assume responsibility as "front line" regulator of all United Kingdom investment and insurance businesses.

Some have seen the origins of the transfer of regulatory authority away from the Bank of England in the various banking failures which have occurred since the passing of the BA 1987, notably BCCI and Barings, and the feeling that the Bank of England could and should have done more to prevent them. However, the government has always denied that any feeling of this kind influenced its decision. Instead the government has argued that the distinctions between different types of financial institution—banks, securities firms and insurance companies—are becoming increasingly blurred, and that in consequence regulation by a plethora of different sector-based regulators was inefficient and merely increased the cost and reduced the effectiveness of regulation and gave rise to confusion in the mind of the public whom the system was designed to protect. **1–017**

In the field of banking regulation the BEA 1998 does little more than provide for the transfer of the Bank of England's functions to the FSA. In the immediate aftermath of the transfer very little has changed in practice, and the transfer of about 500 regulatory staff from the Bank of England to the FSA has ensured that it is still largely the same individuals who are involved in the day to day supervision of United Kingdom authorised banks.

---

[18] The Securities and Investments Board changed its name to the Financial Services Authority. Strictly speaking, therefore, it would be more correct to speak of the FSA continuing to exercise the functions of the Securities and Investment Board.

More substantive changes to the content of the regulatory regime are envisaged in the Financial Services and Markets Bill which we consider later in this chapter.

The impact of international initiatives

1–018 The impact of international initiatives on the United Kingdom's system of banking regulation in recent years has been profound. In the area of capital adequacy, in particular, the need for the United Kingdom to comply with its international obligations has been one of the major factors in the movement away from broad based regulatory discretions towards a system based on prescriptive rules.

International initiatives in banking regulation first began to have a significant influence in the 1970s. Two separate supra-national bodies were involved, the E.U. and the Basle Committee on Banking Supervision.[19]

In the mid 1970s the EEC Commission set to work seriously to make a reality in the banking sector the rights to freedom of establishment and freedom to provide services. The first step in this direction was the Banking Directive 1973, which sought to enshrine these rights specifically for certain categories of banks and quasi-banking institutions. However, this Directive became redundant even before it came fully into force as a result of legal decisions holding that these rights were already provided for in the Treaty itself[20] and had direct effect under the laws of the member states. More significant was the First Banking Directive,[21] which was intended as the first of a series of measures having as their final aim the introduction of uniform authorisation requirements for credit institutions throughout the E.U. The First Banking Directive itself introduced a requirement for member states to require credit institutions to be formally authorised in order to carry on business, and imposed certain minimum conditions which all member states were required to impose. In the United Kingdom this Directive was implemented in the 1979 Act.[22]

1–019 At the same time as these measures were being formulated by the E.U., the Basle Committee had been formed in recognition that the growing globalisation of banking required international co-operation between banking regulators. Unlike Directives produced by the E.U., the pronouncements of the Basle Committee have no legal force and formally their status

---

[19] This is a committee of banking supervisory authorities which was established by the central bank governors of the Group of Ten countries in 1975. It consists of senior representatives of bank supervisory authorities and central banks from Belgium, Canada, France, Germany, Italy, Japan, Luxembourg, the Netherlands, Sweden, Switzerland the U.K. and the USA. It usually meets at the Bank for International Settlements in Basle, where its permanent secretariat is located.

[20] Arts 52, 59 and 60.

[21] Directive 77/780 [1977] O.J. L322/30.

[22] See above para. 1–012. For a detailed analysis of the various E.U. banking initiatives see Dassesse, Isaacs & Penn, *E.C. Banking Law* (1994).

is effectively that of recommendations. The focus of the Basle Committee is on internationally active banks and on containing risk, in particular the risks which banks authorised in one state may pose to banks authorised elsewhere and to the international financial system generally. The primary focus of the E.U., on the other hand, has been the creation of a single market in banking services within the E.U. The E.U. is concerned with minimum regulatory standards not solely for the sake of systemic stability but also for the significant competitive implications of uneven standards. Thus it was clearly recognised that minimum regulatory standards were a necessary prerequisite to requiring a member state (the host state) to allow banks authorised in another member state (the home state) to carry on business in the host state simply in reliance on home state regulation. Similarly, it was also seen as desirable in the interests of a single market that a bank should not find it difficult to compete in a particular host state because domestic banks in the host state are permitted to carry on business on the basis of unduly lax regulation.

The first product of the Basle Committee was the "Concordat" of 1975. **1–020** This contained general guidelines for the division of responsibilities between different national regulators—for example, the host state regulator was to be responsible for the supervision of liquidity of a branch or subsidiary of a foreign bank, and the home state was to be responsible for supervision of solvency. In addition the Concordat made recommendations for practical cooperation in areas such as the sharing of information and inspections of supervised institutions. No specific United Kingdom legislation was required to implement these recommendations, it being sufficient for the necessary adjustments to be made to the Bank of England's supervisory policies and procedures.

The next major development was in the field of consolidated supervision, with the production by the Basle Committee in 1983 of the "1983 Agreement", followed within a month by the E.U.'s First Consolidated Supervision Directive.[23] These documents were at least in part a response to the experience of the West German regulators in supervising subsidiaries of Luxembourg-incorporated institutions, and also to the Banco Ambrosiano affair. The 1983 Agreement clarified a number of aspects of the 1975 Concordat in relation to the division of supervisory responsibilities. It also expressly incorporated the principle of consolidated supervision, making clear in particular that capital adequacy had to be evaluated on a consolidated basis. The first Consolidated Supervision Directive covered much of the same ground as the 1983 Agreement but was much more specific in identifying the types of institution which were required to be included in consolidation. Nevertheless, there was no requirement of consolidation where a banking group was headed by a non-bank holding company.

[23] Council Directive on the supervision of credit institutions on a consolidated basis (Directive 83/350 [1983] O.J. L193/18).

1–021 In 1988 the Basle Committee produced the "Capital Accord". Its main objective was to strengthen the capital position of international banks and to try to limit the extent to which internationally active banks could achieve competitive advantage from inadequate home state capital requirements. The Capital Accord set out an agreed method of measuring capital, an agreed method of measuring risk (calculation of the amount of a bank's risk-weighted assets) and an agreed method of regulating banks' capital which was to impose a minimum permissible ratio (8 per cent) of capital to risk-weighted assets. The Capital Accord was followed in 1989 by two E.U. Directives which closely followed the provisions of the Capital Accord: the Own Funds Directive,[24] which set out rules for the measurement of bank capital, and the Solvency Ratio Directive,[25] which was concerned with the way in which a bank's assets were to be risk-weighted and which imposed the minimum 8 per cent ratio of capital to risk-weighted assets. These measures represented a major step forward in agreeing a common framework for the assessment of bank capital adequacy, although their focus was limited largely to capturing credit risk—other risks, in particular market risk, have been addressed subsequently (see below). These measures were implemented in the United Kingdom simply by means of Bank of England policy changes.

In 1989 the E.U. also adopted the Second Banking Directive.[26] This was a far-reaching measure designed to promote the single European market in banking services. In recognition of its significance member states were given until January 1, 1993 to implement it. Its central provisions required member states to permit banks incorporated and authorised in one member state to carry on business in another member state (by establishing a branch, or on a cross-border basis) without the need for any further authorisation by the host state. The home state was given sole jurisdiction over prudential matters, and the host state's powers were restricted to certain limited controls in relation to liquidity and conduct of business. In the United Kingdom this Directive required substantial changes to the BA 1987, and these were made by the Banking Coordination (Second Council Directive) Regulations 1992.

1–022 The collapse of BCCI in 1991 dramatically highlighted the dangers of fragmented regulatory supervision of banking groups and the urgent need for improvements in international regulatory co-operation.[27] It undoubtedly

[24] Council Directive on the own funds of credit institutions (Directive 89/299 [1989] O.J. L124/16).

[25] Council Directive on a solvency ratio for credit institutions (Directive 89/647 [1989] O.J. L386/14).

[26] Second Council Directive on the co-ordination of laws, regulations and administrative provisions relating to the taking up and pursuit of the business of credit institutions and amending directive 77/780 ([1977] O.J. L322/30) (Directive 89/646 [1989] O.J. L386/1).

[27] For a detailed description of some of the bank regulatory issues that were highlighted by the collapse of BCCI see the various judgments delivered in *Three Rivers District Council and others v. The Bank of England.* The first two judgments are reported at [1996] 3 All E.R. 558 and 634, the judgments delivered by the Court of Appeal are reported at [1996] Q.B. 292 and the judgment of the House of Lords at [2000] 2 W.L.R. 15.

added impetus to moves that were already underway in this respect. Accordingly, in 1992 the Basle Committee produced a document setting out "minimum standards" to be applied in the supervision of banking groups carrying on business in more than one jurisdiction In the same year the E.U. extended the required scope of consolidated supervision of E.U.'s institutions by adopting a new (Second) Consolidated Supervision Directive.[28] This was again implemented in the United Kingdom by appropriate policy changes made by the Bank of England.

In 1991 the Basle Committee produced recommendations in relation to the monitoring and control of large exposures. This was followed in 1992 by the E.U.'s Large Exposures Directive (LED),[29] which set out limits on the maximum permissible exposure to any single counterparty or group of connected counterparties, and on clustering of smaller significant exposures. It also imposed minimum reporting requirements. This Directive also was implemented by policy changes adopted by the Bank of England.

Further developments in capital adequacy came in 1993 with the adoption of the Capital Adequacy Directive (CAD)[30] which formed part of the E.U.'s programme of implementing the single market in investment services, and set out the basis on which the capital adequacy of investment firms was to be measured. However, it was recognised that to the extent that banks were also engaged in investment business the capital requirements for both categories of institution should be the same. The CAD therefore provides that certain types of market risk to which banks are exposed should be subject to the risk measurement techniques set out in that Directive instead of being subject to the requirements of the Solvency Ratio Directive. **1–023**

In 1994 the Deposit Guarantee Directive[31] was adopted, requiring member states to establish deposit guarantee schemes incorporating minimum specified protections. The United Kingdom already had such a scheme under the BA 1987, but the new Directive required certain changes to be made to it by means of secondary legislation.

The Basle Committee made significant amendments to the Capital Accord in 1996, permitting (subject to various conditions) banks to use their own internal risk models to calculate market risks. The E.U. also adopted this approach,[32] although not until 1998, leaving E.U. banks at a competitive disadvantage in the interim. **1–024**

---

[28] Council Directive on the supervision of credit institutions on a consolidated basis (Directive 92/30 [1992] O.J. L110/52).

[29] Council Directive on the monitoring and control of large exposures of credit institutions (Directive 92/121 [1993] O.J. L29/1).

[30] Council Directive on capital adequacy of investment firms and credit institutions (Directive 93/6 [1993] O.J. L141/1).

[31] Council Directive on deposit guarantee schemes (Directive 94/19 [1994] O.J. L135/5).

[32] Directive 98/31 of the European Parliament and the Council of June 22, 1988 amending Council Directive 93/6 ([1993] O.J. L141/1) on the capital adequacy of investment firms and credit institutions ([1998] O.J. L204/13).

Further international developments in banking regulation are inevitable, both within the E.U. and more widely. Within the E.U. perhaps the most significant issue to emerge over the last few years is the problem of ensuring proper supervision of financial institutions which are increasingly organising themselves on a cross-border basis and which are also increasingly conglomerates active in many different financial sectors—banking, insurance, securities trading, etc. There have been suggestions[33] that the only effective means of supervising such groups is to establish a new, central, part-European banking regulatory authority, or to invest such powers in the European Central Bank. Any movement of the Commission towards such a position would of course be extremely politically sensitive. For the moment, the Commission appears to accept that regulation by national regulators is adequate if properly co-ordinated.[34] However, the Commission has made clear that it sees ensuring proper coordination between national regulators as a priority, and that it sees merit in the formulation of a "supervisors co-operation charter" which would clearly assign responsibility for performing different regulatory tasks on a cross-border basis and establish mechanisms for dealing with problems which arise.

1–025 More widely, the major development on the horizon is the prospect of further wide-ranging amendments to the Capital Accord. A review of the Accord is currently under way, and significant amendments in relation to the measurement of credit risk are likely over the next few of years.

The Statutory Framework for Supervision in the United Kingdom

The Need for Authorisation

1–026 Section 3 of the BA 1987 is currently the core provision of the United Kingdom supervisory system since it requires those who provide banking services to be "authorised". Section 3 provides that:

> " . . . no person shall in the United Kingdom accept a deposit in the course of carrying on (whether there or elsewhere) a business which for the purposes of this Act is a deposit-taking business unless that person is an institution for the time being authorised by the Financial Services Authority under . . . this Act"

Any person who accepts a deposit in contravention of section 3 is guilty of an imprisonable offence[35] and section 48 enables the FSA to apply to the

---

[33] See for example *Banking Supervision in the European Community—Institutional Aspects*, the report of a working group of the ECU Institute under the chairmanship of Jean-Victor Louis, 1995.

[34] "The Commission considers that structured co-operation between national supervisory bodies—rather than the creation of new E.U. level arrangements—can be sufficient to ensure financial stability"—*Financial Services: Building a Framework for Action*, a communication of the European Commission, October 28, 1998.

[35] BA 1987, s. 3(2).

court for an order requiring the repayment of any deposits accepted in contravention of section 3.

It is important to note that the prohibition set out in section 3 does not apply in relation to a European Institution relying on the "passport" provisions of Banking Coordination (Second Council Directive) Regulations 1992.[36]

The prohibition on deposit-taking contained in section 3 is wide in scope.[37] It extends some way beyond those institutions which might commonly be regarded as banks to capture institutes which finance their own business materially from deposits or from the interest earned on them. The prohibition has come under increasing scrutiny (and criticism) as corporate entities seek direct access to the international debt and capital markets. This process, known as disintermediation, typically involves the issue of debentures or other securities to raise finance. If the proceeds of such an issue are "received" in the United Kingdom (which will invariably be the case where the issue is in sterling which is required to be cleared through the United Kingdom) it will almost certainly constitute the taking of "deposits" because the issue will be made on terms that the debentures or other securities will be "repaid" and they will not be referable to the provision of property or services or the giving of security. The Financial Services Authority (nor its predecessor, the Bank of England) has not issued any definitive guidance on how many times an entity may issue debentures or other securities in the United Kingdom before its activities will be deemed to be "carrying" on a deposit-taking business. A general rule of thumb, however, is that an entity which is not an authorised institution under the BA 1987, and which cannot otherwise benefit from any of the exemptions under the Act or associated regulations, should not engage in more than three debt issues. **1–027**

Definition of "deposit"

The definition of what constitutes a "deposit" is central to the current supervisory regime and, perhaps unsurprisingly, that term is given a broad meaning by section 5(1) of the BA 1987 which defines a deposit as: **1–028**

> " . . . a sum of money (whether denominated in a currency or in ecus) paid on terms:
>
> (a) under which it will be repaid, with or without interest or a premium and either on demand or at a time or in circumstances agreed by or on behalf of the person making the payment and the person receiving it; and

[36] See below, para. 1–130.

[37] For an analysis of the scope of the prohibition see *SCF Finance Co. Ltd v. Masri (No. 2)* [1987] Q.B. 1002; [1987] 1 All E.R. 175, CA.

(b) which are not referable to the provision of property or services or the giving of security . . ."[38]

On this definition most loans of money are "deposits". The scope of the exclusions referred to below is therefore important.

1–029 Section 5(3) of the BA 1987 explicitly excludes the following payments from the definition of "deposit":

(a) a sum paid by the Bank or an authorised institution (*i.e.* a bank authorised under the BA 1987);

(b) a sum paid by a person for the time being specified in Schedule 2 to the BA 1987[39];

(c) a sum paid by a person other than a person within paragraph (a) or (b) above, in the course of carrying on a business consisting wholly or mainly of lending money[40];

(d) a sum which is paid by one company to another at a time when one is a subsidiary of the other or both are subsidiaries of another company or the same individual is a majority or principal shareholder controller of both of them[41]; and

(e) a sum which is paid by a person who, at the time when it is paid, is a close relative of the person receiving it or who is, or is a close relative of a director, controller or manager of that person.[42]

---

[38] s. 5(2) of the BA 1987 provides that:

"money is paid on terms which are referable to the provision of property or services or to the giving of security if and only if:

(a) it is paid by way of an advance or part payment under a contract for the sale, hire, or other provision of property or services and is repayable only in the event that the property or services is not or are not in fact sold, hired or otherwise provided;

(b) it is paid by way of security for the performance of a contract or by way of security in respect of loss which may result from the non-performance of a contract; or

(c) without prejudice to paragraph (b) above, it is paid by way of security for the delivery up or return of any property, whether in a particular state of repair or otherwise".

[39] BA 1987, Sched. 2 covers a wide range of persons including (i) building societies and insurance companies which are regulated by other statutes, (ii) those that are part of the public sector such as the National Savings Bank and local authorities, (iii) those that are relatively small and are regarded as not posing a major risk to the public, such as school banks and penny saving banks, and (iv) various international or supra-national bodies including the various development banks.

[40] This should generally cover a payment by an overseas bank which is not authorised under the BA 1987.

[41] See BA 1987, s. 2(3) for definition of Shareholder Controllers.

[42] BA 1987, s. 5(4) provides that in relation to paragraph (e) of subsection (3), a sum paid by a partnership shall have the effect as if for the reference to the person paying the sum there were substituted a reference to each of the partners.

Furthermore, BA 1987, s. 5(5) provides that in relation to paragraph (e) of subsection (3) "close relative" in relation to any person means: (a) his spouse, (b) his children and step-children, his parents and step-parents, his brothers and sisters and step-brothers and step-sisters, and (c) the spouse of any person within paragraph (b) above.

Meaning of "deposit-taking business"

Section 6(1) of the BA 1987 defines a business as a "deposit-taking business" if: **1–030**

> "(a) in the course of the business money received by way of deposit is lent to others; or
> (b) any other activity of the business is financed, wholly or to any material extent,[43] out of the capital of or the interest on money received by way of deposit."

There are certain exceptions to the definition of deposit-taking business. Section 6(2) of the BA 1987 provides that a business is not a deposit-taking business if:

> "(a) the person carrying it on does not hold himself out as accepting deposits on a day to day basis; and
> (b) any deposits which are accepted are accepted only on particular occasions whether or not involving the issue of debentures or other securities."

In determining whether a business falls within the definition, regard is to be had not only to the frequency of an institution's acceptance of deposits but also to the characteristics of each such transaction when determining whether deposits are accepted only on particular occasions.[44] It may not be enough for an institution to claim that its business falls within the exemption because the institution rarely accepts deposits if the characteristics of such deposits are very similar.[45]

Exempted persons and exempted transactions

Particular transactions which are exempt from the prohibition contained in section 3 of the BA 1987 are listed in regulations made by the Treasury pursuant to sections 4(4) and (5). The current regulations are the Banking Act 1987 (Exempt Transactions) Regulations 1997[46] (the Exempt Transactions Regulations) which, among other things, exempt from the prohibition of taking deposits certain institutions/persons such as charities, church deposit funds, retail and other co-operative societies and solicitors, subject to certain restrictions. The Exempt Transactions Regulations also exempt **1–031**

[43] In its interpretation of the qualification "to any material extent, the FSA has indicated that it will take into account both the absolute value of the sums involved in the financing of any activity of the business conducted, and the proportion of the total financing of the activity provided by the sums in question.
[44] BA 1987, s. 6(4).
[45] See *SCF Finance Co. Ltd v. Masri (No. 2)* [1987] Q.B. 1002, see also David Lewis , "The Banking Bill: Between Charybdis and Scylla" [1987] 1 J.I.B.L. 49 at 53.
[46] S.I. 1997 No. 817.

the taking of deposits in connection with the issue of certain debt securities (such as the acceptance of a deposit by a person on terms involving the issue of commercial paper or on terms involving the issue of shorter term or longer term debt securities such as medium term note programmes and bond issues), again subject to certain restrictions.

There are also exemptions for deposits accepted by a person regulated under the Financial Services Act 1996 in the course of carrying on specified investment business regulated by that Act.

Territorial scope

1–032 The prohibition on carrying out deposit-taking business laid down in section 3 of the BA 1987 has a territorial scope which reaches beyond the United Kingdom as it applies to deposits accepted in the United Kingdom in the course of an institution's deposit-taking business, whether that business is carried on in the United Kingdom or elsewhere.

There is little guidance as to where a deposit is regarded as "accepted". It is generally thought that this is usually where the deposit is received by or on behalf of the person "accepting" it.

Authorisation and the Statutory Powers of the FSA over Authorised Institutions

The application process

1–033 Section 8(2)(b)(1) of the BA 1987 requires that an application for authorisation must be accompanied by a "statement setting out the nature and scale of the deposit-taking business which the applicant institution intends to carry on, any plans of the institution for the future development of that business and particulars of the institution's arrangements for the management of that business . . .".

Authorisation will only be obtained if the institution in question complies with several specific criteria laid down in the BA 1987 itself and in Schedule 3 to the BA 1987[47] and if the FSA, having exercised its sole discretion, decides to grant authorisation.

1–034 The FSA will not grant an authorisation unless it is satisfied that certain minimum criteria have been fulfilled by the applicant institution. Section 16 of the BA 1987 imposes an obligation upon the FSA to publish statements of principles in which the FSA's interpretation of the authorisation requirements and its practice when exercising its powers of granting, revoking or restricting authorisation are set out. The statement of principles in force at the time of writing were published by the FSA in 1998 (the 1998 Statements of Principles).

[47] See below, para. 1–067.

Other matters relating to applications for authorisation

Section 9(2) of the BA 1987 provides that if the FSA is not satisfied that the criteria specified in Schedule 3 are fulfilled, then authorisation will be refused.[48] Part 4 of the 1998 Statements of Principles states that the FSA will, in accordance with section 9(3A) of the BA 1987, refuse an application made by a credit institution if it appears that any person with which the credit institution may be closely linked will prevent the effective exercise of the FSA's supervision of that institution. **1–035**

Section 10 of the BA 1987 provides that the FSA must give written notice to an applicant of the fact that a grant or refusal of authorisation has been given. If the FSA proposes to refuse an application for authorisation, it is required to state the grounds on which it proposes to refuse such application together with information regarding the applicant's possibility to make written representations to the FSA and the time limits within which such representations must be made.

Revocation and restriction of authorisation

In order to ensure that the interests of depositors and potential depositors continue to be protected after an institution has received its authorisation to carry out deposit-taking business, the FSA has power to revoke or restrict an authorisation if this is perceived necessary to protect those interests. **1–036**

Section 11 of the BA 1987 provides that there are certain situations where the FSA *must* revoke an authorisation and other situations where authorisation *may* be revoked, *i.e.* where the FSA has a discretion as to whether or not to revoke.

The FSA is *obliged* to revoke an authorisation if: **1–037**

(a) a winding-up order has been made against the particular institution in the United Kingdom; or

(b) a resolution has been passed for the voluntary winding-up of such institution in the United Kingdom.

The FSA *may* revoke an authorisation if:

(a) any of the Schedule 3 criteria have not been fulfilled;

(b) the institution has failed to comply with any obligation imposed on it by or under the BA 1987;

[48] The Treasury has the power under s. 26(A) of the BA 1987 to direct the FSA to refuse or defer an application or authorisation made by a credit institution incorporated in or formed under the law of any part of the U.K. in order to implement a decision made by the Council or the Commission of the Communities under Art. 9(4) of the Second Banking Directive (relations with third countries: limitation or suspension of decisions regarding application for authorisations).

(c) the institution, by an actual or potential director, controller or manager, has provided the FSA with false, misleading or inaccurate information;

(d) the institution has contravened any provision of the Financial Services Act 1986 (FSA 1986);

(e) the interests of depositors or potential depositors of the institution are in any other way threatened, whether by the manner in which the institution is conducting or proposes to conduct its affairs or for any other reason;

(f) a person becomes a controller of the particular institution in contravention of section 21 of the BA 1987 or has become or remains a controller after having been given notice of objection;

(g) the institution has not accepted a deposit in the United Kingdom in the course of carrying on a deposit-taking business within the 12 month period beginning with the day of authorisation or if having accepted a deposit within such 12 month period, it has subsequently not done so for any period of more than six months.

1–038 The FSA's power to restrict an authorisation is contained in section 12 and apply if a ground for revocation has arisen but the circumstances of the situation do not justify revocation. Restrictions may be imposed in the form of:

(a) a limit on the duration of authorisation provided such limit does not allow the authorisation to continue in force for more than three years from the date on which it is imposed;

(b) conditions desirable for the protection of the institution's depositors and potential depositors[49]; or

(c) both limits and conditions.

An institution which fails to comply with any requirement or contravenes any prohibition imposed on it by a condition is guilty of an offence and liable on conviction to a fine. Furthermore, non-compliance with a condi-

[49] Conditions may take the form of: (a) a requirement that the institution takes certain steps or refrains from adopting or pursuing a particular course of action, or restricts the scope of its business in a particular way, (b) the imposition of limitations on the acceptance of deposits, the granting of credit or the making of investments, (c) a prohibition on the institution from soliciting deposits, either generally or from persons who are already depositors, (d) a prohibition on the institution from entering into any other transactions or class of transactions, (e) a requirement of the removal of any director, controller or manager, or (f) specific requirements to be fulfilled otherwise than by action taken by the institution.

tion imposed is itself ground for revocation, but such non-compliance does not invalidate any transaction which has been entered into by the institution when acting contrary to such condition.

The FSA's interpretation of sections 11 and 12

In the 1998 Statement of Principles, the FSA has set out its interpretation of section 11 and 12 of the BA 1987 and an explanation of how it will exercise its discretion regarding revocation and restriction of authorisations. **1–039**

Although there are other circumstances in which the FSA can exercise its powers, as a general matter, they are exercisable when the interests of depositors and potential depositors are threatened. The threat might be slight or remote or it may be both immediate and serious.

Generally, the FSA will be reluctant either to revoke or restrict an authorisation in situations where the FSA considers that adequate and speedy remedial steps are likely to be taken by a bank (or its shareholders) by, for example, injecting new capital or appointing new directors. It however, no reasonable prospects of a speedy and comprehensive remedial action seem likely, the FSA will consider revocation even in situations where no matters of immediate concern have arisen. **1–040**

An authorisation would generally be restricted by the imposition of conditions if the FSA considers that there is a reasonable prospect that all relevant criteria for authorisation would be fulfilled again within a reasonable period. Restrictions may also be used by the FSA where it regards it as desirable that the interests of depositors be additionally protected while further information is sought from the particular bank.

Directions

Section 19 of the BA 1987 grants the FSA the power to give directions to an institution which has received a notice restricting or revoking its authorisation. **1–041**

Directions will be given if this seems to the FSA to be desirable in the interests of the institution's depositors or potential depositors and may in particular be in a form similar to the conditions which may be imposed under section 12.

Power to petition for winding-up

Pursuant to section 92 of the BA 1987, the FSA has the power to present a petition to the courts under the Insolvency Act 1986 for the winding-up of an authorised institution or former authorised institution if the institution is unable to pay its debts within the meaning of section 123 or, as the case may be, section 221 of the Insolvency Act 1986 (IA 1986)[50] or if the court is **1–042**

[50] IA 1986, s. 92 provides that an institution which defaults in an obligation to pay any sum due and payable in respect of a deposit is deemed to be unable to pay its debts.

of the opinion that it is just and equitable that the institution should be wound up.

Appeals

1–043 Section 27 of the BA 1987 grants an aggrieved institution the right of appeal to a tribunal against a decision of the FSA to;

(a) refuse an application for authorisation;

(b) revoke an authorisation;

(c) restrict an authorisation;

(d) give directions under section 19 or to vary a direction given to it under that section.

Objections to Controllers

Notification of new or increased control or ceasing to be a relevant controller

1–044 The ability of the FSA to object to prospective controlling shareholders in an authorised institution was originally introduced to protect the United Kingdom banking sector from aggressive foreign or otherwise undesirable take-overs, and from the influence and control of individuals whose interests may be harmful to those of depositors.[51] The FSA's right to object to prospective (and existing) shareholders is contained in section 21 of the BA 1987 which provides that no person may become a minority, a 10 per cent, a 20 per cent, a 33 per cent, a majority or principal shareholder controller, or a parent controller or an indirect controller of an authorised institution unless such person has notified the FSA of his intention.

1–045 Having received such notification, the FSA has up to three months to object to such new or increased control unless the FSA is satisfied that[52]:

(a) the person concerned is a fit and proper person to become the type of controller intended;

(b) the interests of depositors and potential depositors of the institution would not be in any other manner threatened by the person in question becoming the type of controller intended; and

(c) having regard to that person's likely influence on the institution as the intended type of controller, the criteria in Schedule 3 would continue to be fulfilled or if not fulfilled that such person would be likely to undertake adequate remedial action.

---

[51] See Arora, "The Banking Act 1987", Company Lawyer, Vol. 9, No. 2, p. 39.
[52] BA 1987, s. 22.

The FSA can also object to an existing shareholder controller of any description remaining a controller if it appears to the FSA that such shareholder controller is not or is no longer a fit and proper person to be such a controller.

The procedural aspect of the FSA's right to object is reinforced by **1–046**
section 37(A) of the BA 1987 which requires prospective controllers who fall (or will fall) into each of the categories outlined above to give the FSA notice of the intention to become such a controller. The notice must be given prior to the shareholder controller ceasing to hold the relevant interest in the institution. If after ceasing to be such a controller of the institution a person will, either alone or with any associates, continue to be able to exercise a significant influence over the management of the institution or another institution of which that institution is an undertaking, he must include information of such continuing position in the notice to the FSA.

"Shareholder controllers" are defined in section 105 of the BA 1987 as follows:

> A person [who] either alone or with any associate or associates:
> (a) . . . holds 10 per cent or more of the shares in the institution or another institution of which it is a subsidiary undertaking;
> (b) . . . is entitled to exercise, or control the exercise of, 10 per cent or more of the voting power at any general meeting of the institution or another institution of which it is such an undertaking; or
> (c) . . . is able to exercise a significant influence over the management of the institution or another institution of which that institution is such an undertaking by virtue of:
>   (i) a holding of shares in; or
>   (ii) an entitlement to exercise, or control the exercise of, the voting power at any general meeting of, the institution or, as the case may be, the other institution concerned.

The percentage of shares or voting rights held by the shareholder (and **1–047**
his associates) determines whether he is a "minority", a "10 cent", a "20 per cent", a "33 per cent", a "50 per cent", a "majority" or a "principal" shareholder controller. A "minority shareholder controller" is a shareholder controller not falling within (a) or (b) above. A "majority shareholder controller" is a shareholder controller who holds more than 50 but less than 75 per cent of the shares or voting rights and a "principal shareholder controller" is a shareholder controller who holds more than 75 per cent of the shares or voting rights.

A "controller" in relation to an institution means

(i) a managing director of the institution or of another institution of which it is a subsidiary or, in the case of an institution which is a partnership, a partner;

(ii) a chief executive of the institution or of another institution of which it is a subsidiary;

(iii) person who is shareholder controller;

(iv) a person in accordance with whose directions or instructions the directors of the institution or of another institution of which it is a subsidiary or persons who are controllers of the institution by virtue of being a shareholder controller are accustomed to act; and

(v) a person who is, or would be if he were an undertaking, a parent undertaking of the institution.

Powers of the regulator to deal with contraventions

1–048 A person who becomes a shareholder controller in contravention of section 21 is guilty of an offence and liable to imprisonment and/or a fine (section 25).

Furthermore, if a person who has received a notice of objection from the FSA becomes or continues to be a shareholder controller of an institution, the FSA may, in accordance with section 26 of the BA 1987, serve a notice on the person concerned, directing that the relevant shares be subject to one or more of the following restrictions:

(a) any transfer of, or agreement to transfer, those shares or, in the case of unissued shares, any transfer of or agreement to transfer the right to be issued with them shall be void;

(b) no voting rights shall be exercisable in respect of the shares;

(c) no further shares shall be issued in right of them or in pursuance of any offer made to their holder;

(d) except in liquidation, no payment shall be made of any sums due from the institution on the shares, whether in respect of capital or otherwise.

In addition, the FSA may apply to the courts for an order for the sale of the shares in question.

There is a right of appeal to a tribunal against the decision of the FSA to object to controllers.[53]

Solicitation of Deposits

Advertisement regulations

1–049 The BA 1987 recognises the need to protect the public against misleading deposit advertisements. Protection is considered to be especially important in the case of deposit advertisements involving a jurisdiction

[53] BA 1987, s. 27(3).

outside the United Kingdom or another Member State of the European Union which may not be supervised to the same extent as institutions in the E.U. and which may not offer the same protection to depositors.[54]

If a deposit advertisement does not fall within a specified exemption set out in regulations made under the BA 1987,[55] it must include certain information about the deposit-taker, its status and nationality, its assets and liabilities, the deposit protection arrangements of the deposit-taker, the rate of interest payable on the deposit and the currency in which the deposit must be made.

If the FSA considers that a deposit advertisement which has been issued or is proposed to be issued by or on behalf of an authorised institution is misleading, it is empowered to give directions to the institution responsible to address the problem.[56] This power applies to all deposit advertisements, whether or not subject to the Advertisements Regulations.

Information

Effective supervision by the FSA depends heavily on the voluntary **1–050**
provision of financial information by institutions authorised by it, which are obliged to provide the FSA with information relating to almost every area of their activities.

In addition, the BA 1987 includes specific notification requirements that are primarily concerned with changes in the management and shareholdings of an authorised institution.

The obligation to notify the FSA of any new or increased control by a **1–051**
shareholder controller[57] is also reinforced by requiring the relevant institution to notify the FSA:

(a) of any change of director, controller or manager within 14 days of becoming aware of the change,[58] and

(b) annually of the identity of all minority, 10 per cent, 20 per cent, 33 per cent and 50 per cent shareholder controllers, what percentage of shares such shareholder controller holds either alone or with any associates, and what percentage of the voting power at a general meeting of the institution he is entitled to exercise or control the exercise of, either alone or with any associate or associates.[59]

---

[54] There are various other exemptions For example, advertisements by certain insurance institutions are exempt from the Advertisements Regulations as are company prospectuses inviting capital input and numerous other matters concerning applications for shares in, or debentures of a company or invitations to enter into an underwriting agreement with respect to such shares or debentures which comply with the requirements laid down in the CA 1985.

[55] The Banking Act 1987 (Advertisements) Regulations 1988 (as amended) (S.I. 1988 No. 645).

[56] BA 1987, s. 33.

[57] See above, para. 1–044.

[58] BA 1987, s. 36.

[59] BA 1987, s. 36A.

The reporting of large exposures is covered in section 38 of the BA 1987 which provides that an authorised institution must submit reports to the FSA on its large exposures. The authorised institution must give subsequent notification of any exposures that are in excess of 10 per cent of such institution's capital base and prior notice of any proposed exposures in excess of 25 per cent of the capital base.[60] It is not only single exposures that are caught by section 38. Exposures to connected entities (*e.g.* loans to group companies or to companies with common directors) are aggregated for the purpose of measuring the exposure.

1–052 Section 39 of the BA 1987 gives the FSA a general power to obtain information and require the production of documents from an authorised institution which has been served with a written notice requiring such information or documents.[61] Where the FSA has power to require the production of documents from an authorised institution, the FSA can also require the production of such documents from any person who appears to be in possession of them. The FSA can also require a director, controller or manager of an authorised institution to provide the FSA with such information or documents as the FSA may reasonably require for determining whether he is a fit and proper person to hold the particular position which he holds or is to hold. Section 39 also enables the FSA to require an institution to provide a "reporting accountants report".[62]

The FSA is given the right to enter the premises of an institution which has been served with a section 39 notice.[63] The right of entry may be exercised in order to obtain documents or take copies or extracts of documents and require explanations from relevant persons of the particular institution as to the whereabouts of documents which have not been produced in accordance with a section 39 notice. If the requisite documents are not produced then the FSA must be given an explanation as to their whereabouts.[64] The FSA's right of entry which was first introduced in the BA 1987, is also available where the FSA has reasonable cause to believe that a notice under section 39 would not be complied with or that any documents to which the notice relates would be removed, tampered with or destroyed.[65]

[60] For a more detailed explanation of the large exposures requirement, see below, para. 1–141.

[61] See *Price Watherhouse v. BCCI Holdings (Luxembourg) SA* [1992] B.C.L.C. 583 which confirmed the Bank of England can compel the production of documents from an authorised institution even though the documents may be covered by legal professional privilege. See also *BCCI v. Price Waterhouse (No. 2)* [1997] 6 Bank L.R. 216 and *A v. B. Bank (Bank of England intervening)* [1993] Q.B. 311.

[62] See below, paras 1–055–1–058.

[63] BA 1987, s. 40.

[64] BA 1987, s. 41.

[65] BA 1987, s. 40(2).

Investigations

The BA 1987 gives the FSA power, where it appears to the FSA desirable to do so in the interest of the depositors or potential depositors of an institution,[66] to appoint one or more competent persons to investigate and report to the FSA on the nature, conduct or state of an authorised institution's business or any particular aspects of it, or the ownership or control of the institution.[67] **1–053**

Section 42 grants the FSA and its officers wider and more powerful rights of investigation and entry, involving the Police, in cases where the FSA suspects that a person is contravening section 3 (breach of the general deposit taking prohibition)[68] or section 35 (fraudulent inducement to make a deposit)[69] of the BA 1987.

Any person who knows or suspects that an investigation is being or is likely to be carried out under section 41 or 42 of the BA 1987, shall be liable to a maximum of two years imprisonment or a fine or both if he falsifies, conceals, destroys or otherwise disposes of, or causes or permits the falsification, concealment, destruction or disposal of, documents which he knows or suspects are or would be relevant to such an investigation, unless he proves that he had no intention of concealing the facts disclosed by the documents from persons carrying out such an investigation.[70] **1–054**

Accounts and Auditors

The most innovative change introduced by the BA 1987 was to clear the way for auditors to play a greater part in the supervisory process. The Leigh-Pemberton Committee (which was established to report on the system of banking supervision following the collapse of Johnson Matthey Bankers in 1985 and was chaired by the then Governor of the Bank of England, Robin Leigh-Pemberton)[71] noted that if the Bank of England was not to carry out detailed inspections of its own, it must be able to rely on the assistance and co-operation of auditors whose duties necessitate first hand knowledge of an institutions accounts. The FSA regularly draws on this knowledge by requiring auditors to prepare reports (know as "section 39 reports") on particular aspects of their clients business. Aside from strengthening the supervisory regime, this move was intended to be a cost effective one, sparing banks the alternative of facing two largely overlapping enquiries. **1–055**

---

[66] BA 1987, s. 41.

[67] If necessary, such investigation may be extended to such undertakings which are connected with the institution under investigation, including but not limited to, parent or subsidiary undertakings.

[68] See above, para. 1–026.

[69] See above, para. 1–028.

[70] See *Bank of England v. Riley* [1992] Ch. 475.

[71] Cmnd. 9550. Report of the Committee set up to consider the System of Banking Supervision, 1985 (the Leigh-Pemberton Committee).

1–056 The complimentary roles of auditor and supervisor have long been recognised but cooperation between them was largely precluded prior to the passing of the BA 1987 by confidentiality constraints. The BA 1987 overrides an auditor's duty of confidentiality to its client (the relevant authorised institution) by enabling him to pass on information to the FSA concerning the business affairs of his client.[72] Such information must be acquired by the auditor in that capacity and be communicated to the FSA in good faith. Section 39 of the BA 1987, as has already been seen, empowers the FSA to call for such information as the FSA may reasonably require. This power is supported by the right to require an authorised institution to provide a report from an accountant (a section 39 report) containing any information which the FSA requires. The FSA (and previously the Bank of England) has published[73] a comprehensive guidance note on the scope of section 39 reports required by the FSA. That guidance note makes reference to the working knowledge of the authorised institution required to be held by the reporting accountant and the nature of the opinion required to be delivered by him. In forming their opinion, reporting accountants will be expected to consider whether their client has maintained adequate accounting and affiliated records as well as operating the appropriate internal control systems.

1–057 If, during the course of their investigations, the reporting accountants conclude that a return submitted by their client to the FSA contains material errors or omissions, which have not been discovered by management or reported by them to the FSA, the reporting accountants should invite management to bring the matter to the attention of the FSA. If the management declines, the reporting accountants should bring the matter to the attention of the FSA[74] and section 47 of the BA 1987 provides they will not be in breach of any duty of confidentiality by informing the FSA of the matter in question.[75]

1–058 The role of the auditors in the supervisory process was extended further as a result of the collapse of BCCI. The Financial Institutions (Prudential Supervision) Regulations 1996 (the BCCI Regulations)[76] that gave effect in the United Kingdom to the post-BCCI Directive,[77] extended supervision of

[72] The Auditing Guidelines of the Institute of Chartered Accountants impose a professional duty on reporting accountants to report directly to the FSA in the circumstances specified in the guideline. See also the obligation imposed upon reporting accountants under the Accountants (Banking Act 1987) Regulations 1994 (S.I. 1994 No. 524).

[73] See the Chapter entitled, "Reporting Accountants' Reports on Accounting and Internal Control Systems" in the FSA's Guide to Banking Supervisory Policy.

[74] The Auditing Guidelines of the Chartered Institute of Accountants impose a professional duty to report to the FSA. See above, para. 1–056.

[75] See the Chapter entitled, "Reporting Accountants, Auditors and Audit Committees" in the FSA's Guide to Banking Supervisory Policy, which describes the relationship which the FSA has with reporting accountants and auditors.

[76] S.I. 1996 No. 1669.

[77] Directive 95/26 [1995] O.J. L168/7.

financial groups headed by an unauthorised holding company and containing unregulated entities. The post-BCCI Directive provides that where there are "close connections" between a regulated and an unregulated entity (because, for example, they are within the same group) the regulators of the regulated entity should have access to information about the group as a whole in order to provide effective supervision. The information required by the regulator will invariably be obtained from the auditors of the group in question and the BCCI Regulations[78] provide to such auditors the benefit of the same privilege in respect of disclosure to regulators as is extended to auditors of directly regulated entities.[79]

Auditors are required to notify the FSA if they decide to resign or not to seek re-appointment or if they propose to include a qualification to their report on an authorised institution's accounts.[80] Equally, an authorised institution must notify the FSA "immediately" if it proposes to remove an auditor before, or replace an auditor after, the expiry of his term of office.[81]

The Deposit Protection Scheme

Although extensive controls and effective supervision of authorised institutions will minimise the risk of deposit taking institutions experiencing difficulties, it is inevitable that some institutions will fail. Part II of the 1987 Act lays down the framework for a deposit protection scheme to protect depositors in such cases. **1–059**

Under the scheme a fund has been set up and the board of the fund has been granted the power to collect contributions from all institutions authorised by the FSA.[82] The fund is used for repaying "protected deposits".

A "protected deposit" is defined in section 60 of the BA 1987 to mean the liability of an institution to a depositor in respect of: **1–060**

(a) the principal amount of each deposit in an EEA currency which was made by such depositor with a United Kingdom office[83] of the institution before the time when the institution became insolvent and has become due and payable; and

(b) accrued interest on any such deposit up to the time when it became due and payable;

---

[78] reg. 10.

[79] It is rather surprising that this provision is not included in the Financial Services and Markets Bill.

[80] BA 1987, s. 46(1).

[81] BA 1987, s. 46(2).

[82] The BA 1987 also includes various provisions setting out when an authorised institution is obliged to make contributions to the Deposit Protection Fund and the size of such contributions. It must be noted that the DPF is empowered to finance partly by the use of borrowings and not only by contributions from authorised institutions.

[83] With respect to U.K. incorporated institutions, the reference to U.K. offices includes a reference to offices in other EEA States (BA 1987, s. 60(2A)).

provided that the total liability of the institution to the depositor in respect of such deposits does not exceed £20,000 or the sterling equivalent of Euro 22,222 immediately before the time the institution became insolvent, whichever is the greater.[84]

Banking Names and Descriptions

1–061 Banking names and descriptions are regulated by Part III of the BA 1987. As a general rule, no person carrying on any business in the United Kingdom is allowed to use a name or description which indicates or may reasonably be understood to indicate (whether in English or any other language) that the institution is a bank or the person is a banker and that such institution carries out banking business, unless they are authorised institutions under the BA 1987.

Overseas Institutions with Representative Offices

1–062 Overseas institutions which wish to establish a representative office in the United Kingdom must comply with the requirements of Part IV of the Act. "Representative office" in relation to any overseas institution, means premises from which the deposit taking, lending or other financial or banking activities of the overseas institution are promoted or assisted in any way; and "establishment" in relation to such an office, includes the making of any arrangements by virtue of which such activities are promoted or assisted from it. If the institution is to accept deposits in the United Kingdom, "representative office" status will be inappropriate, and full authorisation must be applied for.[85] A representative office is not permitted to accept deposits in the United Kingdom.

An "overseas institution" means a person (other than an authorised institution or any person for the time being specified in Schedule 2 to the BA 1987) established or having its principal place of business outside the United Kingdom, being in either case a person who satisfies one of the following conditions:

(i) that the person's principal place of business is outside the United Kingdom and the person is authorised by the relevant supervisory authority in a country or territory outside the United Kingdom;

(ii) that the person describes himself or holds himself out as being authorised by such an authority in a country or territory outside the United Kingdom;

---

[84] s. 61 of the BA 1987 provides how the Scheme works for deposits held jointly and on trust for beneficiaries.

[85] See *South India Shipping Corp. v. Export-Import Bank of Korea* [1985] 2 All E.R. 219 in which it was held that an overseas bank renting office space in the U.K. that was used only for the purpose of gathering information and maintaining relations with other banks, had a place of business in the U.K.

(iii) that the person uses any name or in any other way so describes himself or holds himself out as to indicate or reasonably understood to indicate (whether in English or any other language) that he is a bank or banker or is carrying on a banking business (whether in the United Kingdom or elsewhere). The Second Banking Directive modifies the definition of authorised institution under section 74 of the BA 1987.

An overseas institution intending to establish a representative office in the United Kingdom must notify the FSA of its intention to do so at least two months before the actual establishment takes place. The FSA is empowered to object to the intended name of such a representative office and require the overseas institution to use another name for its representative office. **1–063**

Furthermore, the FSA has the power to, require an overseas institution which intends to establish a representative office in the United Kingdom to provide any information or documents the FSA may reasonably require. Such requirement must be specified by the FSA in a written notice to the overseas institution in question. The power to require information and documents also applies once the overseas institution has established its representative office in the United Kingdom.

The establishment of a representative office in the absence of the due notification process is a criminal offence. Wherever in the United Kingdom the representative office name is used, the words "representative office" must appear in immediate connection with, and no less prominently than, the name itself. The 1998 Statements of Principles provide that the FSA expects to be informed of any significant proposals or developments regarding the representative office (such as change of address, change of key personnel in the United Kingdom or changes in its role in the United Kingdom).

Restriction on Disclosure of Information

Part V of the BA 1987 lays down restrictions on the disclosure of information by any person who, under or for the purposes of the 1987 Act, receives information relating to the business or other affairs of another person from disclosing such information without the consent of the person to whom the information relates and (if different) the person from whom it was received. **1–064**

The prohibition in section 82 on disclosure of information does not apply to such information that at the time of the disclosure is or has already been made available to the public from other sources or to information in the form of a summary or collection of information so framed as not to enable information relating to any particular person to be ascertained from it.

There are various exceptions to the general rule. The main exceptions are set out in sections 83 and 84. Section 83 enables the FSA to disclose information in any case where such disclosure is for the purpose of enabling **1–065** or assisting the FSA to discharge its functions under the BA 1987. The FSA may also disclose such restricted information in order for it to fulfil its role as a designated agency under the FSA 1986 and its functions as supervisor of money market institutions.

Section 83 also specifically provides that the FSA may disclose restricted information to the auditor of an authorised institution or former authorised institution if it appears to the FSA that disclosure of such information would assist or enable the FSA to discharge its functions or would otherwise be in the interests of the depositors and to such other qualified persons from whom the FSA is seeking advice on any matter of law, accountancy, valuation or other matter if it appears to the FSA that disclosure of such information is necessary to ensure that such qualified person is properly informed with respect to the matters on which his advice is sought.

1–066 Section 84 enables the FSA to disclose restricted information to certain persons or institutions in order to assist such persons or institutions in the discharge of certain functions which are set out in section 84. The persons and institutions to which such information may be disclosed include the Secretary of State and various regulatory bodies such as the Building Societies Commission and the Bank of England. Section 84 also enables the FSA to disclose restricted information to supervisory authorities in other EEA Member States which carry out functions similar to those granted to the FSA under the BA 1987.

Ongoing Requirements for Authorised Institutions

The Criteria for Authorisation

1–067 Under the BA 1987, the Bank of England's authorisation and supervisory powers were based on a distinction between banks and licensed deposit-taking institutions. The BA 1987 abolished that two-tier system.[86] Any institution seeking authorisation to carry on a deposit taking business in the United Kingdom is now subject to a single set of authorisation criteria.

The minimum criteria for authorisation are listed in Schedule 3 to the BA 1987. These are commonly referred to as the "Schedule 3 Criteria". The Schedule 3 Criteria must be satisfied if the FSA is to grant authorisation. It is also the case that they must continue to be satisfied on an ongoing basis failing which the FSA has discretion to revoke the authorisation or to impose conditions or restrictions on it. The Schedule 3 Criteria therefore have major importance for the way in which authorised institutions carry out their business.

1–068 The Schedule 3 Criteria cover the following areas:

(a) the directors, controllers and managers must be fit and proper persons;

[86] See Penn, *Banking Supervision* (1989), Chap. 3.

(b) the business must be directed by at least two individuals;

(c) the composition of the board of directors must consist partly of non-executive directors;

(d) the business must be conducted in prudent manner. Each of the following specific requirements must be fulfilled before an institution may be regarded as conducting its business in a prudent manner:

  (i) the institution must have adequate capital;
  (ii) the institution must have adequate liquidity;
  (iii) the institution must have adequate provisions; and
  (iv) the institution must maintain accounting and other records and adequate systems of control.

  In addition to these specific requirements there are also a number of other considerations, commonly referred to as the "general prudent conduct" requirement. Examples of other relevant considerations listed by the FSA in its 1998 Statements of Principles include:

  (i) the institution's management arrangements (such as those for the overall control and direction by the board of directors, the location of its mind and management and its central direction (which the FSA would expect to be located where the institution is incorporated or formed));
  (ii) the institution's general strategy and objectives;
  (iii) planning arrangements;
  (iv) policies which deal with accounting, lending and other exposures;
  (v) policies and practices on the taking and valuation of security, on the monitoring of arrears, on following up debtors in arrears and interest rate matching; and
  (vi) recruitment, training and remuneration arrangements to ensure that the institution has staff with appropriate skills, experience, incentives and disciplines to carry out its various activities in a prudent manner.

(e) the business must be carried on with integrity and skill; and

(f) the institution must hold certain minimum net assets.

The Schedule 3 Criteria are expanded and interpreted by the 1998 Statements of Principles and the FSA's Guide to Banking Supervisory Policy which compliments and expands upon the 1998 Statements of Principles.

Directors, controllers and managers to be fit and proper persons

Paragraph 1(1) of Schedule 3 requires that every person who is, or is to **1–069**
be, a director, controller or manager of the institution must be a fit and proper person to hold the particular position which he holds or is to hold.

In determining whether a person is a fit and proper person to hold any particular position, regard must be had to his probity, to his competence and soundness of judgment for fulfilling the responsibilities of the position he is to hold, to the diligence with which he is fulfilling or likely to fulfil those responsibilities and to whether the interest of depositors or potential depositors of the institution are, or are likely to be, in any way threatened by his holding that position.

In connection with the evaluation of these standards paragraph (1)(3) of Schedule 3 provides that regard may also be had to whether the individual has committed any offences such as fraud, dishonesty or violence or contravention of any provision of banking, insurance, investments, or other financial services legislation designed to protect members of the public from financial loss due to dishonesty, incompetence or malpractice.

1–070 The 1998 Statements of Principles provide that the standard with which an individual must comply depends upon the specific position that particular person is, or is to be, holding. The standard is very high for the persons with the ultimate responsibility for the conduct of an institution's business. Similarly, the standard to be met by a majority shareholder will be higher than the standard to be complied with by a minority shareholder.

The FSA, in its Banking Supervisory Policy, has confirmed that as a matter of policy the FSA will normally request a comfort letter from any person who controls, or proposes to control, 15 per cent or more of a United Kingdom incorporated institution's voting power, in the context of its assessment of the shareholder controllers[87] of that institution. The reason for this is that the FSA wants to be assured as to the shareholder controller's willingness to stand behind the institution if concerns arise over the institution's solvency and liquidity. The FSA also takes into account in this assessment the willingness (or lack of it) of a shareholder controller to support the institution. A comfort letter involves a shareholder acknowledging a higher level of responsibility to depositors than is implied by strict limited liability as a shareholder. A comfort letter is a statement of intent rather than a legally binding document and is therefore not viewed in the same way as a guarantee. Its existence can, however, help maintain market confidence in a bank during periods of uncertainty. If a United Kingdom incorporated institution has more than one shareholder controller holding more than 15 per cent, the FSA will normally request a comfort letter from each. Exceptionally, the FSA may request a comfort letter from a shareholder holding less than 15 per cent of the institution's voting power.[88]

---

[87] See above, para. 1–044, for description of shareholder controllers.

[88] The FSA has indicated in its Guide to Banking Supervisory Policy that incidences where such a request might be made include (i) where the relevant shareholding appears to confer powers of governance in excess of those that would normally be associated with such a percentage shareholding; and (ii) where significant influence is being exerted, even if the shareholding is not large. There are two main purposes behind a request for a comfort

Business to be directed by at least two individuals

The criterion that the business should be directed by at least two individuals, the "four eyes" requirement, is interpreted by the FSA in its 1998 Statements of Principles, to mean that both individuals must formulate and implement the policies of the institution in question. The responsibility for decision making may riot be split between those two individuals nor may one of them have more responsibility than the other. Day-to-day involvement in the execution and implementation of policy is not required, but the two individuals will be required to be involved in the strategy and general direction as well as have knowledge of and influence the way in which strategy is being implemented through the day-to-day policy. **1–071**

Furthermore, the FSA requires that both individuals must have sufficient experience and knowledge of the business and the necessary personal qualities to detect and resist any imprudence, dishonesty, or other irregularities by the other person.

The individuals who may be accepted for this purpose may be either executive directors or persons who are granted executive powers by and report immediately to the board of directors. If the institution is a partnership, the FSA requires the business to be directed by at least two active partners.

Composition of board of directors

Paragraph 3 of Schedule 3 provides that the FSA may require institutions incorporated in the United Kingdom to appoint such number of non-executive directors as the FSA considers appropriate. The number will depend on the circumstances of the institution and the nature and scale of its operation. **1–072**

The role of such non-executive directors is regarded as particularly important in connection with the audit of an institution. The non-executive directors should therefore preferably be members of the institution's audit committee. In this connection the 1998 Statements of Principles state that even very small institutions should appoint at least two non-executive directors to undertake some audit committee functions.

letter. First, to help the FSA assess a shareholder controller in respect of its shareholding. Secondly, to ensure that the shareholder controller recognises the special nature of a deposit taking business and confirms its acceptance of a moral responsibility to support the bank, should this become necessary, beyond the limited liability attached to its shareholdings. There is, in principle, no limit on the level of expected support given since the shareholder controller undertakes to ensure that the bank continues to meet its obligations. This might result in the shareholder controller being expected to provide liquidity support or to take measures to preserve the solvency of the bank. The scope of a comfort letter encompasses not only the U.K. incorporated bank but also flow of funds from the bank to any solo-consolidated subsidiaries. See generally the Chapter entitled "Comfort Letters" in the Guide to Banking Supervisory Policy.

The FSA attaches considerable importance to the role of non-executive directors, placing particular value on their ability to bring an outsider's independent perspective to the running of the business and in questioning the approach of the executive directors and other management.

Business to be conducted in a prudent manner—(1) capital adequacy

1–073 The main cause of bank failure is insolvency. The risk of insolvency can be greatly reduced if a bank is required to maintain adequate capital.

1–074 **FSA's approach to capital adequacy.** Paragraph 4 of Schedule 3 to the BA 1987, requires that institutions conduct their business in a prudent manner, which includes the maintenance of "own funds" commensurate with the nature and scale of the operations it plans to carry out and adequate to safeguard the interests of its depositors. The amount of own funds must, if the institution is incorporated in the United Kingdom, not be less than five million Euros (or an amount of equal value denominated in another unit of account).[89]

1–075 The basic approach of the capital adequacy framework is that an institution should have sufficient capital to provide a stable resource to absorb any losses arising from the risks in its business. It is based closely on the Capital Accord 1988 and the relevant E.U. Directives. It consists of a quantitative framework for deriving a required level of capital, consisting of three main elements:

(1) a definition of the characteristics an instrument must have to qualify as capital. Capital is divided into tiers according to the characteristics/qualities of each qualifying instrument;
(2) a risk weighting framework which produces risk weighted measures of the relevant risks captured by the framework. An institution is required to hold less capital to support assets with low risk weights than assets with higher risk weights; and
(3) a required capital ratio. This is a ratio of total capital to risk weighted assets and generates a required level of capital for an institution's activity. Both trigger and target ratios are imposed.

The FSA requires United Kingdom-incorporated institutions to comply with these capital requirements on both a solo and a consolidated basis (see below, Chapter 4).

1–076 *(i) Definition of capital.* Capital must have two specific characteristics. It must be available to absorb losses and it must have a certain degree of

[89] Art. 4 of the Second Council Directive on the own funds of credit institutions ([1989] O.J. L124/16) that was implemented in the U.K. by Sched. 3 to the BA 1987.

permanency. Capital is divided into three categories: "Tier 1" (which forms an institution's "core" capital), "Tier 2" (upper and lower) and "Tier 3". Different instruments are allocated to these categories according to the degree to which they are able to absorb losses and the degree of their permanence.

(1) Tier 1 (or "core") capital consists of:

- (a) fully paid-up ordinary share capital/common stock;
- (b) perpetual non-cumulative preferred shares;
- (c) general and other reserves, share premiums and other surpluses;
- (d) retained profit and loss arising during the course of the current year where verified by a bank's external auditors; and
- (e) minority interests arising on consolidation from interests in permanent shareholders' equity (this applies only in calculation of solo-consolidated and consolidated capital base).

(2) Tier 2 (or "supplementary") capital consists of:

- (a) revaluation reserves;
- (b) general provisions;
- (c) certain hybrid capital instruments such as perpetual cumulative preferred shares and perpetual subordinated debt including such debt which is convertible into equity;
- (d) dated preferred shares, convertible subordinated bonds and subordinated term debt with a minimum original maturity of over five years and subject to a straight-line amortisation during the last five years;
- (e) minority interests in Tier 2 preferred shares; and
- (f) certain fully paid shareholders' equity.

Investments in unconsolidated subsidiaries and associates, connected lending of a capital nature and all holdings of other banks' and building societies' capital instruments must be deducted from the aggregate of Tier 1 and Tier 2 capital.

No early repayment of Tier 2 capital can be made without the FSA's prior consent. Consent will only be given where an institution produces a capital plan that shows that the institution will remain above its target ratio for at least two years after repayment.

Furthermore, Tier 2 capital may not exceed Tier 1 capital, Tier 2 subordinated term debt (sometimes referred to, for this reason, as "Lower Tier 2 capital") must not exceed 50 per cent of Tier 1 capital and general provisions must not exceed 1.25 per cent of risk weighted assets.

(3) Tier 3 (or "ancillary") capital consists of:

- (a) short term subordinated debt with a minimum original maturity of two years issued on terms that if the institution's allowable capital falls below its target capital requirements the debt repayments will be suspended; and

(b) minority interests in Tier 3 capital.

Tier 3 capital may only be used to support trading book activities and is therefore applicable to CAD banks only (a CAD bank is a bank with a trading book above the de minimis level.[90]

1–077 *(ii) Risk weighting framework for calculating capital requirements*. The capital adequacy regime provides a framework for a quantitative assessment of various risks, whether they arise in an institution's banking book or trading book. Some of the risks have a different treatment in the banking and trading book, while others are treated in the same way whenever they arise.

Measurement of risk in the banking book

1–078 ***i Credit risk.*** Credit risk is the principal risk addressed in the risk-weighting framework for the banking book. Account is taken of the credit risk on most bank assets both on and off balance sheet and such assets are risk weighted in an attempt to mirror the actual credit risk. As a general rule, unless it can be shown that an exposure merits a reduced risk-weighting under the weighting bands below, it receives 100 per cent risk weighting.

1–079 On-balance sheet assets have been divided into five categories:

0% which includes assets such as cash, claims on or guaranteed by Zone A[91] central governments and central banks, and claims on or guaranteed by Zone B (which comprise all countries not in Zone A) central governments and central banks where denominated in local currency;

10% Certain holdings of government securities attract a 10 per cent weighting as proxy for market risk.[92] This includes holdings of fixed or floating-rate securities with a maturity of one year or less issued or guaranteed by Zone A central governments and by Zone B central governments if denominated in local currency and funded by liabilities in the same currency and claims collateralised by Zone A central governments securities;

20% which includes assets such as certain securities mentioned above with a maturity of over one year, claims on or guaranteed by credit

[90] For a description of the measurement of risk in the trading book see below, para. 1–083.

[91] Zone A countries include the members of the Organisation for Economic Co-operation and Development and those countries which have concluded special lending arrangements with the International Monetary Fund associated with the Fund's general arrangements to borrow, provided they have not rescheduled their external debt whether to official or private sector creditors in the previous five years. Zone B comprises all countries not in Zone A.

[92] See below, para. 1–080.

institutions incorporated in Zone A or Zone B if residual maturity is one year or less, claims on or guaranteed by Zone A public sector entities, and certain holdings of government securities which attract a weighting as a proxy for market risk such as Zone A central government and central bank fixed rate paper with a remaining term to maturity of over one year;

50% which includes loans to individuals fully secured by a first priority charge on residential property;

100% which includes assets such as claims on the non-bank private sector, claims on credit institutions incorporated in Zone B with a residual maturity of over one year, claims on Zone B central governments and central banks (not denominated in the national currency and not funded in that currency), claims on commercial companies owned by the public sector and claims on Zone B public sector entities.

There are a number of circumstances where there is a variation in treatment of assets for calculating risk weighted assets, such as loan transfers and securitisation[93] and collateral and netting.[94]

As noted above, off-balance sheet items are also taken into account. Such items are risk-weighted according to the above rules after having been converted into corresponding on-balance sheet assets. There are four conversion categories:

0% which includes endorsements of bills and other commitments such as formal standby facilities and credit lines with an original maturity of up to one year or which can be unconditionally cancelled at any time;

20% which includes short-term self-liquidating trade related contingent items (such as documentary credits collateralised by the underlying shipments);

50% which includes transaction-related contingent items not having the character of direct credit substitutes (such as performance bonds and standby letters of credit related to particular transactions), note issuance facilities and revolving underwriting facilities and other commitments (such as formal standby facilities and credit lines) with an original maturity of over one year;

---

[93] Assets which otherwise would normally be weighted may be removed from the supervisory balance sheet providing requirements set by the FSA are met—see the discussion of the requirements on loan transfers and securitisation at para. 1–097 below.

[94] Where an exposure to a counterparty is collateralised, a lower risk weight may be applied. The FSA will only recognise certain types of collateral for reduced risk weighting purposes. In addition, the use of netting agreements may reduce exposure to a counterparty. See below, para. 1–123.

100% which includes direct credit substitutes including general guarantees of indebtedness, sale and repurchase agreements and asset sales with recourse where the credit risk remains with the bank and forward asset purchases.

1–080 ***ii Proxies for market risk.*** In the 1988 Capital Accord it was agreed that to reflect the market or investment risks in holdings of government securities, supervisory authorities should be free to apply either a zero or low weight to claims on governments and central banks.

The FSA applies 10 per cent and 20 per cent weight proxies for holdings of certain government and central bank securities in the banking book (these have been included in the five categories detailed above).

1–081 ***iii Foreign exchange risk.*** Annex III of the Capital Adequacy Directive (CAD—Directive 93/6) as amended by the amending Capital Adequacy Directive (CAD2—Directive 98/31) implemented in the United Kingdom on September 30, 1998, sets out the requirements for calculating capital in respect of foreign exchange positions in an institution's banking and trading books.

A bank which has net open positions in foreign currencies either because of foreign exchange trading positions or because of exposures caused by its overall assets and liabilities, is exposed to the risk that the relevant exchange rate or rates might move against it. In accordance with CAD, institutions are set capital charges for foreign exchange position risk in the banking and trading books combined. Non-CAD banks should calculate foreign exchange capital requirements on banking book foreign exchange exposure but are not subject to other trading book capital charges.

The method for calculating the capital requirement for an institution's foreign exchange exposures is to calculate the net open position in each currency and then translate those amounts into the base currency (the currency in which an institutions capital is predominately denominated and in which its statutory accounts are reported) at the prevailing spot rates. The sum of all net foreign exchange long positions and net foreign exchange short positions are then calculated. The overall net foreign exchange open position is the larger of the two. The capital charge is 8 per cent of the overall net foreign exchange open position.

1–082 ***iv Commodity position risk.*** A commodity includes for this purpose any physical product which is or can be traded on a secondary market. It is often the case that commodity markets are less liquid than those for interest rates and currencies and consequently shifts in supply and demand may have a more significant effect on price and volatility than for other types of product. There are three arrangements for measuring and calculating the capital charges for commodity position risk these are:

(1) the internal models approach. A bank may use its internal model as the basis of calculating its capital requirements on its commodity positions. The use of such models is permitted only where a number of qualitative and quantitative standards are met;

(2) the maturity ladder approach. When using the maturity ladder approach, an institution must first express each commodity position in terms of a standard unit of measurement and the position should then be assigned to one of seven maturity or time bands. Under this procedure, a bank can off-set long and short positions in a given commodity which mature on the same day or which mature within ten days of each other, and is not required to include these off-set positions in the maturity ladder calculations. Subject to this, matched long and short positions in each time band incur a capital charge. Once a bank has completed the functions of pre-processings and matching, it may have either a net long or short position in the relevant commodity. A capital charge of 15 per cent applies to this net open position. The same level of percentage charges applies to each commodity. A bank which wishes to have a more commodity specific assessment of its market risk should adopt the models approach; and

(3) the simplified approach. In calculating the capital requirement under the simplified approach, a charge equal to 15 per cent of the overall net open position, long or short, is incurred in respect of each commodity. To guard further against basis risk, interest rate risk and forward gap risk, the total capital charge for each commodity is subject to an additional capital charge equal to 3 per cent of an institution's gross position, long plus short, in the relevant commodity.

Measurement of risk in the trading book. The framework relating to the trading book is only relevant to CAD banks. **1–083**

The trading book includes:

(a) financial instruments held for trading purposes;

(b) exposures due to unsettled transactions;

(c) certain exposures due to repo and reverse repo agreements, securities lending and borrowing; and

(d) certain exposures in the form of fees, commission, interest, dividends and margins, etc., which are directly related to certain items included in the trading book.

i Interest rate position risk. Interest rate risk is the exposure of an institution to loss through movements in interest rates. The CAD framework divides interest rate risk arising in an institution's trading book between general market interest rate risk, and specific interest rate risk. In addition to the interest rate position risk, debt instruments and related derivatives may also give rise to foreign exchange, counterparty risk and/or incremental large exposures capital requirements. **1–084**

The FSA's Banking Supervisory Policy provides that in measuring its positions an institution may net, by value, long and short positions in the same debt instrument to generate the individual net position in that instrument. Instruments are considered to be the same where the issuer is the same, they have the equivalent ranking in a liquidation and the currency, the coupon and maturity are the same. A bank may net by value a long and short position in one tranche of a debt instrument against another tranche of the same instrument only where the relevant tranches rank *pari passu* in all respects, and become fungible within 180 days and thereafter the debt instruments of one tranche can be delivered in settlement of the other tranche.

Unless, a value at risk model[95] approach is adopted, interest rate position risk is divided into "general market risk" and specific risk. Capital requirements for both elements are calculated separately and then aggregated (sometimes referred to as the "building block" approach).

The CAD method for general market interest rate risk is designed to measure the risk, currency by currency, in future cash-flows in the trading book. It makes allowance for institutions to reduce the risks arising from trading activities by hedging long and short positions. Capital is then required to cover those positions which are unhedged or imperfectly hedged.

The "specific" interest rate risk capital requirement relates primarily to the creditworthiness of the issuers of the particular securities concerned.

1–085 ***ii Equity position risk.*** A bank which holds equity positions (whether long or short) in its trading book is exposed to both specific and general equity position risk. A CAD bank is therefore subject to capital requirements for both. Specific equity position risk is the risk that the value of equity positions in individual companies relative to the market may move against the bank. The specific equity position risk capital requirements recognise that individual equities are subject to issuer risk and liquidity risk, and that these risks may be reduced by portfolio diversification. General equity position risk is a risk that the equity market as a whole may move against the bank.

1–086 ***iii counterparty risk.*** In general, counterparty risk is only present in the trading book on deals that are not fully settled. By their nature derivative contracts involve a delay between the transaction date and some future maturity date. The time delay creates two types of risk for that bank, market risk (that the market price will move against the bank, so that when the position matures it will make a loss) and counterparty risk. Counterparty risk in the trading book is the risk that at some future date some party, other than (in the case of a securities transaction) the issuer of the

[95] The use of a value at risk model to measure risk is discussed below, paras 1–089–1–092.

underlying security, fails to complete a contract, resulting in loss for the bank. A bank must hold capital in respect of both market and counterparty risks in its trading book. The counterparty risk weights used for trading counterparties are the same as those used in the banking book. When exposures are collateralised by securities, the risk weight is that applicable to the security.

iv Incremental capital for large exposures. A large exposure is not permitted to exceed 25 per cent of an institution's large exposures capital base (LECB)[96] unless it arises as a result of long securities positions in a CAD bank's trading book, in which case a regime of "soft limits" may be agreed in writing with the FSA. In this case, the bank's LECB may be enlarged to include any Tier 3 capital eligible to support the trading book. If the exposure then exceeds 25 per cent of the enlarged LECB, an incremental capital requirement must be included in the capital adequacy calculation for the excess over 25 per cent. Therefore an exposure which exceeds 25 per cent of the LECB but not 25 per cent of the amended LECB does not result in an incremental capital requirement. The incremental capital requirement applies on a solo (or solo-consolidated) basis and on a consolidated basis. **1–087**

v Underwriting risks. Underwriting is the arrangement under which an institution agrees to buy, before issue, a specified quantity of the securities in a new share or debt security issue (or issue of securities which are new to the market) on a given date and at a given price if no other purchaser has come forward. The purpose is to provide insurance to the company issuing securities against the risk that those securities will be under subscribed. **1–088**

All positions arising from underwriting commitments are treated as part of the trading book, owing to the fact that the nature of underwriting is such that the underwriter's exposure is usually for a very short time. A bank that has an underwriting commitment is subject not only to capital requirements but also to large exposure requirements.

The use of models to measure market risks

i CAD1 models. CAD (referred to in this context as "CAD1" to distinguish it from the amendment to CAD, (CAD2)) allowed the use of computer models in the calculation of capital adequacy requirements for certain very limited purposes. **1–089**

In accordance with CAD1, the FSA allows banks to use their internal models for the purpose of calculating CAD trading book capital requirements for market risk, so as to enable banks with good risk management systems to benefit from more accurate capital requirement than those generated by standard rules. The FSA must formally recognise a bank's

[96] For a detailed description of the rationale for the FSA's policy on large exposures and the obligations imposed upon banks and supervisors see the Chapter entitled, "Large Exposures" in the FSA's Guide to Banking Supervisory Policy.

models prior to their use for the calculation of capital requirements. Banks may perform their own internal risk assessment using models, without prior reference to the FSA. It is only where a bank wishes to use its internal models for the calculation of capital requirements that model recognition is required. The FSA recognises models only where it is satisfied that there are adequate and appropriate risk management systems in place.

The two models eligible for recognition under CAD1 are risk aggregation models and option pricing models. Risk aggregation models are models which summarise and facilitate the management of risk. The types of risk aggregation models that the FSA can recognise for CAD purposes are options risk aggregation models and interest rate sensitivity models.

1–090 A bank may use option risk aggregation models for interest rate, equity, foreign currency and commodity options. These models are used to analyse the aggregate option risk for each underlying instrument and, depending on the type of model, may be used to calculate the capital charge directly, provide inputs for the normal capital calculation or a combination of the two.

A bank which marks to market[97] daily, and manages the interest rate risk on derivative instruments on a discounted cashflow[98] basis, may use sensitivity models to calculate weighted positions for inclusion in the interest rate duration approach. To be eligible for recognition, interest rate risk models must include the following essential elements: cashflow generation, discount factors, net present values and changes in response to shifts in the yield curve.

1–091 Prior to recognition of a CAD1 model certain standards have to be met in both of the following areas:

(1) the mathematics of the model and the underlying assumptions; and
(2) systems and controls including risk management, reporting procedures and limits, staffing issues, reconciliation and valuation procedures, and the setting of capital requirements.

The standards vary depending on the size of the firm, the nature of the business and the models being used. Any models for which recognition is sought must form part of the day to day risk management mechanisms used by the bank. The bank should have the ability to control and monitor its positions through a timely risk management system and should have access to a liquid market in hedging instruments.

1–092 ***ii Internal "value at risk" models.*** CAD2 enabled risk models to be used for more extensive purposes. In accordance with CAD2, models may now be

[97] Marking to market is the practice of revaluing a tradeable asset by reference to current market price.

[98] A discounted cashflow establishes the relative worth of an instrument by discounting the expected cashflows from the instrument to give the net present value.

used to calculate capital charges for interest rate exposure and equity exposure in the trading book and for foreign exchange exposure and commodity exposure in the banking and trading book. Internal models are an alternative to calculations under the standard approach set out above. The use of internal models to calculate market risk capital requirements is intended to allow banks whose risk management is based on an internal model to measure their market risk more accurately than is possible under the CAD standard approach.

The methodology underpinning the internal model approach is "value at risk", a measure which provides an estimate of the worst expected loss on a portfolio resulting from market movements over a particular period of time (10 working days), using data taken from an historical observation period of at least 250 days (unless a shorter observation period is justified by a change in price volatility) at a given confidence level (99 per cent one-tailed confidence level). The forecast maximum loss produced by the model is then multiplied by a factor of at least three (sometimes more)[99] to produce the required amount of capital to be held in respect of the portfolio.

The FSA believes that value at risk is a useful tool for measuring and **1–093**
managing market risk but requires that models should be supported by other forms of risk measurement, such as stress testing, sensitivity analysis and adequate systems for providing information on positions. It is crucial that those responsible for managing the market risk at a bank should be aware of the assumptions and limitations of the bank's internal model.

The use of an internal model to calculate capital requirements for market risks is conditional upon the FSA's explicit prior permission. The FSA must be satisfied that a bank's internal controls, risk management and risk measurement model used to calculate value at risk meet a minimum standard. Risk management refers to the wider environment in which the model operates whereas the risk measurement refers specifically to the internal value at risk model. One of the best assurances of a model's quality is that the bank uses it as an integral part of its own risk management process (although the FSA does not regard this as a sufficient assurance). The FSA therefore attaches great importance to basing capital requirements on the output of a bank's own internal model and not on a parallel model that has been developed specifically to calculate market risk capital requirements.

The FSA will wish to be assured that a bank has considered the impact of **1–094**
material error either in the assumptions underlying the model or in the predicted market moves. Consequently, the FSA will wish to ensure that a programme of stress testing is in place. The results of stress testing should form a key component of a bank's assessment of its capital position. Stress testing is a way of identifying the risk to a bank posed by a breakdown of

---

[99] See below, para. 1–095.

model assumptions or by low-probability events. A bank should use the results to evaluate its capacity to absorb such losses and, if necessary, to identify steps that can be taken to reduce risk by, for example, hedging or reducing the size of any type of exposure. As part of the model recognition process, the FSA will examine a bank's stress testing programme, including the procedures in place to assess and respond to its results. The FSA will wish to see evidence that the bank periodically and actively identifies the full spectrum of worse case scenarios that are relevant to its portfolio. Stress testing results should be communicated routinely to senior management and periodically to the board of directors. A bank will be expected to have the capacity to run stress tests daily. The FSA recognises that more complex stress tests may be conducted at longer intervals or on an ad hoc basis.

1–095 Backtesting is another method of assessing the quality of a model. It compares the model's output—a value at risk forecast—with the corresponding trading outcome. The FSA requires that backtesting should be used as one means of validating internal models. The backtesting system is designed so that the more often a model has under predicted losses in the past, the higher is the capital requirement based on the model. An exception occurs each time a day's loss exceeds the corresponding value at risk measure. The multiplier which is to be applied to the maximum forecast loss depends on the number of exceptions recorded in each rolling period of 250 days. The minimum multiplication factor of three will increase if five or more exceptions are recorded. The extent to which banks meet the qualitative standards may also influence the level at which the FSA will set the multiplication factor.

1–096 ***Credit derivatives.*** "Credit derivatives" is a general term used to describe various swap, option and similar contracts designed to transfer credit risks on loans or other assets from one party to another. Banks may use credit derivatives for a number of reasons including to reduce capital required to support assets on the balance sheet.

The Capital Accord and E.U. Directives do not explicitly cover credit derivatives. In its Banking Supervisory Policy, the FSA has stated that its aim in settling capital requirements for these instruments is to achieve consistency where possible with the capital and large exposures treatment of other similar instruments.

1–097 ***Securitisation and loan transfers.*** The FSA's Banking Supervisory Policy[1] sets out various requirements which must be met if the FSA is to recognise for capital adequacy purposes any purported transfer by a bank of a loan asset. These requirements (the most recent of which were introduced on Decem-

[1] See the Chapter entitled, "Securitisation and Asset Transfers" in the FSAs Guide to Banking Supervisory Policy.

ber 31, 1999) are designed to ensure that the institution has genuinely transferred the risk of the relevant asset.

A transfer of a loan asset through novation is regarded as a clean transfer and the loan is therefore excluded from the selling bank's capital ratio.[2] A legal or equitable assignment, if properly structured, can also achieve an effective transfer of the seller's rights, but not its obligations, and the remedies available to him to enforce those rights. A transfer through an assignment duly notified to the borrower is regarded as clean transfer, provided that the buyer has taken reasonable precautions to ensure that his rights under the transfer are not impaired by an intervening right, for example a right of set-off between seller and borrower.

A silent assignment (where the borrower is not notified) is usually **1–098**
regarded as a clean transfer subject to the following conditions:

(1) the volume of loans to individual borrowers sold on a silent assignment basis is subject to appropriate internal controls; and

(2) the seller must keep under careful review the continuing risks arising from its position as lender of record and therefore the focal point of pressure from the borrower.

If it is not satisfied on these points, the FSA may disregard a transfer of a loan asset through a silent assignment and include it in the calculation of the capital ratio of the seller.

Where a loan asset is funded in whole or in part by a sub-participation, the FSA recognises the transfer of credit risk by excluding it (or the relevant part) from the original lender's capital ratio and including it in the sub-participant's as a claim on the underlying borrower. The sub-participant also faces additional risks since it assumes an exposure to the borrower, but is also at risk to the seller because it relies on the seller to pass through funds received from the borrower.

The sale of a single loan asset, part of a loan or packaging, securitisation **1–099**
and sale of loan asset pools (as well as the transfer of risk under sub-participation agreements) by a bank are excluded from the bank's capital ratio provided that various specific conditions (designed to ensure that the bank has genuinely transferred its risk) are met.

Securitisation involves the additional step of the issue of tradeable paper typically backed by the income stream generated by a discreet portfolio of loan assets. The FSA considers the totality of a bank's involvement when assessing the completeness of the clean break and any residual moral or legal risk to which a securitisation transaction gives rise. An originator of

[2] In a novation, the existing loan between originator and borrower is cancelled and a new agreement between investor and a borrower is substituted. This effectively transfers all the seller's rights and obligations to the buyer.

loans, who continues to administer or service them after they have been transferred, or which has other involvement with the securitisation vehicle, can run significant operational and moral risks. Its continued identification with the loan can mean that the bank's commercial reputation is committed and a completely clean break is therefore not achieved. The FSA has detailed rules dealing with the extent to which such continuing involvement is permissible if the relevant loans are to be treated as having been removed from the balance sheet.

The originating bank may also provide credit enhancement to support a securitisation structure. Depending on the type of credit enhancement, the bank will either be required to deduct the amount of the facility from its capital or include the assets within the bank's risk weighted asset ratio under normal rules as if there had been no securitisation.

1–100 *(iii) Required capital ratio.* When all of a bank's on- and off-balance sheet assets have been risk-weighted it is possible to calculate the amount of capital required to be held by such bank in order to meet potential losses.

1–101 ***i Trigger ratios.*** A bank is required by the 1987 Act to maintain adequate capital at all times. To demonstrate this, banks must meet, on a continuing basis, the capital ratio set by the FSA. This is the "trigger" ratio, the minimum capital ratio for a bank which is acceptable for the purposes of meeting the 1987 Act's criteria. The absolute minimum trigger ratio required by both the Capital Accord and the E.U.'s Solvency Ratio Directive is 8 per cent (*i.e.* a bank must hold an amount of capital equivalent to at least 8 per cent of its risk-weighted assets). However, it is the FSA's practice to set the trigger ratio for most banks significantly above this figure. The size of the trigger ratio applied to any particular bank is ratio based on the FSA's overall assessment of the risk that such bank faces and the quality of its risk management. The trigger ratio is reviewed periodically to ensure that it continues to reflect the bank's risk profile. In the event of a significant deterioration in a bank's risk profile, the FSA may consider increasing the ratio to reflect increased risk. Any breach of a trigger ratio by a bank is a serious matter since it indicates that a bank has insufficient capital safely to support the risks of its business and is therefore unable to satisfy one of the Schedule 3 Criteria.

1–102 ***ii Target ratios.*** The FSA also imposes a target ratio, which will always be somewhat higher than the trigger ratio. The purpose of a target ratio is to act as a warning light that the cushion of capital resources normally considered adequate to prevent an accidental breach of the trigger ratio is being eroded. Banks are generally expected to meet their target ratios at all times. In the event of a planned breach of a target ratio, the FSA's Banking Supervisory Policy requires a bank to demonstrate to the FSA's satisfaction that it has both adequate systems to monitor its position in relation to its target ratio on a continuing basis (as with its trigger ratio) and the ability to restore its actual ratio above target.

Although an institution is required to meet its capital requirements at all times on a continuing basis, the monitoring of capital ratios by the FSA normally takes place using the quarterly and semi annual returns.

Business to be conducted in a prudent manner—(2) liquidity

General. Another major cause of financial difficulties for a bank, often closely linked in practice to a deterioration or perceived deterioration of asset quality, is a lack of sufficient liquidity to meet its day-to-day liabilities. Sufficient liquidity is a precondition of a bank's survival. Accordingly, banking regulators require banks to hold adequate liquid funds to meet their liabilities as they fall due. **1–103**

Liquidity is defined as a bank's ability to meet its obligations as they fall due. A bank's obligations would typically include requirements to repay deposits, requirements to supply committed funds and requirements to make other payments such as cashflows in respect of off-balance sheet instruments, interest payments and other expenses.

The exact level of liquidity required is determined separately for each bank, as it is the view of the FSA that the requirement must take into account each bank's special circumstances (including the nature of its banking activities, the size of the bank, the strength of its management, any potential liquidity problems or other developments which could affect the liquidity of the institution, arising either within its group or other companies connected to the institution). Most of the factors relating to the assessment of capital adequacy will also be relevant when judging the adequacy of liquidity.

The FSA has stated in the 1998 Statements of Principles that it expects every institution to formulate a statement of its "liquidity management policy" and to agree guidelines with the FSA by which adherence to the policy can be assessed. Schedule 3 to the 1987 Act requires banks to maintain adequate systems. Banks must therefore have in place systems which enable them to monitor the liquidity profile on a frequent and timely basis. The adequacy of the systems in place for monitoring liquidity is checked through the section 39 process[3] and through review team visits. The policy statement is in particular required to identity any particular strengths and weaknesses of the institution and analyse its capacity to survive a crisis. The policy statement will be used as the basis for discussions with the FSA with the objective of agreeing minimum liquidity standards for the individual bank in question. **1–104**

A bank must satisfy the FSA on an ongoing basis that it has a prudent liquidity policy, and adequate management systems in place to ensure that the policy is adhered to. A bank should notify the FSA of any breaches of its liquidity mismatch guidelines as soon as they occur.

[3] See below, paras 1–145–1–147.

1–105 **The maturity mismatch approach.** In the majority of cases the FSA monitors a bank's liquidity position through the maturity mismatch approach. In the maturity ladder approach, assets and liabilities are slotted into time bands according to their maturity on a worst case view, with assets (inflows) put in at their latest maturity and liabilities (outflows) at their earliest maturity. This approach is adopted because what is needed is an assessment of a bank's liquidity in a situation when funding sources are unwilling to lend and depositors withdraw their money. A net mismatch figure is obtained by subtracting liabilities from assets in each time band. Mismatches are then measured on a net cumulative basis. This is achieved by cumulating the net positions in each successive time band to arrive at a net overall cumulative mismatch figure. The FSA normally assesses a bank's liquidity position by means of the net cumulative mismatch position expressed as a percentage of total deposit liabilities. The FSA sets recommended guidelines for the maximum percentage for net cumulative mismatches to a percentage of the total deposit. These are known as mismatch guidelines. These prevent banks operating with too large a negative mismatch, and therefore running an excessive risk of not being able to raise sufficient funds to cover the mismatch at short notice. Mismatch guidelines are normally only set for time bands of sight—eight days and sight—one month. Mismatch guidelines are not usually set for longer time bands as over a longer time period, in most cases, banks will have a greater opportunity to raise funds, and therefore a larger negative mismatch is not such a concern.

1–106 **Sterling stock liquidity.** The maturity mismatch approach is unsuitable for United Kingdom incorporated retail banks because their liabilities are dominated by sterling retail deposits which are repayable at call or short notice but which on aggregate are in practice generally stable over time. For these banks, holding an appropriate stock of sterling liquidity against an unexpected loss of funding is more important. For a bank to use this approach, the FSA's written agreement is required. Banks to which this approach applies are still required to monitor their foreign currency liquidity according to the maturity mismatch approach.

1–107 The key element of the FSA's sterling stock liquidity policy is that a bank should hold a stock of sterling liquid assets that can be sold quickly and discreetly in order to replace funding which has been withdrawn owing to some actual or perceived problem with the bank. The objective is that this stock should tide the bank over for a period of five working days, thus providing a breathing space in which the bank can try to arrange more permanent funding solutions. A sterling stock liquidity bank must include in the statement of its liquidity management policy to be agreed with the FSA, its intention to:

(1) maintain an internal limit for its maximum wholesale sterling net outflow over the next five working days (as agreed with the FSA);

(2) hold, as a minimum requirement, a stock of sterling liquid assets sufficient to cover the minimum floor (as agreed with the FSA);

(3) ensure that its sterling stock liquidity ratio is at least 100 per cent; and

(4) notify the FSA of any breaches.

A sterling stock liquidity bank should monitor its compliance with a sterling stock liquidity requirement on a daily basis. Such a bank should ensure that the details of its floor and limits are communicated to the relevant personnel and effectively managed. The floor or limit should not be changed without the prior written agreement of the FSA.

Business to be conducted in a prudent manner—(3) provisioning

Schedule 3, paragraph 4(6) of the BA 1987 requires a bank to have adequate provisions. This requirement applies to all authorised banks except European authorised institutions. This requirement mirrors provisions of the Companies Act 1985 (CA 1985) and requires that an institution adopt a policy on provisioning which covers provisioning for depreciation or diminution in the value of an institution's assets, for liabilities that will or are expected to fall to be discharged and for any losses which it will or expects to incur. **1–108**

The provisioning policy must also include a description of (a) the methods and systems for monitoring the recoverability of loans (e.g. monitoring of the financial health of counterparties, their future prospects, the prospects of the market and geographical areas in which they operate, arrears patterns and credit scoring techniques), (b) the frequency with which provisions are reviewed, and (c) the policy and practices for taking and valuation of security and the extent to which valuation exceeds the balance-sheet value of the secured loans.

The FSA's Banking Supervisory Policy makes clear that, as with all aspects of a bank's business, the board as a whole should have overall responsibility for drawing up and monitoring the policy. A bank's board, or a bank's audit committee, on behalf of the board, must approve the policies, but it is important, however, that one of the executive directors has particular responsibility for the bank's provisioning policies. Also, a member of the bank's senior management team should have responsibility for monitoring implementation of the policy on a day to day basis and for ensuring that all relevant members of staff are aware of the policy. Once the policies are in place, they must be reviewed at least annually to ensure that they are still appropriate for the business the bank undertakes and the economic environment in which it operates. This should be undertaken by a member of the senior management team in the first instance and reviewed and approved by the audit committee or the board. **1–109**

Business to be conducted in a prudent manner—(4) Accounting, other records and systems of control

1–110 Paragraph 4(7) of Schedule 3 requires an institution to keep adequate records and systems of control. Paragraph 4(8) provides that an institution's records and systems will not be regarded as adequate unless they are such as to enable the business to be prudently managed and the institution to comply with the duties imposed on it by or under the BA 1987.

1–111 **Adequate accounting and other records.** In order to ensure consistency and transparency of the information provided by banks and in order to enable comparisons of the financial strength of individual banks, general reporting standards in relation to accounts have been introduced.

The United Kingdom rules are based on the E.U. Directive on the Annual Accounts and Consolidated Accounts of Banks and other Financial Institutions (the Accounts Directive). The Accounts Directive has been implemented in respect of banks in the United Kingdom by regulations made under the Companies Act 1985 (CA 1985). These regulations specify (a) the layout of a bank's balance sheet; (b) the layout of a bank's profit and loss account; (c) the valuation rules to be used by banks; (d) the contents of the notes on the accounts of a bank; (e) provisions relating to consolidated accounts, and (f) provisions relating to publication of accounts and auditing.

1–112 **Systems and internal control.** The strength of the internal control environment[4] is important for banks, as a weak internal control environment can undermine an otherwise sound business. The scope and nature of adequate internal control systems should take account of the size of the business, the diversity of operations, the volume and size of transactions, the degree of risk associated with each area of operation, the amount of control by senior management over day to day operations and the degree of centralisation and the extent of reliance on information technology. A system of internal control should be designed and operated to provide reasonable assurance that all the bank's revenue accrues to its benefit, all expenditure is properly authorised and disbursed, all assets are adequately safeguarded, all liabilities are recorded and all statutory requirements relating to the provision of accounts are complied with and all prudential reporting conditions are adhered to.

It is the responsibility of directors and management to review, monitor and test its systems of internal control on a regular basis in order to ensure their effectiveness on a day to day basis and their continuing relevance to

[4] "Control environment" means the overall attitude, awareness and actions of directors and management regarding internal controls and their importance in the entity. The control environment encompasses the management style, the corporate culture and value shared by all employees.

the business. In many banks an internal audit function assists management by providing an independent review of such systems.

The scope and nature of the specific control objectives which are required for the business to be conducted in a prudent manner should be commensurate with a bank's needs and particular circumstances and should have regard to the manner in which the business is structured, organised and managed, to its size and the nature, volume and complexity of its transactions and commitments. The FSA considers that each bank should address the following control objectives: **1–113**

(a) Organisational structure. A bank should have documented the high level controls in its organisation which define allocated responsibilities, identity lines of reporting for all aspects of the enterprise's operations, including the key controls and giving outline job descriptions for key personnel. The delegation of authority and responsibility should be clearly specified. A bank should also document its risk management framework, setting out how the risks in the business are identified measured, maintained and controlled.

(b) Monitoring procedures. A bank should have procedures in place to ensure that relevant and accurate management information covering the financial state of performance of the bank and the exposures which the bank has entered into are provided to appropriate levels of management on a regular and timely basis.

(c) Segregation of duties. A prime means of control is the separation of those responsibilities or duties which would, if combined, enable one individual to record and process a complete transaction. Segregation of duties reduces the risk of intentional manipulation or error and increases the element of checking. Functions which should be separated include those of authorisation, execution, valuation, reconciliation, custody and recording.

(d) Authorisation and approval. All transactions should require authorisation or approval by an appropriate person.

(e) Completeness and accuracy. A bank should have controls to ensure that all transactions to be recorded and processed have been authorised, are correctly recorded and are accurately processed. Such controls include checking the arithmetical accuracy of the records, checking valuations, the maintenance and checking of totals, reconciliations, control accounts and trial balances and accounting for documents.

(f) Safeguarding assets. A bank should have controls designed to ensure that access to assets or information is limited to authorised personnel.

(g) Personnel. There should be procedures to ensure that personnel have capabilities commensurate with their responsibilities. The

> proper functioning of any system depends on the competence and integrity of those operating it. The qualifications, recruitment and training as well as the innate personal characteristics of the personnel involved are important features to be considered in setting up any control system.

It is a requirement of the Money Laundering Regulations 1993 (MLR 1993) that authorised banks have policies and procedures in place to guard against their business and the financial system being used for the purpose of money laundering.

Integrity and skill

1–114 An institution must carry out its business with integrity, which is defined as a requirement that the institution will observe high ethical standards. Criminal offences such as fraud, other breaches of statute, such as consumer protection, company or banking legislation, as well as non-compliance with recognised ethical standards of conduct such as various codes of conduct, indicate that the business is not carried out with integrity.

An institution's business must also be conducted with the professional skills appropriate to the nature and scale of its activities. The FSA has stated in its 1998 Statements of Principles that "professional skills" cover the general skills which bankers should have when they carry out the business as bankers in relation to (a) accounting, (b) risk analysis, (c) the establishment and operation of systems of internal controls, and (d) ensuring compliance with legal and supervisory requirements and in the standard of the various financial services provided to customers. The level of skill will vary in each individual case and depend upon the nature and scale of an individual institution's business.

Minimum net assets

1–115 A United Kingdom incorporated credit institution must have at the time it is authorised initial capital amounting to not less than five million Euros (or an amount of equal value determined wholly or partly in another unit of account)[5] which it must maintain as a minimum in order for its capital to be sufficient for the purpose of paragraph 4 of Schedule 3 to the BA 1987.

Large exposures

1–116 Experience has shown that large exposures are one of the major causes of bank failure. In the United Kingdom regulation of large exposures is contained in:

[5] Sched. 3 to BA 1987 that implemented Art. 4 of the Second Council Directive on the own funds of credit institutions ([1989] O.J. L124/16).

(a) section 38 of the BA 1987;

(b) the FSA Banking Supervisory Policy implementing the E.U. Directive on the Monitoring and Control of Large Exposures of Credit Institutions (the LED—Directive 92/121);

(c) the FSA Banking Supervisory Policy implementing CAD, which lays down "soft limits" for exposures within the trading book.

Section 38 of the BA 1987 requires an authorised institution, other than one whose principal place of business is outside of the United Kingdom, to notify the FSA in advance of any proposed exposure to any one person exceeding 25 per cent of its capital base and to report to the FSA any actual exposure to any one person exceeding 10 per cent of its capital base. The statutory notification requirements of section 38 of the BA 1987 apply on a solo basis (or, if applicable, on a solo-consolidated basis). The FSA also requires, as a matter of policy, banks to meet the notification requirements on a consolidated basis.

LED

With the implementation of the LED the notification requirements **1–117**
under section 38 of the BA 1987 were supplemented by a prohibition on certain large exposures.

The LED sets limits and reporting requirements at a consolidated level. In implementing it, the FSA decided also to apply these on a solo (or solo-consolidated) basis. There are two primary limits:

(1) an overall limit on the aggregate of large exposures that may be undertaken. A bank must limit the total of its exposures, other than its exempt exposures, to individual counterparties or groups of closely related counterparties exceeding 10 per cent of capital base to a maximum of 800 per cent of the bank's (or the banking group's consolidated) capital base. The total of these exposures should not exceed 300 per cent of a bank's large exposures capital base without the FSA's written approval. The 300 per cent and 800 per cent limits apply whether the exposures arise in the banking or the trading book, since exposures in both books must be aggregated.

(2) a limit on the size of individual exposures. A bank may not incur exposures to an individual counterparty which exceeds 25 per cent of the bank's consolidated capital base (subject to the exception introduced by CAD.

Because of the possibility that the risk assessment of proposed loans to **1–118**
counterparties connected to a bank may be obscured by subjective considerations, the FSA pays particular attention to lending to parties connected to the institution or its management. A bank or banking group's exposures

to all connected counterparties outside the scope of consolidated returns may, when taken together, not exceed 25 per cent of capital base.

The LECB used as the basis for monitoring and controlling large exposures should be calculated as the sum of allowable Tier 1 and Tier 2 capital, less any deductions. An amended LECB, including any eligible Tier 3 capital available to support non-counterparty risk in the trading book, is used if and only if soft limits have been agreed to enable a non-exempt exposure to a single counterparty or to a group of closely related counterparties to exceed the 25 per cent limit as a result of long securities positions in the trading book.

1–119 The LED limits large exposures to both individual counterparties and groups of closely related counterparties. A counterparty will normally be the borrower (*i.e.* the customer of the bank), the person guaranteed (where the bank is providing such a guarantee), the issuer of a security in the case of a security held or the party with whom a contract was made in the case of a derivatives contract.

Certain exposures (*e.g.* short term exposures to other banks, exposures to Zone A central government or central banks, some exposures to Zone B central governments and central banks, and some secured exposures) are exempt from the limitations described above.

CAD

1–120 The implementation of CAD has introduced special rules relating to large exposures within the trading book.

CAD introduced a new feature, soft limits, whereby group large exposures attributable to certain positions held in the trading book are permitted to exceed 25 per cent of the capital base but, if they do so, there are extra capital requirements.[6] A bank to which the CAD regime does not apply is not eligible for the soft limits.

A bank may also enter into exposures which exceed the 25 per cent capital limit in other very limited circumstances.

Foreign exchange

1–121 The FSA has adopted a system for supervising foreign exchange risk which is based on risk based supervision (an assessment of a bank's internal limits in relation to its individual internal controls, risk appetite and capital). This approach largely replaces the Bank of England's previous method of monitoring foreign exchange through a system of foreign exchange guidelines, where it set guidelines for a bank's maximum overnight open position and the bank reported its month-end overnight position, together with any breaches of the guidelines intra-month.

[6] See below, para. 1–117.

Before the FSA will supervise a bank under the risk based approach for monitoring foreign exchange risk, the bank must provide the FSA with information needed for the FSA to assess the adequacy of the bank's internal systems and controls and internal limits. Unless the FSA agrees to supervise a bank under the new risk based approach, a bank is required to operate within its existing foreign exchange guidelines. Under the risk based system for supervising foreign exchange risk, banks are supervised in relation to internally set limits. The FSA assesses the adequacy of internal systems and controls relative to the internally set limits and will consider the extent to which a bank is exposed to foreign exchange risk across all of its businesses.

Fraud

Paragraph 4 of Schedule 3 to the BA 1987 requires that a bank has adequate systems and controls, including systems to protect it against imprudent business or criminal activity, in order to be considered to be conducting its business in a prudent manner. A bank should report promptly to the FSA all significant cases of fraud, either by outside parties or from within it, including serious breaches of internal rules by that bank's own staff. **1–122**

Collateral and netting

The Solvency Ratio Directive, which established the framework within the E.U. for measuring credit risk in the assessment of capital adequacy, recognised the use of collateral for reducing credit risk and bilateral netting[7] for reducing credit risk on interest rate and foreign exchange rate contracts. **1–123**

The requirements set out in the FSA's Banking Supervisory Policy apply to all banks which wish to report on a net basis or use collateral for reducing exposures for capital adequacy or large exposures purposes. The policy applies to all United Kingdom incorporated banks both on a solo (or solo-consolidated) and on a consolidated basis.

In its Banking Supervisory Policy, the FSA's main concern in respect of netting is to ensure that the bank's effective exposure is limited to the net amount under the netting agreement. It is critical that the netting agreement has a well founded legal basis in each relevant jurisdiction, so that the netting process is not invalidated by local law (particularly insolvency law) and that rights of the participants do not revert to being gross claims.

Where collateral is used the FSA seeks to ensure that the collateral agreement is enforceable and the size of the reduction in the capital requirements reflects the value of the collateral provided. **1–124**

[7] Bilateral netting is the netting that takes place between two counterparties.

In order to ensure that there are sufficient unencumbered assets to meet the claims of depositors in a liquidation of a bank the FSA requires that a bank should not give a floating charge over its own assets as security for its own borrowings from banks or other sources.

Where netting is permitted, the reporting should reflect the economic reality of how the bank monitors its exposures to a counterparty and the legal reality. Netting is a term used to describe a process which may involve one of a number of legal techniques. Set-off is the most common. Historically there has been a well established legal right for bankers to be able to set off different accounts of the same customer. Where such a right exists, the FSA is, in principle, prepared to recognise the netting of on-balance sheet items such as loans and deposits. Netting of off-balance sheet items (such as swaps and forward foreign exchange) is generally recognised only where the techniques of netting by novation[8] and close-out netting are adopted and legally enforceable.[9]

Close links

1–125 E.U. supervisors are required by E.U. Directive 95/26 (the Post-BCCI Directive) to refuse authorisation to a credit institution whose structure renders it unsupervisable. The directive as implemented in the United Kingdom by the Financial Institutions (Prudential Supervision) Regulations 1996 made various amendments to the BA 1987. One of the four main provisions of the directive, relating to close links[10] imposed a new obligation upon credit institutions and the FSA. In consequence, the FSA's Banking Supervisory Policy provides that the FSA will refuse authorisation

[8] In netting by novation, obligations between two counterparties to deliver a given amount on a given date are automatically amalgamated with all other obligations to deliver on the same value date. Such netting should have the effect of legally discharging performance of the original obligations and substituting the single net amount as the sole remaining obligation between the counterparties for the relevant value date. Thus a single legally binding new contract extinguishes the former contracts. This technique is used mainly for netting foreign exchange and interest rate contracts.

[9] Close-out netting (often called contractual netting) is a contractual process. It is designed to apply on default of the counterparty, when all outstanding transactions between the counterparties that are subject to the netting agreement are combined and reduced to a single payable sum. There are three stages to the process. Termination, close-out and netting. The loss or cost to each party is calculated according to a prescribed formula, often related to the cost of replacing the transaction by buying an equivalent position in the market at the relevant time. The sums due on both sides may be calculated in or converted into a single currency and netted to one single payment one way or the other. The advantage of this technique is that it allows for risk management on a wider scale than netting by novation. For example, exposures arising from different kinds of product can be netted and different currencies can be netted.

[10] An undertaking is defined as *closely linked* with: (a) any entity which is its parent undertaking; (b) any entity which is its subsidiary undertaking; (c) any entity which is its fellow subsidiary undertaking; and (d) any person in accordance with whose directions or instructions its directors are accustomed to act (*i.e.* an indirect controller as defined in the BA 1987).

(and may revoke authorisation) where a credit institution's "close links" with any other entity prevent effective supervision of the credit institution and requires credit institutions to report the existence of close links with any entity.

Outsourcing

Banks are required adequately to record and control their business. **1–126**
Where the processing which supports a bank's business has been outsourced to another part of the group, or to an external supplier, the FSA's requirements continue to apply with respect to that business. Banks must put into place procedures for monitoring and controlling the outsourced operations.

A bank must make the FSA aware, through its normal supervisory channels, of its intention to outsource a task which, materially, either impacts on its systems and controls or affects its risk profile. During the course of the outsourcing agreement, a bank must make the FSA aware of any material problems encountered with the outsourcing supplier.

Regardless of whether the outsourcing supplier is inside or outside the **1–127**
group, the FSA holds the bank's management responsible for ensuring that the outsourced function is carried out to a proper standard and that the integrity of the bank's systems and controls is maintained. For outsourcing outside the group there must be a right to terminate the contract in the event that the supplier undergoes a change of ownership or the supplier becomes insolvent or goes into liquidation or receivership. A bank must have and regularly review, contingency plans to enable it to set up new arrangements as quickly as possible, with minimum disruption to business, if the contract with the outsourcing supplier is suddenly terminated or the supplier fails.

The FSA requires all banks to have an internal audit function, although it accepts that some banks may wish to discharge this function other than by means of an in-house internal audit department. Although the FSA understands that banks may wish to consult their external auditors for advice on internal audit matters, banks may not outsource outright their internal audit functions to their external auditors or reporting accountants.

Supervision of EEA banks

Credit institutions established within the European Economic Area **1–128**
(EEA) have the right (often referred to as a "passport"), under the Second Banking Directive to carry on business throughout the EEA either by the establishment of branches or on a cross-border basis, subject to meeting certain notification requirements.

The Second Banking Directive details the division of responsibilities of supervisory authorities where an institution carries out activities in a territory of another EEA member state and which activities may be passported.

Division of responsibilities

1–129 Under the Second Banking Directive[11]:

(a) with the exception of liquidity, the home state supervisory authority is responsible for prudential supervision of an institution which carries out relevant activities in the territory of another EEA member state. Supervisory responsibility for liquidity lies with the host country supervisor in co-operation with the home country supervisor. (The "home state" is the member state in which the credit institution is incorporated and authorised. The "host state" is the other member state in which it operates); and

(b) the host state authority retains the right to apply those rules it has itself adopted "in the interest of the general good". The definition of "general good" and the areas of, and the justification for its application have developed with case law. The European Court has held that:

   (i) the principle of the general good could not be applied in areas where there is E.U. harmonisation (the conduct of business rules imposed under the Financial Services Act are an example of rules imposed under the general good principle where there is no E.U. legislation);
   (ii) the principle must be applied in a non-discretionary manner (*i.e.* the host state should not impose measures which are not applied to other banks); and
   (iii) the application of the general good principle must not go beyond what is necessary to obtain it.

Activities that may be passported

1–130 The Second Banking Directive passport is available not just to cover deposit taking but also for carrying out activities. The activities which may be passported are:

(a) acceptance of deposits and other repayable funds from the public;

(b) lending;

(c) financial leasing;

(d) money transmission services;

---

[11] The Second Banking Directive was implemented in the U.K. by the Banking Co-ordination Second Council Directive Regulations 1992 which also amended in part the BA 1987 to reflect the implications of the Second Banking Directive. The procedures to be followed by U.K. institutions passporting out of the U.K. are set out in Part III and Sched. 6 of the Regs. For European institutions passporting into the U.K., the procedures are set out in Part II and Sched. 2.

(e) issuing and administering of payment;

(f) guarantees and commitments;

(g) trading for own account or for account of customers in:

(i) money market instruments;
(ii) foreign exchange;
(iii) financial futures and options;
(iv) exchange and interest rate instruments; or
(v) transferable securities;

(h) participation in share issues and the provision of services related to such issues;

(i) advice to undertakings on capital structure, industrial strategy and related questions and advice and services related to mergers and the purchase of undertakings;

(j) money broking;

(k) portfolio management and advice;

(l) safekeeping and administration of securities;

(m) credit reference agencies; and

(n) safe-custody services.

An institution may only use the passport procedure with the approval of **1–131**
its home state supervisor, which must consider the following before giving approval:

(a) the adequacy of the management to monitor and control the activities of the branch or cross-border activity;

(b) the adequacy of systems and controls to provide management with sufficient information on which to base decisions regarding the branch or cross-border activity;

(c) (for a branch) the presence of relevant skills in the branch for the proposed operations to succeed; and

(d) the financial soundness of the institution as a whole encompassing (at a minimum) capital adequacy, liquidity and the absence of undue concentration of risk.

Passporting rights are available only to credit institutions (and certain other limited categories). A "credit institution" for this purpose is an institution "whose business is to receive deposits or other repayable funds from the public and to grant credits for its own account". Therefore, not all banks authorised under the 1987 Act are credit institutions. An institution may, for example, accept deposits but if they are not accepted from the public or if its business is not to grant credits, it is not a credit institution.

The Process of Ongoing Supervision

The "RATE" Process

1–132 The RATE framework (Risk Assessment, Tools of supervision, Evaluation) is the approach adopted by the FSA for its ongoing supervision of banks. This framework involves undertaking a formal risk assessment of every bank or banking group during each "supervisory period". The length of the period varies according to the risk profile but can be as short as six months for a bank whose risk profile is classified as very high or for a bank undergoing major change, or up to two years or possibly longer, for a bank whose risk profile is low and whose business and control framework are stable.

The formal risk assessment, using nine evaluation factors (capital, assets, market risk, earnings, liabilities, business, controls, organisation and management) is performed by analysing information which the FSA receives during the normal course of its supervision, such as regular prudential returns on the financial position of the bank, or which is acquired through a series of meetings with senior management of the bank. The risk assessment process identifies in a systematic manner the business risks or inherent risks of a bank or banking group, and assesses the adequacy and effectiveness of its controls, organisation structure and management. It also looks at the overall business environment of the bank and the main part of the group, and takes account of those risks which are not inherently quantifiable, including operational, litigation and reputational risk. That assessment is taken into account by the FSA in considering whether the bank continues to meet the minimum criteria for authorisation (Schedule 3 to the BA 1987) and whether specific remedial action is needed, as well as in formulating the supervisory programme for the period ahead.

1–133 After each risk assessment, the FSA feeds back its views on the bank's risk profile to the senior management of the relevant authorised institution. This includes details of any remedial action the FSA is seeking or intends to take, the likely supervisory consequences if this remedial action is not taken promptly and to the FSA's satisfaction (including increasing the bank's capital ratios and, in an extreme ease, revoking the bank's authorisation). The bank will also be informed about the supervisory programme, including which "tools of supervision", such as reporting accountants reports on internal controls, will be used during the supervisory period and the likely timing of their application. In keeping with the risk-based approach, these tools are targeted at areas considered to be of higher risk or to follow-up issues identified during the risk assessment. During the course of the supervisory period the FSA constantly evaluates the information it receives, in particular, the results of applying the tools of supervision.

In practice, the organisation of business and management in a group often does not match its legal structure. In performing a risk assessment, the FSA seeks to understand how the bank's management runs the group from both a business and a control perspective. In identifying business units (an organisational unit which carries on revenue-generating activities and whose revenue is separately identified in the group's management information systems) that should be covered in the risk assessment; the 1998 Statements of Principles state that the FSA normally adopts the approach used by a bank's management.

Consolidation in the context of banking supervision is the technique whereby the activities of all (or some) companies/undertakings within a group are analysed as if the group was one company only, *e.g.* if the capital adequacy ratios are required to be met on a consolidated basis then the group as a whole (*i.e.* a bank and its parent and/or certain subsidiaries) must comply with these ratios on group level. Consolidated supervision may accordingly be defined as the situation where the supervisor monitors whether compliance is achieved at a group level. **1–134**

Consolidated supervision is desirable because there are risks to a bank which arise as a result of its membership of a wider group. These risks include the risk that risks taken by other group companies might undermine the group as a whole, the financial risks taken on by a bank in its links with other group companies, such as inter-group lending, and the reputational risk to a bank if there are losses or other problems elsewhere in the group.[12] At least since the 1974 recession and the subsequent banking crisis, it has become very clear that banking regulators cannot be fully satisfied about the soundness of individual banks unless they can examine the totality of the business of the bank and the wider group of which it forms part, worldwide, through the technique of consolidation. The failure of the Luxembourg-based Banco Ambrosiano Holding in 1982 and BCCI in 1991 and finally Barings in 1995 has confirmed the importance of such consolidated supervision.

The FSA regards consolidated supervision as a compliment to, not a substitute for, solo supervision.

The scope of consolidation

The FSA requires consolidation when the bank in question is itself the parent of companies which conduct one or more of certain specified financial activities. **1–135**

The FSA also requires consolidation where the bank is not the parent company, but is part of a group or sub-group whose business wholly or mainly comprises the above specified activities and the parent of the group or sub-group is itself a financial institution, *i.e.* an institution whose

[12] Although inter-group lending does not show up on consolidated returns, consolidated supervision is relevant to the control of a bank's risks arising from inter-group lending, since its aim is to ensure that the group as a whole is strong enough to cope with the risks run, which otherwise might threaten repayment of inter-group lending.

exclusive or main business is to carry out one or more of the above activities or to acquire holdings in companies that undertake those activities.

The FSA interprets the phrases "mainly" and "main business" to mean the balance of business, *i.e.* it generally requires consolidation when companies carrying out the above activities comprise over 50 per cent of the group or sub-group balance sheet. In determining the balance of the business, the FSA also takes account of the off-balance sheet activities of group companies, and of fee-based services provided by group companies.

1–136 Consolidation extends to all relevant financial companies within the above domain, that is the parent company, its subsidiaries and companies in which the parent or its subsidiaries[13] have a participation. A non-financial subsidiary or participation may be excluded from the consolidation only with the FSA's prior agreement. As provided by Article 3.3 of the second Consolidated Supervision Directive[14] in a limited number of cases the FSA may permit the exclusion from a bank's consolidated returns of subsidiaries or participations which otherwise meet the criteria for consolidation in certain limited cases.

The second Consolidated Supervision Directive[15] contains previous allocating responsibility for consolidated supervision where an authorised institution is part of a wider group containing entities incorporated in other European jurisdictions.

The uses of consolidation

1–137 The FSA's capital adequacy requirements apply on a consolidated as well as on a solo basis.

The FSA states in its Banking Supervisory Policy that it will normally apply the same capital ratio to the group as a whole, as it applies to the principal bank in the group. There are however situations where a consolidated ratio may differ from the solo ratio.

Where a bank fails to meet each consolidated trigger capital ratio, the FSA will consider whether this poses a threat to the bank itself. If the bank is the parent company in the group, the question of whether it continues to fulfil the prudent conduct criterion arises. If the bank is not the parent company of the group, the FSA considers what action is needed to protect the bank. It may also consider whether it continues to fulfil the prudent conduct criterion. The action needed may be, for example, to pursue the controller for a rectification of the capital position, to raise trigger and/or target ratios, to require better liquidity or to restrict lending to other group companies.

[13] As defined in s. 258 of the CA 1985.
[14] Directive 93/30 [1992] O.J. L110/52.
[15] *ibid.*

Consolidated supervision will also be required in connection with large exposures as defined in the LED. A bank must meet the limit and notification requirements in respect of large individual counterparties or groups of closely related counterparties on a consolidated, as well as a solo, basis. **1–138**

Accordingly, banks are required to submit to the FSA consolidated returns covering capital adequacy and large exposures. Such returns must be submitted to the FSA at least twice a year in the case of capital adequacy and at least four times a year in the case of large exposures.

Banks are required to have adequate internal control mechanisms for the production of any data and information which would be relevant for the purposes of supervision on a consolidated basis.

Solo-consolidation

In certain situations, the FSA will allow the inclusion of certain subsidiaries in the calculation and assessment of a bank's individual compliance with the capital adequacy and large exposure requirements. The effect of solo-consolidation is that exposures of a bank to its solo-consolidated subsidiaries are ignored for many capital adequacy and large exposure purposes. **1–139**

Solo-consolidation is a reporting treatment which may be granted for capital adequacy and large exposures reporting. Reporting on a solo-consolidated basis is a substitute for solo (or unconsolidated) reporting. Banks should not report on both a solo-consolidated and a solo basis. In the case of large exposures, the FSA must notify the bank in writing of those subsidiaries which may be solo-consolidated. The aim is to include only those subsidiaries which have a close relationship to the bank, such that it should be possible to wind-up the subsidiary rapidly and repatriate the net assets (to support depositors with the parent). Solo-consolidated subsidiaries must not be a potential source of weakness to the parent.

Solo-consolidation, which results in a subsidiary being treated as effectively a division of a parent bank, will only be allowed if; **1–140**

(a) the subsidiary is at least 75 per cent owned by the bank in question;

(b) either the subsidiary is wholly funded by its parent or all of its exposure to risk is wholly in respect of its parent bank;

(c) the management is under the effective direction of the parent bank;

(d) it is clear that there are no potential obstacles to the payment of surplus capital up to the parent bank, in particular taking account of overseas exchange controls, potential legal and regulatory problems and taxation; and

(e) there is sufficient capital in the bank's own balance sheet to fund its investments in those subsidiaries which are to be solo-consolidated (*i.e.* if the investments were to be deducted rather that solo-consolidated, the parent bank should be left with positive net worth).

Even where all the criteria are met, it is open to supervisors not to permit solo-consolidation. There are additional requirements to those mentioned above where the subsidiary is a bill-issuing subsidiary or an active-trading subsidiary. A United Kingdom authorised bank may not be solo-consolidated with its parent bank.

Periodic Provision of Information

Large exposures notifications and returns

1–141 As outlined earlier in this chapter, a bank must be able to monitor its large exposures on a daily basis. A bank must pre-notify the FSA in writing of all proposed exposures exceeding 25 per cent of its large exposure capital base. A bank must also notify the FSA immediately of any breach of the 800 per cent limit or of any other counterparty limits agreed with the FSA for large exposure purposes. A breach of the 25 per cent limit in particular, other than in the most exceptional circumstances, is sufficient ground for the FSA to consider whether the bank's authorisation should be restricted or revoked. When a breach occurs the FSA will require a bank to agree a timetable to bring the exposure quickly back below 25 per cent or any other agreed limit. The FSA will also require additional capital cover while the breach remains. Such additional capital cover would be significantly higher than would be required for an exposure of 25 per cent or less.

A bank must pre-notify the FSA of all exposures over 10 per cent of its large exposures capital base on a quarterly basis. Such pre-notification must be made before a bank becomes committed to the proposed exposure. Although 10 per cent of the LECB is the normal cut-off level for reporting purposes, the FSA may set reporting thresholds below 10 per cent if it appears to the FSA to be necessary for effective supervision. The FSA may agree a modified reporting process for those banks with an extensive branch network or group structure that renders the correlation of information for large exposures reporting at all times impractical. Before granting this concession, the FSA must be satisfied that the bank's control systems enable it to control the overall size of these exposures and to prevent the actual exposure exceeding the bank's adopted limit for each counterparty.

1–142 In addition, the bank must notify the FSA in advance of its internal limits where they exceed 10 per cent of capital. This is because the statutory post notification requirements cannot be waived. When the concession has been granted, a bank need not report the maximum exposure to a counterparty during a reporting period. However, it must report the actual exposures at the reporting date and the sum of internal limits applying to the particular counterparty plus any excesses where those limits were exceeded during the period. The FSA normally expects to be advised of a bank's plans at least

48 hours in advance to allow time for a discussion of the issues involved. Longer notice should be given if a bank believes a case is likely to raise complex or difficult issues. A nominated senior director has personal responsibility for the accuracy of the large exposure information provided to the FSA.

Capital adequacy returns

The monitoring of capital ratios by the FSA normally takes place using a quarterly (solo) and semi-annual (consolidated) return. However, in the event of a programme of remedial action being agreed (particularly in the case of breaches of the trigger ratio) the FSA may request more frequent information. **1–143**

As outlined below, in Chapter 3, the Schedule 3 requirement to maintain adequate capital must be met on a continuing basis, not just on reporting dates. Where the nature of activities is such that the capital ratio remains stable, the FSA may allow the calculation to be done on an appropriate periodic basis. However, the FSA may require a bank to monitor its capital ratios daily and so a bank should discuss with the FSA what it believes is appropriate in this respect.

Any fall, or anticipated fall, below a bank's target or trigger ratio should be notified to the FSA immediately it becomes known.

Liquidity

A bank must satisfy the FSA on an on-going basis that it has a prudent liquidity policy, and adequate management systems in place to ensure that the policy is adhered to. A bank must report its liquidity position to the FSA quarterly or more frequently as required by the FSA. **1–144**

The accuracy of these returns may be examined by the reporting accountants in the course of their section 39 work. Although the FSA monitors a bank's liquidity profile on a quarterly basis in line with the submission of the above returns, a bank should be able to provide information on a more frequent basis, including on a daily basis where necessary. A bank should notify the FSA of any breaches of its liquidity mismatch guidelines as soon as they occur. The reason for the breach should be given, together with the bank's proposed action to bring its liquidity position back within its guidelines. A bank should also report any breaches of its guidelines retrospectively at the end of each quarter.

A sterling stock liquidity bank should report its sterling stock liquidity position to the FSA monthly. Unless otherwise agreed with the FSA in writing, the return should be completed on a consolidated basis.

The Role of Reporting Accountants

General

As was discussed briefly, earlier in this chapter, the FSA has the power under sections 39(1)(b), 39(6), 39(7) and 8(5) of the BA 1987 to require a bank, certain connected parties or an applicant for authorisation, to **1–145** commission an external report on aspects of their business. Reports are routinely commissioned under section 39 from reporting accountants. Section 39 reports have a supervisory purpose and the decision to commission them is taken by the FSA. The main/routine channel for communication of the reporting accountant's findings is through the bank, which copies the reports to the FSA. Thus, the relationship between the FSA and reporting accountants is described as "trilateral", in that the bank itself is a part of it.

There are two types of report which the FSA routinely requests under section 39 of the BA 1987. These are:

(1) reports on accounting and other records and internal control systems; and

(2) reports on financial returns used for statistical or prudential monitoring purposes.

1–146 Auditors and reporting accountants have a statutory duty to report certain matters to the FSA in its capacity as supervisor under the BA 1987. Section 47 of the BA 1987 offers protection from breach of confidentiality when an accountant communicates information to the FSA in good faith. Reportable matters for credit institutions[16] include matters which give the accountant reasonable cause to believe that there may have been a failure to fill one of the criteria under Schedule 3 to the BA 1987 which is likely to be of material significance, authorisation may otherwise be revoked under section 11 of the BA 1987, where there has been a breach of the BA 1987 which is likely to be of material significance, or continuous functioning may be affected.

The bank retains primary responsibility for keeping the FSA informed, and for bringing matters which are relevant to the FSA's function as supervisor under the BA 1987 to the FSA's attention. This responsibility is not supplanted by the reporting accountants regime, or by the statutory duty for auditors and reporting accountants to report matters to the FSA. There are regular periodical meetings and reporting procedures designed to help banks to meet this obligation. Moreover, banks are expected to bring events or circumstances to the FSA's attention as soon as they have reason to believe that they could have a material effect on the bank or the interest of depositors.

Reporting accountants report on accounting and other records and internal control systems

1–147 The FSA routinely uses its section 39 powers to ask institutions to commission reports on whether the accounting and other records and internal control systems were established and maintained in accordance with the requirements of the BA 1987.

[16] A credit institution is an undertaking whose business is to receive deposits or other repayble funds from the public and to grant credits for its own accounts. Banks are normally credit institutions.

The reporting accountant is required to form an opinion on whether the bank's accounting and other records and internal control systems have been maintained by management during the period examined in accordance with the FSA's interpretation of the requirements of the BA 1987 as set out in the FSA's Banking Supervisory Policy. In forming this opinion the reporting accountant is expected to have regard to the nature and scale of the business undertaken by the bank. The required report includes not only the reporting accountant's opinion on whether the accounting and other records and internal control systems were established and maintained in accordance with the requirements of the FSA Banking Supervisory Policy but also the report is to include descriptions of key risks and controls and an outline of the work which the reporting accountant has carried out. Typically this will be accompanied by "exceptions or control weaknesses" reports.

The FSA has the power under section 39 to require reports not only on **1–148**
authorised banks but also, if it appears to the FSA to be desirable to do so in the interests of the depositors or potential depositors of the bank, on parties connected to the bank.[17]

A section 39 report can cover all areas of business, including money laundering deterrence procedures and internal audit—a "full scope" review. However, more usually the FSA determines one or more areas of the bank's business to be covered by the review in the context of the supervisory programme—the "scope" review. Both the bank and the reporting accountants are encouraged to discuss the scope review with the FSA and to contribute towards the scoping process.

Financial Services and Markets Bill

Overview

In May 1997 the United Kingdom Government announced proposals to **1–149**
introduce legislation to reform the regulation of financial services. The scope of this reform includes the supervision of banks, building societies, insurance companies, friendly societies and investment firms. The draft primary legislation, in the form of the Financial Services and Markets Bill, was released for consultation on July 30, 1998. Following consultation, numerous subsequent amendments and what can only be described as a fairly eventful passage through the House of Lords, the Bill is expected to receive Royal Assent prior to the summer recess in 2000 although at the time of writing the Treasury was considering a further amendment to the Bill relating to the FSA's role in tracking market abuse during takeover battles. The Takeover Panel had previously raised objections to the

[17] "Parties connected to the bank" are listed in s. 39(6) and (7) of the BA 1987. They include the parent, subsidiary and related subsidiary companies.

proposed role of the FSA arguing that the Bill undermined its authority by allowing the FSA to intervene in takeover bids without reference to the takeover Panel's code on takeovers and mergers.

The Financial Services and Markets Bill aims to provide one single legislative framework to replace what is generally viewed as a fragmented and complex system for regulating financial services (including business conducted by Insurance Companies, Building Societies and Banks) in the United Kingdom. Following enactment of the Bill the FSA expects that during the course of 2000/2001 the six statutes governing the regulation of investment business, banking, insurance, building societies and friendly societies will be repealed and replaced by a single regime that will be sufficiently flexible to keep pace with the rapidly developing financial services environment. It has been said that the Bill "represents the most cumulative and thorough overhaul of the United Kingdom financial sector for more than a decade."[18]

FSA to become sole regulator for financial services industry

1–150 Under the Financial Services and Markets Bill, the FSA (formerly called the "Securities and Investments Board") will take over the regulatory responsibilities of the Securities and Futures Authority (SFA), the Investment Management Regulatory Organisation (IMRO) and the Personal Investment Authority (PIA) (the SFA, IMRO and PIA are often referred to as the "self regulating organisations" or "SROs"), the Insurance Directorate of the DTI, the Building Societies Commission, the Friendly Societies Commission and the Registrar of Friendly Societies.

As discussed earlier in this chapter the BEA 1998 has already transferred responsibility for banking supervision to the FSA from the Bank of England. When the New Act becomes law, all organisations which carry on regulated activities will have to be authorised to do so by the FSA.

The FSA's objectives and powers

1–151 The Financial Services and Markets Bill also sets out a number of statutory objectives the FSA is obliged to fulfil. In summary, these are:

(1) maintaining confidence in the financial system;

(2) promoting public understanding of the financial system;

(3) securing the appropriate degree of protection for consumers; and

(4) reducing the extent to which it is possible for a business carried on by a regulated person to be used for a purpose connected with financial crime.

[18] See Peter Johnstone and Mark Jones, "The Financial Services and Markets Bill: An Overview", *European Financial Services Law*, August/September 1999, p. 268.

The Bill equips the FSA with a full range of statutory powers, rather than relying on delegated powers from the Treasury as is the case under the BA 1987.

The Bill gives the FSA significant powers of investigation including the power to enter premises to seize documents (subject to obtaining a warrant). The FSA will be given the authority to investigate the affairs of authorised persons and it will be a criminal offence to obstruct this investigation, to fail to properly reply to reasonable requests for information, to provide misleading information or conceal or to destroy evidence.

Some concerns have been expressed that the concentration of power in **1–152** one body is excessive. Such concerns are heightened by the fact that the FSA is a private company rather than an executive agency of the Government and questions as to whether it is sufficiently accountable in relation to the exercise of its functions and wide discretions. However, having a single regulator could greatly simplify the authorisation and ongoing supervision process for many organisations. In theory it should be easier for a business authorised in one area of financial services to set up operations in another area. Rather than having to undergo fresh authorisation with different regulators, it will be possible to apply to the FSA to extend an institution's permitted business. For example, under the current system some banking groups contain entities regulated by all three SROs as well as by the FSA. Under the new arrangements, they would only need to deal with the FSA.

Types of business to be regulated by the FSA under the Financial Services and Markets Bill

The Government has stated that the scope of regulation under the **1–153** Financial Services and Markets Bill will broadly cover the types of business regulated under the current regimes. To this extent, the provisions under the Bill relating to regulated and prohibited activities connected with banking substantially mirror the provisions currently in the FSA 1986 and the BA 1987. However, the range of activities covered is wider in some respects. For example, mortgage lending may be specifically regulated if the Treasury so determines by implementing regulations.

It seems likely that the territorial scope of the general deposit-taking prohibition (currently contained in section 3 of the BA 1987) will be extended to include accepting deposits outside the United Kingdom if that activity is being carried on from the United Kingdom or in certain cases where the deposit-taker's head office or registered office is in the United Kingdom.

Changes to advertising and promotion regimes

The Financial Services and Markets Bill introduces a new concept of **1–154** "financial promotion". This concept broadly covers the existing separate regimes applying to the marketing of financial products and services by means of unsolicited calls and investment advertisements. Under the Bill, a person must not, in the course of business, communicate an invitation or inducement to engage in investment activity unless they are an authorised person or the content of the communication is approved by an authorised person. This new approach will generally apply to promotions made in the United Kingdom or from the United Kingdom to other countries. The financial promotion prohibition will be subject to various exceptions which, amongst other things are likely to include an exemption for financial promotion which, although available in United Kingdom, is not directed there, addressing some of the problems raised by email and the internet.

The Basle Committee on Banking Supervision: a New Capital Adequacy Framework

1–155 The Basle Committee on Banking Supervision has stated its intention to introduce a new capital adequacy framework to replace the 1988 Capital Accord. A consultative paper was issued in June 1999 and was open for comment until March 31, 2000.

The proposed new capital framework consists of three elements—(a) new minimum capital requirements, (b) a supervisory review process, and (c) effective use of market discipline:

(a) Minimum capital requirements

The Committee's stated aim is to clarify and broaden the scope of the current Accord. With regard to risk weights to be applied to exposures to sovereigns, the committee proposes replacing the existing approach with a system that would use external credit assessments for determining risk weights. It is intended that such an approach will also apply, either directly or indirectly, to the risk weighting of exposures to banks, securities firms and corporates.

(b) Supervisory review of capital adequacy

The proposals seek to ensure that a bank's capital position is consistent with its overall risk profile and strategy. They propose a more tailored capital adequacy requirement with supervisors given the authority to require banks to hold capital in excess of the minimum capital ratios where it is thought desirable. The proposals also stresses the importance of bank management developing credible and clearly defined internal capital allocation methodology which is overseen by senior management, and where necessary subject to supervisory review and intervention.

(c) Market discipline

The Committee has stated a belief that market discipline is an effective tool in promoting safety and soundness in the international banking system. The new framework introduces proposals for disclosures to be made of the market in general about capital levels, risk exposures and capital adequacy.

The E.U. Commission Consultation Document

The European Commission published its own consultation document on the reform of E.U. capital requirements on November 23, 1999. The E.U. consultation document is broadly consistent with the Basle proposals however, it does differ in detail, which is in part a reflection of the fact that the E.U. proposals will affect domestic banks, building societies and investment firms rather than just internationally active banks. **1–156**

The E.C. Commission Consultation Document

The European Commission published its own consultation document on the treatment of F.X. capital requirements in November 1990. This EC consultation document is broadly consistent with the Basle proposals however it does differ in detail, which is an indication of the fact that the EC's proposals will affect domestic banks, building societies and investment firms rather than internationally active banks.

Section II

BANKER AND CUSTOMER

Chapter 2

Banker and Customer

Introduction: New Developments

The Report of the Committee on Banking Services[1]

2–001 At the time that the BA 1987 became law, an independent review into banking services law and practice was set up by the Treasury and the Bank of England.[2] It was not set up because of an urgent need for reform or a strong feeling of public disquiet about the way in which the law operated, but it was felt that it would be valuable to have a full examination of the law relating to domestic banking. The nature of banking has changed beyond recognition since the main statutes, such as the Bankers' Books Evidence Act 1879 (BBEA 1879) and the Bills of Exchange Act 1882 (BOEA 1882), were passed. It has increased greatly in complexity and volume and has been dramatically affected by changes in modern life, particularly the rapid developments of recent decades like the growth of new technology, increasing global communications, and the deregulation of financial services. The Committee had to consider how well the law had withstood the impact of this revolution in banking practice.

The remit of the Review Committee was wide ranging and included matters of banking practice as well as law. It gave priority to four objectives: the need for fairness and transparency in the banker-customer relationship; to maintain confidence in the security of the banking system; to promote the efficiency of the banking system, and to preserve and consolidate the bankers' duty of confidentiality to customers.

2–002 In the result, its Report contained a valuable examination of many aspects of modern domestic banking law, with its diverse legal and practical problems, and a lengthy list of recommendations (ranging from suggestions for reforming the law relating to cheques to suggestions for improvements in the newest payment mechanisms, such as plastic cards, and to recommendations to the government to support and consolidate the duty of confidence owed by bankers). Some of these recommendations would require enabling legislation to give effect to them, and others were to be incorporated in a new code of banking practice. The government of the

---

[1] *Banking Services: Law and Practice*, Cm. 622 (1989) ("the Jack Report").

[2] See Arora (1991) *Company Lawyer* (Vol. 12 No. 7) 127; Stockwell and Petkovic [1989] 3 J.I.B.L. 134.

time, firmly of the opinion that building on competition within a flexible regulatory framework was the most helpful protection for the consumer, responded cautiously to the Report,[3] but it supported the idea of a voluntary code of practice.

The Banking Code of Practice

2–003 A voluntary code of practice[4] was developed by the banks, after a certain amount of controversy.[5] The current version of the Code[6] (it has progressed rapidly through several editions) sets out Key Commitments by banks to customers, including:

- to act fairly and reasonably in dealings with customers;
- to give information on services and products in plain language;
- to help customers understand many of the aspects of banking;
- to have safe, secure and reliable banking and payment systems;
- to correct errors and handle complaints speedily; and
- to consider cases of financial difficulty sympathetically.

Although the Code is voluntary, almost all banks subscribe to it, as do building societies and card issuers, and will comply with it, since the Banking Ombudsman and no doubt the courts[7] will look to it as embodying good banking practice (it has, after all, been drawn up by bankers themselves) in dealing with complaints from customers.

2–004 Many new developments (such as the introduction of the electronic purse and the setting up of the FSA) have been dealt with by successive versions of the Code, and these, such as one of the most innovative aspects of the Code—its way of dealing with problems arising from the use of cards—have followed on from the comments and recommendations of the Jack Committee. Interestingly, each new edition of the Code has incorporated further changes in standards, as a result of a dialogue between consumers and the banks, and of the influence of the Banking Ombudsman. This flexible way

---

[3] In its White Paper, *Banking Services: Law and Practice*, Cm. 1026 (1990).

[4] Jack proposed a self-regulatory code with the threat of a statutory code if necessary, but the threat proved unnecessary. The Code was prepared by the British Bankers' Association, the Building Societies Association and the Association for Payment Clearing Services (APACS). It was adopted in March 1992 and revised in 1994, 1997 and 1999. See Lawson [1992] N.L.J. 346; Campbell [1993] Consum.L.J. 81. A Mortgage Code of Practice has also been issued (Council of Mortgage Lenders).

[5] The first draft attracted the scorn of consumer groups. It was seen as a statement of current (sometimes mediocre) practice; see *Banking Code of Practice—Response by National Consumer Council* (1991) and Duxbury [1991] 3 J.I.B.L. 116.

[6] March 1999.

[7] As in *Barclays Bank v. O'Brien* [1994] 3 W.L.R. 786. See below, para. 3–051.

of changing practice (and, by implication, the law) has produced a number of benefits for bank customers within a relatively short time. Banking services are, as Jack wished, more transparent: information is set out in plain language,[8] for example, banks undertake to explain and offer help if necessary. This allows customers and the Ombudsman to discuss banking services, like charges and interest rates, in an informed, and if necessary critical, fashion with the banks. This apparently gradual process of change may well vindicate the decision to adopt a code of practice for regulation in this fast moving area rather than attempting to set down the law in necessarily rigid legislation.

There have also been modifications which have brought banking practice **2–005**
more into line with Jack's views on consumer protection. These have, on the whole, worked greatly in favour of the customer. For example, there has been a tightening up in the provisions about disclosing information about accounts to outsiders, including to other companies in the banking group[9] and the introduction of similar (not identical) provisions covering loss on all plastic cards to those provided by the Consumer Credit Act 1974 (CCA 1974), and by the banks having to show that the customer acted with fraud or gross negligence to escape liability[10]—this change dramatically reduced customer complaints about "phantom withdrawals" from cash machines (withdrawals from accounts disputed by the customer). This is not to say, of course, that all consumer problems can be dealt with so smoothly. There are still plenty of complaints (see the Reports of the Banking Ombudsman) about inefficiency and the behaviour of banking staff, as well as concern about more serious matters like lending, confidentiality and duties of care.

The Jack Committee's comments and recommendations on specific topics many of which were adopted in the code, the Government's response and the provisions of the banking code will be discussed in the text where appropriate.

The Banking Ombudsman[11]

Consumer pressure was already being felt by banks before the introduc- **2–006**
tion of the new code of banking practice. Partly as a result of an influential report by the National Consumer Council,[12] which emphasised the sheer inequality of power between banks and their customers, the banks set up a

[8] This is also a requirement of the Unfair Terms in Consumer Contracts Regulations, 1999 (UTCCR 1999) (S.I. 1999 No. 2083). See below, para. 3–031.

[9] *e.g.* Banking Code (1999), para. 4.1.

[10] Banking Code (1999), para. 4.15.

[11] See Annual Reports (A.R.s) of the Banking Ombudsman (OBO) and the Jack Report, (see below, Chap. 15). See also two important articles by Morris [1987] J.B.L. 131 and [1992] L.M.C.L.Q. 227; Seneviratne, James and Graham [1994] C.J.Q. 152, James, *Private Ombudsmen and Public Law* (1997) and James [1999] Consum. L.J. 443.

[12] *Banking Services and the Consumer* (1983).

voluntary[13] Banking Ombudsman scheme in 1986. This was one of the first of the financial services Ombudsmen.[14]

The object of the scheme is that any individual or small company[15] (not just customers) can refer disputes with banks to the Ombudsman, who acts as an arbitrator between the individual and the bank. The scheme has obvious advantages for complainants: it is free of charge to the complainant,[16] non-adversarial, informal and speedier than taking legal action. It also has advantages for banks—perhaps less obvious but still considerable. It is not only a useful marketing tool and a "clever tactical response to the threat of setting up a statutory scheme",[17] but also provides a mechanism for clearing up misunderstandings without fuss, and for reaching settlements at an early stage. It may also give banks a good opportunity to consider, and if necessary improve, their own procedures in the light of the Ombudsman's decisions.

2–007 The Office of the Banking Ombudsman[18] is a contractual arrangement between member banks and financed by them,[19] with the objective of facilitating the "satisfaction, settlement, or withdrawal of complaints about the provision of banking services". The scheme consists of three separate organs:

(a) the *Board*, which is composed entirely of bankers elected by member banks, and is responsible for the financing of the scheme. It also appoints the members of the Council, has the final say in the appointment of the ombudsman himself and approves his or her terms of reference;

(b) the *Council*, which acts as a buffer between the board and the ombudsman. It is composed of three bankers, four independent members and an independent chairman[20]; and

(c) the *Ombudsman*[21] and his or her office, which now includes two Deputy Ombudsmen and an Assistant Ombudsman.

---

[13] Almost all banks are members (125—including all the main High Street banks and building societies which have converted to banks).

[14] It was modelled on the Insurance Ombudsman scheme. There are also pensions, unit trust and building societies Ombudsmen. They have developed pragmatically in the United Kingdom and schemes in other jurisdictions, such as Australia and New Zealand, have been modelled on them. U.K. F.S. Ombudsmen are to be amalgamated in 2000. See below, para. 2–021.

[15] Since 1993 including companies with a turnover of less than £1 million.

[16] Costs are, of course, ultimately borne by bank customers in general.

[17] Morris [1992] L.M.C.L.Q. 229.

[18] A company limited by guarantee.

[19] *R. v. Insurance Ombudsman Bureau, ex parte Aegon Life Assurance* [1994] C.O.D. 427: the Insurance Ombudsman is not subject to judicial review because it is a body whose jurisdiction is dependent on contract. This would probably also apply to OBO.

[20] Sir David Calcutt Q.C., who replaced Dame Mary Donaldson in 1994.

[21] David Thomas succeeded Laurence Shurman in 1997.

The Ombudsman has discretion to choose his own procedures. He has developed informal and inquisitorial methods and the basic procedure is straightforward. The complaint[22] may be made in writing, in person or by telephone, and the complainant must waive confidentiality. Once it is clear that the complaint has been taken up with the bank and the parties have reached "deadlock" (the bank's internal complaint mechanisms are exhausted)—which now has to be done within six weeks—the complaint will be screened to ensure that it is within the Ombudsman's terms of reference.[23] The Ombudsman emphasises his role as a conciliator, and the procedure is designed to allow him and the members of his staff to take a proactive role in achieving a fair settlement, acceptable to both parties, before the complaint is investigated. If there is an investigation, this is carried out by an Adjudicator, who considers all the material evidence in detail, and who refers the complaint to an Ombudsman for a final decision if either party requests a review. 2–008

An award of up to a maximum sum of £100,000[24] can be made, and this will bind the bank, though not the complainant who may take the matter further and issue court proceedings, although this is understandably rare.

OBO's independence—criticisms by Jack. When the scheme was set up, the banks were conscious of the risk that the Ombudsman would not be seen as impartial and independent, and they took steps to safeguard the independence of the office—by creating the Council, for example, which was intended to act as a buffer between the Ombudsman and the financing body (the Board) and was set up with a majority of lay members over bankers. All the same, it was not surprising that doubts about independence were expressed by the Jack Committee[25]; the scheme itself was a new type of organisation, the Ombudsman's powers were in some respects limited, and he was financed by bodies he might well have to criticise and adjudicate upon. 2–009

The Jack Report made a number of criticisms regarding certain privileges retained by the banks, which constituted important limitations on the Ombudsman's powers. It commented particularly on the banks' power to withdraw "test cases" at their discretion from the Ombudsman's jurisdiction,[26] and to refuse to disclose documents for the investigation of complaints. These criticisms were taken seriously by the Ombudsman, who,

[22] A complaint must relate to banking services (widely defined). ATMs used to give rise to most complaints, but most now (OBO A.R. 1998/9) concern mortgages, current accounts and lending. They have become more complex (OBO A.R.s, 1992–5).

[23] OBO may not deal with complaints about general bank policies or commercial decisions on lending (unless there has been maladministration, see above, Morris, n. 17.

[24] Increased from £50,000 in 1988. The highest award (to date) was £90,000 (in 1996/7): OBO A.R. 1998/9.

[25] See Chap. 15. Prompted by views of Morris, "The Banking Ombudsman" [1987] J.B.L. 131.

[26] "A quite dramatic power" (Morris [1987] J.B.L. 131 or Jack Committee Chap. 15); used for the first time 1994/5. See also Lord Woolf, *Access to Justice* (June 1995), p. 140.

with the support of the Council and the Board, promptly arranged changes in his terms of reference. The result was that test cases can now be withdrawn from him only with his approval, and he can demand that banks disclose documents for investigation. To date, there have been few test cases,[27] and these have raised issues of legal complexity and importance. The banks, far from abusing the power to withdraw test cases, seem to have resorted to it only when reasonable. It can be argued that it provides a useful safety valve for the banks,[28] as long as its use is controlled by approval from the Ombudsman, and as long as the costs of the complainant are borne by the banks, as they are at present.

The Committee emphasised that the scheme should not only be fair, but be seen to be fair.[29] It recommended the decisions should be made by reference to what is, in the Ombudsman's opinion, "fair in all circumstances". The test, now included in the Ombudsman's Terms of Reference, is reflected in the Banking Code, which commits banks to "act fairly and reasonably in all their dealings with customers."[30]

2–010 The Review Committee also felt doubtful about the independence of the Council. If the Ombudsman was to be independent, a strong and independent body between his office and the banks—by which he is paid—was vital. Jack suggested that the Council should have a larger majority of independent members; again, this suggestion was implemented shortly afterwards. These changes helped to enhance the Ombudsman's independence and authority, and they also indicated a mutual respect between his office and the banks which has been helpful to the growth of the scheme and probably also to the development of the Code of Practice. The Ombudsman has consistently urged improvements in the Code on the banks, which have generally been adopted eventually.

Jack made one important recommendation that was not accepted—to which the Ombudsman himself has been strongly opposed—which was that the voluntary scheme should become compulsory and statutory. This has been overtaken by events and the Government's decision to set up a single compulsory Financial Services Ombudsman scheme.[31]

2–011 **Publicity.** Another pertinent comment made by Jack was that more publicity might have to be given to the scheme in future. Every bank in the scheme must advertise the name, address and phone number of the Ombudsman in every branch (banks are also required by the Code to make copies of it available or to inform customers about how to obtain them, and

[27] *e.g. Sutherland v. Royal Bank of Scotland* (1997) 6 Bank. L.R. 132, C.S. See Morris Little [1997] J.B.L. 82, who criticise the decision reached by the court. They suggest that OBO should have the right to appear as *amicus curiae* at such hearings.
[28] James, *op. cit.*, p. 62.
[29] Jack Report (1989) para. 15.14.
[30] Banking Code (1999) para. 1.1.
[31] Discussed below, para. 2–021.

to ensure that their staff are aware of it). Positive efforts have been made to get the Ombudsman known—he has appeared on television and radio, supplied literature and guidance notes to all sorts of relevant bodies, has an e-mail address and a free telephone helpline.[32] Nevertheless, members of the public are probably still uninformed about both the Ombudsman scheme and the Code. The Ombudsman has found it necessary to urge that banks should give the scheme more publicity, and that bank staff themselves[33] should be more aware of it.

Effect on banking practice. Despite the public lack of knowledge, banking practice is gradually adapting to the Ombudsman's suggestions and to the higher standards required by the Code. His decisions are not formally reported, but the annual reports give a clear and readable account of the complaints made and the decisions reached, as well as lively and apt illustrations from the cases (in which neither party is named). Although the decisions, as is consistent with the informal and pragmatic role of a conciliator, are not regarded as precedents, his views have had an effect on banking practice.[34] Banks, for example, sometimes reach early settlements or compromises with complainants on the basis of considerations he has taken into account in earlier cases, and use his awards as yardsticks.[35] **2–012**

In fact, a number of improvements in banking practice (from the point of view of customers) in the last few years[36] have probably been due, at least in part, to the Ombudsman. For example, he played an active part in the introduction of the Cheques Act 1992 (Ch A 1992), and in dealing with the problem of "obsolete" accounts (where banks have not drawn the attention of customers to the fact that their money has been left in accounts where it is earning a lower rate of interest than it could be in alternative, newer accounts[37]). He is of course assisted by the standards incorporated in the Code of Practice. Although the Code does not have statutory force and parts of it are phrased in general terms, its provisions are a great deal more than mere exhortation, and have to be treated with respect by banks, partly because of the critical publicity they will attract if they fail to follow their **2–013**

[32] See, *e.g.* OBO A.R. 1998/9, pp. 5–6.

[33] OBO A.R. 1993/4, mentions a bank officer who, when telephoned by a complainant, said: "I cannot find a bank in Ombudsman. Have you got a sort code?" See also Seneviratne, James and Graham [1993] C.J.Q. 253 and [1993] Cons. Policy Review.

[34] OBO's terms of reference say he "shall not be bound by any previous decision made by him", but he has been developing a flexibly applied set of precedents: Morris, *op. cit.*, 241, and OBO A.R. 1994/5, para. 11.2. Previously, there was a lack of banking law precedents in the consumer field because few personal account customers could afford to take on the banks in litigation (Deputy Director, N.C.C., *The Independent*, December 8, 1990).

[35] OBO A.R. 1992/3, Case 5A: a complaint about MIRAS, where the customer was assisted by OBO's decision in a previous case.

[36] *e.g.* the tendency to drop entirely some of the more unpopular bank charges: OBO A.R. 1994/5, para. 7.1.

[37] James, *op. cit.*, p. 83. See Banking Code (1999) para. 2.17, 2.18. *Cf. Suriya and Douglas (a firm) v. Midland Bank plc* [1999] Lloyd's Rep. Bank. 103, CA.

own Code of Practice, but also because the Code embodies "good banking practice"[38] and this concept carries the implication that legal duties of care imposed on bankers will take account of it.[39] The Ombudsman may therefore use its provisions authoritatively in arriving at his decisions. Since he also influences the development of the Code itself, an interesting relationship is growing between the Code and the Ombudsman—the fact that the Ombudsman can use the code as an objective yardstick helps to give legitimacy to his practice in the eyes of banks and of the public, and he, in turn, is in a position to urge that improvements are adopted in the periodic revisions of the Code.[40]

2–014 **Conciliation.** A valuable aspect of the scheme is that it helps to short circuit disputes and encourage settlement at an early stage; sometimes the very fact of the intervention of the Ombudsman acts as an incentive to settlement.[41] The role of conciliator, using tactful (it seems) persuasion, is a vital part of his work, and the flexible, persuasive nature of that role is amply illustrated in the cases described in the Annual Reports.[42] The scheme works as alternative dispute resolution.

2–015 **Flexibility and fairness.** The Ombudsman bases his decisions on good banking practice and on law.[43] In many ways, of course—such as the conciliation role he undertakes—his function is unlike that of a court of law, and he certainly takes account of wider considerations than the rules of strict law. For example, banks have sometimes been persuaded to offer *ex gratia* payments to complainants where things had gone wrong but no legal remedy was open to them. In one case, a man who had come to a "full and final settlement" with a bank where one of the £50 notes supplied to him by the bank for his holiday, was a forgery (and he had spent three traumatic

[38] An ambiguous concept: *existing* good practice or something better? The first code was in some respects more pro-customer than existing bank practice (Morris [1992] L.M.C.L.Q. 474). This is partly true also of the revised code (*e.g.* cards, bank charges). But the Director General of Fair Trading saw the new code as a wasted opportunity (*Financial Times*, February 9, 1994), and others (*e.g.* A. Campbell [1994] Consum. L.J. 171) say it does not go far enough.

[39] The standard of care for bankers is the usual one for professionals: *Bolam v. Friern Hospital Management Committee* [1957] 1 W.L.R. 582; see also *Marfani v. Midland Bank* [1968] 1 W.L.R. 956. Practice may be more important than in some professional fields because of the role of commercial usage or custom in banking. *National Bank of Greece v. Pinios* [1990] 1 A.C. 637, is an example, see below, para. 8–008.

[40] See OBO A.R. 1993/4, para. 3.3.

[41] *e.g.* OBO A.R. 1990/2, p. 14 (Mrs E); and OBO A.R. 1994/5, section 3 (early resolution), which gives three examples where a "fair and speedy settlement was achieved before deadlock was reached and without the delay and expense which a full investigation would necessarily have incurred".

[42] *e.g.* OBO A.R. 1992/3, where OBO's personal intervention encouraged a settlement.

[43] Sometimes applying cases by analogy: see OBO A.R. 1992/3, Case 9B, where *Ross v. Caunters* [1979] 3 All E.R. 580 was relied on in a case where a bank delayed in arranging a mortgage protection policy, and the customer died before it was completed.

days in prison in North Africa) was given an extra sum by the bank over and above the modest amount agreed to compensate him for his extremely unpleasant experience because of the intervention of the Ombudsman.[44]

This broad interpretation of his function has allowed him to use a certain elasticity of approach to his Terms of Reference. These state that he is permitted to deal with all types of banking business normally transacted through branches of member banks or by telephone, but not with complaints about *general bank policies* or about *commercial decisions on lending* unless there has been maladministration.[45] Thus, banks are entitled to refuse to grant an overdraft on commercial grounds. But if the bank has done something wrong (in the legal sense—if it was under a duty of care to advise, for example) the Ombudsman will of course feel able to comment on this to the bank, and to point out that as a matter of good banking practice, the bank may not be entitled to rely on the strict legal position. It seems that he may not be inhibited from taking this view even in lending cases if he feels the case merits it. He mentions, for example, that if a customer who was asked by his bank for a business plan for a project produced a plan which was clearly inadequate on the face of it, and the bank did not draw this to his attention so that he went ahead with his project in the reasonable belief that the bank had approved the project, it is likely that the bank would be deemed to have advised negligently, or to have failed in its duty to warn the customer.[46] **2–016**

The Ombudsman has always emphasised the concept of "fairness",[47] and this has distinguished his attitude from the approach which courts would tend to take. His justification is the general principle which underpins the Code that banks should act "fairly and reasonably in all their dealings with their customers" (until recently this was simply a procedural requirement) and the fact that the Ombudsman is required by his terms of reference to reach a decision which is "fair in all the circumstances".[48] The obligation to come to a fair and just resolution of disputes is taken seriously, and he has said that he would like the Code to include a requirement that banks' terms and conditions should be fair in substance.[49] The Unfair Terms in Consumer Contract Regulations 1999 (UTCCR 1999)[50] will help in giving effect **2–017**

[44] OBO A.R. 1992/3, Case 5C.

[45] For "maladministration" as a concept, see Morris, *Five Years On* [1992] L.M.C.L.Q. 227. But see also Walker J.'s comment: "It is not necessarily maladministration for a decision maker to take a wrong view of the law" in *Westminster C.C. v. Haywood* [1996] 3 W.L.R. 563 at 578. (At least in relation to the Pensions Ombudsman, which is a statutory rather than contractual scheme.)

[46] OBO A.R. 1994/5, para. 6.3.

[47] See Reports of the Banking Ombudsman, and Shurman [1994] L.S.G. 25. Though he has to take care to steer a path between flexible adjudication and "palm tree justice". The ombudsmen regard themselves to some extent as modern successors to the old courts of equity (OBO, Seminar at Bristol University, February 8, 1995).

[48] And to consult not only the banking industry but elsewhere (Terms of Reference 14(c)).

[49] OBO A.R. 1993/4, p. 9.

[50] Replacing the UTCCR 1994, see below, para. 3–031.

to this aim. They apply to all standard term consumer contracts in writing, and build a legal requirement of fairness into bank contracts. Banks are having to reappraise the terms and conditions of their standard documents, including mortgages and guarantees, in the light of the regulations.

2–018 The concept of "fairness" does not only apply to banks. Customers who have acted in bad faith or complained about trifling inconveniences will not recover compensation.[51] In one case, for example, compensation was not awarded to a man who had been granted an overdraft to buy a new car abroad, and whose cheques were dishonoured when he tried to use the money to buy shares in a privatisation issue. The Ombudsman decided the customer had acted in bad faith.[52] In other cases, compensation awards have been made but reduced because of contributory negligence by the customer.

2–019 **Statutory scheme?** One important criticism made by the Jack Committee was not accepted. The scheme, unlike the Building Societies Ombudsman scheme,[53] is voluntary and does not have statutory backing. The Committee feared that this would weaken the Banking scheme and that it would give rise to confusion to have two different schemes side by side in two such similar industries—which, indeed, seems particularly curious at a time when banks and building societies are becoming interchangeable. The Committee thought a statutory scheme would be more appropriate for banks because it would offer bank customers a guarantee of impartiality and fairness, as well as ensuring that all banks (including small banks which may represent ethnic minorities) are members. The scheme was not changed to take account of these comments, partly because it was felt by the Ombudsman himself (Laurence Shurman) that introducing a statutory scheme would weaken the effect of the office; since a statutory scheme could not exclude the jurisdiction of the courts, he felt the banks might not regard his awards as binding. He also argued forcefully that the scheme worked flexibly and well and changes could be quickly adopted[54] if they were needed. This would certainly not be the case if legislation were required for every change.[55] The speed with which the banks agreed to the reforms of the scheme suggested by Jack lent weight to this argument.

2–020 The view of the former Ombudsman must be accorded great respect. His position was unique: he had had years of first hand experience of the scheme in practice, and had successfully demonstrated his impartiality

---

[51] OBO A.R. 1992/3, Case 7B.

[52] OBO A.R. 1992/3, Case 7A.

[53] Building Societies Act 1986.

[54] Changes are made on an *ad hoc* basis. Three further changes were made to the Terms of Reference during 1994/5.

[55] It is probable that giving statutory effect to the scheme will have the effect that the scheme will become susceptible to judicial review: see *R. v. Insurance Ombudsman Bureau, ex parte Aegon Life Assurance* [1994] C.O.D. 427.

continuously throughout that time.[56] Nevertheless, the Committee's view that it would be in the public interest for the variety of different schemes in the financial industries to be rationalised was sensible. The schemes were set up on an *ad hoc* basis, and have formed a patchwork of overlapping arrangements whose operation is confusing[57] for complainants, and perhaps even for the Ombudsmen themselves, despite the co-operation which exists between them[58] in sorting out jurisdictional issues and formulating common guidelines.

In any case, the issue has now been settled. The Government has decided to set up a new financial services Ombudsman scheme, amalgamating all the existing financial services Ombudsmen.[59] The new Financial Services Ombudsman is to be a company, and separate from the Financial Services Authority, although there will be a relationship between the two where a complaint reveals the need for supervisory or disciplinary action of some kind. This will almost certainly be an improvement on the present scheme.[60] **2–021**

There are remaining doubts, particularly about the importance of keeping the procedures flexible and informal. The European Convention on Human Rights (now the Human Rights Act 1998) applies, and its provisions were drafted in the context of court procedures, and as the Ombudsman says, it will be a challenge to adapt the Ombudsman methods to them.[61]

Definitions

What is a Bank?

In banking law, the preliminary question of definition is even more important than in many other areas of law because of the reputation of banks for reliability. It is also notoriously difficult to answer. The question has become very much harder to answer in recent years, with the advent of telephone and internet banking as well as banks in supermarkets. The traditional idea of a bank with many local branches dealing with customers face to face (core retail banking) seems odd and out of date. **2–022**

Essentially, however, there are two reasons for wishing to know the answer to the question, "what is a bank?" in law. First, the nature of the relationship between bank and customer has certain distinctive characteristics, which may be presumed to attach to any body that has been identified

56 Morris, *Five Years On* [1992] L.M.C.L.Q. 227 at 233.

57 Some complaints have to be transferred to other ombudsmen each year—397 from OBO in 1994 (OBO A.R., 1994/5, p. 43). A brief survey of them is given by Walker J. in *Westminster C.C. v. Haywood* [1996] 3 W.L.R. 563.

58 Ombudsmen (except those not regarded as impartial: Morris, *Five Years On* [1992] L.M.C.L.Q. 227 at 230) belong to the U.K. Association of Ombudsmen, of which the Banking Ombudsman is chairman.

59 Financial Services and Markets Act 2000, ss. 225–234.

60 See James [1998] P.L. 201.

61 OBO A.R. 1998/9, p. 31.

as a bank. Banks enjoy a number of privileges, both legal and practical. For example, they are given special protection from liability when paying or collecting cheques; they have traditionally been exempted from regulation as moneylenders; they are not compellable to produce their books in court, but may send copies; and trustees may pay trust money into a bank pending investment.[62] The second reason is that the frequent references to banks in statutes[63] may require precise definition. A number of the statutes give definitions of the word "bank" (many more give partial definitions).

Statutory definition

2–023 One might expect to find an authoritative definition of the central concept of banking law in the statute which regulates banks, which is now the BA 1987. As the discussion of the statute above[64] makes clear however, the BA 1987 regulates deposit taking ("authorised") institutions[65] and avoids using the word bank except when referring to institutions using the *name* of bank.[66] Nevertheless, although the BA 1987 does not generally advance the definition of "banker", it has *in practice* clarified the law, because authorised institutions are readily identified. Further, the BA 1987 amended a number of existing statutes[67] by substituting the phrase "authorised institutions" for "banks" or "bankers"; and the tendency since 1987 has been for legislation to refer to "authorised institutions".[67a]

Another clarification is that the BA 1987 restricts the use of banking names and descriptions so that only authorised institutions fulfilling certain specific criteria may call themselves banks.[68] But under the Act, a person may still be described as a banker for various purposes such as taking advantage of a rule of law, international agreement or commercial usage which applies to a person because he is a banker,[69] and institutions still exist which may call themselves banks and are not identifiable by reference to the BA 1987.

---

[62] Lord Denning M.R. listed 12 such privileges in *U.D.T. v. Kirkwood* [1966] 2 Q.B. 431 at 443.

[63] Well known examples are the BOEA 1882 (ss. 60, 73, 79 and 80) and the Cheques Act 1957 (Cheques Act 1957) (ss. 1–4).

[64] See above, Chap. 1.

[65] Compare the E.C. legislation, which is concerned with "credit institutions". The annex to the Second Banking Directive (Directive 89/646 [1989] O.J. L386/1) gives a list of banking activities which is a helpful indication of what might be considered within the scope of modern banking business.

[66] BA 1987, ss. 67 and 69.

[67] *e.g.* the BBEA 1879, the Agricultural Credits Act 1928, the Solicitors Act 1974, the CA 1985, the Building Societies Act 1986 and the IA 1986 were amended by s. 108 and Sched. 6 to the BA 1987.

[67a] "Authorised institutions" are taken to operate as referring to European authorised institutions: Banking Co-ordination (Second Council Directive) Regulations 1992 (S.I. 1992 No. 3218).

[68] BA 1987, ss. 67 and 69.

[69] BA 1987, s. 69(4).

In another respect the Act also fails to provide a complete answer to the problem. A number of important statutes, which include the BOEA 1882 and the Cheques Act 1957 (Ch A 1957), still refer to "banks" and "bankers" and not to "authorised institutions".[70] For the purposes of these statutes, therefore, it is necessary to find a definition. It might be thought that the difficulty could be resolved by turning for guidance to tried and tested definitions in familiar banking statutes, but this is not really helpful. The definition in section 2 of the BOEA 1882, for example, states that "banker" "includes a body of persons whether incorporated or not who carry on the business of banking". Many commentators have pointed out that the circularity of the wording leaves courts with the same question to answer as they started with. It may be, though, that it works reasonably well in practice. Courts are required to have regard to the "business of banking" and to use the common law test, so that a standard has to be used which can alter according to the surrounding circumstances, and which has to be based on the opinions of recognised bankers about their business. The test is therefore flexible and reflects the variety of institutions which might reasonably be called banks at any one time. In banking, where so much law is based on practice, this may often give an effective and sensible answer. **2–024**

A device which has been used for some time is for a statute to empower a government department concerned with particular legislation (generally with the advice of the Bank of England) to draw up a list of the institutions which count as "banks" for the purpose of that legislation. The existence of a number of such lists led to a hierarchy or ladder of banking recognitions, so that the more lists an institution appeared on, the more likely it was to be regarded as a bank. This method of identification has been largely, though not entirely, superseded by the provisions of the BA 1987.

Common law definition

Since the various statutory definitions do not provide a complete answer to the problem of deciding in a doubtful case whether an institution is a bank, the common law definition remains of importance. **2–025**

The first point to make about the common law definition is that, again, there is no complete definition. The cases emphasise, as Salmon J. said in *Woods v. Martins Bank Ltd*,[71] that the question "what is a bank" will be answered differently from time to time and place to place. The nature of banking business at any particular time depends on the surrounding

[70] *e.g.* The BBEA 1879 and the Solicitors Act 1974. See Morrison, Tillet and Welch, *Banking Act 1979* and Penn, *Banking Supervision*.

[71] [1959] 1 Q.B. 55 at 56: "What may have been true of the Bank of Montreal in 1918 is not necessarily true of Martins Bank in 1958". And: "The words 'banking' and 'banker' may bear different shades of meaning at different periods of history and their meaning may not be uniform today in countries of different habits of life": *Bank of Chettinad Ltd of Colombo v. Commissioners of Income Tax, Colombo* [1948] A.C. 378 at 383.

circumstances, and must be a matter of fact as well as of law. This is even more true today, at a time of rapid and accelerating change.[72] Even within the United Kingdom, there is such a wide variety of institutions that are called banks that any general definition would probably be inflexible or so general as to be meaningless. Compare the services and methods of an investment bank or a private bank offering a specialised and personal service with that of a large clearing bank, or even more tellingly, with home or telephone banking. Another good illustration of this point is the changing role of building societies.[73] Their primary purpose used to be the raising of money (*from* their members) to lend long term (*to* their members) for the purchase of residential property,[74] but they have increasingly competed so fiercely with banks (and banks with them, for their market in long term lending on residential property) that their functions have become interchangeable with those of banks; they take deposits,[75] operate current accounts,[76] and offer banking facilities such as payment and collecting cheques for individuals. The result has been that many building societies have changed themselves into banks in law as well—abandoning their mutual status, and have become authorised institutions under the BA 1987. And all banks have changed since *Woods v. Martins Bank* was decided, let alone since the BOEA 1882, still of great importance today, was passed. Similarly, important differences between banking institutions in different countries exist, even for example, between E.C. member states[77] despite the introduction of the single banking market.

2–026 In these circumstances, it is not surprising that English law has not arrived at an exhaustive definition of banking. Instead, the common law has approached the question pragmatically, and answered the question by extracting and listing the characteristics which it regards as typical of the business of banking.

At the heart of the business, of course, is money. A banker is "one that traffics in money"[78] this means, for bankers, borrowing and lending

[72] Clearing banks began offering merchant banking services such as corporate financial advice, capital issue facilities, investment management, loan syndication and acceptance credits in the 1970s (Blair, Allison, Palmer and Richards-Carpenter, *Banking and the Financial Services*, para. 1.3). More recently, they have offered insurance and estate agency services.

[73] See Wurtzburg and Mills, *Building Society Law* (15th ed., 1989).

[74] Formerly, building societies could not be banks: *Re Bottomgate Industrial Co-operative Society* (1891) 65 L.T. 712; *Re Birkbeck Permanent Building Society* [1912] 2 Ch. 183.

[75] Building Societies Act 1986, s. 7; Sched. 8, replaced by Building Societies (Commercial Assets and Services) Order 1988 (S.I. 1988 No. 1141, amended S.I. 1989 No. 839).

[76] Building Societies Act 1986, s. 34, Sched. 8, amended Building Societies (Commercial Assets and Services) Order 1988 (S.I. 1988 No. 1141).

[77] Particularly in retail banking. See Dixon *Banking in Europe* and the Jack Report, Cm. 622 (1989), Chap. 3. Banking practices in the E.C. are closely linked with national habits, despite rapid change in recent years.

[78] Lord Denning M.R. quoted Dr Johnson (1755) to this effect in *U.D.T. v. Kirkwood* [1996] 2 Q.B. 431 at 445. This (as a general statement) includes "bank money", and instruments treated as money, see Mann, *The Legal Aspects of Money*, p. 6.

money.[79] This characteristic does not in itself distinguish the respectable banker from the more dubious moneylender, however, and leaves the problem of definition unsolved. The distinction between the two was the issue that arose in the leading case of *United Dominions Trust v. Kirkwood.*[80]

U.D.T., the plaintiff, was a finance house which described itself as a bank. It was seeking to recover money it had lent to a garage for stocking its business. In order to do so, it had to show that it really was a bank—that it was "bona fide carrying on the business of banking" within the Moneylenders Act 1900[81]; otherwise it would be an unregistered moneylender, not entitled to recover the debt. The court, in the absence of any general definition of "bank", had to examine the firm's business in the light of what it regarded as the essential characteristics of the business of banking in order to decide whether U.D.T. could fulfil the requirement. Lord Denning M.R. gave a list of the usual characteristics of banking business. He said: **2–027**

> "Bankers (i) accept money from, and collect cheques for, their customers and place them to their credit; (ii) honour cheques or orders drawn on them by their customers when presented for payment and debit their customers accordingly, and (iii) keep current accounts[82] in which the credits and debits are entered."

Here, the "deposits" taken by U.D.T. were really short term investments in U.D.T. for which no chequebooks were supplied; secondly, the firm made loans (large numbers of them) but making such loans, without more, would simply establish that it was a moneylender rather than a bank. With regard to the third characteristic, the "current accounts" operated by U.D.T. were not like those run by banks, since the only body which paid money into the account was U.D.T. itself, and it did so in order to pay its customers specific sums of money. Since neither the firm's business of accepting deposits nor its business of loans resembled those characteristic of bankers, it did not seem on the face of it to be a bank.

However, the majority of the court came to the decision that U.D.T. was a bank. After all, said Lord Denning, the *usual* characteristics of a bank are not the *sole* characteristics[83]; the court had to take account also of the **2–028**

[79] "The real business of the banker is to obtain deposits of money which he may use for his profit by lending it out again": *Re Shield's Estate* [1901] I.R. 172, *per* Holmes J. at 182. But lending alone may be insufficient: *Hafton Properties Ltd. v. McHugh* (1986) 59 Tax. Cas. 420, where the alleged bank took no deposits from the U.K. and did not, therefore, "carry on a banking business" in the U.K. for the purposes of s. 54 of the Income and Corporation Taxes Act 1970.

[80] [1966] 2 Q.B. 431 at 447.

[81] s. 6, repealed by the CCA 1974. In Harman L.J.'s words: "Q. When is a moneylender not a moneylender? A. When he is a banker".

[82] It appears unnecessary that there is a deposit account, though a deposit account alone may be sufficient: *Commercial Banking Co. Ltd v. Hartigan* (1952) 86 I.L.T. 109.

[83] [1966] 2 Q.B. 431 at 453.

reputation of a firm amongst ordinary intelligent commercial men. Here, U.D.T. scored well. There was "impressive evidence" that it was generally regarded as a bank in the city of London and by clearing bankers, which could turn the scale in U.D.T.'s favour if there was any doubt. Diplock L.J.'s view was different, and narrower. He was doubtful about the nature and size of the cheque transactions on current accounts held by the firm; there was "a gap in the evidence" as to whether the banking transactions it carried out were more than a negligible part of its business. This gap left room for doubt, but he found, after anxious reflection,[84] that evidence of the firm's reputation could fill that gap, because it was given by bankers and would be based on transactions undertaken by U.D.T. This was enough to establish a prima facie case that U.D.T. was bona fide carrying on the business of banking. In the result, therefore, he agreed with Lord Denning that U.D.T. was a bank.

Harman L.J. dissented. He thought that U.D.T.'s business could not be described as a real banking business, and commented that Lord Denning's judgment seemed to prove that U.D.T. was *not* a bank. He went on to say that reputation alone (though impressive in this case) was not enough without some performance behind it.

2–029 The judgments are illuminating, because they demonstrate the great difficulty of deciding in marginal cases whether institutions are banks or not, and they also make plain the policy issues underlying the decision. All the judges were troubled by the serious consequences of a decision adverse to U.D.T., and were impressed by the commercial reputation of the institution. It was regarded as eminently respectable,[85] and it was felt that it should not be outlawed and be left unable to obtain repayment of debts owing to it.[86]

As we have noted, the characteristics of banking are said to be: accepting money (deposits) from, and collecting cheques for, customers; honouring cheques drawn on them by customers and keeping current accounts. It also seems, from the U.D.T. case, that no one may be a banker who has not a reputation amongst the banking community as a banker. It is difficult to say exactly what this means, beyond saying that it may refer to the prudential reputation of the alleged banker, and possibly to his or her professional skills and range of activities.

2–030 It should be added that there are important aspects which characterise banking in England over and above these[87]: for example, the special relationship of confidence is often mentioned (although it has been much diminished in recent years).[88] If that were to be excluded by, say, contract,

[84] [1966] 2 Q.B. 431 at 473.

[85] *ibid.*, at 453. Not a "ramshackle concern".

[86] Following this decision, s. 123 of the Companies Act 1967 enabled finance houses to be listed as bankers for the purposes of exemption from the Moneylenders Acts.

[87] And an institution may still be a bank though it does not carry out some types of banking business.

[88] See below, Chap. 4.

one would tend to think that the institution to that extent did not resemble a bank. Further, a banker will ordinarily "keep open shop for the receipt of money from all who choose to deposit it with him" so that he or she will accept any customer.[89] However, some institutions which are clearly banks will only accept customers with a certain degree of wealth, or with certain kinds of business, and any bank reserves the right to decline the business of a customer with unsatisfactory references or whose identity cannot be adequately checked.

A subsequent case considered the meaning of the same words of the Moneylenders Act 1990. Harman L.J. in *U.D.T. v. Kirkwood* had expressed the view that the words did not require consideration of the honesty of the transaction, but of whether the business was a *real business of banking*. This point was raised again in the case of *Re Roe's Legal Charge*,[90] where the plaintiffs claimed that they were "bona fide carrying on the business of banking" within the terms of the 1900 Moneylenders Act. The firm had fewer than 200 current accounts, and cleared only a small number of cheques (58 in one month). The defendant did not claim that the transactions were not genuine, but argued that the numbers of accounts was inconsistent with a genuine banking business. **2–031**

Compared with the business of a clearing bank, the firm's business was minuscule, but the Court of Appeal held that that was not the correct test. The question which had to be decided was whether the banking side of the firm's business was negligible in size and number when compared with the rest of the business of that firm. It was held here that the proportion of banking transactions was not negligible in comparison to the lending, and the business could be regarded as a bank.

Ordinarily, therefore, one expects to see a current account, the issue of cheques, and the payment in and collection of cheques. Apart from that, the most that can be said with certainty is that the further the relationship diverges from one involving the features mentioned here, the less likely it is to be one of banker and customer. It may be the case that in a financial conglomerate, where the business is not divided into subsidiary companies, the element of the banking business must be a substantial part of the business, and perhaps *the* substantial part, before the business is that of a "banker".[91] **2–032**

Relationship between statutory and common law definitions

The two definitions do not entirely overlap. Not every deposit taking institution authorised under the BA 1987 will be a bank at common law, because not all operate current accounts. **2–033**

---

[89] *Re Shield's Estate* [1091] I.R. 198.
[90] [1982] 2 Lloyd's Rep. 370.
[91] *U.D.T. v. Kirkwood*, [1996] 2 Q.B. 431.

The common law and statutory definitions can be seen as complementary[92] in the sense that the common law proclaims that a bank is a body engaged in banking business and the Act describes the nature of this business at present. A slightly different way of expressing it might be to say that the Act provides a mechanism whereby the important factual matters (the "business of banking" and the reputation of the institution) can be incorporated into the regulation of authorised institutions. The flexibility of the common law definition may be helpful in deciding whether an institution should be authorised according to the minimum criteria for authorisation.[93] These include the fitness of the individuals who manage the institution, the prudent conduct of the business, and the minimum net assets.

What is a Customer?

2–034 In a practical sense, there is a clear cut answer to this question: almost everybody. As the Jack Report pointed out,[94] the number of bank customers went up from about 30 per cent of the adult population in 1959 to about 90 per cent in 1989. The number may be even larger now.

The legal concept of customer is less clear cut. An understanding of the word is important though, for several reasons. First, the concepts *bank* and *customer* are interdependent, and the one cannot be completely understood without reference to the other: for example, the essential elements of a banker's business are the maintenance of current accounts for customers, and the collection of cheques for the customer.[95]

The meaning of *customer* is also relevant for the purposes of the important banking statutes Banks, for example, may only obtain their characteristic statutory protection under the BOEA 1882,[96] and the Ch A 1957[97] when dealing with cheques if they are dealing for customers.

2–035 It is also necessary to understand the word before looking at the nature of the banker and customer relationship. As we shall see, this relationship is a special one, and the bank and the customer owe each other certain duties—for example, the bank agrees to carry out certain monetary transactions for the customer, and to act as the customer's agent in banking transactions. It is necessary to establish a legal definition of "customer" for

[92] See Ellinger and Lommicka, *Modern Banking Law* (2nd ed.), p. 83.

[93] Set out in Sched. 3 to the BA 1987.

[94] Cm. 622 (1989), para. 2.20. There are 80 million personal current and deposit accounts in the U.K. (OBO A.R. 1998/9, p. 23).

[95] *U.D.T. v. Kirkwood* [1966] 2 Q.B. 431.

[96] *e.g.* BOEA 1882, s. 75 deals with the banker's duty to pay on a cheque which is countermanded, or where the customer is dead. Neither statute gives a definition of the word.

[97] Cheques Act 1957, s. 1 deals with the paying banker's liability regarding endorsements on cheques; Cheques Act 1957, s. 4 with the collecting banker's liability where he receives payment for a customer not entitled to be paid.

this purpose, though there is a danger that this may result in drawing a distinction between customers and non-customers which is more hard and fast than is justified in some areas of the common law, where the boundaries of claims are blurred, and a bank may owe duties to non-customers which are very similar, or even identical, to those owed to customers. If an individual is certainly a customer, certain duties towards him or her will exist unless they are excluded by contract. If he or she is not a customer, however, similar duties towards him or her *may* exist, but it will depend on the precise circumstances of each case. Further, a bank may owe differing duties to different customers, depending on their circumstances and what the bank undertakes to do.

When does one become a customer?

For normal purposes, the main criterion is that a person has opened an account with the bank. Indeed, the first payment into the account or even the acceptance by the bank of an offer to open an account[98] may constitute the person a customer. In the case of *Commissioners of Taxation v. English, Scottish and Australian Bank*,[99] a man opened an account with the respondent bank with a deposit of £20 in bank notes the day before he paid in a cheque which had been stolen from the appellants. During the three subsequent days, he drew three cheques on the bank on which the bank paid. The plaintiffs claimed the stolen money from the bank in an action for the tort of conversion. The bank raised the statutory defence[1]: it would be protected if it could show that it had acted in good faith and without negligence provided that the man was a customer. In the Privy Council's opinion, the duration of the relationship was not of the essence; the distinction was not between an habitué and a newcomer but between a person for whom the bank performs a casual service such as, for example, cashing a cheque for a person introduced by one of their customers, and a person who has an account of his own at the bank.[2] Here, the man had opened an account and was a customer. Since the bank had acted in good faith and without negligence, it was protected. **2–036**

This can be compared with the earlier case of *Great Western Railway v. London and County Banking Co*,[3] where a rate collector, Huggins, who for 20 years had been in the habit of cashing cheques at the bank (which would usually pay some of the money to the district council and the balance to Huggins) had obtained a cheque by false pretences from the plaintiffs which the bank paid him in full. The bank in this case had also raised the **2–037**

[98] *Barclays Bank Ltd v. Okenarhe* [1966] 2 Lloyd's Rep. 87 at 94, *per* Mocatta J. referring to the view expressed by Lord Chorley in the Gilbart Lectures for 1955.
[99] [1920] A.C. 683, PC.
[1] The Australian equivalent of s. 82 of the BOEA 1882, now s. 4 of the Ch A 1957.
[2] *ibid.*, *per* Lord Dunedin, at p. 687.
[3] [1901] A.C. 414.

statutory defence, and it was necessary to establish whether Huggins was their customer. The House of Lords held that, though there had been a number of similar transactions, the bank had collected money on their own behalf, not for him as a customer.

The distinction is between where a bank performs a "casual service"[4] for someone (as for example, where a bank cashes a cheque for a payee with a cheque card from another bank who is not a customer: in this case, the bank has bought the cheque and collects on its own behalf, not for the payee) and where it has some closer connection with a person. That person may not have an account with the bank, although the opening of a current account is usually the most significant factor in deciding whether the connection is close enough (a deposit account[5] or credit card account would probably suffice). The mere deposit of money with a bank, with instructions to transfer it to another bank, does not of itself make the person requesting the transfer a customer of the bank.[6] A person with an account will be a customer even though his or her only connection with the bank was payment into an account opened for the purpose of collecting a single cheque (and even if the cheque has not been collected, so that the "customer" may not draw on the uncleared effect[7]), or if the person is given a cheque book instead of crediting the account.[8]

2–038 A bank may also be a customer of another bank, as where a clearing bank regularly collects cheques sent to it by a non-clearing bank on behalf of that banks' customers, or where a domestic clearing bank collects cheques for a foreign bank.[9]

A case which took a flexible approach to the idea that the opening of a current account is the moment when the banker/customer relationship starts was *Woods v. Martins Bank Ltd.*[10] A young man sought and was given investment advice by a branch manager of the defendant bank. Relying on the advice, he invested money in a financially unsound company which was

---

[4] See also *Tate v. Wilts and Dorset Bank* (1899) 1 L.D.A.B. 286. The mere existence of a contract to purchase a bill of exchange is insufficient therefore to constitute the seller a customer of the purchaser bank.

[5] "There must be some sort of account, either a deposit or a current account or some similar relation": *Great Western Railway Co. Ltd. v. London and County Banking Co. Ltd.* [1901] A.C. 414 at 421, *per* Lord Davey.

[6] *Aschkenasy v. Midland Bank Ltd* (1934) 50 T.L.R. 209; *Kahler v. Midland Bank Ltd* [1948] 1 All E.R. 811, affd [1950] A.C. 24.

[7] *Ladbroke & Co v. Todd* (1914) 30 T.L.R. 433, referred to with approval in *Barclays Bank Ltd v. Okenarhe* [1966] 2 Lloyds' Rep. 87.

[8] A bank crediting a cheque to a "sundry customers' account", does not in itself make the person handing the cheque to the bank a customer: *Matthews v. Brown & Co.* (1894) 10 T.L.R. 386.

[9] *Importers Co. Ltd v. Westminster Bank Ltd* [1927] 2 K.B. 297. See also *Middle Temple v. Lloyds Bank plc & Sekerbank* [1999] Lloyd's Rep. Bank. 50, where the respective liabilities of a clearing bank acting for a foreign bank customer and the foreign bank collecting a cheque for its customer were considered in depth.

[10] [1959] 1 Q.B. 55, approved in *Warren Metals Ltd v. Colonial Catering Co Ltd* [1975] N.Z.L.R. 273.

a customer at that branch, where it had a considerable overdraft. Some weeks later, he opened a current account at the bank and, relying on further advice from the bank manager, invested even more money in the firm. Having lost all his money, he sued the bank and bank manager. The young man's claim was in negligence, but since there was no action at that time for negligent misstatement,[11] the action had to be founded in contract or fiduciary duty. If the plaintiff were to succeed in contract, he had to show that he was a customer of the bank when the advice was given. The judge held that the bank accepted instructions from the plaintiff at the time the first investment was made (the express advice had actually been made earlier than that date, but it was implicitly repeated on that day), and he became a customer on that date. The judge went on to say that if he had not become a customer until later, the bank was nevertheless under a duty, by virtue of a fiduciary relationship, to exercise ordinary care and skill in advising him at that time. It has now become clear that liability for negligent misrepresentation may be owed by banks even to non-customers, so that the finding that the plaintiff was a customer would be correspondingly less important and the existence of a fiduciary relationship would be difficult to support today. It is suggested that it might also be possible to argue now that since Martins Bank was performing "banking" functions for the plaintiff in advising him, there was a contractual relationship; if so, he would have been a customer in any case on account of that relationship.

The primary relationship between banker and customer is contractual,[12] **2–039**
and the bank stands in the position of debtor to the customer in relation to monies deposited when the customer's account is in credit.[13] A person remains a customer, even if he or she is indebted to the bank[14] or if the bank performs functions other than holding money for him or her, such as safe keeping of goods or documents, selling securities, giving investment advice, advising on company takeovers and mergers, selling insurance services and all the other things which, in a era of financial conglomerates, banks will do for their customers. Moreover a bank may hold funds subject to an express or constructive trust or a *Quistclose* trust,[15] and the relationship is still one of banker and customer, though of course not merely debtor and creditor. It is also possible that, in appropriate circumstances, a person who is generally a customer of a bank, might not be considered a customer for a particular purpose, such as those of a statutory provision.[16]

---

[11] Not until *Hedley Byrne v. Heller* [1964] A.C. 465. A claim based on fraud failed; it was held that the manager had honestly believed in the advice he had given.

[12] See below, Chap. 3.

[13] *Foley v. Hill* (1848) 2 H.L. Cas. 28, see below, Chap. 3.

[14] *Clarke v. London and County Banking Co.* [1897] 1 Q.B. 552.

[15] *Barclays Bank Ltd v. Quistclose Investments Ltd* [1970] A.C. 567. See below, paras 9–047 *et seq.*

[16] In *Lloyds Bank Ltd v. E.B. Savory & Co.* [1932] 2 K.B. 122, affd [1933] A.C. 201, Lawrence L.J. (at 140) held that the account holders were not customers of the collecting offices, because each branch is a distinct trading body, so the account holders "might just as well have been customers of some other bank".

Opening an account

2–040 **Identity of customer.** A person may be a customer even though he or she opens an account in an assumed name, since there is no objection, in England and Wales, to a person using whatever name he or she wishes. The bank, however, would now be committing an offence under the money laundering legislation if it did not obtain satisfactory evidence of the person's identity (see below, Chapter 4). But if anyone uses an assumed name purporting to be another existing person, or assumes another name to deceive the bank into thinking that he or she is not the person he or she really is, this may well be fraud, and if the bank (or its officer) is deceived, the contract may be voidable at the bank's option. The obvious risk for the bank is that the account is opened so that cheques payable to the named customer and fraudulently obtained by the person opening the account may be paid in. In this case, the collecting bank would be liable in conversion to the true owner of the cheque, and might not be protected by section 4 of the Ch A 1957, if it has not received payment for a customer.[17]

2–041 Where a person who opens an account is purporting to act with the authority of another person and has no such authority, the contractual relationship of banker and customer between the purported customer and the bank does not come into existence. In *Stoney Stanton Supplies v. Midland Bank Ltd*,[18] the "rogue" forged the signatures of the directors of a company both on the mandate given to the bank and on cheques drawn on the account. The company could not recover as against the bank because it had not become a customer, and since forgery cannot be ratified[19], the company could not ratify what the rogue had done and make the company a customer retrospectively. On general principle, therefore, a request by a person to open an account for another must be met with particular caution, and the authority carefully established in case the account is being opened for fraudulent purposes.

2–042 **Inquiries made by banks.** When a bank opens an account, it normally makes inquiries or obtains references to ensure that the prospective customer is a suitable person for holding an account. If it fails to do so, it runs the risk of being held liable in an action for conversion. The facts in *Ladbroke v. Todd*[20] are a good illustration. A young man wanted to open an account at the defendant's bank, and handed the cashier a cheque which he said he wanted cleared quickly, because "he had to go to Oxford that

---

[17] One situation where the bank would not be liable to the customer, though, is the unusual case where another person has paid funds into the customer's account to which the customer has no right, at least if this is part of a criminal conspiracy (whether or not the customer is implicated). See *Robinson v. Midland Bank Ltd* (1925) 41 T.L.R. 170 at 402.

[18] [1966] 2 Lloyds L.R. 373.

[19] BOEA 1882, s. 24.

[20] (1914) 30 T.L.R. 433, approved in *Commissioners of Taxation v. English, Scottish and Australian Bank* [1920] A.C. 683, PC.

night". The account was duly opened and he obtained the money the following day. It later emerged that the cheque had been stolen from a letter box—it represented an Oxford undergraduate's winnings from Ladbroke's. The bank was sued in conversion and raised the statutory defence[21]: if the bank could show that it had acted for a customer in good faith and without negligence, it would not be liable in conversion. The court held that the man was indeed a customer of the bank, and the bank had acted in good faith. However the bank's defence failed because the inquiries it had made had been cursory and answered incorrectly, and it had been assumed that because the man "was well dressed and well spoken and seemed to be of a class likely to be an undergraduate of Oxford University" he was the payee of the cheque. In these circumstances, the bank had been negligent because it had not made adequate inquiries.

The sort of inquiries a bank should make will depend upon current **2–043**
banking practice.[22] Banking practice has undergone an important change with the introduction of the banking code of practice. The Code requires banks to tell customers what identification banks need to "prove identity. This is important for your security and is required by law."[23] Behind the neutral words lie the stringent identification requirements of the money laundering legislation.[24] Banks (like other institutions) now have to carry out rigorous procedures to identify prospective customers[25] and they have tightened up their procedures for the identification of prospective customers as a result. Banks which fail to conform to these procedures run the risk of criminal penalties. It is likely that in due course they will also be exposed to greater civil liability, since general banking practice will become more stringent as a result.[26]

[21] Which would now be under s. 4 of the Cheques Act 1957.

[22] *Marfani & Co v. Midland Bank Ltd* [1968] 2 All E.R. 573.

[23] Banking Code (1999), para. 4.6.

[24] Money Laundering Regulations, S.I. 1993 No. 1933, made under the Criminal Justice Act 1993 (CJA 1993). Discussed in detail in Chaps 4 and 14.

[25] MLR 1993, regs 7 *et seq.* And if a prospective customer seems to be acting as an agent for some other person, the bank must take "reasonable measures to establish the identity of any person on whose behalf the applicant . . . is acting" (that is, apparently "to use best practice" to do so), MLR 1993, reg. 9(3).

[26] *cf. Marfani v. Midland Bank* [1968] 2 All E.R. 573, *per* Diplock L.J.: the standard of care imposed on a bank has to be interpreted with regard to current banking practice.

ment. The customer was duly informed [illegible] the name, the following [illegible] that the cheque [illegible] stolen from [illegible] [illegible] faith and without negligence, [illegible] could not be liable in conversion. The court held that the [illegible] a customer of the bank [illegible] had [illegible] good name. However the bank's defence failed because the inquiries which [illegible] had been [illegible] and answered [illegible] and it had never [illegible] [illegible] adequate inquiries.

[illegible] inquiries a bank should [illegible] operation of [illegible] 5-043 [illegible] [illegible] decade [illegible] and previous [illegible] procedures [illegible] conform to these procedures [illegible]

[illegible]

Chapter 3

Incidents of the Banker-Customer Relationship

Banking law is not an integral and distinctive body of law in itself, but applies a number of general branches of law, such as contract, tort and trusts law, which are given a distinctive character by their operation in the unique context of banking, and some technical branches of law dealing with typically banking aspects, such as the law of negotiable instruments and of cheques. It is based on law and practice which have grown up over centuries, and as an activity it is so closely bound up with other fields of commerce and with everyday life that it is often at the forefront of legal development. This can be seen from the large proportion of cases which are central to banking law, but which are also leading cases in other fields of law: *Hedley Byrne v. Heller*[1] and *Tai Hing Cotton Ltd v. Liu Chong Bank Ltd*[2] are among examples from tort, and *Lipkin Gorman v. Karpnale*[3] from restitution. **3–001**

Although there are a number of important statutes relating to aspects of banking law,[4] the basic relationship is regulated by the common law of contract. Modern banking is said to have started when merchants deposited their valuables and money with the goldsmiths for safekeeping. In early times this was regarded as bailment (it still is, as far as the custody of valuables is concerned) but once the goldsmiths began to carry out the merchants' instructions about the money they had deposited, the characteristics of the contract changed—they had begun to act as bankers—and the straightforward contract of bailment no longer reflected the reality of the relationship. It was not until the last century that the nature of banking began to be clarified by the courts,[5] and only in the case of *Joachimson v. Swiss Bank Corporation*[6] that it was made clear by the Court of Appeal not only that the ordinary relationship is contractual, but that a single contract[7] governs the general relations between the parties (that is, all the services which a bank is bound to provide if it is asked) though further separate **3–002**

---

[1] [1964] A.C. 465.

[2] [1985] 2 All E.R. 947; [1986] A.C. 80.

[3] [1992] 4 All E.R. 512, HL.

[4] Among them the BOEA 1882, the Ch A 1957 and Ch A 1992, the CCA 1974 and the BA 1987.

[5] *Foley v. Hill* (1848) 2 H.L. Cas. 28, see below, para. 3–004.

[6] [1921] 3 K.B. 110.

[7] *per* Atkin L.J. at 127, (approved in *Tai Hing Cotton Ltd v. Liu Chong Bank Ltd* [1985] 2 All E.R. 947 at 956). Bankes L.J. thought that there was a primary contract, with separate added collateral obligations.

contracts might be entered into for specific purposes, for example where the customer borrows money, or the bank sells securities, or issues credit cards.[8] The contract is formed in the usual way, by offer (usually an offer by the customer to open an account) and acceptance. It was also settled that the relationship is of *implied* contract, so that the terms of the general contract are not usually written, although nowadays of course the terms of banking contracts relating to many specific matters, such as credit cards, invariably are. "The friendly informality of implied contract", as the Jack Committee observed,[9] fitted in well to the more relaxed environment of 80 or 100 years ago, when the law was settled. It was a time when "bank managers knew clients personally and mistakes were relatively rare". Although the climate has changed, the Committee felt that the basic aspects of the relationship are so well established that they do not appear to be in need of clarification, much less reform. Any attempt to codify them (apart from "the special case" of confidentiality) would create more problems than it would solve.

3–003 Although the bank's liability to its customer is primarily contractual, a complex mixture of duties in other fields of law follows from the nature of banking work. The duties of banks and their customers have to be discussed in different contexts. These are primarily (a) in contract (b) in tort (and concurrently in contract and tort), (c) in trusts, and (d) in restitution.

The Nature of the Banking Contract

Debtor-Creditor Relationship as Regards Deposits

3–004 So far as the deposit of money with the banker is concerned, it was settled in *Foley v. Hill*[10] that the ordinary banker and customer relationship is that of debtor and creditor, not trustee and beneficiary. It was held that money paid in by customers is

> "under the control of the banker; it is then the banker's money; he is known to deal with it as his own; he makes of it what profit he can, which profit he retains to himself".[11]

The bank therefore owns the money and merely owes a debt to the customer, to whom it undertakes to repay an amount equivalent to that

[8] *Libyan Bank v. Bankers Trust* [1988] 1 Lloyds Rep. 259 at 272, *per* Staughten J. Standing orders, direct debits, bankers' drafts, letters of credit, automatic cash tills and foreign currency are services banks habitually provide.

[9] Jack Report (1989), para. 2.18.

[10] (1848) 2 H.L. Cas. 28; see also *Midland Bank Ltd v. Conway Corp.* [1965] 2 All E.R. 972. Banks can assume the office of trustee in certain circumstances, see below, Chap. 9.

[11] *per* Lord Cottenham L.C., at 1005. And: "students are taught at an early stage of their studies in the law that it is incorrect to speak of 'all my money in the bank'", *per* Staughten J., *Libyan Bank v. Bankers Trust* [1988] 1 Lloyd's Rep. 259 at 271.

paid in, with or without interest, either at call or at a fixed time. Banks may use the funds they hold as they see fit—they do not have to account to their customers for the use of the money deposited with them—and their customers cannot claim the profits from that use, as they might if banks had fiduciary duties in respect of the deposits.

Implied Terms from *Joachimson v. Swiss Bank Corporation*

As we saw, it was held in *Joachimson v. Swiss Bank Corporation* that there is only one contract between the bank and customer. It was also settled in that case that the contract is not just a simple matter of loan. Atkin L.J. listed a number of implied terms of the contract in a famous passage[12]: **3–005**

1. The bank undertakes to receive money and to collect bills for its customer's account, and it borrows the proceeds and promises to repay them. The bank promises to repay at the branch of the bank where the account is kept (and not at any other branch[13]) and during banking hours[14]
2. The bank promises to repay any part of the amount due against the customer's written order at the branch (though it was not decided whether the order must be in writing)
3. The bank promises not to cease to do business with the customer except on reasonable notice (because cheques may be outstanding for two or three days)
4. The customer promises to exercise reasonable care in executing his written orders so as not to mislead the bank or to facilitate forgery.[15]

The law continues to adapt as practice changes, and for this reason even these implied terms are not written in stone: nowadays we should say that the second and third of these must reflect the widespread use of cash machines and of telephone and internet banking.

---

[12] *Joachimson v. Swiss Bank Corporation* [1921] 3 K.B. 110 at 127, *per* Atkin L.J.

[13] *Clare & Co v. Dresdner Bank* [1915] 2 K.B. 576, *Richardson v. Richardson* [1927] P. 228, *cf. Joseph Leate & Sons v. Direction der Disconto Gesellschaft* (1915) 85 L.J. K.B. 281.

[14] *e.g.* not on statutory bank holidays. Hours of business are published by the Committee of London Clearing Banks from time to time. Normal banking hours may be altered on reasonable notice.

[15] *Joachimson* [1921] 3 K.B. 110 at 127. The case related to the bank account of a partnership. It was held that a demand is a necessary ingredient in a cause of action against a bank, and since no demand had been made before the dissolution of the firm in 1914, the cause of action had not accrued by that time, and the action could not be brought later in the firm's name. For the effect of the outbreak of war on a current account, see *Arab Bank Ltd v. Barclays Bank Ltd* [1954] 2 W.L.R. 1027, HL.

Demand

3–006 **By the customer.** The third of the *Joachimson* implied terms is that the bank's obligation as debtor is to repay[16] the amount due according to the demand of the customer provided there are sufficient funds.[17] Normally a debtor is obliged to seek out and pay the creditor,[18] and the requirement that a demand should be made is exceptional, and characteristic of the banking contract. If customers did not have to make a demand for their money, there would be odd results: the bank would be entitled to tender the amount of the credit balance to the customer at any time and then refuse to honour outstanding cheques, because ordinary debtors have a right to repay their debts at any time.

3–007 Demand is normally made by the presentation of a cheque, but can be made by the issue of a writ by the customer without any previous demand,[19] and, in modern banking, can be made by using a cash machine. A demand is only needed in the case of a current account, not in the case of a fixed deposit which matures at a specified time.[20] If the customer is indebted to the bank, the position is different. In the case of a term loan, the customer is liable from the date at which the loan is repayable, and in the case of an overdraft the rule is that time runs from the date of each advance, where nothing has been agreed to the contrary.[21] In any case, banks usually expressly state that obligations under loans, overdrafts and guarantees arise on demand (in which case the rule in *Joachimson* applies).[22]

3–008 The question of demand by the customer was considered in *National Bank for Commerce v. National Westminster Bank*.[23] A series of unauthorised debits had been made to the plaintiffs' account, and the plaintiffs wrote several letters to the defendant requesting reimbursement of the amount of the debits, and eventually issued a writ. The defendants argued that the plaintiff's demand had taken place when the debits were made. If that were the case, the cause of action would have arisen then, and the claim would have been statute-barred. The judge rejected the argument that the demand was made when the sums were debited. He held that a

---

[16] Payment must be made within a reasonable time. The six year limitation period for actions based on debt (Limitation Act 1980 (LA 1980), s. 5) starts to run from the time of the demand. See also *Re Footman Bower & Co. Ltd.* [1961] Ch. 443.

[17] Further considered below, para. 6–031.

[18] *Walton v. Mascall* (1844) 13 M. & W. 452.

[19] *Joachimson* [1921] 3 K.B. 110.

[20] Nor where the account is being closed and the relationship terminated, nor when the bank is being wound up.

[21] *Parr's Banking Co Ltd v. Yates* [1898] 2 Q.B. 460. The earlier debts would be discharged first because of the operation of the rule in *Clayton's Case* (1816) 1 Mer. 529, see below, Chap. 11.

[22] See *Bradford Old Bank Ltd v. Sutcliffe* [1918] 2 K.B. 833, for a case concerning guarantees. See also the Limitation (Enemies and War Prisoners) Act 1945, ss. 1 and 2, which provides for the suspension of the running of time while a person is an enemy or a prisoner of war.

[23] [1990] 2 Lloyd's Rep. 514

customer who suffered damage as a result of an unauthorised debit would have a claim in damages for breach of contract, and could claim from the bank the amount when the unauthorised debits (ineffective as a matter of law) were left out of account.[24] The unauthorised debits were not effective as demands; the demand to repay was made only when the customer had written the letters demanding repayment, and the claim was therefore not statute-barred.

The corollary of the customer's demand is that where the customer has an overdraft, the bank can also demand repayment, and expect it to be made directly.[25] This is discussed in Chapter 8.

Agency

The debtor and creditor basis of the contract does not account for all the basic aspects of the relationship, even taking into account the implied terms listed above. In *Foley v. Hill* itself,[26] it was stated that there was a "superadded obligation arising out of the custom of bankers to honour the customer's drafts". In fact, there are a number of "superadded obligations" in the contract. These stem from the fact that the banker is also acting as an agent for the customer, and the agency relationship implies more complex duties than those of a debtor to the creditor. These include duties of care and, in some cases, fiduciary duties. An agent must not only obey instructions (unless they are unlawful or contrary to public policy[27]) but must also use reasonable skill and care in carrying them out. Bankers are subject to this common law duty, and also to the statutory duty of care of section 13 of the Supply of Goods and Services Act 1982.[28] The numerous aspects of banking business provide great scope for customers to challenge the way in which banks have performed their duties and litigation is varied and increasing.[29] Fiduciary duties demand even higher standards than duties of care, although the limits of these duties are far from clear. **3–009**

Where a bank is acting as agent, its duties depend partly on what it has undertaken to do, and otherwise may be implied from the circumstances. The law on the duties of agents has recently been set out by the Privy Council in the context of estate agents and illuminates this point: in *Kelly v. Cooper*,[30] Lord Browne-Wilkinson said that agency is a matter of contract, and the rights and duties of the principal and agent are dependent upon the **3–010**

---

[24] Following *Limpgrange v. BCCI International SA* [1986] F.L.R. 36 at 47, *per* Staughten J.

[25] See *Williams and Glyns Bank v. Barnes* [1981] Comm. L.R. 205.

[26] (1848) 2 H.L. Cas. 28. See Chorley [1940] M.L.R. 293, commenting on the effect of *Foley v. Hill*: "Whenever it became necessary to lay down some new aspect of the banker's duty. . . it was found to exist by virtue of a 'super-added obligation'".

[27] *Cohen v. Kittell* (1889) 22 Q.B. 680.

[28] See Steyn J., *Barclays Bank v. Quincecare* [1992] 4 All E.R. 363 at 375–6, and below, para. 5–032.

[29] See Tijo [1997] J.B.L. 350.

[30] [1993] A.C. 205.

terms of the contract between them, whether express or implied. It is not possible to say that all agents owe the same duties to their principals; it is always necessary to have regard to the express or implied terms of the contract.[31] This means that not all agents necessarily owe the *fiduciary duties* often associated with agency; it depends on the terms of the contract. Estate agents, for example, who act for numerous principals, where there may be a conflict of interest between the principals, do not have to reveal information to one of their principals which is confidential to another, because they would be unable to perform their function.

3–011 Some agents are regarded as fiduciaries, however, and must not put themselves in a position where their duty and their interest conflict. Banks are not usually regarded as acting as fiduciaries as far as the normal banker/customer relationship is concerned,[32] but there are situations where they do undertake a fiduciary role. This is particularly true now that banking activities have broadened into many different areas, and are no longer restricted to traditional commercial activities ("core" banking[33]). Banks which act as financial conglomerates may well find themselves in difficult situations, where the interests of their customers conflict with each other and where the interests of customers conflict with those of the bank itself.

3–012 Judicial analysis of the word "fiduciary" in recent decisions has helped to clarify the law, which has been unpredictable because of the loose way in which the word has been used.[34] In *Bristol and West Building Society v. Mothew*, Millett L.J. said:

> "A fiduciary is someone who has undertaken to act for or on behalf of another in a particular matter in circumstances which give rise to a relationship of trust and confidence. The distinguishing obligation of a fiduciary is the obligation of loyalty. The principal is entitled to the single-minded loyalty of his fiduciary. This core liability has several facets. A fiduciary must act in good faith; he must not make a profit out of his trust; he must not place himself in a position where his duty and his interest may conflict; he may not act for his own benefit or the benefit of a third person without the informed consent of his principal. This is not intended to be an exhaustive list, but it is sufficient to

[31] [1993] A.C. 205 at 214.

[32] *National Westminster Bank v. Morgan* [1983] 3 All E.R. 85. In *Woods v. Martins Bank* [1959] 1 Q.B. 55, it was held that a bank was acting as a fiduciary in giving financial advice, but this was, relevantly, a pre-*Hedley Byrne v. Heller* ([1964] A.C. 465) decision; see Chap. 5.

[33] See Cranston, *Principles of Banking Law*, Chap. 1.

[34] "The word 'fiduciary' is flung around now as if it applied to all breaches of duty by solicitors, directors of companies and so forth . . . to say that simple carelessness in giving advice is . . . a breach [of the special duty of a fiduciary] is a perversion of words", *per* Southin J., *Girardet v. Crease & Co* (1987) 11 B.C.L.R. (2d) 361, cited by Millett L.J., *Bristol and West Building Society v. Mothew* [1996] 4 All E.R. 698 at 710.

indicate the nature of fiduciary obligations. They are the defining characteristics of the fiduciary."[35]

The court went on make a further distinction: not every breach of duty by a fiduciary will be a breach of *fiduciary duty*. This expression is properly confined to those duties which are peculiar to fiduciaries, the breach of which attracts legal consequences differing from those consequent upon the breach of other duties[36]; breach of fiduciary obligation connotes disloyalty or infidelity, and although it need not be dishonest, it must be intentional. The duty to exercise reasonable care, however, is not specifically a fiduciary duty; an agent is bound to exercise reasonable care and skill, but failure in this respect does not constitute a breach of fiduciary duty—"mere incompetence is not enough".[37] **3–013**

Conflicts of interest and disclosure or use of confidential information belonging to customers are likely to occur in the context of the bank's duty of confidentiality to its customers.[38] This duty has traditionally been regarded as central to the traditional "core" banking contract, although it has been under attack in recent years, notably because of legislation against money laundering.[39] The duty of confidentiality, whether by virtue of the traditional banker's duty or simply because of the general duty of an agent towards its client,[40] nowadays gives rise to particularly intractable difficulties because of the extensive and varied nature of modern banking business. In the 1980s a process of deregulation of financial institutions took place, including the "Big Bang" of 1986, which abolished the restrictive barriers of the United Kingdom Stock Exchange. This process allowed market forces and competition to play an increased role in shaping the policy and operation of the financial services industry, allowing greater diversification in the industry. Banks were able take advantage of the change by expanding into other profitable areas of activity such as the securities business. Banks **3–014**

[35] [1996] 4 All E.R. 698 at 711–712. See also Lord Browne-Wilkinson's speech in *Henderson v. Merrett* [1994] 3 All E.R. 506 at 543, and Finn, *Fiduciary Obligations,* both cited by Millett L.J. His Lordship went on to refer separately to the situation where a fiduciary deals with his principal, in which case the agent must prove affirmatively that the transaction is fair and that full disclosure has been made.

[36] [1996] 4 All E.R. 698 at 710.

[37] *ibid.*, at 710 and 712. Breach of equitable duty of care attracts the remedy of equitable compensation rather than damages: though "this is merely the product of history and in this context is in my opinion a distinction without a difference. It resembles common law damages in that it is awarded by way of compensation" . . . for loss. (*per* Millett L.J. at 711). See also Capper [1994] Legal Studies 313.

[38] *Tournier v. National Provincial Union Bank of England* [1924] 1 K.B. 461, and Chap. 4 below. In the case of companies, there are statutory prohibitions on "insider dealing" which impose wide restrictions on the ability of persons with insider information (unpublished price-sensitive information) acquired directly or from others to use that information and to deal in the company's securities.

[39] *e.g.* CJA 1993, and MLR 1993, see below, Chap. 4.

[40] It is unclear how far the *Tournier* duty applies to banks performing other functions than "core" banking.

have therefore moved from their concentration on "core" banking and become in effect financial conglomerates offering a range of services including investment banking. Inevitably, traditional banking confidentiality may be threatened by the operation of commercial pressures associated with these developments. One department of a bank may act for a corporate customer whose shares are marketed by the bank, for example, while another department advises investors, and in these circumstances there is a potential conflict of interest between the two customers. The difficulty is increased by the fact that the bank also has interests at stake.

3–015 For these sorts of reasons, the process of deregulation of financial services has, paradoxically, given rise to a simultaneous and corresponding process of *increased* regulation. The FSA 1986 set up systems to protect investors and make the institutions sound. An agency, the Securities and Investment Board (SIB), was set up under the Act, and, with a number of Self Regulatory Organisations (SROs)[41] which authorised their members, regulated the conduct of financial business. These organisations made rules in relation to the conduct of business, and firms had to regulate themselves accordingly in order to obtain authorisation, for example, by having compliance programmes and compliance officers. However, this complicated regime has been altered again by the setting up of the FSA as a single regulator of all financial services, including banks.[42] One of the tasks of the FSA is to rationalise the various existing sets of rules, including the rules designed to prevent conflicts of interests prejudicing customers' interests, and requiring disclosure to customers of the existence of relationships which might conflict with their own.

3–016 The question of how far the duty of disclosure to customers extends has become a serious problem. It seems to be quite impracticable in many cases for conglomerates—"huge international firms with enormous resources that operate on a global scale and offer a comprehensive range of services to clients[43]"—to give full and frank disclosure. Any but the most explicit warning clearly notified to the customer of a possible conflict, may amount to a breach of the duty and expose banks to the risks of liability to account to the customer concerned for the profits made.[44] Methods of "compartmentalizing" different departments of conglomerates by means of what are called *Chinese walls* or information barriers have been devised—that is, a set of policies and procedures which are intended to prevent conflicts of duties[45] and help protect customers against disclosure of confidential

---

[41] *e.g.* LAUTRO (Life Assurance and Unit Trust Regulatory Organization); IMRO (Investment Management Regulatory Organization); FIMBRA (Financial Intermediaries, Managers and Brokers Regulatory Organization).

[42] Replacing SIB, and taking on wider functions. See above, Chap. 1. The draft Financial Services and Markets Bill was published in July 1998. The BEA 1998, transferring the regulatory functions of the Bank to the FSA came into force June 1, 1998.

[43] *Prince Jefri Bolkiah v. KPMG* [1999] 1 All E.R. 517 at 521, *per* Lord Millett.

[44] Under the FSA 1986.

[45] See Pennington, *The Law of the Investment Markets*, and McVea, *Financial Conglomerates and the Chinese Wall*, for discussion of the practical and legal difficulties of Chinese Walls. See Fiduciary Duties and Regulatory Rules, Law Com. No.124, 1992.

information; they may also, of course, protect the bank against claims by customers. These normally involve some combination of: physical separation of departments in order to insulate them from each other (including details like dining arrangements); an educational programme, normally recurring, to emphasise the importance of not divulging confidential information; strict procedures for dealing with a situation where it is felt that the wall should be crossed, and the maintaining of proper records where this occurs; monitoring, by compliance officers, of the effectiveness of the wall, and disciplinary sanctions where there has been a breach of the wall.[46]

The operation of Chinese walls was examined by the House of Lords in the case of *Prince Jefri Bolkiah v. KPMG*.[47] The defendants, a large international firm of chartered accountants, had acted as auditors of the Brunei Investment Agency since its establishment in 1983. Prince Jefri of Brunei was the chairman of the Agency, and for a period of 18 months the firm had also acted for him in private litigation—extensively, since 168 members of the firm had been employed on the work. However, Prince Jefri was dismissed from his position as chairman, and the government of Brunei set up an investigation of the activities of the Agency during the period of his chairmanship. KPMG accepted the instructions of the government, despite the conflict of interest and the fact that it possessed confidential information relating to Prince Jefri's affairs, because the firm was satisfied that the Chinese wall erected around the department carrying out the investigation would protect the interests of the client. Prince Jefri had not been told of these arrangements and, when he discovered them, brought this action to obtain an injunction to restrain KPMG from continuing to work on the investigation. KPMG's defence was that it was only required to make reasonable efforts to protect Prince Jefri's confidential information and that, balancing the competing interests, the precautions it had taken meant that there was no real risk that the information would be disclosed. **3–017**

This was not the view taken by the House of Lords. Lord Millett, considering the firm's duties as those of a solicitor rather than as those of an accountant, first stated the duty to an existing client: the solicitor is a fiduciary, and cannot act both for and against the same client at the same time. He made it clear that there is a distinction between the duties imposed on solicitors and accountants, because auditors' clients are taken to consent to the firm acting for competing clients.[48] Presumably, this may also be true of other financial advisers, like banks, although they were not specifically mentioned. **3–018**

[46] *Prince Jefri Bolkiah* [1999] 1 All E.R. 517 at 529, *per* Lord Millett, quoting Law Com. 124.
[47] [1999] 1 All E.R. 517.
[48] See *Kelly v. Cooper* [1993] A.C. 205, PC.

3–019 His Lordship went on to consider the position here, where Prince Jefri was a *former* client of the firm. He described the question not as a matter of a conflict of interest, which would raise the issue of fiduciary duties,[49] but as the protection of confidential information. It was held that although there is no absolute rule, as in the United States, that a solicitor cannot act for a client with an interest adverse to that of a former client, there is nevertheless a continuing duty to preserve the confidentiality of information disclosed to the solicitor during the relationship. This meant that the plaintiff had to establish first, that the firm was in possession of information which was confidential to him and to the disclosure of which he had not consented, and secondly, that the information was, or might be, relevant to the new matter in which the interest of the other client was, or might be, adverse to his own.[50] These were matters of fact and in most cases would not be hard to prove: the first can readily be inferred and the second is often obvious. The court went on to emphasise that the solicitor's duty to keep information confidential is unqualified; it is *not* enough merely to take all reasonable steps to keep information confidential, and no balancing exercise between the interests of the parties need be undertaken. A solicitor should not without the consent of his or her former client accept instructions unless, viewed objectively, his or her doing so will not increase the risk that information which is confidential to the former client may come into the possession of a party with an adverse interest.[51]

3–020 KPMG therefore had to demonstrate that the precautions it had taken were sufficient to ensure that there was no risk that the information would come into the possession of those now acting for the other party. A Chinese wall might, in principle, be sufficient to eliminate the risk, but the court had to be "satisfied on the basis of clear and convincing evidence that all reasonable measures have been taken to ensure that no disclosure will occur".[52] Here, a Chinese wall had been put in place within the relevant department (the forensic accounting department) and special arrangements had been set up to protect the confidential information by ensuring that nobody who was in possession of the information worked on the investigation. Most of the work was carried out in Brunei, and work in London was done in a separate room with restricted access in a separate building from the department. Separate computer file servers were used, and all electronic information relating to earlier work was deleted from the firm's servers.

3–021 It was not enough. The arrangements were established *ad hoc* and erected within a single department; the teams of staff had a rotating

[49] Examined by Millett L.J. (as he then was) in *Bristol and West v. Mothew* [1996] 4 All E.R. 698.

[50] *Prince Jefri Bolkiah* [1999] 1 All E.R. 517 at 527.

[51] *ibid.*, 529.

[52] Citing Sopinka J. in *MacDonald Estate v. Martin* (1990) 77 D.L.R. (4th) 249 at 269.

membership involving large numbers of staff, many of whom might return to other projects: enforcement would be very difficult. Lord Millett said:

> "In my opinion, an effective Chinese wall needs to be an established part of the organisational structure of the firm, not created *ad hoc* and dependent on the acceptance of evidence sworn for the purpose by members of staff engaged on the relevant work."[53]

Prince Jefri obtained his injunction.[54]

Contributory Negligence

In a number of recent cases, banks taking action against valuers and solicitors for negligence in advising them have been found liable themselves for contributory negligence. The cases were a result of over-enthusiastic bank lending[55] during the late 1980s on the back of a huge property boom. Banks and other lenders lent large sums on the security of property, and, when the perhaps inevitable crash in the property market followed, lost much of the value of their security. In many cases, banks relied on what turned out to be careless valuations from surveyors or faulty advice from solicitors, and sought redress from them. However, the courts, in a series of cases, found that lending decisions by lenders (usually the less responsible lenders) had been made recklessly. The fact that contributory negligence can be pleaded against lenders in this situation was confirmed in the case of *Platform Homes v. Oyston*.[56] **3–022**

Banks and The General Rules of Contract

The general principles of contract law apply to banking contracts, although the rules sometimes have special implications because of the context. Thus the principles governing misrepresentation and undue influence have been significant in recent developments of the law relating to banks taking security over the family home.[57] An outline of some of the rules as they are likely to affect banking is given below.[58] **3–023**

In England, as we have seen, the general banking contract is implied. There are a number of situations, however, where the terms of the contract

---

[53] *Prince Jefri Bolkiah* [1999] 1 All E.R. 517 at 530.

[54] See also *Young v. Robson Rhodes* [1999] 3 All E.R. 524, Ch. D., where the *Prince Jefri* case was considered. It was held that the crucial question was whether the barriers would work, not whether it was created by *ad hoc* arrangements.

[55] "In the heady days of 1988, when the property market was at its height and mortgage lenders were falling over themselves to advance money to house purchasers": *per* Millett L.J., *Bristol and West v. Mothew* [1996] 4 All E.R. 698 at 713.

[56] [1998] Ch. 466, CA, aff'd. [1999] 2 W.L.R. 518, HL.

[57] See below, paras 3–042 *et seq.*

[58] For detailed discussion, see one of the other established texts on contract, such as *Anson's Law of Contract* (Beatson ed., 27th ed.), Treitel, *The Law of Contract* (9th ed.) or *Chitty on Contract*.

(or some of them) are written; for example, it is a universal practice in the United Kingdom for intending customers to be asked to sign a bank's mandate form on opening an account, and this form will contain some terms of the contract. If the customer is given facilities such as a cheque guarantee card or a bank credit card, often supplied by separate subsidiary companies of the bank, the customer then makes a separate agreement on the special terms notified to him or her at the time, and at every renewal. Similarly, term loans are generally made upon express terms notified at the time.

Exclusion Clauses

(1) Incorporation of terms

3–024 The usual contractual principles apply to banking contracts and an exclusion clause must therefore be *incorporated* in the contract if it is to have any effect. In the case of written contracts which are signed, such as credit card agreements, customers are normally regarded as having notice of their terms (*L'Estrange v. Graucob*[59]), including any exclusion clauses, whether they have read them or not. Many banking contracts must be signed by customers who are not aware of their implications.

3–025 In other situations, the term will be incorporated if the customer has notice of it before entering the contract. An instructive case as to the requirement of notice in this context is *Burnett v. Westminster Bank Ltd*,[60] where a bank issued new cheque books containing cheque forms with magnetic ink characters on them for use at a branch which had just become computerised. A warning was printed on the covers of the new cheque books that cheques and credit slips in the books must be used only for the account for which they had been prepared. Mr Burnett had accounts at two branches of the bank, only one of which used the new magnetic ink system. He used one of the new cheques to draw on his account at the uncomputerised branch, but he altered the cheques using ordinary ink. Shortly afterwards, he ordered the latter branch to stop payment, giving the correct number, date and amount of the cheque, and saying that he had altered the address of the branch. However, the cheque had been routed to the former branch because of the magnetic ink coding, and since no one at the branch noticed the alterations, it was paid despite the countermand. The court held that as the relationship between the bank and Mr Burnett predated the introduction of the new cheque books, the bank could not show that he had had notice of the new term. The contract could not be altered unilaterally without notice (and without consideration).

(2) Construction of terms

3–026 Assuming that an exclusion clause has been incorporated in the contract, its meaning must be clear if it is to bind the other party. If there are ambiguities in the wording they will be construed *contra proferentem*—that

[59] [1934] 2 K.B. 394.
[60] [1966] 1 Q.B. 742.

is, against the bank, the party seeking to rely on the clause. Banks are naturally regarded as strong negotiating parties in relation to their customers, and the courts may be inclined to construe terms in their contracts strictly. This was demonstrated by the important decision of the Privy Council in *Tai Hing Cotton Ltd v. Liu Chong Bank Ltd.*[61]

The Tai Hing company had current accounts with three Hong Kong banks, which were authorised to honour cheques bearing certain signatures. A dishonest employee of the company forged some 3,000 cheques over six years, which were paid by the banks. His employers had had no proper financial control and had left him unsupervised. Under the usual implied rules of the banking contract,[62] the customer's account could not be debited on a forgery. The banks' written terms of business, which had been made known to the company when it opened the accounts, stated that monthly statements were deemed to be correct unless the customer notified the bank of any error within a specified period. In one of the contracts the term (a purported *conclusive evidence* clause) read: **3–027**

> "A statement of the customer's account will be rendered once a month. Customers are desired: (1) to examine all entries in the statement of account and to report at once to the bank any error found therein, (2) to return the confirmation slip duly signed. In the absence of any objection to the statement within seven days after its receipt by the customer, the account shall be deemed to have been confirmed."

Tai Hing had not reported any error in the statements. The question was whether the express terms had the effect they purported to have—of making the customer liable if it had made no objection to the statements. **3–028**

The Privy Council said that if the banks wished to impose an obligation on the customer to inspect its account and to make the statements unchallengeable for failure to do so, "the burden of the obligation and of the sanction imposed must be brought home to the customer". This test was "undoubtedly rigorous" but that was because the banks were seeking to exclude rights which the customer would otherwise enjoy. Clear and unambiguous provision was needed if the clause were to bind the customer. The court held, construing the clauses *contra proferentem*, that these terms of business did not amount to conclusive evidence clauses.[63] They did not bring home to the customer the importance of the inspection it had to make, or the conclusive effect of the statements.[64] Lord Scarman (giving the advice of the Board), said that the banks could, if they wished, "increase

[61] [1985] 2 All E.R. 947; [1986] A.C. 80.

[62] See below, Chap. 6.

[63] [1985] 2 All E.R. 947 at 959. For discussion of the other arguments raised, see below, para. 7–031.

[64] And no estoppel could arise from the failure to reply, since there was no duty to reply.

the severity of their terms of business and use their influence, as they have in the past, to seek to persuade the legislature that they should be granted by statute further protection".

3–029 It is possible to conjecture about a form of words which *would* have been effective. If the clauses had said simply "In the absence of such confirmation within . . . days the statement of account shall be conclusive evidence for all purposes of the state of accounts between bank and customer", would this have been sufficient? However, even if the form of words had been effective, the clause would have had to surmount the tests set by the statutory controls on such clauses. In the light of their Lordships' disapproval of the terms in question, it is hard to resist the conclusion that even if they had agreed that the terms were clear, they would have held them unreasonable under the Unfair Contract Terms Act 1977 (UCTA 1977), or now, unfair under the Unfair Terms in Consumer Contracts Regulations 1999 (UTCCR 1999).

(3) Statutory control of contract terms

3–030 **(a) UCTA 1977.** Sections 2 or 3 of UCTA 1977 may be applicable to exclusion clauses in banking contracts. Section 2 provides that, if the bank is "negligent" (in breach of a contractual or tortious duty of reasonable care), then any term excusing the bank from liability for loss or damage is enforceable only if reasonable.[65] Section 3, which applies where a person contracts as a consumer[66] (as a customer would) or on the other's written standard terms of business, provides that any contractual term which attempts to exclude liability[67] will be unenforceable unless it is reasonable. The onus of proving reasonableness is on the bank,[68] and in judging reasonableness, the court will probably have regard to the bank's resources, which are obviously great, and its ability to underwrite its losses by insurance,[69] and to a number of other factors—such as the strength of the bargaining positions of the parties and whether the customer could go elsewhere and bank with others who would not impose such terms.[70]

---

[65] UCTA 1977, s. 2 (2): for loss or damage which is not death or personal injury. The requirement of reasonableness also applies to terms purporting to define the bank's duty, UCTA 1977, s. 13: see *Smith v. Bush* [1990] 1 A.C. 831.

[66] UCTA 1977, s. 12: where he does not make the contract in the course of business, but the other party does.

[67] Excluding liability for loss caused to the customer by breach of contract, allowing the bank to render a contractual performance substantially different from that reasonably expected of it, or rendering none at all in respect of the whole or part of its obligations.

[68] UCTA 1977, s. 11(5).

[69] UCTA 1977, s. 11(4).

[70] Guidelines given in UCTA 1977, Sched. 2 (which, strictly, does not apply to UCTA 1977, ss. 2 and 3, although in practice the courts refer to it). Other factors are: the degree of notice given; whether the customer ought to have known of the term in question; whether the customer received any inducement to agree to it; and whether compliance with any condition imposed on him as a prerequisite to complaining was practicable.

(b) Unfair Terms in Consumer Contracts Regulations 1999 (S.I. 1999 No. 2083). Hitherto, there has been no equivalent in English law of the covenants of good faith or fair dealing in United States law,[71] but the position has been changed by the UTCCR 1999.[72] They were introduced in accordance with an E.C. Directive and will go some way to incorporate civilian ideas of good faith into the English law of contract. They are likely to have a very considerable effect on written banking contracts, like guarantees and mortgages. In giving effect to the Regulations, no attempt was made to organise them with the UCTA 1997 into a coherent whole—indeed, any such attempt would have been a daunting task because of the differing concepts underlying the two pieces of legislation. The Regulations therefore need to be considered separately from the UCTA 1997. 3–031

The Regulations are not limited to exemption clauses, as the UCTA 1997 is, and explicitly have regard to the *fairness* of contractual terms and the *clarity* of the language. They apply in relation to unfair terms in contracts concluded between a seller or supplier and a consumer.[73] 3–032

If a term is unfair, it is not binding on the consumer, although the remainder of the contract may still be valid.[74] A term which has not been individually negotiated is regarded as unfair if, "contrary to the requirement of good faith, it causes a significant imbalance in the parties' rights and obligations under the contract, to the detriment of the consumer. . .".[75–76] If the term has been drafted in advance, it will always be regarded as not having been individually negotiated. The unfairness of a term is assessed taking into account the nature of the goods or services for which the contract was concluded and by referring, at the time of the conclusion of the contract, to all the circumstances attending the conclusion of the contract and to all the terms of the contract or of another contract on which it is dependent.[77] An important exception to this control, however, relates to *core terms*—terms which define the main subject matter of the contract or concern the adequacy of the price or remuneration, as against the goods or services sold or supplied in exchange—which are not assessed for fairness so far as they are in plain and intelligible language.[78]

[71] See the Hon. Sir Anthony Mason (2000) 116 L.Q.R. 66.

[72] S.I. 1999 No. 2083. These Regulations replace those of 1994 (S.I. 1994 No. 3159) (which gave effect to E.C. Directive 93/13 ([1993] O.J. L95/29)). See Law Com. No. 236; Padfield [1995] 5 J.I.B.L. 175; S.J. May 19, 1995, 478; Reynolds (1994) 110 L.Q.R. 1; Brownsword and Howells [1995] J.B.L. 243.

[73] UTCCR 1999, reg. 4(1).

[74] UTCCR 1999, reg. 8. The D.-G. of Fair Trading (and other "qualifying bodies" (UTCCR 1999, reg. 3), which include regulators) may apply for an injunction against a term (UTCCR 1999, regs 10 and 12). The injunction may relate to similar terms used by others. The D.–G. and the other bodies have powers to obtain documents and information (UTCCR 1999, reg. 13).

[75–76] UTCCR 1999, reg. 5(1). The term will then not be binding on the consumer, but the remainder of the contract may still be valid if it can still exist without the term.

[77] UTCCR 1999, reg. 6(1). The four guidelines for assessing good faith given by Sched. 2 to the UTCCR 1994 have disappeared, presumably because they are otiose (since all the circumstances are to be taken into account).

[78] UTCCR 1999, reg. 6(2).

3–033 Schedule 3 to the UTCCR 1999 gives an "indicative and illustrative" list—sometimes called "the grey list"—of seventeen terms which may be unfair. These include: enabling the seller to terminate a contract of indeterminate duration without reasonable notice, enabling the seller or supplier to alter the terms of the contract unilaterally without a valid reason which is specified in the contract, and enabling the seller to alter unilaterally without a valid reason any characteristics of the product or service to be provided. Exceptions however cover suppliers of financial services, who may terminate contracts of indeterminate duration, provided notice is given to the other party, and allowing financial services suppliers to alter the rate of interest payable without notice (the other party is then free to dissolve the contract). In both cases there must be valid reasons.

The original Regulations (UTCCR 1994) have already had a striking effect on bank contracts (as well as the Banking Code), which are now expressed in plain language. Their full effect on the substantive relations between banks and their customers will only become clear with time.[79]

Misrepresentation and Mistake

3–034 In the banking context, these issues tend to arise specifically in the context of real securities and guarantees and they are also discussed in relation to those topics.

Misrepresentation

3–035 A misrepresentation leading to the formation of a contract will probably allow the misrepresentee to rescind the contract and to obtain damages.[80] A misrepresentation is an inaccurate statement of existing fact made by one party to the contract to the other; it must generally be material—that is to say, that it "would affect the judgment of a reasonable person in deciding whether, or on what terms, to enter the contract"[81]—and the misrepresentee must have relied upon it.

Misrepresentation is often used as an additional or alternative plea to a plea of undue influence in attempts to challenge the validity of guarantees or charges by spouses of debtors (or other individual sureties). The misrepresentation may have been made by the bank's representative (as in *National Westminster Bank plc v. Morgan*[82]) or by a third party, normally the

---

[79] The D.-G. of Fair Trading has used his powers extensively, and the Office of Fair Trading publishes case report bulletins. Some cases have reached the courts: see, *e.g. Falco Finance Ltd v. Gough* (1999) 17 Tr. L.R. 526 (Macclesfield); *cf. D.-G. of Fair Trading v. First National Bank plc* [1999] Lloyd's Rep. Bank. 427 reversed by [1999] 2 All E.R. 759, CA.

[80] See Misrepresentation Act 1967, s. 2(1) and (2).

[81] Treitel, *Law of Contract* (9th ed.) 312. The alternatives to an action under the Misrepresentation Act 1967, s. 2(1) are a claim under *Hedley Byrne* [1964] A.C. 465 for negligent misstatement (appropriate if the misstatement has not led to a contract) and for fraud under *Derry v. Peek* (1889) 14 App. Cas 337.

[82] [1985] 1 A.C. 686.

debtor. In that case, the bank's liability depends on whether the debtor was acting as its agent (which is now unlikely) or whether it had constructive notice of the misrepresentation, as in *Barclays Bank v. O'Brien*,[83] where the bank was held by the House of Lords to be fixed with constructive notice of a husband's misrepresentation to his wife who had acted as surety.

Mistake and rectification

Mistake may occasionally provide a defence to an action on a contract. If there is evidence that the contract does not accurately record the intention of the parties—which may happen, for instance, where standard documents are used in special circumstances without appropriate amendment—the document may be rectified to correspond with the true intentions of the parties.[84] **3–036**

In an extreme case, the contract might be avoided if it has been made under a common mistake which is sufficiently fundamental under *Bell v. Lever Bros Ltd.*[85] It is irrelevant in that case whether the mistake was caused by any act or omission of the creditor or by a third party. In *Associated Japanese Bank (International) Ltd v. Credit du Nord SA,*[86] a guarantee would have been avoided for common mistake (the decision was in fact on the construction of the document) because it was essentially different from the guarantee both banks had believed themselves to have agreed; the stringent test of common law mistake would have been satisfied.

In another fraud, the plea of mistake as to identity (which would make the contract void) was raised. In *Citibank NA v. Brown Shipley & Co*,[87] a person purporting to be the agent of a customer of the plaintiff bank arranged, by using telephone calls and forging signatures of persons authorised to operate the account, for that bank to issue a banker's draft. Brown Shipley checked that the draft was genuine, and paid the draft in foreign currencies to the fraudster. The court held that there was a contract between the two banks under which title to the draft passed directly between them. The fraudster had acted as a messenger and was merely a conduit; title had not passed through him, and therefore no mistake as to the "messenger's" identity could make the contract void. This case demonstrates the court's reluctance to support claims for mistake, particularly where, as with many identity mistakes, the claim is between two innocent parties where a successful fraud has been perpetrated, and for which the remedy of rescission of the contract may be adequate. **3–037**

[83] [1993] 3 W.L.R. 786. See below, para. 3–051.
[84] *Joscelyne v. Nissen* [1907] 2 Q.B. 86.
[85] [1932] A.C. 161.
[86] [1989] 1 W.L.R. 255. See further below, Chap. 18.
[87] [1991] 2 All E.R. 690.

Non est factum

3–038 This is a defence of very limited application. Parties to a contract are normally bound by their signatures on a document, whether or not they have understood it—or even read it—but in rare circumstances the court may declare that the contract is void. This may apply if a person has signed a document because he or she is permanently or temporarily unable, through no fault of their own, to have any real understanding of the purport of the document without explanation, whether from defective education, illness or innate incapacity,[88] or because he or she has been tricked into signing.

This is a drastic remedy because the contract is avoided, and this may affect the rights of innocent third parties who have relied on it. From the point of view of a surety it has the great advantage that the contract between him or herself and the bank will be avoided even though the bank has not been involved in any wrongful behaviour. Because it is so drastic, the doctrine of *non est factum* (literally, "it is not his deed") is hedged around with qualifications.

3–039 The following points are relevant in establishing a plea of *non est factum*:

(a) Literate persons of full mental capacity are not normally able to raise the plea. People who are disadvantaged in some way—perhaps because they are blind or illiterate or unable to speak English—are most likely to succeed.

(b) The defence is not open if the signer has been negligent. Thus, where an elderly widow did not read a document and was deceived as to its contents, she was unable to rely on the defence,[89] even though her glasses were broken.

(c) The contract which the signer enters must be fundamentally different from what he or she had thought: it must be of a "nature altogether different". This is not so much a question of the legal nature of the contract as of its practical effect; if A believes he is signing as a witness, for example, that would be fundamentally different from signing as a mortgagor. But it would not be a fundamental difference if A believes he is signing an assignment of a leasehold by way of gift to X, and it is an assignment by way of sale to Y, for A knows that the document involves a disposition of the property.[90] In *Lloyds Bank v. Waterhouse,*[91] Purchas L.J. thought that

---

[88] See *Saunders v. Anglia Building* Society [1971] A.C. 1001 at 1016, *per* Lord Reid. It succeeded in *Lloyds Bank v. Waterhouse, The Independent*, February 27, 1990, where an elderly father guarantor was illiterate (noted Cartwright [1990] L.M.C.L.Q. 338).

[89] *Saunders v. Anglia Building Society* [1971] A.C. 1004.

[90] *ibid. Howatson v. Webb* [1907] 1 Ch. 537, affd. [1908] 1 Ch. 1.

[91] *The Independent*, February 27, 1990.

a guarantor's liability under an all monies' guarantee was fundamentally different from the liability under a loan account for the purchase of a farm, but the point was not resolved.

Estoppel by Convention

The terms of a contract may be changed by what is called "estoppel by convention".[92] Where both parties have acted on an agreed assumption as to the existence of a state of facts or as to the true construction of a document, they are precluded from denying the truth of that assumption,[93] because it would be unjust to allow them, or one of them, to go back on their conduct. In *Amalgamated Investment and Property Co Ltd v. Texas Commerce Bank*,[94] a guarantor guaranteed the debts of a company (D) to whom a bank was to advance money. Subsequently by agreement, the money was advanced to a different company, X, a subsidiary of the bank, which then advanced it to D. The bank assumed that the guarantee covered this situation, but in fact it did not do so, because the guarantee was expressed to be for D's debts to the bank, whereas D's debt was now to X, not to the bank. In these circumstances, a literal interpretation would have defeated the intention of the parties. On the true construction, the court held, the guarantee applied to X, but even if it did not, the company was precluded from denying that the guarantee covered the loan, as both parties had assumed this and had acted on that assumption. **3–040**

The form of the estoppel is unusual because there is no need for a clear and unequivocal representation or promise. The mistake may have been spontaneously made by the person relying on it and the other party may have acquiesced in it. The assumption must be a common one, so that the conduct amounting to reliance and acquiescence was communicated. **3–041**

Undue Influence

Equity will set aside contracts or gifts on the ground that one party has obtained a benefit by reason of the exercise of undue influence over another party.[95] This is a subject of considerable interest to banks because of the possible effect of such a plea on charges or guarantees taken by them. **3–042**

A third party such as a spouse may grant a guarantee or other security to a bank over the family home, often to support borrowing to set up or

[92] Or by promissory estoppel, see *Central London Property Trust Ltd v. High Trees House* [1947] K.B. 130.

[93] *Chitty on Contracts*, para. 3.080; Treitel, *The Law of Contract* (10th ed.), p. 110. See also *Republic of India v. India SS Co. Ltd (No. 2)* (1998) A.C. 878.

[94] [1981] 1 All E.R. 923, affd [1982] Q.B. 84. The same principle was applied in *Norwegian American Cruises A/S v. Paul Mundy Ltd (The Vistafjord)* (1988) 2 Lloyd's Rep. 343. See also *Taylor Fashions Ltd v. Liverpool Victoria Trustee Co Ltd* [1981] 1 All E.R. 897; *Keen v. Holland* [1984] 1 All E.R. 75.

[95] *Allcard v. Skinner* (1887) 36 Ch. D. 145.

maintain a family business. If the business fails and the bank tries to realise the security by taking proceedings for possession of the home, the guarantor may be desperate to challenge the security transaction in order to save the home. One way to do so is by asserting that undue influence was used against them to persuade him or her to grant the security. Sometimes the allegation is that the bank itself has used undue influence against the guarantor, but more often recently it has been claimed that the debtor has used undue influence against the guarantor, and that the bank has in some way become caught up in the situation and should not be allowed to benefit from it.

Requirements of undue influence

3–043 The concept is difficult to define,[96] because of the variety of circumstances which can give rise to it. The courts deal with the difficulty of definition by classifying the relationships where it is likely to arise and allowing potentially vulnerable people to rely on a presumption that they have been subjected to pressure. The three categories of undue influence are:

(a) *"Class 1 cases"*[97]: if a person proves that he or she has entered into a transaction because of *actual* undue influence, that person is entitled to have the contract set aside.

(b) *"Class 2 cases"*: here, the complainant has only to show that there was such a relationship of trust and confidence between him or herself and the other party that it may be *presumed* that the stronger party abused the relationship in inducing the weaker one to enter the transaction. The stronger party must therefore prove that the benefit received by him or her was not obtained by the exercise of undue influence. The cases fall into two categories:

"Class 2(A) cases": relationships of trust and confidence which exist as a matter of law between, for example, parent and unemancipated child,[98] or solicitor and client.[99] If a transaction

---

[96] See *National Westminster Bank v. Morgan* [1985] 1 A.C. 686 at 709, *per* Lord Scarman, who said that there was "no substitute in this branch of the law for a 'meticulous examination of the facts'". Treitel defines it as follows: "where an agreement has been obtained by certain kinds of improper pressure which were thought not to amount to duress at common law because no element of violence to the person was involved" (*The Law of Contract* (10th ed.), p. 378).

[97] See *Barclays Bank v. O'Brien* [1993] 3 W.L.R. 786 at 792, *per* Lord Browne-Wilkinson and *BCCI v. Aboody* [1992] 4 All E.R. 955 at 964, *per* Slade L.J.

[98] *Bullock v. Lloyds Bank* [1955] Ch. 317.

[99] *Wright v. Carter* [1903] 1 Ch. 27. Other examples of such presumed relationships are guardian and ward, fiancé and fiancee, trustee and beneficiary, religious adviser and disciple, doctor and patient.

between such parties takes place, the presumption that there has been undue influence by the stronger party arises automatically.

"Class 2(B) cases": in other cases, such as between banker and customer,[1] or husband and wife,[2] there is no presumption that a relationship of trust and confidence exists, but the complainant may prove that it did exist in the particular case. It must be shown that the weaker party in fact reposed such trust and confidence in the other that the latter was in a position to take unfair advantage of him or her.[3] If the relationship is shown to be of this sort, the presumption arises without any need of evidence that undue influence has been exercised.

Where such a relationship is presumed or proved, the party who benefits from the transaction may prove that undue influence did *not* exist by showing that the transaction was the result of the exercise by the weaker party of "the free exercise of independent will".[4] Generally, this is done by showing that the weaker party had competent[5] independent advice—normally legal advice—before entering into the transaction.[6] But even this may not save the transaction if the influence is particularly strong, and the weaker party does not follow the advice.[7] **3–044**

In addition to proving the existence of such a relationship, it was decided in *National Westminster Bank plc v. Morgan*[8] that it must also be shown that the transaction itself was *manifestly disadvantageous* to the person pleading undue influence. Here, the Morgans faced the loss of their jointly owned home to a building society, and the bank entered into urgent refinancing arrangements with the husband for his business liabilities. The refinancing was to be secured by a legal charge over the house executed by husband and wife. In due course the bank sought possession of the house, and the wife resisted the claim on the ground that the bank manager had exercised undue influence. The House of Lords held that the manager had not assumed a confidential role. Lord Scarman, giving the decision of the court, said that no undue influence could exist unless the transaction was **3–045**

[1] *National Westminster Bank v. Morgan* [1985] 1 All E.R. 821.

[2] *Howes v. Bishop* [1909] 2 K.B. 390; *Bank of Montreal v. Stuart* [1911] A.C. 120; *Mackenzie v. Royal Bank of Canada* [1934] A.C. 468.

[3] See *Tate v. Williamson* (1866) L.R. 2 Ch. App. 55 (financial adviser to undergraduate): *Inche Noriah v. Shaik Allie bin Omar* [1929] A.C. 127 (adviser to elderly person): *Lloyds Bank Ltd v. Bundy* [1975] Q.B. 326 (bank and elderly surety).

[4] *Inche Noriah v. Shaik Allie bin Omar* [1929] A.C. 127 at 136.

[5] *ibid*. The adviser must be in possession of the facts.

[6] *Mackenzie v. Royal Bank of Canada* [1934] A.C. 468 at 474–475.

[7] *Wright v. Carter* [1903] 1 Ch. 27; *Powell v. Powell* [1900] 1 Ch. 243; *Re Coomber* [1911] 1 Ch. 723 at 730.

[8] [1985] 1 All E.R. 821; [1986] A.C. 686. The court rejected the general principle of relief where there was "inequality of bargaining power" proposed in *Lloyds Bank Ltd v. Bundy* [1975] Q.B. 326 at 339 by Lord Denning M.R.

manifestly disadvantageous to the person influenced. There was no manifest disadvantage to the wife in this case, because the transaction saved the home from the building society which would have repossessed it. This requirement has made it more difficult for wives in normal surety situations to establish undue influence and has been criticised.[9]

3–046 After *Morgan* it was uncertain whether manifest disadvantage was a necessary element in all cases of undue influence, including even actual undue influence, where there is often bullying, overbearing behaviour.[10] However, it was held in *CIBC Mortgages v. Pitt*[11] that where actual undue influence is alleged, the requirement of manifest disadvantage is inconsistent with general principle. Lord Browne-Wilkinson said[12]:

> "Actual undue influence is a species of fraud . . . A man guilty of fraud is no more entitled to argue that the transaction was beneficial to the person defrauded than is a man who has procured a transaction by misrepresentation. The effect of the wrongdoer's conduct is to prevent the wronged party from bringing a free will and properly informed mind to bear on the proposed transaction which accordingly must be set aside in equity as a matter of justice".

The question whether manifest disadvantage is still a necessary requirement in *presumed* undue influence cases was not settled in *Pitt*, but Lord Browne-Wilkinson suggested that the limits of *Morgan* may have to be reconsidered in the future.[13]

Undue influence exercised by banks

3–047 It may sometimes be alleged that the bank itself has exercised undue influence. In *Williams v. Bayley*[14] a son gave his bank some promissory notes on which he had forged his father's endorsements. The bank arranged a meeting and made it clear to the father and son that the latter would be prosecuted unless some arrangement was reached. The father, in despair, said "What be I to do? How can I help myself? You see these men will have their money". Then, in consideration for the return to him of the notes (and, it was implied, the dropping of any prosecution) he agreed to give the bank a security for the son's debt. In these disgraceful circumstances, the mortgage

---

[9] See *e.g. Tiplady* 48 M.L.R. 579.

[10] See *BCCI v. Aboody* [1992] 4 All E.R. 955, CA.

[11] [1993] 3 W.L.R. 802.

[12] Disapproving the Court of Appeal's decision in *BCCI v. Aboody*, [1992] 4 All E.R. 955.

[13] In *Dunbar Bank plc v. Nadeem* [1998] 3 All E.R. 876, it was held that manifest disadvantage is still a requirement for presumed undue influence. See also *Barclays Bank v. Coleman* [2000] Lloyd's Rep. Bank. 67, CA, and *Royal Bank of Scotland v. Etridge (No 2)* [1998] 4 All E.R. 705 at 713, CA, discussed below, para. 3–063 where it was said that the presence of manifest disadvantage is a "powerful evidential factor".

[14] (1866) L.R. 1 H.L. 200.

was set aside. On the other hand in *Lloyds Bank Ltd v. Suvale Properties Ltd*[15] a married couple who had themselves defrauded the bank may have been threatened with prosecution (they alleged that they had) to persuade them to give securities for their overdraft, and the Court of Appeal[16] suggested that this would not have been so harsh and unconscionable as to render the securities void. This seems to imply that in civil proceedings on the security, the courts may hold threats by a bank against a wrongdoer to be reasonable, but it is debatable whether any reliance should be placed upon this principle, which comes very close to blackmail (a crime which involves the making of an unwarranted demand with menaces with a view to gain).[17] A demand for security on the threat of prosecution is clearly a demand with menaces, and the bank has a view to a gain. It would therefore have to rely for protection on an argument that the demand is not "unwarranted": it is unwarranted unless the person who makes the demand does so "in the belief (a) that he has reasonable grounds for making the demand; and (b) that the use of menaces is a proper means of reinforcing the demand". While the demand for repayment itself is reasonable, the question seems to be whether the bank official who made the threat believed it to be a proper means to reinforce the demand. The whole subject is, however, fraught with dangers for banks.

A well-known case where the bank was said to have exercised undue **3–048**
influence was *Lloyd's Bank Ltd v. Bundy.*[18] Here the defendant was an elderly farmer, a customer of the bank, who had guaranteed his son's overdraft of £1,500 with the bank, and who had charged his farm as security. When the son's business ran into difficulties the bank called for further security from the son, who said that his father would help. An assistant manager went to the farm, with the forms for increasing the security (whereby the charge would be increased to more than the value of the farm). The documents were executed by the father, who was told that otherwise the bank could not support the business. The Court of Appeal held that the father, who had been a customer for years, had relied on the bank and had placed confidence in it, as the bank knew. He had been a customer for years, and his reliance was clear. (It also appeared, when he gave evidence, that he had some difficulty in understanding all that went on.) In these unusual circumstances[19] it was found that the relationship between the parties was such that a burden was placed on the bank to disprove undue influence, and that it had not done so.

---

15 (1981, unreported). The fraud was "cross-firing"—*i.e.* two persons draw corresponding cheques on different banks or on different branches of the same bank. Since there is a delay in clearing, the credit in each account is temporarily augmented, and in the meantime each of the two customers borrows against the uncleared effects.

16 See the judgment of Oliver L.J.

17 Theft Act 1968 (TA 1968), s. 21.

18 [1975] Q.B. 326.

19 Each member of the court emphasised the unusual nature of the case, and was at pains to stress that undue influence will rarely succeed. Lord Denning M.R.'s decision was based on a wider principle of unequal bargaining power which was rejected by the House of Lords in *National Westminster Bank plc v. Morgan* [1985] 1 All E.R. 821; [1985] A.C. 686.

3–049 The unusual nature of the *Bundy* case was emphasised in *National Westminster Bank plc v. Morgan,*[20] where the House of Lords held[21] that the banker-customer relationship is not normally a fiduciary one, and does not normally give rise to a presumption of undue influence.[22] Here also, the bank manager had called at the family home. The atmosphere had been tense and the husband was "hovering around". Mrs Morgan had made it clear that she had no confidence in her husband's business abilities and did not want the mortgage to cover his business liabilities, and the manager told her that the effect of the agreement was limited to covering the outstanding debt to the building society. This statement was inaccurate, but correctly represented the intention of the manager and the bank. The House of Lords rejected the argument that the wife's reliance imposed a fiduciary duty on the bank to advise the wife to seek independent legal advice, and held that on the facts of the case the relationship between the parties had not "crossed the line" between mere reliance to a position where the banker exercised a "dominating influence". Thus the exceptional characteristics of the *Bundy* case seem to be (a) that Mr Bundy was a customer of long standing, who had come over the years to trust the bank and to rely on it for advice, (b) that he was very elderly and perhaps not fully able to comprehend all that was happening, (c) that he had been specially influenced by previous transactions relating to the guarantee and security between him and the bank, and (d) that his concern for his son was very obvious.

Undue influence exercised by debtors

3–050 Another possibility is that the bank may become involved in wrongful acts of the debtor. This problem has been before the courts frequently in recent years. As mentioned above, debtors required by the bank to give security often ask a spouse or relative to assist in providing it. Typically, when the debtor is engaged in a small business, the only suitable security is a charge over the debtor's family home, and in this case it will probably be necessary to obtain the consent of the spouse to charge the house or to give a guarantee.[23] If the debtor procures the consent of the third party by misrepresentation or by undue influence, the question is whether the security transaction (a contract between the bank and the third party) should be set aside because of the behaviour of the debtor in procuring the third party's consent.

[20] [1985] 1 All E.R. 821; [1985] A.C. 686.

[21] Disapproving Lord Denning's view in *Bundy*.

[22] There may still be a "special relationship" for the purposes of making the bank liable in the tort of negligence, to a person to whom the bank gives advice, see *Woods v. Martins Bank Ltd* [1959] 1 Q.B. 55; *Hedley Byrne & Co Ltd v. Heller & Partners Ltd* [1964] A.C. 465; *Box v. Midland Bank* [1979] 2 Lloyd's Rep. 391; Shea [1986] J.I.B.L. 20, see below, Chap. 18.

[23] See below, Chap. 5.

The House of Lords has established, in *Barclays Bank v. O'Brien,*[24] that the liability of the creditor—that is, whether the security transaction can be impugned by the third party—does not depend on whether the debtor acted as agent for the bank, as earlier cases had held[25] (a highly artificial use of agency in this context[26]), but on whether the bank has been on *constructive notice* of undue influence by the debtor.

In the *O'Brien* case itself, the facts were typical: the bank agreed to extend the overdraft of a company in which the husband had an interest to £60,000, and both husband and wife agreed to a second mortgage of their family home as security for the overdraft. The mortgage was unlimited, and its effect was therefore to secure any liability, including future liability, of Mr O'Brien to the bank, but he told his wife that it was only to secure £60,000, and that even this liability would be released in a short time when the house was remortgaged. The branch manager of the bank sent the documents to another branch to be executed, instructing the bank officers to make sure that both O'Briens were fully aware of the nature of the documents, and that they should be advised that if they were in any doubt they should contact their solicitors before signing. The other branch did not follow the instructions. Mrs O'Brien was given no explanation of the effect of the documents, was not advised to obtain legal advice, and simply signed the documents without reading them. When the company failed and the bank brought proceedings under the charge for possession of the house, Mrs O'Brien resisted the action, claiming that she had been induced to sign the charge by Mr O'Brien's undue influence and by his misrepresentation. The undue influence claim was eventually dropped and the case was decided on the basis of the husband's misrepresentation. The court considered the situation as a whole, however, and attempted to place the liability of banks with regard to wrongful behaviour of debtors, whether by undue influence or misrepresentations, on a principled basis. **3–051**

Lord Browne-Wilkinson, who gave the judgment, made it clear that the law had to be considered in the social context: he recognised the importance of exploiting the wealth tied up in family homes, and did not want to discourage banks from lending because of unnecessary restrictions on them in obtaining security. The courts, though, had to find a balance between that aim and protecting vulnerable people whose emotional involvement and trust in another person might lead to their exploitation. The judgment was primarily concerned with the position of vulnerable wives—even these days, of course, there are marriages where wives entirely depend upon their **3–052**

---

[24] [1993] 3 W.L.R. 786.

[25] *e.g. Bank of Montreal v. Stuart* [1911] A.C. 120; *Avon Finance Co Ltd v. Bridger* [1985] 2 All E.R. 281 and *Kingsnorth Trust Ltd v. Bell* [1986] 1 All E.R. 423. *Cf. Coldunell Ltd v. Gallon* [1986] 1 All E.R. 429; [1986] Q.B. 1184. See also *Midland Bank v. Perry* (1987) 56 P. & C.R. 202; *Midland Bank v. Shephard* [1988] 3 All E.R. 17; *Barclays Bank v. Kennedy* (1988) 58 P. C. & R. 221 and *BCCI v. Aboody* [1992] 4 All E.R. 955.

[26] *Royal Bank of Scotland v. Etridge* [1998] 4 All E.R. 705 at 717 *per* Stuart-Smith L.J.

husbands in financial matters[27]—but the protection of the law was expressly extended to all cases where there is an emotional relationship between individuals, whether they are married, cohabiting or in other relationships such as parent and adult child.[28]

3–053 The protection the court gave to vulnerable wives and other sureties was the recognition that, although the law does not regard the relationship between a married couple as coming within Class 2(A), where undue influence is presumed, a wife may be able to show in any particular case the existence of such a relationship of trust and confidence between her and her husband that it is fair to presume that he abused the relationship in procuring her to enter into the impugned transaction; in effect, she will bring herself within class 2(B). In that case, the burden shifts to the wrongdoer to prove that she entered the transaction freely. As far as the borrower and surety are concerned, the presumption cannot be rebutted by evidence that she understood what she was doing and intended to do it. The borrower must show that she was either free of his (or her[29]) influence or had received independent legal advice, which would have the same effect.[30]

3–054 **The effect on the bank.** Assuming that the debtor's undue influence or misrepresentation has been proved, the crucial question for banks is: when is the security transaction affected by the debtor's wrongful behaviour so that the court will order it to be set aside? The House of Lords held that the creditor bank would be fixed with the wrongdoing, if it had *notice*, actual or constructive,[31] of the wrongdoing (or if the debtor was acting as its agent, though this would be rare). The creditor will be fixed with notice if it knows (through its officers) of facts which put it on inquiry as to the possible existence of the rights of another person and fails to make inquiry or take reasonable steps to verify whether that right does exist. The two factors which may put a creditor on inquiry when a wife offers to stand surety for her husband's debts are: (a) that the transaction is apparently not to the financial advantage of the wife; and (b) there is a substantial risk that, in procuring the wife to act as surety, the husband has committed a wrong entitling her to set the transaction aside.[31a]

[27] The Court of Appeal [1993] Q.B. 109 (*per* Scott L.J.) had found that there was a special equity which protected wives; this was rejected by the House of Lords in favour of the use of the doctrine of notice.

[28] Approving the decision of the Court of Appeal in *Avon Finance Co Ltd v. Bridger* [1985] 2 All E.R. 281.

[29] The wife may be the wrongdoer: see *Barclays Bank v. Rivett* (1997) 29 H.L.R. 893.

[30] *Etridge* [1998] 4 All E.R. 705 at 714.

[31] Including *imputed* notice: *Royal Bank of Scotland v. Etridge* [1998] 4 All E.R. 705 at 719. See *Halifax Mortgage Services v. Stepsky* [1996] 2 All E.R. 277. The use of the concept of notice has attracted criticism. In *Etridge*, it was said: "This is not, we think, a true application of the bona fide defence, but the effect is much the same", *per* Stuart Smith L.J., at 718.

[31a] See further below Chap. 21.

Further, there are some situations (not the typical husband and wife situation) where it is plain that the surety is being exploited (as in the *Burch* case,[32] discussed below). If the transaction is so "extravagantly improvident" that the third party's interest in the transaction is "virtually inexplicable" in the absence of some undue influence, the bank is also put on inquiry.

What must the bank do? It would be absurd to require banks themselves to ask a wife whether her husband has bullied or pressured her into agreeing to act as surety. *O'Brien* therefore requires that banks on inquiry must take reasonable steps to avoid being fixed with constructive notice. Basically, the bank should encourage the wife to seek independent legal advice. In the ordinary case, Lord Browne-Wilkinson stated, banks must insist that the wife attends a private meeting (in the absence of the husband) with a bank official, where she must be told of the extent of her liability, warned of the risk she is running and urged to take independent legal advice. However, if the bank has knowledge of further facts which make undue influence "not only possible but probable"[33] (perhaps, it has been suggested, if the wife is submissive to the husband and has a black eye), the creditor will have to insist that the wife is separately advised. In the *O'Brien* case itself, it was held that the bank had been on inquiry as to the misrepresentation made to Mrs O'Brien by her husband and should have informed Mrs O'Brien of the full scale of her obligation and advised her to seek independent legal advice. Since it had not complied with the reasonable steps necessary to offset the effect of the husband's legal wrong, Mrs O'Brien was entitled to set aside the legal charge on the home. **3–055**

The court's guidance on the important point of how banks could distinguish a transaction where there is a risk of undue influence[34] from a routine joint transaction freely undertaken by both parties was given in *CIBC v. Pitt*,[35] (a companion case to *O'Brien*) where the creditor was aware that the purpose of the transaction, a joint loan to husband and wife, was to finance the discharge of an existing mortgage on their house and the purchase of a holiday home. The situation was different from *O'Brien* in that there was nothing, the court held, to indicate that this was anything other than a normal advance to husband and wife for their joint benefit. It is where a transaction *on its face* favours the husband at the expense of his wife, that the creditor is put on notice, or where there is a secured loan to both, "but the creditor is aware that the purposes of the loan are to pay the husband's debts or otherwise for his (as distinct from their joint) pur- **3–056**

[32] *Credit Lyonnais Bank Nederland v. Burch* [1997] 1 All E.R. 144, see *Etridge* [1998] 4 All E.R. 705 at 719.

[33] [1993] 3 W.L.R. 786 at 799.

[34] See further below, Chap. 21. In *Bank of Scotland v. Bennett* [1999] Lloyd's Rep. Bank. 145 it was held that the fact that the wife supports the family company does not necessarily put the bank on notice.

[35] [1993] 3 W.L.R. 802.

poses",[36] that the bank will be on inquiry and ought to follow the reasonable steps listed by Lord Browne-Wilkinson in *O'Brien*. In *Barclays Bank plc v. Boulter*,[37] the House of Lords made it clear that the burden of showing that the bank is on constructive notice is on the wife, but added that it will usually be easily discharged. She must show that the bank knew that she was a wife living with her husband and that the transaction was not, on its face, to her financial advantage.

3–057 In *O'Brien* and *Pitt*, the court recognised that it is impossible for creditors regularly undertaking everyday commercial transactions to make any reliable investigation of the relationship, and limited their risk of liability by requiring them to act procedurally correctly. The steps listed in *O'Brien* (with the possible exception of the requirement that there should be a personal meeting between a representative of the bank and the surety) are not onerous for banks: as Lord Browne-Wilkinson pointed out, they are the same as the standards set by the Banking Code itself. The most recent version of the Code provides that in cases of guarantees and other types of third party security, banks will advise the third party that he or she might become liable instead of or as well as the principal debtor, advise them whether the security is unlimited or what the liability will be, and advise them to seek independent legal advice before entering into the security.[38] In normal cases, therefore, banks have been provided with a straightforward procedure allowing for swift and efficient commercial decisions.

3–058 Nevertheless, despite the clarity and the practical sense of the judgment, banks have found themselves with problems in some respects. First, the only requirement which might prove onerous for banks was that they should hold a personal meeting with the surety as well as the debtor. This could never have held much attraction for busy banks[39]; not only is it time and labour consuming, but a meeting increases the risk that misleading statements might inadvertently be made to the surety. In fact, it seems to have been quietly dispensed with. The Court of Appeal, in *Royal Bank of Scotland v. Etridge*,[40] doubted whether banks had ever been willing to adopt the procedure: "a personal interview with the wife is likely to expose the bank to far greater risks than those from which it wishes to escape". The court clearly, though rather inexplicably, regarded the reasonable steps

---

[36] [1993] 3 W.L.R. 786 at 810, quoting Peter Gibson J.'s judgment in *Pitt* in the Court of Appeal.

[37] [1999] 4 All E.R. 513.

[38] Banking Code (1999), para. 3.14. And the documentation will contain clear and prominent notice to that effect.

[39] See Lehane (1994) 110 L.Q.R. at 172: "banks' gratitude for the practical guidance . . . may be tempered by the reflection that interviewing officers will need to be alert, during private interviews, for signs that undue influence by a husband is not merely possible but probable . . . What, for instance, is a bank officer to do if, at the end of the interview, the wife says: 'Well, thank you for explaining it all to me, but I completely trust my husband, and have always left business matters to him and will continue to do so'?".

[40] [1998] 4 All E.R. 705.

listed in *O'Brien* as simply an indication of the steps which the bank ought reasonably to take.[41]

Secondly, the guidance relates to the *normal* case. If the bank is aware that undue influence is not only possible but probable, the bank should ensure that the surety receives independent legal advice.[42] More worryingly, if the transaction is so extreme that it is virtually inexplicable why the surety is willing to guarantee the transaction, as it was in *Credit Lyonnais Bank Nederland v. Burch*,[43] the transaction may be at risk even if the surety receives independent legal advice. **3–059**

In *Burch*, a junior employee of a tour operator firm agreed to provide security for the overdraft of her employer, with whom she had "close links" (in the sense of occasionally babysitting for his family and staying with them on holiday) but, from the point of view of the bank, no obvious connection. The security took the form of an unlimited personal guarantee and a charge over her flat in favour of the bank. When, on his default, the bank took proceedings for possession of the flat, the Court of Appeal held that the transaction was so manifestly disadvantageous to Miss Burch—since she had committed herself to a liability far beyond her means and risked the loss of her home and personal bankruptcy to help a company in which she had no financial interest and of which she was only a junior employee—that the presumption of undue influence on the part of the employer was irresistible. The court expressed itself in strong terms: it was a case which shocked the conscience of the court, and gave rise to grave suspicion; it cried aloud for an explanation. In these circumstances, the bank should have realised that the relationship could have developed into one of trust and confidence, with the risk of abuse. It was on constructive notice and had not taken reasonable steps in urging her to take independent advice. Indeed, it was said that even the fact that the surety has taken independent advice might not be enough in such a case to rebut the presumption of undue influence.[44] **3–060**

Burch underlines the resemblance between the doctrine of undue influence and the overlapping contractual doctrines of unconscionability and economic duress,[45] and illustrates how alert lenders must be to the possibility of pressure and overpersuasion—even more alert, indeed, in **3–061**

---

[41] [1998] 4 All E.R. 705 at 719. See also *Banco-Exterior v. Mann* [1995] 1 All E.R. 936, CA, and *Massey v. Midland Bank* [1995] 1 All E.R. 950, CA: "the guidance was intended to strike a fair balance . . . The guidance ought therefore not to be mechanically applied. The relief after all is equitable relief. It is the substance that matters." *per* Steyn, L.J., at 934. *Cf.* Hobhouse L.J., diss., *Banco-Exterior.*

[42] *O'Brien* [1993] 3 W.L.R. 786 at 799.

[43] [1997] 1 All E.R. 144.

[44] *ibid.,* at 155–6, *per* Millett L.J.

[45] *ibid.*, at 181, *per* Nourse L.J. See also *Smith v. Bank of Scotland* (1997) S.C. 111, HL, where the House of Lords decided, in an appeal from Scotland, that *O'Brien* could be given effect in Scotland by means of recognising "the element of good faith" required from a creditor taking a guarantee.

cases where there is no clear relationship between the borrower and surety or mortgagor than in cases where the relationship might make them expect a problem.[46]

Thirdly, the requirement that banks should urge sureties to obtain independent legal advice has proved a fertile area for litigation. What is meant by "independent", for example? Could a lawyer acting for the debtor, or the debtor's company, or even for the bank be independent enough to advise the surety properly? Could the bank be confident that the surety was independently advised if she or he had been interviewed by a solicitor, even if the bank knew that the solicitor acted for the debtor or for the bank itself? What, for that matter, should the nature of the advice given by a lawyer be in such cases? Further, should a guarantee transaction vitiated by undue influence be set aside in its entirety, or only in part (as in *O'Brien* itself)?[47]

3–062 These questions have been answered by a series of cases, culminating in the decision in *Royal Bank of Scotland v. Etridge*,[48] where the Court of Appeal, considering a number of appeals, gathered together the previous decisions[49] and set out a number of rules regulating liability between banks and legal advisers in *O'Brien* cases. Risk of liability for advice rests chiefly on the *legal adviser*, rather than on the bank. In summary, the court's conclusions were:

- Where the wife is advised by a solicitor, the bank is not ordinarily put on inquiry at all. It does not need to question the sufficiency of the legal advice, and it is not important whether the solicitor provides the bank with confirmation that he or she has followed the instructions of the bank.

- It is up to the solicitor (not the bank) to consider whether there is a conflict of interest in giving advice to the wife if he or she is also advising the borrower, or even the bank itself, at least when he or she is acting for the bank "ministerially" (which seems to mean

[46] *cf. Banco-Exterior v. Thomas* [1997] 1 All E.R. 46, CA, where a woman was persuaded by a friend (no sexual relationship) to mortgage her property to support his second hand car business in exchange for a regular income. The bank was not on notice and did not need not make intrusive inquiries, despite the fact that it had been warned of a possible problem by her former solicitor.

[47] See *TSB Bank v. Camfield* [1995] 1 All E.R. 951, CA; *Dunbar Bank v. Nadeem* [1998] 3 All E.R. 876, CA—where a person has a transaction set aside for undue influence he must make full restitution of all he has obtained by the transaction.

[48] [1998] 4 All E.R. 705. See Price (1999) 115 L.Q.R. 8.

[49] *Banco-Exterior Internacional v. Mann* [1995] 1 All E.R. 936; *TSB Bank v. Camfield* [1995] 1 All E.R. 951; *Massey v. Midland Bank* [1995] 1 All E.R. 950, CA; *Bank of Baroda v. Rayarel* [1995] 2 F.L.R. 376, CA; *Midland Bank plc v. Serter* [1995] 4 Bank. L.R. 227, CA; see also *Goode Durrant v. Biddulph* [1994] 2 F.L.R. 551, Ch D; *Allied Irish Bank v. Byrne* [1995] 2 F.L.R. 325, and *Halifax Mortgage Services v. Stepsky* [1995] 4 All E.R. 656. Noted Tjio [1996] J.B.L. 266.

when the solicitor is simply seeing to the formalities of completion of the transaction on the bank's behalf).

- If the solicitor is acting for the wife, he or she is acting exclusively as the wife's solicitor. The bank is not fixed with imputed notice of what the solicitor learns in the course of advising the wife, even if he or she is acting for the bank as well. The solicitor owes the wife a duty of care, but also owes the bank a corresponding duty of care.
- If the wife does *not* see a solicitor, it is normally enough for the bank to urge her to obtain independent legal advice.
- On the other hand, if the bank is in possession of material information which is not available to the solicitor or if the transaction is one into which no competent solicitor could properly advise the wife to enter, the bank will be fixed with constructive notice even if the wife has had legal advice (the *Burch* case).

On the whole, it seems that banks have been given very adequate protection. Provided the wife has seen a solicitor, or been urged to take legal advice, the transaction should be unimpeachable. It is only in the last (*Burch*) situation therefore, or if the bank has actual notice of wrongdoing by the borrower or other material information not available to the solicitor, that the bank need fear challenge. It is true, however, that the *Burch* situation may be a real trap for unwary lenders, and banks should ensure that they satisfy themselves as to the surety's motive for giving security if there is no apparent reason for what may be most imprudent generosity. **3–063**

However, the task of the *solicitor* advising a wife in such cases is unenviable. Above all, the solicitor must be satisfied that the wife is free from improper influence. This means that there must be no "real" conflict of interest; if there is, he or she must decline to act. The solicitor must ascertain whether it is a transaction the surety could be sensibly advised to enter into: that is to say, that the solicitor must not only understand the circumstances of the proposed transaction (this may mean giving financial advice and explaining the commitment involved with a guarantee) but may also need to "probe the stability of the marriage", a task which will need to be done with sensitivity.[50] This puts an enormous burden on the solicitor. The price for wrong or inadequate advice is a negligence action at the suit of the wife. No doubt, the temptation for many solicitors will be simply to say, in the words of Hobhouse L.J. in his dissenting judgment in *Banco-Exterior v. Mann*[51]: "My advice to you is: Do not sign".

There is also doubt whether the surety is adequately protected. The procedural method of distinguishing between a real "victim" and a party to a genuine joint transaction set out in *O'Brien* and *Pitt*, means that a number **3–064**

[50] [1998] 4 All E.R. 705 at 716.
[51] [1995] 1 All E.R. 936.

of victims will still fall through the safety net of constructive notice. After all, the form of the transaction is probably mere accident,[52] and undue influence is just as likely to occur where the transaction appears a quite routine joint transaction as in a guarantee. And even if sureties are taken through the procedures set out in *O'Brien*, it is doubtful whether in practice many of them will be deterred by the meetings with the bank or by the independent legal advice from undertaking obligations which are not to their benefit.[53] If the legal adviser acts incompetently, of course, the surety should be able to recover damages for breach of a duty of care, although this may involve further litigation and will not save the matrimonial home from repossession by the creditor.

O'Brien has not achieved what had been intended and put a stop to the stream of litigation on the subject—far from it. It may be that the firm statement by the Court of Appeal in *Royal Bank of Scotland v. Etridge (No 2),*[54] which has attempted to consolidate the numerous subsequent cases testing the balance of liability apparently established by *O'Brien*, will help to stem the flood; if so, the result should be on the whole reassuring to banks.

Unconscionable Bargains

3–064A Equity can give relief against unconscionable bargains in certain cases where one party is in a position to exploit a particular weakness of the other.[55] The doctrine offers some protection to poor and ignorant persons who are overreached in the absence of independent advice, but has not been well developed in England.[56] In Australia, on the other hand, claims which would have been in undue influence in England have been successfully argued against banks on the basis of unconscionability.[57]

Banks and Tort

3–065 There are a number of ways in which liability in tort may arise, including deceit and defamation, but two of the most typical are conversion and liability for negligent misstatement.

Conversion

3–066 Handling cheques, traditionally the most characteristic part of banking business, has its dangers. If the bank pays the cheque to the wrong person, it may be liable to the customer for breach of contract for not following his

[52] See Cretney [1994] R.L.R. 1; Thomson [1992] Conv. 443, and Fehlberg (1994) 57 M.L.R. 469, who points out that the unsuccessful Mrs Pitt was probably in a more vulnerable position than the successful Mrs O'Brien.

[53] Fehlberg, *op. cit.*, who says that the reality is that, for the sake of the marriage, the wife will feel that she has no choice but to sign, whatever she is told. Such people will probably be those most in need of protection.

[54] [1998] 4 All E.R. 705.

[55] Treitel, *The Law of Contract* (10th ed.), p. 382.

[56] Beatson, *Anson's Law of Contract* (27th ed.), pp. 287 *et seq.*

[57] In *e.g. Commercial Bank of Australia v. Amadio* (1983) 151 C.L.R. 447; *Akins v. National Australia Bank* (1994) 34 N.S.W.L.R. 155.

or her instructions, and to the "true owner" of the cheque (usually the payee)[58] in the tort of conversion, which means wrongfully dealing with another person's property. Conversion (which now arises under the Torts (Interference with Goods) Act 1977) is a strict tort, so that banks would be liable regardless of fault. Statutory defences have been provided for banks because this continued risk of liability would interfere intolerably with banking business.[59]

Liability for Negligent Misstatement

Banks may also be at risk of actions for negligent misstatement. Since 1963, when *Hedley Byrne & Co Ltd v. Heller & Partners Ltd*[60] was decided, it has been clear that if a banker gives advice to a person of a sort which it is reasonable to expect a banker to give, a "special" relationship is created which may give rise to liability in tort. In *Hedley Byrne*, the defendants, a bank, had given a satisfactory reference to the plaintiff about one of their customers, who subsequently went out of business. The plaintiff had relied on the reference and lost money as a result. The House of Lords, in a landmark decision that extended tort liability into the controversial area of pure economic loss, held that a duty of care was owed. The claim would have been successful if the bank had not disclaimed liability.[61] **3–067**

Hedley Byrne liability for banks tends to arise in two particular areas: when banks give inaccurate references for their customers to third parties, and where they give negligent investment advice.[62]

Banks and Liability for Breach of Trust

The bank may owe the "fiduciary" duties of a trustee over trust funds. Some funds may be the subject of an express trust, some of a constructive trust, and some of a "*Quistclose*" trust—a type of trust which arises where money is paid to the bank for a specific purpose. These matters are discussed in Chapter 9. **3–068**

Banks and Liability in Restitution

Restitution or quasi-contract has had an important role in banking law for many years: the discussion in banking textbooks of mistake of fact, or money had and received, is traditional and has been taken for granted. The law in this area has been developing dynamically in recent decades, and **3–069**

[58] To sue in conversion, a person must have either actual possession or an immediate legal right to possession of goods at the time of conversion: *MCC Proceeds Inc. v. Lehman Bros International (Europe)* [1998] 4 All E.R. 675. See below, Chap. 14.
[59] See below, Chap. 5.
[60] [1964] A.C. 465.
[61] The disclaimer might not have been effective after the UCTA 1977.
[62] See below, Chap. 5.

restitution has become fashionable. New cases—notably the House of Lords decision in *Lipkin Gorman v. Karpnale*[63]—and academic discussion are gradually developing and rationalising the old law to deal with modern problems.

[63] [1991] 2 A.C. 548; [1991] 3 W.L.R. 10; see below, Chap. 10.

CHAPTER 4

THE BANKER'S DUTY OF CONFIDENCE

4–001 Many countries have a statutory law relating to banker's duties of secrecy. In England, the law is judge-made,[1] and based on a term implied into the contract between banker and customer. Subject to certain qualifications, a bank may not disclose to any other person any document or other information it has obtained in the course of the relationship with a customer without the consent of the customer.

The duty of confidence raises difficult questions. Naturally, customers would *prefer* information about their accounts to be kept secret, but that does not mean that the preference is necessarily justified. In particular, it is not necessarily self-evident why information should be protected in situations where there is a strong public interest in disclosure. One practical justification for keeping financial information secret, however, is economic. In many cases, it will not conduce to commercial efficiency to have information relating to trading made open to competitors,[2] and, for individual customers also, disclosure of information may have a damaging effect on credit. Less concretely, the courts emphasise that there is a strong public interest in maintaining confidentiality "based on the moral principles of loyalty and fair dealing",[3] and this reflects the fact that many people have strong feelings that they entrust their confidential information to banks (or others) on the understanding that they should respect the wishes of the individual in keeping it private. Customers normally regard their financial information as entirely personal and confidential—so much so that some dislike disclosing it even to their "nearest and dearest"—and resent it being disclosed to strangers, even if the information itself is completely innocuous. This feeling is no doubt based on the need for personal security: knowledge of a person's bank account gives the key to many aspects of his or her day to day life and can be used as a weapon, and a powerful one. Why should customers voluntarily expose themselves to attack by allowing a

---

[1] Though a statutory requirement is contained in s. 82 of the BA 1987, which provides for the confidentiality of information obtained by the Bank of England; see *BCCI (Overseas) Ltd v. Price Waterhouse* [1997] 4 All E.R. 781. See also the Data Protection Act 1998 (DPA 1998).

[2] See *X AG v. A Bank* [1983] 2 All E.R. 464 at 470, 472: the damage which the X company would sustain from a breach of confidence was described as "immediate, irreparable and incalculable"; it would allow "a window into the X company's commercial secrets".

[3] A strong expression of the traditional view is expressed in *Peterson v. Idaho First Nat'l Bank*, 83 Idaho 578, quoted in Huber, *Banks, Fraud and Crime* (Norton ed.), p. 216: "Inviolate secrecy is one of the inherent and fundamental precepts of the relationship of the bank and its customers or depositors."

bank possession of information which it can disclose to potentially hostile strangers unless they have confidence that it will be protected?

4–002 Nevertheless, there may be powerful reasons in favour of disclosure on occasion. If customers behave in a way which threatens others—for example, if they are involved in money laundering the profits of drug trafficking or terrorism—the bank account may provide information about the money laundering and the crime itself[4]; disclosure of the account is a simple and direct method for obtaining evidence. Most would feel that disclosure of personal information is justifiable in such a case, and even jurisdictions which have been well-known for their strong banking secrecy laws have had to make concessions in recent years to international demands that customers' confidential information should be disclosed to investigators for this reason. Similarly, control of banking fraud itself has become a matter of international concern. The closure of the notorious Bank of Credit and Commerce International (BCCI) in 1991 concentrated the attention of regulators on the fact that an important factor in the bank's success over a number of years had been the duty of confidentiality of banks and thcir auditors. Banking regulators now place a strong emphasis on disclosure and transparency. But there must be a balance—even where there is clear public interest in favour of disclosure, private rights need some protection.[5] The Jack Committee was concerned that the balance has moved too far in the direction of disclosure, at a cost to respect for individual rights. The Committee regarded the preservation of the duty of confidentiality as of primary importance; it felt that the duty represents a tradition which should be respected "because its roots go deeper than the business of banking: it has to do with the kind of society in which we want to live".[6]

4–003 As it is expressed in banking law, the duty of confidentiality appears a clear, flexible, and *reasonable* expression of a complex relationship.[7] However, it is very doubtful whether that description, which may have reflected the reality in traditional banking, can now be regarded as remotely accurate. The relationship between banker and customer, in these days of mass banking and computer data processing, bears little resemblance to the gentlemanly, leisured courtesy of banks in the 1920s, at the time of the formulation of the duty. There have been extraordinary developments in

---

[4] An interesting account of developments in banking and money laundering is given by Levi, in *Banks, Fraud and Crime* (see above, n. 3) at p. 29.

[5] See Lord Woolf's remarks in *C v. S* [1999] Lloyd's Rep. Bank. 26 at 29, CA (see also below, para. 4–044).

[6] Jack Report, Cm. 622 (1989), para. 5.26. See also points raised by Goode [1989] J.B.L. 269.

[7] In *Christofi v. Barclays Bank* [1998] Lloyd's Rep. Bank. 208 aff'd [1999] 1 W.L.R. 937, CA (where a wife sued a bank for breach of the duty of confidentiality because the bank informed her husband's trustee in bankruptcy that the caution against the property had been warned off, and the wife's loan was called in) it was held that the limits of the duty must be ascertained in accordance with "common sense": here, the limit was based on the fact that the trustee having a statutory right to the information.

the complexity and speed of communications, and information can be transmitted, stored and exchanged at a rate which was unimaginable then. An obvious example is the use of the internet, which plainly poses a huge (possibly uncontrollable) threat to individual privacy.[8] Another example is the growth of large banking and financial conglomerates performing many different functions for a huge number of customers: not only does this encourage the spread and disclosure of individual confidential information,[8a] it is also unclear how far the banking duty of confidentiality, developed in the context of traditional "core" banking, relates to a bank acting as a financial services adviser.[9]

There are other deeper theoretical problems, not explored in the sensible *Tournier* formulation. The apparently clear definition of the duty of confidentiality in banking and its basis in contract obscure considerable confusion both about the underlying values—the balance between the individual and the public interest—and about the conceptualisation of duties of confidence or confidentiality, which overlap with this one in many other fields of law.[10] **4–004**

The *Tournier* Case

It was first established in *Tournier v. National Provincial and Union Bank of England,*[11] that the bank owed its customer a legal, and not merely a moral, duty of confidentiality, and could not lawfully disclose to third parties information concerning the customer's affairs. Tournier was about £10 overdrawn on his bank account, and he agreed to repay this at the rate of £1 per week. As he then had no fixed address, he gave the bank the name and address of the employers for whom he was about to work. He failed to repay, and the branch manager—trying to find out his private address—telephoned the employers, and in the course of the conversation, disclosed the existence of the overdraft and the default in repayment. He **4–005**

---

[8] See further Hutton [1995] N.L.J. 1810, and below, Chap. 15.

[8a] See above, the discussion of Chinese Walls in Chap. 3.

[9] In *Kaufmann v. Credit Lyonnais Bank, The Times*, February 1, 1995, Ch D, the issue was whether confidential reports about the plaintiff bank, disclosed to a regulator, the SFA, were entitled to public interest immunity (a similar, but not identical, question to that about the banker's private contract duty of confidentiality considered in this Chapter). The position of the SFA was considered by the judge, but although the Bank of England was also a regulator of the institution, its position was simply equated to that of the SFA. The documents, as a class, were not entitled to immunity.

[10] Capper [1994] Legal Studies, 313, quotes Gareth Jones (1970) 86 L.Q.R. 463: "Property, contract, bailment, trust, fiduciary relationship, good faith, unjust enrichment, have all been claimed at one time or another, as the basis of the judicial intervention. Indeed, some judges have indiscriminately intermingled all these concepts. The result is that the answer to many fundamental questions remains speculative." One area of overlap has become clearer: the distinction between fiduciary duties and the duty of confidentiality is being elucidated in cases such as *Bristol and West v. Mothew* and *Prince Jefri Bolkiah v. KPMG*, see above, para. 3–016.

[11] [1924] 1 K.B. 461.

also expressed the opinion that the customer was betting heavily. As a result, the employers refused to employ Tournier after his probationary period. Tournier sued the bank for breach of confidentiality. The Court of Appeal held that it is an implied term of the banker-customer contract that bankers owe their customers a duty of secrecy or non-disclosure, and that in this case, the duty had been breached.

4–006 The majority in the *Tournier* case held that the duty comes into existence along with the banker-customer relationship. The bank must release no information about the customer or his or her account, whether the information is acquired before or after the account was opened or after it ceases, whether obtained directly from the customer or from other sources, and whether the account is in credit or overdrawn. Moreover, information should not be released even after he or she ceases to be a customer (even, probably, after the customer's death).[12]

A duty of confidentiality is characteristic of certain relationships—solicitor and client, and doctor and patient are other familiar examples. Its extent varies in each case, but in the case of the banker it is very marked, according to Bankes L.J., because the credit of the customer depends greatly upon its strict observance.[13] It may be regarded as an aspect of the agency element in the banker-customer relationship which, alongside the debtor/creditor relationship,[14] is central to the relationship. The duty of confidentiality was affirmed by the Court of Appeal in *Lipkin Gorman v. Karpnale,*[15] and is stated in the *Tournier* terms by the Banking Code.[16]

Qualifications to the Duty of Confidentiality

4–007 The duty is not absolute but qualified by four important exceptions. Bankes L.J. said:

> "On principle, I think the qualifications can be classed under four heads: (a) where disclosure is under compulsion by law; (b) where there is a duty to the public to disclose[17]; (c) where the interests of the bank require disclosure[18]; (d) where the disclosure is made by the express or implied consent of the customer".[19]

---

[12] Scrutton L.J. thought that the duty did not extend to knowledge acquired while the banker-customer relation was not in existence, or acquired from other sources.

[13] [1924] 1 K.B. 461 at 474.

[14] *Foley v. Hill* (1848) 2 H.L.Cas.28. Lord Chorley, *Law of Banking* (6th ed.), p. 20, thought the duty implicit in the banker-customer relationship itself.

[15] [1989] 1 W.L.R. 1341 at 1357, *per* May L.J., "the correctness of the principles of law stated by the majority in the *Tournier* case has not been doubted since the case was decided".

[16] Banking Code (1999) para. 4.1.

[17] *e.g.* (citing *Weld-Blundell v. Stephens* [1920] A.C. 956, 965, *per* Lord Finlay) cases where danger to the state or a public duty may supersede the duty of an agent to his principal.

[18] *e.g.* cases where a bank sues a customer for the amount of his overdraft (the amount of the overdraft must be stated).

[19] *e.g.* the "familiar" cases where a customer authorises his banker to give a reference.

Compulsion by Law

Since the duty of confidence is a contractual duty it is subject to the general law.[20] The Jack Report points out[21] that at the time of *Tournier*, instances of compulsion by law were rare; indeed the example given by Bankes L.J.—of a duty to obey an order made by a court under the BBEA 1879—was almost the only one. It is still important today, although it is now only the first of many. Some of these are considered below.[22] **4–008**

(a) Bankers Books Evidence Act 1879. The BBEA 1879[23] was passed to make the proof of banking transactions easier at trial and to absolve bankers from the burdensome duty of being compellable as witnesses in legal proceedings. The rules of evidence normally require the "best evidence" to be called, which, as far as a bank is concerned, would be the verbal testimony of the clerk who had compiled the books. Thus, if there were no specific authority to the contrary, bankers would have to appear as witnesses, even in proceedings to which they are not party.[24] Like any other witnesses, they would also have to answer relevant questions if directed to do so by the court, and to produce their books. The BBEA 1879 therefore provides that a copy of an entry in a banker's book is prima facie evidence of the entry in all legal proceedings.[25] **4–009**

The definition of "banker's books"[26] does not cover correspondence,[27] cheques, paying in slips[28] and bank mandates,[29] although it includes ledgers and other records[30] used in the ordinary business of the bank. Although the phrase "bankers' books" has a Dickensian sound, it has been held to mean any form of permanent record, whether the records are made in writing or by means made available by modern technology. Thus microfilm records of the bank's other records (common for space-saving reasons) are "books",[31] and where records are in electronic form a computer print-out, duly verified, would be sufficient evidence. Books need not be in use every day to be part of the "ordinary business": records kept for occasional reference are included, provided they are in the custody of the bank.[32] **4–010**

---

[20] *Parry-Jones v. Law Society* [1969] 1 Ch. 1 at 9, *per* Diplock L.J. (referring to, *inter alia*, the banker's duty).
[21] Cm. 622 (1989), para. 5.06.
[22] See generally Walker [1983] Crim. L.R. 723; Graham and Walker [1989] Crim. L.R. 185; Feldman [1989] Conv. 389.
[23] See Clayton [1996] J.I.B.L. 117 at 162.
[24] *e.g. Parnell v. Wood* [1892] P. 137.
[25] BBEA 1879, s. 3.
[26] BBEA 1879, s. 9, as amended by the BA 1979, Sched. 6.
[27] *R. v. Dadson* [1983] 77 Cr.App.R. 91.
[28] *Williams v. Williams* [1987] 3 All E.R. 257.
[29] *DB Deniz Nakliyati TAS v. Yugopetrol* [1992] 1 All E.R. 205 at 207, CA.
[30] *e.g.* day books, cash books, account books.
[31] *Barker v. Wilson* [1980] 2 All E.R. 81.
[32] *Idiot's Asylum v. Handysides* (1906) 22 T.L.R. 573.

Under section 7 of the BBEA 1879, a party to legal proceedings (civil or criminal) may obtain from a judge[33] an order to inspect and take copies of any entry in a banker's book for the purpose of the proceedings.[34] The order must normally be served on the bank three clear days before it is to be obeyed, and the bank does not have the protection against production in court until it complies with it.[35] The court has a discretion as to whether to make an order and it will weigh the need to respect confidentiality against the public interest.[36]

4–011 Where an order to inspect the account of a *third party* is sought, the power will be exercised with great caution, and only if the grounds for it are clearly established and "sufficient".[37] For example, the court must be satisfied either that the account in question is in substance that of the person who is a party to the litigation[38] (or, if the application is made after judgment, the judgment debtor) or that the person is so concerned with the account that items in it would be evidence against him or her at the trial.[39] In such a case, notice of the application to the court must be given not merely to the bank but also to the third party concerned.

The established principles of discovery[40] should not be extended by the use of orders under section 7 of the BBEA 1879. For example, the courts' objection to making orders for "fishing expeditions" where there is no real ground for believing that there is a cause of action, but where it is hoped that documents revealed will show one, is also important in applications under the BBEA 1879.[41] Hence, particularly in criminal proceedings, the order must not be used as "an instrument of oppression, which on its face it

[33] Including a magistrate in criminal proceedings, *R. v. Kinghorn* [1908] 2 K.B. 949. Proceedings include arbitrations and proceedings of solicitors' disciplinary tribunals: BBEA 1879, s. 10 (as extended by s. 86 of the Solicitors Act 1974). However, a Commission of Inquiry may not use the rules of the Act for obtaining access to entries in a bank's book: *Douglas v. Pindling* [1996] 3 W.L.R. 242 at 246, PC, *per* Lord Keith of Kinkel (see further below, para. 4–057).

[34] A judge may still order a bank to produce books in court or act as a witness for special cause, BBEA 1879, s. 6. "Bank" means recognised bank, licensed deposit taker, municipal bank, trustee saving bank, National Savings Bank, and the Post Office (in relation to its banking services), BBEA 1879, s. 9.

[35] *Emmot v. Star Newspaper Co.* (1892) 62 L.J.Q.B. 77.

[36] *R. v. Grossman* (1981) 73 Cr.App.R. 302 at 307.

[37] *Arnott v. Hayes* (1887) 36 Ch. D. 731.

[38] Thus inspection of a husband's account may be ordered on the ground that his wife (the party to the litigation) may have been using his account as a cloak for her transactions in securities, the subject of the litigation, *Ironmonger & Co v. Dyne* (1928) 44 T.L.R. 579, or that she has stolen the money and put it in his account, *R. v. Andover Justices, ex p. Rhodes* [1980] Crim. L.R. 644.

[39] See also *South Staffs. Tramways Co v. Ebbsmith* [1895] 2 Q.B. 669 at 674; *Re Marshfield, Marshfield v. Hutchings* (1886) 32 Ch. D. 499; *Pollock v. Garle* [1899] 1 Ch. 1; *DB Deniz Nakliyati TAS v. Yugopetrol* [1992] 1 All E.R. 205, CA.

[40] See below, para. 4–012.

[41] *Williams v. Summerfield* [1972] 2 Q.B. 512. See also *Bhimji v. Chatwani (No. 3)* [1992] 4 All E.R. 912. The court's discretion can be illustrated by *Emmott v. Star Newspaper Co.* (1892) 62 L.J.Q.B. 77, *per* Smith L.J.

might very well be"[42]; it should not extend beyond the true purpose of the issue which a court is considering; it must relate to entries which are relevant,[43] and should be limited in time to the relevant period of the account. It should also be considered whether the prosecution has any real evidence.[44]

(b) Orders for disclosure. Disclosure (or "Discovery") is the pre-trial process by which each party to the action can discover the nature of the other's case and obtain the disclosure of documents and other information. If a bank is party to the litigation, it must comply with disclosure orders. Although the rules have traditionally attempted to limit disclosure,[45] the jurisdiction, as far as fraud cases are concerned, has been extended markedly by judicial decision. In the *Norwich Pharmacal* case, the House of Lords held that non-parties, including banks, who had been mixed up[46] in wrongdoing,[47] could be required to give information to identify the wrongdoers, even though the third party was not liable for the fraud. **4–012**

Norwich Pharmacal has been relied on in later cases, in aid of tracing claims (where property has passed through the hands of a third party), in efforts to tackle the large scale of international fraud.[48] In *Bankers Trust Company v. Shapira,*[49] the plaintiff bank wished to trace the proceeds of two forged cheques, which were alleged to have been paid into the defendant's account with another bank, the Discount Bank (Overseas). The writ had not been served on the two defendants (one could not be found, and the other was in a Swiss prison), but the court ordered the disclosure, by the third party bank, of the state of its customer's account and the documents and correspondence relating to it.[50] The court ruled that a customer who **4–013**

---

42 *Williams v. Summerfield* [1972] 2 Q.B. 512, *per* Widgery C.J.

43 *R. v. Bono* (1913) 29 T.L.R. 635 at 636; *Arnott v. Hayes* (1887) 36 Ch. D. 731; *Howard v. Beall* (1889) 23 Q.B.D. 1; *Perry v. Phosphor Bronze Co Ltd* (1894) 71 L.T. 854.

44 *ibid.*, and see *R. v. Marlborough Street Magistrates' Court Metropolitan Stipendiary Magistrate, ex p. Simpson* (1980) 70 Cr.App.R. 291; *R. v. Nottingham Justices, ex p. Lynn* (1984) 70 Cr.App.R 329. Where a defendant tells the police that he will plead guilty, an order may still be sought, for the accused may not plead guilty at the trial, *Owen v. Sambrook* [1981] Crim. L.R. 329.

45 See Matthews and Malek, *Discovery*, 4.

46 Lord Reid's expression (*Norwich Pharmacal* [1974] A.C. 133 at 174), which, "though expressive, is of uncertain scope": *per* Morritt L.J., *Axa Equity & Law Life Assurance Society plc v. National Westminster Bank* [1998] C.L.C. 1177 at 1183; see also *Mercantile Group (Europe) AG v. Aiyela* [1994] Q.B. 366; and *P v. T Ltd* [1997] 4 All E.R. 200, Ch D.

47 *Norwich Pharmacal Co v. Customs and Excise Comrs.*[1974] A.C. 133. Sir Leonard Hoffmann (1993) 56 M.L.R. 297 at 300 (remarking that allowing litigants to trouble third parties is [so] strongly felt to be un-British) wrote: "Lord Oliver, who was counsel for the unsuccessful Commissioners . . ., once told me that when he died, *Norwich Pharmacal* would be found engraved on his heart".

48 See further Sir Leonard Hoffmann (1993) 56 M.L.R. 297 and Clayton, *op. cit.*, at 117.

49 [1980] 1 W.L.R. 1274; *Dubai Bank v. Galadari* [1990] 1 Lloyd's Rep. 120 at 130, CA; *A v. C* [1981] Q.B. 956.

50 Documents going beyond those which would be "banker's books" for the purpose of a s. 7 order (BBEA 1879).

has been guilty of fraud cannot rely on his or her confidential relationship with the bank, but said that, because it is a "strong thing" for the court to make such an order, good evidence is needed for thinking that the money in the account belongs to the plaintiff.[51] In addition, the plaintiff must give undertakings to pay the bank's expenses and to pay damages to the bank if it becomes liable to anyone as a result of the disclosure, and the documents, once seen, must be used solely for the purpose of following and tracing the money.

4–014 In *Arab Monetary Fund v. Hashim (No. 5),*[52] Hoffmann J., referring to the *Bankers Trust* order, said that the last 20 years have seen "a judge-made revolution in civil procedure"; the courts, under pressure from the increase in cases of commercial fraud, have provided a "panoply of remedies" for plaintiffs. He thought, nevertheless, that the circumstances in which such orders would be given should have limits—if only because there comes a point at which they will no longer be effective.[53] The judge held in this case that the plaintiff must demonstrate a real prospect that the information might lead to the location or preservation of assets to which the plaintiff might make a proprietary claim, and that the balance of convenience between the potential advantage to the plaintiff must be balanced against the detriment for the person against whom disclosure is sought in cost and by way of invasion of privacy. The court refused to grant the order here.

4–015 **(c) Witness summons (subpoena).** In civil proceedings, a party may be made to produce documents by witness summons[54] and there is no defence of confidence. The summons may be set aside if the witness cannot give relevant evidence, or the request was not issued bona fide for that purpose, or if it is oppressive or an abuse of the process of the court.[55]

In *Robertson v. Canadian Imperial Bank of Commerce*,[56] a customer of a bank objected to a *subpoena* requiring the disclosure of some statements of his bank account, which was served on the bank and obeyed without his knowledge. The information revealed that he was overdrawn, and he claimed that the act of the bank was "reprehensible behaviour which

---

[51] [1980] 1 W.L.R. 1278 at 1282, *per* Denning M.R.

[52] [1992] 2 All E.R. 911.

[53] "These orders develop into an international paper chase, in which disclosure of documents by one respondent leads to applications for further information from another respondent and so on. My impression is that these exercises are often non cost-effective . . . the outcome is often no more than a few miserably small sums remaining in disused bank accounts. The bulk of the money has been dissipated in ill-advised commercial speculations": Hoffmann, *op. cit*., at 301. But *cf.* McLachlan [1998] I.C.L.Q. 3 at 31, who points out that £72m. was uncovered in the *Derby v. Weldon* litigation ((No. 6) [1990] 1 W.L.R. 1139, see below, para. 4–025, n. 88).

[54] The term "witness summons" has replaced "*subpoena*" in the High Court: Civil Procedure Rules, rule 34.2.

[55] *Senior v. Holdsworth, ex p. Independent Television News* [1976] Q.B. 23.

[56] [1995] 1 All E.R. 824, PC. See also *Barclays Bank v. Taylor* [1989] 1 W.L.R. 1066, discussed below para. 4–030.

wounded the feelings and injured the pride of the plaintiff in that the credit of the plaintiff depended very largely upon the strict observance of that confidentiality".[57] The Privy Council took the view that the bank was compelled to produce a bank statement to the court under a *subpoena*, and, though not required to withhold the knowledge of the *subpoena* from its customer, it was under no absolute duty to inform him of it; it might do so as a matter of courtesy and good business practice, but at the most would have to use its best endeavours to do so (and here it had done so). There might conceivably be an implied term in a particular banker/customer relationship that a bank should object on the customer's behalf to such a disclosure, although it would be difficult to formulate, and had not been shown to exist in this case.

It used not to be normal to use a *subpoena* to require the production of documents before the hearing (unlike discovery or section 7 orders), but the court has approved the practice of issuing *subpoenas* to compel interlocutory production of documents before the date of trial, provided it can be done conveniently and without injustice.[58] **4–016**

(d) Writs of sequestration. Sequestration is a process invoked by a court when a person (a contemnor) has been found in contempt of court, and has been fined but has not paid, or when the contempt seems likely to continue. The court may issue a writ of sequestration, appointing a sequestrator to take possession of the contemnor's assets, in order to satisfy the fine, or to be retained until the contempt is "purged"—for example by an apology. **4–017**

When a bank knows of the issue of a writ against its customer it must refrain from taking any action which may frustrate the object of the writ (for example, transferring funds out of the country) though it may carry out transactions of an ordinary kind, such as honouring cheques for general business purposes.[59] If in doubt, the bank should inform the sequestrators, in order to protect itself. Thus a bank may be permitted to breach its duty of confidence even without any demand by the sequestrators.[60] Once the sequestrators demand information about the contemnor's property, the request must be answered promptly, fully and accurately, and must reveal whether property is held, or when it was disposed of. The sequestrators are as much entitled to the information as is the contemnor. If the sequestrators demand the transfer of the property, or that it be held to their order, the bank must comply unless someone else may have an interest (for example, the bank under a charge, a joint account holder, or the beneficiary of a trust), or there is doubt whether the property is liable to sequestration. In those cases the bank must explain its failure to comply, so that the

[57] [1995] 1 All E.R. 824 at 827, *per* Lord Nolan.
[58] *Khanna v. Lovell White Durrant* [1994] 4 All E.R. 267.
[59] *Eckman v. Midland Bank Ltd* [1973] 1 Q.B. 519.
[60] *ibid*.

sequestrators may decide whether to seek a specific order from the court. It is contempt of court for any person knowingly to obstruct the sequestrators in carrying out their duty.[61]

4–018 (e) **Garnishee orders.** A judgment creditor whose claim has not been satisfied may use the machinery of the High Court by applying for a garnishee or attachment order against the debtor. The order "attaches" the debt. If a creditor (the garnishor) seeks to attach the debt which the bank owes its customer, the bank (the garnishee) may be ordered to give details of the account as part of the process of attaching the funds in question. The order is usually made *nisi* at first (freezing all accounts of the debtor, unless the order specifies a particular amount) which acts as a demand,[62] (the banker of course is only liable to pay on demand). On full hearing, the order may be made *absolute*, and the bank will have to pay the creditor immediately, unless it gives reasons why it should not be required to do so.

4–019 (f) **Disclosure cross-border.**[63] Banks are now international, indeed global, organisations; they are huge companies with many branches in different countries. Their business is also global: international funds transfers are routine, and virtually instantaneous. Modern business provides huge opportunities for international fraud. If banks are caught in the middle of disputes about international fraud—and they often are—difficult legal and even diplomatic questions may arise.[64] This is a rapidly developing jurisdiction of immense complexity, and only a sketch of some developments can be given here.

4–020 *English courts granting disclosure in aid of foreign legal proceedings.* Courts have powers under the Evidence (Proceedings in Other Jurisdictions) Act 1975 to assist non-English courts in foreign legal proceedings[65] by enabling evidence to be obtained from witnesses by examination (by the court or someone else) in England or Wales,[66] and for the production of documents, inspection of property, and other assistance.[67] Orders under the Act have much in common with witness summonses, but are creatures of statute.[68]

---

[61] *Messenger Newspapers Group Ltd v. N.G.A.* [1984] 1 All E.R. 293.

[62] *Joachimson v. Swiss Bank Corpn.* [1921] 3 K.B. 110.

[63] Helpful articles are: Capper [1996] C.J.Q. 211, McLachlan [1998] I.C.L.Q. 3. See also *Paget's Law of Banking*, Chaps 28 and 29.

[64] See McLachlan [1998] I.C.L.Q. 3 at 7: "A salient feature of this judicial development has been the extent to which it has exposed a potential for serious conflict".

[65] The equivalent provision for criminal proceedings is s. 4 of the Criminal Justice (International Co-operation) Act 1990.

[66] Foreign proceedings include those in other parts of the U.K. and in the European Community.

[67] For criminal cases, see *Bonalumi v. S. of S. for Home Department* [1985] Q.B. 675.

[68] *Boeing Co v. PPG Industries Inc* [1988] 3 All E.R. 839 at 842.

Disclosure for foreign legal proceedings is not always granted. Where foreign legislation is thought to infringe English sovereignty, for example, the Secretary of State may prohibit compliance with foreign rules,[69] and the court will not grant the application if it is satisfied that it is frivolous, vexatious or an abuse of court proceedings.[70] The limitations on the power were considered in the case of *Rio Tinto Zinc v. Westinghouse Electric Corporation*,[71] where the House of Lords said that the court will refuse to allow the procedure to be used for a "fishing expedition". Only direct evidence for use at trial was obtainable, not information which might lead to the discovery of such evidence. The request in this case was phrased in vague terms ("such other director or other person who has knowledge of the facts" and "any memoranda, correspondence or other documents relating thereto"). The request should be strictly construed, and documents must be specified.[72]

Claims of confidentiality or privilege may be raised,[73] under either English or foreign law, and the court has power to limit or even dispense with disclosure in cases where foreign law obligations of confidence are involved (for example, where the banking secrecy of third parties will be breached by disclosure).[74] Courts have a discretion in allowing disclosure in these cases, and have to carry out a balancing exercise. On the one side, there is the desirable policy of assisting a foreign court, and on the other, the court will give great weight to the desirability of upholding the duty of confidentiality in relationships in which it is clearly entitled to be recognised and respected.[75] **4–021**

There might be a problem of balancing interests, for example, where the banker-customer relationship is centred in the United Kingdom and the plaintiff to an action in the USA (or elsewhere abroad) serves a witness summons in the USA on a foreign bank requiring it to disclose documents, including documents held at its London branch. In the case of *X AG v. A bank*,[76] a grand jury *subpoena* was served on the plaintiff,[77] an oil trading **4–022**

[69] The Protection of Trading Interests Act 1980. *e.g. British Airways Board v. Laker Airways Ltd* [1985] A.C. 58.

[70] *Rio Tinto Zinc Corpn. v. Westinghouse Electric Corporation* [1978] A.C. 547 at 634, *per* Lord Diplock.

[71] *ibid.* Lord Denning M.R. (at 561) said that it was the court's "duty and pleasure to do all [it] can to assist in the interests of comity".

[72] Particular documents must be specified, and the court must be satisfied that actual documents exist. It is prepared to edit the request ("carry out a blue pencil exercise"), if necessary, deleting any parts it thinks are excessive; to allow the examination of witnesses shown to have relevant evidence, and the production of specifically identified documents.

[73] s. 3(4) of the Evidence (Proceedings in Other Jurisdictions) Act 1975. In the *Rio Tinto* case, it was the 5th Amendment freedom of a person not to incriminate himself.

[74] *Re State of Norway's Application* [1987] Q.B. 433, CA; *Re State of Norway's Application (No. 2)* [1990] 1 A.C. 723.

[75] *Re State of Norway's Application* [1987] Q.B. 433, CA.

[76] [1983] 2 All E.R. 464. See also *Pharaon v. BCCI (Price Waterhouse intervening)* [1998] 4 All E.R. 455, where BCCI's auditors, Price Waterhouse, were required to disclose documents

company, to produce all the documents relating to any accounts they maintained at the London branch of the defendant bank, which was Citibank (a U.S. bank). The plaintiffs obtained an injunction in London to restrain the bank from producing the documents, because of breach of confidence, and applied to the High Court to continue the injunction. This had the effect of putting Citibank in double jeopardy: if it disclosed the documents, it would disobey the injunction, but if it did not, it would disobey the *subpoena*. Leggatt J., holding that the relationship was centred in London and that English law was the proper law of the contract, was not convinced by the argument that considerations of public policy should necessarily have priority over the private law rule of confidentiality. An English court may, if justified on the balance of convenience, grant and continue an injunction here to prevent disclosure by the London branch of confidential information. In this case, the balance of convenience was between, on the one hand, the fact that continuing the injunction would impede the New York court in its exercise in London of its powers which, by English standards, would be excessive, without in so doing causing detriment to the bank: and on the other hand, the fact that the refusal of the injunction would cause very considerable commercial harm to the plaintiffs. In considering the balance of convenience, the judge thought it was important that the U.S. court would accept the English court's injunction as a defence to its *subpoena.* The balance, he said, clearly favoured the plaintiffs, and the injunction was therefore continued.

4–023 *Obtaining disclosure abroad.* Applications may be made to an English court for the issue of "letters rogatory" or "letters of request"[78] to the appropriate foreign court, which will then be transmitted through government channels, in order to obtain assistance in collecting information for the purposes of an English action. The methods of obtaining the evidence abroad are a matter for the local law concerned.[79] The English courts will

relating to BCCI transactions by subpoena in an action pending in the USA, but were subject to a duty of confidentiality to BCCI and its customers. In this case, where serious wrongdoing was alleged, the public interest in making the documents available outweighed the public interest in preserving confidentiality, provided the disclosure went no further than was reasonably necessary. In *First American Corp. v. Al-Nahyan* [1998] Lloyd's Rep. 213, however, the balance fell the other way, and potential witnesses were protected from oppressive questioning about BCCI's losses despite the importance of cooperating with foreign courts.

[77] X was a wholly owned subsidiary of a Swiss company, with a major branch in New York, which had refused to produce documents to a U.S. Department of Justice investigation into the oil industry, saying they were not subject to the jurisdiction of the U.S. courts.

[78] See also s. 5 of the Extradition Act 1873, which allows a magistrate here, if required by a Secretary of State, to take evidence from witnesses (who may be compelled as if in an ordinary criminal case) to assist in any non-political criminal matter taking place abroad. In conjunction with this, the Secretary of State may seek a s. 7 order (BBEA 1879).

[79] Many countries have signed the Hague Convention, 1970, or have bilateral conventions with the U.K.. It may be easier, in the case of the U.S., to make a direct application to the U.S. court for it to be obtained under 28 U.S. Code 1782. See Matthews and Malek, *Discovery, op. cit.*, 2.77. See also *Panayiotou v. Sony Music Entertainment* [1994] 1 All E.R. 755, and Fellas [1996] N.L.J. 27.

not restrain the party in his or her foreign disclosure exercise, unless the obtaining and use of such disclosure does not comply with local law, or invades the other side's rights, or otherwise amounts to unconscionable conduct.[80]

Traditionally, it was regarded as impossible to order discovery or disclosure against non-parties to the action. As far as domestic jurisdiction in fraud cases was concerned, however, this was permitted in the cases of *Norwich Pharmacal* and *Banker's Trust v. Shapira*.[81] As far as extra-territorial orders are concerned, there has been a dramatic development in the powers of the court in the form of what are known as "*worldwide Mareva injunctions*". Mareva injunctions (freezing injunctions) have been used since 1975 to freeze assets of a defendant pre-trial to prevent the assets being dissipated or removed from the jurisdiction.[82] These have been extended: they may be applied to assets outside England and Wales, and to assets which are not solely owned by the defendant or in the defendant's name. The court has also discretion to make disclosure orders ancillary to the Mareva[83] against a third party like a bank, and this power to make orders designed to ascertain the whereabouts of property may well be more valuable to the plaintiff than the Mareva itself.[84] The power has been extended to include cases where the English court would not have jurisdiction over the substantive dispute.[85] The court has discretion to make "protective orders" in support of substantive proceedings pending in another state; this discretion should be exercised with caution, however, and care should be taken not to make orders which conflict with those of the court seised of the substantive proceedings.[86] A factor in favour of **4–024**

[80] See *e.g. Settebello v. Banco Totta and Acores* [1985] 1 W.L.R. 1050, where letters of request were refused because the plaintiff's allegation that Portuguese law was penal and discriminatory and failed to comply with the standards accepted among civilised nations, would be "deeply embarrassing and indeed offensive to the Portuguese courts": *per* Lord Donaldson M.R.

[81] See above, paras 4–012 *et seq.*

[82] By virtue of s. 37(3) of the Supreme Court Act 1981. See Practice Direction 25. Marevas (freezing injunctions) in the domestic context are discussed below, para. 6–047.

[83] *London and Counties Securities (in liquidation) v. Caplan*, May 5, 1978, decision of Templeman J., unreported, and *Mediterranea Raffineria Siciliana Petroli SpA v. Mabanaft GmbH* (1978) CA. Cited in commentaries, *e.g.* McLachlan [1998] J.C.L.Q. 3 at 9; *A v. C* [1980] 2 All E.R. 347.

[84] The pre-trial order is not limited to examination with regard to local assets, but extends to the defendant's world-wide assets: *Babanaft International Co. S.A. v. Bassatne* [1990] Ch. 13; *Derby & Co. v. Weldon (No. 1)* [1990] Ch. 48; *Republic of Haiti v. Duvalier* [1990] 1 Q.B. 202; *Re BCCI (No. 9)* [1994] 1 W.L.R. 708.

[85] s. 25 of the Civil Jurisdiction and Judgments Act 1982 (*cf. The Siskina* [1979] A.C. 210). The Civil Jurisdiction and Judgments Act 1982 (Interim Relief) Order 1997 extends the effect of s. 25 to states and proceedings outside the Brussels or Lugano Conventions, 1968, 1988. See Dicey & Morris *The Conflict of Laws* (13th ed. Collins 2000), paras 8.018 *et seq.*). See *Credit Suisse Fides Trust v. Cuoghi* [1997] 3 All E.R. 724.

[86] *Credit Suisse Fides Trust v. Cuoghi* [1997] 3 All E.R. 724 at 730, *per* Millett L.J. See also *Van Uden Maritime BV v. Kommanditgesellschaft in Firma Deco-Line* C–391/95 [1999] All E.R.E.C. 258 and *Mietz v. Intership Yachting Sneek BV* C–99/96 [1999] ILPR 541.

granting such an order would be the fact that the defendant is present in England, and so liable to effective enforcement of the order—always providing that the English court does not step on the toes of the primary court.[87]

4–025 Such orders are potentially oppressive for third parties, particularly banks. If a bank where the defendant has an account is served with an injunction, it may be in contempt of court if it obeys his or her instructions, for example by honouring cheques, and it may be in double jeopardy, because it is also bound by the duty of confidentiality to its customer in another country. For this reason, a proviso ("the *Babanaft* proviso") is inserted in the court order to the effect that a third party is bound to comply with the injunction, provided it is *able* to do so[88]; banks (and other third parties) may therefore be able to avoid the double jeopardy difficulty.

4–026 *English courts granting disclosure in the United Kingdom against foreign banks and foreign branches of United Kingdom banks.* The court will not usually make an order directed to a United Kingdom branch of a foreign bank requiring it to produce documents held at the overseas head office relating to transactions which took place there. In an international fraud case, *MacKinnon v. Donaldson, Lufkin and Jenrette Securities*,[89] production of books and papers relating to transactions on the account of a Bahamian company at a New York branch of Citibank (a U.S. bank), was sought against a *London* branch office of Citibank (which was not party to the proceedings). Hoffmann J. held that on principle a court should not, save in exceptional circumstances, impose such a requirement on a foreigner. A *subpoena* was a procedural matter involving an exercise of sovereign authority, and since the bank was foreign and the business had taken place outside the United Kingdom, the order might be seen as an infringement of the sovereignty of the USA,[90] even where the account belonged to a party to the proceedings and disclosure was not unlawful in the foreign state. Banks are in an especially sensitive position, because banks documents are concerned with the business of their customers, and are between different

---

[87] [1997] 3 All E.R. 724 at 735, *per* Lord Bingham C.J.

[88] *Babanaft* [1990] Ch. 13 at 40; *Derby v. Weldon (Nos. 3 and 4)* [1990] Ch. 65 at 78–80; *Baltic Shipping v. Translink Shipping* [1995] 1 Lloyd's Rep. 673. See Practice Direction No. 25 which replaces [1994] 1 W.L.R. 1233. The Order states that "the terms of this Order do not affect or concern any one outside the jurisdiction of this Court until it is declared enforceable or is enforced by a Court in the relevant country and then they are to affect him only to the extent they have been declared enforceable or have been enforced". See also (1991) 54 M.L.R. 329.

[89] [1986] Ch. 482. By *subpoena* and order under BBEA 1879. An application to a New York court for letters of request would have been more orthodox, but might have taken too long. see also *Re Grossman* (1981) 71 Cr.App.Rep. 302.

[90] Hoffmann J. noted that a New York court had followed the same approach in relation to English banks with New York offices, in *Laker Airways v. Pan American World Airways* (1985) 607 F. Supp. 324.

countries, forced to submit to whichever sovereign is able to apply the greatest pressure.[91]

English courts: where information has already been disclosed, can it be used, under foreign compulsion, for another purpose? A different situation arose in *Bank of Crete SA v. Koskotas (No. 2).*[92] The question, which is arising in various forms with increasing frequency, is whether, when confidential information has already been disclosed for one purpose, it can be passed on to another body for another. 4–027

Here, the plaintiff bank was bringing proceedings in England against its former chief executive and others for misappropriation of money. Certain banks with London branches were ordered to disclose information and documents relating to some accounts of their customers on the undertaking that they would be used only for the purposes of this action. However, a special team, appointed by the Bank of Greece, investigating the affair were obliged to prepare reports of their investigations and needed to use the documents. Millett J. held that the court would only authorise a plaintiff *voluntarily* to make use of information for another purpose in exceptional circumstances. But he said that disclosure under compulsion of law is another matter, and the court would not be astute to prevent disclosure for other purposes in a foreign jurisdiction, where it would put the plaintiff in the position of either having to infringe undertakings to the court or be in breach of duties under Greek law. Leave was given for the material to be used for the investigation.[93] 4–028

(g) Disclosure to investigators. The Jack Committee wrote in its Report: "the last two decades have seen a torrent of new legislation, which has become a spate in the past few years, requiring or permitting bankers . . . to disclose confidential information in the public interest."[94] A list of such statutes was given in an appendix to the Report (since that time the list has grown longer). Some of these measures are discussed below. 4–029

Police and Criminal Evidence Act 1984

Under the Police and Criminal Evidence Act 1984 (PACE 1984), the police have extensive powers for investigation into crime where there are reasonable grounds for suspecting that a serious arrestable offence has been 4–030

---

[91] (1985) 607 F. Supp. 324 at 494. The fact that the foreign bank had submitted itself to jurisdiction in the U.K., in the sense of applying to the Bank of England for recognition here, made no difference.

[92] [1993] 1 All E.R. 748.

[93] Millett J. saw disclosure under these circumstances as a potential invasion of *privacy* rather than of confidentiality, because the material had already been disclosed for another purpose. He linked the case to *Marcel v. Commr. of Police of the Metropolis* [1992] 1 All E.R. 72, see below, para. 4–035, n. 22.

[94] Cm. 622 (1989), para 5.07.

committed. They may apply to a circuit judge for an order for access to "special procedure material", which includes bank accounts.[95] The judge has to be satisfied that there are reasonable grounds for believing that a serious offence has been committed, although a prosecution need not be under way. The order is made to the person who is in possession of the material (the bank), and it is made after an *inter partes* hearing, so that the bank may be represented. It was held in *Barclays Bank v. Taylor*[96] that there is no requirement that the bank should inform the account holder of the application[97] (to do so would in some circumstances frustrate the investigation[97a] or be represented at the hearing; and the bank is not bound to make any objection on behalf of the account holder to such an order being made.[98] Further, it made no difference that the person being investigated by the police held one of the accounts involved jointly with his wife, who was *not* under investigation: the joint account had to be disclosed.[99]

Criminal Justice Act 1987

4–031 Section 2 of the Criminal Justice Act 1987 (CJA 1987) gives the Serious Fraud Office (SFO) extensive powers to investigate a serious or complex fraud. Once the Director of the SFO has decided to investigate a case which he or she reasonably believes to involve such a fraud, the person under investigation, or any person who the Director has reason to believe has relevant information, may be given notice that they must answer questions about the investigation.[1] Notices may be directed to bankers to give evidence,[2] or to produce documents. A prosecution need not be under way and there is no restriction to "entries in a banker's book". Failure to comply with such a requirement without reasonable excuse is a criminal offence. It is required that the customer must consent to the disclosure, or the Director or a person designated by him or her must authorise the making of the notice.[3]

---

[95] Under PACE 1984, s. 9(1) and Sched. 1. Access is not limited to entries in a banker's book.

[96] [1989] 1 W.L.R. 1066; [1989] 3 All E.R. 562. Noted Wadsley (1990) 106 L.Q.R. 204.

[97] The bank would have been free to inform him, but Lord Donaldson M.R. said he would have been "surprised and disappointed if they had done so" [1989] 3 All E.R. 562 at 569.

[97a] And could now, under the money laundering legislation (see below, para. 4–042) constitute tipping-off

[98] See also *Robertson v. Canadian Bank of Commerce* [1994] 1 W.L.R. 1493, see above, para. 4–015.

[99] Although this had "the effect of destroying in a technical sense the confidentiality of Mrs Taylor's affairs" [1989] 3 All E.R. 562 at 571, *per* Croom-Johnson L.J.

[1] See *R. v. Director of SFO, ex parte Smith* [1993] A.C. 1; *Re Arrows Ltd (No 4)* [1995] 2 A.C. 75. See also *R. v. Director of SFO, ex p. Saunders* [1988] Crim. L.R. 837. In *Saunders v. U.K.* [1997] 23 E.H.R.R. 313, the European Court of Human Rights held that the use at his criminal trial of documents obtained by D.T.I. Inspectors from him in exercise of their powers of compulsion under s. 432 of the CA 1985 denied him a fair trial and therefore contravened Art. 6(1) of the Convention on Human Rights, because their use tended to incriminate him.

[2] Kirk and Woodcock, in *Serious Fraud—Investigation and Trial* (1992) comment: "Since in fraud cases many witnesses are lawyers, accountants or bankers the extensive use, often the subject of complaint, of notices under s. 2, is not surprising", para. 2.2.1.

[3] CJA 1987, s. 2(10).

The courts have emphasised that the powers of the SFO are not unlimited: the powers of investigation exist to help in solving serious fraud, and should not encroach upon the rights of individuals more than is fairly or reasonably necessary to achieve the purpose for which they were created.[4-5] There is no general power for example to disclose information obtained by the SFO using its compulsory powers to persons who have not specifically been named in the CJA 1987.[6]

Banking Act 1987

Section 41 of the BA 1987 gives the FSA (formerly, the Bank of England[7]) powers to appoint investigators. It was the report by accountants under this section into the BCCI which described the "massive and widespread fraud", and which caused the Bank of England to close down the bank in 1991. Under section 41(10) of the BA 1987, a person's replies may be used in evidence against him.[8] **4–032**

The Authority has other far-reaching powers under the BA 1987, including powers under section 39 to require persons, including accountants, to report on particular institutions.[9] The difference between the two sections is that under section 39 accountants are formally instructed by and report to the bank concerned, whereas under section 41 it is the Authority itself which gives the instructions and receives the report.[10]

Companies Act 1985 and Financial Services Act 1986

Banks may be required to disclose information under various provisions of the CA 1985, relating for example to the investigation of companies and their affairs.[11] If inspectors consider that any person, including a bank, is in possession of information which they believe is relevant to their investigation, they may require him or her to produce documents, to attend before them, and to give them otherwise all reasonable assistance in connection with the investigation.[12] The customer against whom disclosure is allowed **4–033**

[4-5] *Morris v. Director of SFO* [1993] 1 All E.R. 787.

[6] *B & C Holdings v. Spicer & Oppenheim* [1993] A.C. 426.

[7] The supervisory powers of the Bank of England were transferred to the FSA by s. 21 of the BEA 1998, with effect from June 1, 1998.

[8] *cf.* The powers of the SFO under s. 2(8) of the CJA 1987.

[9] See *A v. B Bank (Bank of England intervening)* [1992] 1 All E.R. 778 at 793, *per* Hirst J., where it was held that a BA 1987, s. 39 notice overrode an injunction. The judge added: "Finally, I cannot stress too strongly the importance which should be attached to the Bank of England having, within the limits laid down by the BA 1987 and the general law, unfettered and unimpeded scope for the exercise of their most important public duties of regulation under the BA 1987 in the interests of the public, who are surely entitled to rely on the Bank of England to exercise those powers with integrity".

[10] Report into BCCI, by Bingham L.J. at p. 21. He called the powers "invasive".

[11] ss. 431–453 of the CA 1985, amended by Pt III of the Companies Act 1989 (CA 1989) (Companies Act 1989 (Commencement No. 2) Order (S.I. 1999 No. 142)).

[12] In *Re Mirror Group Newspapers* [1999] 2 All E.R. 641, it was held that inspectors could not place demands on persons that were unreasonable as to the time they had to expend or the expense they had to incur or in any other respect.

must be the company under investigation, or must have consented, or the disclosure must be authorised by the Secretary of State.[13]

The FSA 1986[14] contains similar wide powers with relation to investment schemes and investigations about insider dealing.

Taxation statutes: Taxes Management Act 1970 and the Income and Corporation Taxes Act 1988

4–034 The Inland Revenue has powers to require banks to produce a tax payer's documents. Notice is given to the bank, and the consent of the Board and of a Commissioner are required.[15] It has also other specific powers: for example, it may require banks to give information concerning securities held on behalf of customers,[16] bank interest payable to a customer[17]; and in connection with the transfer of assets abroad.[18]

The Commissioners of Customs and Excise also have wide powers to obtain information and documents from third parties, under the Customs and Excise Management Act 1979, supplemented by the VAT Act 1994.

Insolvency Act 1986[19]

4–035 When a company goes into liquidation, or an individual becomes bankrupt, a liquidator or trustee is appointed, to collect in and distribute the assets of the company or individual to creditors.[20] The liquidator or trustee is given a wide range of powers under the Act in order to obtain all the information necessary to carry out that function effectively. The court, for example, may order any person (including a bank) to give to the office-holder any property to which the company appears to be entitled, and to require *any persons* (including bankers) who it thinks capable of giving information about the company to appear before it for private examination under section 236 (or, for individuals, section 366 of the IA 1986), and may require them to submit an affidavit concerning their dealings with the company, or to produce any books, papers or records (not necessarily the company's books) in their possession or control which relate to the company. This is sometimes called the "Star Chamber Clause", in a

[13] CA 1985, s. 452.

[14] FSA 1986, s. 177.

[15] Taxes Management Act 1970, s. 20; see *R. v. I.R.C., ex p. Taylor (No 2)* [1990] S.T.C. 379, CA (s. 20(2)); *T.C. Coombs & Co v. I.R.C.* [1991] 3 All E.R. 623, HL.

[16] Taxes Management Act 1970, s. 67.

[17] Taxes Management Act 1970, s. 17, amended the Finance Act 1990 and 1988.

[18] Income and Corporation Taxes Act, 1988, s. 745 (amended Finance Act 1990). See *Clinch v. I.R.C.* [1974] Q.B. 76. See also *Royal Bank of Canada v. I.R.C* [1972] Ch. 665 (bond washing transaction not in the ordinary course of business); *NZ Stock Exchange v. I.R.C.* [1991] 4 All E.R. 443; *Wilover Nominees Ltd v. I.R.C* [1974] 3 All E.R. 496; *Cutner v. I.R.C.* [1974] S.T.C. 259; *Essex v. I.R.C.* [1980] S.T.C. 378, CA.

[19] See below, Chap. 24.

[20] An administrator has the general powers of the company as its agent, IA 1986, s. 14, and the bank would not breach a duty of confidence in disclosing information to him or her.

reference to the investigation techniques of the Tudor monarchs. Lord Slynn has commented: "it is plain it is an extraordinary power" requiring a balancing of factors to avoid making an order which is wholly unreasonable, unnecessary or oppressive to the person concerned.[21]

Difficult situations occur where an organisation or body which has powers to obtain disclosure of confidential documents would prefer to take a shortcut by requesting another body to hand it documents which the latter has already obtained using its own powers (perhaps documents belonging to a bank's customer, and seized from a bank).[22]

Money laundering statutes[22a]

Money laundering can be described as the process by which criminals attempt to conceal the true origin and ownership of the proceeds of their criminal activities.[23] Much of the United Kingdom legislation was introduced to implement the European Directive on Money Laundering,[24] which reflects the accepted international view that the most effective way of fighting organised crime is to trace criminals' placement of the proceeds of crime—their efforts to make the (often very large) proceeds of crime appear to have come from legitimate sources: in other words, by attempting to control money laundering at its earliest stages.[25] **4–036**

Among the statutory provisions dealing with money laundering which affect banks, are the following.

---

[21] *B & C Holdings v. Spicer & Oppenheim* [1992] Ch. 342, aff'd [1993] A.C. 426 at 439.

[22] See, *e.g., Morris v. Director of SFO* [1993] 1 All E.R. 788, Ch D, where the liquidators of BCCI requested documents obtained by the SFO from Price Waterhouse, BCCI's auditors; *Re Arrows (No. 4)* [1993] 3 All E.R. 861, CA, where the SFO requested documents from a liquidator, and *Marcel v. Comr of Police of the Metropolis* [1992] 1 All E.R. 72, where documents obtained by the police under PACE 1984 were required for a *subpoena.* See also *Bank of Crete v. Koskotas (No. 2)* [1993] 1 All E.R. 748, discussed above, para. 4–027, and *Re Galileo Group Ltd* [1999] Ch. 100, where disclosure of material obtained under s. 39 of the BA 1987 was sought, and where there was the complication s. 82 of the BA 1987 required confidentiality. The order was not made because failure to remove all embargoed material might be a criminal offence, and a redacted (edited) document might be misleading. See also *B&C Holdings v.Barclays de Zoete Wedd* [1999] B.C.L.C. 86.

[22a] See Cole [1993] 4 J.I.B.L.; Haynes, [1993] 11 J.I.B.L. 454; Haynes, [1994] 2 J.I.B.L. 58; McCormack, (1995) 16 Co. Lawyer 6; Wadsley, [1994] Conv. 275.

[23] Para. 1.03, *Guidance Notes on Money Laundering for the Financial Sector*, revised and consolidated 1997 (Joint Money Laundering Steering Group).

[24] Council Directive 91/308 [1991] O.J. L166/77. The definition of money laundering in the directive is the lengthy one of the Vienna Convention (UN Convention against Illicit Traffic in Narcotic Drugs and Psychotropic Substances, 1988). See Ewing [1991] J.I.B.L. 139 and [1992] J.I.B.L. News, n. 54. English legislation goes further than the Directive in some respects, *e.g.* extending the statutory controls to money laundering of the proceeds of *any serious crime* (optional in the Directive) and making the *mens rea* of the offences created "knowledge or suspicion."

[25] Huber, in *Banks, Fraud and Crime*, p. 223, points out that this is no minor matter, since well in excess of $1 trillion are moved daily among financial institutions.

Drug Trafficking Act 1994[26]

4–037 **Section 50 of the Drug Trafficking Act 1994.** It is an offence to enter into an arrangement which facilitates the retention, or control by or on behalf of another person, of his proceeds of drug trafficking, or which allows the other person's proceeds of drug trafficking[27] to be used to secure funds for him or her, knowing or suspecting that he or she carries on, or has carried on, drug trafficking. The word "arrangement" includes "the retention or control by or on behalf of A of A's proceeds of drug trafficking", or placing funds so obtained at A's disposal, and it is wide enough to include providing banking facilities for a customer. The offence is punishable with up to 14 years imprisonment.

4–038 There is a defence for a person (like a banker) who discloses his or her belief or suspicion to "a constable"[28] as soon as reasonably practicable; there is also a defence of reasonable excuse. No definition is given of what amounts to reasonable excuse (normally it is largely a matter of fact). It would in any case be open to a defendant banker to prove that he or she did *not* know or suspect that the person was carrying on drug trafficking. However, the wording implies that the burden of proof must be discharged by the defendant, and it might be extremely difficult to show, not that he or she had no reasonable cause to suspect money laundering (an objective test) but that he or she did not in fact suspect it.[29]

Bankers are protected against actions for breach of confidentiality by their customers, because disclosures to a constable are not to be treated as a breach "of any restriction upon the disclosure of information imposed by statute or otherwise".[30]

4–039 **Section 52 of the Drug Trafficking Act 1994.** This section creates an offence of failing to disclose knowledge or suspicion of drug money laundering that is gained "in the course of trade, profession, business or employment".

The section makes failure to disclose knowledge or suspicion of money laundering an offence in itself. Its approach is similar to that in section 50,

---

[26] A consolidating Act, repealing and replacing earlier provisions relating to drug trafficking, including sections of the Drug Trafficking Offences Act 1986, for discussion of which, see Feldman, *Criminal Confiscation Orders—the New Law* (1988). The Drug Trafficking Offences Act 1986 also introduced provisions for confiscating the proceeds of drug trafficking, giving the court powers to inhibit dealings with property or to require disclosure of information in such cases.

[27] Defined DTA 1994, s. 1: "doing or being concerned anywhere in the world with producing or supplying, transporting or storing, importing or exporting a controlled drug", etc.

[28] In practice, the National Criminal Intelligence Service (NCIS).

[29] Other criminal statutes require "reasonable cause to suspect", and this was proposed as an amendment during the debates on the Bill in the House of Lords: vol. 540 at 753. Suspicion is a "far less assured state of mind than either knowledge or belief", Feldman, *Criminal Confiscation Orders*, para. 3.09. See also the *Guidance Notes for the Financial Sector*, para. 6.01: "suspicion is personal and subjective and falls far short of proof based on firm evidence".

[30] A change from Drug Trafficking Offences Act 1986, which stated "imposed by *contract*". The new provision repeats the wider wording of the CJA 1993.

however, since a defence of disclosing the information or "other matter in question" is provided. The penalty is less draconian although still very harsh; the maximum is five years imprisonment.

Again, controversially, the *mens rea* of the offence is knowledge or *suspicion* (not "reasonable cause to suspect").

Section 53 of the Drug Trafficking Act 1994. A further important new offence is that of "*tipping-off*" a suspect. If a person (for example a banker) knows or suspects that a constable is acting, or proposing to act, in connection with an investigation which is being, or is about to be, conducted into drug money laundering or that a disclosure has been made to the police, and he discloses to another person (the customer, for example) information likely to prejudice the investigation, he will be guilty of tipping off. The maximum penalty on indictment is five years imprisonment. **4–040**

There are similar provisions dealing with the prevention of terrorism under the Prevention of Terrorism (Temporary Provisions) Act 1989[31] and other legislation.

The Criminal Justice Act 1988 (CJA 1988), has been amended to include parallel provisions to those in the Drug Trafficking Act 1994, but which deal with money laundering of the profits of *all serious crime*. The relevant sections are 93A (which corresponds to section 50), and 93D[32] (which corresponds to section 53). Serious criminal conduct includes all indictable offences and a few others. It therefore includes offences like theft, which normally does not pose the sort of threat or menace to public safety that drug trafficking or terrorism does, and extends the "Big Brother" aspects of the legislation even further. **4–041**

The effect of the legislation

The effect of these changes has been to create what the Government of the time called a "suspicions-based reporting regime".[33] A banker (or any other person) who has a suspicion that a customer has been money laundering must report that suspicion to the police[34] or run the risk of being prosecuted, and, if the "suspect" is later shown to have been money laundering, of having to demonstrate that he or she had no suspicion of that fact. **4–042**

Bankers must also take care not to "tip-off" customers they suspect, and this may cause further problems. First, there is the practical difficulty that if

[31] ss. 11, 12, 13 and 17.

[32] Guidelines as to the operation of CJA 1988, s. 93D have been given by the court: *C v. S* [1999] Lloyd's Rep. Bank. 26, CA, *per* Lord Woolf, M.R., see below, para. 4–044.

[33] HM Treasury Consultation Document on the Directive, May 1992.

[34] The NCIS provides specially designed computer forms for such reports. It is not clear what eventually happens to the information thus stored.

a banker refuses to act for a suspected customer,[35] the customer may not only be offended, but if they are acting criminally, be "tipped-off" by the refusal itself: this might constitute an offence. And, in some situations, banks may have to continue to act for suspected customers, under the directions of the National Criminal Intelligence Service (NCIS), since the NCIS may "advise or instruct the bank as to its future conduct in connection with the customer concerned", and may instruct the bank to continue the relationship in order to make further investigations.[36]

4–043 There is another problem. Many bankers may find it distasteful to have to act as amateur detectives for enforcement agencies in this way, and the disclosure regime may give rise to real ethical dilemmas. Further, there is the fact that the cost of compliance, which probably does not come cheap, is borne by the bank. However, banks may take some small comfort from knowing that customers will find it difficult to take action against them for breach of confidentiality, because of the wide immunity given by the CJA 1988, but this protection may not always work. A salutary example is given in the Guidance Notes,[36a] where bank staff disclosed information about a customer to NCIS and the police made enquiries of the bank manager, who raised the issue with the customer. The customer, a solicitor, was quite innocent and complained to the bank, arguing that it should have made reasonable enquiries internally. The bank paid compensation to the customer, because it had not used sufficient skill and care in dealing with the case rather than having the situation examined by the court or the Banking Ombudsman. The manager was, says the Guidance Notes, "guilty of tipping off", but was not prosecuted.[37]

It is interesting to speculate a little further about the effects of these provisions. Probably, prudent bankers will be zealous in disclosing their doubts to the authorities and many unnecessary reports may be made,[38] which must be time-consuming and costly, not only for banks, but for the NCIS as well. There is also a series of puzzling questions about what happens to the information gathered in this way: how long is it kept and for

[35] If a bank believes a customer is using the account for the purpose of committing a crime, it might be aiding and abetting him or her unless it declines to act.

[36] "If he does any act in contravention of [the Drug Trafficking Act 1994, s. 50 and CJA 1988, s. 93A offence]. He does not commit an offence . . . If (i) the disclosure is made before he does the act concerned and the act is done with the consent of the constable" (Drug Trafficking Act 1994, s. 53, CJA 1988, s. 93A). In any case, the bank should liaise with NCIS to ensure the termination of the relationship does not tip-off the customer or prejudice the investigation in any other way (Guidance Notes, para. 6.27).

[36a] Appendix A, Case 11.

[37] The disclosure shall not be treated as a breach of any restriction imposed by statute or otherwise: CJA 1988, s. 18(4).

[38] The number of reports has increased from about 500 during the year after the Drug Trafficking Offences Act 1986 was introduced to 15,000 during 1994, a fifth of which were found to have some connection with criminal activity. (NCIS, reported in *The Independent*, May 23, 1995); and 16,000 in 1996 ([1997] 94/40 Gazette).

what purposes may it be used—can it be disclosed to other persons or agencies?[39]

Some of the problems were considered in the recent case of *C v. S.*[40] A bank (all the parties in the case were anonymous) disclosed information about a customer to the NCIS. Some time afterwards, a company, C, obtained an order against the bank for the disclosure of the customer's accounts,[41] because it suspected that the customer had been involved in misappropriating vast sums of its money. This put the bank in a most difficult situation, because it was bound to obey the order, but feared that if it disclosed the information it would be subject to criminal prosecution for "tipping-off" under section 93D of the CJA 1988.[42] It therefore asked the NCIS for an assurance that there would be no prosecution if it complied with the order. It did not receive the assurance. The NCIS said that an investigation was being carried out and the tipping-off provisions applied; if the bank disclosed the information, this would, in the view of the NCIS, constitute tipping-off (although it would be for the prosecuting authorities, not the NCIS itself to make the decision as to prosecution). **4–044**

The bank was in a situation of double jeopardy—damned if it disclosed, damned if it didn't. Wisely, it sought directions from the court. After several preliminary skirmishes between the parties before judges *in camera*, the Court of Appeal decided to provide guidance in open court as to the action which should be taken in such cases in the future.[43] The court urged the NCIS to take a more "sympathetic and helpful" attitude in such cases. The NCIS's lack of concern with the bank's difficulties was unwise, partly because it would discourage financial institutions from disclosing suspicions,[44] and also because it would be an abuse of process for a bank disclosing information by order of the court to be prosecuted. **4–045**

In future, the court said, as soon as a financial institution is aware that a order is being sought which might involve disclosure of information which might prejudice an investigation, it should inform the NCIS of the position **4–046**

[39] The DPA 1998 provides a right of access to individuals to personal data, but there is, unsurprisingly, an exemption for data held by law enforcement agencies (DPA 1998, s. 29); in any case, the onus is on individuals to enforce their rights (in the case of data held by NCIS, they may have no idea that any information is held).

[40] [1999] Lloyd's Rep. Bank. 26, CA.

[41] A *Norwich Pharmacal* order.

[42] See above, para. 4–044 *et seq.* The section reads: "a person is guilty of an offence if (a) he knows or suspects that a constable is acting, or is proposing to act, in connection with an investigation which is being, or is about to be, conducted into money laundering; and (b) he discloses to any other person information or any other matter which is likely to prejudice that investigation or proposed investigation." Money laundering here is of the proceeds of serious criminal conduct, not specifically the proceeds of drug trafficking offences".

[43] Lord Woolf referred to the situation giving rise to the case as "highly unusual", but the fact that the court felt it necessary to provide guidelines seems to imply that the court considered that such situations were bound to arise, perhaps frequently, in future.

[44] Perhaps not a very likely result, in view of the stringent penalties which may be imposed if suspicions are not disclosed, see above, paras 4–037 and 4–039.

and of the material. The burden is then on the NCIS: it must identify the material it does not wish to be disclosed and indicate how it would prefer the order to be dealt with. In some cases the problem would not be serious, because the NCIS would not be concerned about the applicant knowing about the investigation, and then the order might be obeyed, subject to an appropriate undertaking to keep the material confidential. In other cases, partial disclosure might be possible and agreed upon. Otherwise, the directions of the court would have to be sought.[45] Importantly, it will be for the NCIS to persuade the court that, were disclosure to be made, there would be a real likelihood of the investigation being prejudiced. If the NCIS were not to co-operate with the institution and any requirements of the court in advancing such a case, the court may presume that no prejudice will occur and make a disclosure order. Lord Woolf emphasised that the court must recognise its responsibility to protect the interests of the applicant, especially when the applicant cannot be heard himself because of all the secrecy of the proceedings. The court, he said, "must have material on which to act if it is to deprive an applicant of its normal rights".

Money Laundering Regulations

4–047 The legislation is supplemented by the MLR 1993,[46] which are set out and explained by the Guidance Notes produced by banks for their own information. The Regulations flesh out the disclosure regime by requiring banks[47] to have systems and training to prevent money laundering. They cover business relationships, "one-off" transactions involving more than a specified amount[48] or linked "one-off" transactions[49]—this is to stop what is known as "smurfing" (placing less conspicuous amounts of money in a number of different institutions). Every bank must maintain identification procedures, record keeping procedures (records must be kept for five years), internal reporting procedures and training procedures. For example, a compliance officer must be appointed to consider any reports made, and decide whether to pass them on to the NCIS.[50] If banks do not install or maintain such procedures, their failure to do so will be taken into account when the Bank of England is considering whether they meet the minimum criteria for authorisation under the BA 1987.[51]

[45] The court gave instructions as to the practicalities and, if necessary, the "stratagems" which should be used in applying to the court ([1999] Lloyds L.R. Banking 26 at 30, CA).

[46] S.I. 1993 No. 1933.

[47] And other businesses which are likely to be used for money laundering, including solicitors engaged in investment business within the meaning of the FSA 1986—see Law Society Guidance for Solicitors; solicitors engaged in conveyancing business, accountants, estate agents, etc., are also vulnerable.

[48] Stated to be 15,000 ECU.

[49] Transactions will not usually be "linked" if there is more than three months between them.

[50] A report made to such a person constitutes a defence for the person suspecting. The Reporting Officer is "expected to act honestly and reasonably and to make his determinations in good faith" Guidance Notes, para. 6.12.

[51] Banking Supervisors are also required to report suspicions to the authorities.

It seems that bankers will have to keep customers' accounts under regular observation in order to satisfy the requirements. As a result, it is likely that the civil standard of care imposed on banks (for example, in satisfying the requirements of section 4 of the Ch A 1957 in identifying prospective customers[52]) will adapt to accommodate the higher standards which are required of banks by the imposition on them of these criminal duties. **4–048**

It is thought that the system of disclosing suspicions about customers will gradually (as customers become aware of what is going on behind the scenes) put a considerable strain on the relationship of bankers with their customers, which should be based on trust, not only with the customer concerned, but generally.[53] The Banking Ombudsman regards the duties on banks under this legislation as "onerous"[54] and states that before a report is made the bank must have *reasonable grounds* for suspicion. It seems, therefore, that banks will have to balance carefully their conflicting duties between customer and authorities[55] if they are to avoid criticism from his Office. **4–049**

Proceeds of Crime Act 1995

The Proceeds of Crime Act 1995[56] strengthens the confiscation provisions of the 1986 and 1988 Acts, which give the court power to make orders confiscating the assets of convicted criminals. The new Act makes the imposition of such orders mandatory on the court in an amount equal to the gross value of the property received by the defendant in connection with the crime. Confiscation of any asset may be ordered, unless the defendant can prove that it was legitimately acquired or the court is satisfied that there would be a serious risk of injustice. **4–050**

In order to use the confiscation powers, investigators and prosecutors must first ascertain what property the defendant has. They may use conventional powers (such as the BBEA 1879) to obtain information but the court may also order the disclosure of information on affidavit to the prosecutor which may be used before the judge when considering confisca-

---

[52] See below, Chap. 14. *cf. Lloyds Bank v. Savory* [1933] A.C. 201; *Marfani v. Midland Bank* [1964] 1 W.L.R. 956.

[53] *cf.* the Guidance Notes, which emphasise: "the integrity of the confidential relationship which has been established *between law enforcement agencies and financial institutions* is considered to be of paramount importance" (para. 6.37: emphasis added.)

[54] OBO A.R., 1994/5, para. 13.2. He goes on to say: "leaving aside any question of malice, a bank has to behave reasonably and not recklessly." He says: "In one such case, the bank first argued that the complaint was outside my jurisdiction, and, later, before my investigation had been completed, paid £2,500 in settlement." (This seems to be a reference to Appendix A, Case 11 of the Guidance Notes referred to above, para. 4-042.)

[55] The requirements and procedures are described in more detail in *Guidance Notes for the Financial Sector.*

[56] See Talbot [1995] N.L.J. 1857.

tion.[57] This provision is wider than section 9 of the PACE 1984, because the application may be made *ex parte*, there is no need for the offence to be a serious arrestable offence, and it need not be the only way to obtain the material. The defendant can also be required to disclose the whereabouts of his or her assets, wherever they may be in the world. The legislation also applies to any "gifts" handed over to a third party.[58]

4–051 The confiscation provisions can affect the rights of creditors of the defendant and bona fide third parties, including banks, particularly if they are unsecured (and probably even if they are preferential) creditors. There is no right to compensation for such third parties if the defendant is convicted, and only a limited right to compensation in the event that the defendant is ultimately not convicted or is pardoned.

Jack's recommendations

4–052 The Jack Committee took the view in 1989 that too many inroads had already been made by legislation into banking confidentiality, particularly with regard to the compulsion of law exception, and recommended that existing statutory exemptions from the duty should be consolidated in new legislation defining the duty.[59] It further recommended that legislation should state that damages for breach of confidentiality should include compensation for distress, embarrassment or inconvenience, regardless of whether financial loss could be proved.[60] The Committee requested that any future exemptions should be made "by reference to this new provision", so that any which had not been so made would not override the central duty.[61]

4–053 The Government was not persuaded to introduce new legislation. It thought the basic framework of the law had worked well, and to change it would risk causing unwelcome difficulties and confusion.[62] Further, it did not accept the Committee's view that there had been a "massive" erosion of the duty—the statutory exceptions had been enacted only after the most careful consideration of all the implications. It is too early to know yet whether success in the fight against drug trafficking, terrorism and serious crime generally will justify the establishment of the new suspicions-based reporting regime, but it is clear that the duty of confidentiality has suffered considerable damage in the struggle.

[57] Courts may also order the disclosure of information held by government departments, make receivership orders to manage assets or realise them to enforce payment of a confiscation order made by the court and make restraint orders preventing any dealing with a defendant's assets (similar to freezing injunctions but giving the prosecution priority over unsecured creditors and not requiring undertakings in damages).

[58] See *The Guardian*, November 1, 1995, which reported that the powers under the earlier legislation had not proved wide enough: only 32 orders had been made, relating to property valued at over £1.7 million.

[59] On the lines set down in the *Tournier* case, see Cm. 622 (1989) paras 5.38–39 and 5.48.

[60] Cm. 622 (1989), para. 5.46.

[61] Probably constitutionally impossible, however, because Parliament is unable to bind its successors.

[62] White Paper, Cm. 1026 (1990), para. 2.12–13.

Duty to the Public

The easiest example of this category to understand is that of a customer who in time of war trades with the enemy.[63] The bank's public duty would require it to disclose knowledge of such behaviour to the authorities. **4–054**

The Jack Committee bracketed exception (b) with exception (a) (compulsion of law) because it regarded this category as residual in that it only seems to cover situations which have not yet been "codified" in statute; in Jack's view, the exception added to uncertainty about the law and was not justified. The Government, however, felt that there was still a need to allow bank officers a discretion to disclose information in the absence of outright compulsion,[64] and refused to provide that it should be deleted.

Despite the difficulty Jack found in envisaging situations where the exception could be used, one or two situations have arisen in recent years where disclosure appeared justified to the court, but would not have been compelled by law, and where the public interest provided the ground for disclosure of confidential information.[65] An interesting question arose in *Price Waterhouse v. BCCI Holdings (Luxembourg)*, although it directly concerned accountants rather than bankers. Price Waterhouse were the accountants who had drawn up a Banking Act Report for the Bank of England on the notorious failure of the Bank for Credit and Commerce International, and they were requested to submit evidence which they had obtained from BCCI to the inquiry held by Bingham L.J. into the bank's failure. The inquiry was private and had no powers to compel witnesses, but the accountants wished to submit the material. Millett J. held that since it was in the public interest, expressed in the BA 1987, for confidential information to be disclosed to the Bank of England so that it could perform its function of supervising banks, there was at least as great a public interest in the disclosure of such information to an inquiry set up to review the bank's past performance in supervision. By giving the Bank of England powers to compel disclosure under the BA 1987,[66] Parliament had chosen to accord greater weight to the public interest than to confidentiality, including banking confidentiality, and that the public interest should be respected and the material disclosed to the inquiry. The judge, Millett J., stated that he had not found the decision easy, since the cases on which he based his decision were based on the public interest in the detection or prevention of wrong-doing, or in preventing a miscarriage of justice. The implication was that the arguments in favour of disclosure in those cases **4–055**

[63] *Weld-Blundell v. Stephens* [1920] A.C. 956 at 965. The example given by Bankes L.J. in *Tournier* [1924] 1 K.B. 461. The Jack Report suggested that disclosure to credit reference agencies might also be by virtue of this exception, see below, para. 4–064.

[64] White Paper, para. 2.15.

[65] In *Libyan Arab Bank v. Bankers Trust Co* [1989] 3 All E.R. 253 at 285, Staughten J. thought (*obiter* and "tentatively") that the Federal Reserve Board, the central banking system in the United States, might have a public duty to perform in obtaining information from banks.

[66] Under BA 1987, s. 39.

are more compelling than those presented in favour of disclosure to improve the supervision of banks.[67]

4–056 Arguably, in this area of law—where private rights may only too easily be pushed aside—the rule of compulsion of law should have been strictly applied. However, the circumstances of the case were special. Not only was BCCI itself notorious and criminal, but the circumstances of its collapse were mysterious and far reaching, and might have involved not only the Bank of England but even the Treasury: the actions of the Bank of England itself had to be investigated by the Inquiry. It was natural, and it is respectfully submitted, correct, that a court would consider that an impartial investigative tribunal should have strong powers to examine evidence (and the evidence, in the case of Price Waterhouse, would be highly relevant) even though these had not been explicitly provided by the Bank of England and the Government when the inquiry was set up.

4–057 Another interesting case is *Douglas v. Pindling*,[68] although this case was decided (by the Privy Council) with reference to the relevant legislation in the Bahamas,[69] rather than by virtue of the *Tournier* case. A commission of inquiry had been established to investigate some dealings in hotels by Sir William Douglas, the plaintiff, at the time when he had been the head of the Government of the Bahamas. The commission required access to the plaintiff's bank accounts, and, when permission was refused, sought production under the BBEA 1879. The plaintiff claimed that this was *ultra vires* of the commission and sought redress for infringement of his constitutional rights, a claim which succeeded before the Court of Appeal of the Bahamas. In the view of the Privy Council, however, the commission had not used the correct mechanism for obtaining production of the accounts. There were no legal proceedings pending to which anyone was a party, and the Act was not suitable for use by an inquisitorial body like a commission of inquiry, whose terms of reference might be extremely wide. Nevertheless, it was important in the public interest that the commission should obtain access to them. Certainly, the personal interest of the customer in the privacy of his or her account should not be lightly interfered with, but a balance must be found between the public interest in the administration of justice—that is, the promotion of the work of the commission of inquiry—and the customer's personal interest. Here, the evidence showed that there had been a number of unconventional features in connection with transactions involving very large sums of public money in which the plaintiff played a prominent part, and the public interest appeared on good grounds to require disclosure and the customer's personal claim had to give way.

4–058 The Jack Committee's hesitation about the open-endedness and vagueness of the public interest exception was entirely justifiable in view of the

[67] [1992] B.C.L.C. 583 at 601. He ordered that there should be no greater disclosure than necessary of the underlying transactions of the bank's customers.
[68] [1996] 3 W.L.R. 242.
[69] Banks and Trust Companies Regulation Act 1965, s. 10.

ease with which private rights of individuals may be overlooked if disclosure by banks is permitted for ill defined reasons. However, the situation has changed in this respect since 1989. The introduction of the money laundering legislation means that banks are not merely *permitted* but *forced* to disclose customers' confidential information, and that for a very vague and ill-defined reason: suspicion of involvement in serious crime and in drug trafficking. By contrast, it is suggested that these two cases indicate a serious judicial effort to consider the balance between the rights of the individuals concerned and the reality of the public interest, and they of course support the eventual decisions by reasoning which is open to evaluation. The comparison with the present situation under the compulsion of law exception is striking: in cases of disclosure under the money laundering legislation now, there is at present no safeguard for individual rights.[70]

In the Bank's Interest

The obvious case here is where the bank is sued in debt by the customer.[71] It must be able to refer to the customer's accounts in order to defend itself, provided that it refers to no more than is necessary. Similarly, if an account is guaranteed, the bank must be able to disclose the extent of the debt to the guarantor when suing him or her, or demanding payment. **4–059**

Another situation, recently tested in the courts, where disclosure may be permitted in the bank's interest, is where a bank is in liquidation. In *El Jawhary v. Bank of Credit and Commerce International*,[72] the liquidators of BCCI sought permission to disclose information relating to customers of the bank for the purpose of discharging their duties and for taking any steps they considered necessary for winding up the affairs of BCCI, and to enable BCCI to plead, prosecute and defend such legal proceedings and comply with discovery. The customers objected to disclosure: they wanted an existing injunction against disclosure to be continued, because the liquidators' claim to disclose was so wide—wider, it was claimed, than was justified by the *Tournier* exception.[73] However, the court was prepared to vary the

[70] *cf.* also PACE 1984: an order from a circuit judge must be obtained before disclosure. Note however that in *Barclays Bank v. Taylor* [1989] 3 All E.R. 563, where Mr Taylor had unsuccessfully claimed that the bank had breached its duty of confidentiality by disclosing his account to the police, he had also unsuccessfully challenged the order obtained by the police by way of judicial review. It is of interest that it was later reported (*The Independent*, January 1, 1990) that criminal proceedings brought against Mr Taylor for fraud collapsed; it seems that the police "misled a judge in order to obtain access to his bank accounts". Mr Taylor was a friend of John Stalker, a former police Deputy Chief Constable, who in 1986 had revealed a "shoot to kill" policy in Northern Ireland, which made him unpopular in the police force.

[71] The example given by Bankes L.J. in *Tournier* [1924] K.B. 461.

[72] [1993] B.C.L.C. 396, Ch D.

[73] "Reasonably necessary for the protection of the bank's interest, either as against their customer or as against third parties in respect of transactions of the bank for or with their customer." *Tournier* [1924] 1 K.B. 461 at 486, *per* Atkin L.J.

injunctions, allowing the liquidators in principle to disclose information, subject to the *Tournier* requirements. This meant that the liquidators would have to consider carefully whether any disclosure would contravene the duty of confidentiality, and if it might do so, to seek the consent of the customer or apply to the court for directions; they must not simply take the easier path and disclose information.[74]

4–060 It seems that the interest of the bank goes beyond defence in legal proceedings and includes attacks, even private attacks, on the bank's reputation or behaviour. In *Sunderland v. Barclays Bank Ltd,*[75] the bank dishonoured the plaintiff's cheques, ostensibly on the ground of insufficient funds, but really because the bank knew she was gambling. She complained to her husband, who was then unaware of the gambling, and he told her to take it up with the bank. She telephoned the bank in his presence, and after a while he took up the phone to add his protests, upon which the bank disclosed the facts of his wife's gambling to him. The court held that this disclosure was in the bank's interests, and that in any case, the customer had impliedly consented. The bank was justified because this was a private attack on the bank's reputation. It is essential for a bank to maintain its reputation.

4–061 Recent developments in communications have extended the use of this exception in other ways, beyond what could have been envisaged in the 1920s. The Jack Committee[76] expressed concern about the implications of these developments, particularly in two areas: first, banks releasing confidential information to companies within their own group; and secondly, the disclosure of information to credit reference agencies.

(1) Banks releasing confidential information to companies within their own group

4–062 Banks are usually not a single entity, but a group of companies, among which may be non-banking subsidiaries such as estate agencies and insurance companies. Release of personal information about customers to other companies in banking groups has become commonplace, and is justified by banks on the two grounds that it is necessary for their protection because customer default is so prevalent, and that customers have impliedly consented to it. It is, however, as the Jack Committee pointed out, a controversial practice—partly because many customers are reluctant to allow that information to be used for marketing purposes, and

[74] [1993] B.C.L.C. 396 at 399, *per* Sir Donald Nicholls, V.-C. Further, there was no obligation on the liquidators to tell the customers of any disclosure made, nor to inform them of others who had become possessed of their information so that customers could "police" the liquidators' activities.

[75] (1938) 5 L.D.A.B. 163.

[76] The Committee regarded exceptions (c) and (d) as linked, although not so inextricably as (a) and (b).

partly because the safeguard of banking confidentiality can hardly be effective if information is widely distributed, particularly to non-banking subsidiaries, although the Committee acknowledged that it is artificial to regard subsidiaries as entirely separate corporate identities.[77] It recommended that banks should be permitted to pass information without customer consent as between banking companies within a banking group, provided that it is reasonably necessary to do so for the specific purpose of protecting the bank against loss in relation to the provision of normal banking services. Banks should not pass information to non-banking subsidiaries, nor use it for the marketing of services.

The Banking Code now gives some protection to the customer by restricting the use by banks of information for marketing purposes without the express consent of the customer. It says: **4–063**

> "nothing about your accounts, nor your name and address will be disclosed to anyone, including other companies in our group",

other than under the four *Tournier* exceptions; and

> "this will not be used as a reason for disclosing information about you or your accounts (including your name and address) to anyone else including other companies in our group for marketing purposes".[78]

The bank itself may "occasionally" bring other services and products to the customer's attention, but the customer will be given the opportunity, when the account is opened and at least once every three years, to ask not to receive this information.[79] Banks may also tell customers about other company's services or products ("host mailing") and if the customer responds positively, he or she may be contacted directly by that company.[80]

(2) Disclosure of information to credit reference agencies[81]

Credit reference agencies[82] make use of computer technology to collect and store data about the credit standing of individuals. Such an agency is defined in statute as: "a person carrying on a business comprising the **4–064**

---

[77] Each corporate entity within the banking group must be regarded as separate for confidentiality purposes, *Bank of Tokyo v. Karoon* [1984] 1 A.C. 45, although in fact information from all has to be collated in order to report large exposures to the Bank of England.

[78] Banking Code (1999): unless customers specifically request it, or give express consent in writing, their names will not be passed to any company, including companies in the banking group, for marketing purposes (paras 2.20 and 4.1). Customers will not be asked to give permission in return for basic services.

[79] Banking Code (1999), para. 2.19.

[80] Banking Code (1999), para. 2.22.

[81] Jack considered this subject under exception (c), but noted that it might also come within the "duty to the public" exception.

[82] For consideration of credit reference agencies, see Crowther Report on Consumer Credit, Cmnd. 4596 (1971); Younger Report on Privacy, Cmnd. 5012 (1972): Lindop Report on Data Protection, Cmnd. 7341 (1978).

furnishing of persons with information relevant to the financial standing of individuals, being information collected by the agency for that purpose".[83] Agencies collect their information from public sources such as court records, as well as providers of credit, and sell it to subscribers. They must be licensed by the Director-General of Fair Trading.[84]

4–065 Banks not only subscribe to such agencies, but also contribute information to them, and this is where potential breaches of confidentiality may arise. It has been accepted for some time (it was by the Jack Report) that banks might reveal "black" information—information about customers who are in default—to agencies. Jack indeed recommended that a new exception to *Tournier* should be created to permit disclosure about debts to approved agencies where there has been "a breakdown of the banker-customer relationship arising through customer default", where "default" would mean that no satisfactory response had been received from the customer within 28 days of formal demand for repayment or where no security has been given.[85] Although the suggestion for a new exception was not accepted in the White Paper, the principle has been included in the Banking Code, which states:

> "information about your personal debts owed to us may be disclosed to credit reference agencies where: you have fallen behind with your payments; and the amount owed is not in dispute; and you have not made proposals satisfactory to us for repayment of your debt following formal demand; and you have been given at least 28 days notice of our intention to disclose.
>
> We will not give any other information about you to credit reference agencies without your consent."[86]

4–066 The real problem, however, arises because of the disclosure of "white" information, where there has been no default by the customer which might justify disclosure. Creditors and the credit industry claim that sharing of white information promotes responsible lending and would be in the public interest—indeed, that it would be in the best interests of borrowers themselves, because it would help prevent them incurring unmanageable debt.[87] The Jack Committee also suggested that banks might try to justify disclosure by reference to the implied consent of the customer.[88] Although the Committee expressed sympathy with the arguments in favour of

[83] CCA 1974, s. 145(8).

[84] CCA 1974, s. 25. An agency's licence may be revoked if it participates in business practices appearing to the Director-General to be deceitful or oppressive, or otherwise unfair or improper.

[85] Jack Report, Cm. 622 (1989), para. 5.45.

[86] Banking Code (1999), paras 4.2 and 4.3.

[87] This was also the view of the Government expressed in the White Paper, *op. cit.*, para. 2.18.

[88] See below, exception (d).

disclosure, however, it strongly recommended that it should only be permitted where the *express* consent of the customer had been obtained. It saw this as a matter of general confidence in the banking system.

The problem of banks providing information to credit reference agencies where the customer is not in default has not disappeared since the Jack Report. The Banking Ombudsman has noted that it "provides a steady source of complaint: either the bank has registered incorrect credit information or it has omitted to update out-of-date information, thereby causing problems to its customer".[89] **4–067**

Customers who are concerned, perhaps because they are not able to obtain credit, may obtain copies of their file from the credit reference agency or apply to the Office of Fair Trading.[90]

The Customer's Consent

The customer may, of course, consent to disclosure. The familiar example of this category referred to by Bankes L.J. is where the customer authorises a reference to the banker.[91] This is normally regarded as authorised by implied consent, though there may be occasions where customers expressly consent to a reference. If the customer expressly prohibits disclosure, the bank must comply with that instruction. **4–068**

A matter which has caused difficulties is telephone disclosure. It is clear that some banks did (and perhaps still do) give information over the telephone to those they believed to be their customers. The bank is justified in giving information to its customer over the telephone, but there is an obvious risk that a person speaking on the telephone may not be the customer. Telephone banking will increase risks in this respect, although procedural checks are made to ensure that it is the customer who is speaking.

Implied consent

As noted above, the Jack Report suggested that the banks might justify disclosure to credit reference agencies by reference to the *implied consent* of the customer, presumably because of the existence of a practice based on that assumption.[92] The Committee was concerned about the use of implied **4–069**

---

[89] OBO A.R. 1994/5, para. 13.3. OBO takes a serious view of these complaints because of the far-reaching effects of registering incorrect data for the customer.

[90] There are two main agencies: see *Which* magazine, November, 1997, p. 49, where it is claimed that the agencies make mistakes and often include financial information about other members of families on customers' files.

[91] See below, paras 5–054 *et seq.*

[92] See the comments of the Court of Appeal in *Turner v. Royal Bank of Scotland plc* [1999] Lloyd's Rep. Bank. 231 at 235, where it was held that the practice of giving references by virtue of the "implied consent" of the customer did not amount to a usage and was not binding. "The proposition that banks can agree among themselves upon a banking practice and put the practice into effect without the knowledge of their customers, and then claim that, because the practice is common to all banks, it is binding upon their customers is, in my judgment, unacceptable" *per* Sir Richard Scott V.-C.

consent of the customer as authority for disclosure, because of its vagueness, and because it might be too tempting for banks "under the spur of competition" to rely on it more than they ought.[93] Jack recommended that in future consent should generally be *express*, and that it must be in writing.[94] The Government's view was less emphatic. It favoured the "fullest possible transfer of credit information, subject to confidentiality considerations", and said that a bank should seek the customer's consent—generally, rather than on every occasion. The bank should explain why this is being done, and give the customer a clear opportunity to object.[95]

4–070 After some tentative movements in the direction of express consent for bankers' references in earlier versions of the Banking Code, the newest version of the Code states that banks will tell customers if they provide bankers' references, and, if a banker's reference is requested, the bank will require the written consent of the customer before it is given.[96]

Data Protection Act 1998

4–071 A change in the law which should provide more protection for customers is the Data Protection Act 1998 (DPA 1998), replacing and extending the Data Protection Act 1984.[97] The protection of the DPA 1998 is not restricted, as was that of the 1984 Act, to information about individuals processed by computer, but includes manual records held within *relevant filing systems*[98] within the definition of data covered by the Act. The DPA 1998 allows *data subjects*[99] the right of access to personal data,[1] the right to prevent processing of the personal data for the purposes of direct marketing[2] to prevent processing likely to cause damage or distress,[3] the right to claim compensation for damage[4] and to challenge wrong data and have it corrected.[5] There is a system of notification, by which *data controllers*[6] must

[93] Cm. 622 (1989), para. 5.33.
[94] Cm. 622 (1989), para. 5.43.
[95] White Paper, para. 2.19.
[96] Cm. 622 (1989), para. 4.5.
[97] Passed to give effect to the Council Directive 95/46 on the protection of individuals with regard to the processing of personal data and on the free movement of such data: [1995] O.J. L281/31.
[98] Which means, roughly, any set of information relating to individuals which though not necessarily automatically processed, is structured in a way that makes information about an individual readily accessible (DPA 1998, s. 1).
[99] A data subject is an individual who is the subject of personal data; personal data is data which relate to a living individual who can be identified from those data or from those data and other information in the possession of the data controller. *Data processing* means: obtaining, recording or holding data or carrying out any operation or set of operations on the data, including organisation, retrieval, disclosure or alignment, combination of the data: DPA 1998, s. 1.
[1] DPA 1998, s. 7.
[2] DPA 1998, s. 11.
[3] DPA 1998, s. 10.
[4] DPA 1998, s. 13.
[5] DPA 1998, s. 14.
[6] A person who makes decisions with regard to specific personal data. A *data processor* processes data on behalf of the data controller.

notify the *Data Protection Commissioner* (replacing the Data Protection Registrar) of their wish to be included on a register of those intending to process personal data. Even if they do not register or are exempted from registration, however, data controllers may be liable if they do not comply with the *Data Protection Principles*.[7]

There are exemptions relating to information held by law enforcement and security services,[8] and also wide exemptions for "special purposes"—journalistic, artistic and literary purposes. Processing of sensitive personal data (relating to race, ethnic origin, political or religious views, health, sexual life, or proceedings for criminal offences[9]) is subject to stricter controls than other personal data.[10] Confidential references given or to be given by a data controller in confidence are also exempted from access by data subjects. **4–072**

The Banking Code states that banks will explain to their customers that they have a right of access under the Data Protection legislation to the personal records held on their computer files.[11]

[7] DPA 1998, s. 4; Scheds 1 and 2.
[8] DPA 1998, ss. 28 and 29.
[9] DPA 1998, s. 2.
[10] DPA 1998, Sched. 3.
[11] Banking Code (1999), para. 4.5.

Chapter 5

Duties of Care

The contractual duty of the bank is to carry out its duties as an agent for the customer. The bank's duty as an agent carries with it a number of other duties, including the duty to carry out its customer's instructions with reasonable skill and diligence. The duty is expressed in statute, in section 13 of the Supply of Goods and Services Act 1982, and also exists at common law. Steyn J., in *Barclays Bank v. Quincecare*,[1] said: **5–001**

> "Prima facie every agent for reward is also bound to exercise reasonable care and skill in carrying out the instructions of his principal . . . There is no logical or sensible reason for holding that bankers are immune from such an elementary obligation. In my judgment it is an implied term of the contract between the bank and the customer that the bank will observe reasonable skill and care in and about executing the customer's orders."

The bank's duties of care may arise not only in contract, but also in tort. Duties of care in tort may be owed to customers concurrently with the duty in contract, or may be owed to non-customers in specific areas, such as banks giving references about their customers to third parties and giving investment advice. Tort duties are based on the liability for negligent misstatement under *Hedley Byrne v. Heller*.[2] **5–002**

Background

Before *Hedley Byrne*, there was no liability in damages at common law for negligent misstatement unless a careless statement which was a term of the contract was breached.[3] *Hedley Byrne*—a ground breaking case—created a new type of liability, for negligent misstatement in tort, based on wide concepts such as "special relationship" or "relationship equivalent to contract" or "voluntary assumption of liability". Principles expressed in **5–003**

---

1 [1992] 4 All E.R. 363 at 375–6. Noted Taylor [1988] L.M.C.L.Q. 441.

2 [1964] A.C. 465.

3 See, *e.g. Midland Bank Ltd v. Seymour* [1955] 2 Lloyd's Rep. 147 at 157. But see *Woods v. Martins Bank Ltd* [1959] 1 Q.B. 55, where it was held that a fiduciary relationship existed, see below (and *Nocton v. Lord Ashburton* [1914] A.C. 932). Fiduciary duties, including equitable (fiduciary) duties of care have received judicial clarification in recent years: see above, para. 3–009.

such broad terms had the potential to provide a foundation for an expansion of liability for economic loss,[4] and, as this became clear, the courts became more cautious in their interpretation of the case because of the fear of indeterminate and unrestricted liability. Eventually the House of Lords held, in *Caparo Industries v. Dickman*,[5] that, when new cases raising issues of new duty areas arose, they should be considered pragmatically on the basis of a *three stage test* of duty or of precedents or analogies from previous cases—what was called the *incremental* approach.[6] As far as liability for negligent misstatement itself was concerned, the court was careful to state the requirements for a duty to arise in specific and limited language.

5–004 In *Caparo*, the question was whether the auditors of a company's accounts were liable to members of the public who might invest in the company, and to individual shareholders. This raised the floodgates issue which has troubled the courts, of indeterminate liability in economic loss cases. The court listed the necessary ingredients for a duty of care in cases of economic loss in a three-stage test: the damage must be *foreseeable*; there must be "*a relationship of proximity*" and the situation should be one in which the court considers it "*fair, just and reasonable*" to impose a duty.[7] The test provides a number of hurdles for plaintiffs to surmount, and gives courts encouragement to ponder the implications of liability in any case.

5–005 The court went on to consider *Hedley Byrne*. The interpretation of the case was important, because a wide interpretation would probably mean that the relationship between the auditors and the plaintiffs was sufficiently proximate for liability, whereas a narrow view could exclude liability. The court's interpretation (in Lord Oliver's words) was that:

> "The necessary relationship between the maker of a statement or giver of advice (the adviser) and the recipient who acts in reliance on it (the advisee) may typically be held to exist where
>
> (1) the advice is required for a purpose, whether particularly specified or generally described, which is made known, either actually or inferentially, to the adviser at the time when the advice is given;
> (2) the adviser knows, either actually or inferentially, that his advice will be communicated to the advisee, either specifically or as a member of an ascertainable class, in order that it should be used by the advisee for that purpose;

---

[4] *e.g. Junior Books Ltd v. Veitchi Co Ltd* [1983] 1 A.C. 520, *Ross v. Caunters* [1980] Ch. 297.
[5] [1990] 2 A.C. 605. See also *Murphy v. Brentwood DC* [1990] 2 All E.R. 908.
[6] Based on *Sutherland Shire Council v. Heyman* (1985) 60 A.L.R. 1 at 43–44, *per* Brennan J.
[7] [1990] 2 A.C. 605 at 620, *per* Lord Bridge.

(3) it is known, either actually or inferentially, that the advice so communicated is likely to be acted on by the advisee for that purpose without independent inquiry; and
(4) it is so acted on by the advisee to his detriment".[8]

The court in *Caparo* had also to take into account the more recent House of Lords decision on *Hedley Byrne* liability, *Smith v. Bush.*[9] In this case, a surveyor negligently valued a house for a building society which was considering granting an advance mortgage to the potential purchasers of the house. It was held that the surveyor owed a duty of care to the *purchasers* (as well as his contractual duty to the building society); since he was not employed by the purchasers, the duty was in tort, not in contract. The important factor in *Smith*, as the court in *Caparo* emphasised, was that the surveyor knew that the purchaser would probably rely on his valuation, and that he knew the purpose of the transaction.[10] In *Caparo*, on the other hand, the relationship was not so close: the relevant statement had not been given for the purpose for which the plaintiff had relied on it (this was the fatal weakness) and it was held accordingly that there was no liability on the auditors.[11] **5–006**

The interpretation of *Hedley Byrne* liability in *Caparo* is well defined, but narrow—so narrow, in fact, that it raises a doubt whether even referee banks would normally fall within the conditions. Under *Caparo*, a bank giving a reference for a customer would only owe a duty to the person for whose benefit the information was provided if it knew the purpose for which it was given, and in order that it should be used for that purpose. In fact, of course, most such cases sufficiently resemble *Hedley Byrne* to make it a precedent itself for the existence of a duty owed by referee banks. However, there might in some circumstances be an opening for a defendant bank to argue that it did not know the purpose for which the reference was given or that the plaintiff would be likely to rely upon it. Whether the argument would succeed would depend on how generously the words were construed. **5–007**

---

[8] [1990] 2 A.C. 605 at 638.

[9] *Smith v. Bush (Eric) and Harris v. Wyre Forest D.C.* [1989] 2 All E.R. 514.

[10] Lord Griffiths stressed that where the advice was not given for the specific purpose of the recipient acting on it, a duty of care would only arise when the "adviser knows that there is a high degree of probability that some other identifiable person will act on the advice" [1989] 2 All E.R. 514 at 536.

[11] *Morgan Crucible Co plc v. Hill Samuel Bank* [1991] 1 All E.R. 148 at 158, *per* Slade L.J. In this case, the CA, distinguishing *Caparo*, refused to strike out an action against auditors. Similarly, in *BCCI v. Price Waterhouse and Ernst & Whinney* [1998] Lloyd's Rep. Bank. 85 ("a most unusual case" involving two sets of auditors). The remarks of Sir Brian Neill ([1998] Lloyd's Rep. Bank. 85 at 96 *et seq.*) summarising duty of care principles in such cases and applying *Caparo* have been referred to and relied upon subsequently (see *Siddell v. Smith Cooper* [1999] P.N. 511 at 526, *per* Clarke L.J.).

Since *Caparo*, there has been a remarkable change of climate. The three House of Lords cases signalling that change[12] have not only relied upon *Hedley Byrne*, but have extended it. This extended principle, based on the *assumption of responsibility* by the defendant, goes beyond the provision of information and advice to include the performance of other services and protects parties who rely on the defendant's "special skill" (which includes special knowledge).[13] It extends to omissions as well as positive acts, at least in the context of professional liability.[14] In some circumstances there may be liability even where the plaintiff has not relied on the defendant, provided that it was the defendant's act or omission which caused the loss to the plaintiff.[15] It again began to seem that *Hedley Byrne* might become the foundation for a general principle for liability for economic loss in tort. As yet, though, it is difficult to detect any single general principle reflecting this in decisions by the courts, certainly in banking cases. This difficulty is well demonstrated by *Wells v. First National Commercial Bank*,[16] where argument for a broader duty of care on the bank based on the authority of "orthodox" *Hedley Byrne* principles (as interpreted in *Henderson v. Merrett*[17]) or alternatively on the more exceptional duty in tort recognised in *White v. Jones*,[18] was unsuccessful.

The law relating to the liability of professional advisers for failure to provide accurate information or correct advice, it has been truly said,[19] is in a state of transition or development.

Concurrent Liability in Tort and Contract

5–008 During the period following the decision in *Hedley Byrne v. Heller*, it was thought that plaintiffs who could make out claims in contract and in tort on the same facts would have *concurrent* claims in both contract and tort open

[12] *Henderson v. Merrett* [1994] 3 W.L.R. 761; [1994] 3 All E.R. 506; *Spring v. Guardian Assurance plc* [1994] 3 W.L.R. 354; *White v. Jones* [1995] 1 All E.R. 691. The test of assumption of responsibility was reaffirmed in *Williams v. Natural Life Health Foods Ltd* [1998] 2 All E.R. 577. See also *Yorkshire Bank plc v. Lloyd's Bank plc* [1999] Lloyd's L.R. 191 at 194. In *Hedley Byrne*, "*voluntary* assumption", but in *Henderson v. Merrett* [1994] 3 All E.R. 506 at 520–1, "an assumption or undertaking of responsibility . . . coupled with reliance by the plaintiff on the exercise by the defendant of due care and skill", *per* Lord Goff. *cf.* Lord Griffiths in *Smith v. Bush* [1989] 2 All E.R. 514 at 534: "not a helpful or realistic test for liability"; and see Barker (1993) 109 L.Q.R. 461.

[13] *Henderson v. Merrett* [1994] 3 All E.R. 506 at 520; *Spring v. Guardian Assurance* [1994] 3 All E.R. 129.

[14] [1994] 3 All E.R. 506 at 521.

[15] *e.g. White v. Jones* [1995] 1 All E.R. 691 where it was held that beneficiaries of a will may recover a legacy lost because of negligence of a solicitor preparing the will.

[16] [1998] P.N.L.R. 552. See Stanton [1998] P.N. 131.

[17] [1994] 3 All E.R. 506.

[18] [1995] 1 All E.R. 691.

[19] A remark of Chadwick L.J. in *Coulthard v. Neville Russell* [1998] P.N.L.R. 276, repeated by Clarke L.J. in *Siddell* [1999] P.N. 511 at 521.

to them and the right to choose which to pursue.[20] A plaintiff might prefer to sue in tort, rather than contract, for example, in order to benefit from a more favourable limitation period[21] or to take advantage of different rules on remoteness of damage, or of a particular defence. By the 1980s, however (as mentioned above), the climate had changed. The courts had become more restrictive in allowing recovery for pure economic loss in tort and were wary of allowing tort to impinge on the strict rules of contract. The view that contract should be protected—that it is primary, and tort fits around the edges, each having a separate domain—underpinned the clear statement by Lord Scarman in *Tai Hing Cotton Ltd v. Liu Chong Bank Ltd*[22] that, in cases where the parties are in a contractual relationship, their mutual obligations in tort could not be greater than those they owed, expressly or impliedly, in contract; plaintiffs who were parties to a contract should found their actions in contract, not in tort. This statement did not go completely unchallenged, but it had a restraining effect on the development of concurrent liability. The interpretation of Lord Scarman's words, indeed, was probably wider than was necessary from the facts of the case, since the court in *Tai Hing* was not considering a straightforward choice between contract and tort. The Privy Council decided not to imply the term in question into the banking contract, and it would have been odd and inconsistent to have allowed a *wider* substantive duty in tort where it would not be justifiable to imply it into the contract.

A striking feature of the change in the approach of the courts in revitalising the *Hedley Byrne* principle has been the recognition of concurrent liability in *Henderson v. Merrett*.[23] The case concerned a complex action against agents who underwrote contracts of insurance at Lloyds on behalf of Lloyds' "names" (members). After a series of catastrophic events which led to unprecedented claims being made on Lloyds' insurance, the names claimed that the underwriting agents had acted negligently. Some claims were brought in contract, others in tort,[24] because of the differing relationships between the names and the underwriting agents—some had contracts, but others only indirect relationships—and the action came before the House of Lords as a preliminary issue about the nature of the duties owed by the agents. The decision of the House of Lords, expressed in a scholarly and thoughtful judgment by Lord Goff, was that the imposition of a tort duty is *not* inconsistent with a contractual relationship between the parties; **5–009**

[20] "The existence of concurrent liability . . . for financial losses is one of the assumptions upon which the modern law concerning the liability of professional persons has been built. This assumption derives from *Midland Bank Trust Co Ltd v. Hett, Stubbs & Kemp* [1979] Ch. 384." Stanton, *The Modern Law of Tort,* p. 6.

[21] *e.g.* the date of accrual of the cause of action in tort (perhaps because of the effect of the Latent Damage Act 1986) might be more favourable than that in contract.

[22] [1986] A.C. 80 at 107, *per* Lord Scarman. Applied in *National Bank of Greece v. Pinios Shipping Co (No 1)* [1989] 1 All E.R. 213.

[23] [1994] 3 W.L.R. 761.

[24] There were also claims for breach of fiduciary duty.

contract and tort actions may co-exist on the same facts. Far from seeing contract as primary, Lord Goff described the law of tort as the "general law, out of which the parties can, if they wish, contract", and referred to Lord Devlin's view in *Hedley Byrne* that "the existence of a contractual relationship is very good evidence of the general tortious duty".[25] For a duty to exist, the plaintiff must have relied on the defendant's assumption of responsibility, and a contract, unless it successfully excludes liability, certainly demonstrates reliance. Even if the parties are in a contractual relationship with the defendant, therefore, as they are in most banking relationships, the plaintiff may now choose to bring the claim in tort if it is more advantageous than the parallel contractual claim.

5–010 The court made it clear in *Henderson v. Merrett* that the tort duties are not *necessarily* the same or parallel to those in contract; the parties may in their contract have modified the tort duties which would otherwise be applicable. Similarly, the court will not assume that the tort claim will be more extensive in substance than the contract claim (as it would have been in *Tai Hing* if the court had accepted it), nor that plaintiffs may use tort to evade contractual exclusions or restrictions.

The Scope of a Bank's Duties: Acting in Accordance with Instructions

5–011 The bank's duty is to obey the mandate promptly—that is, to carry out their customers' instructions promptly and without exceeding their authority—and it seems to be settled that, in general, the duty to observe reasonable skill and care in and about executing the customer's orders is subordinate to obedience to the mandate. This principle may give some help to banks in reconciling their differing duties,[26] but a good deal of uncertainty nevertheless remains about the extent of banks' duties of care. Must the bank obey the customer's instructions to the letter or should it use its knowledge and expertise to interpret them and apply them in a manner which it is aware is in the customer's interest? Should it seek its customer's instructions, or even, sometimes, the instructions of a third party, such as a third party surety? These questions have become particularly important in recent years because banks have emphasised in their marketing strategies the wide range of services available to customers, and customers' expectations, in turn, have been raised. If unsophisticated private customers of banks feel they have been misled by banks' publicity,[27] for example, they may blame banks for losses they have suffered from unsuccessful business

[25] [1964] A.C. 465 at 528; citing Oliver J. in *Midland Bank Trust Co Ltd v. Hett, Stubbs and Kemp* [1979] Ch. 384 at 415.

[26] See *Barclays Bank v. Quincecare* [1992] 4 All E.R. 363; *Lipkin Gorman v. Karpnale* [1989] 1 W.L.R. 1341, CA.

[27] Judges have sometimes commented on the enthusiasm of banks' promotional literature, see, *e.g., Woods v. Martins Bank* [1959] 1 Q.B. 55, and *Williams & Glyns Bank v. Barnes* [1981] Com. L.R. 205.

projects supported by bank lending. The bank's advertising is not likely in itself to ground a claim against a bank, however, unless there are misrepresentations or the bank holds itself out as having within the scope of its business some expertise on which the plaintiff has relied to his or her loss. In *James v. Barclays Bank*,[28] the plaintiff, who ran two farms, complained that the bank had acted as general financial adviser to them and, because it had given negligent advice, they had suffered loss. The Court of Appeal held that the bank's literature showed that it was within the scope of the bank's business to offer comprehensive financial advice to people like the plaintiffs if they asked for it, but this did not suggest that its managers were competent to give farming, as distinct from financial, advice, or that the bank had in fact undertaken the role of general financial, adviser. Here, the plaintiffs had not sought advice, and the bank was not liable.

In *Schioler v. National Westminster Bank Ltd*,[29] it was not the question of **5–012** the bank's literature which was at issue, but the plaintiff's expectations were nevertheless based on the sort of expertise which the bank, an offshore branch of the bank, was regarded as possessing. The plaintiff, a Danish national, had opened an account with the Guernsey branch of the bank, to which her dividends from a Malaysian company were regularly sent. Her account was credited in sterling, with no deduction (as the bank knew) of United Kingdom income tax, because the dividends did not go to England. Some years later, one remittance was sent to Guernsey in Malaysian dollars. The bank had not been given explicit instructions by the customer to cover this contingency. There were no facilities for negotiating drafts in foreign currency in Guernsey and the bank sent it on to London, where income tax was deducted. The plaintiff claimed that the bank had breached its contract by not exercising reasonable care. Mocatta J., however, held that the bank could not be obliged to consider the tax implications for the customer or to consult her before acting in accordance with its ordinary practice; such an obligation would place an impossible burden on banks. The bank was not doing anything unusual in sending the dividend to England, and no alternative method was available. Thus a bank acting according to its normal practice may have no duty to warn the customer or to seek instructions, even if it proposes to act in a way which it knows will cause the customer a loss which the account was set up to avoid.

[28] [1995] 4 Bank L.R. 131.

[29] [1970] 2 Q.B. 719. See also *Cornish v. Midland Bank plc* [1985] 3 All E.R. 513, where a couple borrowed on the security of a mortgage, and the bank continued to advance money to the husband even when (as it knew) the marriage had finished, he had remarried, and she lived abroad. When the property was sold, there was little left for Mrs Cornish, who sued the bank. She claimed that the bank owed her a duty not to conduct her account in such a way as to cause her loss. The bank might have refused new advances to the ex-husband, or sought instructions from Mrs Cornish. The case was decided on a different ground, but it was unlikely that this claim would have been successful.

5–013 In *Redmond v. Allied Irish Bank*,[30] also, it was held that there is no duty on a bank to warn customers of the risk attached to something they wish to do—in this case, of the danger that the plaintiff would have to indemnify the true owner of a cheque if he paid into his account a cheque of which he was not the payee and which was crossed "Not negotiable, payee only", and generally endorsed. In *Williams & Glyns Bank v. Barnes*,[31] where a borrower was seeking a loan for the purpose of purchasing shares in a company, the judge took the view that, in the absence of a specific request from the borrower (if there had been one, he would have been referred to another department), the bank did not owe him any duty to consider the commercial advisability of the loan. The bank did not owe a duty to be careful in the *act* of lending; the only question was whether the bank had been negligent in giving or failing to give advice.[32]

5–014 It might be, however, that *Smith v. Bush*[33] has added an important different aspect to the decision in *Williams & Glyns*. In *Smith*, the House of Lords held that a surveyor owed a duty of care to a borrower who can be foreseen as likely to rely on the implication that if a loan has been granted then the security offered must be valuable, a similar proposition to that argued for in *Williams & Glyns*. This reinforced the decision of the Court of Appeal[34] that a lender, here a local authority, would have owed a duty of care to borrowers, except that a disclaimer had in that case been effective in preventing the duty arising. On this point (the disclaimer) the decision was reversed by the House of Lords.

5–015 Generally, it is evident that the courts have been cautious about increasing the burdens on banks. The emphasis has been on the need for them to carry out their commercial functions effectively without being hampered by the need to fulfil the expectations of customers. However, there are frequent challenges to this view, and courts sometimes take a different approach. In this section, we attempt to give a more detailed description of the banks' duties of care. The variety of factors involved in banking practice means that the cases are very often decisions on the facts, but they do tend to fall into groups relating to the different activities of banks, and it may be helpful to consider them in the following way:

---

30 [1987] F.T.L.R. 264.

31 [1981] Com. L.R. 205.

32 In *Lipkin Gorman v. Karpnale* [1989] 1 W.L.R. 1340 at 1356, May L.J. said "there is nothing in the banking contract which requires a banker to consider the commercial wisdom or otherwise of a particular transaction".

33 [1989] 2 All E.R. 514.

34 *Harris v. Wyre Forest D.C.* [1988] 1 All E.R. 691, (companion case to *Smith v. Bush*) see particularly the comments of Nourse L.J. at 697: should the defendants have recognised the importance which the plaintiffs would have attached to the valuation? (See also *Yianni v. Edwin Evans & Sons* [1981] 3 All E.R. 592.) But see *Saddington v. Colleys Professional Services* [1999] Lloyds L.R. Bank 140 at 143, *per* Balcombe L.J., where the CA indicated (citing *Galoo Ltd v. Bright Grahame Murray* [1994] 1 W.L.R. 1360.) that *Smith v. Bush* was the high water mark of such liability.

(1) paying and collecting cheques—if banks are negligent in their capacities as paying and collecting bankers, they will lose their statutory protection[35];

(2) protecting the customer from fraudulent use of the account;

(3) references (status opinions);

(4) investment and business advice; and

(5) lending and obtaining guarantees—duties to inform or disclose to customers and third parties.[36]

These duties mainly concern customers, but discussion of duty of care in the banking context easily spills over into tort and into concurrent liability.

Negligence in Paying and Collecting Cheques

Negligence in relation to section 4 of the Ch A 1957 and section 80 of the BOEA 1882 is considered in the context of negotiable instruments.[37] **5–016**

Banks paying cheques owe a duty of care to their customers, and this includes reporting forgeries occurring in the administration of the account. This duty has been extended to cover the agent of a customer. In *Weir v. National Westminster Bank*,[38] the customer's agent, a solicitor who held a power of attorney for her, was the sole signatory on her account. The bank negligently failed to detect a forged cheque, and was held to be liable to the solicitor for not informing him of the forgery. If he had known of it, he would have dismissed the clerk responsible and thus have prevented her from carrying out further frauds on his client account. The court held that the solicitor was not, from the bank's point of view, merely an "instrument" by which the principal's account was administered, with no personal interest in the operation of the account, but, as the sole signatory on the account, was proximate enough for the bank to owe him a duty of care to report a forgery to him—a duty similar to the one it would owe the real customer, the principal.

The court made it clear, however, that a bank would not owe a duty of care to an agent who was operating a principal's account at a bank where the agent merely happened to have a personal account (even though the bank might be taken to know his signature). That would impose a wholly disproportionate burden on bankers, who would probably have no idea **5–017**

[35] BOEA 1982, s. 80; Cheques Act 1957, s. 4, see below, Chap. 14.

[36] The doctrine of undue influence is considered in Chaps. 3, 18 and 21.

[37] See Chap. 13.

[38] (1994) S.L.T. 1252; and see *Greenwood v. Martins Bank* [1932] 1 K.B. at 381, where Scrutton L.J. said: "It seems to me that the banker, if a cheque was presented to him which he rejected as forged, would be under a duty to report this to the customer, to enable him to inquire into and protect himself against the circumstances of the forgery".

when they were examining a signature that they were dealing with the pretended signature of a customer who had a quite separate account with them.

5–018 In *TE Potterton Ltd v. Northern Bank Ltd*,[39] it was again a third party, not a customer, who was complaining about the behaviour of a bank. The plaintiff sold cattle to Tansey Farms Ltd, customers of the Northern Bank, the defendant. Tansey paid by cheque, which was presented for payment, but was returned by the bank marked "Refer to Drawer Present Again Alteration req's drawer's conf." (Alteration requires drawer's confirmation.) It was presented again for payment, though without any alteration and without seeking the drawer's confirmation, and was again returned by the Northern Bank, with the same marking, but this time with a line drawn through the words "Present again". Shortly afterwards, Tansey paid for another consignment of cattle by another cheque, which this time was returned after being presented for payment marked with the words "Refer to Drawer". The plaintiff had still not been paid and took proceedings against Tansey, but Tansey went into liquidation; the plaintiff sued the bank, claiming that it had been negligent in dealing with the first cheque.

5–019 In this case, again, a third party plaintiff succeeded in showing that the bank owed it a duty of care. The court held that the queries which Northern raised on the cheque were simply devices to extricate the bank from an awkward situation. The words written on the cheque lulled the plaintiff into a false sense of security and led it to believe that payment was only being withheld for some technical reason. The bank had been playing for time because it did not wish to dishonour Tansey's cheques: it thought (a thought based on previous experience) that Tansey would eventually put it in funds. If it had really wanted to clear up any confusion, it could have done so by a one-minute telephone call to the customer. The bank had deliberately embarked on a course of conduct for its own purposes which was calculated to deceive the payee of the cheque in a manner which might result in financial loss to the payee, when there was no lawful justification for such action on the part of the bank.[40]

5–020 The Court of Appeal in *Wells v. First National Commercial Bank*[41] took a more restrictive view of liability to a payee. Here, Wells was owed money by a Spanish company secured by a charge on property held by the company. The defendant bank agreed a refinancing deal with the company, and for this purpose was given irrevocable instructions by the company to pay Wells the money to discharge the mortgage and pay the debt. The bank discharged the mortgage but did not pay the remainder of the money to Wells, who sued the bank. The court held that the bank did not owe him a duty of care. The decision was based on the ground that to establish a duty

[39] (1995) 4 Banking L.R. 179, High Court of Ireland.
[40] (1995) 4 Banking L.R. 179 at 187, *per* O'Hanlon J.
[41] [1998] P.N.L.R. 552. See Stanton [1998] P.N. 131.

of care in this case would not be a small "incremental" step as required by *Caparo*, but would go a long way to revolutionise English banking law, because it would raise questions about everyday commercial transactions, and it might be used to extend liability of banks to payees in general; this was despite the unusual circumstance that the payment here was "irrevocable". There were, it was said, adequate remedies available to the plaintiff against the customer itself.

The odd aspect of the case is the restrictive view of the *Hedley Byrne* duty. All the requirements of the *Hedley Byrne* duty, even as they were narrowly expressed in *Caparo*, appeared to be satisfied in the unusual circumstances of *Wells*. *Caparo* requires that the defendant knows of the plaintiff as an identified individual, knows of the transaction in which the information would be used, and of the plaintiff's reasonable reliance on the information. In *Wells*, the bank was intentionally making a payment to an identified third party as part of an agreed settlement where, as it knew, the plaintiff was giving up a claim in return. The court did suggest that if the plaintiff had communicated directly with the bank, a relationship between them might have arisen sufficient to found a duty of care, but it is surprising that, even without this addition (which would have been fortuitous[42]) the relationship was not regarded as adequate for *Hedley Byrne* liability to have arisen. **5–021**

A complex situation involving the duty of two collecting banks, an English clearing bank collecting a cheque for a foreign collecting bank, has recently been considered at first instance. It was particularly interesting for banking lawyers, because it was consciously argued as a matter of broad principle in order to give guidance to English clearing banks. In *Middle Temple v. Lloyds Bank plc & Sekerbank*,[43–44] a cheque for nearly £200,000 was drawn by the Middle Temple to pay its insurers, the Sun Alliance Insurance company. Somehow it found its way to Turkey—it had presumably been stolen—and the Turkish bank, Sekerbank, agreed to collect it on behalf of a man who opened an account for the purpose. The cheque was, as most English cheques now are, an "account payee only" cheque, and was not transferable (because of the effect of the Ch A 1992[45]), but it was indorsed on its reverse in writing "Sun Alliance Insurance Ltd", with an indecipherable signature below it—the indorsement was of course a forgery. The cheque was sent to Lloyds for collection, and in due course Middle Temple's account at its own bank was debited with the amount of the cheque, Lloyds was credited with the same amount, and the following day Lloyds credited Sekerbank. Sekerbank's new customer, not surprisingly, **5–022**

[42] Stanton [1998] P.N. 131.

[43–44] [1999] Lloyd's Rep. Bank. 50 at 72. (The claimant was the Honourable Society of the Middle Temple, one of the barristers' Inns of Court. Some members of Lloyds staff, asked afterwards, thought it might have been an organisation involved in freemasonry or a religious sect from the Middle East.)

[45] See below, Chap. 14.

very soon withdrew most of the money from the account. The questions were: how had a cheque made out in favour of the Sun Alliance company been collected by Sekerbank and Lloyds for another person without either bank noticing this, and was either bank liable under section 4 of the Ch Act 1957?[46] What, also, was their liability between themselves?

5–023 Both banks conceded that they had converted the cheque, but contended that they had acted in good faith and without negligence. Their good faith, as usual was not an issue, but the claimant[47] argued that they had both been negligent. The judge, Rix J., held that both banks in this situation were potentially liable for negligence. The duty owed by the foreign bank was not simply delegated to its agent, the clearing bank, because the respective knowledge of the banks about the ultimate customers was not the same.

Basing himself on *Importers Co. Ltd v. Westminster Bank Ltd*,[48] the judge came to the conclusion that the clearing bank acting for a foreign correspondent does not have to establish that the proceeds of the cheque are actually paid to the named payee—that would be too demanding a standard. On the other hand, it could not simply say that it was under no duty at all except to show that it must carry out its duty consistently with the mandate from its foreign correspondent—that would leave the interests of the true owner of the cheque inadequately protected, and would encourage thieves, fraudsters and money launderers to place their cheques through foreign banks.[49] The appropriate test is "whether there is anything in the circumstances which "was noticed or was such that it ought to be noticed". If so, the bank is on inquiry, and has to show that it was not negligent. The judge added, though, that the test must be applied realistically, in view of the large numbers of cheques being handled by a bank each day, and regard must be had to the practice of bankers.

5–024 With this in mind, the judge said that the clearing departments of banks[50] have a highly automated system and do not examine cheques to see if they are being collected for the true owner; indeed, clerical staff dealing with foreign cheques, unlike cashiers at domestic branches, are not even trained in the significance of the "account payee" marking, nor trained to exercise judgment in what is a "factory-like" process, because "judgment impedes automation".[51] The reverse of a cheque is not even looked at, let alone scrutinised. The primary goal is to provide a swift and efficient service at low cost. However, it turned out that even on this basis, Lloyds' service was

[46] Amended by the Cheques Act 1992, s. 3.

[47] Middle Temple was treated as true owner for the purposes of the case.

[48] [1927] 2 K.B. 297; see above, para. 2–038.

[49] [1999] Lloyd's Rep. Bank. 50 at 70.

[50] There were three comparable clearing banks. "Although there are some 11 clearing banks in the U.K., clearing services provided to foreign correspondent banks are some 90 per cent concentrated in the hands of Lloyds, Barclays and Midland, out of which Midland has the largest single share of the business" [1999] Lloyd's Rep. Bank. 50 at 63, *per* Rix J.

[51] [1999] Lloyd's Rep. Bank. 50 at 60. Clearing departments of banks sort and handle cheques "at ferocious speed": [1999] Lloyd's Rep. Bank. 50 at 55.

less careful in respect of its foreign correspondent banks than the other comparable banks. Both Barclays and Midland, though relying on their foreign banks to do what was necessary to ensure that the proceeds of cheques went to the true owner, had regarded themselves as under a duty to inform the foreign banks of the effect of the Ch A 1992 in making cheques non-transferable, and had circularised them, informing them also that the foreign bank should not look to the clearing bank to pick up and make good any error of its own. Further, staff at the other two banks had been asked to keep their eyes open, so far as possible, given the quantity of cheques going through their hands, for types of fraud which had come to their banks' notice.[52] Lloyds, on the other hand, had decided that it had no duty to inform its correspondent banks about the effect of the Ch A 1992 and had not instructed staff to be alert.

It was held that the clearing bank's duty to the true owner would not **5–025** usually extend to checking the identity of the foreign bank's customer, but, on the basis of current banking practice, it does extend to specific types of danger which may come to the bank's notice, such as counterfeit or overstamped cheques. Further, if anything does come to the bank's notice in a particular case, it must make appropriate inquiries: this includes doing so if it appears that a correspondent bank has not carried out its own obligations.

Here, Lloyds had not been justified in assuming that Sekerbank would do **5–026** what was necessary to ensure payment to the named payee. It should have informed Sekerbank of the effect of the Ch A 1992, which had made an important change in English banking law.[53] It did not make any difference to this duty that Sekerbank should have known of the change anyway.[54] Lloyds' negligence, however, had gone further here. Sekerbank, which had never sent any large cheque to Lloyds for collection before, suddenly requested that a cheque for a very large sum, which appeared to be an "entirely English affair" be collected. There were other oddities about the cheque: the "indorsement" on the reverse of the cheque had been written, rather than stamped; Sekerbank had made an inquiry after "fate" of the cheque, which was in itself a perfectly normal occurrence, but here the inquirer had said that Sekerbank's customer was "indeed in a difficult position"—surely an unusual way to describe any large and respectable

[52] [1999] Lloyd's Rep. Bank. 50 at 68. Staff were still not required to look at the reverse of the cheque, and would not be ensuring that the proceeds had been paid into the account of the named payee.

[53] Though banks should have been cautious about the account payee crossing even before the Ch A 1992 ([1999] Lloyd's Rep. Bank. 50 at 71).

[54] From the letter it received from Midland (Midland's letter might have been disregarded because Midland was not used as an agent for collection). The judge's view was that Lloyd's omission was not "causatively relevant". He also remarked that the situation was unlike the case where a bank proves that a plaintiff would have have suffered loss even if it had discharged its duty (*cf. dicta* in the *Marfani* case [1968] 1 W.L.R. 51 particularly, *per* Diplock L.J. at 976, see below, Chap. 14). See also Hooley [1999] C.L.J. 278.

insurance company. The cheque in fact had "emerged from the multitude". It was referred to a senior member of staff for individual attention because of the inquiry after fate, and at this point, different considerations came into play, and greater care should have been taken. The bank could have checked on the bank's previous experience of the foreign bank: indeed, it should have had such information in the computerised system. This would have shown, when the arrival of the cheque was first logged into the computer, that the bank had not used the clearer's services for a considerable time and that on the last occasion the collection had come to grief.[55] Automation, said the judge, brings its advantages as well as its limitations. Lloyds was therefore liable to Middle Temple.

5–027 As far as Sekerbank's own liability was concerned, the judge had no hesitation in finding that it was negligent: it should have known its customer. In fact, it seemed the *grossest* negligence to accept an English cheque payable to an English company in sterling for a large sum of money from a stranger who was not at that time a customer, without the person being asked for, or giving, an explanation as to why he was in possession of such a cheque or wanted a bank which was not his to collect it for him.[56] The bank's foreign relations department had compounded the negligence of the branch by declaring that Sekerbank itself had felt unsure about the cheque. It might have thought it could pass the whole responsibility to Lloyds, but in that case it should have informed Lloyds of the circumstances of the collection.

As between the banks themselves, it was held that, though Lloyds had been negligent as regards the true owner, this did not mean that it was in breach of duty to Sekerbank. It had done what it had been instructed to do. Sekerbank, on the other hand, was making an implied warranty that its customer was entitled to the proceeds of the cheque by sending it forward to Lloyds for collection. Either because of an implied indemnity or because of an implied warranty (the judge thought for both reasons), Lloyds was entitled to be indemnified by Sekerbank against its loss.[57–58]

Protecting the Customer from Fraudulent Use of the Account

5–028 In some situations, banks may have particular difficulty in reconciling their differing duties. The duty to exercise reasonable skill and care demands, a cautious, inquiring approach in protecting the customer from a possible fraud, which can be difficult to reconcile with the bank's strict contractual duty to carry out its instructions promptly in paying cheques.

55 [1999] Lloyd's Rep. Bank. 50 at 73.

56 [1999] Lloyd's Rep. Bank. 50 at 74. The customer had been introduced on the telephone by a person who acknowledged afterwards that he had only seen the customer once in 10 years.

57–58 If the judge had held that Lloyds was not entitled to rely on such an indemnity or warranty, he would have assessed contributions under s. 2(1) of the Civil Liability (Contribution) Act 1978 on the basis that Sekerbank's responsibility for the damage was 75 per cent, and Lloyds was 25 per cent.

What is reasonable depends on the relationship between the agent and the principal, and the facts, as usual in duty of care cases, are crucial. As Parker L.J. expressed it in *Lipkin Gorman v. Karpnale*[59]:

> "That a bank has a duty of care to its customer when carrying out its mandate is beyond doubt, but so to state it advances matters but little, for in each case the question for decision is whether a bank has failed in its duty and there are very many cases . . . essentially [these cases] are no more than decisions of fact, *i.e.* of the application of the law to an endless variety of circumstances."

However, there is some general guidance. An important factor in deciding what banks are impliedly bound to do is the ordinary practice of banks: "a man who employs a banker is bound by the usage of bankers".[60] Other factors are that the standard of the duty is likely to be higher if the agent is paid, or holds him or herself out as having special skills.[61] Some of the advertising of banks, for example, may raise expectations of the public that banks will support and supervise borrowing and repayment, and that may be a factor in considering whether to impose a duty of care. **5–029**

The question whether and how far the bank is obliged to go beyond mere automatic obedience to the mandate if there is a risk of fraud to the customer has been a constant theme in the law. It often arises where there is a fraud on the customer by a person who is an authorised signatory of the account, such as a director of a company or a partner in a firm of solicitors. It arose as a controversial issue in the *Selangor*[62] case, where the bank was found liable at common law and in equity, and both common law duty and equitable duties were sufficiently widely drawn, at least as they were applied in *Selangor* itself, to make liability potentially onerous for banks. The judge, Ungoed-Thomas J., expressed the bank's common law duty in these terms: **5–030**

> "to exercise reasonable care and skill in transacting the customer's banking business, including the making of such enquiries as may, in given circumstances, be appropriate and practical if the banker has, or a reasonable banker would have, grounds for believing that the

[59] [1989] 1 W.L.R. 1341, CA.

[60] *Hare v. Henty* (1861) 10 C.B.N.S. 65 at 77, *per* Willes J. See also *Goodwin v. Robarts* (1875) L.R. 10 Ex. 337 at 346, 352, *per* Cockburn C.J.: "the law merchant is sometimes spoken of as a fixed body of law, forming part of the common law, and . . . [it] is of comparatively recent origin. It is neither more nor less than the usages of merchants and traders in the different departments of trade, ratified by the decisions of Courts of Law, which, upon such usages being proved before them, have adopted them as settled law with a view to the interests of trade and public convenience". See Chorley, 48 L.Q.R. 55, Milnes Holden, *History of Negotiable Instruments in English Law*, p. 32.

[61] *Beal v. South Devon Ry Co* (1864) 3 H. & C. 337.

[62] [1968] 2 All ER 1073; the possible liability of banks for constructive trust was even more controversial, see below, Chap. 9.

authorised signatories are misusing their authority for the purpose of defrauding their principal or otherwise defeating his true intentions".

5–031 Definitions of duty of care may have to be framed in wide terms to be generally applicable, and the meaning of this passage would depend on how it was applied in specific cases, but the objective standard of the "reasonable banker" merely having "grounds" to believe implies a broad base of liability; it could mean that bankers would have to act as amateur detectives.

5–032 Some years later, the question arose in the *Quincecare* case,[63] where a company and its guarantor had been defrauded by the chairman of the company. The company contended that the bank had acted in breach of its implied duty of care because the circumstances of the transaction should have raised questions in the mind of a reasonable banker as to whether the transaction was properly authorised by the customer. The bank's response was that its duty was simply to carry out its customer's instructions promptly. Steyn J. gave expression to the bank's duty in a way which would help to provide practical guidance. After stating that the basic relationship is one of debtor and creditor, he went on to say that as far as the drawing and payment of the customer's cheques is concerned, the relationship is that of principal and agent. In this capacity, the bank owes fiduciary duties to its customer and, like any agent for reward, is bound to exercise reasonable care and skill in carrying out its customer's instructions. He described the balance of the duties owed by banks:

> "[the law] should not impose too burdensome an obligation on bankers, which hampers the effective transacting of banking business unnecessarily. On the other hand, the law should guard against the facilitation of fraud, and exact a reasonable standard of care in order to combat fraud and to protect bank customers and innocent third parties".

5–033 The bank's duty of reasonable skill and care is generally *subordinate* to its other conflicting contractual duties, such as obeying the mandate promptly. Of course, if there is obvious dishonesty, a bank must not shut its eyes to it, and it must not act recklessly in failing to make such inquiries as an honest and reasonable man would make; but if the situation is less clear cut, it is more difficult to give a helpful answer as to the bank's duty. The judge expressed the principle in this way:

> "To hold that a bank is only liable when it has displayed a lack of probity would be much too restrictive an approach. On the other hand,

[63] [1992] 4 All E.R. 363.

to impose liability whenever speculation might suggest dishonesty would impose wholly impractical standards on bankers . . . the sensible compromise which strikes a fair balance between competing considerations is simply to say that a banker must refrain from executing an order if and for as long as the banker is 'put on inquiry' in the sense that he has reasonable grounds (although not necessarily proof) for believing that the order is an attempt to misappropriate the funds of the company . . . And the external standard of the likely perception of an ordinary prudent banker is the governing one".[64]

The facts of any particular case will be vital. Looking at the situation (relevant in *Quincecare*) of the misappropriation of company funds by a director or officer of the company, the judge listed the factors to take into account in approaching the problem: **5–034**

> "the standing of the corporate customer, the bank's knowledge of the signatory, the amount involved, the need for a prompt transfer, the presence of unusual features, and the scope and means for making reasonable inquiries."

One particular factor, however, will often be decisive, and that is:

> "a banker will usually approach a suggestion that a director of a corporate customer is trying to defraud the company with an initial reaction of instinctive disbelief . . . it is right to say that trust, not distrust, is also the basis of the bank's dealings with its customers."[65]

The Court of Appeal in *Lipkin Gorman v. Karpnale*[66] approved Steyn J.'s statements in *Quincecare* and took the same approach. May L.J. thought that any implied term requiring the banker to exercise care in deciding whether to honour a customer's cheque must be limited. The banker's obligation, he said, is "largely automatic or mechanical".[67] In view of the "vast numbers of cheques which are presented for payment every day in this country", it is only when any reasonable cashier would hesitate to pay a cheque at once, and when any reasonable superior would hesitate to authorise payment without inquiry that inquiry should be made. Parker L.J. expressed the duty in this way: if a reasonable and honest banker knew of the relevant facts, would he have considered that there was a serious or real possibility, albeit not amounting to a probability, that its customer might be **5–035**

[64] [1992] 4 All E.R. 363 at 376.
[65] *ibid.*, at 377.
[66] [1989] 1 W.L.R. 1341 at 1356, CA.
[67] *ibid.*, at 1357. See also Rix J.'s comments in *Middle Temple v. Lloyds Bank & Sekerbank* [1999] Lloyd's Rep. Bank. 50 at 55, 67, about the practices of banks' clearing departments, where cheques are sorted and handled "at ferocious speed".

being defrauded by the drawing of the cheque? If so, the banker would be in breach of duty if he continued to pay cheques without inquiry.[68] These statements recognise the commercial pressures on banks in these days of mass banking. The court, concerned not to place an unrealistic burden on banks, took account of the fact that a demanding duty of care would be onerous in view of the vast numbers of cheques presented for payment every day,[69] and disapproved the higher standard suggested by *Selangor*. The Jack Committee considering whether the duties of care imposed on bankers needed strengthening,[70] concluded that the legal position, as expressed in *Lipkin Gorman,* is flexible and strong enough to meet the needs of today.

5–036 An important new factor must be included in the equation. The MLR 1993[71] require banks to "know their customers"—and their customers' accounts—to such an extent that there have been considerable changes in the way in which banks manage their business and monitor accounts. Banks have to be alert to suspicious circumstances to avoid criminal liability and are required to make further inquiry in certain circumstances. Since standard banking practice must inevitably reflect these changes, the duty of care and of inquiry owed by banks where there are suspicious circumstances has surely become stricter, in order to correspond with good banking practice.[72]

Bank References (Status Opinions)

5–037 One of the financial services which banks provide is the giving of "status opinions" or references in respect of their customers. These are usually given without fee to persons who may not be customers of the bank. They may be given to other banks, perhaps when a customer opens an account elsewhere, or to finance companies, prospective trading partners, employers, landlords and others (the *"recipient"* of the reference). Some banks may be prepared to give references directly to the recipient, but most give them only to another bank, through whom the recipient makes the request.[73] Some requests may be made by the recipient directly to the bank, with a request for a reply through the recipient's bank.

---

[68] [1989] 1 W.L.R. 1341 at 1378.

[69] The court said that, in the case of solicitors' accounts, it would "involve the manager of a bank . . . in continually monitoring the personal and client accounts for signs that one of the partners might be abusing his signing powers".

[70] Jack Report, Cm. 622 (1989), para. 6.08.

[71] See Chaps 2, 4 and 14.

[72] See *Marfani v. Midland Bank* [1964] 1 W.L.R. 956.

[73] It is not clear whether it might be more acceptable for the reference to be given directly to the recipient, or for it to be given indirectly, through another bank. See, *e.g. Parsons v. Barclay & Co* (1910) 103 L.T. 196, where the "wholesome and useful habit" to which Cozens-Hardy M.R. referred involved references given to another banker. It is difficult to see why the result should be different, for the bank giving the advice must know that it will often be passed on.

Most references are not signed by the bank and they contain a "disclaimer" to the effect that:

> "This reference/opinion is given without responsibility on the part of the bank and its officers and employees, and is intended for and made available to the named recipient only on a confidential basis, and is not to be passed on to third parties".

Although the recipient may not be charged for the reference, the service is not really gratuitous; the costs are passed on to the bank's customers through the general system of charges. As Lord Devlin said: **5–038**

> "The service that a bank performs in giving a reference is not done simply out of a desire to assist in commerce. It could discourage the customers of the bank if their deals fell through because the bank had refused to testify to their credit when it was good".[74]

Banks are commercial institutions, and provide bank references to gain and keep customers. Directly or indirectly, they receive rewards for the service. This has to be said, because bankers sometimes say that the service is unprofitable and that they would be happy to give it up. This should be treated with scepticism.

Liability to the customer

(a) Duty of confidentiality. An initial question which arises is the justification for the bank departing from the duty of confidence to its customer which normally prevents it disclosing to other people any information, accurate or inaccurate, concerning a customer. One of the exceptions to the duty is that the customer has consented to the disclosure of the information, and it has generally been thought that *implied consent* by customers justifies the practice of giving references—for example, in *Tournier v. National Provincial and Union Bank of England,*[75] Bankes L.J. gave as an example of the case where disclosure is made by express or implied consent "the familiar case where the customer authorises a reference to his banker". **5–039**

If the system is justified by implied consent, then it must surely extend only to the release of the minimum of information. In fact, references are often expressed in what seems to the lay observer to be an oblique and uninformative fashion, such as "He is reliable and trustworthy". If the recipient has a particular credit figure in mind and informs the bank of it, the reference may add "and good for your figures". Where the bank has **5–040**

[74] In *Hedley Byrne & Co Ltd v. Heller & Partners Ltd* [1964] A.C. 465 at 529.
[75] [1924] 1 K.B. 461.

nothing good to say about its customer, it will generally answer in a non-committal fashion, which may be as vague as "We confirm that he has an account with us" (which may be taken as an indication of considerable difficulties with the account) or "He is reliable and trustworthy, but we cannot answer for your figures" (which may mean that there have been no severe problems, but that the bank has no evidence from the account that the customer is good for the credit figure in mind).[76]

5–041 The Jack Committee took a cautious attitude to bankers' references, considering that the practice of giving such references is widely misunderstood. It doubted whether many customers were aware that they had given their implied authority for the bank to respond to enquiries about their private financial affairs.[77] It took the view that disclosure of information with only implied consent cannot be justified generally, but thought there should be a limited exception for bankers' references. The Committee recommended that banks should obtain "express consent in tacit form" by inviting customers in a personal letter to give or withhold a general express consent for the bank to supply opinions on them,[78] that customers should not be put under any pressure to give express consent, and that banks should be required to give a clear explanation of how the system works.[79] The Banking Code, after some years of reluctance, has gone further than this: banks now explicitly undertake to tell customers if they provide bankers' references, and to obtain the customer's written consent before such a reference is given.[80] This approach has recently been strongly taken by the court. In *Turner v. Royal Bank of Scotland*,[81] the Court of Appeal held that the plaintiff (whose bank, without his knowledge, had responded to status enquiries about him on eight occasions and in unfavourable terms) could not be taken to have impliedly consented to the release of his confidential information. The bank's defence that there was a binding bank practice of releasing information which had given rise to an implied consent by the customer was decisively rejected. In order for such a practice to be binding, the usage would have to be notorious, certain, reasonable and not contrary to the law. That was not the case here (the bank took some pains not to publicise the practice) and the fact that the practice was constantly

[76] "From the figures available to us, his resources would appear to be fully committed at present" is code for: the individual's accounts are "at limit or overdrawn and most or all assets pledged in security" and "may also suggest a lack of liquid funds": see *Turner v. Royal Bank of Scotland* [1999] Lloyd's Rep. Bank. 231 at 232. Batchelor (*Financial Times*, April 14, 1992) gives further examples—*e.g.* "undoubted" is the highest praise; "unable to speak for your inquiry" is damning.

[77] Cm. 622 (1989), para. 6.27.

[78] Cm. 622 (1989), paras 5(2) and 6(4).

[79] Agreeing with the Younger Committee (Report of the Committee on Privacy, Cmnd 5012 (1972)) that banks should make the existence and manner of operation of the system clear, and give customers either an opportunity to grant a standing authority for the giving of references, or require the bank to seek their consent on any occasion.

[80] Banking Code (1999), para. 4.1.

[81] [1999] Lloyd's Rep. Bank. 231.

repeated could not make it valid, at least as far as customers who were ignorant of it were concerned.[82]

The Data Protection Act 1984 enables customers to request personal information about them held on computer records for a modest charge. Details of financial transactions are normally held on computer and would therefore be available, but of course, they are already available to customers in the form of regular statements in any case. More personal comment and observations about customers are usually kept by branches on memorandum cards, rather than on computer, and the customer used to have no rights to see those records. Under the DPA 1998,[83] however, customers have rights to see such records held by banks. **5–042**

(b) Liability for incorrect references: defamation and negligence. Banks may be liable for incorrect references both to the customer involved and to the recipient. A customer who has suffered damage because of an incorrect statement would be entitled to sue the bank, either in defamation or in contractual negligence. **5–043**

Defamation. The plaintiff has to show that the report would lower his or her reputation in the estimation of right-thinking people. The bank would then have to *justify* itself by showing that what it said was true; given the bland and non-committal nature of references, this may not be difficult, and if it can do so, the plaintiff may have to argue that the words contain an "innuendo", or suggestion that he or she was not creditworthy. If the bank cannot show the statement is true, it is liable even if it had some grounds for thinking so, unless it can establish *qualified privilege* as a defence. Qualified privilege exists where there is a public interest in permitting people to communicate frankly and freely about matters of which the law recognises that they have a duty to perform or an interest to protect in doing so, provided the statement is made in good faith.[84] Since the recipient of the statement has a common interest with the subject of the reference, the defence may protect the bank (which "publishes" the statement), provided that the maker of the statement bona fide believes in what he says and in the interest of the recipient, and acts without malice or motives of private gain. Malice, although it would be hard to prove[85]—particularly where a bank is concerned—would defeat the defence. **5–044**

Damages would be reduced if, on discovering an error, the bank promptly apologised to the customer and (more importantly) to the recipient, thus mitigating the effect on the plaintiff's reputation.

---

[82] [1999] Lloyd's Rep. Bank. 231 at 236, *per* Judge L.J.

[83] Implementing the Directive on processing of personal data and free movement of such data [1995] O.J. C93/1, see above, Chap. 4.

[84] *Horrocks v. Lowe* [1974] 1 All E.R. 662 at 668, *per* Lord Diplock.

[85] *Spring v. Guardian Assurance plc* [1994] 3 All E.R. 129 at 156, *per* Lord Slynn.

5–045 *Negligence.* In practice it may be difficult to establish lack of reasonable care, if only because references are dealt with in confidence. Taking action in negligence has recently become a real possibility, however, because of the recognition by the House of Lords, in *Spring v. Guardian Assurance plc,*[86] that the writer of a reference owes a duty in tort, or in contract by way of an implied term, to the *subject* of a reference, as *Hedley Byrne* recognised the existence of a duty to the recipient of the reference. If there is sufficient proximity of relationship and it is foreseeable that, if a careless reference is given, it will cause damage to the subject, or if the referee assumes responsibility towards the subject in giving a reference and the subject relies on him or her to exercise due skill and care in giving it, a duty of care exists in preparing and writing the reference.

5–046 *Spring* concerned an employee who was given a "kiss of death" reference by an employer. The court did not spell out how far the duty would apply in analogous situations, but there seems no reason why it should not also apply in the case of bankers' references. The bank has the necessary special knowledge of the customer's financial affairs,[87] and giving such references is regarded as within the "business of banking"; it is not undertaken as a mere social matter. Further, possible injury to the plaintiff is both foreseeable and potentially serious as it was in *Spring*: an unjustified bad reference is likely to damage the subject's credit and future employment prospects.

The central requirement of the duty is that reasonable care and skill should be exercised by the referee in ensuring the accuracy of any facts which either are communicated to the recipient of the reference from which he or she may form an adverse opinion of the subject, or are the basis of an adverse opinion expressed by the referee about the subject.

5–047 *Choice of claims: negligence or defamation?* A customer who has been damaged by an inaccurate bank reference may choose to sue in defamation or negligence or both (in practice both claims will probably be brought). *Spring* makes it clear that the role of defamation is to protect reputation, and this purpose has to be balanced with the competing value of freedom of speech. Defamation has been given a definite and restricted role, and in cases where the plaintiff is claiming damage to his or her livelihood and credit, or where there is no clear evidence of more than carelessness, a claim in negligence must be the appropriate course, particularly since there is no question of having to overcome the difficulty of qualified privilege as in defamation.[88]

5–048 **(c) Liability to recipient.** It is usually considered to be part of the business of a banker to give status opinions,[89] and the Jack Committee took it that

[86] [1994] 3 W.L.R. 354; one of the trio of landmark tort cases mentioned above.

[87] "The skill of preparing a reference in respect of an employee falls as much within the expertise of an employer as the skill of preparing a bank reference fell within the expertise of the defendant bank in *Hedley Byrne*", *Spring* [1994] 3 All E.R. 129, *per* Lord Goff.

[88] *Spring* [1994] 3 W.L.R. 354.

[89] See *Swift v. Jewsbury and Goddard* (1874) L.R. 9 Q.B. 301; *Parsons v. Barclay & Co* (1910) 103 L.T. 196.

this was the case. The Committee suggested though, that many people doubt if the system is of much help to the enquirer. This comment is probably realistic. Banks giving such references not only disclaim responsibility, but are required to formulate their opinions on the basis only of the knowledge they happen to possess at the time of the request, and do not need to make any outside enquiries.[90] Further, people, particularly business people, may be disinclined for credit reasons to let their bank manager know of their financial problems. A reference, therefore, may not be a reliable reflection of the customer's general financial position. Nevertheless, bank references do have advantages: they are speedy and cheap, and the alternatives (trade references or credit reference agency assessments) may also not be completely reliable.[91]

Contract. If the bank gives inaccurate information to a recipient who is its own customer or who has for some reason a contract to be given specific information, it would be in breach of an implied term of the contract (to take reasonable care in the management of the customer's affairs), or perhaps in breach of contract for employing incompetent staff. **5–049**

A misleading precontractual statement made by a party to a contract gives a claim for misrepresentation, but is unlikely in the present type of case. If it occurred, then an action for damages under section 2 of the Misrepresentation Act 1967 might succeed. An action for fraud would only succeed if the representation were signed by the maker,[92] however, and bank references are unsigned.[93]

If a bank *fails* to provide a reference when requested, the customer may be damaged by the implication that there is something for the bank to be silent about, or to hide. **5–050**

Disclaimers. Disclaimers made at the time the reference is given may not be effective at common law, since they are given after the formation of the contract[94] (which contains, as we have seen, an implied term to manage the customer's affairs with due care) and are unsupported by fresh consideration. In any case, it is clear that if the bank has been negligent the provisions of sections 2(2) or 3 of the UCTA 1977 apply, and that the disclaimer must be reasonable. The onus of proving reasonableness is on the bank, and it may be doubted whether disclaimers in the "blanket" form in which they are usually expressed are reasonable. **5–051**

[90] *Parsons v. Barclay & Co Ltd* (1910) 103 L.T. 196.

[91] Batchelors, *Financial Times*, April 14, 1992.

[92] s. 6 of Lord Tenterden's Act (Statute of Frauds Amendment Act) 1828. *Banbury v. Bank of Montreal* [1918] A.C. 626.

[93] *UBAF Ltd v. European American Banking Corp.* [1984] 2 All E.R. 226.

[94] See, *e.g. Olley v. Marlborough Court* [1949] 1 K.B. 532; *Chapelton v. Barry U.D.C.* [1940] 1 K.B. 532.

5–052 *Tort.* It is more likely that the recipient would not be a customer of the referee bank, and would not be in a position to sue in contract. There are, however, two possible tort actions: deceit or negligence.

5–053 *(a) Deceit.* Liability may arise if a statement is made which is not honestly believed by its maker to be true and if another relies on it and suffers loss.[95] It is difficult for any plaintiff to discharge the burden of proof in deceit actions, and in the case of bank references there is an additional hurdle. Section 6 of Lord Tenterden's Act (Statute of Frauds Amendment Act) 1828 provides that a person is not liable for a fraudulent representation concerning the credit, dealings and so on, of another person unless the representation is *written and signed* by the maker or by the maker's authorised agent.[96] It is, of course, in order to obtain this protection that bank references are not usually signed. In *Banbury v. Bank of Montreal*,[97] it was held that the Act applied only to actions for fraud (deceit), and actions in contract and for negligence are therefore unaffected by the requirements of the Act.

5–054 *(b) Negligence.* A recipient of a reference who has suffered damage because of its inaccuracy has been able to claim in tort for negligent misstatement since the decision in *Hedley Byrne v. Heller.*[98] This is a case of importance for banks, therefore, even apart from its importance in creating a new principle of liability in tort. An advertising agency requested a reference (through its own bank) for a company customer of the defendant bank. The defendant supplied the reference, but it was inaccurate: it described the company as responsibly managed and as standing by its commitments, but did not refer to the fact that its account was badly overdrawn. The House of Lords held that banks giving references owe a duty of care, although in *Hedley Byrne* itself the bank had made an express disclaimer of responsibility which prevented the duty arising.

5–055 It is clear, therefore, that banks are subject to a duty of care owed to the inquirer, provided at least that proximity exists between the bank and the inquirer. In other words, the bank must have some knowledge of the purpose of the inquiry (in *Hedley Byrne* it was sufficient that the bank must

---

[95] *Derry v. Peek* (1889) 14 App. Cas. 337 at 374, *per* Lord Herschell: "fraud is proved when it is shown that a false representation has been made (1) knowingly, or (2) without belief in its truth or (3) recklessly, careless whether it be true or false".

[96] Statute of Frauds Amendment Act 1828: no action shall be brought whereby to charge any person upon or by reason of any representation or assurance made or given concerning or relating to the character, conduct, credit ability, trade or dealings of any other person, to the intent or purpose that such other person may obtain credit, money or goods upon unless such representation or assurance be made in writing, signed by the party to be charged therewith. Jack recommended its repeal but the Government refused, because it is still in use, White Paper, Cm. 1026, para. 7.12.

[97] [1918] A.C. 626.

[98] [1965] All E.R. 465.

have known that the inquiry was being made by someone who was contemplating doing business with the bank's customer[99]), and be aware that the information will be communicated to the inquirer, who is likely to rely on it.[1]

It may be that the duty (in tort at least) is merely of honesty rather than of skill and care in preparing and communicating the reference.[2] It is unclear whether the nature of the duty in contract is different from that in tort.[3] Although in either case a bank would of course have a duty not to be fraudulent, a duty in contract might impose higher standards in other respects. In *Hedley Byrne* the House of Lords accepted that if a bank had assumed a duty in tort, it was a duty of care, but the court went on to hold that in fact the bank had not assumed a duty at all, because of the disclaimer. The court therefore did not need to analyse the *nature* of the duty or establish what it would have been reasonable for the bank to do in the circumstances. Lord Hodson, however, gave his views on the nature of the duty. He thought it would be unreasonable to impose on a banker a duty to spend much time and trouble on ascertaining the facts. The banker is "permitted to give an impromptu answer in the words that immediately come to his mind on the basis of the facts which he happens to remember or is able to ascertain from the files."[4] This statement relies on earlier cases, such as *Robinson v. National Bank of Scotland*[5] (a fraud case), where the House of Lords said that the bank had no duty to take reasonable care but only to be honest, although this applied only if the recipient stood "in no special relation" to the banker.[6] Similarly, in *Parsons v. Barclay & Co*,[7] Cozens-Hardy M.R. said "emphatically" that a banker's duty was not "to do anything more than answer the questions put to him honestly from what 5–056

[99] [1965] All E.R. 465, 585, *per* Lord Morris.

[1] *Caparo v. Dickman* [1990] 2 A.C. 605 at 638, *per* Lord Oliver. See *Cypress-Batt Enterprises v. Bank of British Columbia* [1995] 4 Bank L.R. 8, BC Supreme Court: where "a reasonable person in the position of the defendant would not have known the plaintiff was relying on the letter".

[2] The reference does not extend to vouching for the identity of the person with whom an inquirer believes he or she is dealing. In *Gold Coin Joailliers v. United Bank of Kuwait* [1997] P.N.L.R. 217, CA, an impostor introduced himself under a false name to an enquirer and referred him to the bank of the person whom he purported to be. The bank provided its reference in a telephone conversation with the enquirer. It was held that it had not assumed a duty of care to the enquirer as regards the true identity of the person who had arranged for the reference.

[3] See *Henderson v. Merrett* [1994] 3 All E.R. 506 at 520, *per* Lord Goff: the *Hedley Byrne* principle "rests upon a relationship between the parties, which may be general or specific to the particular transaction, and which may or may not be contractual in nature", and at 526, "the relevance of the principle lies in the fact that, as a matter of logic, it is capable of application not only where the services are rendered gratuitously, but also where they are rendered under a contract".

[4] *Hedley Byrne* [1965] All E.R. 465 at 512–513, approving Pearson L.J.'s statements in his Court of Appeal judgment.

[5] (1916) 53 Sc. L.R. 390, HL.

[6] (1916) 53 Sc. L.R. 390 at 392, *per* Lord Haldane.

[7] (1910) 103 L.T. 196.

he knew from the books and accounts before him". These dicta may be explicable on the basis that at the time they were decided there was no general principle of liability for negligent misrepresentation in tort, but they are very benevolent to bankers. If, as is sometimes suggested, this benevolence is justified because the bank is *unpaid* for what it does, it may be argued, as it is above, that in effect there is a payment for the service.

5–057 Even if the duty requires more than mere honesty, however, it may not necessarily be as strict as that suggested in *Spring* for employers, for example—different considerations have to be taken into account. It may be thought that banks acting merely as depositories of money, not as a financial advisers, can only answer reliably as to the funds actually deposited with them, and that it would be unfair to require them to make further inquiries into the financial standing of the customer. Nevertheless, it does not seem unjustified to impose a duty on the bank to be careful in preparing and supplying a reference reflecting the information it does possess, and making clear its limitations.

5–058 *Disclaimer.* Banks' references always contain disclaimers.[8] In *Hedley Byrne* the House of Lords held that a duty of care existed only where it was voluntarily undertaken: it was not imposed by law.[9] Since the referee bank had disclaimed responsibility, the court held that it was not liable—it could not be voluntarily undertaking a duty when in the same breath it said it was not doing so.[10] Since then, however, the position in respect of disclaimers has been affected by the UCTA 1977. Section 2(2) provides that liability for loss, including financial losses,[11] caused by negligence[12] can only be excluded or restricted if the term satisfies the requirement of reasonableness.

5–059 What is *reasonable* of course depends on the facts and on the terms of the disclaimer. Bank disclaimers are written in general terms: they may say, for example that they are "without any guarantee or responsibility on the part of this bank or its officials". If all that the bank owes is a duty of honesty, the disclaimer probably reflects the reality and can hardly be regarded as unreasonable. Disclaimers do not seem to attempt to exclude the duty of honesty, and if they did, would be ineffective even at common

[8] In some cases involving negligent advice where a disclaimer has been omitted, a bank has been held liable: see *WB Anderson & Sons v. Rhodes (Liverpool)* [1967] 2 All E.R. 850; *Box v. Midland Bank* [1979] 2 Lloyd's Rep. 391.

[9] Lord Devlin said "I do not understand any of your Lordships to hold that it is a responsibility imposed by law . . . It is a responsibility that is voluntarily accepted or undertaken . . ." [1964] A.C. 465 at 529.

[10] But see now *Smith v. Bush* [1989] 2 All E.R. 514, HL, where the the argument that in such a case there was no liability in the first place and no negligence which could be subject to the controls of the UCTA 1977 was robustly rejected.

[11] Liability for death or personal injury resulting from negligence (in business matters) cannot be excluded (UCTA 1977, s. 2(1)).

[12] "Negligence" means, in addition to breach of contractual duties and occupiers' duties "the breach . . . of any common law duty to take reasonable care or exercise reasonable skill . . ." (UCTA 1977, s. 1).

law.[13] If, however, the bank owes a duty of reasonable skill and care, the position would be different, and it would be necessary to look at the circumstances to assess the reasonableness of the clause.[14] It would be relevant to consider whether the parties were of equal bargaining power, and what would be the practical consequences of deciding that the disclaimer was unreasonable. It is possible, for example, although unlikely, that banks would simply stop supplying references. Another factor, of course, would be the fact that banks carry out the service without charge.

If the standard "blanket-exemption" disclaimers were held to be unreasonable, it would still be open to banks to phrase their disclaimers more cautiously. Lord Slynn says in *Spring*: "those giving such references can make it clear what are the parameters within which the reference is given such as stating their limited acquaintance with the individual".[15] A disclaimer in the form of a warning, for example, "This information may not be accurate and should not be relied on" or "This information was compiled after a brief reference to the customer's accounts, and should not be relied on as a full and accurate financial report, and no responsibility can be taken . . .") may be effective. **5–060**

There is a further question as to whether a disclaimer would bind a third party to whom the reference was passed by the recipient. It seems unlikely, in view of *Smith v. Bush* and *Caparo*[16] that a referee bank would owe a duty at all to such a person, unless it were informed of the purpose for which it was passed on, of the ultimate recipient and of that person's reliance on it (which is unlikely if the reference is to be confidential). If there were a duty, the applicability of any disclaimer in the reference would again depend upon the requirements of the UCTA 1977. If the reference stipulates that it is confidential, such a disclaimer would probably be effective.

Investment and Business Advice

When a bank gives investment advice it owes a contractual duty to customers and a duty in tort under the principle of *Hedley Byrne*[17] to others, and it must take reasonable care in the provision of the advice. **5–061**

Nowadays, it cannot be doubted that the giving of advice is part of a bank's business, but this was not always so clear. In 1918, in *Banbury v. Bank of Montreal*,[18] a manager gave fraudulent advice to invest in a

[13] *S. Pearsons & Son Ltd v. Dublin Corp.* [1907] A.C. 351 at 353, 362.

[14] Whether it is "fair and reasonable to allow reliance on it, having regard to all the circumstances obtaining when the liability arose or (but for the notice) would have arisen" (UCTA 1977, s. 11(3) and Sched. 2). See also *Smith v. Bush* [1989] 2 All E.R. 514, HL, *per* Lord Griffiths.

[15] [1994] 3 W.L.R. 354 at 385.

[16] [1990] 2 A.C. 605.

[17] [1964] A.C. 465.

[18] [1918] A.C. 626.

company whose account was causing the bank difficulty. The House of Lords held that the bank was not liable because there was insufficient evidence to show that the giving of advice on investments was within the scope of the bank's business, and the bank was therefore acting *ultra vires.* By 1958, however, when *Woods v. Martins Bank Ltd*[19] was decided, Salmon J. could point out that this issue must be a question of fact in each case, and that what may have been true of the Bank of Montreal in 1918 was not necessarily true of Martins Bank in 1958. He had no difficulty in finding that financial advice was within the scope of that bank's business.

5–062 In *Woods*, the bank had held itself out as willing to advise. The plaintiff, a gullible young man[20] with no business experience, sought and took the bank's advice, investing £5000 in a company which had an overdrawn account with the bank (the bank's district office had been pressing the company for reductions in the overdraft). The young man opened an account with the bank, and after further advice, invested more money in the company. The plaintiff lost his money and sued, alleging fraud or negligence. Fraud was not found,[21] but Salmon J. held that the bank was negligent. He found that even though at the time of the original advice the plaintiff had no account with the bank, the plaintiff was a "customer"—there was a contractual relationship because the bank had accepted the plaintiff's instructions. There was, additionally, a "fiduciary" relationship between the parties, which caused the plaintiff to rely upon the bank. While it is unlikely that the relationship between bank and customer would now be regarded as fiduciary,[22] it is clear that if the customer reasonably relies on statements made by officers of the bank the bank owes a duty of reasonable care under *Hedley Byrne.*

5–063 In a first instance case where the legal implications of bank lending were examined in detail, *Williams and Glyns Bank v. Barnes,*[23] a borrower was granted a loan of £1 million for the purpose of purchasing shares in the company of which he was the founder, moving spirit and chairman. The judge took the view that in the absence of a specific request from the borrower (in which case he would have been referred to another department) the bank did not owe him any duty to consider the commercial advisability of the loan or that the company's business was exposed to serious risks. All the bank had done was to lend him the money at his

[19] [1959] 1 Q.B. 55.

[20] So described; in fact, aged 30.

[21] "I think that [the manager] did, in his muddle-headed way, honestly believe in the advice which he gave to the plaintiff" [1959] 1 Q.B. 55 at 60, *per* Salmon J.

[22] After *National Westminster Bank v. Morgan* [1985] 1 All E.R. 821; [1985] A.C. 686. But *cf. Hong Bank of Canada v. Phillips* [1998] Lloyd's Rep. Bank. 343 (Man. Ct. of QB, Canada). For discussion of fiduciary duties and banks, see above, Chap. 3.

[23] [1981] Com. L.R. 205 (abridged). The Banking Ombudsman has no jurisdiction to examine complaints about lending, which is a matter for the commercial judgment of the bank, unless there has been some maladministration. See comments by OBO, A.R. 1994–5, para. 6.

request. It is true that the fact that the defendant was a businessman of full age and competence was a significant factor here; the possibility of a different conclusion if the borrower were naive and lacking in business experience may still exist. In *Smith v. Bush,*[24] a person in modest circumstances reasonably relied on the implication that if a loan has been granted for a property, the property must be valuable, and the House of Lords held that the valuer owed her a duty of care in drawing up the valuation. Where the customer is unsophisticated in financial matters, is not experienced as a business person[25] and has few other sources of advice, it is more likely that a duty of care would be held to exist.

Another court of first instance has recently considered this issue. The action, like so many others, arose out of the wave of reckless lending on the back of the increase in property prices in the 1980s. In *Investors' Compensation Scheme Ltd v. West Bromwich Building Society,*[26] a building society ("the Society"), prompted by an entrepreneurial managing director, developed an innovative scheme for granting remortgages regardless of the reasons for the request for further capital, to borrowers who in the past had experienced difficulties concerning repayment.[27] Its "Home Income Scheme" was directed at retired people owning properties who were living on small incomes. As it was presented, many elderly people would be able to "realise the equity in their homes" by receiving supplements to their incomes, and—again, as it was presented—they would not have to repay during their lifetimes. Provided they were above a certain age (usually 60), they would be able to remortgage their houses up to 40 per cent of value without—this was the unusual feature—having to repay the interest: the interest would be "rolled up" and added to the sum secured, and repaid out of the equity when the property was finally realised. There was, however, the stipulation that if the amount secured by the mortgage reached more than 60 per cent of the value of the property, the borrower would have to make payments to bring it down to that level. The scheme was initiated at the height of the 1980s property boom, and its success depended on the increase in house prices continuing. If prices fell, or even remained stable, the secured sum would reach the "trigger point" quickly. Unfortunately, the Society overlooked the fact that at that time (late 1988) bank base rates of interest had already started to increase[28] and to move the property market towards what soon became a serious crash which would bring the mortgages to a premature end, depriving the investors of the very income for which they had mortgaged their properties. 5–064

[24] [1989] 2 All E.R. 514, see above, para. 5–006.

[25] *cf. Rust v. Abbey Life Assurance Co* [1978] 2 Lloyd's Rep. 386, where the fact that the customer was an experienced businesswoman was irrelevant.

[26] Transcript, January 15, 1999. Reported (edited) in [1999] Lloyd's Rep. P.N. at 496.

[27] Transcript, at p. 4.

[28] On November 11, 1988, Bank base rate of interest was increased from 12 per cent to 13 per cent. The first of these mortgages was completed by the Society on November 29, 1988 (transcript at p. 10).

5–065 There were not only flaws in the scheme itself, but also in the way it was marketed. The marketing had been largely undertaken by an enterprising firm of financial advisers, FPS, who emphasised its benefits. The mortgages could be discontinued at any time, they would free up money which was locked in the property; continued ownership of property would give security and peace of mind, and so on. Many of the statements in the publicity were inaccurate: the scheme was not flexible—it would not be easy to reverse out of the plan—and even in normal market conditions, it could not have been expected that such a mortgage could last longer than between seven and 10 years before the amount secured reached the trigger point,[29] whereas people who had invested in such a mortgage when they were 60 could reasonably have expected to be very much alive and needing their homes even 10 years later. The scheme was being sold by unqualified staff, who were instructed always to be "extremely positive" and who assured potential investors that the mortgages were "sure-fire winners" and would make them "financially secure for the rest of their lives". FPS was warned by the Society in August 1989 that such mortgages had become "excessively risky",[30] but the firm took no steps to warn borrowers of the risks, and went on marketing them for a further two months, simply because it wanted the business.

5–066 Indeed, the whole project was undertaken recklessly. Whereas the normal practice was for building societies to test the performance of new products against historical market conditions and in forecast conditions—normally by making a computer model of the product—neither the Society nor FPS had undertaken any methodical testing in this case. Nor had either of them taken the normal precaution of reviewing the performance of the product as market conditions changed.

5–067 Before long, the scheme was attracting complaints and being investigated. FPS was suspended by its regulator from carrying on investment business in May 1990, and eventually went into liquidation. The elderly investors in the scheme, who had suffered losses, claimed compensation from the Investors' Compensation Scheme (ICS) because they were unable to claim it from the financial advisers; in return, they assigned the benefit of their claims to ICS,[31] who were the plaintiffs in this action (together with some of the individual mortgagors). At issue was the Society's liability to the mortgagors and the ICS, and in order to consider the liability of the Society, it was first necessary to determine FPS's liability. The judge had no difficulty coming to the conclusion that FPS had breached duties in contract (duty of skill and care as an independent financial adviser), tort (concurrent

[29] Transcript at p. 55.

[30] Transcript at 56.

[31] The effect of the assignment was considered as a preliminary issue by the House of Lords in *ICS v. West Bromwich B.S.* [1998] 1 W.L.R. 896.

duty[32]) and statutory duty.[33] He also found that the claimants, financially unsophisticated people, had relied on misrepresentations made by FPS. As far as some claimants were concerned, he upheld claims of undue influence against FPS.

The judge then had to consider the liability of the Society for a similar battery of claims.[34] Some were successful: the Society was a joint tortfeasor, jointly liable for the torts committed by FPS, on the basis that there had been a "meeting of minds" to carry on the enterprise for the joint benefit of each enterpriser,[35] and it was also on notice of the undue influence and the misrepresentations for which FPS had been responsible.[36] However, the Society[37] did not *itself* owe a duty of care in tort to borrowers not to market defective mortgage products, nor alternatively, to advise borrowers as to the financial and other risks to which they would be exposed—or, at least, to advise borrowers to terminate their mortgages once the dangers of the mortgages had become clear.[38] The grounds of the decision were that the mortgage could not be said to be an intrinsically dangerous product[39]: the concept was simply not appropriate in the context of a claim for economic loss. The negligence, if there was negligence, must have arisen from the Society's failure properly to advise applicants, and should therefore be considered in the context of liability for negligent misstatement. In that context, however, there was no sufficient relationship of proximity between the Society and the mortgagors within the meaning of *Caparo*.[40] This conclusion was supported by ample reference to authority, including *Williams & Glyns v. Barnes*,[41] where it had been held that the bank was not under "a duty of care to advise the customer as to the terms, effect or commercial prudence of the transaction of loan which the customer may be about to enter into with the bank"[42]; nor, in these circumstances, where the 5–068

[32] *Henderson v. Merrett* [1995] 1 A.C. 145.

[33] s. 62 of the FSA 1986. But the firm was not liable for breach of a fiduciary duty of loyalty, (because there had been no deliberate decision not to warn the investors) though it was liable for breach of the equitable duty of care and skill of a fiduciary, see *Bristol and West Building Society v. Mothew* [1998] 1 Ch. 18.

[34] WBBS's attempt to deflect liability on to solicitors retained by FPS was unsuccessful, transcript, p. 199.

[35] Transcript at p. 159. But a claim that the B.S. was responsible for enabling and assisting a breach of statutory duty was not made out, and an allegation that it was itself carrying on "investment business" within s. 1 of the FSA 1986 was not pursued (transcript, pp. 160–161).

[36] Transcript at p. 192. The relevant mortgagors would therefore be entitled to rescission of their mortgages, subject to restitution of benefits acquired under the mortgages.

[37] There was no valid distinction between a a bank and a building society in these circumstances: transcript, p. 138.

[38] Transcript at p. 130.

[39] As a tin of chlorinated lime would be: see *Clarke v. Army and Navy Co-Operative Society* [1903] 1 K.B. 155. In any case, these were "ordinary unsecured loans at an unremarkable rate of interest".

[40] [1990] 2 A.C. 605.

[41] [1981] Com. L.R. 205.

[42] Transcript at p. 138.

Society had not had any direct relevant contact with the mortgagors[43] (its express policy was to leave explanations to FPS), nor offered advice to them, had the Society made any "assumption of liability" to them.

5–069 The decision is orthodox and supported by authority. Nevertheless, from a policy point of view, doubts may be expressed about the results. The liability of the Society had to rest on what must be regarded as the *primary* liability of FPS—yet did this reflect the reality? It was the Society which had devised, promoted and which, ultimately, sold the mortgages. It can be strongly argued that the real responsibility lay with the Society. The idea behind the scheme was simply to exploit the property of elderly people. If the law of negligence has the double aim of compensation and of deterrence, as many would assert, it would be coherent to fix legal liability on the Society for both reasons: it would be fair for the Society to have to repay its victims—and perhaps to compensate them for the anxiety and disturbance which they suffered—and it might also help to prevent mortgage lenders in future employing the sort of reckless entrepreneur who devised this scheme.

5–070 There is a further argument for placing primary liability on lenders. Recent decisions have established that banks may be liable for contributory negligence in lending cases[44] to other professionals, such as valuers and solicitors, whose advice has supported lending which caused loss to the lenders. It seems incongruous that the law permits a contributory claim against lenders by professionals although it refuses any direct claim by even unsophisticated borrowers against them on the same facts and for the same imprudent behaviour.

5–071 *Williams and Glyns Bank v. Barnes* was also considered in the first instance decision, *Spindler and Verity v. Lloyds Bank.*[45] A financially naive couple borrowed money from the bank and later claimed that they had suffered loss because they purchased a house as a business venture relying on negligent business advice given by the bank manager. The judge, Taylor J., held that on the particular facts the manager did assume a duty to the borrowers and should have advised with care.[46] In finding that the manager had crossed the line into advising, the judge was influenced by the fact that the borrowers were unsophisticated, and also by enthusiastic statements in the bank's brochure, which said that borrowers could receive "tailor-made" advice for business ventures and "your bank manager will help you to decide how much you can really afford to invest".[47] Two other factors

[43] Other than the signed applications they had made for loans, the offers of advance and the execution of the mortgage documents.

[44] Confirmed by the Court of Appeal in *Platform Home Loans v. Oyston Shipways* [1998] 4 All E.R. 252, CA, affirmed [1999] 2 W.L.R. 518, HL (noted Dugdale (1999) 62 M.L.R. 281).

[45] *The Independent*, September 19, 1995.

[46] On the basis of *Hedley Byrne* and *Cornish* principles.

[47] He "semi-echoed" the comments of Salmon J. in *Woods v. Martins Bank* [1959] 1 Q.B. 55 that it was remarkable that the bank advertised its free advice on business matters and then suggested that it was implausible that customers with a business venture should have sought and obtained such advice.

played a part. Firstly, although the plaintiffs had other sources of advice available to them, it was not implausible that they should have relied on the bank manager, who was well placed to form an accurate picture of their financial position and experienced in financial matters; and secondly, the manager, who had inspected possible houses with them, had been "kindly" and "like an uncle" to them, encouraging them to think that he was assessing the project from their point of view, and not just from the bank's.

Plainly the bank manager had gone to considerable lengths to be helpful and might fairly be said to have assumed the duty of care on behalf of the bank. There was more to justify liability than the Court of Appeal required in *Lloyds Bank plc v. Cobb*,[48] a decision considered in *Verity*, where it was held that the ordinary business of a bank does not include giving advice on the wisdom of commercial projects for which the bank is to lend money, unless there is a request by the customer to do so. Scott L.J. said: **5–072**

> "in order to place the bank under a duty of care to the borrower the borrower must, in my opinion, make clear to the bank that its advice is being sought. The mere request for a loan, coupled with the supply to the bank of the details of the commercial project . . . does not suffice to make clear to the bank that its advice is being sought".

Merely by examining the details of the project the bank does not assume a duty, since the examination is for its own purposes as lender.

Although the *Verity* decision is within accepted *Hedley Byrne* and *Cornish* principles, it is worrying for banks because it shows how fine a distinction there is between examining a project from the point of view of the bank's interest on the one side, and assuming a duty to advise the borrowers carefully on the other. The bank representative must judge the borrowers and his or her own behaviour carefully. If the borrowers are financially inexperienced, the representative should make it clear that the bank is concerned with its own interests, not primarily with the borrowers'. The difficulty may be to reconcile that relatively unhelpful and business like approach with the sentiments expressed in the bank's publicity. **5–073**

Claims can be brought under the principles of *Hedley Byrne* not only for negligent "investment" advice, but for any sort of negligent misstatement made by the bank, upon which the plaintiff reasonably relies. In *Box v. Midland Bank Ltd*,[49] the branch manager of the bank advised the plaintiff that the bank would make an advance to finance a contract. He gave the impression that head office sanction would be a mere formality provided that an ECGD[50] policy was obtained. The plaintiff received a quotation for **5–074**

[48] Unreported, December 18, 1981. See also *James v. Barclays Bank* [1995] 4 Bank L.R. 131.
[49] *Box v. Midland Bank Ltd* [1979] 2 Lloyd's Rep. 391.
[50] Export Credits Guarantee Department: a government department established to promote foreign trade.

an ECGD policy, but for one of a sort which, as the manager ought to have known, would never have been accepted by the head office, and which was duly rejected. The plaintiff was unable to obtain an acceptable policy and, since he had developed the project at considerable cost, got into financial difficulties and became bankrupt. He sued the bank for negligence under *Hedley Byrne*. The bank contended that Mr Box had not received *advice*, but had merely put a proposition to the bank. It was held that that made no difference: the *Hedley Byrne* principle was not limited to negligent advice but applied to negligent statements generally. The bank had failed to take reasonable care—"that is to say the care to be expected of an ordinary competent bank manager". The manager ought to have known that there was never the slightest prospect of obtaining the consent of head office being given without the appropriate policy being obtained, and the bank was liable.

5–075 Another question about the type of statement which might lead to liability under *Hedley Byrne* was raised in *Royal Bank v. Pampellonne.*[51] The branch manager of the bank met the plaintiff twice at unscheduled meetings, and gave him misleading investment information, charging no fee for the service. The majority of the Privy Council considered that, as a question of fact, the manager had *supplied information* in his possession to the plaintiff rather than *advised* him. The majority approved the judge's decision in favour of the bank, because any duty of care was confined to passing on the information accurately. The distinction[52] between information and advice was criticised in a strong dissent by Lord Templeman and Sir Robin Cooke, who suggested that inadequate information is just as useless as negligent advice—indeed, for an unsophisticated person, positively dangerous. Even if the plaintiff made the decision himself, he would obviously rely to some extent on the information given at the meeting, and no meeting where potential investments were being discussed with a banker could be described as merely casual or devoid of serious business purpose. The minority thought that there was a duty of care, on *Hedley Byrne* principles, to do what was reasonable in the circumstances. The manager could have offered to undertake more investigation, or have advised the plaintiff to take other advice; at the least, he could have warned him that he had inadequate information about the investment to enable him to recommend it.

5–076 The decision of the House of Lords in *South Australia Asset Management Corporation v. York Montague Ltd*,[53] may now have some bearing on this issue. Both providing information and advising the plaintiff as to a course

[51] [1987] 1 Lloyd's Rep. 218.

[52] See Clements [1987] P.N. 145, who draws an analogy with consumer magazines: if such a magazine gives "information" about products, the information is certainly relied upon by readers and regarded as advice.

[53] [1996] 3 All E.R. 365.

of conduct may give rise to liability, but the resulting liability for loss may be very different. The House of Lords held that a valuer engaged to provide a valuation of property was providing information upon which a lender could base a decision as to whether to advance a loan secured on the property to a borrower. The valuer was not advising the lender *whether* to advance the loan; there was a distinction between providing information for the purpose of enabling someone else to decide upon a course of action, taking into account a number of other matters, and a duty to advise someone as to what course of action he or she should take. In the case of *advice*, the adviser must take reasonable care to consider all the potential consequences of that course of conduct, and if negligent, would be responsible for all the foreseeable loss consequent on it. If the duty is only to supply *information*, on the other hand, the defendant must simply take reasonable care to see that the information is correct, and if negligent, will be responsible for the foreseeable consequences of the information being wrong. If the duty of the defendant is to give advice about whether to enter into the transaction, he or she is obviously taking on a wider range of risks, and may be liable for greater losses. Banks should be aware, therefore, that even when merely providing information they are under a duty to be careful that it is accurate, albeit a narrower one than that to be careful when providing advice.

It seems then, that as long as the statement made is within the actual or **5–077** apparent authority of the bank official who gives it, and is part of the bank's business, made in circumstances in which it is reasonable for the plaintiff to rely upon it, and contains no effective disclaimer, the bank may be liable if it fails to take reasonable care in making the statement. This is the case whether it is a reference, or investment advice, or some other sort of statement as in *Box v. Midland Bank Ltd*.

Lending and Obtaining Guarantees.

A bank's duty of care in lending money[54] is limited to its *Hedley Byrne* duty **5–078** of liability if its representatives make misleading statements to a borrower. In *Cornish v. Midland Bank*,[55] it was established that a bank which chooses to advise a customer is under a duty not to misstate the advice. But the bank does not owe a duty to advise the customer on the viability of a project, nor to take care in the act of lending. Nor does it owe a duty to a third party concerned in the lending unless it assumes responsibility towards him or her. In *Chapman v. Barclays Bank*,[56] Mr Chapman was the director and shareholder of a company for which Barclays provided overdraft facilities. The bank had withdrawn the overdraft facilities

[54] See generally Cranston, *Banks, Liability and Risk*, 1995. Loans and overdrafts are discussed in Chap. 8, guarantees in Chap. 18 and undue influence in Chap. 3.

[55] [1985] 3 All E.R. 513.

[56] [1997] 6 Bank L.R. 315.

although it knew that the financial assessment on the basis of which it was acting was inaccurate. The company went into liquidation and Mr Chapman claimed damages against the bank for breach of duty of care. He was unsuccessful; although he was the only person with whom the bank had had dealings, he himself was not a customer of the bank. He could not establish, it was held, the necessary proximity between himself and the bank, because no advice had been sought or given, and there were no circumstances from which it could be inferred that the bank assumed any responsibility towards him.

5–079 *A duty to explain the terms of documents or to disclose information?* Banks sometimes explain the terms of security documents and guarantees to those who execute them, particularly if the latter are not business people. If banks do undertake an explanation, they are under a duty not to misstate the effect of the documents.[57] Guarantees are complex documents which are not readily understood. It is likely that many guarantors are unclear about the extent of their obligations when they sign the documents even if an explanation is given.

5–080 One of the most serious misunderstandings—which appears frequently in the cases—is the difference between a "*limited*" and an "*all-moneys*" guarantee (or charge). The former means that the liability of the guarantor is limited to a specified amount of money and the latter that all future lending to the debtor will be secured by that guarantee. The latter carries the serious risk for the guarantor that the debtor may, unknown to the guarantor, simply increase his or her borrowing against the security. In *Cornish v. Midland Bank*,[58] a customer gave a charge to the bank, and was given only a brief—and erroneous—explanation of the effect of the charge. On later challenging the charge, she alleged[59] that the bank had owed her a duty to explain the agreement, (including the fact that it was to cover "all borrowings"), and was in breach of that duty. It was held that, since an explanation had been undertaken, the bank was under a duty to explain properly. However, Kerr L.J. went further and said that although banks might not owe a duty to stranger guarantors to explain the terms and legal effect of guarantees, they might do so to customers.[60] In *Barclays Bank v. Khaira*,[61] however, it was held that the bank owes no duty to explain, either to customers or non-customers.

5–081 Banks, fearing they might incur a duty, might once have preferred to refuse altogether to make any statement about a document to a surety, but they do have to give some information: *Barclays Bank v. O'Brien*[62] and the

[57] *Cornish v. Midland Bank* [1985] 3 All E.R. 513.
[58] [1985] 3 All E.R. 513.
[59] Amongst other things: negligent misstatement/misrepresentation (successfully), undue influence (unsuccessfully), and a breach of duty in the conduct of the account (unsuccessfully).
[60] *O'Hara v. Allied Irish Banks Ltd* [1985] B.C.L.C. 52.
[61] [1992] 1 W.L.R. 623, aff'd April 30, 1992, CA.
[62] [1993] 3 W.L.R. 786, see Chaps 3 and 18.

Banking Code of Practice require that banks must tell private individuals[63] prepared to act as sureties that by giving the guarantee they may become liable as well as the borrower, and they must tell them what the limit of their liability will be (the explanation should not disclose details of the conduct of the account because of the duty of confidentiality to the customer). Further, and importantly, the new version of the Code makes two statements that may considerably affect the liability of a potential surety. First, banks make a clear undertaking not to take unlimited guarantees; and secondly, they warn borrowers that they may require consent from them to disclosure of their confidential information to a potential surety. This seems to imply that banks will be open to challenge from sureties if they have not taken the trouble to obtain that consent where there is material information which might be disclosed to the surety. It may in itself operate as a lever to allow the surety to claim that the bank owes a duty to disclose relevant information about the borrower's account.

Banks owe only a limited duty of disclosure to the surety. They certainly **5–082** do not have to let a guarantor know everything that it is material for the surety to know; this would be commercially impracticable.[64] Moreover, the lender does not need to inform the surety of the state of the debtor's finances: the surety is expected to understand that the reason a guarantee is needed is precisely because financial problems exist. In any case, the bank must be careful not to breach its duty of confidentiality towards its customer, the principal debtor.

In *Levett v. Barclays Bank plc*,[65] it was confirmed that if there is **5–083** something unusual or unexpected in the transaction, this should be disclosed. In particular, a contract between the debtor and the lender making the position of the surety different from what he or she might naturally expect to the disadvantage of the surety should be disclosed by the lender to the surety.

The UTCCR[66] apply to banks' guarantee documents, as to other standard banking contracts, and together with the Code,[67] have had an effect on them. Some of the traditional complex clauses in guarantee documents might well have contravened the "plain English" requirement and run the risk of not being in "good faith",[68] but banks have now simplified their documents and made them more accessible to ordinary bank customers.

---

[63] Banking Code (1999) para. 3.14.

[64] *Hamilton v. Watson* (1845) 12 Cl. & Fin. 109, 8 E.R. 1339.

[65] [1995] 2 All E.R. 615, QBD.

[66] S.I. 1999 No. 2083, replacing S.I. 1994 No. 3159 (giving effect to E.C. Directive 93/13 [1993] O.J. L95/29). *cf.* the view of the editors of *Paget's Law of Banking*, see below, para. 18–004.

[67] The CCA 1974 also regulates contracts of guarantee, mostly with regard to their form: for example, a "health warning" must be given on advertisements for credit secured on the debtor's home. The UCTA 1977 is also relevant with regard to exclusion clauses.

[68] Andrews and Millett, *Law of Guarantees*, App 1, Prec. 1, commentary).

CHAPTER 6

THE PAYING BANK: DUTY TO PAY

Other important duties of banks which relate closely to their specialised activities and the relationships specific to banking business are discussed here. **6–001**

Bankers, as their customers' agents, are under a duty to carry out their instructions within the limits of their authority—that is, the instructions which they have undertaken to honour, either at the time of the original contract or subsequently. This depends on the general "holding out" of the things which bankers will do (for example, the provision of cheques) which arise from the nature of a banker's business, and on any specific undertakings in a particular case. The terms of the contract, express or implied, may of course be altered, provided that adequate notice of the change, and consideration have been given.[1]

Although the basic relationship between banker and customer is a contract of debt, with the bank acting as the depository of the customer's money and repaying when required, banks of course have other functions to perform for their customers, one of the most important of which is to pay third parties on their customer's behalf. Traditionally the customer's instructions to pay have been given by means of cheques drawn on the paying bank. The bank's function as a paying bank is different from its function as a collecting bank, and it owes different duties to its customer and has different defences in the two capacities. Sometimes one bank, or even one branch, may act as both paying and collecting bank in a transaction. If so, the clearing process may be shorter but the two different functions still have to be considered separately. **6–002**

This Chapter considers the relationship between the customer and the bank when it pays a cheque on his or her behalf.

THE PARTIES AND THE PROCESS

Although most of us are familiar with the use of cheques, it is worth describing their operation at this stage in order to be clear about the legal relationships involved. **6–003**

> A draws a cheque on his bank (X branch) to pay B £100. B presents the cheque to her bank (Y branch) to collect it on her behalf. Y

[1] See *Burnett v. Westminster Bank Ltd* [1966] 1 Q.B. 742; [1965] 2 Lloyd's Rep. 218 (see above, para. 3–025).

provisionally credits B's account with that sum and sends the cheque to X through the clearing system. All being well, Y will pay the cheque, B's account will be credited a few days later, and she will be able to draw on the funds.[2] The banks will settle up between themselves through their own bank accounts with the Bank of England.

A is the drawer of the cheque, Y the drawee who pays on his behalf. B is the payee, and Z bank collects the payment on her behalf. Y is therefore the *paying* bank and Z the *collecting* bank.[3]

6–004 Even in this everyday transaction, several contracts are involved:

(a) A is the customer of Y (banker/customer contract);
(b) B is the customer of Z (banker/customer contract);
(c) A and B have a contract by virtue of the cheque; and
(d) Y and Z probably also have a contract as members of the clearing house.[4]

Nature of the Duty to Pay: Cheque as Mandate

6–005 Cheques are an integral part of the traditional business of banking and their use as a mandate[5] is deeply rooted in the banker/customer relationship. Although this Chapter concentrates on this aspect of cheques, it is important to remember that they developed and can still operate as negotiable instruments,[6] so that some references to their characteristics in that respect have to be made, although the law on negotiable instruments will be considered later in the book.[7]

Cheques act as a mandate or instruction to the bank from its customer, who may use them either to obtain repayment of funds from the bank or to pay third parties. It is an implied term of the contract that the bank will repay when its customer's instruction is received at the branch where the account is kept[8] provided there are sufficient funds, and customers wishing

---

[2] Only a few banks, *e.g.* Coutts, return cheques to their private customers these days unless requested.

[3] If the bank is acting on B's behalf and not on its own. If it has given value for the cheque (see below, para. 14–076) it will be presenting the cheque but not collecting it.

[4] *Barclays Bank v. Bank of England* [1985] 1 All E.R. 385 at 390, *per* Bingham J., as he then was.

[5] The concept was first established in England from civilian law by *Young v. Grote* (1827) 4 Bing. 253. "It is a historical accident that the mandate normally takes the form of a bill of exchange", Chorley, "The Cheque as Mandate and Negotiable Instrument", *Journal of the Institute of Bankers*, 1x 392. Note that particular mandates (cheques) have to be distinguished from the *written statement*, also called a mandate, given to the bank at the time of opening the account.

[6] The use of cheques as negotiable instruments is now rare, because of the Ch A 1992, see below, Chap. 14.

[7] See Chap. 13.

[8] *Joachimson v. Swiss Bank Corp* [1921] 3 K.B. 110.

to obtain repayment may use cheques to do so although customers these days are more likely to withdraw their money by means of an automatic teller machine, and to use cheques mainly for the discharge of their debts to third parties.

Considered as a mandate, a cheque is an *authority* to pay which justifies a debit to the customer's account, and if the conditions for payment are fulfilled, it imposes a *duty* on the bank to obey the mandate exactly, and to do so with reasonable care, so that no loss is caused to the customer.[9] Negligence may be a breach of duty in itself, and it may also deprive the bank of its statutory protection against the customer (who may claim in debt or damages) or a third party (who may claim in conversion) where it pays the wrong person. **6–006**

The bank paying within its mandate acts as its customer's agent, so that if a third party is paid, the customer's liability to that party is discharged, and the bank becomes entitled to debit the customer's account. If it acts *outside* the mandate, however—for example by paying a countermanded cheque or on a forgery—it has no authority to debit the account.[10]

Cheques and Third Parties

As we saw, a bank may pay a third party on the instructions of its customer, whose liability to that party is then discharged. A cheque is normally only *conditional* payment and does not constitute discharge until it has been honoured; until then, the acceptance of the tender of the cheque merely entitles the creditor to the transfer of money, and gives the drawer a good defence to an action by the payee on a debt. Once honoured, it is deemed to have been paid at the time of delivery. In some circumstances the question whether the bank itself may owe some sort of duty to the third party may be important. There are several ways in which liability might arise: in relation to the use of the cheque as a negotiable instrument; because the bank might owe a contractual obligation to the third party, or because it might be liable in the tort of conversion[11] to the true owner (usually the payee) of a cheque. There might also be a question of equitable liability where the bank acts as a trustee, or is found by the court to have assumed the liability of a constructive trustee.[12] **6–007**

(1) Negotiable instrument

The fact that a cheque is a negotiable instrument—a specialised form of bill of exchange[13]—means that it may be transferred to another person, who may under certain conditions acquire a better title than the transferor **6–008**

[9] *Lipkin Gorman v. Karpnale* [1989] 1 W.L.R. 1340, CA; *Bellamy v. Marjoribanks* (1852) 7 Exch. 389.

[10] The customer may obtain a declaration to this effect, *Limpgrange Ltd v. BCCI* [1986] F.L.R. 36.

[11] Torts (Interference with Goods) Act 1977.

[12] See below, Chap. 9.

[13] A bill of exchange drawn on a banker payable on demand, s. 73 of the BOEA 1882.

possessed and may be a "holder in due course". A holder of a bill may be in a position to claim, not only against the *drawer* of the cheque, but also against other parties to the bill, such as the *acceptor* who takes primary responsibility for the payment of the bill by signing. As far as cheques are concerned, though, banks are simply *drawees*, who do not have responsibility for payment.[14] They are therefore not liable on cheques to holders or payees.[15]

(2) Claim in contract

6–009 In English law, a third party who has been given a cheque by the customer does not have any contractual claim against the bank, for example as an assignee,[16] who could demand payment from the bank as the legal or equitable owner of the debt. The bank therefore has normally no obligation in contract to the payee. However, the cheque acts not only as an authority from the customer to pay but also as an order to do so, and the bank therefore may be liable to the *customer* for breach of mandate if it does not pay as instructed.

(3) Claim in tort

6–010 The third possibility is liability in the tort of *conversion.*[17] The risk of a claim for conversion is often thought of as a risk run by the collecting bank, but it is also a risk, though a slight one, for the paying bank. There is statutory protection for the paying bank corresponding to that for the collecting bank.[18]

(4) Duties in trust

6–011 An equitable duty might arise where funds which apparently belong to the customer are subject to a trust. Where the bank knows of a trust or agency, it may pay on the trustee's or agent's order unless it knows of a

---

[14] The bank would only accept a cheque "in very unusual and special circumstances": *Bank of Baroda Ltd v. Punjab National Bank Ltd* [1944] A.C. 176 at 188, *per* Lord Wright.

[15] See *Dublin Port and Docks Board v. Bank of Ireland* [1976] I.R. 118.

[16] s. 135 of the Law of Property Act 1925 (LPA 1925). There may be an assignment in Scotland (s. 53 of the BOEA 1882, see Jack Report, Cm. 622 (1989), para. 7.52). A customer in England might assign a cheque by indicating by means other than the cheque itself that an assignment of the debt is intended. If the whole debt is assigned, the bank must pay the assignee, *Walker v. Bradford Old Bank Ltd* (1884) 12 Q.B.D. 511 (*cf. Schroeder v. Central Bank of London Ltd* (1876) 34 L.T. 735). If only part of the debt is assigned, it operates as an equitable assignment, and the assignee may not be able to give a good discharge, *Re Steel Wing Co Ltd* [1921] 1 Ch. 349; *Bank of Liverpool and Martins Ltd v. Holland* (1926) 43 T.L.R. 29; *Williams v. Atlantic Assurance Co Ltd* [1933] 1 K.B. 81; *Walter and Sullivan Ltd v. J Murphy & Sons Ltd* [1955] 2 Q.B. 584; *Re Kent and Sussex Sawmills Ltd* [1947] Ch. 177.

[17] Torts (Interference with Goods) Act 1977. The possibility of claims in quasi-contract or restitution also exists: for money had and received for mistake (of fact), or for waiver of the tort of conversion, if the true owner is entitled to sue in conversion, see Ellinger and Lomnicka *Modern Banking Law* (2nd ed.), pp. 363–4.

[18] See below, Chap. 14.

breach of trust or duty. Generally, the bank should not refuse to pay a cheque on the ground that the funds *might* belong to a third party, and it need not investigate its customer's title to the money, but if it has knowledge of some sort that the customer had no title to the funds, either because they are stolen or because they have been received by mistake, the bank might incur liability as a constructive trustee.

When paying cheques therefore, banks are most likely to risk action from their customers or from third parties in conversion or in trust.

The Customer's Remedies for Breach of Duty by the Bank

If the bank fails to comply with its duty to pay and has wrongly dishonoured a cheque, the customer may sue the bank. The customer's claims are in contract or, in appropriate circumstances, in the tort of defamation, or in both. Usually the damages awarded, whether in contract or in tort, will be greater if the cheque is for a small sum.[19] Although this looks rather odd at first sight, it makes sense, because damage to a person's reputation is greater if he or she is said to be unable to pay smaller rather than larger sums of money. **6–012**

The bank has some defences.[20] It may be able to show, for example, that the conditions for payment were not fulfilled, so that there was no mandate, or the cheque was inadequate as a mandate; the customer's funds may have been insufficient, or the bank may have been forbidden by injunction from paying. Apart from that, there are some common law defences—for example, the customer may have ratified the bank's actions or be estopped from denying the bank's right to debit the account, and an equitable defence available as against the customer, as well as specific statutory protections[21] which may be available in an action by a customer or a third party. **6–013**

(1) Breach of contract

Damages. The aim of damages in contract is to put the plaintiff in the position that he or she would have been in if the contract had been performed. If the bank's action amounts to a breach of contract, the customer will be able to sue for damages as of right, whether any loss has been suffered or not. If there is no actual loss though, only nominal damages (not substantial damages) will be awarded for the breach. If the bank has not honoured a customer's cheque, it can be argued that the customer has suffered no loss merely because of the failure to pay—the argument is that if the cheque had been honoured, the benefit to the customer of the payment would have been offset by the corresponding **6–014**

[19] *Marzetti v. Williams* (1830) 1 B. & Ad. 415.
[20] See below, Chap. 7.
[21] Cheques Act 1957, and the BOEA 1882, ss. 60 and 80. Discussed in Chap. 14.

reduction in the funds in the account, and the customer is therefore financially no worse off because of the non-payment. However, the courts have allowed traders to recover substantial damages for the loss of reputation and hurt feelings, because that loss would be within the contemplation of the banker when a trader opened the account.[22] Such losses were regarded by the courts as too remote[23] in other cases. For this reason, many private customers were unable to establish that they were entitled to substantial damages, because they had to prove special circumstances of which the banker was aware when the contract was made and this would usually be difficult. The distinction between traders and others is now seen to be arbitrary—is a solicitor a "trader", for example?—and it has been held by the Court of Appeal[24] that it is not justifiable: there is no good reason why traders' reputations should automatically be more vulnerable than other peoples'. It seems that claimants will in future be entitled to compensation, both for any actual financial loss and for injury to credit and reputation.

(2) Defamation

6–015 Defamation[25] provides a tort remedy by which a person can protect his or her reputation from attack.[26] It requires that an untrue statement which would lower the plaintiff in the estimation of right thinking persons[27] has been "published" to a third party. Even returning a cheque unpaid to a third party may amount to defamation,[28] but in fact bankers usually write a note on the cheque giving the reason for dishonour, and these words (unless they are *justified* because they are true) may amount to defamation.

Banks naturally try to be cautious in what they write on dishonoured cheques and avoid defamatory phrases but it can be difficult. The words "Not sufficient" or "Insufficient funds" are probably defamatory if they are untrue, and even "Present again" or "Refer to drawer", which look innocent enough, may be defamatory because they may carry an innuendo—an implication going beyond their ordinary meaning—and may be understood by reasonable people as meaning "insufficient funds".[29]

---

[22] *Evans v. London and Provincial Bank, The Times*, March 1, 1917; *Cox v. Cox & Co, The Times*, March 18, 1921; *Gibbons v. Westminster Bank Ltd* [1939] 2 K.B. 882; *Rae v. Yorkshire Bank plc* [1988] B.T.L.C. 35, (domestic customers); *Wilson v. United Counties Bank Ltd* [1920] A.C. 102; *Rolin v. Steward* (1854) 14 C.B. 595 (traders).

[23] On the principles of *Hadley v. Baxendale* (1854) 9 Ex. 354.

[24] *Kpohraror v. Woolwich Building Society* [1996] Bank. L.R. 182; see Enonchong (1997) 60 M.L.R. 412; Loebl [1996] NLJ 25.

[25] Libel, where the defamation is written. See also Chap. 5, bankers' references.

[26] Stanton, *The Modern Law of Tort*, p. 435.

[27] *Sim v. Stretch* [1936] 2 All E.R. 1237, *per* Lord Atkin.

[28] It might not be enough: see Chorley, *Law of Banking*, p. 112.

[29] Some dicta suggest otherwise: see *Flach v. London and South Western Bank Ltd* (1915) 31 T.L.R. 334; *Plunkett v. Barclays Bank Ltd* [1936] 2 K.B. 107. *Sim v. Stretch* [1936] 2 All E.R.

If a cheque is to be dishonoured, the following practical steps may be taken[30]: (a) ensuring that all cheques have been signed by the customer, not by someone with a similar name, and by error debited to the customer's account; (b) ensuring that no postdated cheques have been paid early by error; (c) ensuring that regular credits have not been debited in error; (d) ensuring that the cheque was not drawn with a cheque card; and (e) if it is decided to dishonour the cheque, the least defamatory words possible should be used: if appropriate, "Words and figures disagree", or "Unconfirmed stop received" may be used; otherwise, "Refer to Drawer", which may be defamatory if unjustified, must be used. If a mistake is made, damages will be reduced if there is a prompt and effusive apology to the customer and, more importantly, if the payee or his banker can be contacted, and the mistake explained.[31] **6–016**

Damages. The damages in defamation are either *special* losses flowing directly from the defamatory statement—if, for example, the customer loses a contract with the payee; or are *general*—an amount to compensate the customer for loss to his or her reputation. The amount of damages is a question for the jury (defamation is still often tried by jury), but they must be reasonable in comparison with personal injury awards.[32] **6–017**

Conditions for Payment

It is an implied term of the contract that the bank will repay[33] when its customer's instruction is received at the branch where the account is kept provided there are sufficient funds, there has been no countermand and there is no legal prohibition on payment. **6–018**

1237: it is a question of fact for the jury in every case. Other decisions are: *Jayson v. Midland Bank Ltd* [1968] 1 Lloyd's Rep. 409 (jury found that the words "Refer to Drawer" were defamatory, if unjustified): *Szek v. Lloyds Bank Ltd, The Times*, January 15, 1908 (jury gave no tort damages for "Refer to Drawer"); *Cox v. Cox & Co, The Times*, March 18, 1921 (no damages for "N/S"—meaning "not sufficient"); *Davidson v. Barclays Bank Ltd* [1940] 1 All E.R. 316 ("not sufficient" held to be capable of being defamatory); *Baker v. Australia and New Zealand Bank Ltd* [1958] N.Z.L.R. 907 ("present again" defamatory); *Millward v. Lloyds Bank Ltd*, 1920, unreported ("R/A"—return to acceptor of bill of exchange (a trader)—defamatory); *Frost v. London Joint Stock Bank Ltd* (1906) 22 T.L.R. 760 (slip attached to unpaid cheque saying "Reason assigned" with handwritten words "not stated", not defamatory unless ordinary persons would so understand it. See Paget (11th ed.), pp. 338–339.

[30] See Milnes Holden, *The Law and Practice of Banking*, Vol. 1, pp. 2–152.

[31] Banks now undertake that when they need to tell the customer that one of his or her cheques or other items has been returned unpaid, they will do this either by letter or by other private and confidential means, Banking Code (1999), para. 3.8.

[32] *John v. MGN* [1996] 2 All E.R. 35.

[33] The customer is not bound to accept other than legal tender: Mann, *Legal Aspects of Money* (4th ed.) p. 72, and has a right to have payment in cash, *Libyan Arab Foreign Bank v. Bankers Trust Co* [1988] 1 Lloyd's Rep. 259: even if it means transporting millions of dollars in cash across the Atlantic.

(1) Branch and time

6–019 Unlike other creditors, who may demand payment wherever they find the debtor, bank customers may in strict law only make demand of the bank at the branch where their accounts are kept,[34] despite the fact that banks are corporate personalities which usually have many branches. The strict law has been overtaken on this point, however, by modern life and technology. Nowadays customers regularly demand payment from cash machines at other branches, and from branches of other banks. They also use telephone banking facilities of banks which may have no branches at all.[35] Indeed even the clearing banks are shutting down many of their branches to reduce costs and to compete effectively with internet banking.[35a]

6–020 If the customer keeps accounts at different branches, and has cheque books for the separate accounts, he or she may select which of the branches is to pay. In *Burnett v. Westminster Bank Ltd*,[36] the bank informed its customers that cheques could only be used for the account for which they had been prepared (because it had introduced some cheque books that were designed for use at branches which had become computerised). The instruction was not difficult to see, but the plaintiff nevertheless altered the direction on a cheque drawn on one of his accounts so that it was addressed to the branch where he held another account. After giving his creditor the cheque, he countermanded the payment (at the branch to which he had addressed the cheque). The *other* branch, however, to which the cheque had originally been addressed, ignored the countermand and mistakenly paid the cheque. The court held that the express term by which the bank had attempted to vary the contract did not bind the customer. But even if the term had been binding, the customer might have been successful, because the cheque was probably not a good mandate: his alteration of the address of the branch on the cheque meant that his instruction had not been addressed to the branch which had paid the cheque.[37]

6–021 A customer who has adequate funds in an account at one branch cannot require a demand to be honoured at another branch where his or her account has insufficient funds. This would in effect be to *combine* the accounts, and although the bank is permitted to combine accounts, the customer is not.[38]

---

[34] *Joachimson v. Swiss Bank Corpn* [1921] 3 K.B. 110; *Richardson v. Richardson* [1927] P. 228. See also *Arab Bank Ltd v. Barclays Bank (DCO)* [1954] A.C. 495.

[35] See Cranston, *Principles of Banking Law* (Oxford, 1997), p. 11.

[35a] On April 7, 2000 Barclays caused shock and outrage in rural communities by closing 171 branches.

[36] [1966] 1 Q.B. 742; [1965] 2 Lloyd's Rep. 218.

[37] Though the bank might have been able to counterclaim for damages for the customer's breach of contract.

[38] *Woodland v. Fear* (1857) 7 E. & B. 519; *Garnett v. McKewan* (1872) L.R. 8 Ex. 10. See Chap. 11.

The customer may demand payment only during banking hours, or within a reasonable time thereafter.[39] Countermands, similarly, are only effective if received during those times. Apart from some statutory bank holidays, the bank's opening hours may be set by express agreement or by custom implying a term into the contract. Where a bank is bound to open at a certain time it may unilaterally extend opening hours; thus some banks open on Saturdays,[40] though perhaps for limited purposes. This may become a term of the contract (it depends what is said) but in any case it can be changed by giving notice.

If opening hours are to be extended, it is important to take account of the fact that a paying bank may only be protected by statute (in appropriate situations)[41] if payment is made in the "ordinary course of business". Payment after advertised hours is not "ordinary", though it is possible that, if a bank has extended its hours by public advertisement, payment may be "ordinary" as far as that bank is concerned. Payment within a reasonable time of advertised closing hours may be ordinary, for people may still be in the building and business may be finishing.[42] **6–022**

(2) Form of the cheque

Written demand. An implied term of the contract is that the banker is only normally liable to repay the customer when a demand is made, and repayment will usually be made against the written order of the customer.[43] Traditionally, the demand has taken the form of a cheque, but cheques are now being displaced by alternative methods, such as the use of cards for electronic payments, which, promoted by the banks themselves, have become very well established in practice. **6–023**

Banks may prefer a written demand, but unless there is an express term (perhaps in the original mandate) which says otherwise, it seems that if customers demand repayment of their money they need not do so in writing.[44] However, it is obviously sensible to draw up the mandate in writing anyway: the bank must make sure of its customer's identity because the customer's account cannot be debited in respect of a transaction he or **6–024**

---

[39] *Baines v. National Provincial Bank Ltd* (1927) 96 L.J.K.B. 801: payment five minutes late was acceptable.

[40] The usual (traditional) working week is Monday until Friday (since 1969 not Saturdays).

[41] BOEA 1882, s. 60 and Cheques Act 1957, s. 1.

[42] *Baines v. National Provincial Bank Ltd* (1927) 96 L.J.K.B. 801.

[43] *Joachimson v. Swiss Bank Corpn* [1921] 3 K.B. 110. The "writing" need not be on a cheque form: *Roberts v. Marsh* [1915] 1 K.B. 42. Counsel claimed in *Burnett v. Westminster Bank* [1966] 1 Q.B. 742; [1965] 2 Lloyd's Rep. 218, that cheques written on hard-boiled eggs would be valid; and see A.P. Herbert, "The Egg of Exchange" ("was the cheque hard-boiled? No, milord, it was a fresh cheque.") *More Uncommon Law*; and "The Negotiable Cow", *Uncommon Law* (Methuen). Hedley, *Bills of Exchange and Bankers' Documentary Credits* notes that a bank was willing to honour a cheque written on a paving stone (*The Sunday Times*, February 16, 1975).

[44] At least for all the balance, *Joachimson* [1921] 3 K.B. 110, *per* Atkin L.J.

she has not authorised, and the signature is useful as verification of identity[45]; and in any case the bank is entitled to demand a written receipt.

6–025 **Unambiguous.** An agent who receives instructions which are reasonably capable of more than one meaning and acts bona fide on them, will not be liable for breach of duty if the action taken was contrary to the intentions of the principal.[46] The customer's demand must therefore be "in a form which is clear and free from ambiguity", leaving the banker with no "room for misgiving as to what he is called upon to do".[47]

6–026 The instrument does not need to be in the proper form of a cheque to be a good mandate. Thus, it may not be a cheque because it is not payable on demand[48] (for example, it may be postdated), and it may not even be a bill of exchange (it may be expressed as an authority to pay, for example, rather than as an unconditional order). And even if the instrument is an adequate mandate and therefore provides *authority* to pay, it does not necessarily follow that the bank is *required* to pay. In *Brooks & Co v. Blackburn Benefit Society,*[49] Lord Blackburn said that bankers are bound to pay "cheques properly drawn". In *Griffiths v. Dalton*[50] Macnaghten J. said that a bank was not bound to honour an undated cheque, apparently on the ground that such a bill might be overdue.[51] This may be correct, though the bank would presumably still be entitled to pay, as it is a valid mandate from the customer. But it is submitted that if the mandate is unambiguous, even if it is not a valid cheque, and exposes the bank to no unusual risks,[52] then it must pay, unless the terms of the contract stipulate otherwise.[53] If the bank is exposed to an *unusual* risk (an example might be: where a cheque or draft is negotiated abroad and on which appears a special indorsement in Arabic or other Oriental characters, conveying absolutely nothing to the drawee bank[54]) it is thought that the customer must have given the bank authority to act reasonably for its own protection.

---

[45] Unless the customer is known to the bank. Other forms of verification, like PINs, are increasingly common.

[46] *Ireland v. Livingston* (1872) L.R. 5 H.L. 395. But if the ambiguity is obvious, the agent should probably ask the principal if time permits, *European Asian Bank AG v. Punjab & Sind Bank (No. 2)* [1983] 1 W.L.R. 642 at 656, *per* Robert Goff L.J.

[47] And does not "require exceptional consideration and delay", *London Joint Stock Bank Ltd v. Macmillan and Arthur* [1918] A.C. 777 at 815, *per* Viscount Haldane.

[48] *Orbit Mining and Trading Co Ltd v. Westminster Bank Ltd* [1963] 1 Q.B. 794.

[49] (1884) 9 A.C. 857 at 864.

[50] [1940] 2 K.B. 264.

[51] s.36(3) of the BOEA 1882: if it appears to have been in circulation for an unreasonable length of time. This would affect the ability of the transferor to give perfect title to the transferee.

[52] *London Joint Stock Bank Ltd v. Macmillan and Arthur* [1918] A.C. 777.

[53] Without delay, *e.g.* the bank may not defer payment until it is satisfied that indorsements are genuine, if the bill is "complete and regular" on its face, *Vagliano Bros v. Bank of England* [1891] A.C. 107 (disapproving dicta in *Robarts v. Tucker* (1851) 16 Q.B. 560). ("A banker so very careful to avoid risk would soon have no risk to avoid," at 157, *per* Lord Macnaghten).

[54] See Paget, *Law of Banking* (11th ed.), p. 385, citing *Carlisle and Cumberland Banking Co v. Bragg* [1911] 1 K.B. 489; *Arab Bank Ltd v. Ross* [1952] 2 Q.B. 216.

Other examples of improperly drawn cheques which entitle a bank to refuse to pay are postdated cheques[55]; cheques on which words and figures disagree—in this case, the bank has a mandate to pay according to the words but is not obliged to do so[56]; some banks pay the lower sum of the two; and cheques crossed specially to more than one banker, where the bank has a mandate to pay provided the cheque is not a forgery, but may refuse to pay since it has no protection if it pays the wrong person.[57] 6–027

Postdated cheques. In the case of postdated cheques, the bank has no mandate to pay *before* the date, though it must pay *on* the date.[58] If the cheque is not paid (as it should not be) until its date, the fact that it is postdated does not affect the bank's mandate, although postdating causes inconvenience for banks, because of the risk that the cheque may be countermanded. If it is wrongly paid early, the bank has not observed its mandate, and must be careful not to take that debit into account when it is considering whether it should refuse to honour other cheques on the ground of insufficient funds (one of the checks a bank should make before dishonouring a cheque is to see whether any postdated instruments have wrongly been paid). For these reasons, banks may seek to persuade customers not to postdate cheques. 6–028

Stale cheques. Cheques are generally treated as stale if they are presented more than six months after their ostensible dates of issue (though the period may vary from bank to bank) and it is the custom of banks not to pay them. There is no statutory authority for the practice of not paying them,[59] though the provision that demand bills may become "overdue" after being in circulation for an unreasonable time, for example,[60] may help to explain, if not justify, it.[61] The custom may be so well known that it has become an implied term, which would justify the banks' disobeying their mandates, although it is difficult to establish definitely how long the usage has existed and what the period is, because of the differing practices of banks. If there is a custom, it might amount to this, that the bank may 6–029

55 *Orbit Mining* [1963] 1 Q.B. 794.

56 BOEA 1882, s. 9(2). *cf.* Jack Report, which approved the present "flexible" situation (Cm. 622 (1989), para. 7.49). If only figures are given, the practice is to refuse payment (Encyclopedia of Banking Law, D.21); if only words, the cheque should be paid.

57 BOEA 1882, ss. 79–80.

58 Although "complete and regular on its face", it may not be a valid cheque, since it is not payable on demand, *Hitchcock v. Edwards* (1889) 60 L.T. 636.

59 The limitation period for contract is six years (LA 1980, s. 5).

60 BOEA 1882, s. 36(3). If a bill is thereafter negotiated, subsequent holders take it subject to defects of title affecting their transferors. Few cheques will be negotiable since the Ch A 1992.

61 See *Griffiths v. Dalton* [1940] 2 K.B. 264. Jack considered that banks are at liberty to fix the period they choose, para. 7.51.

refuse to honour a cheque if it is not presented until an unreasonable time after its date.[62] The Jack Committee thought that a rule is required for the sake of certainty for the parties, and suggested that the Code of Practice should set out a minimum period of six months from the date of issue within which a bank should not return a cheque on the grounds that it is out of date. The present code merely states that banks will provide customers with information about out of date cheques.[63]

6–030 **Indorsement.** The fact that an indorsement is missing, or that it may be irregular or forged[64] hardly need concern a paying bank, which is now usually protected by statute.[65]

(3) Sufficient and available funds

6–031 **Sufficient funds.** The banker need honour a cheque only if there are "sufficient funds to meet it"[66] either in a credit balance or in an agreed overdraft at the date when the banker must make payment,[67] although in practice banks are often flexible about this. In a case where the funds were insufficient to pay a standing order on a particular date, it was held that the bank did not need to review the account daily in order to meet it when funds did become available.[68] The customer has no right to combine accounts for funds held at different branches.

If a cheque has been presented for which there are *some*, but not *sufficient*, funds in the account, the bank does not have any obligation to meet it to the extent of the funds that are available—in fact it would probably be in breach of mandate if it did make a part payment, because the mandate is for a specific sum.[69] However, if the payee is aware of the shortfall, and tenders enough to cover payment of the cheque, the bank may be justified in receiving it and (after a delay for clearing if the payment is made by cheque) paying on the customer's cheque.[70] If it does so, it must

[62] If the cheque is dishonoured, the words: "Out of date" or "Stale" on it would not be defamatory.

[63] Banking Code (1999), para. 2.1.

[64] Forged indorsements (unlike forged signatures) do not invalidate a cheque, but merely affect relations between parties.

[65] Discussed below, Chap. 14.

[66] *Joachimson v. Swiss Bank Corpn* [1921] 3 K.B. 110. See also *Whitaker v. Bank of England* (1835) 1 Cr.M. & R. 744.

[67] Giving a cheque which would have the effect of overdrawing the account is considered to be a request for an overdraft which the bank may accept or refuse.

[68] *Whitehead v. National Westminster Bank, The Times*, June 9, 1982.

[69] *Marzetti* (1830) 1 B. & Ad. 415 and Paget, *Law of Banking* (11th ed.), p. 330. Jack points out that such a practice would cause immense practical difficulties for both paying and collecting banks (para. 7.59).

[70] Questions on Banking Practice (10th ed.) No. 417.

be careful not to breach its obligation of confidence to its customer by disclosing information about his or her account to the payee without consent.[71]

If more than one cheque is presented, and it looks as if there are insufficient funds for all of them, they should be paid in the order of presentment; if the first cheque to be presented is too large, then the first for which there are sufficient funds should be paid.[72] This general rule must be observed with due regard to the customer's interests, however, and may be displaced, as it was where delays occurred as a result of a strike of bank-staff and a consequent backlog in processing.[73] If two or more cheques are presented simultaneously, any of them for which there are sufficient funds should be paid. If a choice has to be made between cheques, *smaller* ones should be paid first (because the dishonour of a smaller sum might have a greater effect on the customer's reputation).[74] Now that bank processing systems are computerised, the order in which cheques have been presented should be obvious, and this problem should disappear. **6–032**

The fact that the bank is aware that other cheques will shortly be presented and that there is insufficient for all of them is no reason for it to refuse to pay on a cheque,[75] though if the customer has paid in money to meet a particular cheque ("earmarked" the cheque) the bank may decline to honour another cheque if it has insufficient funds to meet them both, since it must pay the cheque earmarked by the customer[76]—in fact, since the customer has paid the money into the account for a *specific* purpose, the funds may be subject to a *Quistclose* trust.[77] If so, the bank must use those funds to honour the cheque in question; they would not be available for the bank's use by way of combination. Indeed, the bank must honour a cheque which the customer has earmarked by paying in funds previously even if it has mistakenly paid another cheque and left insufficient funds in the account. **6–033**

Available funds. The customer's funds must also be "available" when the cheque is presented, and if they are not the bank may refuse to honour the cheque. Alternatively, the bank may exercise its right of combination without notice (if appropriate), so that, if the funds are not available in the account the customer has chosen, the bank may debit another account[78] to **6–034**

---

[71] *Tournier v. National Provincial Bank Ltd* [1924] 1 K.B. 46; *Foster v. Bank of London* (1862) 3 F. & F. 214.

[72] *Sednaoni Zariffa Nakes & Co v. Anglo-Austrian Bank* [1909] 2 L.D.A.B. 208.

[73] *Dublin Port and Docks Board v. Bank of Ireland* [1976] I.R. 118.

[74] *Sednaoni Zariffa Nakes & Co v. Anglo-Austrian Bank* [1909] 2 L.D.A.B. 208.

[75] *Sednaoni Zariffa Nakes & Co v. Anglo-Austrian Bank* [1909] 2 L.D.A.B. 208.

[76] This is an example of the customer's right of appropriation, discussed below, Chap. 11.

[77] See below, Chap. 9.

[78] Some accounts (*e.g.* trust accounts) may not be so debited, and combination is not possible for all debts (*e.g.* contingent ones). There may also be a right of contractual set-off, and, in insolvency cases, s. 323 of the IA 1986 may be relevant. See below, Chaps 11 and 23.

pay a cheque if it chooses. Similarly, if the customer owes a debt at another branch, the bank may exercise its right of combination of the accounts and refuse to pay on an account which would otherwise be sufficiently in credit, because the *total* indebtedness of the bank to the customer is less than the amount of the cheque. Normally, no notice need be given to the customer of the bank's intention.

6–035 Money, even when it is paid in cash, does not become available at the moment it is paid in or credited to the account,[79] and the bank may refuse to honour cheques until it has had time to carry out the necessary book-keeping obligations.[80] The position regarding cheques is less clear. Cheques which have been paid in but not yet cleared are "uncleared effects" and their proceeds are probably not yet available,[81] so that even if they have been credited provisionally to the account,[82] the bank may decline to meet a cheque because there are insufficient funds in the account.[83] In *A L Underwood Ltd v. Bank of Liverpool*,[84] it was held that the bank is not prevented from dishonouring cheques on the ground of insufficient funds because the account has been provisionally credited with more funds that have not yet been cleared, though it might be different if the bank, intending to "credit cash", agrees to allow the customer to draw against uncleared effects or if some new consideration has been given. Similarly, if the bank has communicated to the customer the fact that the cheque has been credited to the account, it may be bound to pay, because this amounts to a representation which may give rise to an estoppel if the customer incurs expenditure or draws on the account in reliance on it.[85] A note on paying-in slips to the effect that the bank may refuse to pay against uncleared effects may help to confirm that the general rule from the *Underwood* case applies, even if there is evidence of an agreement to the contrary in a particular case.[86]

---

[79] *Capital and Counties Bank Ltd v. Gordon* [1903] A.C. 240 at 249; *Re Mills, Bawtree & Co, ex p. Stannard* (1893) 10 Morr. 193.

[80] *Marzetti v. Williams* (1830) 1 B. & Ad. 415: four hours was an unreasonably long time in 1830.

[81] In *Gordon v. Capital and Counties Bank Ltd* [1902] 1 K.B. 242, CA, the court thought that if the bank credited the account with uncleared effects the customer was entitled to draw upon it. In that case, though, the bank had "credited *as cash*" the effects in question, *i.e.* had allowed the customer to draw against the funds.

[82] Banks provisionally credit accounts with the amount of cheques paid in before they have been cleared; the entry can be reversed if the cheque is dishonoured. Banks should now provide customers with information as to when funds can be withdrawn after a cheque has been credited to the account (Banking Code (1999), para. 2.1)

[83] *contra*, Chorley, *Law of Banking*, p. 72.

[84] [1924] 1 K.B. 775. The question whether the bank had received for value also arose.

[85] *Holland v. Manchester and Liverpool District Banking Co Ltd* (1909) 25 T.L.R. 386; *Akrokerri (Atlantic) Mines Ltd v. Economic Bank* [1940] 2 K.B. 456; *Bevan v. National Bank Ltd* (1906) 23 T.L.R. 65.

[86] See *Westminster Bank Ltd v. Zang* [1966] A.C. 182.

(4) No countermand

The authority of a bank paying a cheque for its customer may, like the authority of any other agent,[87] be revoked by the principal. Such a revocation of authority by the customer is generally called a *countermand*,[88] or *stop*; it is the converse of the bank's duty to honour a valid demand or mandate, and it means that the bank's duty to pay on a cheque is terminated. The bank therefore must not pay if it knows of a countermand.[89] If the bank disobeys the countermand, it does not, strictly speaking, incur liability to the customer (unless it were then to dishonour other cheques because the funds were insufficient), but rather, it has no authority to debit the customer's account for the payment, since it has been made outside its mandate.[90] **6–036**

If the bank does pay wrongly on a countermand it succeeds to the customer's rights, if any,[91] against the payee, and it may have the possibility of recovering the money paid as money paid under mistake of fact from the payee.[92]

The countermand must be sent to the branch which the account is kept. If it is delivered to another branch it may be ignored by the bank.[93] Moreover, a countermand is only effective when the bank, through its servants, actually knows of it. In *Curtice v. London City and Midland Bank Ltd*[94] the stop notice (in a telegram) was put into the bank's mailbox, but was not picked up with the rest of the mail, and not read by the bank's staff until the stopped cheque had been paid. The plaintiff drew a cheque for the whole of what he thought was the balance in his account—assuming that the debit had not been made—and when the bank dishonoured it, he sued in debt. The bank had been negligent in not giving prompt attention to its customer's communications; if it had been careful it would have had actual notice of the stop. The question was therefore whether the bank had had *constructive* notice and was liable because of its negligence. The court held that there was no such thing as a constructive countermand in a commercial transaction of this kind[95] and gave judgment for the bank. It added that the **6–037**

---

87 Except in unusual cases, *e.g.* for an irrevocable power given under the Powers of Attorney Act 1971 and in some cases under the Enduring Powers of Attorney Act 1985.

88 BOEA 1882, s. 75. *Tank Express A/S v. Compagnie Financiere Belge* [1949] A.C. 76 at 79, *per* Lord Wright: payment by cheque is only conditional until the cheque has been cleared, and may be revoked.

89 BOEA 1882, s. 75, or has notice of the customer's death or incapacity, (see below, para. 6–052).

90 *Twibell v. London Suburban Bank* [1869] W.N. 127; *Reade v. Royal Bank of Ireland* [1922] 2 I.R. 22.

91 Like other authorised agents, by subrogation to the rights of its principal. See below, Chap. 16.

92 *Barclays Bank v. WJ Simms, Son & Cooke (Southern) Ltd* [1980] A.C. 677. See below, Chap. 10.

93 *London Provincial and South Western Bank Ltd v. Buszard* (1918) 35 T.L.R 142. Contrast *Burnett v. Westminster Bank Ltd* [1966] 1 Q.B. 742, discussed above, para. 3–025.

94 [1908] 1 K.B. 293.

95 *ibid.*, at 298, *per* Cozens-Hardy M.R.

bank might be liable in damages, but if so, that the measure of damages would not necessarily be the same as that in debt.

6–038 The bank must make sure that the countermand is genuine. It is at risk if it obeys an unconfirmed notice which may not have come from the customer. In the *Curtice* case, the court held that the bank was not bound to obey an unauthenticated telegram; it would have been reasonable and acting in the ordinary course of business if it had postponed paying the cheque until further inquiry could be made.[96] The same presumably applies to telephone countermands. In such cases, therefore, the bank may delay and may mark cheques "Unconfirmed stop received", which is true and should not be defamatory if it turns out that the stop is unauthorised. Generally banks will—and they certainly should—insist upon the customer's signed stop by following mail.

6–039 **Countermand must not be ambiguous.** "If a master chooses to give an order to his servant that bears two meanings, he cannot find fault with his servant for having taken the meaning which it was not in fact intended to bear".[97] Thus, in *Westminster Bank Ltd v. Hilton*,[98] the plaintiff wired a stop order in respect of a post-dated cheque, giving the wrong cheque number, with the name of the payee and the amount of the cheque to be stopped. The cheque with the number he gave had already been paid. When the payee presented the cheque which should have been stopped, the bank assumed from the difference in number and from the date on the cheque (which was post-dated) that it was a replacement cheque, and paid it. The customer sued for negligence. The House of Lords held that the bank had not been negligent, and was not liable. The duty of a bank to pay may conflict with the duty to obey a countermand, and in view of this, it was for the customer to show that the stop had reached the bank in time, and that the stop referred unequivocally to a cheque then in existence, and signed and issued by the customer before the notice to stop.[99] If a cheque was dated after the date of the countermand, for example, the bank might assume that the notice did not apply to it, unless the contrary was clearly brought home to it.

6–040 **Completion of payment.** Obviously, the countermand must be given to the bank before payment of the cheque, and presumably within a reasonable time before presentation for payment, so that the staff in the branch can be notified of the stop. Generally, however, the law does not define when payment has been completed.[1] Difficult questions may arise as to when

[96] [1908] 1 K.B. 293 at 298.

[97] *Curtice v. London City and Midland Bank Ltd* [1908] 1 K.B. 293 at 299, *per* Fletcher Moulton L.J.

[98] (1926) 43 T.L.R. 124.

[99] (1926) 43 T.L.R. 124 at 129–130, *per* Lord Shaw.

[1] Except in the case of payment of cash over the counter on an uncrossed cheque, or one specially presented.

payments using different systems of payment become irrevocable, and modern developments[2] have highlighted and intensified the problems. As far as payment by cheque is concerned, the clearing system allows a certain time during which the payment can be stopped, but the question whether a countermand is still practicable in any particular case depends on banking practice, and whether, in the circumstances of a particular bank's administrative and technical procedures and the procedures of the clearing system, an irrevocable process has been put in hand whereby the payee is allowed to draw upon a credit, or a collecting bank is notified of the credit.[3] It has been suggested that the rules for countermand should be made uniform across the different payment systems, so that the same principle would apply to electronic payments and to cheques. The Jack Committee was not persuaded of the value of such uniformity,[4] and thought that the best rule is simply what is reasonable in the circumstances, which would of course vary according to the different payment systems. They saw no reason why customers should not have the opportunity to have second thoughts, subject to considerations of efficiency, and no reason why banks should not establish practice with regard to countermand by contract but in the light of a standard of best practice allowing customers a period of time for countermand wherever possible, only eliminating it where that is necessary for the efficient working of the system.[5] The Banking Code simply states that banks will provide customers with information about stopping a cheque or other types of payment.[6]

When a cheque guarantee card is used. If the customer has made a payment by cheque using a cheque guarantee card, he or she has in effect undertaken *not* to countermand, because the use of the card constitutes a collateral contract between the bank and the payee.[7] In this case, the bank is bound from the moment the cheque is drawn and delivered to the payee, who takes it in reliance on the card, and the customer is also bound from **6–041**

[2] *e.g.* the proliferation of new payment systems, the speeding up of payment processes and the growing internationalisation of banking, see Jack Report, Cm. 622 (1989), paras 12.01 *et seq.* The White Paper (para. 7.15) points out that the time of completion of payment is important in relation to death and insolvency of customers, court orders, system error and fraud as well as countermand (and bank failure).

[3] In *Momm v. Barclays Bank International Ltd* [1977] 1 Q.B. 790 it was held that the transaction was completed when the defendants accepted instructions to credit the account and computer processes were set in motion, even though the plaintiffs had not been notified of the transfer. It had to be clearly ascertainable by the end of a day whether a payment due to be made on that day had been made or not, *cf. Sutherland v. The Royal Bank of Scotland* [1997] 6 Bank L.R. 132. See also Goode, *Payment Obligations in Commercial and Financial Transactions* for general discussion and Chap. 12 below.

[4] See also Ellinger [1986] L.M.C.L.Q. 178, s. 7; Vroegop [1990] L.M.C.L.Q. 64.

[5] Jack Report, Cm. 622 (1989), Rec. 12(1).

[6] Banking Code (1999), para. 2.1.

[7] It might therefore make the cheque payment unconditional, though Millett J., in *Re Charge Card Services Ltd* [1986] 3 All E.R. 289 at 301, said that the presumption that the cheque was conditional payment was not displaced by the use of a card.

that moment to indemnify the bank. The customer would therefore have no right to order the bank not to pay, because the bank is not merely carrying out its mandate, but also performing its own independent obligation to the payee. Alternatively, the countermand may be (on general agency principles) an effective withdrawal of the bank's authority. In this case the customer may be liable to the bank for damages for breach of the cheque card contract, the amount of the damages being equal to the bank's loss if it had no mandate to debit the account. Clearly the bank's reputation and the whole convenient system of cheque cards would be in jeopardy if banks did obey countermands of such cheques.

6–042 **Who informs the bank?** Only the drawer of the cheque has the power to countermand it. Where several persons have a joint account or joint and several liability, and their mandate to the bank allows some or all to draw cheques (as may be the case in a partnership, or for trustees) and a cheque is drawn by one or more, any of the other parties to the account may countermand the cheque.[8] The signatures of all the signatories are necessary, however, to *remove* the stop.

Finally, although it is only the drawer who has power to countermand, it is thought that if the payee or holder of the cheque informs the bank that it has been lost or stolen, the bank should refuse payment in the meantime, and seek the drawer's instructions, unless it has good reason not to do so. Otherwise it runs the risk of losing its statutory protection if it pays the wrong person, because payment without inquiry in these circumstances may not be in the ordinary course of business or may be negligent.[9]

(5) Operation of law

6–043 There are a number of situations where the bank is not permitted to obey the customer's mandate because it is forbidden to do so by law.

6–044 **(a) Garnishee orders.** A garnishee order is a form of execution of court judgments. A garnishee order *nisi* (or "freezing" order) requires the bank to retain the funds of a customer until the court otherwise orders. If the order is later made absolute at a hearing, the bank will be ordered to pay another person. The bank usually informs the customer of the order, and may open a new account, so that money can continue to be paid in and out for the customer; since the debt must have accrued at the date of the order, the new account is not affected by it.[10]

There may be some points which the bank should bring to the attention of the court making the order. If the account is overdrawn, for example, or

[8] *Gaunt v. Taylor* (1843) 2 Hare 413 (partners).
[9] BOEA 1882, ss. 60 or 80, or Cheques Act 1957, s. 1.
[10] *Heppenstall v. Jackson* [1939] 1 K.B. 585.

if the bank has a right to set-off a debt due to itself,[11] or the account is a trust account (which may not be garnished) or a joint account (which may only be garnished if the debt is a joint debt)[12] the bank should inform the court in an affidavit prepared for the court hearing.

The effect of the order may be that the bank need not pay the customer's cheques from the garnished account on the ground of insufficiency of funds, but this depends on the nature of the order; it can be limited to a certain amount, for example, in which case there may be sufficient funds for other payments. Even if the funds would be insufficient, the bank may obey the mandate if it chooses, but it runs the risk that, if the order is made absolute, the bank will be required to pay the funds to the creditor, and the customer may be unable to meet the debit. **6–045**

(b) Sequestration orders.[13] Have a similar effect, in so far as the bank is obliged to follow the orders of the sequestrator, not the customer. **6–046**

(c) Mareva (freezing) injunctions. The High Court has power to grant injunctions where it appears to the court just and convenient to do so. Mareva[14] injunctions have been developed by the court during the last twenty years in order to prevent defendants making themselves "judgment proof" by disposing of their assets before judgment. These were used initially to stop disposal of assets outside the jurisdiction, and more recently extended to cases where assets might be disposed of within the jurisdiction. They can now be issued pending trial or after judgment, and are normally granted *ex parte* because of the urgency of the situation. The plaintiff has to show a good arguable case[15] and that there is a real danger that the defendant will dispose of assets. **6–047**

As far as banks are concerned, Marevas resemble garnishee orders because they have the effect of stopping dealings with the account, but the order usually extends to all the defendant's assets, and the bank cannot open a new account for the customer. The injunction takes effect as regards the defendant as soon as it is pronounced, but the bank need act only when it has notice of it, and should be told the details of the account and what it is required to do in terms which are as precise as is practicable. It must then do what it reasonably can to preserve the assets of the defendant and is in contempt of court if it disobeys. The court will probably take the precaution

[11] *Tapp v. Jones* (1875) L.R. 10 Q.B. 591.

[12] *Miller v. Mynn* (1859) 1 El. & El. 1075. Matthews [1984] L.M.C.L.Q. 651, discusses freezing of joint accounts by garnishee orders and Marevas.

[13] See also above, Chap. 5.

[14] Supreme Court Act 1981, s. 37 (and see Practice Direction 25). They are named after an early case in which one was issued (1975). See also Atiyah, *Pragmatism and Theory in English Law*, pp. 55 *et seq.*; Capper (1996) 15 *Civil Justice Quarterly*, 211, and Devonshire (1999) 62 M.L.R. 539. See further above, Chap. 5, for discussion of world wide Marevas.

[15] See *e.g. Polly Peck International plc v. Nadir (No. 2)* [1992] 4 All E.R. 782: where a Mareva was sought against a bank.

of requiring the plaintiff to give undertakings to indemnify the bank for its expenses, and the bank may usually exercise any right of set-off.[16]

6–048 **(d) Restraint orders.** Restraint orders under the money laundering legislation and the Proceeds of Crime Act 1995 may also make it impossible for a bank to obey its mandate.[17]

Termination of Mandate

6–049 The basic contractual rules as to termination of contracts apply. The relationship may be terminated by the customer, by the banker, by mutual agreement, or by operation of law.

(1) By the customer

6–050 The customer may terminate the relationship at any time, although the mere withdrawal of a balance will not have this effect; the intention must be made clear. Of course, the customer remains liable for any overdraft. The balance of the account is payable to the customer (on the appropriate period of notice, in the case of deposit accounts) by any method with which the bank is bound to comply,[18] and the obligation of confidentiality on the banker probably continues.[19]

6–051 **Insolvency of customer.** If the customer becomes insolvent, and goes into liquidation or becomes bankrupt, the bank's right to pay is affected. This is considered elsewhere.[20] The bank is entitled to debit the customer's account in respect of necessary expenses and the maintenance of the household.[21]

6–052 **Insanity or death of customer.** The bank's authority is terminated if it has notice of a customer's mental disorder, where it is serious enough to prevent the customer understanding the transaction, which may of course be difficult to determine.[22]

As with a countermand, notice of a customer's death revokes the bank's duty and authority to pay.[23] The notice must be actual, and not constructive, and must be more than a mere rumour, but a report from a reliable source (such as a newspaper, or relatives) should be acted upon. Banks may ask for sight of a copy of the death certificate, for noting in their records.

---

[16] *The Theotokos* [1983] 2 All E.R. 65. Guidelines for banks were given in *Z Ltd v. A* [1982] Q.B. 558, CA.
[17] See above, Chap. 5.
[18] *Libyan Arab Bank v. Bankers' Trust* [1989] Q.B. 728.
[19] *Tournier v. National Provincial Bank Ltd* [1924] 1 K.B. 46.
[20] See below, Chap. 24.
[21] *Re Beavan, Davies, Banks & Co v. Beavan* [1912] 1 Ch. 196.
[22] Admission into hospital is not enough in itself to confirm this.
[23] BOEA 1882, s. 75.

The personal representative is entitled to payment of the money in the deceased's account on production of the probate or the letters of administration.

The effect of death on joint accounts is considered elsewhere.[24]

(2) By the bank

The bank may terminate the relationship, but only on reasonable notice, so that the customer has time to make alternative banking arrangements and protect his or her credit.[25] The period of notice depends on the circumstances, but banks now undertake in the Banking Code that they will not close customers' accounts without giving them at least 30 days notice, unless there are exceptional circumstances.[26] **6–053**

[24] See below, para. 8–018.
[25] *Prosperity v. Lloyds Bank Ltd* (1923) 39 T.L.R. 372.
[26] Banking Code (1999), para. 2.11.

Chapter 7

Paying Bank and Customer: Liability for Unauthorised Debits

Incorrect payments may arise by mistake—for example, where the bank has paid although the customer's account is overdrawn. In such a case, the bank has a mandate and is entitled to debit the customer's account. Other sorts of mistake or fraud, usually by a third party, may happen in several different ways and involve the bank paying without the customer's mandate, so that it is not entitled to debit the customer's account, unless it has a defence at common law, by the equitable defence in *Liggett's Case*, or by statute. **7–001**

The bank may also incur liability to other parties. For example, it may pay a person who is not the true payee of the cheque; this may happen if the cheque has been validly drawn but a necessary indorsement has been forged or is missing or irregular. A bank which pays out on a cheque drawn in favour of A to a person B, who is not entitled to be paid, may be liable to its customer for breach of the mandate to pay A, and liable also as against the true owner of the cheque (A), who may sue in the tort of conversion.[1] The bank, however, has certain statutory protections, and where one of these is applicable it is protected both from its customer's claim for breach of mandate (the bank being entitled to debit the customer's account), and from the claim of the true owner of the cheque.

It is important to remember the dual nature of a cheque as a bill of exchange and as mandate: whether the cheque is a good mandate which gives the bank authority to make a debit is a different question from whether it amounts to a valid cheque within the definition of the BOEA 1882,[2] although in practice the two questions overlap. **7–002**

After a description of the situations in which a bank might make a mistaken payment, this section will continue with a discussion of the defences available to the bank as against its customer and others.

Types of Incorrect Payment

There are several typical ways in which mistaken payment may be made. The bank may have paid on a cheque which did not have the signatures stipulated in the mandate lodged with the bank on a joint or company **7–003**

---

[1] Since payment by cheque is merely conditional payment, A may still claim against the customer on the original debt.

[2] Chap. 14.

account, for example, or overlooked a countermand by the customer and mistakenly honoured a cheque. If the instruction or the countermand was ambiguous and the bank has failed to obey it, the bank may be protected at common law.

Another typical case is where there has been *forgery* of the drawer's signature or of some other part of the instrument (maybe of an indorsement); or some material and unauthorised *alteration* of the cheque. These problems require a little more discussion.

(1) Forgery or lack of authority: drawer's or indorser's signature

7–004 If the signature of the *drawer* has been forged, the cheque is not a mandate, because the customer has not authorised the payment.[3] Prima facie, therefore, the bank is not entitled to debit the account. There is no statutory protection in respect of the forgery of the drawer's signature but common law defences are open to the bank, and are described below.

7–005 If the signature is *unauthorised*[4] the bank has no mandate to pay, and again there is no statutory protection for the bank. As a general rule, the principal is bound by the acts of the agent which are within the agent's actual, or apparent or ostensible authority. Actual authority is expressly conferred by the principal, or is implied from the conduct of the parties or the circumstances of the case; apparent or ostensible authority is the authority the agent appears to others to have. If the person who signs is known to be an agent, purports to sign as agent and the bank's mandate permits it to honour his or her signature, then there is authority and the drawer is liable, but if an agent exceeds the authority given, the drawer is not liable. If the bank is on inquiry, because the circumstances are suspicious, and it has failed to realise that the agent has exceeded his or her authority, there will be no ostensible authority. (The same principles apply to a collecting banker: if sued in conversion by the true owner, authority of an agent is a defence to the bank, but again, negligence would remove the ostensible authority.[5])

If an *indorsement* has been forged (this will be rare now, since most cheques have become non-transferable[6]) the mandate is vitiated. If a bill is

---

[3] It is also not a valid cheque. By s. 24 of the BOEA 1882, a forged or unauthorised signature is "wholly inoperative". A banker is not "bound" to know a customer's signature but a "court would be astute to debar a banker from recovering money he had paid to an innocent person on a forgery of his own customer's signature" (*Questions in Banking Practice*, (11th ed.) No. 25). And see *National Westminster Bank Ltd v. Barclays Bank International* [1975] Q.B. 654 at 678.

[4] *e.g.* a company cheque requiring two directors' signatures which has only one.

[5] For an example see *Lloyds Bank v. Chartered Bank of India, Australia and China* (1928) 44 T.L.R. 534; [1929] 1 K.B. 40. See *e.g.*, *Australia and New Zealand Bank Ltd v. Ateliers de Construction Electriques de Charleroi* [1967] 1 A.C. 86; [1966] 2 W.L.R. 1216; *Midland Bank Ltd v. Reckitt and Others* [1933] A.C. 1; *Reckitt v. Barnett, Pembroke and Slater Ltd* [1929] A.C. 176.

[6] The Ch A 1992 made cheques marked "account payee only" (as most are) non-transferable.

payable to a named payee or order, the bank has no mandate to pay anyone else.[7] In this case, or where the indorser's signature is unauthorised, however, the bank may have statutory protection. These protections are discussed below.

(2) Completion or alteration of cheque without authority

Completion of an *inchoate instrument*—where a cheque is lacking in some material particular, or where it is merely a blank piece of paper with a signature—may cause problems for the paying bank. If an inchoate bill is delivered to a person in order that it may be converted into a bill, it will be treated as a prima facie authority for the possessor to fill it up as a complete bill for any amount, but only if this is done within a reasonable time and it is filled up "strictly in accordance with the authority given".[8] A form of "statutory estoppel" operates to protect a holder in due course to whom the instrument is negotiated after completion, but this will not protect the paying bank, which is unlikely to be either a holder in due course or paying to one, because the payee of a cheque is not a holder in due course.[9] **7–006**

Similarly, if a cheque has been *materially altered* without the assent of the customer[10]—if, for example, the amount of the cheque has been raised—the bank will probably have no mandate to pay. Material alterations include: alteration of the sum payable, the date, the time or place of payment, and any crossing. There is a statutory protection[11] for holders in due course where a bill has been altered and the alteration is not apparent, but again this special protection will not usually apply to the paying banker. A banker who pays the wrong amount is certainly liable to the customer for any excess over the amount named in the original mandate. There is a question, however, whether a banker has any mandate to pay at all to someone who is not a holder in due course when the drawer has not consented to the material alteration. Under the BOEA 1882,[12] the bill is "avoided", which may mean that the cheque is "avoided as a bill of **7–007**

---

[7] This was clearly established in *Robarts v. Tucker* (1851) 16 QB 560; see also *Bank of England v. Vagliano Bros* [1891] A.C. 107. And see the BOEA 1882, s. 24. An unauthorised signature, unlike a forgery, may be ratified, BOEA 1882, s. 24, see below, para. 13–036.

[8] BOEA 1882, s. 20.

[9] BOEA 1882, s. 29 requires the bill to be "negotiated to" a holder in due course, and this does not happen in the case of the original payee, *RE Jones Ltd v. Waring and Gillow Ltd* [1926] A.C. 670.

[10] BOEA 1882, s. 64. See *Flanagan v. National Bank Ltd* (1938) 72 I.L.T. 63 (not a material alteration, *Gairdner v. Walsh* (1855) 5 E. & B. 83, followed); *Re Smith, ex p. Yates* (1857) 2 De G. & J. 191.

[11] BOEA 1882, s. 64: if the alteration is not apparent, the holder in due course may enforce payment of the bill according to its "original tenor". If, *e.g.*, the amount was altered by someone other than the drawer, the holder in due course may sue the drawer for the original amount, and could sue anyone who made the alteration or any subsequent indorser for the full (changed) amount.

[12] BOEA 1882, s. 64.

exchange" but not as a mandate, or it may mean that it is not a valid mandate either. The cases generally suggest the latter, on the ground that the effect of the instrument is wholly changed by any material alteration.[13] If this is the case, the bank, following a material alteration to which the customer has not assented, has no mandate to pay any sum at all, other than to a holder in due course.

If the bank has none of the defences discussed below, it may try to recover the money from the payee, as paid by a *mistake* (if the wrongful payment does not discharge the instrument).[14]

Defences Available to the Paying Bank

7–008 In claims between bank and customer for wrongful payment, some common law defences are available to the paying bank as well as the protections given by statute. There is also an equitable defence (under *Liggett's Case*) which allows the bank to debit the customer's account in some situations, despite incorrect payment.

Statutory Defences

7–009 The common law defences open to the paying bank are described below. The bank is also given statutory protection against action by its customer or a third party. This protection takes the form of a complex patchwork of provisions—sections 60 and 80 of the BOEA 1882, and section 1 of the Ch A 1957. These are likely to come into play when an indorsement on the cheque has been forged or is missing, and they are considered in the context of cheques in Chapter 14.

Ambiguous Mandate or Countermand

7–010 If the principal's authority is ambiguous and the agent reasonably interprets it differently from the principal, the principal cannot deny the agent's authority.[15–16] The customer's instructions must be clear; if they are ambiguous, the bank has a defence. It may be reasonable, however, for the agent to seek clarification if there is an obvious ambiguity or one which a reasonable man would notice, and if time and circumstances allow for the principal to be contacted.[17]

Ratification

7–011 If an agent of the customer, for example a director of a company, has exceeded his or her authority or has no authority but purports to act on behalf of the principal (the company), in drawing a cheque,[18] and the bank

[13] See *e.g. Master v. Miller* (1791) 4 T.R. 367; *Knill v. Williams* (1809) 10 East. 431; *Hall v. Fuller* (1826) 5 B. & C. 750 at 757; *Simmons v. Taylor* (1857) 2 C.B.N.S. 528 at 539, 541, affd (1858) 4 C.B.N.S. 462; *Suffell v. Bank of England* (1882) 9 Q.B.D. 555. *cf. Henfree v. Bromley* (1805) 6 East. 309, and *Imperial Bank of Canada v. Bank of Hamilton* [1903] A.C. 49, PC.

[14] See below, Chap. 10.

[15–16] *Ireland v. Livingstone* (1872) L.R. 5 H.L. 395. See above, para. 6–036.

[17] *European Asian Bank AG v. Punjab & Sind Bank* [1983] 3 All E.R. 508 at 517–518.

[18] *e.g. London Intercontinental Trust Ltd v. Barclays Bank Ltd* [1980] 1 Lloyd's Rep. 241.

has been negligent in failing to realise that the act was unauthorised, it has no authority to debit the customer's account. However, an unauthorised signature may be ratified.[19] Ratification (or adoption) operates retroactively, so that authority is conferred subsequently on the agent, and dates back to the date when he or she made the contract.

The ratification may be express or implied from the circumstances,[20] and may take the form of a simple statement. Unequivocal behaviour indicating an intention to ratify will suffice, provided that the principal, through the agent or otherwise, has received valuable consideration.[21] If the bank, suspecting an irregularity, asks the customer to confirm that all is well, and the customer does so and the bank then pays, this confirmation may be regarded as a ratification or as a mandate to pay—or one may say that an estoppel will arise in relation to the lack of authority.[22] In cases where ratification is impossible, for example where no principal has been disclosed (perhaps also in the case of forgery), estoppel may be relied upon as an alternative, provided that reliance by the bank and detriment can be shown in addition to the confirmation.[23]

The proviso to section 24 of the BOEA 1882 states: "nothing in this section shall affect the ratification of an unauthorised signature not amounting to forgery". This obviously implies that unauthorised signatures, unlike forgeries, can be ratified[24]; there is therefore a distinction between a forgery and an unauthorised signature. It is likely that the proviso reflects the state of the criminal law at the time of the Bills of Exchange Act which distinguished between forgery and signing without authority, and which was changed by the 1913 Forgery Act.[25] The different treatment of the two in the BOEA 1882 (for banking purposes at any rate) might be explained because of the idea of dishonesty; public policy would frown on the **7–012**

[19] BOEA 1882, s. 24. An unauthorised signature on a cheque might be a per pro signature that was outside the limits of the agent's power, or a cheque on a joint account requiring two signatures where only one has been given, *e.g. London Intercontinental Trust v. Barclays Bank Ltd* [1980] 1 Lloyd's Rep. 241; *Lloyds Bank Ltd v. Chartered Bank of India, Australia and China* (1928) 44 T.L.R. 534; [1929] 1 K.B. 40.

[20] *The Bonita, The Charlotte* (1861) Lush. 252. A void contract cannot be ratified, *Ashbury Railway Carriage Company Ltd v. Riche* (1875) L.R. 7 H.L. 653.

[21] It was said in *Greenwood v. Martin's Bank Ltd* [1933] A.C. 51 at 57, *per* Lord Tomlin: "adoption, as understood in English law, requires valuable consideration." There is then no need to prove reliance by the bank or detriment. *e.g. London Intercontinental Trust Ltd v. Barclays Bank Ltd* [1980] 1 Lloyd's Rep. 241 (two directors should have signed, but only one did. The company ratified this.)

[22] See *Vagliano Bros v. Bank of England* [1891] A.C. 107 at 114, 123.

[23] For an example, see *Spiro v. Lintern* [1973] 3 All E.R. 319.

[24] *M'Kenzie v. British Linen Co.* (1881) 6 App. Cas. 82 at 99, *per* Lord Blackburn. Chalmers, the draftsman of the Act, believed that a forged signature could not be ratified, see Chorley, *Law of Banking,* p. 97.

[25] As now under the Forgery and Counterfeiting Act 1981, s. 9(1)(d): a document is false and hence counterfeit, "if it purports to have been made . . . on the authority of a person who did not in fact authorise its making in those terms". See Ellinger and Lomnicka, *Modern Banking Law*, p. 373 and Ellinger [1984] L.M.C.L.Q. 459 at 469.

ratification of a dishonest act, and whereas it is quite possible for an agent to exceed authority inadvertently, it is difficult to imagine an honest forgery. Although from the point of view of the civil law, it really makes little difference whether the person signing is a forger with no authority or has abused the authority given, except as far as ratification is concerned, it seems unnecessary to extend the modern criminal concept to the civil law.[26] It may be helpful in some cases if the principal is prepared to ratify the signature so that it becomes legally a genuine signature.

7–013 If ratification is to be effective, a number of conditions must be fulfilled. The whole of the contract, not merely a part of it, must be ratified; the ratification must occur within a reasonable time of the transaction[27]; the principal must be aware of all the material facts at the time of ratification (though the right to know may be waived); the agent must contract on the basis of acting for a principal,[28] and the principal must exist and have contractual capacity at the time of the transaction.[29]

The Equitable Defence: Liggett's Case

7–014 An equitable defence, which is often considered to be a form of *subrogation*, may sometimes operate in favour of a paying bank which is not entitled to debit the account of its customer because it has made a mistaken payment to a third party. Subrogation can be thought of as "substitution",[30] since one party is substituted for another in relation to certain rights of the other. It is a convenient way of describing a transfer of rights from one person to another without an assignment, or the consent of the person from whom the rights are transferred; it takes place by operation of law in a variety of widely differing circumstances.[31] The doctrine is often explained by saying that one person may stand in the shoes of another in relation to a third party to the extent of the other person's claim.

7–015 Where the paying bank has paid by mistake, it may be able to recover the money from the third party by means of a personal action based on payment under a mistake (of fact).[32] If the payment was made in satisfaction of a debt owed by the customer to the third party, however, the bank may prefer instead to be subrogated to the rights of the third party, by virtue of the case of *B. Liggett (Liverpool) Ltd v. Barclays Bank Ltd.*[33] This

---

[26] *cf. Kreditbank Cassel GMBH v. Schenkers Ltd* [1927] 1 K.B. 826, where a manager used his company's bills in excess of authority. They were held to be forged (*per* Atkin L.J.), and "forgeries within the 1913 Forgery Act" (*per* Scrutton L.J.).

[27] *Metropolitan Asylums Board Managers v. Kingham & Sons* (1890) 6 T.L.R. 217.

[28] *Keighly, Maxsted & Co v. Durant* [1901] A.C. 240; *Spiro v. Lintern* [1973] 3 All E.R. 319.

[29] *e.g.* it cannot operate where a company has not yet been properly incorporated, see *Kelner v. Baxter* (1866) L.R. 2 C.P. 174.

[30] See Mitchell, *The Law of Subrogation*, 1994. Subrogation is discussed below, Chap. 16.

[31] *Orakpo v. Manson Investments Ltd* [1978] A.C. 95 at 104, *per* Lord Diplock.

[32] Under *Barclays Bank v. Simms, Son and Cooke (Southern) Ltd* [1980] Q.B. 677: the claim now also covers mistakes of law, see below, Chap. 10.

[33] [1928] 1 K.B. 48.

means that the bank is taken to have made the payment on the customer's behalf, so that the customer may not dispute the debit. In *Liggett's Case*, a bank, contrary to its mandate, honoured a company's cheques signed by one director only. The cheques were drawn in favour of genuine trade creditors, so that in effect the bank had paid the company's debts. The company disputed the bank's right to debit its account, claiming that the payment by the bank had been purely voluntary, so that at common law it could not recover the payment from its customer. Wright J. held that by virtue of the equitable doctrine[34] the bank was entitled to stand in the place of the creditors who had been paid and it could take advantage of the payment; it was as if the company had merely changed its creditor[35]; it had not increased its liabilities. In order for the doctrine to operate, it must be unconscientious for the customer to retain the benefit of the discharge of debts by a third party (the bank) who has acted in good faith and in the belief that it has the necessary authority.[36] So far as the rule operates, it relates only to banks; there is no general doctrine that a third party who pays another person's debts without authority is entitled to be reimbursed by the debtor.

If the debt is genuinely owing from the customer, the defence of *Liggett's* **7–016**
Case may have an advantage, because it prevents unjust enrichment of the customer and avoids the possibility of several law suits. The bank simply maintains its debit to the customer, and the payee retains the payment.[37] A payee who has to return the payment under the mistake claim, on the other hand, will not only lose the benefit of the payment but also the advantage, in a claim against the customer, of having the cheque.[38] It may be appropriate then, in the commercial context of banker and customer, that the payee, who has received the payment on the strength of what appeared to be the bank's authority to pay, should not be prejudiced by the mistake between the bank and its customer.

A difficulty about the equitable basis of the doctrine, however, is that a **7–017**
bank making a payment without authority seems to be in the position of a volunteer, and it is a maxim of equity that it will not assist a volunteer. And from the point of view of the customer, certainly the intervention may be regarded as objectionable—not unreasonably, it is suggested. It can be argued,[39] though, that it is artificial to think of the bank as a volunteer;

[34] Wright J. did not describe the equitable doctrine as subrogation, but see, *e.g.* Goode (1981) 97 L.Q.R. 254, and Ellinger and Lee [1984] L.M.C.L.Q. 459.

[35] The bank becomes a quasi-lender and the customer is a quasi-borrower. See Ellinger and Lee [1984] L.M.C.L.Q. 459.

[36] *Re Cleadon Trust Ltd* [1939] 1 Ch. 286, see Mitchell, *op. cit.* p. 129. The doctrine does not apply if the payment is made in accordance with a garnishee order nisi: *Crantrave Ltd v. Lloyds Bank, The Times*, April 24, 2000, CA (following *Re Clead on Trust*).

[37] See Goode (1981) 97 L.Q.R. 254.

[38] Although the payee might be able to take advantage of the change of position defence: *Lipkin Gorman v. Karpnale* [1989] 1 W.L.R. 1340, HL.

[39] Ellinger and Lee [1984] L.M.C.L.Q. 459 at 473.

someone acting under a genuine mistake (of fact) in the course of a commercial relationship for which it obtains consideration, as the bank does in this situation, may be intervening but is not truly a volunteer. The bank is also paying within what it believes is a valid mandate and may be said to have apparent authority for making the payment, so far as the payee is concerned, if the debt is genuinely owing. The view that the bank can be taken to have apparent authority is open to criticism,[40] however, on the basis that where a cheque has been countermanded, the bank cannot claim that the customer has represented the bank as authorised to pay, and the courts would be unlikely to hold that the bank's payment amounted to a representation that it was authorised to pay.[41]

7–018 In view of the doubts about the equitable defence and the fact that a bank making an unauthorised payment normally has a claim against the payee in restitution (mistake), which can take account of the merits of the case by the change of position defence, it is thought that banks will not often avail themselves of the equitable defence.

Estoppel

7–019 There are some circumstances in which the bank may be able to defend itself against a challenge by the customer to the debit, by reference to the customer's behaviour. These fall into two types: (a) where the customer's carelessness in drawing up the cheque has facilitated the making of forgery; and (b) where the customer knows of the forgery and has not informed the bank.

These defences of the paying bank operate as estoppels, and they are discussed in the next section.

Duties of the Customer to the Paying Bank

7–020 These estoppels, preventing the customer from disputing the bank's debit in certain circumstances, are founded on duties owed by the customer to the bank which arise from the banking relationship. In *Joachimson*, Atkin L.J. said:

> "the customer, on his part, undertakes to exercise reasonable care in executing his written orders so as not to mislead the bank or facilitate forgery".[42]

Although the estoppels are often referred to as if they were themselves duties, there is an important difference: estoppel has an "all or nothing"

---

[40] See Matthews [1982] J.B.L. 281, and Mitchell, *op. cit*, p. 130. See also Chap. 10.

[41] By analogy with cases where it has been held that mere payment did not constitute a representation that money was owed (*RE Jones Ltd v. Waring & Gillow Ltd* [1926] A.C. 670) or that a cheque was genuine (*National Westminster Bank Ltd v. Barclays Bank International Ltd* [1975] Q.B. 654).

[42] [1921] 3 K.B. 110 at 127.

effect; it either bars the plaintiff's claim completely or it does not work at all.[43] This means that where a party relies on estoppel, any contributory negligence of the other party may not be taken into account.[44] The customer is therefore precluded, because of his or her own behaviour, from pleading that there is no mandate. The essence of estoppel is a representation intended to induce the person to whom it is made to adopt a course of conduct which results in detriment or loss.[45] It operates: (a) if there is a statement of fact, or an omission to speak where there is a duty—mere silence, omission or failure to act cannot amount to a representation on which an estoppel can be based; (b) the other person relies upon that statement or its omission; and (c) he or she suffers detriment from that reliance, or the circumstances are such that it is inequitable to allow the other person to go back on what he or she has said or omitted to say.

The circumstances in which the bank may be able to defend itself against a challenge by the customer to the debit on the ground of the customer's behaviour fall into two types: (a) where the customer's carelessness in drawing up the cheque has facilitated the making of the forgery; and (b) where the customer knows of the forgeries and has not informed the bank.[46] The position of the customer, with regard to the statement of account given by the bank to its customer,[47] which gives rise to disputes and is linked to the discussion about the customer's duties and estoppel, is also considered below. **7–021**

Cheques must be Drawn Carefully, so that Fraud is Not Facilitated

The first of these duties of the customer goes back to the case of *Young v. Grote,*[48] where a customer left blank signed cheques with his wife when he went away. His wife, unaccustomed to business matters, passed one to a clerk to fill out, who filled it out in such a way that he could later fraudulently raise the amount to be cashed. The court held that the "gross negligence" of the customer estopped him from claiming that the bank should not debit his account, and he was held liable for the loss. **7–022**

This principle was accepted by the House of Lords in *London Joint Stock Bank v. Macmillan and Arthur.*[49] Here, one of the duties of the confidential clerk of a firm of merchants was to fill in cheques and present them to **7–023**

[43] That it cannot work partially is shown by *Avon CC v. Howlett* [1983] 1 All E.R. 1073.

[44] *cf.* the position of the collecting bank: s. 47 of the BA 1979, see below, para. 14–043.

[45] *Tai Hing Ltd v. Liu Chong Hing Bank* [1986] 1 A.C. 80 at 110, *per* Lord Scarman.

[46] Maybe even forgery of an indorsement: *Bank of England v. Vagliano* [1891] A.C. 107, although this is unlikely unless the whole cheque is forged, because the customer does not normally have responsibility for it once drawn up and delivered.

[47] See Holden (1954) 17 M.L.R. 41.

[48] (1827) 4 Bing. 253. The case moved away from the commercial principles of negotiable instruments and imported a duty of care into the law, as a reflection of the difference between cheques, which could be regarded as instructions from the customer to the bank, and other negotiable instruments. For many years it was a controversial case: see Beven (1907) L.Q.R. 390. Lord Esher in *Scholfield v. Earl of Londesborough* [1896] A.C. 514 at 543, said it was "the fount of bad argument".

[49] [1918] A.C. 777.

partners for signature. A partner signed one such cheque, which had no words and only the figures "2.0.0." written on it. The clerk then inserted the words "one hundred and twenty pounds" and altered the figures to read "120.0.0". He presented the cheque and was paid in cash. The House of Lords held that the firm had been negligent and was estopped from suing the bank. The customer was bound to take usual and reasonable care in drawing the cheque to prevent forgery. If the cheque is drawn so that it invites "an increase in the amount by forgery if the cheque should get into the hands of a dishonest person, forgery is not a remote, but a very natural consequence of negligence of this description".[50] Despite a suggestion by Lord Shaw that the customer was responsible for any alterations (perhaps even for erasure and substitution) before the cheque was presented to the banker,[51] it was held that the customer's negligence had to be "in the transaction itself, that is, in the manner in which the cheque is drawn".[52] Any wider or more general duty on a customer to avoid negligent harm to the bank was rejected. The narrow test in the *Macmillan* case has never been extended a very warm welcome by leading writers on banking law and the banking community.[53]

7–024 What constitutes negligence? It has been doubted whether leaving a gap[54] after a word like "eight" so that a "y" can be inserted, would be serious enough.[55] Lord Shaw's view in *Macmillan* was not accepted in *Slingsby v. District Bank Ltd,*[56] where the gap was not in the figures, but in the payee's name. The customer made the cheque payable to "John Prust & Co" or order, with a gap between the payee's name and the words "or order". A fraudulent solicitor added the words "*per* Cumberbirch and Potts" (his firm's name) in the gap and succeeded in getting paid. This was held not to be a breach of the customer's duty of reasonable care.[57] If one only looks at the words on the cheque, the decision might be (and has been) criticised, but the principle that a customer would not be in breach if he gives a cheque to an apparently worthy and trustworthy solicitor (or other fiduciary) may be defensible.[58]

[50] [1918] A.C. 777 at 789–790.

[51] Which amounts to saying that the customer is *ipso facto* negligent in not controlling the cheque.

[52] [1918] A.C. 777 at 795, *per* Lord Finlay.

[53] *Tai Hing Cotton Mill Ltd v. Liu Chong Hing Bank Ltd* [1985] 2 All E.R. 947, PC; [1986] A.C. 519, *per* Lord Scarman.

[54] One is probably much more likely to be considered blameworthy for leaving large gaps than for writing words or figures that can be altered, given the ingenuity of forgers.

[55] So said by Bovill C.J. in *Societe General v. Metropolitan Bank Ltd* (1873) 27 L.T. 849.

[56] [1932] 1 K.B. 544, and see *Hall v. Fuller* (1826) 5 B. & C. 750, where the amount was altered, and the customer was not liable.

[57] In any case, the indorsement was irregular so the bank was liable on that ground (pre-Ch A 1957).

[58] *cf. Orbit Mining & Trading Co Ltd. v. Westminster Bank Ltd.* [1963] 1 Q.B. 794, where a company director signed blank cheques and left them with the other director, who paid them into his own account. The collecting bank was not negligent in these circumstances. Presumably the company could not have recovered from the paying bank. See also *Lumsden & Co v. London Trustee Savings Bank* [1971] 1 Lloyd's Rep. 114.

In *Wood v. Clydesdale Bank Ltd*,[59] a deposit receipt was sent by a customer by registered letter overseas, and was stolen, cashed and the customer's account debited. A Scottish court rejected as "fanciful" the argument that by posting it, rather than handing it to the intended recipient, the customer was in breach of any duty to the bank. The *Macmillan* defence will also not succeed if the alteration is "obvious or discoverable by the exercise of reasonable care, or where the state of the cheque raises suspicion of its having been tampered with and payment is made without inquiry."[60] It is thought therefore that the question reduces itself to one of fact in each case. 7–025

The case of *Scholfield v. Earl of Londesborough*[61] demonstrates the reluctance of the courts to extend the *Macmillan* principle beyond the banker/customer relationship. It was held that no duty similar to that of the drawer of a cheque is owed by an acceptor who signs a bill which has been drawn and which the drawer then alters. After all, the acceptor of a bill can refuse to sign if the bill is not drawn in such a way as to exclude all possibilities of fraud.[62] But the case can also be taken as demonstrating the difference between negotiable instruments in general, whose commercial importance depends upon ease of transfer—which implies certainty in payment and freedom from underlying duties—and cheques, which act as an integral part of the relationship between customer (drawer) and bank, the incidents of which may be affected by contractual obligations.[63] 7–026

The view that the *Macmillan* duty is a narrow one was confirmed by the Privy Council in *Tai Hing*, where Lord Scarman said: "their Lordships are in no doubt that the customer owes the bank a duty in drawing a cheque to take reasonable and ordinary precautions against forgery" and rejected the argument that it should be extended.[64] 7–027

Duty to Tell of Known Forgeries

This is the other common law duty owed by the customer to the bank. A case which illustrates the principle clearly is *Greenwood v. Martin's Bank Ltd.*[65] The wife of the bank's customer forged cheques on his account, and 7–028

[59] (1914) S.C. 397.

[60] Paget (11th ed.) p. 345, citing *Scholey v. Ramsbottom* (1810) 2 Camp. 485.

[61] [1896] A.C. 514.

[62] But in *Garard v. Lewis* [1882] 10 Q.B.D. 30, the acceptor was liable for the altered (larger) amount after signing a bill which was largely blank, with only the amount in figures in the margin, and it may be that the *Macmillan* principle applies if the bill is blank and is signed in that form by the acceptor.

[63] This point was emphasised in *Macmillan*; see *e.g.* [1918] A.C. 777 at 799, 803, *per* Lord Finlay.

[64] *Tai Hing Cotton Mill Ltd v. Liu Chong Hing Bank Ltd* [1985] 2 All E.R. 947 at 954, PC; [1986] A.C. 519. Discussed further below, para. 7–031.

[65] [1933] A.C. 51. There is a reciprocal duty on the bank to inform the customer of forgery (*Greenwood* [1983] A.C. 51 at 381, *per* Scrutton L.J.) and see *Weir v. National Westminster Bank plc* (1994) S.L.T. 1251, para. 5–016: if the bank fails to inform the customer of a forgery, and the forger defrauds the customer in some other (unrelated) business, the bank may be liable for loss which could have been prevented but for the failure.

told her husband when he discovered it that her sister needed the money for legal proceedings. He was sympathetic and did not inform the bank of the forgeries. Eight months later, he found out that she had been lying, and he told her that he would inform the bank. His wife killed herself. The court held that, although the bank had been negligent in paying, the reason that it had not been possible to stop the forgeries or recover the money was the failure of the customer to inform the bank on his first discovery, and he was therefore estopped from suing the bank. In this case the prejudice to the bank was that it had been prevented from claiming the money by the concealment, because its possible claim against the husband for the wife's tort (at that time[66]) had been extinguished by the wife's death.

7–029 In *Greenwood*, the customer had known of the forgeries. It seems from *Brown v. Westminster Bank Ltd*,[67] though, that the principle may go rather further than this. The servants of Mrs Brown (a woman of 86) had forged her signature repeatedly (329 times) on cheques drawn on her account over several years. The branch manager called on her on several occasions to ask about the cheques, but she told him at first that she had asked her servant to draw the cheques, and later, simply did not deny that she had drawn the cheques. The plaintiff (Mrs Brown's son, who held a power of attorney for her, brought the action in her name) was estopped from setting up the forgeries against the bank even for the cheques which had passed through the account before the manager had raised the matter. Although there might be some doubt in this case as to the extent of the customer's understanding of events,[68] the bank had certainly made considerable efforts to discover the truth. In some other cases there are *dicta* which suggest that a person may have a duty to inform the bank of forgeries of which they ought to know,[69] but it is difficult to reconcile this suggestion with the fact that estoppel depends upon a statement or representation, which must surely be intentional.[70]

7–030 An older case, *Morison v. London County and Westminster Bank Ltd*[71] is generally thought to have gone too far in suggesting that the failure by the

---

[66] A husband is no longer liable for his wife's tort: Law Reform (Married Women and Tortfeasors) Act 1935. There may be a question from *Greenwood* whether the bank has to suffer loss from the concealment before the estoppel will work. Some kind of prejudice to the bank or inequitable behaviour by the customer is usually needed for estoppel. See *M'Kenzie v. British Linen Co* (1881) 6 App. Cas. 82 at 109, 111, 112; *Pacol Ltd v. Trade Lines Ltd* [1982] 1 Lloyd's Rep. 456; it does not matter that proceedings against the forger would not recover the money—*e.g.* he is bankrupt or dead. See *M'Kenzie* (1881) 6 App. Cas. 82, *Ogilvie* [1896] A.C. 257, *Ewing* [1904] A.C. 806, (*contra*, *Imperial Bank of Canada v. Bank of Hamilton* [1903] A.C. 49 at 57.)

[67] [1964] 2 Lloyd's Rep. 187.

[68] She suffered from some mental disability during the period in question, and the judge found that no reliance could be put on her statements at the trial.

[69] *M'Kenzie v. British Linen Co* (1881) 6 App. Cas. 82 at 92, *per* Lord Selborne; *Morison v. London County and Westminster Bank Ltd* [1914] 3 K.B. 356, *per* Buckley L.J.

[70] In *Greenwood*, Lord Tomlin said that "a representation or conduct amounting to a representation intended to induce a course of conduct" was required for estoppel.

[71] [1914] 3 K.B. 356.

customer to supervise his or her agents or employees might give rise to liability as against the bank. In that case the manager of Morison's business, who had authority to draw cheques for the firm, defrauded the firm of 50 cheques, which he paid into his own bank account. The frauds had gone on for a long time, and some or all were known to the plaintiff and his auditors. Indeed, an arrangement had been reached concerning some of the frauds and the manager was not dismissed despite his actions. Judgment was given for the bank; the "position . . . was such that any suspicion [the bank] ought to have had would have been lulled to sleep by the action of Morison himself".[72] The phrase "lulled to sleep" was seized on in subsequent cases by counsel defending banks as a ground for an argument that negligence gave rise to an estoppel against the customer. But the argument was always rejected,[73] and should now, after the *Tai Hing* case, be regarded as unsustainable. As in *Greenwood*, the bank had lost the chance to proceed against the forger and to recover the money or prevent him from committing later frauds,[74] or at least lost time, during which the forger may have spent all his money, or removed himself or his assets from the jurisdiction. The true explanation of the case is that anyone (customer or not, and whether drawer, acceptor, indorser) who knows that his or her name (or some other detail in respect of which liability exists) has been forged on a bill or cheque, has a duty to inform the bank of it.[75]

Other Duties Owed by the Customer?

In *Tai Hing Cotton Mill Ltd v. Liu Chong Hing Bank Ltd,*[76] the extent of **7–031**
the customer's duties to the bank was considered by the Privy Council. The Tai Hing company had current accounts with three Hong Kong banks, which were authorised to honour cheques bearing certain signatures. A dishonest employee of the company forged some 300 cheques over six years. His employers had had no proper financial system and had left him unsupervised. The question was whether the customer, who had carried on its business in such a negligent fashion, had breached any duty to the bank

[72] [1914] 3 K.B. 356 at 377, *per* Buckley L.J.

[73] See also *Carpenter's Company v. British Mutual Banking Co Ltd* [1938] 1 K.B. 511; *AL Underwood Ltd v. Bank of Liverpool and Martins* [1924] 1 K.B. 775; *Brewer v. Westminster Bank Ltd* [1952] 2 All E.R. 650; (for cases before the *Morison* decision see, *e.g. Bank of Ireland v. Trustees of Evans' Charities in Ireland* (1855) 5 H.L. Cas. 389; *Swan v. North British Australasian Company* (1863) 10 Jur. (N.S.) 102 (though see *Re North British Australasian Company ex p. Swan* (1860) 7 C.B. N.S. 400 at 442, 447); *Vagliano Bros v. Bank of England* [1891] A.C. 107 at 115; *Farquharson Bros & Co v. King & Co* [1902] A.C. 325; *Lewes Sanitary Steam Laundry Co Ltd v. Barclay & Co Ltd* (1906) 11 Com. Cas. 255; *Kepitigalla Rubber Estates Ltd v. National Bank of India Ltd* [1909] 2 K.B. 1010.

[74] See *Fung Kai Sun v. Chang Fui Hing* [1951] A.C. 489.

[75] *M'Kenzie v. British Linen Co* (1881) 6 App. Cas. 82 at 92, 101, 109; *Ogilvie v. West Australian Mortgage and Agency Corpn Ltd* [1896] A.C. 257 at 270; *William Ewing & Co v. Dominion Bank* [1904] A.C. 806.

[76] [1985] 2 All E.R. 947, PC; [1986] A.C. 519.

to take care. If such a duty existed, it would have to be framed more widely than the *Macmillan* and *Greenwood* duties, and to extend to the supervision and control of employees with access to cheques.

7–032 The banks claimed that the law of contract and of tort had developed significantly since the *Macmillan* and *Greenwood* cases. The relationship of banker and customer now gives rise, they argued, to a duty owed by the customer in both contract and in tort to exercise such precautions as a reasonable customer in his or her position would take to prevent forged cheques being presented to the bank. The Privy Council considered these possibilities in turn.

7–033 The contractual question was whether an implied term to this effect existed.[77] The test for that is whether it is *necessary* to imply such a term into the relationship. The court took the view that whereas the *Macmillan* and *Greenwood* duties were plainly necessary incidents of the banker/customer relationship, that in itself demonstrated that it is not a necessary incident of the relationship that the customer should owe his or her banker the wider duty of care. The bank, therefore, could not rely on a defence arising from the customer's lack of supervision of a fraudulent employee, or from the customer's business methods.[78] If the banks wished to look for protection, they could, it was said, either seek to increase the severity of their terms of business, or seek legislative protection. But it did not follow that, because they might need protection, the implied terms of the relationship with their customer should change. Lord Scarman said:

> "The business of banking is the business not of the customer but of the bank. They offer a service, which is to honour their customer's cheques when drawn on an account in credit or within an agreed overdraft limit. If they pay out on cheques which are not his, they are acting outside their mandate and cannot plead his authority in justification of their debit to his account. This is a risk of the service which it is their business to offer".[79]

The court went on to consider whether there was a duty in tort. The argument that there might be a separate tortious duty, which the customer in this case had broken was also rejected:

> "their Lordships do not . . . accept that the parties' mutual obligations in tort can be any greater than those to be found expressly or by necessary implication in the contract".[80]

[77] Banks could make an appropriate duty an express term of the contract, though the attempts to do so in *Tai Hing* were unsuccessful (see Chap. 3). Such an attempt would be subject to the UCTA 1977 and the UTCCR 1999.

[78] Or from his or her failure to read and correct his bank statements, see further below, paras 7–036 *et seq.*

[79] The case has been criticised, for this aspect and others. See, *e.g.*, Ellinger [1986] L.M.C.L.Q. 8.

[80] This principle has been further considered by the House of Lords in *Henderson v. Merrett* [1994] 3 All E.R. 506, see above, Chap. 5.

The Privy Council therefore gave a firm negative answer to the question whether the customer's gross negligence in the way the business is organised is a defence to the bank.[81]

The trouble with this conclusion is that there is an unfairness in the way the law works. The customer may well have been negligent, and many company customers have more than adequate resources to take sensible precautions and set up appropriate systems. In any case, the effect of the negligence is probably a matter of degree and there may be faults on both sides. But, as we have seen, estoppel operates as a complete bar—so that, if a duty were imposed on the customer, he or she would hardly ever have a remedy because the whole claim would be barred. The questions which are asked to establish estoppel—is the bank entitled to debit the customer's account? If not, is the customer estopped from disputing the bank's debit?—produce "all or nothing" replies. **7–034**

It may have been the all or nothing nature of estoppel which has led the courts to draw a "bright line" around the specified kinds of negligent act for which a customer is liable, and to hold that the negligence must be confined to the manner in which the cheque is drawn. No doubt however, the courts, in restricting the duties owed by customers, have also been influenced by the policy consideration that the bank may spread the risk of losses through its system of charges to all customers. It would probably be a better solution, though, to admit contributory negligence as a defence; it would fit more easily into the concept of the duties owed by the customer to the bank and would allow the merits of the case to be considered.

The Jack Committee, considered the state of the law soon after *Tai Hing* had been decided, and heard evidence from bankers who argued that the present law is unjust to them, and that the duties of care on banks had become so burdensome with the increase in banking business[82] that there should be a corresponding increase in the customer's duty. They pointed out that whereas bankers could only detect a fraud being perpetrated by their customer's employees or agents by instituting elaborate and expensive procedures—for which customers would resent paying—substantial business customers with ample resources could have prevented such fraud by the institution of elementary precautions.[83] The Committee agreed that it was unfair that customers who exhibit the degree of negligence shown by the plaintiff in *Tai Hing* should be entitled to sue their banks, and it was impressed by the case for some reform of the law. It favoured a statutory provision which would allow the possibility, in an action against a bank in **7–035**

[81] See also *Yorkshire Bank plc v. Lloyd's Bank plc* [1999] Lloyds Rep. Bank. 191, Q.B.D., where the claimant argued unsuccessfully that the defendant had assumed a duty of care towards it and should reimburse it for the loss it had incurred on paying the cheque, which had been stolen and fraudulently altered..

[82] At that time (after the *Selangor* case, which had imposed higher duties on banks than seemed fair to them, see below, Chaps 5 and 9).

[83] Jack Report, Cm. 622 (1989), para. 6.11.

debt or for damages arising from an unauthorised payment, for the bank to raise contributory negligence as a defence if the degree of negligence shown by the plaintiff were sufficiently serious for it to be inequitable, in the court's view, for the bank to be liable for the whole amount. Further than that, it should be left to the courts to decide on the facts. It would be wrong, for example, to make an arbitrary restriction on the defence to actions by business customers. The White Paper agreed with this recommendation, and undertook that proposals to change the law would be introduced in due course.[84]

Mistakes in the Statement of Account

7–036 Mistakes in the statement (the modern loose-leaf statement has generally replaced the old fashioned passbook) may be in the customer's favour if too much has mistakenly been credited to the account, or in the bank's, if too little. Either party has a right to have the account rectified. The bank, for example, may correct an overpayment by reversing the credit entry. If the customer notices, he or she may object and may claim that the balance is a *"settled account"* or that the bank is *estopped* from changing the entry. If the account has been credited with too little, the customer can demand rectification, and the bank will usually correct the entry.

(1) Statement as "settled account" or "account stated"

7–037 It may sometimes be agreed that the statement shall be conclusive, and if proper notice is given, this may bind both parties,[85] either of whom may then rely on the equitable plea that the statement is a "settled account" (an agreed one) or an "account stated" (an admitted one: there is some ambiguity in the phrases), which are evidence of a debt for the amount stated, and only error or fraud may be shown to rebut the creditor's claim. The question is, therefore, whether the statement, though incorrect, is conclusive evidence against either bank or customer. It seems that neither a passbook nor loose-leaf statements can be regarded as conclusive evidence. Some older cases, which relate to passbooks, have suggested that while the entry in the book itself is not regarded as conclusive, it may become so if the customer fails to rectify it after having the opportunity to do so; his silence could be regarded as an admission that the entries were correct.[86] The great weight of authority, however, is otherwise, and while treating a statement which the customer does not immediately challenge on receipt as

[84] Cm. 1026, para. 17.

[85] See *Bishund Chand Firm v. Seth Girdhari Lal* (193) 50 T.L.R. 465 at 468–469; *Tai Hing Cotton Mill Ltd v. Liu Chong Hing Bank* [1986] A.C. 80. The latter case illustrates the difficulty in an established relationship of making the statement conclusive evidence even by express terms.

[86] *Devaynes v. Noble, Clayton's Case* (1816) 1 Mer. 529 at 572; *Blackburn Building Society v. Cunliffe, Brooks & Co* (1882) 22 Ch. D. 61 at 72.

prima facie evidence, allows either the bank or the customer to show that the entry is in error.[87]

It follows from this, that the customer is not under a duty to check his or her statements,[88] and that an estoppel cannot arise against him from his failure to do so, even if the customer's negligence has facilitated forgery. **7–038**

The most recent decision to this effect is *Tai Hing*,[89] where as noted above, a trusted clerk had defrauded the company customer of a large sum of money by forging or altering cheques, and the fraud had not been noticed by the company. The banks in that case argued, among other things, that clauses in their contracts[90] required the customer to peruse its statements promptly and notify the bank of any errors or irregularities within a specified time. These clauses, it was argued, amounted to "conclusive evidence" clauses, so that if a customer did not notify the bank of any irregularity, it would be evidence that the customer had confirmed the balance on the statement. The Privy Council held that, although banks could impose an obligation on their customers to examine their statements and to make the statements unchallengeable after a fixed time limit, none of the contractual clauses here were sufficiently clear and unambiguous to satisfy the "undoubtedly rigorous" test that the effect of the clause must be brought home to the customer. It is unlikely in the circumstances that, even if the clauses had been drafted sufficiently clearly, the court would have decided that they satisfied the requirement of reasonableness under the UCTA 1977.[91]

The *Tai Hing* decision has settled that the customer has no duty to check his or her bank statements. It is thought that there may be two practical reasons for the decision. First, the bank is able to "spread the risk" of forgery to all customers, through its system of charges. Secondly, if the bank had succeeded in establishing a duty on the customer's part, the doctrine of estoppel would have operated in an "all or nothing" fashion, completely defeating the plaintiff's claim. It would be a better solution to apply the **7–039**

[87] *Commercial Bank of Scotland v. Rhind* (1860) 3 Macq. 643 at 648; *Holland v. Manchester and Liverpool District Banking Co Ltd* (1909) 25 T.L.R. 386; *Vagliano Bros v. Bank of England* (1889) 23 Q.B.D., CA; *cf.* [1891] A.C. 107 at 114, 116; *Kepitigalla Rubber Estates Ltd v. National Bank of India Ltd* [1909] 2 K.B. 1010. *Chatterton v. London County Bank* (1890) *The Miller*, November 3, 1890, p. 394; *Walker v. Manchester and Liverpool District Banking Co Ltd* (1913) 108 L.T. 728; *Brewer v. Westminster Bank Ltd* [1952] 2 All E.R. 650.

[88] *cf.* the U.S. Uniform Commercial Code, ss. 4–406: "It is the customer's duty to discover and report an unauthorised signature or an alteration. If the depositor fails without reasonable excuse promptly to examine the statement and his paid cheques and to report any forgeries, he is estopped after 14 days from disputing the payments." (In England it is not now banking practice to return paid cheques to the customer.) In *Wealden Woodlands (Kent) Ltd v. National Westminster Bank Ltd*, *The Times*, March 12, 1983, McNeill J. refused to bring the law into line with that in the USA. See also *London Intercontinental Trust Ltd v. Barclays Bank Ltd* [1980] 1 Lloyd's Rep. 241.

[89] [1985] 2 All E.R. 947. See above, para. 7–031.

[90] The banks were Hong Kong banks which used express contracts.

[91] UCTA 1977, s. 2(2) or s. 3. And they might also be caught now by the UTCCR 1999.

principles of contributory negligence for attributing liability, rather than to use the artificial method of conclusive evidence clauses or settled accounts.[92]

Although the customer owes no duties to the banker in respect of the statement, the converse is not true. There is probably an implied term that a customer is entitled to regular statements of account.[93] In addition, it is clear that the general principles of estoppel apply to the statement.

(2) Estoppel[94]

7–040 Estoppel operates if there is (a) a statement of fact, or an omission to speak where there is a duty, (b) reliance upon the statement or its omission, and (c) the person relying suffers detriment from that reliance, or the circumstances are such that it is inequitable to allow the other party to go back on what he has said or omitted to say.[95] In *Skyring v. Greenwood,*[96] the bankers (in this case a military paymaster) overcredited an account for five years and the customer drew out the money regularly. After his death, the bankers sought to retain other funds of his, but were held not to be entitled to do so, for the credit entries were statements upon which the customer had relied and he had altered his position by spending more than he would otherwise have done.[96] In *Holland v. Manchester and Liverpool District Banking Co.,*[98] the bank's right to correct an entry was recognised, but it was held that the bank had no right to dishonour a cheque which the customer had drawn on the faith of the uncorrected statements, and it was liable in damages for doing so. It is essential that the customer relies on the incorrect entry; if he or she is unaware of the entry, estoppel cannot operate.[99] Naturally, if the customer knows that the entry was made by mistake, he or she cannot rely upon estoppel—indeed, a person who draws on the account with knowledge of the mistake may be guilty of theft.[1]

"Reliance" and the requirement that it should be inequitable for the bank to demand repayment also generally entails that the customer has changed his position in some way (or not changed it, when otherwise he or she would have done so). In *United Overseas Bank v. Jiwani,*[2] the defendant was wrongly advised of a credit, in circumstances in which he must have

[92] And this was proposed by the Jack Report, Cm. 622 (1989), para. 6.14.

[93] Banks undertake to give regular statements to customers, normally monthly (Banking Code (1999), para. 3.1). From July 1, 1999, statements should be provided at least quarterly for accounts accessible by cards.

[94] See also Chap. 10, which discusses estoppel and the change of position defence in connection with recovery in restitution.

[95] For a clear statement to this effect, see *United Overseas Bank v. Jiwani* [1976] 1 W.L.R. 964.

[96] (1825) 4 B. & C. 281, approved in *Deutsche Bank (London Agency) v. Beriro Co.* (1895) 73 L.T. 669; *R v. Blenkinsop* [1892] 1 Q.B. 43; *Holt v. Markham* [1923] 1 K.B. 504.

[97] For a similar case, see *Lloyds Bank Ltd v. Banks* (1950) 72 J.I.B. 114.

[98] (1909) 25 T.L.R. 386.

[99] *British and North European Bank v. Zalzstein* [1927] 2 K.B. 92.

[1] TA 1968, s. 1.

[2] [1976] 1 W.L.R. 964.

known (and the judge held that he did know—he had queried the balance with the bank) that he was not entitled to it. He used the money towards a purchase which he had already embarked upon and had partly paid for. The court held that he would have gone ahead with the purchase in any case, finding the money elsewhere, and it was not inequitable for the bank to demand repayment. The customer was therefore liable to repay the bank.

In summary, the position is that bank statements are prima facie evidence, but that they may be proved erroneous by either party. The bank's statement may give rise to an estoppel. The customer has no duty to check statements, and cannot be estopped by his or her negligence, though perhaps some behaviour by the customer may amount to a representation sufficient to amount to an estoppel.

Chapter 8

Accounts

Current Accounts

8–001 The current account is still regarded as a basic element in the banker customer relationship. It is thought of as supplying *liquid* funds, and is used for day to day payments in and out. Legally, as has been seen, it is a debt owing to the customer by the bank, not the actual money of the customer. The customer therefore has a right to demand repayment (or, until demand is made, to have a correct statement of the state of accounts between him or herself and the bank). This right is a chose in action, and the customer cannot normally view the bank as a trustee or make use of a tracing order; on the insolvency of the bank, the customer is a mere unsecured creditor. The customer has the benefit of having money kept securely and of having payments made and received by the bank. Banks often now pay interest on current accounts (they used not to), which means that the distinction between current and deposit accounts is being eroded.

8–002 Banks also now charge most customers for their use of a current account, although customers of some banks who keep their accounts above a certain level may not have to pay charges. The Jack Committee recommended—and this was strongly supported by the White Paper[1]—that there should be more transparency about bank charges: full details should be given about the basis of calculating interest and charging for the normal operation of the account, as well as for specific matters like overdrafts. One of the most frequent complaints to the Banking Ombudsman has been interest and charges on current accounts,[2] and the Banking Code now states that banks will give customers 14 days' notice of the amount to be deducted from accounts for interest and charges,[3] a concession made reluctantly by banks because, they said, of the costs of administration. The Code also requires information about how customers' accounts work to be given to them on request, changes in terms and conditions to be notified in advance[4] and notification to be given to customers at least 14 days in advance if charges or debit interest are to be deducted from their accounts.[5]

---

[1] Cm. 1206 (1990), para. 1.31.

[2] See, *e.g.* OBO A.R. (1995), para. 6.1. Bank charges have been heavily criticised by a Government Report (Competition in U.K. Banking by Cruickshank, March 20, 2000).

[3] Banking Code (1999) para. 2.15. Introduced December 31, 1996.

[4] Banking Code (1999) paras 2.12–2.14.

[5] Banking Code (1999) para. 3.4.

A current account may be overdrawn. If a customer draws on an account which has inadequate funds, it is regarded as being a request to the bank for an overdraft.[6] If the customer has an overdraft, the relationship between bank and customer is reversed, and the banker becomes the creditor.

Deposit Accounts

8–003 These tend to be used for longer term deposits. They have a wide variety of different names, such as "savings accounts" or "extra interest accounts", and different conditions, including different rates of interest payable on them. Funds in deposit accounts may be withdrawable on demand, but are often withdrawable only on specified notice or after a fixed time; it depends on the terms on which the contract is made. Because they are less liquid than current accounts, deposit accounts attract higher rates of interest.

The variety of deposit accounts may be confusing for customers, particularly elderly customers. It has been suggested that banks were taking advantage of such customers in their own interest.[7] The Banking Ombudsman has criticised banks for acting unfairly in failing to pay extra interest to customers who were unaware that the rate of interest they were offered on their accounts had been superseded by that on other accounts introduced more recently.[8] The newest version of the Code shows that banks have taken the criticism to heart. They have undertaken to help customers compare interest rates on their savings and investment accounts by sending them a summary of accounts and other information about them, including interest rates, at least once a year. Perhaps more helpfully, they promise to keep interest rates on superseded accounts at the same level as a similar account from a current range or to switch the superseded account to such an account.[9]

8–004 Usually no cheque book is provided for the account (cheque books are specific to an account) and although there may sometimes be a temporary debit balance due to the clearing system, the customer is not allowed to overdraw. This point was emphasised in the case of *Barclays Bank v. Okenarhe*, where Mocatta J. said: "I am quite unable to accept that an overdrawn deposit account is a concept known to the law."[10] The very name means that a deposit of money must have been made.

A deposit account is not a secured debt: again, the relationship of the banker and customer is debtor and creditor, and there is normally no fiduciary relationship between the two parties.

---

[6] See below, para. 8–006.

[7] See James, *Private Ombudsmen and Public Law*, pp. 110–111.

[8] See OBO A.R. (1993/4), para. 6A, though the compensation awarded was reduced by 50 per cent because of the failure of the customers to monitor the account.

[9] Banking Code (1999) para. 2.16. Unless the account is a passbook account with less than £100 in it. *Cf.* the view of the Court of Appeal in *Suriya & Douglas v. Midland Bank* [1999] Lloyd's Rep. Bank. 103 that imposing a term to this effect on banks would be too onerous.

[10] [1966] 2 Lloyd's Rep. Bank. 87 at 94.

Deposit Receipt or Pass Book

In times past, it was normal for the bank to issue the customer with a pass book in which payments and withdrawals were recorded. These could be passed on to other individuals almost as negotiable instruments.[11] Practice has changed now, and these have been replaced by ordinary statements of account, but pass books are still sometimes used.[12] **8–005**

Overdrafts and Loan Accounts

Although the types of facilities for bank financing have been developing dynamically in recent years, particularly for company financing,[13] the two basic methods of borrowing are still by overdraft or by opening a loan account. Overdrafts are a traditional and characteristic method of borrowing in the United Kingdom,[14] normally regarded as suitable for short term borrowing, but banks are increasingly using term loans, and permitting both methods for longer periods. In practice, distinctions between the two are diminishing. **8–006**

The principle of the overdraft is familiar and simple: when the credit balance of a current account is exhausted, the customer may overdraw on the account, provided the bank agrees, expressly or impliedly—for example, from a course of dealing.[15] If a customer draws a cheque when there is no overdraft facility or an insufficient facility to meet it, the bank may treat this as a request for an overdraft; if it accedes to the request, it will normally charge higher interest rates (a "default" rate) on the overdrawn amount.[16] The bank may allow the customer to overdraw up to a certain limit, and if it then refuses to pay or dishonours a cheque within the limit without notice to the customer, it will be liable to the customer in damages.[17] An overdraft is therefore the reverse of a current account in credit, where the banker is debtor, and the customer creditor; when the account is overdrawn, the customer is the debtor.[18]

The alternative is for the bank to open a separate loan account for a customer who wishes to borrow, debit the sum agreed to that account, and credit the same amount to the customer's current account. From the **8–007**

---

[11] *e.g. Evans v. National Provincial Bank of England* (1897) 13 T.L.R. 429.

[12] They are referred to in the 1999 Banking Code, *e.g.* para. 3.3.

[13] See Cranston, *Banks, Liability and Risk* (2nd ed., 1995), and Pennington, *Bank Finance for Companies.* Very large loans are often made by syndicates of banks, with one bank becoming the "lead" bank.

[14] "The transaction is of course of the commonest"; *Rouse v. Bradford Banking Company* [1894] A.C. 586 at 597, *per* Lord Herschell.

[15] *Brooks v. Blackburn Benefit Society* (1884) 9 App Cas 857 at 864; *Cumming v. Shand* (1860) 5 H & N 95.

[16] In *Lordsvale Finance plc v. Bank of Zambia* [1996] 3 All E.R. 156: it was held that the default rate was not a penalty if it is applied only from the date of default.

[17] *Rouse v. Bradford Banking Company* [1894] A.C. 586.

[18] "A payment by a bank under an arrangement by which the customer may overdraw is a lending by the bank to the customer of the money": *Re Hone* [1951] Ch. 85 at 89, *per* Harman J.

customer's point of view, there are advantages and disadvantages attached to both methods of borrowing, although the differences between the two methods are often less striking in practice than they appear at first sight. The interest the customer has to pay on a loan account, for example, may be higher than for an overdraft, and it will probably become payable from the time the account is opened, whether or not the customer makes use of the money, (although this may be offset to some extent by the fact that undrawn amounts are credited with interest as if they were deposits). Interest paid on an overdraft, however, will only be payable on the amount drawn; if the customer may repay an overdraft without giving notice, interest payments will cease if he or she does so. Term loan agreements may often, of course, be terminated by the customer, but usually only on notice. Overdrafts generally have the advantage, therefore, of being more flexible. However, from the customer's point of view, they have the considerable disadvantage that the bank may call for immediate repayment.[19] The two methods also differ in respect of the controls imposed by the CCA 1974, as described below.

Interest

8–008 The rate of interest charged on loans and overdrafts varies—it is usually higher for overdrafts which have not been expressly agreed—and is regarded as a matter of negotiation. Usually nowadays the bank will set out the details in a *facility letter* to the customer.[20]

The practice of banks is to charge *compound interest*, which is added at regular intervals, normally half yearly, to the outstanding balance. This practice was approved by the House of Lords in the case of *National Bank of Greece v. Pinios,*[21] which held that the right to interest (on any account, including loan accounts) arises by virtue of a term implied into the contract by reason of custom or practice of bankers and that banks may capitalise the interest: that is, they may charge compound interest. This right continues until the debt is repaid and does not terminate when the bank makes a demand for the sums outstanding in the account.[22]

[19] Sometimes a loan facility letter states that a loan is for a specific period but repayable on demand; see below, para. 8–010.

[20] The Code of Practice requires banks to tell customers the interest rates applicable to their accounts, when interest will be deducted (or paid) and, on request, to give a full explanation of how interest is calculated must be given (Banking Code (1999), para. 2.1). Customers must be informed of changes in interest rates (Banking Code (1999), para. 2.16).

[21] [1989] 3 W.L.R. 1330, approving *Yourell v. Hibernian Bank Ltd* [1918] A.C. 372. See Kingsford Smith [1990] L.M.C.L.Q. 489. See also *Westdeutsche Landesbank Girozentrale v. Islington LBC* [1996] 2 All E.R. 961, HL, where banks were not permitted to charge compound interest on restitutionary payments from local authorities, and *Whitbread plc v. UCB Corporate Services Ltd, The Times*, June 22, 2000, CA.

[22] Ellinger and Lomnicka, *Modern Banking Law*, pp. 584–585, point out that since banks normally raise the rate of interest when they call up loans, the result of allowing compound interest on the raised rate is that they may "reap a windfall".

Demand

An overdraft is payable on demand, unless the bank has agreed otherwise, and the bank owes no duty to the customer to ensure that it causes him or her no detriment by demanding it.[23] The customer is not in default, however, until there has been sufficient time to obtain the money to repay from another bank, "a time limited to the implementation of the mechanics of payment, a short but adequate period" (here one hour)[24]—although not to raise the money if it is not there—and the bank may be required to honour cheques drawn within the agreed facility before the demand. The bank need not specify the precise amount due[25] and need not use the actual word "demand", but it must give "a clear intimation that payment is required".[26] The demand itself does not necessarily bring the relationship of banker and customer to an end.[27] **8–009**

A case which examined in detail the duties of lending banks is *Williams & Glyns Bank v. Barnes*.[28] The bank lent large sums of money over a period of years to a successful building company and to Mr Barnes himself, who was the founder and moving spirit of the company. In the early 1970s, the building trade went into a slump. By 1974, the company's overdraft had increased to £11 million (Mr Barnes himself owed the bank £1.1 million) and the company failed. After allowing the company a moratorium, the bank appointed a receiver. It also sued Mr Barnes for his debt. Mr Barnes raised an extensive and ingenious series of defences. Among other things, he claimed that the bank was under a duty (implied in contract from a course of dealing) to increase the overdraft to enable the company to remain in a sufficient state of liquidity. Ralph Gibson J. said that an overdraft was repayable on demand unless there was express agreement providing that it should be available for a certain period, or unless the court considered that there was an implied term to the contrary. He held, though, that such a term could not be implied here—there was no reason for the court to consider the relationship between bank and customer with any hostility to the concept of loans or overdraft being repayable on demand. Overdrafts are ordinary commercial contracts and parties are free to determine for themselves what obligations they will accept. A bank might urgently need the money because of commercial misfortunes, and, equally, a customer might obtain better terms from another bank and might wish to repay without notice. He found, however, that the express terms of the **8–010**

[23] *Williams & Glyns Bank v. Barnes* [1981] Com. L.R. 205.

[24] *Bank of Baroda v. Panessar* [1987] Ch. 335 at 349, *per* Walton J. See also *Sheppard & Cooper Ltd v. TSB, The Times*, May 1, 1996. The borrower admittedly could not repay, and it was held that the bank was entitled to appoint receivers 15 minutes after making the demand. And see *Lloyds Bank v. Lampert* [1999] Lloyd's Rep. Bank. 138.

[25] *Bank of Baroda v. Panessar* [1987] Ch. 335.

[26] *Re A Company* [1985] B.C.L.C. 37 at 42, *per* Nourse L.J.

[27] *National Bank of Greece v. Pinios* [1990] 1 A.C. 641 at 684.

[28] [1981] Com. L.R. 205.

facility letter here were inconsistent with the money being repayable on demand, and the bank therefore had to give reasonable notice, since custom would not override an agreement to the contrary. The period of notice would be determined by reference to the commercial use which the bank knew the customer would make of the money; in this case there should be enough time to permit the company to explore other alternatives, probably a maximum of a month.

8–011 Mr. Barnes further argued that the requirement that the loan was repayable on demand was repugnant to the main object of the transaction. Goff J. had held in *Titford Property Co Ltd v. Cannon Street Acceptances Ltd*[29] that a provision that a loan should be repayable on demand was repugnant to an overdraft facility expressed to be for a term of 12 months. In appropriate circumstances, as in that case, this might be an effective argument, but it did not work in *Williams and Glyns*, because the main object of the transaction was to afford the company an opportunity to trade out of its difficulties; an overdraft repayable on demand was not repugnant to that purpose, and nor is it repugnant to public policy. In *Lloyds Bank v. Lampert*[30] where the bank's letter said that it was the bank's "present intention to make the facility available until" a certain date the Court of Appeal said that the words "repayable on demand" in the letter meant what they said. The argument which had succeeded in *Titford* that the words were repugnant to the purpose of the facility was rejected.

The Consumer Credit Act 1974[31]

8–012 A main purpose of the CCA 1974 is to protect consumers borrowing money. Both overdrafts and loans are regulated by the CCA 1974 where the debtor is an individual. The controls apply to "regulated agreements": bank loans and overdrafts are consumer credit agreements[32]—that is, they are agreements whereby one person[33] provides an "individual"[34] with an actual or agreed credit not exceeding £25,000.[35] A bank overdraft is what is called "running account credit": the debtor can receive cash from time to time (up to the limit of £25,000), taking into account credits paid into the account.[36] The CCA 1974 does not affect the bank's right to demand repayment without notice, unless the overdraft was granted for a fixed period.[37]

---

29 May 22, 1975, *Encyclopedia of Banking Law*, Vol. 1, p. 183.

30 [1999] Lloyd's Rep. Bank. 138.

31 This is a necessarily brief account of a highly technical topic. See further, Goode, *Consumer Credit Law*; Guest and Lloyd, *Encyclopedia of Consumer Credit Law*; and Lowe and Woodroffe, *Consumer Law and Practice*, pp. 295–363.

32 CCA 1974, s. 8.

33 Including bodies corporate.

34 Including a partnership or other unincorporated body of persons not consisting entirely of bodies corporate (CCA 1974, s. 189).

35 Raised from £15,000 by the Consumer Credit (Increase of Monetary Limit) Amendment Order 1998 (S.I. 1998 No. 996).

36 CCA 1974, s. 10(3) defines this further.

37 CCA 1974, s. 76.

Overdrafts, unlike loans, are exempt from the most onerous aspects of regulation (from the bank's point of view) under Part V of the CCA 1974.[38] These would effectively make overdrafts impossible to operate, and banks have some privileges in respect of overdrafts with regard to other requirements, such as canvassing.[39] Nevertheless, some written information must be disclosed to overdraft debtors before or at the time when the overdraft is granted[40]: the credit limit, the annual interest rate and the charges, and the conditions under which they may be amended and the procedure to terminate the overdraft (that is, the fact that it is "on demand").

The bank must, during the currency of the overdraft, give its customer on request a copy of any document setting out all or any of the terms of the facility, which is signed by both parties.[41] The bank must also provide statements showing the state of the account at regular intervals (at least annually, though in fact statements are normally provided monthly or quarterly). The sections relating to termination and enforcement of regulated agreements[42] in practice do not usually apply to bank overdrafts, because they apply to early termination or enforcement of agreements for a fixed period (most overdrafts are not made for a specified period) or to termination for breach (overdrafts are repayable on demand, not breach). **8–013**

Loans to individuals are more strictly regulated by the CCA 1974.[42a] The agreement regulations in Part V require creditors to give the debtor certain information, including information about the "true cost of borrowing", so that the debtor can make informed comparisons between different lenders: for example the total charge must be stated as an annual percentage rate (APR).[43] Banks must advertise their interest rates and set them out in a specific quotation given to a customer.[44] The agreement must be in the prescribed form and signed in the prescribed manner, embody all the terms of the agreement (other than implied terms) and be readily legible when presented for signature.[45] A copy should be provided for the borrower,[46]

[38] CCA 1974, s. 74(1)(b), (3) and 3(a) inserted by the BA 1979, s. 38(1). Determination of the Director General of Fair Trading under CCA 1974, s. 74(3).

[39] CCA 1974, s. 49(3).

[40] Determination of the Director General of Fair Trading, with effect from February 1, 1990.

[41] CCA 1974, s. 78(1) and a copy of any other document referred to in the agreement.

[42] CCA 1974, ss. 76, 87 and 98.

[42a] If a customer has several loans and overdrafts with a bank, they will be regarded as one agreement for the purposes of the CCA, if the clear object of the transaction was to provide an overall level of credit: *Story v. National Westminster Bank* [1999] Lloyd's Rep. Bank. 261.

[43] Reflecting annual compounding and the continuing repayment of credit. Lowe and Woodroffe (*op. cit.*, p. 309) describe the difficulties of the calculations. In the case of overdrafts, only the interest rate need be disclosed; the charges can be shown separately.

[44] The Consumer Credit (Advertisement) Regulations 1989, S.I. 1989 No. 1125; Consumer Credit (Quotations) Regulations 1989, S.I. 1989 No. 1126.

[45] CCA 1974, ss. 60–64 and the Consumer Credit (Agreements) Regulations supplementing them set out very detailed requirements.

[46] CCA 1974, ss. 62 and 63.

which must contain a notice informing the debtor of his or her right to cancel the agreement and of the cancellation procedures.[47] Agreements may be varied,[48] and the CCA 1974 also makes provision for termination.[49]

Some Aspects of Joint Accounts

(1) Liability of the parties to the bank

8–014 A joint account constitutes a debt owed to the account holders jointly by the bank.[50] Since there is normally no fiduciary relationship (husbands and wives often have joint accounts, for example) it differs from a solicitor's account or a trust account where the account holder is acting in a representative capacity.

Liability may be either joint, or joint and several, although bank mandates are normally in joint and several form. *Joint liability* means that the account holders make only one promise binding both of them[51]; *joint and several liability* means that they make one promise binding each of them and in addition each makes a *separate* promise binding him or her alone. There is a presumption against the delegation of authority,[52] so that, if there is no express agreement as to who may draw on the account and how many signatures are necessary, liability is joint and both must act jointly in signing cheques; the banker would not be entitled to pay just one party. In most cases, however, the mandate form given by the customers to the bank will clearly show whether one signature suffices, although it is still a question of construction whether the account is joint or joint and several. The fact that the mandate states that either or both parties may sign cheques is not decisive in itself.[53]

8–015 The advantages of joint and several liability of the account holders for the bank are:

(i) if liability is joint, the surviving account holder inherits the debt on the death of an account holder (just as he or she inherits any credit) and the estate of the deceased party is relieved from liability. This

---

[47] Consumer Credit (Cancellation Notices and Copies of Documents) Regulations 1983, S.I. 1983 No. 1557. The Consumer Credit (Agreements) Regulations 1983 (S.I. 1983 No. 1553), which require certain information to be given to the debtor and formal agreement heading and statutory notice warning the debtor of his or her rights, must also be complied with if the loan is to be enforceable.

[48] CCA 1974, s. 82.

[49] CCA 1974, ss. 98, 88 and 76.

[50] Banks undertake in the Code of Practice to give additional information to customers on their rights and responsibilities of joint account holders (Banking Code (1999), para. 2.7).

[51] Joint liability used to mean that if A and B were jointly liable to C, and C sued A, this "exhausted" the rights of C, who could not then sue B, but this was changed by the Civil Liability (Contribution) Act 1978.

[52] *Husband v. Davis* (1851) 20 L.J.C.P. 118.

[53] *Hirschorn v. Evans* [1938] 2 K.B. 801.

might cause a problem for the bank: if all the account holders but one are insolvent and that one dies, the bank would have no effective remedy. Where liability is joint and several, the bank may claim against the estate of the dead account holder.

(ii) if one of the joint parties has a separate account of his or her own, combination[54] is possible against credits in the separate account in respect of debts in the joint account[55] because the party is separately liable for the joint debt;

(iii) in relation to partnership joint accounts, there is the further advantage for the bank that if it wishes to sue a bankrupt partner for partnership debts and liability is joint and several, the bank ranks as a private creditor on the separate claim; whereas, if liability is joint, the bank may claim only after non-partnership (private) creditors of the bankrupt have been satisfied.

(2) Liability of the bank to the parties

There is also the question whether the *bank* owes a duty jointly and severally to the account holders. This problem has sometimes arisen where the bank has paid wrongly. The question is whether, if liability is joint, the other (injured) party can sue the bank separately. **8–016**

In *Brewer v. Westminster Bank Ltd*,[56] two executors of a will held a joint account. One forged the other's signature to cheques, which the bank paid, whereupon the other sued the bank for breach of mandate. McNair J. held that the banker's obligation was a single one to the account holders jointly. This meant that an action on the joint account could only succeed if it was brought by the account holders jointly. Here, where one of account holders could not sue as plaintiff because of his own wrong, the conclusion was that *neither* could sue. (The bank also argued, and this was unsuccessful, that there is an implied term that each customer in a joint account guarantees the other's honesty and will supervise what the other is doing—in other words, that the plaintiff here actually owed a duty to the bank.) The case has not been followed, despite the superficial logic of the decision, and in *Jackson v. White and Midland Bank*,[57] Park J., pointing out that applying the *Brewer* decision would deprive the innocent party of any remedy, said that the bank's agreement with the two customers was to honour cheques jointly drawn and that there was an implied agreement with each of them **8–017**

[54] Or statutory set off on bankruptcy under s. 323 of the IA 1986.

[55] Not the other way around, unless there is a contractual set off clause.

[56] [1952] 2 All E.R. 650.

[57] [1967] 2 Lloyds Rep. 68. See also *Baker v. Barclays Bank Ltd* [1955] 1 W.L.R. 822; *Welch v. Bank of England and Others* [1955] Ch. 508; *Ardern v. BNSW* [1956] V.L.R. 569; *Simos v. National Bank of Australasia Ltd and Guelman* (3d Party) (1976) 10 A.C.T.R. 4; *Catlin* [1983] 1 All E.R. 809. See also Goodhart (1952) 68 L.Q.R. 446, Glanville Williams (1953) 16 M.L.R. 232.

separately not to honour any cheques not drawn by him. In *Catlin v. Cyprus Corporation*,[58] the mandate of a husband and wife's joint account required the signatures of both account holders; the intention was to stop independent action by one of the parties (the husband, in this case: the wife had earlier had a problem with independent action by him and did not want it to recur). After the couple had split up it was found that the bank had negligently allowed the husband to withdraw almost all the money in the account. Bingham J. held that although the bank had made an agreement with the parties jointly, the bank owed a duty to each party separately. In this case, the bank was liable to the extent of the wife's half share of the account.[59]

Brewer now may be regarded as wrongly decided. If the mandate requires joint signatures, the bank is in breach of its mandate if it honours cheques signed by one only, and any of the joint account holders may sue.

It would seem that any joint party may countermand payment of a cheque,[60] subject to the terms of the mandate.

(3) Rights between the bank and the parties

8–018 The ownership of the account, and therefore whether, and on whose behalf, the bank is entitled to pay cheques after the death of one joint account party depends on whether the bank's debt is owned by the creditors as joint creditors, or as tenants in common; and, in the case of joint ownership, whether all account holders own it beneficially. In the normal case, where ownership of the account is joint, the doctrine of *survivorship* applies, and sole legal title vests in the survivor. In the unusual case where the acccount holders are tenants in common, ownership of the debt would pass to the personal representatives of the deceased, and they alone would have authority to deal with the debt (following normal probate or administration procedures).

Normally the parties are not only joint owners at law but also joint beneficial owners, so that the survivor is both legal and beneficial owner, and the bank is entitled to deal with the survivor. Sometimes, however, though both parties are the joint legal owners, one of them may hold the legal title on trust for the other, who is the beneficial owner. In this case, if the survivor is the legal owner, he or she holds the legal title on the other's death on trust for the beneficial owner. On a normal joint account, the presumption (regardless of the terms of the mandate) would be that property is jointly owned, legally and beneficially, so that the bank may pay the survivor, who can give a good discharge for the debt.[61] Even if the

[58] [1983] 1 All E.R. 809.

[59] Taking account of the principle in the *Liggett's Case* [1928] 1 K.B. 348, see above, para. 7–016.

[60] *Gaunt v. Taylor* (1843) 2 Hare 413.

[61] For discussion of these principles, see *e.g. Husband v. Davis* (1851) 20 L.J.C.P. 118; *Marshall v. Crutwell* (1875) L.R. 20 Eq. 328; *Williams v. Davies* (1864) 2 Sw. & Tr. 437; *Re Bishop* [1965] Ch. 450. See also Cullity (1969) 85 L.Q.R. 530.

survivor is merely legal owner, and another person has the beneficial title, therefore, this will not normally concern the bank, unless it knows or has constructive notice of a breach of trust.

The mandate ceases for most purposes on death of the party concerned, but if it allows payment despite the death of one signatory, it can be relied upon as evidence of joint beneficial ownership, and the bank is therefore entitled to pay the survivor. In any case, the mandate should make the question of survivorship and beneficial ownership clear. **8–019**

If there is a clause providing for payment to the survivor, then the bank is obliged to pay the survivor only, not the executors of the dead account holder; if it does pay the executors, it is in breach of contract to the survivor. In rare cases, this can cause difficulties because of the problems of consideration and privity which actually underlie the commonplace arrangement of joint accounts. These problems can be well illustrated by the case of *McEvoy v. Belfast Banking Co Ltd.*[62] A father who was mortally ill had deposited a large sum of money in the joint names of himself and his son, aged 15, stating on the deposit receipt that it was payable to either of them or the survivor. When he died, he left his estate in trust for his son when he attained 25. The bank, however, paid the executors of the estate, who proceeded to lose the money in a business enterprise. The son, some years after he became 25, sued the bank.

The question, of course, was whether the bank had disobeyed the mandate. The bank's argument was that the son, who had been a minor when the account was set up, had not been privy to the contract, but was a third party who could acquire no rights under it (and since he had not contributed to the account either, he had, arguably, also given no consideration). If the bank could succeed in showing that he was not a party to the contract, the bank would have been entitled to pay the executors. **8–020**

In *McEvoy*, it was held that the son's claim was defeated because he had not been a party to the contract between his father and the bank. Lord Atkin's explanation of the relationship between the bank and the son (the third party), however, indicates a possible explanation of the privity problem: his view was that the father was acting as his son's agent in making the contract. The relationship between the contracting parties could be analysed in this way: "Where A deposits money with a bank in the names of self and B, payable to either or survivor, B's right to claim the deposit and sue the bank depends on whether A purported to make B a party to the contract. If he did, he must have either had authority to act as agent, or B must have ratified." In this case, since the son (aged 15), did not have contractual capacity at the time the contract was made, he would have had to ratify the contract later. In Lord Atkin's opinion, however, he had not done so: he had known of the business activities of the executors **8–021**

[62] [1935] A.C. 24.

and had not attempted to claim the money until long afterwards. This privity problem, to which Lord Atkin provided this possible "joint promise" solution, seems now to have been directly settled by the Contracts (Rights of Third Parties) Act 1999. A third party can now enforce a term of the contract if "the contract expressly provides that he may",[62a] or if the term of the contract "purports to confer a benefit on him",[62b] although it can be shown in this case by construction of the contract that the parties to the contract did not intend to confer a benefit on him.[62c]

As far as consideration was concerned, Lord Atkin also found that there could be consideration: there was a difference, he said, between a contract by A with the Bank to pay A and B, and a contract purporting to be made between A and B with the bank to pay A and B. In the latter case, B can sue the bank, because consideration has been given, as far as the bank is concerned.

8–022 **Action by the bank.** If the bank receives a cheque which has only been signed by the deceased party, this should be returned unpaid,[63] marked "Drawer deceased". If it has been signed by both parties, and the survivor is entitled to the contents of the account, the cheque may be honoured. If there is more than one survivor, a fresh mandate should be taken. It is important for the bank to avoid the operation of *Clayton's case*,[64] and an overdrawn account should be stopped (or a term in the original mandate may exclude its operation) in order to preserve the bank's rights against the deceased's estate.

(4) Rights between the parties themselves

8–023 Where the account has been opened in joint names but there is a disparity in the contributions made by the parties, there may be a question as to the rights of the parties when one account holder dies, or on divorce. The bank is entitled to pay the person who has legal title, but this is a question of the equities between the parties themselves. The question must be decided by having regard to the intentions of the parties. It may be that one party has intended to make a gift of the money to the other, or the account may have been put into joint names simply as a matter of convenience.

8–024 In *Marshal v. Crutwell*,[65] for example, the husband was in ill health and the joint account was set up merely to enable the wife to draw the money for necessaries during his illness. The balance therefore accrued, it was

---

[62a] s. 1(1)(a).
[62b] s. 1(1)(b).
[62c] s. 1(2).
[63] BOEA 1882, s. 75.
[64] See below, Chap. 11.
[65] (1875) L.R. 20 Eq. 328.

held, to his estate, and not to his wife. In *Jones v. Maynard*,[66] on the other hand, a case of *inter vivos* benefit, the account was composed of money from the husband, from the wife's small investment income and from the rent of a house jointly owned by husband and wife. The surplus on the account was invested in the husband's sole name. On divorce, it was held that there was a "common purse", and when the spouses had pooled their resources, the husband's earnings became joint property. In *Re Bishop*,[67] money from the joint account was used to buy some shares for the husband alone, some for the wife alone, and some for both of them jointly. It was held that the husband's money belonged to him, not to him in trust for his wife. Each had bought investments with the authority of the other, but for their own benefit and in their own name. In that case, Stamp J. held that an investment purchased by one or the other belonged to the person in whose name it was purchased or invested, who therefore, had the legal ownership.

(5) Bankruptcy of one party

Bankruptcy[68] does not have the same effect as death, because there is no question of survivorship. If one of the account holders becomes bankrupt, the bank should act in relation to a credit account just as if a single account holder is bankrupt, acknowledging the rights of the trustee in bankruptcy to the undivided debt, and should act on the joint instructions of the account holder and the trustee. Where the account is overdrawn, it may be combined with a credit account, if there is one, or otherwise should be stopped to prevent the operation of *Clayton's case*. The bank should open a separate account for the solvent party, and take a new mandate from him or her. **8–025**

Company Customers

This is merely a brief account of aspects of banks' dealings with companies. There is further discussion in other Chapters. **8–026**

A company is a separate legal entity from its shareholders and may make contracts and sue and be sued in its own name. Companies may be limited or unlimited—limited companies may be limited by shares or by guarantee, but most are limited by shares. When a company is formed it is required to register its constitution—its Memorandum and Articles of Association—with the Registrar of Companies. A public company must have "plc" and a private company must have "limited" after its name—the name is important, because the registered name and an address for service of writs must be stated legibly on all business letters, cheques and other documents purporting to be signed by the company.

---

[66] (1951) H.C. 572.
[67] (1965) Ch. 450, approved by *Pettitt v. Pettitt* [1970] A.C. 777.
[68] See below, Chap. 24 for insolvency.

Operation of the account

8–027 A cheque is deemed to have been made by a company if it was made in the company's name or on its behalf, by a person acting under the company's authority.[69] Every company must have its name (in full) on all cheques purporting to be signed by or on behalf of the company, or the officer of the company who signs or authorises the signature will be personally liable if the company does not pay.[70] It is usual to sign "by or on behalf of or on account of the company". If a bank mistakenly prints the incorrect name on a company's cheque form, the signatories may be liable to the holder of the cheque,[71] but the bank may be liable to compensate the signatories.

Powers of the company in dealing with third parties

8–028 Until fairly recently, banks had to make sure that a transaction undertaken with the company was not *ultra vires* (beyond the capacity of the company)—in other words, that it was within the objects and powers of the company as set out in the Memorandum. It might be *ultra vires* for it to borrow money for a purpose not sanctioned by the company's objects clause, for example, in which case the borrowing would be void.

This *ultra vires* rule, which used to bedevil company law, was intended to protect creditors, who would know in their dealings with companies that their money was only at risk if the company was acting within the stated fields of business. In practice, however, it was the creditor who suffered, because of what was known as the doctrine of *constructive notice*: all persons were deemed to know the contents of the Memorandum. If a bank lent money to a company which had no power to borrow, therefore, the bank might not be able to recover the money.

8–029 The reform of the law by section 35 of the CA 1985[72] removed the effects of lack of capacity for those dealing with a company, and section 35A provides that the power of the officers to bind the company or authorise others to do so, is to be deemed free of any limitation under the company's constitution for those dealing in good faith with the company,[73] so that banks are normally protected. Further, there is a presumption of good faith, and so a third party will not be regarded as acting in bad faith simply

---

[69] CA 1985, s. 37.

[70] CA 1985, s. 349. See also *Rafsanjan Pistachio Producers Co-operative v. Reiss* [1990] B.C.L.C. 352. If a bill of exchange is drawn on a company and the drawer writes the wrong name, but it is accepted by a director for the company, the drawer is estopped from suing the director: *Durham Fancy Goods Ltd v. Michael Jackson (Fancy Goods) Ltd* [1968] 2 All E.R. 987.

[71] *Hendon v. Adelman* (1973) 117 Sol. Jo. 631: the bank printed "L. & R. Agencies Ltd", as "L.R. Agencies Ltd".

[72] Inserted by the CA 1989, s. 108.

[73] Including limitations deriving from a resolution of the company or from an agreement between the members of the company or of any class of shareholders. Good faith is presumed: CA 1985, s. 35A(2)(c).

because it knows that an act is outside the powers of the board.[74] The doctrine of constructive notice has been abolished: a third party dealing with a company is not bound to inquire as to its capacity or the authority of directors,[75] and it does not need to check the contents of company documents[76]—indeed, it might be disadvantageous for it to do so, because if a bank sees the Articles, it might be held to have *actual* notice of any restriction or prohibition in them.

Authority of officers dealing with the bank

Another problem for banks remains: a transaction with third parties entered into by officers of the company in excess of authority is not enforceable, though it can be ratified. The company is not bound if those who act for it have no authority, or if there is no ratification. If there is authority, whether actual or ostensible, the bank's protection depends upon principles of agency law, not on Section 35 of the CA 1985.[77] **8–030**

Actual authority may be express or implied: for example, a managing director has *implied* authority to do all the things which fall within the usual scope of that office,[78] which includes authority to borrow or give security. Its existence is a matter of fact. *Ostensible* authority is the authority of an agent as it appears to others. It requires: that a representation was made that the agent had authority to enter the contract; that the third party has relied on the representation; and that the person was authorised to make the representation.[79] Ostensible authority cannot be relied upon where the outsider is aware of some limitation which prevents the authority arising or if it is put on inquiry as to the extent of the individual's authority.[80] Even in this case, however, the company might still ratify the transaction,[81] though this would have to be by special resolution if the third party has notice that the transaction falls outside the company's objects.

Other problems for banks

Among the variety of rules affecting companies which may affect banks are these: **8–031**

[74] CA 1985, s. 35A(2)(b).

[75] CA 1985, s. 35(B).

[76] It is not required to make any judgment as to whether a transaction is for the company's objects or for its benefit, though this might become an issue in case of liquidation, *e.g.* in deciding whether transactions are transactions at an undervalue or preferences.

[77] See *Rolled Steel Products (Holdings) Ltd v. B.S.C.* [1986] Ch. 246.

[78] *Hely-Hutchinson v. Brayhead Ltd* [1968] 1 Q.B. 549.

[79] Farrar's Company Law (4th ed., 1991) p. 374, relying on Lord Diplock's dictum in *Freeman & Lockyer v. Buckhurst Park Properties (Mangal) Ltd* [1964] 2 Q.B. 480.

[80] *AL Underwood v. Bank of Liverpool* [1924] 1 K.B. 775; *Rolled Steel Products (Holdings) Ltd v. BSC* [1986] Ch. 246.

[81] If the irregularity were procedural, the rule in *Royal British Bank v. Turquand* (1856) 6 E. & B. 327 that outsiders need not be concerned with internal irregularities (the indoor management rule) might still protect the bank, unless the bank knew or ought to have known of a failure to adhere to procedures.

8–032 **(a) Financial assistance for share purchase.** The CA 1985 prohibits companies from directly or indirectly giving financial assistance to anyone to help purchase shares in the company, except under certain restricted circumstances.[82] It is possible that the bank may become involved in a dubious transaction of this kind if the funds provided are either held by the bank or advanced by the bank by way of loan or overdraft. The difficulty might arise because the bank might owe a duty of care or might be under a liability for constructive trust, for example, when paying a company customer's cheques[83]; if the directors are acting in breach of their fiduciary duty in ordering a payment, the bank may become liable to compensate the company if the bank knows, or perhaps, ought to know, of the purpose of the payment.

8–033 **(b) Guarantees and loans given to or for directors.** Frequently a bank's customer will be the director of a company or a person connected with a director. If the bank proposes to make an advance to the director, it may call for a guarantee to be given by some other person, and the director may suggest the name of his or her company.

It may be an offence for a company to lend money to its own directors. Provisions of the CA 1985 restrict loans and guarantees given by the company to or for the directors, including shadow directors,[84] of the company, and such transactions may be prohibited, in which case the guarantee is void and the bank may be liable as a constructive trustee if it has knowingly paid out company money for the purpose of the loan. It is therefore dangerous for banks to hold company funds where the company proposes to lend the money to its directors, or to lend money to a company customer knowing that the company will lend the money in turn to a director.

8–034 **(c) Liability as a "shadow director".** A shadow director is defined as a person in accordance with whose instructions the directors of the company are accustomed to act.[85] The risk for a bank is that it may set out a rescue package for a financially troubled company customer which the company follows unsuccessfully, and the bank may become liable for wrongful trading as a shadow director if it has intervened too far in the company's affairs. This is discussed further in Chapter 24.

---

[82] To avoid doubt, a number of transactions are expressly declared to be valid (CA 1985, s. 153(3), (4)) *e.g.* ordinary dividend payments, bonus share allotments, authorised redemptions or purchases of share by the company (CA 1985, ss. 159–181); reductions of capital confirmed by the court under CA 1985, s. 137, certain insolvency transactions, and the lending of money as part of the company's ordinary business; the provision of money to employees as part of an employees' share scheme to enable them to buy fully paid shares; and loans to employees other than directors by way of a trust under which they hold the shares beneficially.

[83] See Chaps 5 and 9.

[84] People in accordance with whose directions the board is accustomed to act.

[85] IA 1986, s. 251; see further below, Chap. 24.

(d) Insolvency. There are a number of special insolvency provisions which affect the bank's relationship with company customers. Again, those are discussed below, in Chapter 24. **8–035**

Partnership Accounts[86]

A partnership is defined as "the relationship which subsists between person carrying on a business in common with a view of profit".[87] Two or more persons who are in such a relationship are, whether they know it or not, partners. Partnerships vary enormously—from a couple of friends running a small corner shop to multi-national commercial conglomerates of accountants or solicitors with hundreds of partners.[88] The Partnership Act 1890 (PA 1980) provides a legal framework for the regulation of partnerships, but partners are entirely free to vary their mutual rights and duties as they wish (the Act does not purport to be a complete code of the law), and there is no need for a formal document or deed of partnership.[89] **8–036**

Not only are there different sorts of partnership, there are different sorts of partners. Solicitors' firms, for example, often have "salaried partners",[90] who may be treated as more than merely employees, but who do not have full partnership ("equity partnership") status.[91] And there may be other members of firms who are not regarded as partners at all, perhaps because their professional rules prohibit them becoming partners in a firm composed of different professionals, but who can in reality be thought of as having partnership status, for example, barristers in firms of solicitors. **8–037**

Partnerships in England do not have legal personality,[92] but can sue and be sued in the firm name. The fact that partners' liability is unlimited has given rise to much heart-searching in recent years, particularly among accountants' firms, which have been found liable in professional negligence in some cases of international company fraud and have had to pay enormous sums in damages.[93]

Operation of the account

In opening a bank account for the firm, the account and the mandate may be in the firm's name (a partnership account) or in the names of the partners (a joint account). In the former case, the bank will require some **8–038**

[86] For authoritative discussion of the law of partnerships, see *Lindley and Banks on Partnership* (17th ed., 1995). For a readable introduction, see Morse, *Partnership Law*, 1997.

[87] Partnership Act 1890 (PA 1890), s. 1(1).

[88] Which prefer to remain partnerships to obtain tax advantages, and because of professional rules.

[89] PA 1890, s. 19.

[90] A solicitor receiving a fixed remuneration rather than a share of the profits, but who is held out by the firm as a partner is treated by the Law Society as a full partner: *Guide to the Professional Conduct of Solicitors* (6th ed., 1993) para. 3.11.

[91] See *United Bank of Kuwait Ltd v. Hammoud* [1988] 1 W.L.R. 1051, and *Nationwide BS v. Lewis* [1998] 3 All E.R. 143.

[92] The position is different in Scots law.

[93] See Freedman and Finch [1997] J.B.L. 387 and Griffiths [1998] CfiLR 157. A draft Bill has been drawn up (January 1999) which will provide for some degree of limited liability for partnerships. See also Birds (2000) 21 Company Lawyer 39.

evidence of the existence of the partnership, such as sight of the articles of partnership, although the signatures on the mandate form are sufficient to bind the signatories as if they were partners in any case. For that reason, all parties are asked to sign the mandate form whatever the name of the account, although those who are partners are bound whether or not this is done. The mandate may limit the authorised signatories to specified partners, and it always states that the liability is to be joint and several.[94]

A partner generally has implied authority to open a bank account in the firm name, and any single partner has the power to withdraw his or her authority and revoke the mandate.[95] Any partner, therefore, may insist on his or her own signature appearing on cheques, whatever the original mandate said, and may countermand a cheque, even if he or she did not sign it. If the firm is dissolved, the mandate is automatically cancelled when the fact of the dissolution is or ought to be known to the bank.

8–039 If one partner has an account in his or her own name, it is not a partnership account, even if it has been used only for partnership funds,[96] and if a bank holds accounts for partners individually, as well as for the partnership, it should always take care when paying a cheque made out to the partnership into a partner's private account and should make inquiries.[97]

Banks' mandate forms always provide for the *joint and several* liability of partners, and this is for two reasons: first, where a partner is bankrupt, this entitles the bank to proceed against his or her personal property equally with the personal creditors (otherwise the bank is postponed to the claims of the personal creditors); and secondly, if there is a debit balance on the firm's account, the bank will obtain the right of combination[98] in respect of credit balances which the partners have on their personal accounts, since the partners are personally liable for the debt.

Liability of partners

8–040 *Lindley and Banks on Partnership* makes the following statement of principle:

> "Every member of a partnership is at the same time a principal and an agent. As a principal, he is bound by what he does himself and by what his partners do on behalf of the firm, provided what they do falls within the limits of their authority; as an agent, he binds them by what he does for the firm, provided he keeps within the limits of *his* authority."[99]

[94] The bank will have to make checks on the identity and credit of the partners for the purposes of the money laundering legislation, see above, para. 2–043.
[95] *Lindley and Banks, op. cit.*, para. 12.51.
[96] *Alliance Bank v. Kearsley* (1871) L.R. 6 C.P. 433.
[97] See, *e.g. Baker v. Barclays Bank Ltd* [1955] 2 All E.R. 571.
[98] See below, Chap. 11.
[99] Para. 3.05.

Partners' liability is unlimited, and the contractual liability of partners to outsiders is joint, unless the partners agree to joint and several liability; each partner is therefore liable for the debts and obligations of the firm incurred while he or she is a partner.[1] This means that the failure of the partnership business may lead not only to bankruptcy of the firm but also to personal bankruptcy of the partners. If one partner alone is sued, the others, as jointly liable parties, must contribute, and each has a right of indemnity against the others.[2]

A concern of banks, as outsiders, is to know whether an individual partner may bind the partnership. Every general partner is an agent of the firm for the purpose of the partnership business, and while acting in the usual business of the partnership, has authority to bind the firm.[3] On ordinary principles of agency law, therefore, a partner may have *actual authority* to act for the firm, in which case the partner is, as a matter of fact, invested with authority by his or her partners, or *ostensible authority*, in which case the principal (the firm) is regarded as having represented that the agent has certain authority.[4] **8–041**

Holding out. A person who represents him or herself or knowingly allows him or herself to be represented as a partner in a particular firm is liable as a partner to anyone who has relied on the representation and given credit to the firm.[5] The representation or action—for example, putting his or her name on the firm's notepaper—must relate to the kind of business carried on by the firm, and must be done in the usual way of carrying on that business,[6] and the third party must not know that the person had no actual authority, and must not believe that he or she was not a partner. Although the firm is bound by the acts of a partner in the usual course of the partnership business,[6a] the other partners may have imposed a prohibition so that he or she has no actual authority, but this is only binding on an outsider if he or she has notice of it.[7] **8–042**

Powers of partners

Only if the firm is a commercial or trading partnership (as opposed, for example, to a professional one such as a firm of accountants or solicitors) do the implied powers of partners include borrowing for the firm, giving **8–043**

[1] PA 1890, s. 9. In tort they are jointly and severally liable, s. 12.
[2] Civil Liability (Contributions) Act 1978, s. 3.
[3] PA 1890, s. 5.
[4] See *United Bank of Kuwait v. Hammoud* [1988] 1 W.L.R. 1051.
[5] PA 1890, s. 5. Partners by estoppel, PA 1890, s. 14. See *Nationwide BS v. Lewis* [1998] 3 All E.R. 143 at 146. "Given credit" probably means having any transaction with the firm: *Lindley and Banks, op. cit.*, para. 5.52.
[6] See *United Bank of Kuwait v. Hammoud* [1988] 1 W.L.R. 1051.
[6a] See *Dubai Aluminium Company Ltd v. Saloam*, *The Times*, April 21, 2000, CA, and *Flynn v. Robin Thompson & Partners*, *The Times*, March 14, 2000, CA.
[7] PA 1890, s. 8. The bank may therefore prefer not to see the partnership deed, because if it does it will have notice of any prohibition.

security,[8] dealing with negotiable instruments,[9] contracting and paying debts on the firm account, borrowing money on the firm's credit,[10] and pledging goods and securities for the business[11]; provided, that is, that the partner is acting in the ordinary course of business.[12] These powers do not extend to giving guarantees for the firm (unless there is a trade custom); to commencing litigation[13] or authorising the use of the firm name for the purpose; to executing deeds; or accepting property in lieu of a money debt owed to the firm.

8–044 In the case of other "non-trading" partnerships, a general partner's powers, which may be extended or restricted by agreement, include drawing cheques,[14] selling and buying goods, employing staff, and giving a good discharge for money received from debtors. Such partnerships have no implied power to borrow, and the bank's mandate form should expressly authorise the making of advances on the signatures of those specified in the mandate. Similarly, the mandate should authorise the signatories to give security over the partnership property, though it is common practice to obtain the signatures of all the partners to such a transaction in any case, to avoid any argument that the transaction was not in the ordinary course of the partnership business. In a trading partnership, all partners would be bound even without written authority, provided the terms of the mandate are not contravened and the borrowing is for and in the ordinary course of business. Partners who are minors may bind the partnership and its assets, though they cannot give securities over their personal assets either for their own debts or for those of the firm.

Partnership property

8–045 The partners are joint owners of all property brought into or acquired by the firm.[15] On the death of a partner, his or her interest passes to the partner's personal representative.

---

[8] *Higgins v. Beauchamp* [1914] 3 K.B. 1192.

[9] But see *Hogarth v. Latham & Co* (1878) 3 Q.B.D. 643.

[10] *Lane v. Williams* (1692) 2 Vern. 277.

[11] *Ex p. Bonbonus* (1803) 8 Ves. 540; *Re Clough* (1885) 31 Ch. D. 324; *Re Bourne, Bourne v. Bourne* [1906] 2 Ch. 427.

[12] See *United Bank of Kuwait v. Hammoud* [1988] 1 W.L.R. 1051 at 1063, *per* Staughten L.J.: the work that solicitors do can be expected to have changed since 1888 (and is changing now) and "elderly cases in the footnotes" of *Halsbury's Laws* should be treated with caution.

[13] *Arbuckle v. Taylor* (1815) 3 Dow 160.

[14] But not other bills of exchange, *Backhouse v. Charlton* (1878) 8 Ch. D. 444. In some firms, this may be inconsistent with the usual course of partnership business, and would be prohibited.

[15] *Popat v. Schonchhatra* [1997] 3 All E.R. 800, CA, considered the nature of partnership interests in property. See also *Joyce v. Morrissey* [1999] E.M.L.R. 233, CA, and *Don King Productions Ltd v. Warren* (1999) 1 Lloyd's Rep. 588, CA.

Unless otherwise agreed, a partner is not entitled to a share of the partnership assets (its "capital") while the business continues.[16] A bank considering the assets of a personal customer who is a partner rarely takes the partnership assets into account, because it is the creditors of the firm who have first claim against the firm's assets, and because it may have to wait a long time until dissolution occurs anyway: partners often agree that the firm will not dissolve on the occurrence of many of the relevant events. If, on the other hand, the customer is the partnership itself, the bank will take the personal assets of the partners into account, because (unless they are limited partners[17] or there is a special agreement with the creditor) their liability is unlimited.

Partnerships may give a mortgage or charge over the firm's property, **8–046** such as book debts, and partners may give a mortgage of their personal property for the firm's debts. A fixed charge may be taken over future book debts,[18] but care must be taken that the charge is properly drawn as a fixed charge; if it is a floating charge it will be ineffective, because it is not possible for the firm or the partners to give a floating charge over their assets.[19] A partner who holds the legal title of property in trust for the others may, if acting within his or her authority, give an effective legal and equitable title.

Complications may arise in the case of land, where there may now be a trust of land under the Trusts of Land and Appointment of Trustees Act 1996 (TLATA 1996).[20] If one partner (or more), acting with authority, actual or ostensible, signs a purported legal mortgage which is not in the correct form for a legal mortgage, the legal interests of the non-signatory partners are not affected, but their equitable interests may be effectively mortgaged in equity. Similarly, one party may pledge deeds of title to partnership property, creating an equitable mortgage; or may pledge negotiable instruments, creating a legal pledge of this personal property.

Partners may assign their share in the assets of the firm or their right to **8–047** profits to another person, who takes no other rights. This enables a partner to mortgage his or her share of the firm's assets. This is rarely done by way of security for bank advances to partners personally, though mortgages as security for advances to the firm itself are common.

---

[16] A judgment obtained against a partner personally cannot be executed against the firm's assets, although a charging order may be obtained against the partner's interest, PA 1890, s. 23(2), and this is a ground to seek dissolution.

[17] Whose liability is limited to the amount of capital contributed: Limited Partnership Act 1907.

[18] See *Siebe Gorman & Co Ltd v. Barclays Bank* [1979] 2 Lloyd's Rep. 142, see Chap. 19.

[19] For technical reasons arising from the Bills of Sale Acts 1878–1891 (BSA 1878–1891).

[20] See below, Chap. 20. PA 1890, s. 22, which applied the doctrine of conversion to partnerships was repealed by TLATA 1996.

Dissolution of partnership

8–048 The partnership may be dissolved when a specific purpose is achieved or becomes impossible; at the expiry of a fixed term; or when a certain event occurs. A partnership at will (that is, for an indeterminate time) may be ended by notice. The partnership is automatically dissolved in certain circumstances—if there is a change in the composition of the firm, by death, retirement or the addition of a new partner; or if a partner becomes bankrupt or an enemy alien, or the partnership becomes illegal in some other way. The articles of partnership may provide that the firm may be ended or its composition changed only "by mutual agreement", in which case unilateral resignation may not be permitted.[21] A partnership may also be dissolved by order of the court[22]—for example if a partner becomes permanently incapable of carrying on (for example, through ill health or mental incapacity), or if a partner (not the petitioner) is guilty of conduct prejudicial to the firm's business, such as dishonesty.

Dissolution does not affect existing liabilities, and limited trading may continue to allow the business to be wound up. People dealing with the firm are entitled to treat all apparent members of the old firm as still being members until they have notice of a change,[23] and in any case, the partners retain authority to bind the firm so far as matters necessary for winding up are concerned.

8–049 The partnership may be replaced by a new one if the remaining or new partners continue to work together, and it is important that the partnership agreement provides for this possibility, because the original terms of the partnership will not necessarily apply to the firm which continues, unless the new partners impliedly adopt them by acting in accordance with them.[24] A bank mandate should also make provision for one partner leaving the firm and may permit the bank to continue to act on the signature of the other parties, although banks normally take a new mandate from the remaining partners in any case and will certainly do so if a new member is admitted.

Third party guarantees or securities, whether given to the firm or for the firm's debts, may also be invalidated by a change in the composition of the firm, unless the guarantee contains terms providing to the contrary.

Events of dissolution

8–050 **(a) Death of a partner.** Death revokes a partner's authority, although the estate of the deceased partner remains liable for anything done while that person was a partner. Where the firm is not dissolved on the death and

[21] *Moss v. Elphick* [1910] 1 K.B. 846.

[22] PA 1980, s. 35.

[23] PA 1890, s. 38. If a partner has been wronged by a dissolution of the firm without his consent and is entitled to damages he is still liable to creditors of the firm for transactions entered into while he was a partner: *Hurst v. Bryk, The Times*, April 4, 2000, HL.

[24] PA 1890, s. 21(1), see *Brooks v. Brooks* (1901) 85 L.T. 453. See also *Sheppard & Cooper v. TSB* [1997] 2 B.C.L.C. 222, CA.

continues to use the dead partner's name in the firm name, the estate is not liable for claims arising after his or her death, and no notification to creditors of the death is necessary to protect the estate. Similarly, a personal security cannot be charged with advances made after the partner's death. The partner's partnership assets go to his or her personal representatives.[25]

On the death of a partner, the rule is that partnership creditors may proceed first against partnership property and personal creditors may proceed first against personal property,[26] but this may be avoided by providing for joint and several liability in the mandate.[27]

Action by the bank. When the death of a partner who has signed a cheque becomes known, the authority of the paying bank to pay on the cheque is revoked, and the bank should return the cheque to the surviving partners for signature.[28] **8–051**

The dead partner's estate is not liable for new debts. If the original bank account is continued, the rule in *Clayton's Case*[29] may have the effect of discharging any past liability for which the partner remains responsible. It is general practice, therefore, where accounts are in debit to rule off the old account and open a new one, even if there is a term in the mandate excluding the operation of the rule. If this is not done, and the rule operates to reduce the debt, then a personal security given by the dead partner may also become ineffective.[30]

The partnership bank account may be continued for a period after dissolution because the surviving partners (or a single survivor) have residual authority to bind the estate of the dead partner; they have implied power to do whatever is necessary to wind up the affairs of the partnership, and this includes the power to mortgage the firm's property where necessary.[31] The bank only needs to take a new mandate if new partners are to be admitted or if there is otherwise to be a change in the authorised signatories. Further, in the absence of any evidence to the contrary, a person dealing with the survivors may assume that a mortgage is granted in the proper course of winding up. There is no duty to inquire.[32] On this principle, even if on dissolution the dead partner's liability is reduced by the operation of *Clayton's Case*, the survivors may still charge partnership property (a share of which belongs to the deceased) so that the estate is **8–052**

[25] PA 1980, s. 20.
[26] *Re Jeffry, ex p. Honey* (1871) 7 Ch. App. 178.
[27] Under PA 1890, s. 9, there is joint and several liability on the death of a partner, but the partnership may expressly negative it.
[28] Some banks may pay on such a cheque, judging the risk to be slight.
[29] (1816) 1 Mer. 529, see below, Chap. 11.
[30] See *e.g. Governors of the Royal Bank of Scotland v. Christie* (1841) 8 Cl. & Fin. 214.
[31] PA 1890, s. 38.
[32] *Re Bourne, Bourne v. Bourne* [1906] 2 Ch. 427.

bound in respect of debts incurred after the death.[33] The share in the security over partnership property for which the deceased partner would have been liable is effective against the estate.

8–053 The bank has no duty to inquire as to the state of indebtedness between the survivors and the dead partner, and payments may, therefore, be safely made to the survivors, unless the bank has actual notice of the state of accounts and has some reason to think that the survivors would not account.

If the surviving partners continue to act as a firm although the old partnership has been dissolved, then strictly, a new mandate is required. The partnership assets must then be distributed, with a share going to the estate of the dead partner unless his or her representatives agree otherwise. Debts of the old partnership may be called in by the bank, though they need not be if the business is prospering. New securities should be taken, unless the old ones make provision for their continuation in these circumstances, by saying, for example: "despite any change in the composition of the firm". Such wording clearly binds the partners who were party to the original agreement, but new partners should be asked to sign a fresh agreement. If new security agreements are taken, there may be a notional repayment and fresh advance, so that the consideration is not past.

8–054 **(b) Retirement of a partner.**[34] The retirement of a partner dissolves the firm unless otherwise agreed. The remaining partners have authority to bind the partnership for winding it up. As when a partner dies, the bank rules off the account. Retiring partners remain liable for debts and claims incurred while they were partners, but not for new ones, except that, in relation to creditors who have been dealing with the firm, the retiring partner has been held out as a partner and will be liable for new partnership debts, and the firm may be bound by the partner's acts, until notice is given.[35]

8–055 **(c) Mental disorder of a partner.** This does not necessarily dissolve a firm, unless the other partners decide to apply to the court for dissolution,[36] but notice of the fact countermands the authority of the remaining partners unless otherwise agreed. If the firm is dissolved, the situation is the same as when a partner has died.

If the disorder is of a sort to make him or her incapable of contracting, the contract is voidable: the partner is not bound by contracts made with the firm by any third parties who are aware of the disorder. If the third

[33] [1906] 2 Ch 427.

[34] See especially the PA 1890, ss. 14, 17(2) and 36. It is common for insurance to be taken out against unexpected liability.

[35] Usually individual notification to existing creditors, and additionally advertisement in the London Gazette, PA 1890, s. 36(2).

[36] Mental Health Act 1983, ss. 94 and 96.

party does not know of the disorder, and there is no reason to know of it, the partner still has ostensible authority to bind the firm.[37]

(d) New partners. When a new partner is taken on, the firm is dissolved unless otherwise agreed. New partners are not liable for anything done before they become partners, unless there is a *novation*, by which the firm's creditors agree to accept the promise of the new partner to assume liability in consideration for discharging a retiring partner, or for some other consideration. **8–056**

If the firm has been dissolved, the bank should stop the old account. It should also take a new mandate when it learns of a new partner, in order to bind that partner and in case there is to be a change of signatories. In that case, or where the firm has been dissolved, all partners must sign the new mandate. If the new partner is not to be a signatory, this is unnecessary, and he or she may sign a new mandate in the name of the firm.

(e) Bankruptcy of a partnership. A number of possibilities are open to bankrupt partnerships, including winding up and joint bankruptcy by individual members of the firm. There are also "rescue" procedures available, such as partnership voluntary arrangement or an administration order. The Insolvent Partnerships Order 1994,[38] permits partnerships to be wound up as though they were unregistered companies, so that the bankruptcy does not necessarily involve the bankruptcy of the partners.[39] After presentation of the petition, any disposition of the firm's property is void unless ratified by the court. On learning of a petition, therefore, any bank account should be stopped, whether it is in the name of the firm or of a partner. With regard to priority, the firm's creditors rank against the assets of the partnership in priority to the individual creditors, whereas both sets of creditors rank equally against assets of individual partners. If a lender has made a loan on the basis that the rate of interest is to vary with the profits, and the borrower becomes bankrupt, the lender may not recover anything in respect of the unpaid interest until the claims of other creditors have been satisfied. **8–057**

Local Authority Accounts

Local authorities must act within their statutory powers,[40] so that officers of the authority must act within its powers and their own authority, which must have been properly issued. An authority is a legal personality and can **8–058**

[37] Where a partner may be of unsound mind, the other partners may apply for an interim injunction to restrain him or her from acting.

[38] S.I. 1994 No. 2421.

[39] There is an attempt to harmonise the insolvency procedures for the partnership and for individual partners if this is necessary: *e.g.* proceedings in relation to both should be considered at the same time: arts 8 and 10.

[40] Local Government Act 1972, Local Government (Miscellaneous Provisions) Act 1976, and the Local Government Act 1985.

open bank accounts in its own name, and may also borrow money for certain purposes. A person lending money does not have to inquire whether the borrowing is legal or regular, or whether it has been used properly, and is not to be "prejudiced by an illegality or irregularity, or by the misapplication or non-application" of the money.[41]

8–059 Some transactions with local authorities have, notoriously, caused problems for banks in recent years. In *Hazell v. Hammersmith and Fulham London Borough Council*,[42] the Council borrowed large sums of money in a legal exercise of its borrowing powers. Some loans were at fixed rates of interest, others at variable rates. The Council, like some other local authorities, then used this borrowing to enter into a number of interest rate "swap" contracts. The Council hoped, by these contracts, based on forecasting movements in interest rates, to reduce the burden of interest payable in respect of the borrowings by the Council.

8–060 A swap transaction works by setting off two different methods of paying interest against each other:

> "one party (the 'fixed rate' payer) agrees to pay the other over a certain period interest at a fixed rate on a notional capital sum; and the other party (the 'floating rate' payer) agrees to pay to the former over the same period interest on the same notional sum at a market rate determined in accordance with a certain formula".[43]

Normally neither party actually pays the sums which it has agreed to pay on the specified date, but instead makes a settlement on a "net payment basis" under which the party owing the greater amount on any day simply pays the difference between the two amounts due to each other. The form of swap which was used here involved an "upfront payment"—one party paying a capital sum to the other, which is balanced by adjustment of their liabilities.[44] This upfront payment was the attraction for the local authorities: if they were "rate-capped", they could effectively borrow money from banks by this means without infringing the statutory controls on their borrowing.

8–061 The House of Lords, however, held that the transactions were *ultra vires* and unlawful, because the Council had neither express statutory power nor implied power to undertake them. Although the Council's functions

---

[41] Local Government Act 1972, s. 172 and Sched. 13: "A person lending money to a local authority shall not be bound to enquire whether the borrowing of money is legal or regular or whether the money raised was properly applied and shall not be prejudiced by an illegality or irregularity, or by the misapplication or non-application of any of that money".

[42] [1992] A.C. 1. See Chatterjee [1996] 4 J.I.B.L. 155.

[43] *Westdeutsche Landesbank Girozentrale v. Islington LBC* [1996] 2 All E.R. 961 at 963, *per* Lord Goff.

[44] *e.g.* A, the fixed rate payer, may make an upfront payment to B, the floating rate payer, and consequently the rate of interest payable by A to B is reduced.

included borrowing, and there was implied power under section 111 of the Local Government Act 1972 to do anything ancillary to the discharge of any of its functions, it could not be said that these transactions could be considered ancillary or incidental to the power to borrow and lend money or that it could be described as "debt management".[45]

Since then, the courts have established that the banks could recover their money from the authorities concerned by virtue of the principles of the law of restitution, since the authorities had been unjustly enriched at the expense of the banks, which were therefore entitled to recover it as money had and received. Although the function of the law of restitution is to restore both parties to the position they were in before they entered into the transaction, it was held by the House of Lords in *Westdeutsche Landesbank Girozentrale v. Islington LBC*, that that did not include the payment of compound interest on the money awarded against the council.[46] **8–062**

It has been commented that the "swaps" cases offer guidelines to local authorities in relation to the use of derivatives; and that "the guidelines have become necessary to emphasise that the ethos of a local authority's activities is far removed from the profit-making ethos of a commercial house".[47] Banks must be aware too that supporting local authorities in speculative activities[48] is imprudent. Other innovative transactions by local authorities in which banks have been involved may be as dangerous for banks as swaps. In *Credit Suisse v. Allerdale B.C.*,[49] the local authority created a limited liability company to assist with the financing of various capital projects for which the authority itself had insufficient funds. The company, which was to purchase and develop a swimming pool and other projects, including carrying on trade in time share accommodation, was set up to avoid the limitations on the expenditure of the authority. Allerdale provided a guarantee for the company to Credit Suisse. The company failed and the bank called in the guarantee. Allerdale's argument, to avoid having to repay the bank, was that it had not had the power to enter into such a scheme.[50] The court agreed and held further—importantly from the bank's point of view—that a third party which contracts with a local authority only obtains protection from statute if the contract is to lend money to the authority.[51] The bank here, in accepting a guarantee from Allerdale, therefore took the risk that the council was acting for an improper motive **8–063**

[45] Which Lord Templeman (at 34–36) described as prudent and lawful activities on the part of the local authority. Swaps, on the other hand, were more akin to gambling: "speculation on a vast and admittedly unlawful scale".

[46] See above, para. 8–008.

[47] See Chatterjee [1996] 4 J.I.B.L. 160.

[48] As derivative transactions, even when hedged, were viewed by the courts.

[49] [1996] 2 Lloyd's Rep. 241, CA.

[50] It had no power under s. 19(1) of the Local Government (Miscellaneous Provisions) Act 1976 to provide time share accommodation; and s. 111 of the Local Government Act 1972 did not enable it to escape the restrictions imposed by Parliament.

[51] Local Government Act 1972, Sched. 13.

and that the transaction might be *ultra vires*, as indeed it proved to be. In the result, the bank was unable to enforce the guarantee against Allerdale.[52]

It is prudent for a bank wishing to conclude a contract with a local authority, to ascertain whether the authority's proposals fall within its statutory powers and to take care that it is not intending to act improperly, in order to avoid falling into the same trap as Credit Suisse.

MARRIED WOMENS' ACCOUNTS

8–064 Women, married or not, now enjoy the same rights in law as men.[53] Problems may occur with accounts of spouses, particularly joint accounts, with lending to married couples, and with one spouse guaranteeing the borrowing of the other. These are discussed in the appropriate Chapters.

MINORS' ACCOUNTS

8–065 Minors (persons below the age of eighteen[54]) may only make valid contracts under certain conditions. Contracts made by minors are void, unless they are for the supply of goods or services that are "necessaries",[55] in which case the minor is bound to pay a reasonable price for goods and services suitable to his station in life and his needs. It is likely in fact that most minors' bank accounts are for necessaries, in this sense, but if not, the bank may not be able to enforce the contract. Banks, therefore, may sometimes be unwilling to open an account in a minor's name, and may prefer to open it in the name of a parent or guardian. The court now has power to order a party to a contract who claims it is unenforceable because he or she was a minor when it was made to transfer to the other party any property acquired under the contract if it is just and equitable to do so.[56]

8–066 A minor also has no capacity to draw or indorse a cheque and can thus never be liable as party to a cheque, even one drawn to pay for necessaries.[57] However, the minor can still be liable to his or her bank for the *debt* created by the cheque, and also to the payee under the contract.

As far as lending to minors is concerned, the law used to be that all contracts with minors "for the repayment of money lent or to be lent" were "absolutely void",[58] even if the bank was advancing money to pay for necessaries. This has been changed, and a contract of loan is treated in the same way as any other contract by a minor.[59] Mortgages granted by minors

[52] See Otton-Goulder [1996] 11 J.I.B.L 266. No remedies in restitution were open to the bank here because nothing had been transferred to Allerdale.

[53] Opening a bank account constitutes a binding contract with the woman who contracts as a *feme sole*: Law Reform (Married Women and Tortfeasors) Act 1935, ss. 1 and 2.

[54] Family Law Reform Act 1969.

[55] *Nash v. Inman* [1908] 2 K.B. 1.

[56] Minors' Contracts Act 1987, s. 3.

[57] BOEA 1882, s. 22.

[58] Infants Relief Act 1874, s. 1.

[59] Minors' Contracts Act 1987. If money advanced to a minor has actually been applied to a lawful debt, such as a purchase of necessaries, the bank may be subrogated to the rights of the lawful creditor, the vendor, and might be entitled to a lien: *Nottingham Permanent Benefit Building Society v. Thurstan* [1903] A.C. 6.

are void, however, because persons under 18 may not hold a legal estate in land.[60]

Banks will therefore be cautious in lending to minors without obtaining guarantees from parents or guardians.

Mental Incapacity

Contracts by patients suffering mental disability are voidable if the other party knew of the facts from which the disorder could be inferred.[61] If the Court of Protection appoints a receiver, dispositions will be void in any case.[62] If a power of attorney is made under the Enduring Powers of Attorney Act 1985, the power may be exercised after the disorder comes into existence, subject to the safeguards of the Act. **8–067**

If a bank advances money to a customer who has no contractual capacity because of mental disorder, subrogation may provide a remedy if the money is used to pay a lawful debt, such as meeting necessary outgoings of the customer's estate.[63]

Trust Accounts

Trustees have the legal title in the trust property (the beneficiaries have the equitable title) and must administer the trust according to the trust deed and their statutory powers and duties.[64] The powers given to trustees differ markedly from one trust to another, and it is important for banks to ensure that any transaction is within the authority of the trustees.[65] **8–068**

Trustees are generally required to act jointly, and the powers to delegate do not extend to the signing of cheques, and therefore a bank should always insist that all trustees sign every cheque.[66] A new trustee may be appointed in place of a retiring trustee under section 36 of the Trustee Act 1925 (Tr A 1925), and the bank will wish to see the deed of appointment and to have him or her sign the mandate. When a trustee dies, the other trustees have power to operate the account for a time.[67] On the death of the last surviving trustee, the account may be operated by his or her personal representatives.

Trustees have some powers of borrowing money[68]: where they have power to apply capital, they may raise capital by mortgage of trust property[69] and have also the power of borrowing. A bank as mortgagee is **8–069**

---

[60] Unless it were in the form of an indemnity. Ss. 1(6) and 19 of the LPA 1925. As to guarantees, see below, Chap. 18.

[61] *Imperial Loan Co v. Stone* [1892] 1 Q.B. 599.

[62] *Re Marshall* [1920] 1 Ch. 284.

[63] *Re Beavan, Davies, Banks & Co v. Beavan* [1912] 1 Ch. 196.

[64] Trustee Act 1925. Powers may also be implied by common law, and the court has statutory and inherent powers to authorise transactions.

[65] See further in Chap. 9 for discussion of banks' liability as constructive trustees.

[66] Except for a charitable trust: Charities Act 1960, s. 34, where at least two trustees may be given general authority.

[67] Tr A 1925, s. 18.

[68] Tr A 1925, ss. 16 and 28 and power may be given in the deed.

[69] Tr A 1925, s. 16.

not concerned to see that the money so raised is wanted by the trust nor that no more than is wanted is raised, nor as to the application of the money.[70]

A bank may permit the trustees to breach the strict terms of the trust if all the beneficiaries (who must be over 18 and mentally capable) consent.[71] A trustee who becomes bankrupt may continue as trustee and his or her trustee in bankruptcy does not take the property held on trust.

Solicitors' Accounts

8–070 Solicitors should place their clients' money in a clients' account to keep it separate from their own office accounts. Strict rules are laid down by the Law Society[72] as to the operation of such accounts by solicitors, but the bank is not required to inquire into any right of a person to any money paid or credited to the clients' account, or to have any knowledge of it.[73]

Executors' Accounts

8–071 When there are two or more executors or administrators,[74] they do, unlike trustees, have power to act on their own. Each may open an account for the estate and they may also countermand cheques drawn by any of them. A personal representative who exceeds his or her powers will be personally liable.

They are entitled to run the businesses of the deceased, but only for the purpose of winding up the estate,[75] and they have power to borrow and to give security.[76]

The bank will normally require that each cheque be signed by at least two executors, and it is prudent for banks to take clear instructions on the mandate to avoid problems, particularly any possible misappropriation. Similarly, any loan sought should be carefully investigated.[77]

---

70 Trustee Act 1925, s. 17.

71 *Saunders v. Vautier* (1841) 4 Beav. 115.

72 Solicitors' Accounts Rules 1995 (amended 1998).

73 Solicitors Act 1974, s. 85.

74 When someone dies intestate, their real and personal estate is held on trust by the personal representatives with the power to sell it: LPA 1925, s. 33(1), TLATA 1996, Sched. 2, para. 5(2).

75 Administration of Estates Act 1925, ss. 25 and 39 (unless there is specific power to do so in the will), *Kirkman v. Booth* (1848) 11 Beav. 273 at 280; *Garrett v. Noble* (1834) 6 Sim 504.

76 Administration of Estates Act 1925, ss. 39–40.

77 The bank should try to ensure that its claim has priority over those of the creditors by requiring their consent to the loan.

Chapter 9

Banks and Some Elements of Trusts

As we have seen, the relationship between banker and customer is founded on the contractual relationship of debtor and creditor. The bank also acts as an agent, however, and if a conflict between the duties arises, the bank will have to reconcile its duty of prompt repayment on the customer's instructions with the duty of reasonable care that agents owe to their principals. Further, since banks are involved with numerous financial transactions which inevitably allow opportunities for fraud, they may be under potentially onerous *equitable* liability with regard to the funds involved. A bank may become affected by rights which third parties have over funds held by the customer in an account. Those third party rights may be legal—for example, an express legal assignment of the funds may have been made. Alternatively, the customer may hold funds in trust for another person, in which case the bank must ensure in dealing with the account that it does not assist in any breach of trust. **9–001**

There are a number of ways in which a trust might affect a bank: the bank itself may be appointed as trustee of a fund, or an account may be subject to a "*Quistclose* trust" where funds are paid into an account for a particular purpose, which may prevent the bank from using the funds for its own purposes. There is also the possibility that the bank may become a *constructive trustee*, or that a fund may be subject to the process of tracing, where the customer has been wrongly paid money by a person with whom he or she had a fiduciary relationship, and where the funds may be recovered from the customer or the bank.[1] These matters are discussed in this Chapter. **9–002**

Banks Acting as Trustees

Banks routinely act as trustees for remuneration,[2] and have departments which specialise in the administration of trusts. In acting as a trustee, a bank must have regard to the trust deed itself (which needs careful attention) to the relevant statutes[3] and to general equitable principles. **9–003**

The standard required of a bank in acting as a trustee was examined by the Court of Appeal in *Nestle v. National Westminster Bank plc.*[4] A fund had

---

[1] The (legal) personal remedy of money had and received (considered below, Chap. 10) may also be available.

[2] The trust deed should contain a charging clause.

[3] *e.g.* Tr A 1925 and Trustee Investments Act 1961.

[4] [1994] 1 All E.R. 122. See Watt and Stauch [1998] Conv. 352.

been entrusted to a bank under a testator's will in 1922. By 1986, when the plaintiff became solely entitled to the estate, the fund was worth about £269,000, but the plaintiff claimed that it would have been worth more than £1.8 million if the bank had managed the trust with proper care. She could show that the bank had misunderstood the nature of the investment clause in the trust, had not taken any steps at any time to obtain legal advice as to the scope of its powers to invest (an "inexcusable failure"[5]) and had failed to conduct periodic reviews of the trust. The court held, however, that these were symptoms of idleness and incompetence, not in themselves enough to give her a remedy or to be breaches of trust. The plaintiff had to be able to point to actual breaches of duty resulting in the loss, not merely to a loss of a chance that she would have been better off if the bank had invested differently, and she had not done so. And although a bank is required to act prudently as a trustee,[6] and fairly and impartially as between the beneficiaries, it would incur no liability for a decision made on wrong grounds or for an untenable reason if it appeared, in the light of later circumstances, that the decision had not been unwise. This standard, which the court itself regarded as "undemanding",[7] does not, it must be said, encourage people with funds to invest to entrust them to banks as trustees.

Banks with Express Notice of Trust Funds

9–004 The customer may hold funds in trust for another person.[8] In this case, the customer (the trustee) is entitled to deposit trust money in a bank account, to borrow money, and withdraw it by cheque, but the beneficiary of the funds has the equitable title to the money. When the bank is dealing with a trust account, it must take care to act in accordance with its mandate, and must ensure that transactions fall within the trustee's authority, or else it may find itself liable to the beneficiaries. If the bank has notice, actual or constructive, of the existence of a trust, it is liable if it is party to a breach of the trust. The problem for the bank is the familiar one—it must reconcile the conflict between the duty of promptly obeying its mandate (failure to do so will make it liable to the customer for breach of contract) and at the same time fulfilling any duty to inquire in order to guard against possible liability for breach of trust. This conflict was described by Lord Cairns in *Gray v. Johnston*[9]:

---

[5] [1994] 1 All E.R. 122, *per* Dillon L.J. at 125.

[6] In *Re Whitely, Whiteley v. Learoyd* (1886) 33 Ch.D. 347 at 355, Lindley L.J. said: "the duty rather is to take such care as an ordinary prudent man would take if he were minded to make an investment for the benefit of other people for whom he felt morally bound to provide." See Kenny [1996] N.L.J. 348, who criticises the decision for not adopting the higher standard of care for professional trustees referred to in the Law Commission *Report on the Powers and Duties of Trustees*, Law Com. No 23 (1982).

[7] [1994] 1 All E.R. 156 at 184, *per* Leggatt L.J.

[8] These comments about trustees are also relevant for others, like executors, who are in a similar position to trustees.

[9] (1868) L.R. 3 H.L. 1.

> "On the one hand, it would be a most serious matter if bankers were to be allowed, on light and trifling grounds—on grounds of mere suspicion or curiosity—to refuse to honour a cheque drawn by their customer, even although that customer might happen to be an administrator or an executor. On the other hand, it would be equally of serious moment if bankers were to be allowed to shelter themselves under that title, and to say that they were at liberty to become parties or privies to a breach of trust committed with regard to trust property, and, looking to their position as bankers merely, to insist that they were entitled to pay away money which constituted a part of trust property at a time when they knew it was going to be misapplied . . . the result of those authorities is clearly this: in order to hold a banker justified in refusing to pay a demand of his customer, the customer being an executor, and drawing a cheque as an executor, there must, in the first place, be some misapplication, some breach of trust, intended by the executor, and there must, in the second place . . . be proof that the bankers are privy to the intent to make this misapplication of the trust funds".[10]

It is only notice of a *breach* of trust which is significant; mere knowledge on the bank's part that a fund is a trust account does not necessarily affect the bank's ability to obey the customer's instructions, or involve the bank in liability. The bank may receive trust funds without incurring liability provided that the funds are placed in a trust account or an ordinary account known to be used for trust purposes by the trustees or that it has received the funds as a bona fide purchaser without notice of any breach of trust.[11] Trust funds in an account cannot be combined with a debit in a non-trust account,[12] for example, and if known trust funds are received into a trustee's personal account, the bank cannot combine the account with the trust account. Notice of breach of trust makes the bank liable (at least) to return what it has received, even if it gave value. **9–005**

In relation to dispositions of the trust fund from the account on the instructions of the customer, the bank has an obligation to obey its customer's orders, and will only be liable if it has notice of breach or trust. The important question for the bank is what amounts to "notice" of breach of trust. If an account is headed with the name ". . . trust account", the bank obviously has actual notice of the existence of a trust. But it is not always immediately apparent from the name of the account: an account **9–006**

[10] Contrast *Re Gross, ex p. Adair* (1871) 24 L.T. 198 at 203; *Re Wall, Jackson v. Bristol and West of England Bank Ltd* (1885) 1 T.L.R. 522, which was approved in *John Shaw (Rayners Lane) Ltd* (1944) 5 L.D.A.B 396.

[11] It is a purchaser if it has given value, *e.g.* where funds are received into an overdrawn account. If it has given no value, it has no title to set up against the customer or beneficiary.

[12] *Re European Bank, Agra Bank Claim* (1872) 8 Ch. App. 41 at 44; *cf. Union Bank of Australia Ltd v. Murray-Aynsley* [1898] A.C. 693.

headed "police account" was held in *Re Gross, ex p. Kingston*[13] to amount to proof that the bank had notice of the fiduciary nature of the account, and the account could not be set off against a personal account. The fact that a customer has more than one account might merely be a matter of personal convenience, and would not in itself be conclusive, but with other indications (like the name of the account, as in *Re Gross*) it might be enough to give the bank warning.

Banks as Constructive Trustees

9–007 Claims in constructive trust have become a frequent feature of commercial litigation, particularly in litigation concerning banks, during the last 20 years.[14] This new dimension in the law reflects the dynamic increase in international commerce and in the speed of modern communications, and as a consequence, the opportunities for international fraud and methods of disposing of its proceeds. Banks form a global financial network and are particularly vulnerable to being used by criminals laundering their profits, who can now dispose of vast sums through the banking system practically instantaneously by electronic funds transfer. The plaintiff's chances of recovering money from a fraudster are usually remote,[15] whereas banks which have handled the money are easily sued and are "deep pocket" defendants with enormous assets if the claim is successful.

9–008 The increase in commercial fraud litigation has raised complex questions about liability. Many of the relevant legal concepts were developed centuries ago and are cumbersome and out of date. The courts (and academics, in numerous contributions to the literature) are now making conscious efforts to analyse and rationalise liability in order to adapt the rules for the very different social and economic conditions of today. Although it is still difficult to give a clear picture and avoid complexity in discussion, the underlying arguments and their implications are becoming more obvious and some of the difficulties are being resolved.

9–009 Constructive trusts are not set up by the intention of the parties, but are imposed by the court because of inequitable or fraudulent conduct. If a stranger to the trust, like a bank, has actual or constructive notice of a breach of trust or fiduciary duties by another and has assisted with the breach or obtained trust property, the court may consider that the stranger, by becoming "involved" in the breach, has become a constructive trustee. The plaintiff must show:

---

[13] (1871) 6 Ch. App. 632.

[14] "A case concerning an express trust is something of a rarity nowadays; constructive trusts, on the other hand, are two a penny." Sir Peter Millett (1995) 9/2 Trust Law International 35 at 36. For helpful discussion of constructive trust, see Oakley, *Constructive Trusts,* 3rd ed. 1997, Chap. 4.

[15] The criminals may be insolvent or may have escaped to "some Shangri La" with numbered bank accounts: *AG for Hong Kong v. Reid* [1994] 1 A.C. 324 at 339.

(1) the existence of a trust[16]: the "trust" need not be formal, but there must be at least a fiduciary duty owed by the so-called trustee with regard to another person's property; for example, company directors may owe a fiduciary duty to the company for this purpose[17];

(2) a breach of trust by the trustee (until *Royal Brunei Airlines v. Tan*,[18] which is discussed below, this was "a *fraudulent and dishonest design* on the part of the trustee");

(3) assistance by the third party or bank in that breach or knowing receipt of a trust fund; and

(4) the third party's knowledge of these three elements.

If a bank has no knowledge or notice,[19] actual or constructive, of the existence of a trust, it is not liable if, acting in good faith, it treats the funds in the account as the absolute property of the customer,[20] and it should not refuse to pay on the ground that the funds might belong to others.[21] This principle, asserted in numerous cases, is necessary, for the bank's duty to obey its customer's instructions and pay on his or her cheques on demand would make the practice of banking excessively difficult if the bank had also to investigate its customer's title to the money. The problem for the bank (and it is a real one[22]) is to know what in practice amounts to knowledge or actual or constructive notice sufficient to put it under a duty to inquire (rather than to obey its mandate promptly), and then to decide how to make appropriate inquiries without unnecessarily offending its customer. **9–010**

It should be noted that the emphasis of this traditional analysis has now been altered by the introduction of stringent duties on bankers (and other professionals) to report suspicious transactions to the police under the **9–011**

---

16 Not necessarily all the details of the trust: *Foxton v. Manchester and Liverpool District Banking Co* (1881) 44 L.T. 406 at 408.

17 Courts have sometimes been very liberal in their interpretation of fiduciary: see, *e.g. Chase Manhattan Bank N.A. v. Israel-British Bank (London) Ltd* [1981] Ch. 105, but see *Brown v. Bennett, The Times,* January 23, 1998 Ch.D., (noted Grantham and Rickett (1998) 114 L.Q.R. 357) where it was held that a misapplication of trust assets was required, not merely a breach of fiduciary duty.

18 [1995] 2 A.C. 378.

19 Gardner (1996) 112 L.Q.R. 56, draws attention to the differences between "knowledge" and "notice" and to the different meanings given to "notice" in this context.

20 *Thomson v. Clydesdale Bank Ltd* [1893] A.C. 282; *Union Bank of Australia Ltd v. Murray-Aynsley* [1898] A.C. 693; *Bank of New South Wales v. Goulburn Valley Butter Co Pty* [1902] A.C. 543.

21 *Callard v. Lloyd* (1840) 6 M. & W. 26; *Tassell v. Cooper* (1850) 9 C.B. 509; *Fountaine-Besson v. Parr's Banking Co and Alliance Bank Ltd* (1895) 12 T.L.R. 121; *Szek v. Lloyds Bank, The Times*, January 15, 1908; *Plunkett v. Barclays Bank Ltd* [1936] 2 K.B. 107; *John Shaw (Rayners Lane) Ltd v. Lloyds Bank Ltd* (1944) 5 L.D.A.B. 396; *Stoney Stanton Supplies (Coventry) Ltd v. Midland Bank Ltd* [1966] 2 Lloyd's Rep. 373.

22 The Jack Report quoted one of its banking consultees: "The first problem the banker has when faced with an apparently unusual cheque drawn on a trust account is how to make appropriate enquiries, evaluate the replies and make a decision as to whether or not to pay, all before 3pm" (Cm. 622 (1989), para. 14.13).

money laundering legislation 1993.[23] It will be recalled that banks are now required to ascertain the identity of their customers, to keep records of transactions and to report suspicious transactions to the authorities. These criminal law duties require banks to know their customers' accounts in more depth than hitherto. Although the implications of the new duties are yet to be worked out, it seems likely that the civil liability of banks for constructive trust, as for negligence, will become more onerous as a result.

When does Liability for Constructive Trust Arise?

9–012 The traditional classification of constructive trusts is derived from Lord Selborne's well-known words in the decision of *Barnes v. Addy*[24]:

> ". . . strangers are not to be made constructive trustees merely because they act as the agents of trustees in transactions within their legal powers, . . . unless those agents receive and become chargeable with some part of the trust property, or unless they assist with knowledge in a dishonest and fraudulent design on the part of the trustees. . . . If those principles were disregarded, I know not how any one could, in transactions admitting of doubt as to the view which a Court of Equity might take of them, safely discharge the office of solicitor, of banker, or of agent of any sort to trustees."

The twofold classification of liability for constructive trust[25] established from these words is:

(a) giving assistance to a dishonest trustee (this used to be known as "knowing assistance", but since the decision in *Royal Brunei Airlines v. Tan,*[26] it should be thought of as "*dishonest assistance*");

(b) knowing receipt of and dealing with a trust fund ("*knowing receipt*").

The elements of the two categories differ with regard to both the acts and the knowledge needed. Indeed, it has become increasingly clear that the two branches of liability are distinct in nature and raise different questions,[27] for example, about the mental state—the "knowledge" or type of fault—of the defendant, and the extent of the liability in each branch. Some

---

[23] See above, Chaps 2 and 4.

[24] (1874) 9 Ch. App. 244 at 251. An article by Harpum (1986) 102 L.Q.R. 114 at 267, provoked the modern discussion.

[25] Aside from the "trustee de son tort" (intermeddling) liability, the basis of which is clearer and which is unlikely to be relevant to banks. See Oakley, *Constructive Trusts*, (3rd ed. Chap. 4).

[26] [1995] 2 A.C. 178 at 392, PC: "'Knowingly' is better avoided as a defining ingredient of the principle".

[27] See Sir Peter Millett (1991) 107 L.Q.R. 71; Birks [1996] L.M.C.L.Q. 1, among others.

of these questions are now being resolved by the courts, although important controversies remain.

The "mental state"

The main controversy about liability in both branches has concerned the mental state of the defendant, and an introductory word about the discussion may be helpful. Lord Selborne's emphasis was on the "knowledge" of the accessory or the recipient, and subsequent discussion naturally concentrated on awareness of the circumstances rather than on moral blame. Recent discussion about what amounts to fault in this context has centred on an analysis of categories of "knowledge" given by Peter Gibson J. in *Baden Delvaux & Lecuit v. Societe General S.A.*[28] The five categories,[29] graduated from dishonesty down to negligence or inadvertence, are: **9–013**

(1) actual knowledge;

(2) wilfully shutting one's eyes to the obvious;

(3) wilfully and recklessly failing to make such inquires as a reasonable man might make ("Nelsonian knowledge");

(4) knowledge of circumstances which would indicate the facts to an honest and reasonable man; and

(5) knowledge of circumstances which would put an honest and reasonable man on inquiry.

The first three categories are forms of actual notice, wilful blindness or failure to appreciate, whereas the last two may be described as "constructive notice" or negligence liability.

This analysis has the merit of illuminating the subtle but important differences in attitude and concentrating argument more closely on the factors which ought to found liability. Its complexity, however, may encourage detailed investigation of states of mind by the courts, which are not only cumbersome but out of place in a context of civil liability where commercial transactions are frequent, rapid and often almost mechanical. Its focus on "knowledge", also, has deflected attention from the fact that liability in these cases is a serious matter, both because of the remedies which can be imposed and because something similar to criminal liability may be at issue here. Recent cases have found it more helpful (in the case **9–014**

[28] [1992] 4 All E.R. 161 at 235 (a knowing assistance case).

[29] Apart from (i), they are in fact descriptions of circumstances from which the court may deduce the state of the alleged trustee's knowledge [1992] 4 All E.R. at 235, *per* Peter Gibson J.

of possible "assistance" liability) to concentrate on the *dishonesty* (broadly speaking) of the defendant rather than on his or her state of knowledge, and the Privy Council has recommended that the *Baden* scale of knowledge is best forgotten.[30] It seems likely, however, that many judges will still find it a useful tool in analysis,[31] particularly with regard to the distinction between behaviour which seems to involve a lack of probity (categories 1 to 3), and honest though negligent behaviour (4 and 5).

9–015 Another factor has been added to the analysis of bankers' knowledge by the duties imposed by the Money Laundering Regulations, mentioned above.[32] The requirement to report suspicions will require banks to familiarise themselves with day-to-day movements on many accounts in order to notice unusual transactions and patterns of behaviour. If a bank does make a report about a suspicious transaction, it may find it difficult to maintain that it did not have the requisite knowledge for civil liability.

Remedies

9–016 The equitable remedies appropriate may be *proprietary*, in which case property rights are affected[33] (rights enforceable against the whole world except a bona fide purchaser for value without notice) and the return of the trust property itself or its traceable equivalent may be ordered; or *personal*, in which case a personal liability to account as a trustee for all the losses caused (which may be more extensive) may be imposed. A plaintiff who can establish a proprietary claim has several advantages; for example, the entire property may be claimed whether or not the defendant is solvent and, in some cases, the plaintiff will be able to take advantage of increases in the value of the property.

---

[30] *Royal Brunei Airlines v. Tan* [1995] 2 A.C. 178 at 392.

[31] See *Heinl v. Jyske Bank* [1999] Lloyd's Rep. Bank. 511, CA, at 523.

[32] See above, Chaps 2 and 4.

[33] In some jurisdictions (*e.g.* USA, Canada and Australia) the constructive trust can be used in commercial cases as a means for claiming the return of property, or compensation ("the remedial constructive trust"). Many English lawyers regard this use as confusing property with obligations, and as a unjustifiable re-ordering of priorities on insolvency. Some would emphasise that the constructive trust, properly so called, is equity's proprietary restitutionary device to redress a wrong in relation to property, and should be viewed as primarily institutional rather than remedial. (See Scott [1993] L.M.C.L.Q. 330; Norman in *Laundering and Tracing* (Birks ed.) p. 102. In *Re Polly Peck International plc (in administration) (No. 5)* [1998] 3 All E.R. 812, CA, an application to bring an action which would order a "remedial constructive trust" to be imposed on the assets of a company in liquidation was refused because there was no prospect that the court would grant the order sought (see Birks, "The end of the remedial constructive trust?" in [1998] Trust Law International). See also the remarks of Lord Browne-Wilkinson in *Westdeutsche Landesbank Girozentrale v. Islington London BC* [1996] 2 All E.R. 961 at 997, HL.

The Two Branches of Liability

(1) Dishonest assistance (formerly "knowing assistance")

Much controversy has centred on what is often regarded as the more serious of the two branches of the *Barnes v. Addy* types of liability, the liability of an assistant or accessory, which should now be called "dishonest assistance".[34] **9–017**

Discussion of the modern development of the law in the context of banking invariably starts with the case of *Selangor United Rubber Estates Ltd v. Cradock (No. 3)*,[35] a case in which the bank had assisted in a breach of trust by making a bridging loan in a complex series of transactions which turned out to be a fraud on a company. Ungoed-Thomas J. held that the bank had owed a duty of inquiry, because it knew of circumstances from which an honest and reasonable banker would have concluded that the payment was to finance a share purchase, and that it was liable both for breach of its contractual duty of care and for constructive trust. Since it was not suggested that the bank had been dishonest, it seemed—to the horror of the banks at the time—that banks and other strangers might be liable in constructive trust as accessories to fraud for no more than negligence.[36] Similarly, in *Karak Rubber Co Ltd v. Burden (No. 2)*[37] a bank was held liable for knowing assistance in circumstances where the bank's branch manager was held to be negligent. These cases gave rise to considerable controversy,[38] and in subsequent cases[39] doubts were expressed about the test used in *Selangor*, and courts began to move away from the extensive liability imposed in that case.[40] **9–018**

The reaction against *Selangor* culminated, in *Lipkin Gorman v. Karpnale*,[41] in the rejection of the view that negligent behaviour alone could found an action for accessory liability and the disapproval of *Selangor* in **9–019**

[34] *Royal Brunei Airlines v. Tan* [1995] 2 A.C. 178. This was the name advocated in the first edition of this book. Cranston, *Principles of Banking Law*, at p. 211, points out the relationship between this liability and other forms of accessory liability in equity such as the receipt of information in breach of confidence, and inducing breach of trust or fiduciary duty.

[35] [1968] 2 All E.R. 1073.

[36] *i.e.* (iv) and (v) of the *Baden* classes of knowledge. See Harpum (1986) 102 L.Q.R. 114 at 152 and Norman, (1992) 12/3 L.S. 332, 337. The decisions were described in the first edition of this work as "insupportable".

[37] [1972] 1 All E.R. 1210. A similar approach was taken in other cases: *e.g. Rowlandson v. National Westminster Bank* [1978] 1 W.L.R. 798; *Baden Delvaux* [1992] 4 All E.R. 235.

[38] They caused "consternation in banking circles": *Quincecare* case [1992] 4 All E.R. 363 at 369, *per* Steyn J., see above, para. 5–030.

[39] Among them *Belmont Finance Corpn. Ltd v. Williams Furniture Ltd (No 2)* [1980] 1 All E.R. 393 and *Re Montagu's Settlement Trusts* [1992] 4 All E.R. 308.

[40] See *Polly Peck International v. Nadir (No. 2)* [1992] 4 All E.R. 769 at 777, *per* Scott L.J., and *Cowan de Groot Properties v. Eagle Trust plc* [1992] 4 All E.R. 700.

[41] [1989] 1 W.L.R. 1340; [1992] 4 All E.R. 512, CA, reversing the decision of Alliott J. [1987] 1 W.L.R. 987.

this respect by the Court of Appeal. *Lipkin Gorman* involved the activities of a partner in a firm of solicitors (the plaintiff) who had authority to draw on the firm's client account with the defendant bank by his signature alone. The partner, Cass, was a compulsive gambler and withdrew money secretly from the account to fund his gambling at the Playboy Club in Mayfair (the defendant). The claim by the solicitors against the bank arose because the bank had some knowledge of Cass's gambling—the manager, for example, had recorded that he did not believe that the gambling was a "controlled activity"—but did not make any inquiry or inform the solicitors of it. The deception was discovered and Cass was convicted of theft. The solicitors brought the action against both the bank and the club.[42] At first instance, Alliott J. held that the bank had breached the duty of care it owed its customer, the solicitors' firm, and that it was also liable to them as a constructive trustee.

9–020 On appeal, the court made it clear that the primary claim should be in contract. It said that it was wrong to equate the duty to inquire where there has been fraud and the bank has known of it with the bank's duty of care. If there was no contractual breach, it was unlikely that liability in constructive trust could arise. Here, on the evidence,[43] the bank had had no reason to believe that there was a serious or real possibility that Cass had been using funds drawn from the account for his own purposes, and it had therefore not even breached its duty of care[44]; *a fortiori* it could not be liable as a constructive trustee. Even if there had been a breach of the duty of care, though, May L.J. said that "nothing less than knowledge, as defined in one of the first three categories stated by Peter Gibson J. in *Baden*" would have sufficed for liability as a constructive trustee.[45] So far as it went, therefore, the case indicated that constructive notice or negligence would *not* suffice for a claim in constructive trust.

9–021 In the case of *AGIP (Africa) Ltd v. Jackson*,[46] Millett J. took the discussion further forward. This was a pattern money laundering case. The chief accountant of the plaintiff (AGIP) fraudulently altered a payment order from AGIP, making it payable to a company which had recently been incorporated, the directors and shareholders of which were the defendants, who were accountants in partnership in the Isle of Man.[47] The payment order was honoured by the banks concerned and the company's account credited with the money. The company's account was closed immediately

[42] The claim against the club for recovery of money had and received, but not the claim against the bank, went to the House of Lords, whose judgment broke new ground in the law of restitution (see below, Chap. 10).

[43] Because allegations against the bank manager had not been pleaded sufficiently explicitly to justify a finding of fraud.

[44] For *Lipkin Gorman* and the contractual duty of care, see above, para. 5–036.

[45] The other two judges did not come to any express conclusion on the point.

[46] [1990] 1 Ch. 265 (Millett J.); affd [1991] Ch. 547, CA.

[47] The case concerned one example of a series of frauds which had been carried out over many years by the accountant, of sums totalling over $10.5m.

after the transfer and the company put into liquidation. Money was then transferred from the account of the defendants' firm in London to its account with a bank in the Isle of Man, and from there overseas to various recipients.

AGIP brought an action at common law for money had and received (money paid under a mistake)[48] and in equity on the ground that the defendants were constructive trustees of the money. The defendants' argument was that they had acted in accordance with the instructions of their clients, and had had no notice of AGIP's claim to the money.

With regard to the equitable claim, the judge's view—which was affirmed on appeal—was that mere constructive notice of the fraud would not be enough to make a third party liable. His approach to the *Baden* categories of knowledge, however, was oblique: while "gratefully adopting" the classification, he warned against over refinement or making too ready assumptions from it. He preferred to see the true basis of liability as *dishonesty*[49]; any failure to make the inquiry which an honest person would have made could only operate as evidence from which the defendant's dishonesty could be inferred, not as a breach in itself. In *AGIP*, the judge found that the defendant accountants who were consciously helping their clients to make arrangements designed to conceal the money from the plaintiffs and investigators must have realised that they were laundering money. They were "at best indifferent to the possibility of fraud. They made no inquiries of the plaintiffs because they thought it was none of their business. That is not honest behaviour".[50] **9–022**

A similar view was taken by the Privy Council in *Royal Brunei Airlines v. Tan*,[51] a case which has authoritatively clarified the law and established the nature of accessory liability in terms of modern requirements. The court held that a third party who dishonestly assists a trustee to commit a breach of trust will be liable to the beneficiary of the trust for the loss. Here, the airline had appointed another company (B.L.T.) to act as its general travel agent and to account to it for all money received from sales of tickets. The effect of the arrangements was that B.L.T. was the trustee for the airline of the money it received for the tickets. In fact, the money was paid into B.L.T.'s ordinary account at its bank, and the defendant (Tan)—who was the managing director and principal shareholder of B.L.T.—used it for B.L.T.'s ordinary business expenses, including keeping down its overdraft—that is, Tan was using the money fraudulently for his own purposes. B.L.T. **9–023**

[48] It was held that the plaintiffs (or the bank) were entitled to bring an action at common law, see further below para. 9–040 *et seq* (for tracing), and Chap. 10.

[49] "There is no sense in requiring dishonesty on the part of the principal while accepting negligence as sufficient for his assistant" *AGIP* [1990] 1 Ch. 265 at 293 (but note that since *Royal Brunei Airlines* it is not essential that the principal is dishonest).

[50] [1990] 1 Ch. 265 at 294–5.

[51] [1995] 2 A.C. 378. The judgment has been warmly praised: it "would have a strong claim to be included in any anthology of great judgments", Birks [1996] L.M.C.L.Q. 1.

defaulted on its payments to the airlines, who sued Tan (B.L.T. was insolvent) to recover the money owed by the company.

The question was whether Tan could be liable as a constructive trustee. Although most of the necessary requirements were fulfilled for liability as an accessory (including not merely knowledge of the trust but dishonesty), the outstanding difficulty was that B.L.T. (the trustee) could not be said to have fraudulently breached its trust to the airline as required by *Barnes v. Addy*,[52] where Lord Selborne stated that the trustee should have "a dishonest and fraudulent design".

9–024 Lord Nicholls, giving the advice of the Privy Council, made two important new statements. First, said that the third party, the accessory—in this case Tan—must be dishonest: that is a necessary and a sufficient condition of his or her liability. Secondly, he said that it is irrelevant—despite the *dictum* in *Barnes v. Addy*—whether the *trustee* acted dishonestly or innocently; for example, a dishonest solicitor might procure a lay trustee to breach the trust unwittingly. In this case (that is, if the trustee is innocent) it is even more important that an accessory should only be liable if he or she is dishonest. Lord Nicholls said that there has been a tendency to construe Lord Selborne's formulation ("the *Barnes v. Addy* straitjacket") as though it were a statute, and this has made it difficult to analyse the underlying concept. The implication is that courts have been struggling to apply concepts like "knowingly" and "dishonest and fraudulent design" without clearly addressing the central question: why should a person who is not a trustee and has not received any trust property be liable at all as a constructive trustee?

9–025 Lord Nicholls set out guidelines as to the meaning of "dishonesty" in this context. He emphasised, no doubt recognising the importance of commercial certainty, that it should be judged objectively,[53] not subjectively, as would be the case for criminal responsibility:

> "acting dishonestly, or with a lack of probity, which is synonymous, means simply not acting as an honest person would in the circumstances. This is an objective standard. At first sight, this may seem surprising. Honesty has a connotation of subjectivity, as distinct from the objectivity of negligence. Honesty, indeed, does have a strong subjective element in that it is a description of a type of conduct assessed in the light of what a person actually knew at the time, as distinct from what a reasonable person would have known or appreciated. Further, honesty and its counterpart dishonesty are mostly concerned with advertent conduct, not inadvertent conduct. Careless-

[52] See *Belmont Finance Corpn Ltd v. Williams Furniture Ltd* [1979] Ch. 250, CA.

[53] Reference was made to *Ghosh* [1982] Q.B. 1053. The test is framed to catch "Robin Hood" or the anti-vivisectionist animal thief, who may believe that his acts are morally correct, but knows that people generally do not think so.

ness is not dishonesty. Thus for the most part dishonesty is to be equated with conscious impropriety. However, these subjective characteristics of honesty do not mean that individuals are free to set their own standards of honesty in particular circumstances. The standard of what constitutes honest conduct is not subjective. Honesty is not an optional scale, with higher or lower values according to the moral standards of each individual. If a person knowingly appropriates another's property, he will not escape a finding of dishonesty simply because he sees nothing wrong in such behaviour."[54]

It seems unlikely therefore that a third party would be liable to the beneficiaries in constructive trust for simple negligence (although the possibility of an action in negligence might still exist[55]). The Privy Council's advice also makes it clear, however, that acting "with reckless disregard for other peoples' rights", as distinct from taking a risk hoping that the outcome will benefit the beneficiaries, or taking a risk where there is genuine doubt about whether a transaction is authorised or not, may be a tell-tale sign of dishonesty.[56] The emphasis the decision places on deliberate and serious misconduct, as well as its clarity, must be welcome to bankers, as to many other professionals who deal with trustees and fiduciaries.[57] **9–026**

Not all the puzzles have been cleared up by *Royal Brunei Airlines*. In *Brinks Ltd v. Abu-Saleh (No. 3)*,[58] a woman admitted that she had accompanied her husband in his car journey to Switzerland with £3m, thinking that he was involved in a scheme for tax evasion. Apparently, she had been unaware that he was in fact engaged in the fraudulent misdirection of gold from the Brinks' Mat robbery. It was held that she was therefore unaware of the facts giving rise to the breach of trust, and she was not liable as an accessory to the breach of trust. This might be considered **9–027**

[54] [1995] 2 A.C. 378 at 389. But in *Heinl v. Jyske Bank* [1999] Lloyd's Rep. Bank. 511, CA, it was held that the "material question is not the objective test whether he ought, as a reasonable businessman, to have appreciated that the funds . . . had been fraudulently procured from the Bank or that there was a real probability that they had been, but the subjective test whether he did indeed appreciate that the funds had been or probably had been so procured", *per* Colman J. at 546.

[55] *ibid.*, at 392. Birks, *op. cit.*, sees this aspect of *Royal Brunei Airlines* as a welcome move away from an anomalous negligence based liability outside negligence towards an alignment of accessory liability with the torts of deceit and conspiracy. See also Lord Nicholls, in *Restitution, Past, Present and Future* (Cornish, Nolan, O'Sullivan and Virgo eds) p. 244: "Dishonest participation in a breach of trust . . . is the equitable counterpart of the common law tort of interfering with contractual relations".

[56] [1995] 2 A.C. 378 at 391. Applied in *Twinsectra v. Yardley* [1999] Lloyd's Rep. Bank. 438 (see particularly 464).

[57] Gardner (1996) 112 L.Q.R. 56, thinks the decision too generous to banks. He argues that in the light of banks' modern role as policemen as a consequence of the MLR 1993, it would be wholesome for them to be regarded as "insurers".

[58] [1996] C.L.C. 133.

an over-generous interpretation of the requirements of dishonest assistance.[59]

(2) "Knowing receipt"

9–028 Liability in knowing receipt is now usually seen as conceptually different from assistance liability,[60] although in many cases the two claims overlap on the facts. If a third party (the bank) has received money which was held in trust knowing that it was trust property and either knowing that it was paid to it in breach of trust or itself having dealt with it in a manner inconsistent with the trust,[61] it will be liable to the beneficiary as a constructive trustee, and may have a personal liability to account as well as the proprietary liability which remains even if the recipient no longer possesses the property. The property right gives the beneficiary a claim which takes priority over claims of unsecured lenders on insolvency.[62]

9–029 **"Receipt".** This is a "receipt based" remedy, and an essential feature is that the defendant acquired the property *beneficially.* This is particularly relevant with regard to banks, who are not normally seen as receiving their customer's money beneficially. In paying or collecting money for a customer, the bank credits the receipt to a particular account as *agent* for the customer,[63] although it may be different if the bank uses the money to reduce or discharge a customer's overdraft.[64] Probably, though, the ordinary operation of an overdrawn account is not enough in itself; the liability may only arise if the banker begins to deal with the overdraft differently from usual—"some conscious appropriation of the sum paid into the account in reduction of the overdraft".[65]

9–030 An example of a "benefit" case is *Neste Oy v. Lloyds Bank plc.*[66] A bank learned that its customer had decided to cease trading and to appoint a receiver. Before the receiver was appointed, the bank received a payment,

---

[59] Noted, Birks [1996] L.M.C.L.Q. 1. See also *Bank of America v. Arnell* [1999] Lloyd's Rep. Bank. 399, where a defendant was not liable for dishonest assistance perhaps because she was under the impression that paying a large sum through her bank account for an acquaintance was to further a tax evasion scheme rather than a breach of trust.

[60] See *Citadel General Assurance Co v. Lloyds Bank Canada* [1998] 152 D.L.R. 411 at 433, *per* La Forest J.

[61] *Gray v. Johnston* (1868) L.R. 3 at 11, *per* Lord Cairns. A mere civil misapplication of the property is sufficient: Clayton, [1993] 5 J.I.B.L. 191 at 192, citing *Polly Peck v. Nadir (No 2)* [1992] 4 All E.R. 769, and *Precision Dippings Ltd v. Precision Dippings Marketing* [1985] B.C.L.C. 385.

[62] Property claims are distinct from obligations (personal claims), although the difference may only become crucial on insolvency: Norman in *Laundering and Tracing* (Birks ed.) p. 100.

[63] In *Bank Tejarat v. Hong Kong and Shanghai Banking Corp* [1995] 1 Lloyd's Rep. 239, a bank which had received funds had the agent's defence (ministerial receipt). See Birks [1995] Trust Law Int. 91.

[64] *AGIP* [1980] 1 Ch. 265 at 292, per Millett J.

[65] Sir Peter Millett, (1991) 107 L.Q.R. 71 at 83.

[66] [1983] 2 Lloyds Rep. 658.

which it credited to the customer's bank account, and which it wished to combine against the customer's other debts. The bank knew no more than the fact of the receivership and the cessation of trading, and that some of the payments from the plaintiff were in advance of expenditure incurred by the customer. It was held that it should have inquired as to the circumstances of the receivership. An inquiry would have revealed that the funds concerned were the subject of a trust in favour of the receivers. The bank, therefore, had knowingly received trust funds. Here the bank was liable although its behaviour could hardly be described as lacking probity or even as grossly negligent. The case seems to be an example of pure constructive liability, applicable because of the benefit to the bank, and its knowledge that some funds were advance payments. Practical questions about the bank's duty to inquire arise. Should the inquiry be made (a) on receipt of the funds? But no other debt might exist then, and so there would be no obvious reason to inquire; and, if the account is overdrawn so that the right to combine arises at that time,[67] it hardly seems reasonable to expect the banker to make inquiry then, because there may never be any intention to exercise the right; or (b) at the time of exercising the right of combination? The insolvency set-off provisions[68] may apply, and it seems unlikely that the operation of the statutory provisions should be impeded by any duty to inquire. In the case of statutory set-off (and combination) it may therefore be more appropriate to inquire at the time at which the funds are received. There is no easy answer.

A rather different situation arose in *Polly Peck plc v. Nadir (No. 2)*.[69] **9–031**
Here, the Court of Appeal held that a bank exchanging Turkish lire for sterling (the Central bank) became entitled to the sterling in its own right, not as banker for the private bank of Nadir, the chief executive of Polly Peck (which became entitled to the Turkish lire) because it could use it for its own commercial gain.[70] It is not easy to see, however, how this situation is any different from any other in which banks exchange currency, and consequently some doubt exists whether the decision, like *Neste Oy*, may be capable of exposing banks in routine transactions to over-extensive liability as constructive trustees.

The problem of what constitutes receipt by a bank has attracted attention **9–032**
in other jurisdictions. Some cases in New Zealand provide examples[71]: banks were found liable where they had closely monitored and controlled

[67] It is, after all, only an accounting position.

[68] Under the IA 1986, see further Chap. 24.

[69] [1992] 4 All E.R. 769.

[70] *ibid.*, at 777, *per* Scott L.J., who considered that the bank's actions in respect of the bulk of the transfers brought it within possible liability for "receipt" rather than for "assistance"; (it was an interlocutory decision).

[71] See *Westpac Banking Corporation v. Savin* [1985] 2 N.Z.L.R. 41; *Anderson v. Chilton* (1993) 4 N.Z.B.L.C. 103; *Westpac Banking Corporation v. Ancell* (1993) 4 N.Z.B.L.C. 103; *cf. Nimmo v. Westpac Banking Corporation* [1993] 3 N.Z.L.R. 218. These cases are discussed by Rickett [1995] Co. Lawyer 35. Bryan [1996] J.B.L. 165 describes the behaviour of banks in these cases as "opportunistic".

overdraft accounts, and perhaps called in a receiver or refused to extend further facilities, causing bankruptcy.[72] The Supreme Court of Canada had occasion to review the law in *Citadel General Assurance Co. v. Lloyds Bank Canada*,[73] and to consider the liability of a bank which had transferred funds between two accounts (one belonging to the company which was defrauding the insurance company plaintiff of trust funds and the other belonging to its parent company) to cover overdrafts in either account and which went on to transfer the balance of any funds in one account to the other account on a regular basis. The court had little difficulty in coming to the conclusion that the bank had itself received a benefit and did not act merely as an agent; its actions went beyond the mere collection of funds and payments of bills on the customer's account. Nor was the bank's argument that it had not received trust *property* because the deposit was simply a debt owed to the customer by the bank successful. The court, relying on Lord Goff's judgment in *Lipkin Gorman v. Karpnale*,[74] held that a debt is a chose in action and therefore property over which (in the court's words) one can impose a trust, or in restitutionary terms, the bank was unjustly enriched at the expense of the plaintiff.[75]

9–033 In fact, possible conflicts of duties are often less perplexing for banks in cases of knowing receipt than where they are making rapid decisions in ordinary commercial transactions, because in many receipt cases the bank is merely deciding whether to exercise its right of set-off, and there is no urgency about the decision.[76]

9–034 **Mental state.** In this branch, as in the other, there has been controversy about the necessary type of knowledge for liability. One orthodox view is that liability is complementary to the bona fide purchaser rule and depends upon constructive notice—that is, upon fault, but only in the sense that the recipient knew or ought to have known that the money was trust money (which could be said to be negligence).[77] A number of cases, for example, appear to hold that constructive notice or knowledge (in the sense of negligence in failing to inquire) is sufficient if the bank itself benefits from the transaction—the usual case being where it applies funds to an over-

[72] Harpum (in Birks, *Frontiers of Liability* (1994) pp. 9 and 19) suggests other examples: setting off a credit balance in what the banker ought to know was a trust account held by the customer, or receiving money for a customer in circumstances where the banker ought to know that the customer is under a fiduciary obligation to use it for a specific purpose and then using it to discharge the customer's overdraft.

[73] [1998] 152 D.L.R. 411.

[74] [1991] 3 W.L.R. 10.

[75] *ibid.*, at 424–5. Bryan, in *Restitution and Banking Law* (Rose ed.) argues that since the bank always receives money for its own purposes, "there is no room for a concept of beneficial receipt on the conventional analysis of the banking relationship . . . [and] recent decisions . . . have overlooked "this axiom of banking law" (Chap. 10).

[76] See *Citadel* [1998] 152 D.L.R. 411 at 436, *per* La Forest J. referring to Harpum (1986) 102 L.Q.R. 114 at 138.

[77] This would include categories (iv) and (v) on the *Baden* scale.

draft.[78] Thus, if a trustee who is overdrawn pays money into his or her account or gives a security under pressure from the banker, the bank will be liable if either it (through its officer) knows that the trust money is used for the purpose, even if the impropriety is not appreciated, or if the circumstances were simply such as to arouse suspicions and the bank has failed to make inquiries. In *Gray v. Johnston,*[79] after referring to the bank's duty to honour mandates, and its duty not to set up third party rights against its customer, Lord Westbury continued:

> "But then it has been very well settled that if an executor or a trustee who is indebted to a banker, or to another person, having the legal custody of the assets of a trust estate, applies a portion of them in the payment of his own debt to the individual having that custody, the individual receiving the debt has at once not only abundant proof of the breach of the trust, but participates in it for his own personal benefit".

And Lord Cairns, having recognised the conflict of duties which might face the banker, said[80]:

> "if it be shown that any personal benefit to the bankers themselves is designed to be stipulated for, that circumstance, above all others, will most readily establish the fact that the bankers are in privity with the breach of trust which is about to be committed".

In the *Neste Oy* case referred to above, the bank was liable although its behaviour could hardly be characterised as lacking probity or even as "gross" negligence.

Some judges, however, have been cautious in imposing constructive trusteeship, emphasising its serious character, and bearing in mind the fact that personal as well as property remedies are available to the plaintiff if liability is established. Megarry V.-C.'s judgment in *Re Montagu's Settlement Trusts*[81] was to this effect. He held that liability was a matter of whether "a **9–035**

---

[78] See *John v. Dodwell & Co* [1918] A.C. 563; *Foxton v. Manchester and Liverpool District Banking Co* (1881) 44 L.T. 406; *A-G v. De Winton* [1906] 2 Ch. 105; *British America Elevator Co Ltd v. Bank of British North America* [1919] A.C. 658; *Reckit v. Barnett, Pembroke and Slater Ltd* [1929] A.C. 176; *Midland Bank Ltd v. Reckitt* [1933] A.C. 1, *contra, Coleman v. Bucks and Oxon Union Bank* [1897] 2 Ch. 243.

[79] (1868) L.R. 3 H.L. 1 at 14.

[80] *ibid.*, at 11.

[81] [1992] 4 All E.R. 308; [1987] Ch. 264; an action by the 11th Duke of Manchester concerning chattels (including "a Van Dyk portrait of the second earl and Queen Katherine (of Aragon's) Trunk") some of which ought to have been selected by the trustees for inclusion in the settlement, but which had not been included, and which had later been sold by the 10th Duke. Megarry V.-C. held that the 10th Duke had not been a constructive trustee because he did not have the requisite knowledge at the relevant time and the trustee's knowledge was not to be imputed to him.

person's conscience is sufficiently affected", and that a want of probity was needed before the court should impose a constructive trust.[82] The necessary degree of knowledge to make a recipient a constructive trustee had to be *actual* knowledge that the property was trust property or knowledge which would have been acquired but for ignoring the obvious or wilfully and recklessly failing to make such inquiries as a reasonable and honest man would have made. Carelessness in making or failing to make such inquiries as a reasonable and honest man would have made would not be enough to amount to want of probity.[83]

9–036 An obvious merit of this approach is that it achieves uniformity of the mental states in knowing receipt and dishonest assistance.[84] As has been suggested, however, it has become increasingly clear that the rationale of the two branches is different, and consistency between the two is therefore less important than the conformity of each with other types of liability. The views of Megarry J. have proved controversial, partly because the traditional approach imposed a more stringent responsibility on recipients, based on notice, and partly because of the recent development of restitution law. The restitution argument is that knowing receipt should be properly understood as a remedy for the restoration of property and liability for receipt should be strict and should, for the sake of consistency, be uniform with the restitutionary remedy of unjust enrichment[85]—now that it has been recognised by the House of Lords in *Lipkin Gorman v. Karpnale*—and liability between the parties made more finely tuned by the recognition of the change of position defence.

9–037 In the *Citadel*[86] case mentioned above, the court surveyed the authorities and considered the arguments. It came to the conclusion that there is a fundamental distinction between accessory liability, which is "fault-based", and recipient liability, which is "receipt-based". Given this difference, a

---

[82] Some argue that the correct mechanism is a *resulting* trust, at least in commercial as opposed to domestic matters, see Birks, *Proprietary Rights as Remedies*, S.P.T.L. 1993.

[83] *i.e. Baden* categories (iv) and (v) would not be enough. Other judges who have taken the same view were Alliott J. in *Lipkin Gorman* [1987] 1 W.L.R. 987 and Steyn J. in *Quincecare* [1992] 4 All E.R. 363. The case has been criticised by Harpum (1986) 102 L.Q.R. 114. Birks and Norman consider that recent cases are unclear as to the precise degree of knowledge on the *Baden* scale required (*Eagle Trust v. SBC Securities* [1992] 4 All E.R. 488, *Cowan de Groot v. Eagle Trust* [1992] 4 All E.R. 700, *Polly Peck* [1998] 3 All E.R. 812, CA; and *El Ajou v. Dollar Land Holdings* [1993] 3 All E.R. 717). See Birks [1993] L.M.C.L.Q. 218, Norman, in *Laundering and Tracing* (Birks ed.).

[84] The Court of Appeal has recently held that the test should be whether it is unconscionable for the recipient to retain the benefits of the receipt (not dishonesty), and that the *Baden* categorisation is not helpful in cases of knowing receipt: *BCCI (Overseas) Ltd v. Chief Labode Onadimaki Akindele, The Times*, June 22, 2000, CA. See also *Houghton v. Fayess, The Times*, February 9, 2000, CA.

[85] See *Underhill and Hayton on the Law Relating to Trusts and Trustees*, (15th ed.), pp. 409 and 415–6 and Hanbury and Martin *Modern Equity*, (15th ed.), p. 300, referred to by Lord Nicholls, in *Restitution, Past, Present and Future* (Cornish, Nolan, O'Sullivan and Virgo eds) p. 238, and Fennell (1994) 57 M.L.R. 39.

[86] [1998] 152 D.L.R. 411, see above, para. 9–032.

lower (though not strict) standard of knowledge should be imposed on recipients, enough to establish the "unjust" nature of the enrichment; restitution must be made if the plaintiff has not consented to the loss of the property, unless a defence (such as bona fide purchase for value) can be established. The Canadian court held that liability must focus on the *defendant's* state of mind, not the plaintiff's. If the recipient of trust property has knowledge of facts which would put a reasonable person on inquiry and fails to inquire as to the possible misapplication of trust property, he or she will be liable. The bank had failed to make the appropriate inquiries of its customer,[87] therefore, and was held to be unjustly enriched.

The way forward?

Lord Nicholls has set out extra-judicially a lucid proposal for the future development of recipient liability.[88] The vigorous development of restitutionary liability has acted as a catalyst for the evolution of a more rational remedial structure,[89] and equity should now follow the law. Pointing out that the law is complex, partly because of the enormously varying circumstances in which the issue arises and the varying types of conduct where liability may be imposed, he considers it doubtful whether one single principle can be devised to accommodate satisfactorily all aspects of the variants. Some form of personal liability less severe than that of a constructive trustee should be imposed where a recipient is innocent or careless: constructive trust "cuts too deeply" because it affords not only a proprietary remedy, but also "swingeing" personal remedies which may require compensation for any loss sustained and paying for any benefits received. Further, a constructive trustee has not undertaken trust obligations. He proposes, instead, that recipient liability: **9–038**

> "should be based on the combination of two separate principles of liability. First, it should cover all third party recipients. This would be a principle of strict liability in that it would apply to every recipient with an impeachable title irrespective of fault, but it would be restitutionary in nature. It would be confined to restoring an unjust gain. Change of position would be available as a defence accordingly. Secondly, dishonest recipients should be personally liable to make good losses as well as accounting for all benefits."[90]

[87] The court did not need to go further and consider whether the bank should be satisfied with any response or only with a reasonable response.

[88] In *Restitution, Past, Present and Future* (Cornish, Nolan, O'Sullivan and Virgo eds, 1998), Chap. 15.

[89] Referring to Harpum, in *The Frontiers of Liability* (Birks, ed.) Vol. 1, p. 17.

[90] Restitution, Past, Present and Future, p. 244.

9–039 This "radical step" could be achieved he suggests, by taking a more restricted view of the ill fitting trust concept.[91] The concept in this context could even be replaced by the recognition that dishonest participation in a breach of trust, whether by receiving trust property or otherwise, is an equitable wrong, rendering the participants accountable in equity: it is "equitable counterpart of the common law tort of interfering with contractual relations".[92]

Tracing and Banks

9–040 Where property has been disposed of by another person, usually by some breach of trust, but perhaps by mistake, the interest of the owner can be followed or traced and is enforceable against the whole world unless and until the property reaches the hands of someone who takes it free of equitable proprietary interests—that is, a bona fide purchaser for value of a legal estate in the property, without notice—actual, constructive or imputed—of equitable interests. Tracing in itself will enable the beneficiaries to recover property which actually remains in the hands of the recipient. Even an innocent volunteer would therefore be liable to restore property if it were still in his or her possession and if the plaintiff could trace it.

Tracing is distinct from constructive trust: although any recipient of property disposed of in breach of trust is in one sense a *trustee* of such property,[93] and the trust property can be traced into their hands, this does not necessarily mean that the recipient will be held to be a *constructive trustee*. Many would say that there would only be good reason to seek the imposition of a constructive trust if the property has depreciated in value or been dissipated while in the hands of the recipient, or if the recipient has obtained some incidental profit, which may be claimed by the beneficiary.

9–041 Tracing is often called a "remedy", but it is now probably accepted that it is better to regard it as a preliminary step, a *process* or means of identifying property[94] which has been passed from one person to another, which may have been mixed with other property, or been replaced, partly or wholly, by other property. Tracing provides rules for following the links in such a chain to the ultimate recipient. This view of tracing has been explained by Millett L.J. in *Boscawen v. Bajwa*[95]:

> "Equity lawyers habitually use the expressions 'the tracing claim' and 'the tracing remedy' to describe the proprietary claim and the proprie-

[91] And by modifying the principle of the Diplock case (*Ministry of Health v. Simpson* [1951] A.C. 251) so that it would apply generally, not merely in the context of deceased persons' estates.

[92] *Restitution, Past, Present and Future*, p. 244.

[93] The beneficiaries' equitable interests must take effect behind a trust of the legal estate.

[94] At least common law tracing: *Agip (Africa) Ltd v. Jackson* [1990] 1 Ch. 265, *per* Millett L.J.

[95] [1995] 4 All E.R. 769 at 776.

tary remedy which equity makes available to the beneficial owner who seeks to recover his property *in specie* from those into whose hands it has come. Tracing properly so-called, however, is neither a claim nor a remedy but a process. Moreover it is not confined to the case where a plaintiff seeks a proprietary remedy: it is equally necessary where he seeks a personal remedy against the knowing recipient or knowing assistant. It is the process by which the plaintiff traces what has happened to his property, identifies the persons who have handled or received it, and justifies his claim that the money which they handled or received (and if necessary which they still retain) can properly be regarded as representing his property. He needs to do this because his claim is based on the retention by him of a beneficial interest in the property which the defendant handled or received. Unless he can prove this, he cannot (in the traditional language of equity) raise an equity against the defendant or (in the modern language of restitution) show that the defendant's unjust enrichment was at his expense."

Tracing is available both at common law and in equity, but the rules in the two jurisdictions differ and have been developed according to circumstances of particular cases. It is perhaps inevitable that, with a pragmatic and fast developing legal system like the common law, the result is alternative claims, neither of which is now seen as entirely satisfactory, rather than a consistent and coherent body of rules. The rules of tracing, like those of constructive trusts, were developed many years ago in the context of traditional family trusts,[96] and have attained their new prominence in the context of the growth of international fraud and the laundering of money. They now have to be adapted for use in the present climate where astronomic sums of money are instantaneously dispatched through the banking system by electronic funds transfer. **9–042**

Tracing at Common Law[97]

The legal owner may follow an asset of which he is deprived[98] into the hands of any person, even if it has lost its form, so long as it can still be identified in its original or converted form.[99] Although money paid into and out of a bank account can be traced, this is possible only if it has not been **9–043**

[96] See Ulph (1995) 9/5 Trust Law International 86.

[97] The common law claim could result in an order for the return of the chattel or payment of its full value; since the Common Law Procedure Act 1854, s. 78, the court has also had discretion to make an order for specific delivery.

[98] This includes a chose in action, such as a bank's debt to its customer, *Banque Belge v. Hambrouck* [1921] 1 K.B. 321; *Lipkin Gorman v. Karpnale* [1992] 2 A.C. 548. McKendrick (1992) 55 M.L.R. 377, says that *Lipkin Gorman* also demonstrates that tracing at law is in principle strict, whereas equitable tracing is arguably fault based or based upon dishonesty.

[99] *Miller v. Race* (1758) 1 Burr. 452; *Banque Belge v. Hambrouck* [1921] 1 K.B. 321; *Re Diplock's Estate* [1947] Ch. 716.

mixed with other money in the account. Further, any attempt to follow the money through the clearing system seems to present insuperable difficulties,[1] because of the requirement that the asset must continue to be identifiable.[2] In the *Agip* case, Millett J. said that it is not possible to trace through electronic transfers at common law, because there is no physical asset, only a "stream of electrons",[3] but the Court of Appeal held that it did not matter that the payment order was an electronic direction by the account holder, not a cheque. However, it was vital to identify the origin of the property, and in *Agip* the origins of the funds could not be identified without tracing the funds through the New York clearing system, where they would have been mixed with other money.[4]

Another limitation on common law tracing is that beneficiaries under a trust cannot use it to follow the trust property (though they can of course trace in equity).

Tracing at common law was permitted in *Lipkin Gorman v. Karpnale*,[5] in the context of the development by the House of Lords of restitution for mistake, and is considered further in the next chapter.

Tracing in Equity[6]

9–044 According to some recent views, this is more sophisticated than tracing at common law, and can more easily be adapted by the courts to meet modern requirements and cope with the ingenious ways in which money launderers are secreting and legitimising their profits. It gives rise to "a proprietary remedy which depends on the continued existence of the trust property in the hands of the defendant".[7] Dissipation of funds will defeat even an equitable tracing claim, but equity does have an advantage in allowing tracing of funds where trust money has been mixed with other money in a bank account, and there are a number of rules which provide for identifying funds in such a case.[8]

---

[1] But see *Banque Belge v. Hambrouck* [1921] K.B. 321.

[2] *Agip (Africa) Ltd v. Jackson* [1991] Ch. 547, CA, and *El Ajou v. Dollar Land Holdings* [1993] 3 All E.R. 717. Followed in *Bank Tejarat v. Hong Kong and Shanghai Banking Corp Ltd* [1995] 1 Lloyds Rep. 239; see Sir Peter Millett (1991) 107 L.Q.R., 71 at 72; Birks (1995) 9/3 Trust Law International 91; and Fennell (1994) 57 M.L.R. 38 at 42: "It is commonly accepted that the rules on common law tracing are exceptionally illogical, difficult to apply in practice and remote from commercial reality".

[3] *Agip (Africa) Ltd v. Jackson* [1990] 1 Ch 265 at 286, *per* Millett J. The plaintiffs (as well as the bank) had title to sue for money had and received in that case because their account had in fact been debited by the bank, although the bank had no valid mandate to do so. The customer would also have title to sue, it was said, if the account had been correctly debited by the bank (at 283). See below, Chap. 10.

[4] [1992] 4 All E.R. 541. See also Smith, *The Law of Tracing*, p. 249 *et seq.*

[5] [1991] 2 A.C. 548. See below, para. 10–029. See also *Bank of America v. Arnell* [1999] Lloyd's Rep. Bank. 399 at 405, 406.

[6] See Oakley [1995] C.L.J. 377.

[7] Sir Peter Millett, *op. cit.*, at 80. In equity, the appropriate relief includes an order to restore an unmixed fund and a declaration of charge.

[8] *e.g. Clayton's Case* (1816) 1 Mer. 572, and *Re Hallett's Estate* (1880) 13 Ch. D. 696.

An important limitation on the use of equitable tracing, however, is that it can only be used where it can be established that a trust or fiduciary duty has been breached,[9] although it is true that the courts have sometimes had little difficulty in finding a fiduciary relationship. A fiduciary relationship has even be found to arise at the time when disputed money was misappropriated or when a mistaken payment was made (as in *Chase Manhattan Bank NA v. Israel-British Bank (London) Ltd*[10]). However, where the property has been stolen by an ordinary thief, who could not be regarded as a fiduciary, equitable tracing cannot be used. Nevertheless, the law is dynamic: there are indications in some recent cases that the equitable rules are being applied generously, so that fraudulently obtained assets in complex money laundering cases can be traced more readily.[11] **9–045**

At present, the law of tracing is full of controversies and confusions. There have been frequent calls for its harmonisation and rationalisation,[12] some by proponents of the common law and others by equity lawyers. Birks points out forcefully that, though claims in equity and common law are different, the exercise of locating value is the same for both. The rules of tracing are simply rules of convenience which solve evidential difficulties, which may hardly be needed in many money laundering cases: they should not, he says, need to be called into play at all when a series of banking movements, however complex, has been motivated by "a well-evidenced intent that A should be enabled to make a payment to Z".[13] **9–046**

Quistclose Trusts[14]

If A pays money to B for a specific purpose, known to B (or of which he or she has constructive notice), the money is "clothed with a trust" for that purpose, and may not be appropriated by B for his own or other uses. In *Barclays Bank Ltd v. Quistclose Investments Ltd*[15] money was paid into a **9–047**

---

[9] *Re Diplock* [1948] 1 Ch. 465. See Oliver [1995] Trust Law Int. 78. The principle was followed recently in *Box v. Barclays Bank* [1998] Ch. D. 185 at 203.

[10] [1981] Ch. 105. See Scott, [1993] L.M.C.L.Q. 330 at 337. There must be some doubt about this case since *Westdeutsche Landesbank Girozentrale v. Islington* [1996] 2 All E.R. 961, although the decision was not overruled. See Watts (1998) 114 L.Q.R. 341 and Friedmann (1999) 115 L.Q.R. 195, where an analogy is drawn between this case and *Banque Financiere de la Cite v. Parc (Battersea) Ltd* [1998] 2 W.L.R. 475, HL (see Chap. 16), where subrogation was permitted for a payment made by mistake.

[11] See *Agip (Africa) Ltd v. Jackson* [1990] 1 Ch. 265, aff'd [1991] Ch. 547, CA and *El Ajou v. Dollar Land Holdings* (1993) 13 All E.R. 717. In the latter case, the precise identification of the plaintiff's funds in each of various accounts was not essential.

[12] *e.g.* Birks (1995) 9/3 Trust Law Int. 91; Sir Peter Millett (1995) 9/2 Trust Law Int. 35, and Ulph (1995) 9/3 Trust Law Int., 86. See also Smith, *The Law of Tracing,* 1997.

[13] Birks, *op. cit.*, at 92.

[14] See Sir Peter Millett (1985) L.Q.R. 269, and Goodhart and Jones (1980) M.L.R. 489. See also *Re Kayford* [1975] 1 All E.R. 604 and *Re Multi-Guarantee Ltd* [1987] B.C.L.C. 257; Re EVTR [1987] B.C.L.C. 646, CA. Mitchell has suggested that the true basis for subrogation in *Boscawen v. Bajwa* [1995] 4 All E.R. 769 might have been a *Quistclose* trust: [1995] L.M.C.L.Q. 451.

[15] [1970] A.C. 567.

company's bank account so that, as the bank knew, the company would be able to meet a dividend payment, and a separate account had been opened for this purpose. When the company went into liquidation, the bank claimed a right of combination for debts which the company owed to it. But the House of Lords held that the company held the money on trust for the recipients of the dividend payments, and if that purpose failed, as it did here when the company went into liquidation, the primary trust was replaced by another trust (a resulting trust) in favour of the person who paid the money in.

9–048 This is an unhappy rule, so far as banks are concerned, for the right to combine or to set-off is a reason for allowing companies to continue with a debt on one account, if money is available elsewhere.[16] Under the *Quistclose* rule, however, the payer of money can defeat the bank's priority on the insolvency of its customer merely by ensuring that the bank knows of the purpose of the payment.[17] On the other hand, third party finance for companies suffering from difficulties is made easier if the third party knows that the bank or receiver or liquidator may not take the money if the company fails before it is paid out.

9–049 Since *Quistclose* trusts are not set up expressly as trusts by the parties, doubts have been expressed about their constitution and implications. It is not always clear who has the power to enforce the trust, for example, or who are the beneficiaries, or even whether it has been properly constituted, since the "purpose" for which such a trust may be established may be expressed in vague terms, as in the case of *Re Northern Developments (Holdings) Ltd*[18] where the principle was expanded considerably. Northern was the parent company of K company, which was experiencing difficulties. In a rescue attempt, a group of banks put up a fund which they paid into Northern's account for the purpose of K's unsecured creditors only. K went into receivership and the banks and K's other creditors were held to be entitled to the money, rather than Northern, or its bank. It would seem that a trust "for all our trade creditors", and "for all our creditors except you, our bank" would be effective.

9–050 Again, in *Carreras Rothmans Ltd v. Freeman Mathews Treasure Ltd*,[19] there was held to be a *Quistclose* trust despite the lack of technical trust language. In this case, the plaintiff had employed the defendant as an advertising agency. The defendant would contract with third party advertising media, and each month the plaintiff would pay the defendant money equal to its fee plus the amount it had paid to the third parties in the last month. When the defendant got into financial difficulties, the plaintiff

---

[16] For combination, see below Chap. 11.

[17] The trust has a similar effect to a secured loan, but does not need to be registered as a charge. See Bridge, (1992) 12 Oxford J.L.S. 333.

[18] Unreported decision of Megarry V.-C., October 6, 1978.

[19] [1985] Ch. 207, noted [1986] 1 J.I.B.L. N–25 and [1985] All E.R. Review, 316.

started to pay money into a "special account" to be used for the sole purpose of settling invoices submitted by the third parties. This was held to create a *Quistclose* trust, and the liquidator of the defendant company was therefore not entitled to the money. The liquidator argued that repayment to the plaintiff offended against the principle of *pari passu* distribution on insolvency, but the court said that this applied only to assets owned beneficially by the company, and that assets subject to a trust were not the company's assets; the account was merely a "conduit" through which the company paid the third parties. The liquidator also argued that the agreement had effectively created a charge on the company's book debts in favour of third parties, which was void for non-registration.[20] The court, however, held that either the arrangement did not constitute a charge but was only a trust, or if it was a charge, there was also a trust, which could be enforced in any case, even if the charge could not be enforced. A further complication was a counterclaim by the liquidator to one month's payments from the plaintiff, which were outstanding at the date of liquidation. It was held that the money was an asset of the defendant at the date of liquidation and the liquidator was entitled to the money. Thus, money as yet unpaid but owing went free of the trust, while money actually paid into the special account was subject to the trust.

In two more recent cases, *Quistclose* trusts have been held to exist. In *Re Branston & Gotthard Ltd*,[21] a stockbroker firm was required by its regulator, the Securities and Futures Authority (SFA), to close its investment business and open a new account, the Client Money Requirement account (CMR) to hold any surplus on client accounts and to meet the expenses of administering the clients' assets. When the firm went into liquidation, the bank wished to combine the firm's accounts. It was held that the money in the CMR account was held on trust for the investor clients of the firm to the extent that the money was required to make good any deficiencies in the money held by the firm. The trust arose for several reasons—among others, because the whole basis of the intervention of the SFA was to protect investors; the account had been opened in a name which clearly showed that it was for the benefit of clients; the firm had accepted that the money in the account was not available to pay the general expenses and liabilities of the firm. There had been a clear intention to create a trust.[22] **9–051**

A more unusual *Quistclose* trust was upheld in *Twinsectra Ltd v. Yardley*.[23] A property entrepreneur was granted a loan on the basis that the money was held on a solicitor's undertaking to retain it until it was applied in the acquisition of property and that it would be used solely for that purpose. The solicitor, however, released the money for the wrong reasons—for the **9–052**

[20] Under CA 1985, s. 395.
[21] [1999] Lloyd's Rep. Bank. 251.
[22] *ibid.*, at 258. Distinguishing *Multi-Guarantee Co Ltd* [1987] B.C.L.C. 257.
[23] [1999] Lloyd's Rep. Bank. 438.

benefit of the entrepreneur and for the payment of his own costs and expenses—and became bankrupt. The Court of Appeal held that although the purpose of the loan ("acquisition of property") fell outside the usual *Quistclose*-type cases, there was no inherent reason why special purpose trusts should not be imposed so long as the terms of the restraint on the borrowers' use of the money were sufficiently certain to be enforceable by the lenders. In principle, the court said, the degree of certainty need be no more than is necessary to enable the restriction on the recipient's use of the money to be identified and enforced, provided that there is, in a commercial setting, some element or circumstance present additional to a simple declaration of purpose to give rise to a fiduciary obligation on the recipient of a loan. This would usually be the requirement that the loan money should be held in a special account separate from the recipient's general funds.[24] Here, "acquisition of property" (before the obligation to repay would arise, which would be in four months) was a sufficiently clear statement of purpose of the loan, although the property to be acquired was not identified. The money was sufficiently segregated from the solicitor's own assets because of the strict rules about solicitors' client accounts. Further, it was not necessary that, at the time of of the loan, there should be an identifiable third party for whose ultimate benefit the payment was made. This decision takes a liberal attitude towards express purpose trusts, which, although banks were not directly affected in the case, has the potential for stretching possible liability for simple loans by banks to amount to express trusts. The requirement that money should be held in a separate account will not be sufficient in itself to allow banks to identify trust funds in these circumstances. It seems that much may rest on the application of the limiting device of "some element giving rise to a fiduciary obligation".

Extent of Banks' Liability for Breach of Trust

9–053 An important question about the rights of beneficiaries under a trust where the trust fund is held by a bank has been considered by the courts several times in recent years. If the trust funds have been used up or dissipated and the trust account is overdrawn, do the beneficiaries have a right to trace their money into the funds of the bank? As we have seen, the courts decided in *Foley v. Hill*[25] that bankers are not trustees for their customers in relation to the taking of deposits but simply owe them debts, so that banks can use deposited funds as their own money. Since *Foley v. Hill*, therefore, ordinary depositors have no priority over the bank's other creditors if the bank becomes insolvent.[26]

[24] [1999] Lloyd's Rep. Bank. 438 at 456, *per* Potter L.J.

[25] (1848) 2 H.L.C. 28. See above, para. 3–004.

[26] As sometimes happens: *e.g.* the collapse of BCCI, see above Chap. 1.

It is an interesting question whether the principle of *Foley v. Hill* applies where the bank itself is trustee of funds—that is, where funds are given to it so that it may act as trustee. This situation must be distinguished from cases where a customer is trustee of funds deposited, and from constructive trusts, in which cases the bank is liable only if it knows (or maybe ought to know) of the customer's breaches of trust. The *Quistclose* trust, considered above, is an example of such a trust; money deposited in a customer's account for a specific purpose may be impressed with a trust, so that it is not available to the customer's creditors on the customer's insolvency. It would seem to follow that the monies would not be available on the insolvency of the bank for the bank's creditors. The question arose in *Space Investment Ltd v. Canadian Imperial Bank of Commerce Trust Co (Bahamas) Ltd*,[27] where some settlements of which the bank was trustee empowered the bank (as trustee) to "deposit" with itself (as banker) money which it had received in trust. At first instance it was held that trust creditors of a bank ranked prior to the unsecured creditors of that bank on the bank's insolvency. The Privy Council, however, decided that *Foley v. Hill* applied even to trust funds held by the bank as trustee. Lord Templeman, who gave the judgment, said,[28] that equity gave no special protection to customers where the bank exercised powers conferred by the trust instrument in good faith. The effect was that, just as with ordinary deposits, the money received as banker was held beneficially by the bank on a debtor-creditor relationship with the beneficiaries. The beneficiaries therefore could not trace their money into any asset (or all the assets) of the bank. The bank continued to have obligations as trustee in respect of the proper management of the account, but not in a proprietary capacity in respect of the money transferred to its general banking business. **9–054**

Lord Templeman went on, however, to make a further controversial,[29] statement about what would be the case if the deposit by the bank been *wrongful*: **9–055**

> "But equity allows the beneficiaries, or a new trustee appointed in place of an insolvent bank trustee . . . to trace the trust money to all the assets of the bank and to recover the trust money by the exercise of an equitable charge over all the assets of the bank . . . that equitable charge secures for the beneficiaries and the trust priority over the claims of the customers . . . and . . . all other unsecured creditors".[30]

[27] [1986] 1 W.L.R. 1072, P.C.
[28] *ibid.*, at 1073–74.
[29] See Goode (1987) 103 LQR 433; Gullifer [1995] LMCLQ 446.
[30] [1986] 1 W.L.R. 1072 at 1074. The reason for the favourable treatment of beneficiaries at the expense of unsecured creditors is that the creditors "voluntarily accept the risk" that the bank may become insolvent.

9–056 Some[31] have taken this statement to mean that a trust beneficiary whose money has been misappropriated by a trustee is able to trace that money into the trustee's overdrawn bank account and recover it by means of an equitable charge. This would mean that the beneficiary of a trust fund held by a bank would be able to trace money (where the bank has acted in breach of trust) into the bank account and, if that provided insufficient funds, trace it *through* the account and into the assets of the bank. If this were the case, it would be unorthodox: conventional doctrines allow the beneficiary to trace into the bank's funds providing that the balance of the account into which the trust money was wrongfully paid has never sunk lower than the amount claimed. The traditional tracing rules, even in equity, have presupposed "the continued existence of the money either as a separate fund or as part of a mixed fund or as latent in property acquired by means of such a fund",[32] whether or not there has been a breach of trust.

9–057 It can be argued that the bank may be regarded as having taken the risk of the loss, since it was aware that the fund was a trust account. However, it would cause difficulties if the bank itself were insolvent, because a problem of priorities would arise: the beneficiary (like a beneficiary of a *Quistclose* trust, where money is deposited with the bank for the specific purpose of being paid to other persons) would in that case have a prior claim to the assets over other creditors of the bank. It would also cast a new light on *Foley v. Hill*.

9–058 Lord Templeman's remarks, which were *obiter*, were treated circumspectly by Lord Mustill in *Re Goldcorp Exchange Ltd*,[33] where a bank disputed the imposition of an equitable charge on funds which it claimed. In this case, customers of a New Zealand company which dealt in gold and precious metals had purchased bullion from the company, which was stored and insured by the company without allocating it to the customers, who simply received certificates of ownership and had the right to take delivery of the bullion on seven days notice. The company became insolvent, and a bank with a debenture over its assets appointed receivers, who claimed the entire assets of the company, including the bullion. The customers claimed that they had proprietary rights in the bullion, and the New Zealand Court of Appeal held that, though they had no proprietary rights in the bullion, the purchase price of the bullion could be traced into the assets of the company on the basis that the company had been a fiduciary and had received the money on trust. This gave the customers a charge over the company's assets ranking in priority to the bank's charge. The Privy Council, however, allowed the appeal, taking the view that this was a simple

[31] *e.g.* Sir Robin Cooke of the New Zealand Court of Appeal in *Liggett v. Kensington* [1993] 1 NZLR 257 (rev'd *sub nom. Re Goldcorp* [1994] 3 W.L.R. 199.

[32] *Re Diplock's Estate* [1948] Ch 465 at 521, CA *per* Lord Greene M.R. See also *Roscoe v. Winder* [1915] 1 Ch. 62.

[33] [1994] 3 W.L.R. 199.

contract of sale, not a trust, and the buyers had not obtained any proprietary interest either in the bullion or in the money paid by them, because they could not acquire title until it was clear to what goods the title related, and here the goods had been unascertained. The Board refused to impose a remedial constructive trust which would be superior to the bank's charge. Lord Mustill said that it was unnecessary to consider the scope and ambit of Lord Templeman's *dictum* in *Space Investments*, because no equitable charge was being imposed in this case.[34]

In *Bishopsgate Investment Management Ltd v. Homan*[35] (where the plaintiffs were the trustees of pension funds whose money had been misappropriated[36]) the Court of Appeal held that recognised equitable principles do not permit tracing through an overdrawn bank account. It seems likely therefore that the traditional rules on tracing are still good law.[37] 9–059

[34] [1994] 3 W.L.R. 199 at 226–7.

[35] [1995] 1 All E.R. 347; see Breslin (1995) Company Lawyer. See also *Style Financial Services Ltd v. The Governor and the Company of the Bank of Scotland* [1996] 5 Bank L.R. 15.

[36] By Robert Maxwell.

[37] See Oliver (1995) 9 Trust Law Int. 78, and Hayton [1994] LMCLQ 449. See also *Box v. Barclays Bank* [1998] Ch. D. 185 at 203.

contrary on one side, that a trust, and the lawyers had not meant [illegible] any impropriety, rather than a trust in the paper or [illegible] taken, because they could not acquire title until it was clear to what ends the [illegible] related, and hence the goods had been unaccounted for. The Bank [illegible] refused to impose a remedial constructive trust which would [illegible] the Bank's charge. Lord Mustill said that it was unnecessary to consider the [illegible] of Lord Templeman's dictum in [illegible] because no equitable charge was being imposed in this case.

In *Nimmo* [illegible] *Westpac* [illegible] where, in pursuing the [illegible] of [illegible] whose [illegible] had been misappropriated, the Court of Appeal held that it [illegible] equitable principles [illegible] tracing through an overdrawn bank account. It seems likely therefore that the [illegible] still good law. 11-59

Chapter 10

Right to Recover Money in Restitution

10–001 As was seen in the last Chapter, tracing may be used to trace what has happened to one's property, to identify the persons who have handled or received it and justify the claim that the money they have handled or received (and, if necessary, which they still retain) can properly be regarded as representing one's own money,[1] so that a right may be asserted to it in priority to other creditors on insolvency (a "proprietary" right).[2] A right to recover money may be asserted, however, not only by a proprietary right, but also by means of a *personal action*[3]—the "action for money had and received" (to recover money paid under a mistake). This is a *restitutionary* right which will allow recovery if the defendant has been unjustly enriched at the claimant's expense. In the banking context, it may be claimed by a paying bank, which has wrongly paid and which wishes to reclaim the money from the payee or from the collecting bank, or by the payer of the money him or herself.[4] It is normally the bank which claims, because if it has made a wrongful payment, it will not be able to debit its customer's account, and will be out of pocket.

10–002 Restitution has been increasingly recognised in English law in the last few decades, and has undergone great development by courts[5] and academic writers (the literature is enormous). It is a dynamic field of law and its fundamental concepts and implications are still being settled. However,

---

[1] See *Boscawen v. Bajwa* [1995] 4 All E.R. 769 at 777.

[2] See above Chap. 9 and generally for this topic, Goff and Jones *The Law of Restitution* (Jones ed., 4th ed., 1993), particularly Chap. 3, and *Restitution and Banking Law* (Rose ed., 1998).

[3] In *Westdeutsche Landesbank Girozentrale v. Islington L.B.C.* [1996] 2 All E.R. 961, *Chase Manhattan Bank v. Israel-British Bank (London) Ltd* [1979] 3 All E.R. 1025 (where it was held that a bank which had paid the same sum twice to the defendant by mistake had a claim *in rem*, it was allowed equitable tracing) was considered, but not overruled.

[4] As in *Lipkin Gorman v. Karpnale* [1991] 3 W.L.R. 10, HL and in *Agip (Africa) Ltd v. Jackson* [1990] 1 Ch. 265, aff'd. [1991] 3 W.L.R. 116. "There are several factors which make it unjust for a defendant to retain the benefit of his enrichment; mistake is one of them": *per* Millett L.J., *Portman BS v. Hamlyn Taylor Neck* [1998] 4 All E.R. 202 at 206. Another is failure of consideration, recently considered in *Goss v. Chilcott* [1996] A.C. 788, PC.

[5] *e.g. Fibrosa Spolka v. Akcyjna v. Akcyjna Fairbairn Lawson Combe Barbour Ltd* [1943] A.C. 32, *per* Lord Wright: "It is clear that any civilised system of law is bound to provide remedies for cases of what has been called unjust enrichment or unjust benefit, that is, to prevent a man from retaining the money of, or some benefit derived from, another which it is against conscience that he should keep"; *Barclays Bank Ltd v. W.J. Simms, Son & Cooke (Southern) Ltd* [1979] 3 All E.R. 522, *per* Goff J., and recently, by the "swaps" cases, see *e.g. Kleinwort Benson v. Lincoln C.C.* [1998] 4 All E.R. 513, discussed below.

"money paid under a mistake of fact", the aspect of what is now restitution, with which this Chapter is concerned, has been recognised as a right of action for much longer—for centuries, in fact[6]—and has traditionally been of great concern to banks. Much of the old law, as well as the new, developed in the context of banking cases.

10–003 The modern application of the claim for mistake can be seen from the case of *Barclays Bank Ltd v. W.J. Simms, Son & Cooke (Southern) Ltd.*[7] A customer of the bank drew a cheque in favour of a building company, but learnt, two days later, that the company had gone into receivership. He telephoned the bank to instruct them to stop payment of the cheque, and confirmed the countermand in writing. When the cheque was presented, a clerk at the bank, overlooking the countermand, paid the cheque. Where the paying bank, as here, has acted without the authority of its customer, it may not debit its customer's account, and it has, of course, no contractual claim against the payee. The question is, therefore, whether it is entitled to recover the payment from the payee. Barclays sued the company for recovery of the money as money paid under a mistake of fact.

By his examination of the authorities and formulation of rules from what was regarded as a notoriously difficult series of cases to reconcile, Goff J. can be said to have established the basis of the modern law.[8] He concluded that a bank which has made a payment under a mistake of fact is prima facie entitled to recover the payment, and here was able to do so. The judge also made it clear that there are several defences open to the payee against such a claim—the payer may have intended that the payee should have the money at all events; the payment may have been made for good consideration (for example, to discharge a debt owed to the payee) or the payee may have changed its position in good faith or be deemed in law to have done so.

10–004 Since that time very important developments in the law, to a remarkable extent as a result of the work of the same judge, have recast the claim of mistake of fact (among other claims) in terms of the law of restitution. Restitution was unequivocally recognised in the law by the House of Lords decision in the case of *Lipkin Gorman v. Karpnale*,[9] a claim by a firm of solicitors against the Playboy Club. A partner in the firm, Cass, had misappropriated large sums of money from the firm's client account at the bank in order to fund his compulsive gambling at the club. These facts, straightforward as they are, gave rise to a range of claims in equity and at common law by the firm against both the bank and the club.[10] By the time

[6] The action dates from the 17th century: Goff and Jones, *op. cit.*, p. 113.

[7] [1979] 3 All E.R. 522. See also *Lloyd's Bank plc v. Independent Insurance Company Ltd* [1999] Lloyds Rep. Bank. 1, CA, discussed below, para. 10–022.

[8] Although not without criticism: see Matthews [1980] N.L.J. 587, and Goode (1981) 97 L.Q.R. 254.

[9] [1991] 3 W.L.R. 10, HL. See Birks (1989) 105 L.Q.R. 352; Watts (1991) 107 L.Q.R. 521; Halliwell [1992] Conv. 124; McKendrick (1992) 55 M.L.R. 377.

[10] Another issue in the case was a banker's draft in favour of the solicitors which was procured by Cass and accepted by the club.

the action reached the House of Lords, the bank (which had won its claim in constructive trust and contract in the Court of Appeal[11]) had dropped out of the picture and the solicitors and the club, both innocent parties, were left to fight out the issue. Since the solicitors conceded any claim they might have had in equity[12] against the club, the issue was determined on common law and, as it turned out, restitution principles. The decision of the House of Lords was that the club, an innocent recipient of stolen money, was obliged to pay an equivalent sum to the true owner because it had been unjustly enriched at the expense of the true owner, subject to a deduction for the amount by which it had changed its position.[13]

Tracing and mistake (of fact/law)

The claim made by the firm against the club in *Lipkin Gorman* had an additional feature, which might have made its success more problematic than the claims between bank and payee like *Barclays Bank v. Simms & Cooke*: the money had not been paid directly to the club by the firm or the bank, but had gone through Cass's hands first. The firm therefore needed to be able to trace the payment from themselves into the hands of the club, the ultimate recipient, in order to bring the claim for restitution. As noted above,[14] two possibilities are open to claimants, tracing in equity or at common law. Since by the time the case reached the House of Lords the defendants had conceded any claim to trace in equity, the firm had to identify their money in the hands of the club by means of common law tracing.[15] **10–005**

The operation of common law tracing in *Lipkin Gorman* was interesting. It was held that the legal title to the money when Cass withdrew it from the bank was with *Cass* and not the solicitors, because of authority which the court was not prepared to overrule.[16] If the firm did not legally own the money, though, it had to be explained how it could trace the money into the hands of the club (the innocent recipients). Lord Goff explained that although the firm did not have title to the *money* itself, it did have title to the *debt* which the bank owed it, by virtue of its deposit of money at the **10–006**

[11] See above, Chap. 9.

[12] [1991] 3 W.L.R. 10 at 27, HL. The case might also have been argued on the basis of "knowing receipt" of the money by the club.

[13] See below, para. 10–029.

[14] See above, para. 9–040.

[15] Assisted by another concession by the defendants, who agreed not to argue that the money was mixed with other money in Cass's hands (which would have defeated tracing at common law). McKendrick points out that the concession is odd: McKendrick, *op. cit.*, 379. The use of common law tracing provokes an interesting comparison with equitable tracing which has been favoured in a number of recent cases, notable among which is *Agip*, [1990] 1 Ch. 265; affd. [1991] 3 W.L.R. 116; see above, Chap. 9. See also Fennell (1994) 57 M.L.R. 38 at 42.

[16] *Union Bank of Australia Ltd v. McClintock* [1922] 1 A.C. 240, PC; *Commercial Banking Co of Sydney Ltd v. Mann* [1961] A.C. 1, PC.

bank. This was a *chose in action* which gave the firm the right to trace the property into its product, the money drawn from the account by Cass, and into the hands of the club. This explanation may enhance the attractions of common law tracing and provide claimants with an improved alternative to equitable tracing where legal title to money paid by banks is in doubt.[17–18]

Although it was held that the club had no complete defence to the claim, since no consideration had been given for the money—the contracts made by the bets at the club were void as gaming contracts[19]—it had changed its position to some extent by losing certain sums to Cass, and therefore would suffer injustice if the money were completely repaid. The solicitors succeeded in part in their claim.

10–007 The principle of *Lipkin Gorman* was applied in the case of *The Trustee of the Property of Jones v. Jones.*[20] After a partnership (a firm of potato growers) had failed to comply with a bankruptcy notice, the wife of one of the partners started dealing in potato futures with money which her husband had drawn from the partnership joint account after the act of bankruptcy. She was remarkably successful and the action was taken by the trustee in bankruptcy to recover not only the principal sum but the profits she had made from her dealings from the firm with which the money had been deposited. Since the original sum drawn from the account belonged to the trustee, the husband had had no title to it and could not confer title on his wife, but the question was whether the money could be traced into the proceeds of the wife's dealings so that the trustee could recover it.

10–008 It was held that the trustee could not trace at equity, because the wife had not been a fiduciary.[21] However, following *Lipkin Gorman*, where the plaintiffs could trace their "property into its product",[22] the chose in action constituted by the deposit of the trustee's money under the terms of the contract between the wife and her brokers belonged to the trustee, and could be traced at common law. There was no problem here in tracing the money: it need not be traced through the clearing system,[23] but could be followed through cheques passed from hand to hand. Nor was there a problem for the trustee in recovering the profits: his right was to the balance standing to the wife's account, whatever that was, not a right to payment of the original amount. The "product" of the property, given a wide interpretation by the court, therefore means not merely property for which the original property has been exchanged, but may include profits made from the property.[24]

[17–18] See Halliwell, *op. cit.*, for a crisp analysis of these aspects of the case; and McKendrick, *op. cit.*, who questions the meaning which should be ascribed to property for common law tracing purposes.

[19] Gaming Act 1845, s. 18.

[20] [1996] 3 W.L.R. 703, CA.

[21] The decision at first instance was reversed on this point.

[22] [1991] 2 A.C. 548 at 573, *per* Lord Goff. In *Jones*, tracing was not related to a claim for money had and received which would, on the facts, have been long out of date, and which would have been a personal claim against the wife, not the brokers.

[23] Which had been a problem in *Agip* [1990] 1 Ch. 265.

[24] [1996] 3 W.L.R. 703 at 714 CA, *per* Nourse L.J.

Money Paid under a Mistake (of Fact or Law)[25]

A bank may pay money to a payee without authority from its customer because of an administrative error, as in *Barclays Bank v. Simms*, or because of forgery of a cheque or an unauthorised signature. If it is not protected by estoppel or some statutory defence, the bank may be unable to debit its customer's account and be liable to the true owner of the cheque, and may then try to recover the amount wrongly paid from the recipient.[26] Conversely, it sometimes happens that a bank has itself been the recipient of money wrongly paid (particularly when it is collecting money on behalf of its customer) and the question of its own liability to such a claim arises. **10–009**

The claim to recover money may be stated in these terms: if one person pays money to another under a mistake of fact, or now of law, which caused him or her to make the payment, he or she is prima facie entitled to recover it as money paid under a mistake.[27] It should be noted that the restitutionary claim is quite different from a claim to set aside a *contract* for mistake, where the question is whether binding obligations in contract exist. The object of the restitutionary claim is simply to prevent the unjust enrichment of the recipient at the expense of the plaintiff. Any restitutionary claim must have the following elements: the defendant must be *enriched*; the enrichment must have been *at the expense of the plaintiff*; it must be shown that there was some "*unjust*" *factor* (some identifiable and principled basis upon which it can be said that the continued retention of the benefit by the defendant is unjust)[28]; and the defendant must not be able to rely upon any recognised defence to the claim.[29] Mistake (or unjust enrichment) simply allows recovery without any examination of fault, until the point at which defences are considered; the claimant can even recover despite its own negligence.[30] **10–010**

[25] Generally, see Goff and Jones, *op. cit.*, Chaps 3 and 4. Sometimes called the action for "money had and received". It is sometimes said that the plaintiff demands repayment of money said to have been "had and received by the defendant to the plaintiff's use." Conversion does not lie for money taken and received as currency: *Lipkin Gorman* [1991] 3 W.L.R. 10 at 14, 25, HL.

[26] If a bank wrongly pays, acting as agent, the customer may sue the payee: *Turvey v. Dentons (1923) Ltd* [1953] 1 Q.B. 218.

[27] Since *Kleinwort Benson Ltd v. Lincoln City Council* [1998] 4 All E.R. 513 the claim is presumably correctly described simply as "money paid under a mistake".

[28] An obligation to make restitution has to flow from the ineffectiveness of the transaction under which the money was paid, not from a mistake or misrepresentation which induced it. In *Portman BS v. Hamlyn Taylor Neck* [1998] 4 All E.R. 202, where a building society had lent money, the solicitors dealing with the advance knew that the borrower required it for a purpose not disclosed to the society and failed to inform the society of the fact. The firm might well have been liable to the society (*e.g.* for misrepresentation), but such claims by the society were statute barred, and therefore the society had made a "hopeless" (at 209, *per* Brooke L.J.) attempt to recover in restitution. The court found the society's claim for restitution of the payment by the firm entirely misconceived: the firm had paid the money on to the borrowers on the instructions of the society, and had not itself been enriched.

[29] McKendrick, *op. cit.*, p. 379.

[30] *Kelly v. Solari* (1841) 9 M & W 54.

10–011 In banking, the sort of mistakes which may allow recovery are:

(a) payment accidentally made on a countermanded cheque;
(b) payment made on a cheque where the drawer's signature is forged;
(c) payment made in the belief that the drawer has sufficient funds in his account;
(d) payment made to the wrong person (for example, if there are two Smiths with accounts at the bank);
(e) overpayment (double credits seem to be quite common); or
(f) payment made by a confirming bank to the beneficiary of a letter of credit, where the bank believes wrongly that the documents are correct.

In these circumstances, the bank will have a remedy in a claim for money paid by mistake.

Conditions for Recovery of Money

10–012 If money paid by mistake is to be recoverable by a bank by way of an action in restitution, the following conditions must apply:

(1) Money must have been paid under a mistake

10–013 Until the decision in *Kleinwort Benson v. Lincoln City Council*,[31] there was a firm rule that the mistake giving rise to recovery had to be a mistake of *fact*, not of *law*.[32] The distinction between the two was notoriously difficult, if not impossible, to draw,[33] and, prompted by a report from the

[31] [1998] 4 All E.R. 513. See Finnis (1999) 115 L.Q.R. 170.

[32] In *Kelly v. Solari* (1841) 9 M & W 54, Lord Abinger said that money paid by mistake of law was irrecoverable. Goff and Jones, *op. cit.* at 142, ascribe the rule to a decision of Lord Ellenborough in *Bilbie v. Lumley* (1802) 2 East 469. See *Kleinwort Benson* [1998] 4 All E.R. 513.

[33] Described in the first edition of this book as "both impossible and pointless". Examples of some of the confusing judicial statements were given (paraphrased): This property is not subject to the Rent Acts (fact)—*Solle v. Butcher* [1950] 1 K.B. 671. The Rent Acts bind the Crown, so that this Crown tenant is protected (law)—*Territorial & Auxiliary Forces Assn. v. Nichols* [1949] 1 K.B. 35. A certain statute exists, affecting a landlord's right to rent (law)—*Sharp Bros & Knight v. Chant* [1917] 1 K.B. 771. A statement about the powers of a company, under a private Act of Parliament (fact)—*Kitson v. Commercial Bank*. The law of foreign state is XYZ (fact) *Andre & Cie S.A. v. Ets. Michel Blanc* [1977] 2 Lloyd's Rep. 166 (in this case Lord Denning, with whom the majority disagreed, said that the distinction between fact and law was illusory, and should be abandoned). We owe you £X while you are away from work (fact)—*Avon CC v. Howlett* [1983] 1 All E.R. 1073. There is a legally enforceable option between us, or between me and another (fact) *Taylor Fashions Ltd v. Liverpool Victoria Trustees Co Ltd* [1981] 1 All E.R. 897. There is a contract between us and we are liable under it to you (fact) *AIP Co Ltd v. Texas Commerce International Bank Ltd*

Law Commission recommending its abolition,[34] numerous criticisms from academic commentators, and a recent change in the law of Scotland,[35] the House of Lords has held that the rule should no longer form part of English law.[36] Lord Goff listed the main criticisms of the rule as: its injustice in allowing the payee to retain a payment which would not have been made but for the payer's mistake, its capriciousness, and the temptation it offered judges to manipulate the distinction in order to achieve a just result in particular cases.

The situation in *Kleinwort Benson* which gave rise to the problem was similar to that in other "swaps" cases.[37] In a swap transaction, the parties agree that there is a notional principal sum on which one party is to pay to the second a fixed rate of interest and the second is to pay the first a "floating" rate (interest calculated by reference to a fluctuating rate set by the market). Only the net difference between the two will eventually (after years) be paid. The attraction for the local authorities in these particular cases was that the banks would make an upfront capital payment in the transaction: in effect, therefore, the local authority was able to borrow money without, apparently, infringing the relevant statutory controls on borrowing. These contracts first came into use in about 1981, and had become widely used and regarded as legitimate by the time the present contracts were made.[38] It was only when the first of the "swaps" cases, *Hazell v. Hammersmith and Fulham L.B.C.*[39] was decided by the House of Lords that it became clear that the local authorities had had no powers under the Local Government Act 1972 to enter such transactions, and that the transactions were void. The banks, which had thereby lost large sums of **10–014**

[1981] 1 All E.R. 923. Goff J. says "where one party has represented to the other that a transaction between them has an effect which in law it does not have" this is factual and can give rise to an estoppel. We are liable (law); we will pay you money (promise, not fact)—*China Pacific S.A. v. Food Corpn of India* [1980] 3 All E.R. 556. Payments under this separation agreement are free of any deduction of tax (law) *Ord v. Ord* [1923] 2 K.B. 432. Whether under a statute a landlord has an obligation to pay for repairs is a question of fact—*Brikom Investments v. Seaford* (*per* Ormrod L.J. "these dichotomies are dangerously neat and apt to mislead. Representations of fact shade into representations of law . . .")

[34] *Restitution: mistakes of law and ultra vires public authority receipts and payments*, Law Com. No. 227, 1994.

[35] *Morgan Guaranty Trust Co of New York v. Lothian Regional Council* 1995 S.L.T. 299.

[36] Criticism was so widely accepted that the defendant local authority in the case made no attempt to defend the rule, but submitted instead that it should be reformulated (*Kleinwort* [1998] 4 All E.R. 513 at 525, *per* Lord Goff).

[37] See Chap. 8.

[38] "There was a general understanding, which was shared by banks and local authorities as regular participants in the money markets, that interest rate swap contracts were within the borrowing and lending powers of local authorities. This understanding appears to have been based upon commercial assumptions which developed within the money markets, not as a result of initiatives taken on legal advice" [1998] 4 All E.R. 513 at 558, *per* Lord Hope.

[39] [1991] 1 All E.R. 545; see also [1994] 4 All E.R. 890, CA and [1996] 2 All E.R. 961, HL. See also *Woolwich B.S. v. IRC (No. 2)* [1992] 3 All E.R. 737, in which it was held that at common law taxes exacted *ultra vires* were recoverable as of right, without the need to invoke a mistake of law by the payer.

money to the local authorities, retaliated by bringing claims for restitution of the money.

10–015 These claims were upheld in *Westdeutsche Landesbank Girozentrale v. Islington L.B.C.*[40] The ground on which recovery in restitution was granted was *absence of consideration*, not mistake[41]; Hobhouse J. held that the lack of knowledge of a statutory provision was a mistake of law, and that he was bound by authority to hold that a mistake of law did not give a right to recover money at common law.[42] In the *Kleinwort Benson* case, however, the House of Lords had to consider the question of principle and determine whether the mistaken assumption as to the law at the time the contracts were entered into would found a claim in restitution. The House had no difficulty in coming to the conclusion that the mistake of law rule should be abrogated.

The question which posed great difficulty in the case, and caused two judges to dissent,[43] was how far the principle of recovery under a mistake of law should extend. All the judges agreed that if one party makes a payment on legal advice which is wrong, that payment may now be recovered. But if the payment was made on an *understanding of the law*—perhaps on the general view taken by lawyers as well as laymen—that was, or seemed to be, correct at the time, but which was later changed by a judicial decision which would have retrospective effect, the position might be different. In *Kleinwort Benson* itself, the payments were made under contracts which at the time were understood by all concerned to be valid and binding, and where it was thought that the payments were lawfully due.

10–016 The argument that the law underlying the mistaken assumption was "settled law" or a common understanding of the law at the time was relied on by the defendant local authorities. The defence was supported by the dissenting judges on two grounds. First, the question was, what sort of "mistake" would ground recovery? It could hardly be said that a payment made where there was an accepted, common view of the law that such a transaction was valid, which was changed later by a court decision (as in the *Hazell* case), was really made under a *mistake.* At the time of the transaction there had been no mistake at all; it was only because of the retrospective nature of judicial lawmaking[44] that it became clear later that the transaction had been *ultra vires* the local authority. In the view of the minority, it was an artificiality to call this a mistake.[45] The further point, a

[40] [1994] 4 All E.R. 890.

[41] The basis of claims for absence or failure of consideration has recently been considered by the Privy Council in *Goss v. Chilcott* [1996] A.C. 788, where it was said that even if the failure of consideration has not been total, recovery will be allowed, at least in those cases in which apportionment can be carried out without difficulty (at 798, *per* Lord Goff).

[42] [1996] A.C. 788 at 931.

[43] Lords Browne-Wilkinson and Lloyd.

[44] The nature of law-making by the courts was considered at length.

[45] [1998] 4 All E.R. 513 at 518, *per* Lord Browne-Wilkinson.

matter of policy, was the question of finality of transactions. It might be years after a transaction that the courts held that the transaction was invalid at the time it was made, and this result would seriously upset the security of commercial transactions.[46]

Nevertheless, the majority came to the conclusion that there had been a mistake, and the mistake had been one of law. In Lord Goff's words: 10–017

> ". . . the payer believed, when he paid the money, that he was bound to pay it. He is now told that, on the law as held to be applicable at the date of the payment, he was not bound to pay it. Plainly, therefore, he paid the money under a mistake of law".[47]

The other judges expressed the view that to take the "commonsense" definition of mistake would be to narrow the meaning of unjust enrichment unduly: "it was to look at mistake in too abstract a way, divorced from its setting in the law of unjust enrichment".[48] Further, it would give rise to doubtful points as to what was believed about the law when the payment was made, and to much scope for argument and arbitrary distinctions in future cases as to what constituted a settled view of the law.[49]

(2) The mistake must have caused the payment

Normally, it seems, the relevant question is whether the payment would have occurred if the payer had not made the alleged mistake (whether the mistake is one of fact[50] or of law[51]). Therefore, if a payment is made under a mistake of law, and the payer is aware that the payment is not due, the payer may still recover the payment provided it would not have been made but for the mistake.[52] This formula is in accord with the general restitutionary approach that the law looks first at whether the payee has been enriched at the expense of the payer. The payee then has the opportunity to raise any defence available, relating to the value given, or any detriment suffered by the payee, which would make it unjust for him or her to have to return the payment. The effect must be that by reason of the mistake the payee has been unjustly enriched. 10–018

---

[46] The problem is compounded by the effect of the limitation period in mistake actions (under s. 32(1)(c) of the LA 1980) which starts to run only when the plaintiff discovers (or could reasonably have discovered) the mistake. This, it was held, would be solved if an appropriately drawn Limitation Statute were passed, which was a matter for the legislature.

[47] Lord Goff [1998] 4 All E.R. 513 at 536, *per* Lord Goff. The conclusion on "settled law" differs from the Law Commission's view.

[48] [1998] 4 All E.R. 513 at 552, *per* Lord Hoffmann.

[49] [1998] 4 All E.R. 513 at 563, *per* Lord Hope; at 553, *per* Lord Hoffmann.

[50] *Barclays Bank v. Simms & Cooke* [1979] 3 All E.R. 522 at 534.

[51] *Nurdin & Peacock plc v. DB Ramsden & Co. Ltd* [1999] 1 All E.R. 941, Ch. D.

[52] *Nurdin & Peacock v. Ramsden* [1999] 1 All E.R. 941, Ch D.

10–019 Since the mistake must cause the payment, it must be a mistake of the *payer*, not of the payee. It is often said that the mistake must be "between" payer (bank) and payee,[53] but the meaning of this is obscure, and perhaps especially obscure in relation to banks. The phrase is understandable where the wrong person is paid, because that is clearly a mistake between payer and payee, but if, say, the drawer countermands a cheque, can it be said that this is a mistake between payer and payee, or only between bank and customer (drawer)? In *Barclays Bank Ltd v. Simms*,[54] it was said that these were mistakes between payer and payee, although they are also, of course, between bank and customer. The bank believed itself obliged to obey the mandate. Goff J. thought that the phrase, which, he said, had been taken out of its original context, had been reformulated in the cases and now meant nothing more "than that the mistake must have caused the payment".[55] Since it seems that the payee need not even know of the mistake,[56] it does not seem to add anything to the understanding of the principles involved to say that the mistake must be between payer and payee. It may well be that all that is needed to make it a mistake "between" payer and payee is that it is sufficiently serious (it is sometimes said that the mistake must be fundamental[57]) to allow it to be said that, but for the mistake, no payment would have been made by the payer to the payee.

10–020 It used to be said that the payer can only recover if the mistake is one which is essential to liability,[58] but this is not necessarily the case. A payment not made to discharge a liability, but made under a mistake for example, of a duty to a third party or even of a moral duty[59], may be recoverable.[60] In *Kerrison v. Glyn Mills Currie & Co*,[61] for example, a payment which was not made to discharge a liability was recoverable.

A *voluntary* payment of the money cannot be recovered: a person who has paid the money intending that the recipient should have it at all

[53] *Westminster Bank Ltd v. Arlington Overseas Trading Co.* [1952] 1 Lloyd's Rep. 211; *Secretary of State for Employment v. Wellworthy* (No. 2) [1976] 1 C.R.B. The phrase is criticised by Goff and Jones, *op. cit.*, p. 115, as a "dogmatic denial" of the right to recover and as unnecessarily invoking privity.

[54] [1979] 3 All E.R. 522 at 536.

[55] *Paget's Law of Banking* (11th ed.), at pp. 360–361 the existence of the "supposed rule" is doubted, but it would be unsafe to assume that the *Simms* case has settled the issue.

[56] *R.E. Jones Ltd v. Waring and Gillow Ltd* [1926] A.C. 670.

[57] *Norwich Union Fire Insurance Society v. Price* [1934] A.C. 455 at 461–3, *per* Lord Wright. Goff and Jones, *op. cit.*, consider that "fundamental" is too strong where there is no contract and the object is simply to avoid unjust enrichment. The mistake must be "vital or material": *Barclays Bank Ltd v. W.J. Simms, Son & Cooke (Southern) Ltd* [1979] 3 All E.R. 522.

[58] *e.g.* dictum of Bramwell B. in *Aiken v. Short* (1856) 1 H & N 210 at 214: "the mistake must be as to a fact which, if true, would make the person paying liable to pay the money; not where, if true, it would merely make it desirable that he should pay the money".

[59] Goff and Jones, *op. cit.*, p. 118, citing *Larner v. LCC* [1949] 2 K.B. 683.

[60] See also Goff J., in *Barclays Bank v. Simms & Cooke* [1979] 3 All E.R. 522.

[61] (1911) 17 Com Cas 41. See also *Kleinwort Sons & Co v. Dunlop Rubber Co* (1907) 97 L.T. 263; *Jones v. Waring & Gillow* [1926] A.C. 870; *Colonial Bank v. Exchange Bank of Yarmouth* (1885) 11 App.Cas. 84.

events[62] should not be able to recover, and a person who has intentionally paid, without reference to the truth or falsehood of the fact—who has declined, for example, to find out more about the fact—is therefore bound, even though he or she has paid under a mistake of fact. The fact that a payer has been *negligent* in paying is normally irrelevant, and the carelessness of the bank in paying a cheque is therefore not usually an issue.[63]

(3) The payment must not be within the mandate

If the payment was within the bank's mandate (its authority) from its customer, the bank cannot recover, because a debt is thereby discharged between bank and customer. This means that the bank has an effective remedy in contract against the customer, and contract rather than restitution governs the claim. The bank is entitled to debit its customer's account and the payment discharges the customer's obligation to the payee on the cheque.[64] **10–021**

Even if the bank pays a cheque where there are insufficient funds in the account, it acts within its mandate because the drawing of a cheque by the customer who has not enough money in the account is regarded as a request for an overdraft.[65] The bank's payment of the cheque is therefore simply an acceptance of the request and the payment is not recoverable by the bank from the third party. The bank's remedy, if one is needed, is again in contract against the customer. If, on the other hand, it pays the wrong payee, it has no mandate from its customer, the customer's obligation to the payee has not been discharged, and the bank should be able to recover the money in restitution.

This aspect of Goff J.'s judgment in the *Barclays Bank* case was considered by the Court of Appeal in *Lloyd's Bank v. Independent Insurance Company Limited.*[66] The bank's customer, an insurance agent, owed a debt to the defendant insurance company. The agent instructed the bank that when it received an electronic transfer from another bank for payment into the agent's account, it should transfer money to Independent's bank by a CHAPS electronic transfer. The transfer did not materialise, but shortly afterwards the agent's representative paid in three cheques to the firm's account at Lloyds, telling the manager that he would like the payment to **10–022**

[62] Or is deemed to have done so: a payment by mistake may be described as voluntary (or not fundamental) where there are other reasons for not allowing recovery (*e.g.* a bookmaker's overpayment in *Morgan v. Ashcroft* [1938] 1 K.B. 49).

[63] *Kelly v. Solari* (1841) 9 M & W 54, *Kleinwort Benson* [1998] 4 All E.R. 513 at 561.

[64] *Barclays Bank Ltd v. Simms & Cooke* [1979] 8 All E.R. 522.

[65] *ibid.* at 542; see also *Lloyd's Bank v. Independent Insurance Co. Ltd* [1999] Lloyds Rep. Bank 1 at 5, CA. Ellinger and Lomnicka, *Modern Banking Law* (2nd ed.), p. 415, express doubts about this reasoning.

[66] [1979] Lloyd's Rep. Bank. 1, CA.

Independent to be made as soon as possible. The manager told him that the payment could only be made when the cheques had cleared. However, the bank mistakenly went ahead and sent the CHAPS payment before all the cheques had cleared. One of the cheques was dishonoured, leaving—as the bank discovered once the payment had been made—insufficient funds in the account to cover the payment made to Independent. Lloyds was therefore suing Independent for repayment.

10–023 The question for the court was whether the payment had been made without the authority of the customer. Here, the agent had, perhaps, authorised the bank to pay Independent the debt owed; if so, the payment had been made for good consideration and the bank could not recover it from Independent. The argument in the case concentrated, therefore, on the question whether the bank had been authorised by the agent. The court concluded from the facts that the bank had had *actual* authority for the payment: the customer's request took the form of instructing the bank to make the electronic transfer, (not, as in the *Barclays Bank* case, of drawing a cheque) and the instruction had not been subject to any condition precedent—it was the bank, not the customer, which had pointed out that the payment could not be made until the cheques had cleared. Since the bank had acted within the authority of the customer, therefore, it could not recover from the payee (Independent).

The bank "boldly"[67] challenged Goff J.'s statement that a claim should fail where *the money is paid by a third party by whom the payer is authorised to discharge the debt* (which was the situation in the Lloyds' case), and, indeed the whole proposition that restitution would not be available where the payment was authorised. It argued that it has never been a rule of law that a bank would be unable to recover because it acted within its mandate. The argument was unsuccessful. The court held that the statement was not only supported by authority, but was a fundamental part of Goff J.'s reasoning, because a payment by a bank would discharge the debt and would provide a good defence to the payee, who could assert that he or she had given consideration for the payment or had changed his or her position in no longer having a remedy against the debtor. It could not be said that a defendant who has given consideration has been unjustly enriched.

10–024 —25 Another important aspect of authority was considered. The question was raised whether the bank had had *ostensible* authority to make the payment on behalf of the customer. Since it was held here that the bank had been acting within actual authority it was not strictly necessary to consider the issue, but the court felt it appropriate to do so, though the views expressed were of course *obiter*. The decision in the *Barclays Bank* case shows the difficulty—indeed, it gave rise to forceful academic criticism of the

[67] [1999] Lloyd's Rep. Bank. 1 at 7, CA, *per* Waller L.J.

decision.[68] The argument is that where the bank wrongly pays a countermanded cheque, it is acting within the ostensible authority of its customer, and the payee may justifiably think that the bank is authorised to make the payment, because the customer has, in effect, held out the bank as his or her agent. As between the bank and the payee, therefore, the payment must be treated as authorised, and the debt as having been discharged (or the payee as having suffered a change in position). The bank would then, unlike in the *Barclays Bank* case, be unable to recover the payment from the payee. In *Lloyds*, it was argued that the payee had relied on the representation of authority by conducting its business on the basis that the payment was valid. The payee would suffer detriment by giving up the cheque to the bank for the payment (if the payment were made by cheque) thereby losing his or her rights against the payer on the cheque, including the right to seek summary judgment. On this point, the court upheld Goff J.'s judgment it said that the bank had not acted with ostensible authority and would have been able to recover the payment. Waller L.J., who gave the leading judgment, said it would be promoting estoppel to a function for which it was not designed, and anyway in this case there was no clear representation or holding out by the customer. The payee had not relied on the bank having authority, but had simply relied on the fact that the money was due, and it did not seem that Independent had suffered any detriment in any case.

Defences

If the plaintiff can satisfy these conditions, there is a prima facie case for recovery of the money. There is no requirement that the defendant should be at fault, and liability is therefore strict. Issues of fault, if there are any, will be relevant when possible defences are considered. **10–026**

There are a number of relevant defences: change of position (recognised by the House of Lords in the *Lipkin Gorman* case), bona fide purchase, ministerial receipt, estoppel and the special defence relating to negotiable instruments. The recognition of the change of position defence should have a substantial effect on the other defences, some of which may become redundant. No doubt decisions in future cases will help to settle the questions.[69]

In *Kleinwort Benson*, the House of Lords held that the honest belief by the payee that he or she is entitled to the payment does not provide a defence to a claim, because it would be so far reaching that it would **10–027**

[68] Goode (1981) 97 L.Q.R. 254, who suggests that if the bank may be considered to be acting within its *apparent* authority recovery by the bank would be more doubtful, but the bank might be able to ground a claim in subrogation (referring also to the U.S. Uniform Commercial Code, Art. 4–07); *contra,* Matthews [1982] J.B.L. 281. Goff and Jones, *op. cit.*, p. 140, comment that the argument was not put to the judge in the case.

[69] It is not clear whether these defences will come to be seen as specific instances of a wider change of position defence, see Sir Peter Millett (1991) 107 L.Q.R. 71 at 82; Birks [1991] L.M.C.L.Q. 473 and Key [1994] L.M.C.L.Q. 421.

swallow up the other defences and exclude the right of recovery in a very large proportion of cases.[70] Nor does the fact that the transaction has been completed provide a defence[71]; if that were allowed as a defence, the result would be one-sided and unjust, and would give effect to contracts which public policy has declared void.[72]

(1) Bona fide purchase[73]

10–028 A recipient who has given consideration for the payment is a bona fide purchaser for value and the payment cannot be recovered. If the payment is made for good consideration particularly—if it is paid to discharge, and does discharge, a debt owed to the payee by the payer, or by a third party by whom he or she is authorised to pay the debt[74]—the bank's claim will fail.

The question of consideration was an important aspect of *Lipkin Gorman* itself: had the Playboy club given consideration for the money it had received from Cass's gambling? It was held that it had not, since the club had no legal obligation to honour the bets (gaming contracts are void[75]) and since the use of chips for gambling (the alternative form of consideration suggested by the club) was merely a convenient mechanism for facilitating gambling. If Cass had used the money instead to buy property, however, a purchaser who had acted in good faith would have had a good defence against the solicitors' claim.

Unlike the new change of position defence, bona fide purchase is a *complete* defence, regardless of the real value of the consideration given.[76]

(2) Change of position

10–029 The decision of the House of Lords in *Lipkin Gorman* was innovative, not only in giving clear authority to unjust enrichment, but also in recognising, for the first time in English law, the existence of a "*change of position*" defence to all restitutionary claims[77]—the defence that the defendant has changed his or her position in good faith in such a manner

[70] [1998] 4 All E.R. 513 at 538, *per* Lord Goff; at 568, *per* Lord Hope.
[71] Argued by Birks (1993) 23 U.W.A.L.R. 195. *contra*, Burrows [1995] R.L.R. 15.
[72] [1998] 4 All E.R. 513 at 541–3, *per* Lord Goff.
[73] See Fox [1996] C.L.J. 547, who discusses the history of the common law rule of bona fide purchase and the currency of money.
[74] *Barclays Bank Ltd v. W.J. Simms, Son & Cooke (Southern) Ltd* [1979] 3 All E.R. 552; [1980] Q.B. 677.
[75] Gaming Act 1845, s. 18.
[76] It has been said that the bona fide purchaser defence has not been subsumed in the defence of change of position: *Lloyds v. Independent Insurance Co. Ltd* [1999] Lloyds Rep. Bank 1 at 13, *per* Peter Gibson L.J. See also *Lipkin Gorman* [1991] 3 W.L.R. 10 at 34, HL, *per* Lord Goff.
[77] The history of the defence goes back to Lord Mansfield's judgment in *Moses v. Macferlan* (1760) 2 Burr. 1005 (see Goff and Jones, *op. cit.*, p. 739.) In *Jones v. Waring & Gillow* [1926] A.C. 670, the defence of change of position was refused.

that he or she would suffer an injustice if called upon to repay the money completely or in part. The injustice of requiring the defendant to repay would then outweigh the injustice of denying the plaintiff restitution.[78] It is unclear how the defence will work in specific cases; in his speech, Lord Goff said that he was anxious not to inhibit the development of the defence on a case by case basis in the usual way. Nevertheless, some aspects may already be commonly accepted and there are some indications as to the way in which the law may develop.

It is clear that the defence will not be available to a recipient who has paid away the money with knowledge of the facts entitling the payer to recover, since the defendant must have acted in good faith, but it was suggested that it should be open to a defendant who, acting in good faith, has paid the money to charity.[79] The mere fact that money has been *spent* is not enough; there needs to be some detriment in the expenditure. For example, if the recipient has used the money for a purchase which would not otherwise have been made, the defence should be available, because he or she has acted to their detriment on the faith of the gift.[80] **10–030**

The change of position defence allows a balance of rights and wrongs to be made. In *Lipkin Gorman* itself, the firm of solicitors was allowed to recover its money to the extent of the club's winnings from Cass, subject to the overall position of the club: Cass's winnings from the club were also taken into account. In *Goss v. Chilcott*,[81] on the other hand, the defence was not allowed. A loan had been made by a finance company on the security of a mortgage. Both loan and mortgage had, as the company knew, been passed on to another person (a brother of one of the borrowers), who in fact was a director of the finance company. This director made alterations to the mortgage which made it unenforceable. The company sought recovery of the loan from the *original* borrowers on the basis of restitution. The claim was successful, and the advice of the Privy Council was that the borrowers had no defence of change of position making it inequitable for them to return the loan, since they had deliberately taken the risk that the other person would be unable to repay the loan. **10–031**

In a first instance "swaps" case, a restrictive view of the change of position defence was taken. In *South Tyneside Metropolitan Borough Council v. Svenska International plc*,[82] the bank and the Council had entered into a "swap" contract,[83] which the bank had backed up with "hedging"

[78] [1999] 3 W.L.R. 10 at 34, *per* Lord Goff.

[79] An example (not given in the case) might be the release of a security (although this could also be regarded as giving consideration).

[80] [1999] 3 W.L.R. 10 at 16, *per* Lord Templeman.

[81] [1996] A.C. 788 at 799.

[82] [1995] 1 All E.R. 545. See also *Scottish Equitable plc v. Derby*, September 30, 1999, QBD, where it was held that no causal link between the receipt of an overpayment and the position of the defendant, so there had not been a material change of position.

[83] See above, para. 10–014.

transactions specifically designed to ensure that it was not exposed to risks. When it later became clear that the swap transation was void, the bank incurred losses on the hedging transactions before it was able to close them. The bank argued that in undertaking the "hedge" contracts relying on the validity of the swap contract it had changed its position. Despite the fact that the bank had acted as a reasonable banker would act, the argument was unsuccessful. It was held that the defence is normally confined to changes taking place after the receipt of property and could not protect a person who had relied on the validity of a contract which was later held to be void.[84]

(3) Ministerial receipt

10–032 The defence of ministerial receipt may now be regarded as a specific example of the change of position defence, although it has its origins in the law of agency. If the payment is to an agent who has passed the money to his or her principal before learning of the mistake, only the principal, and not the agent, can be sued.[85] This rule is of particular relevance to banks, which collect payments acting as agents for their customers.

10–033 For the defence to succeed, the following conditions must be fulfilled. If they are not, both agent and principal may be liable.[86] The bank, of course, must have received the money bona fide (with no knowledge of the mistake, or of any other wrongdoing) because otherwise it would be unconscionable to retain it,[87] and it must have had no notice of the plaintiff's claim before it disposed of the money. It must be able to show that payment to the principal has actually been made.[88] If payment has been made honestly, the bank is not liable, and the fact that the bank thinks it has paid A when it has paid B, or that the principal is unidentified, makes no difference.[89]

The bank must not act as principal during the transaction. If it does so, the fact that the payment has been passed on to the principal does not provide a defence. It is not always clear whether the bank is acting as agent or acting as principal, particularly when it is a "discounting bank" (that is, itself purchasing the payment) as it may be where it allows a customer an overdraft against an uncleared cheque or gives the customer cash.

---

[84] See Jones [1995] Conv. 490.

[85] *Buller v. Harrison* (1977) 2 Cowp 565; *Rahimtoola v. Nizam of Hyderabad* [1958] A.C. 379; *Continental Caoutchouc and Gutta Percha Co v. Kleinwort Sons & Co* (1904) 90 LT 474; *Thomas v. Houston Corbet & Co* [1969] N.Z.L.R. 151; *National Westminster Bank Ltd v. Barclays Bank International Ltd* [1975] Q.B. 654.

[86] *National Westminster Bank Ltd v. Barclays Bank International Ltd* [1975] Q.B. 654.

[87] *John v. Dodwell & Co* [1918] A.C. 563; *Reckitt v. Barnett, Pembroke and Slater Ltd* [1929] A.C. 176; *Larner v. London County Council* [1949] 2 K.B. 683.

[88] More may be required than simply a credit to the account: *Holland v. Russell* (1861) 1 B & S 424.

[89] *Gowers v. Lloyds and National Provincial Foreign Bank Ltd* [1937] 3 All E.R. 55.

(4) Estoppel

Long before the recognition of the change of position defence, a defence of estoppel[90] against a bank trying to recover money paid under a mistake of fact was sometimes available. It has perhaps acted as a precursor, though a limited one, of the change of position defence,[91] and it is likely that as time goes on it will be encompassed in the new defence and lose its separate identity. Until the new defence has been tested by the courts in particular situations, however, such a development remains speculative and the plea of estoppel may still be helpful to defendants. In principle, money cannot be recovered if the payer is estopped from asserting his entitlement to it. In this context estoppel requires: **10–034**

(1) a representation made to the payee, or some breach of a duty owed to him or her by the bank[92];

(2) the payee's reliance on this representation or omission, to his or her detriment or so that it is inequitable for the payer to claim to recover[93]; and

(3) that the payee is not at fault.

Representation. A typical example of a representation by the bank is notification to the recipient (say, by a bank statement) that money has been credited to an account. If the money is then spent, leaving the customer with insufficient funds to repay without hardship, the bank may be estopped from recovering its payment. Much of the difficulty in this area arises from the requirement[94] that the representation which gives rise to the estoppel must be *other than the payment itself.* The mere fact of wrongful payment is neither a representation nor a breach of duty sufficient to give rise to an estoppel. The courts have often made efforts to find statements or actions amounting to representations. **10–035**

Reliance to one's detriment. The payee must have changed his or her position as a consequence of the payment,[95] and this may be difficult to show. The mere fact that the recipient has spent money received wrongly, even if it was paid as the result of negligence on the part of the payer, is not **10–036**

[90] The plea of estoppel is available both to bank and customer in appropriate circumstances: see above, para. 7–019.

[91] See *Lipkin Gorman* [1991] 3 W.L.R. 10 at 32, HL, *per* Lord Goff.

[92] *Skyring v. Greenwood & Cox* (1825) 4 B & C 281.

[93] Where someone has been overpaid, that is hardly a detriment, but it may be inequitable to call on them to repay once they have spent the money: *Avon CC v. Howlett* [1983] 1 All E.R. 1073.

[94] From *Cocks v. Masterman* (1829) 9 B. & C. 902.

[95] *cf.* the change of position defence described by Lord Goff in *Lipkin Gorman*, where the element of "reliance" does not appear.

sufficient to establish any right in the payee to retain the payment.[96] In *Lloyds Bank Ltd v. The Hon. Cecily K Brooks*,[97] the bank overpaid the defendant's account, and sent her statements showing the exaggerated balance. She relied on these and spent more money than she would otherwise have done. The bank could not recover the payment. This would not have been the case if the overcrediting had been of such an amount that the customer must have realised the mistake.

10–037 **Fault.** The payee must not have been at fault (this resembles the "good faith" requirement of change of position). For example, where the defendant has induced the representation by concealing material facts,[98] or where a cheque comes into his or her hands under suspicious circumstances (for example, offered at an unusually deep discount),[99] or where he or she must have realised the mistake, perhaps because of a large, unexpected and unexplained credit to the account, the defence will not succeed. In *United Overseas Bank v. Jiwani*,[1] the defendant, whose account had been credited in error, failed in his defence partly because he could not prove that he had altered his mode of living as a result of the overpayment, but also because the court took the view that he must have realised that the payment was an error.

10–038 Situations where "fault" arises demonstrate another serious difficulty with the operation of estoppel because it is a rule of evidence it does not work *in part.* In *Avon CC v. Howlett*[2] the defendant was overpaid by his employer while on sick leave. Representations were made to him in the form of pay slips showing his supposed entitlement. He showed that he had spent some of the money, and the court accepted that it would be inequitable to demand all of the money back. Since estoppel has an "all or nothing" effect, the employer was able to recover *none* of the money, even that part of the sum overpaid which had not yet been spent. Estoppel therefore works clumsily in comparison with the flexibility of the change of position defence.

(5) Special defence: negotiable instruments

10–039 Perhaps the most technical aspect of the law on this subject relates to the rule in *Price v. Neal*[3] and applied in *Cocks v. Masterman*,[4] that money which has been paid to the holder of a negotiable instrument which has been

[96] (1950) 6 L.D.A.B. 161.

[97] The paying bank does not owe a duty of care to the payee in deciding whether to honour a cheque, at least when it appears to be regular on its face, and does not represent that the payer's signature is genuine: *National Westminster Bank v. Barclays Bank International Ltd* [1975] Q.B. 654.

[98] See *George Whitechurch Ltd v. Cavanagh* [1902] A.C. 117 at 145.

[99] See *National Westminster Bank Ltd v. Barclays Bank International Ltd* [1975] Q.B. 654.

[1] [1976] 1 W.L.R. 964.

[2] [1983] 1 All E.R. 1073. But see *Scottish Equitable plc v. Derby*, September 30, 1999, QBD.

[3] (1762) 3 Burr. 1355.

[4] (1829) 9 B. & C. 902.

negotiated but which has an intrinsic defect[5] (for example, a negotiated bill of exchange with a forged indorsement) cannot be recovered.

The principle here is sometimes said to depend on estoppel,[6] but if so it is an easier form of estoppel to establish than that described above. First, in this case the payment itself is sufficient to establish a representation, and secondly, it may be the case that the payee need not actually have altered his or her position in reliance. Some dicta suggest that it is sufficient if the payee might suffer detriment, and others suggest that it is sufficient simply if the payment has been made. This is apparently on the basis that if the payee is to be able to sue other parties on the instrument, he or she would have to give notice of dishonour. If he or she then is paid, and has to repay, this would cause delay, and the delay is itself a detriment which may affect his or her position.

More recent dicta suggest that as with ordinary estoppel, there must actually be detriment or it must be inequitable to call for repayment.[7] **10–040**

The policy behind the principle relates, no doubt, to the desire of the courts to maintain confidence in the speed and efficiency of negotiable instruments. In the interests of commercial efficacy, payment should be as near certain as possible, and if money paid on a bill could be recovered because of a mistake (especially if there was no obvious defect in the instrument) the risk would probably impair the currency of negotiable instruments. Efforts by some courts to restrict the effect of the principle help to illustrate the link between it and the concept of negotiability. In *Barclays Bank Ltd v. W.J. Simms, Son & Cooke (Southern) Ltd*,[8] Goff J. considered that the reason for the rule is the possibility of prejudice when notice of dishonour is required, and that if no notice has to be given to anyone, or if it is given in reasonable time without loss, the principle will not apply. Since the duty to give notice of dishonour is dispensed with[9] where the drawer of a cheque has countermanded payment, the judge concluded that the defence was not available in that case. The principle will also not apply if the instrument is not a valid negotiable instrument at all (if it has a forged drawer's signature, for example, it is not a bill, and not negotiable)[10]; if the mistake is not about some defect intrinsic to the instrument itself (for example, if it is only about funds in the account)[11]; or

[5] But not forged cheques which are not negotiable instruments at all, see below, Chap. 14.

[6] See *London & River Plate Bank v. Bank of Liverpool* [1896] 1 Q.B. 7, *per* Mathew J.

[7] These propositions are derived from *Cocks v. Masterman* (1829) 9 B. & C. 902; *Mather v. Lord Maidstone* (1856) 18 C.B. 273 at 294; *London v. River Plate Bank v. Bank of Liverpool* [1896] 1 Q.B. 7; *Imperiàl Bank of Canada v. Bank of Hamilton* [1903] A.C. 49; *National Westminster Bank Ltd v. Barclays Bank International Ltd* [1975] Q.B. 654; *Barclays Bank Ltd v. W.J. Simms, Son & Cooke (Southern) Ltd* [1979] 3 All E.R. 522.

[8] [1979] 3 All E.R. 522.

[9] BOEA 1882, s. 50(2)(c).

[10] *National Westminster Bank Ltd v. Barclays Bank International Ltd* [1975] 1 Q.B. 654. According to this argument, the principle does not now apply to cheques, which are normally no longer negotiable (Ch A 1992).

[11] *ibid*.

if the payee is the original payee (because the bill cannot have been negotiated to him or her).

10–041 The principle may simply be another precursor of the change of position defence because the payee would suffer a detriment by giving up a negotiable instrument. As Goode argues,[12] a payee lacking possession has no longer any claim to payment on the cheque itself, which would be determined by summary proceedings, and has no payment either. Any claim he or she wishes to pursue against the drawer must be made with regard to the *original* consideration, which may well be disputed and may take months or years to decide.[13]

[12] Goff and Jones, *op. cit*., pp. 757–758.
[13] Goode, *op. cit*., p. 257.

Chapter 11

The Banker's Lien, Right of Appropriation, and Combination of Accounts[1]

By way of preliminary definition: **11–001**

(a) *the lien* is a right to retain an indebted customer's property while the bank has it, and (if necessary) to sell it to satisfy the debt;

(b) *the right of appropriation* is the right to credit funds to whichever account the bank chooses; and

(c) *the right of combination* is the right to combine separate accounts, usually where one is overdrawn and the other is in credit, so as to take account of the overall state of the indebtedness of the customer to the bank (or of the bank to the customer).

Each of these rights are considered below separately, but they often work in tandem. For example, where a bank receives a cheque from an indebted customer for collection each right may play a part. First, by virtue of the lien, there is a right to retain the cheque and realise its value by collecting the proceeds; secondly, there is a right to appropriate the proceeds to whichever of the customer's accounts the bank chooses; and thirdly, there is a right to combine accounts if, say, the proceeds are paid into a credit account whilst the customer has another account in debit. All of these rights are subject to contrary agreement, but they arise by operation of law.

The Banker's Lien

(1) The nature of the lien

Like other types of lien, a banker's lien gives the bank the right to retain in its possession property belonging to another until its claims against that other have been satisfied. Unlike other types of lien, it carries with it the right to sell the property.[2] This makes it akin to a pledge, and it is **11–002**

---

[1] See Goode, *Legal Problems of Credit and Security ("LPCS")* (2nd ed., 1988); Wood, *English and International Set-off* (1989); Derham, *Set-off* (2nd ed., 1996); Paget's *Law of Banking* (11th ed., 1996); McCracken, *The Banker's Remedy of Set-off* (3rd ed., 1998).

[2] *Rosenburg v. International Banking Corpn* (1923) 14 Lloyd's Rep. 344 at 347; see also *Halesowen Presswork & Assemblies Ltd v. Westminster Bank Ltd* [1971] 1 Q.B. 1 at 33–4, CA, reversed on other grounds at [1972] A.C. 785, HL. This is usually regarded as a settled point, but questioned by Everett & McCracken, *Banking and Financial Institutions Law* (1992), pp. 336–338.

sometimes referred to as an "implied pledge."[3] Like a pledge it depends on possession of the property which it affects, it is a legal (not merely an equitable) right, and does not require registration, whether under the Bills of Sale Acts 1878 (BSA 1878)[4] or under the CA 1985.[5] But unlike a pledge, which is created by consensual agreement, the banker's lien arises by operation of law and derives from banking custom and practice which became part of the Law Merchant.[6]

(2) Circumstances in which the lien may arise

11–003 In the leading case of *Brandao v. Barnett*[7] it was said that "Bankers . . . have a general lien on all securities deposited with them as bankers by a customer, unless there be an express contract, or circumstances that show an implied contract inconsistent with lien."[8]

11–004 **(a) All securities.** This means "paper securities"[9] so, for example, gold coins deposited for sale by the bank would not be subject to a lien. The lien has been held to apply (*inter alia*) to share certificates,[10] an order for payment of money to a particular person,[11] and it probably extends to insurance policies.[12] The lien also applies to bills of exchange[13] and in this context it has particular significance, because a bank which has a lien on a cheque is deemed to be a holder for value of the cheque to the extent of the sum for which it has the lien.[14] There seems to be no reason in principle to exclude any class of document which represents valuable property, with the important exception of deeds to land. In *Wylde v. Radford*,[15] Kindersley V-C said "what is intended is such securities as promissory notes, bills of exchange, exchequer bills, coupons, bonds of foreign governments, etc".[16] He appears not to have considered deeds to land as falling within these types of securities, although the case has been explained on the basis that

---

[3] See, for example, *Brandeo v. Barnett* (1846) 3 C.B. 519 at 531.

[4] BSA 1878, s. 10 (which requires registration of various classes of documents creating security over personal chattels).

[5] See CA 1985, s. 395 (which requires registration of various classes of company charges) and compare *Trident International Ltd v. Barlow*, July 30, 1999, unreported, CA, in which a contractual possessory lien was held not to be registrable, even though coupled with a contractual power of sale.

[6] *Brandeo v. Barnett* (1846) 3 C.B. 519 at 530; *Davis v. Bowsher* (1794) 5 Term Rep 488 at 491.

[7] (1846) 3 C.B. 519.

[8] (1846) 3 C.B. 519 at 530.

[9] *Davis v. Bowsher* (1794) 5 Term Rep 488 at 491.

[10] *Re United Service Co Johnstone's Claim* (1870) 6 Ch. App. 212 at 217.

[11] *Misa v. Currie* (1876) 1 App. Cas. 554 at 567, 573.

[12] See *Re Bowes, Earl of Strathmore v. Vane* (1886) 33 Ch. D. 586, where on the facts no lien was held to arise in view of the existence of an express memorandum of charge (see further below, para. 11–005).

[13] See below, para. 11–008.

[14] See s. 27(3) of the BOEA 1882; see below, para. 11–012.

[15] (1864) 33 L.J. Ch. 51.

[16] (1864) 33 L.J. Ch. 51 at 53.

an accompanying memorandum made it clear that no security was in fact intended to be given on the land in question.[17] In practice deeds to land are usually only deposited with a bank as security pursuant to a consensual agreement or for safe-keeping and in either case, as we shall see, there is no room for a lien to arise.

(b) Deposited with them as bankers. The question of what constitutes the business of banking is examined elsewhere.[18] Whatever a banker's business may be, the securities must come to him in the course of it for the lien to arise. Goods or securities deposited for safe-keeping are generally not regarded as held in the course of a banking business because they are only left with the bank as bailee, not for any other purpose.[19] But much depends on whether the bank is instructed to do anything with the securities whilst holding them for safe-keeping. If, for example, it holds bonds and is to present them for payment or to collect interest on them, these are things which can be regarded as part of the banking business and so a lien may arise.[20] It would be different if the customer merely arranges for dividends on shares to be paid to the bank which happens to hold the share certificates.[21] 11–005

Collection of cheques being part of normal banking business, a lien may arise over a cheque received by a banker as its customer's agent for collection of the cheque.[22] Similarly, a bank collecting a bill as agent for another bank may claim a lien on the bill for monies owed to it by the other bank.[23]

(c) Inconsistent agreements. The existence of a consensual security is inconsistent with a lien arising by operation of law. So if there is a pledge, charge or mortgage on the property in question, this destroys an existing lien or prevents one arising.[24] If a consensual security is given for a specific debt which is later discharged by repayment, the customer is entitled to the return of the property, even if the customer is still indebted to the bank.[25] But if he does not ask for its return, and the property is left in the hands of the bank in the ordinary course of business, a lien may later arise.[26] It has 11–006

17 *Re London and Globe Finance Corpn* [1902] 2 Ch. 416 at 420, *per* Buckley J. In *United Bank of Kuwait v. Sahib* [1996] 3 W.L.R. 372, in which the Court of Appeal held that a simple deposit of deeds to land can no longer give rise to an equitable charge by reason of section 2 of the Law of Property (Miscellaneous Provisions) Act 1989 (LPMPA 1989), it was not argued that the Bank could claim a lien on the deeds.

18 See above, Chap 2.

19 *Leese v. Martin* (1873) LR 17 Eq 224 at 235.

20 *Re United Service Co Johnston's Claim* (1870) 6 Ch. App. 212.

21 See Paget's *Law of Banking* (11th ed., 1996), p. 527.

22 *Barclays Bank Ltd v. Astley Industrial Trusts Ltd* [1970] 2 Q.B. 527 at 538–9.

23 Compare *Johnson v. Robarts* (1875) 10 Ch. App. 505.

24 *Re Bowes, Earl of Strathmore v. Vane* (1886) 33 Ch. D. 586; *Wylde v. Radford* (1864) 33 L.J. Ch. 51.

25 Compare *Wilkinson v. London and County Banking Co* (1884) 1 T.L.R. 63.

26 *Re London and Globe Finance Corpn* [1902] 2 Ch. 416.

been suggested[27] that if a consensual security relates to a specific debt, a lien might arise over the same asset in respect of another debt after repayment of the specific debt, even if both debts originally existed at the same time. No case establishes this, and the fact that a consensual security is expressed to cover only one of two or more existing debts might be treated as negativing any intention that the asset should later be the subject of a lien for any other debt which existed when the consensual security was created.

11–007 It would seem that if a consensual security for a specific debt is realised, any surplus from the proceeds of sale after satisfaction of the debt for which the security was given would be subject to the banker's right of combination[28] (unless that right had been excluded or lost). So even if the bank cannot rely on any rights arising by virtue of a lien so as to claim the surplus proceeds, it may combine the account into which the proceeds have been paid with another overdrawn account to achieve the same result.

An agreement excluding the bank's right of appropriation[29] may also be inconsistent with the existence of a lien. Thus, there may be an agreement to "freeze" the debit balance on an account[30] so that an appropriation of any credit to that account reducing the debit balance would be a breach of the agreement. Such an agreement may also prevent any lien arising in respect of the indebtedness on that account.

(3) Priority accorded by the lien

11–008 The banker's lien is liable to be defeated by anyone with a prior legal right. Thus the bank must have obtained possession of the property in question with the consent of the legal owner.[31] If, for example, the true owner of a cheque has a claim to its return on the ground that it was given by mistake, the bank cannot rely on a lien to defeat the claim.[32]

However, the banker's lien is itself a legal, not merely an equitable, right. On general principles, therefore, it can be relied upon to defeat the rights of an equitable owner of the property on which it arises, if the bank is in the position of a bona fide purchaser for value without notice of the rights of the equitable owner.[33] So there cannot be a lien over assets which are, to the bank's knowledge, held on trust (whether actual, constructive or a

[27] See Paget's *Law of Banking* (11th ed., 1996), p. 528.
[28] See below, paras 11–038 *et seq.*
[29] See below, paras 11–036 *et seq.*
[30] As in *National Westminster Bank Ltd v. Halesowen Presswork Ltd* [1972] A.C. 785.
[31] *Cuthbert v. Robarts, Lubbock & Co* [1909] 2 Ch. 226 at 233.
[32] Nor would the bank be able to rely on a right of combination in respect of the proceeds of the cheque: see below, para. 11–051.
[33] Purchase of a legal interest for value without notice being an "absolute, unqualified, unanswerable defence" against the claims of any prior equitable owner: *Pilcher v. Rawlins* (1872) 7 Ch. App. 259 at 269. For a more recent application of the principle see, for example, *MCC Proceeds Inc v. Lehman Bros International, The Times*, January 14, 1998, CA.

Quistclose[34] trust). In *Siebe Gorman & Co Ltd v. Barclays Bank Ltd*,[35] the bank sought to rely (inter alia) on its lien on bills of exchange which it held for collection. But the bills had been assigned to a third party and it was held that the lien was ineffecive against the assignees for indebtedness arising after the date when the bank received notice of the assignment, because from that date the bank was aware that the customer no longer had title to the bills.

In the case of a floating charge on property, which does not include a provision preventing subsequent dispositions or which is not known to contain such a provision, it is not thought that knowledge of the existence of the floating charge would prevent a lien from arising.[36]

(4) Liens over money paid to a bank and contingent liabilities

In some cases the courts have referred to a bank having a "lien" over **11–009**
money paid into a customer's account.[37] These were probably intended to be references to the banker's right to combine such money with the customer's indebtedness on other accounts, the development of which was influenced by the banker's lien.[38] Strictly speaking a banker cannot have a lien over money paid to it. In the past the reason for this was said to be that the bank cannot have rights over its own money, and the bank is the legal and beneficial owner of such money because the banker-customer relationship is merely one of debtor-creditor.[39] Thus in *Halesowen Presswork & Assemblies Ltd v. Westminster Bank Ltd* Buckley L.J. stated[40]:

> "No man can have a lien on his own property and consequently no lien can have arisen affecting that money or that credit . . . a banker has a general lien on all securities deposited with him . . . [but] . . . the term "securities" . . . does not. . . extend to the banker's own indebtedness to the customer."

More recently, however, it has been held by the House of Lords in *Re Bank* **11–010**
of Credit and Commerce International SA (No 8)[41] that it is possible for a bank to take security by way of a charge on cash deposited by its customer

---

[34] See *Barclays Bank Ltd v. Quistclose Investments Ltd* [1970] A.C. 567, discussed above, Chap. 9.

[35] [1979] 2 Lloyd's Rep 142. See also the equivalent principles in cases concerning the banker's right of combination, see para. 11–051.

[36] Compare *English & Scottish Mercantile Investment Co v. Brunton* [1892] 2 Q.B. 700.

[37] See, for example, *Misa v. Currie* (1876) 1 App. Cas. 554 at 565, 569 and 573.

[38] See below, para. 11–040.

[39] *Foley v. Hill* (1848) 2 H.L. Cas. 28; *Joachimson v. Swiss Bank Corpn* [1921] 3 K.B. 110 esp at 127, *per* Atkins L.J.: "The proceeds . . . are not to be held in trust for the customer, but the bank borrows the proceeds and undertakes to repay them".

[40] [1971] 1 Q.B. 1 at 46; approved in the House of Lords [1972] A.C. 785 at 802, 810; and cited with approval by Millet J. in *Re Charge Card Services* [1987] 1 Ch. 150 at 174. See also the judgment of Lord Denning in the *Halesowen* case [1971] 1 Q.B. at 33, commenting that a lien on the proceeds of a cheque "is no true lien", but a right of combination or set-off.

[41] [1997] 4 All E.R. 568.

with itself. Nevertheless it was accepted[42] that it is a misuse of language to speak of a bank having a lien over its own indebtedness to a customer because the word "lien" refers to a right to retain possession and a debt, being a chose in action, is not capable of possession.

So in the case of a cheque, a lien only exists while the bank has possession of the cheque itself, but when the proceeds are received the banker's only rights are either to appropriate the proceeds to reduce or discharge indebtedness on a particular account, or to an account in credit and then to combine the accounts.

11–011 In some of the older cases the courts considered whether a bank can claim a right to retain a credit balance on its customer's account if the customer has contingent liabilities outstanding to the bank, being liabilities which will only become actual liabilities at a future date or on the happening of a future event—such as is the case if the bank discounts or accepts bills for a customer which are payable at a future date, or if the customer has given the bank a guarantee of the liabilities of a third party. The banker may wish to retain a credit balance on the customer's current account to meet the contingent liability on the bills or under the guarantee. The courts have held that the bank cannot do so: it has no right to retain a sum of money which is actually due against a sum of money which is only becoming due at a future time.[43] Although the courts often referred to the claim to retain the credit balance as a claim to a "lien," for the reasons explained above, it is not strictly correct to speak of a lien in respect of a bank balance. These cases are also more properly regarded as attempts to assert a right of set-off and they are examples of the application of the principle that there can be no right of set-off in respect of contingent liabilities, save in insolvency when set-off is mandatory.[44]

(5) Liens over cheques and bills

11–012 In the context of cheques and bills of exchange given to the banker for collection, there are three main reasons for the bank to invoke a lien as set out below.

11–013 **(a) Security.** While the bank is holding a cheque or bill payable to its customer it has some security for non-payment of a debt owed to it by its customer. However, the lien is in many ways the least useful of the bank's potential rights for various reasons. First, the bank ordinarily has a duty to present cheques for collection within a reasonable time,[45] so cheques are

---

[42] [1997] 4 All E.R. 568 at 576c, *per* Lord Hoffmann.

[43] *Jeffryes v. Agra & Masterman's Bank* (1866) LR 2 Eq 674 at 680; *Bower v. Foreign and Colonial Gas Co Ltd, Metropolitan Bank, Garnishees* (1874) 22 W.R. 740. For dicta to the contrary, see *Bolland v. Bygrave* (1825) 1 Ry & M 271 (NP).

[44] See *Baker v. Lloyds Bank Ltd* [1920] 2 K.B. 322 and see below, para. 11–039 and chap. 23.

[45] BOEA 1882, s. 45(2).

not usually in the bank's possession for long. In the ordinary course of events therefore, when cheques are deposited for collection, the right of appropriation of the proceeds is more important than the lien itself.

The fact that the lien is dependent on actual possession also limits its usefulness. When a cheque or bill is cleared "it cease[s] to be a negotiable instrument, and also cease[s] to be in the possession of the bank. Any lien of the bank on the cheque must thereupon have come to an end."[46] Similarly, if the cheque is dishonoured and the bank returns it to the customer, for example, for the purposes of litigation, this also destroys the lien.[47] This is because the lien arises by operation of law and cannot be maintained by agreement, as is necessarily involved if a cheque is delivered to the customer for such a specific purpose. Even if the cheque is later returned by the customer to the bank to enable the bank to sue on it, no new lien arises because the bank is not given possession in the course of its business as banker but in order to sue.[48] So if a bank is to return to its customer an item which is the subject of a lien, it would have to protect its position by taking in substitution some form of express security such as a pledge with a trust receipt by which the customer acknowledges that he holds the item, or the proceeds of its sale, on trust for the bank.[49] **11–014**

It is unclear whether a lien on a cheque can exist if the customer appropriates the proceeds of the cheque to a particular debit item. If the lien can exist in those circumstances but the appropriation prevents it being exercised, the bank could not be a holder for value or a holder in due course, nor could it collect the cheque for its own benefit, so the lien would have no real effect.[50]

(b) The bank as holder for value. By section 27(3) of the BOEA 1882, where the holder of a bill has a lien on it arising either from contract or by implication of law, he is deemed to be a holder for value to the extent of the sum for which he has a lien. This is so whether the bank receives the cheque for collection on its own behalf or as the customer's agent, for the role of the bank as an agent for collection is not inconsistent with this status.[51] As a holder for value the bank can sue the parties to a dishonoured **11–015**

---

[46] *Halesowen Presswork & Assemblies Ltd v. Westminster Bank Ltd* [1971] 1 Q.B. 1 at 46, *per* Buckley L.J.

[47] *Lloyds Bank v. Dolphin* (1920) 3 L.D.A.B. 230.

[48] *Westminster Bank v. Zang* [1966] A.C. 182 at 205 (where it was conceded that the bank lost any lien by returning the cheque to the customer's solicitors).

[49] See, for example, Lingard, *Bank Security Documents* (3rd ed., 1993), pp. 423 *et seq.*

[50] Although it is possible that the bank may qualify as a holder for value by giving value in some other way: see s. 2 of the Cheques Act 1957 which refers to a bank which "gives value for, or has a lien on" a cheque.

[51] On the "dual capacity," see *Barclays Bank Ltd v. Astley Industrial Trust Ltd* [1970] 2 Q.B. 527.

cheque even if the cheque, given to it for collection, is not indorsed to the bank.[52]

11–016 **(c) The bank as holder in due course.** If the bank is deemed to have given value for the cheque and also takes it in good faith without notice of any defect in its customer's title, it will also qualify as a holder in due course,[53] in which case it has good title, even against the "true owner" or against the customer's trustee in bankruptcy or liquidator.[54] Whether the bank loses its lien if it becomes a holder in due course is largely academic, because even if it does, it obtains rights which are as effective as the lien.

11–017 A question arises whether the bank can have a lien on a cheque received for collection if, when the cheque is received the customer's account is not overdrawn but the cheque is "credited to cash"[55] before the cheque has been cleared. If a cheque which has been credited provisionally in this way is dishonoured, the account can be debited again and the bank may wish to sue the drawer of the cheque. But if the customer has not indorsed the cheque the bank can only sue if it took the cheque for value or has a lien on it.[56]

11–018 It was formerly thought that the bank would be a holder for value of a cheque credited to cash. This appeared to be the effect of *Capital and Counties Bank Ltd v. Gordon*,[57] which concerned the bank's defence against the true owner. For this purpose it now matters little whether the bank is a holder for value or not, because of the protection afforded to the collecting bank by section 4 of the Ch A 1957. The modern view, established in *A. L. Underwood Ltd v. Bank of Liverpool; Same v. Barclays Bank Ltd*,[58] is that merely crediting to cash does not make the bank holder for value, and it must follow from this that neither does merely crediting to cash entitle the bank to a lien, because if it did the bank would be deemed to be a holder for value.[59]

If the bank does in fact have a lien on a cheque, it has been said that it does not lose the lien by allowing the customer to draw against the proceeds, but it is treated as releasing the lien to that extent.[60]

---

[52] Cheques Act 1957, s. 2; and see *Westminster Bank v. Zang* [1966] A.C. 182 (where the argument centred on the question whether the bank had given value for the purpose of Cheques Act 1957, s. 2 so that it could sue on a cheque given to it for collection even if the cheque was not indorsed to it; on the facts it was held to have given no value); *Midland Bank Ltd v. Reckitt* [1933] A.C. 1 and *Barclays Bank Ltd v. Astley Industrial Trusts Ltd* [1970] 2 Q.B. 527.

[53] Within BOEA 1882, s. 29.

[54] *Re Keever* [1967] Ch. 182.

[55] See above, para. 6–035.

[56] Cheques Act 1957, s. 2; and see above, n. 52.

[57] [1903] A.C. 240. See also *Sutter v. Briggs* [1922] 1 A.C. 1 at 14.

[58] [1924] 1 K.B. 775 at 803 *et seq.*; and see *Westminster Bank Ltd v. Zang* [1966] A.C. 182. This view appears to be reflected in s. 4(1)(b) of the Cheques Act 1957.

[59] According to the *Underwood* case the bank will only have given value if it has agreed to allow the customer to draw against the uncleared effects, in which case it becomes academic whether the bank also has a lien, because the fact that the bank has given value for the cheque gives it the right to sue on it under Cheques Act 1957, s. 2.

[60] *Halesowen Presswork & Assemblies Ltd v. Wesminster Bank Ltd* [1971] 1 Q.B. 1 at 33–4, *per* Lord Denning M.R. reversed in the House of Lords on other grounds, see [1972] A.C. 785.

(6) Garnisheee orders and liens

Debts owed to a customer by a third party (the "garnishee") may be attached by a creditor, who has sued the customer to judgment, in satisfaction of the judgment debt. The court can order the garnishee, here the bank, to pay "any debt due or accruing due to the judgment debtor."[61] A "debt due" is one which has become payable, and a debt is "accruing due" if a debt exists but is not payable until a future time.[62] So a bill of exchange which is payable at a future date is attachable,[63] and cheques, by definition payable on demand,[64] are also affected. But any bill deposited with the bank over which the bank has a lien is unaffected by the order, and the order can only attach debts owed at the time it is made, so cheques received after the date of the order for credit to a customer's account are not subject to it.[65] If the bank has collected the cheque, the proceeds are attachable, but subject to the banker's right of combination.[66] **11–019**

If the bank credits the account to cash before the cheque is cleared, *obiter dicta* in *Jones v. Coventry*[67] suggest that the amount credited would be affected by a garnishee order. But this probably reflects the incorrect interpretation of *Capital and Counties Bank Ltd v. Gordon*[68] already mentioned that in such cases the bank has given value, so that the credit amounts to a debt due to the customer on demand. After the *Underwood* case[69] it seems that the credit entry is simply reversible if the cheque is dishonoured, and in the interim the customer cannot sue for the debt, unless there is an agreement to allow him to draw against uncleared effects. Therefore the better view is thought to be that in the absence of such agreement no debt is due until the cheque has cleared.[70] **11–020**

(7) Liens in bankruptcy

In bankruptcy or liquidation, there is a statutory right of set-off.[71] But a bank may also assert its separate common law lien and this will give it the same priority against the trustee in bankruptcy or liquidator as it had **11–021**

[61] RSC, Ord. 49, r. 1; CCR, Ord. 30. r. 1.

[62] *Tapp v. Jones* (1875) L.R. 10 Q.B. 591; *Webb v. Stenton* (1883) 11 Q.B.D. 518, CA.

[63] *Hyam v. Freeman* (1890) 35 Sol Jo 87, holding that the order can be made before the bill matures, suspending execution until maturity and restraining the judgment debtor from dealing with the bill in the interim.

[64] BOEA 1882, s. 73.

[65] *Heppenstall v. Jackson, Barclays Bank Ltd Garnishee* [1939] 1 K.B. 585.

[66] *Tapp v. Jones* (1875) L.R. 10 Q.B. 591; see below, para. 11–038.

[67] [1909] 2 K.B. 1029 especially at 1041, 1044. But on the facts of this case it was held that the sum in question, due under a retirement pay warrant under s. 141 of the Army Act 1881, was not affected because no debt existed until the warrant was paid by HMPG. Until then it retained the protected character of retirement pay.

[68] [1903] A.C. 240; see above, para. 11–017.

[69] [1924] 1 K.B. 775; see above, para. 11–017.

[70] As has been held in Australia, see *Bank of New South Wales Ltd v. Barlex Investments Pty Ltd* (1964) 64 SR (NSW) 274.

[71] IA 1986, s. 323 (bankruptcy) and the Insolvency Rules 1986, r. 4.90 (IR 1986) (liquidation).

against the customer. In *Re Keever, a Bankrupt, ex p. Cork v. Midland Bank Ltd*[72] a bank was given a cheque for collection on the day before a receiving order was made, not knowing of the act of bankruptcy. The bank received the proceeds on the day the receiving order was made, and claimed that it was entitled to apply the proceeds to the customer's overdrawn account. Under the Bankruptcy Act 1914, the title of the trustee in bankruptcy related back to the first available act of bankruptcy, and as a result the trustee claimed that the cheque and its proceeds belonged to him. However, section 45 of the Bankruptcy Act 1914 protected "Any contract, dealing, or transaction by or with the bankrupt for valuable consideration" if it took place before the date of the receiving order and without notice of an act of bankruptcy. It was held that the bank fell within this provision. The "dealing" was the receipt of the cheque (which was before the receiving order), and this was for valuable consideration because the bank had a lien. A separate ground in the bank's favour was that it was a holder for value[73] and received the cheque before the date of the receiving order.[74]

11–022 Under the bankruptcy scheme established by the IA 1986, bankruptcy commences on the day of the bankruptcy order.[75] The property vests in the trustee when later appointed[76] but his appointment relates back to the commencement[77] and covers all property vested in the bankrupt at the commencement (subject to some exceptions).[78] The trustee's title is subject to the rights of others, whether they are secured or not.[79] Any disposition of property or payment made by the bankrupt in the period between the date of the bankruptcy petition and the appointment of the trustee in bankruptcy is void, unless made with the consent of, or ratified by, the court.[80] But this does not affect property received before the bankruptcy order if the person who received the property did so in good faith for value and without notice of the petition.[81] It seems, therefore, that the principle of *Re Keever* is still relevant, since it helps to show "value" but that now the last stage at which a lien may arise is immediately before the making of the bankruptcy order (rather than the receiving order, as before).

11–023 It is specifically provided that if a bankrupt incurs a debt to a banker or other person by making a payment after the bankruptcy order (for example by drawing on his overdrawn account) this is deemed to occur before the bankruptcy order, and is not subject to the trustee's rights unless the bank

[72] [1967] Ch. 182.
[73] Under BOEA 1882, s. 27(3), see above, para. 11–015.
[74] This would not have protected the bank if the cheque had been received after the receiving order: see *George Barker (Transport) Ltd v. Enyon* [1974] 1 W.L.R. 462.
[75] IA 1986, s. 278.
[76] IA 1986, s. 306.
[77] IA 1986, s. 307.
[78] IA 1986, s. 283.
[79] IA 1986, s. 283(5).
[80] IA 1986, s. 284(1).
[81] IA 1986, s. 284(4).

had notice of the bankruptcy (presumably the petition) before the debt was incurred.[82] It seems, therefore, that (a) the banker can prove for such a debt, and (b) the lien or right to appropriate or to combine accounts could arise in relation to it, or (c) statutory set-off under section 323 of the IA 1986 will apply. Subject to this, no lien can arise for debts incurred after the bankruptcy order.

Rights of Appropriation

(1) Introduction

Funds may come into the banker's hands by way of cash deposit, from the collection of a cheque, from a telegraphic or electronic transfer, or from the realisation of securities held by a customer.[83] A customer with more than one account may wish to *appropriate* the funds to whichever account he or she pleases, or to repay a particular debit item *within* a particular account. Whether the customer may do so depends on the rules of appropriation, which may be summarised as follows: **11–024**

(a) Unless otherwise agreed (for example, by express agreement in the bank mandate), the customer has a right to specify to which account a credit is to be applied.[84] This is the case even if one account is in debit and another is not. Similarly, the customer has the right to appropriate *within* a particular account,[85] and may, for example, demand that a particular credit item should be used to meet a particular cheque which has been or is to be drawn.[86] The fact that the customer has a right to appropriate funds so as to discharge a particular debit item means that for these purposes it is not always correct to regard the overall debt on an account, or on a number of accounts, as a single undivided debt. For this limited purpose the account is made up of a series of individual debits and credits. This could affect the banker's right to combine the customer's accounts,[87]

[82] IA 1986, s. 284(5).

[83] Not being securities which the bank has realised on its own account (such as by virtue of a power of sale in a mortgage or charge), in respect of which the bank alone is entitled to approriate the proceeds to whichever part of the customer's indebtedness it thinks fit: *Re William Hall (Contractors) Ltd* [1967] 1 W.L.R. 948.

[84] *Simson v. Ingham* (1823) 2 B & C 65 at 72; *Deeley v. Lloyds Bank Ltd* [1912] A.C. 756 at 783; *Re Footman Bower & Co Ltd* [1961] Ch. 443 at 448.

[85] *Farley v. Turner* (1857) 26 LJ Ch 710; *W.P. Greenhalgh & Sons v. Union Bank of Manchester* [1924] 2 K.B. 153 esp at 155, 157–8.

[86] In *W.P. Greenhalgh & Sons v. Union Bank of Manchester* [1924] 2 K.B. 153, the court proceeded on the basis that there had been an equitable assignment to a third party of bills paid to the bank by its customer, entitling the third party to sue. This is unusual, except perhaps if there is a trust, in which case the beneficiary may have a complaint against the bank, as trustee (compare *Barclays Bank Ltd v. Quistclose Investments Ltd* [1970] A.C. 567, discussed above, Chap. 10), but a similar conclusion was reached in *Re Marwalt Ltd* [1992] B.C.C. 32.

[87] See below, para. 11–038.

but in practice if all that happens is that the customer appropriates a payment to a specific account, whilst the bank should appropriate the funds to that account, there is nothing to stop it thereafter exercising its rights of combination, which may well have the same effect as if it had originally appropriated the payment to the account of its choice. The position would be different in the (perhaps unlikely) event that the bank has taken a security for a particular debt, because if the customer appropriates a payment in to that particular debt, the debt is discharged and the customer would be entitled to have the security released.

(b) The customer may show his intention by a course of dealing or by other circumstances indicating his intent to the banker[88] but a mere private act such as making an entry in his own books is insufficient.[89]

(c) If the customer does not appropriate the credit item, then the banker may do so.[90] As we have commented in the context of the banker's lien,[91] the right to appropriate the proceeds of a cheque is often a more useful right to a banker than the lien which he has on cheques which he receives for collection, because the lien is lost when the cheque is cleared and ceases to be in the possession of the bank.

(d) The banker may appropriate to a statute-barred debt, since such a debt still exists and is merely unenforceable by action.[92]

(e) There are House of Lords dicta which appear to support the view that once the bank has credited a given account the appropriation is final.[93] If so, when the customer has more than one account, by making a credit entry on one of the accounts the banker will have made the appropriation (although it may later be able to exercise rights of combination or set-off). But some earlier cases suggest that an appropriation is final only when communicated to the debtor,[94] and more recently it has been held that until the credit to a particular account has been communicated to the customer, it remains only a provisional (or "prima facie") appropriation and does not exclude the bank (and, presumably, not the customer) from making a different appropriation.[95]

---

[88] *Nash v. Hodgson* (1855) 6 De G M & G 474 at 486–7.

[89] *Manning v. Westerne* (1707) 2 Vern 606.

[90] *Simson v. Ingham* (1823)2 B & C 65; *Cory Brothers & Co v. Owners of Turkish Steamship Mecca, The Mecca* [1897] A.C. 286 at 293.

[91] See above, para. 11–013.

[92] *Mills v. Fowkes* (1839) 5 Bing NC 455; *Williams v. Griffith* (1839) 5 M&W 300; *Re Footman Bower & Co Ltd* [1961] 1 Ch. 443 at 446–7.

[93] *Deeley v. Lloyds Bank Ltd* [1912] A.C. 756.

[94] *Simson v. Ingham* (1823) 2 B & C 65 at 73–4; *London and Westminster Bank v. Button* (1907) 51 Sol Jo 466; *Cory Brothers & Co v. Owners of Steamship Mecca, The Mecca* [1897] A.C. 286 at 292.

[95] *Julian Hodge Bank Ltd v. Hall* [1998] C.C.L.R. 14, CA.

(f) If on a current account there is no specific appropriation by either banker or customer to a specific debit item, a *default rule* established in *Clayton's Case*[96] applies. This is examined below.

(g) Special rules apply if the customer is liable to make payments under two or more agreements regulated by the CCA 1974. The customer has a statutory right to appropriate payments towards satisfaction of one or more of the agreements in such proportions as he thinks fit, but if he makes no appropriation and one or more of the agreements is a hire-purchase, conditional sale or consumer hire agreement, or an agreement in relation to which security has been provided, the payment must be appropriated to each in the proportion they bear to one another.[97]

(2) The default rule: *Clayton's Case*

If neither the customer nor the banker specifically appropriates a payment, and it is merely credited to a current account, there is a presumption that: **11–025**

(a) when the account is in credit, the first sum paid in is the first to be drawn out; and

(b) when the account is overdrawn, a payment in is appropriated to the earliest debit item on the account which caused the account to become overdrawn, so that debit item is wholly or partly discharged.

This "default rule" is usually referred to as "the rule in *Clayton's Case*."[98] In that case Clayton had an account with a banking partnership. Devaynes, one of the bank's partners died, and at the time the bank owed Clayton £1,713 in respect of the credit balance on Clayton's current account. Under the principles of partnership law, Devaynes was jointly liable with the surviving partners only for debts of the partnership existing at the date of his death,[99] so his liability became "fixed" at that date. However, Clayton and the bank continued to operate the account for a year, during which time more than £1,713 was paid in and drawn out. The bank then failed, and Clayton attempted to sue Devaynes' estate. It was held that the sums paid out of the account since Devaynes' death had discharged the debt which the bank had owed to Clayton at the time of Devaynes' death, and the "new" debt created by credits paid in since that time, was not the **11–026**

---

[96] *Devaynes v. Noble, Clayton's Case* (1816) 1 Mer 529.

[97] CCA 1974, s. 81.

[98] *Devaynes v. Noble, Clayton's Case* (1816) 1 Mer 529. For a recent example of the application of the rule see *Omar v. Omar*, November 29, 1996, unreported Blackburne J., New Law Transcript No. 2961118803.

[99] See PA 1890, s. 36(3).

responsibility of the estate. Although on the facts the bank was the debtor, the rule is the same if the customer is the debtor, where it is normally of more importance.

(3) The application of *Clayton's Case*

11–027 The rule is often significant for banks. Three particular cases may be mentioned.

(a) Money may be advanced on a security which relates to a specific debt. If money then passes through the account, the specific debt will be discharged, and the security rendered ineffective. This problem may be overcome if the security is not for a specific advance, but secures "all monies" to be advanced, for then as long as there is a debt it is covered by the security. Even so, if the bank learns that a second or subsequent mortgage or other security has been given over the same assets to another creditor, the bank will not take priority over the second creditor's security for any new lending after receipt of notice of the later security (unless the second creditor agrees to postpone the priority of its security, or the bank has the right to tack further advances).[1] Thus in *Deeley v. Lloyds Bank Ltd*[2] the bank, which had a mortgage as security for an overdraft, heard that its customer had given a further mortgage to a third party, but continued the account nevertheless. The House of Lords held that the rule in *Clayton's Case* applied, so that the payments into the account after the date on which the bank received notice of the further mortgage had discharged the overdraft in existence at that date. To the extent that the bank had permitted new borrowing after receipt of notice of the further mortgage, that borrowing was secured by the bank's mortgage but subject to the priority of the third party's mortgage. As there was insufficient equity in the property after discharging the sums due under the third party's mortgage, the bank lost its security. The appropriate way for the bank to prevent the default rule from operating was to "rule off" (or stop) the account, thereby fixing the debit balance, and to open a separate account for subsequent transactions.[3]

(b) If, as in *Clayton's Case* itself, a partner or other joint account holder dies or becomes bankrupt, or if in some other way his or her liability

[1] See *Hopkinson v. Rolt* (1861) 9 H.L. Cas 514; and s. 94 of the LPA 1925 (mortgages on land). The same principles apply to security on other assets, such as a charge on book debts: see *Siebe Gorman & Co Ltd v. Barclays Bank Ltd* [1979] 2 Lloyd's Rep 142 at 164–5. On tacking, see below in relation to mortgages of land.

[2] [1912] A.C. 756.

[3] [1912] A.C. 756 at 785; and see to the same effect *Siebe Gorman & Co Ltd v. Barclays Bank Ltd* [1979] 2 Lloyd's Rep 142 at 164. The bank may require the new account to be kept in credit or, if borrowing is to be permitted and the bank is not prepared to lend unsecured, it may seek additional security from the customer.

becomes "fixed," then that fixed debt may be reduced by the operation of the rule, leaving the bank with a remedy for the new debt only against the remaining debtors.[4]

(c) Where the liability of a guarantor becomes fixed or determined, payments through the principal debtor's account may discharge the debt for which the guarantor is liable. The total amount of the debt may remain the same, but it will be a *new* debt, for which the guarantor will not be liable.[5] If, for example, the guarantor has guaranteed a given sum, his liability becomes fixed on the first occasion that the debit balance on the principal account reaches that amount, and thereafter by operation of the rule in *Clayton's Case*, the guarantor's liability is reduced by credits paid in, even if further sums are withdrawn so that the account remains overdrawn. This may be avoided if the guarantor guarantees all debts of the debtor subject to a limitation on the amount recoverable from him, rather than guaranteeing a specific sum.[6]

There remains some doubt whether notice of death or incapacity of a guarantor determines the continuing nature of a guarantee.[7] If it does, by operation of the rule in *Clayton's Case* the guarantor's liability may be discharged if the principal debtor's account is not stopped when notice of the guarantor's death is received.[8] The safe course is, therefore, for the bank to rule off the principal debtor's account when it receives notice of the guarantor's death, and to open a new account in the same way as discussed above.[9] This has been held effective to avoid the possible application of *Clayton's Case*, and not to breach any duty owed by the bank to the guarantor which might otherwise discharge the guarantee.[10]

These are only specific instances of the many cases in which the rule requires some caution on the part of bankers. Banks usually take care to make an express appropriation if the operation of the default rule will prejudice its interests. It may be added that there are some occasions on which the rule is peculiarly *beneficial* to bankers. One such instance **11–028**

[4] For an example, see *Royal Bank of Scotland v. Christie* (1840) 8 Cl & F 214, where an overdrawn partnership account was allowed to continue after the death of a partner, and his estate was discharged from liability as a result.

[5] See for example *Re Quest Cae* [1985] B.C.L.C. 266 at 270; *BCCI v. Simjee*, July 3, 1996, unreported, CA.

[6] *Ellis v. Emmanuel* (1876) 1 Ex D 157.

[7] It was said not to do so in *Bradbury v. Morgan* (1862) 1 H & C 249 and *Harris v. Fawcett* (1873) 8 Ch. App. But the point was expressly left open by the Court of Appeal in *Re Sherry, London and County Banking Co v. Terry* (1883) 25 Ch. D. 692.

[8] This was held to be the case in *Coulthart v. Clementson* (1879) 5 Q.B.D. 42, but this decision was criticised in *Re Silvester* [1895] 1 Ch. 573 and *Re Crace* [1902] 1 Ch. 733 (both first instance decisions).

[9] Modern bank guarantee forms usually expressly permit the bank to do so.

[10] *Ellis v. Emmanuel* (1876) 1 Ex D 157.

concerns floating charges, which may be invalid where liquidation occurs within 12 months of the date of creation of the charge, except to the extent that the charge is given for consideration.[11-12] So if a bank to which a company is indebted takes a floating charge for past advances, the charge will be vulnerable. But if the account is continued after the charge is taken, a position may quickly be reached by virtue of *Clayton's Case*, in which the "old" debt is replaced by "new" debt, so that the security is saved.[13]

11–029 A second instance where the rule is of advantage to banks concerns advances for wages and salaries. Debts incurred to pay wages and salaries are given preference in the distribution of assets on insolvency if they arise within four months of bankruptcy or liquidation.[14] If the bank advances money to the customer for the purpose of paying such debts, and the money is used for that purpose, the advances enjoy this preferential status. So if the bank makes advances from time to time to the customer on a wages account, it can preserve its status as a preferential creditor for the full amount of the advances on that account by ensuring that sufficient credits are transferred to the wages account from time to time to cover advances made more than four months previously. By operation of the rule in *Clayton's Case*, those credits will be treated as having discharged the earliest debits, so that the outstanding balance consists entirely of advances which qualify for preferential status.[15] A separate wages account does not necessarily have to be opened. The effect of *Clayton's Case* may still be that non-preferential debts in the current account are paid off first.[16] But the opening of a separate account makes the position clear.[17] The bank must not, however, insist on credits sufficient to cover the amount of wages cheques being made to a deposit account before it allows the wages cheques to be drawn on the wages account, because in that event the deposit and wages account may be regarded as operating as one account with the result that the bank is not entitled to be treated as making any loan for which it can claim preferential status.[18]

[11-12] IA 1986, s. 245 (the successor of s. 322 of the Companies Act 1948 (CA 1948) and s. 617 of the CA 1985).

[13] *Re Yeovil Glove Co Ltd* [1965] 1 Ch. 148 at 172–3.

[14] See ss. 175, 328 and 386 and Sched. 6 to the IA 1986. There is a limit of £800 per employee.

[15] See *Re James R Rutherford & Sons Ltd* [1964] 1 W.L.R. 1211; *Re Yeovil Glove Co Ltd* [1965] 1 Ch. 148.

[16] See *Re Primrose (Builders) Ltd* [1950] 1 Ch. 561 where it was argued by the liquidator that by requiring funds to be paid into the company's account shortly after allowing payment of wages cheques the bank was indicating an intention to appropriate the credits to meet the debits created by payment of the cheques. It was held that this arrangement was merely evidence of an attempt by the bank to ensure that the company's overdraft did not increase, not of any appropriation.

[17] As was said by Plowman J. in *Re Rampgill Mill Ltd* [1967] 1 Ch. 1138 at 1143A.

[18] *Re E J Morel (1934) Ltd* [1962] 1 Ch. 21.

(4) Where the default rule does not apply

The rule is merely a presumption, and it may be displaced by evidence of some contrary agreement or of circumstances from which a contrary intention is to be presumed.[19] As the rule was formulated in the context of current accounts as a convenient method of determining the order of appropriation of payments, it is not easily rebutted in that context. Thus in *Deeley v. Lloyds Bank Ltd*[20] the bank argued, and it was accepted by the Court of Appeal, that the bank must be taken to have intended to appropriate credits received after notice of the later security to discharge the customer's unsecured debts (leaving the bank with security for the remainder), but the House of Lords held[21] that on the evidence the bank had overlooked the existence of the further security, and as a result no such intention could be inferred. Therefore the rule in *Clayton's Case* applied. **11–030**

In less conventional circumstances it seems that the courts are now prepared more readily to infer a contrary intention. Thus, in *Barlow Clowes International Ltd v. Vaughan*[22] a business which had taken deposits of about £100 million from 11,000 would-be investors collapsed, leaving assets which were quite inadequate to repay them in full. Its liquidators, left with the task of apprortioning the remaining money contributed by the investors among them, were in doubt as to whether it was appropriate to apply the default rule in *Clayton's Case* or some other rule. The money had been deposited over a period of time and mixed in bank accounts from which payments into investments, like gilt-edged stock, had been made at times. Prima facie the default rule applied. However, the default rule would have the arbitrary effect in these circumstances that payments made into the accounts by the earlier investors would have been treated as dissipated by payments out of the accounts. On that basis the only investors likely to recover their contributions would have been the later ones. A possible alternative method of administering the assets was to allow all the claimants to recover proportionately to their investment (*pari passu*).[23] The court expressed hesitation about the operation of the default rule; although its use might be convenient in the case of normal bank current accounts, it was inconvenient and arbitrary in its effects here. It held that the rule should not be used in the circumstances of this case either because the depositors were contributing to a common fund in which they were all to participate,[24] **11–031**

---

[19] *Cory Brothers & Co v. Owners of Turkish Steamship Mecca, The Mecca* [1897] A.C. 286 at 295–6; *Re Hallett's Estate, Knatchbull v. Hallett* (1880) 13 Ch. D. 696 at 728, 739, CA; *Deeley v. Lloyds Bank Ltd* [1912] A.C. 756 at 771.

[20] [1912] A.C. 756; see above, para. 11–027.

[21] [1912] A.C. 756 at 773, 784.

[22] [1992] 4 All E.R. 22.

[23] A third suggested alternative, of a "rolling charge" or the "North American method" (by which each debit to the account is attributed to all the depositors so as to reduce all their deposits pro rata) was considered impracticably complex and expensive.

[24] [1992] 4 All E.R. 22 at 31b, *per* Dillon L.J.; at 41d, *per* Woolf L.J.; at 45d–g, *per* Leggatt L.J.

or because even if no such collective investment had been intended, the misapplication of the investments had created a "common pool" which had caused the investors to suffer "shared misfortune."[25] Therefore the claimants should be allowed to recover proportionately. The default rule was a rule of convenience, to be used where the parties had no other intention ("express, inferred or presumed"), where its application would not be impracticable, and would not result in injustice.[26]

11–032 Against this background the following specific examples are cases in which the rule in *Clayton's Case* does not apply.

11–033 **(a) Between trustee and beneficiary.** Where a trustee pays money belonging to a beneficiary into the trustee's own account, mixing it with his or her own funds, and subsequently withdraws funds for his or her own purposes, there is a presumption that the funds first withdrawn are not the trust funds but the trustee's own funds—because the trustee is presumed to be acting honestly and drawing his or her own money from the account before resorting to the money held on trust.[27] This rule protects both the trust funds for the benefit of the beneficiaries, and the trustee from claims of a possible breach of trust for misusing trust money. If *Clayton's Case* applied the first funds to be paid in, which might be trust funds, would be treated as the first funds to be withdrawn. This situation is to be distinguished from cases in which funds belonging to *two or more beneficiaries* are paid into an account, and part of the trust moneys are drawn out. In these circumstances, prima facie the default rule will apply as between the beneficiaries to determine whose money was withdrawn if there is a deficiency.[28] But as we have seen from the *Barlow Clowes* case, this prima facie presumption is readily rebutted in appropriate circumstances.

11–034 **(b) Separate accounts.** The rule does not apply to separate accounts at the bank, even if they are at the same branch. Thus credits to one account cannot be regarded as discharging debits on another.[29] But if the accounts, although entirely separate, are operated together in such a way that they are in reality a single account, the rule can apply.[30]

11–035 **(c) Stopped accounts.** The rule does not apply to a stopped account, because payments in and out do not take place. By "ruling a line" under an

---

[25] [1992] 4 All E.R. 22 at 41e–22h, *per* Woolf L.J.

[26] [1992] 4 All E.R. 22 at 42f, *per* Woolf L.J. The court acknowledged the convenience of the rule for bank accounts, although Leggatt L.J. commented that the acclaim and application of *Clayton's Case* has not been universal during the 175 years since it was devised (at 43a/b).

[27] *Re Hallett's Estate* (1880) 13 Ch. D. 696. The rule of appropriation is here merging into the rules on equitable tracing.

[28] As in *Pennell v. Deffell* (1853) 4 De GM & G 372; see also *Hancock v. Smith* (1889) 41 Ch. D. 456 at 461; *Re Diplock's Estate, Diplock v. Wintle* [1948] Ch. 465 at 554.

[29] *Bradford Old Bank Ltd v. Sutcliffe* [1918] 2 K.B. 833, where an argument that credits to a current account discharged debits on a loan account was rejected (see at 839, 843, 847).

[30] *Re E J Morel (1934) Ltd* [1962] Ch. 21.

account, and starting a new account,[31] the bank evinces an intention not to make an appropriation to the debits on the stopped account. Sometimes a bank will continue to allow credits to be made to an account, but debits will not be permitted (such an account is often referred to as a "frozen" account). In such a case the default rule would apply, but is unlikely to be of significance because the debit balance will simply be reducing, as if it were a reducing loan account.[32]

(d) Contrary agreement. An example of express contrary agreement is to be found in *Westminster Bank Ltd v. Cond.*[33] There a customer's account was guaranteed. Demand was made of the guarantor, which would normally "fix" his liability, so that continuation of the debtor's account would cause the old debt to cease to be covered by the guarantee. However, the guarantee form contained a term that the bank might continue the account after demand without discharging the guarantor's liability, and this was held to be effective. Similar terms often appear in bank security documents, and sometimes in joint account mandates so as to protect the bank against the default rule operating to its prejudice on the death, retirement or bankruptcy of one of the joint account holders. But bankers are reluctant to rely upon these clauses, and the general practice is still to stop the account and open a new one. This may be because of uncertainty about the decision in the *Westminster Bank* case, but it seems to be unnecessary. **11–036**

(e) Accounts which are not current or "running" accounts. The rule in *Clayton's Case* applies only to current accounts, on which there is a "running" balance. It will not, therefore, apply in circumstances where there has been a course of dealing between parties by a number of entirely separate transactions.[34] Nor will it apply to loan accounts on which there is merely a reducing debt. There is also some authority that the rule only applies to banking accounts.[35] **11–037**

---

[31] As stated in *Deeley v. Lloyds Bank Ltd* [1912] A.C. 756 at 785.

[32] See *E J Morel (1934) Ltd* [1962] Ch. 21 at 30–1, where Buckley J. treated a frozen current account as in the nature of a loan account.

[33] (1940) 46 Com Cas 60.

[34] *Cory Brothers & Co v. Mecca Turkish SS (Owners), The Mecca* [1897] A.C. 286.

[35] "We see no justification for extending that rule beyond the case of a banking account:" *Re Diplock* [1948] Ch. 465 at 555, *per* Lord Greene M.R. But compare *Barlow Clowes International Ltd v. Vaughan* [1992] 4 All E.R. 22 at 28j, *per* Dillon L.J. "That rule will apply to the appropriation of payments between any trader and his customer where there is an account current or running account". Support for the latter view can be found in *Re Footman Bower & Co Ltd* [1961] 1 Ch. 443, where the default rule was applied to a trading account.

Combination of Accounts (Banker's Set-off)

(1) The nature of the right and its significance

11–038 Combination (or "consolidation") refers to the right of a bank to set one account off against another of the same customer in order to determine the total state of indebtedness between customer and bank.[36] It is used in many diverse transactions and is of enormous importance in modern banking practice.[37] It has the benefit, from the bank's point of view, of enabling the bank to reduce or extinguish the customer's overdraft from a credit balance held by the same customer on a deposit account or another current account, and to that extent it may help the bank to avoid being a unsecured creditor on the customer's insolvency.

11–039 Although it is frequently called set-off, the right of combination is to be distinguished from set-off proper, because set-off presupposes the existence of a claim, the value of which is reduced or extinguished by deducting from it the value of a *separate* cross-claim. Separate cross-claims which are sufficiently closely connected may qualify for *equitable set-off*, where one is set off against another in a judgment (usually at the discretion of the court).[38] By virtue of the statutory rules for *set-off in insolvency*, an account must be taken of sums due to and from the insolvent and any particular creditor arising from their mutual dealings, and the creditor can only prove in the bankruptcy or liquidation for any net balance due to him.[39] The banker's right of combination differs fundamentally from these forms of set-off because the bank does not assert a separate claim; its liability to the customer is the net amount of the combined balance, taking both accounts into consideration as if there were in fact only one single account.

11–040 The right of combination is also to be distinguished from the banker's lien. Some cases refer to the right of combination as a right of lien, but although its development may have been influenced by the banker's lien,[40] the right of combination cannot be a lien in the strict sense because a lien is a right of possession. By definition there cannot be a possessory right over a chose in action, such as the content of a bank account.[41]

11–041 These distinctions were summarised in *Halesowen Presswork and Assemblies Ltd v. Westminster Bank Ltd*[42] by Buckley L.J. in the following terms:

---

[36] This definition from the first edition of this book was cited with approval by Otton J. in *Re K* [1990] 2 All E.R. 562 at 566.

[37] *e.g.* in "swaps" and netting transactions. See *The Law and Practice of International Banking.*

[38] See *Hanak v. Green* [1958] 2 Q.B. 9.

[39] See IA 1986, s. 323 (bankruptcy) and IR 1986, r. 4.90 (liquidation), fomerly Bankruptcy Act 1914, s. 31(a); CA 1948, s. 317(b).

[40] See *National Westminster Bank Ltd v. Halesowen Presswork & Assemblies Ltd* [1972] A.C. 785 at 810G, *per* Lord Cross.

[41] See above, para. 11–009.

[42] [1971] 1 Q.B. 1; reversed on other grounds in the House of Lords, *sub nom., National Westminster Bank Ltd v. Halesowen Presswork & Assemblies Ltd* [1972] A.C. 785.

"... the situation is not, in my judgment, a situation of lien at all. A lien postulates property of the debtor in the possession or under the control of the creditor. Nor is it a set-off situation, which postulates mutual but independent obligations between the two parties. It is an accounting situation, in which the existence and amount of one party's liability to the other can only be ascertained by discovering the ultimate balance of their mutual dealings. . ."[43]

So analysed, the right of combination is particularly significant if a court order, such as a garnishee order[44] or freezing injunction,[45] is served on a bank at a time when there is a credit balance on one of the customer's accounts but an overdraft on another. It follows from the nature of the right, that such orders can only affect any net credit balance remaining after the accounts have been combined, for otherwise there is no debt due from the bank to the customer to be attached by a garnishee order[46] and no asset of the customer's which is frozen by the injunction.[47]

In *Re K*[48] the position was held to be the same in a case where a restraint order had been made under section 8 of the Drug Trafficking Offences Act 1986 preventing a customer dealing with a credit balance on an account. Otton J. held that the bank was entitled to a variation of the order so as to permit it to exercise its right of combination, otherwise the rights of the bank would be severely undermined and the Drug Trafficking Offences Act 1986 would have the effect of depriving the bank, which had acted in good faith and in ignorance of the tainted source of the money, of its rights. There was nothing in the Drug Trafficking Offences Act 1986, which provided expressly or by implication that the bank's vested rights should be extinguished. He added that, despite the fact that banks might be able to **11–042**

43 [1971] 1 Q.B. 1 at 46E (and see to the same effect, at 33G, *per* Lord Denning M.R.), approved in the House of Lords on this point: see [1972] A.C. 785 at 802D, *per* Viscount Dilhorne and at 810F, *per* Lord Cross. See also *Re Charge Card Services* [1987] 1 Ch. 150 at 174, where Millett J. also described set-off as needing "mutual but independent obligations capable of being quantified and set-off against each other."

44 See above, para. 11–019.

45 Formerly known as "*Mareva*" injunctions, following *Mareva Compania Naviera SA v. International Bulk Carriers SA "The Mareva"* [1980] 1 All E.R. 213 in which the High Court jurisdiction to grant an injunction restraining the defendant from disposing of any assets was developed.

46 *Tapp v. Jones* (1875) LR 10 Q.B. 591 at 593, holding that rights of set-off can be exercised in respect of debts owed to the garnishee when the order was made, but not in respect of debts arising after the order. The same applies if at the date of the garnishee order the garnishee has a cross-claim against the judgment debtor which amounts to an equitable set-off on the basis that it is closely connected with the transaction giving rise to the debt which would otherwise have been attached: *Hale v. Victoria Plumbing Co Ltd* [1966] 2 Q.B. 746.

47 For this reason standard forms of freezing injunction contain an express proviso that they do not affect a banker's right of set-off: see annex to *Practice Direction—Interim Injunctions*, supplementing Part 25 of the *Civil Procedure Rules* 1998. If such proviso is not included the bank can apply to the court to vary the order so as to permit combination: *Oceania Castelana Armadora SA v. Mineralimportexport, The Theotokos* [1983] 1 W.L.R. 1302.

48 [1990] 2 All E.R. 562.

exercise a right of combination in these circumstances without resorting to the court, it would be prudent to apply to the court for a variation of the order, for the avoidance of doubt.

11–043 The fact that the right of combination is merely a method of establishing what is due between banker and customer also means that strictly speaking it is not necessary for any entries to have been made on the customer's account for the bank to exercise the right. It has been held to be enough that the banker evinces an intention to invoke the right.[49]

(2) Scope of the right

11–044 The leading case is *Garnett v. McKewan*,[50] in which it was decided that a bank may combine two current accounts without giving notice to the customer, even if the accounts are maintained at different branches. The customer had drawn cheques on an account in credit held at one branch of the bank, at a time when he was overdrawn on an account held at another branch. Without notice to him, the bank combined the balances which left an over all debit balance, so the bank dishonoured the cheques. It was held that the bank was entitled to do this.

11–045 Some doubt was cast on the decision in *W P Greenhalgh & Sons v. Union Bank of Manchester Ltd*[51] in which Swift J. stated that if a customer has two accounts, this implies an agreement to keep them separate. This was finally rejected in the *Halesowen Presswork* case.[52] In the Court of Appeal, Lord Denning said that on the contrary "You have to find an arrangement to keep them separate. The mere opening of two accounts does not do it."[53]

11–046 The position was summarised by Mocatta J. in *Barclays Bank Ltd v. Okenarhe*[54] as follows:

> "As regards the case in which the customer has separate running current accounts at each of two branches of a bank, it is plain that the general principle is that the bank is entitled to combine the two accounts. There is clear authority for this in the case of *Garnett v McKewan*. The learned Barons, in giving their judgments in that case, emphasised, of course, as one would have expected, that there was no right of combination in relation to accounts maintained with a banker by one person but in two different capacities, for example, one account

---

[49] *National Westminster Bank Ltd v. Halesowen Presswork & Assemblies Ltd* [1971] Q.B. 1 at 19, *per* Roskill J., who held that the bank had evinced the necessary intention by proving in the customer's liquidation for the net balance due. This point was not challenged on appeal.

[50] (1872) LR 8 Ex 10. See also *Re European Bank, Agra Bank Claim* (1872) 8 Ch. App. 41 decided on the same day in a different court.

[51] [1924] 2 K.B. 153 at 164.

[52] See above, para. 11–041, n. 42.

[53] [1971] 1 Q.B. 1 at 35; approved by Lord Kilbrandon in the House of Lords: see [1972] A.C. 785 at 819F.

[54] [1966] 2 Lloyd's Rep 87 at 95.

> might be a personal account of the customer and the other might be a trust account. Further, it was made clear by Baron Bramwell that the right to combine did not arise if there was an agreement between the customer and the banker that the two accounts should be kept separate, or if such an agreement should be implied from their conduct. Furthermore, in the case the learned judges dealt with what, at first sight, might seem the apparent anomaly that the customer cannot without specific agreement of the bank draw on account A a sum in excess of his balance on that account which is less than the combined balance at account A and account B. The limitation on the customer's rights, in other words, the inability of the customer without specific agreement to combine accounts, is explained as necessary to business efficacy. It would make the task of the banker impossible if every branch was expected to know the state of the customer's account at every other branch."

It seems, therefore, that the rights arise by implication of law.[55] It also seems clear that no prior notice needs to be given to the customer before the right is exercised. As was said in *Garnett v. McKewan*[56] "it might be proper or considerate to give notice to that effect, but there is no legal obligation on the bankers to do so . . . The customer must be taken to know the state of each account. . .". If notice were given, it might render the right to combine useless, since the customer would then have the opportunity to withdraw the credit balance unless the notice took immediate effect. Whether it may do so has not been decided, but even if it is possible to give notice taking immediate effect it seems that the bank should nevertheless honour any cheques drawn by the customer before he received notice.[57]

Both *Garnett v. McKewan* and the *Okenarhe* case show that the accounts may be at different branches of the bank; the customer is regarded as having one contract with the bank,[58] not with each of the branches at which he or she has an account. **11–047**

(3) Agreement not to combine accounts

The right of combination is available unless there is an express or implied agreement to the contrary.[59] It has been held that where a customer has a loan account and a current account, there is an implied term that the bank will not combine the two accounts, otherwise the customer could never be **11–048**

[55] Goode (LPCS) p. 169 suggests the right to combine accounts is a special form of contractual set-off arising by implied agreement.

[56] (1872) LR 8 Ex 10 at 13.

[57] See the *Halesowen* case [1972] A.C. 785 at 810, *per* Lord Cross.

[58] See *Joachimson v. Swiss Bank Corpn* [1921] 3 K.B. 110, above Chap. 3.

[59] In this respect the right is similar to equitable set-off, which can likewise be excluded by agreement: *Coca-Cola Financial Corporation v. Finsat International Ltd* [1996] 3 W.L.R. 849.

sure that cheques drawn on the current account would be met.[60] The same has been held to apply in the the case of a frozen account, which may be treated as akin to a loan account.[61]

It is not clear whether accounts which are held in different countries, or accounts denominated in different currencies, can be combined but the courts may find it easy to imply an agreement to keep such accounts separate.[62]

11–049 An agreement to keep accounts separate can, however, be terminated in some circumstances without notice. For example, in the *Halesowen* case,[63] the bank froze the overdrawn account of a company and agreed to allow another account to operate on a credit basis only for four months "in the absence of materially changed circumstances in the meantime." The bank continued this arrangement despite a meeting of the creditors of the company to consider going into liquidation, the holding of which would have justified the bank treating the circumstances as having changed sufficiently to terminate the arrangement. On a resolution being passed for the voluntary winding up of the company, the bank sought to combine the accounts, which led to a dispute with the liquidator as to the ownership of a cheque which had been paid in to the credit account on the day the winding up commenced. It was held that the agreement had come to and end when the company went into liquidation, because that made the objective of the agreement impossible, which had been to keep the company in business so that it could be sold as a going concern. The bank was, therefore, entitled to combine the accounts, without giving notice to the customer.

11–050 The *Halesowen* case also made it clear that if the bank had not been able to use the banker's right of combination, it would nevertheless have been required to set the accounts off against each other by virtue of the rules of statutory set-off in insolvency which were held to be mandatory in the sense that the parties cannot contract out of them.[64] It follows that an agreement not to combine accounts will end on the customer's insolvency.

Insolvency of the customer is usually treated as terminating the banker-customer relationship. An event which does not automatically put an end to the on-going nature of the relationship, such as receivership or administra-

[60] *Buckingham v. London & Midland Bank Ltd* (1895) 12 T.L.R. 70; *Bradford Old Bank Ltd v. Sutcliffe* [1918] 2 K.B. 833 at 847; *National Westminster Bank Ltd v. Halesowen Presswork & Assemblies Ltd* [1972] A.C. 785 at 809, *per* Lord Cross.

[61] See *Re E J Morel (1934) Ltd* [1962] Ch. 21 and see also the discussion in the *Halesowen* case, above.

[62] See Goode (LPCS) at 170–172; Paget at 535 & 537, where it is pointed out that an account held in a different country may be subject to a different proper law (which may not recognise the right of combination); and see also Horrigan, "Combining Bank Accounts in Different Currencies" (1991) 65 ALJ 14.

[63] [1972] A.C. 785, see above, para. 11–041.

[64] See above, para. 11–041, n. 42. In the *Halesowen* case it was held that the opening of the second account and the making of payments into it by the company constituted "mutual dealings" for the purpose of the set-off provisions in the insolvency legislation.

tion, would not have the same effect on any agreement to keep the customer's accounts separate. But in the *Halesowen* case Lord Cross agreed with the view which Buckley L.J. had expressed in the Court of Appeal[65] that a bank can give notice terminating with immediate effect an agreement to keep accounts separate, although it should honour cheques drawn by the customer before receipt of notice.[66]

(4) Other cases in which combination is not permitted

The banker's right of combination cannot be exercised over credit balances which, to the bank's knowledge, are not held in the customer's own right but are funds to which a third party has a proprietary claim. **11–051**

For example, funds which are known to be trust funds may not be combined with a debit balance on an account held for the customer in his personal capacity.[67] The same applies if money is known to have been deposited with the bank by the customer for a specific purpose,[68] or to have been paid into an account by mistake of fact.[69] Similarly, money which represents the proceeds of a debt which has been assigned to a third party can also fall outside the scope of the right of combination once notice of the assignment has been received by the bank.[70] In such cases the bank is disabled from exercising its right of combination once it has notice (actual or constructive) that the funds are held by the customer for, or are subject to the claims of, a third party.[71]

The right does not entitle the bank to combine a debit balance on a joint account with a credit balance on a sole account of one of the parties to the joint account.[72] Similarly, a bank has no right to combine a partner's private **11–052**

---

[65] [1971] 1 Q.B. 1 at 47.

[66] [1972] A.C. 785 at 810; there were only three other members of the House of Lords (one of their Lordships having been taken ill during the hearing), none of whom expressed a view on the point.

[67] *Re Gross* (1871) 6 Ch. App. 632; and see the *Halesowen* and *Okernarhe* cases, above.

[68] *Stumore v. Campbell & Co* [1892] 1 Q.B. 314; *Barclays Bank Ltd v. Quistclose Investments Ltd* [1970] A.C. 567; *Neste Oy v. Lloyds Bank Plc* [1983] 2 Lloyd's Rep 658. Combination would be permissible if no agreement has been reached as to the purpose for which the funds are held, or if the funds are not sufficiently identifiable because they have been mixed with other funds: *Peacock AG v. Anglo-Corporation Ltd*, February 12, 1997, Unreported, CA, New Law Transcript No. 297022501.

[69] Such monies being recoverable by the payer, subject to the recipient making out a defence of change of position: *Lipkin Gorman v. Karpnale Ltd* [1991] 2 A.C. 548 at 579. Once the bank knows of the mistake it may be treated as holding the funds as a constructive trustee for the payer: see *Westdeutsche Landesbank Girozentrale v. Islington LBC* [1996] A.C. 669 at 715, *per* Lord Browne-Wilkinson.

[70] *Re Marwalt Ltd* [1992] B.C.C. 32. If the debt to the bank accrued due before notice of the assignment was received, or if it is closely connected with the debt which has been assigned, combination may still be possible: see *Business Computers Ltd v. Anglo African Leasing Ltd* [1977] 1 W.L.R. 578 (dealing with equitable set-off); *Marathon Electrical Manufacturing Corp. v. Mashreqbank*, May 13, 1997, Unreported, Com Ct.

[71] In *Union Bank of Australasia v. Murray-Aynsley* [1898] A.C. 693, PC, the bank was held to have been entitled to exercise its right of combination because it did so without knowing that funds deposited were trust funds.

[72] *Re Willis, Percival & Co, ex p. Morier* (1879) 12 Ch. D. 491.

account with the partnership account, even though the partner's liability on the partnership account is joint.[73] If, however, a bank requires (as it usually does) a mandate to be signed by the partners which provides for them to be jointly and severally liable for any borrowing, then the debt is not merely a joint debt of the partners as partners, but is also a separate personal debt of each individual, so the private account could be combined with the partnership account.

11–053 It might be thought that customers could circumvent the bank's right to combine accounts by opening accounts in the names of nominees, and to some extent this is true. The courts have held that banks may not combine such an account with the account of a customer on mere suspicion—or even if there is an arguable case—that the customer is operating the accounts in the names of nominees, for this would throw upon the person who is suspected of being a nominee the need to take action to recover money which is prima facie his own.[74] But the bank can combine such accounts if there is clear and indisputable evidence that they are being operated by nominees of the same person.[75] In *Re K*,[76] the problem of a nominee opening accounts was raised in a different context. The bank's customer made substantial deposits into two deposit accounts and then requested an overdraft from the bank, which was agreed. The customer, who had in fact been acting for her brothers, gave her brothers a mandate over the accounts. All three were subsequently charged with drug dealing offences and a restraint order was made prohibiting dealing with the accounts.[77] The case against the customer was not taken further—and she relinquished all claims to the accounts—but one of her brothers was convicted, and the Crown applied for a confiscation order against the accounts in credit. The bank applied for a variation of the order to allow it to combine the accounts, which would pay off the overdraft. It was held that the bank's fundamental right to combine accounts (by which it was carrying out an accounting exercise, not asserting a claim over the moneys) was not affected by the restraint order.

11–054 As in the case of the banker's lien, there is no right of combination for contingent liabilities.[78] This distinguishes the right to combine accounts

---

[73] *Watts v. Christie* (1849) 11 Beav 546 at 555.

[74] *Bhogal v. Punjab National Bank* [1988] 2 All E.R. 296; *Uttamchandami v. Central Bank of India* (1989) 139 NLJ 22 (cases of equitable set-off).

[75] *Re Hett Maylor & Co Ltd* (1894) 10 T.L.R. 412; explained in *Bhogal v. Punjab National Bank* [1988] 2 All E.R. 296 at 301 as "a very plain case where the nomineeship of one account was known to both parties and undisputed." Similarly, in *Bhogal v. Punjab National Bank* [1988] 2 All E.R. 296, Lloyd L.J. held the evidence of nomineeship would have to be clear "either on the face of it, or by distinct admission, or otherwise without the need for any further enquiry."

[76] [1990] 2 All E.R. 562 (in which the bank also had a contractual right of set-off under the terms of a letter of "lien").

[77] Under the Drug Trafficking Offences Act 1986, s. 8.

[78] *Jeffryes v. Agra & Mastermans Bank* (1866) LR 2 Eq 674 at 680 (see also above, para. 11–009); *Bower v. Foreign & Colonial Gas Co Ltd; Metropolitan Bank, Garnishees* (1874) 22 W.R. 740.

from the rules for statutory set-off on insolvency which require both actual and contingent liabilities to be taken into account.[79]

(5) Customer's right to combine?

A customer is entitled to instruct the bank to combine two or more accounts, unless there is an agreement that they will be kept separate.[80] But so long as the customer has more than one account, he has no right to rely on the combined balances, for example by presenting a cheque at one branch where he has insufficient funds and demanding that the bank pay it because there are funds in an account kept elsewhere, even though the bank is entitled to combine such accounts as a reason to refuse to pay. This "apparent anomaly", as it was described in the *Okernarhe* case,[81] was justified in *Garnett v. McKewan*[82] on the ground of business efficacy, since the bank could not be expected to know the state of a customer's account at every other branch, whereas the customer can be expected to know the state of his various accounts. So it is for the customer to transfer the necessary funds between his accounts to ensure there are sufficient funds available in the account on which he draws his cheques. **11–055**

(6) Duty to combine?

In some circumstances it seems the bank is obliged to combine the customer's accounts. If a bank holds security for a general balance on two or more accounts, it cannot appropriate the security to discharge the debit balance but should first combine the accounts to ascertain the combined balance.[83] By parity of reasoning it would seem that if there are multiple accounts, it is probable that a bank wishing to exercise its right of combination must combine all of them. It probably cannot combine a debit balance on a No. 1 account with a credit balance on a No. 2 account, but leave untouched a debit balance on a No. 3 account which represents, for example, a preferential or secured debt.[84] Similarly, if a customer has two current accounts, and draws a cheque generally (that is, not referring to a particular account)[85] there may be a duty on the bank to combine the customer's accounts.[86] **11–056**

---

79 See *Re Charge Card Services* [1987] Ch. 150 at 170; *MS Fashions Ltd v. BCCI SA (No 2)* [1993] Ch. 425, CA, affirmed by the House of Lords: [1997] 4 All E.R. 568; *Stein v. Blake* [1996] A.C. 243 at 252E–H.

80 *Halesowen Presswork & Assemblies Ltd v. National Westminster Bank Ltd* [1971] 1 Q.B. 1 at 34E, *per* Lord Denning M.R.

81 See above, para. 11–046.

82 (1872) LR 8 Ex 10. See also *Woodland v. Fear* (1857) 7 El & Bl 519.

83 See *Mutton v. Peat* [1900] 2 Ch. 79.

84 Compare the *Halesowen* case [1971] 1 Q.B. 1 at 34E, CA. The contrary view expressed by Buckley J. in *Re E J Morel (1934) Ltd* [1962] Ch. 21 was disapproved in *Re Unit 2 Windows Ltd* [1985] 3 All E.R. 647.

85 Rare nowadays, because of the use of printed cheque forms with account numbers on them.

86 See Chorley, 70. It is not thought that this obligation would extend to accounts held at different branches.

11–057 On termination of the relationship of banker and customer, if the customer has more than one account, and one is in debit, the bank will need to combine the balances to ascertain what sum is due. If for some reason a bank does not take steps to combine accounts on its customer's bankruptcy or winding-up, the mandatory provisions of the IA 1986 will compel it to do so by way of statutory set-off of mutual debts in ascertaining the sum, if any, for which it may prove.[87]

(7) Agreement to combine accounts

11–058 The right of combination can be extended by agreement. Such agreement need not be in writing; it could, for example, be inferred from a course of dealing between the bank and its customer. But the bank will usually require a document to be signed (often called a "letter of set-off"), to evidence the agreed terms.

In *Re Charge Card Services Ltd*[88] a provision contained in a factoring agreement gave the factoring company a right to retain such amount as it decided from sums credited to the insolvent company's factoring account, as security for sums which might become chargeable as a debit to the account. The liquidator of the company argued this provision was void on the ground that it gave the factoring company a right of set-off which was more extensive than permitted under the statutory rules for set-off in insolvency, but Millett J. held that the right of retention was "not a matter of set-off but of account."[89] This provides support for the view that by express agreement a banker can be accorded a right to set-off against credit balances sums for which the customer is contingently liable.

11–059 Banks often require letters of set-off to be signed when monies are specifically placed on deposit as security for a customer's liabilities on other accounts. There is some doubt whether such arrangements may be construed as creating a charge over the deposited cash which, in the case of a limited company, would be registrable. For this reason applications are often made to register such arrangements as company charges.[90] There is also often included in such agreements a so-called "negative pledge" clause, by which the customer agrees not to deal in any way with the cash deposited (whether by assignment, mortgage, charge or otherwise) without the bank's prior written consent, and agrees that any purported dealing without such consent is ineffective. Such clauses have been upheld as effective.[91]

---

[87] *National Westminster Bank Ltd v. Halesowen Presswork & Assemblies Ltd* [1972] A.C. 785, HL.

[88] [1987] Ch. 150.

[89] [1987] Ch. 150 at 173G.

[90] Under the CA 1985, s. 395. In *Re BCCI SA (No 8)* [1998] A.C. 214 at 227E/F, Lord Hoffmann stated (*obiter*) that the decision in *Northern Bank Ltd v. Ross* [1990] B.C.C. 883 suggests an obligation to register is unlikely to arise.

[91] *Linden Gardens Trust Ltd v. Lenesta Sludge Disposals Ltd* [1994] 1 A.C. 85, HL.

Section III

PAYMENT

CHAPTER 12

PAYMENT METHODS

Recent developments in technology and practice have tended to focus attention on basic questions of definition and principle which may have been implicit in the law rather than systematically addressed. Money laundering on a large scale, for example, facilitated by effective, instantaneous communications and payments systems, has been a factor in bringing home the need for careful analysis of concepts of property, obligations and priority—analysis which is taking place through developments in the law of constructive trust, tracing and restitution. Equally, the developments in the technology introduced by banks in recent decades have illustrated that concepts like *money* and *payment*, which have typically been treated pragmatically by the common law, need more thoughtful examination when they are applied to methods of electronic payment. Decisions by the courts and work by academic commentators[1] have clarified the issues so that the important problems can be identified and coherent solutions developed. **12–001**

Money

> "Economists have probably spilled more printers' ink over the topic of money than any other, and while monetary theory impinges on almost every conceivable branch of economic analysis, confusion over the meaning and nature of money continues to plague the economics profession."[2] **12–002**

Forms of money have progressed from "seashells, to spices, to precious metal coins, to the tokenised currency we use today"[3] Today, however, we use a variety of methods to make payments—currency is one of them, but banks are concerned with many others, including electronic money. Payments can now be made by computer checkout machines in shops, by

---

[1] *e.g.* Goode, *Commercial Law* (2nd ed.), pp. 489 *et seq.*; Goode, *Payment Obligations in Commercial and Financial Transactions*. See also Geva, *The Law of Electronic Funds Transfers*; Chorafas, *Electronic Funds Transfers*, and Mann, *Legal Aspect of Money*. See also Vroegop [1990] L.M.C.L.Q. 64

[2] Davidson, Post Keynesian Macroeconomic Theory (1994), at 86, quoted by Stern [1998] CfiLR 217 at 226.

[3] Hutton (1995) NLJ 1810, quoted by Stern.

automated teller machines, by electronic funds transfers, by the "electronic purse" and by "digital cash", involving the internet. It is a question (which commentators are beginning to address[4]) how far these financial innovations can be regarded as "money" in a legal sense. These new forms of payment are considered in Chapter 15.

12–003 Lawyers are chiefly concerned with money as currency, as a means of satisfying obligations, rather than thinking of it more broadly, as economists might. With this in mind, money[5] can be thought of either as *physical* money or as *intangible* money. Physical money[6] (such as bank notes and coin used as currency) is of enormous importance for routine small payments; cash remains the dominant method of payment, although its use is gradually declining.[7] The creditor normally has a right to payment in legal tender[8]—according to the statutory requirement of legal tender at any particular time—although most people are now content to receive payment by one of the methods we shall be considering in this section. Where payment is in cash, few legal problems usually arise.

Intangible money is a different matter, and it is intangible money that gives rise to most of the problems with which banks are concerned. Intangible money can take the form of a generic claim to payment, such as for damages or for debt (unlike claims for specific assets or funds of the defendant); or a specific claim, where there is a particular intangible, such as a bank deposit, which is held for the claimant under a trust of some sort.

Although the concept of money is of course central to banking, it is often less crucial to modern banking law and practice than problems of payment and payment methods.

---

[4] See Stern, *op. cit.,* and works cited there.

[5] What follows is based on Goode's discussion of the subject. He quotes the view of Dr F. Mann in his authoritative work, *The Legal Aspect of Money*: "It is suggested that, in law, the quality of money is to be attributed to all chattels which, issued by the authority of the law and denominated with reference to a unit of account, are meant to serve as universal means of exchange in the State of issue", (at p. 8).

[6] Physical money has five important legal characteristics: the value of the money is its *face* value, not its intrinsic value; it is *given or borrowed or used to discharge an obligation,* not bought or exchanged; it is fully *negotiable*, so that a person who obtains it in good faith and for value obtains a good title; a creditor may *demand money in discharge* of the debt owed; and it is a *fungible*—legally interchangeable with any other unit of account. From the last of these, Goode concludes that a creditor's right to be paid is a purely personal right: he is *owed* money, he does not *own* it.

[7] In the U.K. cash still accounts for around three-quarters of all payments APACS, *Annual Review* (1999), p. 27.

[8] There is some doubt: Goode thinks that it would be "absurd" for this requirement to be taken literally when a large sum of money is at stake, and there are dicta in the cases (*e.g. The Brimnes* [1975] 1 Q.B. at 768, *per* Cairns L.J.) which agree with this view, but Staughten J. came to a different conclusion in *Libyan Arab Foreign Bank v. Bankers' Trust Co.* [1989] Q.B. 728, when he held that a customer had a right to receive payment in cash—even though it amounted in that case to $292m.

Payment[9]

The concept of payment—of discharging money obligations—is difficult and relatively unfamiliar to common lawyers. The law provides no real definition, although section 59 of the BOEA 1882 states that payment in due course discharges a bill or cheque. The Act goes on to describe what constitutes payment in due course, but does not define at what point payment occurs.[10] Indeed, when referring to cheques or other forms of payment, we usually mean the *process* of payment rather than the conclusive point or action which finalises payment. The fact that payment is not necessarily a single event is not so evident from normal cash transactions, where there are likely to be problems only if there is a delay between tender and acceptance.[11] **12–004**

It is easy, for example, to confuse *payment* with the *tender of payment* by the debtor. If the debtor offers, or tenders, payment, the debt is not discharged, although the debtor has a good defence if sued: he or she may pay the money into court with a plea of tender.[12] The debt is actually discharged, however, only when the creditor accepts the payment. Similarly, the parties may, by contract or course of dealing, mean something different by payment than its usual legal meaning. If they agree on payment by cheque, for example, this does not necessarily mean that payment is made by giving the cheque: it is only made when the cheque has been honoured,[13] although the date of payment will be deemed to have been the time of the delivery of the cheque.[14] Until then, the payment of a cheque, bill of exchange or a letter of credit is normally *conditional*,[15] so that the payment obligation will revive if the instrument is not honoured, whereas payment by credit or charge card is normally *absolute*, and the debtor is discharged if the creditor accepts the card.[16] **12–005**

---

[9] See B. Geva, *The Law of Electronic Funds Transfers*; Goode, *Commercial Law* (2nd ed., 1983), Chapter 17; and Goode, *Payment Obligations in Commercial and Financial Transactions*; Arora, *Electronic Banking and the Law* (2nd ed.); Brindle and Cox, *Law of Bank Payments*.

[10] Goode's view is that payment in the legal sense means a gift or loan of money or any act offered and accepted in performance of a money obligation; money must therefore feature in some way, either as physical money or because the obligation itself is a money obligation (*Commercial Law*, p. 501).

[11] See Vroegop [1990] L.M.C.L.Q. 64, who cites *Chambers v. Miller* (1862) 13 C.B.N.S. 125 and *Balmoral Supermarket Ltd v. Bank of New Zealand* [1974] 2 N.Z.L.R. 155.

[12] See *TSB v. Welwyn Hatfield DC* [1993] 2 Bank L.R. 267 at 271–2, *per* Hobhouse J. "The difference between tender and payment is that more than a mere tender of money is required to effect a payment. Payment discharges the liability but tender does not".

[13] Although Vroegop ([1990] L.M.C.L. 64) suggests that the cases hesitate between two possible moments when payment is completed: when a cheque is cleared (which is logical if a cheque is regarded as a payment mechanism) or when it is handed over (which is more appropriate if it is regarded as a negotiable instrument).

[14] *The Brimnes* [1975] 1 Q.B. 929.

[15] *Alan (WJ) & Co v. El Nasr Export and Import Co* [1972] 2 Q.B. 189; *EDF Man v. Nigerian Sweets and Confectionery Co.* [1977] 2 Lloyd's Rep. 50. *cf. Sibree v. Tripp* (1846) 15 M.&W. 23.

[16] *Re Charge Card Services* [1987] Ch. 150, aff'd [1989] Ch. 497.

12–006 Similarly, it is not always clear from the way we talk *which* party is paying *whom*: when a payment is credited to a customer's account, for example, it is "payment" in one sense, because it constitutes payment between debtor and creditor (so that the debtor is discharged), but in another sense it is not, because the *bank* has yet to pay its customer—it is its customer's debtor. Completion of the one payment may have to be considered as a separate event from the completion of the other. And it may be important to distinguish between the point where the payment of money is completed and the point where the money is *available* to the customer, which again may occur at a separate moment.[17] No doubt the confusion arises because concepts appropriate to the simple payment of cash—where all the significant moments (tender, acceptance, availability of funds) probably occur at the same, or nearly the same, time—are stretched to make them apply to the more complex world of modern payment mechanisms.

12–007 Thus the uncertainties about payment are more obvious when payment is made through the banking system[18]; apart from anything else, such transactions are complex because of the multiplicity of parties. Even at its simplest, the debtor pays by the agency of his or her bank, and the payment is received by the bank of the creditor and then credited by that bank to the appropriate account. Frequently other banks are also involved—if correspondent banks are used, or if one of the banks is not a settlement member of the clearing association. The uncertainties tend not to obtrude when payment is by cheque, however, because the rules governing the use of cheques themselves are clear, and the clearing process, which is subject to well defined rules (the Clearing Rules) established by the banks, has mechanisms to limit the ambiguities and resolve the difficulties which arise.

Payment Systems[19]

12–008 Before going on to consider the various new types of payment, it may be helpful to give an outline of the payment systems[20] on which they depend.

[17] See, *e.g.*, *A/S Awilco of Oslo v. Fulvia S.p.a. Di Navigazione of Cagliari, The Chikuma* [1981] 1 W.L.R. 314.

[18] See *R. v. Preddy* [1996] 3 All E.R. 481, HL, where it was held that a person who obtained a mortgage advance by deception did not commit an offence under s. 15 of the TA 1968, because he had not "obtained another's property by deception". His deception involved the debiting of the lender's bank account and the crediting of his own by means of fraudulent statements to the lender. This meant that the chose in action (debt) of the bank to the lender was extinguished and another chose in action (of another bank to the defendant) came into existence; the defendant did not obtain the *lender's* property by the deception. In that case, the transaction had been effected by CHAPS, but the same would be true if it had been by cheque (at 491, *per* Lord Goff). (The section was amended by the Theft (Amendment) Act 1996). See also para. 15–063.

[19] Detailed descriptions of payment systems can be found in Brindle and Cox, *op. cit.*, Chap 3 and Paget, *op. cit.*, Chap. 19. See also Giovanoli in *Cross-Border Electronic Banking*, at p. 205, for a helpful explanation of payment and netting systems.

[20] Goode sees a developed payment system structure as having "four key components: an

Payments through banks are dealt with according to whether they are made by "paper" or by electronic means. This Chapter is primarily concerned with the various electronic systems.[21]

With the aid of advanced technology, banks have developed these systems to a high level of technical efficiency. The distinguishing characteristic of an electronic funds transfer system is said to be that the inter-bank communication of payment instructions is by electronic means, for example by magnetic tape, disc or telecommunication link, even though the original instruction is on paper.[22] The two United Kingdom electronic systems are BACS and CHAPS,[23] which are the main systems designed to be used by banks for the inter-bank transfer of funds. Personal account holders do not have direct access to the systems.

The organisation with responsibility for payment systems in the United Kingdom is the *Association of Payment Clearing Services* (APACS), which was set up in 1985.[24] It is an umbrella association for the three autonomous clearing companies: **12–009**

- the Cheque and Credit Clearing Company, which deals with bulk "paper" clearings[25];
- BACS (Bankers' Automated Clearing System) Ltd, which deals with the bulk electronic clearings; and
- CHAPS (Clearing House Automated Payments System) Clearing Company Ltd,[26] which deals with high value same-day electronic clearings.[27]

---

interbank communications network for the on-line electronic transmission of large-value (wholesale) payment orders and associated messages; a clearing house for the physical exchange of paper-based payment orders (bills, cheques, bank giro payments) and the netting of matured payment obligations; an automated clearing house for the batch processing of large-volume off-line, mainly low-value (retail) payment orders stored in magnetic form on tapes and diskettes; and the involvement of the central bank as the vehicle for settlement of dealings between the banks participating in the clearing (settlement banks) by means of transfers in the books of the central bank, where all settlement banks hold an account." *Commercial Law*, p. 505.

21 Cheque payments and payments by card are discussed below, in Chaps 14 and 15.

22 Geva, *op. cit.*, para. 1.03[4].

23 Another important method of paying electronically is by EFTPOS (electronic transfer at the point of sale) such as SWITCH cards. ATM (automated teller machines) also use electronic payment (see below, Chap. 15).

24 There are currently 29 member banks of APACS.

25 The Cheque Clearing is for physical exchange of sterling paper-based debit payment orders (cheques and other instruments, direct debit vouchers), a high-volume clearing system for payments of relatively small value; the Credit Clearing is a similar system for paper-based credit collections (credit transfers, credit card vouchers, etc.).

26 Formerly CHAPS and Town Clearing Company Ltd. The Town Clearing, a high value, same-day paper clearing in the City of London, ceased operation in February 1995.

27 There are other clearings for foreign currency.

12–010 In this context, it is important to mention the international communications system, SWIFT (Society of Worldwide Interbank Financial Telecommunications), which transmits instructions for payment, although it does not act as a clearing system, since it has no settlement rules for its members.

These systems depend upon a series of interdependent contracts, between individual banks and the companies, between banks and their customers, and between the banks themselves.

Cheque clearing

12–011 Problems with regard to payment of cheques between banks are governed by the Clearing Rules. Payment of a cheque as between the paying and collecting banks is made at a different time from when final payment is made between the payer and the payee.[28] If a cheque is presented through the cheque clearing, payment is made between the two banks when they finally agree on the net balance payable by the one to the other on settlement of business between the accounts maintained by the banks at the Bank of England. The "In" and "Out" totals of the day's business are agreed between them, and the Bank of England makes a transfer of the net difference to the credit of one bank's account and to the debit of the other bank's account with it.[29] When the paying bank reserves the right to dishonour the cheque or other instrument, payment between the banks is complete only when settlement is effected between them, and if the cheque or instrument is dishonoured the paying bank has the right to recover the amount paid from the collecting bank.[30] Payment is not made finally by the drawer to the payee or holder until the expiry of the time under the General Clearing Rules within which the cheque may be dishonoured by the branch of the drawer's bank at which his or her account is kept.[31]

BACS

12–012 These letters stand for Bankers' Automated Clearing System; the name is used both for the system and the operating company. BACS was the first electronic system for clearing (established in 1968) and is the largest single automated clearing house in the world.[32]

[28] In *Sibree v. Tripp* (1846) 15 M. & W. 23 and *Camidge v. Allenby* (1827) 6 B. & C. 373, it was established that the point of time when payment of a debt is made, either absolutely or conditionally, depends upon the intention of the parties, and in order to ascertain those intentions the terms of the transaction must be looked at as a whole.

[29] *Pollard v. Bank of England* (1871) L.R. 6 Q.B. 623.

[30] *Banque de l'Indochine et de Suez S.A. v. J.A. Rayner (Mincing Lane) Ltd* [1982] 2 Lloyd's Rep. 476.

[31] Paras 12(a) and (b)—that is, 12 noon of the day following that on which the cheque is received at that branch after presentation through the clearing: *Barclays Bank plc v. Bank of England* [1985] 1 All E.R. 385.

[32] The number of transactions dealt with by BACS has increased steadily; in 1999, it processed more than 3 billion items (an increase of 6.6 per cent over 1998). APACS, *Annual Review* (1999), p. 12. Bill and other payments initiated via telephone and internet banking was the fastest growing BACS application, A.R. (1999) p. 27.

It deals with the bulk processing of payments in three forms: standing orders (an instruction from a customer to make a regular payment of a specified amount to a named creditor); customer credits (credits made direct to a customer's account, often the payment of wages, salaries and pensions) and direct debits (a pre-authorised debit on the payer's account initiated by the payee).[33] Compared to CHAPS, it is high-volume and low value, and it takes longer—it has a three day cycle, and is no faster than ordinary paper clearing. BACS Users' Manuals and agreements between BACS members provide the rules.

The payment cycle takes this form: data must be submitted by members[34] **12–013** by telecommunication link[35] to the main processing centre in Edgware before 12 p.m. The data (the input data) are processed overnight and the relevant credits and the corresponding debits (the output data) are recorded on individual tapes or disks for each member bank or building society and are sent to them on the second day by courier or telecommunication link. On that day, the banks process the data and adjust customers' accounts accordingly by the opening of business the next day. Balances owing between the banks are struck on the third day, after payment instructions take effect, and the Bank of England is informed by BACS of the settlements which need to be made between accounts of the banks.

CHAPS

The acronym CHAPS stands for the Clearing House Automated Pay- **12–014** ments System. It is the United Kingdom's same-day payments system, a guaranteed irrevocable nationwide electronic sterling credit clearing and settlement system, used mainly for high-value payments.[36] The value of the items cleared is enormous: in 1998, it was over £41,500 billion.[37]

The system became operational in 1984, and now functions on a nationwide basis through the head offices of the clearing banks, which are connected by computer terminals to their principal country branches. Several hundred other banks obtain indirect access for their customers by using one of the full members as agents. The members exchange payment messages across a British Telecom network. There is no central clearing

[33] See discussion of bank giro payments,

[34] Members may sponsor other (non-personal) customers, for whom they are responsible, and who must submit their data by 9 p.m., or to the City of London collection centre by 5 p.m.

[35] From 1999, all input to BACS was received via telecommunications (BACSTEL).

[36] There used to be a limitation of £10,000 on the minimum payment and a maximum limit of £100,000, but both limits have now been removed. The other high value clearing (the Town Clearing, which was a manual system operating in the City of London) was closed in 1995.

[37] APACS *Annual Review* (1998): an increase of 15.2 per cent over 1997; there are 18 million. payments annually. A new product called CHAPS euro is now being offered for euro-denominated payments to handle payments to other CHAPS euro members or cross-border payments to any other bank connected to TARGET, the European real-time gross settlement system.

system; each bank has a standardised piece of software, known as a *gateway*, which acts as the interface or routing device between that institution's internal banking system and the CHAPS network as a whole. The computer terminals at the head offices (and some other branches) of each settlement bank feed instructions through the gateway, which records the value of all incoming and outgoing payments for its bank.

12–015 In the past the Bank of England used to be involved at this stage, by posting the multilateral net amounts to the members' settlement accounts, but this has now been changed to allow *real-time gross settlement* (RTGS). The reason for the change was the problem of the risk caused by balances between banks fluctuating quickly and unpredictably during the day; if net transfers from one bank were greater than incoming transfers from other members, the bank would be left exposed.[38] In order to give efficient protection against the risk, the new system enabling banks to settle accounts in "real time" has been introduced: each CHAPS payment is settled at the Bank of England before it is sent to the receiving bank. The Bank is therefore able to check that the sending bank has sufficient funds in its account at the Bank before the transaction is completed. If it has, the Bank will confirm this, and the sending bank's message, which has meanwhile been waiting at the gateway, is released automatically to the receiving bank. This system has the additional advantage that the Bank of England is able to keep the flow of funds smooth by providing extra funds if necessary (intra-day liquidity)[39] for banks which do not have sufficient funds in their accounts.[40]

12–016 The CHAPS payment instruction comprises the name of the payee, the amount of the payment, the special sorting code number of the payee's bank and the branch to which payment is to be made, and the payee's account number. Similar information must be given about the payer's account so that the account may be debited on the computerised record of the accounts of the paying bank's customer and so that the payee can be informed. The payer may include in the payment instruction certain additional information for the benefit of the payee about the reason for payment or the transaction to which the payment related.

12–017 A payment instruction made through CHAPS may be altered, abandoned or cancelled at any time prior to it being released through the gateway. Although payment is probably not made until the payment instruction is accepted by the receiving bank, the paying bank cannot amend or counter-

[38] Banks used limits (net sender limits), raising or lowering them at their discretion, to control the payments they made, in order to guard against this risk.

[39] By purchasing high-quality assets under sale and repurchase agreements, which the banks later repurchase.

[40] As well as providing a "circles processing" facility for simultaneous settlement of payments which can be set off against each other which is intended to avoid the "gridlock" problem with RTGS systems—see Encylopaedia of Banking Law, DI (583).

mand the payment once it is transmitted through the gateway and has been acknowledged (formally).[41]

Although a payment instruction sent to the head office of a paying bank cannot be countermanded or recalled once it has entered the system, the instruction will not be released for transmission until it is checked and authenticated by a senior member of the staff of the paying bank. The payment is then transmitted to the head office of the receiving bank whose own computer will immediately credit the payment to the payee's account. Simultaneously, the receiving bank's computer will transmit the information contained in the payment instructions to its branch where the payee's account is held so that a print-out made by the terminal at that branch may be sent to the payee.

SWIFT[42]

SWIFT (Society of Worldwide Interbank Financial Telecommunications) **12–018** is a non-profit making communications network which is used for international bank payments. Unlike BACS and CHAPS, which have both communications networks and settlement systems, it does not have specific settlement rules for the participants. It works by passing messages, which constitute payment instructions between banks, by special SWIFT link or telex. The banks of the member countries have national terminals connecting with one of three main international centres, which are interlinked and interchangeable. Messages are normally expected to arrive within one day (although the entire process may be as short as 20 seconds[43]), unless the difference in time zones makes this difficult. Security is provided by encoded security numbers, and because the banks have harmonised forms and the system is attuned to the special needs of banks, the system is regarded as the safest way to effect transfers.[44]

Legal Roles of Banks Making a Funds Transfer

Vroegop's approach in discussing a direct credit transaction[45] is to **12–019** describe it as a series of steps, and it may be helpful to introduce this section by adopting her analysis:

(1) The payer's bank sends a message to the payee's bank.

[41] Or now, since the introduction of RTGS, as soon as the request is received by the Bank of England: *cf.* Paget, *op. cit.*, p. 299 or acted upon. It was held in *R v. King* [1992] 1 Q.B. 20, CA, that a CHAPS instruction was a "valuable security" within TA 1968, s. 20: this would imply a property right and would have serious implications. See further Brindle & Cox, para. 3–72.

[42] The current system (since 1990) is SWIFT II.

[43] Geva, *op. cit.*, para. 4.03.

[44] Ellinger [1986] L.M.C.L.Q. at 194.

[45] [1990] L.M.C.L.Q. 64. A direct debit transaction can be analysed in the same way, but the initiative comes from the payee, so the transaction begins with the payee's bank. She suggests that the difference is immaterial.

(2) The payee's bank receives the message.

(3) The payee's bank completes processing the message.

(4) The payee's bank makes the funds available to the payee.

(5) The payee's bank advises the payee that the funds are available.

Another way of describing the process, using the terminology frequently adopted, is:

> A debtor, X, transmits an instruction to his bank to credit a sum of money to the account of his creditor, Y; this instruction is a *payment order*; X is the *sender* and X's bank is the *receiving bank* of the payment order. Y is the *beneficiary*.[46]
>
> X's bank may *execute* its customer's order by issuing an instruction to Y's bank (usually a different bank) to credit Y's account in the amount requested; the instruction from the bank is also known as a *payment order*.

The series of transactions is known as the *funds transfer*. X is the *originator*, his bank is the *originator's bank*, Y is the *beneficiary* and her bank is the *beneficiary's bank* or the *receiving bank*.

12–020 The simplest model is an *in-house payment*, where the payer and payee bank at the same branch of the same bank, but this is relatively unusual. A slightly more complex situation is where the payer and payee bank at the same bank, but at different branches. Even more complex—and more usual—is where they bank at different banks. Frequently, a number of other banks may also be involved; in foreign transactions, the principal banks may use correspondent banks, and, if they are not themselves members of the system concerned, may use settlement members to act for them in using the system. These would be *correspondent or intermediary banks*.

It has already been mentioned that uncertainties about payment, which have hitherto been relatively unnoticed because of the contractual relations of the parties and the rules of the clearing system, may cause more significant problems in the context of funds transfer, because of the speed and complexity of the transactions. One reason for the problems is that legal consequences depend upon the roles of the banks involved in a particular transaction, which may vary with the circumstances. There may, for example, be a number of intermediary banks through whom the payment instruction between the paying bank and the receiving bank is remitted, particularly if it is an international payment.

---

[46] These terms derive from Article 4A of the Uniform Commercial Code (promulgated 1989) and UNCITRAL Model Law on International Credit Transfers (adopted 1992), and are used by Goode, *Commercial Law*, p. 507.

The roles of the banks concerned in funds transfers (where the legal capacity in which a bank is acting varies according to the circumstances of the transaction) are largely governed by bilateral contracts between the banks—for example, a member of the clearing may agree to act as agent for a non-member bank—or by multilateral contracts between members of a particular system, for example, BACS or CHAPS, in which case, all the members are bound by the rules and are deemed to have contracted with each other.[47] As far as English law is concerned, a funds transfer is regarded as a single transaction, rather than one involving a series of successive bilateral operations,[48] and the relationships between the banks, it seems, are governed by the principles of agency.[49] It is not always clear, however, which bank is the agent and which the principal. It may be important to establish whether a given bank or other intermediary is the agent of the debtor or of the creditor,[50] particularly for determining the point at which the debtor loses the ability to cancel or vary a payment instruction, and for deciding the time at which payment has been received. **12–021**

The view expressed by Webster J., who had to consider the interaction of several banks in *Royal Products Ltd v. Midland Bank Ltd*,[51] that the relationships between banks are governed by the rules of agency rather than by the law of negotiable instruments[52] or the rules on assignment,[53] helps to cast some light on the questions. In this case, the judge had to consider the roles of the paying bank and of correspondent banks in a funds transfer transaction. The facts were that the plaintiffs were customers of Midland bank, whom they instructed to transfer funds by cable to an account they held at the Bank of Industry, Commerce and Agriculture (BICAL) in Malta. Midland cabled National Bank, its correspondent in Malta, to pay the money to BICAL. National knew that BICAL was in difficulties, but had been informed by the Central Bank of Malta that it would be open on the following day, and National therefore credited the money to a suspense account in the name of BICAL. However, as it turned out, BICAL ceased **12–022**

[47] Under the principle of *Clarke v. Dunraven* [1897] A.C. 59.

[48] Unlike the position in the USA, for example, where Article 4A of the Uniform Commercial Code takes a "segmented" approach: Geva, in *Cross-Border Electronic Banking: Challenges and Opportunities*, p. 21.

[49] *ibid.*

[50] See King (1982) 45 M.L.R. 369.

[51] [1981] Com. L.R. 93.

[52] It was held in *The Brimnes* [1973] 1 All E.R. 769 that a funds transfer instruction in the form of a telex could not be regarded as a negotiable instrument; and see Ellinger [1986] L.M.C.L.Q. 178 (and Ellinger and Lomnicka, *Modern Banking Law* (2nd ed.)), who demonstrates that money transfer orders do not conform to the requirements of s.3 of the BOEA 1882, because they are not "payable on demand", and, at least in the case of bank giro credits, are not "payable to the order of a specified person or bearer" or expressed as a formal instruction by the payer to the transferring bank.

[53] The question whether the instruction could amount to an assignment of the funds concerned was considered by the Jack Committee in the context of giro transfers. It concluded that it was not an assignment, see below, para. 14–105.

business the following day. The plaintiffs were unable to retrieve their money and claimed it on the grounds (amongst others) that their instructions had not been carried out, that the National were their agents and were in breach of their duty of care to them, and that the Midland itself owed them a duty of care and was liable for National's negligence.

12–023 The judge considered the roles of the banks in the transaction and the function of the payment instruction given to the National bank. The Midland bank, first, was the *paying bank*, and was acting as an agent for the customer.[54] The customer's instruction was to be regarded:

> "simply as an authority and instruction from a customer to its bank, to transfer an amount standing to the credit of that customer with that bank to the credit of its account with another bank, that other bank being impliedly authorized by the customer to accept that credit by virtue of the fact that the customer has a current account with it, no consent to the receipt of the credit being expected from or required of that other bank, by virtue of the same fact."[55]

12–024 In this case, the bank was held to be providing this service as part of its normal banking operations, since no separate fee was charged. The payment instruction was simply an instruction to transfer money standing to the credit of one account of the customer to that of another; as far as the customer was concerned, it was similar to a transfer which was carried out within the bank or between two branches of the same bank. The Midland owed the customer a duty of care and might be liable vicariously for the breach of that duty by any servant or agent to whom it delegated the carrying out of the instructions.

The National, the *correspondent bank*, had acted as the agents of Midland, but not of the plaintiffs. The plaintiffs, as Midland's customers, had not given Midland any authority which would have had the effect of creating privity of contract between themselves and National.[56] National therefore did not owe the plaintiffs a duty of care. In principle, the plaintiffs might have been able to claim against *Midland*, as their agent, which might be liable for any breach of duty by National, as a bank to which it had delegated the carrying out of its instructions, but the judge found here that there was no evidence of any breach of duty by National.

12–025 It seems therefore that a customer in the United Kingdom[57] wishing to claim for the negligence of a correspondent bank would normally have an

[54] If a bank transmits a funds transfer order for a person who is not a customer, as may sometimes happen in giro payments, for example, it may have no privity of contract and therefore owe no duty of care (unless in tort) to the payer. It may also run the risk of losing its protection under s.4 of the Cheques Act 1957, for which it must be acting "for a customer".

[55] [1981] Com. L.R. 93 at 198.

[56] See Vroegop (1990) L.M.C.L.Q. 547, who argues that an exception to the privity rule should be created. This may have been achieved by statute: the Contracts (Rights of Third Parties) Act 1999.

[57] The position is different in the USA: see Ellinger, *op. cit.*

action only against his or her own bank, and only for its own negligence (if that can be shown) and not against the correspondent bank directly.[58] Banks normally exclude liability for the negligence of their correspondent banks, however, and it may be that the only practicable means of establishing a claim would be either to show that the paying bank had been negligent in its selection of the correspondent—which is unlikely to succeed if a reputable bank is chosen—or to establish that the exclusion clause itself is unreasonable under the UCTA 1977 or unfair under the UTCCR 1999.

A "money-back guarantee" to refund payers making cross-border credit transfers has been introduced by the Cross-Border Credit Transfer Regulations 1999.[59] Banks handling cross-border credit transfers involving consumers and small and medium business enterprises where the transfers are less than 50,000 Euros in currencies of the European Union are now liable to reimburse the originator (payer) with the amount of the transfer (up to 12,500 Euros) and interest and charges if a transfer order is not credited to the account of the payee after it has been accepted by the originator's bank. The originator's bank can claim reimbursement from any correspondent bank in certain circumstances.

The position of the *receiving bank*, though it is still that of an agent, may **12–026**
be more difficult to ascertain, because it acts on the instructions of the paying bank in crediting the payee's account, but at some point becomes the payee's debtor in holding the funds. The transaction may therefore be completed as between the banks but not yet completed as between the receiving bank and the payee. In some transactions it may not be clear whether the receiving bank is acting as the payee's agent and within the payee's authority. For example, a bank may sometimes accept payment even when the payee does not know that a payment is to be made, and the bank must then be acting at the request of the payer or the payer's bank, rather than the payee. Is the payee, who may be unwilling to accept the payment, *bound* to accept it because the payment has been accepted by the bank acting as the payee's agent? It seems that the bank is acting as its customer's agent if it acts within the customer's actual or ostensible authority. If it does not, it may be that it is acting as the agent of the payer,[60] or more likely, as the sub-agent of the payer, in view of the decision in the *Royal Products* case: if there is no contractual relationship between payer and correspondent bank, it is probable that there is also no privity between payer and payee's bank. Failing a contractual remedy, the payer would have to sue in restitution[61] or tort.

[58] See also *Calico Printers' Association Ltd v. Barclays Bank Ltd* (1931) 36 Comm. Cas. 71, aff'd at 197.

[59] S.I. 1999/1876 implementing Directive 97/5/EC, Art. 8, based on UNCITRAL Model Law on International Credit Transfer (1992).

[60] Brindle and Cox, *op. cit*, para. 2.65.

[61] For money paid under a mistake. *Agip (Africa) Ltd v. Jackson* [1990] Ch. 265, aff'd [1991] Ch. 547, concerned an electronic funds transfer.

The position of the payee with regard to the paying bank is that there is no contract between them and any claim would have to be founded in tort.[62]

Legal Problems of Payment

12–027 In modern commercial transactions, payment is normally made by some kind of bank transfer of funds by paper or electronic means. As Goode says, a bank's unconditional undertaking to pay (in countries where banks are reliable) is regarded as the equivalent of cash.[63] It is important to bear in mind, though, that the transfer is accomplished, not by transferring actual currency, but simply by the banks making debits or credits in the appropriate accounts, and by striking a balance at the end of the day between the total of amounts transferred amongst themselves (or by settling accounts in real time).[64] It causes confusion to think of bank payments as real *transfers*, since intangible money, unlike cash, does not pass by delivery.[65]

Two separate but linked problems cause particular difficulty when electronic payment methods are used. The first—which mostly affects the customer in relation to the bank—is the question of countermand, and the second—which often concerns banks—is the question of completion of payment.

Countermand

12–028 Customers have long had the right (as a matter of banking practice and of law[66]) to have second thoughts and stop the payment of a cheque, provided it is practicable to do so. Cheque clearing, however, is relatively lengthy—it takes three or four days—and lends itself to the possibility of countermand.[67] Other, newer, payment systems do not usually allow a similar lengthy period during which a payment can be stopped.

At what point in the process of payment in the different systems does payment become irrevocable? The latest possible point would obviously be when payment is completed, but it may well be at some point before that.

---

[62] *Hedley Byrne v. Heller* [1964] A.C. 465, under the principle of assumption of responsibility, as explained by *Henderson v. Merrett Syndicates Ltd* [1995] 2 A.C. 145; see above, Chap. 5.

[63] See also *Mardorf Co. v. Attica Corpn.* [1977] A.C. 850 at 879, *per* Lord Salmon: "Payment orders are regarded in the banking world as the equivalent of cash", although Lord Fraser of Tullybelton said: "that only means that the payment order was something on which a member bank could safely rely and act" (at 884).

[64] See above, para. 12–015.

[65] It is probably more accurate to speak in terms of the transfer of *value* from payer to payee—Encyclopaedia of Banking Law, DI (303).

[66] The mandate of the bank which acts as agent of the customer is withdrawn by the countermand; and see BOEA 1882, s. 75.

[67] Though the customer may not countermand a cheque when a cheque guarantee card has been used with the cheque, because the bank's obligation arises as soon as the card is used.

The system may be governed by express contracts which provide for countermand: BACS, for example, which operates a three day cycle, allows for countermand, which must be made to BACS through a member bank not directly by the customer. It must be received by BACS before 11 a.m. on the second day of the clearing cycle.[68] A CHAPS payment message used to be considered irrevocable once there had been an acknowledgement[69] (which is automatic and built into the process) by the paying bank (although this may now have changed).[70]

The Jack Committee took the view that problems with countermand can be dealt with pragmatically. As long as the time when the payment becomes irrevocable is made clear, the actual time allowed to the debtor for stopping the payment is not particularly important. Still less is it vital to have one uniform rule as to when payment is complete for all different systems; given the variety of systems, that would be unnecessarily rigid. The Committee recommended simply that the Code of Practice should require banks to make customers aware of the different countermand rules applying to payment systems.[71] The White Paper, agreeing that some explanation should be given in the Code, thought that no artificial period should be built in to systems to permit countermand; the customer may have a right to countermand, depending on the terms of the contract, but any such right is limited, and should be limited, to what is practicable within the existing rules. The Banking Code now includes the requirement that banks will provide customers with details of how their accounts operate, including information about how and when they may stop a cheque or countermand other types of payments.[72] **12–029**

An E.C. Recommendation now relates to countermand of card and electronic transactions. The holder of a product allowing for remote access to a bank account (for example payment cards and phone- and home-banking applications) or of an electronic money product (that is products through which electronic value is stored) must not countermand any order which the holder gives by means of that product, except where the amount was not determined when the order was given.[73]

[68] Brindle and Cox, *op. cit.*. para. 2.66.

[69] A "Logical Acknowledgment" (LAK).

[70] Since the introduction of real time gross settlement: a message is probably irrevocable as soon as the sending bank's settlement request is received: Brindle and Cox, *op. cit.*, para. 2.66.

[71] Jack Report, Cm. 622 (1989) Rec. 12(1).

[72] Banking Code (1999), para. 2.1. Article 4 of the E.C. Directive on Settlement Finality (see below, para. 12–044) states that a payment order may not be revoked either by an institution which participates directly in a payment system or a third party as against the other direct participants in that payment system after the moment defined by the rules of that payment system.

[73] Recommendation 97/489 [1997] O.J. L208/52, Art. 5(d).

Completion of Payment

12–030 A more intractable problem, perhaps, is the question of completion of payment in the different payment systems. Despite the fact that, as the Jack Committee noted, the concept of payment is all pervasive and does not depend upon the medium of payment, there is no generally accepted legal definition, either in this country or overseas.[74]

A number of factors contribute to make this an important and general problem:

- problems can arise in several different contexts—on the insolvency of a bank; in cases of fraud; in a dispute whether a payment has been made on the contractual date of payment, or where there is a system error or failure;
- a great deal of money frequently depends upon the decision: if a bank crashes, for example, the answer to the question whether payment has been completed will affect many large payments;
- in view of the enormous number of international funds transfers, it is highly desirable to have limits which are consistent with those of other jurisdictions.

Whereas banking practice and the convenience of both banks and their customers may be the deciding considerations for the question of countermand, therefore, the decision as to whether a payment has been completed should if possible depend upon general principles, and only secondarily upon considerations of banking practice.

12–031 Goode's view, which is supported by the decided cases, and which was favoured by the Jack Committee is:

> "payment could be regarded as complete at the point where the payee's bank (or its agent in the clearing), having actual or ostensible authority to accept payment on behalf of the payee, accepts a transfer of funds from the paying bank (or its agent in the clearing) for the payee's account—provided that the transfer is or has become unconditional."[75]

In most cases, difficulties are resolved by contractual provisions, either between the two relevant parties or by the terms of the general contract

[74] Jack Report, Cm. 622 (1989), para. 12.14.

[75] Goode, *Payment Obligations in Commercial and Financial Transactions*, and *Commercial Law*, p. 512, where it is expressed as "payment by the debtor to the creditor becomes complete at the moment when the creditor's bank unconditionally accepts that the creditor is its creditor for the amount in question". The principle where both parties bank at the same bank is the same, and the difference is merely that the transaction is entirely in-house and does not involve any clearing process, any payment order or any correspondent relationship.

governing the system involved. Even so, problems still arise; in charterparty cases, for example, where payment of the hire has to be made by a certain contractual date (the "value" date), and there is dispute as to whether the payment has been completed by that date. The desire for strict performance in these cases may often of course be connected with the fact that market conditions may have made the bargain less satisfactory for the payee, who would prefer not to continue the contract. The courts, for reasons of commercial certainty and predictability,[76] tend to emphasise the importance of strictly observing the terms of the contract.

In *The Brimnes*,[77] the question was whether the payment of hire under a charterparty had been made before the value date, either by a telex instruction to credit the owners' account or by the bank's decision to credit the owners' account; and, if by the latter, whether the notice of withdrawal had arrived before the credit had been made. The court rejected the argument that payment had been made by the telex itself operating as a negotiable instrument, and held that the payment was made when the decision was taken to credit the owners' account (and debit the paying bank's account). This had occurred at some time during a specified hour on the relevant day, but probably after the charterers had received the notice of withdrawal. But the court held that in any event the owners were entitled to withdraw the vessel because the charterers had not made the payment in time. **12–032**

In the case of *The Laconia,*[78] the House of Lords had to consider whether the owners of a ship, who had refused a late payment of hire as soon as they were informed that it had been made, had a right to withdraw the ship. The question was whether the fact that a payment had been received or accepted *by the bank* constituted payment to the owners. The House held that the bank had only a limited authority to act on behalf of the owners.[79] It was acting "ministerially"—without any intention or capacity to affect legal relations with third parties—and could not have rejected the payment out of hand; it was therefore provisionally processing the payment while seeking the owners' directions. The owners had a right to refuse the payment once it had not been made punctually, although they might waive the default if they chose to accept the late payment, or if they did not give notice within a reasonable time that they had rejected it.[80] Here the **12–033**

[76] *A/S Awilco of Oslo v. Fulvia SpA di Navigazione of Cagliari, The Chikuma* [1981] 1 W.L.R. 314.

[77] *Tenax Steamship Co. Ltd v. The Brimnes (Owners)* [1973] 1 W.L.R. 386; affd [1975] 1 Q.B. 929. See also *Zim Israel Navigation Co Ltd v. Effy Shipping Corporation, The Effy* [1972] Lloyd's L.R. 19.

[78] *Mardorf Peach & Co v. Attica Sea Carriers Corp.*[1977] A.C. 850.

[79] Although in some circumstances, as perhaps in *The Brimnes*, bankers may have authority to accept late payments (*per* Lord Wilberforce).

[80] See *TSB Bank of Scotland Ltd v. Welwyn Hatfield District Council* [1993] 2 Bank L.R. 267, where a local authority knowingly retained a payment for three weeks in its account and used it. It could not claim that payment had not been completed because it had dealt with the money as its own.

payment order was refused and was reversed the next day by a counter order. The receipt of the money by the bank could not in itself operate as a waiver of the right of withdrawal, and nor could the actions of processing of the payment by the bank, which were "private acts internal to the bank... not communicated to the charterers",[81] and in any case did not demonstrate a final decision by the bank. The bank was simply the nominated place at which the hire could be paid.

12–034 It seems, therefore, that the bank may be regarded as accepting a payment on its customer's behalf if it has authority to do so; when it has such authority, the payment is made when the bank has decided to accept the payment, provided that the decision by the bank to accept is unconditional. However, if the bank has no actual or implied authority to accept the payment, it cannot be said to be accepted until the customer knows of it and accepts it.[82] What amounts to authority must depend on the circumstances and on the practice of banks.

The question of whether the decision by the bank is *unconditional* came up in *The Chikuma,*[83] where the contract stated that payment must be made in cash. It was held that the date of payment (by an Italian bank) was the date of the "value date" when interest would accrue, not the date, several days earlier, when the funds became available to the owners, because until the value date, payment was not unconditional: the fact that no interest could be paid on it meant that it was not equivalent to cash.

12–035 The formulation that it is the unconditional decision of the bank, within its authority, to accept the payment does not necessarily resolve all the difficulties. It can still be impossible to state exactly at what stage during the banking process the decision to accept the funds was taken and to decide what actions by the bank demonstrate that the bank has taken its decision to accept the payment; sometimes this may be before the payment is credited unconditionally to the payee's account.[84] For example, in *The Brimnes*, the decision by the bank to debit one account and credit the other constituted the payment, but it was not possible to decide precisely when the decision was taken, although it was probably made during one specific hour.

---

[81] [1977] A.C. 850 at 886, *per* Lord Fraser of Tullybelton.

[82] It seems therefore that in the case of *Rekstin v. Severo Sibirsko Gosudarstvennoe Akcionernoe Obstchestvo Komseverputj* [1933] 1 K.B. 47, where it was held that a payment could not have been received until its arrival had been communicated to the customer, the bank had had no authority to accept the payment. *Momm* [1977] 1 Q.B. 790 at 800, *per* Kerr J., described the facts of *Rekstin* as "very unusual", and said that not only had there been no final appropriation to the credit of the relevant account, but the payees "knew nothing of the proposed transfer, that there was no transaction . . . underlying it, and that the delegation had accordingly never assented" to the credit. (See also Webster J. in *Royal Products Ltd v. Midland Bank* [1981] 2 Lloyd's Rep. 194 at 199.)

[83] *A/S Awilco of Oslo v. Fulvia SpA di Navigazione of Cagliari, The Chikuma* [1981] 1 W.L.R. 314.

[84] See Geva [1990] J.I.B.L. 108.

However, the case of *Momm v. Barclays Bank International*,[85] which dealt with an in-house transfer of funds, is helpful in providing a further test. (In-house transactions are particularly interesting, because there is no movement of funds between banks, and the different roles of the bank are blurred; this means that analysis requires decisions of principle—about *when* completion has taken place, for example[86]). *Momm* concerned a German bank, Herstatt, which had agreed to transfer money in sterling to the plaintiffs. Herstatt instructed a London branch of the defendants to transfer the money to the account of the plaintiffs, who also had an account at that branch. After the money had actually been credited to the plaintiffs' account and debited from Herstatt's account, the Herstatt bank failed. The payment was processed by computer during the night, and on the following morning Barclays, who had not informed the plaintiffs of the entries in their accounts, cancelled the entries and reversed them, as the bank occasionally did with in-house payments. In these circumstances, Kerr J. held that commerce requires that it should be clearly ascertainable by the end of a day whether a payment due on that day has been made or not. The transaction in this case had been completed on the day when the defendants had accepted the instructions to credit the plaintiffs' account. The defendants were not entitled to reverse the transaction the next day. In coming to the conclusion that the bank had completed the payment by then—and without making any communication to the payee—the judge said that the reaction of both lawyers and bankers would be that payment had been made by the end of the day. He went on: **12–036**

> "I think that both would say two things. First, that in such circumstances a payment has been made if the payee's account is credited with the payment at the close of business on the value date, at any rate if it was credited intentionally and in good faith and not by error or fraud. Secondly, I think they would say that if a payment requires to be made on a certain day by debiting a payor customer's account and crediting a payee customer's account, then the position at the end of that day in fact and in law must be that this has either happened or not happened, but that the position cannot be left in the air. In my view, both these propositions are correct in law".[87]

The statement gives a measure of certainty, although it may not settle the whole question. Much depends, as in *The Brimnes*, on the facts and on the practice of banks. Not only are the details of a complex series of **12–037**

[85] [1977] 1 Q.B. 790. See also *Libyan Arab Foreign Bank v. Manufacturers' Hanover Trust Co (No. 2)* [1989] 1 Lloyd's L.R. 609.

[86] See Goode, *Payment Obligations in Commercial and Financial Transactions*, p. 116, cited in *Sutherland* [1997] Bank. L.R. 132 Sc. at 140.

[87] [1977] 1 Q.B. 790 at 799–800.

transactions difficult to establish with certainty but the technology is constantly changing. The relevance of technological development was considered by the court with reference to the *Momm* case, in another first instance decision, *Sutherland v. Royal Bank of Scotland*.[88] In *Sutherland*, two cheques were issued payable to Mr and Mrs Sutherland, customers of the bank, on the account of the company of which Mr Sutherland was a director. Since the account of the company was held at the same branch, the transaction was an "in-house" one. Mr Sutherland paid the cheques, together amounting to more than £17,000, into the Sutherlands' account, and withdrew £10,000 from the account in cash. On the same day, the cheques were paid and the sums were credited to their account and debited to the company account. On the next day, the bank discovered that a receiver had been appointed for the company, and it promptly reversed the entries. The customers disputed the reversing of the entries, claiming (relying on *Momm*) that payment was complete as soon as some executive action to process the transaction was taken, or in other words, when the book-keeping entries had been made by the bank. The bank argued that that would mean, at least unless the pursuers could show some *decision* to pay which was reflected in the entries, that the accounting entries would be equivalent to payment, which could not be right.

12–038 The case came before Lord Penrose, who distinguished the present practice of banks from that obtaining at the time of *Momm*. Although by 1974 (the time of *Momm*), banking payment systems had been computerised, he said, the method was relatively cumbersome. In particular, it required punched cards prepared in the branch to be sent to the bank's central computer to be fully processed overnight. Ledger sheets would be produced for each customer for dispatch back to the branch in the morning. The result of this was in practice that the branch would only have a complete picture of any customer's account on the day following the transaction. This differed from the previous manual system, where the bank could be flexible during the day, and could reverse entries if necessary when accounts were reviewed before the close of banking hours on that same day; decisions could be made by the bank without the customer knowing and without any reversal of entries appearing on the statement. It would therefore be clear whether a payment had been made by the end of the day. Banks' practice, however, has changed again. The "cumbersome procedures" described in *Momm* have been replaced by on-line and networked computer systems, which enable a bank to review the whole spectrum of transactions continuously during the day, just as a branch would have done under the old manual system. The judge thought that the accounting entries were not themselves conclusive of payment: the important consideration

88 [1997] 6 Bank. L.R. 132, Sc. The issue had been considered by the Banking Ombudsman, who decided in favour of the customers, but the bank withdrew it, with his consent, and referred it as a test case (the first one) to the courts.

was *when* the bank decided to pay, and the entries would merely be an important stage in the completion of transactions where the decision has already been taken. The entries cannot be divorced from the surrounding circumstances. The question was whether the bank was irretrievably committed to give effect to the transaction, where it was beyond the power of the branch to alter the treatment of the transaction on the critical day.

The effect of *Momm*, according to the judge, was that for a time the right which banks had formerly had to alter book-keeping entries was limited. Although the judge endorsed the proposition in *Momm* that it should be clearly ascertainable by the end of the day whether a payment due to be made on that day was in fact made, it might be that for some reason the decision could be made on the following day. Here, it was possible (not decided, because the facts of the case were still to be established) that there had been some inadvertency by the bank which would allow the bank under the rules of the clearing house to reverse the payment on the following day. **12–039**

The decision shows the importance of banking practice to the question of principle. Arguably, though, it ignores the commercial need for coming to a clear and workable line signifying completion of payment, which *Momm* had provided. It may, therefore, give opportunity for further, perhaps unnecessary, doubts—and therefore litigation—about the rules. **12–040**

View of the Jack Committee

The Jack Committee recognised that the terms of the contract governing the payment system often provide for completion of payment, but nevertheless concluded that a legal definition of completion of payment would be highly desirable in order to give a basis of certainty where no other provision existed, and recommended that it should be enshrined in primary legislation, with the addition that the rules should be subject to modification by contract by the parties.[89] As regards the terms of the definition, the Committee favoured Goode's "authoritative view" set out above. **12–041**

The payment would generally be complete when a transfer of funds in the books of one bank has taken place.[90] Where a transfer is between two accounts at the same bank, payment should be regarded as complete when the bank has taken the decision to treat the instructions for transfer as irrevocable. There would be no necessity, on this formulation, for the receiving bank to have actually credited the account of its customer, although, if it had, that would amount to objective evidence that the decision to accept the transfer had been made. Similarly, informing the customer that the transfer had been made would be evidence of the decision, not a necessary act to complete the payment. **12–042**

[89] Jack Report, Cm. 622 (1989), Rec. 12(2).

[90] Which, in the case of settlement members of the clearing, would happen between accounts at the Bank of England.

12–043 The Government's response to the recommendation was unenthusiastic. It considered that, although greater legal certainty was desirable, the introduction of legislation to define when a payment is complete would be premature, in view of various possible international initiatives.[91] Once the various domestic and international developments have been considered further, the Government would consider whether a working group should be convened by the Bank of England to consider the implications of the proposed definition.[92]

12–044 The Commission of the European Union has also been concerned about completion of payment in order to encourage effective cross-border payment systems, which it regards as essential to the smooth functioning of the internal market. A Directive on settlement finality[93] was adopted by the European Parliament and Council in 1998, Article 5 of which states that a payment order may not be revoked either by an institution which participates directly in a payment system, or a third party as against the other direct participants in that payment system after the moment defined by the rules of that payment system. Member States will therefore, it seems, be required to fix some definite point after which the payment may not be revoked.

Other legal problems connected with electronic payments

12–045 To a considerable extent, the electronic funds transfer systems involve the same or similar risks to the participating banks as occur when acting on a conventional payment authorisation (for example, as embodied in a cheque or credit transfer instruction). No doubt rules of existing law can be used to resolve many of the problems which may arise from the nature of an electronic transfer of funds[94] but the courts may have to adapt the law to the new payments methods. However, both technology and the contractual arrangements concerned are becoming increasingly sophisticated—for example, some would say that the new systems are in many ways more secure and reliable than traditional paper methods,[95] and the contractual

[91] *e.g.* the UNCITRAL Working Group on International Payments.

[92] Cm. 1026, para. 7.13ff.

[93] Directive on Settlement Finality in Payment and Securities Settlement Systems, 98/26 EC. Introduced to reduce the risk of settlements unravelling (and possible systemic failure) because of the approach of some of the Member States to netting and to reduce disruption by insolvency proceedings against a participant in a payment or securities settlement system. "Netting" or set-off means the conversion into one net claim or one net obligation of claims resulting from payment orders with the result that only the net claim can be demanded or the net obligation be owed. It greatly reduces the number of settlement transactions needed to process a number of payments. The Directive also applies to real time gross settlement payment systems (like CHAPS). It relates to both debit and credit transfers.

[94] *e.g.*, Cheques Act 1957, s. 4, which provides protection for a bank which in good faith and without negligence collects payment for a customer who has no title or a defective title to an instrument, seems to extend to credit transfers, since it applies to any document issued by a customer of a banker which, though not a bill of exchange, is intended to enable a person to obtain payment from that banker of the sum mentioned in the document, Cheques Act 1957 s. 4(2)(b).

[95] See Andrews, in *Cross-Border Electronic Banking*, at p.76, who points out that the "tendency is to assume that, in establishing a computer based system, all risks must be dealt with in a highly secure manner . . . partners try to plug security gaps that were never plugged before".

arrangements governing the electronic systems include detailed measures to protect security and cover the risks involved, and are normally made between large commercial parties (individual consumers are not concerned), where there is no particular imbalance of negotiating power. For these reasons, there may be less reason for the introduction of specific legislation dealing with payment than in some other fields.

Specific legal issues which may have to be resolved in connection with new forms of payment are considered below, in Chapter 15.

Chapter 13

Negotiable Instruments

The law of negotiable instruments[1] looks unfamiliar to those accustomed to English common law. Not only is the language of the law difficult for modern students, but the concepts on which the law is based are unfamiliar, although we are comfortable enough with the practical application of the ideas in everyday life: we pass bank notes around, for example, without thinking twice about the sophistication of the medium we are using. Negotiable instruments have evolved from the custom and practice of merchants, recognised by the common law rather than part of it, and the law seems technical. Nevertheless, the basic principles are coherent and, as regards bills of exchange, have been consolidated with consistency and clarity in the BOEA 1882.[2] Bills of exchange have remained important commercially, particularly in international trade, and their principles underpin the law of cheques and are woven into the law and practice of banking. An understanding of negotiable instruments is still important for bankers and banking law students. **13–001**

Instruments

An instrument is a document which embodies in physical form an obligation to pay. It may be called a documentary intangible, which is a type of *chose in action*; this means that the obligation is only enforceable by taking legal action, not by taking possession of the property, as one might do with a tangible or corporeal thing (a *chose in possession*). The *holder* of the instrument however is entitled to claim payment, by action if necessary, and may pass the instrument to another holder by delivery and, where appropriate, indorsement (signature); there is no need for any formal assignment or for notice to the debtor. Not all documents amount to instruments; what is recognised in law as an instrument at any one time may be difficult to determine and depends on mercantile usage and statute. The functions of such documents vary, but they are usually connected with financial obligations.[3] **13–002**

---

[1] There are a number of authoritative works on the subject: see Chalmers and Guest on *Bills of Exchange*, and Byles, *Bills of Exchange*. See also Chaps 18 and 19 in Goode, *Commercial Law* (2nd ed.); and James, *Richardson's Guide to Negotiable Instruments* (8th ed., 1991), an admirably clear introductory text. Professor Shea provided a detailed analysis and assessment of the law in a consultation paper for the Jack Committee (Cm. 622 (1989) App. A).

[2] By Sir Mackenzie Chalmers.

[3] Not all—see Shea, *op. cit.*, para. 2.6.

Negotiable Instruments

13–003 An instrument which does not merely embody a claim to payment but can give a holder a better claim to payment than the previous holder is called a *negotiable* instrument.[4] This is the distinctive characteristic of negotiability. Negotiation must be distinguished from *transfer*. If the instrument is merely transferred, the transferee cannot obtain a better title than his or her predecessor.

In many transactions negotiable instruments take the place of cash and they have many of the characteristics of cash.[5] They express the obligation they represent with certainty and accuracy; they are short and easily comprehensible[6]; they are easily transferable, and a person giving value for a negotiable instrument and receiving it in good faith may obtain an unchallengeable title to the instrument—in other words, may become a *bona fide transferee for value*, having full legal title to the document and the rights which it represents—even though the transferor's title is defective; even if, for example, it has been obtained by fraud.

13–004 And, like cash, negotiable instruments have another great advantage for the holder: the transaction is *autonomous*—that is to say, independent of the underlying transaction. While the instrument is current, the underlying transaction is suspended and is only revived if the instrument is dishonoured. This means that the holder of the document, having a right to sue on the document itself, has the advantage of being able to take summary proceedings[7] on it so that no inquiry need be made into the rights and wrongs of the underlying contract.[8] In a claim on a bill of exchange or cheque the court will refuse to take into account any counterclaim or set off[9] arising on the underlying transaction unless there are "truly exceptional circumstances".[10] The recipient therefore has confidence that he or she is receiving or will receive full value.

13–005 Although defences relating to the underlying contract normally have no place in proceedings concerning the instrument, there are defences available on the separate contract formed by the transaction on the instrument

[4] An exception to the principle *nemo dat quod non habet* (one does not give what one does not have).

[5] Negotiable instruments are not legal tender. Coinage Act 1971: gold coins (made by the Mint) are legal tender for any amount; other coins for stated amounts; Currency and Bank Notes Act 1954, amended by the Currency Act 1983: bank notes issued by the Bank of England in England and Wales are legal tender.

[6] See Goode, *op. cit.*, p. 518; Shea, *op. cit.*, para. 2.10.

[7] Under Order 14 of the Rules of the Supreme Court.

[8] Shea lists the implications: the underlying obligation is reduced to a certainty (no unquantified claim to damages), the evidence is reduced; burden of proof of payment is transferred to the defendant; counterclaims are excluded (Shea, *op. cit.*, para. 2.2 D).

[9] *Nova (Jersey) Knit Ltd v. Kammgarn Spinnerei GmbH* [1977] 1 W.L.R. 713.

[10] *Cebora S.N.C. v. S.I.P. (Industrial Products Ltd* [1976] 1 Lloyd's Rep. 271 at 278–279, *per* Sir Eric Sachs. He added that the court should be really careful not to whittle away the rule of practice by introducing unnecessary exceptions to it under the influence of sympathy-evoking stories.

itself such as fraud or illegality[11] or failure of consideration. The courts also have a discretion to order a stay of execution in an action on a bill, but it will very rarely be exercised and usually only in disputes between immediate parties to the bill.[12]

There are many varieties of documents traded in the world's money markets for which negotiability is claimed.[13] Documents are recognised as negotiable instruments by mercantile usage[14]; they include bank notes, bills of exchange and cheques (which are a type of bill of exchange), bearer bonds, debentures payable to bearer, dividend and interest warrants, share warrants payable to bearer, certificates of deposit, Treasury bills and bankers' drafts. Instruments which are not negotiable include postal orders, child benefit orders, money orders, registered share certificates, registered debentures, letters of allotment, insurance policies and documents of title to goods such as bills of lading. Promissory notes[15] are negotiable instruments and are governed by the BOEA 1882, but they differ from bills of exchange in that they constitute a promise by one person to pay another, rather than an order to someone else (like a bank) to pay the other.

Bills of Exchange

Bills of exchange are an important type of negotiable instrument, **13–006**
although their importance in domestic transactions has reduced drastically since the corresponding increase in the use of cheques. Both are regulated by the BOEA 1882, although there are a number of other statutory provisions relating specifically to cheques, as will be seen in the next Chapter. Bills are still of vital importance, however, in international trade, where they may be called "acceptances".[16] The Jack Committee recommended a number of detailed changes to the provisions of the BOEA 1882, including the introduction of a new "Negotiable Instruments Act".[17] The

---

[11] BOEA 1882, s. 30(2): "fraud, duress, or force and fear, or illegality".

[12] See *Jade International Steel Stahl und Eisen GmbH v. Robert Nicholas (Steels) Ltd* [1978] 3 W.L.R. 39.

[13] See Jack Report, Cm. 622 (1989), para. 8.04 and Shea, *op. cit.*

[14] Which may give rise to uncertainty until the custom is acknowledged by the courts, *Goodwin v. Robarts* (1876) 1 App. Cas. 476; see Holden, *The History of Negotiable Instruments in English Law*. In *Kum v. Wah Tet Bank Ltd* [1971] 1 Lloyd's Rep. 439 at 444, Lord Devlin said: "There must be proof in the first place that the custom is generally accepted by those who habitually do business in the trade or market concerned. Moreover, the custom must be so generally known that an outsider who makes reasonable enquiries could not fail to be made aware of it. The size of the market or the extent of the trade affected is neither here nor there."

[15] Bank notes are a form of promissory note, although an odd one, because the Bank of England is no longer bound to pay its notes in gold coin (Gold Standard Act 1925, s. 1(2)), so that the holder will merely receive other notes in payment (see Goode, *Commercial Law*, pp. 491 and 519).

[16] See Shea, *op. cit.*, para. 2.1.

[17] With the caveat that the present Act "is so well drafted and is so clear, concise and well understood by those who use it, that its language and style should as far as possible be retained in the new statute" Jack Report, Cm. 622 (1989), para. 8.06.

Government decided that there was no need for a new Act at present, but that it would introduce some of the recommendations (with regard to "avals" for example, legislation on dematerialised instruments and notice of dishonour by electronic communication) when time permits.[18]

Definition

13–007 A bill of exchange is defined by section 3(1) of the BOEA 1882, as:

> "an unconditional order in writing, addressed by one person to another, signed by the person giving it, requiring the person to whom it is addressed to pay on demand or at a fixed or determinable future time a sum certain in money to or to the order of a specified person, or to bearer".

13–008 The definition sets out the requirements in a nutshell, and therefore provides the best focus for explanation and analysis. It may be helpful to start by describing the parties in the straightforward type of transaction:

> a bill is an order by *one person* to *another*, requiring that person to pay money to a *third person*, or to bearer.

The order is written and signed by A (the *drawer*), and is usually addressed to his or her bank (B) (the *drawee*). B is instructed to pay C (the *payee*) money. B (the bank) may pay out of A's account, and, when it does so, it discharges its debt to A to the extent of the payment made to C.

These are the bare bones of the transaction. The issues are expanded below.

13–009 **Acceptance.** The drawee, B (the bank here), will probably be asked to *accept* the bill as well as pay it. If B accepts the bill by signing it, he or she will take primary responsibility for its payment. Cheques, however, are not usually accepted; the bank merely acts as drawee and is not therefore liable to the payee for the money (although it may breach its contractual duty to A, its customer, if it does not pay on his or her instructions).

13–010 **Negotiation.** A bill may order the payment to be made at some future date, and the payee, C, may not wish to wait until the date of its maturity and may prefer to sell it to someone else, probably at a discount. A bill which has been accepted by a reliable person or institution, such as a bank, will provide assurance of payment at maturity, and C will be able to negotiate its sale (which will almost certainly be at a discount because ready money is given for a right of payment in the future) to another person, D.

[18] Cm. 1026, Annex 6.

Order or to bearer. If the bill is payable to *order* (A will have specified that payment should be made to C or to order), C will have to indorse (sign) the bill to D to give a good title. C then becomes the first *indorser* of the bill and D becomes *indorsee* or *holder*. If he or she has taken in good faith and for value and the bill itself is in order, D will become *holder in due course* (the holder in due course obtains title free of any equities—the equivalent of *bona fide purchaser for value*). D may in turn sign the bill and deliver it to E, and it may be passed from E to another and so on. When the bill matures, the current holder will be entitled to receive payment, either from B, the acceptor, or from one of the other parties. **13–011**

If the bill is a *bearer* bill (that is, it is not payable to any specified person), there is even less difficulty about negotiation, because the right to payment passes with the physical possession of the bill: it vests in the person who is the current holder without any need for indorsement. This means that even a thief will be able to obtain payment from the acceptor on such a bill.

Accommodation Party. A person who adds his or her name to the bill in order to *accommodate* a friend (usually) gratuitously is called an accommodation party, and is liable to a holder for value (even though the holder knows he or she is an accommodation party), but has the defences open to the party accommodated.[19] Since the accommodation party has not given value, however, he or she is not primarily liable for the bill, and payment by the drawer also discharges it. **13–012**

The Form of the Bill

The definition given in section 3 of the BOEA 1882 includes a number of other requirements that a bill must satisfy: it must be unconditional, in writing, signed by the drawer, it may be payable on demand or at "a fixed or determinable future time" and the amount must be certain in money. These requirements are discussed below. If the document does not satisfy all of these, it will not amount to a bill of exchange and the transferee will not obtain all the rights granted on the negotiation of a negotiable instrument, although the document may still have some limited legal effect; a conditional instrument may be valid and lawful evidence of the debt or the legal rights it invokes, and the rights embodied in the instrument may be assignable. **13–013**

Unconditional order. This means that there must be no qualification which would make payment uncertain or give rise to cumbersome inquiries.[20] For this reason, a bill which specified "pay C when he passes his exams" would **13–014**

---

[19] BOEA 1882, s. 28. This type of transaction is woven into the stories of Trollope's *Framley Parsonage* and *Phineas Finn*.

[20] "Unless they are to be treated as unconditionally payable instruments . . . which the seller can negotiate for cash, the seller might give credit", *Nova (Jersey) Knit Ltd v. Kammgarn Spinnerei GmbH* [1977] 2 All E.R. 713 at 721, *per* Lord Wilberforce.

not be valid even if C did pass his exams; one which said "pay C's estate on C's death" however, would be—death is not uncertain, although the time at which it happens, of course, is.

An instrument which requires as a condition of payment the signing of a receipt by the payee on the front or reverse of the document is not a negotiable instrument. In *Bavins and Sims v. London and South Western Bank*[21] the plaintiff received an instrument in the form of a cheque which read: "Pay to . . . provided the receipt form at the foot is duly signed and dated". The instrument was stolen from the plaintiff, an indorsement forged on it and the receipt form signed. In an action by the plaintiff against the collecting bank, it was held that the instrument was not a cheque; it depended upon the receipt being signed and was not therefore an unconditional order.

13–015 Where, however, the condition or requirement embodied in the cheque is not to be fulfilled by the drawee bank, but is a direction addressed to the *payee*, the order is unconditional for the purposes of the Act. In *Nathan v. Ogden*[22] a cheque drawn in the ordinary form contained a clause requiring a receipt on the back of the cheque to be signed by the payee. The court held that the condition requiring the payee's signature on the receipt was addressed to the payee alone, and not to the bank; consequently in this case the instrument was a cheque. Similarly in *Thairlwall v. Great Northern Railway Company*[23] a dividend warrant contained a note that it would not be honoured after three months of the date of issue. The court held that the instrument was a cheque and the note did not make the order conditional, since the words were merely a definition of what was considered a reasonable time within which the warrants were to be presented for payment, and it was in any case only a direction to the payee to present the cheque within that time.

A cheque may further provide that the instrument must be presented for payment within a certain period. This does not make the instrument conditional, but once the given period has expired, the payee cannot insist on payment of the cheque as against the drawer, although the debt represented by it still remains owing.

13–016 An order requiring payment from a particular account or fund would not be valid, because there might be inadequate funds when payment was required. An unqualified order to pay, however, coupled with an indication of a particular fund—for example, a bill worded "pay C £x and debit my savings account"—would be valid.[24]

There must be a clear *order* to pay; even if the expression of the order is courteous, it must be a requirement and not a request. In *Little v.*

---

[21] [1990] 1 Q.B. 270.
[22] [1905] 94 L.T. 126.
[23] [1910] 2 K.B. 509.
[24] BOEA 1882, s. 3(3).

Slackford[25] an instrument in the form "please to let the bearer have £7 . . . and you will oblige your humble servant . . . ," was held to be a mere request and not a demand on the bank.

In writing. Writing includes typewriting and printing,[26] although in practice this may be discouraged by banks because of the ease with which typewritten or printed cheques can be fraudulently altered. The writing does not have to be in ink, but a customer who writes a cheque by hand would probably facilitate fraud by drawing it in pencil, and might therefore be negligent; the bank would probably return it unpaid. The writing does not have to be on paper,[27] although it must not be written on metal.[28] **13–017**

Addressed by one person to another. There must be one person as drawer, and another, usually a bank, as drawee. The drawee must be named with reasonable certainty[29] and may be an individual or a company. There may be one drawee or joint drawees, but not drawees in the alternative or in succession.[30] **13–018**

If the drawer and drawee are the same person, the holder may treat the instrument either as a bill of exchange or a promissory note.[31] Since the head office and branches of a bank constitute one legal entity, a *banker's draft*, which is drawn by one branch of a bank on another branch, is not a cheque, because it is not addressed by one person to another, but is a form of promissory note.

Signed by the drawer. A bill or cheque, to be a valid instrument, must be signed by the person giving it (the drawer) or a person authorised by him or her. The instrument is not complete until the drawer has signed it, so that a cheque form which is otherwise complete is not a valid cheque until signed by the drawer or his or her agent. The "mark" of a person who is illiterate is a satisfactory signature. Under the BOEA 1882[32] an agent or official of an organisation may have the power to draw cheques on behalf of the organisation. In the case of large companies and corporations it may be possible, after giving an indemnity to the bank, to draw instruments in the form of cheques which bear a printed facsimile reproduction of the signature of one of its officials. **13–019**

A forged signature or one given without authority makes the bill invalid, although in certain circumstances a person may nevertheless incur liability on it.[33]

[25] (1829) 1 M. & M. 171.
[26] BOEA 1882, s. 2.
[27] See above, para. 6–023.
[28] Coinage Act 1870, s. 5.
[29] BOEA 1882, s. 6(1).
[30] BOEA 1882, s. 6(2).
[31] BOEA 1882, s. 5.
[32] BOEA 1882, s. 91(1).
[33] See below, paras 13–036 and 18–063 *et seq.*

13–020 **To pay on demand.** A bill is payable *on demand*[34]—that is, immediately—either when it is expressed to be payable, or when it is payable at sight or on presentation, or when no time for payment is expressed.[35] Payable *at sight* means that it is payable when it is seen for acceptance or for payment. (This differs from payable *after sight*.)[36]

13–021 **At a fixed or determinable future time.** A bill may be said to be payable at a fixed period after date or sight. If it is after sight (for example, 90 days after sight) this means that it becomes mature and therefore payable only on the day which is 90 days after acceptance or protest for non-acceptance. Similarly, if it is payable at a fixed period after an event which is bound to happen (even if the date of it is uncertain), it is valid.[37] An event which is not certain to happen, like a marriage, is a contingency, and a document specifying a contingency is not a valid bill. If acceptance of a bill is the event, for example, this is a contingency which makes the document invalid as a bill.[38]

In *Williamson v. Rider*,[39] a majority of the Court of Appeal came to the conclusion that an instrument expressed to be payable "on or before" a particular date is not valid because the phrase does not state a fixed or determinable time: the words give the payer an option to repay on any day of his choosing before the date. This strict view was followed by a later Court of Appeal in *Claydon v. Bradley*.[40]

13–022 If the bill is said to be payable at a fixed period after date, and the bill is undated, this is not fatal, because a holder may insert the "true date of issue".[41] If the wrong date is inserted, a holder in due course may still obtain payment, on the date which should have been inserted, not on the incorrect date. Dates on a bill are presumed to be correct unless the contrary is proved.[42]

A bill which is ante-dated or post-dated is not invalid,[43] and a post-dated cheque is therefore valid as a bill, though it is not a true cheque because it is not payable on demand.

13–023 **A sum certain in money.** A bill or cheque may be drawn or negotiated for any sum of money but it must be for a certain sum, which normally is

[34] A cheque must be payable on demand, BOEA 1882, s. 73. See further, Chap. 14.
[35] See below, para. 13–044.
[36] BOEA 1882, s. 10(1).
[37] BOEA 1882, s. 11.
[38] "At 90 days D/A" (which was taken to mean "90 days after acceptance") was a contingency: the Court of Appeal held that there was no maturity date: *Korea Exchange Bank Ltd v. Debenhams (Central Buying) Ltd* [1979] 1 Lloyd's Rep. 540.
[39] [1963] 1 Q.B. 89. Criticised, *Byles on Bills of Exchange*, p. 18; Hudson (1962) 25 M.L.R. 593.
[40] [1987] 1 W.L.R. 521.
[41] BOEA 1882, s. 12; similarly where a bill is to be paid at a fixed period after sight and the date of acceptance has been omitted, the holder may insert it.
[42] BOEA 1882, s. 13(1).
[43] BOEA 1882, s. 13(2).

expressed both in words and figures.[44] Section 9 of the BOEA 1882 permits the sum to be paid with interest or in instalments. An instrument which orders anything to be done in addition to the payment of money, however, is not a bill of exchange.[45]

It seems that a sum payable in "units of account"[46] would not be regarded as sufficiently certain at the time the bill is issued. The Jack Committee considered that a preferable formulation in the BOEA 1882 would be "a certain or ordinarily determinable sum", which would cover doubtful cases.[47] The White Paper accepted that the BOEA 1882 should be modified, but preferred a narrower description: "a monetary unit of account established by an inter-governmental institution".[48]

To or to the order of a specified person or bearer. A bill or cheque must specify the person who is entitled to be paid—the *payee*, who may be a particular named person, or the *bearer*, the person in possession of the instrument. If the bill is an *order bill*—for example if it states "pay A" or "pay A or order"—the person named may present the instrument for payment or may negotiate it to another person.[49] In the latter case there must be an intention to transfer the property, coupled with the delivery of the instrument. If an order bill has been made non-transferable, however, by words such as "pay A only", or "not transferable" it may not be negotiated. **13–024**

Section 7 of the BOEA 1882 requires that the payee must be named or indicated "with reasonable certainty", and it depends on the facts what this is in any particular case. It is clear, though, that the payee's full name need not be given. There may be joint payees (each must be indicated with reasonable certainty) and even alternate payees.

A bill may be payable to an office-holder, such as "The Manager of United Football Club"; but the use of an expression such as "cash" or "pay cash or order" probably means that it is not a valid cheque although it may operate perfectly well as a direction to the bank.[50] "Pay cash or order" on an instrument causes difficulties because, despite the use of the words "or order", there is no specified person, and it is not a bill or cheque.[51] If the words used are simply: "pay cash", it is treated as a bearer cheque. **13–025**

---

[44] This is not specifically required by the Act, which, however, does say that if there is a discrepancy the sum in words is the amount payable, BOEA 1882, s. 9(2).

[45] BOEA 1882, s. 3(2).

[46] Such as ECUs.

[47] Cm. 622 (1989).

[48] White Paper, Cm 1026, para. 6.4. The Government did not accept Jack's further recommendation to change the law to include notes on which interest is paid at a floating rate (FRNs), because, it said, they are very rare.

[49] In *Chamberlain v. Young* [1893] 2 Q.B. 206, it was held that an instrument which was made payable to " . . . order" (the blank had not been filled in) must be construed as being payable to "my order", that is, to the order of the drawer and was a valid bill when indorsed by him.

[50] See below, Chap. 14.

[51] *North & South Insurance Corporation v. National Provincial Bank* [1936] 1 K.B. 328. But the bank (here) acted within its mandate in paying it.

13–026 **Bearer bill.** A bill is payable to bearer when it explicitly says "pay bearer" or when the last or only indorsement is an *indorsement in blank*—that is, when the last indorser has simply written his or her signature on the back of the bill without specifying any person to whom the bill is to be transferred.[52] A bearer bill, as mentioned above, has the effect that any person in possession of the bill may transfer it without indorsement. A bona fide transferee obtaining the bill, even from a thief, has good title to it, and the acceptor, if acting in good faith, obtains a good discharge by payment to him or her.[53] There are obvious risks in such a bill.

13–027 **Fictitious payee.** Another situation where the bill can be treated as payable to bearer is more complex. Section 7(3) of the BOEA 1882 states that "where the payee is a fictitious or non-existing person", the bill can be treated as payable to bearer. These words have given rise to problems of interpretation. The problem is that a specified payee who is fictitious or does not exist can obviously not obtain payment, nor, for that matter, genuinely indorse the bill; a later holder of the bill will therefore not be able to obtain payment either. If the bill is treated as a bearer bill, however, indorsement is not necessary, and a later holder may be paid. The rule therefore reflects the emphasis put on the currency of negotiable instruments.[54]

However, it has proved difficult to say what the phrase means, and whether, indeed, the two expressions—non-existent and fictitious—are synonymous. The law has to be explained by examination of the cases.

13–028 The leading case is *Bank of England v. Vagliano Brothers*.[55] Vagliano was a firm of merchants in London who banked with the Bank of England, and were in the habit of accepting bills which were drawn payable at the Bank. Among the firm's foreign correspondents was one Vicuna, who, in the course of business frequently drew bills on Vagliano in favour of Petridi and Co, a firm in Constantinople. A clerk of Vagliano, Glyka, forged a series of bills which purported to be drawn by Vicuna on Vagliano in favour of Petridi & Co, and obtained Vagliano's acceptance of the forged bills. When Vagliano had accepted the forged bills, Glyka indorsed them by forging Petridi & Co's signature, and presented them at the Bank of England when they matured; the bank paid them over the counter to Glyka and then debited Vagliano's account. When the fraud was discovered, Vagliano brought an action to determine whether the bank was entitled to debit their account. The majority of the House of Lords held that under the

[52] BOEA 1882, s. 8(3).

[53] BOEA 1882, s. 59.

[54] And the commercial importance of the courts not having to consider "the history of every negotiable instrument, in itself perfectly genuine, in respect of the person who drew it and the person who issued it." *Clutton v. Attenborough* [1897] A.C. 90 at 93, *per* Lord Halsbury, L.C.

[55] (1891) A.C. 107.

circumstances Petridi & Co were *fictitious payees*—they existed, but the firm had never been intended by the real drawer, the clerk, to have any rights; the use of its name was merely a pretence and the transaction was entirely fictitious. The case should therefore be treated as coming within section 7(3) of the BOEA 1882, so that the Bank had been entitled to treat the bills as payable to bearer, and payment over the counter to the person who presented them had discharged the bills.[56] From the majority decision, it seems that the case indicated that the real or fictitious character of the payee depended on the actual intention of the person who drew the bill with regard to the transaction; the existence or not of the payee was a less important consideration. The dissenting minority, however, considered that the payees, as a real and existing firm, could not be fictitious, because the fact that the forger did not intend that the bills should be paid to that firm could not affect the fact that it existed.

The implications of the liberal interpretation of "fictitious" in *Vagliano* have been limited by subsequent cases. In *Clutton v. Attenborough*,[57] decided soon afterwards (which concerned cheques rather than bills of exchange) unlike *Vagliano*, the payee of the instruments really did not exist. A clerk in the accounts department of the plaintiffs had fraudulently told them that work had been done on their account by a person called Brett, and induced them to draw cheques payable to the order of Brett. When the cheques had been signed by the plaintiffs, the clerk obtained possession of them, and indorsed them in Brett's name. He negotiated them to the respondents who took them in good faith and they were paid by the plaintiff's bankers. When the plaintiffs discovered the fraud, they brought an action to recover the amount of the cheques as money paid under a mistake of fact. The House of Lords held that the payee specified by the drawer was fictitious or non-existent, although the drawer, who had drawn the cheques in the belief and with the intention that they should be payable to the order of a real person, was unaware of it. The bank was entitled to pay on them. The argument that a person of the name of Brett might exist and that the bill should therefore not be regarded as fictitious (and a bearer bill) was received without enthusiasm. **13–029**

In *Vinden v. Hughes*,[58] on the other hand, a cashier filled in a number of cheque forms with the names of customers of his employer as payees and obtained his employer's signature as drawer. He then forged the signatures of the payees by way of an indorsement and discounted the cheques to an innocent third party, who obtained payment from the drawer's bankers. Here it was held that the payees could not be regarded as fictitious or non- **13–030**

[56] It was also considered that Vagliano could not contend that the payments by the bank were unauthorised since they had accepted the bills and had advised the bank that they had done so.

[57] [1897] A.C. 90.

[58] [1905] 1 K.B. 795.

existing, because at the time the cheques were drawn, the drawers in fact intended identifiable persons, namely, certain of their customers, to be the payees, in the belief that they owed the sums represented by the cheques to those persons; the drawers had not used the names of the payees only by way of pretence. The bank had therefore not been entitled to pay on the cheques which had forged indorsements. The judge, Warrington J., distinguished *Clutton v. Attenborough* on the ground that the payee in that case was a non-existent person. He also distinguished *Bank of England v. Vagliano*, because in that case the House of Lords had been dealing with the case where there was no real drawer, and the use of the name of the firm as payee (rather than the firm itself) was a fiction.

13–031 The importance of treating such a bill as payable to bearer arises from the fact that it enables any person receiving the bill to disregard an indorsement purporting to be that of the payee which in fact is forged, an effect which can be helpful for banks. In cases where the payee is a real person, known to the drawer of a cheque (for example, his or her customer), however, the decision of the House of Lords in *North & South Wales Bank Ltd v. Macbeth*,[59] shows that the defence is unlikely to be helpful. In the *Macbeth* case, White fraudulently induced Macbeth to draw a cheque in favour of "Kerr or order". Kerr was an existing person known to Macbeth, and Macbeth, although misled by White as to the use to which he would put the cheque, fully intended that Kerr should receive the money. White obtained the cheque, forged Kerr's indorsement and paid the cheque into his account with the appellant bank. On discovering the fraud, Macbeth brought an action in conversion against the bank. The bank argued in defence that the payee was a fictitious person within section 7(3) of the BOEA 1882, and that the bank had been entitled to pay because the cheque was payable to bearer. The House of Lords held that the subsection did not apply, because the drawer of the cheque, Macbeth, had intended that a real person known to Macbeth, namely Kerr, should receive the amount of the cheque, and it could not be said, therefore, that the payee of the cheque was fictitious.

13–032 The subsection does not operate, therefore, if the drawer intends a real person to be the payee; the payee is not regarded as fictitious and the cheque remains an order cheque.[60] In fact, however, it would rarely happen that a person drawing a cheque would not intend it to be payable to an identifiable payee, because the drawer of a cheque normally has no reason to make it out to a person who does not exist (unlike the drawer of a bill, who might be able, as in the *Vagliano* case, to cheat the acceptor).

---

[59] [1908] A.C. 137.

[60] *North & South Wales Bank Ltd v. Macbeth* [1908] A.C. 137; *Vinden v. Hughes* [1905] 1 K.B. 795.

Issue of a Bill

This is the first delivery of the complete bill to a person who takes as holder, who will usually be the payee.[61] The delivery need not be actual in the sense of physically handing over the bill, but may be constructive—the drawer may inform the payee that the cheque is being held on the payee's behalf. Delivery must either be by the drawer or by his or her agent, and it may be conditional, although if the bill is in the possession of a holder in due course, unconditional delivery is conclusively presumed.[62] **13–033**

Incomplete Instruments

A bill of exchange, cheque, or a promissory note which lacks a material particular[63]—such as the amount, the name of the payee or the place of payment—is called *inchoate* in the BOEA 1882, and is not in itself valid. It may, however, be converted into a bill if it has a signature—a simple signature on a blank piece of paper will suffice—and it must be delivered by the person who signed it in order that it may be converted into a bill.[64] **13–034**

The signature can be used as the drawer's, the acceptor's or an indorser's, and any holder who has it has authority to fill in the omission(s) as he or she pleases, although it must be filled in according to the authority given and within a reasonable time if it is to be enforceable against the person who gave it. If it is completed, it is treated as if it had never been defective, and even if it has not been filled in according to the authority, a person who takes it as a holder in due course[65] can enforce it; putting such a note into circulation therefore has dangers.[66]

Altered Instruments

If a bill has been *materially altered* without the assent of all the parties who are liable on it, it is avoided except as against a person who has assented and subsequent indorsers.[67] The Act lists the following as material alterations: the **13–035**

[61] BOEA 1882, s. 2.

[62] BOEA 1882, s. 21.

[63] The date is less important: the bill is valid even if undated, BOEA 1882, s. 3(4). (Jack saw no need to change this: Jack Report, Cm. 622 (1989), para. 8.13.) If the name of the drawee is not inserted but the instrument is otherwise complete, it is a valid promissory note made by the person who signed it initially, *Mason v. Lock* [1939] L.T. 696.

[64] BOEA 1882, s. 20.

[65] The payee cannot be a holder in due course, because it has not been negotiated to him or her. A person taking a blank signed paper or incomplete bill could hardly take as holder in due course in any case, Byles, *op. cit.*, p. 38.

[66] Bills used to be stamped, and the section provided that the paper could only operate as an authority for an amount covered by the stamp. The words were repealed by the Finance Act 1970.

[67] BOEA 1882, s. 64. *Slingsby v. District Bank Ltd* [1932] 1 K.B. 544; *Attwood v. Griffin* (1826) 2 Ry. & Mood. 425; *Koch v. Dicks* (1932) 49 T.L.R. 24. See Hudson [1975] J.B.L. 108. Alteration of the payee's name on a cheque is a material alteration: *Smith v. Lloyds TSB Group plc* [2000] 1 W.L.R. 1225, QBD..

date, the sum payable, time and place of payment,[68] but the list is not exhaustive. Altering the business effect of the instrument would be material.[69]

However, if the alteration is not apparent, a holder in due course is protected and may enforce the bill as if it had not been altered. It can be a tricky question whether an alteration is apparent or not—the onus of proof that an alteration is not apparent lies on the holder, who must show that it would not be apparent to an intending holder scrutinising it with reasonable care.[70]

Forgery

13–036 The criminal definition of forgery, which probably holds good also for the BOEA 1882, is: the making of a false instrument with the intention of inducing someone to accept it as genuine and thereby to act to his own or another's prejudice.[71]

No title can be passed through a forgery; the signature is wholly inoperative[72] and gives no right to enforce payment, give a discharge on the bill or even to retain the bill. A person who possesses a bill with a forged signature, however, is by no means in such a hopeless position as appears at first sight, because he or she may well obtain rights against other parties to the instrument who are *precluded* or estopped from setting up the forgery as a defence. This is discussed further below.

13–037 As far as companies are concerned, the situation is rather different. The rule is that third parties can usually rely on the ostensible authority of the directors and other officers in their dealings with a company,[73] but if a bill of exchange is a forgery (by an officer of the company, for example), it seems that the company is not bound, because the document is invalid[74]; the rule that third parties can rely on the ostensible authority of directors of a company is displaced.

---

[68] And, where a bill bas been accepted generally, the addition of a place of payment without the acceptor's assent.

[69] *Suffell v. Bank of England* (1882) 9 Q.B.D. 555.

[70] *Woollatt v. Stanley* (1928) 138 L.T. 620.

[71] s. 1 of the Forgery and Counterfeiting Act 1981 (the current definition for the purposes of criminal law). No guidance is given in the BOEA 1882 but Scrutton L.J. assumed in *Kreditbank Cassel GmbH v. Schenkers* [1972] 1 K.B. 827 that the court should look at the then current statute, the Forgery Act 1913. The Forgery and Counterfeiting Act 1981 definition makes no distinction between forgery and unauthorised signature. The distinction would be relevant for the purposes of s. 24 of the BOEA 1882, which provides that forgery invalidates the instrument, but that an unauthorised signature may be ratified, See above, para. 7–011. Jack thought that there was no reason to change the law to provide that a person whose signature was forged should be able to ratify the forgery, Jack Report, Cm. 622 (1989), para. 8.24.

[72] BOEA 1882, s. 24.

[73] *Royal British Bank v. Turquand* (1856) 6 E & B 327; that is, provided everything appears externally to be in order, they have no notice of any irregularity, and the transaction is not one absolutely prohibited by the constitution of the company nor exceeding the limitations on the powers of the directors in the constitution.

[74] *Kreditbank Cassel GmbH v. Schenkers Ltd* [1927] 1 K.B. 826. Goode, *op. cit.*, pp. 566–567, criticises this exception.

Signing on Another's Behalf

Where a person authorises another person to sign for him as his or her agent, the authority is usually limited. This can be done by writing "per pro" by the signature, and this means that anyone taking the bill is warned of the risk that the agent may be exceeding his or her authority; if the agent does exceed the authority given, the principal is not bound.[75] Banks paying on "per pro" signatures should ensure that the written mandate covers them when they do so. **13–038**

An exception to this provision relates to companies. A bill which is made, accepted or indorsed by or on behalf of a company by a person acting under the authority of the company is deemed to have been made, accepted or indorsed by the company.[76] This includes ostensible authority as well as actual authority, and a director with ostensible authority seems to be able to bind the company under the CA 1985 but not under the BOEA 1882.[77]

If a person indicates when signing a bill that the signature is on behalf of someone else, or in a representative capacity, he or she will not be personally liable.[78] Provided this is clear, the actual words may be insufficient. For example, if a person wrote "Director" after his or her name, this would suffice when the cheque was a company cheque but if it were not, he or she would be personally liable.[79] **13–039**

How the Parties Use the Bill

The parties who sign a bill undertake liabilities which interlock and can be thought of as a chain of liabilities and rights. A transaction with a bill payable at a future date to a specified payee who specially indorses it to another person can be described in stages in this way: **13–040**

> A draws the bill on B, to pay C, and delivers it to C; the bill is payable "60 days after sight";
>
> C, wishing to receive payment immediately, negotiates the bill to D for an immediate (reduced) payment; C writes on the back of the bill "Pay D" and signs it;
>
> D presents the bill to B for acceptance; if B accepts it, B may write: "Accepted, payable at X branch," date, and sign it; the bill will

---

[75] BOEA 1882, s. 25: this is a *procuration* signature. A principal may ratify an unauthorised signature.

[76] CA 1985, s. 35.

[77] Because the words of BOEA 1882, s. 25 appear to apply to companies as well as natural persons, see Byles, *op. cit.*, p. 69.

[78] BOEA 1882, s. 26.

[79] *Bondina Ltd v. Rollaway Shower Blinds* [1986] 1 All E.R. 564 at 566. In deciding whether the signature is of the principal or personally of the agent, the construction most favourable to the validity of the instrument must be adopted. See also *Maxform S.p.A. v. Mariani and Goodville Ltd* [1981] 2 Lloyd's Rep. 54.

mature 60 days after the date of acceptance; if B does not accept it, it is dishonoured for non-acceptance, and D may immediately seek payment from A or C;

D then negotiates the bill to E, who may in turn negotiate it to F; who may negotiate it further;

when the bill reaches maturity, the holder, say G, should present it immediately to the acceptor for payment (if G does not, the liability of the other parties is discharged);

if B pays, the bill is discharged and B should cancel A's signature on it;

if B does not pay, the bill is dishonoured by non-payment and G should serve notice of dishonour as soon as possible on A, C, D, E and F and seek payment from the other parties; if any of them pays, the bill is not discharged, because that party has a right to sue the other parties on the bill; the bill is only discharged when there are no more parties liable on it.

These are the parties in this transaction:

A is the *drawer*;

B the *drawee*, later the *acceptor*;

C is the *payee*; when C indorses the bill to D, C becomes the first *indorser* (D is the first *indorsee*);

D is the second *indorser* (E the third, F the fourth);

Whichever of C, D, E, F and G possesses the bill is the *holder* of it at that time;

D, E and F may be *holders in due course*, but C, the payee cannot be, because bills are not *negotiated* to the payee.

The relationships between these parties, the problems which might arise and the appropriate defences must be examined in a little more detail.

13–041 First, a point about capacity and the parties to a bill: generally, any person (including bodies corporate) with capacity to contract may sign a bill; liability is co-extensive with the right to contract.[80] Any person with contractual capacity who signs the bill will be bound as an indorser to a holder in due course, even if he or she receives no value for it.[81] A person whose signature has been forged[82] does not incur liability; indeed, the

[80] BOEA 1882, s. 22(1). Diplomatic immunity may be claimed.
[81] BOEA 1882, s. 56. He or she becomes an "accommodation party" see above, para. 13–012.
[82] BOEA 1882, s. 24.

forgery of the drawer's or an indorser's signature, as will be seen, invalidates the instrument as a bill so that a later holder cannot obtain a good title to it, although he or she is given certain personal rights (by estoppel) against other parties. A plea of *non est factum* will allow a party to escape liability, but is unlikely to succeed, even if a person has innocently signed a folded document. Other contractual defences such as misrepresentation or undue influence do not affect the title to the bill, so that although they provide the victim with a defence against the guilty party, they are not effective as a defence against a holder in due course.

(1) Drawer[83]

A, the drawer, makes and issues the bill. At first, therefore, he or she has the primary responsibility for payment to the holder of the bill. This primary responsibility continues if the bill is not accepted, as in the case of cheques, where the bank (the drawee) does not accept the cheque. Similarly, if the drawee refuses to accept the bill (dishonours the bill by non-acceptance), the drawer is the party primarily liable. **13–042**

The drawer guarantees to future parties that the bill will be accepted and paid, or, if dishonoured, that he or she will compensate anybody who has had to pay on it.[84] The drawer cannot claim by way of defence against a holder in due course that the payee does not exist or have capacity to indorse the bill. This is an estoppel, a personal liability, rather than a claim by virtue of the bill, and is parallel to that of the acceptor under section 54(2) of the BOEA 1882, which is discussed below.

(2) Drawee/acceptor[85]

B is initially the *drawee* of the bill. In England, unlike Scotland, that has the negative meaning that B has no liability on the bill so that any funds B has available for the payment are not automatically assigned to the holder of the bill from the time when the bill is presented to him or her. The holder has therefore no recourse against B (except that B may well be liable to A, the drawer, in contract—this will depend upon their agreement). A bank, for example, does not normally accept cheques; accordingly, if a bank does not pay on a cheque, it would incur no liability on it to the payee,[86] but may be liable for breach of mandate to its customer, the drawer. In **13–043**

[83] BOEA 1882, s. 55. The drawer is not always the buyer as one might expect; in some cases (see *e.g.*, *Jade International* [1978] Q.B. 917) the *seller* draws the bill (the seller is also the payee) and the buyer accepts it.

[84] The drawer, like the indorsers, may limit or negate his or her own liability to the holder (by writing "sans recours" on it, as in *Clifford Chance v. Silver* [1992] 2 Bank. L.R. 11, CA.

[85] BOEA 1882, ss. 53 and 54. If the drawee is a fictitious person (*e.g.* a non-existent bank), the holder may treat the document as a bill of exchange or as a promissory note, BOEA 1882, s. 5(2).

[86] Although it may be liable to the true owner in conversion (usually the payee), see below, Chap. 14.

England, B is only liable on the bill once he or she has *accepted* the bill by signing it (the mere signature of the drawee on the bill is sufficient[87]). B then becomes primarily liable on the bill, and unless some defence is available—a general contractual defence like lack of capacity, *non est factum* or lack of consideration; or some defence on the bill like its invalidity or discharge because of some material alteration—B must pay the holder when the bill matures.

13–044 Not all bills need acceptance.[88] A bill which is payable *after sight*, as in the model above, has to be accepted in order to fix the maturity of the instrument, and if the bill expressly requires acceptance, or if it is payable at some place different from the place of residence or business of the drawee, it must also be presented for acceptance before it is paid. Otherwise, acceptance is not necessary—demand bills or bills payable *at sight* do not need to be presented for acceptance before payment, although it may be advantageous for the holder to obtain the signature of another party on the bill. As mentioned, cheques are not normally accepted.

If a bill is to be accepted, it must be presented to the drawee; acceptance cannot be assumed.[89] If an acceptor fills up the bill, he or she does not have a duty to be careful in doing so that no fraudulent alterations are made, unlike the drawer of a cheque,[90] where the instrument depends on the contractual relationship between bank and customer, and commercial transferability is less significant.

13–045 Once the bill has been accepted, there is no *necessity* to present it for payment when it matures: the acceptor has a duty to pay anyway. But it is safer for the holder to present it then, because otherwise the liability of the other parties, the drawer and indorsers, is discharged.

The acceptor's liability is to pay the bill to the holder, and payment in due course (that is, in good faith, on the maturity of the bill and without notice of any defect in the bill[91]) by the acceptor discharges the bill. Further, the acceptor may not raise certain defences on the bill against a holder in due course seeking payment. Section 54(2) of the BOEA 1882 provides a statutory *estoppel* in favour of such a holder; it operates as a personal liability undertaken by the acceptor and does not relate to the validity of the bill itself. The acceptor may not dispute the existence and capacity of the drawer; that the drawer's signature is genuine; and that the payee exists and has capacity to contract (there is no estoppel as to the genuineness of the *payee's* indorsement, however, even if as sometimes

[87] BOEA 1882, s. 17. Acceptance may be qualified, but if the holder does not agree to the qualification, the bill is dishonoured; similarly, if one of the other parties does not consent to it, he or she is discharged from liability on the bill (BOEA 1882, ss. 19 and 44).
[88] BOEA 1882, s. 39.
[89] *E.D. & F. Man v. Miyazaki* [1991] Lloyd's Rep. 154.
[90] *Scholfield v. Earl of Londesborough* [1896] A.C. 514; *cf. London Joint Stock Bank v. Macmillan and Arthur* [1918] A.C. 777; see above, Chap. 7.
[91] BOEA 1882, s. 59.

happens, it was already on the bill before it was accepted). In effect, the acceptor is guaranteeing the liability of the prior parties—the drawer and payee—and what is on the bill when it is accepted, to a future holder.

In most cases, the bill will have been negotiated smoothly and the holder will have the benefit of a real title to it and receive payment. There is a problem where a person takes the bill after the forgery of an indorsement, however. Such a transferee cannot have good title (that is, have a real right) to the bill, because the forgery breaks the chain of indorsement, the links in the title between the acceptor or drawer and the later possessor, and the "bill" becomes a nullity thereafter. Where a bill has a forged indorsement, therefore, the holder will not be able to sue the acceptor and drawer on the bill itself. The holder is not entirely without remedy, however, because he or she can sue any person who has indorsed the bill after the forgery.[92] **13–046**

If a bill which requires acceptance is *dishonoured by non-acceptance* by the drawee (because of refusal, where the drawee cannot be found or avoids the presentment, or because presentment is excused on the ground that the drawee is dead, bankrupt, fictitious or has no capacity[93]) the holder immediately obtains the right of recourse and does not need to wait until the date of maturity. He or she must serve notice of dishonour on other parties and seek payment from one of them.

(3) Payee

C, the payee, is the person who is named in the bill as the person to whom it is payable. Because he or she is a specified person, this is an *order* bill, not a *bearer* bill, and can be negotiated only by signature (indorsement) as well as delivery. C, like later indorsers, may indorse it *in blank*, that is, by mere signature without specifying any particular person, and in this case it becomes payable to bearer. If a person is named, the indorsement is *special* and that person must sign the bill in turn for it to be validly negotiated to another person. The indorsement forms part of the chain which passes the title. A bill indorsed in blank may be converted back into an order bill (unlike a bill which starts off as a bearer bill) by a later special indorsement. **13–047**

C, as payee, is a holder of the bill, but cannot become *holder in due course*[94] because the bill was not actually negotiated to him or her.[95] If C

[92] By BOEA 1882, s. 55(2)(c) an indorser engages that at the time of his indorsement the bill was valid and subsisting. And any indorser who took the bill after the forgery is regarded as giving new currency to the bill—as in effect a drawer (etc.) of a new bill.

[93] BOEA 1882, s. 41.

[94] See below, para. 13–058.

[95] *R.E. Jones Ltd v. Waring & Gillow* [1926] A.C. 670. By BOEA 1882, s. 29(1), a holder is a person to whom the bill has been negotiated; by BOEA 1882, s. 31, negotiation requires transfer by indorsement where necessary, and delivery; BOEA 1882, s. 21(2) seems to include a holder in due course among remote, not immediate parties. The case has been criticised because it denies the payee the rights to which he or she was previously understood to be entitled: see Byles, *op. cit.*, p. 232.

negotiates the bill to another person and it is then negotiated back to C, however, C may become holder in due course.[96]

(4) Indorser

13–048 C, as payee, becomes an indorser ("backs" the bill) when he or she signs the bill (usually on the back) and delivers it to D. Since D is named, this is a *special* indorsement, and the bill can only be properly negotiated by D signing it before it is delivered. If D merely signs it, it becomes, as has been seen, a bearer bill, though it can be changed back into an order bill by subsequent special indorsement. The person to whom the bill is delivered is a *holder* (at least) and acquires certain rights by virtue of that status.

The indorser becomes liable to pay the indorsee and subsequent holders if there is default in payment. The indorser and the drawer are, similarly, potentially liable to parties who are subsequent to themselves, and their liability is secondary to that of the acceptor. Like the drawer, the indorser becomes estopped under section 55(2) of the BOEA 1882 from denying certain matters to a holder in due course. In effect, C is guaranteeing the bill as he or she signed it, and may not deny that the signature of the drawer and previous indorsers were genuine and that the bill was then a valid bill.

The bill may be restrictively indorsed[97]: "pay A only" is an example of such an indorsement. In this case the bill becomes non-negotiable.[98]

13–049 Sometimes a bill is indorsed where it is not necessary for the purpose of creating the chain of indorsements, but where it may be desirable for the person taking the bill to have another name on the bill—effectively, another guarantor of payment, who is backing the bill. In many other European systems of law, the signature is recognised as an *aval*[99]: a person who signs in this capacity, known as an *avaliste*, may be liable to all parties, prior as well as subsequent, if payment is not made; the avaliste may also limit liability, for example, may act as guarantee for only one particular party. This concept is not recognised in English law,[1] or at least is uncertain.[2] It seems that at present such a signature would be regarded as that of an ordinary indorser[3] rather than as a guarantor, and that although no consideration has been given and the indorsement is unnecessary from the point of view of transfer of title, he or she is liable like any other indorser. The Jack Report recommended that the concept be recognised,

---

[96] *Jade International Steel Stahl und Eisen GmbH v. Robert Nicholas (Steels) Ltd* [1978] Q.B. 917.
[97] BOEA 1882, s. 35(1).
[98] BOEA 1882, s. 8(1).
[99] And in Art. 30, Geneva Convention providing a Uniform Law for Bills of Exchange and Promissory Notes, 1930.
[1] *G. & H. Montage v. Irvani* [1990] 2 All E.R. 225.
[2] Shea, Jack Report, Cm. 622 (1989), App. A, para. 8.9.
[3] Under BOEA 1882, s. 56.

and the Government agreed to introduce an amendment to the BOEA 1882 to do so.[4]

(5) Holder

A holder is the payee or indorsee who is in possession of the bill, or, in the case of a bearer bill, the bearer. It is the holder who prima facie has the right to be paid on the instrument, and payment to the holder discharges the bill.[5] Three different grades of holder are designated in the BOEA 1882, with differing rights and liabilities, and the term has therefore certain complexities. The three grades are: a mere *holder*; a *holder for value*; and—best of all—a *holder in due course*. **13–050**

(a) Mere holder. Any holder has the advantage of being presumed to be a holder in due course. If the holder is shown not to have given value, though, the claim may not succeed. The holder may also retain possession of the bill, may sue on it in his or her own name,[6] and give a good discharge to the drawer or acceptor who pays in due course[7]; thus the holder has a good title to the bill as against third parties. The holder is also entitled (among other things) to insert the date of issue or acceptance if it is lacking and convert an order bill into a bearer bill by indorsement in blank. **13–051**

(b) Holder for value.[8] A holder for value is in a better position than a mere holder, because consideration has been given. The BOEA 1882 does not give any definition of such a holder, but it is clear that he or she cannot obtain any better title than the transferor, whereas the title of a holder in due course is unimpeachable. There is a presumption that a holder has given value on a bill unless the contrary appears at least probable.[9] If there has been fraud, duress or illegality, though, the burden of proof is shifted, and the holder has to prove that value was given after the fraud or illegality.[10] **13–052**

Value is the equivalent of consideration in general contract law, and section 27(1) of the BOEA 1882 states that value may be any consideration which is sufficient to support a simple contract; subsection 27(1)(b) of the **13–053**

[4] Cm. 622 (1989), para. 8.16; Cm. 1026, para. 6.8.

[5] BOEA 1882, ss. 38 and 59. In the case of a bearer bill, this means that if the acceptor pays even a thief in good faith, the acceptor obtains a good discharge.

[6] BOEA 1882, s. 38(1).

[7] BOEA 1882, s. 38(2).

[8] The Jack Report's recommendation that this category should be abolished in order to avoid the need for consideration as a test of negotiability (Cm. 622 (1989), para. 8(4)) was not accepted.

[9] Byles, *op. cit.*, p. 243.

[10] BOEA 1882, s. 30. Negligence would not amount to notice of fraud, although it might indicate wilfully shutting one's eyes to the fraud, which may be. Proof of full value having been given is strong evidence of good faith; inadequacy of consideration, not normally a matter for the court, may be evidence of bad faith; see Byles, *op. cit.*, p. 245.

BOEA 1882 states, however, that an *antecedent debt or liability* is deemed to be valuable consideration, whether the bill is payable on demand or at a future time. The words "antecedent debt or liability" imply that past consideration would in some cases be sufficient to support a contract on a bill, although it does not suffice for simple contracts.[11] An application of the rules on value which may be unexpected is that it is not necessary that the *actual* holder has given value, in order to be holder for value; value may have been given at any time.[12] A holder for value may sue any of the parties on the bill, except that, fairly enough, such a holder who is the donee of the bill may not sue the person who gave it to him or her.

13–054 Such an antecedent debt or liability, however, must probably be the liability of the promisor, not of a stranger to the bill. In the case of *Oliver v. Davis and Woodcock*, for example, Davis was lent money by the plaintiff, and persuaded a Miss Woodcock to send the plaintiff her cheque to repay him, but she changed her mind and stopped her cheque before it was paid. When the plaintiff sued her on the cheque, she claimed that she had received no consideration from the plaintiff for her cheque. Her defence was successful: it was held that an "antecedent debt" did not include the debt of a third party (Davis), and the plaintiff had given no consideration.[13]

13–055 *The banker's lien.*[14] A provision of particular relevance for bankers is Section 27(3) of the BOEA 1882:

> "where the holder of a bill has a lien on it arising either from contract or by implication of law, he is deemed to be a holder to the extent of the sum for which he has a lien".

A bank receiving a bill or cheque for collection may be collecting it for its customer, or it may be acting on its own behalf, in which case it may be a holder for value, if the cheque is negotiable (this is very unlikely nowadays, though).[15] If the customer is indebted to the bank, and the bank receives a bill or cheque for collection for him or her, the bank has a lien over it and is therefore a holder for value, provided it is acting in the course of its business as banker—for example collecting the cheque—and does not have it for an unusual purpose. As a holder for value (or a holder in due course as it will probably be) it can sue the parties to a dishonoured cheque even if

---

[11] But *cf.* Goode, *Commercial Law*, p. 538.

[12] BOEA 1882, s. 27(2): where value has at any time been given for a bill, the holder is deemed to be a holder for value as regards the acceptor and all parties to the bill who became parties prior to such time.

[13] [1949] 2 K.B. 727; *contra*, *Diamond v. Graham* [1968] 1 W.L.R. 106; see also *Hasan v. Willson* [1977] 1 Lloyd's Rep. 431, and Byles, *op. cit.*, p, 248.

[14] See above, Chap. 11.

[15] Since the Cheques Act 1992, cheques marked "account payee" are not negotiable (or even transferable); see below, Chap. 14.

the cheque, given for collection, is not indorsed to the bank.[16] The bank then has an alternative defence to an action in conversion brought by a "true owner" to that given by section 4 of the Cheques Act 1957.[17]

If a bank has a lien on a cheque which is dishonoured, but returns it to the customer (for example for litigation), this destroys the lien, and, if the cheque is then redelivered to the bank so that it can sue,[18] no new lien arises, because the bank has been given possession of it in order to sue, not in the course of its business as banker.[19] **13–056**

The banker's lien exists if at the time the cheque is received the customer is indebted to the bank and the customer does not appropriate it to some other payment or account.[20] A question arises whether there is a lien if a cheque is paid in to the customer's account and *provisionally* credited to the account ("credited to cash"[21]) before it is cleared (this is normal banking practice).[22] If the drawer's cheque is dishonoured, the account can be debited again. The bank may sue the customer or the drawer on the cheque, even if it does not wish to allow an overdraft or an increase in the overdraft, by virtue of section 2 of the Cheques Act 1957, if it takes for value or if it has a lien,[23] and the problem is therefore, whether it obtains a lien or becomes a holder for value by "crediting to cash". Banks have a good alternative defence against a claim in conversion by the true owner of a cheque in the form of section 4 of the Cheques Act 1957, and the holder for value defence is therefore less important, but the answer may still affect the bank's right to sue on the cheque and other matters, such as the garnishing of the account. It used to be thought that a bank would be a holder for value in this case,[24] but the modern view, established in *A.L. Underwood Ltd v. Bank of Liverpool: Same v. Barclays Bank Ltd*,[25] appears clear: merely crediting to cash does *not* make the bank holder for value, because the credit entry may be reversed and therefore no value is given. Similarly, the bank does not have a lien. It might be different if the bank were to allow the customer to draw against uncleared effects, though, **13–057**

[16] Cheques Act 1957, s. 2.

[17] See below, Chap. 14.

[18] The redelivery of a security to the customer for a specific purpose, for example, as agent for the bank, could not give rise to a lien. The security would have to be expressly taken as a pledge, and released by Trust Receipt, because the lien arises by operation of law in particular circumstances, see above, Chap. 11.

[19] *Westminster Bank Ltd v. Zang* [1966] A.C. 182 (see below, Chap. 14).

[20] See above, Chap. 11.

[21] See above, para. 6–035.

[22] Regardless of whether the bank receives as agent for collection or for value, and whether the cheque is indorsed by the customer.

[23] For an example of a case where a bank was holder for value to the extent of a lien over an overdraft, see *Midland Bank Ltd v. Reckitt* [1933] A.C. 1; see also *Barclays Bank Ltd v. Astley Industrial Trusts Ltd* [1970] 2 Q.B. 527.

[24] *Capital and Counties Bank Ltd v. Gordon* [1903] A.C. 240. See also *Sutters v. Briggs* [1922] 1 A.C. 1 at 14.

[25] [1924] 1 K.B. 775; and see *Westminster Bank Ltd v. Zang* [1966] A.C. 182. A reflection of this view appears in the Cheques Act 1957, s. 4(1)(b).

because this might amount to the giving of value,[26] although it would not create a lien.

13–058 (c) **Holder in due course.** This is the top grade of holder, the person who benefits from the negotiability of a bill by obtaining a title free of defects, which may be a better title than that of his or her predecessor.[27] The holder in due course may acquire a good title from a thief, or where the bill has been obtained by fraud or where the consideration on the bill has failed, and, if a signature on the bill has been forged, may have a claim against earlier parties by way of estoppel.[28] Every holder is presumed to be a holder in due course.[29]

There is a sub-species of holder in due course: one who acquires the bill from a holder in due course has all the rights of such a holder, provided that he or she is not actually a party to any fraud or illegality affecting it.[30]

13–059 Section 29(1) of the BOEA 1882 states the conditions which must be fulfilled in order to become a holder in due course:

> "A holder in due course is a holder who has taken a bill, complete and regular on the face of it, under the following conditions, namely,
>
> (a) that he became the holder of it before it was overdue, and without notice that it had been previously dishonoured, if such was the fact:
>
> (b) that he took the bill in good faith and for value, and that at the time the bill was negotiated to him he had no notice of any defect in the title of the person who negotiated it."

The person must be a *holder*: section 1 of the BOEA 1882 provides that the holder is the payee or indorsee of a bill or note who is in possession of it, or the bearer thereof. The payee is a holder, but cannot be a holder in due course because the bill has not been *negotiated* to him or her.[31]

13–060 The bill must be *complete and regular on the face of it*: the bill must be a valid bill and must have been issued; and the "face of it" includes the back of the bill. It must be complete, and so all material information must be on the bill, such as the name of the payee, the amount payable, the necessary

---

[26] See *Underwood* [1924] 1 K.B. 775 at 804 at 805.

[27] Any other holder may acquire an unchallengeable title provided the bill has no defects, but that would not be an exception to the *nemo dat* rule.

[28] Under BOEA 1882, ss. 54 (acceptor) and 55 (drawer and indorsers); see above, paras 13–040 *et seq.*

[29] BOEA 1882, s. 30; unless there has been fraud, duress or force and fear or illegality in the drawing or negotiation of the bill, in which case the holder may still show that value has been given in good faith for the bill.

[30] BOEA 1882, s. 29(3).

[31] *R.E. Jones Ltd v. Waring & Gillow Ltd* [1926] A.C. 670; unless it has been negotiated back again to the payee: *Jade International* [1978] Q.B. 917.

indorsements (the date is only essential if for example, the bill is payable "after date"). If the bill is inchoate, a holder has the right to complete it,[32] but will not be a holder in due course (it may be negotiated to a holder in due course once it is complete). It must also be regular: the first indorsement should be strictly in conformity with the name of the payee, for example.[33] If there is anything suspicious about it, the person who takes it will not be a holder in due course, although the bill may be valid.

Before it was *overdue*: in the case of a time bill (due on a particular day) it will be overdue if it is not presented for payment on the day it falls due; if it is payable on demand, presentment must be within a reasonable time,[34] which is a question of fact. An overdue bill can still be negotiated, but the holder will not be holder in due course.

The holder must have *no notice of previous dishonour*: bills may be dishonoured for non-payment or for non-acceptance. If a cheque is dishonoured, the bank will normally write some phrase indicating dishonour on it, such as "refer to drawer", and the dishonour will therefore be very obvious. **13–061**

The holder must have taken the bill *in good faith*: this is a question of honesty, not of negligence, unless the transferee took the bill under such circumstances that the conclusion must be that he or she was dishonest.[35]

And for *value*: the academic view has been that, unlike a holder for value, where value can have been given at any time on the bill, a holder in due course must have given *value personally*,[36] because of the wording of the section which is: "he took the bill in good faith and for value".[37] The Court of Appeal did not take this view in *Clifford Chance v. Silver*,[38] however, where it was held that Clifford Chance, who were solicitors acting as stakeholders in a property transaction and had not themselves given value on a cheque which was indorsed to them, were nevertheless holders in due course of the cheque because value had been given by an earlier holder. It seems, therefore, that the courts will prefer to have consistency for all holders rather than to make the standard of holder in due course more difficult to attain. **13–062**

Without *notice of any defect in title*: this means either a defect due to acts of the immediate predecessor or of a prior holder. Both "particular notice",

[32] BOEA 1882, s. 20.

[33] *Arab Bank Ltd v. Ross* [1952] 2 Q.B. 216.

[34] BOEA 1882, s. 45 and s. 36(3).

[35] *Jones v. Gordon* (1877) 2 App Cas. 616. Bills were bought at a massive undervalue. The difference is between honest blundering and knowing in one's secret mind that there was something wrong and deciding not to ask questions lest the suspicion become a certainty: at 629, *per* Lord Blackburn.

[36] Goode, *op. cit.*, p. 543. See also Hitchens [1993] J.B.L. 571. The Jack Report recommended that the requirement for consideration should be abolished as a test of negotiability (Cm. 622 (1989), para. 8.16); this was rejected by the White Paper.

[37] Whereas BOEA 1882, s. 27(2) states that where value has at any time been given for a bill the holder is deemed to be a holder for value.

[38] [1992] 2 Bank. L.R. 11.

which is knowledge of particular fact avoiding the bill, and "general" or "implied notice", which is knowledge of some illegality or fraud but without knowledge of precise details, will suffice, but notice here means *actual* notice, not constructive notice. Being put on inquiry because of constructive notice is a very different question from a wilful and fraudulent absence of inquiry into the circumstances when they are known to be such as to invite inquiry.[39]

The Effect of Forgery on the Parties

13–063 A forged signature on a bill may be that of the drawer, an indorser or of the acceptor. The effect of a forgery can be described as follows.

13–064 **Forgery of drawer's signature.** The bill is invalid. If it is accepted, however, the acceptor (and any later indorsers) will incur liability by virtue of the estoppel which is provided by section 54 of the BOEA 1882 (or section 55), because the signature "guarantees" the instrument as it existed when it was signed and gives a protection to a later holder.[40]

13–065 **Forgery of an indorsement.** In this case, the bill is valid but the title of holders after the forgery will be invalid. The indorsements form a chain of liability on the bill, so that if one has been forged, the chain is broken.[41] The person in possession has not derived title from the signatures of the parties before the forgery and cannot claim on the bill against them; the rights of the "holder" of the bill[42] depend on section 55 of the BOEA 1882. The holder would be able to sue any party who had signed the bill after the forgery, because such an indorser is estopped under that section from denying that the bill is valid, and the instrument acquires currency from the signatures after the forgery. As an example:

> A draws a bill payable to C, accepted by B. It is issued to C, who indorses it specially in favour of D and negotiates it to D; D similarly indorses it specially to E, and negotiates it to E. X steals it and forges a special indorsement by E in favour of F and delivers it to F, who indorses it and delivers it to G.

13–066 X's indorsement is a forgery and cannot be a link in the chain. F has therefore no right to transfer the bill, and neither has G; E may claim it

[39] *Baker v. Barclays Bank Ltd* [1955] 1 W.L.R. 822 at 834, *per* Devlin J.

[40] See above, para. 13–042.

[41] Banks have statutory protection in the case of forged indorsements; see Chap. 14. Only forgery of an essential indorsement—*i.e.* one which forms a link in the chain of indorsements—is important. If a non-essential signature has been forged it simply means that that signatory (who may have added his or her name as an extra guarantee, as an aval) is not liable.

[42] He or she is regarded as a holder because the bill has in effect been "reissued" by an indorser signing it after the forgery.

back from him. G's rights depend on the estoppels in sections 54 and 55 of the BOEA 1882; here, she has a claim against F under section 55 of the BOEA 1882, but not against A or B; nor against those indorsers (C and D) who indorsed it before the forgery.

If B, who might well be a bank, paid G despite the forged indorsement, B could find that it has to make a second payment to the true owner (here, E).

Forgery of the acceptor's signature. This does not affect title on the bill, but simply means that the bill has not been accepted. **13–067**

A person whose signature has been forged may represent the forged signature to be his or her own. If a subsequent holder is thereby induced to take the instrument believing the signature to be genuine, the representor will be estopped from setting up the forgery and may become liable on it. A person may be estopped by mere non-disclosure of a forgery from relying on it where there is a duty of disclosure, as there is between banker and customer.[43]

Dishonour of a Bill

Notice of dishonour

Bills which require presentment for acceptance[44] will be *dishonoured by non-acceptance* if the drawee refuses to sign the bill or cannot be found. **13–068**

All bills (except those which have been dishonoured by non-acceptance) have to be presented for payment. If payment is refused or cannot be obtained on maturity, the bill is *dishonoured by non-payment*. The acceptor, if there is one, is the person primarily liable on the bill, and if the acceptor pays on it, the bill is discharged. The bill must be presented promptly: the rules are strict, and if they are not adhered to, the drawer and indorsers are discharged even if they suffer no loss. The bill must be presented on the due date at a reasonable time, on a business day, and at the right place.[45] Even if it is known that the bill will be dishonoured, it should be presented, so that the drawer and indorsers become liable on it.

If a bill is dishonoured in either of these ways, the holder has a right of immediate recourse against other parties on the bill. In order to enforce the bill against them, the holder must give notice of dishonour to prior parties. Notice does not need to be in writing, but the words must identify the bill and clearly state that it has been dishonoured.[46] Notice must be given within a reasonable time of the dishonour (and it must not arrive before the dishonour has happened). **13–069**

---

[43] *Greenwood v. Martins Bank* [1932] 1 K.B. 371.

[44] See above, para. 13–044.

[45] BOEA 1882, s. 45. Delay is excused under certain circumstances beyond the control of the holder (s. 46).

[46] BOEA 1882, s. 49. In some circumstances notice need not be given.

It is safest for the holder to serve notice individually on the drawer and on all previous indorsers because any person who is not advised of the dishonour is discharged, but notice may be served on any party, and it will normally be passed along the chain because any parties failing to pass it on would remain liable but lose their own right of recourse.

Noting and protesting

13–070 This is optional for inland bills, but must be done for foreign bills.[47] It is an internationally recognised means of obtaining legal proof of dishonour. Noting is cheap and extends the time during which a protest may be made. The holder gives the bill to a notary public who presents the bill for acceptance or payment; if it is still unobtainable, the notary may *note* it by attaching a piece of paper to the bill giving details of the dishonour. If the bill is still not honoured, the notary will draw up a *protest* (a formal certificate evidencing the dishonour) and sign it (it takes effect from the time of noting in order to comply with the strict time limits in the Act BOEA 1882).

Damages on dishonour

13–071 The BOEA 1882 specifies the damages a holder may recover on dishonour of a bill: the amount of the bill, expenses of noting and protest if necessary, and interest.[48]

Discharge of a Bill

13–072 A bill is normally discharged by payment in due course.[49] If the bill is paid at or after its maturity[50] by the acceptor, in good faith and without notice of any defect in the title, to the holder, it will be discharged. The obligation then ceases to exist and all rights of action on the bill are extinguished. If another party, the drawer or an indorser, pays, however, the holder could still sue the acceptor,[51] and, although the party who has paid is discharged, the bill is not. In this case, the holder of the bill may prefer to renegotiate it.

13–073 There are other methods of discharge: the bill may be discharged by the acceptor becoming the holder of it[52]; or by renunciation by the holder of his

[47] Jack recommended that a procedure of certification should be retained, but made voluntary and simplified.
[48] BOEA 1882, s. 57. Interest is paid from the time it was presented if it is a demand bill, otherwise from its maturity.
[49] BOEA 1882, s. 59.
[50] The acceptor may pay before maturity, but the bill is not discharged and may be reissued.
[51] Except where the bill is signed by an accommodation party (under BOEA 1882, s. 28(1)), BOEA 1882, s. 59(3), *Coats v. The Union Bank of Scotland Ltd* (1929) S.C. (HL) 114 at 127, *per* Lord Atkin. See Mitchell, *The Law of Subrogation*, p. 60.
[52] BOEA 1882, s. 61.

or her rights as against the acceptor; this must be at or after maturity, unconditional and in writing unless the bill is given up to the acceptor.[53] Or a bill may be cancelled: this must be intentional and apparent from the bill[54]; and if the bill has been materially altered without the consent of all the parties liable on it, it is avoided, except as far as any party who has consented is concerned and subsequent indorsers.[55]

When the bill has been paid in due course, the obligation of the seller on the underlying contract, which has been suspended during the currency of the bill (if as is normal, the bill was given as conditional payment[56]) is extinguished. If the bill is not paid in due course, the obligations under the contract revive.

[53] BOEA 1882, s. 62.
[54] BOEA 1882, s. 63.
[55] BOEA 1882, s. 64; and except where the alteration is not apparent and the bill has come into the hands of a holder in due course.
[56] *Alan (W.J.) v. El Nasr Export & Import Co.* [1972] 2 Q.B. 189; *E.D.F. Man v. Nigerian Sweets and Confectionery Co* [1977] 2 Lloyd's Rep. 50.

CHAPTER 14

CHEQUES

Cheques are still important in the banking relationship, although their use is being steadily displaced by other forms of payment.[1] For many people, using cheques now seems a cumbersome method of payment by comparison with plastic cards. For the banking industry, too, they involve much laborious and now unnecessary work. As a result, the industry has willingly taken advantage of the revolution in technology and acted to overcome legal and practical obstacles in the *truncation* of cheques,[2] to enable the payment of cheques by electronic means, and this has now been partially introduced into cheque clearing.[3] **14–001**

This Chapter will look at cheques in their function as negotiable instruments rather than as mandates, or instructions, from the customer to the paying bank. As a species of bill of exchange, cheques are regulated primarily by the BOEA 1882, and the rules set out above[4] relating to bills are therefore generally relevant for cheques. The discussion in this present chapter, however, will concentrate on their distinctive character. Cheques have diverged in a number of ways from bills of exchange; they received special treatment even in the BOEA 1882, and since then separate legislation has been needed to deal with them (the Cheques Act 1957 and 1992). The reason for the divergence is that their function as a mandate from the customer to his or her bank has made them an integral part of the banking relationship, and different characteristics have grown up from this. Customers use them mainly in order to instruct their bank to pay either themselves or other people, and vast numbers of cheques are still used daily in these ways, despite the many other methods of obtaining money and of payment which are now available. Cheques are now only rarely used as negotiable instruments—one example is where a person without a bank account is the payee of a cheque and indorses it to a person with a bank **14–002**

---

[1] The use of cheques and paper credits for payment transactions has declined by almost 22 per cent in the last seven years as a whole—automated payments have increased by 62 per cent and the use of plastic has more than doubled: APACS, *Yearbook of Payment Statistics* (1998), p. 44.

[2] BOEA 1882, s. 74, inserted by the Deregulation (Bills of Exchange) Order 1996.

[3] APACS, *Yearbook* (1998), p. 44.

[4] See above, Chap. 13.

account in order to obtain payment—and even this occurs relatively infrequently now that the vast majority of adults have bank accounts.[5]

14–003 The fact that cheques have largely lost their use as negotiable instruments was recognised by the Cheques Act 1992. The purpose of this Act, which was a result of the comprehensive survey of banking law and practice of the Jack Report,[6] was to reduce cheque fraud. The negotiability of cheques increases the risk of fraud by multiplying possible holders and at the same time makes it difficult or impossible for the banks to detect it. The Cheques Act 1992 established the use of non-transferable cheques by giving the words "account payee" on cheques that effect.

The Nature of Cheques

14–004 The specialised function of cheques has resulted in distinctive legal characteristics. The starting point is the basic definition, set out in section 73 of the BOEA 1882: a cheque is a bill of exchange drawn on a banker payable on demand. A bill of exchange, as has been seen, is defined in section 3 of the BOEA 1882.[7] The effect of combining section 73 with section 3 is that:

> "A cheque is an unconditional order in writing, signed by the person giving it, requiring the bank to whom it is addressed to pay on demand a sum certain in money to, or to the order of, a specified person or bearer.

A valid cheque must also be supported by valuable consideration,[8] and have been delivered (issued).

14–005 The requirement that there should be a "specified payee" or that payment should be ordered to bearer has sometimes posed difficulties in relation to cheques, which are often drawn in varied ways, some of which actually make them invalid as a bill of exchange. A cheque payable to "cash or order", for example, does not satisfy the requirements of section 3 of the BOEA 1882, because there is no specified payee ("cash" is not a specified person), and the cheque cannot be an instrument payable to "bearer",

---

[5] 95 per cent of adults held a bank account in 1997: APACS, *Yearbook* (1998), p. 48. But see Macleod: The plight of the unbanked payee (1997) 113 L.Q.R 133. It is reported that the F.S.A. (See Chapter 1) will force "banks for the poor" to reopen: *The Independent*, February 22, 1999.

[6] Cm. 622 (1989).

[7] See above, Chap. 13.

[8] *Lipkin Gorman v. Karpnale* [1991] A.C. 548, [1991] 3 W.L.R. 10; [1992] 4 All E.R. 512. See also *AEG v. Lewis, The Times*, December 29, 1992: a fitter carried out repairs on a domestic gas appliance and was given a cheque by the householder's daughter, who later stopped the cheque because her father was dissatisfied with the repairs. The Court of Appeal, by a majority, held that the cheque was invalid because no consideration had been given and the fitter had not had implied authority to accept her cheque as releasing her father's obligation.

because the words "or order" contradict that implication. The result is that the instrument is not a bill of exchange and therefore not a cheque. In the normal banking situation, however, this is unimportant because the instrument still works as a mandate from customer to banker and a person may obtain payment on it.[9] It is treated as not needing indorsement by the person paying it in—that is, as a bearer cheque.

Differences between bills of exchange and cheques

Cheques, unlike bills, are not normally used to obtain credit. The important differences between the two instruments are: **14–006**

- a cheque must be drawn on a banker, whereas a bill may be drawn on any person;
- a cheque is payable on demand, whereas a bill may be payable in the future;
- a cheque is not accepted, and the drawer remains primarily liable on it;
- a cheque can be crossed, whereas a bill cannot;
- there are a number of statutory provisions which protect a bank dealing with a cheque, whether the bank is paying or collecting it; and
- the drawer of a cheque is not discharged by failure to present a cheque, as would happen in the case of failure to present a bill, unless the delay causes the drawer injury.[10]

Banking and the Operation of Cheques

It may be helpful to repeat the model used in Chapter 6 above as a reminder of the relationships between the parties: **14–007**

> "A draws a cheque on his bank (X branch) to pay B £100. B presents the cheque to her bank (Y branch) to collect it on her behalf. Y provisionally credits B's account with that sum and sends the cheque to X through the clearing system. All being well, Y will pay the cheque, B's account will be credited a few days later, and she will be able to draw on the funds. The banks will settle up between themselves through their own bank accounts with the Bank of England.

[9] *North and South Insurance Corpn. Ltd v. National Provincial Bank Ltd* [1936] 1 K.B. 328; *Cole v. Milsome* [1951] 1 All E.R. 311; *Orbit Mining and Trading Co Ltd v. Westminster Bank Ltd* [1963] 1 Q.B. 794; [1962] 3 W.L.R. 1256; [1962] 3 All E.R. 565. Such an instrument is covered by ss. 1(2)(a) and 4(2)(b) of the Cheques Act 1957, see below, para. 14–045.

[10] BOEA 1882, s. 74.

A is the *drawer* of the cheque, Y the *drawee* (bank) who pays on his behalf. B is the *payee*, and Z bank *collects* the payment on her behalf. Y is the *paying bank* and Z the *collecting bank*.[11]

14–008 Several relationships are involved:

- A is the customer of Y (banker/customer contract) and Y, the paying bank, must obey his mandate[12];
- B is the customer of Z (banker/customer contract) and Z, the collecting bank, is under a duty to present cheques on her behalf to the paying bank;
- A and B have a contract by virtue of the cheque; and
- Y and Z probably also have a contract as members of the clearing house.[13]

If the cheque drawn by A[14] is not correctly handled, there are a number of ways in which the banks concerned might be liable:

(a) if Y, the *paying* bank, does not pay according to its mandate, for example, it will be liable to A in contract; this is described in the chapters about the paying bank and the mandate above.[15] If it pays the wrong person, it may also be liable to the *true owner* of the cheque (who will probably be the payee, B) in the tort of conversion, not in contract. Conversion is discussed below (para. 14–015.

(b) similarly, if Z, the *collecting* bank, has collected the payment for the wrong person, it may also be liable to the true owner, again in conversion. Alternatively, the victim can claim against the bank for money had and received by a claim that is known as "waiving the tort" of conversion (nowadays this is in restitution).[16] Sometimes, depending on the facts, a claim for constructive trust may even be available.[17]

The clearing process

14–009 It is important to know how banks deal with cheques, and particularly how the process of cheque clearing works, to understand how these contracts interact and the technicalities of the law of cheques. The brief

[11] If the bank is acting on B's behalf and not on its own. If it has given value for the cheque (see below, para. 14–076) it will be presenting the cheque but not collecting it.

[12] See above, Chap. 6.

[13] *Barclays Bank v. Bank of England* [1985] 1 All E.R. 385 at 390, *per* Bingham J. see below, para. 14–015.

[14] If the cheque has not been drawn by A, but forged by C, the paying bank will not be able to debit A's account, unless one of the defences discussed above in Chap. 7 is available—*e.g.* A may be estopped because he has drawn the cheque in such a way as to facilitate fraud.

[15] See above, Chaps 6 and 7.

[16] Both claims are often made: one might be successful and not the other (*e.g.* there is no defence of change of position in conversion). The claim in restitution (money had and received) is for the proceeds of the cheque rather than the value of the instrument. See above, Chap. 10 for discussion of some other aspects of restitution.

[17] See above, Chap. 9.

account below is mainly taken from the description by Bingham J.[18] in a case where he acted as arbitrator between the banks and the Bank of England (*Barclays Bank v. Bank of England*[19]). The banks wished to ascertain the extent of the responsibility of the paying and collecting banks in the clearing process.

Vast numbers of cheques are presented daily for payment.[20] Traditionally, they have been transported physically from the collecting bank, exchanged centrally and delivered to the paying bank. Cheque clearing is a centralised process for presenting cheques to the banks which are to pay them. The system, which was reorganised in 1985, consists of an umbrella organisation, the Association for Payment Clearing Services (APACS), with twenty three member banks and building societies, which has overall responsibility for the clearing process, and three companies which operate the three different clearings used in England under its auspices for different methods of payment. Cheques are dealt with by the Cheque Credit and Clearing Company (the other two companies are CHAPS Clearing Company Ltd and BACS Ltd[21]), owned by the banks and building societies which are members of it; at the moment, there are 13 direct members, but among them they act as agents in the process for several hundred other financial institutions.[22] The banks send the cheques they have received for collection to a central address (the clearing house)[23] where they are sorted and sent to the banks on which they are drawn. **14–010**

The clearing house had its origins as a meeting house for the outdoor clerks of the banks; they could meet there, exchange cheques and settle up amongst themselves without having to deliver the cheques arduously by foot to each individual bank.[24] If millions of cheques have to be physically dispatched around the country the centralised system obviously saves time and money.

Truncation of cheques. In 1989, the Jack Committee recommended that this efficient but cumbersome process should be curtailed by sending the information electronically.[25] This process of truncation has become common practice in most European countries, but although the banks in England had developed a truncation system,[26] there were obstacles to its **14–011**

[18] See below, para. 14–015.

[19] [1985] 1 All E.R. 385.

[20] In 1998, 2.2 billion cheques were processed through the clearing system, with a total value of more than £1,400: APACS, *Annual Review* (1998), p. 11.

[21] Discussed in Chap. 12. The Town Clearing, which formerly operated within the City of London and dealt with high value cheques, was abolished in 1995.

[22] See *Importers Company Ltd v. Westminster Bank Ltd* [1927] 2 K.B. 297.

[23] Now at Goodman's Fields in London.

[24] Daily clearings are believed to have evolved around 1770 from the practice of bank clerks exchanging cheques in, or near, the Five Bells, a tavern in Dove Court, Lombard Street: APACS, *Yearbook* (1995), p. 50.

[25] Jack Report, Cm. 622 (1989), paras 7.38 *et seq.* See Vroegop [1990] L.M.C.L.Q. 244.

[26] Inter Bank Data Exchange (IBDE).

introduction. Section 45 of the BOEA 1882 required that bills "must be presented for payment"—which means physically presented[27]—at the place named in the bill, which, in the case of cheques, is the paying branch. There were other difficulties. The paying bank would be unable to examine cheques to detect forgeries and would therefore be at risk of paying on forged cheques, although as a matter of fact, checking on signatures by paying banks has now become very limited; it is usually only done for high value cheques because it would be impossible to carry out checks on the huge numbers of cheques now presented daily.

14–012 In 1996, the law was amended to allow for the truncation of cheques.[28] A bank may now specify an address[29] at which cheques drawn on it may be presented for payment. The cheque is then deemed to have been presented "at the proper address". Another change in the law permits the presentation of the cheque by means of electronic or similar message, which sets out the "fundamental features" of the cheque[30]: that is, the serial number, the sorting code of the drawee bank, the number of the account on which the cheque is drawn and its amount. Nevertheless, the drawee bank has the right to demand that the cheque is presented physically—a right it may use, for example, if it suspects fraud, or where a cheque has been indorsed (this would be rare now).

A provision has also been introduced in the Code to cover disputes between banks and customers about payment of a cheque. Customers now have the right to receive the original, or a copy of a cheque within a reasonable period of time as evidence. Banks also undertake to recredit the customer's account if necessary.[31] The system has been partially implemented by the banks.[32]

14–013 **What happens when a cheque is cleared.** B has received the cheque from A, and she takes it to her bank, Z, for collection. What must Z do with the cheque when it acts for B as collecting bank?

14–014 Z must take reasonable steps to obtain payment of the cheque by presenting it for payment, and credit the proceeds to B's account or notify B that payment has been refused. Further, the cheque must be presented for payment in accordance with section 45 of the BOEA 1882, the effect of which is that it must be presented for payment by Z[33] within a reasonable

[27] *Barclays Bank* [1985] 1 All E.R. 385.

[28] Deregulation (Bills of Exchange) Order 1996, S.I.1996 No. 2993 inserted a new s. 74 into the BOEA 1882.

[29] By a notice published in the London, Edinburgh and Belfast Gazettes.

[30] New s. 74B of the BOEA 1882.

[31] Banking Code (1999) para. 3.6, BOEA 1882, s. 54(2) and Cheques Act 1992, s. 3 have also been amended to allow cheques to be used as receipts.

[32] It is unlikely to be taken further until decisions about the euro have been taken: APACS, *Annual Review* (1997), p. 11.

[33] As B's agent, or by B herself.

time of its issue[34] and at a reasonable hour on a business day, at the proper place, (the drawee's, the paying bank's, place of business—the address is on the cheque). As we have just seen, the information on the cheque may now be transmitted by electronic methods. The traditional procedure, which often still takes place, however, is as follows:

Day 1:

(a) Z, the collecting bank, (a branch of W bank), receives A's cheque for £100 from B. Z stamps (crosses) the cheque with its own name; it provisionally credits B's account with £100, but B cannot withdraw the funds or earn interest on them yet because, unless there is a special arrangement, she does not receive value until the cheque is cleared;

(b) Z usually encodes the cheque: it notes on the cheque in magnetic ink the sum payable on it (adding this to the numbers of the cheque, the branch, and the account which are already written in magnetic ink at the bottom of the cheque);

(c) the cheques Z has received during the day will be sorted into bundles—a separate bundle for each bank; the bundles will be taken to W bank's clearing department;

Day 2:

(d) any omitted encoding is done at the bank's clearing department; the bundles from all branches are amalgamated and sorted into boxes; the only inspection of cheques is to ensure that they have the magnetic ink characters, are free of staples, and are unfolded;

(e) the boxes are taken to the clearing house; they are given to employees of the appropriate paying bank or placed in racks reserved for that bank; they are not inspected;

(f) they are taken to the clearing department of the paying bank (in the example, X bank, of which Y is a branch); the cheques for payment are fed into a *reader-sorter machine*, which sorts the cheques into bundles for appropriate branches; it checks the amounts charged against X by the various presenting banks and corrects them if necessary; it records the details of the magnetic characters, which are sent to the computer

[34] As a demand bill. Otherwise A is discharged, under s. 45(2) of the BOEA 1882. (Within a reasonable time of its indorsement to make an indorser liable.) What is a reasonable time is a question of fact and depends upon usage (it is normally 6 months).

centre where branch accounts are kept. There is no consideration of the validity or payability of the cheque yet. The bundles are delivered to the individual branches;

Day 3:

(g) each cheque received by Y branch is inspected to decide whether it is technically in order (for example, properly signed and dated, with numbers and figures corresponding and no alterations) and whether there is any reason why it should not be honoured (for example, lack of funds, countermand or injunction). If the cheque is to be paid, it is cancelled and A's account will be debited at the end of this day and the computer entry will take effect; if it is not to be paid, it will be sent by first class post back to W, and then to Z, and the computer entry will be reversed;

(h) the banks settle up between themselves: they pay the net balances owing and their accounts at the Bank of England are credited or debited appropriately. This is actually done on the basis of the computer projected entries, and it is assumed that all cheques will be honoured. Adjustment to account for any cheques which are in fact dishonoured has to be done later.

The process therefore takes three days, although the banks usually allow four days for clearing before customers may draw on the funds. The Banking Code requires[35] that customers are given details of the relevant dates: this one is sometimes known as the "fate date", and the "value date", when interest may be paid (or charged) will be one or two days earlier. Each bank sets its own fate and value dates.

14–015 If only one branch of a bank is both collecting and paying bank, the process is obviously shorter, and the cheque is regarded as paid at the moment the branch does any act indicating its decision to pay the cheque or not.[36] In the case of one branch of a bank collecting and another branch of the same bank paying, the cheque is not sent to the clearing house but is dealt with by the clearing department of the bank itself.

The banks are, of course, responsible for the cheques during this process. The question of which bank is responsible at the different stages was examined in *Barclays Bank plc v. Bank of England*[37] by Bingham J., acting as arbitrator. He concluded that the presenting bank's responsibility to its customer is discharged only when the cheque is physically delivered to the paying branch for decision whether it should be paid or not.

---

[35] Banking Code (1999) para. 2.1.
[36] *Momm v. Barclays Bank Ltd* [1977] Q.B. 790; Brindle and Cox, *op. cit.*, paras 4.38 and 4.154.
[37] [1985] 1 All E.R. 385.

Crossings on cheques

One of the distinctive aspects of cheques is the fact that they, unlike bills, are usually crossed. The effect of crossings in general is to reduce the possibility of fraud. A person seeking payment of a crossed cheque has to have a bank account (and is presumably known to the bank) and the cheque will take several days to clear, during which time a fraud may be discovered. Crossing cheques as a practice started as a custom of the Clearing House: the name of the collecting bank would be written between two lines on each cheque so that it could be identified by the paying bank.[38] The practice has changed over time, and there are a number of crossings and other additions, like the words "account payee", made to cheques. The meanings of these are not self-evident, and some explanations need to be given. **14–016**

Cheque crossings are regulated by the BOEA 1882.[39] A crossing is described as two parallel lines drawn diagonally across the face of the cheque, sometimes with the words "& Co."[40] written between them. This amounts to an instruction to the paying bank by the drawer to make payment only through another bank, so that the cheque cannot be paid over the counter. If the name of the bank is added (a *special* as opposed to a *general* crossing), the payment must be made through the named bank.[41] **14–017**

Nowadays crossings are normally printed on cheque forms by the bank. The drawer may, however, *open* the crossing, by striking it out, writing "pay cash", and initialling the amendment.[42] This alteration of the mandate might not protect the bank from a "true owner"[43] since the BOEA 1882 does not contemplate the "opening" of a cheque in this way, but the bank would probably be entitled to an indemnity from its customer, and it can debit his account. If a crossing is altered by some other person the alteration will be unlawful, because it is a material part of the cheque.[44]

The bank primarily affected by crossings is the paying bank: if it pays the wrong person, it runs the risk of liability to its customer and to the true owner. If the cheque is crossed and the paying bank pays another bank, as **14–018**

---

[38] Byles, *op. cit.*, p. 285, Goode, *Commercial Law*, p. 582.

[39] BOEA 1882, ss. 76–81.

[40] Originally used where the drawer did not know the name of the payee's bank, Goode, *op. cit.*, p. 582.

[41] BOEA 1882, s. 76(2). The White Paper accepted the Jack Committee's recommendation (Cm. 622 (1989), para. 7(3)) to abolish the special crossing (Cm. 1026, para. 5.5).

[42] *Smith and Baldwin v. Barclays Bank Ltd* (1944) L.D.A.B. 370 at 375. The Committee of London Clearing Bankers recommended to banks (November 7, 1912) that no opening of cheques be recognised unless the full signature of the drawer is appended to the alteration, and then only when presented for payment by the drawer or his or her known agent. In practice, banks will usually accept an initialling.

[43] *Smith v. Union Bank of London* (1875) L.R. 1 Q.B.D. 31; s.10 of the Crossed Cheques Act 1876: a banker paying a crossed cheque in contravention of the crossing is liable to the "true owner" of the cheque, (Byles, *op. cit.*, p. 285).

[44] BOEA 1882, s. 78. The holder of a crossed cheque may cross it specially, BOEA 1882, s. 77(3). An unauthorised alteration may make it a forgery within the Forgery and Counterfeiting Act 1981, s. 1.

required by section 79 of the BOEA 1882, the bank is protected by section 80 of the BOEA 1882,[45] provided it has acted in good faith and without negligence, and the bank and its customer are treated as if they have paid the true owner. If a bank has paid another banker a bearer cheque (where the risk for the bank is always less in any case) according to the crossing, the bank is protected if the holder turns out to be a thief.

14–019 **"Not negotiable".** These words are rarely used now, because most cheques, since the Cheques Act 1992, are not transferable at all, and therefore not negotiable. The meaning of the words "not negotiable" added to a crossing on a cheque,[46] is that the cheque is transferable but not negotiable (section 81 of the BOEA 1882), so that the transferee cannot have a better title than the transferor and takes subject to equities. A "not negotiable" marking (whether with or without a crossing) on other bills of exchange makes them not transferable at all, so that only the original payee may be paid. A "not negotiable" marking on an uncrossed cheque probably has the same effect.

A cheque may also be marked "not transferable",[47] in which case it is valid only as between the immediate parties and is not negotiable.

14–020 **"Account payee".** The phrase "account payee only" has become of considerable importance since 1992. The words (and other similar expressions sometimes used on crossed cheques) are not recognised by the BOEA 1882, and used to be regarded simply as a direction to the *collecting bank* as to how it deals with the money after it has received it[48]; unlike crossings, they did not affect the paying banker. The legal effect of the phrase was doubtful, particularly because the drawer of the cheque has no contractual relationship with the collecting bank. The implication was probably not that the cheque became non-transferable,[49] but that the collecting bank might be negligent if it received payment for someone who was not the named payee, so that the protection of section 4 of the Cheques Act 1957[50] was not available.

The effect of the words has been strengthened by the Cheques Act 1992, which inserts a new section 81A into the BOEA 1882. Collecting banks are now required to ensure that cheques with the words *account payee* (or "a/c payee") or *account payee only* are not transferable, but only valid as between the parties.[51] They should be paid in only for the account of the payee of the cheque.

---

45 See below, para. 14–032.

46 Authorised by BOEA 1882, s. 76(b).

47 BOEA 1882, s. 8(1).

48 *Akrokerri (Atlantic) Mines Ltd v. Economic Bank* [1904] 2 K.B. 465; *A.L. Underwood Ltd v. Bank of Liverpool and Martins* [1924] 1 K.B. 775.

49 *National Bank v. Silke* [1891] 1 Q.B. 435. See Jack Report, Cm. 622 (1989), para. 7.17.

50 See below, para. 14–045.

51 Jack's view was that the most efficient way to introduce a non-transferable instrument was to replace the cheque by the "bank payment order" (to be introduced by a Cheques and Bank Payment Orders Act), which would not be transferable. (Cm. 622 (1989) Recs 7(1) and (2)). The Government found little support for this recommendation.

This means that cheques with these words—the vast majority, because banks now have the words preprinted on cheque forms—are not merely not negotiable, but not transferable at all, so that a person who obtains possession of the cheque and who is not the payee does not obtain any title to it. This puts the collecting bank unequivocally in the position of ensuring that it pays the correct payee; if it does not, it will be at risk of losing its protection under section 4 of the Cheques Act 1957.[52] Banks must therefore make careful enquiry before paying out to a third person on such a cheque.[53] **14–021**

It was feared that making cheques non-transferable by using the "account payee" device would impose an unreasonable burden on the *paying* bank,[54] which would have no way of ensuring that it was the payee who was receiving the payment. This objection has been met by providing specifically in the Cheques Act 1957 that the paying bank's protection under section 80 of the BOEA 1882 covers cheques with "account payee" on them.[55]

Oddly, it seems that one side-effect of the change to non-transferable cheques may be that collecting banks themselves will often lose one of their means of protection against claims by victims of fraud, since they will not be able to become holders in due course of such cheques (an alternative defence, where the bank has given value, to the statutory protection under section 4 of the Cheques Act 1957).[56] **14–022**

The Paying Bank

The paying bank is under a duty to its customer to act according to his or her mandate.[57] If it pays wrongly, it has certain defences as against its customer, as seen in Chapter 7, where the common law defences such as estoppel were described. The bank has no contractual duty towards third parties, such as the payee or the true owner of the cheque, though it may be liable in conversion or restitution,[58] and is given statutory protection against action by a third party (and by its customer, in the appropriate circumstances). **14–023**

---

52 The Cheques Act 1992 provides (s. 3) for collecting banks to have protection under s. 4 in handling such cheques.

53 In *Middle Temple v. Lloyds Bank plc & Sekerbank* [1999] Lloyd's Rep. Bank. 50, where the respective duties of a foreign correspondent bank and an English clearing bank acting for it who between them had negligently collected an "account payee only" cheque were considered; see above, Chap. 5.

54 See the Jack Report, Cm. 622 (1989).

55 Cheques Act 1957, s. 2. For BOEA 1882, s. 80, see below, para. 14–032.

56 Ellinger (1992) J.B.L. 15; Brindle and Cox, *op. cit.*, p. 240. See below, 14–076.

57 See above, Chap. 6.

58 That is, by "waiver of the tort".

The tort of conversion

14–024 Conversion[59] is wrongfully interfering with the right to possession of a chattel.[60] Liability is strict, so that, if a cheque has been stolen, the bank would be liable for dealing with it even innocently; and the bank, as a "deep pocket" defendant, will be more attractive to sue than the actual wrongdoer. Prima facie, therefore, the risk of liability for banks dealing with cheques is great; whenever a cheque is wrongly dealt with, the true owner may claim against the collecting or paying bank or both, depending upon the facts. The banks would find it impossible to carry on their daily business if they had no protection against such widespread liability. This is the reason that statutory defences were provided for banks paying and collecting on behalf of their customers.

14–025 **Measure of damages in conversion.** The measure of damages for conversion would normally be the value of the article converted, and the article would be the chattel—in this case, the cheque. This poses a problem, because a cheque merely has the value of a small piece of paper. The courts have held, though, in a series of decisions, that the measure of damages is the face value of the cheque.[61] This will often achieve a fair result, although there must be occasions when the face value of the cheque may not be the real measure of loss—if the cheque has been given where the drawer's account is overdrawn, for example, the cheque, whatever its *face* value, may have no real value at all. If the cheque has been materially altered, however, it is a nullity, and the claimant cannot recover the face value in an action for conversion.[61a]

14–026 **Liability to the true owner.** There is reference in the BOEA 1882 to the "true owner" although it is not defined.[62] It is usually, but not always, obvious who is the true owner. Once the cheque is issued, the payee will be the first true owner. If the cheque has been made out to bearer, the bank is entitled to pay the person in possession, whoever it is, provided the bank is not on notice of any suspicious circumstances. If the cheque is negotiated, the holder in due course, if there is one, will be the true owner. However, it is not necessary for the person in possession to show that he or she is the *owner* of the cheque, but merely to establish a "sufficient proprietary right". In *Bute*

---

[59] Conversion now arises under the Torts (Interference with Goods) Act 1977.

[60] *MCC Proceeds v. Lehman Bros* [1998] 4 All E.R. 675 at 685, *per* Mummery L.J.

[61] Including *Morison v. London County and Westminster Bank Ltd* [1914] 3 K.B. 356, *Underwood v. Bank of Liverpool* [1924] 1 K.B. 775. See also *Smith v. Lloyd's TSB Group plc* [2000] Lloyd's Rep. Bank. 58, where it was held that the payee of a cheque which had been materially altered (by the alteration of the name of the payee) could not recover the face value of the cheque from the collecting bank which had converted it because the cheque was a nullity under s. 64 of the BOEA 1882..

[61a] Under s. 64 of the BOEA 1882. See *Smith v. Lloyds TSB Group plc* [2000] Lloyd's Rep. Bank. 58.

[62] BOEA 1882, ss. 79(2) and 80.

(Marquess) v. Barclays Bank Ltd,[63] McGaw, the manager of some of the plaintiff's sheep farms whose employment had ended, received some warrants for payment of sheep farm subsidy from the Department of Agriculture who had not been notified that the employment had ended. The warrants were payable to McGaw, but the words "for the Marquess of Bute" were also written on them. McGaw paid them into his own account and drew out the money later. It was held that the warrants were payable to the Marquess through McGaw. The Marquess, as the person entitled to immediate possession, had sufficient title to sue in conversion. In *Lipkin Gorman v. Karpnale,*[64] solicitors had been defrauded by their partner of a banker's draft payable to themselves. The partner indorsed it to a casino and gambled away the proceeds. It was held that the solicitors had title to require the delivery of the draft to them, and they succeeded in that part of their claim against the casino.

However, a claim for conversion of goods is a common law action, and is **14–027** not maintainable by a person who only has an equitable interest in goods as against another who has acquired the legal title to them, as a bona fide purchaser for value without notice of the prior equitable claim, because the equitable interest has then been overreached and extinguished. A person with an equitable title who also has *actual possession* or the right to immediate possession of the cheque is in a different position, however, and in that case will be the true owner.[65]

Statutory defences open to the paying bank

This protection takes the form of three provisions (sections 60 and 80 of **14–028** BOEA 1882, and section 1 of the Cheques Act 1957) which together form a complex and ill-fitting patchwork of defences. Because these come into play when an indorsement on the cheque has been forged or is missing, they have become of much less importance since most cheques became non-transferable in 1992, but the provisions still exist and are still relevant for those cheques which may be transferred.

Most cheques are *order* cheques,[66] made out by the drawer to a specified person. In the case of an order cheque, if the bank has paid a person who is not the payee of the cheque, the question whether the bank has paid correctly and the cheque has been discharged depends upon whether the cheque has been negotiated properly[67]—that is, by *indorsement* (signature) and delivery to a third party. If an indorsement on the cheque is invalid[68] or

[63] [1955] 1 Q.B. 202; [1954] 3 W.L.R. 741; [1954] 3 All E.R. 365.
[64] [1991] 3 W.L.R. 10; [1991] A.C. 548; [1992] 4 All E.R. 512.
[65] *MCC Proceeds* [1998] 4 All E.R. 675 at 691, *per* Mummery L.J.
[66] As opposed to bearer cheques, which can be transferred without indorsement, and where the bank may usually safely pay the holder.
[67] Under BOEA 1882, s. 31(3).
[68] The requisites for valid indorsement are set out in BOEA 1882, s. 32.

missing, the bank has no mandate from the drawer to pay the holder and is also liable in conversion to the true owner.

14–029 Years ago, when the use of cheques became popular, it became evident that it was impossible for banks to scrutinise all indorsements properly. The paying bank, for example, does not usually know the payee and could not verify his or her signature, let alone that of any subsequent holder. It would have been impossible for banks to carry on their business effectively if they were constantly at risk of action even when they were acting quite properly. The statutory protections modifying banks' duties were therefore introduced.

14–030 **(a) Section 60, Bills of Exchange Act 1882.** This section provides that where an order cheque has a *forged or unauthorised indorsement*, the bank may be protected—provided it paid in "good faith and in the ordinary course of business",[69] the bank is deemed to have paid in due course. The cheque is then discharged,[70] and the customer's debt to the third party is also discharged and the customer's account may be debited. Assuming that the bank has acted in good faith,[71] the main question is what amounts to "the ordinary course of business". Generally, this is a question of banking practice at the time and what is reasonable in the particular circumstances, and it is not possible to lay down firm rules. It has been held[72] that it is not the same as "negligence", so that a bank could be negligent yet still act in the ordinary course of business. Paget[73] cites *Brighton Empire and Eden Syndicate v. London and County Bank*,[74] where the bank cashed an order cheque drawn by a customer, even though an indorsement had been forged by an employee whose handwriting was well known to the bank. The court held that even if failure to recognise the handwriting was negligence, the bank was protected. Nevertheless, negligence must be an indication that the circumstances are not "ordinary" and in any case negligence may indicate a lack of "good faith". In *Auchteroni & Co. v. Midland Bank Ltd*,[75] Wright J. said that where the circumstances were suspicious "the taker of the instrument is not acting in good faith if he shuts his eyes to the fact presented to him and puts the suspicions aside without further inquiry".

(i) Paying an obviously suspicious person would not be in the ordinary course of business. In the *Auchteroni* case, the question (which

[69] Protection where an indorsement is *missing* is provided by BOEA 1882, s. 80, see below, para. 14–032.

[70] Under BOEA 1882, s. 59: "payment made [at maturity] to the holder thereof in good faith and without notice that his title to the bill is defective".

[71] Defined as "where [a thing] is in fact done honestly, whether it is done negligently or not": BOEA 1882, s. 90.

[72] In a case where the paying bank was also the collecting bank (when the bank must bring itself within the protection afforded to the collecting bank as well): *Carpenters' Company v. British Mutual Banking Company* [1938] 1 K.B. 511.

[73] (11th ed.), p. 384.

[74] *The Times*, March 24, 1904.

[75] [1928] 2 K.B. 294.

involved a bill of exchange, not a cheque) was whether there was payment "in due course" under section 59 of the BOEA 1882. A fraudulent person presented the bill to the paying bank and was paid cash over the counter. The court held that this was unusual and infrequent, but not so unusual that it deprived the bank of its protection under the section. Payment to an obviously suspicious person, such as a tramp, postman or office boy would render the bank liable, however, according to Wright J.

(ii) Payment after hours[76] might also be out of the ordinary course of business, but a few minutes makes little difference, especially if the bank pays to persons already in the building at close of business.[77]

(iii) Payment of an uncrossed cheque to a stranger who presents the cheque through the post and asks for cash to be sent to him or her, would be suspicious, and not "ordinary".

(iv) Payment "under advice" (by open credit) occurs when a branch at which the account is not kept cashes cheques for a customer of the bank on request. This is presumably within the ordinary course of business.

If the bank paid an uncrossed cheque marked "not negotiable", section 60 of the BOEA 1882 would not protect it since only the original payee may be paid. A crossed cheque with the "not negotiable" marking but without the "account payee" marking is still transferable, and section 60 could apply, provided that payment is made to a banker. **14–031**

Section 60 of the BOEA 1882 does not protect the bank if the bill also suffers from other defects, such as a material alteration in the amount. In *Slingsby v. District Bank*[78] a fraudster altered the payee's name to include his own, and then indorsed the cheque. It was held that the cheque was avoided by virtue of section 64 of the BOEA 1882 because it had been materially altered, and the bank was not protected: "this invalidity comes before any question of indorsement".[79]

(b) Section 80, Bills of Exchange Act 1882. This section applies to crossed cheques paid according to the crossing to a banker,[80] "in good faith and without negligence". If the bank pays the wrong person, it is protected and it may debit the account of its customer, the drawer. Since the cheque is **14–032**

---

[76] See above, Chap. 6.

[77] *Baines v. National Provincial Bank Ltd* (1927) L.J.K.B. 801.

[78] [1932] 1 K.B. 544.

[79] [1932] 1 K.B. 544 at 559, *per* Scrutton L.J. See also *Smith v. Lloyds TSB Group plc* [2000] Lloyd's Rep. bank. 58.

[80] Or, if the cheque has been crossed "specially", a specified banker or his agent for collection, who must be a banker.

discharged, no party can be liable on it, and the true owner cannot sue the bank for conversion, although the true owner still has a remedy in conversion against the person whom the bank actually paid. The customer is discharged from any debt for which the cheque was given if the cheque comes into the hands of the payee. The cheque must be paid "without negligence", but since the bank is making payment to another banker, negligence would be rare.[81]

The converse of section 80 is section 79 of the BOEA 1882, which provides that if the bank does *not* pay according to the crossing, it is liable to the true owner (it would also be in breach of its mandate to its customer, who would also still be indebted to the payee). This applies even if the cheque is a bearer cheque, though usually the holder will then be the true owner. It has the effect of displacing section 60 of the BOEA 1882, for payment of a crossed cheque other than to another banker is clearly not "in the ordinary course of business".

14–033 **(c) Section 1, Cheques Act 1957.** Under certain conditions, section 1 of the Cheques Act 1957 protects a bank which pays a cheque which is not indorsed or is irregularly indorsed from claims by the true owner and its customer. It also provides that the instrument is discharged by the payment, so that the bank can debit its customer's account. It applies in the following circumstances:

(i) to a banker acting in good faith and in the ordinary course of business;

(ii) who pays a cheque drawn upon him, or any instrument issued by a customer which is a mandate for payment[82] (or the banker's own demand draft);

(iii) where the cheque is not indorsed, or is irregularly indorsed.[83]

14–034 Again, the important question is what amounts to acting "in the ordinary course of business". What was said in relation to section 60 of the BOEA 1882 above would also apply here, so that paying a crossed cheque to someone other than a banker would not be protected. However, the

[81] If an indorsement is bad or missing, BOEA 1882, s. 80 protects the bank. There is an overlap between the sections: payment of a crossed cheque with a forged indorsement is also protected under BOEA 1882, s. 60 and Cheques Act 1957, s. 1. Paget, *op. cit.*, p. 389, criticises the overlap between the sections: Cheques Act 1957, s. 1 did not, unlike Cheques Act 1957, s. 4, completely restate the bank's protection and there are confusions as to the wording of Cheques Act 1957, s. 1 which might have been avoided if it had done so.

[82] A document "intended to enable a person to obtain payment from" a bank would include, *e.g.* a postdated cheque.

[83] A cheque with a forged indorsement may be regarded as "not" indorsed or as "irregularly" indorsed (by BOEA 1882, s. 24 the signature is inoperative). Whichever it is, the bank is protected under BOEA 1882, ss. 60 and 80.

Committee of London Clearing Bankers has also laid down[84] certain rules of practice, and it is likely that if a bank failed to comply with these it would not be acting "in the ordinary course of business". These were issued because there were still situations where it was considered prudent for banks to examine indorsements despite the statutory protection. It is obviously very likely that if a bank fails to comply with the rules of practice, it does not act "in the ordinary course of business", but in general, as far as paying banks are concerned, indorsements on cheques or other instruments need otherwise not be examined.[85]

It is sometimes said that section 1 of the Cheques Act 1957 made indorsements unnecessary, but this statement should be treated with reserve. If a cheque is negotiable, an indorsement will still be necessary to transfer title from a payee A to an indorsee B. If the cheque has been correctly indorsed, B will become the holder and will be able to sue the drawer or prior indorsers if the cheque is not paid. But the effect of the section is that, provided the bank complies with its requirements, it is protected if the cheque has not been correctly indorsed and the bank pays B, who has no title. It may debit the account of its customer, the drawer, who is discharged from any debt owed to A for which the cheque was given, and the true owner cannot sue the bank for conversion. Since the cheque is discharged, no party can be liable on it, but the true owner still has a remedy in conversion against B. It is therefore better to say that, provided the bank acts in the ordinary course of business, it does not need to check indorsements, rather than to say that indorsements are unnecessary on negotiable cheques. In any case, the wide use of non-transferable cheques since the Cheques Act 1992 means that indorsements are now rare. **14–035**

The statutory protections: Jack's view

The Jack Committee considered the protection given to paying banks and concluded that the provisions, though necessary, were not clear or wholly consistent. The differing prerequisites, "good faith", "without negligence" and "the ordinary course of business" do not fit coherently together, and the concept of the "ordinary course of business" is uncertain because it is so **14–036**

---

[84] Memorandum of September 23, 1957. Where indorsements are to be examined, BOEA 1882, ss. 32–35 apply.

[85] This includes "house debits" (where the branch in question pays its customer A and debits its customer B). The rules go on to list the exceptions, where indorsements *should* be examined; these are (i) instruments which are combined cheque and receipt forms, but only if marked with a bold outline letter "R" on the face of them; (ii) traveller's cheques; (iii) bills of exchange (those which are not cheques), (iv) promissory notes; (v) cheques and other instruments cashed at the counter (including those cashed under open credits). Where indorsements are to be examined, ss. 32–35 of the BOEA 1882 apply. There are too many complicated rules on indorsements, many deriving from custom, to mention here. Reference might be made to Thomson's *Dictionary of Banking*, under the entry for "Indorsement". To give one of hundreds of examples: if the payee is "Mr John Brown" an indorsement "Mr John Brown" is not acceptable (he should indorse "John Brown").

dependent on particular circumstances. The Committee proposed that it should be removed and the other protections available to the paying bank should be brought together in one statute and made subject to the condition that a bank has acted in good faith and without negligence.[86] The effect of the Cheques Act 1992, however, in drastically reducing the numbers of indorsed cheques, has made the introduction of further legislation unnecessary.

The Collecting Bank

14–037 The collecting bank may also be liable in conversion (or restitution) to the true owner of the cheque. The defences open to it depend upon whether it acted for its customer or for itself. Again the provisions of the Cheques Act 1992 have made an effect on the way in which the law operates—the defence of holder for value may not normally be available to banks since cheques are generally not negotiable.

Collecting and discounting

14–038 When a bank collects a cheque for its customer, it acts as an agent for the customer. If it has given value for the cheque, however, it may be acting on its *own* behalf; if so, it is said to *discount* the cheque. In this case, it takes it as a party to the cheque (subject to the provisions of the Cheques Act 1992), as a holder for value (or, probably, as a holder in due course) and itself has title to the cheque.[87]

Banks may be acting both for their customers and as holders.[88] In this case, both defences—section 4 of the Cheques Act 1957[88a] and as a holder of the cheque (probably of a holder in due course)—are open to the bank. If it qualifies as a holder for value or in due course, the bank may gain the advantage of being able to claim the cheque even if it has acted negligently, whereas negligence would prevent it from claiming protection under section 4. This section of the chapter will look first at the relationship between the collecting bank and its customer, and its liability towards third parties, and then at the bank as a holder for value.

---

[86] Jack Report, Cm. 622 (1989), para. 7.26.

[87] A holder in due course is a party to whom the bill (cheque) has been negotiated when it is complete and regular on its face; before it is overdue and without any notice of any dishonour; in good faith and without any notice of a defect in the transferor's title; and for value (s. 29 of the BOEA 1882). See above, Chap. 13.

[88] *Barclays Bank Ltd v. Astley Industrial Trusts Ltd* [1970] 2 Q.B. 527, although it seems a little odd. Milmo J. said (at 538): "It is moreover a commonplace occurrence for a banker to allow credit to a customer against an uncleared cheque. A banker who permits his customer to draw £5 against an uncleared cheque for £100 has given value for it but is it to be said that in consequence he is no longer the customer's agent for the collection of that cheque?".

[88a] Discussed below, para. 14–045.

Duties of collecting bank to customer

When a cheque is given to a collecting bank, it must be presented for collection[89] within a reasonable time. This means that where the paying bank is in the same town, the collecting bank should present it on the business day following receipt.[90] If the paying bank is elsewhere, the cheque should either be presented or forwarded on the following business day.[91] If the bank fails to present the cheque within the time allowed, it is liable to its customer for any loss.[92] Cheques today are normally presented through the clearings, but a collecting bank which is not a member of the clearing house may forward the cheque to another branch or to an agent of the bank, which will act for it in clearing the cheque and will have the same time for presentation after the cheque has been received.[93] A bank may specially collect by special presentation to another bank (not through the clearings) and the paying bank may hold the cheque until the day after receipt and pay then.[94] Where authorised by custom, a bank may present a cheque by post.[95] **14–039**

If a collecting bank delays in presenting a cheque so that the cheque is dishonoured—for example, there are insufficient funds available or the drawer is insolvent (or the drawee bank is insolvent), the collecting bank will be liable if its customer suffers loss.[96] **14–040**

If a cheque is dishonoured, the bank must inform its customer as soon as reasonably possible, so that he or she can give notice of dishonour to the drawer and others; the bank will be liable for losses arising from any delay. The bank itself may give notice of dishonour as agent, but rarely does—the usual practice is to return the cheque to the customer. Notice of dishonour must be given by the customer within a "reasonable time"[97] and this means (a) where they live in the same place (postal district perhaps)[98] it must be sent so that it arrives on the day following dishonour, and (b) otherwise must be sent on the day following dishonour if there is a post, and otherwise sent by the next post. If, however, bank or branch A acts as clearing agent for bank B, then each in the chain is allowed the same time;

[89] The meaning of "for collection" (within s. 2 of the Cheques Act 1957) is not confined to collection for the payee's own account: *Westminster Bank v. Zang* [1966] 2 W.L.R. 110.

[90] *Alexander v. Burchfield* (1842) 7 Man.. & G. 1061; *Forman v. Bank of England* (1902) 18 T.L.R. 339.

[91] *Hare v. Henty* (1861) 10 C.B.(N.S.) 65; *Heywood v. Pickering* (1874) L.R. 9 Q.B. 428.

[92] *Lubbock v. Tribe* (1838) 3 M & W 607.

[93] *Prideaux v. Criddle* (1869) L.R. 4 Q.B. 455.

[94] *Bailey v. Bodenham* (1864) 16 C.B.(N.S.) 288.

[95] s. 45, rule 8 of the BOEA 1882.

[96] *Forman v. Bank of England* (1902) 18 T.L.R. 339.

[97] BOEA 1882, s. 49, r. 12.

[98] In *Hamilton Finance Co Ltd v. Coverley Westray Walbaum and Tosetti Ltd* [1969] 1 Lloyds Rep. 53. Mocatta J. had to decide "the fascinating question whether for the purposes of [BOEA 1882] s. 49 . . . Upper Brook Street Mayfair is in the same place as Seething Lane E.C.3." He held that it was.

so that A has the time allowed to inform B and B has the time to inform its customer, who has the time allowed to give notice to the drawer, and so forth.[99]

14–041 The collecting bank has no duty to warn its customer of risks in the transaction. In *Redmond v. Allied Irish Bank*,[1] the bank's customer paid in to his own account cheques which were payable to other people and crossed "not negotiable—a/c payee only". It turned out that they had been misappropriated, and he sued the bank for negligence in failing to advise him that the cheques constituted a risk to him, but it was held that the bank was under no duty to warn him of the risk.[2]

Collecting bank and third parties

14–042 At common law, the bank is liable to the true owner of a cheque or bill in the tort of conversion if it pays another person.[3] Liability is most likely to arise when an order cheque[4] has a missing or forged indorsement, and a person who is not entitled to it presents it to the bank. The bank is not discharged by payment and may be liable to the true owner in conversion. Conversion, which arises under the Torts (Interference with Goods) Act 1977, is a "strict liability" tort, inasmuch as innocence or taking care does not provide a defence. Alternatively, the bank may be able to recover the money from the person to whom it has been paid by an action at common law for money had and received (restitution).[5]

Contributory negligence

14–043 The collecting bank, unlike the paying bank,[6] may plead contributory negligence by the plaintiff. In *Lumsden & Co. v. London Trustee Savings Bank*[7] the plaintiffs brought an action for the conversion of some cheques. The court accepted the view[8] that the Law Reform (Contributory Negligence) Act 1945 applied not only to actions for negligence, but also to other torts, including the tort of conversion, so that if the plaintiffs are contributorily negligent in facilitating a fraud the damages recoverable by them should be proportionally reduced. In the *Lumsden* case the plaintiffs' damages were reduced by 10 per cent because the court held that while the

[99] BOEA 1882, s. 49, r. 13.

[1] [1987] F.L.R. 367; [1987] F.T.L.R. 264.

[2] A decision on these facts might be different since the Cheques Act 1992.

[3] Or in restitution.

[4] If the cheque is a *bearer* cheque, the presenter is the holder and the bank is protected if it pays in due course under BOEA 1882, s. 59. The cheque is discharged.

[5] *e.g. National Westminster Bank Ltd v. Barclays Bank International* [1975] 2 W.L.R. 13 (forgery); *Barclays Bank v. Simms & Cooke* [1979] 3 All E.R. 522 (countermanded cheque). See above, Chap. 10.

[6] See above, Chaps 6 and 7.

[7] [1971] 1 Ll. Rep. 114.

[8] Advanced by Milnes Holden.

bank was negligent in not fully establishing its customer's credentials when his account was opened, the plaintiffs had also been negligent in leaving spaces on the cheques in question which allowed unauthorised additions to be made to the payee's name. However, the Torts (Interference with Goods) Act 1977 (possibly inadvertently) abolished the defence of contributory negligence in such cases. The decision, however, was restored by the BA 1979.[9]

Section 47 of the BA 1979 gives the *Lumsden* decision statutory force: **14–044**

> "In any circumstances in which proof of absence of negligence on the part of the banker would be a defence in proceedings by reasons of s. 4 of the Cheques Act 1957, a defence of contributory negligence shall also be available to the banker notwithstanding the provisions of s. 11(1) of the Torts (Interference with Goods) Act 1977."

Statutory Protection of the Collecting Bank

In its role as agent of the customer, the bank is not acting on its own account and cannot claim to be a holder of the cheque in its own right. The risk it runs of liability for conversion would make banking business impossible, and for that reason section 4 of the Cheques Act 1957 was enacted to provide protection for collecting banks. **14–045**

The section[10] states that:

4(1) Where a banker, in good faith and without negligence,-

(a) receives payment for a customer of an instrument to which this section applies; or

(b) having credited a customer's account with the amount of such an instrument, receives payment thereof for himself,

and the customer has no title, or a defective title, to the instrument, the banker does not incur any liability to the true owner of the instrument by reason only of having received payment thereof.[11]

4(3) A banker is not to be treated for the purposes of this section as having been negligent by reason only of his failure to concern

[9] The position is not completely restored, because the paying bank cannot plead the defence of contributory negligence if it is sued for conversion.

[10] Formerly in the BOEA 1882, s. 82, which, however, applied only to crossed cheques and was limited to cases where payment was received by the bank for the customer. Section 4 of the Cheques Act 1957 also applies to banks acting in their discounting role.

[11] Cheques Act 1957, s. 4(2) states that the section applies not only to cheques, but to any document issued by a customer which is intended to obtain payment from the banker. This covers instruments made out to "cash or order" which are not bills of exchange (*North & South Insurance Corporation v. National Provincial Bank* [1936] 1 K.B. 328, see above, para. 14–005), any document issued by a public officer intended to enable a person to obtain payment from the Paymaster General, etc.; and any draft payable on demand drawn by a banker upon himself (a banker's draft, see below, para. 14–086).

himself with absence of, or irregularity in, indorsement of an instrument.

14–046 The bank must fulfil the requirements of section 4(1) of the Cheques Act 1957 to claim protection, and it must therefore satisfy the court that it is a *bank* and that it has *received payment for a customer*. In most cases now there is no difficulty in practice for the bank in establishing that it is a bank and that it was receiving payment for a customer,[12] but the requirements mean that the court can consider whether the bank has acted negligently at the stage of opening an account as well as at the later stage of collecting the cheque.

14–047 **Good faith.** Providing there is no problem about the above requirements, the bank has then to show that it acted in *good faith*. This is a separate requirement from showing that it has not been negligent, but in practice, the bank is most unlikely to have any difficulty in demonstrating this.[13]

Without negligence. Negligence is a different matter. What amounts to negligence is the all important question, and each case turns on its own facts. This is not a common law duty of care as such, but a specialised statutory form of liability for negligence. Since it takes the form of a qualified immunity from liability at common law, the burden of proof is on the bank.[14]

Standard of care

14–048 The standard of care for the bank has to be ascertained by reference to the practice of reasonable men carrying on the business of bankers and endeavouring to do so in such a manner as may be calculated to protect themselves and others against fraud.[15] The practice of bankers is the normal guide; in the case of *Marfani v. Midland Bank Ltd*,[16] Diplock L.J. said:

> "What the court has to do is to look at all the circumstances at the time of the acts complained of, and to ask itself, were those circumstances such as would cause a reasonable banker, possessed of such information about his customer as a reasonable banker would possess, to suspect that his customer was not the true owner of the cheque."

---

[12] *Ladbroke v. Todd* (1914) 30 T.L.R. 433. The definitions of "bank" and "customer", are discussed above, in Chap. 2.

[13] Byles, *op. cit.*, p. 320), says there appears to be no reported case where good faith has been called in question. Ellinger and Lomnicka, *Modern Banking Law*, p. 515, cite one (*Lawrie v. Commonwealth Trading Bank of Australia* [1970] Qd. R. 373); even then, the bank was successful.

[14] *Marfani v. Midland Bank Ltd* [1968] 2 All E.R. 573 at 579, *per* Diplock L.J.; [1968] 1 W.L.R. 956 at 972.

[15] *Lloyds Bank v. Savory* [1933] A.C. 201 at 221, *per* Lord Warrington of Clyffe.

[16] [1964] 1 W.L.R. 955.

Banking practice may not always be followed, because the fact that it has been sanctioned by long usage does not necessarily mean that it is good practice.[17] The standard of care, in any case, is always a matter of fact, and since the practice of banks necessarily changes over time, the standard will change accordingly; cases from decades ago will not necessarily be a good guide. The view taken by the court of the duties of the bank in *Lloyds Bank Ltd. v. E.B. Savory and Co.*,[18] in the 1930s, was more demanding than that of Diplock L.J. **14–049**

There are a number of statements to the effect that the standard is a high one, but judges just as frequently state that banks are not expected to be amateur detectives, and that making a thorough inquiry into the history of each cheque would render banking business impracticable.

Causation

If the cheque or circumstances surrounding the transaction are unusual or suspicious enough to put the bank on inquiry, it may lose the protection of the section if it fails to make inquiries or to obtain a satisfactory explanation. There is a difference of view in the authorities as to whether a bank may protect itself by showing that, if it had inquired, it would not have been told the truth. Some consider that this is irrelevant[19]; others that the defence is open to the bank.[20] Further, the section does not establish a normal duty of care, but provides a special statutory protection against conversion. This means that if the bank cannot show that it was not negligent, it may be liable in conversion whether or not the negligent behaviour was the cause of the customer's loss. **14–050**

Types of Negligence

The words of section 4(1) of the Cheques Act 1957, making the bank liable for negligent acts refer only to the act of collection but in fact the obligation on the collecting bank to take care applies from the beginning of its relationship with the customer for whom it collects the cheque. The bank may have been negligent either in the course of collecting a cheque **14–051**

[17] *Lloyd's Bank v. Savory* [1933] A.C. 201. See also *Turner v. Royal Bank of Scotland* [1999] Lloyd's Rep. Bank. 231 at 235, 236. But *cf.* Diplock L.J. in *Marfani* [1968] 1 W.L.R. 956 at 975: "I venture to think that this court should be hesitant before condemning as negligent a practice generally adopted by those engaged in banking business". And it would not necessarily be the same standard as the "ordinary course of business" (applying to paying banks) of Cheques Act 1957, s. 1, although failing to comply with the ordinary course of business may often amount to negligence.

[18] [1933] A.C. 201. See below para. 14–063.

[19] See, *e.g. Lloyds Bank v. Savory & Co* [1932] K.B. 122 at 148, *per* Greer L.J., CA; [1933] A.C. 201 at 203, *per* Lord Wright, *Thackwell v. Barclays Bank* [1986] 1 All E.R. 676 at 684, *per* Hutchison J.

[20] *e.g. Baker v. Barclays Bank Ltd* [1955] 1 W.L.R. 822 at 836, *per* Devlin J., *Marfani* [1968] 2 All E.R. 573, *per* Diplock L.J.

for a customer or in circumstances related to the collection (it is obviously under an obligation to see that everything is apparently in order when it receives the cheque for payment and presents it for collection), or in the antecedent circumstances, for example in a failure to make proper checks on opening the account. The bank is not concerned only with the customer's apparent respectability, but with all matters which may be relevant to the possibility of his or her using the account to obtain payment of cheques to which he or she has no title.

14–052 **(a) in collecting a cheque.** A bank's decision as to whether it can properly accept a cheque for collection has to be made at the time when the cheque is handed in at the counter, when it is received by post, or soon after that, before the cheque and paying-in slip are separated and the cheque is sent forward to the clearing house. Very often there is no indication from the face of a stolen cheque that it has been misappropriated, and the bank must be alert to possible warnings that it might have been. For example, if a person who is known to be an agent pays in to his or her own account a cheque drawn by a third party in favour of the principal[21] (a director of a company, perhaps, may pay a cheque payable to the company into his or her private account) or if a cheque is indorsed *per pro*[22] the principal by the agent.[23]

14–053 In *A.L. Underwood Ltd v. Bank of Liverpool and Martins*,[24] the sole director of a company indorsed a number of cheques payable to the company and paid them into his own account instead of the company's account, which was at another bank. The bank collected the cheques for him without inquiring whether the company had a separate bank account. The bank was sued in conversion on behalf of a holder of a debenture in the company. The court held that the bank was not protected because the fact that an agent was paying his principal's cheques into his own account was unusual enough to put the bank on inquiry, and that the director had behaved, and had been treated by the bank, as if he himself were the company.

14–054 In the case of *Orbit Mining and Trading Company Ltd v. Westminster Bank Ltd*,[25] on the other hand, a bank was held not to have been negligent where a director paid company cheques into his own account. E, a director of the plaintiff company, was trusted by the other director, W, who signed blank company cheque forms and left them for E to use while he went

---

[21] As in *Bute (Marquess) v. Barclays Bank* [1955] 1 Q.B. 202; [1954] 3 W.L.R. 741; [1954] 3 All E.R. 365.

[22] *Per procurationem*, see s. 25 of the BOEA 1882.

[23] See *Midland Bank Ltd v. Reckitt and Others* [1933] A.C. 1 and *Penmount Estates Ltd v. National Provincial Bank Ltd* (1945) 89 Sol. Jo. 566.

[24] [1924] 1 K.B. 775.

[25] [1963] 1 Q.B. 794.

away. E would fill them in, usually making them payable to cash,[26] sign the cheques and pay them into his own account. When the frauds were discovered, the company sued the bank in conversion. It was held by the Court of Appeal that the bank had not been negligent. The bank did not know that E was employed by the company, and was not negligent not to have known. In Harman L.J.'s words, which reflected the practice of banks at the time (which may have changed since the introduction of the money laundering regulations requiring banks to "know their customers")[27]: "It cannot at any rate be the duty of the bank continually to keep itself up to date as to the identity of a customer's employer". The bank had to be judged on the provision it had made for the proper scrutiny of cheques paid in for collection and on the actual scrutiny which was made in a particular case, and, on that basis, it was not negligent here.

Other situations where banks should be alert to possible misappropriation of cheques include fiduciary relationships in general, because a fiduciary may be well placed to steal a cheque and forge the signature of the principal as drawer, or to sign as drawer in excess of authority and fraudulently insert his or her own name as payee, or that of the principal, adding a forged or unauthorised indorsement. Banks should make more inquiries when collecting a cheque indorsed to a customer with a dubious banking record[28] and, of course, should be alert if the cheque on its face gives rise to suspicion; for example, a customer might present a cheque for a large sum payable to a third person or a cheque payable to a public official and apparently indorsed by that official. Since the Cheques Act 1992, banks have had to be particularly cautious in accepting a cheque marked "account payee only" for a person other than the payee specified, and they should do so only if they are quite satisfied with the explanation given. **14–055**

It might be enough to alert a bank if a customer presents a cheque which, although it appears otherwise satisfactory, is for a sum quite out of proportion to the amounts the bank is accustomed to collect for that customer. The bank will obviously be more at risk if it does not follow its own internal rules, although this is not a conclusive factor in itself.[29] **14–056**

Sometimes the surrounding circumstances are enough to put the bank on inquiry. In *Thackwell v. Barclays Bank plc*,[30] A.J., a director of A.J. Ltd, took a cheque for a very large sum payable to A.J. Ltd to the bank to pay it in. At the bank, he met another person, S, and they asked the assistant **14–057**

---

[26] Usually by putting the word "cash" between the printed words "pay" and "or order", but the bank was not negligent in paying on this direction ("pay cash or order"), which, it was held, was infrequently but regularly used; it was the practice of banks to pay on such instruments, although they were not cheques, see above, para. 14–005.

[27] See below, para. 14–069.

[28] *Motor Traders Guarantee Corpn. Ltd v. Midland Bank Ltd* [1937] 4 All E.R. 90.

[29] See also *Lumsden & Co v. London T.S.B.* [1971] 1 Lloyd's Rep. 114.

[30] [1986] 1 All E.R. 676.

manager to allow them to use an office. S appeared some time later with two cheques drawn on the account of A.J. Ltd, one of which was payable to the plaintiff, T, and the other payable to S. The first cheque had apparently been indorsed by T, and the second by S—but both indorsements were obviously written by the same person. The manager did not check the plaintiff's signature on the first cheque or compare the indorsements. It was discovered later that S had forged T's signature and that the transaction had formed a part of a fraudulent hire purchase transaction designed to raise capital for a gold mining company owned by the plaintiff, T. It was held that the circumstances in which the cheques had been presented for collection were so unusual and out of the ordinary course of business that the bank should have made further inquiries.[31] However, the bank escaped liability despite its negligence because the judge found that T had been a party to the fraudulent refinancing scheme[32] and it was against public policy for T to recover in conversion. The bank could rely on the defence of illegality (*ex turpi non oritur actio*).

14–058 *Checking indorsements.* Collecting banks used to be at risk because of the negotiability of cheques, which entailed the necessity of checking indorsements. Section 4(3) of the Cheques Act 1957 provided for collecting banks similar protection in this respect to that provided by section 1 for the paying bank:[33] "a banker is not to be treated for the purposes of this section as having been negligent by reason only of his failure to concern himself with absence of, or irregularity in, indorsement of an instrument".

14–059 The no-negligence defence under section 4 of the Cheques Act 1957 is not identical to the "ordinary course of business" defence for the paying bank under section 1 of the Cheques Act 1957, but, even so, failing to comply with the ordinary course of business must often amount to negligence. In this context, the ruling of the London Clearing Banks on September 23, 1957, which sets out cases in which indorsements are still required is important although it would apply only to non-account payee only cheques. These are: (a) if the payee's name is misspelt or he or she is incorrectly designated, and there are circumstances to suggest that he or she is not the person to whom payment is intended to be made (failure to inquire would in any case surely amount to negligence); (b) if the cheque or other instrument is collected for an account other than that of the original named payee, indorsement will be required (so-called "third party"

[31] In *Thackwell*, the bank had omitted to check indorsements, one of which turned out to be irregular, and the bank might have been assisted by Cheques Act 1957, s. 4(3). The words of the section read "by reason only of his failure" to check indorsements, and the decision supports the alternative view that Cheques Act 1957, s. 4(3) does not *necessarily* protect a bank if indorsements are absent or irregular if there have been other circumstances which ought to have put the bank on inquiry. See Stanton [1986] P.N. 190.

[32] S had been convicted of criminal charges, and T acquitted.

[33] See above, para. 14–033.

cheques): this requirement is, in fact, a very major exception to the rules about indorsement—the question of indorsement only arises if the original payee does not present the cheque, but this means that indorsements are needed *whenever* he or she does not do so[34]; (c) instruments payable to joint payees must be indorsed if they are to be credited to an account to which all payees are not parties; (d) combined cheque and receipt form marked "R" must be indorsed, as must bills of exchange, promissory notes, travellers' cheques and instruments payable by banks abroad.[35]

In all these classes of case, therefore, the collecting bank must ensure that a negotiable cheque is properly indorsed, or it will be liable to the true owner unless it is also the paying bank in the transaction and has the protection of section 1 or section 80 of the BOEA 1882, or unless it is a holder in due course. **14–060**

(b) Negligence in opening and carrying on an account. Although there may be no indication when the cheque is paid in that there has been a misappropriation, it may be that the bank should have made some inquiry when the account was opened which would have shed light on the transactions undertaken by the customer.[36] When a potential customer wishes to open an account, the bank has an opportunity to make some investigation into credit worthiness and reliability, and it should seek certain information from and about that person which might help to avoid later problems. The nature of the inquiries which should be made reflects banking practice, as one would expect, and, accordingly, has changed over time.[37] **14–061**

Important changes in banking practice have been introduced as a result of the money laundering legislation, with which banks are obliged to comply and which are described below.[38] The Banking Code, reflecting these requirements, states that banks will tell customers what identification they need to prove identity.[39] These changes have required banks to carry out strict checks on the identity of prospective customers, and these stricter standards, which with no doubt have a corresponding effect on the banks' duties, are considered below. **14–062**

---

[34] This does not apply if the cheque has been specially indorsed to the customer who presents the cheque for his or her account (if the cheque is payable to A, in other words, and A has indorsed it to B, who presents it).

[35] This fourth class also applies to paying banks, see above, para. 14–034, n. 85.

[36] *Commissioners of Taxation v. English Scottish and Australian Bank* [1920] A.C. 683 at 688, *per* Lord Dunedin.

[37] See *Marfani Co. Ltd v. Midland Bank Ltd* [1968] 1 W.L.R. 956, *per* Diplock L.J. at 972: "Cases decided 20 years ago, when the use by the general public of banking facilities was much less widespread, may not be a reliable guide to what the duty of a careful banker in relation to inquiries, and as to facts which should give rise to suspicion, is today".

[38] S.I. 1993 No.1933, made under the CJA 1993, both giving effect to the E.U. Money Laundering Directive (Directive 91/308 [1991] O.J. L166/77).

[39] Banking Code (1999) para. 4.6.

14–063 The leading cases illustrate how the courts have interpreted changing banking practice: in 1932, for example, a reference introducing a customer would not necessarily have sufficed.[40] In *Lloyds Bank v. Savory,*[41] the bank, knowing that the customer was a stockbroker's clerk (and therefore might handle, and have the opportunity of stealing, his employer's cheques) failed to inquire about his employers. Further, it failed to obtain information about the employment of another customer's husband (married women were of course less likely to be independent and in employment themselves at that time than they are now, and a bank would "generally inquire or somehow learn about her means and circumstances, and, if she was living with her husband, something about him and his occupation or position in life"[42]). Both the customers had given references which appeared satisfactory. The court took account of the bank's own internal rules on the point, and these emphasised the importance of being cautious in opening new accounts.[43] It found that the bank had been negligent when it permitted these customers to pay in to their own accounts cheques made out by the employer in favour of a third party.

14–064 More recently, in 1968, the Court of Appeal considered a bank's
—065 responsibility in checking on a prospective customer in *Marfani Co. Ltd v. Midland Bank Ltd.*[44] Here, a man (K) asked the bank if he could open an account with them. He said his name was "Eliaszade" and gave the names of two referees. He was not asked for identification nor about his employment. The next day he paid in a cheque for £3,000 in favour of Eliaszade, which was specially cleared by the bank, though it had not been asked to do so. The following day, one of the named referees (A) who was a respected customer of the bank and had introduced a number of customers, was asked about Eliaszade, and said that he had known him "for a time" and that, in his opinion, he was all right for the conduct of a bank account. Nothing was heard from the other referee. K, who had stolen the cheque from the plaintiffs, drew out the money from the account and left the country. It turned out that A had met K (as Eliaszade) on only a few occasions. The plaintiffs brought an action against the bank for conversion of the cheque. The bank claimed the protection of section 4 of the Cheques Act 1957, for which, of course, it had to establish that it had not been negligent.

It was held that, judged by the current practice of careful bankers, the defendants had not been negligent when they opened the account for K. The reference which they had received from a respected customer sufficed, and to have made further inquiries was not likely to have led to the

[40] ". . . it is unfortunately common knowledge that persons of respectability, well introduced, may still commit frauds." *Lloyds Bank v. Savory* [1933] A.C. 201 at 233, *per* Lord Wright.
[41] [1933] A.C. 201.
[42] *Savory* [1933] A.C. 201 at 239, *per* Lord Wright.
[43] *Cf. Motor Traders Guarantee Corporation Ltd v. Midland Bank* [1937] 4 All E.R. 90.
[44] [1968] 1 W.L.R. 956.

detection of the theft; it would merely have offended the potential customer.[45] Cairns L.J. gave a warning, though, that, if the bank here had exercised sufficient care, it was only just sufficient and the decision should not encourage any relaxation of the rules that the banks had established. The court's view may have reflected the enormous increase in the use of bank services since the 1930s and the consequent impracticability of banks being familiar with their customers' circumstances as they had been decades before.

Other cases take a stricter view of the bank's duty. In *Lumsden and Co. v. London Trustee Savings Bank*[46] Donaldson J. held that the bank was negligent in not fully establishing the customer's credentials when the account was opened. The bank had trusted the customer because he said he had professional qualifications and he appeared respectable. The duty to enquire is a continuing one, and arises every time a transaction occurs which is apparently out of harmony with the description of the customer's business or occupation given by him or her or is otherwise inconsistent with the normal manner of conducting his or her account.[47] The implication of this decision is that the bank must at all times be cognisant through all its officers, present and future, who may be concerned with collecting cheques for any customer, of information about the customer which the bank obtained at the time the account was opened. It is to be treated as having this knowledge for all time, whether it was in fact aware of it at the time of collecting or not. **14–066**

This stricter attitude of the courts is also illustrated by *Baker v. Barclays Bank Ltd.*[48] In that case Baker and Bainbridge were trading in partnership under the name "Modern Confections". Bainbridge misappropriated nine cheques amounting to about £1,160 payable to the partnership. He indorsed the cheques and handed them to one Jeffcott, an insurance agent, who paid them into his account at Barclays Bank for collection. Jeffcott further paid in cheques payable to Bainbridge personally, who had indorsed them. The bank manager was assured that Jeffcott was paying in cheques for his friend Bainbridge who was the sole proprietor of Modern Confections and who had just begun in business and was using Jeffcott's bank account temporarily before opening one of his own. The manager was satisfied with the explanation and never asked to see Bainbridge. In an action for conversion by the other partner, Baker, the bank was held to have been negligent in not making further and fuller enquiries. Devlin J. gave two reasons for his decision: firstly, that the bank was not protected by the statute[49] because the explanation given by Jeffcott to the bank manager **14–067**

[45] [1968] 1 W.L.R. 956 at 976, *per* Diplock L.J.
[46] [1971] 1 Ll. Rep. 114.
[47] See also *Nu-Stilo Footwear Ltd v. Lloyds Bank Ltd* [1956] 7 Legal Decisions Affecting Bankers 121.
[48] [1955] 1 W.L.R. 822.
[49] BOEA 1882, s. 82 at that time.

was not one which should have satisfied him, and, as Bainbridge was not a customer of the bank but was using another customer's account, the bank manager should have made enquiries about Bainbridge personally. Secondly, the bank was not a holder in due course of the cheques because Bainbridge was guilty of fraud in his dealings with the cheques and the bank had not discharged the burden of proving that it had given value for them. It seems to have been accepted that the standard of care to be shown by a collecting bank will become more exacting if the amount of the individual cheques and the number of indorsed cheques passing through the account is substantial or increasing.

14–068 The banker's duty of care and inquiry operates more strictly when the first large cheque which is indorsed in favour of a customer is presented for collection, and may be less stringent where a number of small cheques, indorsed in favour of its customer, are presented for collection over a considerable period of time. In *Crumplin v. London Joint Stock Bank Ltd.*,[50] where the court gave judgment in favour of the bank, the judge stated that it can only be a question of fact in each case whether the payment into an account for collection of a second or third (or even subsequent) small cheque should give rise to suspicion, so that if the collecting bank does not make the inquiries as to its customer's title, it will lose the defence under section 4 of the Cheques Act 1957. Furthermore, the bank cannot assume that a transaction by its customer is legitimate simply because it is similar to other such transactions which have occurred over a substantial length of time. The conclusion to be reached from an examination of the decisions is that banks are always required to take reasonable precautions, and, in determining what precautions are called for in a particular case, the current prevailing practices of the banking community are taken into account. The courts are not bound by the standards set by the banks for themselves, but will work out with the benefit of hindsight what a reasonable and competent banker would have done in the circumstances.

Modern banking practice: money laundering requirements

14–069 As we have already seen, the practice of banks, both when opening an account and during the lifetime of the account, has undergone change since the time of *Marfani*. The stringent requirements of the money laundering legislation,[51] which may be summed up as "the bank must know its customer", have affected banking practice in ways that will correspondingly alter the standards with which banks must comply in claiming the protection of section 4 of the Cheques Act 1957.

14–070 **(a) Verifying identity.** The statements of the Banking Code mentioned above are underpinned by the MLR 1993, which require the bank to take

[50] (1913) 30 T.L.R. 99.
[51] See above, Chaps 2 and 4.

"reasonable measures to establish identity", according to the best banking practice for the time being applicable to the circumstances.[52] Identity must be verified whenever a bank account is to be opened,[53] or when a "significant" one-off transaction or series of linked transactions is undertaken.[54] As soon as reasonably practicable,[55] the bank must request "satisfactory evidence" of the identity of an applicant for business; if this is not produced, the transaction must not proceed. Satisfactory evidence means "evidence which is reasonably capable of establishing that the applicant is the person he claims to be, and the person who obtains the evidence is satisfied . . . that it does establish that fact".[56]

The Guidance Notes published by the banks for protection against money laundering[57] provide a practical interpretation of the regulations and give examples of good practice.[58] No doubt courts will also use the Notes as a basis for assessing what may reasonably be expected of banks, when considering whether they have been negligent within the meaning of section 4 of the Cheques Act 1957. **14–071**

The information required is the true name(s) used and the correct permanent address, including post code. The Notes state that the best identification documents possible should be obtained from the prospective customer[59]—those which are the most difficult to obtain illicitly. Documents should be obtained from reputable sources; no one form of identification can be fully guaranteed as genuine. The name used should (ideally) be verified by reference to a document from a reputable source bearing a photograph, if possible a current passport. Separate verification of the current permanent address of the person should be obtained, by, for example, checking the Voters' Roll, making a credit reference agency **14–072**

---

52 MLR 1993, reg. 9(3). Banks are also required to keep records of transactions for five years, MLR 1993, regs 12 and 13.

53 If money laundering is known or suspected, and details of the transaction are reported to the authorities (National Criminal Intelligence Service (NCIS)), identity must always be verified.

54 Banks are also required to maintain the procedures for one-off transactions (MLR 1993, reg. 5). Special provision is made for cases where payment of more than 15,000 ECU (or linked transactions amounting to that sum or more) are undertaken. Banks may use a limit such as £10,000 if they prefer.

55 This has reference to all the circumstances of the relationship, including the nature of the transaction, the geographical locations of the parties, whether it is practical to obtain the evidence before commitments are entered into; and the earliest stage at which there are reasonable grounds for believing that the total amount payable by an applicant is 15,000 ECU or more, if appropriate.

56 MLR 1993, reg. 11(1).

57 Money Laundering Guidance Notes for the Financial Sector, revised and consolidated 1997, issued by the Joint Money Laundering Steering Group.

58 Banks which do not follow the recommended procedures are not only likely to be committing an offence, but may also be refused authorisation by the Bank of England. The Guidance Notes are standards against which the adequacy of a bank's systems to counter money laundering will be assessed, para. 2.23.

59 If the account is to be in joint names, where the surname and/or address of the account holders differ, all should be checked, Guidance Notes, para. 4.38.

search, requesting sight of a recent utility bill or checking a telephone directory. An introduction from a respected customer may be of assistance, but cannot replace the other checks. (The inquiries made in *Marfani*, it seems, would be quite inadequate). In less standard cases—if an account is to be opened by a foreign resident, by company customers, or by post, for example—procedures are slightly different and may be more exacting. If an account is being opened for another person, particularly where that fact has not initially been disclosed to the bank, measures should be taken to obtain information as to the identity of the other person.[60]

The continuing supervisory role is emphasised in the Guidance Notes. The bank must ascertain the nature of the customer's business with the bank at the outset and should update the information as appropriate.[61] Changes to the customer's name, address and employment details should be recorded.[62]

14–073 **(b) further duties on banks in monitoring accounts.** Banks will probably also find it necessary for their own protection to make further investigations of their customers' affairs, including credit checks. Under the MLR 1993, however, they are also required to exercise a continuing supervisory role in respect of customers' accounts, since the law now requires financial institutions to report suspicions of money laundering[63] to the authorities. It is obviously difficult to assess what amounts to *suspicion* of a customer, particularly since this is a subjective standard: this seems to imply that, in cases where money laundering has actually taken place, the bank or its officers may have to discharge the burden of proof in showing that they did *not* suspect it. The way to avoid committing an offence is to be alert to disclose suspicions to the NCIS, taking care, however, not to "tip-off" the customer, which is also an offence.[64] This involves setting up systems and training for staff. In most institutions there will be a reporting officer, to whom reports of suspicions are made, and whose responsibility it is to consider them and, if appropriate, to pass them on to NCIS.

14–074 The Guidance Notes provide a list of suspicious transactions[65] for banks to use in checking their customers' accounts and deciding which transactions should be reported. Suspicious transactions include:

---

[60] In the case of client accounts which are opened by solicitors, accountants, etc., the client is the person opening the account, but in some cases, banks are also required to verify the identity of the underlying clients.

[61] Para. 4.02.

[62] Para. 4.06. See also para. 7.05, and Case 5, App. II: "On-going monitoring of bank accounts is recommended. . ."; and Case 6: "it is essential to know your long standing banking customers, and monitor transactions against the expected pattern of transactions".

[63] Resulting from any serious crime, CJA 1993, MLR 1993.

[64] See above, para. 4–042.

[65] At Appendix I.

> "unusually large cash deposits made by an individual or company whose ostensible business activities would normally be generated by cheques and other instruments[66] . . .
> substantial increases in cash deposits of any individual or business without apparent cause . . .[67]
> any individual or company whose account shows virtually no normal personal banking or business related activities, but is used to receive or disburse large sums which have no obvious purpose or relationship to the account holder and/or his business . . .[68]";

and, in the case of financial institution employees and agents,

> "changes in employee characteristics, *e.g.* lavish life styles or avoiding taking holidays[69] . . .
> [and] changes in employee or agent performance, *e.g.* the salesman selling products for cash who has remarkable or unexpected increase in performance[70]".

It seems, therefore, that the procedures for detecting suspicious behaviour will involve banks in a certain amount of amateur detective work. At the least, an up to date knowledge of the employment and routine of customers is now an essential part of banking practice. The courts' standards for negligence in dealing with accounts, including the rule expressed in *Orbit*[71] that banks have no need to keep themselves informed about customers' employment, will have to adapt in response. **14–075**

Bank as Holder for Value

As mentioned above, banks which have discounted cheques (obtained them on their own behalf by giving value for them) have always been able to argue that they were holders in due course of the cheque. This claim gives them the right to claim the cheque against a person suing in conversion, and, as true owner, to sue the paying bank in conversion if the paying bank pays someone else. The argument is open to discounting banks whether or not they might also be able to claim the defence of section 4 of the Cheques Act 1957.[72] It is doubtful, though, whether in the case of a standard cheque, this argument will still be open to banks, as a consequence **14–076**

---

[66] 1a.
[67] 1b.
[68] 2c.
[69] 5a.
[70] 5b.
[71] [1963] 1 Q.B. 794.
[72] A discounting bank is protected under the provisions of Cheques Act 1957, s. 4 (by subsection (1)(b)—a banker who, having credited a customer's account with the amount of such an instrument, receives payment for himself).

of the Cheques Act 1992. Cheques are, as has been seen, normally not negotiable or even transferable now and it seems that banks, like other persons taking account payee cheques, cannot normally be holders for value of such instruments.[73]

14–077 When a cheque is negotiable, a bank will have the status of a holder if it gives value for the cheque itself or if it has a lien over it.[74] Section 2 of the Cheques Act 1957 covers this situation by allowing a bank which has given value to treat it like a bearer cheque, so that if indorsements are lacking, the bank still has title to it. The bank therefore does not need to make sure that the cheque has been indorsed to it. The section states that a banker who gives value for, or has a lien on, a cheque payable to order which the holder delivers to him for collection without indorsing it, has such (if any) rights as he would have had if, upon delivery, the holder had indorsed it in blank. The question is, therefore, whether a bank has *given value* or *has a lien on* a cheque.

14–078 A bank is regarded as having *given value* when there has been an express or implied agreement[75] that the customer may overdraw on a cheque before it is cleared, or when the bank permits the customer to draw against the proceeds or pays cash to the customer against the value of the cheque before it has been cleared. It seems clear that the bank does not give value when it "credits the cheque as cash"—that is, when it merely provisionally credits the amount of the cheque to the customer's account before it has been cleared, as banks normally do.[76] A bank has a *lien*[77] over a customer's cheque when the customer is indebted to the bank and when the cheque comes into its hands in the ordinary course of business. In this case, the bank can claim under the section to be a holder for value (or holder in due course, if the bank can show that it took the cheque, complete and regular on its face, in good faith and for value) even if the cheque has not been indorsed.

14–079 The courts had to consider the provisions of section 2 of the Cheques Act 1957 in detail in the case of *Westminster Bank v. Zang.*[78] The case concerned a cheque for a gambling debt made out by Zang to Tilley. Tilley paid it into the account of his company, not into his own account, without indorsing it to the company, as he should have done. When the bank presented it for payment to Zang's bank, it was dishonoured and returned.

---

[73] See Pagets Law of Banking, p. 249.
[74] BOEA 1882, s. 27.
[75] *e.g.* by course of business.
[76] *Capital and Counties Bank v. Gordon* [1903] A.C. 240 decided that, by crediting as cash, a bank had given value; this led to the Bills of Exchange (Crossed Cheques) Act 1906: payment was received for a customer notwithstanding that the account was credited before payment was received. *AL Underwood v. Bank of Liverpool* [1924] 1 K.B. 775; *Westminster Bank Ltd v. Zang* [1966] A.C. 182 held that the bank did not give value when crediting as cash. See above, para. 6–035.
[77] The banker's lien is a form of security, see above, Chap. 11.
[78] [1966] A.C. 182.

Tilly decided to sue Zang for the debt, and his solicitors requested the return of the cheque from the bank, which handed it over on the solicitors' undertaking to return it on demand. After some months, Tilly decided not to proceed with the action and the cheque was returned to the bank, which brought an action itself against Zang. There were difficulties for the bank in doing so. First, it could not rely on section 4 of the Cheques Act 1957 to protect it as a collecting bank, since it had not collected the cheque for its customer when it received it for the second time, but for itself (it wished to sue on it). Secondly, the cheque had not been indorsed to the bank, which on the face of it, therefore, had not become the holder of the cheque—*unless* the bank was able to rely on section 2 of the Cheques Act 1957. If it could do so, it could assert that it had taken the cheque as a bearer cheque and it would not matter that Tilley had not indorsed it. To rely on the section, it had to show that it had either *given value* for the cheque or had a *lien* on it.

The question of a *lien* was dealt with briefly: although the bank might have had a lien over the cheque when the cheque was first paid in, because the company's account had been overdrawn at that time, the bank had lost its lien by allowing the cheque out of its possession when it was given to Tilley's solicitors, and could not have a lien on it when it was returned.[79] The bank had therefore to show that it had *given value* for the cheque. The bank argued unsuccessfully that the fact that it had credited the payment provisionally to the company's account meant that it had given value. Nor could it show that there was an agreement, express or implied, that the company should be allowed to draw against uncleared effects, or that it had allowed the customer to draw cash over the counter against the uncleared cheque. It was held, therefore, as a matter of fact, that no value had been given. In all the bank was unsuccessful in its claim. **14–080**

The case cast light on other aspects of section 2 of the Cheques Act 1957. In order to succeed, the bank would have had to show that the *holder* had delivered the cheque to it *for collection*. These points, which were not decisive in the case, were settled in the bank's favour. It was held that Tilley was the holder, even though he had paid the cheque in for his company's account. The words of the statute were not ambiguous, and there was no reason to construe the section restrictively. Similarly, the cheque had been given to the bank for collection, even though the collection was not for Tilley's own account, but for that of the company: *for collection* therefore includes *collection for another person*, as well as for the holder's own account. **14–081**

The court also considered the question of indorsement. Section 2 of the Cheques Act 1957 provides that a lack of indorsement is not fatal if a bank is collecting a cheque, provided value is given or it has a lien. This provision **14–082**

[79] See above, Chap. 11.

may cause prejudice to the drawer of the cheque, because the cheque with the payee's indorsement cannot then function as a *receipt* for the payment. Although section 3 of the Cheques Act 1957 assists the drawer to some extent by making the cheque itself, even without an indorsement, prima facie evidence of payment,[80] it would not always be satisfactory as proof of payment. Lord Denning M.R.[81] had expressed the view that the legislature could not have intended this result. He preferred to interpret section 2 of the Cheques Act 1957 by reference to the explanatory Memorandum of the Committee of London Bankers of 1957,[82] which recommended to bankers that certain indorsements should be routinely checked by banks despite the words of the section. Banks, he considered, should only be allowed to disregard indorsements if a cheque is credited for the account of the payee. The House of Lords did not accept this liberal interpretation of the section, which they regarded as unambiguous. Although in practice banks should take account of necessary indorsements if a cheque is collected for the account of a person who is not the payee, the words of section 2 of the Cheques Act 1957 mean that there is no statutory requirement that they should do so.

Bank Acting as Both Paying and Collecting Bank

14–083 If a crossed cheque drawn by one customer is paid in by another customer at the same branch, the payee customer's account should be credited, rather than cash paid.[83] But the bank may make a "house debit", so that it debits the account of the drawer and credits the account of the payee, effectively paying him or her cash. There is no obligation to do this, for as agent for collection, the bank would have the normal time allowed (the following business day).[84] If the cheque is not crossed, the bank ought to pay the customer as it would pay any other holder, that is, on demand.

Paying and collecting bank and third parties

14–084 Although section 60 of the BOEA 1882 protects a bank paying a cheque in the ordinary course of business if an indorsement is forged or unauthorised, it seems that this does not apply to a bank which is both collecting and paying bank.[85] However, the bank may still be protected as

[80] Cheques Act 1957, s. 3 states: an unindorsed cheque which appears to have been paid by the banker on whom it is drawn is evidence of the receipt by the payee of the sum payable by the cheque.

[81] In the Court of Appeal decision.

[82] Circular of September 23, 1957, based on the recommendations of the Mocatta Committee (the Committee on Cheque Indorsements), Cmnd. 3 (1956). See above, para. 14–059.

[83] BOEA 1882, s. 79.

[84] *Boyd v. Emmerson* (1834) 2 Ad. & El. 184.

[85] *Carpenter's Co. v. British Mutual Banking Co. Ltd* [1938] 1 K.B. 511, esp. 533. See also Megrah (1966) 29 M.L.R 72, commenting on *Universal Guarantee Pty Ltd v. National Bank of Australasia Ltd* [1965] 1 Lloyd's Rep. 525; [1965] 2 All E.R. 98.

paying bank by section 80 of the BOEA 1882, and by section 1 of the Cheques Act 1957, and as collecting bank by section 4 of the Cheques Act 1957.

Cheque Guarantee Cards

The customer acts as agent of the bank in creating a collateral obligation on the part of the bank to pay the cheque if the conditions are satisfied. They are discussed with other cards, in Chapter 15. **14–085**

Instruments Analogous to Cheques

Bankers' drafts

These are instruments drawn by a bank on a bank which are often used for payments made overseas or for property transactions. A banker's draft which is drawn by a bank on itself[86] is not a cheque because it does not satisfy the requirements of section 73 of the BOEA 1882 (a cheque has to be drawn *on another person* which is a bank), but it can be treated by the holder as either a bill of exchange or a promissory note.[87] Bankers' drafts are often thought of as more secure than cheques and usually operate in a similar way; they go through the cheque clearing systems. **14–086**

Payment orders

These instruments are not cheques, in this case because they are not *drawn on banks*. They are usually drawn on a Government department, such as the Paymaster General's Office. They are again similar to cheques for clearing purposes. **14–087**

Statutory protection for banks

Both bankers' drafts and payment orders are brought within the protection of the Cheques Act 1957. Section 4(2) states: **14–088**

> This section applies to the following instruments, namely, . . .
>
> (b) any document issued by a customer of a banker which, though not a bill of exchange, is intended to enable a person to obtain payment from that banker of the sum mentioned in the document;
>
> (c) any document issued by a public officer which is intended to enable a person to obtain payment from the Paymaster

---

[86] A bankers' draft which is drawn by one bank *on another* does conform to the requirements of a cheque.

[87] BOEA 1882, s. 5(2).

General or the Queen's and Lord Treasurer's Remembrancer of the sum mentioned in the document but is not a bill of exchange;

(d) any draft payable on demand drawn by a banker upon himself, whether payable at the head office or some other office of his bank.

5 The provisions of the Bills of Exchange Act 1882 relating to crossed cheques shall, so far as applicable, have effect in relation to instruments (other than cheques) to which the last foregoing section applies as they have effect in relation to cheques.

The Jack Report recommended that these instruments[88] should be equated to cheques.[89] In the view of the White Paper, it would be a useful tidying up of the law to state clearly in legislation that such instruments are to be treated as cheques for all purposes.

Bank Giro[90] Credits

14–089 Although traditional methods of transferring money, namely, cash, cheques, bills of exchange and bankers' drafts, will undoubtedly continue to be used for many years yet as a means of settling payment obligations, the last 20 years have seen a revolution in the development of methods of transferring money from one person to another, and from one place to another. Whilst the fully automated systems of money transfers (CHAPS in the United Kingdom on a national basis, and SWIFT on an international basis) have been operational for a number of years, partially automated systems—which are credit transfer and direct debit systems—are of considerable and increasing importance.[91]

14–090 A giro system for the direct transfer of money between bank accounts has existed for more than 90 years in Europe, where it was developed by the co-operative banks alongside the traditional payment facilities provided by the commercial banks. In Britain the pressure for the introduction of a credit transfer system gradually increased. Only about one in four people held bank accounts in the 1950s, and thus there was considerable scope for the banks to attract further customers, especially among people making small payments regularly. Finally, the commercial banks were forced by the threat

[88] And dividend warrants, which are specifically covered by s. 95 of the BOEA 1882.

[89] Jack Report, Cm. 622 (1989), paras 7.11 and 7.12.

[90] From the Greek word for circle. See generally Geva, *The Law of Electronic Funds Transfers* (1992) s. 1.03; Brindle and Cox, *The Law of Bank Payments*, paras 3–4, 3.34 *et seq*.

[91] 1,736 million direct debits were processed in 1998, an increase of 9.6 per cent over 1997, and 934 million direct credits were processed, an increase of 6.9 per cent over 1997: APACS, *Annual Review* (1998), p. 13.

of the introduction of a National Giro system by the Post Office in 1968 to consider favourably the introduction of a credit transfer system. The interest expressed by the Radcliffe Committee[92] in a low-cost national system for transferring money and credit, and its recommendation that unless the banks provided such a service the Post Office should do so, provided an impetus. In 1969 the banks committed themselves to extend and develop a system of credit transfers.[93]

Even in the United Kingdom, credit transfer was not an entirely new **14–091** concept, since the banks had run a standing order service since the nineteenth century to facilitate the payment of fixed amounts at regular intervals and also a traders' credit system by which firms paid their employees salaries by transfers to the credit of the employees' bank accounts. In 1961 these facilities were extended to all kinds of payments and to persons who were not customers of a bank.

So far as direct debits were concerned, there was no continental precedent and on its introduction it was unique to the United Kingdom. It came into operation as an addition to the credit clearing service in 1970.

Operation of the system

Whereas a cheque allows the creditor to *draw* the money from the **14–092** account of another person (who must be a customer), a giro credit is a paper instruction by one person (not necessarily a customer of a bank) to *send* money from the paying bank through the banking system to another. This may be done by individual money transfer or, on a regular basis, by standing order. Conversely, a direct debit is the transfer of funds from one bank to another under a general mandate given by a debtor to a creditor where the transfer is effected by the creditor initiating a payment by the debtor's bank to his or her own or by collection from the debtor's bank to the creditor's bank.

The system enables a person to make payments through his or her bank, **14–093** either to other customers of the same bank or to those of other banks. Generally, the credit transfer system may not appear to have any great advantage over the cheque system for a person with a bank account—a giro form is more cumbersome to fill out than a cheque—although a person not possessing a bank account who wishes to avoid sending cash or postal or money orders through the post may find it particularly valuable. He or she may go into any bank and, by filling up a transfer form and paying cash over the counter, ensure that payment is made to the credit of the payee's bank account. The system has the great advantage for companies and other large organisations of permitting bulk payments to be made efficiently. The system is less vulnerable to fraud than using cheques, because, once the

[92] Report of the Committee on the Working of the Monetary System, Cmnd. 827.
[93] Girobank is a member of APACS.

form has been delivered to the paying bank, the operation takes place directly within the banks. The main risk from fraud is, by and large, that from bank employees themselves.

Giro credits or debits are carried out by the banks either by traditional "paper" methods or electronically, even though the original instruction is on paper. The distinguishing characteristic of an electronic funds transfer system is that the inter-bank communication of payment instructions is by electronic means, for example, by magnetic tape, disc or telecommunication link.[94]

14–094 **(a) Individual money transfers.** When payment is made by credit transfer, the payer initiates the transfer of funds[95] by giving written instructions for it to his or her bank on a credit transfer form provided by the bank (or by a transferee, such as utilities like water or gas companies). The form must authorise the paying bank to make a payment to the credit of the account of a specified person with the same or another bank. The standard credit transfer form has spaces for details of the payee's name, the name of his or her bank and the branch where the account is kept, the bank account number and, of course, the amount to be transferred. The payer (debtor) may draw a cheque for the total amount payable to the paying bank, or may pay in cash. When the paying bank receives the form and the money, the information on the credit transfer form is encoded in magnetic ink at the bottom of the form. The forms are passed through the bank's clearing house in London, where they are sorted automatically into bundles to be presented to each collecting bank and are delivered to the central Clearing House,[96] (or they may be dealt with by one of the settlement member banks).

14–095 The credits must be delivered to the collecting banks by 11 a.m. on the second day of the clearing cycle, and must be accompanied by dockets listing the amount of each credit transfer. The rules—"the Bankers' Clearing House Credit Clearing Rules", which contractually bind the participants[97]—lay down the procedure where there is an error on the dockets, where the docket is sent to the wrong collecting bank or where a credit transfer listed on a docket cannot be found.

The credit transfer is finally credited to the payee's account by the collecting bank on the third day of the cycle. The docket control vouchers have to be returned to the presenting bank by 8.15 a.m. of that day, and the

[94] Geva, *The Law of Electronic Funds Transfers* (1992), s. 1.03[4]. In the U.K. they are dealt with since 1985 by BACS Ltd, under the auspices of APACS, an unincorporated association composed of banks and building societies.

[95] Not a transfer in reality, since the banks concerned simply settle between themselves by adjusting their accounts with each other at the Bank of England.

[96] Operated by the Cheque and Credit Clearing Company Ltd, which also deals with cheques.

[97] The "settlement members", who may also act as agents in clearing for many other banks and building societies ("indirect clearers").

figures must be faxed to APACS by the settlement members. A disagreement between the banks will be sorted out later. Final settlement takes place on the same working day across the accounts of the banks at the Bank of England.

(b) Standing orders. Regular payments of fixed amounts (such as monthly rent or mortgage payments) can be made by standing order. The payer has again to fill out a form giving details of the relevant accounts and informing the bank of the dates and amounts of the payments to be made. These forms (unlike those for individual transfers) usually include a specific clause giving the bank authority to debit the payer's account. The form, with a cheque for the total amount, is delivered to the paying bank, and the payment is made electronically, through the BACS system.[98] **14–096**

The system is advantageous to enterprises which have to make a large number of payments regularly for varying amounts to different payees (wages and salaries to employees and debts owing to creditors), and which can do so by sending instructions to their banks with details of the intended transfers accompanied by a single cheque for the total amount to be transferred. The payee no longer receives a cheque, which has to be presented for collection, but instead obtains payment by the amount transferred to his or her bank being credited to his account, and will simply be informed by the bank that this has been done.

(c) Direct debits. This is a term used to describe payments which are made by a bank out of its customer's account to a third person (not an individual) which instructs the bank to transfer the amount involved to its own bank.[99] This will, of course, only be done if the customer of the paying bank gives it a mandate for the purpose. The system has shown a considerable increase in popularity in recent years, as customers take on more regular commitments. **14–097**

In order to make payments by the direct debit system, the creditor or originator has to be sponsored by one of the banks or building societies operating the scheme. The payment is initiated by the payee and because of the possibility of fraud the banks will extend direct debiting facilities only to payees of high financial standing who can be relied on to act properly. In all cases the creditor (originator) must sign an undertaking to indemnify all the banks involved in the direct debiting scheme against claims which may arise from debits initiated by the initiator which are erroneous or unauthorised. The payment is effected, like payment of standing orders, through the BACS system.

---

[98] Described above, Chap. 12.

[99] The system has its own set of rules: *The Originator's Guide and Rules to the Direct Debiting Scheme*, a new edition of which was launched in 1997: APACS, *Annual Review* (1998), p. 13.

14–098 All organisations using the direct debit system are given an identification number which must be included in the details of all debits which they initiate. The creditor (originator) must obtain a direct debiting mandate from its debtor authorising its bank to honour debits initiated by the creditor, and this must be sent to the debtor's bank, usually at least 14 days before the first debit is made. The form must contain the debtor's signature and must indicate the name of the creditor, the amount to be debited, which may be fixed or variable, and the dates upon which payments are to be made, if they are periodic. The debtor must also be given notice—14 days, unless a shorter period is agreed—of the first debit, and of later debits if the amount or date is changed. The paying bank is entitled to reject a direct debit (if the payer has insufficient funds to meet the order, for example) without any possibility of an action against the bank for wrongful dishonour. If the debtor's bank refuses to pay, the creditor is informed automatically. If an error is made—for example, funds are withdrawn from the debtor's account on the wrong date or after the authority has been cancelled—the debtor is entitled under the terms of the scheme to a full and immediate refund.

14–099 Although mistakes do happen, there should be little risk of fraud, because payment can only be made in accordance with the written mandate given by the payer to the paying bank authorising the payee to draw against the payer's account, which specifies the payee, the amount to be debited (unless it is variable) and the time of payment (if it is a periodic payment).

14–100 The commonest type of fraud will be when the initiator makes an unauthorised debit on the payer's account. This may occur if there is a general mandate for the payment of variable sums which does not specify the amount or the dates of the debit. In this situation the paying bank would be protected by its mandate from the payer and it would be entitled to debit the payer's account. This is, in theory, guarded against by the requirement that the originator should notify the payer before initiating a debit against the account, although where the originator is perpetrating a fraud, this step will certainly be omitted. In this situation the payer might be able to recover the amount paid from the originator as money paid under a mistake or in an action for fraud; or might recover from the collecting bank if it had paid the money out negligently or in the unlikely event of bad faith. In this situation the payer's position would be the same as if the payment had been made by cheque.

14–101 In the operation of direct debits there is unlikely to be a significant risk of forgery of the direct debit vouchers or unauthorised use of computerisation facilities in an originator's name, since the only person who can receive the benefit of the transfer of funds by direct debit is the person named in the mandate given by the payer as authorised to initiate debits, unless there is a fraud by some employee of a company drawing funds from another person by direct debit. In this case, the victim and its bank might be entitled to recover the money paid from the collecting bank as money paid under a mistake from the recipient company or from its bank.

A person who has authorised another to initiate direct debits on his or her account can revoke the original mandate to the originator and its bank at any time before payment is made under it, by giving notice of intention to revoke to his or her bank and to the holder of the mandate, even if the originator has given the payer's bank the notice required by the terms of its mandate. Direct debits notified to the paying bank subsequent to the revocation will be returned unpaid. If the paying bank does make payment, it cannot debit its customer's account because the customer has revoked its authority to do so; the paying bank may be able to recover amounts wrongly paid from the payee. The revocation of an authority to initiate a direct debit may involve the payer in liability for breach of contract as between him or herself and the originator, but the revocation is nonetheless effective as far as the paying bank is concerned. **14–102**

While the authority is effective, that is, before a revocation, there is authority that a direct debit gives the originator the same certainty of payment as a cheque. In *Esso Petroleum v. Milton*,[1] the defendant was licensed by Esso to manage two petrol stations and paid for all his supplies of petrol, supplied by Esso, by direct debit; his account was normally debited two days after a delivery. Mr Milton became dissatisfied with Esso's stringent terms of business and cancelled the direct debit mandate he had made to the bank, just after he had received nine deliveries of petrol for which he had not yet been debited. Esso claimed that the court should order the outstanding payment to be made by summary judgment, as it would be if payment was by cheque—in other words, without any examination of the merits of Mr Milton's counterclaim in contract against Esso. The court agreed with Esso: it held that payment by direct debit is equivalent to a claim arising on a dishonoured cheque, and, as with a cheque, must be treated as equivalent to "deferred instalments of cash" and requiring unconditional payment, rather than as simply providing credit.[2] It was held that the direct debit system has become the modern mechanism for handling sales on a large scale (Mr Milton's annual purchases of petrol amounted to £5 million), and has taken over from the use of cheques to that extent. Sir John Balcombe said: **14–103**

> "This is essentially a question of policy. As the evidence shows . . . modern commercial practice is to treat a direct debit in the same way as a payment by cheque, and, as such, as the equivalent of cash. The fact that a cheque is, technically, a negotiable instrument, is for this purpose irrelevant. . . It is its equivalence to cash which is the essential feature of a direct debit."[3]

[1] [1997] 1 W.L.R. 938, CA, Simon Brown, J. dissented on this point. See also *Mercedes-Benz Finance Ltd v. Clydesdale Bank* (1996) S.C.L.R. 1005.

[2] *Nova (Jersey) Knit Ltd v. Kammgarn Spinnerei G.m.b.H.* [1977] 1 W.L.R. 713 at 721, *per* Lord Wilberforce.

[3] [1997] 1 W.L.R. 938 at 953.

The decision has been criticised[4] on the basis that the analogy drawn between direct debits and cheques is flawed. Direct debits are not transferable and there is no need to provide the extra protection of being able to obtain summary judgment on the instrument as well as being able to sue on the underlying contract. The effect is that the creditor has the benefit of an exclusion clause being implied into the contract, and this is unfair.

14–104 The main differences between credit transfer and direct debit are:

(1) Credit transfers are initiated by the payer—a "push" by the debtor—whereas direct debits are made on the instruction of the payee—a "pull"—by the creditor;

(2) In the case of credit transfers the payer need not necessarily be a customer of the bank, but in a direct debit the payer must have an account out of which the payment is made;

(3) In the credit transfer system no restrictions are placed on the payees to whose accounts payments may be made where as a limited class of payees only may initiate direct debits.

The legal character of giro payments

14–105 The bank giro services have been developed entirely by the banking community and are not established or regulated by statute. Consequently, the law relating to them must be derived by applying the general principles of common law and equity to the relevant banking practice.

A credit transfer form does not contain a direct order by the payer to the paying bank for payment, nor an acceptance of the order by the bank, and so it cannot be said that there is a direct relationship between the paying bank and the payee similar to the relationship between the acceptor and the payee of a bill of exchange, and the payee cannot sue the bank for breach of contract if it does not effect the transfer. Indeed, the payee is not normally aware of the credit transfer until his bank notifies him or her that payment has actually been made.

14–106 The most important problem in the field of credit transfers is to establish the exact stage at which payment can be said to have been made to the payee—that is, when does the payment become both effective and irrevocable? The earliest possible moment that this could happen is when the payer hands the completed credit transfer voucher to the paying bank, together with the necessary cash if he is not a customer of the bank. If it could be shown that the payee becomes an *assignee* of that part of the payer's credit balance or that the paying bank becomes a *trustee* for the benefit of the payee of the appropriate amount out of the payer's credit balance, it might

[4] See Hooley [1997] C.L.J. 500.

be argued that the initiation of the credit transfer constitutes a transfer of funds to the payee.

It is unlikely that an assignment takes effect,[5] and it was held in *Esso v. Milton*, as noted above, that, far from the payment becoming irrevocable immediately and the payee being entitled to sue the paying bank for the amount involved, payment by direct debit resembles payment by cheque. This means that the instruction operates as a mandate by the payer to pay a certain sum of money, and does not take effect as an assignment of a corresponding part of the drawer's credit balance at the drawee bank.[6] Similarly, it would be most unlikely that it would be held that there is a trust unless there is evidence of a *Quistclose* trust.[7]

The Jack Committee, considering whether it was necessary to introduce **14–107**
statutory provisions of some kind, concluded tentatively that giro credits are a matter of contract, and typically, of three separate contracts, the first between transferor and paying bank, the second, between paying bank and receiving bank, and the third, between receiving bank and transferee.[8] The transferring bank receives the mandate and acts as the agent of the payer. The position of the receiving bank may vary, and it depends upon the facts whether it acts as the agent of the payer or of the payee.

The Committee took a relaxed view about the lack of clarity in the general legal analysis of such payments; it concluded that the system has in fact worked well and there is no need for statutory intervention, although it would be helpful for customers to have their rights and obligations spelt out.

Travellers' cheques

Even nowadays, travellers' cheques are widely used, because of their **14–108**
familiarity and the security they offer, although their use is being displaced by plastic cards. Payment may be obtained from any of the many and various institutions worldwide which accept such cheques. They are unusual as negotiable instruments because they are not really cheques at all; they are conditional and therefore do not fall within section 3 of the BOEA 1882.[9] The issuer of a travellers' cheque undertakes to pay a specified sum

---

[5] The requirements of legal assignment under the LPA 1925, s. 136(1) would not be fulfilled in practice in any case because notice in writing must be given to the debtor (the bank) by the assignee (the payee). Nor would a transfer normally amount to an equitable assignment, because it is unlikely that any intention to make an assignment could be detected from the words of the forms used: see *Chitty on Contracts*, pp. 33–316; Jack Report, Cm. 622 (1989) para. 7.75. The White Paper on Banking Law and Services, Cm 1026, Annex 5, para. 5.19 said that legislation to make it clear that bank giro credits are not assignments would be introduced.

[6] BOEA 1882, s. 53(1).

[7] See *Barclays Bank Ltd. v. Quistclose Investments Ltd* [1968] 1 All E.R. 613 and *Re Kayford Ltd* [1975] 1 W.L.R. 279; see above, Chap. 9. See also *Mercedes-Benz* (1996) S.C.L.P. 1005, where, in a Scottish case, it was held that no trust arose.

[8] Cm. 622 (1989), para. 7.76.

[9] Three different patterns are common: two orders and one promise: see Stassen 95 S.A.L.J. 182.

of money to the order of the purchaser of the instrument, on certain conditions. The purchaser signs the "cheque" when it is bought, and countersigns it when it is cashed. The important condition is that the counter signature must match the original signature. The counter signature may be regarded as a first indorsement, giving the holder a good title, and the instruments are usually classified as being negotiable instruments by virtue of mercantile usage.[10]

14–109 The valuable aspect of such cheques, from the traveller's point of view, is that the issuer, often a bank, undertakes to replace them even if their loss has resulted from the purchaser's negligence.[11] This promise to replace them can be excluded by contract: for example, if the original purchaser loses them because of negligence before they have been counter signed.[12] It would be inconsistent with the purpose of the cheques, and the undertakings and publicity of the issuers, however, to allow issuers to go back on their promises unless the conditions have been clearly spelt out, and it has been made clear in the cases that negligence will not be found too easily.[13]

---

[10] Paget (11th ed), p. 257, Ellinger and Lomnicka, *Modern Banking Law*, p. 331. *Chitty on Contracts*, para. 33.147–33.158: the principles of the BOEA 1882 apply, *mutatis mutandis*.

[11] *El Awadi v. Bank of Credit and Commerce International SA* [1990] 1 Q.B. 606.

[12] *Braithwaite v. Thomas Cooke Travellers' Cheques Ltd* [1989] Q.B. 553.

[13] *Fellus v. National Westminster Bank plc* (1983) 133 N.L.J. 766, *El Awadi* [1990] 1 Q.B. 606. It is not clear who bears the onus of showing negligence; in *Fellus*, it was the bank, in *Braithwaite* ([1989] Q.B. 553), the traveller. See Pugh-Thomas [1989] 2 J.I.B.L. 75.

CHAPTER 15

CARDS AND NEW TECHNOLOGY[1]

For bank customers, one of the most familiar manifestations of new technology is the "plastic revolution". Plastic cards, introduced thirty years ago, have become of enormous importance to banks and to their customers,[2] who find them convenient and time saving to carry and use. There are now many varieties of card performing different functions, some regulated by the provisions of the CCA 1974, some too new to have been envisaged by the drafters of that massive piece of legislation. Their use has thrown up a number of novel legal problems, which focus on liability for theft (cards lend themselves to fraud), misuse or loss. The law and practice governing the use of cards is a mixture of common law, the provisions of the CCA 1974 and other consumer protection statutes. The decisions of the Banking Ombudsman,[3] based on the standards of the Banking Code as well as the law, also play an important part in regulation. **15–001**

At the moment, despite these exciting developments, we are still a long way from the cashless society: about three quarters of all transactions are cash transactions.[4] However, dynamic progress in producing new cards and other technology is happening all the time[5]; the variety of cards is expanding as well as the frequency of their use. The newest type of card now is the *chip card*[6]: the addition of a computer chip converts a card into a smart card, with greater security (it is hoped) and new uses—for example, as an *electronic purse*. Trials of chip-based credit, debit and ATM cards have also been taking place, and these cards are shortly to be produced commercially. Apart from cards, there are many other important innovations. Home banking by telephone is now familiar and popular. *Electronic* **15–002**

---

[1] See Arora, *Electronic Banking and the Law* (2nd ed.), Brindle and Cox, *Law of Bank Payments*, (2nd ed., 1999) Chapter 6, Stephenson, *Credit, Debit and Cheque Cards, Law and Practice*, Sayer, *Credit Cards and the Law*, Reed [1994] J.I.B.L. 451. For discussion of the 1974 Consumer Credit Act, see Diamond, *Commercial and Consumer Credit—An Introduction*, Goode, *Consumer Credit Legislation* and Guest and Lloyd, *Encyclopedia of Consumer Credit Law*.

[2] The first credit card was introduced in the U.K. by Barclays in 1966, though the original "store card" was introduced in 1915 in the USA (Sayer, *op. cit*, p. 1). In 1999, there were 5.45 billion transactions on plastic cards with a total value of over £259 billion (an increase of 14 per cent over 1998). There are 118 million bank and building society cards in issue: APACS Plastic Card Review, 2000.

[3] And the Building Society Ombudsman.

[4] See APACS, *Annual Review* (1998) p. 27. There are 10 billion cash transactions of under £1 in value each day, p. 28.

[5] And, thanks to "technology push", are unstoppable: Reed, *op. cit.*, p. 462.

[6] See below, para. 15–069.

commerce—banking on the internet[7–8]—is also a reality and a real threat to traditional branch-based banking.

15–003 These developments have their sinister aspect. Confidentiality, or rather the lack of it, is a serious worry, and problems in providing adequate security are the main obstacles to the introduction of electronic commerce in banking transactions. An unprecedented amount of information is being generated and data can be accumulated easily and comprehensively[9]—and illicitly—on computer. Security of personal data held on computers and on files is being tightened up to some extent by data protection legislation.[10] Further, measures regulating electronic commerce are being considered, within the E.U.[11] and worldwide,[12] to promote security and regulation. These include measures to promote the legal recognition of electronic signatures in electronic commerce and to improve the security of the communications, for example by the introduction of a voluntary licensing scheme for providers of encryption services.[13] Both the integrity of data, which is vital in many forms of electronic commerce, and its confidentiality need to be considered.[14] Nevertheless, the issues of regulation remain enormous, if only because security measures proposed by Governments have their own risks: systems allowing government agencies and the police to access computers and decode messages have obvious "Big Brother" implications.[15]

Plastic Cards

15–004 The varieties of card, though bewildering at first sight, can be grouped into four or five discrete types. Classification is important because the legal implications are complex, and in some cases vary for different types of card. Regulation by the Consumer Credit Act 1974 (CCA 1974) depends upon whether a card can be classified as a card which is the subject of a *credit agreement* (credit agreements are regulated in detail by the CCA 1974) or as a *credit token* (in which case liability for misuse is controlled by the CCA 1974). For this reason, it is necessary to be clear about how particular cards

[7–8] Electronic Data Processing (EDI) is beginning to be used—*e.g.* a set of EDI implementation guidelines covering the entire payment cycle has been produced (APACS, *Annual Review* (1997), p. 32)—but has not yet been widely adopted by business; international trade is still conducted largely on paper, because of the difficulty of complex manual processes and the large numbers of interested groups involved in adopting electronic commerce (APACS, *Annual Review* (1997), p. 22).

[9] Hutton [1995] N.L.J. 1810; Walden [1994] 12 J.I.B.L. 506.

[10] Data Protection Act 1998, with effect from March 1, 2000. It replaces the Data Protection Act of 1984.

[11] *e.g.* Communication of the Commission on Encryption and Electronic Signatures (COM (97) 503).

[12] *e.g.* UNCITRAL (the United National Commission on International Trade Law) developments.

[13] See DTI statements April 27, 1998, (1998) *Company Lawyer*, (June) 161.

[14] *ibid.*, at 162.

[15] See, *e.g.*, *The Independent*, March 3, 1999.

operate, even though many of the controls of the CCA 1974 have now been extended, more or less, to other cards by the Banking Code.[16] "Multi-function cards" are increasingly issued, but it is still necessary to distinguish between the separate functions on such cards because the legal characteristics of transactions relate to the particular function which is used.

After a description of cards in current use and their distinctive characteristics, this Chapter will consider their legal implications, and then give a brief outline of some other innovative types of technology being used, or about to be used, in banking transactions. **15–005**

(1) Credit cards[17]

These are cards (such as Visa and Mastercard) which allow customers to buy on credit—the card may be produced at a shop which has agreed to accept payment by means of the card—and to obtain cash advances at a bank or through an automated teller (cash) machine (ATM), with the use of a personal identification number (PIN). Credit cards are also frequently used in transactions carried out over the telephone. **15–006**

With "normal" credit cards, there are *three parties*[18] (the card holder, card issuer and the retailer), and three autonomous contracts. The retailer, who may have to seek authorisation from the issuer if the amount exceeds the limit agreed between the two, is reimbursed by the card issuer, who deducts a service charge. The agreement between card holder and issuer is classified as a *credit agreement* and is regulated by the CCA 1974. Customers receive regular statements and may pay the balance in full or in part, subject to a certain minimum. Interest is payable on outstanding balances. Although many card holders pay off the whole balance each month in order to avoid paying interest, there is no obligation to do so.

Other cards which operate on similar lines are *budget cards*, where customers agree to pay a fixed amount into their card account each month, and *store cards* which are issued by particular companies or retail groups for use at their own outlets, such as John Lewis cards, which are *two party* credit cards, since card issuer and store are the same.[19] A two party card is issued by or on behalf of the supplier and can be used only on the issuer/supplier's premises. **15–007**

---

[16] The Code gives brief definitions of the types of card. The present discussion does not include "pre-payment" cards, which store value on the card (see below, para. 15–069). Some sections of the CCA 1974, such as ss. 56, 66 and 75 are not extended to all payment cards (see below, para. 15–028).

[17] There were 1.3 billion credit and charge card transactions in 1999, an increase of 10 per cent over 1998 (APACS, *Plastic Card Review* (2000)).

[18] There is often a fourth, the "merchant acquirer", who arranges to receive the credit card slips from the retailer, making the appropriate payments to the retailer less a handling discount, and which recruits retailers to the card scheme (Stephenson, *op. cit.*, p. 4). See also Brownsword and MacGowan [1997] N.L.J. 1806.

[19] This is a form of credit sale agreement, so that the sale contract is governed by the Sale of Goods Act 1979 (or by the Supply of Goods and Services Act 1982, if it is for services or mixture of goods and services), Stephenson, *op. cit.*

Among the reasons for the continued popularity and proliferation of credit cards are the number of incentives (like no fee and cash benefits) and the variety of types offered; for instance, there are *gold* cards for wealthier customers and *affinity* cards, which enable the issuer to make a donation to the linked organisation—often a charity—every time the card is used. These have become very popular; successful examples are Royal Society for the Protection of Birds, Open University and Manchester United Football Club credit cards.[20]

(2) Charge cards

15–008 These are cards, often called travel and entertainment cards, (such as Diners' Club, American Express and some "gold" cards) which, though similar to credit cards, are not classed as credit cards, because the total balance outstanding has to be repaid regularly on the due date. They are therefore not covered by the most onerous requirements of the CCA 1974,[21] although they may be *credit tokens*[22] if they are used for obtaining cash advances.

(3) Debit cards

15–009 Debit cards (such as Switch and Visa Delta)[23] were introduced in 1987 and have become increasingly popular, particularly for smaller payments. They function like cheques,[24] by debiting a bank account by EFTPOS (electronic funds transfer at the point of sale), and can be used to obtain cash or make payments at a point of sale like a supermarket. Two new on-line debit cards (Visa Electron and Solo), which require authorisation for every transaction, have been introduced[25] for customers who might otherwise not be allowed cards, and have also proved popular.

15–010 The Electronic Funds Transfer at Point of Sale (EFTPOS)[26] system is now widely used in retail and business premises. The card has a black magnetic stripe on its back with information encoded on it. When a transaction takes place, the card is "swiped" through a card reader terminal in the supplier's premises, which reads the magnetic stripe. The information and the details of the transaction may be sent to a central processing point (if it is an "on-line" system and the supplier's terminal is in communication with the bank's central computer) where the validity of the card is

---

[20] Worthington in, *Payments—past, present and future* (APACS) p. 61.

[21] Exempt by virtue of s. 16(5)(a) of the CCA 1974 and Reg. 3(1)(a)(ii) of the Consumer Credit (Exempt Agreements) No. 2 Order 1985, (S.I. 1985 No. 757).

[22] See below, para. 15–032.

[23] Transaction volumes grew by 20 per cent during 1999 to 2 billion. The total number of debit cards in issue is 46 million (APACS, *Plastic Card Review* (2000)).

[24] They are not subject to the BOEA 1882.

[25] In 1996 and 1997 respectively.

[26] See Chorafas, *Electronic Funds Transfer,* and Brindle and Cox, para. 4.19. The point of sale system operates in the same way as a CHAPS terminal does within the CHAPS system.

authenticated and then the terminal produces a voucher for the customer to sign. The customer's account may be debited very shortly after a transaction, though details may be stored on magnetic tape for the day.

Debit cards come within the ambit of the Banking Code, but they may not be regulated by the provisions of the CCA 1974 which relate to *credit agreements*, at least if there is no provision in the agreement for the card to be used against an overdraft, although this point is undecided and not clear from the wording of the CCA 1974.[27] It is doubtful, also, whether a debit card agreement is a *credit token agreement*, because it does not involve the extension of credit directly, although it can be argued that credit is (briefly) provided because of the delay in payment.[28] If the card has been used against an overdraft granted to the customer, however, it seems that the card may be regarded as a *credit token*,[29] and in this case some statutory protection against liability for loss and misuse would be available to the debtor.[30] The extra protection of connected lender liability[31] accorded to consumers using credit cards does not apply to those using debit cards.[32] **15–011**

(4) Automated teller machine (ATM) cards (cash cards)

"Hole in the wall" machines are electronic funds transfer (EFT) machines, first introduced in 1967,[33] and now very familiar to bank customers. They are used to obtain cash and other services, such as allowing the customer to make balance enquiries and order cheques, and customers activate them by inserting the cash card (a variant of a debit card). Banks have reciprocal arrangements allowing their customers to use any ATM in a shared network, and many ATMs nowadays are sited in places away from bank branches, like supermarkets, stations and even football grounds. ATMs therefore are convenient and flexible to use, but **15–012**

[27] Paget, *op. cit.*, pp. 64 and 311, sees the wording of s. 14(3) of the CCA 1974 as indicating that debit cards would be providing credit because a third party is supplying cash, goods or services in connection with a credit token. Goode (*Consumer Credit Legislation*, para. I [549.3], on the other hand, considers that the fact that debit cards could not have been envisaged by the Act (they did not exist when it was drafted) should be conclusive. Some banks treat debit cards as regulated by the Act in the same way as credit cards even if the customer has no agreed overdraft facility: Paget, *op. cit.*, p. 64.

[28] See Arora, *Electronic Banking and the Law,* (2nd ed.) p. 115.

[29] CCA 1974, s. 14(1), see below, para. 15–032. A credit-token is a card, a check, a voucher or some other "thing" which is issued to an individual, provided it is issued by someone in the business of making regulated credit agreements. Cheques are not included, however, because the bank's undertaking is to pay the cheque, not to supply cash, goods or services, Guest and Lloyd *Encyclopedia of Consumer Credit Law*, para. 2–015.

[30] CCA 1974, ss. 83 and 84, see below, para. 15–037.

[31] CCA 1974, s. 75 (nor "deemed agency" under CCA 1974, s. 56). See below, para. 15–041.

[32] Because by CCA 1974, s.187(3) (the "EFTPOS amendment", inserted by s. 89 of the BA, 1987), an EFTPOS arrangement is not a "pre-existing arrangement" (within CCA 1974, s. 12(b) or (c)) which would make it a DCS agreement, see Stephenson, *op. cit.*, p. 142.

[33] The U.K. machines were the first in the world. There are now more than 28,000 cash machines in Britain. In 1999, about £108 billion was withdrawn from ATMs in more than 1.9 billion transactions (APACS, *Plastic Card Review* (2000)).

have the slight financial disadvantage for the customer, as compared to cheques, that the customer's account is usually debited the same day.

15–013 Banks need a clear mandate for machine transactions as well as for paper ones. The method which banks use for authenticating instructions for cash machines is the use of the PIN (the customer's Personal Identification Number) together with the customer's card. The customer inserts his or her card into the machine, which reads the data encoded on the magnetic stripe on the back of the card, and then keys in his or her PIN. Only if the correct PIN is used with the card will the machine be activated. The data is captured and used to debit the account automatically. The apparent security of the operation has proved less than effective in practice, and the main problems with card machines have related to the lack of security, and the difficulty of establishing whether particular transactions were genuine.[34]

Cash card agreements do not normally fall into the category of regulated credit agreements under the CCA 1974, but if a cash card is used against an overdraft or if it is used at another bank's machine (unless the other bank is an agent of the customer's bank), it may be a *credit token,* in which case its use will bring it within the ambit of the CCA 1974.

(5) Cheque guarantee[35] scheme

15–014 Cheque guarantee cards (or, more frequently now, the cheque guarantee *function* of cards—"standalone" cheque guarantee cards are not usually seen nowadays) are not used for payment, like the other cards described here. They are issued by banks or building societies to be used with a cheque book to guarantee a payment made by cheque up to the limit specified by the card. If they are used in accordance with the conditions of use, the cheque will be honoured by the bank even if the account has insufficient funds. There is no possibility of countermanding a cheque used with a cheque card, because the bank's obligation comes into existence at the time the card is used.

15–015 The agreement is not a credit card agreement, although in some circumstances a card may be used to obtain short-term credit, and may be a *credit token*—for example, if it is used against a current account with an agreed overdraft facility in which case some provisions of the CCA 1974 apply to its use.[36]

Eurocheque cards are specific cheque guarantee cards which can be used either with special eurocheques to pay for goods or services, or by

[34] See below, paras 15–055 *et seq.*

[35] There is no real guarantee: see Brindle and Cox, *op. cit.*, para 4–14. See also Evans L.J., *First Sport Ltd v. Barclays Bank* [1993] 3 All E.R. 789 at 795: "[t]he bank's undertaking that payment of the cheque is 'guaranteed' does not mean that its contract with the payee . . . is strictly a contract of guarantee. It is a separate and independent obligation which is not dependent in any way upon default by the customer. . .".

[36] Cheque cards do not come within ss. 56 and 75 of the CCA 1974, because cheque card arrangements cannot be DCS agreements, see below, para. 15–034.

themselves to withdraw cash from machines, in the United Kingdom and abroad.

(6) Multifunction cards

Many cards now are "*multifunction*" cards: one card combines a number of functions, so that it may for instance be a debit card, cash (ATM) card and cheque guarantee card combined. These provide savings and ease of administration for banks, and increased convenience for customers. The Jack Report pointed out, however, that they may leave customers exposed to increased risk: if a card is stolen and the PIN is known, the thief can use it over its full range of functions, leaving the customer deprived of all means of payment except cash. The Committee recommended[37] that customers who do not want all the functions should be free to choose to have functions blocked off, and that if a card is compromised, the customer should have no liability for the unauthorised functions unless he or she is fraudulent. The Banking Code, however, simply provides that card issuers will tell customers if a card has more than one function, although it also states that banks will not issue Personal Identification Numbers (PINs) where requested not to do so,[38] and banks undertake to allow customers to choose their own PINs.[39] **15–016**

The Contractual Basis

The use of credit (and other three party[40]) cards is governed by three contracts.[41] These are between the card issuer (the creditor, usually a bank) and the card holder (debtor); between the holder and the retailer (supplier); and between the retailer and the issuer. **15–017**

These contracts are independent of each other, and in each the parties are acting as principals, not as agents. The agreements between card issuer and card holder and between card issuer and supplier are standard form contracts, and on the face of it, banks can include any terms they wish in the contracts to which they are party, since they are in effect dictating the terms. However, the contract terms are subject to the general law of contract (for example, if there has been a misrepresentation), and to the provisions of the CCA 1974, the UCTA 1977 and the UTCCR 1999. In certain circumstances, the terms may give rise to criminal liability under the Trade Descriptions Act 1968, the Consumer Protection Act 1987, and some provisions of the CCA 1974.

---

[37] Jack Report, Cm. 622 (1989), para. 11.11.
[38] Banking Code (1999), para. 3.12.
[39] *ibid.*, para. 3.11.
[40] Charge cards and EFTPOS.
[41] *Re Charge Card Services* [1987] Ch. 150, *per* Millett J., aff'd [1988] 3 All E.R. 702. The terms of the contracts are considered in detail by Brindle and Cox, *op. cit.*

15–018 **(a) Card issuer and card holder.** This relationship is governed by the terms of the contract between the parties, which typically contains terms stating that the card remains the property of the issuer and that its issue may be cancelled at any time; that the holder must not exceed the credit limit; that the issuer is not liable for a retailer's refusal to accept a card, and that the issuer may vary any card conditions on notice.[42] This will invariably be a standard term contract, and the issuer must take account of the general law, the provisions of the Banking Code and the control exercised by the Ombudsman. Generally, therefore, the contract must be in plain language[43] and the written terms and conditions should be fair in substance.[44]

15–019 **(b) Card holder and retailer.** This is likely to be a contract to supply services or a sale of goods contract.[45] Retailers are entitled to discriminate between cash and credit card purchasers if they wish,[46] although a retailer who refuses to take a card if the logo is displayed on the shop premises may be committing an offence.[47]

15–020 **(c) Retailer and issuer.** Usually a standard form contract. The issuer agrees to discharge the amount due under the contract between retailer and holder subject to the deduction of an agreed discount.[48] If the retailer accepts payment by plastic card for the goods or services, he or she will be reimbursed by the issuer, who will in turn be repaid by the holder. It may well be a term of the contract between the issuer and the retailer that, unless there is some irregularity, the retailer will not refuse to accept the card.

The effect of payment by card

15–021 The legal implications of credit cards were considered by the courts in *Re Charge Card Services Ltd,*[49] where the question was whether it is the retailer or the holder who is ultimately responsible for the price of the goods or service on the default or insolvency of the card issuer, Charge Card Services Ltd provided cards for obtaining petrol and other motoring products from the garages (the retailers) who had entered into the Charge Card scheme

---

[42] Subject to the Banking Code (1999), para. 2.12.

[43] UTCCR 1994, reg. 7; Banking Code (1999), para. 2.9.

[44] UTCCR 1994, reg. 8; Banking Code (1999), para. 2.9.

[45] But Stephenson, *op. cit.*, points out that s. 2(1) of the Sale of Goods Act 1979 states that the goods should have been bought for a money consideration, and there is some doubt (see Diamond, *Commercial and Consumer Credit—An Introduction*) whether goods bought with credit cards satisfy this requirement.

[46] Monopolies and Mergers Commission: Credit Cards (Price Discrimination) Order 1990, (S.I. 1990 No. 2159). This does not apply to the use of debit cards, Brindle and Cox, *op. cit.*, para. 4–38.

[47] Under the Trade Descriptions Act 1968 or the Consumer Protection Act 1987.

[48] See Brownsword and MacGowan [1997] N.L.J. 1806.

[49] [1987] Ch. 150, aff'd [1988] 3 All E.R. 702.

(in fact, a credit card scheme). The card holder could buy goods or petrol by producing the card and signing a sales voucher, and the garage would be reimbursed for the transaction by the card company. The company in turn would be paid by the card holder. The company's own finances were arranged through a factoring agreement with another company,[50] and the litigation arose when this other company went into liquidation. At the time of the liquidation, the company owed money to the garages. The question was whether the garages could recover that money from the customers rather than having to claim in the company's insolvency (in which case they would recover only a dividend). The customers, however, who would still be liable for their own debts to the card company, naturally thought that they had already paid with their cards. The answer to the question whether the retailer or the customer was liable on the default or insolvency of the card issuer depended on whether the payment by card was *absolute* payment or whether it was regarded as *conditional* payment, like payment by cheque or by letter of credit.

Millett J. held that payment by the customer by credit card was absolute payment,[51] and the risk of the insolvency of the card issuer fell on the garages, not on the customers. In card transactions, therefore, plastic cards work like cash: retailers cannot turn to the customers for recovery on the card issuer's default or insolvency (unless express terms of the contracts provide that the payment is conditional) but must claim against the issuer or in the insolvency. The judge's reasoning emphasised the commercial relationship between the card issuer and the retailer. In the case of card payments, he pointed out, it is the relationship between the issuer and the retailer which is central to the transaction, and contractual arrangements already exist between them at the time of the transaction. The relationship between the card holder and the retailer, on the other hand, is likely to be ephemeral: the retailer may well not even know the address of the card holder. Moreover, although the customer benefits from the use of the card by obtaining credit, the retailer also benefits in a number of ways: by obtaining better security (probably), the convenience of having one debtor instead of many, and the prospect of extra trade. The judge also pointed out that if the customer were liable to pay the retailer on the default of the issuer, the terms of the customer's contract would be more onerous than those of the others, because the liability would be to repay immediately the **15–022**

[50] By assignment of debts.

[51] This has the effect that the debt is extinguished. In *Customs and Excise v. Diners Club Ltd* [1989] 2 All E.R. 385 at 394, *per* Woolf J.: "When a member becomes indebted to the retailer on a card being accepted, not only is the liability of the cardholder to the retailer extinguished but so also is the debt, albeit that the debt is replaced by a new debt due from the member to Diners or CSL . . . because any other result would be inconsistent with both sets of bilateral contracts when read as a whole, and in particular it is inconsistent with the different obligations owed by the member to the retailer before he uses his card to those which he owes the credit card company under his contract with that company after he has used the card".

whole of the full face value of the voucher, whereas the retailer can deduct its commission.

15–023 The operation of *cheque guarantee cards* has also featured in litigation. They work in a different way from credit cards, because their purpose is not to make a payment, but to "guarantee"[52] a payment made by cheque up to the limit specified by the card, provided it is used in accordance with the conditions of use. The effect of using the card is that the cheque will be honoured by the bank even if there is not enough money in the account. The conditions of use of the card usually include the requirement that the cheque should be signed in the presence of the payee; that the cheque should be drawn on a cheque form with the code number shown on the card; that the card should still be in force, and that the card number is written on the reverse of the cheque by the payee.

There are four contractual relationships supporting the transaction: between buyer and seller under the contract of sale; between buyer as drawer of a bill of exchange and seller as payee of the bill; between buyer as customer and his or her banker; and between buyer's bank and seller.[53] The last of these is a unilateral contract, brought into effect by the use of the card, which conveys to the retailer an offer by the bank which, if accepted, establishes the contract between them even though the acceptance is not communicated to the bank.[54]

15–024 The legal implications of cheque cards were considered by the House of Lords in the criminal case of *R. v. Charles*.[55] Here, the card holder's account was overdrawn but he ignored the bank manager's instruction not to use the card and drew several cheques for gambling, using the card to guarantee each of them separately. Since the bank had to pay according to the guarantee, he had cheated it of the funds, and he was prosecuted for obtaining a pecuniary advantage by deception.[56] It was held that a contract between the retailer and the bank comes into existence when a card holder uses the card, so that a direct contractual right to payment from the bank of the cheque is given to the payee by the use of the card, provided that the use of the card by the drawer is within his or her actual or ostensible authority. The card holder therefore was making a representation that he had the authority of the bank to enter into the contract on its behalf and that it would pay the cheques without question. Since the card holder did not have that authority in this case, he was guilty of the offence. There is some difficulty about the nature of the deception here, since the defendant did not in fact mislead the casino manager; the question was whether his *silence* could amount to an actual representation. What was more, the

[52] Strictly, not a guarantee, see above, para. 15–014, n. 35.
[53] *First Sport Ltd v. Barclays Bank* [1993] 3 All E.R. 789 at 798, *per* Sir Thomas Bingham M.R.
[54] *ibid.*, *per* Evans L.J.
[55] [1977] A.C. 177; [1977] 3 All E.R. 112.
[56] TA 1968, s. 16.

representation, if there was one, was *true*: the bank would pay. This is a situation where the drafting of the legislation is too narrow and precise to accommodate modern types of fraud without distortion.[57]

A further question arose in the civil law context of a dispute between a bank and a retailer about a fraudulent payment by a cheque used with a cheque guarantee card. In *First Sport Ltd v. Barclays Bank plc,*[58–59] this statement was written on the card: "This card may only be used by the authorised signatory . . ." A thief obtained goods from a retailer by giving a cheque which was accepted by the retailer on the presentation of a cheque card. The bank refused to pay the cheque because the signature was forged, although the forged signature agreed with the signature on the card, and all the other conditions on the card had been complied with. Neither signature, of course was the real signature of the authorised signatory, which had apparently been removed from the card and replaced by the thief's signature. The Court of Appeal had to decide, on the construction of the statement on the card, which of the two innocent parties, bank and retailer, had to bear the loss. The majority of the court decided that the words were simply a warning to the retailer, not a condition that payment would not be made if the card was not presented by the account holder. Furthermore, the bearer—even a thief—had ostensible authority to convey the bank's offer, provided at least that the retailer had no reason to believe that he or she was not the authorised signatory. Read as a whole, the bank's conditions encouraged the belief that the bank would accept liability, and thereby held out anyone able to fulfil the conditions as having the authority to bind it.[60] The dissenting judge, Kennedy L.J., disagreed on the question of authority. The bank, he thought, had not held itself out so as to be estopped from denying the authority of the thief and had not intended to shoulder the whole of any loss. **15–025**

All the same, it is no doubt true that the banks would not undertake liability if they did not benefit overall from such transactions. If they offer a "guarantee", it is not surprising that retailers rely on the bank's undertaking as giving an assurance of payment, whatever the reason for the default by the card holder. It is not unreasonable in these circumstances, to require banks to make the extent of their liability quite clear. In fact, Barclays have changed (indeed, at the time of the litigation, had already changed) their standard conditions to read: "provided . . . it [the cheque] is signed . . . in the presence of the person whose signature appears on the card."[61] This form of words should protect banks from the problem arising again by simply placing the risk of loss on the retailer. **15–026**

[57] See further below, para. 15–062.
[58–59] [1993] 3 All E.R. 789.
[60] [1993] 3 All E.R. 789 at 798. *per* Sir Thomas Bingham M.R.
[61] Hitchens (1994) 57 M.L.R. 811. The present wording is promulgated under the Standard Cheque Card Scheme, which is administered by the Cheque Card Committee of APACS (see Brindle and Cox, *op. cit.*, pp. 465 and 468).

15–027 Kennedy L.J. agreed with another argument raised by the bank. It claimed that the card should only operate to guarantee the payment of a *valid* cheque (the wording of the condition was "payment of one personal cheque . . . is guaranteed"). The "cheque" here had a forged signature, and was therefore not valid—it was "a mere sham piece of paper".[62] This argument was dismissed by Sir Thomas Bingham on the basis that "complex concepts derived from the Act [BOEA 1882]" which might be used in the context of a dispute between a paying bank and a collecting bank should not be imported into the present situation, where a reasonable seller would not have regarded the cheque as a mere sham. On this point, the dissenting judgment seems preferable. The view that forged cheques are valid in some contexts but not in others surely makes an artificial distinction which could lead to unnecessary technicality in the law.[63]

Consumer Credit Act Implications for the Use of Cards

15–028 In the United Kingdom, unlike some other jurisdictions,[64] there is no general regulation of card or EFTPOS use by legislation. Nevertheless, important controls are provided over many aspects of some types of card (not all) by the CCA 1974, which governs both the negotiation and some of the substantive provisions of agreements. Precontractual regulation of credit card agreements under the Act takes the form of controlling advertisements,[65] canvassing, and quotations given to prospective customers.[66]

Card issuers

15–029 Banks issuing credit cards[67] to private individuals come within the definition in the CCA 1974 of persons carrying on a consumer credit business.[68] They must therefore be licensed by the Director-General of Fair Trading, and must satisfy the Director that they are fit to engage in that

[62] see BOEA 1882, s. 24 and Kerr J., *National Westminster Bank Ltd v. Barclays Bank International Ltd* [1974] 3 All E.R. at 836.

[63] Hitchens, *op. cit.*, at p. 815, points out that a person who takes a cheque *without* a cheque guarantee card "will find only too quickly that the legal meaning of a cheque containing a forged drawer's signature will become relevant".

[64] *e.g.* Electronic Funds Transfer Act 1978 (U.S.); Payment Cards Act 1984 (Denmark). The E.U. is also taking initiatives with regard to credit cards, such as the Recommendation regarding payment systems and in particular the relationship between cardholder and card issuer of November 17, 1988); and the protection of consumers obtaining credit, such as the Consumer Credit Directives (Directive 87/102 [1987] O.J. L42/48 and Directive 90/88 [1990] O.J. L61/14.

[65] Consumer Credit (Advertisements) Regulations 1989 (S.I. 1989 No. 1125).

[66] Consumer Credit (Quotations) Regulations 1989 (S.I. 1989 No. 1126).

[67] But not other types of cards, (*e.g.* charge cards), which are not issued under regulated credit agreements.

[68] Any business so far as it comprises or relates to the provision of credit under regulated consumer credit agreements, CCA 1974, s. 189(1).

activity.[69] Their fitness will be continually monitored, so that if there is any doubt about their suitability, or that of their employees, agents or associates, the licence may be varied, suspended or revoked.[70] For example, business practices which appear to the Director "to be deceitful or oppressive, or otherwise unfair or improper (whether unlawful or not)",[71] including, probably, high pressure selling, might attract scrutiny.

Consumer credit agreements

A personal credit agreement is between an individual[72] and any other person by which credit of any amount is given, not exceeding £25,000.[73] *Credit* includes a cash loan and any other form of financial accommodation.[74] Since consumer credit card agreements (though not charge card agreements, which require the credit to be paid off in one single amount for each period and which are exempt[75]) come within the definition of credit agreement, they are regulated agreements,[76] and therefore fall within the scope of nearly all the provisions in the CCA 1974. **15–030**

The credit card may be used to finance a transaction between the debtor and creditor, which may or may not form part of the credit agreement, or to finance a transaction between the debtor and a third person. In these cases, the agreement is known as a *debtor-creditor-supplier* agreement.[77] A consumer credit agreement may be a *restricted-use* or an *unrestricted-use* credit agreement. If the credit is given in such a way as to leave the debtor free to use it as he or she chooses[78] (for example, cards which allow a debtor to obtain cash advances), the agreement is for unrestricted-use credit. In a restricted-use credit agreement, the creditor can ensure that the payment is made for a particular purchase or transaction—for example, the creditor pays the price directly to the supplier. Purchases of goods or services by credit card would be restricted-use.[79]

[69] CCA 1974, s. 25(1).

[70] CCA 1974, ss. 31–33.

[71] CCA 1974, s. 25(2)(d).

[72] Which includes a partnership or other unincorporated body of persons not consisting entirely of bodies corporate, CCA 1974, s. 189(1).

[73] The credit limit is the maximum credit balance which is allowed during a period, disregarding any provision for temporary excess, CCA 1974, s. 10(2). It is the total charge for credit which is considered, not the cash price of the goods or service. The Act differentiates between "fixed-sum credit" (where the amount is fixed) and "running account credit", where the debtor may use an account up to an agreed limit; the account may be drawn on repeatedly, provided the indebtedness is cleared, or reduced, regularly. (More usually thought of as "revolving credit".)

[74] CCA 1974, s. 9(1).

[75] CCA 1974, s. 16, art. 3(a)(ii) of the Consumer Credit (Exempt Agreements) Order 1989 (S.I. 1989 No. 869).

[76] CCA 1974, s. 8(3). Section 189(1) of the CCA 1974 defines a regulated agreement as "a consumer credit agreement or consumer hire agreement, other than an exempt agreement."

[77] See below, para. 15–034.

[78] CCA 1974, s. 11(3).

[79] Goode, *op. cit.*, III [19].

Credit token agreements

15–031 Plastic cards may function as *credit tokens*, whether or not the particular card agreement amounts to a regulated credit agreement. A credit token agreement is a "regulated agreement for the provision of credit in connection with the use of a credit token" (section 14(2) of the CCA 1974); some provisions of the Act relate specifically to credit tokens.

15–032 **Credit token.** A credit-token can be thought of as "a piece of paper or plastic which unlocks the door to credit".[80] The definition given in section 14(1) of the CCA 1974 is that a credit-token includes a card, check, voucher, coupon, stamp, booklet, form or other document or thing (but not a cheque[81]) given to an individual by a person carrying on a consumer credit business, who undertakes:

(a) that on production of it (whether or not some other action is also required) he will supply cash, goods and services (or any of them) on credit

[this can be called a *two party credit card*,[82] where the creditor is the same person as the supplier, like a store card] or

(b) that where, on the production of it to a third party (whether or not any further action is also required), the third party supplies cash, goods and services (or any of them), he will pay the third party for them (whether or not deducting any discount or commission), in return for payment to him by the individual

[this is a *three party credit card* like Visa or Mastercard, where the creditor and the supplier are two different persons].

15–033 A card may be used as a credit token even though the agreement under which it has been issued does not amount to a credit token agreement and vice versa. Thus, where the issuer does not carry on a consumer credit business, the card may be a credit token—for example, a cash card used to obtain money from an ATM may be a credit token[83] (if it is used against an agreed overdraft or from an ATM belonging to another bank[84]) even though it is not issued under a credit token agreement.[85] In that case, the

---

[80] Goode, *op. cit.*, I [549.1]

[81] Cheques are not included, because the bank's undertaking is to pay the cheque, not to supply cash, goods or services, Guest and Lloyd, *Encyclopedia of Consumer Credit Law*, para. 2–015

[82] Although the creditor may be treated legally as playing the two different parts for the purpose of the debtor-creditor-supplier relationship.

[83] CCA 1974, s. 14(4).

[84] And the other bank is not acting as agent for the card holder's bank.

[85] A debit card might also be a credit token, and there is debate as to whether the debit card agreement might sometimes amount to a regulated credit token agreement; see further Paget, *op. cit.*, pp. 64 and 311, n. 18.

provisions of the CCA 1974 relating to credit tokens apply, (for example, those relating to the supply of unsolicited credit tokens) but not those relating to credit token agreements. Equally, if the card issuer does carry on a consumer credit business, a card may be issued under a credit token agreement though the card itself—a cheque guarantee card, for example—may not be a credit token.

Debtor-creditor-supplier (DCS) and debtor-creditor (DC) agreements

The concept of a debtor-creditor-supplier agreement expresses the idea **15–034**
of a *business connection* between the creditor and the supplier.[86] This idea is based on some "pre-existing arrangements between them"[87] and is not easy to express neatly in legal terms. It includes not only normal three party credit cards but also cards where the creditor and supplier are the same person, such as store cards, because the creditor is then effectively performing the two separate functions of issuer and supplier.[88] The definition includes credit cards used to obtain goods and services from a third party (*restricted-use*), but does not include credit cards used to obtain cash from a third party (these are *unrestricted-use*), nor credit cards used to obtain cash withdrawals from the card holder's own bank (DC transactions). A debtor under a DCS agreement may obtain better protection than one under a DC agreement, and most importantly obtains the advantage of *connected lender liability* under section 75 of the CCA 1974.[89] Cheque card, cash card and debit card agreements are not classed as DCS agreements because they are not regulated consumer credit agreements.[90]

[86] The Crowther Committee's concept of a "connected loan" (Committee on Consumer Credit, Cmnd. 4596, paras 6.2.22 *et seq.*). A connected loan is where the creditor also acts as the supplier of goods or services, or where an advance is made under the terms of regular financing arrangements between creditor and supplier of goods or services for the purposes of financing purchases by one of the supplier's customers. The connection may be an "arrangement"—*i.e.* less than a formal contract, CCA 1974, s. 187.

[87] CCA 1974, s. 12. A DCS agreement is a regulated credit agreement which is *restricted-use* (within CCA 1974, s. 11(1)(a), or (b) if made by the creditor under pre-existing arrangements, or in contemplation of future arrangements, between himself and the supplier; or which is *unrestricted-use* if made by the creditor under pre-existing arrangements between himself and a person (the supplier) other than the debtor in the knowledge that the credit is to be used to finance a transaction between the debtor and the supplier (CCA 1974, s. 12).

[88] Because CCA 1974, s. 12 defines one form of DCS agreement as "a restricted-use credit agreement which falls within section 11(1)(a)"; that subsection states that such an agreement can be "to finance a transaction between the debtor and the creditor, whether forming part of that agreement, or not"; see Stephenson, *op. cit.*, para. 3.12.

[89] The distinction also affects other provisions, *e.g.* concerning cancellation, canvassing and disclosure.

[90] Cheque card agreements are not used to obtain credit, and CCA 1974, s. 187(3) provides that they are not to be considered DCS agreements; similarly the "EFTPOS" amendment (CCA 1974 s. 187(3)(A)), inserted by the BA 1987, provides that debit card agreements are not "arrangements" within CCA 1974, s. 187(1) and (2) (at least when used in EFTPOS transactions, see Paget, *op. cit.*, p. 64).

Protection for card holders

15–035 The CCA 1974 is weighted towards protecting card holders against liability for loss, theft or use without authorisation of the card,[91] and inhibits the exploitation by banks and other card issuers of the great difference in bargaining power between themselves and their customers.

It is a criminal offence, for example, which may have implications for the renewal of the issuer's licence, although it does not affect the validity of the contract, to give a credit token to a person who has not asked for it. A request for a card must be in writing and signed by the person making it, unless there is already a credit token agreement in existence or it is given in renewal or replacement for one previously accepted.[92] The exceptions are obviously sensible, in view of the enormous numbers of cards which are renewed more or less automatically each year. A further protection is that any card sent to a person (even a replacement card) must be *accepted* by the debtor: in other words, the debtor will not become liable on it until it is signed, or a receipt for it is signed or until it is first used.[93] This means that the debtor does not run the risk if the card falls into the wrong hands before he or she receives it.

15–036 The CCA 1974 also makes an attempt to protect minors, who are obviously vulnerable in respect of the use—and abuse—of cards. It is prohibited[94] to send documents with a view to financial gain to a minor, inviting him or her to borrow money, obtain goods on credit or hire, obtain services on credit or to apply for information or advice on borrowing money. An issuer may show that he or she did not know and had no reasonable cause to suspect that the person was a minor.[95]

The CCA 1974 is strict with regard to the *formalities* of a credit card agreement. For example, it is an offence to canvass debtor-creditor-supplier agreements off trade premises; the document embodying the agreement must be in a prescribed form; and some agreements are cancellable.[96] These provisions are too lengthy and complex to examine in depth here, and reference should be made to a specialist work if further information is required.[97]

Liability for loss, theft and use without authorisation

15–037 On the face of it, the card holder could be made liable for whatever the contract provides, even for loss where the card has been stolen and used by an unauthorised person. The CCA 1974 provides important protection for debtors against such onerous liability being imposed on card holders.

[91] But not cards under exempt agreements (CCA 1974, s. 16), *i.e.* charge cards.
[92] CCA 1974, s. 51(3).
[93] CCA 1974, s. 6.
[94] CCA 1974, s. 50.
[95] CCA 1974, s. 50(2).
[96] CCA 1974, s. 49.
[97] See above, para. 15–001, n. 1.

Section 83 of the CCA 1974 applies to all cards used as a *credit facility*,[98] and provides simply that the debtor under a regulated consumer credit agreement shall not be liable to the creditor for any loss arising from the use of a credit facility by another person not acting, or to be treated as acting, as the debtor's agent.[99]

In principle, therefore, a card holder using a card to obtain credit cannot be made liable for losses due to misuse unless he or she has allowed, deliberately or not, someone else to use the card. **15–038**

Section 84 of the CCA 1974 acts as a partial exception to section 83 of the CCA 1974, and might provide the issuer with a little comfort. It states that the contract may provide that the debtor is liable for loss to the issuer from use of the credit token to the extent of £50 (or the credit limit if lower) up to the time that the creditor has been given notice that it has been lost or stolen,[1] unless the debtor has allowed someone else to have possession of the credit token.[2] The issuer must provide details of the name, address and telephone number of a person to whom the notice is to be given; in practice, useful organisations exist which will notify card issuers of loss on behalf of card holders.

The effect of the two sections together is that the card holder will not be liable at all for loss incurred after he or she has notified the issuer of the loss of the card unless the card has been used by someone else with the holder's consent, but the contract may provide that the holder is liable for a maximum of £50 for loss incurred before notification. **15–039**

Importantly, if it is asserted that the card holder allowed another person to use the card, or that the use occurred before the creditor was given notice, the onus of proof lies on the *creditor*, not the card holder.[3]

These provisions only apply to the theft or loss of the actual card, so if the card has been *counterfeited*, the situation is not covered by section 84 of the CCA 1994, and the debtor cannot be made liable at all. **15–040**

The CCA 1974 by no means protects all card holders in all situations. Its protection with regard to loss or theft, as we have seen, operates where there has been misuse of a *credit facility* (that is, where it has been used against an overdrawn account) and cards which are not used to obtain credit are not included. This raises intricate legal questions, because liability depends on the type of card used and the way it is used; as regards

[98] The words "credit facility" mean that a card which is not a credit card—*e.g.* a cash card—is not covered if it is misused against a current account in *credit*.

[99] Only in the case of a commercial agreement, but it would be difficult to imagine a credit card agreement which is *not* commercial. The provision does not apply to instruments to which Cheques Act 1957, s. 4 applies.

[1] CCA 1974, s. 82(3) or is for any other reason liable to misuse; notice takes effect when received and may be oral, but if the agreement requires it does not take effect unless confirmed in writing within seven days (CCA 1974, s. 82(5)).

[2] Even if it has been given to another person for a different purpose from that for which it was used or for safekeeping.

[3] CCA 1974, s. 171(4)(b).

different types of card liability this is therefore inconsistent and difficult to predict.[4] The uncertainty and possible unfairness of this complexity of liability was criticised by the Jack Report.[5] The Banking Ombudsman tried to bring some clarity to the operation of the Act with regard to cards by giving guidance in his Annual Reports as to how it might affect card holders' liability and by giving a series of detailed examples.[6] However, many of the difficultes have become far less obtrusive in practice, because of the provisions of the Banking Code, which has introduced standards of good practice relating to *all* payment cards.[7] These provide similar protection for card holders as that given by the CCA 1974, although there are still areas of difference between the ambit of the CCA 1974 and that of the Code. These are considered below.

Connected lender liability[8]

15–041 An innovative provision of the CCA 1974, and one which gives considerable protection to consumers, is section 75, which allows a card holder to claim against the *card issuer* for any misrepresentation or breach of contract by the *supplier* of goods.[9] The section, which is based on the idea of a "business connection" between the creditor and the supplier, applies only in the case of a *regulated agreement*—that is, only where the price of the goods is more than £100 and less than £30,000,[10] and only if the cardholder is an individual, not a company. It applies to credit cards,[11] but not to charge cards, nor to debit cards used in EFTPOS transactions.[12]

The section states that if the debtor (the card holder) under a DCS agreement has a claim in respect of a misrepresentation or breach of contract against a supplier "he shall have a like claim against the creditor, who, with the supplier, shall accordingly be jointly and severally liable to the debtor".[13] It has effect only in the case of a debtor-creditor-supplier

[4] *e.g.* cash cards used in ATMs may be credit tokens when used to draw against overdrafts, see below, para. 15–058.

[5] Cm. 622 (1989) para. 10.41.

[6] OBO A.R. 1990–91, para. 10.06.

[7] See further below, para. 15–046.

[8] See Campbell [1996] 12 J.I.B.L. 527, Gidney [1996] N.L.J. 762.

[9] CCA 1974, s. 56 is similar in some respects, see below, para. 15–045.

[10] See S.I. 1983 No. 1571 (Consumer Credit (Increase of Monetary Amounts) Order 1983).

[11] It applies to DCS agreements under CCA 1974, s. 12(b), where the creditor and supplier are not the same person, but not to agreements under CCA 1974, s. 12(a).

[12] CCA 1974, s. 187(3) (BA 1987, s. 89): EFTPOS is excluded from CCA 1974, s. 187(1) and (2). It makes no difference whether the agreement is a DCS one or not.

[13] This would not include claims for breach of statutory duty or in tortious negligence.

agreement,[14] and there must therefore be a pre-existing arrangement ("arrangement" implies something less formal than a contract.)[15]

The card company may therefore be liable for loss, including even consequential loss, to the card holder. For example, where a person uses a credit card to buy electrical equipment which turns out to be defective and blows up the house, causing injury to the family, the card company could end up paying for the whole loss, although it will of course have a right to be indemnified by the supplier. Because the liability is joint and several, the card holder can elect to sue the company without taking steps against the supplier first. **15–042**

The reason for this provision was the view[16] that although the two contracts made by the card holder—one with the supplier and the other with the card company—are independent of each other, the supplier and the card issuer are in a joint venture. This means that in some respects the card holder is vulnerable in comparison with the other parties. Card holders who purchase defective goods, for example, would have no right to refuse immediate payment to the card issuer, whereas they might be able to withhold payment to the supplier until the goods were replaced or the defect remedied.

Card issuers regard connected lender liability with understandable dislike. They object particularly to the fact that a claim for loss due to misrepresentation or breach of contract against the supplier may be far greater than merely compensation for defective goods or for the amount of the credit supplied; as we have seen, it may even include damages for personal injury resulting from use of defective goods. Issuers have raised a number of other arguments against the operation of the section.[17] For example, does a *second* card holder, authorised by the main card holder, also have a "like claim"? It would be inconsistent with the "consumerist" spirit of the provision that he or she should not do so, but the existence of such a claim (based, perhaps, on agency) seems doubtful. **15–043**

Another question which has been raised is whether connected lender claims can be brought against a card issuer when the defaulting supplier is abroad. The Banking Ombudsman's view has been that the section does not apply to credit card transactions abroad.[18] If this were correct, the card **15–044**

14 See above, para. 15.034.

15 Made with the intention that the supplier and the creditor will at some later stage be providing for the supply of cash, goods or services to be financed by a consumer credit agreement, CCA 1974, s. 187. Campbell, *op. cit*, p. 528, notes that the display of the relevant sign ("*e.g.* "Visa") indicates that such a pre-existing arrangement may exist. Merchant supplier agreements will probably fall within this requirement; see Gidney [1996] N.L.J. 762, who comments that the alternative view would not conform with the requirements of art. 11, of the Consumer Credit Directive (Directive 102/87 [1987] O.J. L42/48).

16 Stemming from the view of the Crowther Committee in para. 6.6.20 of its 1971 Report.

17 The Director General of Fair Trading considered them in his Reports on Connected Lender Liability, March 1994 and May 1995, and recommended some limited changes (see Campbell, *op. cit*, p. 531).

18 Goode, *op. cit.*, considered that card issuers should be liable for foreign supply contracts under CCA 1974, s. 75; the Office of Fair Trading was also of this view (I [1591].

holder would have to seek satisfaction against the supplier in the foreign court, with all the difficulties that would entail. However, the Court of Appeal has held,[19] that connected lender liability of card issuers does indeed extend to extra-jurisdictional claims. The parties had been induced to purchase timeshares in holiday apartments in Portugal and Spain (which, in one of the cases, did not actually exist) by the vendors' representations. The purchasers had paid partly by credit card and claimed that the misrepresentations by the vendors gave rise to *like claims* under section 75 of the CCA 1974 against the card issuers. The card issuers argued that, since the claims against the suppliers could only be brought in Portugal and Spain, like claims against the issuers would also have to be brought in those countries. The Court of Appeal, however, decided that it is the *claim* which must be "like", not the *remedy*, and so a different remedy could be sought from the supplier from that sought from the issuer. In any case, the court said, the use of the word "like" in fact presupposes some differences. The court brushed aside any idea that Parliament had intended to enact any "jurisdictional requirement" in respect of the section.[20]

15–045 Similar to section 75 of the CCA 1974, and in some respects affording even wider protection—because there are no monetary limits to the claim—is section 56 of the CCA 1974. This section relates only to antecedent negotiations[21] which are "deemed to be conducted by the negotiator in the capacity of agent of the creditor as well as in his actual capacity". The cardholder may therefore recover damages from the issuer for any misrepresentations made in antecedent negotiations by the retailer as the "deemed agent" of the issuer.[22] Unlike section 75 of the CCA 1974, it applies only to *precontractual* matters; it would not cover a claim for breach of contract unless there had been a breach of a precontractual statement which had been incorporated into the contract. There are other differences: for example, section 56 gives rise to a separate liability, not a joint and several liability, and so there is no provision for the supplier to indemnify the card issuer.

The Banking Code and Cards

15–046 The Banking Code deals with all payment cards which may be used to pay for goods and services or to withdraw cash. It contains similar standards about opening an account and the terms and conditions of a card account

---

[19] *Jarrett v. Barclays Bank plc; Jones v. First National Bank plc; First National Bank plc v. Peacock* [1997] 6 Bank. L.R. 66.

[20] Or CCA 1974, s. 56. The court held that the timeshares were not to be classed as tenancies of immovable property, and thus within Art. 16(1) of the Brussels Convention (Civil Jurisdiction and Judgments Act 1982, s. 2), but as personal statutory rights conferred by the CCA 1974 on a debtor under a debtor-creditor-supplier agreement. ". . . a robust, some would say wrong-headed, interpretation" of the law. Robertson, in Brindle and Cox, *op. cit.*, para. 5–62.

[21] Which are any negotiations conducted by the supplier in relation to a transaction financed or proposed to be financed by a debtor-creditor-supplier agreement within CCA 1974, s. 12(b) or (c), s. 56(1)(c).

[22] This has the effect that "the debtor is spared the niceties of agency law on the difficult issues of usual and apparent authority", Stephenson, *op. cit.*, p. 151.

to those for customers with ordinary bank accounts. As we have seen, the Code does not have the force of law, although in practice its provisions are likely to be recognised as the standard to which banks should conform—it can be regarded as "soft law".

One of the most important ways in which the Code has shown its value to bank customers is by extending a good deal of the protection provided by statute for card holders of certain cards to those of any payment cards.[23] For example, there are similar provisions to those in the CCA 1974 on the issuing of cards: **15–047**

- cards will be issued only when requested or to replace cards that have already been issued;
- issuers will comply with requests from customers not to issue PINs (*personal identification numbers*)[24];
- PINs will be advised only to the customer and will be issued separately from cards;
- banks should emphasise to customers that they should keep their card safe and the PIN secure at all times to avoid fraud;
- customers will be able to choose their own PIN[25]; and
- card issuers should provide a written record or statement of account of all payments and withdrawals made.[26]

Liability for loss or theft

The Code provides that issuers will bear the full loss if the card has not been received by the customer, or if faults have occurred in the machines or system used which cause customers to suffer direct loss, unless the fault was obvious or advised by a message or notice on display. It also goes quite a long way to protect the card holder against other loss or theft. Card issuers will bear the full loss for all transactions not authorised by the customer after the issuer has been told of the mishap—unless the customer has acted fraudulently or, maybe, with "gross negligence".[27] Customers' liability for transactions not authorised by them will be limited to a maximum of £50 in the event of misuse before the card issuer has been notified that a card has been lost or stolen or that someone else knows the PIN. **15–048**

[23] Except *prepayment* cards, such as telephone and photocopying cards. The newest edition of the Banking Code (1999) includes "electronic purses" (see below, para. 15–069), which are generally treated like other cards, but there is a warning that, since they "contain" money, they should be treated with care, like cash in a wallet (Banking Code (1999) para. 4.13).

[24] Banking Code (1999) para. 3.12.

[25] *ibid.*, para. 3.11 (from July 1, 2000).

[26] *ibid.*, para. 3.2.

[27] *ibid.*, para. 4.16.

15–049 One of the most helpful provisions of the Code, from the card holder's point of view, is that, in cases of disputed transactions, the burden of proving fraud or gross negligence or that a card has been received by a customer lies on the *card issuer* (although the customer is expected to co-operate with the issuer's investigations).[28] This is similar to the position under the CCA 1974. It is quite likely that the difficulty of discharging this burden has persuaded banks not to claim in doubtful cases and that this is the main reason for a striking reduction in the number of cases of "phantom withdrawals" from cash machines taken to the Ombudsman in the last few years.[29]

Card holders must be told that they have to notify issuers if the card has been lost or stolen or that someone else knows their PIN, and to do so as soon as reasonably practicable after they find out. The issuer must give a place and telephone number where the mishap can be reported at any time, and undertakes to take action to prevent further use of the card.

Differences between Act and Code

15–050 Although the protection provided by the Code is broadly similar to that provided by the CCA 1974, there are still some differences between the CCA 1974 and the Code with regard to liability for loss, which mean that the technical differences between types of cards are still relevant and produce unnecessary and unjustifiable complexity in the regulation of cards.

15–051 **(a) Gross negligence.** Sections 83 and 84 of the CCA 1974 protect the card holder unless he or she has authorised the use of the card. The Code is more restricted. It states that the card issuer will not be liable if the card holder has been *fraudulent* and also, probably, will not be liable if the card holder has been *grossly negligent*. Gross negligence is an unusual concept in English law.[30] Some examples of what the banks suggest would amount to gross negligence are suggested in the Code. It would be grossly negligent for card holders to keep their cheque book and cards together; to allow other persons to use their card and PIN; not to take "reasonable steps" to keep the card safe and the PIN secret at all times; to write the PIN down on the card or on anything usually kept with it; to write the PIN down without making a reasonable attempt to disguise it, or not to destroy any PIN advice promptly on receipt.[31]

15–052 The Ombudsman considers that gross negligence means "if not recklessness, something more than mere carelessness".[32] He gives some illustrations in his Reports: disclosing the PIN to another member of the family; leaving

[28] Banking Code (1999), para. 4.15.
[29] From 36.2 per cent of the total complaints to OBO in 1991–92 to 6.5 per cent in 1995–96.
[30] See Reed, *op. cit.*, p. 457.
[31] Banking Code (1999) para. 4.8.
[32] OBO A.R. 1992–93, para. 12.3.

bags containing the card and written records of the PIN in a locked car or even at one's side while reading in a library might also suffice, if there has been no attempt to disguise the PIN.[33] He emphasises, though, the statement in the Code that the careless action by the cardholder must in fact have *caused* the loss.

(b) Limitation on amount of compensation. The Code makes it plain—again, unlike the CCA 1974—that compensation for losses is limited to any amounts wrongly charged to customers' accounts and any interest on those amounts.[34] Consequential loss is not recoverable. This has been strongly criticised by the Ombudsman in recent Reports.[35] He considers that it is an unfair term which does not comply with the UTCCR 1999 and should be omitted. 15–053

Crime and Banking Technology

One of the most troublesome aspects of the use of cards is the amount of fraud[36] to which they give rise. Levels of fraud in plastic card payment are high, and, although they were reduced by initiatives taken by the banking industry in the last few years,[37] they have been rising again recently. The problem is exacerbated by cross-border fraud and the development of the Single European market as well as the potential risks in the new developments in payment like "electronic commerce".[38] 15–054

ATMS (cash machines)

Disputed transactions from ATM machines (which, like debit cards, are covered by the Code of Practice and may come within some sections of the CCA 1974) caused considerable problems in the past.[39] The main difficulty with ATMs has been that of authenticating the instructions of the customer. 15–055

[33] OBO A.R. 1995–96, Cases 12A and 12B.

[34] Banking Code (1999) para. 4.12.

[35] *e.g.* OBO A.R. 1992–93, para. 12.6; OBO A.R. 1995–95, para. 12.12.

[36] The Jack Committee was particularly troubled about the counterfeiting of cards. It recommended that s. 5(5) of the Forgery and Counterfeiting Act 1981 should be amended to cover plastic cards, and a provision included to make it an offence to possess or sell information that could be used in the manufacture of counterfeit cards with intent to defraud. (Jack Report, Cm. 622 (1989) para. 11.18; Rec. 11(5)) .

[37] APACS reported that plastic card fraud losses, which had been falling until 1995, despite a substantial growth in the volume and amount of transactions, have started to increase (£189 million in 1999—an increase of 40 per cent over 1998) (APACS, *Plastic Card Review* (2000)). Losses from counterfeit cards, particularly, have increased. Professor Levi, commissioned by the Home Office and APACS, published a report on plastic card fraud in 1998.

[38] See below, para. 15–068.

[39] Jack noted that disputed ATM transactions occurred on average about once an hour across the country: Jack Report, Cm. 622 (1989) para. 10.07.

15–056 Banks need a clear mandate for machine transactions as well as for paper ones[40]: indeed, the Jack Report recommended that standards of good practice should be introduced to make clear the bank's "principal and general duty to observe its customer's mandate" (which is not clearly recognised in the terms of contracts with banks, nor, for that matter, in the Banking Code). The method which banks use for authenticating instructions for cash machines is the use of the PIN (the customer's Personal Identification Number) together with the customer's card.[41] The system can only be activated if the correct card and the correct PIN are used together. However, there are a number of ways in which the security of a PIN may be prejudiced: another person may obtain knowledge of both card and PIN by intercepting them in the post, or by intercepting one of them and obtaining the other by some other means (the PIN may be intercepted and the card may be stolen, lost or borrowed); another person may obtain knowledge of the PIN by watching the cardholder keying it in to the machine, or may be told the number by the cardholder. Problems with the transaction may also arise if the EFT malfunctions during use, or if there is a fraud within the bank.[42]

15–057 For several years disputes about cash machine transactions formed the greatest proportion and were the most intractable of the complaints dealt with by the Banking Ombudsman. The banks tended to emphasise how secure cash machines are,[43] and if a customer asserts that he or she is not responsible for the withdrawal of a sum debited to their account, the Ombudsman can only take account of any facts which can be objectively confirmed, including the "audit trail" of the transaction provided by the bank. In some cases this reveals the problem—a breakdown of equipment, perhaps—and the dispute can be satisfactorily settled. Often, however, nothing conclusive can be established and the Ombudsman has felt constrained to decide the dispute against the customer whose card has been used. In some cases, of course, this was fair; cases are recorded, for example, where the customer becomes aware during the investigation that the card has been stolen by a member of his or her own family. But there were also transactions where, as it later became clear, withdrawals had been made fraudulently but it was simply very difficult to establish that there had been a fraud. Whatever the truth about individual transactions, however, a great deal of distress could be caused to customers by these so-called "phantom withdrawals".[44]

---

[40] See Reed [1994] J.I.B.L. at 453.

[41] Jack was concerned that a PIN is less personalised than a signature and allows greater room for fraud and misuse, and thought that banks should accept a wider responsibility for the social consequences of the systems they have introduced.

[42] This has been known: OBO refers to a fraud by engineers working on ATM machines in the Clydesdale Bank.

[43] "The level of fraud at ATMs is extremely low: in 1997 fraud committed at a cash machine accounted for just 6.7 per cent of the total plastic card fraud losses": APACS, *Paypoints—Cash Machines*.

[44] See "Losing at Cards", National Consumer Council (1985).

A card used as a credit token (or in other situations where the CCA 1974 applies) provides protection for the customer because liability is generally limited to £50, although the complexity of the law makes this sometimes difficult to predict.[45] The Jack Committee's proposal to extend the limitation of customers' liability to the use of other cards was taken up in the Banking Code[46] and, together with the fact that the Code places the burden of proving fraud or gross negligence by the card holder on the bank, has had the welcome result of allowing banks and card holders to settle claims more easily, and indeed to deter banks from claiming at all in many cases.[47] **15–058**

All the same, this reduction in complaints has not removed all the Ombudsman's concern about losses for cash card transactions. He has pointed out that *someone* has to pay; if it is not the cardholder, the general body of customers will ultimately have to pay for the bank's loss. He has repeatedly urged banks to introduce further security at ATMs. The technology, in the form of cards with computer chips in them,[48] or "biometric" cards—cards which can only be used by recognition of a unique physical characteristic such as the cardholder's thumb or voice print—is now available.[49] The difficulty about introducing more advanced technology was that the cost for banks of extending the appropriate security methods to the network of machines, would probably outweigh the losses caused by fraud.[50] It is also true, though, as the Ombudsman points out, that there are other factors to consider beyond the direct savings which may be achieved, such as the increase in banking business to which the use of cash machines has contributed. Lower level technology, such as video cameras or laser engraved photographs on cards might be more widely used, and even the monitoring of suspicious patterns of withdrawal is not as widespread as it could be.[51] **15–059**

---

[45] The Banking Ombudsman set out the principles on which he acted in applying the Act in OBO A.R. 1990–91, para. 10.06.

[46] Banking Code (1999), paras 4.14 and 4.15. Banks take all liability for loss where faults in the ATMs have occurred which were not obvious or subject to a warning notice at the time of use: para. 4.12.

[47] Not all the Committee's proposals were taken up: the recommendation that, in cases where no clear decision could be reached, the loss should be apportioned between the parties was not accepted, and nor was the recommendation that consequential loss should be recoverable by the customer.

[48] Which have their own memory and may have details of the customer's current account balance and a line of credit (which can be recharged when used up); these are now being introduced: see below, 15–069.

[49] The Jack Report (Cm. 622 (1989) paras 10.09 and 10.15), which also suggested the use of a "biometric" identification technique, *e.g.* fingerprint, palmprint, voice recognition, retina scan, vein or saliva analysis, pointed out that there may be some reservations about their social acceptability. Siting ATMs in lobbies to which only customers can gain access reduces the risk of the customer being robbed.

[50] OBO A.R. 1993–4, sec. 10.

[51] OBO A.R. 1995–96, paras 12.4 and 12.5.

However, banks are now introducing chip cards in order to improve security and more than 12,000 ATMs have been upgraded to read chipcards.[52]

Other cards

15–060 The courts have had opportunities to consider how the established principles of criminal law apply to the problems posed by cards. The House of Lords held in *Metropolitan Police Commissioner v. Charles*[53] that a person who uses a cheque card to support a cheque makes a representation that he or she has the actual authority of the bank to enter on its behalf into a contract that the bank will honour the cheque on presentment for payment. In *Charles*, the card holder ignored the manager's instruction not to use the card. Since he had no authority from the bank to use it, he was guilty of an offence of obtaining a pecuniary advantage by deception.[54] Similarly, in *R. v. Lambie*,[55] where a card holder had used her credit card to obtain goods when her account was overdrawn and she had been asked to return the card, the House of Lords held, following *Charles*, that the card holder had made a representation to the shop that she had the actual authority of the bank to enter into the transaction and that the bank would honour the voucher signed by the holder on presentment for payment. Since she had had no such authority, she was guilty of dishonestly obtaining a pecuniary advantage by deception.[56] The cases have been criticised,[57] because it is doubtful whether it is really a representation by the card holder which induces the shop to accept the credit card as payment. In *Lambie*, for example, it was evident that the reason for taking the card was not the defendant's standing at the bank, but simply the fact that the shop had an agreement with Barclaycard. Any representation she made was not therefore the real cause of the defendant obtaining the pecuniary advantage. The court's broad interpretation of the requirement of inducement in order to bring this conduct within the ambit of deception offences has been influenced by the widespread scale of credit card fraud,[58] and no doubt also by the simple fact that most lay people would regard the conduct of the defendant as fraudulent.

15–061 The novelty of use—or misuse—of credit and cheque cards has given rise to problems in interpreting and applying other statutory offences in relation

[52] APACS Annual Review 1999, p. 17. Most of the bank "infrastructure" is expected to be upgraded by 2002.

[53] [1977] A.C. 177; [1976] 3 W.L.R. 431; [1976] 3 All E.R. 112, HL(E). See also *R. v. Gilmartin* [1983] 1 All E.R. 829: in the generality of cases under ss. 15 and 16 of the TA 1968, the courts should proceed on the basis that by the giving of a cheque the drawer impliedly represents that the cheque will be paid when presented on or after the date specified (at 835, *per* Goff, L.J.).

[54] TA 1968, s. 16.

[55] [1982] A.C. 453, HL.

[56] TA 1968, s. 16(1).

[57] For summary of criticism, see Sayer, *op. cit.*, p. 120.

[58] [1982] A.C. 453 at 460, *per* Lord Roskill, HL.

to them. In *R. v. Kassim*,[59] a defendant who opened a number of accounts with a bank using a false name and address and obtained cheque books and a credit card, withdrew large sums of money from the accounts (and became overdrawn) and used the credit card. He was found guilty of "procuring the execution of valuable securities", contrary to section 20(2) of the Theft Act 1968 (TA 1968). The House of Lords quashed the conviction, holding that "execution" of a document in this context meant acts done to or in connection with a negotiable instrument, and did not include "giving effect to" it by carrying out the instructions it might contain, such as the delivery of goods or the payment of money. A bank paying a cheque or a credit card company paying on a card voucher is not, therefore, executing a valuable security. Lord Ackner[60] recognised the difficulty of fitting the new transactions into the old formulas—the retailer may well not care whether the card holder is exceeding the authority given by the bank, for instance, provided the conditions on the card are satisfied, and it may therefore be difficult to establish an operative deception—but disliked overstraining the words of the statute.

Bank payment and theft

The problem of overstraining the definitions of offences was considered by the House of Lords in *R. v. Preddy*,[61] in the context of a CHAPS payment (though the same problem would have arisen if the payment had been by cheque[62]). The crime in this case was mortgage fraud—a fashionable activity in the 1980s, when many people, including criminals, were trying to take advantage of the huge rises in property prices. The defendant had lied to building societies so that he could obtain advances from them to purchase property which could be resold at a higher price. He was charged with an offence under section 15 of the TA 1968: dishonestly obtaining property belonging to another. The difficulty was that the advance had been paid to him, quite normally, through the bank, and this raised the question: had he actually obtained property belonging to a building society? Lord Goff's analysis separated the different stages of the bank transaction: the credit in the *lender's* bank account which was to be transferred was a debt, a chose in action, owed by the bank to the lender. When payment of the advance was made to the defendant, the *defendant's* bank account in another bank, was credited with the advance. His bank then owed him a debt. But what had happened was that the chose in action belonging to the lender had simply been extinguished and a new chose in action owed to the defendant by his bank had come into existence. It could not properly be 15–062

[59] [1991] 3 All E.R. 713, HL. See also *R. v. Beck* [1985] 1 All E.R. 571, and *R. v. King* [1991] 3 All E.R. 705 (which concerned a CHAPS payment).
[60] [1991] 3 All E.R. 713 at 721.
[61] [1996] 3 All E.R. 481. See also para. 12–006.
[62] *ibid*., at 491, *per* Lord Goff.

said that the defendant had "obtained property belonging to another". Lord Goff said: "In truth, section 15(1) is here being invoked for a purpose for which it was never designed, and for which it does not legislate".[63]

15–063 The description by the House of Lords of the genesis of section 15 of the TA 1968 is illuminating. The narrowness of the definition in the section (a broader definition in was considered and rejected[64]) was compared to the broader approach in of Scots law, where there is a common law offence of fraud, which is simply: "the bringing about of some definite practical result by means of false pretences".[65] The same problem would not have arisen in Scotland.[66]

As a result of *Preddy*, Parliament hastily amended the TA 1968 by creating a new offence of dishonestly obtaining a money transfer by deception, which applies to payments made by cheque and electronic transfer.[67]

New Technology

15–064 Technological advance has continued at breathtaking speed since the introduction of plastic cards, and banks and banking have been revolutionised by the new developments.[68] Some of these are familiar to customers—"home" or telephone banking, for example, has been available for over 10 years. Similarly, many card holders buy services and goods over the telephone or Internet by using their cards.[69] Other developments, poised for introduction, will complete the transformation from the traditional banker-customer relationship which the Jack Committee described as characterised by the informal world of implied contract into the new world of high technology.

Other developments, less familiar to ordinary customers, have been happening behind the scenes: the introduction of electronic systems for payment of cheques (truncation), for example, and the use of CHAPS, with real time gross settlement now a reality.[70]

"Remote" banking

15–065 The first telephone banking service was launched in 1989. These services, some of which have no branches, deal with customers over the telephone. The customer is connected by telephone, maybe through an operator or via

[63] [1996] 3 All E.R. 481 at 490.
[64] By the Criminal Law Revision Committee, 1966.
[65] [1996] 3 All E.R. 481 at 487, *per* Lord Goff citing *Gordon on the Criminal Law of Scotland*, p. 588.
[66] Lord Jauncey, a Scots Law Lord, said: "Building societies may, however, derive some small comfort from the fact that in Scotland common law and common sense rather than Parliamentary wisdom still prevail", [1996] 3 All E.R. 481 at 497.
[67] By the Theft (Amendment) Act 1996.
[68] See also Encyclopaedia of Bank Law DI (3004) *et seq.*
[69] Transactions which are subject to the CCA 1974 and the Banking Code provisions in the usual way. These transactions are obviously particularly vulnerable to fraud.
[70] See Chap. 12.

a personal computer, or by choosing from recorded menus on the phone by dialling numbers. The service has now become popular, because of its convenience for paying regular bills and transferring money between accounts.[71] There is always some kind of security check, which may be by the use of PINs or by password, dates, addresses or other details, but in fact there has been a significant rise in the levels of fraud in transactions where the card is not present, and greater authorisation controls are being developed by banks.[72] Generally, apparently, the amount of security depends on the complexity of the service provided; most conversations are recorded, but customers are recommended by the Consumers Association to keep a personal record of transactions.[73]

Telephone banking also increases the opportunities for criminals to gain access to the banking system. The guidance Notes on money laundering say that the procedures to confirm identity of customers should be "at least as robust as those for face-face-verification[74]

As yet, no legal controls exist for home banking systems, except in so far as they are subject to the normal rules of bank transactions—transactions must be authorised by the mandate of the customer—and by the general rules of contract. The terms of the contracts are of course established by the banks. They differ, but most of the contracts do not limit the customers' liability, and some contain exclusions: for example, banks may refuse to accept liability for inaccuracy of information. Some of the terms may therefore be invalid under either the UTCCR 1999 or the UCTA 1977.[75] **15–066**

The Jack Committee's view was that there was a need for a secure means of authenticating instructions and that banks should take responsibility for certain minimum standards of security in their authorisation procedures, so as to provide an acceptable degree of protection for the customer.[76] Similarly, the Ombudsman[77] has expressed concern about the possibility of customer's confidentiality being breached when personal information is passed over the phone. Customers should be cautious in using the telephone and ensure that they are in fact speaking to an official of the bank before giving confidential information about their financial affairs. **15–067**

---

[71] Many customers describe themselves as "very satisfied" with their bank's service, although they report more mistakes on their current accounts: *"Which"* magazine, May 1996, p. 50. The Banking Ombudsman (OBO A.R. 1994–5, para. 2.17) also has "an impression that [telephone banking] generates proportionately fewer complaints than branch banking".

[72] (APACS): *Paypoints: Card Fraud*.

[73] *"Which"* magazine, May 1996, p. 52.

[74] Guidance Notes for the Financial Sector (Banks) para. 4.75.

[75] The Consumer's Association, (in "*Which*", May 1996,) comments adversely on some of these terms, and proposes that the standards now limiting customers' liability in the case of payment cards should be extended by the Banking Code, for the sake of consistency and fairness, to the contracts governing home banking systems.

[76] Jack Report, Cm. 622 (1989) para. 10.15.

[77] OBO A.R. 1994–5, para. 2.17

Banking on the Internet

15–068 The internet is a worldwide network of computer networks.[78] Reed,[79] who considered the implications of technological innovations in banking in depth, has described the development of electronic banking from electronic funds transfer between banks, through consumer use of EFT services, both now well-established, to telephone banking and, now, to internet banking. The internet can be used simply as a new method of access to existing services, regulated by legislation in some jurisdictions, and presumably by contract, consumer protection legislation (such as the CCA 1974, the DPA 1998 and the UTCCR 1999) and the Banking Code in the United Kingdom. Organisations are developing payment initiatives by the internet and new products such as interactive television are on offer: it has even been reported that microwave ovens with banking facilities are being developed.[80] Home P.C.-based banking is already expanding enormously[81] as ownership of P.C.s grows and as suitable security procedures are developed.[82]

At the moment, there are risks that customers who use the Internet to purchase goods with cards, without using security features, risk having their card details being intercepted by a thief and used for unauthorised transactions.[82a] It is also possible for fraudsters to set up as sellers on the internet and advertise on it, and then to disappear without trace—with information obtained from unwary users. Card issuers are developing secure systems to protect transactions.[83–84]

15–069 **Digital cash.** An even more recent development is digital cash.[85] Instead of issuing coins and notes, a bank transfers a number of digital cash units to a customer's storage device, which may be a disk storage device attached to a P.C. (or a smart card). The units can be transferred by the customer to a supplier's storage device, either physcially or at a distance.[86] Reed argues that a "digital cash issuer" or "payment system provider" (an institution set up specifically to effect such payments) may not need to be regulated as

---

[78] See Terrett, *A Lawyer's Introduction to the Internet, in Law and the Internet—Regulating Cyberspace* (Edwards and Waelde eds. 1998), and Brindle and Cox, *op. cit.*, Chap. 5.

[79] In *Legal Regulation of Internet Banking: a European Perspective* (1996).

[80] *The Independent,* February 20, 1999.

[81] The volume of remote banking payments is expected to rise to over 190m. by 2008 (APACS Payments Markets Briefing, 1999).

[82] Cryptography is the cornerstone of all payment systems and key to the development of electronic commerce (APACS, *Annual Review* (1997) p. 33). See also the Electronic Communications Act 2000.

[82a] In such cases, where the card holder has not lost possession of the card, it is likely that he or she is protected by s. 83 of the CCA 1974 if the card transaction is covered by the Act, see above, para. 15–037.

[83–84] A secure electronic transaction payment system protocol known as SET: APACS, *Paypoints—Paying over the Internet.*

[85] See also Encylopaedia of Banking, D1 (3004 *et seq.*) and Stern, [1998] Cfi. LR 21 at 225.

[86] Reed, *op. cit.,* 1.

a bank, because the digital cash is in the custody and control of the customer, not the depository. The cash could not be regarded as a deposit, therefore, and would fall outside the requirements of the legislation for institutions accepting deposits,[87] and outside credit licensing regulations.

Reed's discussion of Internet banking concludes:

> "Internet banking law poses interesting new challenges to banks, particularly in two areas with which they already have some familiarity:
>
> - convincing their supervisory authority that offering new internet banking services does not involve excessive risk to the bank's solvency; and
> - drafting suitable account terms which minimise these risks, and at the same time are not rendered unenforceable by consumer protection legislation.
>
> Banks will be less familiar with the challenges posed in a third area, that of regulation by the laws of countries other than their home jurisdiction. The global nature of the Internet means, however, that a bank's internet activities are potentially regulated by every jurisdiction in the world."[88]

Traditional banks, indeed, are already finding that there is another problem with internet banking: its popularity poses a great competitive threat to their core banking and branch based activities. The trend is for our familiar banks to reduce the numbers of their branches ever more drastically and to adopt new technologies with enthusiasm.[88a]

Chip cards[88b]

(a) the "Electronic Purse". This is an instrument with a computer chip embedded in it which can be "charged" by a bank with part of its customer's current account balance or a line of credit, enabling it to be used for, and to record, a series of transactions until the available balance is exhausted. The card can then be recharged.[89] It will also store the customer's PIN, and provide the verification for it when the card is to be used in a machine. It will allow customers to buy goods at participating retailers' and purchase other services (such as telephone calls, bus rides and **15–070**

[87] BA 1987, s. 5, at that time.

[88] Reed, *op. cit.,* at p. 39.

[88a] The editor of the *Encyclopedia of Banking Law* (Hooley) points out that the *U.D.T. v. Kirkwood* definition of a bank seems singularly unsuitable to modern banking practice and will need to be reformulated before long (para. 3065).

[88b] Chip card roll-out officially commenced in the U.K. in spring 1999. By the end of 1999 there were about 4m. chip cards in issue, 80,000 chip terminals deployed at point-of-sale, and more than 12,000 ATMS, with chip readers: APACS, *Annual Review* 1999, p. 17.

[89] The units transferred are heavily encrypted electronics tokens which it is claimed are unforgeable: Reed, *Legal Regulation of Internet Banking,* 1.

car parking). It will store such further data as will allow it to handle all forms of payment for a customer; its use is not limited to EFT applications.[90]

It is expected that customers will find that the electronic purse is more convenient to carry and use than cash, and it may offer the first real alternative to cash for lower value payments. Many "electronic purse" schemes are being set up around the world, and, although there is no product operating on a national basis in the United Kingdom as yet, localised pilot schemes have been tried in Britain: for example, the "Mondex" electronic purse pilot in Swindon which started in 1995.

15–071 There are a number of potential problems in using the electronic purse: possible disputes between customer and bank, if the record of balances and transactions on the card differs from that held by the bank, for example, and between bank, retailer and customer about the accuracy of transaction data recorded on a card by the retailer's terminal. There may also be doubt as to the customer's right to countermand a payment instruction; and the obvious and tricky problem that if a card is lost, the stored value on it will also be lost, in the same way as cash would bc.[91] Thc Banking Codc recommends customers to treat their electronic purses like cash in a wallet, because any money left in the purse at the time it is lost or stolen will be lost in the same way as it would be if a wallet were lost. It goes on, however, to provide the same assurance of limiting customers' liability for such loss to £50 (unless they have acted with fraud or gross negligence) as banks provide for ordinary cards.[92]

15–072 **(b) The ICC Project (Integrated Circuit Card Project).** Chip-based credit, debit and ATM cards have also been tested in Northampton and Dunfermline and are being introduced.[93] They will help to reduce fraud, particularly counterfeiting (an increasing problem) and will allow issuers to offer new services to customers. It is important, however, to ensure that cards are *interoperable*: that is, that all cards are usable in the same card slot in each terminal, so that card holders will get at least the same level of service as that provided to holders of ordinary magnetic stripe cards.[94]

[90] Jack Report, Cm. 622 (1989), para. 11.24. "Universal prepayment cards like Mondex combine the features of smart cards and cybermoney in one instrument and the ability to make secure unlimited value transfers through every competing communication channel (telephone, Internet and card networks as well as face to face) in up to five currencies provides direct competition initially for retail but eventually for wholesale payments": Wood, in *Payments—past, present and future,* APACS, 20.

[91] For discussion of Mondex, see Hooley, Payment in a Cashless Society, Ch. 13 in B.A.K. Rider (ed.) *The Realm of Company Law* (1998), pp. 245–252, quoted in Sealy and Hooley, *Commercial Law—Text, Cases and Materials*, pp. 736–741.

[92] Banking Code (1999), para. 4.13.

[93] From early 1999. APACS Press Release, July 8, 1998. Apparently the new cards will still carry a magnetic stripe alongside the microchip so that the cards can still be used in places where chip technology is not yet used.

[94] APACS, *Annual Review*, (1997) p. 14.

Chapter 16

Subrogation and Subordination

Subrogation[1]

The idea of subrogation "embraces more than a single concept in English law. It is a convenient way of describing a transfer of rights from one person to another, without assignment or assent of the person from whom the rights are transferred and which takes place by operation of law in a whole variety of widely differing circumstances".[2] The doctrine is often explained by saying that one person may "stand in the shoes" of another in relation to a third party; this is generally to avoid unjust enrichment. The right operates in some situations where one party, A would otherwise have no enforceable rights against C. B has some right against C, and because there is some relationship between A, B and C, A may be able "to stand in B's shoes" and enforce its own claim against C as though A were B. Subrogation is increasingly seen as basically a restitutionary remedy (not a cause of action in itself[3]) to avoid C's unjust enrichment.[4] Millett L.J.[5] expressed it in this way: 16–001

> "It is available in a wide variety of different factual situations in which it is required in order to reverse the defendant's unjust enrichment. Equity lawyers speak of a right of subrogation, or of an equity of subrogation, but this merely reflects the fact that it is not a remedy which the court has a general discretion to impose whenever it thinks it just to do so. The equity arises from the conduct of the parties on well-settled principles and in defined circumstances which makes it unconscionable for the defendant to deny the proprietary interest claimed by the plaintiff. A constructive trust arises in the same way. Once the equity is established the court satisfies it by declaring that the property

---

[1] See Mitchell, *The Law of Subrogation* (1994) and Goff and Jones, *The Law of Restitution* (4th ed., Jones, ed. 1993), Ch. 31.

[2] *Orakpo v. Manson Investments Ltd* [1978] A.C. 95 at 104, *per* Lord Diplock.

[3] *Boscawen v. Bajwa* [1995] 4 All E.R. 769, CA.

[4] *Banque Financiere de la Cite v. Parc (Battersea) Ltd* [1998] 1 All E.R. 737, HL: "Distinguished writers have shown that the place of subrogation on the map of obligations is by and large within the now sizeable corner marked out for restitution" at 741–2, *per* Lord Steyn, citing Goff and Jones, *op. cit.*, Birks, *An Introduction to the Law of Restitution*, Burrows, *The Law of Subrogation*, and Mitchell, *op. cit. Banque Financiere* has been criticised for taking a too generous view of unjust enrichment principles, see Bridge [1998] J.B.L. 323.

[5] As he then was.

in question is subject to a charge by way of subrogation in the one case or a constructive trust in the other."[6]

16–002 The rights gained by A in this way may be either personal or proprietary.[7] For example, A may be able to sue C in debt, or may be able to enforce against C a security held previously by B. Whatever the amount of A's claim, however, A cannot recover more than B's entitlement.[8]

A common example of subrogation is the right of an insurer who pays a loss to stand in the shoes of the insured in respect of the insured's right of action against any party responsible for the loss.[9] Some of the principles of the doctrine of subrogation have been worked out in the context of insurance law. For example, the principle from insurance that the subrogator is under a duty not to destroy or prejudice any right or remedy to which the subrogatee becomes entitled has been extended to apply to the conduct of an encumbrancer, or mortgagee, who is paid off by a subsequent encumbrancer.[10]

Subrogation and Securities

16–003 If C owes money to B, who holds a mortgage or charge as security for the debt, and if A advances money which discharges the mortgage, A has a personal right of indemnity from C, and will also be subrogated to B's rights as mortgagee, so that A will have a proprietary right. Traditionally, it has been said that the mortgage is "kept alive"[11] in equity for A's benefit.[12] This was sometimes regarded as an example of contractual subrogation: that is, of subrogation arising pursuant to a contract between A and C to advance money to B,[13] but it is now said to be an *equitable* remedy to reverse or prevent unjust enrichment which is not based upon any agreement or common intention of the party enriched and the party deprived.[14]

---

[6] *Boscawen v. Bajwa* [1995] 4 All E.R. 769 at 777, HL.

[7] See *Lord Napier and Ettrick v. Hunter* [1993] 1 All E.R. 385 HL, and *Banque Financiere* [1998] 1 All E.R. 737.

[8] See Mitchell, *op. cit.*, p. 43 and authorities cited there.

[9] If the insured obtains recovery from the wrongdoer and unconscionably retains that payment as well as receiving a payment from the insurer in respect of the loss, the insurer has a right to recover its payment by way of an enforceable equitable proprietary lien or charge from the damages: *Lord Napier and Ettrick v. Hunter* [1993] 1 All E.R. 737.

[10] *Faircharm Insurance Ltd v. Citibank International plc* [1998] Lloyd's Rep. Bank. 127, CA. It seems, though, that in the context of insurance law, subrogation is "a contractual arrangement . . . founded upon the common intention of the parties": *Banque Financiere* [1998] 1 All E.R. 737 at 749, *per* Lord Hoffmann.

[11] A phrase which should be handled with some care: see *Banque Financiere* [1998] 1 All E.R. 737 at 749, *per* Lord Hoffmann.

[12] *Butler v. Rice* [1910] 2 Ch. 277; *Ghana Commercial Bank v. Chandiram* [1960] A.C. 732.

[13] See *Orakpo v. Manson Investments Ltd* [1978] A.C. 95 at 104, 120.

[14] *Banque Financiere* [1998] 1 All E.R. 737 at 744–5, *per* Lord Hoffmann.

The question whether the payment must be *intentional* arose in *Boscawen v. Bajwa.*[15] It was argued that it was sufficient if the claimant's money had been used to discharge someone else's debt, whether or not this was intended. Here, the purchase for which a bank mortgage was intended fell through, but the money was used by a third party (the vendor's solicitor) to pay off the existing mortgagee of the property (a building society) without the knowledge of the bank. It was held that in some circumstances a mortgage may be kept alive, as was the building society's here, so that A, the bank here, can be subrogated to B's rights, even where A discharged the mortgage without intending to do so or to obtain the benefit of the security by subrogation. The intention could be that of the third party who paid the mortgage without the knowledge of A.[16] **16–004 –005**

In *Banque Financiere de la Cité v. Parc Ltd*,[16a] the question related to a subordination agreement,[17] a "postponement" letter. The plaintiff bank (BFC) advanced a large sum of money to an ailing company (Parc) to enable it to pay off part of a loan secured by a first charge on its property. It was an express condition of the advance that other companies in the group to which Parc belonged, including one called (for short) OOL,[18] would postpone any demand for repayment of loans they had made to Parc until BFC had been repaid. This would provide BFC with a "a negative form of protection"[19] from the claims of other companies in the group who were creditors. However, BFC had not ensured that OOL itself was a party to the agreement. It turned out that it was not a party, and had not authorised the transaction; it was therefore not bound by it. **16–006**

Thus, when Parc became insolvent, BFC lost the priority it had been given under the postponement letter because OOL was not bound by it. BFC therefore claimed a restitutionary remedy against OOL—that its charge should be subrogated to that of OOL's security against Parc (now effectively the first charge). OOL's defence was that there had been no mutual intention that BFC should have priority, and that if BFC took OOL's place, it would have a *better* right than it would have had if the postponement letter had been binding. The House of Lords held that in the absence of subrogation, OOL would be enriched at the expense of BFC, and BFC would fail to obtain that priority over intra-group indebtedness which was an essential part of the transaction under which it had lent the money (the reality, Lord Steyn said, was that OOL was enriched by the **16–007**

[15] [1995] 4 All E.R. 769, CA.

[16] *ibid.*, at 781, *per* Millett L.J. (See also *Re TH Knitwear* [1988] 1 All E.R. 860 at 867, *per* Slade L.J.)

[16a] [1998] 1 All E.R. 737.

[17] Subordination is discussed below, para. 16–017 *et seq.*.

[18] Omnicorp Overseas Ltd. Parc and OOL were members of the same group, which was controlled by R and H, Swiss nationals. The lending arrangement was structured in this way to avoid disclosure requirements under Swiss banking regulations.

[19] [1998] 1 All E.R. 737 at 742, *per* Lord Hoffmann.

money advanced to Parc[20]). The enrichment would be unjust, and the mistake or neglect by BFC to take elementary precautions to safeguard its interest did not itself undermine the ground of restitution.[21] Nor was it necessary (approving Millett L.J.'s views in *Boscawen*) that there should have been any mutual intention that BFC should have priority.

16–008 The court's response to the other defence put forward by OOL (that BFC would obtain a better ranking against Parc than it had bargained for) was that subrogation to a security should not be seen as "keeping the charge alive" for the benefit of the plaintiff. This was merely a metaphor, and in fact, the charge is discharged—it ceases to exist. What actually happens is that the plaintiff's legal relations with the defendant are regulated by the court *as if* the benefit of the charge had been assigned to him or her in order to avoid unjust enrichment. The plaintiff would not necessarily be treated in the same way in all respects as the party to which it was subrogated. Here, consistently with that principle, the charge was not "kept alive" for BFC, but subrogation was used as a *personal* remedy as against OOL, not a property right as against other creditors. This would not give BFC greater rights than it had bargained for; all that would happen would be that OOL would be prevented from being able to enrich itself to the extent that BFC's money paid off the earlier charge. BFC obtained a restitutionary remedy of subrogation as against OOL.[22]

Subrogation and Marshalling

16–009 The equitable doctrine of marshalling holds that if creditor 1 has a separate security over different assets, a and b, and creditor 2 then takes a second security over asset b, and if creditor 1 realises asset b before it realises asset a, then, after creditor 1's security rights have been satisfied by payment out of assets, creditor 2 will be subrogated to creditor 1's security rights over asset a. This is not to say that creditor 1 must have any concern about creditor 2. Creditor 1 may realise whichever of the assets it chooses, and is entitled to be satisfied in full if it is fully secured. But if a secured asset remains, or part of the proceeds of a secured asset remain, creditor 2 is entitled to stand in the shoes of creditor 1 in respect of that asset or its proceeds, even if his or her original security was over another asset taken by creditor 1.[23]

---

[20] [1998] 1 All E.R. 737 at 740. By looking at the realities of the transaction, the court was in effect "piercing the corporate veil".

[21] [1998] 1 All E.R. 737 at 741, *per* Lord Steyn.

[22] Bridge [1998] J.B.L. 323, has criticised the decision because the "extravagant expression of unjust enrichment" may cause commercial chaos unless the scope of the decision is limited by future cases (perhaps by viewing the decision as a matter of piercing the corporate veil). He argued that the House of Lords did not sufficiently scrutinise the precise position of BFC, and took no account of the distribution rights of other creditors of the company on insolvency, creating a danger that the beneficiary of a postponement contract will be overcompensated.

[23] *Wallis v. Woodyear* (1855) 2 Jur. N. S. 179; Goode, *Commercial Law,* p. 696.

Subrogation and Guarantors

If A is a guarantor for C's obligation to B and pays off C's debt or performs the obligation (or part of it), A has a right to be reimbursed or indemnified by C, and is also subrogated to B's security rights against C to the extent of the payment. If A's liability under the guarantee (and the amount paid) did not cover the whole of B's claim, A acquires a proportionate interest in the securities and the claims against the co-guarantors. It is irrelevant whether A was aware of the existence of the securities at the time of the contract, and indeed, A is even entitled to security taken after the guarantee, and receives a windfall to this extent.[24] A guarantor or surety who pays a debt which is a preferential debt in bankruptcy or liquidation will achieve the same priority by subrogation that the creditor would have had.[25] **16–010**

If B, say a bank, has been fully paid, there will be no objection to this, but where it has been only partially paid, it may object to sharing the security with the guarantor, and to the guarantor's claims against the co-guarantor. It is, therefore, common for banks to include in their guarantees a term excluding the guarantor's right of subrogation until such time as the bank itself has been fully paid.[26]

A particular instance of the right of subrogation by a surety exists in relation to a bill of exchange. If a bill is dishonoured, a drawer or other person liable upon the bill (an indorser) may be subrogated to securities provided by the acceptor to the holder. A buyer of goods, for example, may have provided a security to his bank and the seller may draw a bill upon that bank and discount the bill with the bank upon "recourse" terms (thus putting himself in the position of surety). If the buyer fails to pay, the bank may either have recourse to its securities or to the seller, and in the latter case the seller has recourse to the securities.[27] **16–011**

There are limitations upon subrogation in such cases, however. First, the surety must have paid the bill, or declared his or her willingness to do so.[28] Secondly, the securities in question must have been given by the debtor (or possibly a co-surety) in order to cover the debts underlying to the bills in

---

[24] *Deering v. Lord Winchelsea* (1787) 2 B. & P. 270; *Aldrich v. Cooper* (1803) 8 Vest. Jun. 382; *Craythorne v. Swinburne* (1807) 14 Ves. 160; *Mayhew v. Cricket* (1818) 2 Swans. 185; *Stirling v. Forrester* (1951) 3 Blig. 575, 590; *Yonge v. Reynell* (1852) 9 Hare 819; *Forbes v. Jackson* (1882) 19 Ch. D. 615; *Ghana Commercial Bank v. Chandiram* [1960] A.C. 732. The principle is given statutory expression in the Mercantile Law Amendment Act 1856, s. 5. See *Ellinger* (1986) J.B.L. 399 and the Australian cases cited there.

[25] *Re Lamplugh Iron Ore Co*. [1927] 1 Ch. 308.

[26] Sometimes, indeed, even other separate rights of the guarantor against the debtor are subordinated to the bank's rights, see below, Chap 18.

[27] *Duncan, Fox & Co v. North and South Wales Bank* (1880) 6 App.Cas. 1. See also *Aga Ahmed Isphany v. Crisp* (1891) 8 T.L.R. 132, JC; *Jowitt & Sons v. Union Cold Storage Co.* [1913] 3 K.B. 1.

[28] *Re Howe, ex p. Brett* (1871) L.R. 6 Ch. App. 838 at 841; *cf. Re a Debtor* [1976] 2 All E.R. 1010; *Buckeridge v. Mercantile Credit Ltd* (1981) 147 C.L.R. 654.

question.[29] This is a question of construction of the contract, and is generally easy to establish in the case of the principal debtor. But if other parties are in the position of co-sureties, it may be difficult to establish any right to subrogation to their rights,[30] unless they clearly are co-sureties.

Subrogation and Agents

16–012 The normal rule is that if an agent (A) borrows money for a principal (C) without authority to borrow, the agent is liable[31] but the principal is not. If it is a bank which is using the money to discharge the debts of C (its customer) to another person (B), however, there is authority to the effect that the bank is subrogated to B's rights against C, and may claim from C (that is, it may debit C's account) notwithstanding its want of authority. In *B. Liggett (Liverpool) Ltd v. Barclays Bank Ltd*[32] a bank, contrary to its mandate, honoured a company's cheques signed by one director only. The cheques were drawn in favour of trade creditors, who received payment. The company sued the bank, which would normally have been liable to re-credit the company's account, but it was held, in effect, that the bank was subrogated to the trade creditors whose debts were paid. This result avoided the unjust enrichment of the company.[33] In many cases of this sort, the principal will ratify the transaction, but if he or she does not, and if the payment can be identified as having paid a debt of the customer (and this will often be a simple matter where an unauthorised cheque is in question) subrogation is possible.[34]

Subrogation and Invalid Contracts

Companies

16–013 Subrogation used to be of some importance before the law on *ultra vires* transactions was reformed, in situations where a company's borrowing was not authorised by the objects clause of the company. The lending bank was entitled to subrogation in respect of the loan itself,[35] and, if it had taken securities for the loan (assuming that the company had power to give securities for lawful debts), might enforce its own security.[36] If it had no security of its own, the bank could only claim as an unsecured creditor.[37]

[29] *Duncan, Fox & Co. v. North and South Wales Bank* (1880) 6 App.Cas. 1.
[30] See *Scholefield, Goodman & Sons Ltd v. Zyngier* [1985] 3 All E.R. 105; [1986] 1 A.C. 562, PC.
[31] On a warranty of authority.
[32] [1928] 1 K.B. 48.
[33] See also *Re Cleadon Trust* [1939] Ch. 286.
[34] The case is discussed above in Chap. 10, in the context of *Barclays Bank v. Simms Son & Cooke (Southern) Ltd* [1980] Q.B. 677, *per* Goff. J.
[35] *Neath Building Society v. Luce* (1889) 43 Ch. D. 158.
[36] *Cunliffe Brooks & Co. v. Blackburn and District Benefit Building Society* (1884) 9 App.Cas. 857, affirming (1882) 22 Ch. D. 61.
[37] *Re Wrexham Mold and Connah's Quay Railway Co.* [1899] 1 Ch. 440.

Mentally disordered persons

If a bank advances money to a mentally disordered customer who has no contractual capacity, subrogation may provide a remedy if the money is used to pay for a lawful debt, such as meeting necessary outgoings of the customer's estate.[38] **16–014**

Minors

It used to be the case that all contracts with persons under 18 years of age "for the repayment of money lent or to be lent" were "absolutely void".[39] Where money was lent to an infant under a contract void for that reason, however, lenders might be subrogated to the rights of a creditor of the infant, for example in respect of securities held by the creditor or if the money advanced was actually applied to a lawful debt, such as a purchase of necessaries.[40] **16–015**

Statutory Subrogation

This may happen on individual or company insolvency. The principle is that on insolvency a person who pays the debts of preferential creditors may stand in their shoes, and be treated as a preferential creditor itself.[41] **16–016**

Subordination Agreements

"Subordination is a transaction whereby one creditor (the subordinated creditor) of the borrower agrees not to be paid until another creditor (the senior creditor) is paid in full".[42] The reason a creditor is willing to surrender rights of priority is normally to enable the company to persuade another creditor to provide the necessary extra investment to keep the company solvent; this will probably benefit the creditors as well as the company. Similarly, companies can often only continue trading with the financial support of a parent or associated company, which may agree to enter subordination agreements to support them.[43] The subordinated creditor may be an ordinary creditor or a preferential creditor surrendering its preference, or may be a secured creditor under a fixed charge, surrendering priority to the holder of a floating charge. **16–017**

---

[38] *Re Beavan, Davies, Banks & Co. v. Beavan* [1912] 1 Ch 196; *Lloyd v. Coote and Ball* [1915] 1 K.B. 242. Interest and commission are not recoverable.

[39] s. 1 of the Infants' Relief Act 1874, repealed by Minors' Contract Act 1987.

[40] *Re National Permanent Benefit Building Society* (1869) 5 Ch. App. 309 at 313; *Lewis v. Alleyne* (1888) 4 T.L.R. 560.

[41] See below, Chap. 24.

[42] Wood, *Law and Practice of International Finance,* p. 403. See also Goode, *Commercial Law*, pp. 663 *et seq*.

[43] See Vinelott J., *in Re Maxwell Communications Corpn. plc. (No. 2)* [1993] 1 W.L.R. 1402 at 1416.

16–018 Subordination agreements are widely used[44] and are recognised in many jurisdictions.[45] As far as English law is concerned, however, it has been unclear to what extent subordination agreements were affected by the *pari passu* provisions of bankruptcy law, which require equal treatment of unsecured creditors in order to prevent some creditors obtaining an unfair advantage over others.[46] If the subordination affects only the two immediate parties, it appears unobjectionable in principle—in any case, the *pari passu* principle does not apply to secured creditors, who can realise their security without regard to insolvency—but a full subordination agreement, which purports to affect the rights of third parties would raise problems. If creditor 1 agrees with creditor 2 that the latter will take priority over the former, this priority is a personal right, and it should not be asserted against the debtor or his or her trustee or liquidator. First, there is the practical reason that the liquidator might be obliged to consider whether the contract between the two creditors is valid, and secondly, the fact that the liquidator would have to consider the position of any creditors which are not party to the agreement: the agreement might state that creditor 1 ranks equally with creditor 2, who would, therefore, stand ahead of creditor 3, who might otherwise be ahead of creditor 2. It is most unlikely that creditor 3 will be happy to comply with such an arrangement, set up by an agreement to which he or she was not party. The liquidator would not know whom to pay first.

16–019 However, it certainly may be agreed as a mere private matter between creditors that distributions received by the subordinated creditor should be handed over to the senior creditor for application to the senior debt. Such a variation of priorities by agreement between two parties binds the debtor, whether or not the debtor has consented.[47] In this case, it may be that the subordinated creditors are subrogated to the claims of the senior creditors which the former have paid.[48] It should be observed that "seniority" refers to the position between the creditors: so far as the liquidator is concerned, the "senior" creditor may still have its original priority. Subrogation would not affect the priority of the subordinated creditor in the liquidator's eyes.

16–020 In *Re Woodroffe's (Musical Instruments) Ltd*,[49] a company had granted a fixed and floating charge to the bank, and had later granted Mrs Woodroffe a floating charge: this was expressed to be subject to and rank immediately after the bank's charge. What caused the problem was that Mrs Woodroffe's floating charge crystallised,[50] making it a fixed charge. This would

[44] Wood, *The Law of Subordinated Debt* gives a detailed survey of techniques used in practice.

[45] In *Re Maxwell Communications Corpn. plc* [1993] 1 W.L.R. 1402 there is a survey of authorities in several jurisdictions: South Africa, U.S.A. and Australia.

[46] In particular by dicta in *Halesowen Presswork & Assemblies Ltd v. National Westminster Bank Ltd* [1971] 1 Q.B. 1 interpreting s. 31 of the Bankruptcy Act 1914.

[47] *Cheah Theam Swee v. Equiticorp Finance Group Ltd* [1992] 1 A.C. 472, PC.

[48] Wood, *op. cit.*, p. 411.

[49] [1985] 2 All E. R. 908; [1986] Ch. 366.

[50] See Chap. 19.

normally give it priority over the bank's floating charge (which had not crystallised), but what effect did the statement that Mrs Woodroffe's charge was subject to the bank's charge have? The court held that by virtue of that term, the floating chargeholder, the bank, took priority as between itself and the fixed chargee (Mrs Woodroffe), but, as against the preferential creditors, the priority of the floating charge was unchanged. The eventual order of priority was therefore as follows: (i) the floating chargeholder (bank) to the extent of the claim of the fixed chargeholder (Mrs Woodroffe), (ii) the preferential creditors, (iii) the floating chargeholder (bank) for the balance of its claim, and (iv) the fixed chargeholder (Mrs Woodroffe).

At first sight it appears that a mere contractual provision agreed between the debenture holders, the bank and Mrs Woodroffe, allowed the bank to "leapfrog" over the preferential creditors. It has been suggested,[51] however, that the case is best understood as a situation where the floating chargeholder (the bank here) is *subrogated* to the position of the fixed chargeholder, (Mrs Woodroffe's crystallised charge) so that the former collects from the liquidator *in the right of the latter* the amount due to her. Thus, it is not really a question of the floating chargeholder being able to leapfrog over the preferential creditors, but of it being able to claim in the right of the fixed chargeholder and only to the same extent. **16–021**

It is not certain if one should really regard this as a case of subordination, because the floating chargeholder gained no rights against preferential creditors. There was no dispute between the fixed and floating chargeholders as to their priority *inter se,* and the floating chargeholder "stood ahead" of the preferential creditors only to the extent of the debt secured by the fixed charge. It makes no difference to preferential creditors how the chargeholders arrange matters between themselves, so long as those arrangements do not alter the sums of money payable to preferential creditors. Suppose that the question has to be considered by a liquidator: it is submitted that he or she should normally (unless given a direction by a court as happened in *Re Woodroffe's)* pay the fixed chargeholder first, then the preferential creditor, and then the floating chargeholder, though it would be different if the liquidator or receiver had the consent of the fixed chargeholder (as in fact seemed to be the case in *Re Woodroffe's*), so that he or she could pay the floating chargeholder first, as the creditors had agreed.[52] **16–022**

A similar, though not identical, issue arose in *Re Portbase Clothing Ltd*,[53] and was treated differently. In that case, it had been agreed by a deed of priority that a fixed charge in favour of the bank should be subject to a **16–023**

[51] Goode, *Legal Problems of Credit and Insolvency,* (1st ed.) p. 55; (2nd ed.) p. 98.

[52] The liquidator should take these steps even if the agreement between the chargeholders has the effect of an assignment, for unless the cross-assignment is of debts of equal amounts, they will be equitable in nature, and only a legal owner could give a good discharge. The written consent of the legal owner, or the court order, solves the problem for the liquidator.

[53] [1993] B.C.L.C. 796, Ch D.

floating charge in favour of trustees of a pension fund. There were also preferential creditors in competition with both, whose claim, under the IA 1986,[54] would be prior to any charge which, as created, was a floating charge (as the trustees' was here), but not to a fixed charge.

16–024 Here, if it were not for the deed of priority, the assets of the company would go first to satisfy the fixed charge in favour of the bank, and secondly to the preferential creditors, although there would not have been enough to satisfy their claims. The question was what effect the deed of priority had on the ranking. In the view of Chadwick J., the floating charge had to rank before the fixed charge—that is, the debt secured by the floating charge should be satisfied out of the proceeds of the charged asset before the proceeds were paid to the fixed charge holder. As between the two chargeholders, therefore, the liquidator would have to pay the floating charge first. However, the judge went on to say that, since the IA 1986 provides that a charge which, as created, was a floating charge is ranked behind the preferential creditors, the preferential creditors here had to rank before the floating charge. Overall, therefore, the preferential creditors came first, then the floating chargeholder and lastly the fixed chargeholder. Chadwick J. rejected the argument that the fixed chargeholder should hold the proceeds of its security *on trust* for the floating chargeholder, so that the floating chargeholders were to be treated as having become entitled, by assignment or subrogation, to the security which the bank would otherwise have had as against the unsecured creditors. If this argument had prevailed, presumably the floating chargeholder would have jumped ahead of the preferential creditors by virtue of subrogation (arguably as in *Re Woodroffe's)*, in which case, the fixed chargeholder would (presumably) have been relegated to third place.

16–025 The result in *Re Portbase* differed from that in *Re Woodroffe's*, partly because of the construction of the deed of priority. Chadwick J. pointed out that there had been no *agreement* between the chargeholders in *Re Woodroffe's*; the statement in Mrs Woodroffe's charge simply acknowledged the position—that the bank's charge was first in time and that she had notice of it. Secondly, the effect of the change in the IA 1986 which made preferential creditors rank in priority to holders of a floating charge as created made an important difference. After 1986, a floating charge *as created*, like Mrs Woodroffe's could not simply jump ahead because it had crystallised and therefore become fixed. Also, Chadwick J. in *Portbase* seemed to look at the situation from the point of view of the liquidator paying out of the property available to particular creditors according to the legislative provisions and the requirements of the contracts to which the company was a party or of which it had notice, rather than with regard to the arrangements between the creditors. In fact, he viewed the result as in

[54] IA 1986, s. 175(2).

accordance with the policy underlying the legislation. The interests of the preferential creditors should be protected over those of the floating chargee, he thought, because for example, their debts include the remuneration of employees of the company who have contributed to the company's business.[55] This result has been strongly criticised by Professor Goode, in whose view the *Re Woodroffe's* decision did justice to everyone,[56] and who saw the *Portbase* result through the other end of the telescope—the result put the *preferential creditors* in a more favourable position by allowing them to jump ahead of the fixed chargeholder. In his view, applying the subrogation analysis—allowing the floating chargeholder to enforce the fixed chargeholder's priority directly—would achieve the result intended by the priority agreement without disturbing the position of the preferential creditors.

Subordination of the rights of creditors between themselves seems unobjectionable in principle, though it causes problems in practice. It has been unclear, however, whether a subordination which would affect third parties was possible in English law, unless it were done by way of legal assignment of the whole of the debt, or by trust, both of which are certainly possible[57]—indeed, the machinery of a trust deed for achieving subordination of debt is very common.[58] However, there are problems with using assignment. Suppose that creditor 1 assigns its debt to another person. If creditor 1 claims to have a preferential debt, it could assign its debt to creditor 2 in return for an assignment of creditor 2's non-preferential debt. The assignee has the same priority as the assignor and can assert its assignment against a liquidator, who must consider the validity of the contract. Problems arise, though, if the amounts of the debts differ, because an assignment of *part* of a debt can only be an equitable assignment, and an equitable assignee cannot give a good discharge to the liquidator. **16–026**

The difficult question, however, has been whether such an arrangement could be achieved by *contract*. One situation where the question might arise is where a company issues debentures or bonds by which it subordinates the rights of a class of bondholders to other creditors. Bonds may be traded and may come into the hands of new holders. This in itself causes no problems, for since the terms of the bonds are known, the transferees can have no greater rights than the original holders. The real problem is to determine what the effect of such an agreement is on the insolvency of the debtor. **16–027**

[55] [1993] B.C.L.C. 796 at 805.

[56] *Principles of Corporate Insolvency Law,* p. 170.

[57] In *Re British & Commonwealth Holdings plc. (No. 3)* [1992] 1 W.L.R. 672, Ch D, an arrangement by which the claims of holders of loan stock were subordinated to the claims of other creditors by trust deed was held to be a valid subordination.

[58] See *Re Maxwell Communications Corpn. Plc.* [1993] 1 W.L.R. 1403 at 1405, *per* Vinelott J., Ch D.

16–028 This situation was considered by the court in *Re Maxwell Communications Corpn. plc*.[59] The question was whether liabilities to bondholders were effectively subordinated to the company's liabilities to other unsecured creditors. In this case the arrangement was simply a contractual undertaking not to prove in the debtor's winding-up[60]; there was no machinery of trust or assignment by which the subordination could be effectively achieved, for the practical reason that the relevant issues were governed by Swiss law, which does not recognise trusts (although it does recognise the effectiveness of subordination provisions). Vinelott J. came to the conclusion that the legislative provisions requiring that creditors should be dealt with *pari passu*[61] were designed to protect the interests of the liquidator and the general body of creditors which might be unfairly prejudiced if other creditors could override the statutory provisions by contract among themselves. However, this public policy consideration was not a good reason for denying a creditor's right to waive or vary its right to prove in the insolvency.[62] Nor would it be particularly onerous for the liquidator to have to "look behind" a creditor's proof to see whether its debt is postponed to other creditors' debts; there are other situations where the liquidator is required by statute to do exactly that. The judge robustly acknowledged the realities of the situation: not to recognise subordination by a direct contract, when the same result can be achieved by trust or assignment, would represent, he thought, a triumph of form over substance.[63]

59 [1993] 1 W.L.R. 1402, Ch D.

60 The situation differed in this significant respect from *Re British and Commonwealth Holdings* [1992] 1 W.L.R. 672, a decision of the same judge.

61 IA 1986, s.107; CA 1948, s. 302; IR 1986, r. 4.181; see further below, Chap. 24.

62 Considering that dicta in *Halesowen Presswork & Assemblies Ltd v. National Westminster Bank Ltd* [1971] 1 Q.B. 1 to the effect that there could be no contracting out of statutory set-off (under the Bankruptcy Act 1914, s. 31, now under the IA 1986, s. 323, and the IR 1986, r. 4.90) did not compel him to conclude that contractual subordination was rendered void by the insolvency legislation [1993] 1 W.L.R. 1402 at 1416, Ch D.

63 [1993] 1 W.L.R. 1402 at 1417, Ch D.

Section IV

GUARANTEES AND SECURITIES

Chapter 17

Introduction to Securities and Banks[1]

Banking business is not only about borrowing money from customers—it is vital for banks to lend the money they borrow in order to make a profit. A maxim of bankers is: "borrow short and lend long"; the longer the term of the loan, the greater the interest rate. Business needs credit[2] so that it has capital to invest in equipment, staff, and premises, and it often relies on bank lending to supply it. Banks have developed sophisticated and flexible types of lending to fulfil corporate needs.[3] Individuals need finance as well as companies, however, particularly to buy homes, and during the past two decades banks have enthusiastically competed in the mortgage market which supplies that credit. 17–001

When a bank lends money, it needs to ensure that it will be repaid, and the chances are that it will require support for the loan in the form of *security*, from which it can recover its money if the borrower defaults. In this context, the normal feature of security is that it gives the holder of the security a claim over assets (either the debtor's or those of a third party) to support the payment of the debt—the debt itself is merely a personal claim between the parties to the transaction. Security gives a *proprietary* or *real* right,[4] a right as against the rest of the world, which secures the performance of the obligation because the creditor may seize the property on default by the debtor and sell it to satisfy the debt. On insolvency, the secured creditors are in a privileged position because their real right permits them to realise their security from the secured assets before the estate is wound up and the remaining assets distributed. Unsecured creditors have merely an ordinary claim for debt, and recover a proportionate share (that is, they are entitled *pari passu*) of whatever remains 17–002

---

1 See Finch (1999) 62 M.L.R. 633.

2 Goode, *Commercial Law* (2nd ed.) p. 706, defines credit as: "financial accommodation of some kind; the provision of a benefit (cash, land, goods, services or facilities) for which payment is to be made by the recipient in money at a later date".

3 For corporate debt financing, see *Farrar's Company Law* (4th ed.) p. 260: "The emphasis is on flexibility through individual contracting. Short term debt can be rolled over into medium term finance, bonds can be converted into equity and interest separated from principal. It is a world of syndicated loans, convertibles and swaps characterised by flexibility, diffusion of risk and rapid trading of commercial paper. Some of these developments are tax driven to take advantage of tax loopholes in national tax regimes and tax havens. Three common forms taken by the new corporate debt financing are negative pledges, debt defeasance and subordinated debt."

4 Compare guarantees, where one person agrees to answer for some existing or future liability of another provides a personal claim against the promisor (although a guarantee may well be backed up by real security). See below, Chap. 18.

of the debtor's property. They are likely to be left fighting for the crumbs of what is left—even those, like the Inland Revenue, which are *preferential* creditors on insolvency.[5] Secured creditors not only have a far greater chance of receiving full payment, but have greater rights of enforcement and the right to trace their debt into its proceeds if necessary.[6] The use of security also allows banks to acquire a measure of intervention and control over the affairs of a problem company, particularly by appointing a receiver.

17–003 Security may take a number of different forms. Some, like the mortgage, the charge, and the pledge, are *consensual*—they arise by agreement of the parties; others, like the lien, arise by the *operation of law*.[7] Some, again like mortgages, are *proprietary*, whereas others are *possessory*, in which case the creditor takes physical possession of the property until the debt is paid—pledge is the obvious example.[8] As pledgee, the creditor has an implied right to sell the property on default. There is no need for registration, and the creditor is completely protected against any fraud by the debtor. There is the obvious disadvantage though that the possession of the asset (machinery for example) may be of no use to a creditor like a bank, while the debtor may be unable to carry on his or her business without it. However, the use of the pledge has been extended by allowing the creditor to take merely *constructive* possession of the property. In this case the debtor may retain the property and can deal with it, but delivers the relevant documents of title (for example the bill of lading) to the bank. The bank can then release the documents back to the borrower under a *trust receipt.* The debtor holds the documents of title, and may deal with the property, while the trust receipt acknowledges that the customer holds the property as the bank's agent or trustee,[9] so that, if the property is sold, the bank obtains the proceeds of sale. This provides a good protection for the bank on the debtor's insolvency, but is unlikely to be effective against fraud by the debtor. Pledge also has the disadvantage that it cannot be used to take security over choses in action, such as the debt owed by an overdrawn customer to the bank, because they are intangible, and cannot be physically possessed. For security purposes, choses in action are *assigned* to the creditor by way of security. Negotiable instruments, however, (which give rights of title to property rather than simply being evidence of contractual rights in it) and some transportation documents, such as bills of lading, may be pledged.

---

[5] See further below, Chap. 24.

[6] See on this point and generally Prentice in Gower, *Principles of Modern Company Law* (6th ed.) 1997. See also Pennington, *Corporate Insolvency Law*, (2nd ed., 1997).

[7] This is important with respect to company charges, see below, Chap. 19.

[8] The earliest form of security: Goode, *op. cit.*, p. 643.

[9] Another form of pledge used by banks is *field warehousing,* where the goods are stored in an independent warehouse. See further on these uses of pledge, Ellinger and Lomnicka, *Modern Banking Law* (2nd ed.), pp. 683 *et seq.*

Similarly a lien,[10] like a pledge, allows the creditor possession of goods. It gives a right by contract or operation of law to a person who already has custody of property to detain the property until payment—for example, where goods have been given to the creditor for repair. In this case, however, there is normally no power of sale (the banker's lien is an exception). **17–004**

Proprietary, as opposed to possessory, securities allow the debtor to retain possession and use of the goods. The normal ways to achieve this are by means of mortgage or charge over property, which are frequently used by banks over any kind of property. The property may be *personal property*, such as shares, life insurance policies, or book debts; or *real property,* in the form of land. Equitable mortgages and charges can be created over after-acquired property and even an agreement to create a mortgage or charge takes effect in equity as a security and is immediately effective when the asset intended to be subject to it is acquired by the debtor.

Although the words mortgage and charge are often used interchangeably, there is an important difference between them.[11] A mortgage is a *conveyance* of property which gives a legal estate, and the mortgagee is therefore in the position of a purchaser, but with the essential difference that the mortgagor retains a right of redemption. The mortgagee has the right of possession (and also the right of foreclosure, although it is very rarely exercised nowadays), but normally takes advantage of the right only on default. A charge in the sense it is used here acts merely as an incumbrance on the property and, although it gives the chargee certain rights over the property, does not affect the ownership or allow a chargee to foreclose or take possession; the chargee must apply to the court for an order for sale or for the appointment of a receiver, and will be paid from the proceeds of sale.[12] A charge may be fixed or floating. A floating charge is normally created only by companies,[13] and relates to a changing fund of assets rather than to a specific asset. It has no effect until one or more specified events occur, at which time it becomes crystallised or fixed and attaches to the asset which form the security. In the meantime, the debtor is able to use the property, and even to dispose of it. **17–005**

Much legal creativity has been devoted to developing varieties of security and this has no doubt assisted commerce by encouraging the provision of credit. Equity has proved particularly inventive in supplying flexible instruments which could be adapted to apply to numerous types of assets, making it possible to create securities over choses in action such as book debts and **17–006**

[10] Liens may be of different types. Examples are: maritime liens; equitable liens in favour of unpaid vendors of land; liens securing the rights of trustees, agents and other fiduciaries like solicitors; and the banker's lien, see above, Chap. 11.

[11] Mortgages and charges over land are discussed in Chap. 21.

[12] *Swiss Bank Corpn. v. Lloyds Bank Ltd* [1980] 2 All E.R. 419 at 425, *per* Buckley L.J.

[13] See below, Chap. 19.

over assets which may be acquired in future.[14] Assets over which security may be taken include: shares in a partnership or company, life insurance policies, present and future book debts, contractual pension rights, copyright and patent rights to be taken in the future, interests under trusts and expectations under the wills of living persons.

17–007 Apart from these established forms of security, which provide good protection for the lender, there are other transactions which give rise to what amounts to a privileged position on insolvency but which are not necessarily regarded as security interests, such as the right of set-off—a right which is much used by banks.[15] And apart from those, a number of other types of "quasi-security" exist, which are not formally classified as security, but which vest, or attempt to vest, some type of proprietary control over assets of the debtor in the creditor. These are designed to put the creditor in a position superior to that of other unsecured creditors in the event of insolvency.[16] Among these are retention of title clauses,[17] *Quistclose* trusts,[18] and negative pledge clauses.[19] The increasing sophistication of instruments to achieve this end now provides a challenge both for the ingenuity of legal draftsmen and for the logical powers of the courts, and these "queue jumping" arrangements may be effective under certain conditions. They pose a particular threat to unsecured creditors, because they reduce the assets available on insolvency and they are usually "invisible" to outsiders. Other transactions giving similar benefits, such as hire-purchase and instalment credit, are regarded as sales rather than as creating rights of security. It is often hard to distinguish between a sale transaction and a security transaction and the court may have to make difficult decisions as to the legal nature of such transactions.[20]

17–008 It is vital, if the security is to have its intended effect, that it is correctly created by the debtor in favour of the creditor. It is also vital, in the case of many securities, that once created, they are *perfected,* usually by registration,[21] which binds third parties by giving them notice of the security and plays an important part in ranking the claims on the property.

---

[14] See Pennington [1985] 6 Co. Law 641 who gives an interesting survey of the development of security. Equity provided not only the equitable charge, but also the equitable mortgage, whereby an agreement to give a legal mortgage is regarded as giving the lender an immediate equitable interest in the assets over which it will acquire a legal interest when the mortgage is executed.

[15] Set-off may be contractual, equitable or imposed by statute; see further above, Chap. 11 and below, Chap. 23.

[16] See Millett (1985) 101 L.Q.R. 271; Bridge (1992) 12 Oxf. J.L.S. 358, and Belcher and Beglan [1997] J.B.L. 1. See also Oakley [1996] C.L.J. 377, for an interesting consideration of equitable claims and their priority on insolvency.

[17] See below, Chap. 20.

[18] See above, Chap. 9.

[19] See below, Chap. 19.

[20] See *Curtain Dreams plc v. Churchill Merchanting Ltd* [1990] B.C.C. 341; *Welsh Development Agency v. Export Finance Co. Ltd* [1992] B.C.C. 270.

[21] Or by possession of the property physical or constructive, or notice to the debtor.

It is obvious that unsecured creditors get a raw deal on insolvency.[22] Cranston rightly points out that it is not always realised that security law raises important issues of social policy: it is often said that banks, relying on the security they hold, are willing to lend in risky situations (such as on derivatives markets, or to small businesses which may have inadequate management and financial expertise).[23] The policy advantages underlying the legal encouragement for creditors taking security are said to be first, that it reduces the cost of credit, and secondly, that if a business becomes precarious, lenders, with the reassurance of security, may encourage attempts to rescue the enterprise—for example, they can afford to allow the debtor time to repay, and may help to re-organise the debtor's financial commitments and the business itself. If there is one lender or a group of lenders in control, rational policies for the survival of the business—such as selling it as a going concern—are more likely to be taken than if there are a number of creditors fighting over it.[24] It is doubtful how far these arguments have real weight. The reality is that the lender uses—and often realises—the security primarily or entirely for its own benefit. Similarly, it is also often suggested that unsecured creditors, unlike secured creditors, voluntarily accept the risk of the insolvency of the company, and therefore do not take the trouble to bargain for the extra security. This superficially attractive idea overlooks the fact that most unsecured trade creditors are not in a position to bargain, whereas institutions like banks hold all the negotiating cards in their hands, particularly when the debtor is in deep water financially. **17–009**

[22] See *Borden (U.K.) Ltd v. Scottish Timber* [1981] Ch. 25, CA, *per* Templeman L.J. See also Pennington (1985) *Company Lawyer* (Vol. 6 No. 1) 9 at 21: "The policy problems associated with charges over classes of a company's assets, whenever acquired, are of course part of the larger general problem whether creditors who are sufficiently astute or economically powerful should have power by contract to earmark particular slices of a company's assets for the satisfaction of their claims before those of other creditors".

[23] The same point is forcefully made by Bridge (1994) 110 L.Q.R. 340. See also Gower, *op. cit.*, p. 818. Grylls [1994] 10 J.I.B.L. 391 proposes the abolition of the floating charge, the "all-embracing safety net" for the bank to remedy the balance and consequently (it is argued) to encourage the viability of the company.

[24] Cranston, *Principles of Banking Law* (1997) p. 432.

It is obvious that unsecured creditors get a raw deal in insolvency. [illegible] Commercially [illegible] and time [illegible] a [illegible] important [illegible] of social pattern [illegible] often [illegible] which [illegible] they hold [illegible] In [illegible] companies [illegible] small business [illegible] which may [illegible] financial expertise. The policy advantages [illegible] proceedings [illegible] creditors [illegible] are [illegible] first [illegible] of credit and [illegible] a business [illegible] precautions [illegible] the [illegible] security may encourage them [illegible] the enterprise [illegible] for example, they can [illegible] the [illegible] and may [illegible] commitment and [illegible] If [illegible] a company [illegible] policy [illegible] the survival of the business [illegible] [illegible] these [illegible] [illegible] [illegible] that the [illegible] of the [illegible] company, and [illegible] [illegible] trade creditors are [illegible] accounting [illegible] [illegible] directly.

See [illegible] Cmnd. [illegible] [illegible] [illegible] with [illegible] of accounting [illegible] company [illegible] [illegible] the [illegible] of the [illegible] [illegible] [illegible] [illegible] the [illegible] of the company.

CHAPTER 18

GUARANTEES

A guarantee[1] is an accessory contract by which the promisor undertakes to be answerable to the promisee for the debt, default or miscarriage of another person, whose primary liability to the promisee must exist or be contemplated.[2] The responsibility of the guarantor is secondary to the principal obligation, and is, in principle at least, co-extensive with it.[3] While banks naturally prefer real securities, guarantees, which create a *personal* obligation between bank and guarantor, are also important. They are widely used in dealings with companies; they are taken from the directors or associates, who are then unable to hide behind the limited liability of the company, and banks often take them in dealings with groups of companies, from other companies in the group. Guarantees are also frequently taken from individuals to support lending to other individuals. Familiar examples are guarantees of young customers' overdrafts given by parents, and a spouse's guarantee of the business borrowing of the other spouse. Bankers normally prefer a person giving a real security to give a guarantee as well, particularly directors of small companies, because it entails a personal commitment to pay the debt. Sometimes a cash deposit is taken from the guarantor on terms that it must not be withdrawn, to ensure that the guarantor is not a "man of straw", and so that the bank has an immediate right of recourse against the deposit if the guarantee is determined. **18–001**

As contracts, guarantees are governed by the general rules of contract, but statutory controls are also important—section 4 of the Statute of Frauds 1677[4] requires guarantees to be evidenced in writing, and the CCA 1974 provides that if a guarantee is given at the request of a debtor in relation to an agreement regulated by that Act, it must be in writing, in the prescribed form and properly executed[5]; if it is not, it can be enforced **18–002**

---

[1] See further *Halsbury's Laws* (4th ed.), Vol. 20, *Rowlatt on Principal and Surety*, Andrews and Millett, *The Law of Guarantees* (1994) and Phillips and O'Donovan, *The Modern Contract of Guarantee* (2nd ed., 1992). For guarantees given by banks, see Vol. 2 (performance bonds). Guarantees are as old as the Pyramids and can be traced in the earliest laws: Philips and Donovan, at p. 8.

[2] *Halsbury*, para. 101. A "guarantor" may sometimes be distinguished from a "surety", on the basis that sureties are said to give a real security for another's debt, but in practice the terms are used interchangeably.

[3] See Johan Steyn (1974) 90 L.Q.R. 246.

[4] See below, para. 18–014.

[5] CCA 1974, ss. 189 and 105 *et seq*.; Consumer Credit (Guarantees and Indemnities) Regulations 1983 (S.I. 1983 No. 1556).

against the guarantor only by order of the court. The CCA 1974 also controls extortionate credit agreements, which may be re-opened at the instance of the surety.[6]

18–003 Other statutory controls which affect the content of bank guarantees, as they do other contracts, are the UCTA 1977,[7] (although in practice it has had little effect on guarantees) and the UTCCR 1999.[8] The UTCCR 1999 apply in relation to unfair terms in contracts concluded between a seller or supplier and a consumer,[9] and probably therefore apply to bank guarantees, which are standard form contracts. Banks seem to come within the definition of *supplier*—"a natural or legal person who, in contracts covered by these Regulations, is acting for purposes relating to his trade, business or profession . . .".[10]

18–004 Any contractual term, unless—an important exception—it defines the main subject matter of the contract or concerns the adequacy of the price or remuneration, as against the goods or services sold or supplied in exchange, so far as it is in plain and intelligible language,[11] must not be unfair. If a term is unfair, it is not binding on the consumer,[12] although the remainder of the contract may still be valid. A term which has not been individually negotiated is regarded as unfair if, contrary to the requirement of good faith, it causes a significant imbalance in the parties' rights and obligations under the contract, to the detriment of the consumer. . ."[13] If the term has been drafted in advance, it will always be regarded as not having been individually negotiated. The unfairness of a term is assessed taking into account the nature of the goods or services for which the contract was concluded and by referring, at the time of the conclusion of

---

[6] CCA 1974, ss. 137–139.

[7] UCTA 1977, s. 3. See further above, Chap. 3.

[8] S.I. 1999 No. 2083, replacing S.I. 1994 No. 3159 (which gave effect to E.C. Directive 93/13 [1993] O.J. L95/29). See above, Chap. 3.

[9] UTCCR 1999, reg. 4(1).

[10] UTCCR 1999, reg. 3(1). The wording under the superseded UTCCR 1994 was "a person who supplies goods or services and who, in making a contract to which the Regulations apply, is acting for purposes relating to his business" (UTCCR 1999, reg. 2(1)). The new wording may settle doubts (see *Chitty on Contracts* (27th ed.), Vol. 2, para. 42–078 and *Paget's Laws of Banking* (11th ed.), Chap. 35) as to whether a bank is supplying a service in taking a guarantee from a person who is a third party to the borrowing contract—the suggestion is that the *guarantor* is the supplier of the service, not the bank, in which case the Regulations would only apply if the bank were (as no bank could be) a *consumer*—"a natural person who is acting outside his business". And see *Bayerische Hypotheken- und Wechselbank v. Dietzinger* [1998] 2 C.M.L.R. 499, ECJ, where it was held that the Directive on Consumer Protection (Directive 85/577 [1985] O.J. L372/31) extended to guarantees and that the grant of a credit facility was the provision of a service.

[11] UTCCR 1999, reg. 6(2).

[12] The D.-G. of Fair Trading (and other "qualifying bodies" (UTCCR 1999, reg. 3, Sched. 3), which include regulators) may apply for an injunction against a term (UTCCR 1999, regs 10 and 12). The injunction may relate to similar terms used by others. These bodies have powers to obtain documents and information (UTCCR 1999, reg. 13).

[13] UTCCR 1999, reg. 5(1). The term will then not be binding on the consumer, but the remainder of the contract may still be valid if it can still exist without the term.

the contract, to all the circumstances attending the conclusion of the contract and to all the terms of the contract or of another contract on which it is dependent.[14] Further, written terms of such a contract must be expressed in "plain, intelligible language".

Schedule 3 of the UTCCR 1999 gives an "indicative and illustrative" list—sometimes called "the grey list"—of 17 terms which may be unfair. These include: enabling the seller to terminate a contract of indeterminate duration without reasonable notice, enabling the seller or supplier to alter the terms of the contract unilaterally without a valid reason which is specified in the contract, and enabling the seller to alter unilaterally without a valid reason any characteristics of the product or service to be provided.[15] **18–005**

The full implications of the UTCCR 1999 will certainly be far-reaching but will only become clear with time. Banks are taking the requirements of the UTCCR 1999, as far as plain language is concerned,[16] at least, into account in the terms of their standard guarantee forms,[17] and into the standards of the Banking Code. Suggestions as to the possible substantive effects of the UTCCR 1999 are made in this Chapter as appropriate, and summarised at the end, where standard bank guarantee clauses are set out.

For brevity, the bank's customer (the debtor) will be referred to as D, the guarantor or surety as G, and the bank as B.

Guarantees and Indemnities

A *guarantee* must be distinguished from an *indemnity*.[18] A guarantee is a *secondary* or *collateral* liability, where G agrees with B that if D does not meet a legally binding obligation owed by D, G will meet it. Thus, G's liability is dependent on D's obligation, and liability only arises on D's default. If D is not liable, therefore—perhaps because he or she is a minor—G is not liable. **18–006**

Liability under an indemnity is *primary*. G undertakes to meet a legally binding obligation to B. G's liability does not depend on D's obligation (D may or may not owe a legally binding obligation to B), nor on D's default. If, say, D were not liable on the debt because she was a minor, G would still be liable to B.[19]

14 UTCCR 1999, reg. 6(1). The four guidelines for assessing good faith given by Sched. 2 of the UTCCR 1994 have disappeared, presumably because they are otiose (since all the circumstances are to be taken into account).

15 Specific exceptions in the UTCCR 1994 for terms allowing financial services suppliers to alter a rate of interest unilaterally have not been included in the new UTCCR 1999.

16 UTCCR 1999, regs 4 and 6.

17 Barclays Bank won a "Crystal Mark" for plain English for its new guarantee forms.

18 See *Davys v. Buswell* [1913] 2 K.B. 47.

19 *Birkmyr v. Darnell* (1704) 1 Salk 27; *Moschi v. Lep Air Services Ltd* [1973] A.C. 331; *Yeoman Credit Ltd v. Latter* [1961] 2 All E.R. 294; *Heald v. O'Connor* [1971] 2 All E.R. 1105; *Argo Carribean Group Ltd v. Lewis* [1976] 2 Lloyd's Rep. 286; *General Produce Co v. United Bank Ltd* [1979] 2 Lloyd's Rep. 255.

18–007 It is a matter of construction in each case whether a contract is one of indemnity or of guarantee, and it is often difficult to distinguish the two. In practice banks use the terms as if they were synonymous,[20] but it is important to separate them for several reasons. A guarantor is liable only if D is liable, and only to the extent that D is liable; a guarantor is liable only if D defaults, but an indemnifier is liable for his or her own actions; guarantees have to be evidenced in writing,[21] but indemnities may be oral or may arise by implication—for example, between principal and agent, where the agent is entitled to an indemnity for expenses properly incurred in carrying out his or her tasks.

18–008 The distinction used to be more important because of the rules in relation to companies acting *ultra vires* and to minors, where, if the principal contract were void, voidable or unenforceable,[22] G would not be liable under the guarantee.[23] If G had assumed the *principal* liability, on the other hand, he or she would continue to be liable. These problems are much less likely to occur now, since statute has changed the law concerning these two situations concerning the capacity of the principal debtor. First, the *ultra vires* rules relating to the powers of companies, were changed by the CA 1985[24]; this extended the protection bestowed on third parties (like banks) dealing with companies. Secondly, the law with regard to minors has been changed[25]: a guarantee is no longer unenforceable against the guarantor for the reason alone that the principal is a minor. In fact, if it were not for the Statute of Frauds, there would not be much need to consider the often artificial distinction between guarantees and indemnities,[26] because the question is really what G has undertaken to do in any particular contract: this may be to agree to a guarantee or to an indemnity, or to a form of liability intermediate between the two, for example where G has agreed to become liable not only on D's default, but even if D is not liable.[27]

---

[20] For a discussion of the difference, see *Moschi v. Lep. Air Services Ltd* [1973] A.C. 331, *per* Lord Diplock.

[21] Statute of Frauds 1677, s. 4.

[22] Or illegal, or if it had been repudiated.

[23] A clause protecting the bank's position against lack of capacity of a company or minor might read: "notwithstanding that D, being a limited company, corporate or unincorporated body or committee, may have exceeded its borrowing powers or that the borrowing from the bank may be *ultra vires*, or that D, being a person lacking in contractual capacity, shall not be liable in law to repay B, or that for any other reason the bank shall have no legal remedy against D for all or any part of the liabilities heretofore mentioned".

[24] CA 1985, ss. 35, 35A and 35B, inserted by CA 1989, the effect of which is that a third party dealing with a company need not concern him or herself with the company's capacity to enter into a transaction.

[25] By the Minors' Contracts Act 1987, s. 20. This Act repealed s. 1 of the Infants' Relief Act 1874. The previous common law rules now apply.

[26] Unless D's debt is illegal, in which case it would contravene public policy to allow G to agree to indemnify B: *Swan v. Bank of Scotland* (1836) 10 Bli. (N.S.) 627, and see CCA 1974, s. 113(1–2).

[27] See *General Produce Co v. United Bank Ltd* [1979] 2 Lloyd's Rep. 255.

However, problems may arise because the intentions of the parties are not clear. The use of the one word rather than the other is not conclusive, because the parties may not have understood the need to distinguish between the two—indeed, very likely they have not even considered the matter. If D is not contractually bound to B, and G and B know this, the contract may be construed as an indemnity.[28] If the agreement is oral, there may be a tendency to treat it as an indemnity in order to save it.[29] If G receives a payment for the promise, the obligation may be construed as independent, that is, as an indemnity.[30] It has been said that arrangements are to be strictly construed, and that no liability should be imposed on G which is not clearly provided for.[31] **18–009**

In any case, bank guarantee forms usually make the position clear, by including what is known as a *principal debtor* clause.[32] The guarantee generally begins by stating that G guarantees D's liabilities, and then, typically, includes a clause stating that the bank may recover from G as a separate and independent stipulation all sums of money which may not be recoverable from D[33]; this is the "principal debtor" clause.[34] In this case the extent of G's obligations is clear. If G guarantees the payment by D, then G is liable if D defaults, in the sense of not paying at the proper time or on demand, and, though the clause does not state simply that G is to be liable as an indemnifier for the debt, G also bears primary liability.[35] Effectively, the clause is a hybrid. **18–010**

Even if there is a principal debtor clause in the agreement, however, it may not save the contract, if the purported guarantee is a wholly deficient document, as it was in *State Bank of India v. Kaur*,[36] where the document was not a sufficient note or memorandum for the purposes of the statute, and could not be a guarantee: it lacked a date, a signature by a witness, G's signature (although there was a cross and letters spelling out her name) and **18–011**

---

[28] *Lakeman v. Mountstephen* (1874) L.R. 7 H.L. 17.

[29] See *Guild & Co v. Conrad* [1894] 2 Q.B. 885.

[30] See *e.g. Goulston Discount Co Ltd v. Clark* [1967] 2 Q.B. 493.

[31] See *First National Finance Corpn. Ltd v. Goodman* [1983] B.C.L.C. 203.

[32] See, for the effect of a principal debtor clause on insolvency set-off, where security has been taken over bank deposits, *MS Fashions Ltd v. BCCI International S.A. (No. 2)* [1993] Ch. 425 and *cf. Re BCCI International S.A. (No. 8)* [1996] B.C.L.C. 20. See Chap. 23.

[33] "On the footing of a guarantee whether by reason of any legal limitation or incapacity on or of D or any other fact or circumstance and whether known to G or not".

[34] *e.g. Barclays Bank Ltd v. Trevanion* (1933) The Banker 98, where the clause said "As a separate and independent stipulation G agrees that all sums of money which may not be recoverable from the undersigned on the footing of a guarantee whether by reason of any legal limitation disability or incapacity on or of the principal or any other fact or circumstance and whether known to B or not shall nevertheless be recoverable from the undersigned as sole or principal debtor(s) thereof " ("principal debtor" clause). See also *Credit Suisse v. Allerdale B.C.* [1995] 1 Lloyd's Rep 315 at 366, *per* Colman J. There are also clauses in bank guarantees which allow the bank to discharge D while leaving G liable. Discussed below, para. 18–053.

[35] See *Halsbury*, *op. cit.*, para. 109.

[36] [1996] 5 Bank. L.R. 158, CA.

other information. However, it was not a valid indemnity either—apart from anything else, there was no indication of the person to be indemnified.[37]

18–012 The bank may prefer to have an indemnity, though G (if it is explained to him) may be unwilling to agree to this. It is possible that a court would regard a principal debtor term as unreasonable under the UCTA 1977.[38] A clause of this kind might in any case be within the ambit of the UTCCR 1999, (unless it were exempted because it defines the main subject matter of the contract[39]). If it is unfair, it will not be binding on G.

Requirements of Guarantees or Indemnities

General Contractual Requirements

18–013 As with any other contract, there must have been offer and acceptance and intention to create legal relations.[40]

Writing

18–014 Guarantees, but not indemnities, must be evidenced in writing.[41] Section 4 of the Statute of Frauds 1677 requires that there is either[42] a written agreement signed by the person to be charged or his agent, or a note or a memorandum of an oral agreement similarly signed. G's signature is usually witnessed, sometimes by two bank officials, but this is not strictly necessary.

A material alteration (an alteration which goes to the essence of the contract[43]) of a guarantee which has not been agreed by all the parties will avoid the guarantee.

---

[37] *cf. M.S. Fashions Ltd v. BCCI SA (No. 2)* [1993] Ch. 425, CA, where the primary indemnity overcame the deficiencies in a document called a guarantee.

[38] See *Standard Chartered Bank Ltd v. Walker* [1982] 3 All E.R. 938 at 943, *per* Lord Denning M.R..

[39] UTCCR 1999, reg. 6(2).

[40] See *Kleinwort Benson Ltd v. Malaysia Mining Corp. Bh.* [1989] 1 All E.R. 785; for letters of comfort, see below, para. 18–097.

[41] s. 4 of the Statute of Frauds 1677 merely makes the agreement unenforceable and an oral agreement can therefore be relied upon as a defence: *Re a Debtor (No. 517 of 1991) The Times*, November 25, 1991. There may be more than one document, but either all must be signed by the guarantor or his or her agent or one document must refer to the other (which is signed) and the terms must be clear from both together: *Elias v. George Sahely & Co. (Barbados) Ltd* [1983] 1 A.C. 646 (Statute of Frauds 1677, s. 2).

[42] The operation of these alternatives was considered in *Elpis Maritime Co. Ltd v. Marti Chartering Co. Inc. (The Maria D.)* [1992] 1 A.C. 21, HL. See also *Clipper Maritime Ltd v. Shirlstar Container Transport Ltd (The Anemone)* [1987] 1 Lloyd's Rep. 546. The signature may be in pencil: *Lucas v. James* (1849) 7 Hare 410.

[43] *Lombard Finance Ltd v. Brookplain Trading Ltd* [1991] 2 All E.R. 762. See also *Raiffeisen Zentralbank Österreich AG v. Crosseas Shipping Ltd* [1994] Lloyd's Rep. 164. Where an alteration is made in pencil to a document which is printed, typed or in ink, the most natural inference to draw is that it was not an operative and final alteration, and does not alter the substance of the document, *Co-operative Bank v. Tipper* [1996] 4 All E.R. 366, Ch D.

Construction

The same principles of construction which apply to other contracts apply to guarantees. The court attempts to establish what may fairly be inferred to be the intentions of the parties and to give effect to it. Where the words of a guarantee are ambiguous, the guarantee will be construed *contra proferentem*—that is, against the bank.[44] 18–015

Construction of express terms.[45] The guarantor is liable only for what has actually been agreed.[46] If G guarantees advances up to £1000, for example, and B advances £1500, G is liable for £1000.[47] Similarly, if G has agreed to guarantee a given mortgage debt and "any further advances", and the debt increases because the term is extended and the interest rate increased, G is not liable for the increase as "further advances".[48] Another example is the phrase "due or owing" in a guarantee referring to debts owed by D. This phrase exposes the bank to the risk that if D does not owe the sum guaranteed it cannot be recovered from G.[49] This result can be avoided if G guarantees to pay not what is *due and owing* from D but *all moneys unpaid* by D including interest. 18–016

Equally, G is liable for what he or she has agreed even if the result is harsh, unless there has been some contractual defect such as misrepresentation. In *First National Finance Corporation v. Goodman*,[50] G and his co-directors guaranteed an advance by a bank to their company, renewable after a year. The guarantee covered G's liability to B or its successors and assigns or any company with which it might amalgamate. After a year G ceased to be connected with the company, and the bank merged with another bank (the plaintiff). This would normally discharge G from the guarantee. The company subsequently borrowed more money, and, when it was wound up, the second bank sought to make G liable on his guarantee. The court held that, because of the terms of the guarantee, G was liable, 18–017

[44] Extrinsic evidence may sometimes be introduced to explain a guarantee, see *e.g. Perrylease Ltd v. Imecar A. G.* [1988] I W.L.R. 463; but perhaps only to supply the details of a complete document: *State Bank of India v. Kaur* [1996] 5 Bank. L.R. 158.

[45] See Andrews and Millett, *op. cit.*, p. 61.

[46] See *Hyundai Shipbuilding and Heavy Industries Co. Ltd v. Pournaras* [1978] 2 Lloyd's Rep. 502; *First National Finance Corpn. Ltd v. Goodman* [1983] B.C.L.C. 203.

[47] Note that if G agrees to guarantee payment of a bill of exchange for £1000, and the bill is drawn for a greater amount than that, he or she has no liability at all, because the instrument is a different thing in law from what was agreed.

[48] *Burnes v. Trade Credits Ltd* [1981] 2 All E. R. 122. See also *Lloyds and Scottish Trust Ltd v. Britten and Another* (1982) 44 P. & C. R. 249.

[49] See *Re Moss, ex p. Hallet,* where G's liability was "to pay interest so long . . . as any principal money remains due", it was held that on D's bankruptcy his liability for interest ceased and accordingly G's liability for interest also ceased [1905] 2 K.B. 307.

[50] [1983] B.C.L.C. 203.

even though the result was harsh. G should have given notice to determine the guarantee when he left the company.[51]

18–018 **Conclusive evidence clauses.** Banks attempt to avoid disputes as to the amount of liability by including a "conclusive evidence" clause in the guarantee. This will be to the effect that a copy of D's account signed by an officer of the bank is conclusive against D, and therefore apparently conclusive against G, of the amount due.[52] It is unlikely that the courts' acceptance of such terms in earlier cases, on the ground of the high standing of bankers in the commercial world—the standing of bankers "is so high that their work is to be trusted"[53]—would be repeated now.[54] The character of the banking relationship has undergone many changes, and it has become clear, as a matter of common experience, as well as from the statements of consumer organisations and from the reports of the Banking Ombudsman, that banks, like other businesses, make mistakes. In any case, "conclusive evidence" terms in this context must be open to question under the UTCCR 1999.[55]

Most bank guarantees contain a jurisdiction clause stating that the contract is to be governed by English law.[56]

Consideration

18–019 Because liability is contractual, consideration or a deed[57] is required. The consideration need not be stated in the document,[58] although it normally is. Past consideration—such as a past advance—is insufficient. Whatever the

[51] In such cases, although UCTA 1977 will not assist G (since B has not attempted to exclude liability or to render a performance substantially different from that expected), the provisions of the UTCCR 1999 may do so if the clause is regarded as unfair, under the general principle of unfairness in reg. 4(1).

[52] "In the event of any action or other proceeding brought against G upon this guarantee, a copy of D's account (or of the account for the preceding six months if the account shall have extended beyond that period) signed by the manager for the time being of the branch or office at which the account shall be kept, or by some other officer of the bank, shall be conclusive evidence against D of the amount for the time being due to B from D."

[53] *Bache & Co. (London) Ltd v. Banque Vernes et Commerciale de Paris* [1973] 2 Lloyd's Rep. 437; *R.D. Harbottle (Mercantile) Ltd v. National Westminster Bank Ltd* [1978] Q.B. 146.

[54] See *Tai Hing Cotton Mill v. Liu Chong Hing Bank Ltd* [1986] A.C. 80, *per* Lord Scarman. Prima facie, UCTA 1977 applies to such a clause, because there is a duty to give a correct account, and a conclusive evidence clause excludes or restricts liability for breach of the duty, s. 13 of the UCTA 1977. See also *Westpac Banking Corp. v. Sugden* (1988) N.S.W. Conv. R. 55–377: it was held that such a clause went far beyond what was needed for the protection of the bank.

[55] As "excluding or hindering the consumer's right to take legal action or exercise any other legal remedy, particularly by . . . unduly restricting the evidence available to him or imposing on him a burden of proof which, according to the applicable law, should lie with another party to the contract": UTCCR 1999, Sched. 3, para. 1(q).

[56] See further Andrews and Millett, *op. cit.*, p. 64.

[57] The requirement that a deed should be sealed was abolished by s. 1(1)(b), of the LPMPA 1989 (see also *Firstpost Homes Ltd v. Johnson* [1995] 4 All E.R. 355, CA).

[58] Mercantile Law Amendment Act 1856.

consideration is, it must not be a sham: thus, if it is for "further advances", it must be shown that the advances have been made.[59] A nominal consideration may be provided by the bank, but usually the bank takes advantage of the rule that as long as consideration moves from B it need not move to G, and consideration therefore takes the form of the bank either stating that it will continue to afford banking facilities to D, or demanding repayment from D and then promising to forbear from suing him or her for a time. The court may infer that a forbearance has been given, even if there is no express statement to that effect.[60]

Capacity

Persons who are actually incapacitated by drunkenness cannot give guarantees (because it is usually obvious to the other party), and nor can the mentally unsound—certainly not once the other party becomes aware of the incapacity; such contracts are voidable at the option of the person who lacked capacity. A guarantee given by a minor is not enforceable, although a guarantee given to support a principal contract made by a minor is not necessarily unenforceable.[61] **18–020**

In the absence of a special trade custom in particular cases, a partner has no implied authority to give a guarantee,[62] and the signature of all partners is required to bind the partnership. Partners who sign will be personally liable on the guarantee.[63]

A company guarantee is normally authorised by a resolution of the board (unless a particular director is given power to grant guarantees).[64] A company cannot back out of its guarantees on the ground that it lacked capacity to give the guarantee. It may argue that the directors giving the guarantee lacked authority to do so, but the bank will be protected if it has acted in good faith.[65]

---

[59] See *Provincial Bank of Ireland v. Donnell* [1934] N.1. 33 (where the bank had no intention of making further advances); *Burton v. Gray* (1873) 8 Ch. App. 932 (£1000 to be lent to C within seven days, but sums falling short of that lent to him); *Bank of Montreal v. Sperling Hotel Co. Ltd* (1973) 36 D.L.R. (3d.) 130; *Royal Bank of Canada v. Salvatori* [1928] 3 W.W.R. 501, PC; *National Bank of Nigeria v. Awolesi* [1964] 1 W. L. R. 1311 (if guarantee refers to existing account, opening a new one is not sufficient.) See also *U. D. T. Ltd v. Beech* [1972] 1 Lloyd's Rep. 546 at 551 (block discounting facilities are not "banking facilities" where the latter are promised.).

[60] *Glegg v. Bromley* [1912] 3 K.B. 474 at 491.

[61] Minors' Contracts Act 1987, s. 2.

[62] *Brettel v. Williams* (1849) Exch. 623.

[63] *Re Smith, Fleming & Co., ex p. Harding* (1879) 12 Ch. D. 557.

[64] The directors are either given a bank guarantee form referring to that resolution, to which in turn the resolution refers; or the board may be provided with a bank form of guarantee containing space for the resolution, which all the directors sign. In either case the Company Secretary certifies these as genuine resolutions of the company.

[65] *e.g.* by CA 1985, s. 35A(1); *Royal British Bank v. Turquand* (1855) 5 E. & B. 248.

18–021 In the case of group guarantees, difficulties may arise if new members are to join the group, and the guarantee is to be extended to them. In that case (a) either the original agreement must allow for the addition of new guarantors and all the original members must agree to the addition of the new member, or the new member must sign a separate guarantee; and (b) there must be consideration for the new member or the obligation must be created by deed; and (c) the new member (if it is a company, for example) must follow the procedures which are appropriate in its case. In *Ford & Carter Ltd v. Midland Bank Ltd*,[66] five companies in a group gave mutual guarantees to the bank. Later, another member of the group purported to enter the transaction, and also gave a security. The memorandum endorsed on the guarantee was signed by two officers of the company, one of whom was finance director of the parent company, but none of the initial signatories signed again. The guarantee and security failed for two reasons: first, there was no resolution of the board of the new member, and secondly, there was no agreement by the original five members that the parent company had the authority to introduce a new party to the guarantee in this way. The consent of the original signatories had to be obtained.

18–022 Local authorities may only enter into contracts, including guarantees, to the extent that they have been given the power to do so by statute. If they go beyond that, they will be acting *ultra vires*, and third parties like banks taking such guarantees from them will not be protected as they are if they take guarantees from companies. In *Credit Suisse v. Allerdale B.C.*, for example, a guarantee to support lending to a company set up by a local authority to promote leisure activities was outside the statutory powers of the authority and was void.[67]

Mistake and non est factum

18–023 If it can be shown that both parties have made a fundamental mistake relating to the subject matter of a contract (a common mistake), the contract will be void.[68] This is a severe consequence, and common mistake has been hard to show at common law,[69] although it has sometimes proved easier to obtain a more flexible remedy at equity.[70] The principles relating to common mistake were considered and applied in a guarantee case, *Associated Japanese Bank (International) Ltd v. Credit du Nord SA*.[71] Here, a

[66] (1979) 129 N.L.J. 543.

[67] (1995) 1 Lloyd's Rep. 315; see also *Credit Suisse v. Waltham Forest L.B.C.* [1996] 4 All E.R. 176. See above, Chap. 8.

[68] It may also be that a mutual or unilateral mistake will prevent there being agreement: *Halsbury, op. cit.*, para. 121.

[69] See *Bell v. Lever Bros* [1932] A.C. 161.

[70] *Solle v. Butcher* [1950] K.B. 671, CA. Equity makes a contract flawed by a fundamental mistake voidable. It may be rescinded on appropriate terms.

[71] [1989] 1 W.L.R. 255. See further above, Chap. 3.

bank agreed a sale and leaseback arrangement for four engineering machines with B, whereby B would raise a large sum of capital and repay the bank by way of rent. The bank required a guarantee for B's obligations under the contract, and this was provided by Credit du Nord. As it turned out, there were no such machines in existence; B had defrauded the banks. In an action by the Associated Japanese Bank, the defence of common mistake was considered by Steyn J., who came to the conclusion that, as a matter of construction, the guarantee included an express or implied condition precedent that the machines existed, which had not been fulfilled. He went on to say that a contract will be void if a common mistake by both parties makes the subject matter of the contract essentially and radically different from that which both parties believed to exist at the time the contract was executed, provided that the party seeking to rely on the mistake had reasonable grounds for entertaining the belief on which the mistake was based. Here, therefore, since the fact that the machines did not exist made the guarantee essentially different from the guarantee both banks had believed themselves to have agreed, the stringent test of common law mistake would have been satisfied and the guarantee would have been void. Though it will be rare that such a mistake will avoid a contract, banks should take care that they take adequate measures to assess a security or the subject matter of a transaction.

Similarly, the doctrine of *non est factum* may occasionally operate to make a guarantee void. Where a person who signs or executes a contract is, for permanent or temporary reasons—for example, illiteracy or blindness—not capable of reading and sufficiently understanding the document, so that the transaction is essentially different in substance or in kind from the transaction intended,[72] and the signer has not been careless, the transaction may be void. An example is the case of *Lloyds Bank v. Waterhouse*,[73] where an illiterate farmer signed a guarantee of a loan made to his son by the bank. The Court of Appeal upheld the farmer's defence of *non est factum*. **18–024**

Undue influence and misrepresentation

Other contractual defects may affect guarantees taken by banks. Developments in the law concerning undue influence and misrepresentation (in *Barclays Bank v. O'Brien*[74] and *C.I.B.C. v. Pitt*[75]) have attempted to clarify the law for banks taking guarantees from individuals and set out a procedure on which banks may normally rely when they do so. **18–025**

The problem arises where a debtor wrongfully persuades a third party to give a guarantee on his or her behalf by using undue influence or by misrepresenting material facts. This may happen where the debtor and the **18–026**

[72] *Gallie v. Lee* [1971] A.C. 1004, *per* Lord Wilberforce.
[73] [1993] 2 F.L.R. 97.
[74] [1993] 3 W.L.R. 786. These cases are discussed in Chaps 3 and 21.
[75] [1993] 3 W.L.R. 802.

third party are in a close relationship with each other and the guarantee is given as much for personal and emotional reasons as for financial considerations, as may happen with a married couple. The bank itself may be directly concerned in such behaviour,[76] and it also runs the risk that the courts may decide that it has been involved indirectly, by having been on actual or constructive notice of the wrong (or, possibly, that D has acted as agent for the bank). If so, the guarantee may be vitiated. *Barclays Bank v. O'Brien* sets out the principles on which the courts will act in reaching that decision. A bank will have constructive notice[77] of a possible wrong when there is a relationship of trust and confidence. In the case of spouses, for example, it will be on constructive notice if a wife offers to stand surety for her husband's debts because of two combined factors: (a) the transaction is on its face not to the financial advantage of the wife; and (b) there is a substantial risk in transactions of that kind that, in procuring the wife to act as surety, the husband has committed a legal or equitable wrong that entitles the wife to set aside the transaction.

18–027 If a bank is put on inquiry of undue influence or of misrepresentation in this way, it must take "reasonable steps" to bring home to the wife the risk she is running by standing as surety and to advise her to take independent advice. Lord Browne-Wilkinson said:

> "the bank should insist that the wife attend a private meeting (in the absence of the husband) with a representative of the bank at which she is told of the extent of her liability as surety, warned of the risk she is running and urged to take independent legal advice." [78]

18–028 In the normal situation, therefore, a bank which has constructive notice of undue influence or misrepresentation by a debtor over the surety should take care to follow the "reasonable steps" prescribed by *O'Brien* in taking a guarantee and it should then be able to rely upon the validity of the guarantee. This does not seem to impose a harsh burden on banks; indeed, most banks, like Barclays itself, had already introduced similar procedures (except for the interview with the surety) before the judgment in *O'Brien*. Moreover, in subsequent cases, the courts have tended to decide that, if a wife is not properly or independently advised, it is likely to be the responsibility of the solicitor advising her rather than that of the bank,[79] and in this case the bank's guarantee or charge would be valid, although the solicitor might be liable in damages. Only in extreme cases is there likely to be a problem for the bank.[80] The large number of cases testing the *O'Brien*

---

[76] See, *e.g. Lloyds Bank v. Bundy* [1974] 3 All E.R. 757.

[77] The House of Lords' understanding of constructive notice is "very radical" in this context: Chitty, *op. cit.*, Vol. 2, para. 42.019.

[78] [1993] 3 W.L.R. 786 at 798.

[79] *Bank of Scotland v. Etridge* [1998] 4 All E.R. 75, see further above, Chaps 3 and 21.

[80] As in *Credit Lyonnais v. Burch* [1997] 1 All E.R. 144.

formula is a sign, however, that many guarantors are unhappy with the law, and, arguably, are inadequately protected by the present regime.[80a]

The Banking Code requires banks to follow similar procedures to those set out in *O'Brien* (except that it does not require the bank to have a separate interview with G). It states[81] that banks will: **18–029**

> "encourage guarantors to take independent legal advice to make sure that they understand their commitment and the potential consequences of their decision. All the documents guarantors are asked to sign should contain this recommendation as a clear and prominent notice."

Banks also undertake to advise guarantors that by giving the guarantee they may become liable instead of or as well as the debtor, and that they will tell them the limit of their liability. These undertakings also affect the bank's duty of disclosure to the surety and are considered further below.

In the newest versions of the Code, there is an important addition. Paragraph 3.14 states uncompromisingly: "An unlimited guarantee will not be taken."[82] This undertaking, if respected, will help to prevent many of these cases. In fact, it may, by making the extent of the surety's obligation clear, be more effective in protecting guarantors than the *O'Brien* case and the Code; it can be argued that the "reasonable steps" are not very effective in protecting vulnerable sureties, who are often unwilling to take the independent advice even if they receive it, and in the case of wives, might be better protected by legislation safeguarding the matrimonial home.[83] **18–030**

Characteristics of Guarantee Contracts

Single and continuing guarantees

Guarantees may be limited to a single transaction, but most bank guarantees are intended to cover a series of transactions (for example on a fluctuating overdraft balance) spread over a period of time. These are *continuing guarantees*. A *single* guarantee would be discharged by the first advance up to the agreed limit and G would be liable only for that sum. This is risky for the bank, because the operation of *Clayton's Case* on an **18–031**

[80a] See the trenchant comments of Bryan, considering the Australian Courts' revival of the "special equity" or tenderness to wives doctrine of *Yerkey v. Jones* (1939) 63 C.L.R. 649 ([1999] L.M.C.L.Q. 327 (*Garcia v. National Australia Bank* (1998) 155 A.L.R. 614)).

[81] From individuals. Banking Code (1999) para. 3.14 (and the Mortgage Code, para. 4.2).

[82] See further below, para. 18–033.

[83] See Ellinger and Lomnicka, *Modern Banking Law,* p. 124. See also Fehlberg [1994] 57 M.L.R. 467 and [1996] 59 M.L.R. 675, who argues that the distinction made between wives acting as sureties (*O'Brien*) and those acting jointly with their husbands in agreeing to a charge (*Pitt*) is unlikely to protect vulnerable wives (though it will probably protect banks) because the form of the transaction is normally accidental.

active current account might have the effect of discharging the guarantee.[84] A continuing guarantee, on the other hand, covers all debts on the account and could not be discharged in that way. Continuing guarantees may give rise to difficulties, though, if G is given the right to determine the guarantee on notice.[85]

18–032 Whether a guarantee is single or continuing is a question of construction of the agreement to determine the intention of the parties.[86] In cases of ambiguity, the court will generally lean in favour of construing the guarantee as a specific rather than a continuing one, in deference to the *contra proferentem* canon of construction. Traditional forms of guarantee express the guarantee so that it covers the "ultimate balance" of the account, whatever that may be at any time. The words "continuing security" may be used in addition. A clause might say:

> "and this guarantee shall be a continuing security applicable to the ultimate balance that shall become due from D to B from time to time and at any time"

or might now state that G will continue to be bound regardless of any changes in the amount or nature of D's liabilities, G's death or mental illness or any other matter.[87]

Continuing security clauses may not satisfy the requirements of the UTCCR 1999.[88]

Limited and unlimited ("all monies") guarantees

18–033 In most guarantees, there is an extensive clause (the "whole debt" clause), whereby G promises to become collaterally liable for any liabilities of D. Such a clause might say (in the traditional form):

> "I hereby guarantee all advances, liabilities, bills and promissory notes whether made, incurred or discounted before or after the date hereof, to or for D, either alone or jointly with other persons together with interest, commission and other banking charges including legal charges and commission".[89]

---

[84] See above, Chap. 11.

[85] *BCCI v. Simjee* [1997] C.L.C. 135 at 137, *per* Hobhouse L.J., CA and see further below, para. 18–080.

[86] *cf. Westminster Bank Ltd v. Sassoon* (1926) L.D.A.B. 19.

[87] From Barclays' guarantee form, para. 3.

[88] One of the examples of terms which may be regarded as unfair is a term "irrevocably binding [the guarantor] to terms with which he or she had no real opportunity of becoming acquainted before the conclusion of the contract": UTCCR 1999, Sched. 3, para. 1(i); or perhaps under UTCCR 1999, Sched. 3, para.1 (b). See Chitty, *op. cit.*, Vol. 2, para. 42–079, and Stafford [1995] S.J. 478.

[89] See *Ellis v. Emmanuel* (1876) 1 Ex. D. 157.

Or in "plain language" form:

> "This guarantee is a guarantee of the full amount of all customer liabilities without limit."

A guarantee in these terms is unlimited, but it is common for guarantees phrased like this to be followed by another (traditional) term to the effect:

> "Provided that the amount for which G shall be liable shall not exceed £X and interest on such sum or on such less sum as may be due at the rate of Y from the date of D's default until payment."

Or, in newer terms:

> "However, the total amount you have to pay . . . will not be more than the specified amount plus interest . . ." [90]

Here, the guarantee is *limited*, notwithstanding the whole debt clause. (If the guarantee is to be *unlimited*, the proviso need only be deleted and initialled by the parties.)

Doubts about the fairness of unlimited guarantees have often been expressed.[91] The fact that D may increase the debt against the security of the guarantee may result in G eventually having to pay far more than he or she had contemplated, and even where the meaning of the "all monies" clause is explained clearly to G, it may not be understood. D's power to increase the debt without the knowledge of G may also encourage him or her to mislead G as to the effect of the guarantee.[92] As mentioned above, a new guideline has been introduced in the Banking Code stating not only that banks will advise guarantors of what the limit of their liability will be, but also, strikingly, that "an unlimited guarantee will not be taken".[93] **18–034**

If such a term is now included in guarantees given by individuals, it is possible that it may be considered unfair and be invalid under the UTCCR 1999, unless it is regarded as a term "which defines the main subject matter of the contract".[94] It seems unlikely, however, that courts would consider that clauses providing for unlimited liability define the main subject matter of the contract, if only because the new provision of the Code indicates that banks themselves consider that it can safely be omitted. **18–035**

Guarantor and Debtor

G's contract, the contract of guarantee, is with B. D's obligation (the principal obligation) is also owed to B. G and D are not necessarily in a contractual relationship at all. Unless the guarantee provides to the **18–036**

[90] Barclays' guarantee, para. 2.1.
[91] See *e.g.* Sir Peter Millett [1998] 114 L.Q.R. 214 at 220.
[92] As happened in *Barclays Bank v. O'Brien* [1992] 3 W.L.R. 593.
[93] Banking Code (1999), para. 3.14.
[94] UTCCR 1999, reg. 3(2)(a). This is Paget's view (*op. cit.*, p. 635). If it does define the main subject matter, it will not fall to be assessed, provided that it is in plain, intelligible language.

contrary, however, the guarantee, because it is accessory to the principal obligation, will be determined if the principal obligation is changed without the guarantor's consent or if the principal obligation itself is determined.

If G has been requested by D[95] to give the guarantee and pays the whole of what is due to B under the guarantee,[96] he or she is entitled to an indemnity from D[97] and is subrogated to the rights of B in relation to that debt,[98] and to any securities[99] held by B (even if the securities are acquired by B after the guarantee is taken) unless it has been agreed otherwise with B, or the securities also secure further advances by B. Generally, unless there is agreement to the contrary, G may only enforce the right to an indemnity against D once G's liability is *fixed* or has *accrued*[1]—for example by B calling on the guarantee or by G giving notice to determine his or her liability for the future.[2] Once the liability is fixed, G may wish to reduce the liability contingent on D's default by paying the amount due to the bank, and to require D to indemnify him or her.

18–037 Even where B has not demanded payment (and, exceptionally, even where G's liability has not yet accrued[3]), however, G has equitable remedies—of "exoneration"—to require D to pay off the debt.[4] This is demonstrated by *Thomas v. Nottingham Incorp. Football Club Ltd*[5] where G guaranteed a football club's overdraft with Lloyds Bank. G gave notice to B to determine the guarantee, and then called on D to pay off the overdraft and thus reduce G's liability. The bank had ruled off the account in the usual way (to avoid the effect of *Clayton's Case*) and opened a new one. The debt in the old account, therefore, simply remained as before. The guarantee stated, as most do, that G was liable only when D was in default and demand had been made by B and not complied with. Here, since no demand had been made, D's argument was that G's liability was merely contingent and the payment was officious and voluntary. G therefore had no right to call on D to repay. But the court held that it was unreasonable that a guarantor should always have the cloud of liability hanging over him, and he had a right in equity to have the overdraft paid off, even though no

---

95 This is essential: *Owen v. Tate* [1976] Q.B. 402; *The Zuhal K* [1987] F.TL.R. 76. The request may be actual or constructive. But see Andrews and Millett, *op. cit.*, pp. 304 *et seq.*, for commentary on *Owen v. Tate*.

96 *Ewart v. Latta* (1865) 4 Macq. 983; *Re Howe, ex p. Brett* (1871) 6 Ch. App. 838. Even if the guarantee continues and G pays the amount owing to date, *Davies v. Humphreys* (1840) 6 M. & W. 153.

97 *Ascherson v. Tredegar Dry Dock & Wharf Co. Ltd* [1909] 2 Ch. 401.

98 *Wilkinson v. London & County Banking Co*. (1884) 1 T.L.R. 63.

99 Mercantile Law Amendment Act 1856, s. 5. See *Forbes v. Jackson* (1882) 19 Ch. D. 615; *Duncan, Fox & Co v. North and South Wales Bank* (1880) 6 App. Cas. 1.

1 *Morison v. Barking Chemicals Co. Ltd* (1919) 122 L.T. 423.

2 In which case G remains liable for debts which D has already incurred if D defaults.

3 *Halsbury, op. cit.*, para. 241.

4 G may take *quia timet* proceedings to exonerate him or herself against D.

5 [1972] Ch. 596. See also *Watt v. Mortlock* [1964] Ch. 84; *Tate v. Crewdson* [1938] Ch. 869, and *Stimpson v. Smith* [1999] 2 All E.R. 833.

demand had been made.[6] If D cannot repay, he may become bankrupt, of course, in which case B will call upon G, so that the course of action adopted in *Thomas's Case* may not be advantageous to G. Nevertheless, this equitable right may be a useful weapon for G.

Terms in guarantees often restrict G's right to sue D until the "ultimate balance" is paid to the bank, but it seems that such terms are not intended to prevent the sort of action brought in *Thomas's Case*, since the result of the action was that the bank was repaid, to which, of course, it could have no objection. If, on its true construction, a term does prevent a person from demanding that his or her liability is discharged, however, the term may be contrary to the UTCCR 1999 because it is unfair, or it may be unreasonable under the UCTA 1977.[7] Such a term might perhaps be reasonable if a term loan, not repayable earlier, had been made to D. **18–038**

Guarantor and Bank

Liability under the Guarantee

Since the contract of guarantee is accessory to the main contract,[8] the most important principle governing liability is that *G's liability is co-extensive with D's*. It is therefore necessary to ascertain the extent of D's liability in order to determine the extent of G's. If there is some contractual defect in the main contract, which makes it void, voidable or unenforceable, the guarantee cannot normally be enforced. A number of equitable principles have developed to protect guarantors by discharging them from liability if their rights might be prejudiced by the creditor's conduct, although many of these are excluded by banks' guarantee forms.[9] **18–039**

When liability arises

G is liable on a guarantee only if D is liable on the debt and to the same extent. Modern guarantee forms usually require G to pay *on demand*, and otherwise G is liable on D's default. In traditional bank guarantees, for example, which make G liable if D does not make "due payment", D's liability on a term loan would arise if the term has expired or if D has repudiated his or her obligations. On an overdraft, liability arises if D has repudiated his or her obligations, or if demand has been made for **18–040**

[6] Goff J. at 606. See also *Stimpson v. Smith* [1999] 2 All E.R. 833. Peter Gibson J. commented (at 838) that the provision in a guarantee that there should be a demand is for the benefit of the guarantor, and, as such, can be waived by the guarantor.

[7] UCTA 1977, s. 3(2)(b), on the ground that the contract enables B to "render a contractual performance substantially different from that which was reasonably expected of him." But it is unclear if such a term relates to B's performance at all.

[8] *Moschi v. Lep Air Services Ltd* [1973] A.C. 331.

[9] See Paget, *op. cit.*, p. 621. The UTCCR 1999 may affect the validity of some of the excluding terms.

repayment and D has failed to repay. Once D is in default, B may proceed directly against G without making any further demand from D.[10] The bank must be careful that G's liability for any debit item is not discharged by the effect of *Clayton's Case*,[11] or (with a relatively dormant account) that it is not time-barred.[12]

18–041 It is more common for the agreement to state that G must pay "on demand". In this case (a) B has no cause of action against G until D has defaulted and B has made demand of G; and (b) the statutory limitation period for suing G[13] does not start to run against the bank until it makes demand.[14] The means by which demand may be made (for example, that it must be in writing and is deemed to have been made within a certain time of posting, whether received or not) are usually specified. It is not necessary for the bank to specify the exact amount in the demand.[15]

18–042 Where there is a "principal debtor" clause, G has *primary* liability, and this is not contingent on the making of a demand in writing, even if G has expressly stipulated that there should be one.[16]

Once a demand is made of G, this "call" fixes G's liability at that time, and no further debits may be made to D's account, unless notice is given to G at the time when the demand is made that there may be further outstanding items, such as cheques not yet cleared. G cannot be called upon to pay or be in default for not doing so unless B tells G of the amount of his or her liability.[17] If requirements are specified which restrict the rights of G to exercise legal remedies (an example might be a clause that a demand will be treated as being properly served on G at noon on the day after it was posted if it was sent by post to an authorised address, even if it is not delivered or is returned undelivered), the term may fall foul of the UTCCR 1999.[18]

---

[10] Newer guarantees, drawn up in "plain language", may state that G guarantees that all customer liabilities will be paid or satisfied. Customer liabilities are defined as "any money and liabilities which the customer now owes us or may owe us in the future in any way", including liabilities depending upon events which may or may not happen.

[11] See above, Chap. 11.

[12] Under the LA 1980: *Parr's Banking Company Ltd v. Yates* [1898] 2 Q.B. 460, holding that time begins to run when a debit item is made, and is not paid. This must presuppose a default in D in not repaying. Paget criticized this decision: 1 L.D.A.B. 278, and see Paget's Law of Banking (11th ed.) p. 521. See *Wright v. New Zealand Farmer's Co-Operative Assn. of Canterbury Ltd*. [1939] A.C. 439, and Andrews and Millett, *op. cit*., p. 168.

[13] For contracts of suretyship, as for other contracts, this is six years (UCTA 1977, s. 5), and for liability on deeds, 12 years (UCTA 1977, s. 8).

[14] See *Bradford Old Bank v. Sutcliffe* [1918] 2 K.B. 833.

[15] *Bank of Baroda v. Panessar* [1987] 1 Ch. 335.

[16] *M.S. Fashions Ltd v. BCCI SA (No. 2)* [1993] Ch. 425, CA.

[17] *Banbury Foods Pty. Ltd v. National Bank of Australasia Ltd* (1984) 58 A.J.L.R. 199 (HC of Australia).

[18] UTCCR 1999, reg. 5(1), Sched. 3, para. 1(b).

Interest and costs of enforcement

If G guarantees all D's liabilities interest payable by D is included, whether that is expressly provided or not. If G does not guarantee all D's liabilities, it is a matter of construction how far G is liable.[19] **18–043**

The question whether G is liable for costs is a matter of construction of the guarantee and of the main contract, but if B brings a fruitless action against D without giving notice to G (so that G has no opportunity to intervene) G remains liable on the guarantee but is not liable for the cost of the action.[20]

G's Rights under the Guarantee

G is not only liable under the guarantee, but has rights under it as well, which generally arise at the time the guarantee is given. The rights are of two kinds: those which protect G from prejudicial dealing by B; and rights of subrogation, allowing G to stand in the shoes of B.[21] **18–044**

Discharge of G by appropriation[22]

Generally, in the absence of express agreement, the bank retains the normal rights of appropriation as against D and G and need not appropriate between accounts or, within an account, to the secured part of the account, in a way which will be favourable to G. While D's accounts are in operation, therefore, B has no duty to apply monies received for D to a particular account which has been guaranteed.[23] Payments may even be placed in a new account, provided that there is no agreement with G not to open a new account.[24] In any case, if G guarantees the "ultimate balance" owed by D, all D's cash deposits are available if D defaults, and appropriation is not relevant, even though G may complain if D withdraws cash deposits earlier. It has been suggested that, on an ultimate balance guarantee, it is wrong to open a new account especially for such deposits if the effect would be to deprive G of the benefit of them.[25] **18–045**

D, of course, retains the right to appropriate payments between accounts as he or she chooses, unless there is an agreement otherwise with the bank. In that case the bank presumably need not consider G's interests and could

---

[19] See Andrews and Millett, *op. cit.*, p. 135.

[20] *Baker v. Garrett* (1825) 3 Bing. 56.

[21] See Andrews and Millett, *op. cit.*, pp. 278 *et seq.* G has a right, even before demand, to pay off the debt to B and sue D: see also *China and South Sea Banking v. Tan* [1990] A.C. 536 at 545, *per* Lord Templeman, PC.

[22] See above, Chap. 11.

[23] *Williams v. Rawlinson* (1825) 3 Bing. 71; *Re Sherry* (1884) 15 Ch. D. 692; *Deeley v. Lloyds Bank Ltd* [1912] A.C. 756.

[24] See the cases in the previous note. Contrast *National Bank of Nigeria Ltd v. Awolesi* [1964] 1 W.L.R. 1311.

[25] *Re Sherry* (1884) 25 Ch. D. 692 at 706, *per* Cotton L.J.

place the funds in a new account. After all, if B refuses, D could deposit the money elsewhere, and that would not assist G.

Variation or release (indulgence) to D or to a co-surety[26]

18–046 An indulgence given by B to D or to a co-surety, or any variation[27] of the contracts of D or the co-surety prejudicial to G will probably discharge G from both existing and future liabilities under the guarantee.[28]

One form of variation is for B to *release* D, which has the effect of extinguishing the debt and which normally discharges G.[29] The effectiveness of a provision preserving B's rights in the contract depends on what G has undertaken to do. If G has agreed to pay "D's debts", and the agreement between B and D is binding,[30] G is no longer liable because the debt has ceased to exist and the agreement preserving the bank's rights no longer preserves anything.[31] If G has only undertaken to pay such sums as D originally agreed to pay, however, a release of D would not release G. In principle, even an implied reservation of rights may preserve B's right in an appropriate case, where an examination of the factual matrix or objective setting justifies the court in implying such a reservation, but such cases will probably be rare.[32]

18–047 On the other hand, the bank may simply waive its rights by agreement not to sue D, rather than releasing him or her. In this case, B's rights against G may be preserved by agreement.[33] If the bank enters into what looks like a release of D's debt but there is a term in the release preserving rights against G (a "reservation of rights"), the words of release may be construed as a "mere covenant" not to sue D,[34] rather than as a release, and this would not discharge G.

Where there is a novation, by which a new debtor is substituted for D and D is released, G is discharged, because G has not undertaken liability for the new debtor's debts, and D's debts are discharged.[35]

18–048 The situation is different, of course, where B permits D to enter some transaction which does not affect G's liability under the guarantee. If G

[26] As to co-sureties, see below, para. 18–071.

[27] The rule in *Holme v. Brunskill* (1878) 3 Q.B.D. 495.

[28] *Ward v. National Bank of New Zealand* (1883) 8 App. Cas. 755 at 763; *Holme v. Brunskill* (1878) 3 Q.B.S. 495; *Webb v. Hewitt* (1875) 3 K. & J. 438; *Swire v. Redman* (1876) 1 Q.B.D. 536; *Pledge v. Buss* (1860) John. 663.

[29] *Perry v. National Provincial Bank of England* [1910] 1 Ch. 464. Unless it is procured by fraud, D is insolvent or dissolved as a company, or G becomes liable as principal.

[30] Accord and satisfaction, whereby D's debt is discharged in return for some consideration.

[31] See *Commercial Bank of Tasmania v. Jones* [1893] A.C. 313 at 316, PC.

[32] *Finley v. Connell Associates (a firm), The Times*, June 23, 1999, QBD; following *Watts v. Aldington*, unreported, December 15, 1999, CA, which concerned a creditor and a number of joint debtors.

[33] *ibid.* See also *Price v. Barker* (1855) 5 E. & B. 760.

[34] *Green v. Wyn* (1869) 4 Ch. App. 204 at 206; *Re Whitehouse* (1887) 37 Ch.D. 683 at 694; *Duck v. Mayeu* [1892] 2 Q.B. 511, 514.

[35] *Commercial Bank of Tasmania v. Jones* [1893] A.C. 313; *Bradford Old Bank Ltd v. Sutcliffe* [1918] 2 K.B. 833.

guarantees one account and B allows D to open another account, this probably does not discharge G. G remains liable on the first account, whether or not he or she is liable for debts on the other one. But if there is an express or implied agreement that D is to have only one account, and B then allows D to open another account, this would be a variation affecting G's liability and G would be discharged.[36] Other similar arrangements affecting G's liability may have the same effect[37]; for example, it may have been arranged that statements of the first account will be sent to G at regular intervals, so that he or she can observe the extent of D's liabilities and the risk involved. In that case, it could be argued that it had been impliedly agreed that B would not open a second account for D.[38]

Where it is contemplated that B will hold securities and B releases them in a way that prejudices G, G may be discharged,[39] not because of any prejudice, but because of the implied or express agreement that the securities will not be released.[40] **18–049**

A binding agreement to give time (any time, however short) to D will discharge G,[41] even if it does not prejudice him or her.[42] However, an agreement in the principal contract whereby D's liability is allowed to fluctuate—for example, for D's overdraft to fluctuate within an agreed limit—does not seem to affect the guarantee, and nor does any *non-contractual* indulgence, such as an indication by the bank that it will not sue D, or the bank merely *giving* time to D (which is not a variation of the contract).[43] In any case, bank contracts of guarantee permit B to give time to D without discharging G.

Right to D's defences and set-offs

Once payment has been demanded of G, G has all the legal and equitable rights of D as against B.[44] G is entitled to insist on a rigid adherence to the terms of the obligation by the creditor and cannot be made liable for more than he or she has undertaken.[45] **18–050**

---

36 *National Bank of Nigeria Ltd v. Awolesi* [1964] 1 W.L.R. 1311. The consideration was the continuation of "the existing account".

37 See, *e.g.*, *Guinness Mahon & Co. v. London Enterprise Investments Ltd.* [1993] Bank. L.R. 185; *Howard de Walden Estates Ltd v. Pasta Place Ltd* [1995] 22 E.G. 143.

38 Similarly, where securities deposited by D are no concern of G's, but the parties have contemplated that securities would be deposited before further advances are made, G may be discharged if they are not provided, see *Royal Bank of Canada v. Girgulis* (1980) 98 D.L.R. (3d) 335.

39 Perhaps only to the extent of the value of the security; *Rose v. Aftenberger* (1970) 9 D.L.R. (3d) 42; *Wulff v. Jay* (1872) L.R. 7 Q.B. 756.

40 See *Wulff v. Jay* (1872) L.R. 7 Q.B. 756 at 766; *Re Wolmershausen* (1890) 62 L.T. 541.

41 *Polak v. Everett* (1876) 1 Q.B.D. 669; *Rouse v. Bradford Banking Co.* [1894] A.C. 586 at 590, 594.

42 See *Ward v. National Bank of New Zealand* (1883) 8 App. Cas. 755 at 763.

43 *Overend Gurney & Co. v. Oriental Finance Corpn.* (1874) L.R. 7 H.L. 348.

44 *Bechervaise v. Lewis* (1872) L.R. 7 C.P. 372, where G was only liable when B had paid the promised consideration to D.

45 See, *e.g.* *First National Finance Corporation v. Goodman* [1983] B.C.L.C. 203.

If B breaches the principal contract with D, it affects the guarantee. If the breach is a repudiatory one, so that D is entitled to terminate the contract, G is discharged, except in so far as rights have already accrued under the contract. Even a non-repudiatory breach of the principal contract may discharge the guarantor, provided it amounts to a not insubstantial departure from a term of the principal contract embodied in the guarantee either expressly or by implication.[46] Otherwise, a non-repudiatory breach[47] allows G to use D's claim for damages as a set-off against a claim by B on the guarantee, but does not discharge G.

If there is a breach of contract by D, though, G remains liable.[48]

18–051 If D has a right of set-off arising out of the same transaction as the principal debt, the effect of which is to reduce or extinguish the debt, G can rely on it to reduce his or her personal liability on the guarantee.[49] If G is only liable for B's debt, this must be calculated by looking at the *overall* state of indebtedness of D to B, and so any sum which D has deposited with B before his or her default can generally be deducted from G's liability. Traditional bank guarantees state that G secures the "ultimate balance" of D's account, and the bank must therefore combine all D's accounts (even if they are held at different branches) to determine the extent of G's liability.[50] If there is an agreement between B and D that accounts will not be combined, the agreement should also bind G, although it could not survive D's insolvency, because the mandatory insolvency set-off provisions then apply.[51] Assuming that there is no "ultimate balance" clause, then, if G guarantees one account, he or she may still rely upon any deposit which the bank holds for D in another account.

---

[46] *National Westminster Bank v. Riley* [1986] B.C.L.C. 268 at 275–276, CA.

[47] *e.g.* wrongfully dishonouring a cheque or a direct debit. See also *Bratley v. Skipton B.S.*, December 10, 1999, CA, where a lender exercised its right of sale over mortgaged property, but did not obtain full value for the property. This was held to be a breach of its duty to the borrower (under Sched. 4 of the Building Societies Act 1986) but since it was only a breach of warranty, it did not discharge the guarantor. The Building Society had to give credit to the guarantor for the difference in prices.

[48] See, *e.g. Moschi v. Lep. Air Services Ltd* [1973] A.C. 331; *Hyundai Heavy Industries Ltd v. Papadopoulos* [1980] 2 All E.R. 29, HL. Where G guaranteed D's obligation to pay by instalments, and D breached the obligation, it was held that B's acceptance of the breach was not a variation of the main contract which would discharge G from his obligations, because G's liability is to ensure that D performs his or her obligations under the main contract. In other words, G's liability extends not only to D's "primary" obligation to repay B, but also to D's "secondary" liability to pay damages to B for breach of the primary obligation: *Moschi v. Lep. Air Services Ltd* [1973] A.C. 331.

[49] See *Ashley Guarantee v. Zacaria* [1993] 1 W.L.R. 62, CA, where it was held that a mortgagor guarantor's claim for equitable set-off for an unliquidated sum (or even a cross-claim for a liquidated sum) could not be used to defeat the mortgagee's claim for possession of the guarantor's property. See also *National Westminster Bank plc v. Skelton* (Note) [1993] 1 W.L.R. 72, CA and *Sun Alliance Pensions Life & Investments Services Ltd v. RJL and Anthony Webster* [1991] 2 Lloyd's Rep. 410.

[50] *Re Sherry, London and County Banking Co. v. Terry* (1884) 25 Ch.D. 692 at 706.

[51] See below, Chap. 23.

Right to securities[52]

If G pays B, he or she is *subrogated* to B's rights against D, and may claim securities[53] belonging to D which are held by B, even if the securities have been acquired by B after the guarantee is taken, provided they are held in respect of the guaranteed debt. This right may be, and usually is, excluded by agreement between G and B, or between B and D (an example of the latter would be where B takes the security as a continuing security for all advances without closing D's account). Again, it is possible that a term restricting or denying G's right to claim securities held by B may be vulnerable to challenge under the UTCCR 1999.[54] **18–052**

Indulgence clauses in guarantees

Much of this is academic so far as banks are concerned, since bank guarantees are phrased in terms which allow B to make the widest variations in D's liabilities under the principal contract. A traditional example allows B **18–053**

> "full discretionary power, without any further consent from G, and without in any way affecting G's liability under this guarantee, to renew any advance, and to hold over, renew or give up in whole or in part and from time to time any (bills, securities, etc.) or to make any other arrangement with D in respect of (bills, securities, etc.) held by B, and to grant time or indulgence or consideration to D or to compound with D or release D from any liability, or to vary the term or the interest rate of any liability of D to B."

In a "plain language" guarantee, this might be expressed[55]:

> "From time to time the bank may:
> provide D with any credit or facilities; vary, cancel or refuse any credit or facilities; give D time to pay any money owing to B; make any

[52] "Security" here has been given a wide meaning by the courts (Andrews and Millett, *op. cit.*, p. 310): *e.g.* a sum of money standing to D's credit appropriated to a particular purpose under a contract is a security in this sense: see *Re Sherry* (1884) 25 Ch. D. 692.

[53] Mercantile Law Amendment Act 1856, s.5. See *Forbes v. Jackson* (1882) 19 Ch. D. 615; *Duncan, Fox & Co v. North and South Wales Bank* (1880) 6 App. Cas. 1. G also has a right of *marshalling* the securities in the hands of B once a demand has been made of it, to ensure that B does not act so as to deprive G of the due portion of D's estate: see Andrews and Millett, *op. cit.*, p. 291.

[54] As inappropriately excluding or limiting the legal rights of the consumer *vis-à-vis* the seller or supplier or another party in the event of non-performance or inadequate performance by the seller or supplier of any of the contractual obligations which the consumer may have against him, UTCCR 1994, reg. 4(1), Sched. 3, para. 1(b). It may also be within the ambit of the UCTA 1977, s. 3, in which case the bank would have to demonstrate that it was reasonable.

[55] Barclays' guarantee form, para. 5.3.

other arrangement, compromise or settlement with D or any other person; take or deal with any security, guarantee or other legal commitment for D's liabilities; or release, enforce or not enforce B's rights under any such security, guarantee or commitment.

18–054 Although indulgence clauses may be effective at common law,[56] statutory controls may apply. First, the effect of the UCTA 1977 cannot be taken for granted. If it does apply, the term must be shown to be reasonable,[57] although it is difficult to imagine that a court would hold that a provision enabling the bank to be lenient to D is unreasonable; to do so seems to imply that banks would always be bound to pursue remedies against debtors, however hopeless the debtor's position. Nevertheless, it may be that indulgence clauses could be challenged under the UTCCR 1999 on the general ground that they cause "a significant imbalance" in the rights and obligations of B and G arising under the contract to the detriment of G,[58] since unfairness (here to G) is the crucial factor for these Regulations.

18–055 If there is an effective indulgence clause, it must cover what happens. In *Burnes v. Trade Credits Ltd*,[59] a guarantee covered the original mortgage and "any further advances". B extended the term of D's mortgage and increased the interest rate. On the face of it, this would have discharged G, but the contract allowed B to give "any indulgence or consideration" to D. It was held here, however, that G was discharged, because a further advance usually meant furnishing money for a specific purpose, not merely repaying the original sum, and the extension of the term was also not a further advance. The indulgence clause did not require G "to shoulder an added liability", and the bank's action was a variation of G's liability rather than an indulgence to D.

Duties of the Bank

With regard to securities

18–056 If B has failed to deal with a security as it should, equity may intervene[60]; the bank's rights in dealing with a security are not unfettered. However, the bank is not obliged to take steps to realise its security, even though G may be entitled to the securities if G pays B and may be prejudiced if the

[56] See *Perry v. National Provincial Bank of England* [1910] 1 Ch. 464; *Union Bank of Manchester Ltd v. Beech* (1865) 3 H. & C. 672, though see *Boultbee v. Stubbs* (1811) 18 Ves. 20.
[57] Under UCTA 1977, s. 3.
[58] UTCCR 1999, reg. 5(1).
[59] [1981] 2 All E.R. 122.
[60] Chitty, *op. cit.*, Vol. 2, para. 42–063.

security loses its value.[61] The guarantee usually specifies that B is under no obligation to realise any securities held.[62]

If the bank does take steps to realise the security, however, it must take reasonable care to obtain a proper price.[63] In *Standard Chartered Bank v. Walker,*[64] it was held that a bank-appointed receiver of D's property is under a duty of reasonable care towards G to secure a good price, and the bank may be liable for the receiver's failure to do so.[65] If a security is taken from D which is contemplated by the parties when G enters the agreement, and B fails to register it, G is prejudiced and is released to the extent of any loss suffered.[66] The *Walker* case dealt with the disposal of D's assets, which directly and necessarily concerns G, and affects his or her liability in a way which the parties must have contemplated. But it seems that B cannot be subject to a duty to register a security which was not contemplated when G entered the guarantee, and which is no concern of G's. A provision in the contract protecting B should therefore be effective[67] and unaffected by the UCTA 1977,[68] and, for the same reason, unaffected by the provisions of the UTCCR 1999. **18–057**

Wider duty of care to guarantor?

There have been attempts to broaden the duty owed by the bank to the guarantor to include a duty of care and skill; for example, in *Standard Chartered Bank v. Walker*,[69] Lord Denning suggested that the bank owed a wider duty of care in negligence. But the authorities generally have taken the opposite approach and such attempts are unlikely to be successful. It was held in *Bank of India v. Trans Continental Commodity Merchants*,[70] where G guaranteed performance of twelve foreign exchange contracts by D, that it was no defence to G to argue that the bank was negligent in not ensuring that D actually signed the contracts. Bingham J. said: **18–058**

[61] *South Sea Banking Ltd v. Tan Soon Gin* [1990] A.C. 536, PC. It was suggested there (at 545) that G could avoid the consequences of a creditor's failure to deal with securities which were declining in value by paying off the debt and obtaining a transfer of the securities to him (see Andrews and Millett, *op. cit*., p. 85).

[62] It seems unlikely that refraining from selling could be affected by the UCTA 1977; s. 3(2)(b) should not apply, since the bank is not "rendering" a contractual performance to G substantially different from that which he reasonably expects. Similarly, in the light of the courts' unwillingness to impose a wider duty of care on creditors (below, para. 18–058) it may be unlikely that such a term would be regarded as unfair under the UTCCR 1999.

[63] *Cuckmere Brick Co. Ltd v. Mutual Finance* [1971] Ch. 949.

[64] [1982] 1 W.L.R. 1410.

[65] See *Palk v. Mortgage Services plc* [1993] 2 All E.R. 481 and *Downsview Ltd v. First City Corpn. Ltd* [1993] A.C.295, PC, discussed below, Chap. 21.

[66] *Wulff v. Jay* (1872) L.R. 7 Q.B. 756. Andrews and Millett, *op. cit*., suggest that recovery is *pro tanto* because the breach is regarded as a simple breach of the guarantee, not as a repudiatory breach (p. 239).

[67] See *Bauer v. Bank of Montreal* (1980) 110 D.L.R. (3d.) 424, where such a clause was held not to be an exemption clause, or unreasonable.

[68] B seems not to be "rendering a contractual performance" within UCTA 1997, s. 3(2)(b).

[69] [1982] 1 W.L.R. 1410.

[70] [1982] 1 Lloyd's Rep. 506, approved [1983] 2 Lloyd's Rep. 298 at 302.

"The true principle is that while a surety can be discharged if the creditor acts in bad faith towards him, or is guilty of concealment amounting to misrepresentation, or causes or connives at the default of the debtor in respect of which the guarantee was given, or varies the term of the contract in such a way as to prejudice the surety, other conduct on the part of the creditor, even if irregular, and even if prejudicial to the interests of the surety in a general sense, does not discharge the surety."

18–059 In *National Bank of Greece v. Pinios Shipping Co*,[71] the defendant guarantors claimed that B was under a duty of care to see that the managing agent of a vessel had not under-insured the vessel. The claim (in both contract and tort) was unsuccessful. The agent was subject to the direction of B, but B had not directed or interfered with him. If it had done so, a duty might have been imposed by the court.

18–060 The Privy Council considered the question of the creditor's duties in negligence in *China & South Sea Bank Ltd v. Tan*,[72] and held that the defence of a surety does not rest on contract or tort but on equitable principles. Lord Templeman said: "the tort of negligence has not yet subsumed all torts and does not supplant the principles of equity or contradict contractual promises".[73] Equity may intervene where the security is surrendered, lost, not properly perfected or altered in its condition by reason of what has been done by the creditor, but otherwise the creditor is entitled to decide freely whether to sue D or G, to realise the security or do none of these. The bank here owed no duty in tort to G to exercise reasonable care in the realisation of security and was not liable for allowing it to decrease in value. Although in appropriate cases the court may intervene to protect a guarantor on equitable principles, therefore, the occasions when it will do so are specific and limited in nature.

Duties of explanation and disclosure

18–061 **Explanation to G by B.** The terms of standard guarantees are technical, and banks may try to explain them to potential guarantors, particularly those who are not business people. Generally, however, banks are not under a duty to give any explanation as to the meaning or effect of a guarantee,[74]

---

[71] [1989] 1 W.L.R. 185. See also *Barclays Bank plc v. Quincecare Ltd* [1992] 4 All E.R. 363, where it was held that B owed no duty to G to act reasonably to ensure that a loan is applied for the purposes for which it was given. In *American Express International Banking Corpn. v. Hurley* [1985] 3 All E.R. at 571, Mann J. said that an exclusion of liability for negligence had to be expressly conferred; in this case, the claim against B succeeded, because B was vicariously liable for its agent.

[72] [1990] A.C. 536, PC. See also *Downsview Ltd v. First City Corpn. Ltd* [1993] A.C. 295, PC.

[73] [1990] A.C. 536 AT 543, PC.

[74] *Barclays Bank v. Khaira* [1992] 1 W.L.R. 623 (reversed, but not with respect to this point: [1993] F.L.R. 345).

although this general statement must now be qualified: if there may be undue influence or misrepresentation affecting an individual guarantor, banks are required to follow the procedures, including explanation to the guarantor, settled by *Barclays Bank v. O'Brien*[75] and the Banking Code. In any case, if a bank *does* undertake an explanation, it is under a duty not to misstate the effect of the documents.[76]

In *Cornish v. Midland Bank*,[77] a customer who gave a charge to the bank later contested the charge, asserting among other things that the bank had breached a duty to explain the agreement to her. Only Kerr L.J. considered this issue, and he expressed the view that banks might well owe a duty to customers to explain the terms and legal effect of guarantees, and that evidence of banking practice would support the view that bankers themselves recognise that "their proper professional standards would not be consistent with mere silence on their part in such situations".[78] This suggestion has not been followed by a subsequent case on the point.[79] **18–062**

The UTCCR 1999 require that contracts to which they apply (which probably include bank guarantees) should be drafted in "plain intelligible language". This should have an important effect in making the terms of bank guarantees more accessible.

Duty of disclosure to G by B. Guarantees, unlike insurance contracts, are not contracts *uberrimae fidei* (of the utmost good faith), and the bank and the guarantor are at arms' length. The legal position has therefore been that there is only a limited duty of disclosure owed by the bank to the surety, (again, modified by *Barclays Bank v. O'Brien*[80]).Unless otherwise agreed, G is entitled to a statement of his or her own liability at any time, and if the guarantee is a regulated agreement under the CCA 1974 the bank must provide a certain amount of information to G if G makes a written request—a copy of the executed agreement, a copy of the security, and details of the accounts between B and D—otherwise it may not enforce the security. However, a bank should not reveal excessive detail concerning D's account, because of the duty of confidentiality it owes to D, though there is in such a case implied consent to *necessary* disclosure. If G has guaranteed a certain sum, and D's debt is less than that sum, G may be told the exact sum. If D's debt exceeds that sum, G may be told simply that the guarantee is being fully relied upon. **18–063**

The bank does not have to let G know everything that is material for him or her to know as surety; this would be commercially impracticable.[81] Banks may in an appropriate case (for example if D's circumstances have **18–064**

[75] [1993] 3 W.L.R. 786, see paras 18–025 and 18–068.
[76] *Cornish v. Midland Bank* [1985] 3 All E.R. 513.
[77] [1985] 3 All E.R. 513.
[78] *O'Hara v. Allied Irish Banks Ltd* [1985] B.C.L.C. 52.
[79] *Barclays Bank v. Khaira* [1992] 1 W.L.R. 623, CA.
[80] See below, paras 18–025 and 18–068.
[81] *Hamilton v. Watson* (1845) 12 Cl. & Fin. 109, 8 E.R. 1339.

changed) take some action from a sense of moral obligation, such as making demand on D, or arranging a tripartite meeting at which, with D's consent, the matter may be discussed with G. However, the bank is under no duty to inform the surety of the state of the debtor's finances: the surety is expected to understand that the reason a guarantee is needed is precisely because financial problems exist.

18–065 In *Hamilton v. Watson*,[82] the House of Lords held that a bank had no duty to inform a substitute surety that the bank had, on the death of a surety, previously asked the debtor for payment or fresh security and had obtained neither. The surety should have asked if he wished to know. Lord Campbell,[83] however, expressed this view:

> "I should think that this might be considered as the criterion whether the disclosure ought to be made voluntarily, namely, whether there is anything that might not naturally be expected to take place between the parties who are concerned in the transaction, that is, whether there be a contract between the debtor and the creditor, to the effect that his position shall be different from that which the surety might naturally expect. . ."

18–066 From time to time, arguments have been put to the court that the situation between B and D is so unusual and unexpected that B should disclose information to D. But it has been said that even if the bank knows of suspicious transactions by D which indicate that he or she may be using the account for purposes not contemplated by G, there is no duty to tell G.[84] In *Royal Bank of Scotland v. Greenshields*[85] the court stated that the bank need not disclose unless (i) it is asked a specific question, or (ii) the bank misleads G by volunteering half the truth, or (iii) in the bank's presence G makes a statement or gives some indication which demonstrates that he or she entirely misunderstands D's position.[86]

18–067 The duty of disclosure owed by banks to guarantors was recently examined by the English courts in the first instance decision of *Levett v. Barclays Bank plc.*[87] An elderly couple were persuaded to allow some Treasury stock to be used as security for a loan to two "rogues",[88] on the

---

[82] (1845) 12 Cl.& Fin. 109.

[83] (1845) 12 C1. & Fin. 109 at 118.

[84] *National Provincial Bank of England v. Glanusk* [1913] 3 K.B. 335. D was G's agent, using the account for improper purposes. In fact, the bank had no suspicions about this. See also *Cooper v. National Provincial Bank Ltd* [1945] 2 All E.R. 641 (D's husband was an undischarged bankrupt with power to draw on the account, and D had stopped about a dozen cheques; no duty to tell G). See also *Westminster Bank Ltd v. Cond* (1940) 46 Com. Cas. 60; *cf.. Commercial Bank of Australia v. Amadio* (1983) 57 A.L.J.R. 358 at 361.

[85] (1914) S.C. 259 but *cf. Lloyds Bank Ltd v. Harrison* (1925) 4 L.D.A.B. 12.

[86] See also *Smith v. Bank of Scotland* (1997) S.C. 111, HL.

[87] [1995] 2 All E.R. 615, QBD.

[88] One, particularly convincing, was a solicitor, who was later struck off the Roll.

express condition that it was not to be sold, but to be returned before the date of its maturity. The bank arranged for the Levetts to be given independent legal advice, and explained to the solicitor the nature of the bank's forms. It did not mention that the facility letter from the bank to the borrowers had made it clear that the loan was actually to be repaid out of the sale of the stock (the repayment date for the loan was the date on which the Levetts' stock would mature). Consequently the advice given by the solicitor to the Levetts was, to say the least, inadequate.

The judge[89] considered whether the bank should have disclosed this information to the Levetts or their solicitor. He cited Lord Campbell's dictum in *Hamilton v. Watson*,[90] emphasing that it is well established that a bank's duty to disclose must not be too onerous, and concluded that banks are under a duty to disclose to a surety contractual arrangements between the principal debtor and creditor which make the terms of the contract "something materially different in a potentially disadvantageous respect from those which the surety might naturally expect".[91] Here there had been a "contractual arrangement" in the facility letter from the bank to the borrowers, that the method of repayment would be by the use of the realised proceeds from the Levett's stock. This meant that the bank would certainly go first against the securities. The terms of the guarantee were therefore "automatically unusual" and different in a potentially disadvantageous respect from what the guarantors were entitled to expect, and had caused loss to the Levetts, who would have had nothing more to do with the guarantee if they had known the undisclosed facts. It is prudent for banks to consider, therefore, whether any unusual or unexpected arrangement in the principal transaction by way of a formal contract or not, which might affect G ought to be disclosed to G. **18–068**

Other recent developments

The fact that banks could not disclose information about D's account without breaching their duty of confidence to D has been an incentive to banks to keep prudent silence towards the surety. Banks have now, however, made a change in their policy in respect of confidentiality. The Banking Code states that banks may ask debtors to consent to the disclosure of their confidential financial information to the guarantor or his or her legal adviser,[92] and this statement may help to open up the traditional duties of disclosure to challenge in the courts or by the Ombudsman. If D's consent is not obtained, and the bank finds itself unable to disclose a relevant fact about the account to a guarantor who suffers loss because of entering the transaction, a court may consider that **18–069**

[89] Michael Burton Q.C. sitting as a Deputy Judge of the High Court.
[90] (1845) 12 Cl. & Fin. 109 at 118–9; 8 E.R. 1339 at 1343–1344.
[91] [1995] 2 All E.R. 615 at 630, QBD.
[92] Banking Code (1999), para. 3.14.

the bank has been remiss. It is possible, therefore, that banks will find that their duty of disclosure to guarantors becomes more extensive, because they will have to consider routinely whether information about D's account should be disclosed to a potential guarantor and whether they should seek D's consent to disclosure. This may come to be regarded as normal practice, and as a result, eventually, as imposing a duty on banks. Although the Code gives no indication as to the nature of the information which might be disclosed, the obvious fact that the bank should be in a position to disclose is that D's financial situation is worse than G was aware, if that is the case.

18–070 The change of emphasis in the Code is interesting in light of the decision of the House of Lords in a Scottish appeal, *Smith v. Bank of Scotland*,[93] where it held that though the effect of the *O'Brien* case should be the same for sureties in Scotland as in England, this result should be founded in Scotland upon the requirement of good faith rather than achieved by way of the doctrine of constructive notice.[94] Although generally the guarantor (in Scotland, the cautioner) is expected to look after his or her own interests and make such inquiries as are necessary or appropriate, that rule is subject to exceptions based on the requirement of good faith. If the creditor, the House said, misleads the guarantor either by a positive representation or by silence, it will be acting in bad faith and may be unable to enforce the contract.

18–071 The reasoning of the court is interesting for English as well as Scots lawyers. The principles and general rules of guarantees were said to be the same in both jurisdictions, and Lord Clyde thought that, on a broad policy basis, the same considerations are applicable in both.[95] The House was influenced by the practical advantages of having similar rules on this area of law in both jurisdictions. Courts in England may also be influenced by the approach that the bank's non-disclosure or silence about D's account might be a breach of a duty, particularly, it is submitted, in view of the innovative "good faith" requirement of the UTCCR 1999 and the provisions of the Banking Code mentioned above.

Guarantees by More than One Person (Co-Sureties)

18–072 The rights of a surety must not be put in danger. If they are, the surety is entitled to be discharged. If one guarantor has to pay an unfair proportion of the debt, for whatever reason,[96] the other guarantors must indemnify him

[93] (1997) S.C. 111, HL.

[94] The duty arises if the circumstances are such that if a reasonable man would believe that because of the personal relationship between D and G, G's consent may not be fully informed or freely given. If the duty arises, B must take certain steps (as in *O'Brien*) to ensure that it remains in good faith so far as the proposed transaction is concerned.

[95] (1997) S.C. 111 at 119, HL.

[96] See, *e.g. Ellesmere Brewery Co. v. Cooper* [1896] 1 Q.B. 75; *Scholefield Goodman & Sons Ltd v. Zyngier* [1985] 3 All E.R. 105, PC and s. 1(1) of the Civil Liability (Contribution) Act 1978.

or her.[97] This right of a co-surety is known as the equitable right of "contribution". Any change in a guarantor's liability may discharge the other co-sureties because their right to contribution may be affected.

One effect of this principle is that the consent of existing parties is required if a new guarantor is to be added, and if this is not forthcoming the new guarantor is not bound by the agreement. Further, a guarantor may be discharged if a condition of the contract, express or implied, to the effect that there should be other sureties, is not fulfilled. If, for example, G1 agrees to sign provided that G2 and G3 do so,[98] and G2 or G3 do not sign, Gl is discharged from the guarantee.[99] Thus, in *National Provincial Bank of England Ltd v. Brackenbury*,[1] four persons were to be joint and several guarantors. After three had signed, the bank advanced the money, but the fourth guarantor died before signing. Although this was a "hard case for the bank, and a curious result of the equitable doctrine", the guarantee was unenforceable. The same rule applies if the signature of one of the guarantors is forged.[2] This aspect of the doctrine in fact may not be equitable at all, but a simple application of the contractual principle that where A's liability under a contract is subject to a condition precedent, the prescribed event must occur in order to make him or her liable.[3] **18–073**

If one of the guarantors alters the terms as regards him or herself in a material way when signing, the others are discharged because the condition precedent to their liability is not fulfilled.[4] And, similarly, if the guarantors sign the guarantee and one or more of the terms affecting any of the guarantors is subsequently materially changed, or if a guarantor is discharged from liability by the bank, all of them are discharged, unless the guarantee provides otherwise, or all agree at the time.[5] **18–074**

The original agreement should therefore provide for the addition of new members, or that the consent of all should be obtained, or that a separate guarantee should be taken from any new party. Where there are to be joint or joint and several guarantors, no money should be advanced until all have **18–075**

---

[97] If the bank sues one guarantor only (whether liability is joint and several or joint) that one would probably join the others in the action, since they must indemnify him or her to the extent of their share.

[98] On either joint or joint and several guarantees.

[99] *Evans v. Bremridge* (1855) 15 L.J. Ch. 102 aff'd. (1856) 266 L.J. Ch. 334; *Hansard v. Letherbridge* (1892) 8 T.L.R. 346. This must be more than a mere stipulation in the contract for the provision of additional security; there must be some evidence to show that the parties regarded it as an essential term: *Byblos Bank SAL v. AL Khudairy* (1987) B.C.L.C. 232.

[1] [1906] 22 T.L.R. 797.

[2] *James Graham & Co (Timber) Ltd v. Southgate Sands and Others* [1985] 2 All E.R. 344.

[3] See *James Graham & Co (Timber) Ltd v. Southgate Sands and Others* [1985] 2 All E.R. 344, *per* O'Connor L.J.

[4] *Ellesmere Brewery Co. v. Cooper* [1896] 1 Q.B. 75.

[5] See *Ward v. National Bank of New Zealand* (1883) 8 App. Cas. 755; *Smith v. Wood* [1929] 1 Ch. 14. That the contract may provide to the contrary is shown by *Perry v. National Provincial Bank of England Ltd* [1910] 4 Ch. 464.

signed in the same terms. Similarly, no alteration of the terms of discharge or accommodation should be made for any guarantor unless all agree, whether originally or at the time.

18–076 Multi-party guarantees may be several (that is, quite separate and independent), joint (that is, there is a single obligation, each guarantor being liable for the whole amount guaranteed) or joint and several. The advantage of joint and several liability for the bank is that, on the death of a joint guarantor, liability passes to the other joint guarantors by survivorship, and not to the deceased's estate. Joint and several liability is to be preferred, although there is nothing wrong with several guarantees, except that a single document may be more convenient.[6]

Determination of the Guarantee

18–077 The guarantee may be discharged by payment by G of the debt guaranteed; by performance by D, which discharges D; by agreement, express or implied, between B and G; or by expiry of the period of the guarantee.

The determination of the guarantee means that G is excused from future liabilities incurred by D, *not* from liabilities which have already accrued, although many guarantors seem to misunderstand the position. In *Westminster Bank Ltd v. Sassoon*[7] the guarantee stated: "This guarantee will expire on June 30, 1925". When demand was made of G three months after that date, she claimed that her liability had ceased on that day, not merely for the future, but entirely. The court, however, construed the words in the usual way to mean that the expiry of the guarantee did not discharge G from liabilities of D already accrued.

18–078 One way in which G's liability may be gradually discharged, however, is by the operation of the rule in *Clayton's Case*[8] on D's current account, because the debts for which G is liable will have become "fixed" at the time the guarantee was determined and diminish as money is paid into the account. This may be prevented if the guarantee contains an appropriate term,[9] or, alternatively, the bank may close D's current account, and open a new one for him or her. In practice, it seems that banks do both. In *Re Sherry*,[10] it was held that the bank had a right to close D's account on the

[6] A several surety may also have a right of contribution, although this may only be to the extent that the release of one surety prejudices the other surety: *Ward v. National Bank of New Zealand* (1883) 8 App. Cas. 755; *Whiting v. Burke* (1871) 6 Ch. App. 342, see *Chitty on Contract* (27th ed.), para. 42.061. A document embodying an apparently several guarantee given by G3 seems, if it is on the same terms as others, not to be "several" at all, but only a separate piece of paper embodying a joint and several (or a joint) liability with Gl and G2.

[7] (1927) 5 L.D.A.B. 19.

[8] See above, Chap. 11.

[9] *e.g.* "G's liability for the amount due from D at the time when the guarantee is determined shall remain notwithstanding any subsequent payment into or out of the account by or on behalf of D." See *Westminster Bank Ltd v. Cond* (1940) 46 Comm. Cas. 60, where such a clause was held to be effective.

[10] (1884) 25 Ch. 692. See also *Deeley v. Lloyds Bank Ltd* [1912] A.C. 756.

determination of the guarantee, and that, even on D's death, the closing of the account was effective to protect against the discharge of D's debt. Bank forms usually state this right expressly. As already noted, however, the bank must combine existing accounts on D's default if the guarantee secures the ultimate balance, and must combine accounts on D's insolvency.

Determination by revocation by the guarantor

Even if a guarantee is for a specified time, G may revoke it by giving reasonable notice,[11] unless it is expressly or impliedly irrevocable.[12] A guarantee may be impliedly irrevocable if it is given for a single lump sum consideration,[13] because the consideration for the guarantee is said to be indivisible. In that case, D may be allowed to continue to draw on the account up to the maximum sum agreed, notwithstanding G's protests, if alternative security cannot be arranged. A guarantee to secure a fluctuating overdraft would not be impliedly irrevocable. Express terms making guarantees irrevocable may now fall foul of the UTCCR 1999.[14] **18–079**

Bank guarantee forms generally allow G to withdraw by giving a fixed period of notice. Three months is a common period, and it is always stated that notice must be in writing. At the end of the period of notice, the extent of G's liability will be established and G will be informed of it. It is still a contingent liability depending on D's default unless the guarantee states otherwise. The period of notice enables the bank to consider whether further securities should be arranged, or whether it should make demand of D, thus fixing G's liability immediately, rather than waiting until the notice expires. **18–080**

Difficult questions may arise if the bank is required under the guarantee to make a demand but has not done so by the end of the notice period. It was held in *National Westminster Bank plc v. Hardman*,[15] where no demand had been made on D by that time, that G was not liable even in respect of sums due before notice had been given. This decision was distinguished by the Court of Appeal in *BCCI v. Simjee*,[16] where the wording of the document was different from that in *Hardman*. The guarantee stated that G's liability could be determined and crystallised by notice (except as regarded unascertained or contingent liabilities), and the court held that, although G's liability crystallised at the end of the notice period, his undertaking to pay continued until the demand was made. Much therefore **18–081**

[11] *Offord v. Davies and Another* (1862) 12 C.B. (N.S.) 748.
[12] *Morrison v. Barking Chemicals Ltd* (1919) 122 L.T. 423.
[13] *Lloyd's v. Harper* (1880) 16 Ch. D. 290 (irrevocable on both sides—D was admitted as an underwriter to Lloyds for his life—so that the bank could not dishonour the agreement and refuse to provide D with the sum agreed).
[14] See UTCCR 1999, Sched. 3, para. 1(i).
[15] [1988] Fin. L.R. 302. The editor of Paget regards this decision as questionable: *Law of Banking* (11th ed.), p. 636.
[16] [1997] C.L.C. 135, CA.

depends on how clearly the bank expresses the continuing nature of the obligation to pay.

18–082 In any case, it may be that G will agree not to withdraw if the consequences of a demand upon D are explained to him or her, because it is (probably) permissible for D to continue to increase the debt in the period of notice. If D abuses this right, and particularly if G's fears that D will do so are made known to the bank, it might be ethical for the bank, perhaps with G's consent, to fix G's liability by making demand of D.[17]

Occasionally the bank may allow G to determine the guarantee without notice, subject to payment by D of any outstanding cheques drawn by D and dated on or before the date of determination. In such a case G is allowed, or may be requested, to discharge his or her existing liability by making a payment to the bank, which will be held in a suspense account in case of D's default.

18–083 **Determination by G's death, lack of mental capacity or by change in constitution of a partnership.** It has been held that, if G dies, notice of the death given to B (not the death itself) ends the guarantee, and G's estate therefore remains liable for any new debts until notice is given to B by the personal representatives.[18] It seems probable that constructive notice is not sufficient for this purpose, and that the bank must have actual notice of G's death.[19] However, bank guarantees may provide otherwise. They often say that the liability of G's estate continues until the personal representatives actually give notice of their intention to determine the guarantee, and a normal period of notice is required. If G's liability was irrevocable the personal representatives are still bound. Thus, a guarantee of a single lump sum advance, which is impliedly irrevocable, would be unaffected by G's death.[20] It seems that death has no effect if the bank is not told, if the guarantee is irrevocable, or if there is any term to the contrary.

18–084 When banks learn of the death of a guarantor, they frequently inform the personal representatives of the guarantee and of their right to determine it. It is unnecessary for the bank to demand payment from D in order to fix the liability of G's estate unless there are special circumstances. If D is the personal representative (whether there are others or not), for example, it would be necessary, because in that case D faces a conflict of interest of which B is aware.[21] Similarly, if G's estate is left on trust to another person, the bank cannot claim against the estate in respect of future advances if it knows this.[22] In these cases the normal procedures are followed: payment is

[17] It has been said that B must behave "equitably" towards G (*Holland v. Teed* (1848) 7 Hare 50), but this is doubtful.

[18] *Bradbury v. Morgan* (1862) 1 H. & C. 249; *Harriss v. Fawcett* (1873) 8 Ch. 866.

[19] *contra, Coulthart v. Clementson* (1879) 5 Q.B.D. 42, but see *Re Silvester, Midland Railway Co. v. Silvester* [1895] 1 Ch. 573, and *Re Crace, Balfour v. Crace* [1902] 1 Ch. 733 at 739.

[20] *Lloyd's v. Harper* (1880) 16 Ch. D. 290.

[21] D may be tempted to increase the debt, knowing that the loss falls on G's estate.

[22] *Harriss v. Fawcett* (1873) 8 Ch.App. 866.

demanded from D, other securities are taken if possible, the account is closed and a new one opened where appropriate.

If G loses contractual capacity, the guarantee will be determined for the future.[23] It is thought that, as with death, notice to the bank would be required, and many bank forms provide for this.[24]

Where G is a co-surety, the departure of G (by death or resignation, for example) will discharge the other sureties for the future, unless otherwise agreed. If G is a partnership, the dissolution of the partnership will end the guarantee for the future, but the personal liability of the partners in the original partnership for existing debts remains. The original partners may agree either that the partnership will not be dissolved, or that their liability for the future continues in any case, but a new partner will not be bound by the guarantee, and a new guarantee from that partner will therefore be necessary. **18–085**

Where there are multiple guarantors under a joint guarantee, the operation of the doctrine of survivorship discharges the liability of G's estate on G's death, and the liability passes to the surviving co-sureties. If liability on the guarantee is joint and several, on the other hand, the normal rules apply, for the estate is severally liable. **18–085A**

Determination by revocation by one joint guarantor (co-surety)

Where there is a joint, or joint and several guarantee, the withdrawal of one joint guarantor ("co-surety") may[25] terminate the further liability of all the guarantors,[26] unless otherwise agreed. It does not terminate liability for existing debts. In *Beckett v. Addyman*[27] it was held that the death of a joint and several co-surety did not release the others from future liability. It may be different however, where G does not die but withdraws. **18–086**

It seems that any co-surety may give reasonable notice to withdraw, unless the contrary is agreed expressly, or, as noted above, impliedly.[28] As this may have the effect of terminating the further liability of all of the guarantors, the bank should ask the others for fresh security when it receives the notice, or should make demand of D to fix the liability of all parties.

---

[23] *Bradford Old Bank Ltd v. Sutcliffe* [1918] 2 K.B. 833.

[24] *ibid*.

[25] It is not clear if this is so, nor if there is a difference between joint, or joint and several, liability; see *Egbert v. National Crown Bank* [1918] A.C. 903 (see below, n 26).

[26] It has been held that a provision for withdrawal on the giving of notice by "the undersigned," meant that all the co-sureties had to give notice in order to entitle any to resign: *Egbert v. National Crown Bank* [1918] A.C. 903. An appropriate phrase to use instead is "all or any of the undersigned".

[27] (1882) 9 Q.B.D. 783.

[28] See *Kalil v. Standard Bank of South Africa* [1967] 4 S.A. 550, AD.

18–087 The contract may provide for one co-surety to give notice to withdraw without the withdrawal affecting the liability of co-sureties.[29] In that case, the liability of the one who withdraws is fixed on the expiry of the period of notice, and if the liability was joint, he or she is liable for the whole of the debt at the time. This is another term which may run the risk of being regarded as unfair under the UTCCR 1999 because it might be said to create a "significant imbalance in the parties' rights and obligations. . . to the detriment of the consumer."[30]

If there is such a term and it is effective, it is possible for all of the parties to agree to apportion the debt, though none is obliged to do so. If apportionment is agreed, either consideration is required to release the departing guarantor from a part of the liability or the release must be done by deed. One way to provide consideration is to take new guarantees from the remaining guarantors in return for continuing the account, and to take a new several guarantee from the departing guarantor on the same consideration, but limiting the amount for which he or she is liable. In such a case, D's account will be ruled off and a new one opened,[31] unless the withdrawing guarantor pays off thc amount of his or hcr liability (which may often be a condition of apportionment).

18–088 The release of a co-surety may be a variation discharging the other parties, but the contract may provide for the bank to agree to release one co-surety (that is, to allow one to withdraw), without discharging the others.[32] If the bank exercises this power, there may be no point in ruling off D's account and opening a new one, but the departing guarantor may be required to pay off a share of the indebtedness as a condition of the bank's agreement.

Determination by the bank

18–089 If the bank demands repayment from D and D defaults, this fixes G's liability, and will terminate the guarantee as a continuing obligation, unless otherwise specified. The account is ruled off.

Normally, if the bank releases D, this also releases G, not only from future obligations, but from all obligations.[33] An appropriate clause in the agreement, however, gives the bank the right to release or modify D's obligations without discharging G.[34] The same rules apply to the release by

---

[29] Bank guarantees invariably do this.

[30] UTCCR 1999, reg. 5(1). See Chitty, *op. cit.*, Vol. 2, para. 42–079.

[31] Because of the effect of *Clayton's Case* (1816) 1 Mer. 572.

[32] That is, the bank "shall have full discretionary power, without any further consent from [any co-surety], and without in any way affecting the liability under this guarantee [of any co-surety] to release any security and to discharge or grant time or indulgence to or compound with any person liable jointly with or as surety."

[33] *Samuel v. Howarth* (1817) 3 Mer. 272; *Perry v. National Provincial Bank of England Ltd* [1910] 1 Ch. 464.

[34] *ibid.*

the bank of a co-surety, provided of course, in either case, that such a term is effective despite the UTCCR 1999.

Determination by change in the constitution of D or B, or by death

If the constitution of either D or B changes, the liability of G may be discharged. Thus a company may be liquidated,[35] or a partnership may be dissolved because a partner is lost or added, and in this case G's guarantee would end for the future, since the guarantee only covers the debts of the original partnership, unless otherwise agreed.[36] If the constitution of B changes, for example by amalgamation with another bank, the guarantee is discharged, because G's promise was given to another person.[37] In all these cases, contrary provision is usually made in bank guarantee forms. For example, the term "the bank" may be defined so as to include "the bank's successors and assigns" and it may be stated that the guarantee is enforceable "notwithstanding any change in the name of the bank, and shall enure for the benefit of any banking company with which the bank may become amalgamated and to which the bank shall assign it." **18–090 –094**

If D dies the guarantee is determined for the future, for G does not promise to guarantee debts incurred by D's personal representatives, unless otherwise agreed.

Insolvency of Guarantor

If G becomes bankrupt or goes into liquidation, G's liability, even if it is contingent, is a provable debt,[38] but G will not be liable for D's future debts, unless they are debts incurred by D pursuant to an obligation entered by him or her before commencement. Although it is not necessary to make demand of D in order to prove for G's debt, it is advisable to do so, so that G's liability is not contingent and in order to ascertain more clearly the amount for which G is liable.[39] **18–095**

Insolvency of Debtor

D's bankruptcy or liquidation does not affect G's liability to B.[40] If G pays B in full, G may prove in D's insolvency. The bank will close D's account when it discovers D's insolvency, since D can then incur no new **18–096**

[35] Or a company may be dissolved under CA 1985, s. 653.

[36] PA 1890, s. 18.

[37] See *First National Finance Corpn. v. Goodman* [1983] B.C.L.C. 203. The mere change of name by a corporation does not affect the guarantee: CA 1985, s. 28(7).

[38] IA 1986, s. 382(3); IR 1986, r. 13.12(3) (companies).

[39] See further below, Chap. 24.

[40] Other effects of insolvency upon guarantees are noted below. The effect of a voluntary arrangement was considered in *Johnson v. Davies* [1998] 2 All E.R. 649, CA. It was held that a voluntary arrangement may have the effect of releasing G from liability, but this depends upon whether, as a matter of construction, having regard to the surrounding circumstances and taking into account also any terms which could properly be implied, it constituted an absolute release. It did not in that case. See also *Raja v. Rubin* [1999] 3 All E.R. 73, CA.

debts to the bank, and G's liability will be fixed. The normal practice is for the bank to prove first against D, and if there are insufficient assets, then claim against G. The problem of double-proof may arise on insolvency, and this is discussed below.[41]

Bank Guarantee Forms

18–097 Many references have been made already to the terms in a bank's guarantee form. Forms vary greatly, of course, between one bank and another, and according to the circumstances, whether G is an individual, a minor, or adult; whether he or she is to accept joint and several liability with another person; whether liability is to be limited or not, and so on. The general structure may however be summarised as follows. (The suggested effect on particular clauses in guarantees with individuals of the UTCCR 1999 is indicated.)

(a) The consideration clause[42];

(b) The "whole debt" or "all monies" clause, whereby G guarantees all types of D's liabilities, and the ultimate balance of his or her accounts, and any expenses of the bank in connection with D's debts or recovery under the guarantee. This clause is less likely to be encountered without any limitation in individuals' guarantees now because of the new standard in the Banking Code.[43] It may be that the "all monies" clause would be regarded as unfair within the UTCCR 1999[44];

(c) The proviso to the "whole debt" clause whereby G's liability, notwithstanding (b), is limited to a stated figure;

(d) The continuing security clause, which has the effect that G is not discharged when D's overdraft first reaches the figure limited, and that the operation of *Clayton's Case* is excluded.[45] Again, this clause may not satisfy the requirements of the UTCCR 1999;

(e) The demand clause, whereby G must pay on written demand. The clause may provide for "machinery" for the demand (for example, it may be deemed to be made 48 hours after posting). If the clause "excludes or restricts the consumer's right to take legal action or exercise any other remedy by . . . unduly restricting the evidence available to him or imposing on him a burden of proof which, according to the applicable law, should lie with another party to the contract",[46] it may be invalid under the UTCCR 1999;

[41] See below, para. 24–165.
[42] See above, para. 18–019.
[43] Banking Code (1999), para. 3.14. See above, para. 18–033 *et seq.*
[44] UTCCR 1999, reg. 5(1). See above, para. 18–035.
[45] See above, Chap. 11.
[46] UTCCR 1999, Sched. 3, para. 1(q).

(f) The determination clause, whereby G is allowed to give notice to determine liability for the future, and which indicates how events such as his or her death may be dealt with;

(g) The variation and release clause, whereby the bank is allowed to vary the contract or release D, co-sureties or securities, (or not to do so) without discharging G; to agree to compositions, arrangements and so on made by D, and to prove against D on insolvency and receive dividends. This term also seems to run the risk of being held unfair[47];

(h) The clauses preventing G from competing with the bank, either in taking security from or suing D or proving against him or her on insolvency. Such clauses may infringe the Regulations by excluding G's rights to exercise legal remedies[48];

(i) The constitutional change clauses, providing that the guarantee is effective notwithstanding any change in the bank's constitution or the dissolution of D if D is a partnership, on D's bankruptcy, liquidation or death;

(j) The continuation clause, whereby B is entitled to continue D's account after determining the guarantee or to open a new one; this also prevents *Clayton's Case* operating to reduce the debt;

(k) The conversion-to-indemnity clause, so that G will be liable even if D is not liable as principal debtor. This clause may also be within the ambit of the UTCCR 1999 if it is regarded as unfairly increasing G's possible liability;

(l) The additional security clause, stating that this guarantee is additional to other guarantees given by G to B, if there are any, and that the bank has a lien on any securities of G which come into its hands. This term may not satisfy the Regulations if it is construed as increasing G's liability under the bank's lien at common law;

(m) The part-payment clause, whereby payments received from G may be put in a suspense account, and not applied so as to discharge D's liability. Again, if the effect of this is onerous as regards G, the term may fall foul of the general test of fairness;

(n) The conclusive evidence clause, to avoid disputes as to the extent of D's liability. This may fall within an example on the "grey list" of the Regulations by excluding the consumer's right to take legal action by unduly restricting the evidence available to him[49];

---

[47] UTCCR 1999, reg. 5(1). See above, para. 18–054.

[48] UTCCR 1999, reg. 5(1), Sched. 3, para. 1(q). If they are expressed as exclusion or limitation clauses, they may also contravene the UCTA 1977, s. 3(2).

[49] UTCCR 1999, Sched. 3, para. 1(q).

(o) The joint and several liability clause if the guarantee is or may be for multiple guarantors (and who may be released and so forth, as in (g) above);

(p) The currency conversion clause, if the guaranteed indebtedness is or may be in a different currency;

(q) The choice of law clause. Even this apparently innocuous term might be unfair if used to deny G a remedy which is available in one jurisdiction but not the other;

(r) The retention clause, whereby the bank keeps the right to retain the guarantee or securities for a certain time after determination, (perhaps six months or even two years) in case, say, D has repaid B, but D's payment is a preference, or is made after a realisation of assets under a floating charge which is subsequently avoided by the liquidator. In addition, it is stated that G is not discharged if payments from D turn out to be invalid (though this is probably the case anyway). This seems generally fair, but may be unfair if an onerous liability on G results in particular circumstances; it must be borne in mind though, that the fairness of the term has to be tested as at the time of the conclusion of the contract[50];

(s) The general waiver clause, whereby G waives all or any of his rights against B or D so far as may be necessary to give effect to any of the provisions of the guarantee. This is put in just for good measure. If a term is invalid under the UTCCR 1999, however, it is unlikely that this waiver will save it.

Letters of Comfort

18–098 Guarantees or indemnities are legally binding contracts. A letter of comfort, however, is not susceptible of precise definition. The significant characteristic of many letters of comfort is that they are understood not to be legally binding, because they lack either consideration or intention to create legal relations or both. Such a letter may be in the form of a guarantee, but stated to be binding "in honour only, as a gentleman's agreement". Letters of comfort are often given by parent companies in respect of subsidiaries, perhaps foreign subsidiaries, and amount to an indication of the parent company's intention to support its subsidiary in its business ventures, usually up to a certain limit. A letter of comfort may be given simply because the parent has a policy of not giving guarantees, or because financial or legislative constraints prevent it from doing so.

18–099 In *Kleinwort Benson Ltd v. Malaysia Mining Corpn.*,[51] a parent company, which had previously been unwilling to enter into a guarantee on behalf of

[50] UTCCR 1999, reg. 6(1).
[51] [1989] 1 All E.R. 785.

a subsidiary, stated in a letter of comfort for the subsidiary that "It is our policy to ensure that the business of (the subsidiary) is at all times in a position to meet its liabilities to you. . .". It was held by the Court of Appeal that this gave rise merely to a moral responsibility, not a binding promise as to future conduct. Since it is intentionally not legally binding, the value of such a letter depends entirely on the standing of the parent company in the business and financial world.

There is, however, a danger in always assuming that what is called a "letter of comfort" is not legally binding. In fact, so-called letters of comfort are phrased in many different ways, and some may be binding guarantees or other obligations,[52] some binding in some respects, and others entirely ineffective in law.

[52] See *Chemco Leasing S.P.A. v. Rediffusion Ltd.* [1987] 1 F.T.L.R. 201, CA, where a valid option was created, subject to a requirement of acceptance within a reasonable time.

CHAPTER 19

COMPANY SECURITIES

Securities given by companies[1] differ from those given by individuals in a number of respects. First, most securities given by companies are subject to registration under the CA 1985 as well as to registration under other provisions relating to different types of property, such as land, ships and aircraft, whereas the only securities individuals are required to register, generally speaking, are chattel mortgages.[2] Secondly, a company[3] can create a floating charge over its assets so that it remains free to deal with the asset until specified events occur, (such as liquidation), when the charge "crystallises" and the secured creditor obtains priority over all creditors except preferential creditors and those with fixed charges. Thirdly, an individual's charge or mortgage must not provide that it shall never be redeemed or contain any other unreasonable terms (such as non-redeemability for a very long time or on onerous conditions). This is usually expressed by saying that there may not be a clog on the equity of redemption.[4] A company, however, may create an irredeemable debenture,[5] or one redeemable only on the happening of a contingency, or after the expiration of a certain time, though a bank is unlikely to take a perpetual debenture[6] as security from a company. **19–001**

Another characteristic difference between company and individual securities used to be that banks and other third parties taking company securities were at risk that it might be outside the powers of the company to grant security. The effect of the doctrine of *ultra vires* for banks lending to **19–002**

---

1 See further Gough, *Company Charges* (2nd ed. 1996); Penningon, *Bank Finance for Companies* (2nd ed.), Burgess, *Corporate Finance Law* (7th ed.); and established texts on Company Law, such as Pennington, *Company Law* (7th ed., 1995); Gower's *Principles of Modern Company Law* (6th ed., 1997) (the chapter on company charges is contributed by Prentice); Palmer's *Company Law*; *Farrar's Company Law* (4th ed., Farrar and Hannigan eds); *Halsbury's Laws* (4th ed.) paras 1250 *et seq.*.

2 Under the BSA 1878–91.

3 Individuals do not create floating charges because such a charge would be likely to fall within the scope of the BSA 1878–91 which do not apply to companies. Until its abolition in 1986, the reputed ownership doctrine, which applied on bankruptcy but not liquidation, also inhibited the practicality of individuals creating floating charges.

4 Though company charges are not exempted from this rule: *Jarrah Timber & Wood Paving Corporation v. Samuel* [1903] 2 Ch. 1 at 11, CA.

5 By virtue the CA 1985, s. 193; *Bloomer v. Union Coal and Iron Co.* (1873) L.R. 16 Eq 383.

6 A debenture which is irredeemable or redeemable only on the happening of a contingency: CA 1985, s. 197 (although it is possible that a bank loan (and security) will not be repayable for a specific period). Banks as corporations may issue their own perpetual bonds or debentures.

companies was that any transaction which was not reasonably incidental to the attainment of the objects specified in the company's Memorandum of Association was void. Banks therefore had to ensure that the transaction was within the company's objects. The doctrine was to all intents and purposes abolished by the CA 1985[7] and needs little discussion now. Problems of directors exceeding their authority are also reduced, because any transaction by the directors is deemed, in favour of a person dealing in good faith with a company, to be within the powers of the company and within the scope of the directors' authority.[8]

Company Charges

Debentures

19–003 A *debenture* is the distinctive form of security which may be created by companies.[9] The word "debenture" is used in the CA 1985,[10] but the definition is vague: "'Debenture' includes debenture stock, bonds and any other securities of a company, whether constituting a charge on the assets of the company or not".[11] Chitty J. said that "a debenture means a document which either creates a debt or acknowledges it, and any document which fulfils either of these conditions is a 'debenture'".[12] Generally, however, people use the word "debenture" as if it means *secured* debenture,[13] and for present purposes, since we are concerned with securities, a debenture is a document which creates a debt or acknowledges a debt or promises to advance money, thus creating a debt, possibly on a contingency, and which provides for security to be given for that debt.[14] The rights given to the debenture holder are a matter of contract and the company's Memorandum and Articles. Debentures come in many forms; for example, they can be registered or bearer, single or series, and perpetual or redeemable. Bank debentures are normally *all monies* debentures: that is to say, they secure not only existing loans but all present and future loan advances on the company's current account. The kind of debenture with which we are concerned here is a single redeemable debenture taken by the bank as security for a debt. The typical terms of a bank debenture are set out later in this Chapter.[15]

---

[7] s. 35 (implemented by CA 1989, s. 108).

[8] Banks may risk breaching their duty of care (see above, Chap. 5) or being liable as constructive trustees (see above, Chap. 9) if they deal negligently or knowingly with directors exceeding their authority.

[9] Pennington, *Company Law*, p. 556, although they may also be granted by clubs and occasionally by individuals: *Halsbury's Laws*, p. 1250.

[10] *e.g.* CA 1985, ss. 190–197.

[11] CA 1985, s. 744.

[12] *Levy v. Abercorris Slate and Slab Co* (1887) 37 Ch. D. 260 at 264.

[13] Gower, *op. cit.*, p. 323, points out that though in practice few problems occur because of the lack of definition, this may change because of the "invention of a remarkable array of new and highly sophisticated types of securitised loan investments", some, but not all of which, unquestionably are debentures.

[14] This working definition would not cover *e.g.* an unsecured bond issue.

[15] Below, para. 19–061.

Fixed and Floating Charges

A charge may be created over assets in which the debtor has an existing interest, provided that the obligation is not contingent. Existing property is understood to include *potential* property: that is, property not yet in existence but "growing" out of property in existence which is owned by the debtor,[16] for example, wool growing on sheep, apples on trees. Similarly for rights "growing" out of existing contracts: if payment is to be made for a house when it has been built, the builder cannot sue for the money until there has been substantial completion at least, and it may seem that the debt does not yet exist. But for the purpose of security interests, the debt is considered to be a present, rather than a contingent or future, debt, because there are legal obligations on both sides which, if fulfilled, will inevitably result in the debt becoming due. The only contingency is the possibility that either party may break the contract, and legally this is irrelevant. **19–004**

A charge may also be expressed to cover *future* property, in which case it can have effect in equity, though not at law.[17] An inchoate security interest exists from the date of agreement, and an equitable charge attaches when the property described comes into existence, without the need for further action; for priority purposes, it relates back to the date of creation of the security interest. **19–005**

Company charges may be either *fixed* (or specific) charges, which may be legal or equitable, or *floating* charges, which are necessarily equitable.

Fixed charges

A fixed charge is one which, when it is made, immediately attaches or "fixes on ascertained and defined property or property capable of being ascertained or defined".[18] If the charge is by way of mortgage of goods, for example, property in the goods will pass immediately to the mortgagee. If the charge is a true charge,[19] the asset is immediately encumbered by it even though the ownership does not pass. In either case, the right and ability of the owner to continue to deal with the asset is immediately affected. Normally, provided the charge is properly registered,[20] subsequent **19–006**

---

16 See Goode, *Commercial Law* (2nd ed.) p. 682, referring to *G & T Earle Ltd v. Hemsworth R.D.C.* (1928) 140 L.T. 69; *Norman v. Federal Commissioner of Taxation* (1963) 109 C.L.R. 9; *Hughes v. Pump House Hotel Co Ltd* [1902] 2 K.B. 190.

17 See *Holroyd v. Marshall* (1862) 10 H.L. Cas. 191 at 220: "At law property, non-existing, but to be acquired at a future time, is not assignable; in equity it is so": *Tailby v. O.R.* (1888) 13 App. Cas. 523; *Re Lind* [1915] 2 Ch. 345.

18 *Illingworth v. Houldsworth* [1904] A.C. 355 at 358, *per* Lord MacNaghten.

19 CA 1985, s. 396(4) refers to either mortgages or charges. A true charge does not involve a transfer of ownership or possession and can be created by contract or by declaration of trust. If the "charge" is properly a *mortgage*, ownership is transferred, although possession remains with the mortgagor.

20 And no exceptions to the *nemo dat* rule apply.

purchasers cannot obtain good title to the property. Even if it is sold, the proceeds will belong to the chargeholder. Typically, a fixed charge is taken over land or over specified chattels as a legal or equitable charge or mortgage. The company will be unable to deal with the property except with the debenture holder's consent.

Floating charges

19–007 A floating charge, on the other hand, is one which, while it creates a kind of immediate security right (which is "ambulatory and shifting in its nature" and "hovers" over the designated assets[21]), creates no immediate change of title to or encumbrance upon the assets. Crucially, the company is free to continue to dispose of the assets (maybe subject to conditions or restrictions) until certain events occur, such as the appointment of a receiver, when the charge fastens on or attaches to the existing assets of the designated type. There is, nevertheless, an immediate security right or proprietary right in the chargeholder[22] in two senses: first, even before the charge becomes fixed, the chargeholder may apply to the court for the appointment of a receiver[23] if its security is in jeopardy, and secondly, a priority is established between creditors, so that, for example, a first floating charge will ordinarily take priority over a later one. A floating charge may be taken over land, goods, or choses in action, or over any or all of them simultaneously.

19–008 From the point of view of a lender's priority over other creditors, a fixed charge will almost always be preferable to a floating charge. However, whether a particular charge is fixed or floating depends not on what the parties have chosen to call the charge, but on what they have in substance created. In *Re Yorkshire Woolcombers Association,*[24] Romer L.J. said that a floating charge had the following characteristics:

> "(1) If it is a charge on a class of assets of a company present and future. (2) If that class is one which in the ordinary course of the business of the company would be changing from time to time; and (3) If you find that by the charge it is contemplated that, until some future step is taken by or on behalf of those interested in the charge, the

[21] *Illingworth v. Houldsworth* [1904] A.C. 355 at 358, *per* Lord MacNaghten. It has often been pointed out that judges like describing floating charges in terms of metaphor.

[22] *Evans v. Rival Granite Quarries Ltd* [1910] 2 K.B. 979 at 999.

[23] *Re Borax Co* [1901] 1 Ch. 326.

[24] [1903] 2 Ch. 284 at 295 (aff'd *sub. nom*: *Illingworth v. Houldsworth* [1904] A.C. 355).

company may carry on its business in the ordinary way so far as concerns the particular class of assets I am dealing with".[25]

In practice, it seems that the last of these characteristics is the vital one; even if the charge only covers existing assets or the assets are not to be replaced on sale, it will still be a floating charge if that requirement is satisfied.[26] The essential point is that a floating charge allows the company unencumbered control of the asset and liberty to deal with it.[27]

The advantage of a floating charge[28] is therefore that the company can continue to deal with the unencumbered asset in the ordinary course of business and give good title to a purchaser without having to discharge the security, and, at the same time, the bank has the assurance that the charge will *crystallise*—attach as an encumbrance—when one of certain specified events occurs which might threaten the repayment of the debt by the company. The chargeholder also has some measure of control over the activities of the company it may be able to participate in management decisions and the company may have to report to it.[29] When the charge crystallises it becomes a fixed charge, and the debenture holder may enforce the charge against the debtor company by the appointment of a receiver.[30] If the creditor has a floating charge covering substantially the whole of the company's assets (and banks normally make sure that they do have such a charge), it has the further important advantage that it may block the appointment of an administrator by appointing an administrative receiver,[31] who will realise that security on behalf of that creditor, whereas the function of an administrator is to act in the interests of *all* the creditors of the company. Another advantage of floating charges is that assets covered by company charges (unlike those covered by an individual's charge[32]) need not be specifically described; "all our business and assets" is **19–009**

[25] See also *Evans v. Rival Granite Quarries Ltd* [1910] 2 K.B. 979 at 999, *per* Buckley L.J.: it "is not a future security; it is a present security, which presently affects all the assets of the company . . . not a specific mortgage of the assets, plus a licence to the mortgagor to dispose of them . . . but a floating mortgage applying to every item . . . but not specifically affecting any item until some act or event occurs or some act on the part of the mortgagee is done which causes it to crystallize into a fixed security". See also *Government Stock and Other Securities Investment Co v. Manila Ry. Co* [1897] A.C. 81 at 86; *Illingworth v. Houldsworth* [1904] A.C. 355 at 358; *Driver v. Broad* [1893] 1 Q.B. 744 at 748; *Hubbuck v. Helms* (1887) 56 L.J. Ch. 536 at 537; *Re Atlantic Computer Systems plc* [1991] B.C.L.C. 606, CA; *Re Atlantic Medical Ltd* [1992] B.C.C. 386; *Re G.E. Tunbridge* [1995] 1 B.C.L.C. 34; *Re Cimex Tissues Ltd* [1995] 1 B.C.L.C. 409; *Re ASRS Establishment Ltd, The Times,* November 17, 1999, Ch D; *Re Coss Lett (Contractors) Ltd* [1999] 1 B.C.L.C. 205, CA.

[26] *Re Bond Worth Ltd* [1979] 3 All E.R. 919; [1980] Ch. 228. See also the comments of Hoffmann J. in *Re Brightlife* [1987] Ch. 200 at 213–4.

[27] *Siebe Gorman & Co. v. Barclays Bank Ltd* [1979] 2 Lloyd's Rep 142.

[28] For criticism of the bias of the law towards secured creditors, and a suggestion that floating charges should be abolished, see Grylls [1994] 10 J.I.B.L. 391.

[29] *e.g.* the cessation of business, see below, para. 19–012.

[30] Usually under the terms of the charge, and by the court's inherent power, if not.

[31] See below, Chap. 24.

[32] BSA 1878–91.

sufficient.[33] A fixed charge would be more advantageous for the creditor, though, if an administrator is appointed, because the administrator may freely dispose of assets subject to a floating charge, whereas the court's authorisation is needed to dispose of an asset subject to a fixed charge.

19–010 Despite their benefits floating charges have disadvantages. The most serious is that the company may dissipate all the assets before the charge has crystallised or may create fixed charges over the assets which rank in priority to the floating charge. Chargees try to prevent companies doing this by including restrictions (*negative pledge clauses*) in debentures which prohibit the assignment of the property and the creation of any mortgage or charge ranking in priority to the floating charge. Negative pledges are binding on the debtor company. There is an unresolved doubt, however, as to whether such clauses can protect chargees by binding future lenders.[34] A company will still have apparent authority to deal with the asset despite the floating charge, and it seems that a negative pledge clause can only be a contractual covenant limiting the actual authority of the company, and cannot create a security right in the asset, nor bind a purchaser without notice of it.[35]

19–011 Another potential disadvantage for the chargee is that floating charges may be invalidated if they are created at a time which would give an unfair preference to the chargee on insolvency, and this is less likely with fixed charges. Further, on insolvency, floating charges are subordinate, not only to fixed charges, but also to the claims of preferential creditors. Even though it is possible for borrowers to grant floating charges over single assets or over a single class of assets, therefore, creditors prefer to take fixed charges if the asset is valuable, easily identifiable and not subject to regular change or turnover.

The ideal combination for a secured creditor is a fixed charge over all appropriate assets together with a general floating charge. The document creating the charge is generally worded so that it will apply to all a company's assets for the time being and to its whole undertaking (that is, its whole business and goodwill), and specific assets are often additionally identified as the subject of a fixed charge.

Crystallisation of floating charges

19–012 Crystallisation is the process by which a floating charge attaches specifically and finally to all the items of the class of mortgaged assets which the company owns at that date or subsequently acquires if future assets are

---

[33] Otherwise, listing the assets may be impossible or at least extraordinarily time-consuming.

[34] See below, para. 19–051.

[35] The company remains full owner of the asset and has power to dispose of it; at most the effect of a clause on a subsequent chargeholder would be to make it liable for the tort of inducing a breach of contract. The effect of notice of such clauses on priorities is discussed below.

within the scope of the particular charge.[36] After crystallisation the charge is fixed, and the company can no longer deal with the property charged except as subject to the charge.

The charge may be made to crystallise by the following events, all of which in some way reflect the termination of the company's right or ability to manage the assets in question: **19–013**

(1) if winding up commences (compulsory[37] or voluntary[38]);
(2) if a receiver is appointed out of court[39] or the creditor takes possession of the assets subject to the charge[40];
(3) if the chargor ceases to carry on business[41] or disposes of the whole of its undertaking or assets with a view to the cessation of trading.[42]

In these cases the charge crystallises as a matter of law. It is established, however, that other contractual provisions may cause the charge to crystallise[43] —say, by giving a notice, or even "automatically" (by failure to repay money on demand, for example).[44] This may happen before any of the events which trigger off crystallisation as a matter of law occur, and it is often called *automatic crystallisation*.

Subsequent equitable chargees may be put at a disadvantage[45] by automatic crystallisation, since they may have no way of knowing that the charge has crystallised. This would affect equitable chargees rather than legal ones, because a chargee taking legal title, relying on the ostensible authority of the directors, would take free of the crystallised charge as a bona fide purchaser without notice. **19–014**

Floating charges and unfair advantage in insolvency

It is tempting for unsecured creditors (particularly if they are directors of the company) to try to obtain security for their debts when it looks as if the insolvency of the company may be imminent. In order to prevent creditors **19–015**

[36] *Farrar's Company Law,* (4th ed.) p. 635. To crystallise is to "settle and fasten on the subjects of the charge within its reach and grasp": *Illingworth v. Houldsworth* [1904] A.C. 355 at 358, *per* Lord MacNaghten.

[37] *Re Colonial Trusts Corpn. Ex p. Bradshaw* (1879) 15 Ch. D. 465 at 472.

[38] In *Re Roundwood Colliery Co* [1897] 1 Ch. 373.

[39] *Evans v. Rival Granite Quarries* [1910] 2 K.B. 979. Receivers may also be appointed by the court.

[40] *Re Hamilton's Windsor Ironworks, ex p. Pitman & Edwards* (1879) 12 Ch. D. 7007 at 7010.

[41] *Re Woodroffes (Musical Instruments) Ltd* [1986] Ch. 366.

[42] *Hubbuck v. Helms* (1887) 56 L.J.Ch. 536.

[43] See Goode, *L.P.C.S.*, pp. 35–40.

[44] *Re Woodroffes (Musical Instruments) Ltd* [1986] Ch. 366; *Re Brightlife Ltd* [1987] 2 W.L.R. 197. Automatic crystallisation seems to have been generally accepted since the decision of Hoffman J. in *Re Brightlife*. But this proposition is not altogether straightforward—the wording of express automatic crystallisation clauses is very important.

[45] For discussion of the disadvantages of automatic crystallisation, see Lightman and Moss, pp. 47 *et seq*. See also *Fire Nymph Products Ltd v. The Heating Centre Pty. Ltd*. (1992) 7 A.S.C.R. 365, CA, NSW.

obtaining an unfair advantage over other creditors in this way, section 245 of the IA 1986 provides that where a company creates a floating charge,[46] the charge is invalid *if it was created within 12 months of the commencement of the insolvency, unless the company was able to pay its debts at the time the charge was granted or except in so far as money has been paid or goods or services*[47] *supplied to the company at the same time or after the charge was created*. In the case of a person connected with the company[48] the period is two years, and the charge may be invalid even if the company was able to pay its debts at the time the charge was created. The operation of section 245 of the IA 1986 must be considered together with provisions concerning transactions at an undervalue and preferences.[49]

19–016 It is only the *charge* which is invalidated; the debt is unaffected, and the creditor may claim as an unsecured creditor. In any case, there is no difficulty with a charge if the company was solvent at the time, or if the charge is for a genuine consideration—the charge may be partially saved, in fact, because it is only invalid so far as money has not been paid or goods supplied. The consideration given may be consideration which reduces the company's debts, and therefore, if a bank is granted a charge because it has paid a creditor of the company directly (instead of paying the company), or if a guarantor has paid money to a bank to discharge a debt owed by the company, and the guarantor has been given a charge, these would be protected, even if they were done in pursuance of a previous agreement.[50]

The words "at the same time as" in section 245 of the IA 1986 have been interpreted strictly by the courts.[51] Even though the bank pays the money to the company in advance of the execution of the debenture on the faith of a promise to execute a debenture, the transaction is not protected unless the interval is trifling.[52] The bank should therefore take care not to advance money until the company has actually executed the debenture.

19–017 If a creditor attempts to avoid the rule by entering into a transaction purporting to advance money to the company secured by a charge, on the understanding that the "new" loan will be used to pay off an old debt of the same amount, the courts may look on it as a sham, and therefore invalid,

---

[46] At a time when it is insolvent, or if it becomes insolvent as a consequence of creating the charge, or after the presentation of a petition for an administration order. Section 245 of the IA 1986 does not apply to fixed charges. See Gower, *op. cit.*, pp. 374–5, who questions the policy of exempting fixed charges from this limitation.

[47] Goods and services supplied cannot be valued at an exorbitant price; they are valued at a reasonable market price, IA 1986, s. 245 (6).

[48] *i.e.* a director, shadow director, associate of one of these, or an associate of the company. A shadow director (IA 1986, s. 251) is one in accordance with whose directions the company is accustomed to act, and it is not inconceivable that this may in some circumstances apply to a bank, if it is in the position of a dominant creditor.

[49] IA 1986, ss. 238–241; see further below, Chap. 24.

[50] See *Re Orleans Motor Co Ltd* [1911] 2 Ch. 41. The security may also cover the interest payable (up to 5 per cent).

[51] More strictly than the equivalent provision before 1986 used to be construed.

[52] *Power v. Sharp Investments Ltd.* [1994] B.C.L.C. 111, CA.

because the consideration is past.[53] An example is *Re G. T. Whyte & Co. Ltd*.[54] The bank made an advance to the company, using a bank subsidiary as agent to make the payment and take security. Later, the subsidiary called in the advance, and the bank provided a replacement advance of a fixed amount, not accounted for in an active current account, and secured this with a floating charge. Ten months later the company was wound up, and the liquidator challenged the charge. The bank claimed that it had advanced fresh money at the time of the charge, but the court held that, having regard to the way the loans had been arranged between the bank and its subsidiary, the two loans could not be regarded as being made by separate entities. Thus the bank was treated as having entered a paper transaction to substitute its own "old" debt with apparently "new" debt, which would be secured, and the charge was therefore void. In such cases, the validity of the charge will depend on the facts, and on whether the transaction was in any sense genuine. In *Re Matthew Ellis Ltd*.[55] a company owed about £2000 to a partnership, including X, and X advanced £3000 to the company in return for a floating charge. £2000 was used to pay the partnership to discharge the existing debt, and the balance of the money went in cash to the company. The security was held to be enforceable by X as to the full £3,000. The company had some prospect of succeeding, and to do so it needed goods. The partnership was the only firm which would provide it with goods on credit, and the court took the view that if X did provide the goods, it was right that it should be secured. The transaction, therefore, was "genuine", since it was a real attempt to keep the company in business, and not merely arranged to protect a desperate creditor.

Banks enjoy a singular advantage because of the effect of the "first-in, **19–018**
first-out" rule in *Clayton's Case* on current accounts. This is that the normal operation of a current account will gradually eliminate the "old" debt in the account because of new payments in, even though the total amount of debt remains constant or even reduces. The subsequent withdrawals from the account are then seen as "new" debt, representing money advanced to the company after the creation of the charge, even though the total debt remains constant.[56] If the terms of the charge cover later loans, therefore, the bank may make loans after the creation of the charge which will have the benefit of the security, even if it is under no obligation to do so,[57] provided that the cash advance is to benefit the company, not merely a way of substituting a better security for the creditor. This may entirely nullify the effect of section 245 of IA 1986.[58]

[53] See, *e.g. Re Destone Fabrics Ltd* [1941] 1 All E.R. 545; [1941] Ch. 319.

[54] [1983] B.C.L.C. 311.

[55] [1933] Ch. 458.

[56] *Re Yeovil Glove Co Ltd* [1965] Ch. 148 (in relation to s. 322 of the CA 1948). See also *Re Thomas Mortimer Ltd* (1925) 4 L.D.A.B. 3.

[57] *Re Yeovil Glove Co Ltd* [1965] Ch. 148.

[58] A "startling result": *Yeovil Glove* [1965] Ch. 148 at 172, *per* Harman L.J.

A creditor which realises its security before liquidation cannot be forced to repay, because the underlying debt is not affected, and the payment to the creditor discharges the company's liability.[59]

Charges Over Book Debts[60]

19–019 *Book debts* (often nowadays included in the term *receivables*) are attractive as security, although there may be problems in dealing with them because they are a highly fungible and fluctuating asset, and enforcement may be tricky.[61] Nevertheless, the courts have gradually developed the law to the point at which it is perfectly possible to take fixed or floating charges over book debts, and banks often do so.[62]

19–020 Book debts are debts owing to the company which arise out of the normal carrying on of its business. They can be described as debts which would appear in the books of the company, if these are well-kept,[63] but in practice, there is uncertainty about what is included in the concept of book debts. On one view:

> "The distinction to be drawn is probably between debts accruing to the company in the course of carrying on the business for which it was formed, and debts which are merely incidental to carrying on that business, or which, although *intra vires,* are totally unconnected with it".[64]

If, for example, a company set up to make goods sells goods to C, C's debt is a book debt of the company. But if the company deposits money with a bank to secure an advance to the bank, the debt owed by the bank may not be a book debt (it depends on the construction of the debenture), since it is

---

[59] *Re Parkes Garage (Swadlincote) Ltd* [1929] 1 Ch. 139; *Mace Builders (Glasgow) Ltd v. Lunn* [1987] Ch. 191, CA (relating to the former provision).

[60] See generally Oditah, *Legal Aspects of Receivables Financing*, referred to by Rose L.J., *Re BCCI SA* (*No.8*) [1996] 2 All E.R. 121 at 123: "The discovery in comparatively recent times that the right to receive payment of a debt is a saleable commodity has been of enormous commercial and economic importance".

[61] Oditah, *op. cit.*, p. 2.

[62] See Pennington [1985] 6 Co. Lawyer 9, for a discussion of the development of such charges.

[63] *Shipley v. Marshall* (1863) 14 C.B. (N.S) 566 (a "debt connected with and growing out of the plaintiff's trade"); *Dawson v. Isle* [1906] 1 Ch. 633 ("debts accruing in the ordinary course of trade and entered in the book"); *Independent Automatic Sales Ltd v. Knowles and Foster* [1962] 3 All E.R. 27 ("a debt arising in due course of a business . . . [which] would or could in the ordinary course of such a business be entered in well kept books relating to that business"). See also *Annangel Glory Cia Naviera SA v. M Goldetz* [1988] 1 Lloyd's Rep. 45 (contract lien on sub-freights); *E.Pfeiffer Weinkellerei-Weineinkauf Gmbh v. Arbuthnot Factors Ltd* [1988] 1 W.L.R. 150 (retention clauses); *Lovell Construction Co. Ltd v. Independent Estates plc (in liq.)* [1994] 1 B.C.L.C. 31.

[64] Pennington, *Company Law*, p. 641.

incidental to carrying on the business, and does not arise from the carrying on of the business itself.[65]

Fixed charges over book debts. A fixed charge encumbers the asset, and the company can only deal with it with the creditor's consent, whereas a floating charge allows the company liberty to deal with the asset. For a long time, it seemed unlikely that book debts could be the subject of an effective fixed charge, because of their inherently fluctuating nature, and there was some doubt as to whether it was possible to word a clause in sufficiently certain terms to create a valid fixed charge over future book debts when they come into existence.[66] However, it was demonstrated by the case of *Siebe Gorman & Co. Ltd. v. Barclays Bank Ltd.*[67] that fixed charges over book debts are unexceptionable,[68] provided that the debtor is prevented from dealing with the debts. In that case, the bank took a debenture which charged by way of fixed charge (as it was described) all book debts and other debts owing to the company then or in the future. The company agreed not to assign or charge any money received in respect of such debts to any other person unless the bank gave its written consent, and to pay such money into the company's account with the bank. The company later assigned some bills held by the bank (book debts for this purpose) to the plaintiffs by way of sale, although it could only validly sell them if the charge were floating. The bank claimed that the charge was an effective fixed charge, and that it was entitled to retain the proceeds of the bills as against the plaintiffs. Slade J. held that the charge was truly a fixed charge, because the restrictions on assignment and the requirement to pay to the bank alone removed the essential element of a floating charge, the debtor's freedom to dispose of the asset.[69] The way in which it works is that each debt as it arises is regarded as subject to a fixed equitable charge under the 19–021

[65] In *Re Brightlife* [1986] B.C.L.C. 418 at 421, Hoffmann J. held that a credit balance at the bank was not a "book debt or other debt" because it is not natural usage for businessmen or accountants to describe it as a debt (although it is in law) rather than as "cash at bank" (at 154); see also *Re Permanent Houses (Holdings) Ltd* [1988] B.C.L.C. 151 and *Northern Bank Ltd v. Ross* [1991] B.C.L.C. 504, CA, NI.

[66] Similarly, there would be no theoretical problem in creating a charge over a company's stock in trade, but such a charge would be impracticable because of the administrative difficulties for the bank in keeping control over the constant sale of stock.

[67] [1979] 2 Lloyd's Rep. 142. See Pennington [1985] 6 Co. Lawyer 9; Pearce [1987] J.B.L.18; McCormack [1987] 8 Co. Lawyer 3.

[68] Although there has been criticism: see Berg [1995] J.B.L. 433, who considers it unsound because a fixed charge should normally prohibit the company from dealing with the asset, which would be impossible in the case of book debts because it would immediately cut the company off from its cash flow.

[69] See also *Evans Coleman & Evans Ltd v. R.A. Nelson Construction Ltd* (1959) 16 D.L.R. (2d.) 123; *Re Keenan* (1986) 2 B.C.C. 98 at 970, CA, NI; *Re Armagh Shoes Ltd.* [1984] B.C.L.C. 405; *Re Brightlife* [1987] 2 W.L.R. 197; *Re A Company (No 005009 of 1987) ex p. Copp* [1989] B.C.L.C.13; *Re Atlantic Computer Systems plc* [1992] Ch. 505; *Re Atlantic Medical Ltd* [1993] B.C.L.C. 386.

debenture.[70] The proceeds of specifically charged debts may become held on constructive trust for the secured lender.[71]

19–022 It is helpful to compare the terms of the charge in *Re Brightlife*,[72] which distinguished *Siebe Gorman*. In that case, the charge (again described as a fixed charge) in favour of a non-bank creditor had left the company free to pay the receipts into its own bank account, where they would be mixed with the company's own money and would be at the company's free disposal. Despite a provision that the company was not permitted to sell, factor or discount its debts,[73] the company really had the freedom to deal with the debts as it wished. It was held that the restrictions were consistent with the company's freedom to deal with its assets, and that that freedom is characteristic of a floating, not a fixed, charge.[74]

19–023 The lender must be careful, therefore, in drafting the clause. It is not enough simply to impose a restriction preventing the company from dealing with the debts before they are paid (for example by factoring[75] or discounting[76] them); the debenture must also restrict the company from dealing with the proceeds of book debts. A bank creditor will find it easier to draft an effective fixed charge, because of the control it will be able to exercise over the account; it need only prohibit dealings with the debts charged, arrange for payment to the bank, and prohibit withdrawals without its consent.[77] A non-bank creditor should arrange for payment of the debts to the creditor or his or her nominee or a bank, or at least prohibit the use of funds paid into the company's bank account.

19–024 Some doubt has been cast on the clarity of the distinction between fixed and floating charges over book debts by some later cases. In *Re Atlantic Computer Systems plc*[78] the Court of Appeal found that charges over book debts were fixed, despite the fact that the company was free to deal with the

[70] *Siebe Gorman* [1979] 2 Lloyd's Rep 142 at 158, 165.

[71] *Barclays Bank v. Willowbrook International Ltd* [1987] B.C.L.C. 717n, CA.

[72] [1986] B.C.L.C. 418.

[73] In *Oakdale (Richmond) Ltd v. National Westminster Bank* [1996] B.C.C. 919, an imaginative (though unsuccessful) attempt was made to claim that a requirement in a debenture for the bank's consent to factoring, discounting, etc., book debts subject to a fixed charge was void under Arts 85 and 86 of the E.C. Treaty. It was held that the bank needed control for its charges of book debts to be effective because of the transient nature of book debts, and the requirement was what any lender in the market would have regarded as necessary.

[74] See Millett L.J.'s remarks (*obiter*, because the parties had conceded that the charge in issue was a fixed charge) in *Royal Trust Bank v. National Westminster* [1996] B.C.C. 613 at 619, CA, that "a contractual right in the chargor to collect the proceeds and to pay them into its own bank account for use in the ordinary course of business is a badge of a floating charge".

[75] A factor is one who, pursuant to a continuing relationship with a supplier of goods or services to trade customers purchases debts from time to time arising in respect of supplies to those customers: Goode, *Commercial Law*, p. 802. See also Salinger *Factoring Law and Practice*.

[76] Discounting debts is selling them (usually in blocks) at a discount for collection on behalf of the creditor: Goode, *op. cit.*, p. 656. See also Oditah, *op. cit.*

[77] As in *Re Keenan* (1986) 2 B.C.C. 98 at 970, CA, NI. See also *Re Double S Printers Ltd* [1999] 1 B.C.L.C. 220, CA.

[78] [1990] B.C.C. 859, CA. See also *Re Atlantic Medical Ltd*. [1992] B.C.C. 653.

proceeds of the debts until the chargee might choose to intervene, because the rights of property assigned by the charges were not "ambulatory", but were rights under specific existing contracts, which included rights to future instalments. This seems to blur the clear distinction between assets within the control of the company with which it can deal, characteristic, according to *Siebe Gorman* and *Re Brightlife*, of floating charges, and those subject to a fixed charge, which cannot be dealt with without the consent of the chargee.

"Convertible" fixed charge. In the controversial decision of *Re New Bullas Trading Ltd.*,[79] the Court of Appeal went rather further. In that case, the efficacy of a "convertible charge" was at issue. The contract was drafted to create a *fixed* charge over the book debts and a *floating* charge over their proceeds. To achieve this, the clause dealt separately with the different aspects: all money representing proceeds received from book debts was to be paid into a bank account as the chargee might require with a specified bank, and the chargor was required to deal with the money as directed by the chargee; in the absence of any such direction, the proceeds would be released from the fixed charge and subjected to the floating charge. It was held, on the basis that the intention of the parties should prevail unless there was good reason to the contrary, that the debts were subject to a fixed charge while uncollected, and the proceeds should be subject to the bank's general floating charge when realised. This arrangement had benefits for the bank in giving it priority by virtue of the fixed charge where it would be effective, and a floating charge where it would not, whereas a charge which "as created" was floating would be postponed on insolvency to the claims of preferential creditors. **19–025**

The decision has been strongly criticised; it is not clear whether it is possible to detach the proceeds of debts from the debts themselves—indeed, it seems an unreal distinction to make, because once the proceeds are received, the debt no longer exists.[80] If no true distinction between the book debt and its proceeds exists, then the case casts doubt on the requirement of *Siebe Gorman* and *Re Brightlife* that a fixed debt over debts can only be valid if the debtor is prevented from dealing with the debt. It has also been observed that the policy implications of the decision are **19–026**

[79] [1994] B.C.C.36. See also *Re Brumark Investments Ltd Commissioner of Inland Revenue v. Agnew* [2000] 1 B.C.L.C. 353 NZ CA. For recent comment see Gregory and Walton (1999) 115 L.Q.R. 14.

[80] See Millett L.J.'s comment in *Royal Trust Bank v. National Westminster,* [1996] B.C.C. 613 at 618: "although it is obviously possible to distinguish between a capital asset and its income, I do not see how it can be possible to separate a debt or other receivable from the proceeds of its realisation." Lightman and Moss (*op. cit*, p. 36), argue that if there is such a distinction, so that the debts exist while they are uncollected but are extinguished on payment (at which time the company acquires a new asset in the form of the moneys paid by the debtor), the agreement over the money should be treated as separate from the charge over the debt and not relevant to it.

undesirable, because it enables creditors taking security over book debts to "drive a coach and horses" through the statutory provisions protecting the priority of preferential creditors.[81]

19–027 **"Charge-back"**. As we have seen, banks often require debtors to give fixed and floating charges over book debts, and this can be in the form of what is known as a *"charge-back"*, a device which has become popular in recent years. The benefit of the bank account into which the debts are paid is charged to the bank by the company by way of security Additionally, banks may require a company to agree that withdrawals from the account are not to be made until it has discharged its liability to the bank. This is known as a *"flawed asset"* agreement.

19–028 The "charge-back" device is widely used, but was initially held (at first instance) to be logically impossible and not to achieve the result intended. The point for the creditor of taking a mortgage or charge is that it will take priority over the rights of other creditors on insolvency; the creditor can recover the debt intact instead of having to take a dividend or proportionate share of whatever remains of the estate. The security gives the chargee a *property* right in the asset charged. Even an equitable charge, though it is not an immediate transfer of property, affects the property rights so that eventually a transfer of ownership can take place if the liability has not been discharged.

The argument about the "charge-back" device is that it purports to affect a company's bank account, in other words, the debt owed to the company by the bank. A debt is simply a *contractual obligation*, not a property right. The bank only owes a debt to the customer, who can hardly *sell* the debt to the bank, its debtor (though it could sell it to a third party): if the debt is "sold" or assigned to the bank, the debtor, the transaction simply has the effect of releasing the debtor from liability.[82]

19–029 This view—that it is conceptually impossible for a customer to create a charge over its own bank account in favour of the bank—was taken by Millett J. in *Re Charge Card Services Ltd,*[83] in a decision which gave rise to a lively controversy,[84] and caused consternation among members of the banking community. Banks pointed out vigorously that such charges had

---

[81] See Bridge (1994)110 L.Q.R. 340, who sees the charge as "a simple device to keep out the preference creditors"; and Goode in (1994) 110 L.Q.R. 492, in a powerful critique of this decision and that of *Re Atlantic Computers* [1992] Ch. 505. The decision was supported by Berg [1995] J.B.L. 433, in a reply to Goode.

[82] The argument was first propounded by Professor Goode, in *Legal Problems of Credit and Security* (1st ed., 1982), pp. 86–89, and is further explained in the 2nd ed., pp. 124 *et seq.*

[83] [1987] 2 All E.R. 150.

[84] Criticised by Wood, in (*e.g.*) (1987) 8 Co. Law 265; Oditah [1992] J.B.L. 541, and the editor of *Paget, op.cit.*, pp. 553–4. See also *Welsh Development Agency v. Export Finance Co. Ltd* [1992] B.C.C. 270 at 284, *per* Dillon L.J., who expressed reservations. The decision was analysed and supported by Shea [1986] 3 J.I.B.L 192, and supported by Goode: *L.P.C.S.* (2nd ed., 1988) p. 125.

been widely used for some time, and had given rise to no particular difficulties. In *Re BCCI SA (No. 8)*,[85] the Court of Appeal noted the criticism, but came to the same view about charge-backs as the decision in *Charge Card*. In the *BCCI* case, there could not even be an effective insolvency set-off because the arrangement was tri-partite (so there could be no mutuality[86]), in that the loan was advanced to the company customer, but repayment was secured by the deposit of money with BCCI by a third party, the director of the company.[87]

The House of Lords took a different view when the *BCCI* case was appealed.[88] Lord Hoffmann, giving the judgment of the court, agreed that the arrangement was effective contractually, as a flawed asset, but went on to disagree with the "conceptual impossibility" view and to hold that a charge-back arrangement could and did amount to a valid charge. He was clearly impressed by the policy arguments. He pointed out that other jurisdictions had simply introduced legislation to validate such charges,[89] and said that the courts should be very slow to declare a practice of the commercial community to be conceptually impossible. Plainly, the court would have been unwilling to carry the theory to the extent of incommoding established practice.[90] **19–030**

However, Lord Hoffmann also made some telling theoretical points. An equitable charge, he said, is a species of charge, which is a proprietary interest granted by way of security. Proprietary interests confer rights *in rem* which, subject to questions of registration and the equitable doctrine of purchaser for value without notice, will be binding upon third parties and unaffected by the insolvency of the owner of the property charged. But he pointed out that the holder may only resort to the property for the purpose of satisfying a liability due to it, and the owner of the property retains an equity of redemption to have the property restored to him or her when the liability has been discharged, and retains title subject to the bank's charge. A chose in action or right has always been recognised as property; a charge over it can certainly be granted to a third party.[91] The only difference in **19–031**

[85] *Re BCCI SA (No. 8)* [1996] 2 All E.R. 121. The argument also relies on dicta (*per* Buckley L.J.) in *National Westminster Bank v. Halesowen Presswork* [1970] 3 All E.R. 473, that a lien cannot exist over a debtor's own indebtedness to the creditor.

[86] IR 1986, r. 4.90. See also *Tam Wing Chuen v. BCCI Hong Kong Ltd (in liq)* [1996] 2 B.C.L.C. 69, PC.

[87] Here it was, unusually, the bank which was insolvent, and it was the depositor, not the bank, who would have benefited if the set-off had been valid. A "flawed asset" clause, which would work contractually (merely stating that a bank need not repay the deposit until the customer's debt is repaid, or some such arrangement, without a right expressed to set off the deposit) would be satisfactory in the normal situation—where the *customer*, not the bank, is insolvent.

[88] *Re BCCI (No. 8)* [1996] 2 All E.R. 1211 (also cited as *Morris v. Agrichemicals Ltd)* [1997] 4 All E.R. 568.

[89] *e.g.* Hong Kong, see *Tam Wing Chuen* [1996] 2 B.C.L.C. 69 PC.

[90] Goode (1998) 114 L.Q.R. 178, has criticised Lord Hoffmann's approach as entirely result-driven and producing a fiction in the law.

[91] No view was expressed by the court as to whether such a charge is registrable.

granting such a charge to a debtor (the bank) would be a slight difference in realisation, which the bank could effect merely by making the appropriate book entries.

19–032 It seems, therefore, that the court analysed the proprietary rights in the asset, not as one single unit, "ownership", but as a bundle of rights (it is respectfully submitted correctly), some of which, or at least one, the equity of redemption,[92] remain with the customer, even though others are passed to the bank, the debtor, when the charge is created. The bank can be said to own some of the proprietary rights[93]—enough to give it an effective security right on insolvency (and that is the nature of an equitable charge)—but not enough for it to describe itself as "owner", unless and until the customer is in default.[94]

Assignment of Securities

19–033 Since a security is a property right, it may be assigned, and the normal rules applying to assignments apply.[95] Bank forms usually make this clear by expressly providing that the debenture enures for the benefit of the bank's successors and assigns. Where a customer changes banks, assignment by the former bank to another is rare; the usual procedure is for the company's new bank to arrange for discharge of the old debenture and to take and register a new debenture.

If a bank takes security in the form of an irrevocable authority from a company entitling the bank to require the company's debtors to pay directly to the company's bankers, this authority will create a charge over the book debts concerned, which will be void if not registered.[96] If the debts are absolutely assigned[97] to the bank by way of repayment of the advances to

[92] See *Re George Inglefield Ltd* [1933] Ch. 1, where the distinctions between a sale and a security transaction (mortgage) are described as: the right of the mortgagor to get back the security until foreclosure; the right of the mortgagor to be repaid any profit recovered from realising the security; and the mortgagee's right to recover any loss on the realisation from the debtor.

[93] It is submitted that this split ownership distinguishes the charge-back from the grant of a lease to oneself. In the case of the charge-back, the bank, a separate person, is given some of the proprietary rights in the asset. In the case of a freeholder granting a lease to himself, on the other hand, all the proprietary rights (including the potential rights of a tenant) would be held by *one* person, and not split.

[94] Goode emphasises that one cannot *owe* what one *owns*, an expression which neatly exposes the difference between obligations and property; but the clarity of the distinction seems to depend upon regarding ownership as a unit rather than as a bundle of rights, and does not allow for "the flexibility of the concept of the equitable charge, by which the chargee obtains an equitable proprietary interest in the charged asset, without becoming its legal or beneficial owner" as argued by Calnan (1998) 114 L.Q.R. 174.

[95] *e.g.* under s. 136 of the LPA 1925.

[96] *Re Kent and Sussex Sawmills Ltd* [1947] Ch. 177. It was admitted that the debts in question were book debts: the question was whether it was a charge.

[97] "Absolute" here means without proviso for redemption: a mortgage of a chose in action can be made by an assignment which is "absolute" in another sense, so that it can be a legal assignment, within the meaning of s. 136 of the LPA 1925, even though it is undoubtedly registrable because there is a proviso for redemption. There must be an outright sale, not just a mortgage, to escape registration.

the company, however, this will be a sale of the debt, not a charge,[98] and of course would not be registrable.

Discharge of Securities

If the customer ceases to be indebted to the bank, the security interest is terminated and the customer may demand that the security be vacated. Banks often wish to retain the security for their own protection, however, and include a clause in the debenture stating that the bank may retain the security for contingent liabilities. Also, where an overdraft is secured, banks try to ensure that the security is not discharged inadvertently: the original debt might be discharged by the operation of *Clayton's Case*.[99] Banks avoid this result by using *all monies* debentures which cover all debts from time to time in the account. **19–034**

If the legal title of an asset has been transferred to the bank, it may continue to hold the legal title when the security interest has been terminated, though it holds it on trust for the customer until retransfer. With a mortgage of registered shares, for example, the shares will have to be re-transferred to the mortgagor, and until they are, the legal rights will remain with the mortgagee. With a mortgage of registered land, the entry on the land register has to be corrected, and until that is done the mortgagee retains its legal charge. If the security is registered at the companies register, the entry may be removed if the company makes a statutory declaration in the prescribed form to the registrar, who will enter a memorandum of satisfaction on the register.[1] **19–035**

There may be a clause in the debenture that the bank may refuse to vacate its legal title to an asset or its legal charge over land even for unaccrued liabilities,[2] and in that case its security interest would be protected even against a subsequent purchaser.

Registration of Charges[3]

Most company charges (including mortgages) must be registered with the registrar of companies under section 395 of the CA 1985; strictly, the statutory obligation is to deliver to the registrar the details required within **19–036**

---

[98] It is a question of interpretation whether the instrument is an outright assignment, *Welsh Development Agency v. Export Finance Co. Ltd.* [1992] B.C.L.C. 148; *Lloyds & Scottish Finance Co. Ltd v. Cyril Lord Carpet Sales Ltd* [1992] B.C.L.C. 609.

[99] (1816) 8 L.J. Ch. 256, see above, Chap. 11

[1] CA 1985, ss. 403.

[2] Or, if it has an equitable interest, it might refuse to agree to the removal of a caution from the register.

[3] Part IV of the CA 1989, which was to introduce sweeping changes to the law on registration (in Part XII of CA 1985) on the lines of Art. 9 of the American Uniform Commercial Code, has not come into force and is unlikely to do so in the immediate future. On the proposed changes, see the Report of the Committee on Consumer Credit (Crowther Committee Report), Cmnd 4596 (1971), Diamond Report, *Security Interests in Property* (1989), and Goode, *Commercial Law* (2nd ed.).

21 days of the charge's creation.[4] The purpose of registration of company charges is to *perfect* the security—to make the security interest effective as against third parties and prevent the company fraudulently charging the same asset to more than one creditor. Company registration is not a *priority point*—it does not guarantee the chargee priority from the date of registration—but it still has some effect on priorities between charge holders, first because it gives notice of the existence of the charge, and secondly because, if a charge is not registered, it will become void as against the liquidator, administrator and other creditors, and thereby lose its priority.[5]

An unconditional agreement to create a charge in future creates a present equitable charge, and this is registrable.[6] The later charge need not be registered,[7] but if the later charge is registered and the earlier one is not, the later charge is valid.[8] A conditional agreement—to execute a charge if called upon to do so—is not an existing equitable charge, and is not registrable.[9]

Registrable Charges

19–037 Section 396(1) of the CA 1985 states that the charges[10] which must be registered are the following (the list is exhaustive[11]):

(a) a charge for the purpose of securing any issue of debentures.[12]

(b) a charge on uncalled share capital of the company.

(c) a charge created or evidenced by an instrument which, if executed by an individual, would require registration as a bill of sale. This covers certain chattel mortgages or charges if they are in writing.[13]

---

[4] For strong criticism of the existing system of registration, see Goode, *Commercial Law* (2nd ed.), p. 703.

[5] Property which is already subject to a charge when the company acquires it is still registrable, but the consequence of non-registration is merely that the company and its officers may be fined, not that the charge is void: CA 1985, ss. 400 and 409.

[6] See *Property Discount Corpn. Ltd v. Lyon Group Ltd* [1981] 1 All E.R. 379.

[7] *Re William Hall (Contractors) Ltd* [1967] 2 All E.R. 1150.

[8] *Re Columbian Fireproofing Co Ltd* [1910] 2 Ch. 120.

[9] *Williams v. Burlington Investments Ltd* (1977) 121 Sol. Jo. 424; *Re Gregory Love & Co.* [1916] 1 Ch. 203. Such an "inchoate" security right, however, may be affected by the insolvency rules concerning preferences, see below, Chap. 24, and *Re Jackson & Bassford Ltd.* [1906] Ch. 467; *Re Eric Holmes (Property) Ltd* [1965] Ch. 1052.

[10] It may be hard to differentiate between a sale and a charge: see *Welsh Development Agency v. Export Finance Co. Ltd* [1992] B.C.C. 270; *Chow Yoong Hong v. Choong Fah Rubber Manufactory* [1962] A.C. 209.

[11] *Re Bond Worth* [1980] Ch. 228 (referring to CA 1948, s. 95(2)). Goode, (*op. cit.*, p. 704), regards this *numerus clausus* approach as too narrow.

[12] "Issue" refers to a series of debentures, and means that a single bank debenture is not covered by this provision.

[13] Some goods are exempted, *e.g.* identified goods to be imported: BSA 1890, s. 1. An individual need not register charges of particular book debts, hence (e) in the list.

(d) a charge on land (wherever situated) or any interest in it, but not including a charge for any rent or other periodical sum issuing out of the land.

(e) a charge on book debts of the company. This refers to fixed charges.[14]

(f) a floating charge on the company's undertaking or property. This would include floating charges over book debts.

(g) a charge on calls made but not paid.

(h) a charge on a ship or aircraft, or any share in a ship.[15]

(i) a charge on goodwill, on a patent or a licence under a patent, on trademark or on a copyright or a licence under a copyright.[16]

Non-Registrable Transactions

For various reasons, the following are not registrable. **19–038**

Charges which have not been "*created by the company*" are not registrable. A charging order made against the company's property has not been "created by the company" and is therefore not registrable.[17] Rights which arise through the operation of law, such as liens[18] (including a bank's lien over securities deposited with it in the way of banking[19]) and equitable or statutory set-off, are not registrable for the same reason.[20] A chargee whose charge is void because it has not been registered may sometimes claim that it has a lien over the property which has revived if the charge has proved void for non-registration. A lien arising by operation of law, however, is destroyed by the granting of some contractual security right, so that if a person with a lien, such as an unpaid vendor, takes a legal mortgage over the asset, the lien disappears and it does not revive if it turns out that the mortgage is void.[21] Similarly, where title deeds were deposited (as they used to be) to create an equitable mortgage, which might have been registrable, the lien over the deeds could not co-exist with the mortgage.[22]

---

14 See above, para. 19–006.

15 These must also be registered in other registers.

16 Patents and trademarks must also be registered in other registers.

17 *Re Overseas Aviation Engineering (G.B.) Ltd* [1963] Ch.24.

18 See *Re Hamlet International plc (in administration); Trident International v. Barlow* [1999] 2 B.C.L.C. 506, CA.

19 See above, Chap. 11.

20 *e.g.* an unpaid vendor's lien for the price of land sold—*London and Cheshire Insurance Co Ltd v. Laplagrene Property Co Ltd* [1971] Ch. 499—or a solicitor's lien over title deeds, etc., for costs.

21 *Burston Finance Ltd v. Speirway Ltd* [1974] 3 All E.R. 735.

22 *Re Molton Finance Ltd* [1968] Ch. 325; *Wallis and Simmonds (Builders) Ltd* [1974] 1 All E.R. 561 (title deed deposited by company acting as surety. Depositing deeds now has this effect only if the requirements of s. 2, of the LPMPA 1989 are complied with: *United Bank of Kuwait v. Sahib* [1996] 3 All E.R. 215.

19–039 Charges over *choses in action* not specifically mentioned in Section 391 of the CA 1985[23] are not registrable. This means that charges over stocks and shares owned by the company are not registrable unless the charge is floating. The chargee normally registers its title to registrable shares, or takes physical possession of bearer certificates (the absence of the documents would warn others). Charges over life policies are not registrable; if the charge (or assignment) is legal, the life office concerned is notified, and notification gives priority; equitable charges are created simply by taking physical possession of the policy. A deposit of bills of exchange by way of security does not amount to a registrable charge of the company's book debts.[24]

19–040 Charges over *chattels* which are subject to one of the exemptions for individuals are also not registrable: for example, charges over goods in foreign parts or at sea, over identified imported goods, or goods represented by documents of title used in the ordinary course of business. Charges which are purely possessory, like pledges of goods, are not registrable, even if the goods are subsequently released to the pledgor by way of *trust receipt*,[25] which usually specifies that the proceeds of goods belong to the lender, even though the proceeds are actually a book debt of the company: the book debt is deemed to be no more than a consequence of the non-registrable right (the pledge). If the goods had already been validly sold[26] on to another person at the time of the pledge, however, the reference to the proceeds of sale in the trust receipt could only operate as a charge, which would be void if not registered.[27]

19–041 A *Romalpa (reservation of title) clause*[28] may be effective in relation to non-mixed goods, in which case it is *not* registrable, because it is not a charge: but in relation to mixed goods (the products of the original goods and others) or the proceeds of sale, such a clause might operate as a floating charge, and in that case would be registrable. An arrangement which creates a *Quistclose* trust, where a debtor of a company pays money to the company's account with a bank specifically so that the money should repay creditors of the company, may not create a charge, but even if it does, there is a trust as well, which is not registrable.[29]

---

[23] *i.e.* the uncalled share capital, calls made but not paid, floating charges, charges over book debts, goodwill, patents, licences, trademarks, and copyrights.

[24] CA 1985, s. 396(2). See *Chase Manhattan Asia v. Official Receiver* [1990] 1 W.L.R. 1181, PC (promissory note). Discount houses in the City of London may borrow on the security of negotiable instruments, for example (Pennington, *Company Law*, p. 643).

[25] *Re David Allester Ltd*. [1922] 2 Ch. 211.

[26] It will be valid, *e.g.*, if the lender knows of the sale, because the exception to the *nemo dat* rule in s. 25 of the Sale of Goods Act 1979 will operate.

[27] *Ladenburg Co v. Goodwin Ferreira & Co Ltd* [1912] 3 K.B. 275.

[28] See below, Chap. 20.

[29] *Carreras Rothman Ltd v. Freeman Mathews Treasure Ltd* [1985] Ch. 207.

Book debts and registration

Book debts may be payable now or at some future time. In either case, they can be charged and the charge is registrable. For example, hire-purchase agreements can be charged by way of deposit as security for a loan: this is a charge over the book debts due under the agreements, even if they are payable in future.[30] **19–042**

It is possible to create an equitable charge, though not a legal charge, over *future* property.[31] In *Tailby v. Official Receiver,*[32] where the House of Lords accepted that the assignment of future debts was possible, it was said that an inchoate security interest exists from the date of agreement, and an equitable charge attaches when the debt comes into existence without the need for further action, and, for priority purposes, relates back to the date of creation of the security interest. Charges over potential debts are also registrable because the property is deemed to have present existence.

However, fixed charges over a *contingent* book debt, which is an obligation which may become a debt on the occurrence of a certain future event,[33] is not registrable; contingent debts are not "book debts" for this purpose. A debt is contingent if under the terms of a contract it may or may not arise if there is some contingency or condition or event, other than breach of a presently enforceable obligation, upon the occurrence or non-occurrence of which the existence of the debt depends. Until the event occurs, the existence of the debt remains hypothetical. Thus, it has been held that a charge over an existing contractual right (to the benefit of an export credit insurance policy) was not registrable where no book debt existed at the time, even though a book debt might have come into existence if the policy money became payable.[34] **19–043**

Since fixed charges over future book debts *are* registrable, a difficult distinction exists. Book debts which may arise in the future under trading contracts not yet entered into are merely hypothetical, and it might seem that they are contingent on all sorts of eventualities, and should be treated in the same way as contingent debts. Yet it has been said that charges over future debts of this kind are registrable, on the ground that they are not contingent.[35] That they are not contingent is, it is respectfully submitted, an **19–044**

---

[30] *Independent Automatic Sales Ltd v. Knowles & Foster* [1962] 3 All E.R. 27. This must be distinguished from a sale (at a discount) of the agreements, which is a common form of financing: see *Re George Inglefield Ltd* [1933] Ch. 1; *Lloyds and Scottish Finance Ltd v. Prentice* (1977) 121 Sol.Jo. 847.

[31] See *Holroyd v. Marshall* (1862) 10 H.L. Cas. 191 at 220 "At law property, non-existing, but to be acquired at a future time, is not assignable; in equity it is so": *Tailby v. O.R.* (1888) 13 App. Cas. 523; *Re Lind* [1915] 2 Ch. 345.

[32] (1888) 13 App. Cas. 523.

[33] See Oditah, *op.cit.*, p. 30, and authorities cited there.

[34] *Paul and Frank Ltd v. Discount Bank (Overseas) Ltd* [1967] Ch. 348.

[35] See *Independent Automatic Sales Ltd v. Knowles & Foster* [1962] 3 All R.R. 27; *Paul and Frank Ltd v. Discount Bank (Overseas) Ltd and the Board of Trade* [1967] 1 Ch. 348.

odd view. In *Paul and Frank Ltd. v. Discount Bank (Overseas) Ltd.*,[36] Pennycuick J. took the view that contingent debts are non-registrable. The examples he had in mind concerned debts under contracts of insurance, guarantee and the like. These are clear examples of contingent debts, but it is submitted that debts which may arise under contracts which may or may not ever be entered into are just as much contingent as debts arising under contracts of guarantee. Indeed, they are more contingent, since the contracts in question may not ever be entered into. Yet the result of the view criticised is that one is compelled to say that a debt which arises under a contract that may not ever be entered into is not contingent, and a debt which may arise under a contract which has been entered into is contingent. It is submitted that both are contingent, and that either both are registrable or neither are registrable. The preferable view, it is submitted, that despite *Paul and Frank Ltd. v. Discount Bank (Overseas) Ltd,* both should be registrable,[37] and the phrase "book debts" should be interpreted to include all future and contingent book debts.[38] It is advisable to register in cases of doubt.[39]

Method and Effect of Registration

19–045 Strictly speaking, the statutory obligation is to deliver to the Registrar of Companies the *prescribed particulars of the charge* together with the instrument (if any) by which it is created or evidenced, rather than to register it.[40] This must be done within 21 days of the creation of the charge, using a form which must show the prescribed particulars: the company name, the date and description of the charge instrument (or the date on which property already subject to a charge was acquired), the amount owing on the security, names, addresses and descriptions of the chargees, and a short description of the property charged.[41] One of the main problems about the registration system is the "invisibility" of registrable charges during these 21 days, during which subsequent lenders may obtain a

---

[36] [1967] Ch. 348. The obligation to register extends to a charge over a debt under a future contract which will be a book debt when that contract is made, but not to a charge of an existing contract under which no book debt presently subsists, even if a book debt may arise under that contract at a later date.

[37] In *Property Discount Corpn. Ltd v. Lyon Group Ltd* [1981] 1 All E.R. 379 it was said that a charge over property part of which did not yet exist was registrable.

[38] CA 1985, s. 396(1)(e). See Oditah, *op.cit.*, p. 31, for discussion of this case and these views, expressed in this passage in the first edition of this book. He regards the distinction as not illuminating in the discussion of present and future receivables.

[39] Paget, *Law of Banking* (11th ed.) p. 552, suggests that the safest course is always to register a charge over a debt.

[40] CA 1985, s. 395(1).

[41] On the form, and not by way of cross-referencing to other attached documents: *R. v. Registrar of Companies, ex p. Central Bank of India* [1986] 1 All E.R. 105; [1986] Q.B. 1114. If the form submitted to the registrar does not contain the prescribed particulars, the registrar has no discretion to accept a late re-submission, though he or she may correct "obvious clerical or typing errors" without returning the form.

clear search only to find their charges postponed to another charge with priority.

19–046 Although the duty to register is placed upon the company, any "person interested" in the charge may register it and recover the fees from the company.[42] It is a wise precaution for the bank itself to undertake registration, because it is the bank which will suffer the penalty of the charge being void if it is not registered. The registrar keeps a register of charges which contains the prescribed particulars[43] and issues a certificate of registration of the charge.[44] The instrument of charge is returned to the company, which must keep a register of charges at its registered office.[45]

A charge is created (and the 21 day period begins to run) when it is executed by the company, and not at the later date when the money is first advanced.[46] If there is an agreement to give a legal mortgage later, the agreement creates an immediate registrable equitable charge, but even if time for registration of that charge expires, the legal charge, if it is executed at a later date, is valid and can be registered within 21 days of its execution.[47]

19–047 If the particulars are not delivered in time (and this includes cases where defective particulars are delivered) or if there is an omission or misstatement of any particular, then a further charge may be taken, though it may be subject to securities taken by others in the meantime. Alternatively, the bank may apply for an extension of time to the court, which has a discretion to extend the time or to rectify the misstatement "on such terms and conditions as seem to the court just and expedient".[48] Orders will be made subject to a condition to the effect that it is made without prejudice to the rights of parties acquired during the period between the date of creation of the charge and the date of its actual registration.[49] It seems that the court takes a liberal approach, since it always imposes the condition protecting creditors, and possibly only negligence which is serious and gives rise to a suspicion of deliberate delay would debar an extension.[50] If a mistake is

---

[42] CA 1985, s. 399.

[43] CA 1985, s. 401.

[44] A copy of this must be endorsed on any debenture subsequently issued by the company which is secured by that charge: CA 1985, s. 402.

[45] CA 1985, ss. 406–7. This also applies to foreign companies with a place of business here, but in that case the register should be kept at the principal place of business, CA 1985, s. 409.

[46] *Esberger & Son Ltd v. Capital and Counties Bank Ltd* [1913] 2 Ch. 366.

[47] *Re Columbian Fireproofing Co Ltd* [1910] 2 Ch. 120.

[48] If the mistake was "accidental or due to inadvertence or to some other sufficient cause, or is not of a nature to prejudice the position of creditors or shareholders. . . . or that on other grounds it is just and equitable to grant relief": CA 1985, s. 404. "Sufficient cause" can be shown by demonstrating, for example, confusion between different officers: *Re Kris Cruisers Ltd* [1949] Ch. 148.

[49] See *Re Ehrmann Bros Ltd* [1906] 2 Ch. 697; *Exeter Trust Ltd v. Screenways Ltd* [1991] B.C.C. 477, CA. Exceptionally they are not: see *Re Fablehill* [1991] B.C.C. 590, where the directors of the company had taken no steps to ensure that the company registered, and had registered a charge in their own favour.

[50] Or misleading behaviour by a bank, see *Re Telomatic* [1994] 1 B.C.L.C. 90.

discovered, an application for an extension should be made immediately; the court will look askance at a chargee who deliberately delays.[51] Normally, an order will not be made after the company has gone into liquidation[52] or where a winding up petition has been presented or is imminent,[53] unless the circumstances are exceptional.[54]

Certificate conclusive

19–048 When the charge is registered (or, strictly speaking, where the prescribed particulars have been delivered in time) the registrar delivers a certificate of registration, which is conclusive evidence that the requirements as to registration have been satisfied.[55] Once the certificate has been issued, compliance with section 395 of the CA 1985 cannot be challenged.[56] The registrar has no discretion to accept a late submission, and acts *ultra vires* if he or she does so, but the certificate still cannot be challenged. There would be an exception for fraud—for example, where an attempt is made to deceive the registrar by deliberate falsification of the date.[57]

Effect of Non-Registration

19–049 If a charge is not registered, it becomes void against the liquidator, the administrator, or any creditor of the company.[58] "Creditor" here means secured creditor[59] or an execution creditor who has completed execution; it does not include an unsecured creditor unless the company is in liquidation (or possibly while the company is in administration). However, a purchaser, as opposed to a creditor, may be bound by an unregistered charge, unless he or she acquires an overriding legal title or can claim an estoppel.[60]

The company's personal obligation or contract to repay the money remains enforceable,[61] and the money secured by the charge in fact

[51] *Victoria Housing Estates, Ltd v. Ashpurton Estates, Ltd* [1982] 3 All E.R. 665; [1983] Ch. 110.
[52] *Re Eric Holmes (Property) Ltd* [1965] Ch. 1052; *Re Mechanisations (Eaglescliffe) Ltd* [1966] Ch. 20.
[53] *Victoria Housing Estates, Ltd v. Ashpurton Estates Ltd* [1982] 3 All E.R. 665; [1983] Ch. 110.
[54] See *Re R. M. Arnold & Co Ltd* [1984] B.C.L.C. 535, where there appeared to be no unsecured creditors to be prejudiced, and where priority between secured creditors needed to be established.
[55] CA 1985, s. 401(2). See *National Provincial and Union Bank of England v. Charnley* [1924] 1 K.B. 431.
[56] *National Provincial & Union Bank of England v. Charnley* [1924] 1 K.B. 431; *Re Mechanisations (Eaglescliffe) Ltd* [1966] Ch. 20; *Re Eric Homes (Property) Ltd* [1965] Ch. 1052; *Re C. L. Nye Ltd* [1971] Ch. 442; *R. v. Registrar of Companies, ex p. Central Bank of India* [1986] 1 All E.R. 105; *Exeter Trust Ltd v. Screenways Ltd* [1991] B.C.C. 477, CA.
[57] In the *Central Bank* case [1986] 1 All E.R. 105, the court left open the possibility of challenge by judicial review.
[58] CA 1985, s. 395, as amended by the IA 1986. Professor Goode, *op. cit.*, p. 704, regards the sanction of avoidance as too drastic, particularly when creditors may well have given full public notice of their charge in some other register.
[59] *Re Telomatic Ltd.* [1994] 1 B.C.L.C. 90 at 95, Ch D. See also *Re Ayala Holdings Ltd* [1993] B.C.L.C. 256.
[60] *Stroud Architectural Systems Ltd v. John Laing Construction Ltd* [1994] B.C.C. 18. See Goode, *op. cit.*, p. 721.
[61] See *Re Cosslett (Contractors) Ltd* [1997] 4 All E.R. 115, CA.

becomes immediately payable, regardless of any term originally allowed.[62] The unregistered charge even remains effective against the company itself, if it is not in liquidation, and no other secured creditor claims priority.[63] It has been held, therefore, that if the debenture holder seizes and realises the asset in question before liquidation begins, the liquidator may not demand the return of the proceeds.[64]

Priorities of Charges

Certain types of property, such as land, are subject to other registration requirements as well, and even if a particular charge has been registered under the CA 1985 and apparently has priority, that priority may be lost because of non-compliance with, for example, the Land Registration Act 1925 (LRA 1925). Here only the effect of the CA 1985 is considered. **19–050**

Provided that the charge is registered within twenty-one days, it has priority according to the date of its creation. Non-registration affects priorities by rendering the charge void against the liquidator, unsecured creditors in the liquidation and an administrator, and thus defeats priorities otherwise established.[65]

Notice and Priorities

Registration (delivery of particulars) affects priorities by giving notice of the existence of the charge,[66] and non-registration may defeat an existing priority. There is no system of priority notices, however, as there is for land registration. **19–051**

It is an important and unresolved question as to what aspects of charges registration gives notice. It seems that registration may only be notice of the existence of the charge, not of its contents,[67] which may include, for example, a *negative pledge*.[68] It is uncertain therefore whether a chargee with a registered floating charge who wishes to protect its interest over

---

62 CA 1985, s. 395(2).

63 See *Independent Automatic Sales Ltd v. Knowles & Foster* [1962] 3 All E.R. 27 (company not a proper party to proceedings to have charge declared void).

64 *Mace Builders (Glasgow) Ltd v. Lunn* [1986] Ch. 459; [1986] 3 W.L.R. 921, CA, applied in *Power v. Sharp* [1992] B.C.L.C. 636, CA.

65 This is the effect of CA 1985, s. 395.

66 A subsequent purchaser or mortgagee has constructive notice of the matters which would come to his or her notice through "such enquiries as ought reasonably to be made by him": LPA 1925, s. 199(1) (Encl.(1113)); which would include a search at the Companies Registry, but not an inspection of the debenture itself, *Siebe Gorman* [1979] 2 Lloyd's Rep. 142. See also *Snell on Equity* (29th ed., 1990) pp. 51–2; *Palmer's Company Law*, Vol. 2, para. 13.127.

67 See *Siebe Gorman & Co. Ltd v. Barclays Bank Ltd* [1979] 2 Lloyd's Rep. 142.

68 *Cf. Ian Chisholm Textiles Ltd v. Griffiths* [1994] 2 B.C.L.C. 291 at 303. See also *Griffiths v. Yorkshire Bank plc* [1994] 1 W.L.R. 1427, where Morritt J. said that a restriction does not affect priorities as a matter of property law, but may have a contractual result (at 1435). But see Goode's comments in *Commercial Law*, pp. 741 and 742, nn. 59 and 66. See now also *Linden Gardens Trust Ltd v. Lenesta Sludge Disposals Ltd* [1993] 3 All E.R. 417, HL.

other creditors can do so successfully by a negative pledge, because, although it is binding between the two parties, it can only affect third parties who have notice of it. Although the existence of a negative pledge is usually noted in the particulars filed with the registrar of companies, it is not one of the particulars which *must* be filed, and other creditors, who need not examine the register, may not be aware of its existence. It may be that negative pledge clauses are now so common that if details of the pledge are noted on the register and an inspection would reveal them, a person who did not investigate would be held to have constructive notice and would not be able to rely upon the company's apparent authority to grant the charge. In reality, negative pledges in both fixed and floating charges are now so common that people in commercial life would be very surprised not to find them, especially in a bank debenture form. If the position has been reached when commercial people would expect to find a particular provision in most charges, the prospective chargees ought to be taken to have "factually inferred" constructive notice of such a provision if they do not at least make the reasonable inquiry of searching the Companies Register. It seems almost to amount to turning a blind eye to disregard the prevalence of such clauses.[69] Some take the view, however, that it is an unreasonable extension of equitable concepts to impose constructive notice on lenders in these cases.[70] It is also argued that since creditors are not obliged to search the register, it is unfair to expect them to be on inquiry for notification of particulars which companies are not required to include in the register.[71]

19–052 *Fixed charges*, whether legal or equitable, encumber the asset and rank ahead of floating charges, over later fixed charges and, in winding-up, over the preferential creditors. Since a floating charge is designed precisely for the purpose of allowing dealings with the assets to which it applies, mere knowledge (actual, or by registration) of the existence of a floating charge does not prevent a subsequent sale, charge or other disposition of the asset, and a subsequent fixed charge, whether equitable or legal, would take priority over a prior floating charge unless the fixed charge was granted outside the ordinary course of the company's business to a chargee with

[69] This argument is put by Farrar (1974) 38 Conv. 315, and appears in *Buckley on the Companies Acts* (14th edn., 1981), p. 625. It is not accepted by Goode, *op. cit.*, pp. 718–9, by Pennington, p. 577, or by Gower, p. 475. The treatment in the Encyclopedia, E (1113) is somewhat ambiguous. There is also a question whether purchasers would now have "factually inferred" notice of a fixed charge over future book debts, which have become common since the decision in *Siebe Gorman & Co. Ltd v. Barclays Bank Ltd* [1979] 2 Lloyd's Rep. 142.

[70] See Lightman and Moss, *The Law of Receivers of Companies* (2nd ed.) pp. 41 *et seq.*, and authorities cited there.

[71] Goode, *Commercial Law* (2nd ed.) p. 716.

notice of the earlier charge.[72] Some fixed charges do not require registration, unlike floating charges, which must all be registered.[73]

19–053 As between fixed charges, the established common law rule is that as between attached charges of the same kind (for example, legal charge versus legal charge) the first in time prevails; and as between attached charges of different kinds (legal versus equitable), a legal charge will prevail over the equitable charge, even if the legal charge attaches after the equitable charge, provided that the legal charge is taken bona fide, for value and without notice of the prior equitable charge. Registration, of course, gives notice of prior charges, so that there should not be a purchaser "without notice". But the bona fide purchaser rule would still operate if the charges are both created before the prior equitable one is registered, because notice is given only on delivery of particulars, and cannot work retrospectively.

19–054 **Floating charges.** A subsequent floating charge will not have priority over an earlier floating charge relating to the same assets even if the later charge attaches first,[74] unless the earlier debenture expressly allows the company to create later charges in priority over specified assets.[75]

With regard to dealings with third parties, a company whose property is subject to a floating charge has "an implied business licence", under which it may carry on business and effect transactions with the property without the consent of the chargee.[76] The effect is that the charge does not affect third parties while it continues to float.[77] Rights of set-off between the company and a third party debtor may continue to accrue, therefore, and will affect a floating charge covering the debts in question, even if the third party knows of the charge.[78] Probably even an (unknown) crystallization would not affect this position, since the company would still have apparent authority to deal with the debtor. Similarly, rights of lien arising before crystallization may be asserted against the floating charge, and if a party contracts for possession of assets for a purpose which may give rise to a lien, the relevant priority date is the date of the contract, not the date at which possession is actually taken if that is later.[79]

---

72 *Fire Nymph Products Ltd v. The Heating Centre Pty. Ltd* (1992) 7 A.C.S.R. 365 at 367; Lightman and Moss, *op. cit.*, p. 42.

73 See above, paras 19–037 *et seq. e.g.* a charge over a debt which is not a book debt, or over stocks and shares.

74 *Re Benjamin Cope & Sons Ltd* [1914] 1 Ch. 800.

75 *Re Automatic Bottle Makers Ltd* [1926] Ch. 412; *Re Household Products Co Ltd* (1981) 124 G.L.R. (3d.) 325. See Gough, *op. cit.*, p. 275.

76 Gough, *op. cit.*, Chap. 12.

77 Goode, *L.P.C.S.*, p. 84, who goes on to say that crystallisation does not work retrospectively and the subordination of some interests consequent on it is not always easy to explain and has never been fully analysed by the courts.

78 See *Biggerstaff v. Rowatt's Wharf Ltd* [1896] 2 Ch. 93; *Rother Iron Works Ltd v. Canterbury Precision Engineers Ltd* [1974] Q.B.1.

79 *George Barker (Transport) Ltd v. Eynon* [1974] 1 All E.R. 900.

19–055 **Floating charges over book debts.** Normally, priorities over choses in action are determined by the rule in *Dearle v. Hall*[80]—that is, by the order in which notice is given to the debtor. But that rule cannot apply to floating charges over book debts, "for the floating chargee, having impliedly authorised the subsequent fixed charge, cannot jump ahead by being the first to give notice to the debtor after the charge has crystallised".[81] Nevertheless, the debtor would be entitled to a good discharge if he or she paid the first legal assignee to give notice, and there is no reason to prevent the floating chargee from attempting to perfect its priority position through notice.[82]

19–056 **After crystallization.** The floating charge becomes fixed and has priority over subsequent interests. After crystallization, the company has no right to deal with property subject to the charge, though if it does do so, the priority of the first charge probably remains unless a bona fide purchaser takes without notice.[83]

Future Property

19–057 As we have seen, an agreement to give security over future property is not recognised at law as creating a security interest but it is recognised in equity,[84] and, although there is no property to which anything can have attached, a present security right is created. The significance of this is first, that if a subsequent creditor[85] takes a similar agreement from the same debtor, the first creditor will take priority if an asset comes into existence; and secondly, the security interest automatically attaches to property which is acquired later without new value being given.

Priorities in future property between a chargeholder and a subsequent purchase-money financier

19–058 Normally, A's prior charge over future property would defeat B's later charge. However, if the debtor borrows money from B to finance the purchase of the asset and gives B security over the asset, it seems right that B should have priority over A. This may happen, depending when B's

---

[80] (1828) 3 Russ. 1.

[81] Goode, *L.P.C.S.* (1st ed.) p. 43, citing *Ward v. Royal Exchange Shipping Co Ltd* (1887) 58 L.T. 174; *Re Ind Coope & Co Ltd* [1911] 2 Ch. 223. The rule in *Dearle v. Hall* is impracticable and inefficient when applied to a continuous flow of dealings in receivables and a large number of debtors: Goode, *op. cit.*, p. 705. See also Oditah: "It is a poor reflection on our law that in this day and age an account debtor should be treated as a kind of public register of notices of assignment," *op. cit.*, at p. 3. See also Brown [1995] 1 J.I.B.L. 3, who comments on the "genuine practical problems" in giving notice to each subsequent debtor.

[82] According to Gough, *op. cit.*, p. 278.

[83] Goode, *L.P.C.S.*, p. 90.

[84] See *Holroyd v. Marshall* (1862) 10 H.L. Cas. 191.

[85] A "purchase-money creditor" may be an exception, see immediately below.

security is taken. If B's security is created before the debtor agrees to buy the asset, B's security rights will attach to the asset when the debtor acquires his or her rights in it, and will take priority over A's charge,[86] but if the debtor acquires the asset and *later* grants security to B, A's charge should take priority, because there will have been time for it to attach while the debtor had the unencumbered asset. If so, B's charge can only attach subsequently, and A therefore has priority. It used to be thought that A's charge would have priority even if the purchase and A's charge took place *simultaneously*, because there was thought to be a moment of time between the two during which the debtor could charge the asset, and in that case, A's charge would fasten on the asset before B's. *Abbey National Building Society v. Cann*[87] decided that there is no such intervening moment, and it is likely, therefore, that in these circumstances B's charge would be regarded as ranking in priority.

Waiver of Security Interests

A bank may ask a secured creditor to waive its security rights in the bank's favour as a condition of making further advances to the company, or the bank itself may be asked to waive its rights.[88] Where a floating charge is involved, the bank may not be willing to give a waiver, but may be prepared to give a certificate that nothing has happened which as yet has caused the charge to crystallize. If such a *certificate of non-crystallization* is given, then it should be expressed as a statement that the bank is not aware of any crystallizing event, not as an absolute statement that no crystallization has taken place. **19–059**

If a waiver is given, it is revocable by reasonable notice, unless it is made by deed or for valuable consideration (in which case it is a binding agreement, not a waiver) or unless the party to whom it is given relies on it and the party giving would be estopped from retracting it because it would be inequitable to do so.[89] Thus, once the other party has advanced money on the strength of the waiver, retraction would be impossible in relation to any transactions covered by the waiver. If a secured lender were to waive its rights and later to assign the debt and security to another person, that other person would be bound by the waiver, because the assignee's rights can be **19–060**

---

[86] See *Wilson v. Kelland* [1910] 2 Ch. 306; *Re Connolly Bros Ltd (No. 2)* [1912] 2 Ch. 25; *Security Trust Co. v. The Royal Bank of Canada* [1976] A.C. 503.

[87] [1991] 1 A.C. 56. In *Cann*, the House of Lords overruled *Church of England Building Society v. Piskor* [1954] 1 Ch. 553, in which it had been held that there was a moment of time (*scintilla temporis*) between the purchase and the charge being created. But see Goode, *op. cit.*, p. 724.

[88] Goode, *L.P.C.S.*, p. 54. See above Chap. 16, particularly the discussion of *Re Woodroffe's* and *Re Portbase Clothing*, where a particular problem of priorities was occasioned by a fixed chargee agreeing to subordinate itself to a floating charge where there were preferential creditors in a liquidation.

[89] See Treitel, *The Law of Contract* (10th ed.) pp. 98 *et seq.*

no greater than those of the assignor; he or she takes " subject to equities".[90]

Standard form Debentures

19–061 Banks generally have standard forms,[91] normally of the *all monies* type, at least where the debenture secures an overdraft rather than a specific loan. These normally include the following clauses[92]:

(a) The company agrees to pay on demand existing or future debts or liabilities on any account, whether it is solely or jointly liable, and whether as principal or surety; it also agrees to pay charges, interest and any costs to the bank.[93]

(b) The company charges certain property with repayment of the debts specified. Generally there is a legal fixed charge over any freehold and leasehold property, and perhaps over fixed machinery, if any; these assets will be specified in a schedule. A fixed equitable charge can be taken over any similar property which may be obtained in future (a charge taken over future property must be equitable). Fixed charges, which may be legal or equitable, are taken over uncalled or unpaid capital, over shares in and securities of subsidiaries, over book debts, and over goodwill. Finally, a floating security is taken over the "undertaking" of the company and all its other assets not already charged, either existing or which may afterwards be acquired.[94]

(c) There are generally prohibitive clauses:

   (i) a negative pledge clause, prohibiting the creation of liens or securities ranking equally or ahead of this one;
   (ii) a clause stating that the bank is to hold all title deeds in relation to land, and that the company agrees to execute legal charges in relation to equitably charged property when called on to do so;
   (iii) the company agrees not to dispose of the undertaking or any part of it unless the bank consents;

---

[90] Goode, *L.P.C.S.*, p. 53, noting that it may be different in the case of land.

[91] These are standard form contracts, but will not be governed by the UTCCR 1999, since companies cannot be consumers (who must be "natural persons", reg.2). Similarly, the Banking Code does not apply to transactions with corporate customers.

[92] Following the model in the Encyclopaedia, I (921).

[93] This covenant to repay on demand (a) does not affect the existence or nature of debts, so that if the debenture is released, the separate debt is still actionable: *Barclays Bank Ltd v. Beck* [1952] 2 Q.B. 47; and (b) does not change the terms of loans previously granted for fixed terms, unless this is made clear: *Williams and Glyn's Bank Ltd v. Barnes* [1981] Comm. L.R. 205.

[94] This is included so that the bank may then block the appointment of an administrator for the company (if for no other reason). See further below, Chap. 24.

(iv) clauses setting out prohibitions against the company dealing with (selling, factoring, discounting or assigning) charged debts, except for getting them in and paying them into the bank account; the company agrees to execute an assignment in such form as the bank reasonably requires if called on to do so.

(d) A "crystallisation" or "realisation" clause, specifying the events on which the bank debt is repayable and the security becomes enforceable. Relevant events may be:

(i) a demand for repayment made by the bank;
(ii) a breach of the prohibitive clauses or failure to repay interest or capital as agreed (perhaps for 14 days);
(iii) a petition for winding up is presented;
(iv) a receiver is appointed by another creditor;
(v) distress is levied or any form of execution issued;
(vi) the company ceases to carry on substantially the whole of its business.

(e) Provision for the bank to appoint a receiver and manager (or administrative receiver), whose powers are extensively described and include realising the assets secured including the whole business and managing the company; the receiver will be described as the company's agent, not the bank's.

(f) Provision for distributing the proceeds of realisation.

(g) An irrevocable power of attorney appointing the bank as agent to do what is necessary to enforce the debenture and to appoint others as substitute agents.

(h) The company agrees:

to repair and maintain land and insure all the property, and to allow the bank to remedy the failure if there is default (the bank's costs will also be secured);
not to lease property or accept surrenders of leases unless the bank consents;
to pay all debts as they fall due, and inform the bank of any proceedings against it. It also agrees to keep its records in good order and to supply copies of accounts and notices of meetings to the bank.

(j) It is stated that the security is in addition to existing securities, not in substitution for them, and that it is a continuing security[95] and

[95] A "continuing security for all debts liabilities and obligations from time to time of the company to the Bank".

unaffected by payment of any monies to the bank, so that *Clayton's Case*[96] will not operate to reduce the original debt and replace it with a new one which is not secured.

(k) The bank is given power to close the account and to open a new one (if it learns of other charges, for example) and is deemed to do so in any case (again, so that *Clayton's Case* will not affect its claim as against another mortgagee). It may combine accounts if there is a credit balance in another account of the company.

(l) The company certifies that the charges do not contravene the Memorandum or Articles.

(m) There may be administrative provisions about interpretation, the making of demands, service of documents and so forth.

Company Stocks and Shares as Security

19–062 In the present context, the word "securities" is used to refer to documents representing choses in action, such as stocks and shares, and bonds or debentures. Other forms of tradeable securities include certificates of deposit, bank bills, and American depository receipts. These are all capable of providing *security* in the usual legal sense by way of mortgage, charge or pledge, to support lending.[97] Here, we examine two kinds of company shares, bearer or registered, and their use as security.[98] Banks generally deal in "quoted" securities, which are dealt on the Stock Exchange.[99] Shares in quoted companies are easily valued, though the valuation of shares in private companies is more difficult, and the security value is more doubtful, because they are difficult to sell.

Traditional paper transactions are rapidly giving way to electronic or computerised transactions—a process known as *dematerialisation*—and dematerialised securities may also be charged by way of legal or equitable mortgage. There is a brief outline of the new Stock Exchange electronic system at the end of the Chapter.

Bearer securities

19–063 Negotiable instruments are documents of title to a chose in action, capable of transfer by delivery, or by delivery and indorsement, which make the transferee the legal owner of a perfect title to the chose in action,

---

96 (1816) 8 L.J. Ch 256, see above, Chap. 11.

97 It is thus possible to speak of "taking security over securities".

98 Or "collateral" security.

99 See Milnes Holden, *The Law and Practice of Banking* (8th ed.) Vol. 2 (*Securities for Bankers' Advances*), Part IV. The CA 1948 restrictions on the transfer of "unquoted" shares, has been repealed (Companies Act 1980, Sched. 4), so that private companies are not now obliged to include such restrictions in their Articles of Association.

regardless of any defects in the transferor's title.[1] If the instrument (or "security") is capable of being transferred by delivery alone, it is a *bearer* security. Bearer securities do not name a payee or holder; they generally contain an order or promise by the drawer to pay "Bearer", and do not require registration to perfect the transferee's title against the drawer. The obvious risk to the owner of bearer certificates is that a thief could transfer good title to an innocent purchaser.

If bearer securities are delivered to a bank by way of security for a fresh advance, they are taken for value. If they are taken as security for a past advance, the consideration must be expressed as being for continuing the account, though if a bill of exchange is deposited as security, the bank takes for value if the customer is in debt to the bank at the time, because past consideration is good consideration for liability on a bill.[2]

The bank has no duty to inquire as to the ownership of securities deposited as security,[3] though it might not take in good faith if facts exist which put it on enquiry.

The bank becomes legal owner when the security is delivered to the bank **19–064** if it is intended to create a mortgage, or pledgee otherwise—bearer stock is made available as security by way of pledge rather than mortgage.[4] In either capacity, the bank has the right of sale, and so there is no need to specify which is intended, though if the security is not sold outright to the bank to discharge liabilities, a Memorandum of Deposit may refer to the receipt of the security "by way of security". The banker has a lien[5] for the customer's debts (and an implied right of sale), even if the securities are not deposited by way of security but for some other function of a banker's business.

Delivery may be *constructive:* bonds or debentures, for example, may be held by a depository or clearing house. If a third party acknowledges the title of another person (the bank) to the instruments and agrees to hold them for that person, that is sufficient delivery to transfer legal title. Internationally traded securities, for example, may be held by clearing houses. Realisation of the security is also achieved by delivery.[6]

Security over bearer certificates is easy to take, realisation is simple, and the bank faces no risks as to the customer's title because the security is negotiable.

---

1 Provided that the transferee takes a document which is complete and regular on its face, for value, in good faith, and without notice of any defect in his transferor's title. See further Chap. 13.

2 BOEA 1882, s. 27.

3 See *London Joint Stock Bank Ltd v. Simmons* [1892] A.C. 201, where the customer was a stockbroker who pledged bonds belonging to his clients, and *Lloyds Bank Ltd v. Swiss Bankverein Ltd* (1913) 108 L.T. 142, where the court held that a negotiable instrument is not to be impressed with vendor's lien, implied trust or constructive notice. Contrast *Colonial Bank v. Cady and Williams* (1890) 15 App. Cas. 267, where the instruments were not negotiable.

4 Milnes Holden, *op. cit.,* p. 191.

5 See Chap. 11.

6 The provisions of the CCA 1974 do not apply to pledges of documents of titles (CCA 1974, s. 114) or to bearer bonds: BA 1979, s. 38(2).

Registered stocks and shares

19–065 A holder of stock or shares is given a certificate (in the traditional system[7]) and the names of stockholders or shareholders are entered on a register kept by the company. Legal title is transferred, not by delivery of a document alone, but by a proper transfer followed by registration. A new certificate is issued in favour of the transferee.

Whether the bank has legal or equitable title, it must take reasonable care on realising the shares to obtain a proper price for the property.[8]

Legal and Equitable Title

Legal mortgage

19–066 A legal mortgage is effected by transferring stocks or shares (usually by means of a stock transfer form,[9] to the bank) subject to an agreement that they will be transferred back to the borrower when the advance is repaid.[10] In fact, transfer is usually to a nominee company (a subsidiary) of the bank, which makes it easier to carry out duties, for example concerning the use of the bank's seal, expecially on re-transfer. The share certificate is not a negotiable instrument,[11] but a certificate under the company seal is prima facie evidence of legal title to the shares.[12]

If the bank acquires legal title as a bona fide purchaser without notice, it will defeat any equitable title in the normal way; but if the bank has actual or constructive notice of the existence of an equitable owner, it will take subject to his or her rights.[13] In order to acquire legal title, the proper method of transfer must be used[14] and the bank must be registered[15] as legal owner (not mortgagee) with the company. Until it is registered, the bank only has an equitable title, and the company is not bound to give any

[7] See below, para. for the CREST (electronic) system.

[8] *Bishop v. Bonham* [1988] 1 W.L.R. 742, CA. This is on the basis of the "*Cuckmere* principle" (*Cuckmere Brick Co. Ltd v. Mutual Finance Ltd* [1971] Ch. 949, CA see below Chap. 21).

[9] Where legal title is to be obtained by registration, a document (transfer form) must be used, notwithstanding anything in the company's articles, CA 1985, s. 183. Even if the articles prescribe a certain form of transfer, a "stock transfer form" may often be used, Stock Transfer Act 1963, though it can only be used for fully paid up registered securities, *ibid*, s. 1.

[10] Banks normally create a separate nominee company, (rather than have personal nominees in the bank) into whose names the securities are transferred. It is essential for the bank to keep accurate records of transactions, Milnes Holden, *op. cit.*, p. 165.

[11] *Swan v. North British Australasian Co. Ltd* (1862) 7 H & N 603.

[12] CA 1985, s. 186. Not of equitable title: *Shropshire Union Railways and Canal Co. v. R.* (1875) L.R. 7 H.L. 496.

[13] See *Colonial Bank v. Cady and Williams* (1890) 15 App. Cas. 267 where executors signed blank transfers and gave them to stockbrokers for sale. The brokers pledged them to a bank for their own purposes. The court held that the bank was put on inquiry as to the brokers' authority. This was distinguished in *Fry v. Smellie,* [1912] 3 K.B. 282. See also *Société Général de Paris v. Walker* (1885) 11 App. Cas. 201; *Moore v. North Western Bank* [1891] 2 Ch. 599.

[14] See below.

[15] Company articles always require them.

recognition to the rights of an equitable owner.[16] Registration alone, though, is not enough to confer legal title unless the proper method of transfer is used,[17] which includes the requirement for the signature of the registered owner or of his or her authorised agent.

A Memorandum of Deposit is often taken by the bank, even when a legal mortgage is created, to show that the transfer is by way of security only.

The advantages of taking legal title are first, that registration protects against later titles; secondly that registration defeats an earlier unknown equitable title; and thirdly, that the bank has full control over the securities, since it is able to sell without recourse to the courts, and is entitled to all rights such as bonus shares, rights issues, dividends, and votes. The disadvantages or risks of legal title (apart from those arising from the slight risk of a forged share transfer) include the fact that the registered shareholder may be under obligations affecting the person with legal title, such as liability for calls on unpaid shares or on winding-up.

Forgery. A forgery on a transfer will confer no legal title even though the bank has the share certificate and obtains registration, because the certificate is only prima facie evidence of title. In this event, the true legal owner may bring an action for rectification of the register if the company disputes the title. However, the company is estopped from denying the truth of any statement in the share certificate as against a person who acts on the faith of it and suffers loss.[18] If a thief steals a certificate, forges a transfer and obtains registration, and the bank relies on the new certificate showing the thief as owner, the bank therefore has a remedy against the company. But if the thief steals the old certificate, produces it with a forged transfer to the bank, and the bank obtains registration, the bank has no remedy against the company, because its loss was caused by the use of the forged transfer, not by relying on the company's statement. Furthermore, if the bank obtains registration and sells the shares on to another person, the buyer has a remedy against the bank for selling him or her what it did not own. 19–067

In this latter case, where the shares have been sold on, the buyer might take action against the company, on whose new certificate naming the bank he or she relied. Here, the company would have a remedy against the bank, because the company had relied on the transfer form sent in by the bank, which is taken to have made an implied promise to indemnify the company.[19] The issue of the new certificate to the bank does not assist the bank, because that has been obtained by the bank's own misrepresentation, and so the bank cannot rely on it as against the company.[20] In all these

[16] CA 1985, s. 360.

[17] *Powell v. London and Provincial Bank* [1893] 2 Ch. 555, 566.

[18] *Balkis Consolidated Co. v. Tomkinson* [1892] A.C. 396.

[19] *Sheffield Corporation v. Barclay* [1905] A.C. 392; *Bank of England v. Cutler* [1908] 2 K.B. 208; *Oliver v. Bank of England* [1902] 1 Ch. 610.

[20] See especially *Sheffield Corporation v. Barclay* [1905] A.C. 392.

cases, the original "true" owner may have the register rectified, and will suffer no loss.[21] Any dividends received by the bank belong to the true owner.

There are risks, therefore, in dealing with a person whose signature is unknown, even if he or she has the share certificates, and the clearest possible identification is required. It may be added that there is no substantial risk from a forgery of the share certificate itself, as opposed to forgery of a signature, since when the bank sends the certificate in for registration, the company will identify the forgery, unless it is negligent.

Equitable mortgage

19–068 It is not uncommon for the bank to remain content with equitable title because of the speed and convenience of obtaining it. This may be done first merely by a memorandum evidencing the security right; secondly by taking possession of the certificates (this is preferred); or, thirdly, by a reliable third party agreeing to hold them for the bank. A Memorandum of Deposit may be used to establish the purpose for which the bank has the certificates and setting out the terms of the mortgage. The memorandum may cover all securities deposited, or only those mentioned in a schedule. In either case, it is stated to be a continuing security for all monies from time to time owing and on any account; this prevents *Clayton's Case*[22] from discharging both the debt and the security. Also, where the securities belong to a third party surety, appropriate terms will be included, similar to those included in guarantees,[23] for example, entitling the bank to vary arrangements with the debtor. Other terms give the bank a power of sale, the right to demand the execution of further documents if required to perfect the bank's title, the right to substitute equivalent securities on redemption,[24] and perhaps a clause entitling the bank to "re-pledge" the securities as security for re-financing operations.[25] Where a memorandum is signed by two parties it should be joint and several, so that it covers not only joint holdings and liabilities, but also separately owned holdings and separate liabilities.

19–069 Realisation on default would have to be effected by application to the court for sale or foreclosure,[26] unless the bank has protected itself. To avoid

[21] If the company discovers the forgery before registration, the bank cannot compel the company to register the bank's title: *Simm v. Anglo-American Telegraph Co.* (1879) 5 Q.B.D. 188.

[22] (1816) 1 Mer. 572. See above, Chap. 11.

[23] See Chap. 18.

[24] The originals may be transferred to a nominee company for administrative purposes, and if it handles large volumes, it may be administratively difficult to keep the originals separate.

[25] Another reason for providing for substitute securities.

[26] See *Harrold v. Plenty* [1901] 2 Ch. 314. There is a duty of care on the bank on realising the shares, however, in so far as it must take reasonable care to obtain a proper price for the property. *Bishop v. Bonham* [1988] 1 W.L.R. 742 CA.

that, one or more of the following may be done: first, the owner may sign a transfer form, leaving other details blank[27]—this is the normal practice; secondly, an irrevocable power of attorney may be taken which enables the bank to sell as agent, or thirdly, the Memorandum of Deposit may be taken by deed: in that case, there will be a power of sale under the Law of Property Act 1925, Section 101.

As we have mentioned, it may be sensible to take equitable title using a blank form—if, for example, the articles require that a signed transfer is taken, but a stock transfer form cannot be used because the shares have not been fully paid.[28] If the bank has a transfer form (or power of attorney, or deed giving a statutory power of sale) which has already been executed, it may in the event of default or insolvency simply insert its own name, register, and become legal owner.[29] The advantage of using a blank transfer form was explained by Millett J. in *Macmillan Inc. v. Bishopsgate Investment Trust (No. 3)*[30]: the bank can avoid the inconvenience and the commercially unacceptable procedures of registration at the time the money is advanced, knowing that it can later, without recourse to the legal owner, obtain a legal interest in the shares which will give it priority over an earlier equitable interest even if it had actual notice of that interest at the time when it advanced the money.[31]

Of course, if the bank has only an equitable title, it may be defeated by a **19–070**
bona fide purchaser for value and without notice of the bank's rights,[32] but the possession of the certificates is some protection against that happening. It is not a complete protection, because there is a procedure for a registered owner to obtain a replacement certificate on certifying the loss or destruction of the originals. It is difficult for the bank to protect itself against this slight risk, because the company is entitled to disregard any equitable interests,[33] and does not need to note on its records that the bank has the certificates, (though it may be prepared to do so) so that there is no need to make duplicates available to anyone else. However, a "stop notice"[34] may be served on the company, requiring the company to give the bank (or another equitable owner) eight days warning of intention to

[27] The efficacy of blank transfers was approved in *Ireland v. Hart* [1902] Ch. 522 at 527.

[28] A stock transfer form may only be used for fully paid up registered securities: Stock Transfer Act 1963, s. 1(4). Where shares are traded on the Stock Exchange, a different form is provided. See S.I. 1979 No. 277 and Stock Transfer Act 1982.

[29] Otherwise, the trustee or liquidator may execute the transfer or the court may order a sale of the shares and payment of the bank's share of the proceeds to the bank.

[30] [1996] 1 All E.R. 585.

[31] If a deed of transfer is used, the details (including the date) must not be left blank because this would not be a valid deed and the bank would be left with only equitable title, see *Powell v. London and Provincial Bank* [1893] 2 Ch. 555.

[32] See *Coleman v. London County and Westminster Bank Ltd* [1916] 2 Ch. 353; *Fry v. Smellie* [1912] 3 K.B. 282; *c.f. Colonial Bank v. Cady and Williams,* (1890) 15 App. Cas. 267. See also *Macmillan Inc. v. Bishopsgate Investment Trust plc.*

[33] CA 1985, s. 360.

[34] Under the Rules of the Supreme Court.

transfer the shares and allowing time for notice to be given to the purchaser or for an injunction to be obtained. This requires the expense and delay of an application to the court, however, and as the purpose of taking an equitable title is to save time and expense, it rather defeats the object of the exercise. Another risk is that the company may claim a lien over the shares for debts owed by the registered owner to the company. This risk, which does not exist for fully paid shares of a public company,[35] is avoided by the bank sending a "notice of lien" to the company, after which no new rights of lien effective against the bank may be acquired.[36] Apart from these risks, the equitable title should assure priority to the bank in the event of the registered shareholder's insolvency.

It is administratively simple, cheap and private to take equitable title, it does not expose the bank to any liability on the share obligations, and does not affect the customer's legal title. Nevertheless, there are disadvantages. These include, first, the risk that the customer will fail to pay calls and will be deprived of title—this would defeat the bank's title; secondly, defeat by a *prior* equitable title; thirdly, fraud by the registered shareholder leading to a bona fide purchaser obtaining good legal title through duplicate certificates (again, this would defeat the bank's title); and, fourthly, the issue of bonus of rights issues to the registered shareholder, and not to the bank. In particular, on a rights issue, as mentioned below, the increase of allotted shares will tend to depress the price of all shares. Although the Memorandum taken by the bank entitles it to new issues, a risk remains until the certificates come into its possession.

As stated earlier, the bank can avoid the difficulty of having to make an application to the court for sale by taking an executed transfer form, an irrevocable power of attorney or a Memorandum under deed.

Rights Issues and Bonus Issues

19–071 A rights issue or issue of bonus shares may have a serious effect on the value of the bank's security if the bank is unaware of it.

On a rights issue, where the company issues new shares to existing shareholders, usually on favourable terms,[37] letters of allotment may be used instead of provisional certificates. (Provisional certificates, usually negotiable by delivery and often called "scrip",[38] may be issued where shares are not fully paid). The letters of allotment may be personal to the allottee, but more often may be renounced in favour of someone else within

[35] CA 1985, s. 150 prohibits liens or charges in favour of a public company unless for partly paid shares or where the company's business includes moneylending.

[36] *Bradford Banking Co. Ltd v. Henry Briggs, Son & Co. Ltd* (1886) 21 App. Cas. 29; and see *Mackereth v. Wigan Coal and Iron Co. Ltd* [1916] 2 Ch. 293.

[37] No shareholder can be compelled to take more shares: CA 1985, s. 16.

[38] "Scrip" is a word used by some to indicate that the certificate is of a provisional nature and by others to refer to bonus issues.

a certain period.[39] A rights issue increases the number of shares available, and this has the effect of decreasing the value of the shares. It is important for the bank, therefore, that the allottee either sells his or her rights or buys the new issue: otherwise (if he or she simply renounces) the existing shareholding will decrease in value with no corresponding gain elsewhere.[40] Rights issues in public companies will be saleable. There are also risks to the bank in partly paid shares: either of forfeiture by non-payment of instalments where the bank has only equitable title, or of liability for payment where the bank has legal title.

Bonus shares are fully paid issues allotted to existing members. These will be issued to the bank, if it is the legal owner, and to the registered shareholder if the bank has an equitable security. Again, the price will fall, and again the bank is at risk until it obtains the new certificates.

The Memorandum of Deposit will expressly extend the charge to cover bonus shares and rights issues.

Dematerialisation

Rapid developments in technology have made the paper-based system described above seem cumbersome, and dealings in stocks, like other financial dealings, are becoming computerised—a sign of the dramatic changes taking place in commercial and financial practice. The CREST system, a wholly electronic system,[41] which is voluntary and which provides for title to securities to be evidenced and transferred without a written instrument, became operational for securities listed on the Stock Exchange in July 1996.[42] Normally, a company can enter classes of shares in the system only where its articles of association permit the holding of uncertificated shares and their transfer electronically. The consent of the shareholder is also required. A company participating in the system must enter on its register of members how many shares each member holds in uncertificated and in certificated form.[43] **19–072**

Entry on the register of shares in uncertificated form is prima facie evidence of title to the shares.[44] The transfer of title to the shares is effected by an "Operator" (approved by the Treasury) by an authenticated **19–073**

[39] The allottee completes the form of renunciation contained in the letter and delivers it to the transferee, who completes the form and lodges it with the company. If the allottee is committed to the purchase, the usual transfer forms are used, with the letter of allotment merely filling the role of the as yet unissued share certificate.

[40] There is usually a warning on the rights issue documents.

[41] On aspects of dematerialisation in banking, see *Cross-Border Electronic Banking* (Norton, Reed and Walden eds, and *Gore-Brown on Companies* (Boyle & Sykes eds, 44th ed.) paras 16.3 and 16.15; *Palmer's Company Law,* 6.707; and Gower, *Principles of Company Law* (6th ed.) pp. 337 *et. seq.* CREST replaces the earlier unsuccessful TAURUS system (and will replace the TALISMAN system).

[42] Uncertificated Securities Regulations 1995, S.I. 1995 No. 3272, under CA 1989, s. 209.

[43] reg. 19(1).

[44] reg. 20. It is evidence of such title as would be evidenced if the entry related to shares held in certificated form.

"operator-instruction". The company must then register the transfer and notify the Operator that it has done so by an authenticated "issuer-instruction".[45] Until the transfer is registered, the transferee has only an equitable title in the security. There is provision for limited compensation to be paid to those suffering loss if unauthorised instructions are given.

Legal mortgages under the CREST system are by transfer from the stock account of the mortgagor to that of the mortgagee; this requires that the transferee be a member or sponsored member of CREST.[46]

Equitable mortgages can take place where shares are held by a nominee: the mortgagor instructs the nominee to hold the designated stocks for the mortgagee. No transfer takes place between the CREST accounts of the mortgagor and mortgagee, since the legal title remains in the nominee.[47]

[45] reg. 23. A transfer must be registered within two hours.
[46] *Palmer's Company Law, op. cit.,* 6.802.
[47] *ibid.,* 6.803.

CHAPTER 20

RESERVATION OF TITLE CLAUSES[1]

It has become common in recent years for sellers of goods to sell them on terms that property in the goods will not pass to the buyer until the price is paid, and if the goods are sold before they are paid for, the proceeds will belong to the original seller. The aim has been to avoid the more complicated procedure involved in taking and registering a charge,[2] because the seller asserts *ownership*, not a *security* right. Since the seller retains the property in the goods, the buyer cannot "return" a charge to the seller.[3] Reservation of title clauses (retention clauses) have not been used in contracts with individual traders, first, because an individual's charges over specific book debts are not registrable,[4] and secondly, because the doctrine of reputed ownership in bankruptcy[5] prevented them from operating effectively in any case—goods *apparently* belonging to the debtor were regarded as part of his or her property. However, the doctrine of reputed ownership has been abolished,[6] and retention clauses may become more commonly used in sales to individuals. **20–001**

Retention clauses have had a chequered history: the courts have been loath to deny ordinary principles of law, but have tended to regard such clauses with disfavour. In the first place, they act as an "invisible" type of security, since they are not registrable as charges, and this may be regarded as an unfair advantage against which others cannot protect themselves;[7] and in the second place, difficult questions about part-payments by the buyer, and windfall profits from capital appreciation of the goods or from mixing with other goods, have had to be dealt with. **20–002**

---

[1] See generally McCormack, *Reservation of Title* (1990).

[2] Under CA 1985, s. 395.

[3] See *Armour v. Thyssen Edelstahlwerke AG* [1991] 2 A.C. 339, Sc: a retention clause does not constitute a security because title has not passed, but does in effect give the seller an extra security.

[4] Though a general assignment of book debts is registrable. Also because even though individuals do not need to register a charge over goods (receivables) from a sale, a charge over the original goods must be registered as a Bill of Sale, and for technical reasons this is often impracticable.

[5] Bankruptcy Act 1914, s. 38.

[6] By the IA 1986.

[7] See Gough, *Company Charges* (2nd ed., 1995), p. 567 for discussion of reform: "a false appearance of credit-worthiness is created because the company is in possession of property that it does not own".

20–003 The efficacy of retention clauses was considered in *Aluminium Industrie Vaassen B. V. v. Romalpa Aluminium Ltd*[8] (generally called "the *Romalpa Case*", from which retention clauses have acquired the title "Romalpa clauses"). The clause in that case provided that legal ownership remained in the seller until payment in full; that the products of the goods were held by the buyers as "fiduciary owners" (bailees) and should be stored separately from other stock on the supplier's behalf as "surety" for the remainder of the price; and that the products might be sold by the buyers as agent for the original sellers. On the buyer's insolvency, it was held that the plaintiff seller could assert ownership of goods (unmixed with other goods, as it happened) in the buyer's hands at that time, as against the receiver. A fiduciary relationship existed because the buyer was bailee and agent, and this entitled the plaintiff to trace.[9] The court was prepared to imply a term that the proceeds of sale belonged to the original seller.

It all depends on what is said in the particular clause. Since the *Romalpa Case* it has been held that if a clause refers to "equitable and beneficial" ownership remaining with the seller, this implies that legal title passes to the buyer, and the agreement therefore constitutes a registrable charge.[10] It is a question of construction whether the buyer acts in a fiduciary capacity or for him or herself.[11]

20–004 It is necessary to consider the position relating to (a) the original goods, if they remain identifiable, (b) new or "mixed" goods, made from the goods in question, and other goods, which may have been the property of the buyer, or some other seller, and (c) the proceeds of sale of the original goods, or of the mixed goods. Strictly speaking, a "simple" reservation of title clause for original goods as used in *Romalpa* is not now seen as making the agreement a security agreement, because the seller simply retains the ownership in the goods rather than having a property right in goods belonging to another person.[12] The "extended" clauses used in the other situations, however, might be regarded as giving rise to a charge in favour of the seller rather than the retention of the title in the goods by the seller.

---

[8] [1976] 1 W.L.R. 676.

[9] *i.e.* to apply for a tracing order to follow his or her property into the proceeds of sale, and to claim the latter; see above, Chap. 9 for tracing.

[10] *Re Bond Worth* [1979] 3 All E.R. 919; [1980] Ch. 228. Other cases distinguishing *Romalpa* have found that a charge had been created, particularly when an "extended" reservation of title clause is litigated; see: *E. Pfeiffer Weinkellerei-Weineinkauf GmbH & Co. Arbuthnot Factors Ltd* [1988] 1 W.L.R. 150; *Tatung (UK) Ltd v. Galex Telesure Ltd* (1989) 5 B.C.C. 325; *Re Curtain Dream* [1990] B.C.C. 341; *Compaq Computer Ltd v. Abercorn Group Ltd* [1993] B.C.L.C. 603. The charge may be said to be created by virtue of a transfer of the property in the goods to the buyer for a *scintilla* of time, followed by the grant back by the buyer of the charge to the seller. Doubts have been expressed as to whether this can still be done—since *Abbey National Building Society v. Cann* [1990] 2 W.L.R. 832, a *scintilla* of time may no longer exist, because the transaction may be single and undivided: see Gregory, (1990) 106 L.Q.R. 550.

[11] *E. Pfeiffer Weinkellerei-Weineinkauf GmbH & Co. Arbuthnot Factors Ltd* [1988] 1 W.L.R. 150.

[12] See Goode, *Commercial Law* (2nd ed.), p. 654.

Original goods

The easiest case relates to the original identifiable goods (as appears from the *Romalpa Case* itself). A seller who provides goods to the buyer and retains the legal title may assert ownership of the goods or proceeds so long as they—goods or proceeds—remain identifiable. In the *Romalpa Case*, however, the receiver had sold the original goods, and the proceeds of sale were in a mixed fund, to which there were other claimants, and tracing was appropriate. **20–005**

Another important case is *Clough Mill Ltd v. Martin,*[13] where the plaintiffs supplied yarn to be used in the manufacture of fabrics. The risk was to pass on delivery but ownership was to remain with the seller. If payment was overdue, re-possession was permitted. Payment became due if any act or proceeding was taken in relation to the buyer's solvency. If the yarn was incorporated into any other property, this was also to become the original seller's property, so that his rights extended to the product of the original goods. The company's receiver claimed that this was a charge and was void against him for non-registration. The argument on appeal was only about the original goods (which remained identifiable),[14] and it was held that title was in, and remained in, the sellers; the buyers had therefore never had property over which they could confer a charge. The plaintiffs were entitled to damages.

Problems which were considered by the court related to what the parties had intended as to their respective rights where part-payments had already been made by the buyer, and where the value of the goods had appreciated. The court held, in relation to the original goods, that it depended whether the contract was still in existence when the goods were sold. If the repudiatory breach by the buyer had not been accepted by the seller, and the seller had therefore seized the goods and sold them while the contract still subsisted, the intention of the parties under the terms of the contract was (a) that he could sell only enough to discharge the balance of the price still owing from the original buyer and (b) that if he sold more, the proceeds belonged to the original buyer. But if the sale took place when the original contract had been *terminated*—that is, discharged for breach—then the seller had sold his own goods free of any implied contractual restraints, and could keep any profit, although he had to repay the buyer for any part of the purchase price already paid. Further, an agreement might specify, though this agreement did not, that the seller would keep legal title as trustee for the buyer, so that any balance received by the seller on resale, after discharging his or her liability for the price, belonged to the buyer. **20–006**

[13] [1985] 1 W.L.R. 111.

[14] Though there are *obiter dicta* concerning "new" goods manufactured from a mixing of the original goods with others, see below, para. 20–008.

Mixed goods

20–007 Frequently, goods are supplied so that they can be mixed with other goods, and in this case, the original product loses its identity. In *Borden (U.K.) Ltd v. Scottish Timber Products Ltd*[15] the original goods became mixed with other goods, and it was held that they ceased to be identifiable. There was no provision for separate storage of the mixed product, or provision for ownership in the mixed product remaining with the original seller.[16] The retention clause failed.

The contract may provide, however, that legal ownership of the mixed goods passes directly to the original seller, or it may provide merely that he or she has a proprietary right in equity (so that in effect he or she would seek to trace on bankruptcy of the buyer). An essential element of tracing in equity is some fiduciary element.

20–008 In *Clough Mill Ltd v. Martin*, although the product of the original goods and other goods was not in issue on appeal, the court considered the matter *obiter*. One question was whether an agreement that title in mixed or new goods should pass directly to the seller necessarily amounts to a charge. The title to the *original* goods could not remain in the seller once the identity of those goods was destroyed, and title to the *mixed* goods must vest in someone. In the normal course of events, without the retention clause in the contract, title would vest in the buyer. The effect of the clause, however, was that the seller had owned the original goods and now owned the product; the buyer therefore, never owned the new goods and could not charge them. This was not a charge.

20–009 But this gives rise to a difficult problem, because the new goods are the product, not only of the seller's goods, but also of goods belonging either to the buyer or to other sellers—conceivably, the seller's goods subject to the retention clause are only a minor part of the new goods. In that case, the seller will obtain a windfall—the full value of the new goods. In the court's view, it would need the clearest possible words to show that it had been intended that on termination of the contract the seller would gain such a windfall. This, it is submitted, is undoubtedly correct. What buyer would have agreed that a seller of, say, 100th part of the new goods should obtain

---

[15] [1979] 3 All E.R. 961; [1980] 1 Lloyd's Rep. 160.

[16] Retention clauses failed in *Hendy Lennox (Industrial Engines) Ltd v. Grahame Puttick Ltd* [1984] 2 All E.R. 152, where there was no attempt to deal with mixed or manufactured goods, no express obligation to store new goods separately, and no mention of "fiduciary" obligations; in *Re Andrabell* [1984] 3 All E. R. 407, where the clause had these defects and also provided for property to pass after payment for each consignment (in *Romalpa,* it was only on full payment of all debts), where there was no provision for the supplier to have any benefit against a sub-purchaser, no provision for the buyer's sub-sale as agent for the supplier, no obligation to keep the proceeds of sale separate, and credit given to the buyer showed that in the meantime it could use the proceeds as it saw fit; and in *Four Point Garage Ltd v. Carter* [1985] 3 All E.R. 12. See also *Re Peachdart Ltd* [1983] 3 All E.R. 204; *Specialist Plant Services Ltd v. Braithwaite* [1987] B.C.L.C. 1; *Modelboard Ltd v. Outer Box Ltd* [1992] B.C.C. 945, Ch D.

title to the whole? The court concluded that the clause must have been intended to create either a trust or a charge. A trust (where the seller had legal title to the property, which he held in trust for the buyer to the extent of any windfall profits) seemed unlikely, because any seller with a *Romalpa* clause should suspect that other suppliers of goods might also have agreed a *Romalpa* clause with the buyers, and they could not *all* have the same rights as trustees in the mixed goods. Therefore the parties must have intended to create a charge, which would be void if not registered. The clause in this case, therefore, was effective in relation to *unmixed* goods, but would not have been effective in relation to *mixed* goods, had any been in issue.

For a seller, there are at least two theoretical ways around the decision: **20–010** the first is to say expressly that all mixed goods and their windfall profits do indeed belong to the seller. No properly advised buyer would agree to this, but it may be that the small print of many supply contracts is rarely examined with care. The second is to say that it is intended to create a trust. But the trust option may not be effective as a way of dealing with mixed goods. If supplier A and supplier B both supply goods to a company, which mixes the goods, and both A and B rely on a retention clause under which both claim legal title to the mixed goods, how could this ever be given effect? It may be that they would become joint legal owners, though legal ownership is said to depend on intention, and clearly neither the company nor either seller intended joint ownership. If the only way one can envisage a trust in this situation is by ignoring the intention of the parties as expressed in their clause, it is doubtful whether the court would agree.[17]

Despite the difficulties with mixed goods and their proceeds, it might be **20–011** possible, as has been seen, to draft an effective retention clause relating to unmixed goods and their proceeds, although the clause would have to be drafted to deal with the separate "storage" of the proceeds of sale, and a restriction on their use. It may be (depending on the facts, including the nature of the process to which the goods are subjected, and the length of time since the sale) that the seller's retained property in the original goods has disappeared and been replaced by a title in the finished product. This title would be a charge by way of security for the payment of the price of the original goods, and should therefore be registered.[18]

"All liability" clauses

It has been argued that there is a distinction between (a) "single **20–012** contract" retentions clauses, whereby the seller reserves title until the goods delivered under the single contract in question have been paid for, and (b)

[17] See *Clough Mill Ltd v. Martin* [1985] 1 W.L.R. 111 at 120, *per* Goff, L.J.

[18] *Modelboard Ltd v. Outer Box Ltd* [1992] B.C.C. 945 Ch D. See also Oditah, *Legal Aspects of Receivables Financing*, p. 91.

"all liabilities" clauses, whereby title is retained so long as *any* liability of the buyer to the seller under this or other contracts is not discharged.[19] The reasoning is that if there is truly a retention of title as opposed to a charge, and the seller recovers the goods, he or she must refund the purchase price to the buyer; where more than one contract between them is involved, however, the seller would not wish to do this, and the conclusion must be that the clause was intended to create a charge. If, for example, the seller sells two lots of goods, both at £1000, and the buyer pays for the first contract, but not the second, the seller may (under the clause) seize both lots of goods and sell them. If £1,200 is received, the seller may use this to satisfy his or her claim to £1,000 of damages for breach of the second contract, but would have to refund the price of the first lot of goods, because there has been no breach of that contract; the seller would therefore be left with only £200. Since the seller is better off if the clause creates a charge, this should be said to have been the intention of the parties.

20–013 The House of Lords[20] in the case of *Armour v. Thyssen Edelstahlwerke AG,*[21] however, did not distinguish "all liability" clauses from other clauses. In both cases, there were conditions to be fulfilled, and the condition that all debts owing must be paid did not differ in substance from a ordinary condition that the price of goods had to be paid—in which case, for example, the market value might have gone up in the meantime, so that the goods were worth more: the extra value would then belong to the seller.[22] The clause did not create a charge.

Recovery where the buyer is subject to insolvency procedure

20–014 There is no legal impediment to recovery by the supplier of goods where the buyer is bankrupt or in liquidation,[23] or in administrative receivership.[24] When there is an administration order, no recovery can be made without a court order or the permission of the administrator.[25] There is no legal impediment to recovery by the seller when there is a voluntary arrangement.

---

[19] See Jones and Goodhart (1980) 43 M.L.R. 489; Goodhart (1986) 49 M.L.R. 96.

[20] And appear inconsistent with the reasoning in *Clough Mill Ltd v. Martin* [1985] 1 W.L.R. 111 (a "single contract" case), though see Goodhart (1986) 49 M.L.R. 96.

[21] [1991] 2 A.C. 339.

[22] *ibid*., at 353, *per* Lord Keith of Kinkel.

[23] See *Canon (Scotland) Business Machines v. GA Business Systems Ltd* [1993] B.C.L.C. 1194.

[24] But see *Lipe Ltd v. Leyland DAF* [1994] 1 B.C.L.C. 84, CA.

[25] IA 1986, ss. 10(1)(b) and 11(3)(c). "Hire purchase" agreements include retention of title agreements (see s. 10(4); see also *Barclay's Mercantile Business Finance Ltd v. Sibec Developments Ltd* [1992] 1 W.L.R. 1253. The administrator may be able to sell the goods with a court order, subject to satisfying the conditions set out in IA 1986, s. 15.

Chapter 21

Land as Security[1]

Bankers deal with land as a form of security, and this Chapter primarily considers that aspect of the subject, though it begins by briefly outlining the nature of interests in land. Land—realty or real property—is distinguished from personalty or personal property. It is an excellent form of security even where most of the value is in buildings rather than the land itself, for buildings can be insured, and all of it often, though not invariably, increases in value. Banks use mortgages of land as security for both individual and business customers, although this Chapter concentrates on its use for personal customers.[2] **21–001**

Lending in the 1980s—property speculation and crash

Home lending is low risk for the lenders (and rates of interest on such loans are correspondingly low), because borrowers normally strain every nerve to repay the loan to save their home,[3] and because property tends to keep or increase its value. This was particularly true in the 1980s, when there was a period of rapid increase in the value of property.[4] During that period, banks increased their lending to personal customers for loans secured by mortgages on the family home in enthusiastic competition with building societies.[5] Provided there remained enough "equity" in the home (the value in the property remaining available to the owner after repayment of loans secured on it) to act as a cushion, there was no risk to the lender **21–002**

---

[1] See, for further reference, the Encyclopaedia, Section E, and Megarry and Wade, *Law of Real Property,*(6th ed., Harpum), to Megarry, *Manual of the Law of Real Property*, (6th ed.), Cheshire and Burn, *Modern Law of Real Property*, (13th ed.), or Gray, *Elements of Land Law*, (2nd ed.). There have been proposals by the Law Commission for reform (*e.g. Transfer of Land: Land Mortgages*, Law Com. No. 204, 1991), but it was announced (March 19, 1998) that these will not be implemented, at least at present.

[2] Company charges are discussed in Chap. 19.

[3] See Salter, in Cranston, *Banks, Liability and Risk*, (2nd ed.) p. 113.

[4] See comments by judges; *e.g.* "the 1980s gallop for gold"—*Britannia B.S. v. Pugh* [1997] 2 F.L.R. 7 at 8, *per* Ward L.J, and "in the sharply rising property market of 1988, it looks as if [lenders] were desperately eager to join the party"—*First National Commercial Bank v. Andrew S Taylor Commercial Ltd* [1997] P.N.L.R 37, *per* A. Thompson Q.C. In *Nationwide v. Bulmer Radmore* [1999] Lloyd's Rep. P.N. 241 at 282, Blackburne J. said: "the demand for finance was triggered by a number of factors including relaxed Bank of England lending guidelines, the entry into the mortgage market of banks and centralized lenders, the announcement of the ending of double MIRAS relief" (mortgage interest relief at source) "and a general growth in the economy".

[5] See Cranston, *Banks, Liability and Risk*, particularly Chaps 3, by Salter, and 4, by Hill.

while property prices were stable or increasing. At the end of the 1980s, however, there was a crash in the property market followed by a period of serious recession, which was an unpleasant shock to borrowers and to lenders. The consequent reduction in the value of houses meant that the equity available in a property often disappeared completely, to be replaced by what became known as "negative equity"—in other words, the value of the home reduced to a level which would not even repay the lender (or lenders) completely. Controversy about bank lending and taking security over homes reached an unprecedented level as a result, and had its effect on the law of mortgages. Together with other factors (including the issue of the Banking Code[6]) this stimulated the banking industry into producing a Code of Practice for mortgage lending.[7] The Code applies only to personal customers and it is voluntary, but it will no doubt act as guidance for the Ombudsmen[8] and the courts as to the standards of good practice in making mortgage decisions. The standards of the Code are set out in ten "key commitments" which are intended to provide safeguards for customers.[9]

21–003 One of the results of the property crash was a flood of litigation. Lenders who had suffered losses took action against valuers and solicitors[10] where they thought there might have been negligence in their advice or actions. These cases have produced some interesting decisions on the boundaries of duties in negligence and fiduciary duties[11] and on the principles of awarding damages.[12] Another interesting result has been the recognition of the fact that lenders themselves contributed to their losses by their negligent, even reckless, lending. It is often stated that lenders owe no duty of care simply by their lending (although they may do so if they make some negligent misstatement when they lend[13]), but it is now firmly established that they may be *contributorily* negligent.[14] In *Platform Homes v. Oyston Shipways*,[15] the lender (like many others at the time) was operating a system of "non status" loans—in other words, lending against the security of the property alone, without making any real investigation into the borrower's credit-

[6] See above, Chap. 2.

[7] The Mortgage Code, issued by the Council of Mortgage Lenders, obtainable from the Council and from lenders.

[8] The Banking Ombudsman and the Building Societies' Ombudsman (in future, the Financial Services Ombudsman).

[9] Controversy about aspects of mortgages has not abated, see OBO A.R. 1998/99.

[10] *e.g. Barclays Bank v. Weeks Legg & Dean* [1998] P.N.L.R. 729, CA; *Zwebner v. The Mortgage Corporation* [1998] P.N. 769, CA.

[11] *e.g. Bristol & West B.S. v. Mothew*, see above, para. 3–012.

[12] *e.g. South Australia Asset Management Co.* [1997] A.C. 191, see above, Chap. 5.

[13] See above, Chap. 5, discussion of *Williams & Glyns Bank v. Barnes* [1981] Com L.R. 205 and *Hedley Byrne v. Heller* [1964] A.C. 465, HL.

[14] Law Reform (Contributory Negligence Act) 1945, s. 1; *Forsikringsaktieselkapet Vesta v. Butcher* [1986] 2 All E.R. 488.

[15] [1999] 2 W.L.R. 518, HL, affirming CA: see Dugdale (1999) 62 M.L.R. 281. See also, *e.g.*, *Mortgage Express Ltd v. Newman & Co.* [1996] P.N.L.R. 603; *Midshires Mortgage Services v. Parry* [1996] P.N.L.R. 494; *First National Bank v. Andrew S. Taylor Commercial Ltd* [1997] P.N.L.R. 37.

worthiness or circumstances. The theory was that if not too high a proportion of the value (often, as here, 70 per cent) was lent, there would be a "cushion" of equity in the property, and the loan would be recoverable out of the proceeds of sale of the property if the borrower defaulted.[16]

In *Platform Homes*, unfortunately, the property was badly overvalued by the defendants, and when the crash and the inevitable default happened, the lenders lost a large sum of money. It was held that the lenders had contributed by their negligence to their own loss, first because they had not checked the borrower's application form (there were omissions by the borrower which would have alerted them to important facts) and secondly, because of their policy of lending 70 per cent of the value of the property. A reduction of 20 per cent was made to their damages. **21–004**

Environmental liability

A further modern problem for those taking mortgages of land is the possibility of liability for environmental pollution affecting land used as security,[17] particularly under the Environmental Protection Act 1990 and the Environment Act 1995 and the Pollution Prevention and Control Act 1990.[18] Banks might be affected in several different ways[19]: as mortgagees, for example, they run the risk that, after a mortgage or charge is taken, the property might drastically lose value because of contamination and, potentially, fine and clean-up costs.[20] Liability can attach even to "innocent" landowners or occupiers (including perhaps banks) in certain circumstances: section 78 of the Environmental Protection Act 1990 states that the person primarily liable is the person who caused or knowingly permitted the contaminating substances to be in or under the land,[21] and the current owner[22] or occupier[23] may be liable where, after reasonable inquiry, no such **21–005**

[16] From Lord Hobhouse's speech, [1999] 2 W.L.R. 518 at 526, HL.

[17] See *e.g.*, Norton, Auerback and Gaba, *Environmental Liability for Banks*, (1995); Jarvis and Fordham, *Lender Liability*, (1993). See also *Re Celtic Extraction Ltd* [1999] 2 B.C.L.C. 555, CA, where a liquidator successfully claimed that a waste management licence could be disclaimed as onerous property under s. 178 of the IA 1986.

[18] The 1999 Act (and Regulations) will eventually replace the 1995 Act. See also the ground-breaking U.S. legislation: the Comprehensive Environmental Response Compensation and Liability Act 1980 (CERCLA or Superfund) and the Resource Conservation Recovery Act (RCRA).

[19] Also, perhaps, by putting in a receiver, or controlling the borrowing company in some way so that they become regarded as shadow directors, *e.g.* by controlling the majority of the voting shares of the borrower or controlling the board of directors of a borrower. See below, Chap. 24.

[20] Processes prescribed under the legislation have to comply with the "Best Available Techniques" in order to obtain permits (Pollution Prevention and Control Act 1999, giving effect to European Council Directive 96/61 [1996] O.J. L257/26, which substitutes this test for the "best available techniques not entailing excessive costs" (BATNEEC) test).

[21] s. 78F(2), inserted by the Environment Act 1995.

[22] Defined, s. 83A(9) of the Environmental Protection Act 1999.

[23] Not defined, but generally a person who exercises a degree of control over the land rather than possessing exclusive rights of occupation (*e.g. Wheat v. Lacon* [1966] A.C. 552).

person can be found.[24] Although mortgagees not in possession are excluded from the definition of owner, there are situations where mortgagees may become owners, as when they go into possession, or when they find themselves in possession by default—for example, the borrower may abandon the property and send the keys to the lender.

Banks should therefore take environmental factors—potentially polluting elements relating to the land—seriously into account when making lending decisions, and make appropriate enquiries and investigations into the land before committing themselves.[25]

The Nature of Interests in Land

21–006 People talk of "owning" land, but our system of land law relates back to a system of "tenure" (which has little significance now) where different persons held rights in the same land, all deriving title ultimately from the Crown. Even today, the theory is that the Crown owns the land and the subject is allowed merely the use of it, by owning a bundle of rights in the land, termed an estate in land.

Estates and Interests in Land

21–007 In modern times there are two forms of *estate*, freehold and leasehold.[26] Different persons may have rights in the same land: one may be the freeholder and another a leaseholder, for example, or one may be the legal owner, and another an equitable owner, or two or more persons may own the land jointly, so that they have the same, or similar, rights.

Freehold estates

21–008 The term "freehold" means that the freeholder owes no obligations to a superior tenant in respect of his or her holding. The normal freehold estate is the "*fee simple absolute in possession*"—a phrase which is a relic of the old law, transformed by extensive legislation in 1925. "*Fee simple*" now means an estate in the land which can endure indefinitely.[27] It may pass under the will of the freeholder or on his or her intestacy, or the freeholder may sell or give it to someone else (*alienate* the land). "*Absolute*" means that it is not conditional or determinable in any way, and "*in possession*" means either in actual physical possession or having the right to receive

[24] Environmental Protection Act 1999, s. 78F(4) and (5).

[25] A helpful account of possible measures is contained in Chap. 6 of Norton, *op. cit.*, contributed by Sykes.

[26] LPA 1925 s. 1(1).

[27] "Simple" meant that the estate could be inherited by the general heirs of the freeholder, as opposed to an "entailed" estate, where some kind of descent, perhaps to male heirs only, was specified. The TLATA 1996 (para.5, Sched. 1) makes it impossible to create an entailed estate.

rents or profits[28]: a freeholder who has leased his property is still in possession.

A leasehold estate

This means that the tenant derives the estate from a superior tenant, who may be a freeholder or another leaseholder, to whom the tenant owes obligations, such as to pay rent, to repair, and to give up possession when the lease expires. The person who grants the lease is the *landlord (or lessor)* and the person who receives it is the *tenant (or lessee)*. The freehold interest continues throughout the lease, and the freeholder has the reversion. **21–009**

A leasehold is referred to in the legislation as a *term of years absolute* (although it may last for less than a year).[29] This means that it is to last for a fixed period, unless it ends earlier by forfeiture for breach, or by operation of law. Realistically, the only leases which are useful as security are fixed term leases of a certain duration, which have a certain capital value. A lease, as an interest in land, must be distinguished from a mere licence, or the permission to remain on land that a hotel guest, for example, would have. A tenant may grant another person a leasehold interest of a lesser term: this is a sub-lease or underlease. **21–010**

Generally, a tenant pays rent, a periodical payment, to the landlord, although sometimes a lease may be granted for a single payment (a premium). There are a number of other obligations, which are of concern to lenders, since the landlord may have a right to determine or forfeit the lease if they are broken, which would deprive the bank of its security.

Apart from freehold and leasehold estates, other rights or *interests* in land are recognized by law or equity, and, though they are normally not valuable enough to be granted as security in their own right, they may be important to a mortgagee because they are owned by another person and adversely affect a security interest. For example, there are *easements*[30] (rights of an owner of land over the lands of another, such as rights of way or of light or to a flow of water) and *rent charges*[31] (annual or periodic sums charged on or issuing out of land, other than rent under a lease, or sums payable by way of interest). **21–011**

Legal and Equitable Rights

Historically, the two systems of courts in England, the courts of law and of equity, would recognise different types of right in land, so that a court of law might recognize the rights of A to a certain piece of land, while a court **21–012**

[28] LPA 1925, s. 205.
[29] LPA 1925, s. 205.
[30] LPA 1925, s. 1(2)(a).
[31] LPA 1925, s. 1(2)(b). But no new rent charges may be created and existing ones will be extinguished in the 60 years from 1978: Rent Charges Act 1977.

of equity might recognize the superior rights of B to the same land. When the dual system of courts was abolished (in 1873–5[32]) the courts continued to apply both sets of rules, which operate as a complement to each other. Thus it is possible for one person to be recognized as the *legal* owner while another is regarded as the *equitable* (or *beneficial*) owner. The legal owner (or trustee) holds the legal title in trust for the beneficiary (equitable owner), and the latter is entitled to the profits from use of the land. One can think of the legal owner having the "paper" title, while the beneficiary has the "real" or beneficial title. The trustee has to manage the trust property for the benefit of the equitable owner.

21–013 Equitable titles can be created by will, or can be created by a person in his or her lifetime, who declares him- or herself irrevocably to be a trustee for the benefit of another (in the case of land, the declaration is invalid unless evidenced in writing).[33] Another common way to create an equitable title—not necessarily by design—is to omit the formalities which are required by law to dispose of an interest in land, such as a deed. In that case, the attempted disposition will be invalid as regards the legal interest, but will effectively dispose of an equitable interest, thus "splitting" ownership. Since 1989, this can only happen where there is a contract in writing which satisfies the provisions of section 2 of the Law of Property (Miscellaneous Provisions) Act 1989 (LPMPA 1989).[34]

21–014 If the legal and equitable ownership of property is separate, the legal owner may dispose of the legal interest and an equitable owner may dispose of his or her equitable interest. The legal owner can create either legal or equitable mortgages, whereas the equitable owner can create only equitable mortgages. A trustee, as legal owner, may therefore validly dispose of the land to a third party, such as a mortgagee, provided the appropriate requirements are satisfied: the trustee may be permitted to sell by the terms of the trust deed, for management or investment purposes, or where it is necessary to sell in order to distribute the proceeds of sale to the beneficiaries; or it is possible that adult beneficiaries may consent to the trustee's disposition. Statutory provisions may also allow sale; for example, where there is a "trust of land" under the TLATA 1996,[35] a purchaser or mortgagee (a mortgagee is in the same position legally as a purchaser) may take legal title from at least two trustees or a trust corporation, and the trustees can give a good receipt to a bona fide purchaser or mortgagee for

[32] Judicature Acts 1873–5.

[33] LPA 1925, s.53.

[34] Discussed below paras 21–042 *et. seq.*

[35] s. 1 of the TLATA 1996 provides that a trust of land means any trust of property which consists of or includes land. Before January 1, 1997, this would have been a "trust for sale", governed largely by rules set out in the LPA 1925. In theory, this was a trust of the proceeds of sale of the land (the doctrine of conversion). As to TLATA 1996, see Hopkins [1996] Conv. 411, Oakley [1996] Conv. 401; Barnsley [1998] C.L.J. 123; Clements (1998) 61 M.L.R. 56; Ferris and Battersby [1998] Conv. 62 generally Megarry and Wade (6th. ed., Harpum).

the proceeds of sale.[36] This is called "overreaching" the beneficiaries' rights.[37] The beneficiaries will be left to their remedies against the trustee for any breach of trust which has taken place.

Since 1925, only two legal *estates* in land (freehold and leasehold) may exist. Any of the *interests* mentioned above to which there may be legal title if they are granted over a legal estate may also be held in equity.

Co-Ownership

Where two or more people hold an interest in land in possession at the same time, they are said to be *co-owners* of the land. The increased status of women in society has led to a huge increase in the number of domestic properties held in co-ownership in recent years, and sole ownership is correspondingly rarer. Co-owned land must be held on trust, and legislation (the TLATA 1996) attempts to reflect the changed social needs of the owners of domestic property and to remedy defects in the existing law,[38] including its complexity. The Act has replaced the old "trust for sale" by the "trust of land".[39] The basic principle is that the trustees have the powers of absolute owners,[40] but they must also act as trustees in respecting the rights of the beneficiaries under the trust. **21–015**

There are two forms of co-ownership, *joint tenancy* and *tenancy in common*. The only form of legal co-ownership is by way of joint tenancy. Equitable co-ownership may be by joint tenancy or by tenancy in common. **21–016**

A *joint tenancy* exists if two or more persons each own the whole interest, and do not have distinct and separate shares in it, so that none is entitled to exclusive possession of any part of it. The most significant characteristic is that there is a right of *survivorship*: that is to say, when one of the co-owners dies, the others automatically succeed to the rights of the deceased because their interest in the whole property is concurrent with that of the deceased co-owner.

There may not be more than four legal joint tenants of land.[41] It is not possible for one tenant to sell or mortgage his or her *legal* rights, for the legal joint tenancy cannot be severed,[42] but a joint tenant may sell or mortgage his or her *equitable* rights. If this is done, it severs the equitable joint tenancy, so that between the new tenant (or a mortgagee) and those **21–017**

36 LPA 1925, ss. 2(1)(I) and (ii) and (1A) and 27, as amended by TLATA 1996, Sched. 3.

37 The overreaching rules apply to both registered and unregistered land "Overreaching is the process whereby existing interests are subordinated to a later interest or estate created by a trust or power": *State Bank of India v. Sood* [1997] Ch. 276, *per* Peter Gibson L.J., referring to Harpum [1990] C.L.J. 277.

38 See (1989) Law Com. No. 181.

39 TLATA 1996, s. 1. The creation of strict settlements has also been abolished.

40 TLATA 1996, s. 6.

41 Tr A 1925, s. 34(2) (amended by TLATA 1996, s. 25(2); Sched. 3, para. 3) limits the number of trustees to four.

42 LPA 1925, ss. 34(1) and 36(2).

remaining, there is an equitable tenancy in common (though still an equitable joint tenancy between those who remain, if there is more than one). The bankruptcy of a joint tenant also severs the equitable joint tenancy.

21–018 A *tenancy in common* exists where two or more persons own land (or other property) in undivided shares: that is, each simply has a share in the land, though that share is not identifiable in the sense that the land is divided up. The shares may be equal or unequal. There is no right of survivorship, so that if one co-owner dies, his or her share does not go to the others, but passes to the personal representatives, who dispose of it according to the co-owner's will or the rules of intestacy. There cannot be a legal tenancy in common; if the legal estate is co-owned, the co-owners (trustees) must hold as legal joint tenants on trust for the equitable owners.

21–019 The principles for settling disputes about occupying, mortgaging and selling the property are now largely set out in the TLATA 1996. For example, the Act creates a statutory right for beneficiaries to occupy the land, where the purposes of the trust allow for this, provided that the property is suitable and available for occupation.[43] The trustees may exclude or restrict the entitlement of one or more, but not all, of the beneficiaries who have a right to occupy, but only if they act reasonably in doing so. The trustees can also impose conditions (such as paying expenses on property) on beneficiaries, and generally have power to balance the interests of the co-owners. Similarly, if the trustees wish to sell the property, they must consult and give effect to the wishes of the majority of the beneficiaries of full age as far as those wishes are consistent with the general interest of the trust[44]; if the trustees sell the land without consultation, or if they ignore the consultation, they are acting in breach of trust. From the mortgagee's point of view, however, the important point is that a purchaser (or a mortgagee) is only concerned to see that there are two of the necessary consents.[45]

21–020 If there is a conflict, a trustee or person having an interest in the property[46] may apply to the court to resolve the dispute under section 14 of the TLATA 1996.[47] The court has wider powers than under the previous law and may make any order relating to the exercise by the trustees of any of their powers as it thinks fit.[48] Section 15 sets out four factors which the

[43] TLATA 1996, s. 12. Formerly, the interest of a co-owner, in theory at least, was in the proceeds of sale, rather than in the land. The terms in which the right of occupation are defined have been criticised, see Barnsley, *op. cit.*; Kenny *op. cit.* and Martyn (1997) 61 Conv. 254.

[44] TLATA 1996, s. 11(1).

[45] TLATA 1996, s. 10 and s. 16(1), (except where land is held on charitable ecclesiastical or public trusts).

[46] TLATA 1996, s. 17: any trustee or beneficiary of the proceeds of the sale of land.

[47] It has power to make an order relating to any of the functions of the trustees: TLATA 1996, s. 14(2). It can declare the nature and extent of a claimant's interest in property, and can authorise transactions which would otherwise be in breach of trust.

[48] TLATA 1996, s. 14(2).

court must take into account in making an order: the intention of the person who created the trust; the purposes for which the property is held; the welfare of any minor occupying, or who might reasonably be expected to occupy, the property as his or her home (reflecting the increasing social importance placed on the interests of the family); and the interests of any secured creditor (such as a mortgagee) of any beneficiary.

It remains to be seen how the courts will balance the interests of the family as against those of the creditors,[49] although it seems likely that the interests of children may be taken into account as an independent factor; possibly they may sometimes even outweigh the interests of a mortgagee.

These rules do not apply in cases of bankruptcy, which is governed by section 335A of the IA 1986.[50]

For potential mortgagees, there may be no real change: a legal mortgage granted by two or more legal joint tenants is effective to transfer the equitable interest of a co-owner under the trust.[51] Any single co-owner may mortgage his or her *equitable* rights in the tenancy (a joint tenancy is severed by a mortgage and becomes a tenancy in common). In this case, a bank mortgagee may apply to the court for an order for sale of the share of the property if need be, but the court may not be prepared to order a sale. **21–021**

Dealing With Land

Registered and unregistered land[52]

In England and Wales, we are moving to a system whereby title to land is registered, so that each parcel of land has a file in the land registry and a file number by which it is referenced. The name of the owner of the legal estate (the proprietor) is registered, together with any other interests which may affect the land, such as mortgages or equitable interests. All areas of England and Wales have now been designated as areas of compulsory **21–022**

---

[49] *TSB Bank v. Marshall* [1998] 3 E.G. 208, the first reported case under these sections of TLATA 1996, indicates that the principles established by case law under s. 30 of the LPA 1925, which was replaced by these sections, will still be relevant (s. 17 of the Married Womens' Property Act 1882 has not been affected by TLATA 1996.)

[50] Inserted by TLATA 1996, Sched. 3, para. 23. See below, Chap. 24.

[51] TLATA 1996, s. 16(1). By taking advantage of the overreaching provisions of the L.P.A, and paying the proceeds of sale to two trustees or a trust corporation. Section 16 of the TLATA 1996 applies only to unregistered land; for registered land, the purchaser must rely on entries in the register. This means that the problem for mortgagees of a possible overriding interest still exists (as in the *Boland* case, see below).

[52] Registration is considered below paras 21–101 *et seq*. Electronic conveyancing is to be introduced over the next few years.

registration,[53] so that on a *registrable disposition*[54] the property will come within the system and must be registered within two months.[55]

21–023 The Land Register has three parts to it: first, the *Property Register*, which describes the property and its location; secondly, the *Proprietorship Register*, which describes the owner and his or her rights; and thirdly, the *Charges Register*, which describes rights such as mortgages affecting the land. The public has a right to inspect the Register and any documents other than leases or charges, which are referred to in it, subject to payment of a fee.[56]

The Land Register and the Land Registry (for *registered* land) should not be confused with the Land Charges Register and Registry which deal with certain rights (including mortgages) over *unregistered* land, which is not yet within the registration system.

The sale of land

21–024 A purchaser of land—or a mortgagee, which is in the same position—must be sure of obtaining a good title to the land. The purchaser must check that the vendor owns the property in question and what, if any, incumbrances exist. In registered land, incumbrances may be overriding interests (which are not mentioned on the register, but which bind the purchaser) and minor interests, which will bind the purchaser only if they are entered on the register.In unregistered land, a purchaser is bound by adverse legal interests, or by adverse equitable interests which are protected by registration as land charges or not overreached by the sale. The value of the property could easily be reduced or disappear entirely because of an incumbrance, and the procedures for purchase and mortgage, and those for protection of the transaction when it has been completed, are therefore vitally important.

21–025 Usually, the purchaser makes an offer to buy the property "subject to contract" which the vendor accepts; at this point, no contract is created and the purchaser has no mortgageable interest. The solicitors for the purchaser then investigate the title of the vendor by examining the Land Register, in the case of registered land, or by *deducing* title from the title deeds—documents relating to past dealings in the land—for unregistered land. In the latter case, the obligation on the vendor is only to show a good title at least 15 years back, unless the parties agree to a longer period. This does not give a guarantee of good title in the vendor, but it does protect the

[53] Land Registration, England and Wales: The Registration of Title Order 1989 (S.I. 1989 No. 1347). All conveyances taking effect after December 1, 1990 must be recorded in the Land Register.

[54] s. 1 of the Land Registration Act 1997 substitutes new s.123 into LRA 1925, and increases the number of transactions giving rise to compulsory registration.

[55] The Registrar has a discretion to extend the period for a good reason: s. 123A of the LRA 1925, substituted by s. 1 of the Land Registration Act 1997. See s. 123A(5) of the LRA 1925 for the effect if no application for registration has been made after two months.

[56] LRA 1925, s.112(1), substituted by Land Registration Act 1988, s.1(1).

purchaser from equitable interests not registered or disclosed in the documents, and he or she will take free of these.[57]

21–026 When good title has been shown, finance has been arranged and when a list of questions about the property ("inquiries before contract") and inquiries made of local authorities have been answered to the satisfaction of the purchaser and his or her solicitor, the parties exchange contracts, which must be in writing and must incorporate all the terms which the parties have expressly agreed in each document.[58] The contracts must be signed by or on behalf of each party to the contract. They bind the parties, and the purchaser becomes the owner of the property in equity and has a mortgageable interest in it. The purchaser's solicitor prepares a *transfer* (for registered land) or *deed of conveyance* (for unregistered land), and this is given to the vendor to sign. On the day of completion, this is handed to the purchaser or the purchaser's solicitor in return for the rest of the purchase price. Where the finance is provided by mortgage, the lender transfers the money in exchange for an instrument of mortgage of the land, so that the conveyance takes place simultaneously with the mortgage.[59] In the case of unregistered land, the purchaser becomes the legal owner on completion; in the case of registered land, the purchaser only becomes the legal owner when the transaction is registered and he or she becomes *registered proprietor*.

Leasehold estates

21–027 Whereas freeholds are *conveyed*, leaseholds are *granted* (or *created*) by a freeholder or leaseholder, or are *assigned*, if they already exist, by one leaseholder to another. A leaseholder may grant a lease by granting a term which is less than his or her own (an underlease). This is a separate estate, carved out of the greater estate. If the whole term is granted, the lease is assigned.

A legal lease exceeding three years must be created by deed,[60] whereas equitable leases exceeding three years can be created in writing, and need not be by deed. Only the legal owner can create a legal lease, so if an equitable owner grants a lease by deed, it is still an equitable lease. All legal assignments of legal leases must be by deed, and equitable assignments must be in writing.

---

[57] Where a purchaser cannot discover an equitable title as a legal charge because it is concealed behind the root of title, the purchaser is bound by the interest but entitled to compensation: Law of Property Act 1969, s. 25.

[58] LPMPA 1989, s. 2.

[59] *Abbey National Building Society v. Cann* [1991] 1 A.C. 56. It used to be thought that the transfer must take place before the creation of the mortgage (even if only by a fraction of time—*scintilla temporis*). See further below, para. 21–122.

[60] LPA 1925, s. 52(1).

Mortgages[61]

Taking a Mortgage

21–028 Mortgages convey some title in the land to the mortgagee, who has the benefit of the mortgage as security for a loan. A mortgage has the same effect legally as a purchase, but in the case of a legal mortgage the land is not actually conveyed to the mortgagee; the transaction is accomplished by demise or by charge by way of legal mortgage, and the mortgage gives the mortgagee rights to enable it to take swift action to realise the property if there is default. The mortgagor has the advantage of obtaining a loan, often for a long period, at a relatively low rate of interest, which allows him or her, typically, to purchase property, to finance a business project, or to make some expensive home improvement. The mortgagor may continue to use the property as his or her own unless or until the mortgagee takes possession, or exercises the right of sale or another remedy.

21–029 The mortgagee must be satisfied that the property is good security—that is, that the value of the property is adequate for the debt and that there are no incumbrances affecting the mortgagee's title to the property. The mortgagee will require searches to be made (by the solicitor), including a bankruptcy search against the borrower, and for details of planning permissions given (which might have run out), and will require the local authority development plan to be inspected, in case there are proposals for compulsory purchase of property in that area.

21–030 Mortgages in standard form for personal customers must fulfil the requirements of the UTCCR 1999 with regard to plain language and fairness.[62] The Code of Mortgage Lending issued by the banks[63] is designed to set standards of good mortgage lending practice, and commits lenders to the promise that: "all written terms and conditions will be fair in substance and will set out your rights and responsibilities clearly and in plain language, with legal and technical language used only where necessary".[64]

Second mortgages

21–031–21–038 Any number of mortgages may be granted over the same land to the same or different mortgagees. There may be problems of priorities between the mortgagees,[65] and a sale by the first mortgagee under its statutory powers extinguishes the title of the subsequent mortgagees, who are only

[61] The Law Commission proposed reforming the law of mortgages in 1991: Law Com. No. 204, *Transfer of Mortgages* (see Wilkinson [1992] Conv. 69), but the proposals have not yet been adopted.

[62] Replacing UTCCR 1994, see above, Chap. 3. Mortgages are exempted from the provisions of the UCTA 1977.

[63] See also Butt, *Plain Language and Conveyancing* [1993] Conv. 256.

[64] para.5.1.

[65] See further below, paras 21–101 *et seq*.

entitled to the surplus proceeds, if there are any. Despite the disadvantages, second mortgages were common during the 1980s, because the rising property values at the time tended to leave surplus value in the land.

Legal Mortgages

Methods of Creation

There may be a legal mortgage of a legal estate[66] or of legal interests.[67] Since 1925, legal mortgages[68] may be granted in two ways, neither of which involves a transfer of the mortgagor's title[69]: **21–039**

(1) by way of *conveyance of a legal estate*. Freeholders may grant a lease of land for a term of years[70] absolute, subject to a provision for "cesser on redemption": that is, that the lease is terminable when the loan is repaid. Leaseholders may grant a sub-lease for a lesser term[71] than remains to the mortgagor. Because the mortgagee is granted a lease, it has the power to go into possession immediately, but obviously the right is rarely exercised.

(2) the mortgagor may execute a deed stating that the land is being *charged "by way of legal mortgage"*. There is no conveyance of the legal estate, but in terms of the mortgagee's protection, powers and remedies in case of default, the charge method has the same effect as if (for freehold) a 3000 year lease had been granted or (for leasehold) a term less by one day than the mortgagor's term had been granted.[72] This method is normally used, because it is simpler,[73] and can be used for either freehold or leasehold and for a mortgage of parcels of land comprising both interests.[74]

For a legal mortgage of registered land, the Land Certificate must be surrendered on registration and a Charge Certificate is returned. Legal mortgages of unregistered land may be protected by deposit of the title deeds, and the first mortgagee has a right to the deeds.[75] Mortgages protected in this way are not registrable, but other mortgages are registrable land charges. **21–040**

[66] The legal fee simple absolute in possession or the legal term of years absolute.
[67] Some, like easements, are unsuitable, because they have little value.
[68] Governed by the LPA 1925, s. 85.
[69] Since 1925 an attempt to create a mortgage by transfer results in a lease for 3000 years (freehold) or a term ten days less than that expressed to be assigned (leasehold), LPA 1925, s. 85.
[70] Commonly 3,000 years.
[71] LPA 1925, s. 86. Commonly less by one day only.
[72] LPA 1925, s. 87.
[73] It does not require the long forms usually used with leases, although most modern charges add a long list of covenants to the required form.
[74] Called a "compound" mortgage.
[75] LPA 1925, s. 85(1) and s. 86(1).

In law, the conveyance and the granting of a mortgage occur simultaneously[76] on the day of completion. If money is to be advanced earlier, therefore, the bank may only obtain an equitable mortgage, which is contractual in origin, and can extend to property which the mortgagor does not own at the time when the mortgage is created. The mortgage takes effect when the mortgagor acquires the property.

Equitable Mortgages

21–041 A mortgage of an equitable interest has to be equitable, but it is also quite possible to create an equitable mortgage over a legal estate or interest. The use of equitable mortgages must have declined in recent years, however, because of the effective abolition of the most common type by legislation in 1989.[77] Before that time, they used to be quite common, even for legal estates—as against short-term loans, perhaps; or arranged in haste, pending a legal mortgage; or for customers not wanting the record of a registered charge, even one which has been discharged, appearing against the property; or sometimes for customers simply wishing to avoid the expense of a legal mortgage. Equitable mortgages may be simpler to take than legal mortgages, and (with registered land) more easily discharged. Disadvantages, such as the lack of a statutory power of sale,[78] may be overcome by special terms.

Methods of creation

21–042 Traditionally there were four ways to create an equitable mortgage,[79] although the use of the first, by deposit of deeds with the mortgagee, has been effectively abolished by statute. In all types, the money must actually have been advanced by the mortgagee, for while the property may be future,[80] the consideration must be executed.[81]

21–043 Banks may ask the customer to sign a Memorandum of Deposit, both to show that the documents are held as security, rather than, for example, for safe-keeping, and because it contains an undertaking by the customer to execute a legal mortgage if called on to do so. It will probably also contain useful terms such as an irrevocable power of attorney, which enables the mortgagee to sell a legal estate if the mortgagor had one. In addition, if the memorandum (or any of the types of equitable mortgage described here) is

[76] *Abbey National Building Society v. Cann* [1991] 1 A.C. 56.

[77] LPMPA, 1989.

[78] Which exists for mortgages created by deed: LPA 1925, s. 101(1).

[79] The first method (deposit of deeds) did not create a registrable land charge (for unregistered land) but all the others do. With registered land all methods create a minor interest, requiring protection on the register by caution or notice.

[80] *Re Clarke, Coombe v. Carter* (1887) 36 Ch.D. 348.

[81] See *Rogers v. Challis* (1859) 27 Beav. 175; *Holroyd v. Marshall* (1862) 10 H.L.Cas. 191; *Tailby v. O.R.* (1888) 13 App.Cas. 523.

in the form of a deed, the mortgagee is entitled to all the powers given by section 101 of the LPA 1925, which include the power of sale.

(1) The first method (now effectively abolished by the LPMPA 1989, which took effect on September 27, 1989) used to be by *deposit of title deeds* or, for registered land, *deposit of the Land Certificate*.[82] There was no need for a written agreement or memorandum,[83] although a Memorandum of Deposit was commonly taken.

Section 2 of the LPMPA 1989, however, provides that a contract for sale or other disposition of any "interest in land" (this includes a mortgage) must be in writing, contain all material terms and be signed by each party.[84] Both parties may sign on the same document, or there may be two documents, each signed by one of the parties, but if both do not sign, the transaction will be a nullity. It was decided by the Court of Appeal in *United Bank of Kuwait v. Sahib*[85] that equitable mortgages by deposit of title deeds are contractual and that the section applies to them. In order to be safe, banks must therefore ensure that the contract creating the mortgage is in writing and fully complies with the requirements of the section.

However, some mortgages of this type created before 1989 will continue to exist for some years yet, and so far as these are concerned, the position is that the mere delivery of deeds is not sufficient to create the security interest; there must have been an intention to do so (which might be shown by the Memorandum). In respect of unregistered land this form of mortgage was not a land charge and could not be registered, but the possession of the deeds would normally ensure priority.

(2) An equitable mortgage may be made by way of *equitable charge*. This needs only a signed written memorandum identifying the property concerned, and indicating that the mortgagor intends his or her property to be security for money advanced; it can be very simple.[86] An equitable charge requires only the signature of the mortgagor.[87]

(3) Where money has been advanced, and a mortgagor agrees to execute a legal mortgage or charge for the money, equity regards the

[82] See LRA 1925, s. 66.

[83] Under LPA 1925, s. 40, part performance of an oral contract (by depositing the deeds: see *Russel v. Russel* (1783) 2 Bro CC 268) was effective to evidence the contract (see *Re Wallis and Simmonds (Builders) Ltd* [1974] 1 All E.R. 561).

[84] See *Firstpost Homes Ltd v. Johnson* [1995] 4 All E.R. 355: a printed or typed name is not a signature under the Act LPMPA 1989.

[85] [1996] 3 W.L.R. 372. Section 40 of the LPA 1925 has been superseded by s. 2 and ceases to have effect (LPMPA 1989, s. 8). See Thompson, [1994] Conv. 465, and Hardcastle (1995) 139 S.J.246.

[86] *London County & Westminster Bank v. Tompkins* [1918] 1 K.B. 515.

[87] It involves the creation of a security interest (depending on LPA 1925, s. 53) rather than an agreement to create a legal mortgage (which would have to comply with s. 2 of the LPMPA 1989, see Emmet on Title, 25.116.

other person as having an immediate equitable mortgage (equity regards as done that which ought to be done).[88] Such a mortgage must also comply with the requirements of section 2 of the LPMPA 1989 if created after September 27, 1989.

(4) If the estate or interest is equitable, the whole property may be *transferred* (unlike a legal mortgage[89]) subject to a proviso that it will be returned to the mortgagor on repayment. This must be in writing, but need not be by deed, and needs no special form of words if the meaning is plain.[90]

Bank Forms for Equitable Mortgages

21–044 These tend to be much simpler than for legal mortgages, though, for practical reasons, they are often made by deed.[91] They will probably include terms to this effect:

21–045 **(a) Covenant to repay and charge.** This is usually a charge, though it may be a conveyance (method four, above). The charge may extend to property not yet owned by the mortgagor, which may be the subject of an equitable mortgage, often for company customers.[92]

21–046 **(b) Covenant to execute a legal mortgage.** Consideration for this is usually expressed in the form of provision of banking facilities, because equity will not assist a volunteer even where there is a deed.

21–047 **(c) Power of attorney.** The bank is given an irrevocable power of attorney to execute the legal mortgage or to execute a conveyance of the legal estate. Alternatively, there may be a declaration that the borrower holds the legal title as trustee for the execution of a legal mortgage and the bank has the power to remove him or her and appoint new trustees instead.

21–048 **(d) Protecting the charge.** It is stated that (for registered land) no-one else is to be registered as proprietor and the costs of putting a caution on the register are to be deemed to be properly incurred (and therefore to be a secured debt).

21–049 **(e) Right of possession.** The bank is to have the same right to possession as it would have if the charge had been a legal mortgage created by way of a demise for 3000 years.

---

[88] *Ex p. Wright* (1812) 19 Ves. 255; *Parker v. Housefield* (1834) 2 My. & K. 419; *Swiss Bank Corpn. v. Lloyds Bank Ltd* [1979] Ch. 584, [1980] 3 W.L.R. 457, CA.
[89] The method was left unchanged by the LPA 1925. It is a conveyance, not a charge.
[90] LPA 1925, s. 53.
[91] *Re White Rose Cottage* [1965] Ch. 940.
[92] See Chap. 19.

PROTECTION OF THE MORTGAGOR

The right of redemption

A maxim of equity is "once a mortgage, always a mortgage."[93] This is not literally true, but means that the purpose of the mortgage is simply to provide security. The courts are concerned (to this limited extent at least) to protect the mortgagor, who is seen as being in a vulnerable position because of his or her need for money, and they insist on the mortgagor's right to *redeem* the property by paying off the principal, interest and costs, whatever kind of mortgage it is, and even though there is a date for redemption stated in the mortgage which has already passed. The right to redeem is not restricted to the mortgagor. Any person interested in the equity may redeem.[94] This includes a spouse and other connected persons (for example, former spouses and co-habitees). **21–050**

Even if the mortgagee would prefer to keep the mortgagor tied in to the mortgage—perhaps because it provides a good rate of interest—courts allow the mortgagor to exercise the equitable right to redeem: generally speaking, it is not possible to "clog the equity of redemption". The equity of redemption is itself seen as a proprietary interest, capable of being disposed of like any other interest. However, there are some cases where the equity can be extinguished as outlined below.

First, the mortgagor may give it up ("release") it to the mortgagee; the mortgagee may go into possession and stay in possession for 12 years; the mortgagee may sell or agree to sell the land on the mortgagor's default; or the mortgagee may foreclose. **21–051**

Secondly, there is a statutory exception which relates to companies. A company's debenture may contain conditions making the debenture irredeemable or redeemable only on the happening of a remote contingency or on the expiration of a long period.[95]

Thirdly, some reasonable restrictions on the right to redeem may be permitted. The types of restrictions normally found are set out below.

(a) clauses giving the mortgagee some "collateral advantage". A "collateral advantage" confers an advantage on the mortgagee in addition to the payment of interest on the loan.[96] A mortgagor who is a garage proprietor **21–052**

[93] *Samuel v. Jarrah Timber and Wood Paving Corpn. Ltd* [1904] A.C. 323 at 329.

[94] See Megarry and Wade, *op. cit.* at pp. 19–141 *et seq.*

[95] CA 1985, s. 193.

[96] These clauses may also be struck down under the separate "restraint of trade" doctrine, which can apply even if there is no security. In this case, the clause, to be valid, must be reasonable not only between the parties but from the point of view of the public interest, and it may sometimes be required that the clause is no wider than is needed to protect a proprietary interest. It seems probable that the doctrines converge to a large degree. See generally Treitel, *The Law of Contract*, (10th ed.) pp. 415 *et seq.*; Beatson *Anson's Law of Contract* (27th ed.) p. 359. Such clauses may also be anti-competitive under Art. 85 of the E.C. Treaty.

or publican, for example, may "tie" him or herself to a petrol company or brewery for a period as an additional obligation, in return for the mortgage.[97] If the clause is unconscionable[98] or restricts the right to redeem, it may be struck out. The court will look at the reality of the situation—whether the clause makes the right to redeem illusory, for example.[99] A collateral advantage may be more reasonable when the mortgage is granted after the property has been acquired, because the mortgage and the advantage can be seen as distinct. An advantage is more likely to be seen as fair if it ceases with the mortgage.[1] A modern court is likely to distinguish between ordinary commercial transactions and those involving oppression, however, so that a tie made on fair commercial terms which continues after redemption may be upheld in appropriate cases.[2]

It is possible, however, that the validity of such arrangements may be challengeable under Article 85 of the Treaty of Rome.[3]

21–053 **(b) postponements of redemption (prohibitions on repayment).** Postponement of the right to redeem may be permissible if it is not unreasonable, undue or oppressive, or if the mortgagor is a company. If a commercial borrower with an existing mortgage who is not under any pressure transfers its mortgage to an "arms length" mortgagee to secure a better rate of interest, and asks for the term to be fixed at, say, 40 years, to ensure that the repayments are spread over a period and will not be called in at any time, a prohibition on repayment would be reasonable.

21–054 **(c) provisions requiring additional sums to be paid (premiums, or penalties, or index-linking clauses).**[4] A premium on prepayment requires the borrower to pay the mortgagee a sum of money for the privilege of early repayment. Whether true premiums are enforceable (where there is a security) depends on all the facts: the relative strengths of the parties,[5] the availability of independent legal advice, the size of the premium, and so on. If there is no security, a premium cannot be a "clog" on the equity of redemption, and it is enforceable unless it amounts to a "penalty". It may be a penalty if it is payable on default, and it is not a genuine pre-estimate of the likely losses.[6] An example of a "genuine pre-estimate" might be the compensation clauses found in some term loans where the lending bank

---

[97] See *Esso Petroleum Co Ltd v. Harper's Garage (Stourport) Ltd* [1968] A.C. 269.
[98] *Multiservice Bookbinding Ltd. v. Marden* [1979] Ch. 84.
[99] *Knightsbridge Estates Trust Ltd v. Byrne* [1939] Ch. 441 (affirmed [1940] A.C. 613).
[1] As in *Biggs v. Hoddinott* [1898] 2 Ch. 307.
[2] *Kreglinger v. New Patagonia Meat and Cold Storage Co Ltd* [1913] A.C. 25.
[3] Megarry and Wade, *The Law of Real Property* (6th ed., Harpum ed.), paras 19.131.
[4] See Beatson, *Anson's Law of Contract*, (27th ed.) p. 587.
[5] See *Cityland and Property (Holdings) Ltd v. Dabrah* [1968] Ch. 166.
[6] See *Re Anglo-Danubian Steam Navign. and Colliery Co* (1875) L.R. 20 Eq. 339; *Re Phillips ex p. Bath* (1884) 27 Ch.D. 590; *Booth v. Salvation Army Building Assn. Ltd.* (1897) 14 T.L.R. 3l; *Cato v. Cato* (1972) 116 Sol Jo. 138.

funds itself in the interbank market for a fixed period, and where the loan provides for repayments to become due at periods matching the bank's funding periods. Losses may occur if early repayment causes a mismatch of interest rates, and a term providing for the prepayer to compensate the bank for such losses might therefore not be objectionable. A provision for an increase in the rate of interest which is not related to possible losses would be a penalty, although there may be ways to require a payment to be made which avoid this effect: for example, fixing a high rate of interest at the outset and then reducing it for prompt payment.

Undue influence, misrepresentation or other contractual wrong

A mortgage may be set aside if there has been some contractual defect such as *non est factum* (this would be rare), or where one party exerts undue influence over, or makes some misrepresentation to, the other party.[7] Banks may be responsible themselves for such behaviour, but it is unlikely, particularly now that reputable lenders must be aware of the risks. What is much more likely is that a mortgage might be challenged, and perhaps set aside,[8] where the bank has notice (actual or constructive) that undue influence or misrepresentation has been exercised by a borrower over another person who is a party to the mortgage, or acting as surety for the borrower. This has been an important issue in numerous cases in the past decade or more, and the House of Lords' guidance to lenders was given in the case of *Barclays Bank v. O'Brien*[9]; the guidance was intended to be authoritative, but the case has been the subject of a vast amount of judicial consideration and interpretation. Banks can and should protect themselves by taking reasonable steps to ensure that any third party who may be vulnerable to a legal wrong such as undue influence receives independent legal advice. **21–055**

Individuals frequently approach banks with requests for loans and prepared to use their family property to secure the loan. In order to charge the property, it is necessary to obtain the consent of other persons with an interest in the property, such as a spouse. The spouse may be willing to agree to the proposal, but it is not easy for banks to distinguish between straightforward transactions in which both parties are willingly participating and transactions where one of the parties has been intimidated or over persuaded into agreement. Recognising that requiring banks to inquire whether there has been undue influence would be onerous and would **21–056**

[7] See *Lloyds Bank v. Bundy* [1975] Q.B. 326 and *National Westminster Bank v. Morgan* [1983] 2 All E.R. 85, discussed above, Chap. 3.

[8] The mortgage may be set aside in its entirety: *TSB v. Camfield* [1995] 1 All E.R. 951 CA; but see *Dunbar Bank v. Nadeem* [1997] 1 F.L.R. 318.

[9] [1994] 4 W.L.R. 786. See above, Chaps 3 and 18. The court recognised that there may also be situations where the mortgagor acts as the mortgagee's *agent* in wrongfully procuring the consent of another party to the transaction.

inhibit lending, the House of Lords held, in *C.I.B.C. Mortgages v. Pitt*,[10] that the question whether the bank has notice of some contractual wrong depends on what the transaction looks like on its *face*. In the case of a normal joint mortgage, where there are no other suspicious factors, the bank is not regarded as being put on inquiry. Normally, banks are on notice only where a transaction is not for the financial advantage of one of the parties[11] (typically a wife, although it might be a cohabitee, elderly parent or, indeed, any other person). In such a case, the bank should follow the "reasonable steps" described by Lord Browne-Wilkinson in *Barclays Bank v. O'Brien*: that is, to advise the mortgagor or surety in a private interview that he or she should obtain independent legal advice.[12] If there are actual suspicious factors—where, for example, one of the parties is obviously intimidated by the other—then the bank should *ensure* that the vulnerable party receives independent legal advice.

21–057 The risk that one party is behaving wrongfully is normally less obvious to the bank in mortgage transactions than when the spouse is acting as a surety, although in fact it is just as likely that people will be overpersuaded into signing mortgages as signing guarantees, and the wrongful behaviour is likely to produce the same result—that is, the victim may lose the right in the property. Some first instance decisions held that a transaction might be "on its face" not to the advantage of one of the parties if a loan is sought jointly by husband and wife for a "family" company, and the wife holds some interest in the company; in this case, it was thought, the bank could not simply take it for granted that the loan was truly for their joint purposes. The wife's interest in the company must be a real one, and must be in proportion to the liability she is being asked to assume.[13] Further, the financial advantage for the wife which should be taken into account has been held in these cases to be her "direct" advantage, not any indirect benefit she might gain from her husband's prosperity.[14]

21–058 If there are striking[15] and relevant features about the relationship or the behaviour of the parties (if one party is unable to speak English, for example, or the couple come from a culture where wives traditionally rely on their husbands in financial matters[16]) the bank should be alert to the

---

[10] [1994] 4 All E.R.433—the companion case to *Barclays Bank v. O'Brien* [1974] 4 W.L.R. 786.

[11] See, *e.g., Barclays Bank v. Sumner* [1996] E.G.C.S.96.

[12] *Barclays Bank v. O'Brien*, [1994] 4 W.L.R. 786 and the Banking Code (1999), para. 3.14; see above, Chaps. 3 and 18.

[13] *Goode Durrant Administration v. Biddulph* [1994] 2 F.L.R. 551 (the wife's share of any profit would be 2.5 per cent, whereas she ran the risk of personal liability for a large sum); *cf. Britannia BS v. Pugh* [1997] 2 F.L.R. 7, where development properties and home were jointly owned by husband and wife. See also *Bank of Cyprus (London) Ltd v. Markou* [1999] 2 All E.R. 707. But see now *Bank of Scotland v. Bennett* [1999] Lloyd's Rep. Bank. 145, CA.

[14] This element seems to distinguish the "financial advantage" for the wife of *O'Brien* and *Pitt* from "manifest disadvantage" of presumed undue influence (see above, Chap. 3).

[15] See *Allied Irish Bank v. Byrne* [1995] 2 F.L.R. 325.

[16] *e.g. BCCI v. Aboody* [1992] 4 All E.R. 955; *Dunbar Bank v. Nadeem* [1997] 1 F.L.R. 318.

possibility that these features may later be regarded as putting the bank on notice of undue influence. On the other hand, the mere fact that one party has taken the lead in negotiating the transaction is not enough to put the bank on inquiry.[17]

Banks should also be aware that in some extreme cases, lenders have been regarded by the court as being on notice where the relationship between the parties was not obviously a relationship of trust and confidence, but where there was some unconscionable behaviour. In *Credit Lyonnais Nederland v. Burch*[18] and *Steeples v. Lea,*[19] transactions were set aside where junior employees (in the first case a young employee) had provided guarantees, together with mortgages over their property in favour of their employers. In both cases, the Court of Appeal regarded the transactions as manifestly disadvantageous to the employee and the bank as being on constructive notice. It seems therefore that in cases where there is no good reason, emotional or financial, why a person (like an employee) is willing to act as surety, the bank should at least ensure that the vulnerable party receives independent legal advice. **21–059**

In *Royal Bank of Scotland v. Etridge*,[20] the Court of Appeal laid down guidelines for the division of responsibility between banks and solicitors in *O'Brien* cases. It seems that the main risk to the bank is from the *Burch* kind of case: although the bank is normally entitled to assume that a solicitor who is asked to advise the wife will discharge his or her duties fully and competently, the bank cannot make any such assumption if it knows or ought to know that it is false. If the bank is in possession of material information which is not available to the solicitor, or if the transaction is such that no competent solicitor could properly advise the wife to enter into it, the fact that the wife has been advised by the solicitor will not prevent the bank from being fixed with constructive notice. Where the lender is aware of facts which make the arrangements special or unusual in some way, it must at least ensure that these facts are known to the solicitors. Where a lender, for example, was aware that a widowed sister was charging her house to assist her brother and that she would not herself be able to afford the monthly repayments on the mortgage (the brother agreed to be a surety for the repayments), the lender was on constructive notice of the sister's trust and confidence in her brother and under a duty to take reasonable steps to satisfy itself that she was freely entering into the agreement; it should have informed the solicitors advising her of her situation, but failed to do so. The fact that the solicitors knew the circumstances made no difference, because the lender was not aware of that at the time.[21] **21–060**

[17] *Britannia BS v. Pugh*, [1997] 2 F.L.R. 7.

[18] [1997] 1 All E.R. 144, CA ("a case which shocked the conscience of the court", *per* Millett L.J.).

[19] [1998] 1 F.L.R. 143.

[20] [1998] 4 All E.R. 75.

[21] *Northern Rock B.S. v. Hazel Archer* [1999] Lloyds L.R. Bank, CA.

21–061 Nevertheless, it is thought that the *O'Brien* case and its later interpretations have generally had the effect that a transaction which seems like a routine joint mortgage for a normal purpose[22] where there are no obvious suspicious factors should pose no risk for banks. If there are reasons for doubt, ensuring that the vulnerable party obtains independent legal advice should protect most transactions.

Statutory regulation of credit

21–062 The CCA 1974 applies to mortgages given to individuals if the credit does not exceed £25,000[23] and if none of the exemptions apply; given the financial limit, the Act would primarily affect second mortgages. If the Act applies, the agreement must be in a specified form, and the mortgagor must be given a seven day period in case he or she wishes to change his or her mind. The mortgage may generally only be enforced on a court order.[24]

21–063 The court also has power under section 137 of the CCC 1974 to re-open extortionate credit bargains made by banks and finance companies[25]; in this case, there is no restriction as to the size of the loan. A loan is extortionate if it requires the debtor or a relative of his or hers to make payments which are "grossly exorbitant or . . . otherwise grossly contravene the ordinary principles of fair dealing".[26] A number of factors, including age, experience, business capacity, state of health and the degree of financial pressure the debtor was under should be taken into account.[27] Courts seem to be reluctant to find even high levels of interest extortionate,[28] and it is unlikely that banks would be vulnerable to this liability.

The Rights and Remedies of the Mortgagee

21–064 A mortgagee has rights it may exercise even without default by the mortgagor, such as taking possession. But rights which can be exercised without default merge into the remedies of the mortgagee on default, because bank mortgages normally permit the bank to make demand at any time,[29] and thus to "manufacture" a default.[30]

---

[22] See *C.I.B.C. Mortgages v. Pitt* [1994] 4 All E.R. 433.

[23] Consumer Credit (Increase of Monetary Limits) Order 1983 (S.I. 1983, No. 1878) (as amended by S.I. 1998 No. 996).

[24] CCA 1974, s. 126 and 173(3).

[25] Not building societies.

[26] See *Wills v. Wood* [1984] C.C.L.R. 7, and *Davies v. Direct Loans Ltd* [1986] 1 W.L.R. 823.

[27] CCA 1974, s. 138(3).

[28] See, *e.g.*, *A Ketley Ltd v. Scott* [1980] C.C.L.R. 37, where it was held that an annual rate of interest of 48 per cent was not extortionate. But the UTCCR 1999 may be effective in some cases: see *Falco Finance Ltd v. Gough* [1999] 17 Tr.L.R. 526

[29] Even after the death of the mortgagor: *Barclays Bank Ltd v. Kiley* [1961] 2 All E.R. 849.

[30] If a company is in administration, a mortgagee is not entitled to exercise its powers of sale or take any other steps to enforce its security against the company without the consent of the administrator or leave of the court: IA 1986, s. 11(3). See *Re Atlantic Computer Systems plc* [1990] B.C.C. 857 for guidance as to the basis on which the court will exercise its discretion, and see Chap. 24.

The right to possession

A legal mortgagee is entitled to possession of the property as soon as the security has been executed—"even before the ink is dry on the mortgage",[31] even though there has been no default. An equitable mortgagee probably has the same right if the mortgage includes a covenant for a legal mortgage and a power of attorney.[32] **21–065**

Possession is achieved by taking the management of the estate out of the mortgagor's hands, even if the mortgagor is still in physical occupation[33]—oddly, and unsatisfactorily,[34] if the mortgagor is absent, even temporarily, the mortgagee may take possession even of a dwelling house without a court order.[35] It is a criminal offence, however, for anyone to threaten violence against a person who is present on any premises, in order to gain entry.[36] If the mortgagor is on the premises, a court order must be obtained[37] if it is a dwelling house. Where an action for possession is brought, any co-occupier must be joined as a party.

Banks normally prefer not to go into possession of mortgaged property. **21–066** It is not only administratively inconvenient to do so, but it means that the mortgagee is liable for any negligence which causes damage to the property, and is under a strict duty to account to the mortgagor for profits and rents. In addition, the mortgagee may be liable in other ways—for nuisance, for example, or even possibly for environmental damage.[38] Since these problems may be avoided by appointing a receiver, who is the agent of the *mortgagor*, banks regard the appointment of a receiver as a better remedy than going into possession.

Banks used to exercise their right to take possession rarely, therefore, **21–067** unless there was a default. The drop in property values in the 1980s, however, meant that it became more common for banks to take possession, in order to let the property and wait for an upturn in the market. This would cause serious problems for mortgagors, who would still have to pay the bank any shortfall between the amount received from the rent and the payments required under the mortgage, as well as their own housing costs.

Problems of this sort in domestic lending come before the courts because, where the land includes a dwelling house, the right to take

---

31 *Four-Maids Ltd v. Dudley Marshall (Properties) Ltd* [1957] Ch. 317; *National Westminster Bank v. Skelton* [1993] 1 W.L.R. 72. Unless the mortgagee gives notice of intent to take possession the mortgagor has many of the normal rights of a full owner, such as the right to rents or to sue for trespass, LPA 1925, s. 98 and s. 141.

32 Encyclopaedia, E(501); *Barclays Bank Ltd v. Bird* [1954] Ch. 274.

33 *Noyes v. Pollock* (1886) 32 Ch.D. 53.

34 See Megarry and Wade, *op. cit.,* para. 19–074.

35 *Ropaigealach v. Barclays Bank,* [1999] 2 W.L.R. 17. There is a lacuna in the protection for dwelling houses given by s. 36 of the Administration of Justice Act 1970. See Dixon [1999] C.L.J. 281.

36 Criminal Law Act 1977, s. 6.

37 See below, para. 21–066.

38 See further above, para. 21–005.

possession has been qualified by statute,[39] and the court has a discretion to adjourn proceedings for possession if it appears that the mortgagor is likely to be able to pay any sums due or to remedy any fault within a reasonable period.[40]

21–068 Account can be taken of a mortgagor's proposal to pay off the arrears, often by selling the property,[41] provided that the mortgagor has prospects of being able to clear the arrears within a reasonable time.[42] In *Palk v. Mortgage Services Funding plc*,[43] the mortgagee wished to take possession of the property in order to rent it out until the market improved. The mortgagor, who had to pay the shortfall between the rent and his repayments, however, made a successful application to the court for the property to be sold instead. Other cases have taken a more traditional and restrictive approach, particularly of course, where it has seemed from the facts that the mortgagor is merely trying to postpone the evil day.[44] An order will not be suspended simply to enable the borrower to obtain a better price for the property, and where the mortgagor would not be able to discharge the mortgage fully even by selling, the mortgagee's rights are of primary importance.[45]

Sale

21–069 The power of sale is the most important remedy. There are statutory rights of sale, though standard forms also contain an express power or modifications to the statutory power.[46] The statutory power is given for mortgages made by deed,[47] and may be exercised on default by the mortgagor—that is, the power of sale must have *arisen* (where money is due) and have *become exercisable* (for example, where an instalment is due).

---

[39] Administration of Justice Act 1970, s. 36; Administration of Justice Act 1973, s. 8.

[40] *Cheltenham and Gloucester Building Society v. Norgan* [1996] 1 W.L.R. 343, CA.

[41] *Royal Trust of Canada v. Markham* [1975] 1 W.L.R. 1416. See further *Target Home Loans Ltd. v. Clothier* [1994] 1All E.R. 439; *National & Provincial Building Society v. Lloyd* [1996] 1 All E.R. 630, CA; *Bristol and West Building Society v. Ellis* [1996] 73 P. & C.R. 158, CA.

[42] *First National Bank v. Syed* [1991] 2 All E.R. 250, CA; *Town & Country Building Society v. Julien* [1992] 24 H.L.R. 312, CA.

[43] [1993] Ch. 330, CA: under s. 91(2) of the LPA 1925, see below para. 21–076. See also *Barrett v. Halifax B.S.* [1996] 28 H.L.R. 634. In *Albany Home Loans Ltd v. Massey* [1997] 2 All E.R. 609, CA, it was held that there was an equitable jurisdiction to refuse to make a possession order against a husband who had defaulted where the wife was disputing the claim under *Barclays Bank v. O'Brien*, [1994] 4 W.L.R. 786. The possession order could only have taken effect against her husband, at least for a time, and if he were invited back by the wife, he might be in contempt of court.

[44] See *Cheltenham and Gloucester Building Society v. Krausz* [1997] 1 All E.R. 21 and *Cheltenham and Gloucester B.S. v. Booker* [1997] 29 H.L.R. 634, noted, A. Kenny [1998] Conv. 228.

[45] *Cheltenham and Gloucester Building Society v. Krausz*, [1997] 1 All E.R. 21.

[46] Where the mortgagee is unable or unwilling to rely on the statutory power, it may apply to the court for an order for sale under LPA 1925, s. 91.

[47] LPA 1925, s. 101(1).

Sale can be of the whole or of parts of the property; it can take place by auction or private contract, and it may be subject to such conditions as the mortgagee thinks fit. The power of sale may be exercised by "any person for the time being entitled to receive and give a discharge for the mortgage money",[48] and the conveyance on sale may be made in the name of either mortgagor or mortgagee,[49] though the latter is more common. **21–070**

The statutory power *arises* "when the mortgage money has become due," (for example, on the contractual date of redemption or on default of repayment on demand) but does not become *exercisable* until one of the following conditions has been met[50]: **21–071**

(1) demand for payment followed by the default continuing for three months; or

(2) interest remaining in arrears for two months; or

(3) breach of some covenant (other than payment of principal and interest).

The statutory power may be varied, extended or wholly excluded by the mortgage,[51] and banks normally exclude the statutory restrictions. Express clauses[52] may extend the power as between bank and purchaser, so that the power is exercisable at any time (at least, once the bank has made demand of the mortgagor). In fact, purchasers have statutory protection from verifying that the power has become exercisable,[53] and have a remedy in damages against the person exercising the power if they are injured by an unauthorised or improper exercise of it.[54] The protection will not operate, however, if they become aware of any impropriety,[55] and inserting an express clause may help to avoid claims that the power has been improperly exercised. **21–072**

There may be other rights in the mortgage—relating, for example, to the sale of chattels in the property, or with a company mortgage, to the separation and separate sale of fixtures. In leasehold mortgages there may **21–073**

---

48 LPA 1925, s. 106(1).

49 LPA 1925, ss. 88 and 89.

50 LPA 1925, s. 103. The court has also power to order a sale, but if the mortgagee's statutory power of sale has arisen and is exercisable, the court will only order sale in exceptional circumstances: *Arab Bank plc. v. Merchantile Holdings Ltd* [1994] 2 W.l.R. 307. See also below paras 21–074 *et seq.*

51 LPA 1925, s.101(34).

52 *e.g.* "Section 103 of the LPA 1925 shall not apply to this security but the statutory power of sale shall as between the bank and a purchaser from the Bank arise on and be exercisable at any time after the execution of this security provided that the Bank shall not exercise the said power of sale until payment of the moneys hereby secured has been demanded but this proviso shall not affect a purchaser or put him on inquiry whether such demand has been made."

53 LPA 1925, s. 104.

54 LPA 1925, s. 104(2).

55 *Lord Waring v. London and Manchester Assurance Co Ltd* [1935] Ch. 310.

be terms allowing the mortgagee to sell by granting leases at a premium,[56] or allowing the mortgagee to charge the mortgagor for the landlord's obligations to leaseholders. It is desirable to retain and exercise the statutory power, for this has the effect of discharging not only the mortgagee's own mortgage, but also any subsequent incumbrance, without the consent of the incumbrancer, thus giving the purchaser clear title.[57]

21–074 **Protection of the mortgagor**. The mortgagee, though not in other respects a trustee of the power of sale, owes a limited duty—an equitable duty, not a duty in tort[58]—to the mortgagor and to any guarantor of the mortgagor's debt, but not to a beneficiary under a trust of whose interest it has notice,[59] to take reasonable care to obtain the true market value of the property at the date on which it decides to sell.[60] The mortgagee may exercise the power of sale even though the mortgagor has agreed on a sale which would produce enough to pay the whole mortgage debt,[61] but if the mortgagor tenders the whole sum, that will prevent sale by the mortgagee. The mortgagee may not sell to itself, because that would amount to foreclosure.[62]

21–075 Although the expression of the duty is narrowly defined, courts have nevertheless sometimes taken a broader view of the mortgagee's duties. In *Palk v. Mortgage Services Funding plc*,[63] Sir Donald Nicholls V.C. said that once a mortgagee takes steps to exercise its rights and its security it must act fairly towards the mortgagor, including taking reasonable care of the property and taking reasonable care to maximise the mortgagor's return from it. He implied that the mortgagee should not act in "a cavalier fashion".

21–076 *Palk* was one of the cases following the collapse of property prices in the late 1980s when the "negative equity" of many properties prompted banks into taking possession of properties to let them with a view to sale when the market improved. The court has discretion, in the case of a dwelling house, to order a sale and to adjourn the possession proceedings[64] if it considers

---

[56] *i.e.* not for a regular rent.

[57] LPA 1925, s. 104(1).

[58] *China & South Sea Bank Ltd v. Tan Soon Gin* [1990] A.C. 53, PC. *Cf.* the view of the Court of Appeal in *Standard Chartered Bank v. Walker* [1982] 3 All E.R 938, that a duty of care existed. See Berg, [1993] J.B.L. 213. See also *Medforth v. Blake* [1999] 3 All E.R. 97 at 111, *per* Sir Richard Scott, V.-C. (who did not think the distinction was material: it does not matter "one jot whether the duty is expressed as a common law duty or as a duty in equity." But it might make some difference, *e.g.* with regard to issues of limitation) and Chap. 24.

[59] *Parker-Tweedale v. Dunbar Bank* [1991] Ch.12.

[60] *Downsview Nominees Ltd v. First City Corp.* [1993] 2 W.L.R. 86, PC; *Cuckmere Brick Co. Ltd. v. Mutual Finance Ltd* [1971] Ch. 949. The mortgagee does not have a duty to take steps to preserve the value of the security in the exercise of its security rights ahead of obtaining possession of and control of the property subject to the mortgage: *AIB Finance Ltd v. Debtors* [1998] 2 All E.R. 929.

[61] *Duke v. Robson* [1973] 1 All E.R. 481.

[62] *Farrar v. Farrars Ltd* (1889) 40 Ch. D. 395, CA.

[63] [1993] Ch. 330, CA, see above, para. 21–068. See also Dixon [1998] Legal Studies 278.

[64] LPA 1925, s. 91(2); Administration of Justice Act 1970, s. 36, Administration of Justice Act 1973, s. 8.

that the mortgagor is likely to be able within a reasonable period to pay any sums due. In *Palk*, the court permitted a sale in the mortgagor's interest at a depressed market price against the wishes of the mortgagee by virtue of this discretion. This approach, however, may be out of line with other decisions which take a less generous approach to the problems of the mortgagor,[65] although it has since been applied: in *Polonski v. Lloyds Bank Mortgages Ltd*,[66] the mortgagee wished to delay sale of the property in order to allow the price to improve, but the owner wished to sell because of unpleasant housing conditions affecting her children. It was held, following *Palk*, that she could accept an offer to purchase the house which left a considerable shortfall in the repayments to the mortgagee. In some respects, this is a sensible decision: not only because it can be said to show sound social and family values, but also because of the likelihood that, in cases where there is real hardship, the mortgagor will simply leave the property and return the keys.[67]

Proceeds of sale. The mortgagee is trustee of the proceeds and to avoid breach of trust must pay in this order: **21–077**

(1) prior incumbrancers;[68]

(2) costs of sale;

(3) moneys payable under the mortgage agreement;

(4) any subsequent mortgagee, which pays itself, then subsequent mortgagees, then the mortgagor; and then

(5) the mortgagor.

If a search of the Land Register, or (with unregistered land) the Land Charges register, for other incumbrances has been made, and, through no fault of its own the bank had no notice of a subsequent mortgagee, and paid any surplus to the mortgagor or another incumbrancer, the bank is not liable.[69]

Equitable mortgages. The statutory power of sale covers equitable mortgages if they are made by deed and if the mortgagor is the legal owner of the property. If the equitable mortgage has not been made by deed, there is no power to transfer the legal estate, though the mortgagee may transfer good equitable title. In that case, therefore, an equitable mortgagee of a **21–078**

[65] See *Krausz* [1997] 1 All E.R. 21 and *Booker* [1997] 29 H.L.R. 634.
[66] *The Times*, May 6, 1997. See Thompson [1998] Conv. 125.
[67] See Thompson, *op. cit*.
[68] LPA 1925, s. 105.
[69] Tr A 1925, s. 30(1) says the trustee is only liable for "his own wilful default."

legal estate must apply to the court for an order of sale.[70] An irrevocable power of attorney may be taken separately, but again, it must be made by deed if it is to transfer the legal title.[71] A declaration of trust by the mortgagor that he or she holds legal title for the mortgagee, coupled with a power in the bank to remove the trustee and appoint another person would be effective.[72] With registered land, however, the bank probably may not sell the legal estate while the mortgage remains equitable, and it must first become legal mortgagee (which the mortgage usually allows) by registering the charge.[73]

The purchaser obtains good title to the whole estate, subject only to mortgages prior to those of the mortgagee who sells. The sale extinguishes the security of the selling mortgagee, and any mortgages with lower priority.[74]

Action for foreclosure

21–079 Foreclosure is a draconian remedy: a judicial procedure by which the mortgagee obtains the land freed from the mortgagor's equity of redemption. The right to foreclose arises, generally, only once the legal date of redemption has passed. Foreclosure is rarely sought, and can only be obtained in an action brought by a legal mortgagee or an equitable mortgagee who is entitled to a legal mortgage.[75] All other incumbrancers must be parties, and must be satisfied.

If an order is made, it extinguishes the title of the mortgagor so that for all purposes the mortgagee is entitled to the mortgagor's rights in the property. The court may,[76] and generally will, order a sale instead, to establish the price of the property, and to prevent the mortgagee receiving a windfall.

Appointment of receiver[77]

21–080 Receivers may be appointed under a statutory power by the court, or under an express power. In deciding whether to appoint a receiver, the mortgagee owes no duty to the mortgagor or to guarantors.[78] If the mortgage is by deed, there is a statutory right to appoint a receiver in order to collect income from the property, but the appointment cannot be made

[70] The court has power under ss. 90 and 91 of the LPA 1925. The court can vest title in the purchaser, or appoint a person to convey the land or vest a term in the mortgagee so that it can sell as if it were a legal mortgagee.

[71] Powers of Attorney Act 1971, s. 52 of the LPA 1925

[72] The bank appoints a nominee who is willing to convey the legal title.

[73] LRA 1925, ss. 59(2) and 106(2); Encyclopaedia, E(586) n. 8. This step is unnecessary for unregistered land: *Re White Rose Cottage* [1965] Ch. 940.

[74] LPA 1925, ss. 88, 89 and 104.

[75] *Re Owen* [1894] 3 Ch. 220.

[76] LPA 1925, s. 91.

[77] See further Chap. 24.

[78] *Shamji v. Johnson Matthey Bankers Ltd* (1994) L.D.A.B. 396.

until the statutory power of sale has become exercisable.[79] Both the statutory power and this restriction may be varied, extended or excluded, and it is normal for mortgages to provide for the appointment of a receiver.[80]

The receiver is given powers in the name of the mortgagor to take possession of the property, and to deal with it, for example by selling, leasing or mortgaging it. If (unusually) there is an equitable mortgage with no express power to appoint a receiver, the court has inherent power to appoint one.

Banks usually appoint receivers in connection with company or individual **21–081** business mortgages, but the procedure has advantages for the bank even with an individual domestic mortgage: the bank does not have the administrative burden of realisation of the property, and the receiver's costs are recouped from the assets of the mortgagor. Above all, receivers are not regarded as the agents of the bank, unless it interferes with them and gives them directions,[81] and negligence by the receiver is usually not the responsibility of the bank, although it may agree to indemnify the receiver.

The receiver, like the mortgagee, owes certain specific duties in equity, both to the mortgagor and to subsequent incumbrancers.[82] He or she must apply the proceeds of sale in the order provided by statute.[83]

Other rights of the mortgagee

The right to additional property: a mortgage of land includes fixtures,[84] and **21–082** anything affixed later becomes subject to the mortgage.[85] Similarly, if the mortgagor of leasehold property acquires a new lease or the freehold reversion, the new interest becomes subject to the mortgage.[86]

The right to documents of title: where the mortgage is registered, the **21–083** mortgagee has a Charge Certificate. In unregistered land, a first legal mortgagee is entitled to all the title deeds,[87] though the mortgagor is entitled to inspect them and make copies at his or her own expense.[88] An equitable mortgagee is not entitled to them unless this is stipulated (except where the mortgage is—or was—made by deposit of deeds[89]).

---

[79] LPA 1925, s. 109.

[80] LPA 1925, s. 101. Of a receiver and manager "at any time after the bank shall have demanded payment of any moneys hereby secured or if requested by the Mortgagor . . ."

[81] See Chap. 24.

[82] *Downsview Nominees Ltd v. First City Corpn. Ltd* [1993] A.C. 295, PC, *per* Lord Templeman, pp. 312 *et seq.*;(*cf. Standard Chartered Bank Ltd v. Walker* [1982] 3 All E.R. 938.) See also *Medforth v. Blake* [1999] 3 All E.R. 97.

[83] LPA 1925, s. 109(8).

[84] For a discussion of fixtures, see Megarry and Wade, *The Law of Real Property* (6th ed) paras. 14–311 *et seq.*

[85] *Reynolds v. Ashby & Son* [1904] A.C. 466.

[86] *Leigh v. Burnett* (1885) 29 Ch.D. 231; *Chelsea Estates Investment Trust Co Ltd v. Marche* [1955] Ch. 328.

[87] LPA 1925, ss. 86 and 87.

[88] LPA 1925, s. 96.

[89] Before the LPMPA, see above, para. 21–043.

21–084 **Granting and surrendering leases**. The mortgagee has a statutory power to grant leases not exceeding 50 years[90] if it is in possession and the mortgage does not prohibit it. Either mortgagee or mortgagor, if entitled to exercise the power of leasing, may for that purpose accept the surrender from a tenant of all or part of a leasehold interest which is part of the mortgaged property.[91] A business tenant often has a statutory right to renew his or her lease, and the landlord's duty to renew it cannot be excluded by the mortgage.[92]

21–085 **The right to protect the property**. Bank mortgages should contain terms concerning maintenance of the property and insurance, although even without express terms, there are common law and statutory powers to restrain deliberate damage, to do necessary repairs, and to insure against fire.[93] Express provision is desirable, though, because only *necessary* repairs may be charged to the mortgagor. If the mortgagee goes into possession to effect the repairs, it must account strictly for what is done, and it is more sensible to appoint a receiver, as we have noted above. The statutory right to insure against fire only exists if the mortgage is by deed, and is only to the extent of two-thirds of reinstatement value, and does not cover other risks. Again, express provision should be made.

21–086 **The right to tack**. Tacking or consolidation is the right of a secured lender to add further monies to the security, so that those monies are also secured. This is discussed further below.[94]

Leasehold Mortgages: Special Features

The nature of the leasehold interest: forfeiture

21–087 Mortgages of leasehold property are not entirely straightforward for lenders. Not only will tenants owe obligations to their landlord which probably include duties affecting the value of the property, like the duty to repair, but also the landlord may be entitled to forfeit the lease—that is, to end the lease prematurely by re-entering the premises—and, in that case, naturally, the security vanishes. Banks should be aware that leases are not always suitable for mortgage purposes.

21–088 The landlord may forfeit the lease if the tenant does not pay rent or denies the landlord's title, or if there is a covenant giving a right to forfeiture on breach, and a breach takes place. The landlord must prove that he or she is entitled to forfeit the lease, however, and there is a heavy burden of proof on the landlord.[95] The court may grant the tenant equitable

[90] For agricultural or occupation purposes, LPA 1925, s. 99.
[91] LPA 1925, s. 100.
[92] Landlord and Tenant Act 1954, s. 36.
[93] LPA 1925, s. 101.
[94] See below, para. 21–141.
[95] Megarry and Wade, *op. cit.,* para. 14–129.

relief against forfeiture on the ground of non-payment of rent, and there is statutory relief against forfeiture on other grounds.

If the bank discovers that the rent has not been paid, it should pay the arrears itself and try to realise the security, in case the landlord demands the rent from the tenant (this is usually allowed by the terms of the lease) and brings an action for possession. If this happens, the tenant may pay all arrears of rent and get the proceedings stayed, or claim relief in equity. If it is just and equitable, and if the tenant pays the rent and the landlord's expenses, the court will give relief and reinstate the lease. This can be done normally within six months of the order for possession,[96] but relief is discretionary and may not always be given (for example, it may not be granted if the landlord has agreed to lease the property to another person). **21–089**

For breaches other than non-payment of rent, the landlord must serve a statutory notice,[97] specifying the breach, its remedy, and any compensation sought; if this is not done, the forfeiture is void. The tenant must be given a reasonable time, usually three months, to comply with the notice, and if he or she does not do so, the landlord may enforce the forfeiture by action.

The right of the landlord to forfeit may cause difficulties for banks although the tenant or mortgagee[98] can apply to the court for relief, and the court may make an order vesting the whole or part of the premises in the applicant, on any conditions it thinks fit.[99] If an order is granted, the effect is as if the lease had never been forfeited. However, it may not be possible for the bank to apply to the court in time to stop the forfeiture, because it may not know of the breach before the landlord entered the premises, and in that case it would be too late for the bank to apply to the court. Procedural rules, however, now require the landlord to file the particulars of the claim for service on the mortgagee,[1] and provide some protection for them in respect of leasehold property. **21–090**

Prohibitions on assignment[2]: The tenant is free to mortgage or assign the property unless the lease contains prohibitions on such actions, as many do. If there is a prohibition, it is a contractual matter between landlord and tenant; this means that if the tenant does mortgage the property, the landlord may be able to forfeit the lease for breach of the covenant, with **21–091**

[96] It is more complicated that this, and sometimes a longer period is allowed. See Megarry and Wade, *The Law of Real Property* (6th ed.) para. 14–130. The main statutes governing this are the Common Law Procedure Act 1852 and the County Courts Act 1984.

[97] Under LPA 1925, s. 146.

[98] Under LPA 1925, s. 46(4).

[99] The mortgagee has to take a new lease, and becomes directly responsible to the landlord. This is not the equivalent of foreclosure, because the mortgagor still has the equity of redemption against the new lease.

[1] See Megarry and Wade, *op. cit.*, para. 14–144.

[2] See generally, Megarry and Wade, *op. cit.* para. 14–259. *et seq*. It is a matter of construction of a lease whether a prohibition in it affects the mortgage. Often the prohibition is against "assignment, underletting or parting with possession" of all or any part of the premises.

the consequences noted above. Relief is unlikely to be available, because such a breach can hardly be "remedied" if the mortgagee insists on the security.

21–092 A prohibition may be absolute or conditional. An absolute prohibition prevents assignment or other transactions, and the landlord cannot be compelled to consent. A conditional prohibition usually requires the landlord's consent as the condition of the transaction. In this case, statute requires that the landlord shall not unreasonably withhold his consent.[3] Moreover, under section 1(3) of the Landlord and Tenant Act 1988, the consent must be given within a reasonable time,[4] and the tenant must be given written notice of the decision. If the consent is conditional, the tenant must be informed what the conditions are, and if consent is refused, of the reasons for refusal. These requirements make it easier to overcome wilful obstruction by the landlord, and make mortgages of leases more generally attractive to banks.

In non-residential leases, the landlord and tenant may expressly specify circumstances in which the landlord may refuse consent to assignment or impose conditions.[5] The refusal of consent or imposition of conditions will be valid as against a mortgagee.

Transfers of Mortgages

21–093 A mortgage can be assigned, though it is not common for banks to assign domestic mortgages. It may be done if the mortgagor prefers to assign the debt and mortgage to a third party rather than to redeem the mortgage by repayment; a bank faced with such a request must comply.[6] Naturally, the bank is repaid simultaneously. Similarly if a third party, B (a guarantor, for example) pays A's debt so that the mortgage is discharged without any reconveyance, surrender or release, the mortgage may be assigned to B.[7] Or if the customer wishes to obtain mortgage finance from another lender, the new lender may pay the bank directly, and take a transfer of the mortgage. This gives the new lender the advantage of preserving the priority of the original mortgage, but the disadvantage is that the new mortgage is subject to the terms of the old mortgage unless they are subsequently varied—this might be a reason why the lender would refuse the transfer.

21–094 With any assignment, there may be difficulty if the mortgage is an *all monies* mortgage securing an overdraft, because the security would cover all

[3] Under the Landlord and Tenant Act 1927, s. 19. A term requiring the tenant to offer to surrender the tenancy to the landlord before assigning or entering another transaction seems to be effective: consent is not required (but it has the same effect as if it were, since the landlord may refuse the surrender) and it is not subject to a reasonableness test, *Bocardo S.A. v. S. & M. Hotels Ltd* [1980] 1 W.L.R. 17; *Alder v. Upper Grosvenor Street Investment Ltd* [1957] 1 W.L.R. 227.

[4] *Midland Bank v. Chart Enterprises* [1990] 2 E.G. 59; *CIN Properties v. Gill* [1993] E.G. 152.

[5] Landlord and Tenant (Covenants) Act 1995, s. 22

[6] LPA 1925, s. 95.

[7] Though not in all cases, see LPA 1925, s. 95(2).

the debts of the mortgagor to the assignor, but (unless it is varied with the consent of the mortgagor) not all the debts between mortgagor and assignee. If the mortgagor does agree, this variation probably constitutes a novation—the mortgage is discharged and a new one created.

With registered land, a transfer of a registered charge must be by deed in a prescribed form.[8] The assignment is only complete on the registration of the transfer. If this is not done, the transferor remains proprietor, though the assignee has a good equitable right.

With unregistered land, legal mortgages may be transferred by deed, which transfers the debt, the security right, and all associated remedies.[9] There is a simple statutory form of transfer.[10] An equitable assignment of a legal mortgage must be made in writing, and for valuable consideration,[11] but the assignee can only give a good discharge for the debt if it is in the form of a deed. It used to be possible to transfer a mortgage made by deposit of title deeds merely by delivery of the deeds to the transferee,[12] though a Memorandum was desirable for evidential purposes, but the requirements of section 2 of the LPMPA 1989 must now be complied with.[13] **21–095**

For perfection purposes—that is, to create a complete legal assignment, with legal title in the assignee—notice must be given to the mortgagor. Strictly speaking it is unnecessary to obtain the mortgagor's consent to a transfer, but nevertheless, it is desirable to obtain it, because the statement in the deed reciting the amount of the debt binds the mortgagor, who might otherwise contest it.[14] It also prevents the mortgagor from relying on any defect (such as misrepresentation) which might make the mortgage voidable, or from asserting that the mortgage is void.[15] **21–096**

Sub-Mortgages

A mortgagee may mortgage the rights which it has under the mortgage[16] —create a "mortgage of a mortgage"—in order to raise money, as an alternative to assigning the debt outright or to calling in the debt. The bank (the sub-mortgagee or sub-chargee) then has the double security of the personal liability of both the original mortgagor and the original mortgagee on their covenants to repay, and it has the interest in the land as well. Sub- **21–097**

[8] LRA 1925, s. 33(1); Land Registration Rules 1925.
[9] LPA 1925, s. 114(1).
[10] LPA 1925, Sched. 3. The transfer may be made by separate instrument, or it may be endorsed on the original mortgage instrument. A legal assignment may use some other form, if by deed: LPA 1925, s. 52(1).
[11] LPMPA 1989, s. 2.
[12] *Brocklesby v. Temperance Permanent Building Society* [1895] A.C. 173.
[13] See above, para. 21–043, and Encyclopedia, E 359.
[14] See *De Lisle v. Union Bank of Scotland* [1914] 1 Ch. 22l; *Turner v. Smith* [1901] 1 Ch. 213.
[15] See further Encyclopedia, E 361.
[16] The first mortgage is referred to as the "head mortgage."

mortgages are not very commonly encountered by banks. They may be legal or equitable, and are made by way of assignment of the mortgage, with a proviso for redemption.[17] If, say, a mortgage company gives a floating charge to its bankers, the crystallization of the charge operates as an equitable assignment of the mortgages held by the company, and therefore as a sub-mortgage.[18] The rights under the assignment are perfected by giving notice to the original mortgagor, and the sub-mortgagee will have the rights and powers of the original mortgagee.

Discharge of Mortgages

By redemption

21–098 The mortgagor (or any person who has an interest in the mortgaged property[19]) has the right to redeem the mortgage—that is, to pay off the mortgage. Bank mortgages are often repayable on demand and, unless otherwise agreed, the mortgagor may repay when he or she wishes.[20] Some loans for fixed periods may require a premium for early repayment.[21]

By release

21–099 It is possible to release the mortgage without redeeming the debt—for example, (a) if only part of the property is to be released, and if the rest is of sufficient value to cover the debt (the debt may have reduced, or the property increased in value); or (b) if substitute security is to be given; or (c) if the mortgagor wishes to sell and the property is of insufficient value even to repay incumbrances which have priority over the bank's mortgage—in this case the bank may as well agree, because prior incumbrancers can always exercise their power of sale.

By lapse of time

21–100 The mortgagee's right to sue for the principal and to enforce the mortgage may become time barred if action is not taken within 12 years of the date on which the right to receive it accrues.[22] In the case of loans

[17] For the form of the sub-mortgage see the Encyclopaedia, E 383–385.

[18] See *Sowman v. David Samuel Trusts Ltd.* [1978] 1 All E.R. 616; *Barrows v. Chief Land Register* [1977] C.L.Y. 315.

[19] *e.g.* subsequent mortgagee, tenant, (subrogated) surety for the mortgagor, spouse with right of occupation. See Encyclopedia, E 453.

[20] In the case of an endowment mortgage (where a life assurance policy is taken out when the mortgage is created by the mortgagor, who pays regular premiums to the insurance company, and the mortgage is redeemed by one lump sum payment when the policy matures), it is necessary for the bank to execute a deed of re-assignment of the policy to the borrower and to notify the life office. See Barnsley, *op. cit.* p. 603.

[21] Which may be structured as a reduced rate for timely payment, to avoid the "penalty" rule, see above, para. 21–054.

[22] LA 1980, ss. 8 and 20.

repayable on demand, however, time begins to run from the making of the demand.

PRIORITIES AND MORTGAGES

A number of interests may co-exist in the same property. The mortgagee will want to ensure that it has an effective security that can be realised without challenge from others with interests in the property, such as other secured lenders and occupiers. The rules on priorities organise the different interests into a ranking, so that each party can ascertain which interests are prior, and which subordinated, to his or hers. The system of land registration, by which properties and interests in property are centrally registered and can be examined, allows priorities to be organised for this purpose. The process of changing to compulsory land registration is not yet complete, and there are still two systems of conveyancing in operation. Both systems recognise and protect the rights of third parties in land, such as mortgagees, but they do so in different ways, and therefore need some description. First registered land is described. **21–101**

Title and Protection of Interests in Registered Land

Registration[23] is intended to simplify conveyancing and make it easy to examine all the relevant information about the rights affecting a particular property. The register is open to the public and is being computerised.[24] The Land Register has three parts to it: **21–102**

(1) the *Property Register*, which describes the property and its location; it refers to a filed plan of the property, and gives a title number for the estate in the land. More than one estate may be registered for a property—for example, a fee simple and a leasehold—and will be entered separately;

(2) the *Proprietorship Register*, which describes the owner and his or her rights (any restriction on the power of the proprietor to deal with the property, such as a trust or bankruptcy, will be recorded); and

(3) the *Charges Register*, which sets out incumbrances, that is, third party rights such as mortgages or restrictive covenants affecting the land.

---

[23] Mostly set out in the LRA 1925 (as amended) and the Land Registration Rules 1925.

[24] A joint working group of the Law Commission and the Land Registry has produced a consultation document: "Land Registration for the 21st Century" (Law Com. No. 254) proposing a new Act to place land registration on a new footing—especially in view of likely moves to electronic conveyancing (noted (1998) 62 Conv. 438) and [1998] N.L.J. 1348) The Law Commission proposed a fundamental structural reform of the law of mortgages because of the complexity, confusion and artificiality of the present law; see *Transfer of Land: Land Mortgages*, Law Com. No. 204 (1991), but this has been shelved.

21–103 The registered proprietor has a title, which is shown in the Proprietorship Registers and is given the *Land Certificate* showing that title. The Land Certificate is a copy of the entries on the Register and provides documentary evidence of the title. If the land is mortgaged, the Land Certificate is replaced by a *Charge Certificate* which is normally taken by the mortgagee, in which case the Land Certificate is returned to the Registry.

21–104 **Freehold title**. The best grade of title is *absolute freehold title* which is a guarantee of title.[25] It vests an estate in fee simple in the registered proprietor. This is subject, as we shall see, to incumbrances and other entries on the register and to overriding interests.[26] The first registered proprietor is also subject to any equitable rights of which he or she has notice,[27] even if they are not protected by entry on the register.

If the owner has been able to give the Registry some evidence of title, not conclusive, but enough to show that he or she is in possession of the land or in receipt of rents and profits, the owner may have a certificate of *possessory freehold title*. This gives no guarantee that there are no other rights affecting the land, and it is subject to claims by others with better rights, but a freeholder may convert this into a certificate of absolute title after 12 years.[28]

The third kind of title—*qualified*—is extremely rare, and means that the title is subject to some reservation and is therefore granted subject to interests arising before a specified date or arising under a specified instrument. Such land would be bad security.

21–105 **Leasehold title**. A leasehold title may be registered as *absolute*; *good*; *possessory*, or *qualified*. These are similar in effect to those relating to freehold title, except for *good leasehold title*, which is given to a leaseholder who shows a good lease except for the fact that the freeholder's title is not absolute because no evidence of the quality of the freehold title is available. An absolute title may be given after 10 years in possession by the leaseholder (or his or her successors) or if the superior title is registered later and is absolute.

Mortgages and Registration

21–106 Obviously, the mortgagee will obtain the best security from property where the mortgagor has absolute title. Even this may not be satisfactory, however, if it is subject to other interests in the land—where there is an entry in the Charges Register, a *minor interest* noted on the register, (unless it is an overreachable interest which will be overreached by the mortgage),

[25] Unless the register has to be rectified.
[26] LRA 1925, s. 5.
[27] As defined by LRA 1925, ss. 198 and 199.
[28] LRA 1925, s.77.

or an *overriding interest*. Registration in the Charges Register or entering the interest on the register as a minor interest will, first, give notice to, and therefore priority over, subsequent purchasers of the land; and secondly, determine priorities between parties with interests in the same land.[29]

The search period. The mortgagee must inspect the register before taking the mortgage in order to check title and ascertain whether adverse interests are registered or noted on it, and therefore the mortgagee makes an *official search* of the register. The search is guaranteed as accurate, and the mortgagee will be compensated for loss caused by an error.[30] The search has the additional effect of giving a "priority period" of 30 working days to the searcher, provided that an application for registration of the mortgage is submitted within that time. If any entry by another person is made in the register during the priority period, it will be postponed to that of the person who made the earlier official search. This is no hardship to the party whose interest is postponed, because the fact that a search is being made is entered on the Register, and will itself be discovered by a search.[31] **21–107**

Entries in the Charges Register

Legal mortgages and charges must be registered within two months of their creation or they will have no effect at law.[32] They appear in the Charges Register, as do leases of the land and certain incumbrances, like rights of way. Anything in the Charges Register binds a purchaser or mortgagee. **21–108**

On registration, the mortgagee must either produce the Land Certificate or the Land Certificate must already be lodged with the registrar. In return for the Land Certificate, the registrar returns a Charge Certificate to the applicant. If the mortgage is a second mortgage, the Charge Certificate shows details of the earlier charge. A mortgage which is not registered as a legal mortgage is treated as an equitable mortgage[33] and should be protected as a minor interest.

As between two registered mortgages, priority is generally determined by the order of registration, and not by order of creation.[34]

---

[29] The normal order of priority may be changed by agreement between the various incumbrancers and the proprietor, usually by a "deed of priority" which varies the charge. The alteration is entered on the register, provided that all the Charge Certificates are presented to the Registrar: LRA 1925, ss. 31 and 64.

[30] LRA 1925, s. 83(3).

[31] Land Registration (Official Searches) Rules 1993, r.3; the rules also make provision for searching by telephone, in person or by fax, etc.

[32] LRA 1925, s. 26; see *Barclays Bank plc v. Zaroovabli* [1997] 2 W.L.R. 729.

[33] LRA 1925, s. 106.

[34] LRA 1925, s. 29.

21–109 **The effect of non-registration.** If an interest such as a legal mortgage is not registered, it will not take effect as a legal interest.[35] The unregistered transaction has effect only as a minor interest, needing protection by notice or caution.

A recent decision, *Barclays Bank v. Zaroovabli,*[36] shows that the bank must be careful to ensure that mortgages are registered. If a mortgagor grants a lease over the property despite a prohibition in the mortgage, the mortgage normally has priority.[37] It was held in *Zaroovabli*, however, that if a lease[38] is granted over registered land before the mortgage has been registered it takes effect as an overriding interest[39] and has priority over the mortgagee's interest. This is because the mortgage acts only in equity before registration; the legal title takes effect when the title is registered. Even if the lease is initially contractual and becomes a statutory lease later, and the mortgage has been registered before it becomes statutory, it remains binding on the bank. The reason is that a contractual term has given the status of irremovability to the tenant, and the statutory lease must be at least as effective in binding a mortgagee as a contractual term. If the mortgagee applies promptly to register the mortgage, as it should, there will normally be little or no opportunity for the mortgagor to grant a lease over the property before registration, since registration is effective from the date of application.

Minor interests

21–110 This category covers a residual class of interests—that is, any interests in registered land that are not protected by registration as legal titles or legal charges, and which are not overriding interests.[40] Minor interests must take effect in equity.[41] In certain cases, a minor interest may become an overriding interest (where a person with a minor interest is in actual occupation of the property, for example[42]), and, conversely, an overriding interest may sometimes be converted into a minor interest by noting on the register. Purchasers and mortgagees take free of any minor interests not protected by an entry on the register. A mortgagee must therefore inspect the land register before taking the mortgage to see if there are prior mortgages or other rights, and must protect its own mortgage by registration.

---

[35] If the area is a compulsory registration area, as, since 1990, it must be: LRA 1925, s. 123(A)(5), substituted by the Land Registration Act 1997, s. 1.

[36] [1997] 2 W.L.R. 729.

[37] Even if the tenancy became protected, the mortgage had priority, *Britannia Building Society v. Earl* [1990] 1 W.L.R. 422, CA; but see also *Quenell v. Maltby* [1979] 1 W.L.R. 318, CA.

[38] For a term not exceeding 21 years.

[39] Under LRA 1925, s. 70(1)(g).

[40] LRA 1925, s. 3(xv).

[41] LPA, s. 2(1).

[42] See further below, para. 21–119.

Entries protecting such interests may appear in the Proprietorship Register or the Charges Register.[43] They are notices, inhibitions, cautions, or restrictions. These should be investigated by potential mortgagees before the mortgage is taken. Mortgages which are not registered charges[44] may be protected by notices and cautions in the following ways: **21–111**

(1) by a *notice* in the Charges Register[45]: which can be entered only if the mortgagee has the Land Certificate or where it is on deposit at the Land Registry, for example where there is a prior registered charge.[46] As the name implies, a notice gives notice, and anyone taking an interest in the land takes it subject to the rights it protects. Statutory rights of occupation under the relevant family legislation are protected by notices.

(2) by a *caution* lodged by any person interested in the registered land or in any charge.[47] This does not require production of the Land Certificate and can be done unilaterally by the person lodging it. Cautions against the land appear in the Proprietorship Register, and against charges in the Charges Register. Cautions give no priority against a purchaser.[48] The only protection is a right to object to dealings if anyone attempts to deal with the land in a way that would affect the register, or if the proprietor attempts to remove or "warn off" the caution; in that case, the registrar must inform the person who has lodged the caution, who then has 14 days in which to act—for example, by seeking an injunction—and during that time no change will be made to the register. A mortgagee whose mortgage is protected by a caution has the protection, though, that if a later transaction is proposed, the mortgagee will be notified by the registrar. It will then be able to place a notice on the register (which will preserve its priority) or register its own first mortgage,[49] since the Land Certificate has to be produced for the new transaction. This will give the mortgage priority because the first in time prevails until another interest is registered. If a purchaser's search fails to disclose the existence of the caution, the caution protects the cautioner's interest against the later interest (the purchaser may be

---

[43] s. 54(1).

[44] Before the LPMPA 1989, an equitable charge could be created simply by deposit of the land certificate with the mortgagee: see *Bank of Kuwait v. Sahib* [1996] 3 All E.R. 215, CA. The Land Registry will no longer accept applications to enter a notice of deposit of a land certificate or charge certificate and those already entered on the register (before April 3, 1995) operate as cautions: Land Registration Rules 1995 (S.I. 1995 No. 140) para. 4.

[45] LRA 1925, ss. 48–52.

[46] LRA 1925, s. 64.

[47] LRA 1925, ss. 53–56.

[48] *Barclays Bank Ltd v. Taylor* [1974] Ch. 137.

[49] *Re White Rose Cottage* [1965] Ch. 940, CA, describes methods of protection available to equitable mortgagees.

indemnified by the registrar[50]). On the other hand, if the registrar does not warn the cautioner of a subsequent charge, it seems that the cautioner's right is lost, because a caution is merely a procedure, not an interest in the land, and docs not confer any kind of priority. In that case, it is the cautioner who may claim an indemnity from the registrar.[51] Thus, while a caution gives reasonable protection, it is not as satisfactory as a notice.

21–112 The other two forms of protection do not protect mortgages. These are *inhibitions*,[52] which are court orders or directions by the registrar forbidding dealings with the land, either absolutely, or until a certain time, or event, and which are routinely used in bankruptcy cases to prevent the registered proprietor from disposing of his or her land; and *restrictions*,[53] which prevent dealings until a specified condition has been met (for example under a trust) and are usually made by application of the registered proprietor.

21–113 **Priority between minor interests and later legal interests.** A minor interest which is not overriding may be defeated by a subsequent purchaser or mortgagee if:

(a) the trustees have power to dispose of the property subject to the equitable interest—for example, by *consent*, by the *terms of the trust deed*, by *overreaching*, or by *court order*. The subsequent legal purchaser will take priority whether he or she knows of the prior equitable title or not;

(b) if the minor interest is not protected by an entry on the register, it will not bind a transferee or grantee of a legal estate for valuable consideration, whether or not he or she has notice of it.[54] Only an entry on the register serves to give notice to any legal transferee or grantee.[55]

21–114 **Priority between minor interests.** As between minor interests, they take priority in order of time of creation,[56] if the "equities are equal". An equitable mortgage, including one which is equitable because it has not been registered, takes priority as a minor interest over a later equitable mortgage, even if the latter is protected by a notice[57] or by a caution,[58]

[50] *Parkash v. Irani Finance Ltd* [1970] Ch. 101.
[51] *Clark v. Chief Land Registrar* [1994] 3 W.L.R. 593.
[52] LRA 1925, s. 57.
[53] LRA 1925, s. 58.
[54] LRA 1925, s. 20(1).
[55] Different considerations may apply in cases of unconscionability (or fraud): see *Lyus v. Prowsa Developments Ltd.* [1982] 1 W.L.R. 1044.
[56] *Dearle v. Hall* (1828) 3 Russ.1, LPA 1925, s.137(1).
[57] *Mortgage Corporation v. Nationwide Credit Corporation* [1994] Ch. 49.
[58] *Barclays Bank Ltd v. Taylor* [1974] Ch. 137.

provided, of course, that the equities are equal. In cases (which must now be increasingly rare[59]) of equitable mortgages where the Land Certificate has been deposited with a mortgagee, the fact that the Certificate is not available protects the mortgagee against any transaction for which its production is required, because no purchaser could obtain legal title.

Overriding interests

Overriding interests, which are set out in section 70(1) of the LRA 1925 constitute a very important category of rights in registered land. They are not entered on the register, but they nevertheless bind any purchaser or a mortgagee of registered land, even though he or she does not know of them. They are considered to be rights which would become obvious to any purchaser who goes to look at the property, but in fact some types of overriding interest could quite well remain undiscovered even then.[60] For that reason, they are of particular significance to mortgagees. **21–115**

Important classes of overriding interests are rights of persons in actual occupation (section 70(1)(g) of the LRA 1925)—the most important class; certain liabilities to repair (for example, highways, embankments, sea walls); legal easements and profits[61]; local land charges unless protected by entry on the register; leases[62] granted for a term not exceeding 21 years.[63] **21–116**

A statutory right of occupation arising under the relevant family legislation is expressly declared not to be an overriding interest, and must therefore be protected by entry on the register.[64]

Right of persons in actual occupation. This is the most difficult and important class of overriding interests, and appears in section 70(1)(g) of the LRA 1925. This reads: **21–117**

> "the rights of every person in actual occupation of the land or in receipt of the rents and profits thereof, save where enquiry is made of such person and the rights are not disclosed."

Thus the owner of an equitable interest who is in actual occupation is protected, even though his or her interest is not noted on the register. For this purpose, the person who claims the overriding interest must be able to

---

[59] Because of the LPMPA 1989, s. 2, see above, para. 21–042.

[60] Gray, *op. cit.* p. 199.

[61] But see *Celsteel Ltd v. Alton House Holdings Ltd* [1985] 1 W.L.R. 204, where an equitable easement was regarded as falling within the scope of the LRA 1925, s. 70(1)(g). Section 144 provides that new overriding interests can be created: applied in *Thatcher v. Douglas* (1995) 146 N.L.J. 282, CA.

[62] Not an agreement for a lease: *City Permanent Building Society v. Miller* [1982] Ch. 840, though the tenant may fall within (a), being in occupation.

[63] See also Land Registration Act 1986, s. 4.

[64] Family Law Act 1996, s. 31(10)(b).

show both points: that he or she has a *right* subsisting in registered land, and that he or she is in *actual occupation*, which existed at the time the mortgage was granted.[65] If the bank has properly protected its mortgage, it is not concerned with other rights arising subsequently.

21–118 *(a) right in the land*. The right must be of a proprietary nature,[66–67] but equity does not require a formal disposition and may hold that there has been a trust in a beneficiary's favour. Even some oral arrangement may suffice to confer rights in the case of a trust implied by law.

Questions about such rights frequently arise between spouses or cohabitees. A trust may be implied if a couple acquire a home in the name of one of them with the joint intention of sharing the ownership between them: it depends on the intentions of the parties and may be rebutted by evidence of contrary intention. It may be inferred that such an agreement was made either at the time of acquisition (particularly if the purchase money, or part of it, has been provided by the person who does not have the legal title), or subsequently[68] (for example, contributions to buildings or improvements[69]). The courts tend to look for evidence of a financial contribution to the purchase or subsequent maintenance of the home.[70]

21–119 *(b) actual occupation*. There is no statutory definition of "actual occupation", and it is not immediately clear what it means. The House of Lords has said that occupation is a matter of fact, not law, and means simply physical presence.[71] It has also been said that it must take a form and subsist at a time which allows a purchaser to make purposeful and fruitful inquiry before the transaction is completed.[72] It would seem that it ought to mean occupation of some degree of permanency, and that a temporary absence, say on holiday, would not prevent the person concerned from asserting actual occupation. Although occupation need not be continuous or uninterrupted, however,[73] an equitable owner who merely happens to

---

[65] *Abbey National Building Society v. Cann* [1991] A.C. 56. Some other rights (*e.g.* local land charges, under LRA 1925, s. 70(1)(I)) will take effect as overriding interests as long as they are in existence at the date of the *registration* of the charge.

[66–67] A mere licence to occupy the land will not suffice, *Strand Securities v. Caswell* [1965] Ch. 958, CA; *Nationwide Anglia B.S. v. Ahmed* [1995] 70 P. & C.R. 381. In *Wallcite Ltd v. Ferrishurst Ltd* [1999] 1 All E.R. 977, it was held, disapproving *Ashburn Anstalt v. Arnold* [1989] Ch. 1, that a person does not need to be in occupation of the whole land to which his or her right extends in order to claim that he or she is in actual occupation.

[68] See *Winkworth v. Edward Baron Development Co. Ltd* [1986] 1 W.L.R. 1512, CA; [1987] 1 All E.R. 114, HL.

[69] See *Hussey v. Palmer* [1972] 1 W.L.R. 1286. (The mother-in-law of the legal owner spent money for extension to house for her accommodation: trust in her favour found.)

[70] See *Gissing v. Gissing* [1971] A.C. 886; *Heseltine v. Heseltine* [1971] 1 W.L.R. 342; *Pettitt v. Pettitt* [1970] A.C. 777. See also *Lloyds Bank v. Rosset* [1991] 1 A.C. 107, which imposed "extreme limitations on the fuller realisation of the many forms of contributory activity which are now excluded from the ambit of constructive trust", Gray, *op. cit*., p. 431.

[71] *Williams & Glyns Bank v. Boland* [1981] A.C. 487 at 504 *per* Lord Wilberforce.

[72] *Abbey National B.S. v. Cann* [1991] 1 A.C. 56 at 88, *per* Lord Oliver.

[73] *Chhokar v. Chhokar* [1984] F.L.R. 313, CA.

stay in the property on the day of the mortgage, but who normally lives elsewhere, is probably not in actual occupation.[74] Actual occupation may be vicarious or symbolic: a caretaker or representative of a company, for example, may occupy on behalf of an employer, though this would probably not be true of mere casual employees.

Can the lender protect its mortgage?

Mortgagees' concerns about protecting mortgages by registration have concentrated, naturally enough, on the possibility that an occupier of the property may have a right in the property. The problem for the mortgagee arises where there is only one legal owner (trustee), because if the property is mortgaged by *two* trustees, the *overreaching* provisions apply, and the transaction defeats the rights of an equitable joint tenant, or tenant in common, even though in actual occupation of the land[75]—a mortgage granted by two trustees is safe from challenge.[76] Where there is only one trustee, however, and there are other persons who may have beneficial interests, the bank should protect its mortgage by making appropriate inquiries to ascertain whether there is any person in actual occupation whose interest in the property would override the mortgage. **21–120**

An occupier's rights can only defeat the mortgage if the occupier is in actual occupation *at the time when the mortgage is granted*. The importance of this point is that if the property is bought with the mortgage (an *acquisition* mortgage) there will usually be no time for anyone to have obtained an equitable right in the land from the new legal owner because the purchase and the mortgage happen at the same time. On the other hand, if the mortgage is granted at some later stage, for some lending which may or may not be related to the property (a *post-acquisition* mortgage), there will have been more time for people to have obtained a right in the property, and the risk to the lender is greater. **21–121**

The fears of banks as far as *acquisition* mortgages are concerned were put to rest by *Abbey National Building Society v. Cann*.[77] In that case, an elderly mother claimed an overriding interest in her son's property on the basis that she was in actual occupation of it when the mortgage was granted. If the court upheld her claim, it would give her priority over the **21–122**

[74] It does not mean a "mere fleeting presence", [1991] 1 A.C. 56, at 93, *per* Lord Oliver.

[75] *City of London Building Society v. Flegg* [1988] A.C. 54. In this case, two trustees sold a property without the consent of the wife's elderly parents who lived there. The decision of the Court of Appeal that the interest of the parents could not be overreached despite the sale by two trustees was reversed on appeal by the House of Lords. The Law Commission has proposed (Law Com. No 188, 1989) that the interests of beneficiaries in actual occupation should not be overreached unless their consent was obtained.

[76] Provided the trustees are acting *intra vires*, a disposition by them overrides the equitable interest of the beneficiaries, whether capital money arises or not, provided that if it does, the money is dealt with in accordance with the LRA 1925: *State Bank of India v. Sood* [1997] 1 All E.R. 169, noted Thompson [1997] Conv. 135.

[77] [1991] 1 A.C. 56.

rights of the building society which had provided her son with some of the funds for purchase of the property. The House of Lords held that she had not been in actual occupation of the property at that time.[78] However, even if she had been in actual occupation, she would not have been able to claim priority over the building society; this is because the purchase of the property and the granting of the mortgage are treated as happening simultaneously and as constituting one indivisible transaction.[79] This meant that her son had granted the mortgage precisely at the time of the purchase and could not have given her any equitable rights in the property. There was in law no intervening moment between the purchase and the mortgage in which her rights could arise, and anyway the only right to which the son would be entitled was the right to the equity of redemption: no equitable right to the property could have been carved out of that. This decision means that it is most unlikely that equitable owners will be in a position to challenge a mortgagee's priority by asserting that they were in actual occupation at the time when the property was purchased.[80]

21–123 Banks may still have concerns about *post-acquisition* mortgages, however. In these cases, other people have had the opportunity to obtain an equitable interest and to occupy the property. This was brought home to banks by the decision of the House of Lords in *Williams and Glyn's Bank Ltd. v. Boland,*[81] where the wife of the legal owner had contributed to the purchase price, and the parties (it was held) had intended to share ownership in equity. The husband, however, mortgaged the house and used the money for his business. The House of Lords held that the wife had an overriding interest, and could successfully claim priority over the mortgage transaction. The bank should have made inquiry of her, and, if her interest had been disclosed, should have asked her to join in the mortgage or to waive her rights.

21–124 Since *Boland*, banks have become practised at making prudent inquiries of potential occupiers—after all, not a very onerous task[82]; surveyors, for example, can be asked to look for evidence of occupation. If the bank can discover whether anyone lives in the property other than the legal owner, then that person should be asked whether he or she has any interest in the

[78] The relevant date in this case—unlike that for other overriding interests—is the date of the completion of the purchase and the mortgage, not of the registration of the mortgage (Lord Oliver, at 87). See also *Lloyds Bank v. Rosset* [1989] Ch. 350.

[79] That is, there was no fraction of time—no "*scintilla temporis*" during which the title was transferred to the legal owner, before the mortgage can be created: *Church of England v. Piskor* [1954] Ch. 553 overruled.

[80] *Emmet on Title*, para. 25.035, suggests that the reasoning in *Cann* [1991] 1 A.C. 56, applies only where the mortgage loan finances or helps finance the purchase of the property, and, arguably, would not extent to cases where a mortgage completed simultaneously with the purchase was to secure a business overdraft of the mortgagor.

[81] [1981] A.C. 487. See also *Hodgson v. Marks* [1971] Ch. 892, where the equitable owner was the original owner and the registered proprietor was a lodger.

[82] The fears created by *Boland* have proved to be "greatly exaggerated": *Barnsley's Conveyancing Law and Practice* (4th ed., 1996, Thompson ed.) p. 362.

land. If the answer is yes, the bank should ask the person to join in the mortgage, or at least to waive his or her rights in writing.[83] One situation, however, which might still be a trap for a mortgagee is the risk that there has been a purported grant of a tenancy to a person not in occupation. It is hard to guard against this risk.[84]

The courts in fact, have given further support to mortgagees. It has been held that the equitable owner may be estopped from challenging the mortgage transaction if he or she knew or must have known of the sale, and has not disclosed his or her interest, nor joined in the mortgage or agreed to waive his or her rights in writing; in that case, the equitable owner's interest does not have priority over the mortgage.[85] This approach by the courts goes some way to allay the fears of lenders, though again it applies particularly where a mortgage is granted at the time of the acquisition of the property, when it is probably obvious that extra funds are needed. This was endorsed in the *Cann* case.[86] **21–125**

The principal remaining cause for worry for lenders (apart from the situation where the equitable owner's consent is vitiated by undue influence or misrepresentation[87]) is the case where the property is mortgaged by the legal owner without the knowledge of an equitable owner in occupation. Here, the *Boland* decision could still cause problems for banks in taking a mortgage, particularly if a fraudulent legal owner makes it difficult to discover who has equitable rights in the property and what they are.[88] The legal owner should be asked, of course, but may not tell the truth. And there may be other sorts of fraud by the legal owner: for example, he or she might have forged the signature of the equitable owner to a waiver or to the mortgage deed. This *apparent* consent is no protection for the mort- **21–126**

[83] It seems that inquiry need not be made of children (all minors, even if married or cohabiting), who may have an interest in the property: *Hypo-Mortgage Services Ltd v. Robinson*, *The Times*, January 2, 1997. There is a summary of the case at [1997] 2 F.L.R. 71.

[84] See *Emmet on Title*, para. 25.037; unless the tenant can be said to have impliedly consented to the mortgage or helped to mislead the mortgagee.

[85] *Paddington v. Mendelsohn* (1985) 50 P. &C.R. 244; *Equity and Law Home Loans Ltd v. Prestidge* [1992] 1 W.L.R. 137, CA. (A controversial case where consent to a second mortgage was imputed to an occupier who had known of the original mortgage, but did not know of the second one, see Thompson [1992] Conv. 206.) This "estoppel" against the occupier is similar in unregistered land: *Bristol & West Building Society v. Henning* [1985] 1 W.L.R. 778. See Welstead [1985] C.L.J. 354 for criticism.

[86] This was endorsed in the *Cann* case [1991] 1 A.C. 56. Lord Oliver (at 76) said that the equitable owner (the mother) must have known funds were needed from somewhere to meet the shortfall and must be taken to have impliedly authorised her son to create a charge.

[87] Where the bank may have constructive notice of the defect: *Barclays Bank v. O'Brien* [1993] W.L.R. 786, see further above, para. 3–18 and paras 21–055 *et seq*.

[88] See, *e.g.*, *Skipton Building Society v. Clayton* (1993) 66 P. & C.R. 223, where the mortgagees were the victim of an "unscrupulous fraud" by the mortgagors.

gagee.[89] The best way for the mortgagee to protect itself against this risk is to have all those in occupation of the property physically attend for the signing of the agreement, and this may sometimes be a wise precaution.

21–127 Another way for the bank to avoid a problem, if there is or might be an occupier with an equitable right, could be to request the trustee (the legal owner) to appoint a co-trustee[90]; if both trustees sign the mortgage, the bank will be protected from any third party rights not entered on the register, even if it knows of the existence of beneficiaries. There is the risk, however, that it might be claimed that the bank did not act in good faith,[91] if it knew that the appointment was made to defeat the equitable rights of the occupier, and if so, the equitable rights might override the bank's title.

21–128 If there has been fraud, the bank's remedies are to sue the proprietor—who may be insolvent—on his or her personal obligation to pay; to obtain a charging order on the proprietor's beneficial interest in the property and then apply for sale; or to apply to the court as a person interested under the trust of land for a sale[92] under section 14 of the TLATA 1996. This is possible in theory, because the mortgage would be an effective mortgage over the equitable interest of the proprietor (it would sever any equitable joint tenancy),[93] but, since a sale would affect the other equitable tenant in common, the court may not be willing to make such an order. Indeed, since lenders are now aware of the problem, the court may look askance at any lender who has not taken the precaution of inquiring of persons in occupation (and of spouses) and of seeking their consent where necessary.

21–129 Rather oddly, it seems that in some cases even the consent of the occupier may not be enough. In *Woolwich Building Society v. Dickman,*[94] the plaintiff building society had obtained the consent of the tenants to the transfer of the property. It turned out that the occupiers were protected

---

[89] *Winkworth v. Edward Baron Development Co. Ltd.,* [1986] 1 W.L.R. 1512, CA. The forgery will be grounds for rectification to obtain removal of the charge, s. 82 of the LRA 1925. The mortgagee may find it possible to show that a solicitor acting in the transaction was negligent or in breach of fiduciary duty in not ensuring that the documents had been properly signed: *Zwebner v. The Mortgage Corpn. Ltd* [1998] P.N. 769, CA, but *cf., Cox & McQueen* [1998] 3 All E.R. 213.

[90] Now under the TLATA 1996, s. 14.

[91] See Encyclopaedia of Banking Law, E 185, which considers that the effect of *Peffer v. Rigg* [1978] 3 All E.R. 745 may be to add a requirement of good faith to the provisions of the LRA 1925; see also Gray, *Elements of Land Law*, p.190 *et seq.* The editors of the Encyclopedia consider that appointing another trustee in these circumstances would amount to a breach of trust under ss. 6(5) and 6(6) of the TLATA 1996 by the trustee making the appointment, and the bank might then be considered a constructive trustee.

[92] *First National Securities Ltd v. Hegerty* [1985] Q.B. 850 and *Ahmed v. Kendrick and Ahmed* [1988] 2 F.L.R. 22. But see *Penn v. Bristol and West Building Society* [1995] 2 F.L.R. 938, Ch D, where the court refused to sever the joint tenancy. It was held that the contract for sale and the conveyance were forgeries and the whole transaction was a sham, because the vendor (who had forged his wife's signature) and the purchaser had colluded to defraud the building society; see also *Cedar Holdings v. Green* [1981] 1 Ch.129, CA.

[93] See above, para. 21–017.

[94] [1996] 3 All E.R. 204

tenants, and when the building society sought possession of the property, it was unsuccessful, because it could not deny the contractual rights of the tenants. The tenants' consent had no effect on the mandatory rights they enjoyed. It may be that the decision here turned on the fact that the occupiers were tenants under the Rent Acts[95] and therefore entitled to special protection. However, the decision is a worrying one for banks, whose mortgage would not have priority in such cases.

Title and Protection of Interests in Unregistered Land

Proving title and checking for adverse interests is more complicated for unregistered land than for registered land. Title is shown by an indefeasible chain of transactions for a period of at least 15 years,[96] starting from what is known as a good "root of title". Many third party interests are registered in the Land Charges Register as "land charges",[97] and, unlike in the land registration scheme, they are registered against the name of the *proprietor*, not the *land* (this can make the register unreliable). There are six classes of land charges, known as classes A to F, and the method of protection depends upon the type of the mortgage. The most relevant classes of land charges are: **21–130**

> C (i) legal mortgages not secured by the deposit of documents relating to the legal estate of the property[98]; (iii) equitable charges, which includes equitable mortgages where the mortgagee does not have the title deeds to the property and (iv) estate contracts;
>
> D (i) restrictive covenants and (iii) equitable easements; and
>
> F: a spouse's charge under the Family Law Act 1996.

These classes do not cover all third party interests. For example, most legal rights, including legal mortgages protected by deposit of the title deeds, are not registrable, nor are equitable mortgages protected by deposit of the title deeds, and nor, importantly, is an interest under a trust of land.

Mortgages and Registration

Registration is deemed to give actual notice to others,[99] and notice prevents a subsequent purchaser from obtaining title free of the incumbrance. If an equitable mortgage is registered before a legal mortgage is taken (whether the legal mortgage is registered or not) it takes priority **21–131**

95 Rent Act 1977, s. 98(1).
96 LPA 1925, s. 23.
97 Under the Land Charges Act 1972.
98 LPA 1925, s. 2(4).
99 LPA 1925, s. 198(1).

over the legal mortgage. Conversely, a purchaser is not normally bound if he or she has notice, even actual notice, of an interest which has not been registered.[1] Unlike registered land, it does not matter that the interest holder was actually in possession or occupation of the land.[2]

Registration, of course, does not prevent the subsequent purchaser or mortgagee suing the vendor or mortgagor, or rescinding the contract, if the vendor has misrepresented the existence or extent of any interest.[3]

21–132 **Searches and priority notices.** A "priority notice" can be registered at least 15 days before the creation of a land charge. This system allows a rapid sequence of transactions. For example, a purchaser may agree to grant a restrictive covenant. If he or she is to raise the money by mortgage from a bank, the sale, the grant of the covenant and the mortgage will in practice take place only moments apart. To enable the vendor to protect the covenant against the mortgagee (in effect a purchaser, against whose interest the covenant would be void if it were not registered) the vendor gives a "priority notice" to the registry at least 15 days before the covenant is created; the covenant will then take priority over the mortgage if it is registered within 30 days of the priority notice being entered.

21–133 Searches of the register may be made in person or by official search; the latter is conclusive in favour of a purchaser (in respect of the persons specified, and if the land is correctly described). Protection is also given against incumbrances registered in the interval between search and completion, provided completion takes place within 15 days of the date of the certificate, and no priority notice has been entered. If the registry is negligent, it may be sued.[4] There is a scheme allowing compensation for a purchaser who fails to discover a registered land charge of a person not revealed by the root of title and subsequent conveyances. Since charges are registered against names and may appear against the name of a previous owner, or may not be correctly given, a failure to discover is quite possible.

21–134 **The effect of non-registration**. If registrable interests are not registered the interest is generally void against a subsequent purchase for value, which includes a subsequent mortgage, whether it is legal or equitable,[5] and whether or not the subsequent interest is itself registered anywhere[6]; this covers classes A, B, C (i)-(iii) and F. However, estate contracts, restrictive

---

[1] *Midland Bank Trust Co. Ltd. v. Green*, [1981] A.C. 513; *Coventry Permanent Economic B.S. v. Jones* [1951] 1 All E.R. 901 at 904; *Hollington Bros. Ltd v. Rhodes* [1951] 2 T.L.R. 691 at 696.

[2] *City of London Building Society v. Flegg* [1988] A.C. 54; *Hollington Bros. Ltd. v. Rhodes*, [1951] 2 T.L.R. 691.

[3] Law of Property Act 1969, s. 24.

[4] *Ministry of Housing v. Sharp* [1970] 2 Q.B. 223. But see s. 10(6) of the Land Charges Act 1972—where the applicant does not check that the particulars supplied are those requested.

[5] Land Charges Act 1972, ss. 4–7.

[6] Contrast registered land, see above, para. 21–109.

covenants, equitable easements and inland revenue charges (classes C (iv) and D (i)-(iii)) are void only against subsequent purchasers of a legal estate "for money or money's worth",[7] while bankruptcy petitions and receiving or vesting orders[8] are void only as against a subsequent purchaser of a legal estate without notice of a petition.

Unregistered land and trusts of land

Equitable interests under trusts of land—which are very common, since all co-owned land is held on trust—are not registrable as land charges. Two trustees (or a trust corporation) have the power to dispose of land subject to the trust to a bona fide purchaser of a legal estate, including a mortgagee, thus *overreaching* even the equitable title of a person in occupation.[9] A legal mortgage may, therefore, safely be taken from two trustees of unregistered land if the bank does not know of bad faith. **21–135**

If there is only one trustee, however—say, the husband—and the wife has an equitable interest,[10] the husband cannot give a good receipt for capital money, and the overreaching provisions do not apply. On the other hand, the doctrine of the bona fide purchaser does apply, so that the interest of a purchaser or mortgagee who has no notice of the wife's equitable interest will take priority over her interest.

The important question, therefore, is as to what counts as *notice*. It may be actual or constructive. *Actual notice* (or knowledge) of the equitable interest is, of course, binding, and a prospective mortgagee should seek the equitable owner's consent. Registration is deemed to constitute actual notice,[11] but trust interests are not registrable, and therefore notice cannot come from registration. *Constructive notice* includes matters the purchaser is deemed to know or would have discovered if he or she had made the usual searches.[12] This is more difficult, and implies that the purchaser must search not only the title deeds and the register but must inspect the property itself. In *Hunt v. Luck*,[13] a purchaser was held to have notice of the rights of a tenant; to be safe, he should have made inquiry in respect of third party rights in the property, and if necessary, have physically inspected it. **21–136**

[7] Where some kind of financial value can be put on the price (*e.g.* not a transaction in consideration of marriage), although the court will not inquire into its adequacy; see *Midland Bank Trust Co. Ltd v. Green* [1981] A.C. 513.

[8] Which are registrable as pending actions or as writs and orders in the Register of Pending Actions, not the Land Charges Register.

[9] LPA 1925, s. 27(1); TLATA 1996, s. 16.

[10] It must be a property interest, not a contractual right like a licence. In *Lloyds Bank v. Carrick* [1996] 4 All E.R. 630, CA, a widow who contributed the whole purchase price had only a contractual claim against her brother-in-law who, having bought the property on her behalf, was a bare trustee. Since the claim was specifically enforceable and related to unregistered land, it should have been registered as an estate contract; it had not, and the widow had no claim in constructive trust.

[11] LPA 1925, s. 198(1).

[12] From the title deeds and from the land itself: LPA 1925, s. 199(1)(ii).

[13] [1902] 1 Ch. 428; *cf. Caunce v. Caunce* [1969] 1 W.L.R. 286, Ch D.

21–137 This precaution includes inquiry into the rights of a spouse and of other occupiers[14] in the property. In *Kingsnorth Trust Ltd v Tizard*[15] a building society was dishonestly told by the mortgagor that he was single, but when the agent for the society visited the property there was evidence of occupation by children. The mortgagor then said he was separated from his wife—this was true, but she lived nearby and came in each day to look after the children. The court held that the building society, through the agent, knew of the wife's existence and should have made inquiry about her rights. The agent should not have prearranged a visiting time, which would enable a fraudulent mortgagor to arrange for his wife to be absent, and the fact that the mortgagor had lied about his status was surely a suspicious occurrence, which indicated that he might be seeking to conceal the rights of his wife. The safe course for the lender is therefore to make inquiry of any occupant whose existence is known rather than to rely on statements of the mortgagor. Generally, the position now seems to resemble that applicable to registered land,[16] and reflects (in part) the changes in social attitudes which have taken place in recent decades.

21–138 A legal owner (the trustee) has power to mortgage his or her own equitable title. If the mortgage is defeated by an occupier's equitable claim, therefore, the legal owner may still mortgage his or her equitable title, thus severing the equitable joint tenancy if there is one. The bank (which is then in the position of an equitable co-owner) may apply for a sale of the property under section 14 of the TLATA 1996. Such an order is in the court's discretion, however, and it is unlikely that the court will make such an order if it would cause hardship to the other equitable co-owner.[17] The court is probably more likely to make an order for sale if the equitable co-owner does not occupy the property.

Mortgages: Other Priority Matters

Statutory right of occupation: Family Law Act 1996[18]

21–139 Section 30 of the Family Law Act 1996 gives "matrimonial home rights" to spouses (this protection of the Act for wives against third party interests in the home does not extend to cohabitants). It applies where, first, one spouse is entitled to occupy the home by virtue of either a beneficial estate or interest or contract or any enactment which gives the spouse the right to

---

[14] See *Hodgson v. Marks* [1971] Ch. 892, and *Williams & Glyn's Bank v. Boland* [1981] A.C. 487 (registered land).

[15] [1986] 1 All E.R. 54.

[16] Although the range of rights that may be protected by actual occupation is wider where the title is registered—Megarry and Wade, *op. cit.*, para. 6–048.

[17] See *Lloyds Bank v. Semmakie* [1993] 1 F.L.R. 34, *Thames Guaranty Ltd v. Campbell* [1985] Q.B. 210, and *First National Securities Ltd v. Hegerty* [1984] 3 All E.R. 641.

[18] In force October 1997 (S.I.1997 No. 1892); replaces Matrimonial Homes Act 1983.

remain in occupation; and secondly, the *other* spouse is not so entitled. It is the rights of the other spouse which are protected by the legislation. He or she cannot be evicted or excluded by the first spouse except by leave of the court. This right of occupation has the effect of an equitable charge on the land. The charge only affects a third party purchaser or mortgagee, however, if it is registered as a Class F land charge (for unregistered land) or protected by a notice (for registered land). It is expressly stated that it is not an overriding interest.[19] If there is such a charge, and it is protected, then the mortgagee should ask for its withdrawal or take a written postponement of priority from the protected spouse.

This is a quite separate right from the equitable rights under a trust of land which may be overreached, and which, if not overreached, are protected under section 70(1)(g) of the LRA 1925 in registered land, or by the doctrine of notice in unregistered land.

The wife's statutory rights of occupation do not always provide protection. The court has a discretion to take account of the circumstances of a third party (purchaser or mortgagee) and give priority to the rights of the third party over the charge to the third party if it considers that in all the circumstances it is just and reasonable to do so.[20] This preserves the decision of the Court of Appeal in *Kaur v. Gill*,[21] where the wife's rights were subject to those of a purchaser whose need for housing (he was blind) were said to be greater than hers. In certain circumstances, therefore (though these are unlikely to benefit mortgagees) the wife's rights are not fully protected, even if they are registered. **21–140**

Tacking

Tacking is the right of a secured lender to add further monies to the security so that the further monies are also secured.[22] In certain circumstances, the further advances will be tacked on to the original mortgage (whether it is legal or equitable) and have the same priority, thus squeezing out the rights of intervening legal or equitable mortgages. In any case, bank mortgages usually provide that the mortgage secures any further advances.[23] **21–141**

In *unregistered land* the right to tack is restricted to the following situations—if **21–142**

(a) the original mortgage *obliges* (not merely permits) the mortgagor to advance further money[24]: this would not apply where a bank gives an

[19] Family Law Act 1996, s. 31(10)(b).
[20] Family Law Act 1996, s. 34(2).
[21] [1988] 3 W.L.R. 39.
[22] As to the effect of tacking on priority between competing charges, see *Macmillan Inc. v. Bishopsgate Trust (No 3)* [1995] 3 All E.R. 747, *per* Millett J.
[23] *e.g.* "all moneys and liabilities which shall for the time being . . . be due owing or incurred . . ."
[24] LPA 1925, s. 94.

overdraft limit secured by mortgage, since there is no obligation to maintain the limit, which remains repayable on demand.[25] But some large term loans are made in terms of a *commitment* by a bank, entitling the borrower to draw-down certain amounts at certain periods if he or she chooses. A security over subsequent draw-downs would have priority over subsequent incumbrances. Notice will not prevent tacking in this case; or if

(b) the original mortgagee does not know of later mortgages when it advances the money.[26] Registration of the subsequent mortgage as a land charge, after the original mortgage, and after the last search by the mortgagee, does not give notice to a mortgagee whose mortgage secures a current account or further advances (but searching is advisable, in case the "subsequent" mortgage was in fact granted before the original mortgage, although it was registered after it). Actual notice binds the original mortgagee, and subsequent incumbrancers ought to give written notice when their mortgages are made; or if

(c) by arrangement, the subsequent mortgagees *subordinate* their securities to the original mortgagee.[27]

21–143 With *registered land*, there are special statutory rules for charges: first, any obligation to advance further monies is entered on the register, so that subsequent incumbrancers know of it and take subject to further advances.[28] Secondly, where there is no obligation but the charge covers further advances, the land registry is obliged to notify the proprietor of the charge of proposed entries affecting its priority, (so that it may decide whether to advance further sums or not).[29] Thirdly, a subordination agreement may be entered by deed, and put on the register.[30]

21–144 If the original mortgage is protected by notice or caution, but not registered, further advances have no priority over subsequent registered mortgages (which, once registered, take priority not only over further advances but also over the earlier mortgage protected by a caution). Further advances probably have no priority if the original mortgagee has notice of the subsequent mortgage (whether registered or not) even through entries on the register.[31]

21–145 Notice generally prevents tacking of further advances, and if a bank mortgagee receives notice of a subsequent mortgage, and the debt secured

[25] *Hopkinson v. Rolt* (1861) 9 H.L.C. 514.
[26] See *Macmillan Inc. v. Bishopsgate Trust (No 3)* [1995] 3 All E.R. 747.
[27] See Chap. 16.
[28] LRA 1925, s. 30.
[29] *ibid*.
[30] LRA 1925, s. 31.
[31] LRA 1925, ss. 29, 30, 48, 49 and 55 and Land Registration Rules 1925, r. 218.

is an overdraft on a current account, it should, as normal procedure, rule off the account and open a new one, which should either be kept in credit or secured by alternative security. This procedure avoids the effect which the rule in *Clayton's Case* would have in reducing the size of the secured debt.[32] Otherwise, the effect of *Clayton's Case* would be that transactions through the current account would continually replace the original debt with new debt; this would mean that, although the total amount outstanding would remain the same or even increase, the bank would be making "further" advances, and these would have no priority once the bank had notice of a subsequent incumbrancer. Since the rule in *Clayton's Case* is merely a rule as to the presumed intention of the parties, it can be rebutted,[33] either by an express term or by the opening of a new account.[34]

Leases

If a *mortgagee* grants a lease otherwise than under the statutory power, the lease is subject to the mortgagor's right to redeem, except in the unlikely case that the tenant[35] is a bona fide purchaser who may defeat the equity of redemption. A lease granted by the *mortgagor* otherwise than under the statutory power will be subject to the mortgage unless the tenant is a bona fide purchaser, and the mortgage is not properly protected.[36] **21–146**

A lease granted by the *mortgagor* in breach of a prohibition and without the consent of the mortgagee does not bind the mortgagee[37] unless the agreement to lease was made before the mortgagor acquired title to the land. Although it seemed that this might cause a problem if the lease were granted immediately the property was acquired (since the mortgage would only take effect after the acquisition and the grant of the lease, and the lease would therefore take priority over the mortgage[38]) the decision of the House of Lords in *Abbey National Building Society v. Cann,*[39] made it clear that where property is acquired with a mortgage, the title passes and the mortgage is granted in the same indivisible transaction; this implies that a **21–147**

32 See above, Chap. 11.

33 *Deeley v. Lloyds Bank* [1912] A.C. 756.

34 Sufficient terms would include: "the rule in *Clayton's Case* shall not only apply to the secured debt," or "money paid in or carried to the mortgagor's credit on any current account shall first be appropriated towards and have the effect of discharging the most recent debit items on the said current account(s)." Cautious banks also break the account, though it seems unnecessary.

35 Who will generally know that he or she is dealing with the mortgagee or otherwise have notice of the mortgagor's rights.

36 See *Citibank International plc. v. Kessler* [1999] 2 C.M.L.R. 603, CA, where a mortgagor who was returning to Germany was refused permission by the bank mortgagee to let his English property. It was held that the Art. 48, E.C. (right to freedom of movement) did not prevent the bank refusing consent.

37 *Dudley and District Benefit Building Society v. Emerson* [1949] Ch. 707.

38 See *Rajapakse v. Fernando* [1920] A.C. 892; the same rule applies to registered land: *Woolwich Equitable Building Society v. Marshall* [1952] Ch. 1.

39 [1991] 1 A.C. 56.

lease cannot be granted before the creation of the mortgage, and that it will be the mortgage which takes priority, provided it has been registered.[40]

Other Registers

21–148 Whether the land is registered or not, there are a variety of other charges which may exist over property and must be considered by mortgagees, for example: (a) *Company charges*[41]; (b) *Local Land Charges*[42]: these relate to government land charges which may be imposed by public authorities upon land under statutory powers relating to health, housing, highways and town and country planning, for example; (c) *Commons and town and village greens*[43]; and (d) *Agricultural charges*[44]: charges given by farmers over farming stock and agricultural assets.

Bank Forms for Legal Mortgages

21–149 Bank forms are now written in "plain English": the language, therefore—if not the concepts—should be easier to understand; this increased transparency will surely prove to be a great advantage for modern mortgagors in understanding and, if necessary, questioning the obligations which they have undertaken. Here, we have set out the traditional clauses of a typical mortgage and have added a "plain English" version in italics to illustrate how a modern mortgage may set out its terms.[45]

Repayment

21–150 **Personal liability to repay principal and interest.** Banks' mortgage forms may secure (a) a fluctuating overdraft, (as with business mortgages) or (b) a loan for a fixed amount, as in the home mortgage business undertaken by banks in recent years. Financing by secured term loans is becoming more common, especially with larger businesses. The customer is usually obliged to repay on demand by the bank,[46] and there is sometimes a covenant to this effect:

> The mortgagor hereby covenants . . . that he will on demand in writing repay all monies, interest, bank charges, and other sums which from time to time and for the time being . . . be due or owing or incurred to

---

[40] *Barclays Bank v. Zaroovabli* [1997] 2 All E.R.19.
[41] CA 1985, s. 395, see above, Chap. 19.
[42] Local Land Charges Act 1975, s.10.
[43] Commons Registration Act 1965.
[44] Agricultural Charges Act 1928.
[45] These "plain English" illustrations are taken from the Mortgage Terms and Conditions 1999, kindly supplied by the National Westminster Bank.
[46] Even term loans may contain "material change of circumstances" clauses which make them resemble demand loans.

> the Bank by the mortgagor whether actually or contingently and whether solely or jointly with any other person and whether as principal or surety including interest discount commission or other lawful charges and expenses . . .,[47]

with the security then taken over the sums so covenanted to be paid (it may be omitted, since the obligation exists anyway[48]):

In the case of a home mortgage, the customer will also agree to repay amounts of principal and interest from his or her account at certain intervals (usually one month), but this agreement can be informal and may not be part of the actual mortgage, because the bank always retains the right to demand repayment. The bank's right to interest may be expressed to be at a fixed or a floating rate, expressed by some terms such as: **21–151**

> and including interest . . . which shall be computed and compounded according to the usual mode of the Bank both after and before any demand is made or judgment is obtained hereunder.

> *Details about monthly repayment are given, and information about notice of changes in payment which has to be given by the mortgagor; immediate repayment is required if the whole debt is not repaid when the property is sold*[49];
>
> *The bank is allowed to make changes to monthly repayment, because of changes in interest rate or for other reasons*[50];
>
> *Details about interest charges are given, including when it is payable and what on*[51]*; and of changes in interest rates and the possible reasons*[52];
>
> *Information about early repayment of the mortgage is set out, including a possible extra charge; and about making extra monthly repayments*[53];
>
> *The mortgagor is required to contact the bank straight away if he or she has problems paying.*[54]

There are other terms about giving notices to the mortgagor; about the bank's expenses, which must be paid in full by the mortgagor; and about endowment, pension or other policies, if appropriate.[55] **21–152**

47 Terms may be included as to the making of demand by letter to the last known place of business or abode, and the time at which the demand is deemed to be made.

48 With registered land, it is implied by the LRA 1925, s. 28, unless there is a negativing clause, and with unregistered land it is implied by law: *Sutton v. Sutton* (1883) 22 Ch.D. 511 at 515. The right is preserved by the CCA 1974.

49 Term 3.

50 Term 4.

51 Term 5.

52 Term 6: *e.g.* a change in bank base rates, in the actions of the bank's competitors, or in the cost to the bank of raising money.

53 Terms 9 and 10.

54 Term 21.

55 Terms 11, 12 and 13. Other terms relate to changes in the accounting year(7); and tax relief—notification to bank of loss of right to claim it (8).

Ownership of Property/Charge

21–153 **Type of charge.** The simplest method is to say that the mortgagor as beneficial owner "hereby charges by way of legal mortgage" the property described in a schedule.

> The mortgagor as beneficial owner hereby charges by way of legal mortgage ALL that the property referred to in the schedule hereto . . . as a continuing security for the payment or discharge of demand of all monies and liabilities hereby covenanted to be paid or discharged by the mortgagor.

21–154 The mortgagor covenants expressly as beneficial owner[56]: this is an implied promise that the mortgagor has the power to convey the property, that the mortgagee is entitled to possession, that the mortgagor will execute further documents to perfect the mortgagee's title if required, and, in the case of leaseholds, that the lease is valid and that all obligations under it have been and will be performed.[57]

21–155 **"All estate" clause.** A mortgage will pass to the mortgagee the rights the mortgagor has power to convey.[58] No problem should arise where the mortgagor is sole legal and beneficial owner, but if others have equitable rights in the property the mortgagee should seek the participation of those others. A joint legal owner may not create an effective legal charge but may charge his or her own equitable interest, if any, severing any equitable joint tenancy. A mortgagee who cannot obtain the agreement of co-owners, but who agrees to take security over whatever interest the mortgagor has will probably purport to charge the whole beneficial interest anyway; a cautious lender may specify expressly that a charge is over the whole interest of the mortgagor, whatever that may be.[59] In addition to the charge in that form, the mortgage may assign to the bank the beneficial interest of the mortgagor in the property and the proceeds of sale subject to cesser on redemption.

21–156 The mortgage may state that if the title is not registered, no person, including the mortgagor, is to be registered as proprietor without the bank's consent; and if the title is registered, that the Land Certificate must be given to the bank (if it is not deposited with the Land Registry) so that the bank can register the charge;

---

[56] The mortgagor may covenant as trustee or personal representative, if that is appropriate, in which case, the implied covenant is that he or she has not done anything to prevent the mortgage operating according to its terms.

[57] LPA 1925, s. 76.

[58] LPA 1925, s. 63.

[59] This is expressed as a conveyance, because this is possible where the interest is equitable. It could be expressed as a charge.

The mortgagor confirms that he or she is the owner of the property as described in the mortgage deed; that the property is free from any rights or obligations in favour of others; and that the mortgagor is registered, or entitled to be registered, with absolute title;

and that, to the best of the mortgagor's knowledge, all the information he or she has given the bank concerning the mortgage application is true and complete, and he or she will tell the bank in writing as soon as anything changes before completion;

It is stipulated that the bank's first legal charge must be preserved at all times, and the mortgagor will not grant any subsequent charges over the property and any policies without first getting the bank's written permission.[60]

Upkeep of the Property

The mortgagor is required to insure the property and keep it in good repair, in default of which the bank is permitted to do so[61]; the costs will then constitute a secured debt; giving the bank power to apply insurance moneys either to repairing the property or to discharging the debt; 21–157
The bank is permitted to make payments on which the mortgagor is liable, without affecting his or her liability under the security.

The mortgagor must keep the property insured properly, giving the bank the power to settle all insurance claims.[62]

The property must be a single private home, lived in by the family as the main home, and its use must not be changed—for example, it must not be used for business—without the bank's written permission.[63]

The property must be kept in good repair and condition; if it is not, the bank can have the work done and charge the mortgagor for it, and add the charge to the debt, with or without taking possession of the property.[64]

Other responsibilities relating to the property are set out: 21–158

obligations must be kept to, charges must be paid, the bank must be informed of any disputes about the property, for example with neighbours, and of any notices about the property like planning enforcement orders or notices of road improvements; no development of the property which needs planning permission is to be undertaken, nor any substances to be kept which might be dangerous or cause pollution.

[60] Term 1.
[61] See *Colonial Mutual Insurance Co. Ltd v. ANZ Banking Group (N.Z.) Ltd* [1995] 1 W.L.R. 1140, PC.
[62] Term 14.
[63] Term 15.
[64] Term 16.

21–159 If the mortgagor does not comply with these terms, the bank may carry out work, and charge the mortgagor for the cost.[65]

The mortgagor must not leave the property unoccupied for four weeks or more without telling the insurers. If the property deteriorates while the mortgagor is away, or if the mortgagor does not follow the insurer's instructions, the bank may take possession of the property and arrange to sell it, even if the repayments are up to date.[66]

The mortgagor must allow the bank to send agents to inspect the property at any reasonable time (without necessarily taking possession of the property).[67]

Granting Leases

21–160 The mortgagor's power to grant or accept surrenders of leases is excluded unless the bank consents.[68]

The bank's statutory powers of sale are extended, so that it can grant leases of the whole or any part of the property and on terms which it thinks fit.[69]

The mortgagor may not let the property, or allow anyone else to occupy it, without the written approval of the bank.[70] *The bank is permitted to give a tenancy of the property without the need of keeping to the restrictions in section 99 of the Law of Property Act 1925.*[71]

Power of Sale

21–161 There is an immediate power of sale after demand.[72]

The bank is permitted to remove and sell chattels in order to facilitate sale, and to pay the net proceeds to the mortgagor.[73]

The money owed is treated as due 28 days after the date of the mortgage, and the bank can exercise its powers of sale at any time, so that any

---

[65] Term 17.

[66] Term 18.

[67] Term 20.

[68] Mortgagors in possession have such powers by the LPA 1925, ss. 99–100.

[69] Any mortgagee has some powers of leasing by the LPA 1925, s. 99, but only for agricultural leases less than 50 years, or building leases less than 999 years, and subject to certain conditions.The powers can be increased in the mortgage deed: LPA 1925, s. 99 (14).

[70] Term 19.

[71] Term 23(c).

[72] Excluding the LPA 1925, s. 103 (which prohibits sale for a three months period after default). This term is normally included, but, although it probably binds the mortgagor contractually, it may not be effective against other incumbrancers: Encyclopedia, E 555.

[73] Some agreements for individual mortgagors will say that the bank is to have no right of set off or retention of these proceeds against the debt, to prevent the term being construed as a chattel mortgage, and void for non-registration as a bill of sale. But probably the absence of the qualification does not create a chattel mortgage, in which case combination with the proceeds would be possible, although an individual mortgagor might well object to this.

purchaser from the bank can assume that the bank has good title to the property. The bank may sell the property even if it has not taken possession of it, and without the restrictions of section 103 of the Law of Property Act 1925.

There is an extended list of events which could trigger repossession, including: **21–162**

failure to pay two or more monthly repayments or breach of other conditions; where a bankruptcy order has been made—or the bank thinks that one is likely to be made—against the mortgagor; where a person is applying for a court order against the mortgagor to do with the property which the bank thinks could endanger its rights, or the mortgagor allows a third party to gain an interest in the property or trying to sell the property.[74]

The bank may ask for a court order for possession and evict the mortgagor and anyone else who is there and sell the property (or use other powers given to mortgage lenders, including appointing a receiver or letting it[75]*); if the proceeds are less than the mortgagor's debt, he or she must pay the bank the shortfall.*[76]

The mortgagor must sign and (if necessary) seal any document and do anything else the bank considers reasonable to help it to use our powers under the mortgage and to make good and preserve its rights.

If the bank takes possession of the property, any of the mortgagor's belongings left in it will be stored or sold by the bank (at the mortgagor's expense).[77]

Power to Appoint a Receiver

The clause provides that a receiver and manager of the property may be appointed after demand or on the mortgagor's request; for the payment and powers of the receiver; it excludes the bank's liability for moneys not actually received by it; and declares that the receiver's costs are a debt which is also charged on the property: **21–163**

The bank may also appoint a receiver, who will be the mortgagor's agent and have all the powers in the terms and conditions as well as the statutory powers.[78]

---

[74] Term 22.
[75] Without the restrictions in the LPA 1925, s. 99.
[76] Term 23.
[77] Term 25.
[78] Terms 24 and 23(c).

Consolidation/Appropriation Powers

21–164 The bank may *consolidate* mortgages (insist that if one is redeemed, all must be[79]), although, in fact, banks normally take an *all monies*[80] mortgage, so that, generally, the bank would not need to take separate mortgages.

The security is said to be a continuing security notwithstanding any settlement of accounts, so that it does not prejudice any security previously given or relating to other property, and is not replaced by subsequent security. The bank is permitted to close the account and open new accounts if it learns of a subsequent disposal or incumbrance of the property, and to declare that no money paid into the new account shall discharge any part of the amount due under the closed account[81]; if an express power to combine accounts is given (as it may be to avoid doubt) it will specify that no notice to the debtor is required beforehand[82]:

> *The bank may choose which part of the debt it applies the payments to.*[83]
> *The mortgage is security for the debt and also for any other money the mortgagor owes the bank. The bank will not release any security it holds until the debt has been paid (continuing security).*[84]

Appointing Bank as Attorney

21–165 The mortgagor irrevocably appoints the bank and the receiver as the joint and several attorneys of the mortgagor with power to execute deeds, so that there is no need to apply to the court in disposing of the property:

> *The mortgagor is said to appoint the bank (or its receiver) as his or her attorney, who is authorised to act in the name of the mortgagor and can receive money due to him or her to do with the property, and can enforce his or her rights to do with the property (or management company).*[85]

Miscellaneous Conditions

21–166 The (company) mortgagor certifies that a company charge does not contravene the Articles or Memorandum of the company; this acts as an express[86] warranty of authority by the directors, so that they are personally

---

[79] LPA 1925, s. 93, excludes consolidation unless the contrary is expressed.

[80] Banks are committed not to take unlimited (or "all monies") *guarantees* (Banking Code (1999) para. 3.14, Mortgage Code para. 4.2), but do not make the same promise with regard to mortgages.

[81] This is to prevent *Clayton's Case* (see above, Chap. 11) from operating to discharge the debt. Sometimes an account is "deemed" to be opened.

[82] This right exists anyway: see above, Chap. 11.

[83] Terms 2(d) and (f). The bank may also divide the mortgage account into different parts—for tax reasons, or to charge interest at different rates or if different repayment terms apply, for example; and presumably also for appropriation of payments.

[84] Term 28.

[85] Term 27.

[86] One would be implied, anyway.

liable in damages if it is false, and if the company is not bound by the charge.

"Mortgagor" (and "bank") are defined so as to include successors in title. There may be other interpretative provisions.

The "plain language" mortgage contains a variety of other terms:

> *The mortgage is to remain in force even if the mortgagor becomes bankrupt, mentally incapable, or dies.*
>
> *The bank will not lose its rights under the mortgage even if it does not enforce them, or if it makes mistakes or gives the mortgagor wrong or incomplete information; if the mortgage is released before the debt is paid in full, the remainder of the debt must still be paid, even if the bank has given the mortgagor a receipt which says that he or she has paid in full.*
>
> *Transfer: the bank has the right to transfer the mortgage to a new lender without the mortgagor's permission, but the mortgagor's rights and obligations will remain the same against the new lender. The mortgagor may not transfer the mortgage or delegate any rights or obligations under it.*
>
> *Guarantors: if a guarantor gives a guarantee of the mortgage he or she takes on all the responsibility for the mortgage; everything in the terms and conditions also applies to the guarantee. It is stipulated that the guarantor's obligations will not be affected by the fact that the bank has lent the mortgagor further money, taken further security, given the mortgagor time to pay, or done or not done anything. Each guarantor must get independent legal advice.*[87]
>
> *Releasing confidential information: the bank may ask for relevant information about the mortgagor from other organisations if he or she applies for extra borrowing, and may exchange information about him or her with other companies in the bank group, or to third parties under certain circumstances. This includes credit reference agencies, if the mortgagor is in default.*[88]

[87] Term 30. See above Chap. 18, for discussion of "indulgence clauses" in guarantees.
[88] Term 26. See above, Chap. 4 for discussion of the banker's duty of confidentiality.

liable in damages if [illegible] sales, and if the company is not [illegible] the charge.

Mortgagors [illegible] interests subsequent to [illegible]. There may be other interpretative provisions. The [illegible] mortgage contains [illegible].

The mortgage [illegible] remains in force even if the mortgagor [illegible] becomes bankrupt, mentally incapable or dies.

The bank will not lose its rights under the mortgage [illegible] even if [illegible] makes [illegible] changes [illegible] mortgage [illegible] incomplete [illegible] of the [illegible] of foreign law [illegible] even if the bank [illegible] the mortgage or a receipt which [illegible] further [illegible] the right [illegible] the bank [illegible] whether [illegible] mortgage [illegible]. The mortgage [illegible].

[illegible] all the [illegible] for the mortgage [illegible] obligations [illegible] and the bank [illegible] that the bank [illegible] the [illegible] remedies [illegible].

[illegible] powers [illegible] of the [illegible] covenants [illegible] mortgagor is in default.

[illegible] See above, Chap. [illegible] for discussion of [illegible] intelligence [illegible].
[illegible] See above, Chap. [illegible] for discussion of the banker's duty of confidentiality.

CHAPTER 22

LIFE ASSURANCE[1]

In a contract for life assurance, the insurer promises, in consideration of payment (usually regular payments in the form of premiums), to make an agreed payment to a particular person or persons on the death of the insured.[2] There must be some link with the life or death of the assured person, but modern courts, reflecting the changing nature of insurance, take a broad approach to the nature of the link.[3] **22–001**

Life assurance policies are of interest to bankers for two separate reasons. First, if a customer is indebted to the bank, say by way of a 25 year mortgage loan, the life policy (even a simple temporary insurance policy) preserves the bank's position if the customer dies. Secondly, if the policy has a surrender value, the assured person's contractual right to that value is good security, since it is easy to value, transfer and realise, and the value increases with the premiums paid. In both cases, the benefit of the policy is *assigned* to the bank by way of security. Valuation (by asking the insurer) and realisation (by surrender) of the policy are both simple. For these reasons, life policies are regarded by bankers as a very satisfactory form of security,[4] although it is sometimes said that a bank's reputation may be damaged if it is obliged to realise a policy which has been taken out to make provision for the assured's dependants.[5] Accident policies, which have no surrender value, and retirement annuity policies, which are not surrenderable or assignable, are not useful for security. **22–002**

The main legal problems are as to the insurable interest, the doctrine of *uberrima fides*, the effect of crime, and suicide. Contracts of insurance are excluded from the effect of the UCTA 1977, so that there is no requirement for terms to be reasonable within that statute. There is no such **22–003**

---

[1] See further Milnes Holden, *The Law and Practice of Banking* (8th ed., 1993,) Vol. 2, p. 133; Clarke, *The Law of Insurance Contracts*, MacGillivray on *Insurance Law*, Colinvaux, *Law of Insurance* (7th ed.). For discussion of conflicts of laws problems, see Clarke, *op. cit.*, Chap. 2.

[2] Insurance Companies are regulated under the Insurance Companies Act 1982, as amended; the enforceability of contracts issued by unauthorised insurance companies is regulated by the FSA 1986 (s. 132, see also *Bates v. Barrow Ltd* [1995] Lloyd's Rep. 680.) See also the Policyholders Protection Acts 1995 and 1997.

[3] The meaning of "life insurance" was considered in *Fuji Finance Inc. v. Aetna Life Insurance Co. Ltd* [1996] 3 W.L.R. 871, CA, where the policy holder was able to switch the investment under the policy from one fund to another and managed thereby to increase its surrender value from £50,000 to over £1m in six years. It was held that it was life insurance under the Life Assurance Act 1774, s. 1. See comment by Clarke, *op. cit.*, 1–1D.

[4] Milnes Holden, *op. cit.*, 135.

[5] *ibid.*, p. 136.

exclusion from the requirements of the UTCCR 1999, however, and terms of insurance contracts with a consumer which have not been individually negotiated may be struck down as unfair if, contrary to the requirement of good faith, they cause a significant imbalance in the rights and obligations of the insured to his or her detriment.[6] Some of the "severer" aspects of insurance contracts[7] (such as the absolute nature of the obligation to disclose material facts and the effect of breaches of warranty) might contravene the UTCCR 1999 although there is the possibility that the courts might regard them as defining the main subject matter of the contract, so that their fairness would not need to be considered unless they were not expressed in plain language.[8]

Insurable Interest

22–004 For reasons of public policy—to prevent "moral hazard"[9] and gambling and murder—life assurance may only be created to benefit a person who has a pecuniary interest in the life of another person (the *assured*).[10] Moreover, where there is such an interest, the amount recoverable under the policy may not exceed the amount of that interest.[11] The rule is satisfied so long as the insurable interest exists when the policy is made, even if it ceases afterwards.[12] If the rule is broken, the policy is void and confers no rights, and no premiums are recoverable,[13] although it is probably unlikely that a reputable insurance company would seek to insist upon this rule to avoid payment to an innocent third party assignee such as a bank.

22–005 The following individuals have insurable interests in the following persons: (i) spouse, in spouse[14]—the amount of interest here is unlimited; (ii) creditor, in debtor, to the amount of the debt[15]; (iii) surety or guarantor, in principal debtor, to the amount of guarantee; (iv) employer, in

---

[6] See further above, para. 3–031.

[7] See *Chitty on Contract*, II, 39.052.; the point is also made that the "severer terms" derive from the general principles of insurance law, rather than the specific terms of the insurance contract, although it is not easy to see why that should exempt them from the ambit of the UTCCR 1999 any more than terms of similar contracts, such as guarantee contracts.

[8] UTCCR 1999, reg. 3(2). See Treitel, *Law of Contract* (10th ed.), p. 250. Other terms which might fall foul of the UTCCR 1999, include terms permitting the insurer to terminate the policy at any time; terms requiring the insured to forfeit premiums if the policy is avoided; terms providing that the insurer's agent is the agent of the assured for the purpose of completing the proposal, and terms restricting the insured's access to a judicial remedy, for example, shortening the limitation period. See Clarke, *op. cit.*, para. 19–5A, and *Encyclopedia of Insurance*, Kluwer, B 4.3–36.

[9] See Clarke, *op. cit.*, 4–2A.

[10] Life Assurance Act 1774, s. 1.

[11] See *Fuji Finance Inc. v. Aetna Life Insurance Co. Ltd* [1996] 3 W.L.R. 871, CA.

[12] *Dalby v. India and London Life Ass. Co* (1854) 15 C.B. 365.

[13] See *Harse v. Pearl Life Ass. Co.* [1904] 1 K.B. 558. Premiums are recoverable if the assured is misled by the insurer: *Hughes v. Liverpool Victoria Legal Friendly Soc.* [1916] 2 K.B. 482.

[14] *Griffiths v. Fleming* [1909] 1 K.B. 805 (husband, in wife); *Reed v. Royal Exchange Assurance Co.* (1795) Peake Add.Cas, 70 (wife, in husband).

[15] *Anderson v. Edie* (1795) 2 Park's Mar. Ins. (8th ed.), 914.

employee[16]; (v) trustee, in life of the beneficiary[17]; (vi) dependent child, in parent[18]; (vii) litigant, in life of the judge.[19] There is no insurable interest between siblings or other relatives, or from parent in the life of a child, unless there is some pecuniary interest in a particular case.[20] A banker has an insurable interest in the life of a person indebted to him, and could take out a policy over that life, but this would be unusual.

The rule that the beneficiary must have a pecuniary interest applies to the original contract of insurance itself, not to subsequent assignments. This means that the rule can be avoided in one of two ways: A (the assured) may insure his or her own life, for his or her own benefit and subsequently assign the benefit of the policy moneys to B (the beneficiary)[21]; or, alternatively, A may insure his or her own life and make a declaration of trust, appointing a trustee to hold the policy for B's benefit. B may then assign his or her rights as assignee or as beneficiary under the trust. **22–006**

The Duty to Disclose

Certain classes of contracts, including insurance contracts, are said to be contracts *uberrimae fidei,* which means "of the utmost good faith". This means that parties to such contracts have a duty to disclose any material facts which affect the insurance.[22] A material fact is one which would have had an effect on the mind of a prudent insurer in weighing up the risk and fixing the premium,[23] and is a question of fact in each case,[24] provided that it must be shown that the insurer was induced by the misrepresentation or non-disclosure of that fact to make the policy on the relevant terms.[25] If a material fact is not disclosed, the insurer may avoid the contract, and refuse to pay. Examples of material facts are failing to disclose that a number of other insurers had declined the risk of life assurance,[26] and failing to **22–007**

[16] *Hebdon v. West* (1863) 3 B & S 579.

[17] *Tidswell v. Ankerstein* (1792) Peake, 151.

[18] *Howard v. Refuge Friendly Soc.* (1886) 54 L.T. 644 (not a child being supported).

[19] This is not uncommon where there may be a lengthy trial.

[20] See *Halford v. Kymer* (1830) 10 B & C 724 (parent, in child); *Evanson v. Crooks* (1911) 106 L.T. 264 (sisters).

[21] For the validity of this, see *Ashley v. Ashley* (1829) 3 Sim. 149.

[22] See *Banque Keyser Ullman S.A. v. Skandia (UK) Insurance Co. Ltd* [1990] 1 Q.B. 665, CA, aff'd. [1991] 2 A.C. 249 for consideration of the insurer's duty of disclosure.

[23] *Pan Atlantic Insurance Co. Ltd v. Pine Top Insurance Co. Ltd* [1995] 1 A.C. 501 at 508, *per* Lord Goff; explained *St Paul Insurance v. McConnell* [1996] 1 All E.R. 96, CA.

[24] See s. 18(2) and (7) of the Marine Insurance Act 1906, which were said to be generally applicable in *Locker and Woolfe v. Western Australian Insurance Co Ltd* [1936] 1 K.B. 408, and see *Pan Atlantic Insurance Co. Ltd v. Pine Top Insurance Co. Ltd* [1995] 1 A.C. 501.

[25] *Pan Atlantic Insurance Co. Ltd v. Pine Top Insurance Co. Ltd* [1995] 1 A.C. 501. This is a new requirement for non-disclosure (as opposed to misrepresentation) cases (see Birds and Hird, 59 M.L.R. 285). If the requirement takes the form that there is a presumption that the statement or omissiont has induced the contract (as suggested by Lord Mustill in *Pan Atlantic*), there is unlikely to be a radical change in practice.

[26] *London Assurance v. Mansel* (1879) 11 Ch. D. 363.

disclose doubts about the assured's mental health, (which might have made him suicide prone).[27]

22–008 Proposal forms often contain a list of specific questions, and an untrue answer is a misrepresentation entitling the insurer to avoid the policy,[28] if the fact is material and induces the insurer to make the policy. However, the policy often goes further and provides that the truth of statements made is a condition of the insurer's liability. That provision extends the duty to disclose to include replies which state facts which are non-material.[29] The fact that there is a list of questions specifically asked does not exclude the duty to disclose other material facts: the duty would have to be expressly excluded by the insurer.[30] Facts which need not be disclosed include those the insurer should already know, or which reduce the risk, which both parties have equal means of knowing, or general topics of speculation, or facts the disclosure of which is waived, or facts which the assured does not know (such as a hidden illness).

Any material changes which occur between the date of the proposal and the policy date must be disclosed,[31] but the fact that the insured warrants the truthfulness of his or her statements does not mean that the insured's answers in the proposal form are to be read as importing promises as to the future. That would depend upon the construction in the particular case, and if the insurer wishes to include a continuing warranty of that kind, it would have to stipulate for it in clear terms.[32]

22–009 The difficulty with the rule of disclosure is that matters which the assured thinks are not relevant may be relevant to the hypothetical "prudent insurer". The presence of questions on the form may make the assured think those are the only points requiring any comment, whereas, if the proposal forms make accuracy a condition, even insignificant errors may vitiate the policy, and, if there is an omission, the insurer can avoid the policy even though, as it happens, the omission was irrelevant to the cause of the claim[33] (although not to the making of the policy[34]). All of this may

[27] *Lindenau v. Desborough* (1828) 8 B & C 586.

[28] See *Gerling Konzern v. Polygram Holdings* [1998] 2 Lloyd's Rep. 544, QBD.

[29] See *Dawsons Ltd v. Bonnin* [1922] 2 A.C. 413. Or, conversely, the form may restrict the duty to disclose, so that the policy is avoided only for wilful failure to disclose or positive misrepresentation.

[30] In *Woolcott v. Sun Alliance and London Ins. Ltd* [1978] 1 W.L.R. 493, a house purchaser obtained a building society mortgage, and the society gave him a form for insurance purposes. He answered all the questions asked without disclosing a conviction for armed robbery several years before. When his house was later damaged by fire, the insurers were held to be justified in refusing to pay. The conviction related to dishonesty and this was a material fact.

[31] *Canning v. Farquhar* (1886) 16 Q.B.D. 727, where the assured was seriously injured after making his proposal.

[32] *Hussain v. Brown* [1996] 1 Lloyd's Rep. 627, CA, because it is a "draconian" term.

[33] *e.g.* a potential suicide fails to disclose mental ill-health, but dies in an aeroplane crash.

[34] See *Pan Atlantic* [1995] 1 A.C. 501 where the House of Lords decided that the statement or omission must have induced the making of the policy on the relevant terms.

affect the bank's security, because insurance companies usually, from reasons of economy, postpone carrying out thorough checks until the time when a claim is made. If the assured fails to disclose a fact to the insurer, he or she is also unlikely to disclose it to the bank. Some insurers have stated that they will not rely on the disclosure rule, others will not rely on it against innocent assignees, and many have agreed to make clear on the proposal form the duty to disclose material facts.[35]

The Effect of Murder and Suicide

Murder and unlawful killing

It is a principle of public policy that no-one may benefit from his or her own unlawful act. A murderer, for example, may not make a claim on the life of his or her victim.[36] In cases of unlawful killing other than murder[37] the Forfeiture Act 1982 gives the court a discretion to allow recovery where it thinks just, and this may be applied in some cases.[38] **22–010**

Suicide

Suicide is not a crime in England.[39] Most policies will state what will occur in case of suicide,[40] but, if not, the rule is still that laid down by *Beresford v. Royal Insurance Co. Ltd*[41]: that it is against public policy for a sane suicide to take the benefit of an assurance. A finding by the coroner that the assured took his or her life while the balance of his or her mind was temporarily disturbed will allow recovery,[42] unless the policy states otherwise.[43] It is not clear whether the public policy rule would override any contrary provision in the agreement,[44] but presumably no insurer would **22–011**

---

[35] See the Statement of Long-Term Insurance Practice, 1986 (Association of British Insurers and Lloyd's). There is an insurance ombudsman, established 1981, for the status of whom, see *R. v. Insurance Ombudsman Bureau, ex. p. Aegon Life Assurance Ltd* [1995] L.R.L.R. 101. In 1995, another insurance ombudsman was established: the Personal Investment Authority Ombudsman assumed jurisdiction over investment insurance within the FSA 1986.

[36] *Amicable Society v. Bolland* (1830) 4 Bli. N.S. 194; *Cleaver v. Mutual Reserve Fund Life Assn.* [1892] 1 Q.B. 147.

[37] *i.e.* for manslaughter, or murder reduced to manslaughter by reason of provocation or diminished responsibility.

[38] Possibly, *e.g.*, where a wife, under provocation, kills her husband and then herself. The children might be allowed to recover as next of kin under a policy in favour of the wife. In *Re S* [1996] 1 W.L.R. 235, it was held that the benefits payable under a joint policy to a husband who killed his wife could be held in trust for the son of the marriage.

[39] Suicide Act 1961, s. 1.

[40] *e.g.* assignees, or perhaps all parties, may be protected if suicide does not occur within the first few years of the policy.

[41] [1938] A.C. 586. The Forfeiture Act 1982 does not apply to suicides, because it applies only to killings of "another".

[42] See *Moore v. Woolsey* (1854) 4 E & B 243.

[43] See *Ellinger & Co v. Mutual Life Insurance Co Ltd* [1905] 1 K.B. 31.

[44] See the discussion in *Beresford v. Royal Insurance Co Ltd* [1938] A.C. 586 at 607, *per* Lord Atkin.

refuse to pay, particularly to an assignee, like a bank, where the policy allows for payment to a sane suicide.

22–012 It is a crime to aid and abet suicide,[45] and the benefit of the policy of a person who takes part in a suicide pact will be subject to forfeiture,[46] but the court has a discretion whether to order forfeiture. Where one partner in a suicide pact survived a series of attempts, but the other did not, for example, the court expressed sympathy with the survivor and ordered total relief against forfeiture.[47]

The Beneficiary

22–013 Where a life policy is used for security, the assignment to the bank is taken from the person who is entitled to the benefit, who may or may not be the life assured: that is, the *beneficiary*, to whom monies payable under a policy are payable or who is entitled to the surrender value. The beneficiary must be 18 years of age, or the assignment will be ineffective. Because the life assured would be entitled to surrender the policy and claim the surrender value, the bank should ensure that both life assured and the beneficiary join in the assignment, unless there has been a trust set up by the assured who makes himself or herself a trustee for the beneficiary. In this case, both the capital monies and the surrender value payable under the policy belong to the beneficiary, who must always join in the assignment. (An important consideration is that if there is a trust, the trustee is under an obligation not to let the policy lapse, for that is a breach of his or her duty to the beneficiary.[48]) If it is only the policy monies which are in question, only the beneficiary need be party to an assignment.

22–014 If a husband or wife effects an insurance on his or her life which is expressed to be for the benefit of the other or for their children or both, a trust is created and an interest immediately vests in the person or persons named, who must be a party to the assignment,[49] so that the policy money will not form part of the estate of the assured and may not be used to pay off his or her debts. In other cases, a trust is created only if there are express words not merely making the monies payable to a particular person, but pointing to the conclusion that the insurance money is to be a fund to which the person named is to be entitled.[50] The use of words such as "held in trust" is quite clear.

A policy may either name the beneficiary (the person to whom the benefits are payable) or identify him or her by reference to a description such as "my wife", or "my wife and children".

---

[45] Suicide Act 1961, s. 2.

[46] Forfeiture Act 1982.

[47] *Dunbar v. Plant* [1997] 4 All E.R. 289, CA.

[48] *Re Sinclair's Life Policy* [1938] Ch. 799.

[49] Married Women's Property Act 1882, s. 11.

[50] *Re Webb, Barclays Bank Ltd v. Webb* [1941] Ch. 225; see also *Perrin v. Dickson* [1930] 1 K.B. 107; *Re Sinclair's Life Policy* [1938] Ch. 799.

Where the beneficiary is named—for example, "my wife Jane"—then if there is a trust the interest is vested in her and she will not cease to be entitled to whatever rights she or her estate may have if there is a divorce or if she predeceases her husband.[51] Where, however, the beneficiary is only identified by a description, not by name, the person must correspond with the description at the time the policy monies become payable. Thus, if the description is "my wife", and the wife at the time the policy was taken out has divorced or died, no monies would be payable to her or her estate.[52] And in the case of a trust "for my wife and children", there may be difficulties: the children, depending on their ages, may not have contractual capacity, or it may not be clear which children are included—for example, there may be children from another marriage, or if the trust is in favour of "my children", it is possible that there may be more children subsequently who would not be bound by an assignment. Such points affect the security value of the policy. If there might be any doubt as to the entitlement of the beneficiary named, he or she should be asked to join in the mortgage.[53] **22–015**

If the parties agree jointly and severally to pay the premiums, one party—for example, a husband—is entitled to a lien on the policy monies after the death of his wife to the extent of the premiums paid by him since her death.[54]

Non-payment of Premiums

The customer will covenant to pay the premiums, and the security covers these as well (in case the bank has to pay them). When taking the security, the bank will obtain the current premium receipt. The risk of non-payment of premiums may be reduced if they are paid by standing order through the bank account. If the customer has insufficient funds to arrange this, the bank can continue to pay premiums, if the insurance is near maturity, or, if the policy allows this, convert the policy into a fully paid one.[55] This will be stated by the charge forms, though the mortgagee has a right to safeguard its own security in any case. **22–016**

The effect of non-payment depends on the terms of the policy. With some policies, the assurance is "renewable" (that is, it may continue only so long as premiums are paid), and with others the policy may be "continuing", but subject to forfeiture if the premium is not paid. In either case, a period of grace is usually allowed. With the renewable type, payment within the period of grace is usually allowed, even after the assured's death, **22–017**

[51] *Cousins v. Sun Life Assurance Society* [1933] 1 Ch. 126, approving *Prescott v. Prescott* [1906] 1 I.R. 155.

[52] See *Re Browne's Policy, Browne v. Browne* [1903] 1 Ch. 188.

[53] Where there may be undue influence, it is sensible for the beneficiary to be independently advised, preferably by a lawyer, see above, Chap. 3.

[54] *Re Smith's Estate, Bilham v. Smith* [1937] Ch. 636; *Grabiner v. Brew* (1964) 108 Sol.Jo. 1030.

[55] But if the policy holder becomes bankrupt, the bank cannot prove for future unpaid premiums: *Deering v. Bank of Ireland* (1886) 12 App. Cas. 20.

subject to deduction of the premium. With the continuing type, the payment may be made within the period of grace unless the policy states otherwise, even if the assured has died.[56] Some policies provide for conversion to fully paid policies (for a smaller amount) if there is default in payment of the premiums.

Method of Assignment

22–018 Where the beneficiary is a different person from the assured, the assignment is taken from the beneficiary, unless the contract provides to the contrary.[57] Problems of undue influence must be considered.[58] Minors will not be bound by the assignment, so that a policy to "wife and children" would be good security for the wife's share only. Company insurances of the lives of directors do not require registration on assignment by way of charge.[59] It should be noted that policies in which age is not admitted may be vitiated if the insured has made a misrepresentation as to age, and banks should be careful to obtain a birth certificate from the customer and an admission from the insurer before the insurance is taken.

The assignment may be either legal or equitable, although no legal assignment is possible if this is prohibited by the policy.[60] An agreement to assign in those circumstances would be effective between assignor and assignee, but might be ignored by the insurer.

Legal Assignments

22–019 The effect of a legal assignment of a life assurance policy is that after the insurer receives notice of the assignment, it must only pay the assignee, who can give a good discharge without the agreement of the assignor. As legal assignee the bank has the power to surrender or sell the policy, and to give a good discharge to the insurer for payment of the monies, and as assignee, it may sue in its own name.[61] The insurer is entitled to any defences, set-offs or counterclaims which existed between itself and the assured before notice.[62] The bank may take the assignment as security for a fixed sum, but it is generally for *all monies* and the customer convenants to repay all advances on any account, including interest, and as a continuing security.[63]

[56] *Stuart v. Freeman* [1903] 1 K.B. 47.
[57] This is occasionally the case.
[58] See above, Chap. 3.
[59] Under the CA 1985, s. 395.
[60] This is uncommon.
[61] Policies of Assurance Act 1867, s. 1.
[62] Policies of Assurance Act 1867, s. 2.
[63] To avoid the effect of *Clayton's Case*: see above, Chap. 11.

The Policies of Assurance Act 1867 requires that the assignment be signed and witnessed.[64] It need not be made by deed, though deeds are often used. The assignment may be effected on the policy itself, or by separate instrument.[65] The insurer must be informed in writing of the date and effect of the assignment,[66] at its principal place for business, which must be stated on the policy.[67] The assignment is not complete as a legal assignment until notice has been given.

The priorities between successive assignees are regulated by the order in which notice is received by the insurer, but only if an assignee has no notice of any prior assignment at the time of contracting.[68] Notice may be actual or constructive.[69] If the policy has not been produced to the assignee by the assignor, this may amount to constructive notice of a previous assignment,[70] and may indicate that the bank has not taken sufficient care to make inquiries. Where the policy has not been produced, therefore, the bank should not make any further advances in reliance upon the security unless it has full details of any prior assignees,[71] or unless some reasonable explanation for the absence of the policy is given.[72] Assuming that the bank has no notice of prior assignees and that it gives notice to the insurers, its legal charge defeats prior equitable assignees (if they have not given notice to the insurers) and subsequent legal or equitable assignees. As a matter of procedure, the insurers should be asked before further advances are made whether there is any outstanding incumbrance.[73] If the account is a current account, it should be closed to prevent the operation of the rule in *Clayton's Case.* **22–020**

Equitable Assignments

Given the simplicity of taking a legal assignment, that is the preferred method except in special cases, but life assurance policies, like other choses in action, may be informally assigned[74]—simply by an oral agreement, by **22–021**

---

[64] The requirements of the Policies of Assurance Act 1867 are different from those of s. 136 of the LPA 1925 because the assignee is also required to be entitled to receive the policy *in equity* at the time when an action is brought. This goes further than the LPA provision in making the assignment subject to the equities. Since s. 136 of the LPA 1925 is stated not to affect the provisions of the Policies of Assurance Act 1867, however, it is better for the insurer to obtain a discharge from the assignor as well as the assignee, to be on the safe side. For discussion of this confusing statutory situation, see MacGillivray, *op. cit.*, 24–76.

[65] Policies of Assurance Act 1867, s. 5.

[66] Policies of Assurance Act 1867, s. 3.

[67] Where a written receipt is required, a small fee is payable, the Policies of Assurance Act 1867, ss. 4 and 6—maximum 25p. A convenient practice is for the bank to give duplicate notices to the insurer, which returns one copy as a receipt.

[68] Possibly the time of giving notice to the insurer.

[69] *Newman v. Newman* (1885) 28 Ch. D. 674; *Re Weniger's Policy* [1910] 2 Ch. 291.

[70] *Spencer v. Clarke* (1878) 9 Ch. D. 137.

[71] Either from the insurer or the customer.

[72] *e.g.* that it has been destroyed by fire and it is proved that a fire has occurred.

[73] Because of the requirements of the Policies of Assurance Act 1867 noted above.

[74] Though an assignment of an equitable interest must be in writing (LPA 1925, s. 53(1)(c)), so an assignee under a previous equitable assignment or a beneficiary for whom a policy is held on trust must assign it in writing, see Colinvaux, *op. cit.*, para. 16.39.

written memorandum,[75] or by deposit of the policy with intent that it be security.[76] The last of these is the safest, though there is still a risk that the assured may declare that the policy has been lost and obtain a replacement from the insurer. A Memorandum of Deposit could be (but rarely is, it seems) taken in the usual way to explain the purpose of deposit. If so, it should be by deed and contain a promise by the assured to make a legal assignment if called on to do so. This may give the bank a power of sale on default.[77] In addition, the bank may take an irrevocable power of attorney entitling it to sell in the name of the assignor. If no Memorandum is taken, the document is not by deed, and there is no separate power of attorney, realisation could be effected only by application to the court.

22–022 Earlier legal assignments have priority over equitable assignments. As with legal assignments, the priority between competing equitable assignees is determined by actual or constructive notice of prior assignments, or, where there is no notice, by order of notice to the insurer.[78] The bank will have priority over the assignor's liquidator or trustee.[79]

---

[75] *Myers v. United Guarantee and Life Ass. Co.* (1855) 7 De G. M. & G. 122.

[76] See *Spencer v. Clarke* (1878) 9 Ch. D. 137. Banks may hold life policies simply for safe-keeping; this does not operate as security, even if the owner subsequently borrows money from the bank, see Colinvaux, *op. cit.*, para. 16.40.

[77] Under the LPA 1925, s. 101.

[78] Although the insurer has no obligation to note formally on its records any equitable interest, it may do so, but notice should be given in any case, even if it is disregarded.

[79] *Re Wallis, ex p. Jenks* [1902] 1 K.B. 719.

Section V

INSOLVENCY

Chapter 23

Set-off in Bankruptcy and Company Liquidation

Set-off[1] allows a debtor to reduce the debt by an amount owed to him or her by the creditor—to "set off" one debt against the other. There are different types of set-off, most of which affect banks[2]; set-off on insolvency is regulated by section 323 of the IA 1986 (for individual bankruptcy) and rule 4.90 of the Insolvency Rules 1986 (IR 1986) (for winding-up of companies), which operate in a similar way. These provisions apply to English bankruptcies or liquidations, whatever the nationality of the individual or company, and displace other forms of set-off which have not been executed before the insolvency.[3] **23–001**

An explanation of how set-off on insolvency works is: **23–002**

> "Bankruptcy set-off . . . affects the substantive rights of the parties by enabling the bankrupt's creditor to use his indebtedness to the bankrupt as a form of security. Instead of having to prove with other creditors for the whole of his debt in the bankruptcy, he can set off pound for pound what he owes the bankrupt and prove for or pay only the balance."[4]

When the conditions of set-off are satisfied, it is treated as *self-executing*—that is, having taken place automatically on the bankruptcy date or the date of winding up. The original claims are extinguished and only the net balance remains owing one way or the other.[5]

Nature of Statutory Set-off

Section 323 of the IA 1986 provides that an account between the parties is to be taken **23–003**

> "where before the commencement of the bankruptcy there have been mutual credits, mutual debts or other mutual dealings between the

---

[1] See Goode, *Principles of Corporate Insolvency Law* (2nd ed.) particularly Chap. 8 and *Legal Principles of Credit and Security* (2nd ed.) Pennington *Corporate Insolvency* and Derham, *Set-Off*.

[2] See above, Chap. 11.

[3] Goode, *Principles of Corporate Insolvency Law*, p. 177.

[4] *Stein v. Blake* [1995] 2 All E.R. 961 at 964; [1996] A.C. 243 at 246, *per* Lord Hoffmann.

[5] *Stein v. Blake* [1995] 2 All E.R. 961. See also *Re BCCI SA (No. 8) (Morris v. Agrichemicals)* [1997] 4 All E.R. 568 at 573, *per* Lord Hoffmann.

bankrupt and any creditor of the bankrupt proving or claiming to prove for a bankruptcy debt".

Mandatory

23–004 Insolvency set-off is mandatory, and cannot be excluded by contrary agreement. Thus, in *National Westminster Bank Ltd v. Halesowen Presswork and Assemblies Ltd*,[6] the bank had agreed with its customer to freeze an overdrawn account and not to reduce the debit balance in the absence of "materially changed circumstances". On the customer's winding-up, the bank wished to combine accounts despite the agreement. The House of Lords decided that the agreement did not apply once the customer had gone into liquidation. However, a majority of judges expressed the view, albeit *obiter*, that such an agreement could not apply in any case where the customer was bankrupt or in liquidation, because insolvency set-off[7] was mandatory, and could not be excluded by prior agreement. This rule may cause problems for rescuing companies in difficulty[8]—it was thought that it would prevent contractual subordination agreements, for example, though it now appears that this is not the case.[9]

Mutual Dealings

23–005 The claims must arise between the same parties and in the same right. The statute expresses this by saying that the debts or claims must be *mutual*. To allow set-off where there is no mutuality would be to allow the parties to subvert the fundamental principle of *pari passu* distribution among creditors on insolvency[10] by agreement among themselves.

23–006 **Claims must be between the same parties.** In *Re BCCI SA (No. 8)*,[11] the shareholders of a company secured a loan made to the company by BCCI by making deposits with the bank equal to the amount of the loan and charging them to the bank (by a *charge back* arrangement[12]). On BCCI's liquidation, it was held that the company's debt could not be set off against the deposits[13] because the shareholders were separate persons from the *company*, the principal debtor. The shareholders did not owe money to

---

[6] [1972] A.C. 785. See also *Coca Cola Financial Corp v. Finsat Int. Ltd* [1996] 2 B.C.L.C. 626.
[7] At that time under the Bankruptcy Act 1914, s. 31.
[8] See *National Westminster Bank Ltd v. Halesowen Presswork and Assemblies Ltd* [1972] A.C. 785 at 824, *per* Lord Kilbrandon, cited by Vinelott J., *In re Maxwell Communications Corpn. Plc* [1993] 1 W.L.R. 1403 at 1410. See also Goode, *Principles of Corporate Insolvency Law*, p. 178.
[9] *Re Maxwell Communications Corpn. plc*. [1993] 1 W.L.R. 1403 see Chap. 16.
[10] See below, Chap. 24.
[11] [1997] 4 All E.R. 568, HL.
[12] See above, Chap. 19.
[13] *Morris v. Agrichemicals Ltd* [1997] 3 W.L.R. 909, affirming in this respect the CA decision reported as *Re BCCI International SA (No 8)* [1996] 2 B.C.L.C. 254.

BCCI themselves; they had merely secured the company's debt. It would have been different if the security document had created a personal liability on the shareholders which included a principal debtor liability. In that case, they themselves would have owed the debt to the bank as principal debtors, and then they could have set off their claim against the claims made by the bank.[14] As it was, BCCI could recover its loan in full from the company, leaving the shareholders to prove in the insolvency. The shareholders were in fact the beneficial owners of the company, and felt the result to be unjust; they seemed (to themselves) to be economically the same as the company. The distinction may indeed seem artificial, particularly because it is normally an incidental matter whether a personal liability and a principal liability is created by the documentation. The important thing from the bank's point of view is normally the *real* security, and the personal liability is merely additional. It is difficult to avoid the distinction, however, in view of the separate legal personality of the company from its shareholders and the requirements of set-off.[15]

Claims must be of similar types. The two claims to be set off should be, broadly speaking, of the same type: a simple debt cannot be set off against a proprietary claim, for example. As with combination, no set off is available between a personal debt on the one hand and a joint account or a trust account, on the other.[16] Further, it must be possible for the two claims to resolve themselves into money payments, so that a claim for the return of goods could not rank as a set-off,[17] (though damages might be claimed instead, which could be set off). Only debts which are provable on insolvency can be set off[18]; secured debts cannot be included in the calculation, unless the creditor chooses to prove the debt in the liquidation.[19] **23–007**

However, the two claims need not be of exactly the same type. The section refers not merely to mutual debts but to *mutual dealings*—a wider term. The purpose of insolvency set-off is to enable justice to be done **23–008**

[14] As was the case in *MS Fashions Ltd v. BCCI International SA* [1993] B.C.L.C. 280; [1992] B.C.C. 571, where a reference to the liability of the depositor being that of principal debtor was construed as creating a personal liability.

[15] *Morris* [1997] 3 W.L.R. 909, *per* Lord Hoffmann.

[16] See above, Chap. 11. On joint debts see *Watts v. Christie* (1849) 11 Beav. 546; *Re Willis, Percival & Co., ex p. Morier* (1879) 12 Ch. D. 491, and *BCCI v. Prince Fahd Bin Salman Abdul Aziz Al-Saud* [1997] B.C.C. 63. See also the *Halesowen* case [1972] A.C. 785 at 808–9, *per* Lord Simon: "I prefer to say that money is paid for a special (or specific) purpose so as to exclude mutuality of dealing within section 31 [of the Bankruptcy Act 1914] if the money is paid in such circumstances that it would be a misappropriation to use it for any other purpose than that for which it is paid". A problem with claims in different rights may sometimes arise from the rules relating to constructive trusts, see above, Chap. 9.

[17] *Rolls Razor Ltd v. Cox* [1967] 1 Q.B. 552.

[18] At least as far as a claim by a creditor against an insolvent company or person is concerned (the position is not so clear if it is the claim by the insolvent which is in issue): Lord Hoffmann, *Morris* [1997] 3 W.L.R. 909 at 929.

[19] *Re Norman Holdings Co. Ltd* [1990] 3 All E.R. 757. See below, Chap. 24.

between the parties,[20] and the right is therefore wider than the common-law right of combination. Statutory set-off allows an unliquidated claim to be set off against a liquidated debt. Similarly, a future debt, or even, often, a contingent liability, may be set off against a present debt, and a contractual claim may be set off against a claim under a different contract or a non-contractual claim.[21] The important thing is that there is a sufficiently close link.[22]

23–009 An example of a *future* liability is the case where a customer with an outstanding loan payable at sometime in the future becomes bankrupt.[23] An immediate proof may be made for the debt, or if the bank has some credit balance on another account, this may be set off. The debt is owing at present, though only repayable in the future.

23–010 A *contingent* liability is one which arises out of an existing legal commitment or state of affairs, but which is dependent on the happening of an event which may or may not occur.[24] An example of a contingent liability is that of a customer who indorses and discounts a bill to the bank and who then becomes bankrupt. The bank may at some future date have to proceed against the customer, but until maturity the customer's liability is merely contingent: there is no present debt. Similarly, the obligation of a guarantor is contingent unless the principal debtor has defaulted.

23–011 As far as contingent debts are concerned, it might be difficult to ascertain the amount owed, but the legislation deals with this problem by providing that if a contingent debt does not bear a value which is certain, the trustee must *estimate the amount*, and this is the amount provable[25] unless the creditor appeals.[26] Where it is the *solvent* party (the creditor) who owes the contingent debt, therefore, the claim may be taken into account as if it were certain, and be set off automatically. Where it is the *insolvent* party whose debt is contingent, however, it is not possible to apply the rules in this way, because it would be unfair to have the bankrupt's liability to pay advanced merely because the trustee wants to wind up the estate.[27] The solvent party

[20] "It arose to prevent the injustice of such a man having to pay in full what he owed in respect of such dealings while only receiving a dividend on what the bankrupt owed him in respect of them." *per* Lord Cross in the *Halesowen* case [1972] A.C. 785 at 813.

[21] See *Hichens, Harrison, Woolston & Co v. Jackson & Sons* [1943] A.C. 266.

[22] *British Anzani (Felixstowe) Ltd. v. International Marine Management (UK) Ltd.* [1980] Q.B. 137. The Crown can set off against a claim from a government department a claim due to a different department, and a person owing money to a government department can set off money owing to him or her by a different department, but set-off cannot be claimed against debts for taxes, duties or penalties: *Re D.H. Curtis (Builders) Ltd* [1978] 2 All E.R. 183. Nor can a "misappropriation of assets" by a director be set off against a debt due to him: misappropriation is not a dealing, see *Manson v. Smith* [1997] 2 B.C.L.C. 161.

[23] s. 382(3) of the IA 1986 expressly provides that it is immaterial whether a debt is "present or future" and such a debt is a "bankruptcy debt", which can be set off. For an example of a "future" debt see *Rolls Razor Ltd v. Cox* [1967] 1 Q.B. 552 (debt repayable in instalments).

[24] Goode, *Principles of Corporate Insolvency Law*, p. 87.

[25] IA 1986, s. 322(3).

[26] *e.g.* under IA 1986, s. 303.

[27] *Stein v. Blake* [1995] 2 All E.R. 961 at 965, *per* Lord Hoffmann.

is entitled to prove for his or her claim in full without the debtor's contingent claim being set off against the claim.

If loans are supported by guarantees from third parties which do not make them liable as principals, and the bank becomes insolvent,[28] the guarantors' liability is contingent unless the bank has already demanded payment. If their claims are contingent, they cannot be set off against those of the creditor, the bank, and on the bank's insolvency the guarantors will have to prove for their claims against the bank. If the security agreement includes a principal debtor clause, on the other hand, the guarantors will be jointly and severally liable with the principal debtors, so that their liability will be certain, not contingent, and can be set off against the amount owed to the bank.

Preferential Debts

Banks may be preferential creditors in some insolvencies—for example, if an insolvent company's wages account is overdrawn.[29] Preferential debtors are in a privileged position on bankruptcy or winding up, because they are paid before unsecured creditors. For preferential debts, the position as regards set off is the same as for other debts and they must also be set-off against credit balances held by the bank. It may well be that the bank is owed both preferential and non-preferential debts. In such a case, where the bank would like to be able to pick and choose how to set off the claims, it would gain the greatest advantage from setting its claim off against the non-preferential debt first, leaving the largest possible preferential debt for proof in bankruptcy. In *Re Unit 2 Windows Ltd*,[30] however, Walton J. held that the correct solution was to apply the credit balance rateably between the preferential and a non-preferential debts; if, for example, the preferential debt is twice the size of the non-preferential debt, then two-thirds of the credit balance will be allocated to the former. It is submitted that this is, as the learned judge said, the "only logical and sensible solution".[31] **23–012**

It is submitted that this situation is different from that in *Re William Hall (Contractors) Ltd*,[32] and should be distinguished from it. In that case, a secured creditor realised its security and then *appropriated* the money to a non-preferential debt in an account containing both a preferential and a **23–013**

[28] As with the BCCI litigation mentioned above para. 23–004. In *MS Fashions Ltd v. BCCI International S.A. (No. 2)* [1993] Ch. 425, the third parties had agreed to be principal debtors (though the documentation was not a normal guarantee). See also *Re BCCI International S.A. (No. 8)* [1996] B.C.L.C. 20, *sub. nom. Morris v. Agrichemicals Ltd* [1997] 3 W.L.R. 909.

[29] See below, Chap. 24.

[30] [1985] 3 All E.R. 647. It was, he said, "an austere point of law" (at 648).

[31] In *Re E. J. Morel (1934) Ltd* [1962] Ch. 21, however, Buckley J. suggested *obiter* that the credit balance must first be set-off against the preferential debt. This dictum was disapproved in *Re Unit 2 Windows Ltd* [1985] 3 All E.R. 647.

[32] [1967] 2 All E.R. 1150.

non-preferential debt.[33] The bank has a right of appropriation of moneys received to any debt it chooses,[34] unless it has agreed otherwise with its customer.[35] Further, it is established that a debt remains preferential even though it is not kept in a separate segregated account,[36] and thus has to be regarded as a separate debt, subject to different rules. Both these rules imply that individual debit items in a single account are separate debts. *Re William Hall (Contractors) Ltd* follows these rules. It shows that where the bank relies properly on the right of appropriation to an account rather than on the right of combination or the right of statutory set off, it can simply act in accordance with that right without being constrained by considerations relevant to other rights. It seems, therefore, that *Re William Hall (Contractors) Ltd* is unaffected by the decision in *Re Unit 2 Windows Ltd.* However, the *Hall* decision does not mean that the bank, once it has appropriated money to any account, may subsequently combine accounts so that it pays off a non-preferential debt. The appropriation must be made when the money is received, because, according to the principle, debts are discharged at the moment of appropriation. It is further submitted that the appropriation principle has nothing to do with the question whether the bank is secured, or not.[37] Unless otherwise agreed expressly, or by implication, the right of appropriation is a general right, not confined to cases of realisation of securities. It may be added that the bank, as usual, is well placed to take advantage of the way these technical rules operate.

[33] So far as appears, it seems to have been a single account.
[34] *Devaynes v. Noble, Clayton's Case* (1816) 1 Mer. 572.
[35] *Westminster Bank Ltd v. Cond* (1940) 46 Com. Cas. 60.
[36] See, *e.g. Re Primrose Builders Ltd* [1950] Ch. 561.
[37] Though *Re William Hall (Contractors) Ltd* [1967] 2 All E.R. 1150 relied on older cases concerning the rights of secured creditors.

Chapter 24

Insolvency and Banks

In this Chapter, the processes of corporate and individual insolvency are considered, with comments on their effect on banks. 24–001

Insolvency means inability to pay debts. It often results in the *liquidation* or *winding-up* of a company, which means the end of the company's existence and the disposal of all its assets; or in the *bankruptcy* of an individual, which involves the disposal of some of the assets of the individual, but leads to his or her eventual rehabilitation. The main provisions affecting both types of insolvency[1] are to be found in the IA 1986 and the IR 1986.

One of the innovative aspects of the IA 1986 was its requirement that insolvency practitioners—that is, liquidators, administrators, administrative receivers, supervisors of voluntary schemes, and trustees of individual bankrupts ("office holders") other than the official receiver—must be professionally qualified.[2] The provisions of the Act[3] are designed to ensure that insolvency practitioners are not only competent, but also independent. They are now required to be qualified, licensed[4] and "bonded"—that is, they must provide sufficient security.[5]

Banks are normally *secured creditors* and can therefore realise their security outside the insolvency. Nevertheless, they may be concerned with an insolvency in a number of ways—and of course, they may themselves sometimes be insolvent.[6] Among the most important concerns for banks on an insolvency of a customer are their possible liability as shadow directors, particularly for wrongful trading; the effect of vulnerable transactions like preferences on charges and guarantees; the effect of the rule against double proof on guarantees; and the effect of operating a bank account where 24–002

---

[1] Introduced following the Report of the Cork Committee in 1982 (Insolvency Law and Practice, Cmnd 8558). The precursor of the IA 1986, the Insolvency Act 1985, introduced some of the concepts, For detailed reference, see Pennington, *Corporate Insolvency* (2nd ed., 1997), Muir Hunter, *Personal Insolvency*, Grier and Floyd, *Personal Insolvency*, and, for insolvency generally, Totty and Moss, *Insolvency*.

[2] See Finch [1998] JBL 334.

[3] IA 1986, ss. 388–398.

[4] By a recognised professional body, IA 1986, s. 390(2).

[5] In practice, insolvency practitioners are accountants, and are members of firms authorised to conduct investment business under the FSA 1986: Grier and Floyd, *Personal Insolvency*, p. 60. There has been considerable public concern about the level of remuneration received by insolvency practitioners. Guidance on remuneration has been given by the court: *Mirror Group Newspapers v. Maxwell* [1998] 1 B.C.L.C. 638 at 647, *per* Ferris J.

[6] As in the notorious case of BCCI, see above, Chap. 1.

dispositions by the customer are void. These, as they concern both company and individual customers, are discussed below, in the context of both winding up and bankruptcy.

24–003 Banks are also concerned, of course, with the *realisation of their securities*,[7] which may be carried out in different contexts and by different officers. The remedies of the bank become *exercisable* not only on breach by the customer of its obligations, but also whenever the bank's charge or debenture permits, which is normally for non-repayment on demand, whether or not there is a breach. The remedies are:

(i) to sue for debt, or for damages if there is a breach of contract;

(ii) to apply to the court for an order for foreclosure, or for sale of the asset; the court will normally prefer sale, in order to prevent the mortgagee getting a windfall from foreclosure (which makes the mortgagee the owner of the asset);

(iii) to sell without reference to the court under an express or implied power: powers of sale are implied for mortgages[8] but must be given expressly for other forms of security, such as floating charges;

(iv) to present a winding-up petition;

(v) above all, as far as companies are concerned,[9] there is the remedy of receivership.

24–004 Banks are also often involved in *rescues* of companies—for example, where a company has had cash flow problems, but, in the bank's opinion, its assets exceed its liabilities and its position is not hopeless. If a rescue succeeds, it is for everybody's benefit, including the bank's.[10] This philosophy of rescuing companies is of recent origin: it developed, ironically enough, from the rescue by the Bank of England of failing banks in the early 1970s (the "lifeboat" operation).[11]

Some of the four "régimes", or courses of action available on company insolvency give effect to the policy of the IA 1986 in encouraging this rescue culture. These régimes are: winding up; receivership; administration, and voluntary arrangements. The insolvency régimes available for individuals are voluntary arrangements and bankruptcy.[12] Much of this Chapter is

---

[7] Aspects of realisation are also discussed in other relevant Chapters—*e..g.* Chap. 21, dealing with land.

[8] LPA 1925, s. 103.

[9] Receivers are not usually appointed for individuals, except to realise land.

[10] See Lingard, *Corporate Rescues and Insolvencies* (1989). The Government has initiated a Review of Company rescue and Business Reconstruction Mechanisms (September 1999).

[11] Lingard, *Corporate Rescues and Insolvencies* (1989) p. 35.

[12] Banks may appoint receivers for mortgaged property, but receivership is not considered an insolvency régime. Administrators are not appointed for individuals.

concerned with the winding up of companies and the bankruptcy of individuals, but first other régimes, receivership, administration and voluntary arrangements, are considered.

Insolvency Régimes Other than Liquidation or Bankruptcy

Receivership

Receivers manage the business, realise the assets and distribute the proceeds to pay off the debenture holders, returning any unrealised assets to the company. Bank debenture forms will always expressly allow the bank to appoint a receiver on default or in other stated circumstances, and will give receivers wide powers so that they can manage the business of the company effectively. The receiver appointed under a fixed charge or a partial floating charge is called simply a "receiver".[13] An "*administrative receiver*"[14] is a particular type of receiver, whose function is governed by special and distinctive rules,[15] and who can be appointed by a secured creditor who has a floating charge which, together with any other charges, covers substantially the whole of the company's property.[16] An administrative receiver has wider powers of management than other receivers, and also has the power to veto the making of an administration order, which, as we shall see, is important from the point of view of a secured creditor like a bank. **24–005**

Because it may be advantageous to be able to sell the company (or parts of it) as a going concern, the security generally covers the company's whole undertaking. Under the debenture or the general law, the receiver will have the right to manage the company's business and to dispose of all the assets, and often will "hive off" part of the company—that is, form a new subsidiary company, transfer such parts of the company's assets and business as will form a viable new undertaking to the subsidiary, and sell the shares in the subsidiary to the highest bidder, who will thus obtain a debt-free business. **24–006**

A receiver cannot be a body corporate, nor an undischarged bankrupt.[17] Only an insolvency practitioner can be an administrative receiver.[18]

---

13 See IA 1986, s. 29.

14 A receiver used normally to be a receiver (to collect the rents and profits of the property) and manager (to manage the property). The administrative receiver is the statutory name for this individual: Goode, *op. cit.* p. 205.

15 Pennington, *op. cit.* p. 495.

16 See IA 1986, s. 29(2)(b), and *Re Croftbell* [1990] B.C.L.C. 844.

17 IA 1986, ss. 30 and 31.

18 IA 1986, s. 230(2) and Part XIII. Section 393 of the IA 1986 sets out the criteria for appointment as insolvency practitioners—in practice accountants authorised as fit and proper persons, with the required education, training and experience.

Appointment[19]

24–007 The court has an inherent power to appoint a receiver.[20] Appointment by this method is slow and expensive, particularly because frequent applications to the court for directions have to be made. It does not apply to administrative receivers.

Alternatively, and usually, it is the debenture holder who makes the appointment, when it is entitled to do so by the terms of the debenture and in the manner authorised by it.[21] Before the appointment is made, the bank should check (a) that the charge is valid; (b) that the appointment is valid in other respects (for example, that the demand specifies the correct amount, if this is required by the debenture[22]); and (c) that there are sufficient assets to cover the receiver's fees and expenses. An administrative receiver cannot be appointed while an administration order is in force.[23]

24–008 The appointment of a receiver must be in writing[24] although it need not necessarily be made by deed, even if the receiver is to transfer a legal estate in company land.[25] It takes effect when it is received and accepted (even tacitly) by the receiver within the permitted time.[26] Acceptance of an appointment must be made by the receiver or his or her agent by the end of the business day next following the receipt of the letter[27] and must be confirmed in seven days.[28] Joint receivers may be appointed, and are subject to similar rules[29]; the appointment must declare whether they must act together or may act separately.[30] Concurrent appointments under different debentures are probably possible: in this case, the second administrative receiver waits on the sidelines until the prior administrative receivership has been completed. This allows for a smooth continuation of the process if necessary.[31]

---

19 See IR 1986, Part 3.

20 Supreme Court Act 1981, s. 37(1). On a winding up it can appoint the official receiver, IA 1986, s. 32.

21 Lightman and Moss, *op. cit.*, at 8, suggest that consideration should be given as to whether the terms of the debenture are wide enough to cover modern forms of communication, *e.g.* fax, telex etc.

22 The precise sum may not be specified, because it may be impracticable to do so; in *Bank of Baroda v. Panessar* [1987] Ch. 335, "all moneys due" was acceptable. See also *NRG Vision Ltd v. Churchfield Leasing* [1988] B.C.L.C. 624.

23 IA 1986, s. 11(3)(b).

24 LPA 1925, s. 109(1).

25 *Windsor Refrigerator Co Ltd v. Branch Nominees Ltd* [1961] Ch. 375.

26 IA 1986, s. 33(1). Handing an appointment letter by a bank's head office to a receiver's assistant who is to take it to a branch office of the bank is not sufficient; appointment would take place when the branch manager handed the letter to the receiver: *R.A. Cripps & Sons Ltd v. Wickenden* [1973] 2 All E.R. 606, though it may be otherwise if the receiver expressly appoints an agent to receive and accept.

27 IA 1986, s. 33(1).

28 IR 1986 3.1(1).

29 IA 1986, s. 33(2) and IR 1986, r. 3.1(2).

30 IA 1986, s. 231.

31 See Goode, *op. cit.*, p. 208.

The debenture holder is normally entitled to make the appointment once the payment has been *demanded* from the borrower. Bank overdrafts or ordinary advances are normally repayable on demand, and even term loans may contain a term entitling the bank to demand repayment if in its opinion a "materially adverse" change in the position of the borrower has occurred.[32] Where the debtor is required to pay on demand, a default[33] is easily engineered by the bank making a demand and then giving the debtor a very short time to get the money. It is established[34] that the debtor need not be given time to negotiate a deal which might produce the money, but only be allowed time to implement whatever reasonable mechanics of payment are needed, assuming funds are available. Thus, in *R.A. Cripps & Son Ltd v. Wickenden*,[35] the demand was made at 10.45 a.m. and the default was held to have occurred by 12.30 a.m. One reason that banks require overdrafts and advances to be repayable "on demand" is to allow them to appoint a receiver very swiftly. **24–009**

To reduce the risk of challenge by the company or its liquidator on the ground that the appointment is invalid[36] (in which case the receiver would have to be withdrawn and then reappointed[37]) the directors may be formally asked by the bank to request it to appoint a receiver. If the appointment proves invalid, perhaps because the debenture itself is invalid or because of a faulty method of appointment, the person "by whom or on whose behalf the appointment was made" may be required to compensate the receiver against any liability,[38] although the receiver will usually take an indemnity anyway in case the appointment is invalid. **24–010**

After appointment, an administrative receiver must give notice to the company and publish the fact of his or her appointment, and within 28 days send a notice to all the creditors of the company of whose addresses he or **24–011**

32 Even in the domestic mortgage market, where a "term" (of say, 25 years) is used (it may be merely to calculate the repayment schedule).

33 The debenture need not provide that the default is a breach of contract, but only that it is an event entitling the appointment of a receiver.

34 *R.A. Cripps & Son Ltd. v. Wickenden* [1973] 2 All E.R. 606. See also *Brighty v. Norton* (1862) 3 B & S 305 at 312; *Toms v. Wilson* (1863) 4 B & S 442 at 453; *Moore v. Shelley* (1883) 8 App. Cas. 285 at 293; *Massey v. Sladen* (1868) L.R. Ex. 13; *Windsor Refrigerator Co Ltd v. Branch Nominees Ltd* [1961] Ch. 374; *Bank of Baroda v. Panessar* [1987] 2 W.L.R. 208. No time at all may be necessary, if it is clear that the funds are not available: *Sheppard & Cooper Ltd v. TSB Bank plc* [1996] 2 All E.R. 654. In *Lloyds Bank plc v. Jeffrey Lampert* [1999] Lloyds Rep. Bank. 138, the argument that the "more liberal approach" taken in Canada and Australia should be considered by the appellate court was rejected as academic on the facts of the case.

35 [1973] 3 All E.R. 606.

36 The receiver would be liable to repay money received, and may be a trespasser (though, if invited by the company, not until the invitation is withdrawn, or the liquidator challenges him or her): *Ford and Carter Ltd v. Midland Bank Ltd* (1979) 129 New L.J. 543. The appointor might be a joint tortfeasor. Both might even be held liable as constructive trustees, see Lightman and Moss, *op. cit.* p. 94.

37 *Cripps v. Wickenden* [1973] 2 All E.R. 606.

38 IA 1986, s. 34.

she is aware.[39] Notice of the appointment of a receiver or manager must appear on every invoice, order for goods or business letter on which the company's name appears, issued by or for the company or the receiver or manager.[40] On appointing a receiver or manager, or obtaining an order for appointment, the debenture holder must notify the registrar of companies within seven days, and the appointment will be registered in the register of charges[41] in order to warn others who may deal with the company.

The bank must not act in bad faith when it appoints a receiver—it must not act solely to prevent the enforcement of an existing receivership, for example,[42] or appoint a receiver who it has reasonable grounds to believe is incompetent[43]—but it has no duty to consider such matters as whether a company might be able to finance itself in the near future.

Removal

24–012 An administrative receiver may resign or be removed by the court, and must vacate office if he or she ceases to be a qualified insolvency practitioner[44] or when an administration order is made.[45] Although it used to be common for debentures to provide for the removal of a receiver by the debenture holder, the independence of the insolvency practitioner is now confirmed to the extent that an administrative receiver may only be removed by order of the court, not by the debenture holder or by the appointment of a liquidator.[46] When a receiver or manager ceases to act, he or she must inform the registrar[47]—in the case of an administrative receiver, 14 days is allowed for notification.[48]

Once a receiver has enough funds to pay off the debt and his or her own expenses, he or she should cease managing the company's assets, and any remaining assets should be handed back to the company.[49] Documents should also be returned as appropriate: those brought into existence in the discharge of the receiver's duty to the company; those brought into existence in the discharge of the duty to the debenture holder; and those brought into existence for the carrying out of the receiver's own duties retained by him or her.[50]

[39] IA 1986, s. 26 and IR 1986, r. 3.2.
[40] IA 1986, s. 39.
[41] CA 1985, s. 405.
[42] *Downsview Nominees v. First City Corp.* [1993] A.C. 295.
[43] *Shamji v. Johnson Matthey Bankers Ltd* (1994) L.D.A.B. 396.
[44] IA 1986, s. 45.
[45] IA 1986, s. 11(1)(b).
[46] IA 1986, s. 45(1). But liquidation may affect the receiver's powers: see s. 44.
[47] IA 1986, s. 45(1)(b). No time is specified.
[48] IA 1986, s. 45.
[49] *Rottenberg v. Monjack* [1993] B.C.C. 371.
[50] *Gomba Holdings U.K. Ltd. v. Minories Finance* [1988] 1 W.L.R. 1231.

Powers and duties

The powers of the administrative receiver derive from the debenture under which he or she is appointed, which include the very extensive statutory powers,[51] unless these are varied or excluded by the debenture. A variety of duties are imposed on an administrative receiver, including managing the business, realising the assets and distributing the proceeds,[52] and also concerning notification of his or her appointment, the taking of statements about the affairs of the company, the making of a report on the receivership, and the calling of a creditor's meeting.[53] 24–013

The statutory powers cover most of the eventualities which might occur in management of the business or realisation of the assets covered by the security, but can be extended or restricted by the debenture.[54] The powers of an administrative receiver are wider than those of other receivers: an administrative receiver may carry on the company's business generally, not just for the purposes of winding-up, and has power to transfer the whole or part of the company's business or property to a subsidiary.[55]

Debentures normally provide that receivers act as the agents of the company. The fact that a receiver is regarded as the company's agent reduces the possibility of claims in negligence against the debenture holder for any wrongdoing by the receiver.[56] The effect is, however, that administrative receivers have two sets of powers: first, the powers to manage and realise the security, which are exercised on behalf of the *debenture holder* and unaffected by the company's liquidation; and, secondly, powers to conclude contracts on behalf, to engage staff and run the business, which are exercised on behalf of the *company*. The powers exercised on behalf of the company are subordinated to those exercised on behalf of the debenture holder. In acting on behalf of the company, the receiver can act only within the powers given by the memorandum of association to the company, but a third party dealing with a receiver in good faith and for value is not concerned to inquire whether the receiver is acting within his or her powers.[57] 24–014

Administrative receivers can, as agents, bind the company,[58] though that does not mean that they owe all the duties of agents to principals, such as the duty to take instructions.[59] Although an administrative receiver's powers 24–015

[51] Listed in IA 1986, Sched. 1.

[52] Like a liquidator, the receiver must distribute the proceeds according to the order laid down by law. See further below, para. 24–155.

[53] See the IA 1986, Part III, and IR 1986, r. 3.3.

[54] IA 1986, s. 42(1).

[55] Pennington, *Corporate Insolvency Law*, p. 495.

[56] The company has (by contract) to pay the receiver's fees and cannot dismiss him or her. Making the receiver the company's agent is "primarily a device to protect the . . . debenture holder", *Gomba Holdings (U.K. Ltd v. Minories Finance)* [1989] 1 All E.R. 261 at 263, *per* Fox L.J.

[57] IA 1986, s. 42.

[58] IA 1986, s. 42(3).

[59] *Re B. Johnson & Co (Builders) Ltd* [1955] 2 All E.R. 775; [1955] Ch. 634.

do not necessarily supersede the powers of the directors legally, they probably do supersede them in practice, because he or she is acting as agent of the debenture holder. Usually, in any case, the administrative receiver is also made manager of the company by the debenture, in which case the appointment does suspend the powers of the directors.[60] Although directors do retain powers which are not inconsistent with the powers of the receiver,[61] the powers of an administrative receiver under the IA 1986 are so extensive that it may be true to say that an administrative receiver with those powers will be a manager in any case, and that the powers of the directors are automatically suspended.

24–016 Unlike ordinary agents, receivers are personally liable on any contract entered into by them in carrying out their functions,[62] although (except in the case of employment contracts) the contract may provide otherwise. If the receiver is sued, he or she may have a right to an indemnity from the company under the contract or by statute.[63]

The appointment of an administrative receiver by the debenture holder does not automatically have the effect of dismissing the employees (although an appointment by the court will do so) and the appointment does not affect the company's liability for existing contracts. An administrative receiver is not personally liable on contracts entered into by the company before his or her appointment, nor if the realisation of assets prevents the company from carrying out its contracts (for example, if goods for sale cannot be made, or if vehicles are disposed of, so that contracts to carry cannot be performed), though the company itself may be liable for damages for breach of contract, or specific performance may be ordered.[64] However, while the receiver may freely realise assets subject to the charge, he or she must act within the scope of his or her authority and in good faith.[65] No contract should be broken in such a way as to damage the company's goodwill, for example, unless with leave of the court, for the receiver owes a duty to the company not to diminish its goodwill.[66] The court's leave will not be given merely because there is an advantage to the debenture holder.[67] Thus, the receiver might be liable to the company, though not to the third party involved.[68] Administrative receivers are also

[60] *Reid v. Explosives Co Ltd* (1887) 19 Q.B.D. 264; *Re Foster Clark Ltd's Indenture Trusts* [1966] 1 All E.R. 43.

[61] *e.g.* they continue to be responsible for keeping accounts under the CA 1985. The law as to the extent to which the directors have the right to bring proceedings in the name of the company is unsettled, Lightman and Moss, *op. cit.*, pp. 14 *et seq.*

[62] IA 1986, s. 44(a) and (b). Contracts already in existence are not terminated unless the receiver does something inconsistent with the contract, *e.g.* selling the property concerned, see *Edwin Hill v. First Federal Finance Corpn. plc* [1989] 1 W.L.R. 225.

[63] IA 1986, s. 44(1)(c).

[64] See *Airlines Airspares Ltd v. Handley Page Ltd* [1970] Ch. 193; *Freevale Ltd v. Metrostore (Holdings Ltd* [1984] Ch. 199.

[65] *Welsh Development Agency v. Export Finance Co. Ltd* [1992] B.C.L.C. 148.

[66] *Kernohan Estates Ltd v. Boyd* [1967] N.I. 27.

[67] See *Re Newdigate Colliery Co Ltd* [1912] 1 Ch. 468.

[68] *Airlines Airspace Ltd v. Handley Page Ltd* [1970] Ch. 193.

personally liable on contracts of employment "adopted" by them in carrying out their functions[69] but in this case, they cannot contract out of liability on the adopted contracts. The contract is adopted by the receiver unless he or she terminates or repudiates it within fourteen days of his or her appointment.[70]

A receiver's power as agent to bind the company to new contracts (and, in that sense, his or her right to manage) ceases on liquidation.[71] However, the receiver's powers to manage the company's assets for the purpose of realisation and to deal with the secured assets are unaffected.[72] **24–017**

Dealings with third parties. Administrative receivers have powers to dispose of property[73]; they may borrow and create mortgages or charges to fulfil their functions properly. A person dealing with an administrative receiver in good faith and for value does not need to inquire if the receiver is acting within his or her powers.[74] **24–018**

If other creditors have securities with priority, an administrative receiver may ask the court to authorise a sale of the assets in question.[75] A sale may be ordered provided that other secured creditors receive at least the market price available in an unforced sale. An unauthorised disposal of secured assets would, it seems, give good unencumbered title to a bona fide purchaser for value,[76] but the administrative receiver would clearly be liable to the other secured creditors.

Liability for negligence

The actions of receivers may affect not only the debenture holder, but also the company and a number of others, including other creditors of the company, and officers and members of the company. The receiver's *primary* duty is to the debenture holder, but questions often arise as to whether and how far that duty should be balanced against liability to other parties. The courts have traditionally regarded the receiver's duties to the company whose agent they are as limited. If a receiver sells in circumstances where **24–019**

---

[69] IA 1986, s. 44 caused considerable difficulties—it would have burdened receivers with onerous liabilities—and the Insolvency Act 1994 (effectively a "statutory overruling of *Nichols v. Cutts*" [1985] B.C.L.C. 322, *per* Nicholls L.J., *Re Atlantic Computer Systems plc* [1992] Ch. 505) was passed to alter its effect. See also Lord Browne-Wilkinson, *Powdrill v. Watson* [1995] 2 A.C. 394 at 44.

[70] The view of Goode, *op. cit.*, p. 254, considering Lord Browne-Wilkinson's judgment in *Powdrill v. Watson* [1995] 2 A.C. 294.

[71] IA 1986, s. 44(1)(a) (administrative receivers); the same is true at common law of any receiver: see cases in the next note.

[72] *Gosling v. Gaskell* [1897] A.C. 575 (compulsory winding-up); *Thomas v. Todd* [1926] 2 K.B. 511 (voluntary winding-up); *Sowman v. David Samuel Trust Ltd* [1978] 1 All E.R. 616.

[73] IA 1986, s. 42(3).

[74] IA 1986, s. 42(3).

[75] IA 1986, s. 43.

[76] IA 1986, s. 42(3).

the sale may cause loss to the company without any advantage to the debenture holder, there is a strong argument that the receiver should delay the sale until a more favourable time for the company, but the law restricts the receiver's duties to the company to taking proper care to obtain the best price reasonably obtainable when actually selling the secured assets.[77] Otherwise, it is often said that the receiver must merely act in good faith with the purpose of obtaining repayment for the debenture holder.

24–020 Some cases have suggested—on the basis that the duties owed to the company, are tortious[78]—that receivers might owe a more general duty in tort to the company.[79] However, the advice of the Privy Council in *Downsview Nominees Ltd v. First City Corp. Ltd*,[80] expressed by Lord Templeman, was that receivers exercising the power of sale owe the same duties to the mortgagor as are owed by the mortgagee exercising the same power, and the receiver's duties to the company and others are not owed in tort but are equitable,[81] and are specific and limited. This view has been strongly criticised,[82] and other judges have expressed different views: in *Palk v. Mortgage Services Funding plc*, it was suggested that wider duties should be imposed on mortgagees (and, by implication, receivers).[83]

24–021 The Court of Appeal recently examined the issue of receivers' duties to the mortgagor in *Medforth v. Blake*.[84] The receivers of a pig farming business failed to obtain freely available discounts on pig food. In their defence to the pig farmer's complaint about their way of managing the business, they claimed that they owed him as mortgagor merely a duty to exercise their powers in good faith, which they had done, they said, since there had been no conscious or deliberate impropriety. This defence fell on stony ground as far as the Vice-Chancellor was concerned. Sir Richard Scott V.-C. said that to limit the receivers' duty to that extent offended commercial sense. Why should they not be liable for managerial incompe-

---

[77] *Cuckmere Brick Co. Ltd v. Mutual Finance Ltd* [1971] Ch. 949 (considering the duty owed to guarantors of the company's debts).

[78] *Cuckmere* [1971] Ch. 949.

[79] *Standard Chartered Bank Ltd. v. Walker* [1982] 3 All E.R. 938. See also *American Express International Banking Corpn v. Hurley* [1985] 3 All E.R. 564, *Tse Kwong Lam v. Wong Chit Sen* [1983] 3 All E.R. 54 and *Knight v. Lawrence* [1991] B.C.C. 411.

[80] [1993] A.C. 295. See also *China and South Sea Bank Ltd. v. Tan Soon Gin* [1990] 1 A.C. 536, again *per* Lord Templeman, and *Parker-Tweedale v. Dunbar Bank plc* [1991] Ch. 12.

[81] This seems to make little difference to the remedy, which is for the equitable duty of skill and care rather than for a fiduciary duty, and is assessed on a compensatory basis: *Bristol and West B.S. v. Mothew* [1996] 4 All E.R. 538.

[82] See *e.g.* Goode: ". . . in policy terms the result is profoundly unsatisfactory." (*Principles, op. cit.*, p. 242); Goode considers that the mortgagee would be adequately protected by a rule that it is entitled to put its own interests first (*Commercial Law*, p. 691). See also, for detailed analysis of Lord Templeman's reasoning, Lightman and Moss, *op. cit.*, pp. 120 *et seq.*

[83] [1993] Ch. 330 at 63, *per* Sir Donald Nicholls V.-C. (see also Chap. 21). And see *Standard Chartered Bank Ltd* [1982] 3 All E.R. 938: as Goode, *Commercial Law*, pp. 863–4, points out, it is this case (rather than *Downsview*) which is binding.

[84] [1999] 3 All E.R. 97.

tence? A unanimous Court of Appeal concluded that a receiver managing property[85] does owe duties to the mortgagor. These duties are equitable and not tortious—although the court's view was that it makes no difference in reality whether the duties are based in tort or in equity, because they are flexible and depend very much on the particular facts of the particular case. In principle though, the duties were described as follows:

> "(1) A receiver managing mortgaged property owes duties to the mortgagor and anyone else with an interest in the equity of redemption.
> (2) The duties include, but are not necessarily confined to, a duty of good faith.
> (3) The extent and scope of any duty additional to that of good faith will depend on the facts and circumstances of the particular case.
> (4) In exercising his powers of management the primary duty of the receiver is to try and bring about a situation in which interest on the secured debt can be paid and the debt itself repaid.
> (5) Subject to that primary duty, the receiver owes a duty to manage the property with due diligence.
> (6) Due diligence does not oblige the receiver to continue to carry on a business on the mortgaged premises previously carried on by the mortgagor.
> (7) If the receiver does carry on a business on the mortgaged premises, due diligence requires reasonable steps to be taken in order to try to do so profitably."[86]

The court added that the concept of good faith should not be diluted. Breach of a duty of good faith requires some dishonesty or improper motive, some element of bad faith.

With regard to other potential claimants, such as other creditors or officers of the company, there is only a duty (of good faith and on occasion a duty of care) owed by the receiver to persons with an interest in the equity of redemption.[87] **24–022**

In exceptional cases, if the debenture holder treats the receiver as its own agent—for example, by giving him or her instructions or by interfering in the process of realisation—the receiver may be regarded in law as its agent,

---

[85] The management of the property is independent of the power of sale, not merely ancillary to it ([1999] 3 All E.R. 97 at 112).

[86] [1997] 3 All E.R. 97 at 111.

[87] *Burgess v. Auger* [1998] 2 B.C.L.C. 478; *Lathia v. Dronsfield Bros.* [1978] B.C.L.C. 321. Persons with an interest in the equity of redemption are the mortgagor, a guarantor, or "the person entitled to the next ranking interest in the equity of redemption, who may be a subsequent mortgagee, a person subrogated to the right of a subsequent mortgagee or the mortgagor": *Burgess v. Auger* [1998] 2 B.C.L.C. 478 at 482, *per* Lightman J.

whatever the debenture says,[88] and the bank may be liable if the receiver is negligent. It is common for receivers to refer back to those who appointed them—indeed, unrealistic to expect them not to do so—and the implications of this are of some concern to banks, for it is difficult to say when exactly expressions of opinion, concern, advice, or desire become "interference".[89] The bank is entitled to an indemnity from the receiver for any liability so caused under an implied term in the contract, and bank debenture forms also provide for an express indemnity from the receiver for his or her negligence where this can be agreed.

Receivers and liquidation

24–023 Very frequently, liquidation follows the appointment of an administrative receiver—so much so that people often talk as if receivership were synonymous with liquidation—but in law, the two regimes are different. On the appointment of the liquidator the administrative receiver's powers of agency and management cease, though this does not mean that the receiver normally becomes the agent of the debenture holder.

A receiver may be appointed after liquidation commences,[90] but to save costs the court often appoints the liquidator as receiver in a compulsory winding-up, and the debenture holder's receiver can only take possession of the company's assets if authorised by the court. The court always has power to remove a receiver, but it will not normally do so where the receiver has been appointed and is in possession before the liquidator takes office, unless it is to the debenture holder's advantage.[91]

24–024 In windings up by the court, the liquidator may take into his or her custody "all the property and things in action to which the company is or appears to be entitled",[92] but a receiver who was appointed before the liquidator may still (without the court's permission) take or retain and dispose of the property comprised in the debenture and use the company's name for the purpose of agreeing a sale, and the debenture holder is still entitled to use a power of attorney to effect a transaction, such as a conveyance.[93] If the receiver was appointed after the liquidator, however, the court's permission is needed if the receiver is to dispose of the assets.[94]

In a voluntary winding up, the agency rights of a receiver cease, but his or her rights to take and dispose of assets are unaffected by the appointment

[88] *American Express International Banking Corpn v. Hurley* [1985] 3 All E.R. 564 (following *Standard Chartered Bank Ltd v. Walker* [1982] 3 All E.R. 938) where a bank debenture holder claimed against a director on his guarantee, but the director was able to rely on negligence because, on the special facts, the receiver was the agent of bank.

[89] Active intervention is required: *National Bank of Greece v. Pinios* [1990] 1 A.C. 637 at 648, *per* Lloyd L.J.

[90] *Re Northern Garage Ltd* [1946] Ch. 188.

[91] *Re Joshua Stubbs Ltd* [1891] 1 Ch. 475; *Re Henry Pound, Son and Hutchins Ltd* (1889) 42 Ch.D. 402.

[92] IA 1986, s. 144.

[93] *Gosling v. Gaskell* [1897] A.C. 575; *Sowman v. David Samuel Trust Ltd* [1978] 1 All E.R. 616.

[94] *Re Henry Pound, Son & Hitchins Ltd* (1889) 42 Ch. D. 42.

of a liquidator (whichever was appointed first) unless the court gives a contrary direction.[95] The court also has powers to appoint a special manager.[96] It seems unlikely that these powers would be exercised in such a way as to prevent a receiver from carrying out his or her functions.

Administration

Administration[97] was introduced by the Insolvency Acts 1985–86. It was designed to help in rescuing ailing companies by giving a breathing space to facilitate the rehabilitation of a company in difficulty or to improve the prospects of beneficial realisation of its assets or business. The management of the company is placed by the court in the hands of an authorised insolvency practitioner as administrator, who acts as an external manager of the company, and is an officer of the court.[98] The administrator acts as agent of the company in exercising his or her powers, which are therefore limited to the powers conferred on the company by its memorandum of association, and has the protection of an officer of the company.[99] The purpose of the appointment is to provide a moratorium on claims against the company—as long as the order is current, it prevents winding up or the appointment of an administrative receiver—so that the business is preserved as long as possible, allowing an opportunity for proposals for recovery to be made.[1] **24–025**

If an administration order is to be made, the court must be satisfied that the company is or is likely to become unable to pay its debts and that the order is likely to achieve one of four purposes set out in the IA 1986.[2] The effect of the order is that actions against the company are frozen: no winding up petition can proceed, any administrative receiver must vacate office and any other receiver must do so if required,[3] and no steps can be taken to enforce any security or to repossess goods, no other proceedings and no execution or legal process may be commenced, or distress levied, without the administrator's or the court's consent.[4] This "freeze" is at the **24–026**

[95] Under IA 1986, s. 168(3).

[96] IA 1986, s. 177.

[97] See Fletcher, Higham and Trower, *The Law and Practice of Corporate Administration* (1994) for a detailed account of the law.

[98] *Re Atlantic Computers plc*. [1992] Ch. 505.

[99] See *Re Home Treat* [1991] B.C.L.C. 705.

[1] To achieve the survival of the company as a going concern or the approval of a composition or scheme of arrangement under the IA 1986, Pt. I, CA 1985, s. 425, etc.; IA 1986, s. 8(3).

[2] IA 1986, s. 8. The test for "likely to achieve" has been established as that "there is a real prospect that the purpose will be achieved", see *Re Harris Simons Construction Ltd* [1989] 1 W.L.R. 368; *Re Primlaks (U.K.) Ltd.* [1989] B.C.L.C. 734; *Re S.C.L. Binding Services Ltd* [1990] B.C.L.C. 98; *Re Rowbotham Baxter Ltd* [1990] B.C.L.C. 397; *Re Chelmsford City Football Club (1980) Ltd.* [1991] B.C.C. 133.

[3] IA 1986, s. 11(1) and (2). Receivers' remuneration is a charge on, and paid out of, the charged property: IA 1986, s. 11(4).

[4] The Court of Appeal has given guidance as to the proper course for administrators in considering whether to consent, see *Re Atlantic Computer Systems plc* [1992] Ch. 505. As to the powers of the administrator to act without the court's approval, see *Re Charnley Davies Ltd* [1988] 4 B.C.C. 152.

heart of the administration procedure,[5] and it is designed to allow the company a respite during which proposals for reorganisation can be put to the creditors.

24–027 Secured creditors who hold a floating charge (provided that that charge and any fixed charges cover together substantially the whole of the company's assets) may block the appointment of an administrator by getting in first and appointing an administrative receiver. They may wish to do this, because the administrator exercises his or her powers on behalf of the general body of creditors rather than for the benefit of the secured creditors, and under an administration the creditors will only be able to realise their security if they have the consent of the administrator or of the court.[6]

A floating charge may be realised as the administrator wishes,[7] and the administrator becomes responsible for paying preferential creditors.[8] The administrator's remuneration, expenses, and some other debts are paid in priority to the debt of a floating charge holder[9]—another reason for banks to refuse to agree to the appointment.

24–028 Holders of fixed charges cannot block the appointment of an administrator, and the securities may be realised by the administrator (a) by agreement with the fixed charge holder[10] or (b) by application to the court, where the court agrees that this will promote the purposes of the administration. In the latter case, the fixed charge holder should receive at least the market price which could be obtained in an unforced sale (any deficiency because of a forced sale must be made up).[11] There is no similar "market-value" provision in respect of floating charges.

24–029 Prudent banks take fixed charges which are as extensive as possible and take a floating charge as well over the remaining property and over the whole "undertaking" (even if this is only a residual security[12]). This allows the bank to appoint an administrative receiver, because it has a charge over substantially the whole of the company's assets, and it can therefore step in and block the appointment of an administrator. This happens in the following way[13]: when an application is made to appoint an administrator,

[5] See *Re Atlantic Computer Systems plc* [1992] Ch. 505.

[6] IA 1986, s. 11(3)(c) and (d).

[7] Although the floating charge holder has the same priority over the proceeds of realisation when the administration has been completed as it had over the original property: IA 1986, s. 15(4).

[8] IA 1986, s. 11(5). Although there is no preferential status for the purpose of administration, the administrator must bear in mind the prospective status of preferential creditors after discharge of the order, and take care that there is no ground for complaint under IA 1986, s. 27 about unfair prejudice: see Goode, *op. cit.*, p. 279.

[9] IA 1986, s. 19(4).

[10] See IA 1986, s. 11(3)(c), (d).

[11] IA 1986, ss. 11(5) and (6).

[12] "Lightweight" floating charges, see *Re Croftbell* [1990] B.C.L.C. 844, and Oditah [1991] J.B.L. 49.

[13] Under IA 1986, s. 9.

the court must give notice to anyone entitled to appoint an administrative receiver, and a copy of the petition must be served on him or her at least five days before the hearing.[14] Therefore the bank has five days in which to decide whether to appoint an administrative receiver. If one is appointed, the court will dismiss the petition, unless the debenture holder has consented to the administration order, or the charge is invalid for some reason.[15] If one is not appointed, the court is free to grant the administration order, and this will (a) prevent the bank from realising the asset, except with the consent of the administrator, (b) permit the administrator to dispose of assets subject to a floating charge, and (c) permit the administrator to sell assets subject to a fixed charge if the court allows. Although the bank will not lose its security rights, therefore, it may only be entitled to the proceeds of realisation, which are paid out at the administrator's discretion, if at all.

Perhaps surprisingly, banks by no means always block the appointment of administrators, although they usually take floating charges so that they have the option to do so if they wish. Goode[16] lists several possible reasons for this: the bank may consider that the freeze on creditors' remedies outweighs the disadvantages of the order, or it may prefer criticism of the management from creditors to be directed at the administrator, not the bank's receiver; it may have adequate security and be prepared to wait; the amount due to the bank may be too small to justify appointing a receiver, or the charge may seem vulnerable; or the bank may have been allowed to nominate the administrator or have confidence in his or her management abilities. **24–030**

Nevertheless, banks with a floating charge often do refuse to consent to the appointment of an administrator, and in that case the collapse of the company subsequent to the receivership will be inevitable. The fact that only five days are given for the decision may also mean that receivers are appointed precipitately; this may bring about the very collapse that the appointment of an administrator was designed to avoid. This can be compared with the position of an individual bankrupt who, if he or she is insolvent, may apply to the court for an interim order for an individual voluntary arrangement supervised by an insolvency practitioner[17]; this, unlike company administrations, cannot be prevented by a secured creditor. **24–031**

[14] IR 1986, rr. 2.6 and 2.7. In practice, if the persons served with the petition consent, the court is willing to make the order immediately after the presentation of the petition if this is justified in all the circumstances: see Fletcher, Higham and Trower, *op. cit.*, para. 1.36.

[15] *e.g.* contravening the "12 months rule" under IA 1986, s. 245.

[16] Goode, *op. cit.*, p. 293. He describes research by Homan and Rajak indicating that administrations may be helpful in some cases. See also Gower, *Principles of Modern Company Law* (6th ed.), pp. 818–819, who suggests that banks have tried to be sensitive to criticisms that they may act prematurely in deciding to put companies into receivership, and also that banks have gained confidence in administrators as professionals.

[17] Under IA 1986, s. 253.

Voluntary Arrangements

(1) Company voluntary arrangements[18]

24–032 Debtors and their creditors may be able to come to some compromise—a composition, arrangement or assignment—with each other. A *composition* is an agreement of creditors not to take action against the debtor, in return for part payment (a dividend) of their debt or payment over a period. An *arrangement* (a wider term used for any voluntary scheme) with a debtor company might be by reorganisation of the company's share capital, whereby creditors convert some debt into equity. An *assignment* involves transfer of the company's property to the creditors or their nominee. All the creditors benefit from avoiding the delays and expense of liquidation, but a contractual scheme of this kind requires individual negotiation and the consent of each creditor, and for this reason the scheme under the IA 1986,[19] by which creditors may be bound by the decision of the creditors' meeting even without their consent, is more likely to be effective. A proposal for a scheme can be made (not necessarily when the company is being wound up) by directors, the liquidator, or the administrator to the company and its creditors. A *nominee,* who must be an insolvency practitioner, is appointed to implement the scheme. No meeting of creditors under a voluntary scheme can approve a proposal which affects the rights of a secured creditor to enforce its security, nor one which affects the priority of a preferential debt or causes any preferential creditor to be paid an amount proportionately less than other preferential creditors unless the creditor affected agrees.

24–033 Although the requirements are simpler and the procedure quicker than under earlier legislation,[20] there will still be delays which may lead to the death of the company. Such schemes are most likely to be advantageous in conjunction with the appointment of an administrator, whose appointment freezes all proceedings against the company, so that creditors are prevented from petitioning for winding up, and holders of fixed or floating charges from realising their securities.

(2) Individual voluntary arrangements

24–034 The IA 1986[21] also introduced a scheme for voluntary arrangements for individuals (compositions in satisfaction of their debts) with their creditors.

---

[18] The Insolvency Bill 2000 provides for the introduction of a new scheme for small company voluntary arrangements. There is intended to be the option of a moratorium to give the management time to produce a rescue plan.

[19] In IA 1986, ss. 1–7.

[20] The former procedure (under CA 1985, s. 425) requiring among other things class meetings of creditors, was little used, because it was slow, complicated and fairly expensive. Class meetings are not required now.

[21] IA 1986, Part VIII (ss. 252–263). See remarks of Lindsay J. about individual Voluntary Arrangements in *Re a Debtor (No 14010 of 1995)* [1996] 2 B.C.L.C. 429.

It has been a success,[22] effectively superseding earlier statutory provisions,[23] which have the disadvantage that they do not prevent dissenting creditors presenting a bankruptcy petition. For individuals, as compared to companies, there is a substantial advantage to the procedure, because the court has wide powers to grant an interim order staying actions or executions against the debtor's property or person[24]; during this moratorium no bankruptcy petition may be presented or proceeded with. Even an interim order, which lasts only for 14 days unless extended on the application of the nominee, may be extremely valuable in allowing the debtor to reorganise his or her affairs. Voluntary arrangements are appropriate where some trust can be placed in the debtor to carry on his or her own affairs (with day to day management of a bank account for carrying on business if appropriate) without the detailed control of the supervisor.

A debtor, or, more likely, an insolvency practitioner on his or her behalf, **24–035**
may propose a composition or scheme to the creditors under which the practitioner (the *nominee*), is to supervise the implementation of the agreement. To prevent abuse, it is required that the debtor must genuinely intend to make a proposal, must be an undischarged bankrupt or in a position to petition for his or her own bankruptcy, and must not have made a previous application in the past 12 months. The nominee (who usually becomes the supervisor of the scheme) must be a qualified insolvency practitioner and must be willing to act. The position is demanding,[25] becausc it needs responsibility on the part of the nominee, whose duty is to act as an honest broker between the debtor and creditors and other interested parties, such as the debtor's wife, particularly if the matrimonial home is involved.[26] Nominees also have to be careful in dealing with debtors themselves, who may well be evasive and "economical with the truth".[27]

---

[22] See Grier and Floyd, *Personal Insolvency, A Practical Guide*, para. 1.06.

[23] *e.g.* for deeds of arrangement under the Deeds of Arrangement Act 1914, amended by the IA 1986, Sched. 14.

[24] IA 1986, ss. 252–254. Although there are some actions which may proceed: *e.g.* a landlord may enforce his rights: *McMullen v. Cerrone* [1994] B.C.C. 25, *Re A Debtor (No 13A10 of 1994)* [1996] B.C.C. 57; and the rights of a receiver in respect of assets under the Drug Trafficking Offences Act 1986 are not affected: *Re M, The Times*, April 17, 1991.

[25] Guidelines for nominees issued by the Technical Committee of Society of Practitioners in Insolvency, 1991, cited by Totty and Moss, *op. cit.*, para. F1.03. See also *Re a Debtor, ex p Bank of Ireland (No 222 of 1990)* [1992] B.C.L.C. 137: a practitioner whose report is badly deficient may become personally liable in costs. In *King v. Anthony* [1998] 2 BCLC 5147, CA, it was held that there is no private law right of enforcement for breach of statutory duty against the supervisor of a voluntary arrangement. There are statutory means of enforcing duties of supervision under IA 1986, s. 263.

[26] See *Re a debtor (No. 48810 of 1996)* [1999] 2 B.C.L.C. 571, where the possible claims of a wife were considered by the court. It was held that her entitlement under an order of the matrimonial court might be overriden by possible collusion by the husband and friendly creditors in setting up the voluntary arrangement.

[27] See *Re A Debtor (No. 14010 of 1995)* [1996] 2 B.C.L.C. 429.

24–036 Before the interim order ceases to have effect, the nominee must submit a report (for which the debtor must provide details of his or her debts, liabilities and assets) saying whether the creditors should be called to a meeting to consider the proposals. The proposals must be serious and viable, not merely a means of postponing the making of a bankruptcy order.[28] If the report is approved, the interim order is extended. The court may discharge the order if it is satisfied that the debtor has not complied with his or her obligations under this provision,[29] or that it is inappropriate to call a meeting of creditors.

The crucial advantage of the statutory scheme is that, if a meeting is called and approves the proposal, all those who had notice of the meeting and were entitled to vote at it are bound as parties to the arrangement, whether they attended and voted or not. It is important to make sure that all the creditors are notified, however, even creditors who are thought to be fully secured, because any creditors who have not been given notice of the meeting are *not* bound by its decisions and may serve a statutory demand on the debtor.[30]

24–037 As with company voluntary arrangements, the decisions of the meeting must not affect the rights of secured or preferential creditors without their consent. A proposal or modification which fails to respect the rights of a secured creditor may be overturned because it unfairly prejudices the interests of the creditors, or for material irregularity in relation to the meeting.[31] In fact, secured creditors may consent, either because they have some connection with the debtor or because the value of the asset secured is inadequate and the arrangement offers the most favourable opportunity of at least partial repayment. Modifications to the proposal may also be suggested: banks often put forward standard modifications to proposed schemes. For example, it may be proposed that contributions towards repayment are to be made by the debtor over a period of time, usually three years; in such a case, banks usually require that the period should be a minimum of five years.

24–038 If the meeting approves the proposals, any bankruptcy petition stayed by the interim order is deemed to have been dismissed. If the debtor is an undischarged bankrupt, the court may give such directions with respect to the conduct of the bankruptcy as it thinks fit, including annulling the bankruptcy order.

---

[28] *Hook v. Jewson Ltd* [1997] 1 B.C.L.C. 664.

[29] The court has given guidance to nominees in this respect: *Re A Debtor (No 14010 of 1995)* [1996] 2 B.C.L.C. 429, *per* Lindsay J.

[30] *Re A Debtor (No 64 of 1992)* [1994] B.C.C. 55 and *Re A Debtor (No 40010 of 1996)* [1997] 2 B.C.L.C. 144.

[31] IA 1986, s. 262(1)(a) or (b), see *Re Primlaks (UK) Ltd (No 2)* [1990] B.C.L.C. 234; *N.W.Bank v. Scher* [1998] B.P.I.R. 224; *Re Naeem* [1990] 1 W.L.R. 48; *Re Cranley Mansions Ltd* [1994] 1 W.L.R. 161; *Re Bradley-Hole (A Bankrupt), ex p. Knight* [1995] 1 W.L.R. 1097; *Doorbar v. Alltimes Securities Ltd* [1996] 1 W.L.R. 456, CA; *Tager v. Westpac Banking Corpn* [1997] B.C.L.C. 313. See also *In Re Debtor (No. 638 of 1994), The Times*, December 3, 1998, Ch D.

The question has arisen whether approval of a voluntary arrangement precludes a creditor from taking steps *outside* the arrangement, to enforce its claim against a guarantor or co-debtor. The question is important, because if a voluntary arrangement does not have that effect, creditors have a neat way of circumventing the arrangement by claiming against other parties liable, who in turn will be able to claim an indemnity from the debtor. This may prejudice the other creditors, and therefore the whole arrangement. It was held, in *Johnson v. Davies*,[32] that the words of the statute[33] do not impose the arrangement on a dissenting creditor. An arrangement should be treated as consensual and the question whether it has the effect of discharging co-debtors or guarantors is a matter of construction. The court was not prepared to imply a term into the arrangement to prevent creditors taking steps against co-debtors.[34] The judge acknowledged that arrangements would work better and that it would be a "convenient and tidy result" to prevent creditors proceeding against co-debtors, but said that it would not be *necessary* to do so in order to give efficacy to the arrangement (the test for implying a term). It will therefore depend on the construction of the voluntary arrangement in any particular case whether the arrangement has this effect or not. This result, although said by the court to be desirable from the point of view of policy, because it will not discourage creditors from approving voluntary arrangements, leaves considerable doubt as to the effectiveness of arrangements where there are co-debtors. The uncertainty of the result in any particular case seems to have left the door open for increased litigation. **24–039**

Company Liquidation

Winding up may be carried out in two ways: first, winding up by the court (*compulsory winding up*) and secondly, the more common form of *voluntary winding up*—which may be by way of *members' winding up* (broadly, where the company is solvent), or *creditors' winding up*. Compulsory winding up normally starts with a petition by a creditor, and voluntary winding up starts with a resolution by the company. **24–040**

---

[32] [1998] 3 W.L.R. 1299, CA. See also *Raja v. Rubin* [1999] 3 All E.R. 73, CA, and *Comrs. of Inland Revenue v. Adam* [1999] 2 B.C.L.C. 730, which concerned a company voluntary arrangement.

[33] IA 1986, s. 260(2) provides: "the approved arrangement—(a) takes effect as if made by the debtor at the meeting, and (b) binds every person who in accordance with the rules had notice of, and was entitled to vote at, the meeting (whether or not he was present or represented at it) as if he were a party to the arrangement". In the view of Chadwick J., the implication of the legislation (and the legislative history) is that voluntary arrangements should be treated as "consensual deeds of arrangement" rather than as "a substitute for compositions or arrangements in bankruptcy proceedings" ([1998] 3 W.L.R. 1299 at 1310). It would therefore be "contrary to authority to hold that the rights of creditors against co-debtors would be affected by anything in proposals for a voluntary arrangement, which only took effect by reason of . . . a "statutory binding".

[34] Although it was willing to imply a narrower term—that creditors bound by the proposal will take no steps to enforce their debts *against the debtor* while the debtor is complying, or has complied, with his or her obligations under the arrangement: [1998] 3 W.L.R. 1299 at 1307.

Compulsory Winding up (by the Court)

24–041 **Grounds for petition.** Petitions may be presented in circumstances laid down in section 122 of the IA 1986,[35] the most commonly used of which is that the company is unable to pay its debts. Several tests are provided,[36] among them that the company has failed to comply with a statutory demand, that there has been an unsatisfied execution by a judgment debtor, that it is shown that the value of the company's assets is less than its liabilities ("asset test"), or "proved insolvency"—that the company cannot pay its debts as they fall due. This is a question of fact, and a bank with a standard type of charge will be in a position to demonstrate swiftly to the court the fact (if it is one) that the company cannot pay its debts by making a demand of the company, and if it is unsuccessful, appointing a receiver and seizing the relevant assets.

24–042 The winding up petition must be advertised in the London Gazette not less than seven business days after it is served on the company and not less than seven business days before the date appointed for the hearing of the petition unless the court directs otherwise.[37] The publication of the petition will be serious for the company and may cause damage to its business—for example, the bank will probably stop it operating its bank account. If the presentation of the petition is an abuse of the process of the court, the court will order that the petition is not to be advertised.[38]

24–043 **The petition.** At the hearing of the petition, the court may make a winding-up order or any other order it thinks fit.[39] In reaching its decision the court will have regard to the wishes of the creditors,[40] and may order a meeting of creditors to be summoned to determine the wishes of the majority.[41] After the presentation of the petition and before a winding-up order is made, the court may "freeze" the position, by appointing a provisional liquidator.[42]

---

[35] As to who may petition, see IA 1986, s. 124. There are other statutory provisions—*e.g.* petitions in relation to banks may be presented by the Bank of England under BA 1987, s. 92(1). As to unregistered companies, see IA 1986, s. 221(5) and as to partnerships, see Insolvent Partnerships Order 1994 (S.I. 1994 No. 2421).

[36] By IA 1986, s. 123. See *Re a Company* [1985] B.C.L.C. 37 and *Re a Company (No. 0012209 of 1991)* [1992] 1 W.L.R. 351.

[37] IR 1986, r. 4.11. See *Re a Company* [1985] B.C.L.C. 37; *Re a Company (No. 0012209 of 1991)* [1992] 1 W.L.R. 351

[38] See, *e.g. Re a Company (No. 003079 of 1990)* [1991] B.C.L.C. 235; *Re a Company* [1985] B.C.L.C. 37; *Re a Company (No. 0012209 of 1991)* [1992] 1 W.L.R. 351; *Re a Company (No. 004502 of 1988) ex p. Johnson* [1992] B.C.L.C. 70 and *Re a Company (No. 004415 of 1996)* [1997] 1 B.C.L.C. 479.

[39] IA 1986, s. 125: *e.g.* order any action or proceeding against the company to be stayed, dismiss the petition, adjourn the hearing conditionally or unconditionally, or make an interim order (IA 1986, s. 126).

[40] And "contributories"—members or past members of the company (Pennington, *op. cit.*, pp. 25–26, citing IA 1986, s. 124(1)).

[41] IA 1986, s. 195.

[42] IA 1986, s. 135.

The order removes the powers of the directors to dispose of property, and is intended to preserve the status quo and prevent the assets of the company being dissipated, or possibly, to protect a public interest. It can be draconian in effect, however, because it may kill the business, and there is little potential for redress if it turns out that the petition was unfounded.[43]

After commencement. In compulsory windings up the commencement date is the time of the presentation of the petition.[44] After the commencement, the company ceases to carry on business, except so far as is necessary to carry on the beneficial winding up of the company. The powers of the directors cease.[45] The employees are automatically dismissed,[46] although the liquidator may re-employ some of them temporarily. Proceedings against the company may be affected, as are dispositions of the company's property, and any attachment, sequestration, distress or execution put in force against the estate or effects of the company is void.[47] **24–044**

The Official Receiver is *ex officio* liquidator.[48] Where the court has made a winding-up order, the official receiver, who has the same powers as a receiver and manager appointed by the court, becomes the liquidator and continues as liquidator until another person is appointed in his or her place.[49] The official receiver must decide whether to call a meeting of creditors, must investigate the affairs of the company and the causes of its failure, and must report to the court. **24–045**

The official receiver has powers to investigate the conduct of company directors who may be unfit to be concerned in the management of the company; for example, he or she may apply to the court for the *public examination* of persons connected with the company,[50] where questions about the company's promotion or management may be put to them in order to enforce claims or initiate criminal proceedings against them or others. The official receiver may also seek a court order for the *private examination*[51] of officers of the company or others, like bank managers or solicitors, who may have information about the company's affairs.[52] **24–046**

The liquidator[53] may be appointed by a meeting of creditors.[54] The functions of the liquidator are to get in and realise the assets of the company, and to distribute them to the company's creditors. Liquidators **24–047**

[43] *Re Forrester and Lamego* [1997] 2 B.C.L.C. 155 at 158.

[44] IA 1986, s. 129.

[45] *Fowler v. Broad's Patent Night Light Co* [1893] 1 Ch. 724; *Measures Bros Ltd v. Measures* [1910] 2 Ch. 248.

[46] *Re General Rolling Stock Co., Chapman's Case* (1866) L.R. 1 Eq. 346.

[47] IA 1986, s. 128. If a judgment creditor has issued execution against company property in a voluntary winding up, or has attached any debt, it may keep the benefit of the execution or attachment only if the process was complete before winding up commenced.

[48] See *Re Minotaur Data Systems Ltd, Official Receiver v. Brunt* [1999] 2 B.C.L.C. 766, CA.

[49] IA 1986, s. 136.

[50] IA 1986, s. 133.

[51] Under IA 1986, s. 236.

[52] Liquidators and other office holders have the same power, see below, para. 24–060.

[53] See below, para. 24–055.

[54] Or of contributories, IA 1986, s. 139.

have wide powers, some of which are subject to the sanction either of the court or of the committee of creditors.

24–048 **Final general meeting of creditors.** If it seems to the liquidator that the winding-up of the company is for practical purposes complete, he or she summons a final general meeting of creditors to receive the report and to determine if the liquidator should be released.[55]

24–049 **Dissolution.** When the registrar of companies is informed that the winding-up of a company is complete, the notice is registered and the company is normally dissolved three months later.

Voluntary Winding up

24–050 Voluntary winding up is more common than winding up by the court because it is quicker and less expensive. A company may be put into liquidation by its members by passing a resolution for a winding-up in general meeting.[56]

A *members' voluntary winding up* presupposes that the company is solvent. The directors make a "statutory declaration of solvency" not more than five weeks before the winding up resolution is passed. This must be based on reasonable grounds; if it is not, the directors will be liable for penalties.[57] If it then seems to the liquidator that the company's debts will not be paid in full within the period stated in the declaration, the liquidator must convert the liquidation into a *creditors'* voluntary winding up,[58] with the meeting having the normal powers of a creditors' meeting (for example, to appoint a committee).

24–051 A *creditors' voluntary winding up* also depends on a resolution being passed by the company. Within 14 days of the resolution, a meeting of creditors which the directors must attend and preside at must be advertised and called to consider the resolution. The company meeting and the creditors' meeting may nominate a liquidator; in case of conflict, the creditors' choice of liquidator prevails. The creditors and the company may appoint a committee, which may permit the continuance of some or all of the directors' powers,[59] which, unlike in a compulsory winding up, do not automatically cease. The sanction of the committee (or of the court) is required for the liquidator to exercise certain of his or her powers—for example, to pay any class of creditors in full or to make any compromise with creditors[60]—and if the liquidator disposes of company property to a

[55] Under IA 1986, s. 174.
[56] IA 1986, s. 84(1).
[57] IA 1986, s. 89(4).
[58] IA 1986, ss. 95–96.
[59] IA 1986, s. 103.
[60] IA 1986, s. 165 and Sched. 4.

person connected with the company, he or she must give notice to the committee.[61] Apart from this, the main function of the committee is to act as a more coherent and manageable body than the whole body of creditors, better able to monitor the progress of the winding up.

Once the winding up resolution has been passed, it must be advertised in the London Gazette within fourteen days,[62] and a copy must be sent to the Registrar of Companies within fifteen days.[63]

After commencement. Winding up commences at the time of the passing of the resolution.[64] The company must cease to carry on its business except so far as is necessary for its beneficial winding up, although its corporate status and powers continue until dissolution.[65] Actions against the company are not automatically stayed, however; the liquidator has to apply to the court for a stay to any pending action and show good cause for a stay to be granted. **24–052**

The liquidator. Except where the committee's sanction is needed, a liquidator may exercise any of the powers given to liquidators in a compulsory winding up,[66] and must use his or her own discretion in the management of the estate and in its distribution among the creditors, though he or she may apply to the court for directions.[67] **24–053**

Dissolution. Once the company's affairs are fully wound up, the liquidator draws up an account showing what has occurred, and calls separate meetings of the company and the creditors at which it is explained and considered. A copy of the account and a return as to the meetings is sent to the registrar of companies to register. The company is dissolved after three months unless the court defers the date.[68] **24–054**

Functions and Powers of Liquidators

The liquidator's functions are to get in and realise the assets of the company, to distribute them to the company's creditors and, if there is a surplus, to the persons entitled to them.[69] Liquidators are given wide **24–055**

[61] IA 1986, s. 167(2).
[62] IA 1986, s. 85.
[63] IA 1986, s. 380.
[64] IA 1986, s. 86.
[65] IA 1986, s. 87.
[66] The liquidator is an officer of the company for the purposes of the CA 1985 (*Re X Co. Ltd* [1907] 2 Ch. 92).
[67] IA 1986, ss. 168 and 112.
[68] IA 1986, ss. 106 and 201.
[69] IA 1986, s. 135. Mostly specified in IA 1986, ss. 165–167. The substantive rules governing the powers and duties of liquidators are largely the same, whether the winding-up is compulsory or voluntary, but there are procedural differences between the two: Pennington, *op. cit.*, p. 98.

powers, and are generally expected to act independently, although some of their powers are subject to the sanction either of the court or of the committee of creditors.

They are responsible for swelling the assets of the company by disposing of property and collecting in all the debts, bringing actions to establish and enforce liabilities, and recovering sums owed by the directors or the officers of the company, for example if they have behaved improperly. Liquidators must challenge invalid transactions (those which are beyond the powers of the directors, made by unauthorised agents, transactions at an undervalue, or voidable preferences). They have powers to disclaim onerous property.[70] They may not, of course, dispose of assets owned by another person[71] or subject to a trust,[72] and secured creditors may not be prevented from realising their secured assets, although the liquidator will naturally scrutinise the securities to make sure they are valid.

24–056 Liquidators may apply to the court for directions[73] in relation to any particular matter—a power which may be useful not only where there is doubt as to their powers or duties, but where they face obstruction. Similarly, any person aggrieved by the liquidator's acts or decisions may apply to the court, which may confirm, reverse or modify the act or decision complained of.[74] The court is usually most unwilling to interfere with a liquidator's discretion, provided it is exercised reasonably and in good faith.[75] Nevertheless, liquidators owe the company at least some fiduciary duties; these probably are liability for behaviour amounting to fraud,[76] for misapplication of the assets of the company (for example, paying debts in the wrong order), for admitting and paying an invalid claim,[77] and for making a secret profit from their position. The liquidator's safeguard, if in doubt about his or her duties, is to apply to the court.[78]

Liquidators may only resign in restricted circumstances,[79] but can be removed by the court (or by a meeting of creditors called for the purpose[80]) if they have been guilty of misconduct, even in the sense of failure to carry

---

[70] IA 1986, s. 178. See *Hindcastle Ltd v. Barbara Attenborough Associates Ltd* [1997] A.C. 70; *Re Park Air Services, Christopher Moran Holdings Ltd v. Bairstow* [1999] 2 W.L.R. 396. And see *Re Celtic Extraction Ltd* [1999] 2 B.C.L.C. 555, CA; where it was held that a waste management licence under the Environmental Protection Act 1990 could be disclaimed by the official receiver as liquidator.

[71] *e.g.* subject to hire-purchase, or a retentions clause.

[72] *Re Kayford* [1975] 1 All E.R. 604.

[73] IA 1986, ss. 168 and 112.

[74] IA 1986, s. 168(5).

[75] *Leon v. York–O-Matic* [1966] 3 All E.R. 277.

[76] *Knowles v. Scott* [1891] 1 Ch. 717; *Re Hills Waterfall Estate and Gold Mining Co* [1896] 1 Ch. 947.

[77] *Re Windsor Steam Coal Co. (1901) Ltd* [1929] 1 Ch. 151; *Pulsford v. Devenish* [1903] 2 Ch. 625.

[78] IA 1986, s. 168 and s. 112.

[79] IA 1986, s. 172.

[80] IA 1986, ss. 172 and 168.

out duties or to show the necessary vigour,[81] or where it is in the interests of the creditors to do so—for example, where there is a conflict of interest.[82]

Powers to deal with property

In a *compulsory winding up*, all the company property is taken into the custody or control of the liquidator[83] and the court may direct that all or part of the property vest in the liquidator.[84] In a *voluntary winding up*, the company's corporate powers continue until it is dissolved although it ceases business.[85] There is no need to vest the company's property in the liquidator because he or she is appointed to act for the company[86] and exercises its powers over property. The powers of the directors cease except as the liquidator permits,[87] and questions as to the powers of directors to deal with property become a problem of agency and of ostensible authority (directors lose their ostensible authority on the Gazetting of the liquidation). **24–057**

The liquidator in any winding up has power to sell or mortgage company property and may open a bank account for the purpose of winding up (the bank closes the company's bank accounts and sends the liquidator any credit balances remaining on them). The liquidator may open a separate bank account at a local branch of a bank for carrying on the company's business, but has to be authorised to do so by the Department of Trade and Industry.[88] Accounts should be kept separate, so that cheques issued by the company before the liquidation are not paid out of the liquidation bank account, and so that the company's funds are not mixed with those of other companies with which the liquidator is dealing. **24–058**

In either form of liquidation, liquidators may "hive off" the company's assets by forming a new company, and transferring to it the old company's assets and business. The new company may pay for its acquisition of property and goodwill by an issue of shares to the liquidator, who holds the shares as an asset of the old company, and who may be able to sell the "hived off' new company and its business as a going concern, unencumbered by debt (it is not responsible for the debts of the old company). By this means, a better price may be obtained than by piecemeal realisation of parts of the company's assets.

---

[81] See, *e.g. Re Keypak Homecare Ltd* [1987] B.C.L.C. 409.

[82] *Re Corbenstoke (No. 2)* [1990] B.C.L.C. 60, where the liquidator was a debtor of the company, a former trustee of the company and a shareholder's trustee in bankruptcy—an "impossible" conflict of interest.

[83] IA 1986, s. 144.

[84] IA 1986, s. 145.

[85] IA 1986, s. 87.

[86] IA 1986, ss. 165 and 167 and Sched. 4, Part II, para. 5 and Part III, paras 6, 7, 9 and 13.

[87] IA 1986, s. 103.

[88] Funds received by a liquidator must be paid into the Insolvency Services' account at the Bank of England, unless the Secretary of State for Trade and Industry sanctions the use of a local bank account, IA 1986, s. 411; Sched. 8; Insolvency Regulations 1994 (S.I. 1994 No. 2507), regs. 5 and 6.

Liquidator's powers to investigate and seize property

24–059 Liquidators (like trustees) have wide powers to seek a court order to take possession of property, books, papers, or records to which the debtor is or appears to be entitled, which are in the possession or control of the debtor or someone else.[89] Office holders who seize or dispose of the wrong property are given protection provided that they had reasonable grounds to believe that they were entitled to seize or dispose of it; they also have a lien on property or its proceeds for their expenses of sale or seizure,[90] although they are liable for losses they negligently cause to the property. Liens on books, papers and so forth cannot be enforced against the liquidator except those liens which give a title to property and which are held as such.[91]

Persons who are or have been officers, or who have taken part in the formation of the company within the past year, or are or were employees, must provide the office holder with such information as he or she may reasonably require, and attend on him or her.[92]

24–060 The office holder has a particularly powerful weapon for investigation[93]: he or she may apply to the court under section 236 of the IA 1986 for a *private examination* or the production of documents or an affidavit. This may be used against both company insiders, such as directors, and outsiders, such as bankers. Although the courts attempt to prevent the power being used as an instrument of oppression or as a "fishing expedition to obtain" information, it is a very strong power, and has given rise to extensive litigation.[94] The courts have increasingly set limits on its use, and are likely to refuse an order if the office holder has an improper motive in applying. In *Re PFTZM*,[95] for example, the court refused to grant an order to liquidators who were acting oppressively in attempting to obtain admissions from officers of a finance company that they had acted as shadow directors of the company, in order to obtain evidence which could

[89] IA 1986, ss. 234 and 365.

[90] IA 1986, ss. 234(3–4) and 304(3–4).

[91] IA 1986, ss. 246 and 349. See *Re SEIL Trade Finance Ltd* [1992] B.C.C. 538

[92] IA 1986, s. 235.

[93] Like administrators, administrative receivers and the Official Receiver. Trustees have similar powers, see below, paras 24–093 *et seq*.

[94] It is known as the "Star Chamber" clause. See further above, Chap. 4. Application is often made *ex parte*, and an order may be obtained without even showing a prima facie case against the person. The examinee has no privilege against self-incrimination (but see *Saunders v. U.K.* [1998] 1 B.C.L.C. 362, ECHR, which relates to the similar powers of the SFO). See *Cloverbay Ltd (joint administrators) v. BCCI International SA* [1991] 1 All E.R. 894; *Bishopsgate IM v. Maxwell* [1992] B.C.C. 214; *Re Polly Peck International plc No. 2* [1992] B.C.L.C. 1025; *Re B & C Holdings* [1992] B.C.L.C. 641; *Wallace Smith Trust Co. Ltd (in liq.) v. Deloitte Haskins & Sells* [1996] 4 All E.R. 403. Among recent cases are: *Re Murjani* [1996] B.C.L.C. 272; *Re James McHale Automobiles Ltd* [1997] 1 B.C.L.C. 273; *Re Galileo* [1998] 1 All E.R. 545; *Re Sasea Finance (in Liq)* [1998] 1 B.C.L.C. 559; *Re Maxwell Communs. Corp plc (No. 3)* [1995] 1 B.C.L.C. 521; *Re BCCI (No. 12) Morris v. Bank of America* [1997] 1 B.C.L.C. 526; *B & C Holdings v. Barclays de Zoete Wedd* [1999] 1 B.C.L.C. 86.

[95] [1995] B.C.C. 161.

be relied upon in court. The court may also, in appropriate cases, and with caution, require that documents are "redacted" (edited) to omit material whose disclosure is unnecessary, undesirable or unlawful.[96] Information or documents subject to legal professional privilege may be protected to some extent[97]; this protection may cover legal advice given in documents held by bankers. It is unlikely, though, that a banker would be able to exercise a lien over documents which the office holder wished to examine,[98] and the fact that the person to be examined will have to undertake a heavy burden of work in order to respond to the inquiries will not in itself prevent the court from requiring the production of documents or an oral examination.[99]

The courts are more protective of outsiders like bankers, who have not **24–061** been guilty of any misconduct, than of company insiders. They are less likely, for example, to order them to attend an oral examination, as opposed to disclosing documents.[1] Nevertheless banks, like others, have few, if any, arguments to set against the exercise of the power, and may well have to undertake the burden of the work and the responsibility for the cost of complying with orders under section 236 of the IA 1986.

Personal Liability of Company Directors

The whole point of forming a limited company is that the *company*, not **24–062** its members or managers, should be liable if the company becomes insolvent. There are numerous exceptions to this principle, however, some of which have developed as a response to the fact that limited liability can be abused, and these make directors liable to compensate either the company itself, or persons dealing with the company who suffer loss. When an insolvent company is wound up, the exceptions may assume considerable importance.

Fraudulent and wrongful trading

Fraudulent trading. Directors (and others) may be civilly and criminally[2] **24–063** liable for fraudulent trading. The IA 1986[3] provides that when it appears in a winding up that the company's business has been carried on[4] with intent

[96] *Re Galileo* [1998] 1 All E.R. 545, where disclosure of the requested material was prohibited by s. 82 of the BA 1987. Redaction might have been possible (the court considered the practicalities of redaction) but, in this case, what was left would have had so little value to the liquidator that he could not be said reasonably to require it.

[97] See *Re Murjani* [1996] B.C.L.C. 272 and *Re Ouvaroff* [1997] B.P.I.R. 712.

[98] *Re Aveling Barford* [1989] B.C.L.C. 122 (solicitors' lien); *Brereton v. Nicholls* [1993] B.C.L.C. 593.

[99] *British and Commonwealth Holdings plc v. Spicer and Oppenheim* [1993] B.C.L.C. 168.

[1] Moss, Insolvency Intelligencer, June 11, 1998, p. 41.

[2] CA 1985, s. 458.

[3] IA 1986, s. 213.

[4] In *Re Sarflax Ltd* [1979] 2 W.L.R. 202, it was held that a company which effectively closed down its business by ceasing to trade and transferring its assets to its parent company to which it was indebted, was "carrying on" the business.

to defraud its creditors or for any other fraudulent purpose, the court may, on the liquidator's application,[5] order any persons who were knowingly parties to carrying on the business in that way to make contributions to the company's assets. There must have been some dishonesty in carrying on the business before personal liability will be imposed, but even one act of dishonesty is sufficient.[6] A director who has no reason to believe that the company will be able to pay its creditors in full by the time when their debts become payable or within a short time afterwards will be guilty,[7] but not an optimistic but stupid director. The court may include a punitive element in the amount of contribution it orders.[8]

A creditor of the company may be a party to the fraudulent trading, and the court may order that its liability to contribute to the assets is charged against its own rights against, or security interests in, the company, and that its rights rank behind all the other debts.[9]

24–064 **Wrongful trading.** Although liability for fraudulent trading is helpful in restraining over-enthusiastic directors, there have been numerous scandals where it has seemed to the public that company directors deliberately allowed their companies to run into debt, but where it has been difficult to prove fraud. The IA 1986 therefore includes a separate provision[10] relating to "wrongful trading", which is designed to prevent directors escaping liability if they have been acting on the unreasonable belief that "there is light at the end of the tunnel".[11] It applies if a director (including a non-executive director or shadow director of the company) "knew or ought to have concluded" at some time before the commencement of winding up that there was no reasonable prospect that the company would avoid going into insolvent liquidation.[12] The court may, on the application of the liquidator, make similar orders to those for fraudulent trading.

24–065 The second requirement—whether the director "ought to have concluded"—extends liability to cases where directors have been negligent; no dishonesty is required. In this case, the court will consider the steps the defendant should have taken as compared with those which would have been taken by a reasonably diligent person with the level of skill, knowledge and experience which may reasonably be expected of a person carrying out

[5] IA 1986, s. 213(1) and (2).

[6] *Re Gerald Cooper Chemicals Ltd* [1978] 2 Ch. 262.

[7] *Re a Company (No. 001418 of 1988)* [1991] B.C.L.C. 197.

[8] *Re A Company (No. 001418 of 1988)* [1991] B.C.L.C. 197.

[9] IA 1986, s. 215(4).

[10] IA 1986, s. 214.

[11] *Gore-Brown on Companies* (Boyle and Sykes eds) para. 35.4.2, referring to the Cork Report, *op. cit.*

[12] See *Re Produce Marketing Consortium Ltd* [1989] 3 All E.R. 1; *Re DKG Contractors Ltd* [1990] B.C.C. 903; *Re Purpoint Ltd* [1991] B.C.C. 121; *Re Sherborne Associates Ltd* [1995] B.C.C. 40. See also *Re Oasis Merchandising Services Ltd* [1995] B.C.C. 911, aff'd [1997] B.C.C. 282; *Re Farmizer (Products) Ltd* [1995] B.C.C. 926.

the director's functions in relation to the company, together with any additional general knowledge and experience which the director in question actually has. Directors are therefore expected to have a minimum level of skill, which will vary from company to company, and within the company, depending on the position the director holds, and they cannot defend themselves by pleading abnormal stupidity. Directors who actually have a *greater* degree of skill than the minimum, however, must exercise it; they cannot plead that they did what acceptable, but less skilled, directors would have done.[13]

The section also provides a defence for the protection of directors who, having realised that the company has no reasonable prospect of avoiding insolvent liquidation, do what they can to avoid loss to creditors, perhaps in the face of opposition by other directors. No order can be made against directors who, knowing of the prospect of insolvent liquidation, took every step that they ought to have taken with a view to minimising the potential loss to the creditors.[14] However, directors who are concerned about the company cannot necessarily escape liability by resigning, since they must still show that they have taken every step which they ought to have taken.[15] **24–066**

Banks may have reason for anxiety about the provisions because there is a danger that they may in certain circumstances become shadow directors of companies they are supporting financially. This is discussed further below.[16] Parent companies are also likely to be particularly affected, given the universal presence of nominated directors on the board of the subsidiary company.

Guarantees[17]

It is common for banks to take guarantees from directors, often secured over the personal property of the directors, especially in small private companies where the directors are often the major, or the only, shareholders. On default, the bank may ignore the guarantee and other third party securities and seek its remedies under its company securities, or by proving for debts against the company, and if it is then unsatisfied, it may proceed against the directors. Alternatively, the bank may proceed immediately against guarantors. In relation to public companies, guarantees from directors may also be taken, but are rarer, unless other companies in the group act as directors. To this extent, the "limited liability" achieved by the corporate structure is often an illusion when dealing with liability to banks. **24–067**

[13] IA 1986, s. 214(4).
[14] IA 1986, s. 214(3).
[15] IA 1986, s. 214(3).
[16] See below, para. 24–072.
[17] See above, Chap. 18.

Liability for other wrongful acts

24–068 There are numerous other ways in which directors may become personally liable for their acts.[18] They may be liable for tort—for example, for negligent misstatement, if they obtain a loan by negligent or fraudulent misrepresentation or they have assumed personal responsibility for negligent advice by the company[19]—or for *misfeasance*[20]: that is, breach of any fiduciary or other duty.[21] The directors' duties include acting in the best interests of the company, exercising their powers for the proper purposes, exercising care and skill in the management of the company's property and business, and duties of loyalty and good faith (for example, avoiding conflicts of interest, or making secret profits). Effectively, these proceedings may be taken to recover for any loss suffered by the company, including negligence. The court may order restoration of money or property, or the contribution of a compensating sum to the company's assets.

24–069 If a company's borrowings are *ultra vires*, if the board of directors have no authority to act, or if particular directors borrow without authority, then the directors who have expressly or impliedly warranted their authority (the very fact that directors negotiate on behalf of the company impliedly represents that they have authority to do so) are liable for *breach of warranty of authority*. For example, a director is liable if he or she negotiates a loan to the company and this causes the company to exceed a borrowing limit in the memorandum.[22] Even if a company which has entered an *ultra vires* transaction can rely upon section 35 of the CA 1985 for protection,[23] the directors are probably still liable on their warranty of authority, because the section merely prevents the company from relying on lack of power or authority as a defence against the other party; it does not validate the transaction.

24–070 Directors may be disqualified under the Company Directors Disqualification Act 1986 because they have been found guilty of an offence of fraudulent trading[24] or of any other fraud in relation to the company,[25] for

---

[18] One way in which directors may become personally liable is by signing a bill of exchange in their own names while acting for the company, unless there is an indication that the signature is on behalf of the company, *e.g.* by using words such as "for", "per pro," or "for and on behalf of," or by signing "as agent for the company": BOEA 1882, s. 26; CA 1985, s. 37.

[19] See *Williams v. Natural Life Health Foods Ltd* [1998] 2 All E.R. 577, H.L.

[20] Summary application to court under the IR 1986, r. 7.1(1) and r. 7.3(2), against persons responsible for the management and administration of the company's affairs who have committed breaches of their fiduciary (etc.) obligations in carrying out their functions.

[21] IA 1986, s. 212.

[23] *Weeks v. Propert* (1873) L.R. 8 C.P. 427; *Chapleo v. Brunswick Permanent Building Soc.* (1881) 6 Q.B.D. 696; *West London Commercial Bank v. Kitson* (1883) 12 Q.B.D. 157.

[23] See above, para. 8–029.

[24] Under CA 1985, s. 458, or (the Company Directors Disqualification Act 1986, s. 10) IA 1986, s. 213.

[25] Company Directors Disqualification Act 1986, s. 4.

wrongful trading[26] or for other offences,[27] and where disqualified persons act, they may be personally liable. They also commit a criminal offence.[28] If a company itself "commits" an offence, the directors or other officers are also guilty of the offence if they consented to it, or connived at it, or it was a result of their neglect.[29]

Provision is made in the Company Directors Disqualification Act 1986 to prevent "phoenix" companies being set up—that is, to prevent people involved with insolvent companies starting up new companies under a similar name to the insolvent company, relying on the fact that the previous name is well known, where the public may be unaware that the original company has gone into liquidation. A person who was a director or shadow director of a company which has gone into insolvent liquidation in the 12 months before liquidation, therefore, is not permitted to be a director or concerned in the promotion, formation, management, or in carrying on a business conducted by another company if the other company uses a name by which the liquidated company was known, or a name so similar to that company's name that it suggests an association with it, for a period of five years after the liquidation except with the consent of the court.[30] **24–071**

Banks as Shadow Directors

It is possible that banks may be liable under some of these provisions (particularly for wrongful trading) as "shadow directors"[31]: that is, persons in accordance with whose directions or instructions the actual directors of the company are accustomed to act.[32] Shadow directors are those who "remain backstage", or "in the shadows" and who may try to evade legal liabilities by doing so. When companies are in difficulty, and come cap in hand to the bank, it is not unknown for directors to accept the instructions of the bank. There is some risk that banks may find that they are regarded as shadow directors if they take this responsibility too far and become involved with the management of companies. Great care must therefore be exercised, for a bank would be a clear target for a liquidator. A bank might be expected to have a considerable degree of skill, and if it is a shadow director, it must attempt to minimise loss to all the creditors, not just to itself. There could be real dangers here. **24–072**

---

26 Under IA 1986, s. 214: the Company Directors Disqualification Act 1986, s. 10.

27 Company Directors Disqualification Act 1986, ss. 5, 6, 8 and 11.

28 Company Directors Disqualification Act 1986, s. 13.

29 Company Directors Disqualification Act 1986, s. 14, in relation to offences concerning disqualification orders.

30 IA 1986, s. 216.

31 IA 1986, s. 214(7). As to the interpretation of shadow director (relating to s. 22(5) of the Company Directors Disqualification Act 1986) See *Secretary of State for Trade and Industry v. Deverell and Hopkins, The Times*, December 21, 1999, CA.

32 IA 1986, s. 251. Professional advisers are excluded, but this probably does not apply to a bank creditor.

24–073 A person does not become a shadow director merely because the directors of the company act on advice given by him or her in a professional capacity, or because he or she has power to appoint one or more directors of the company or nominate persons whom its board of directors is obliged to appoint as directors.[33] Banks should be careful to phrase their discussions with directors in terms of "advice" rather than instruction, perhaps merely informing the company of the terms upon which it is prepared to continue its support, or refraining from calling in loans, and enforcing security without actually giving instructions to the company.

24–074 The issue of banks as shadow directors came before the court as a preliminary issue in *Re a Company (No. 005009 of 1987), ex p. Copp*,[34] and the possibility that a bank might become one was not ruled out: Knox J. said that the plea was not obviously unsustainable, although he did not give his reasons for refusing to strike out the claim, in case these might cause embarrassment to the trial judge. When the case was tried (as *Re M.C.Bacon*[35]), however, the issue did not come before the court for decision, and it was said by the judge[36] that the allegations had been "rightly abandoned". So far as it goes, this comment indicates scepticism about the possibility of banks becoming shadow directors in the context of normal lending and enforcing security.

24–075 Indeed, it seems now fair to say that the courts are showing caution about ascribing responsibility as shadow directors to banks. In *Re PFTZM*,[37] where the liquidators of an insolvent company were trying to establish that the officers of a finance company had acted as shadow directors, the judge found that they had not. He distinguished between cases where the directors of the company were accustomed to act in accordance with the directions of others, and cases where the creditor made terms for the continuation of credit in the light of threatened default. The directors of the company had been quite free to take the offer or leave it.[38] The board of directors of the company had not "ceded its management autonomy" [39] to the finance company, whose actions were simply directed to trying to rescue what they could out of the company, using their undoubted rights as secured creditors, and acting in defence of its own interests.

From a policy point of view, there are good reasons for the courts to be cautious. Ascribing responsibility as shadow directors too readily to banks would be likely to inhibit them from attempting to rescue or stave off the

[33] See *Kuwait Asia Bank EC v. National Mutual Life Nominees Ltd* [1990] 3 All E.R. 404; *Re Hydrodam (Corby) Ltd* [1994] 2 B.C.L.C. 180, and *Re Tasbian Ltd (No 3)* [1993] B.C.L.C. 297, where the Court of Appeal held that it was arguable that a person controlling the company's bank account was a shadow director.

[34] [1989] B.C.L.C. 13.

[35] [1990] B.C.L.C. 324.

[36] [1990] B.C.L.C. 324 at 326, *per* Millett J.

[37] [1995] B.C.C. 161.

[38] [1995] B.C.C. 161, *per* H.H. Judge Paul Baker, Q.C.

[39] See Gower, *Company Law*, p. 154.

insolvency of companies in difficulties, and would probably lead to the earlier collapse of many companies, and to the collapse of some which might have been saved, given the tendency of banks in that situation simply to enforce their securities, and to appoint receivers.

Individual Bankruptcy

The purpose of bankruptcy is not to punish debtors but to protect them from their creditors, as well as to protect the creditors themselves from an unseemly scramble for the assets. **24–076**

The petition

The process begins with a petition to the court made by one of a number of people: by the debtor, by a creditor or creditors jointly, or by the supervisor of, or a person bound by, an approved voluntary arrangement.[40] **24–077**

Debtor's petition. A debtor may view bankruptcy as a refuge from creditors, and may bring a petition him- or herself. The only ground is that the debtor is unable to pay his or her debts.[41] The petition must be accompanied by a statement of the debtor's affairs. **24–078**

Creditor's petition. A creditor who petitions must do so in respect of debts owed by the debtor which meet the requirements set out in the IA 1986. Debts must be equal to the "bankruptcy level" (a statutory minimum figure, at present £750), for a liquidated sum payable to the creditor either immediately or at some certain future time (this excludes contingent and unliquidated debts), they must be unsecured, and must be debts which the debtor is either unable to pay or has no reasonable prospect of being able to pay. The debtor's inability to pay a particular debt can be shown either by the petitioning creditor serving a demand on the debtor requiring payment (a *statutory demand*) which is not complied with,[42] or by the execution of a judgment debt by the creditor which is unsatisfied. The requirements for a statutory demand are more flexible than they used to be,[43] to avoid spurious technical arguments from debtors, who now have to show that they suffer some real prejudice from a defect in the statutory **24–079**

---

[40] IA 1986, s. 264. Formerly, in criminal bankruptcy cases, it would have been made by the Official Petitioner, but criminal bankruptcy is to be abolished on a day to be appointed (CJA 1988, Sched. 16).

[41] IA 1986, s. 272.

[42] See *Re A debtor (No. 544/5D/98)* [2000] 1 B.C.L.C. 103.

[43] In *Re A Debtor (No. 1 of 1987)* [1989] 2 All E.R. 46, CA, Nicholls L.J. set out principles (approved in *Re Smith (a Bankrupt) ex p. Braintree D.C.* [1990] 2 A.C. 215). See *e.g. Re A Debtor (Nos 49 and 50 of 1992)* [1995] Ch. 66; *Re A Debtor (No. 51- SD- 1991)* [1992] 1 W.L.R. 1294; *Re A Debtor (No. 490-SD–1991)* [1992] 1 W.L.R. 507; *Re A Debtor (No. 657-SD–91)* [1993] B.C.L.C. 180.

demand, although a demand drawn up by a bank, for example, should certainly not be slipshod.[44]

24–080 **Secured creditors.**[45] A creditor who holds security over the debtor's property[46]) may only petition if it is willing to surrender the security for the benefit of all the bankrupt's creditors[47]; or does not make the petition in respect of the secured part of the debt, and gives an estimate of the value of the security at the date of the petition (the secured and unsecured parts of the debt are treated as separate debts)[48]; or realises the security and then petitions if there is a deficit after deducting the amount realised.[49]

24–081 **After the petition and before the bankruptcy order.** In the interval between the petition and the bankruptcy order, proceedings and execution against the debtor may be stayed[50]; certain dispositions and dealings with the debtor's property may be affected[51] from the date of the petition (if a bankruptcy order is subsequently made) and an interim receiver of the debtor's property (the official receiver) may be appointed if it is necessary for the protection of the debtor's property.

The bankruptcy order

24–082 The court must be satisfied when it makes an order[52] that the debt on which the petition is based is either payable at the time of the hearing and has not been paid (or secured or compounded), or that it is a debt which the debtor has no reasonable prospect of being able to pay when it falls due. The petition may be dismissed if the court is satisfied that the debtor is able to pay all his or her debts, including contingent and prospective liabilities, or that he or she has made an offer to secure or compound for a debt on which the petition is based, that acceptance of the offer would have required the dismissal of the petition, and that the offer has been unreasonably refused.[53]

---

[44] Nor designed to defeat a fair settlement in some way: in *Re Mordant* [1995] B.C.C. 209, a building society set in motion bankruptcy proceedings against a husband with a view to thwarting the award of a lump sum payment to the wife in pending proceedings. Because it was trying to take advantage of different sets of proceedings in different courts and taking care not to tell the wife it was doing so, it was ordered to pay the wife's costs.

[45] See further below, para. 24–151. Security means mortgage, charge, lien or other security, though not a lien on books, papers or other records unless they are documents of title to property and held as such, IA 1986, s. 383(2) and (4).

[46] This does not include third party securities. IA 1986, s. 383(2).

[47] IA 1986, s. 383(3).

[48] IA 1986, s. 269(2).

[49] IA 1986, s. 267(2).

[50] IA 1986, s. 285. There is special provision for a landlord's rights to rent, IA 1986, s. 347.

[51] See below, paras 24–136 *et seq*.

[52] Special procedures are available for small estates, and these may result in a court sponsored voluntary arrangement, or a certificate for the summary administration of the estate, IA 1986, ss. 273–276.

[53] IA 1986, s. 271. *Re A Debtor (No. 2389 of 1989)* [1991] Ch. 326; *Re A Debtor (No. 32 of 1993)* [1994] 1 W.L.R. 899.

Annulment. The court has powers to annul a bankruptcy order in certain cases (even after an apparent "discharge").[54] 24–083

Effect of bankruptcy

The bankruptcy commences when the order is made,[55] and continues until discharge. If there has been an interim receivership,[56] it is terminated by the bankruptcy order. Notice that the order has been made must be sent to the Chief Land Registrar for registration in the Register of Writs and Orders affecting land, and the order must be advertised in a local paper and must be gazetted.[57] A trustee will probably be appointed if there are assets to be distributed but if there is no appointment or the trustee does not accept the appointment by the time specified in the certificate of appointment,[58] the official receiver is trustee. The bankrupt's estate vests in the trustee, and after the bankruptcy order no person who has a provable debt can take action against the bankrupt before discharge unless the court gives leave.[59] Bankrupts themselves may bring actions, however, (provided the actions do not relate to their property), and they have capacity and authority to retain a solicitor for the purpose.[60] 24–084

The trustee. Where there are assets to be realised for the benefit of creditors, a trustee, who must be a qualified insolvency practitioner, will probably be appointed. The appointment may be made by a meeting of creditors or by the Department of Trade and Industry or the court.[61] 24–085

The official receiver. The official receiver will become receiver and manager of the estate if there is no trustee, and has a duty to protect the bankrupt's estate and any property which may be claimed for the estate by the trustee. The official receiver may sell or dispose of any goods which may diminish in value, and is protected if he or she wrongly, but not negligently, seizes property not belonging to the debtor.[62] The official receiver investigates the conduct and affairs of the bankrupt, who must co-operate (the penalty is contempt of court) and provide him or her with specified information, and attend when reasonably required. The official receiver may report to the court, and may apply to the court for the public examination of the bankrupt in court at any time before the discharge of the bankrupt.[63] 24–086

---

[54] IA 1986, ss. 282 and 260–261.
[55] IA 1986, s. 278.
[56] IA 1986, s. 286.
[57] IR 1986, r. 6.34.
[58] IA 1986, s. 292.
[59] IA 1986, s. 285.
[60] *Nelson v. Nelson, The Times*, January 8, 1997.
[61] IA 1986, ss. 292–297.
[62] IA 1986, s. 287.
[63] And is obliged to do so if required to do so by the creditors, unless the court orders otherwise, IA 1986, s. 290. As to the official receivers immunity from suit, see *Mond v. Hyde* [1998] 3 All E.R. 833, CA.

24–087 **Final meeting of creditors.** Once it appears to the trustee (this does not apply to the official receiver) that the administration of the estate is for practical purposes complete, he or she summons a final general meeting of creditors to receive the trustee's report of the administration and to decide if he or she should be released.[64]

Discharge

24–088 The effect of discharge is that the bankrupt is released from all the bankruptcy debts to which he or she was subject at the commencement or to which he or she became subject because of an obligation incurred prior to commencement.[65] It normally occurs automatically three years from commencement,[66] although the court may suspend the running of time for a period or until specified conditions are fulfilled.

Discharge does not affect the right of a secured creditor to enforce its security for a released debt, nor the right of an unsecured creditor to prove in the bankruptcy for a bankruptcy debt, and the trustee may continue to carry out his or her unfulfilled functions, for example in relation to the estate. Similarly, the bankrupt's liability for criminal penalties such as fines, debts arising under family or domestic proceedings, debts incurred by fraud, and damages in respect of personal injuries are not affected. The bankrupt's release does not release any other person (such as a partner, or co-trustee or surety for the bankrupt) from their liabilities.[67]

Bankruptcy offences and penalties

24–089 There are numerous offences[68] which a bankrupt may commit and for which he or she may be fined or imprisoned, some of which require an intent to defraud or to conceal the state of his or her affairs. They include failure to disclose property or its disposal, or to hand over property to the trustee, or concealment, removal or failure to account for loss of any debt or property; failure to deliver up books and records; misinforming the trustee; fraudulently disposing of property; obtaining credit exceeding £250 and not revealing that he or she is bankrupt; engaging in business under a different name without disclosing it; carrying on business without proper accounts.

24–090 **Disqualification from public office.** An undischarged bankrupt is disqualified from being elected to, sitting or voting in the House of Lords or the House of Commons. Elected members of the Commons must vacate their seats at the end of a period of six months disqualification.[69]

---

[64] IA 1986, ss. 315–319.
[65] IA 1986, s. 382.
[66] IA 1986, ss. 278–280. One of the reforms of the 1986 Act.
[67] IA 1986, s. 281(7).
[68] IA 1986, ss. 350–362.
[69] IA 1986, s. 427.

Functions and Powers of Trustee

The debtor's property vests automatically in the trustee in bankruptcy.[70] Trustees must get in, realise and distribute the estate in accordance with the IA 1986, using their own discretion[71] and co-operating with the official receiver. They may summon a general meeting of the creditors at any time and must do so if requested to do so by the creditors.[72] A meeting of creditors may establish a committee to exercise various functions like those of the committee in a winding up. Trustees may exercise some of their powers[73] without sanction and others with the consent of the committee or the court; if consent is required, however, it must be given in relation to specific actions; it cannot merely be a general permission. If trustees act without permission, their acts may be ratified by the court (or by the committee, if they act in an emergency and seek ratification promptly). Third parties like banks who deal with trustees in good faith and for value are protected in any case, since they are not concerned to see that consent has been given.[74] **24–091**

Every bankruptcy is under the general control of the court, which has full power to decide all questions of priority and of law and fact, and which may give binding directions to the bankrupt.[75] The trustee may apply to the court for directions, and, if the bankrupt or a creditor or any other person is dissatisfied with decisions of the trustee, he or she may apply to the court, which may give the trustee such directions as it thinks fit. If the trustee has negligently misapplied money or property of the bankrupt or is guilty of misfeasance or breach of fiduciary duty,[76] the court may order the trustee to restore or account for the money or property.[77] The trustee may be removed by the court or by a meeting of creditors summoned specially for the purpose.[78] **24–092**

Investigation and seizure of property. The bankrupt must deliver up books, records, and papers to the trustee,[79] must give the trustee any information reasonably required (for example about property he or she has acquired, or any increase in income) and must attend on the trustee at such times and do such acts as he or she reasonably requires.[80] This applies even after discharge, and it is contempt of court not to comply.[81] The trustee, unlike a **24–093**

[70] By IA 1986, s. 306.
[71] IA 1986, s. 305(2).
[72] Listed in IA 1986, s. 314 and Sched. 5.
[73] IA 1986, s. 314(3).
[74] IA 1986, s. 314(7).
[75] IA 1986, s. 363.
[76] See *Re Corbenstoke (No. 2)* [1990] B.C.L.C. 60, where there were impossible conflicts of interest.
[77] IA 1986, s. 304.
[78] IA 1986, s. 398: see *Re Sankey Furniture Ltd, ex p. Betts* [1995] 2 B.C.L.C. 594.
[79] IA 1986, s. 312(1–2).
[80] IA 1986, s. 333.
[81] The trustee is treated as a receiver appointed by the High Court, and is therefore an officer of the court (to which he or she may apply for assistance).

liquidator, has powers to break in and enter premises and to issue a search warrant.

Third parties like banks, who hold property for the bankrupt must pay or deliver any of it which is part of the estate and which they are not entitled to retain to the trustee.[82] A bank can, of course, exercise a right of lien or set-off, or a valid security right under a pledge, and if it has a receiver in possession, can retain possession. If goods are held by way of pledge or other security, however, the trustee may serve a notice to inspect them and may redeem them in any case.[83] Interference with the trustee taking control of the estate is contempt of court.

24–094 Office holders who seize or dispose of the wrong property are given protection provided that they had reasonable ground to believe that they were entitled to seize or dispose of it. They have a lien on the property or its proceeds for their expenses of sale or seizure,[84] although they are liable for losses they negligently cause to the property. There are provisions enabling trustees to disclaim onerous property.[85]

The powers of the trustee include the draconian power to apply to the court for a private examination or production of documents (under section 366 of the IA 1986) and, like other office holders, they may thereby compel disclosure of confidential information by banks and other third parties.[86]

The bankrupt's estate

24–095 Individuals, unlike companies, must be allowed the necessities of life for themselves and their families, and the IA 1986 accordingly provides for the bankrupt to retain some assets.

24–096 **(a) Property originally owned.** The bankrupt's estate[87] immediately vests in the trustee or the official receiver without any conveyance, assignment or transfer.[88] The estate does not include property held on trust for another person,[89] nor property subject to the rights of a third party such as a hirer of goods, a tenant of property, or a secured creditor (unless the secured creditor has given up its rights in accordance with the rules[90]).

The estate also does not include tools, books, vehicles and other items needed for the bankrupt's employment; or clothing, bedding, furniture,

---

[82] IA 1986, s. 312(3).
[83] IA 1986, s. 311(5).
[84] IA 1986, s. 234(3–4), 304(3–4).
[85] IA 1986, ss. 315–321. See *Hindcastle Ltd. v. Barbara Attenborough Association Ltd* [1988] 1 All E.R. 737, *per* Lord Nicholls.
[86] See above, para. 24–060.
[87] IA 1986, s. 283. See *Bristol Airport plc v. Powdrill* [1990] Ch. 744 at 759, CA, and *Re Landau (A Bankrupt)* [1998] Ch. 223.
[88] IA 1986, s. 306.
[89] IA 1986, s. 283(3).
[90] Under IA 1986, s. 269.

household equipment and provisions which the bankrupt and his or her family need for basic domestic use,[91] although the trustee can claim even that property if it is too valuable, by serving a notice and buying a reasonable replacement. This duty has priority over the obligation to distribute the estate to creditors.[92]

When property has been recovered after an order has been made setting aside transactions,[93] such as preferences or transactions at an undervalue, it is treated as falling within the bankrupt's property.

(b) After-acquired property.[94] Property acquired by the bankrupt after the commencement of the bankruptcy does not automatically vest in the trustee, but may be claimed by the trustee serving notice, and the property will then vest in the trustee, whose title relates back to the time when the bankrupt acquired the property. If a bona fide purchaser for value has acquired the property without notice of the bankruptcy, however, or a banker has entered into a transaction in good faith and without notice, the trustee has no remedy against him or her or others deriving title through him or her. **24–097**

(c) Income payments.[95] The trustee may apply to the court for an "income payments order" claiming any income (including payments from the carrying on of any business or from any office or employment) earned by the bankrupt. The order must not reduce the bankrupt's income below what appears to the court necessary for meeting the reasonable domestic needs of the bankrupt and his or her family.[96] **24–098**

(d) The bankrupt's house. The bankrupt's dwelling house, which is often the most substantial asset in the estate, is liable to be sold by the trustee. This may be done by application to the court[97] under section 14 of the TLATA 1996,[98] which allows any person having an interest in the property to apply for an order relating to the exercise of the powers of the trustees. **24–099**

A new section,[99] (335A), in the IA 1986 gives the court the power to make such order as it thinks just and reasonable, having regard to the following factors: **24–100**

---

[91] IA 1986, s. 283(2).

[92] IA 1986, ss. 308–309.

[93] Under IA 1986, ss. 284, 342, 343, 344, 346, 347 and 425. With regard to property confiscated under the CJA 1988 or the DTA 1994, see Muir Hunter, *Personal Insolvency* para. 3–147.

[94] IA 1986, s. 307.

[95] IA 1986, s. 310.

[96] This may even include private school payments if a child would be placed at disadvantage if moved at the time: *Re Rayatt, The Times*, May 4, 1998.

[97] To the court which has jurisdiction in bankruptcy, s. 335A of the IA 1986. In *Zandfarid v. BCCI* [1996] 1 W.L.R. 1420, it was held that where the wife of a debtor was taking proceedings under s. 30 of the LPA 1925 for a share of the matrimonial home, it was not an abuse of process for the creditor to waive its security in order to be able to proceed under the bankruptcy regime. The approach of the court would be the same in either case.

[98] Replacing LPA 1925, s. 30, which has been repealed.

[99] Inserted by TLATA 1996, Sched. 3, para. 23.

(a) The interests of the bankrupt's creditors;

(b) Where the property includes a dwelling house, which is the home of the bankrupt or the spouse or former spouse of the bankrupt, these factors must be taken into account:

  (i) the conduct of the spouse, so far as it has contributed to the bankruptcy;

  (ii) the needs and financial resources of the spouse;

  (iii) the needs of any children.

(c) All the circumstances of the case, other than the needs of the bankrupt.

24–101 After one year, beginning with the vesting of the estate in the trustee (and trustees in many bankruptcies will not be in a position to consider sale of the family home until a year or more after starting to deal with the property) the court is to assume that the interests of the bankrupt's creditors outweigh all other considerations, unless the circumstances of the case are exceptional.

The court will probably allow the sale of the property at the instance of the trustee, and will almost certainly do so if a year has passed since the property has vested in him or her. The only way in which the bankrupt's family can avoid sale after a year, is to demonstrate that there is some "exceptional circumstance" justifying delay of the sale. Although by case law under the earlier legislation, that was difficult to establish (it was not an exceptional circumstance, for example, that the wife and children will be evicted, or that the bankruptcy expenses would exceed the proceeds of sale,[2] these are indications that there will be a more flexible approach which will work to the benefit of families and the detriment of banks under the new provisions.[2a]

24–102 Some judges have been sympathetic to the hardship caused to the bankrupt's family.[3] In *Re Mott*,[4] Hoffmann J. held that the fact that the bankrupt's mother, who lived in the home, was elderly and sick constituted extreme hardship, and in *Re Raval*,[5] the serious mental illness of the wife which might have been exacerbated by enforced rehousing, prompted the court to delay the order for possession and sale for six months. Again, in *Judd v. Brown*,[6] the serious illness of the wife and the likely adverse effect

[1] *Re Citro* [1990] 3 All E.R. 952, CA.

[2] *Trustee of Estate of Bowe (A Bankrupt) v. Bowe* [1997] B.P.I.R. 747.

[2a] See *Mortgage Corporation v. Shaire*, *The Times*, March 21, 2000, Ch D.

[3] See *Re Holliday* [1981] 2 W.L.R. 996, CA, where a husband petitioned for bankruptcy to prevent a wife obtaining a property order on divorce and the court held that sale would be delayed until the children were 17.

[4] [1987] C.L.Y. 212. See also *Claughton v. Charalamasons* [1999] 1 F.L.R. 740; *Re Bremner (a bankrupt)* [1999] 1 F.L.R. 912.

[5] [1998] C.L.Y. 324 (from transcript).

[6] [1997] B.P.I.R. 470; [1997] C.L.Y. 3015, *per* Harman J. The case also raised the possibility of the wife's equity of exoneration (which might increase the amount of the wife's claim). For the equity of exoneration see further *Re Pittortou* [1985] 1 All E.R. 285, and Grier and Floyd, *Personal Insolvency*, p. 112.

of even a postponed order for possession were held to be exceptional circumstances and it was said that an order for possession or sale of the house ought not to be granted. Another reason for delaying sale is that the court may allow time for legal proceedings to be brought by a spouse who might have a good chance of buying out the trustee if the claim succeeds. This plea is unlikely to be successful, however, unless proceedings are imminent and the chances of winning the action are high.[7]

If the spouse of the bankrupt is not a co-owner of the property, his or her matrimonial home rights[8] are protected by the IA 1986, which provides that where the rights of a non-owner spouse are a charge on the estate or interest of the other spouse (who is bankrupt), the charge continues to exist and binds the trustee.[9] Such a charge must exist at the time of the petition; no new rights of occupation can arise after that. If the trustee wishes to sell the property, therefore, he or she should first negotiate with the spouse to purchase the spouse's claim in the property. **24–103**

Where the house is occupied by the bankrupt or the spouse or former spouse and the trustee is unable for some reason to realise the property for the time being, the trustee may end his or her supervision and administration of the property by applying to the court for an order charging the property. The house then vests in the bankrupt again subject to the charge and the estate (the creditors) have the benefit of the charge.[10] If the bankrupt were to sell the house, the charge would bind the purchasers, who should pay the trustee. This provision may be useful where there are exceptional circumstances allowing the family to remain in the home, or where the trustee does not have adequate funds to litigate with the bankrupt's spouse. **24–104**

Where premises are occupied by a bankrupt on condition of payment by him or her towards liability under a mortgage or other outgoings, the bankrupt does not acquire any interest in the property by virtue of making the payments.[11]

Invalid Transactions

There are a number of provisions in the Act designed to prevent abuse by debtors and to achieve a fair distribution of a debtor's property among the creditors,[12] by giving the court power to set aside transactions made by debtors which would allow some creditors to obtain an unfair advantage over others.[13] **24–105**

[7] See *Re Gorman (A Bankrupt)* [1990] 1 W.L.R. 616; cf. *Re Lowrie* [1981] 3 All E.R. 353. See also *Trustee of Estate of Bowe* [1997] B.P.I.R. 747.

[8] Under part IV of the Family Law Act 1996 (with effect from October 1, 1997).

[9] IA 1986, s. 336(2).

[10] IA 1986, s. 313.

[11] IA 1986, s. 338.

[12] *Re Paramount Airways Ltd (in liq.) No. 2* [1993] Ch. 223 at 230, 233, *per* Nicholls V.-C.

[13] These include IA 1986, s. 245, dealing with the invalidity of floating charges in some circumstances, which is discussed above in Chap. 19.

Transactions at an Undervalue

24–106 If a debtor company[14] or individual[15] *makes a gift to or enters a transaction with another party whereby the debtor receives no consideration, or, alternatively, receives a consideration which is significantly less in value in money or money's worth*[16] *than the consideration it provides*, the transaction will be set aside if it takes place within a limited period before the winding-up or bankruptcy, and at a time when the debtor is unable to pay its debts or if it becomes unable to do so as a result of the transaction.[17] In the case of a company debtor, the period is two years, and in that of an individual debtor it is five years, before the date of the petition for bankruptcy if the debtor was insolvent at the time of the transaction; for individuals, transactions at an undervalue made within two years before the petition are set aside whether the individual was solvent at the time or not. In both company and individual insolvency, inability to pay debts is presumed if the transaction is with a connected person of a company[18] (which includes a shadow director) or an associate, unless the contrary is proved.[19]

24–107 In the case of a company debtor, there is a possible defence: the court will not make an order if the company can show that it entered the transaction in good faith and for the purpose of carrying on its business, if there were reasonable grounds for believing that the transaction would benefit the company at the time it did so.[20]

The court looks at the whole of the transaction between the parties, not merely at the consideration stated. The liquidator has to show that there was a significant difference between the values of the consideration received by the debtor and that given by the debtor by making a comparison between the two values, in money or money's worth, from the company's point of view.[21] It may not be easy to identify the consideration, bearing in mind that past consideration is not good consideration, although it may be that the continuation of banking facilities would be regarded as a

[14] IA 1986, ss. 238–240.

[15] IA 1986, ss. 339–341. For consideration of the jurisdiction (geographical) of these provisions, see *Re Paramount Airway Ltd (in liq.) (No 2)* [1993] Ch. 223, CA.

[16] The consideration of marriage for an individual debtor is an undervalue, s. 339(3)(b).

[17] IA 1986, s. 240.

[18] A director or shadow director of the company, an associate of these, or an associate of the company: IA 1986, s. 249.

[19] "Associate" is widely defined; it includes spouses, relatives, partners (and their spouses or relatives), trustees who may benefit under a trust, employees (including directors), and controllers of companies. Two companies are associates if the same person controls both, or controls one and his or her associates the other, and in other cases, IA 1986, s. 435.

[20] IA 1986, s. 238(5).

[21] *Re MC Bacon Ltd* [1990] B.C.L.C. 324 applied in *National Bank of Kuwait v. Menzies* [1994] 2 B.C.L.C. 306 at 319, CA and *Agricultural Mortgage Corporation plc v. Woodward* [1995] 1 B.C.L.C. 1 at 5, CA; see also *Re Kumar* [1993] B.C.L.C. 548; *Arbuthnot Leasing International Ltd v. Havelet Leasing* [1990] B.C.L.C. 802 and *Philips v. Brewin Dolphin Bell Lowrie Ltd* [1999] 2 All E.R. 844, CA. In *National Westminster Bank plc. v. Jones, The Times*, July 7, 2000, Ch D, it was held that a transaction prejudicing only one creditor may be set aside.

benefit provided to the company. It may also be difficult to assess the monetary value of transactions in which banks are involved, such as charges and guarantees, and to see whether they are "significantly less" than the consideration given by the debtor. The benefit in taking and granting a charge may appear intangible, or too unpredictable to value accurately.[22]

In *Re M.C. Bacon*,[23] a company secured its overdraft by a debenture shortly before its liquidation. Millett J. held that the statutory provision is concerned with the depletion of the company's assets. Granting a debenture is not a gift, however, nor is it without consideration. The consideration given to the company consisted of the bank's forbearance from calling in the overdraft and its honouring of cheques and making fresh advances to the company during the continuance of the facility. Alternatively, assessed by the standard of the second requirement—that the consideration provided by the company might be significantly less than that provided by the creditor—the mere creation of a security over a company's assets does not deplete them, and therefore does not come within the requirement. The judge's view was that the company's appropriation of the assets to the secured creditor may adversely affect the rights of other creditors in the event of insolvency, but does not deplete the company's assets or diminish their value. The mere fact that the company loses the ability to apply the proceeds otherwise than in satisfaction of the secured debt is not something capable of valuation in monetary terms and is not customarily disposed of for value. In this case, the transaction did not fall within the requirements of the subsection. **24–108**

This view is reassuring for banks. It is supported by Professor Goode, who sets out illustrations from a hypothetical balance sheet to demonstrate the correctness of the judge's argument that the net balance sheet figures of a debtor company would be unchanged by granting a debenture.[24] Nevertheless, the judge's reasoning has given rise to some doubt.[25] By granting the debenture, the company has "lost the ability to apply the proceeds otherwise" (as the judge described it): this could be taken to be an economic disadvantage which might in other contexts be regarded as consideration. Moreover, the view that the section is concerned with "the depletion of a company's assets" and "from the company's point of view" might be said to emphasise a rather technical "balance sheet" approach to the section, rather than emphasising that the concern of the law may be justifiably regarded as the depletion of the company's assets from the point of view of the unsecured creditors, as well as from the point of view of the company itself, since giving security to one of the creditors adversely affects the rights of the others. **24–109**

[22] See Goode, *Legal Problems of Credit and Security*, p. 207.
[23] [1990] B.C.L.C. 324.
[24] Goode, *P.C.I.L.*, p. 370.
[25] See Paget, *Law of Banking* (11th ed.), p. 210.

Guarantees. A guarantee may amount to an undervalue on the insolvency of the guarantor if it is given within the relevant period, and the *guarantor has either received no consideration* or *the transaction is for a consideration significantly less than the value of the consideration given by him or her*. The transaction may satisfy the second of these requirements (but probably not the first, because the guarantor does not usually receive the consideration in any case) in that the consideration may be that *the debtor* is afforded time to pay. In the case of a guarantee, the value of the consideration will be extremely difficult to assess, because so much will depend upon the creditworthiness of the guarantor at the time the guarantee is given (which is the relevant time for assessing whether there has been an undervalue, not the date when the guarantor becomes liable).

24–110 If the guarantor is a company, the bank will be protected by the defence in section 238(5) of the IA 1986 if the guarantor entered the transaction "in good faith and for the purpose of carrying on its business" and that at the time there were reasonable grounds for believing that the transaction would benefit the company. For example, a transaction where one company in a group gives a guarantee and security to a bank on behalf of another company in the group,[26] or promotional offers made at a nominal consideration, or free, which would otherwise be undervalues, may be protected by this provision. This reflects the aim of the prohibition of undervalues—to prevent transactions which are unfair, not those which merely might have been negotiated on more profitable terms for the company.[27] If the guarantor is an individual, however, the defence will not operate, and if neither the guarantor or the debtor has received any, or adequate, consideration, a guarantee given within six months of the bankruptcy of the guarantor is vulnerable.

Voidable Preferences

24–111 A preference is given *where an insolvent debtor does anything* or *suffers anything to be done which has the effect of putting one of his or her creditors or guarantors into a position if the debtor is eventually wound up or is bankrupt which will be better than if that thing had not been done*. Insolvency means that if the company is unable to pay its debts at the time, or becomes unable to pay its debts because of the preference or that an individual was insolvent (that is, is unable to pay debts as they fall due or the value of assets is less than the amount of liabilities, taking into account contingent and prospective liabilities. The debtor must have been influenced by a desire to put that person into a better position, and the action must have taken place within a limited period before the winding up or bankruptcy.

[26] *Charterbridge Corpn. Ltd v. Lloyds Bank Ltd* [1970] Ch. 62, though see *Rolled Steel Products Ltd v. B.S.C.* [1986] Ch. 246.

[27] Pennington, *op. cit.*, p. 225.

The rule applies even if the debtor believes him or herself to be solvent. A transaction can be set aside for this reason if the act or forbearance took place less than six months before the start of the winding up or bankruptcy, or less than two years if the preference was given to a connected person (of a company, which includes a shadow director), or given to an associate (of an individual bankrupt). In certain circumstances—where the person who receives the preference is connected with or an associate of the company debtor, or is an associate of the individual debtor[28]—the motive to prefer is presumed.[29]

Third parties have a defence against the transaction being set aside: the order must not prejudice any interest in property they have acquired from someone other than the debtor if they acquired it in good faith and for value.[30] A third party who has notice of the relevant circumstances[31] will be presumed not to be in good faith. **24–112**

Preferences require a recipient, an effect, and a motive. The *recipient* of the preference is a creditor or guarantor of the debtor's liabilities. It is not necessary that the person preferred is the person paid; for example, a debtor may make a payment to a bank to reduce a guarantor's liability to the bank, in which case it is the guarantor who is preferred.[32] The *effect* occurs where the debtor does or allows anything to be done which has the effect of putting the recipient into a better position. The use of the word "preference" does not mean that the debtor must literally prefer one creditor over another, only that the creditor "preferred" has its position improved over what it would have been otherwise. The *motive* to be shown is that the debtor was influenced in deciding to give it by a desire to produce the effect of a preference.

This requirement—influenced by a desire to prefer—is a striking reformulation of the motive (which used to be *dominant intention* to prefer), and the meaning of *desire* in this context was considered in depth in the case of *M.C.Bacon Ltd*.[33] The judge, Millett J., emphasised the novelty of the test, and pointed out that the word "desire" introduces a subjective element, although its existence may be inferred from the circumstances. The mere fact that the debtor *knows of* the effect of the transaction is not in itself enough; the debtor must positively wish to improve the creditor's position in the event of his or her own insolvency and this desire must have **24–113**

---

[28] IA 1986, ss. 249 and 435.

[29] IA 1986, ss. 239(6) and 340(5).

[30] IA 1986, ss. 241(2), as amended by the Insolvency (No. 2) Act 1994, s. 1(1).

[31] Probably actual notice—Pennington, *op. cit.* p. 232.

[32] See below, para. 24–118.

[33] [1990] B.C.C. 78. See also *Re Fairway Magazines Ltd* [1993] B.C.L.C. 643, and *Re Ledingham-Smith (a bankrupt)* [1993] B.C.L.C. 635, and *Re Agriplant Services Ltd* [1997] 2 B.C.L.C. 598. See also *Re Exchange Travel (Holdings) Ltd (No. 3)* [1996] 2 B.C.L.C. 524 (where it was not a preference: the debtor's concern was that the store would look "more like a morgue than a market" in its final weeks of trading just before Christmas); and *Re Lewis's of Leicester Ltd* [1995] B.C.C. 213.

influenced the decision, although it need not have been the only or the decisive influence.[34] In *Re MC Bacon* itself, where, as we saw above, a company secured its overdraft by a debenture shortly before its liquidation, the debenture was not set aside as a preference because the directors had not been influenced by any other desire than to avoid the bank calling in the overdraft and to continue trading. Their actions were not influenced by a desire to improve the bank's position in the event of the company's insolvency. It is still possible, therefore, for a bank to provide assistance to an ailing company by taking a charge or guarantee, provided the company is actuated only by proper commercial considerations.[35] The same is presumably true as far as individual debtors are concerned.

24–114 Normally, payment to secured creditors will not be a preference, because payment makes no change in the value of the assets available to the general body of creditors on insolvency; the secured creditor is still entitled to payment or to enforce its security on insolvency. However, there are one or two situations where payment to a secured creditor may be vulnerable. If the payment exceeds the value of the security; if the security would have been void (for example, for non-registration); and where the security is a floating charge, and at the time of the payment, there is not enough to repay the preferential creditors, who have priority over the floating chargeholder.[36]

24–115 An act or forbearance may be a preference even if the action or omission is done by order of a court[37]—this may be to prevent debtors acquiescing in legal actions by particular creditors; but it is not a preference if a company exercises a right of set-off against one of its creditors which is indebted to the company, and this results in the creditor being paid.

The fact that in certain circumstances—where the person who receives the preference is connected with the company debtor—the motive to prefer is presumed may pose a particular risk for banks. "Connected person" includes *shadow directors*, and banks may sometimes be regarded as shadow directors[38] of companies with which they have been involved financially—say, if they have taken some part in management decisions, as banks frequently do. In that case even the advance of further funds in a rescue would be deemed to be a preference and the bank would have to prove the contrary.

24–116 **Powers of the court.** Once it is established that a preference is wrongful, the court has a wide jurisdiction to restore the company to the position it would have been in if the transaction had not taken place. It may make a variety

[34] See discussion in Keay [1999] C.fi. L.R. 198.
[35] [1990] B.C.L.C. 324 at 336.
[36] Goode, *P.C.I.L.*, p. 395.
[37] IA 1986, ss. 239 and 340.
[38] See above, para. 24–072.

of orders[39]: for example, that the property or its proceeds be re-transferred or vested in the company or the trustee, that security given by the debtor be released or discharged, or that payments be made to the debtor.

The court may also make orders against persons who are not the ones preferred. If, say, the debtor paid a debt to its bank, thus releasing a guarantor from liability, the court may order the *bank* (which has not been preferred) to repay, and the *guarantor* whose obligations were released or discharged to be under new or revived obligations if appropriate. The obligation can be charged on property if necessary, and the charge may be given the same priority as the security which has been released or discharged. The court may make orders as to the extent to which a person, affected by orders relating to property or imposing obligations, is to be allowed to prove in the liquidation or bankruptcy in respect of debts or liabilities arising in this way.

There is protection, however, for third parties (which would include **24–117** banks in some situations) who have obtained an interest in property where the transaction is set aside by the court: an order made by the court must not prejudice any interest in property which was acquired by a third party in good faith and for value or prejudice any interest deriving from such an interest.[40]

Guarantees. On the *guarantor's* insolvency, the guarantee may be a **24–118** preference if it was given during the relevant period and at a time when the guarantor was unable to pay its debts, or became unable to pay the debts in consequence of giving the guarantee. Although it seems unlikely that a guarantee would be taken from the guarantor if it is unable to pay its debts, this may be a possibility in company inter-group guarantees.

For the guarantee to be set aside, it would be necessary for the bank to be the guarantor's creditor (or guarantor), which would be unusual; the nature of the transaction is that the bank is normally the *debtor's* creditor, not the guarantor's. For this reason, it is unlikely that many guarantees would amount to preferences. Moreover, the guarantee would only be invalidated if it were to put the bank in a "better position" in the guarantor's insolvency, whereas, again the likelihood is that, unless secured, it puts the bank in a better position as against the *debtor*, not the guarantor.

On the *debtor's* insolvency, the problem is that if the debtor, contemplat- **24–119** ing insolvency, pays money to the bank with the intention of favouring the guarantor, that intention is enough to amount to a preference, even though there is no intention to prefer *the bank*.[41] Further, if the guarantor is

[39] IA 1986, ss. 241 and 342.

[40] IA 1986, ss. 241(2) and 342(2). Formerly the third party was also required to have taken it "without notice of the relevant circumstances": this was altered by the Insolvency Act (No. 2) 1994.

[41] There may be such an intention: see *R.F.P. & C.H. Matthews Ltd* [1982] Ch. 257.

connected with, or an associate of, the debtor (as a member of a group may be) the debtor's intention to prefer the guarantor is presumed. Nevertheless, it is the bank and not the guarantor which must refund the payments.[42]

As third party, the bank may have the defence mentioned above that the order must not prejudice any interest in property acquired by it from someone other than the debtor if it acquired the interest in good faith, for value and without notice of the relevant circumstances,[43] which would normally be the case. A bank creditor who innocently receives money from a debtor into an overdrawn account (since that is "for value") where the debtor intends to prefer a guarantor or surety is probably protected by this provision. If the bank is not innocent, however, and has to repay the money, the court could order the guarantor's obligations to revive.

24–120 If there is a preference, it seems that the payment to the bank is valid and the guarantor has been discharged from liability unless and until the guarantor's liability is *revived* by the court. Most bank forms, however, expressly provide that the guarantor *remains* liable, and that the bank may retain the guarantee for a period of six months, or for two years if the guarantor is connected with the debtor (this is in order to avoid problems of proof). If the bank has merely been holding the guarantor's securities without having a personal promise to repay from the guarantor, the bank may have given up the security at the end of the six month period, and, if so, the court may renew the security.

Invalidity of Floating Charges under Section 245

24–121 It will be recalled that floating charges (not fixed charges) are subject to a rule under which they may be void to the extent that they are not given for fresh consideration. This is considered in Chapter 19 above.

Transactions Defrauding Creditors (Fraudulent Undervalues)

24–122 The IA 1986 also invalidates "fraudulent undervalues".[44] These are transactions (with either company or individual debtors) at an undervalue where the purpose of the transaction is either to put assets beyond the reach of a person who is making, or who may make, a claim against the debtor, or to prejudice the interests of a person claiming in some other way. There is no need to prove actual fraud or dishonesty, only the existence of one of these two purposes. In the case of a company, it is thought that the purpose must be the purpose of those who make the decision to enter the transaction (directors or other persons with some sort of authority). Unlike ordinary transactions at an undervalue, there is no limitation as to the time

---

[42] *Re T.N. Barling & Co. Ltd* (1937) unreported, *Re Lyons, ex p. Barclays Bank Ltd v. Trustee* (1934) 152 L.R. 201; *Re Conley* [1938] 2 All E.R. 127.

[43] IA 1986, ss. 241(2), as amended by the Insolvency (No. 2) Act 1994, s. 1(1).

[44] IA 1986, ss. 423–25.

when the transaction was made. Further, application may be made even outside insolvency, in which case the classes of people who may apply for an order are much wider, and include any person prejudiced.

These provisions are important because they are so far reaching. They may allow a speedy application to the court to prevent assets being removed from the jurisdiction (like a Mareva (or freezing) injunction). They may be used to set aside a transaction where one company in a group of companies disposes of assets to another in the group, or to a nominee, and the transfer was not for bona fide commercial reasons, or to prevent a debtor giving assets to members of his or her family,[45] so that in the event of bankruptcy the assets will remain in the family. **24–123**

In *Agricultural Mortgage Corpn v. Woodward*,[46] the owner of a farm set up his wife as tenant of the farm at a market rent in order to preserve the farm from possession and sale by the bank: the fact that she was there as a sitting tenant reduced the value of the property by more than a half, and made it much less likely that the bank would be able to recover the debt and its costs from the property. This put the parties in a "ransom" situation, giving a benefit to the wife which was greater than the value in money or money's worth than the consideration she had given, and which prejudiced the position of the bank. The transaction was set aside. **24–124**

If a fraudulent undervalue is proved, the court can make an order to restore the position and to protect the interests of those who are, or who are capable of being, prejudiced.[47] The orders which the court may make are similar to those in relation to ordinary transactions at an undervalue or preferences, and with the same protection for parties who were not parties to the transaction and who acted in good faith and for value.

Avoidance of Assignments of Book Debts by Individual Bankrupt

If an individual engaged in business makes a general assignment of his or her existing or future book debts and is subsequently adjudged bankrupt, the assignment is void as against the trustee as regards any book debts which were not paid before the presentation of the petition unless the assignment was registered.[48] This provision does not apply to debts due at the date of the assignment from specified creditors or becoming due under specified contracts, or included either in a transfer of a business made in **24–125**

---

[45] See *Midland Bank v. Wyatt* [1997] 1 B.C.L.C. 242.

[46] [1995] 1 B.C.L.C. 1; see also *Barclays Bank v. Eustice* [1995] 2 B.C.L.C. 630.

[47] See *Arbuthnot Leasing International Ltd v. Havelet Leasing Ltd (No. 2)* [1991] 1 All E.R. 591; *Pinewood Joinery v. Starelm Properties Ltd* [1994] 2 B.C.L.C. 412; *Agricultural Mortgage plc v. Woodward* [1995] 1 B.C.L.C. 1; *Barclays Bank plc v. Eustice* [1995] 2 B.C.L.C. 630; *Chohan v. Saggar* [1993] B.C.L.C. 661; *Aiglon Ltd v. Gau Shan Co Ltd* [1993] B.C.L.C. 1321; *National Bank of Kuwait SAK v. Menzies* [1994] 2 B.C.L.C. 306, CA; *Agricultural Mortgage Corpn plc v. Woodward* [1995] 1 B.C.L.C. 1.

[48] Under the BSA 1878, IA 1986, s. 344. Unregistered charges over company property are also void.

good faith and for value, or in an assignment of assets for the benefit of creditors generally.

Extortionate Credit Transactions[49]

24–126 Where a debtor (company or individual) has been provided with credit, the liquidator or trustee may apply to the court for an order on the ground that the transaction was extortionate, provided that it was entered into during the three years before the commencement of liquidation or of the individual's bankruptcy.[50] It will be extortionate if, having regard to the risk accepted by the provider of the credit, either the terms of it are such as to require grossly exorbitant payments to be made (even conditionally), or it otherwise grossly contravenes ordinary principles of fair dealing. It is open to the provider of credit to prove that the transaction is not extortionate.

24–127 If the transaction is extortionate, the court has a wide power: it may set aside the whole or part of the obligation, vary its terms or the terms of any security, require sums of money to be paid to the office holder, or security to be surrendered, or direct that accounts be taken between any persons.

A debtor or the trustee cannot re-open the same transaction as an extortionate credit transaction under the CCA 1974,[51] since both provisions serve the same purpose.[52]

The Bank and the Debtor's Dispositions

24–128 There are provisions of the Act designed to prevent dispositions of the debtor's property between the presentation of a bankruptcy or winding-up petition and the assets coming under the control of the trustee or liquidator. These start from the principle that such dispositions are void, but that they may be validated by the court. The principles which the courts follow in exercising their discretion in giving validation orders can be seen from the cases. There are some puzzles, however, about the effect of the provisions on banks in particular circumstances, because of the difficulty of establishing what is a disposition in the context of the operation of bank accounts.

Companies

24–129 Section 127 of the IA 1986 provides, "*in a winding up by the court, any disposition of the company's property . . . made after the commencement of the winding up is, unless the court otherwise orders, void.*"

Problems for banks, as far as companies are concerned, arise from the fact that in a winding up by the court the order is ante-dated to the date of

[49] IA 1986, ss. 244 and 343.
[50] Or the making of an administration order.
[51] CCA 1974, s. 139.
[52] IA 1986, s. 343(6).

the presentation of the petition; this means that there is a gap or hiatus between the presentation of the petition and the winding up order. The directors of the company are still able to exercise their powers, including their power to use the company bank account, during this period, but their transactions will be invalid if a winding up order is later granted. If that happens, the bank will not be able to recover any payment it has made on behalf of its customer unless the court has either *validated* the transaction beforehand or is willing to ratify it retrospectively. (This is not a problem with a voluntary winding up, because the powers of the directors cease on the passing of the winding up resolution, and there is no hiatus.)

Banks should therefore refuse to allow transactions on company accounts **24–130** after the presentation of the winding up petition unless there is an order of the court. The company account should be frozen and cheques presented for payment returned marked "Winding up petition presented". (It is, of course, a serious libel if this is incorrect). If the bank decides to continue the account without an order, it should freeze the old account, and insist that subsequent dealings are dealt with on a separate account taking personal assurances from the directors that payments out will relate to new business, and not be used to discharge pre-liquidation debts. Once a winding up order is made, the account will be stopped entirely, and the liquidator will be paid the credit balance. If the petition is dismissed, the account may be continued as normal if the bank has not already called in the debt.

If the bank does allow a transaction on the account, the court may be **24–131** willing to exercise its discretion in favour of the bank, because it will not want to paralyse the trade of the company unnecessarily.[53] If, for example, the liquidator wishes to continue trading in order to permit a better realisation of the company's assets, the court may validate transactions made in good faith and for the purpose of carrying on the company's business. However, it will also be concerned about the interests of the unsecured creditors, because it may be unfair to them if the bank is allowed to receive payments or to incur new, provable, debts. The court may therefore be willing to grant approval provided that the old account is frozen, in which case all new transactions will take place on a new account, in respect of which the bank will not be able to take advantage of combination or insolvency set-off. If a "validation order" is made, it will normally be on condition that continued trading is at a profit, and for the benefit of creditors generally.[54] The standard form of order permits

[53] See *Re Wiltshire Iron Co.* (1868) 3 Ch.App. 443 at 446–7, *per* Cairns L.J.

[54] See *Gray's Inn Construction Co Ltd* [1980] 1 All E.R. 814. In *Denney v. John Hudson & Co Ltd* [1992] B.C.L.C. 901, the Court of Appeal set out guidelines for the use of the court's discretion. See also, *e.g. Re J Leslie Engineers Co Ltd* [1976] 2 All E.R. 85; *Re McGuinness Bros (UK) Ltd* [1987] 3 B.C.C. 571; *Re Sugar Properties (Derisley Wood) Ltd* [1988] B.C.L.C. 146; *Re Fairway Graphics Ltd* [1991] B.C.L.C. 468; *Re a Company (No. 00687 of 1991)* [1992] B.C.L.C. 133; *Re Rafidain Bank* [1992] B.C.L.C. 301.

payments in and out of bank accounts and dispositions in the ordinary course of business.[55] Indeed, the court may be willing to sanction some transactions retrospectively if the bank has acted in good faith and without negligence—for example, if it was not aware of the petition before the Gazetting of the petition.

24–132 Not all operations on bank accounts will be caught by the prohibition against dispositions. For example, although it is a disposition for the company to grant a charge over its assets, it is not a disposition for assets which are already subject to a charge to be realised and paid over to the bank or to pay money into a bank account (even one which is overdrawn), because the money is only being applied in accordance with the charge to which it was already subject.[56] This is the case even if the charge is a floating one, because the bank is treated as having an immediate beneficial interest in the charged assets. Nor is it a disposition for a company to complete a contract which is specifically enforceable, although if the contract is conditional or voidable, a waiver, confirmation or variation of the contract may be a disposition.[57] If the contract is not plainly specifically enforceable, it is prudent to seek the approval of the court before the performance.

24–133 Any deposit into an overdrawn account is caught as a disposition, because there is a transfer of the funds to the bank.[58] In *Re Gray's Inn Construction Co. Ltd*,[59] an account (which was overdrawn) was continued between the time of the petition and the order, with payments in and out being made. The Court of Appeal held that both payments in and out were dispositions, and therefore void if they were not validated by the court. Payments would not be validated if the validation might result in any creditor being paid in full while others received only a dividend; this might happen if the bank benefited from a payment into an overdrawn account which discharged a debt. Here, the court validated credits received up until the day after the petition was advertised, but not a credit received four days later. Credits to the account made after the bank should have known of the liquidation from the advertisement in the Gazette, therefore, were not allowed to reduce the overdraft. Sums paid out for pre-liquidation debts were recoverable from the bank, but only if recovery could not be obtained from the recipients, from whom recovery should first be sought.

24–134 It has been held that payments into a bank account in *credit* are not dispositions of the company's property, because the funds do not reduce a debt owed to the bank. In *Re Barn Crown Ltd*,[60] a cheque was paid into a

---

[55] Pennington, *op. cit.*, p. 104.

[56] *Re Margart Pty Ltd, Hamilton v. Westpac Banking Corpn* [1985] B.C.L.C. 314, approved by Vinelott J. in *Re French's (Wine Bar) Ltd* [1987] B.C.L.C. 499.

[57] *Re French's (Wine Bar) Ltd* [1987] B.C.L.C. 499.

[58] And the bank acquires a lien over—that is, a property interest in—a cheque when it is deposited.

[59] [1980] 1 All E.R. 814.

[60] [1995] 1 W.L.R. 147.

company customer's account after the order to wind up the company. The judge took the view that the collection of the cheque by the bank was *not* a disposition within section 127 of the IA 1986. In collecting a payment, a bank simply "credits the customer's account with the amount of the cheque, and, if the account is already in credit . . . All that happens between the customer and the banker is an adjustment of entries in the statement recording the accounts between them".[61] The judge considered at some length, but did not follow the analysis of bank collection by Goode,[62] whose reasoning is: the bank receives the cheque in the first place as the agent of the customer, at which point there is nothing in the nature of a disposition by the customer; when the bank receives the payment and in turn surrenders the cheque, however, there is an exchange of property for payment, which does amount to a disposition. Further, when the funds are credited to the customer's account, they become the property of the bank and the customer obtains a debt in return, and this is another, though technical, disposition. Professor Goode's analysis, in the judge's view, would require a "transformation" of the property rather than a disposition and would appear over-technical and out of line with ordinary English usage.

In a very recent case, the judge made a positive attempt to deal with the issue—in an area where, as he said, the authorities are in disarray[63] and the state of the law is uncertain—on a principled basis. In *Coutts & Co. v. Stock,*[64] Lightman J. took a purposive, and narrower, view of the section, emphasising that section 127 operates as part of the statutory scheme designed to prevent the directors of a company, when liquidation is imminent, from disposing of the company's assets to the prejudice of its creditors. It does not "bite", he said, when the disposition can have no impact on the creditors. **24–135**

In *Coutts,* the company's account was in credit at the time the winding up petition was presented, but the bank went on to honour cheques drawn in favour of third parties so that, by the time the order was made, the account was badly overdrawn. The issue here was confined, the judge held, to the impact of section 127 on the creation of, and subsequent increases in, the debtor's overdraft with the bank. This was unlike the situation in *Gray's Inn,* where the question was as to the validity or voidness of payments received by the bank and applied in *reduction* of the overdraft,[65] and unlike

[61] [1995] 1 W.L.R. 147 at 195–6, *per* Judge Rich Q.C. The bank is acting as agent, not disponee or disponea (relying on *Re Mal Bower's Macquarie Electrical Centre Pty Ltd* [1974] 1 N.S.W.L.R. 254 at 257–8, *per* Street C.J.; *Re J Leslie Engineers Co Ltd* [1976] 2 All E.R. 85, *per* Oliver J. and *Re Loteka Property Ltd* [1990] 1 Qd R 322 at 328, *per* McPherson J.).

[62] *P.C.I.L.* (1st ed.), pp. 187–8.

[63] Referring not only to the English cases but to the Commonwealth decisions mentioned above.

[64] [2000] Lloyds' Rep. Bank. 14.

[65] The judge distinguished the further point raised in *Gray's Inn* as to whether payments out were dispositions by the company or the bank on the basis that they were not fully argued (differing from Goode's view as expressed in P.C.I.L. (2nd. ed.,) at p. 430, is stated above, see para. 24–134).

cases[66] where payments had been made by the bank which reduced the company's *credit* balance.

The section, he said, does not change what has happened—it merely denudes any disposition of legal effect, and therefore does not invalidate any liabilities assumed by a company, nor preclude a company incurring or continuing to incure liabilities (for example for rates, electricity or the services of employees). An increase in the company's overdraft over the period between presentation of the petition and the making of the order for winding up is therefore outside the ambit of the section. Nor does the section have any impact on the use, consumption or exhaustion of assets—the use and even exhaustion of the overdraft limit by the company is not a disposition within the section.

The presentation of the petition does not affect the bank's mandate from its customer to honour cheques (it would be a breach of contract by the bank "with the most serious repercussions for the bank and the company"[67] if it did not pay) and the loan made by the bank to the customer in honouring cheques is not invalidated by the winding up order.[68] In the judge's analysis, the bank is making a loan to the company and paying the payee as agent of the company of the money loaned. The disposition is therefore a disposition of the bank's money to the company, but it is also a disposition by the bank as agent for the company to the payee. The liquidator can therefore recover the payment from the *payee*, but not from the bank.

Accordingly (if this careful analysis is accepted in future cases) it seems that a bank would not be vulnerable under the section if it is dealing with a company's payments as an agent. The real danger to the bank remains where the money is applied in reduction of an overdraft. Lightman J. quoted the words of Buckley L.J. in *Gray's Inn*:

> "but as soon as [the bank] credits the amount collected in reduction of the customer's overdraft, as in the ordinary course of business it has authority to do in the absence of any contrary instruction from the customer, it makes a disposition on the customer's behalf in its own favour discharging pro tanto the customer's liability on the overdraft."[69]

[66] Such as another very recent case, *Hollicourt (Contracts) Ltd v. Bank of Ireland* [2000] Lloyd's Rep. Bank. 21, and, presumably, *a fortiori,* unlike the *Barn Crown* case, where there was a payment into a company's account in credit.

[67] [2000] Lloyd's Rep. Bank. 14 at 17.

[68] If the bank is said to be paying its own money to the payee of the cheque by way of a loan to the company, the transaction still does not come within s. 127, because there is no disposition of the company's property, only of the *bank's.* The liquidator would not be able to recover the payment from either the payee or the bank.

[69] *Gray's Inn* [1980] 1 W.L.R. 711; [1980] 1 All E.R. 814, CA.

Individual Bankrupts

After the bankrupt's property[70] has vested in the trustee, the bankrupt has no power to dispose of it except with the consent of the court,[71] and dispositions by the bankrupt become a question of whether the trustee has given authority for the transaction or not. However, the trustee may not be appointed until after the bankruptcy order or perhaps after a meeting of creditors (the official receiver may be appointed to safeguard the bankrupt's property pending the trustee's appointment[72]). The IA 1986 therefore makes provision, in section 284, for dispositions made by the bankrupt before the trustee's appointment similar to that for dispositions by companies.[73] **24–136**

Any disposition of property or payment by the bankrupt during the period between the petition and the time when the estate vests in the trustee is void unless it is made with the consent of the court or subsequently ratified by the court. Where a payment is void the person paid holds the sum for the bankrupt as part of his or her estate.[74] "Disposition" is not defined, but as with companies, may include payments by the bankrupt into his or her overdrawn bank account, (which is in favour of the bank) as well as payments from an account in credit to third parties.[75] It seems that it does not include payments into an account in credit. **24–137**

A defence is available to third parties (like banks) under section 284(4) of the IA 1986: a person who received property or a payment before the commencement of the bankruptcy in good faith, for value and without notice that the petition has been presented[76] is protected against claims by the trustee.[77] Since bankruptcy petitions, unlike winding up petitions, need not normally be advertised, many people, (including banks), who deal with the bankrupt will not have notice of the petition, and their transactions will be protected under subsection (4). **24–138**

The next subsection provides a further protection especially for banks: if the bankrupt has incurred a debt to a banker (or other person) by making a payment which is void, the debt is deemed to have been incurred before the bankruptcy order unless the banker had notice of the bankruptcy before the debt was incurred, or it is not reasonably practicable for the payment to be recovered from the person to whom it is made (section 284(5) of the IA **24–139**

[70] IA 1986, s. 283.

[71] IA 1986, s.183.

[72] IA 1986, s. 287.

[73] IA 1986, s. 284(1). The wording is similar to that of IA 1986, s. 127, making void dispositions of a company's property made after the presentation of a winding-up petition.

[74] IA 1986, s. 284(2).

[75] *Re Gray's Inn Construction Co* [1980 1 All E.R. 814 which relates to company dispositions.

[76] And someone who derives an interest in the property from someone else whose interest is already protected.

[77] Or in respect of any interest in property which derives from an interest in respect of which there is, by virtue of this subsection, no remedy (IA 1986, s. 284(1)(b)).

1986). The second part of this defence is rather problematic, because it is not clear in what circumstances it will operate, except that it seems that the insolvency of the recipient will probably make it not "reasonably practicable" to recover it from the recipient.[78]

(1) Payments without notice of the petition

24–140 **Payment into an overdrawn account.** It seems that a payment into an overdrawn bank account after the petition is void as a disposition unless it is ratified by the court. However, as has been seen, a person who receives property or payment before the bankruptcy order in good faith, for value and without notice that the petition has been presented is protected by section 284(4) of the IA 1986. If the account is overdrawn, therefore, or if the debtor owes debts on other accounts to the bank, the bank probably takes payments in for value and is protected if it has no notice or suspicion[79] as to the petition.

24–141 **Payment from an account in credit.** If after the petition the debtor pays money from an account in credit to a third person, this is prima facie a payment made by the bankrupt, and therefore void. It seems therefore that the trustee can recover the payment from the bank.[80] Even payments made in ignorance of the petition seem to require ratification by the courts (as do those by company debtors after the start of winding up). The bank would however, be able to prove for the debt in the bankruptcy, since its payment would be protected by section 284(4) of the IA 1986 provided it was made in good faith.

24–142 **Payment from an overdrawn account.** If, on the other hand, the account is overdrawn at the time of a debit this is not a disposition of the *bankrupt's* property, but of the *bank's* property, and the question is not whether the trustee can recover it from the bank, but simply whether the debit was validly made; if it was, the bank can prove for the debt in the bankruptcy. If the debt was incurred before the commencement of the bankruptcy the bank probably may prove for it.

(2) Payments made with notice of the petition

24–143 **Payment into an account.** This may vest in the trustee if it was credited before the start of bankruptcy, or otherwise may be after-acquired property, if the trustee gives notice.

---

78 See Muir Hunter, *op. cit.*, para. 3–158 and Paget, *Law of Banking* (11th ed.) p. 226: it was "widely regarded as unsatisfactory and obscure" when used under the Bankruptcy (Amendment) Act 1926, from which the present phrase was derived.

79 It is uncertain whether the notice must be actual or whether, as under the old law, it need not be express or precise: see Paget, *op. cit.*, 225.

80 But see analogous cases on company liquidation, above, paras 24–134 *et seq.*

Payment from an account. This is where section 284(5) of the IA 1986 may protect the bank. It applies if a bankrupt has "incurred a debt to a banker" by making a payment which is void before the bank had notice of the bankruptcy order, or if it is not reasonably practicable for the payment to be recovered from the payee. The debt is then deemed to have been incurred before the bankruptcy order, and the bank may prove for it. However, the wording does not make it clear whether it was intended that it should apply to accounts in credit or to overdrawn accounts. **24–144**

Account in credit. Where the account is in credit, however, no debt is incurred to the banker (although, of course, the banker *debits* the account), and the defence apparently does not apply. If this is the case, a payment from a credit account, if it is a disposition of the bankrupt's property,[81] requires the court's ratification before the debit can be made and is not protected by section 284(5) of the IA 1986. It seems, then, that the protection given by the subsection can only refer to debits which leave the account overdrawn, so that a debt to the banker is incurred. **24–145**

Overdrawn account. In relation to an overdrawn account, the debit represents a debt incurred after the start of bankruptcy, which would normally not be provable,[82] but, presumably, in this case, the bank would be protected by section 284(5) of the IA 1986. However, even here, the wording of the subsection is problematic: the bankrupt must have "incurred a debt to a banker" for the defence to be available to the bank, but a payment from an overdrawn account is normally regarded as a payment of the *bank's* money, not of the bankrupt's money.[83] If it is the bank's money, the payment would not come within the section (it would be a debt to the bank incurred by the bankrupt after commencement and the bank would not be able to prove for it in the insolvency). However, it is difficult to see what other possible application the section could have, given that it apparently does not apply to accounts in credit either. If the subsection does operate in this situation, the bank would be protected (unless it had notice of the bankruptcy order) because the debt would be deemed to have been incurred before the start of the bankruptcy. **24–146**

(3) Payments after the vesting order

Debits after the vesting order are not provable, and any dealing with the property is a dealing with the trustee's property, or with after-acquired property. **24–147**

---

[81] It may not be, by analogy with the cases on winding up of companies, see above, paras 24–134 *et seq.*

[82] IA 1986, s. 382.

[83] See above, para. 24–135, the views of Lightman J. in *Coutts & Co. v. Stock* [2000] Lloyd's Rep. Bank. 14.

PROVABLE DEBTS AND PRIORITIES

24–148 The first duty of the liquidator or the trustee is to creditors who can prove their debts. A person who wishes to establish rights as a creditor must complete a proof of debt—even a secured creditor[84] must show the liquidator proof of the debt and security.[85]

24–149 **The *pari passu* principle.** All creditors, both of companies[86] and of individuals,[87] of the same rank are paid rateably according to the size of their debt. Creditors with a valid security and preferential creditors obtain an advantage over other creditors, but a mere contractual provision having the effect of giving the creditor an advantage in winding up over other creditors is void,[88] although an agreement between creditors for one to subordinate itself to another may be enforceable between the creditors involved. The *pari passu* principle does not affect non-contractual rights such as the right of combination or of lien. Where there are mutual debts, the rules of statutory set-off operate[89] and the debts have to be set-off and, if there is a balance, are provable to the extent of the balance.

In both voluntary[90] and compulsory[91] windings up, the liquidator pays the company's creditors (after costs and expenses) *pari passu*, except for secured creditors and preferential debtors,[92] with any surplus going to the members of the company according to their rights under the Articles or otherwise.[93] In individual bankruptcies, the trustee distributes dividends amongst the creditors (except secured creditors) in respect of the bankruptcy debts which they have proved,[94] again after payment of costs and expenses, and of the debts of preferential creditors. Any surplus is returned to the debtor.

24–150 **Provable debts.** Debts or liabilities are provable if they are owing before commencement of the bankruptcy or liquidation, and interest on them may be claimed in some circumstances. "Liability" means an obligation to pay money or money's worth,[95] but it makes no difference whether the obligation is present or future, certain or contingent, whether the amount is fixed or liquidated, or is capable of being ascertained by fixed rules or as a

---

[84] IR 1986, rr. 4. 75(1)(g) and 6.98(1)(g).
[85] IA 1986, s. 322 and 411 and Sched. 8.
[86] IA 1986, s. 107.
[87] IA 1986, s. 328(3).
[88] See *British Eagle International Airlines Ltd v. Compagnie National Air France* [1975] 1 W.L.R. 758.
[89] See above, Chap. 23.
[90] IA 1986, s. 165(5).
[91] IA 1986, ss. 143, 167, 168 and 175 and IR 1986, rr. 4. 179—184 and 181.
[92] IA 1986, ss. 107 and 175.
[93] IA 1986, s. 107.
[94] IA 1986, s. 165.
[95] IA 1986, s. 382(4) and IR 1986, r. 13.12(4).

matter of opinion.[96] Where a debt is not certain in value, the liquidator,[97] or trustee[98] makes an estimate of its value, which is the amount provable, although it may be revised later.

Debts in foreign currency are converted into sterling at the official rate of exchange prevailing on the date the debtor went into liquidation.[99] Rent and periodical payments may be proved so far as due and unpaid up to the date winding up commenced or the bankruptcy order was made.[1]

Secured Creditors

24–151 The rights of secured creditors[2] are not affected by insolvency, and creditors like banks holding a valid security normally rely on their security. A secured creditor may only petition for bankruptcy,[3] if it is willing to give up the security,[4] or values it and claims for the unsecured part of the debt, in which case the secured and the unsecured parts of the debt are regarded as separate.[5]

The liquidator or trustee will require proof of the debt from the creditor[6] and particulars of the security, including the value placed on it by the creditor. If the creditor fails to disclose the security in the proof, it must surrender the security for all the creditors unless the court excuses it for inadvertency or honest mistake.[7]

24–152 If the secured creditor is content to rely upon its security, it need not prove in the bankruptcy at all, but it has several other options. It can rely on the security as sufficient to cover the amount owing to it, and defer realising it until later, in which case the liquidator would have to redeem it, if he or she wishes to do so, by paying the whole amount owing to the creditor secured on that property. Alternatively, the creditor may realise the security and claim as an unsecured creditor for any balance of the debt, or it may give up the security and prove for the whole debt. Fourthly and lastly, the creditor may wish to value the security and prove for the balance,[8] running the risk, if the valuation is too low, that the liquidator or trustee will redeem the asset at the value placed on it. The creditor may call on the liquidator or trustee to say if he or she will redeem,[9] and the liquidator has six months to decide whether to do so.

---

[96] IA 1986, s. 382(3) and IR 1986, rr. 13 and 12(4).
[97] IR 1986, r. 4.86.
[98] IA 1986, s. 322(3); or the court: IA 1986, s. 303.
[99] IR 1986, rr. 4.89 and 6.111.
[1] IR 1986, rr. 4.92 and 6.112.
[2] "Security" is defined widely in IA 1986, s. 383(2) to include mortgages, charges, liens and other security.
[3] IA 1986, ss. 267 and 269.
[4] See *Zandfarid v. BCCI* [1996] 1 W.L.R. 1420.
[5] IA 1986, s. 269(2).
[6] IR 1986, rr. 4.75 and 6.98.
[7] IR 1986, rr. 4.96 and 6.116.
[8] IR 1986, rr. 4.88 and 6.109.
[9] IR 1986, rr. 4.97 and 6.117.

24–153 Generally speaking, the bank's choice is between realisation of the asset and valuation. It is rare to surrender the security, and banks will normally only waive the proof if the value of the security is obviously sufficient to cover the debt. It is sensible to obtain valuations of securities over land, when realisation may be slow, unlike shares or life policies, which are easily realisable.

Third party securities are not assets of the debtor and are irrelevant; only those securities which would augment the assets or estate of the debtor need be taken into account.[10] But if the debtor and a third party jointly own an asset which is jointly charged to a creditor, then the security must be taken into account.[11] Liens count as securities, and must be taken into account.[12]

Preferential Debts[13]

24–154 Preferential debts are certain specific debts arising not later than certain "relevant dates" before the insolvency.[14] Examples (they are listed exhaustively in the IA 1986[15]) are as follows:

(1) certain deductions for income tax which the employer ought to have made from wages and salaries in the 12 months before the relevant dates;

(2) value added tax payable in the six months before the relevant dates;

(3) certain social security contributions[16] due from the debtor in the 12 months before the relevant date;

(4) certain contributions to occupational pension schemes[17] which the debtor should have made;

(5) amounts payable for wages or salary (including various payments such as holiday pay and sick pay), incurred in the four months before the relevant date, if they do not exceed a sum made by order (presently £800).

This last category is most important for banks because it includes debts for money advanced for the purpose of paying such wages, and means that

---

[10] *Re Turner, ex.p. West Riding Union Banking Co* (1881) 19 Ch. D. 105.

[11] *Re Rushton* (a bankrupt) *ex p. National Westminster Bank Ltd v. O.R.* [1972] Ch. 197.

[12] IA 1986, s. 383(2).

[13] See Keay and Walton [1999] C.fi. L.R. 84.

[14] *e.g.*: voluntary arrangements—the date of approval of the arrangement; compulsory winding up—the date of the appointment of a provisional liquidator, or, if none, the date of the winding up order; receiverships—the date of the appointment of the receiver; bankrupts—the date of the bankruptcy order (unless there is an interim receiver appointed, in which case it is that date).

[15] IA 1986, s. 386 and Sched. 6.

[16] Under Social Security Contributions and Benefits Act 1992.

[17] Under the Pension Schemes Act 1993.

a bank which advances money to an insolvent employer for the payment of wages becomes a preferential creditor to the extent it has done so.[18]

Priority of Distribution

Companies

Creditors with fixed charges are paid from the proceeds of the secured assets.[19] If the secured assets are insufficient to satisfy the secured debts of creditors, they fall into the class of unsecured creditors to the extent of the shortfall. **24–155**

(1) *Expenses*: in the case of a voluntary winding up, the expenses of winding up (including the liquidator's remuneration) are payable in priority to all other claims.[20] In a compulsory winding up, the court has a discretion to order payment of expenses in the priority it thinks fit[21];

(2) *Preferential creditors*[22]: preferential debts rank equally among themselves after the expenses of winding up and are paid in full; if the assets are insufficient to meet them, they abate in equal proportions[23];

(3) *Holders of floating charges*: to the extent of the assets covered by their charges (bank floating charges normally cover all assets) even if they crystallise before liquidation[24];

(4) *Unsecured creditors*: rank *pari passu* (in proportion to their claims);

(5) *Interest on debts*[25]: the capital of the unsecured or preferential debts is paid first, and then any surplus is applied in paying interest on the debts for the periods during which they have been outstanding since the company went into liquidation. All interest ranks equally, regardless of the ranking of the unsecured debts. The rate of interest is the greater of the statutory rate[26] and the rate which would be applicable to the debt apart from the winding up. Thus, with a bank overdraft on which the bank set a standard rate, the standard rate would be payable if it is higher than the statutory rate. Secured creditors will already have taken interest on their debts;

---

18 See further below, paras 24–159 *et seq*.
19 Validity and priority of charges are discussed above, in Chap. 19. If the assets in question are sold by the receiver instead, his or her expenses would be paid first.
20 IA 1986, s. 115.
21 IA 1986, s. 156: for detailed rules of priority of expenses see the IR 1986, rr. 4.218–220.
22 IA 1986, ss. 107 and 175.
23 IA 1986, s. 175.
24 If "as created" the charge was floating: IA 1986, s. 251. See above, Chap. 19.
25 Payable under IA 1986, s. 189.
26 Under the Judgments Act 1838, s. 17, on the day liquidation commenced.

(6) *Members of the company*: if any assets remain. The division at this stage depends on the Articles or on subordination agreements. For example, preference shareholders might have preference as to capital, taking ahead of the "equity" shareholders.

Individuals

24–156 The bankrupt's estate is subject to the rights of secured creditors which have not been surrendered.[27] The priorities are as follows:

(1) *Replacement property*: if the trustee has sold exempted property of the bankrupt and replaced it with cheaper items,[28] the cost of buying replacement goods has priority over any distribution;

(2) *Expenses*: of the bankruptcy and of a final meeting before making a distribution[29]; money must be retained by the trustee for this purpose. In small bankruptcies, the expenses often take up most of the estate[30];

(3) *Preferential debts*: which are the same as in company insolvency, rank equally between themselves and are paid in full or abate in equal proportions between themselves.[31] Advances by a bank for wages also become preferential[32];

(4) *Ordinary unsecured creditors*: rank equally between themselves and if not paid in full, abate proportionally[33];

(5) *Interest*: is paid on both preferential or ordinary debts for the period since bankruptcy commenced; the preferential debts have no priority in this respect[34];

(6) *Deferred debts*: the spouse of the bankrupt (if a creditor at the commencement of the bankruptcy)[35];

(7) *The bankrupt*: receives any surplus.[36]

Distributing the Estate

24–157 When the trustee or liquidator has sufficient funds in hand he or she declares and distributes a dividend among the creditors according to this list of priorities, and keeping enough money in hand for payment of the

[27] IA 1986, s. 283(5). With individual debtors, there are no floating charges.
[28] IA 1986, s. 308, see above, para. 24–096.
[29] IA 1986, s. 324(1) and 331(4).
[30] In *Mirror Group Newspapers v. Maxwell* [1998] 1 B.C.L.C. 638, Ferris J., prompted by public concern about the levels of office holders' remuneration, explained the duties of office holders in that respect.
[31] IA 1986, s. 328(2).
[32] See below, para. 24–159.
[33] IA 1986, s. 328(3).
[34] IA 1986, s. 328(4–5).
[35] IA 1986, s. 329.
[36] IA 1986, s. 330(5).

expenses of the bankruptcy. Property which cannot be readily or advantageously sold may, with the committee's permission, be divided amongst the creditors. He or she gives notice of the dividend and of how it is proposed to distribute it, with details of the debtor's assets or estate, making provision for disputed proofs and claims, and for people who have not had enough time to establish their proofs because they live at a distance. Creditors who have not proved before the dividend cannot disturb the dividend, but may be compensated in priority to others in future dividends.

When all the estate has been realised, or as much of it as can be realised **24–158** without needlessly protracting the liquidation or trusteeship, the office holder gives notice of intention to declare a final dividend, or that no dividend or further dividend will be declared. After this final date (which the court may postpone) the liquidator or trustee defrays any outstanding expenses of the insolvency out of the estate. Any surplus goes to members of the company or to the bankrupt.[37]

Banks and the Insolvent Customer

Wages Accounts: Statutory Subrogation

If the bank has preferential status, it ranks equally with other preferential **24–159** creditors (the main ones are normally the Inland Revenue or Customs and Excise) and, if the assets are insufficient, the claims of all preferential creditors abate rateably in proportion to their claims. The fact that one of the preferential claims is for *employees' wages* in the four months before the bankruptcy is of particular significance for banks, because a creditor who advances money for the payment of wages is also given preferential status to the extent of the advance—that is, it is subrogated to the preferential position of the employees—providing that the money advanced is used for that purpose.

Because of this provision, banks have developed the practice of operating **24–160** special *wages accounts*. Although this is not necessary in law,[38] it is done (a) for administrative purposes, (b) to prevent the operation of the rule in *Clayton's Case* from eliminating the preferential debt from the ordinary (and more active) current account,[39] and (c) to avoid argument about the purpose for which the money was advanced. The general practice as to wages accounts is for drawings for remuneration to be recorded only on this account, and for a debit to be cleared by being transferred to the current

[37] IA 1986, s. 330, IR 1986, r. 4.186.

[38] See *Re Primrose (Builders) Ltd* [1950] Ch. 561.

[39] See *Re Rampgill Mill Ltd* [1967] Ch. 1138, where the bank failed to keep a separate wages account, and, although the court accepted the bank's preferential status for £5,000 applied to wages, the bank lost its preference to the extent of £3,000 because of the rule in *Clayton's Case.*

account when it loses its priority after four months so that the wages account gives an up to date picture of the bank's preferential status.

It is not essential for the bank to set up an account for the purpose, provided that it can show that the money was actually used for payment of wages.[40] If it can do this, it seems that there is a presumption that the banker advanced money for that purpose, even if it was not advanced from a special account,[41] and this relieves the bank from having to show that it made a particular advance for this purpose only—a difficult thing to prove, if there is simply a general account. Accordingly, the bank need not have the intention to achieve preferential creditor status.

24–161 It is essential, however, that there is an *advance*. In *E. J. Morel (1934) Ltd*[42] a company operated a wages account on terms that the credit in the current account was always to exceed the debit in the wages account; that wages would be paid by debit from the wages account, and that old debts (over four months old) in the wages account would be moved to the current account. This arrangement was set up because there was a third account, heavily in debit, which had been frozen. Buckley J. held that the way this account was operated meant that the accounts were completely interdependent and really had to be regarded as a single account, because the bank would not meet a cheque on either account without considering the combined position of the two accounts taken together, and the combination of the accounts always left the company in credit overall. It followed that overall there was no "advance" made by the bank which could be preferential. In other words, this was a book-keeping arrangement to disguise the fact that wages were paid by the company, not by the bank. It is submitted, with respect, that given the way this account was operated, this conclusion was unavoidable. The problem arose because the bank froze that account and opened a new current account which was closely tied to the wages account instead of maintaining, stabilising, and gradually reducing the overdraft on the current account.[43] A different conclusion would probably be reached if the current account were not so "tied" to the debit on the wages account. Indeed, sometimes the wages account is not opened until the company is overdrawn on the current account, and the bank simply attempts to stabilise or gradually reduce the overdraft there, while opening a wages account for preferential treatment of wages payments. Here there is no problem, because the bank is clearly advancing its own money.[44]

24–162 An agreement which ties together the current and wages accounts closely will not be subject to the principle in *Morel's* case, however, provided that

[40] Hence, companies are often asked to certify this, showing employees' names, amounts paid, etc.

[41] *Re Rampgill Mill Ltd* [1967] Ch. 1138.

[42] [1962] Ch. 21.

[43] See Ryder (1961) J.B.L. 278.

[44] Strictly, not an advance if made by way of overdraft, but the distinction appears not to be significant in this context.

the current account remains overdrawn. Thus, in *Re James R. Rutherford & Sons Ltd*[45] transfers were made weekly to the wages account from the overdrawn current account, on condition that the company should repay the earliest advances made for wages on that account.[46] On the company's liquidation, it was held that not only the debit on the wages account, but also the debits to the current account made when the transfers to the wages account occurred, had preferential status. The difference between the facts here and those in *Morel's* case was presumably that in *Morel's* case the balance on the two accounts in question was never a debit balance, while in *Rutherford's* case it was. In the former case the bank advanced nothing, while in the latter it did. It is submitted that this is correct.

Appropriation of payments within an account may also give rise to doubt. **24–163** In *National Provincial Bank Ltd v. Freedman and Rubens*[47] a company's overdraft had increased to an extent which aroused the bank's concern, and the bank refused to meet cheques drawn for wages unless the same amount was paid into the account at the same time. On the company's liquidation, the liquidator claimed that there had been no advances, for the bank had merely exchanged cash for the cheques paid in each week, discharging the most recent debits. The court rejected the argument. The payments in, on normal principles, discharged the *oldest* liabilities first, not the current debits, as the liquidator argued. *Clayton's Case* operated here to the bank's advantage.[48]

If a customer is in debt to the bank, the bank may appropriate payments **24–164** received to whichever account it chooses (if they have not been specifically appropriated by the customer to meet a particular liability), and may subsequently combine accounts.[49] If the bank appropriates when the credit is first received, it appears from *Re William Hall (Contractors) Ltd*[50] that it may appropriate the money entirely to the non-preferential debt, if it chooses. But in *Re Unit 2 Windows Ltd*[51] it was held that a credit balance on a third account (as in *Rutherford*) must be apportioned between the debit balance which represents advances to the company to enable it to make payments to its employees which would have been preferential debts if unpaid, and the amount of those debit balances which represent other advances.

[45] [1964] 1 W.L.R. 1211.

[46] As would happen anyway, by virtue of *Clayton's Case*, unless the account was used for other purposes. See *Re Yeovil Glove Co Ltd* [1963] Ch. 148.

[47] (1934) 4 L.D.A.B. 444.

[48] See Chap. 11. *Clayton's Case* was expressly the ground for the decision in *Re Primrose (Builders) Ltd.* [1950] Ch. 561, on very similar facts to the case just discussed.

[49] Chap. 11.

[50] [1967] 2 All E.R. 1150.

[51] [1985] 3 All E.R. 647.

The Rule Against Double Proof

24–165 It is a rule of equity that the insolvent estate should not be compelled to entertain more than one proof in respect of the same debt—that is, that two creditors may not prove in respect of what is, in effect, the same debt—so that there is no doubling up of dividends.[52] This rule against double proof may be troublesome to banks from time to time, especially in relation to guarantees. Briefly, the effect of insolvency on guarantees is as follows.

24–166 When it discovers the debtor's insolvency, the bank will stop his or her account, and the guarantor's liability will be fixed. The normal practice is for the bank to prove first against the debtor, and if there are insufficient assets, to sue the guarantor. This gives the bank two sources of funds.

However, guarantors sometimes pay sums to the bank before the start of the insolvency in order to reduce their own later liability. In this case, the bank can only submit a proof against the debtor for the amount unpaid. The bank may prefer, however, to prove in the debtor's insolvency for the whole debt, and only to have recourse to the payments made by the guarantor if it is not fully paid.[53] If so, the bank should take certain steps.

24–167 First, the bank must ensure that the guarantor's payments are not credited to the debtor's account; if they are, they will be appropriated to the debtor's debts (because of the operation of *Clayton's Case*[54]), and will reduce or even discharge the debtor's liability and, correspondingly, the bank's claim. The guarantee therefore normally permits the bank to place payments by the guarantor in a separate "suspense" account, so that the payments are not appropriated to the debts.

24–168 Secondly, the bank should also ensure that the guarantor cannot prove for his or her contingent liability in competition to itself. For this reason, bank guarantees normally contain (a) a "whole debt" clause, and (b) a contractual agreement to prevent the guarantor proving in competition.

(a) The clause states that the guarantor guarantees the debtor's *whole debt* rather than a specific sum. A limitation on the guarantor's liability is added as a proviso if desired.[55] Where the guarantor is responsible for the whole debt, the debtor's liability is regarded as *undivided*; because of the rule against double proof, two persons cannot prove for the same debt,[56] and the guarantor must give way to the bank. This allows the bank to prove

---

[52] See *Barclays Bank Ltd v. TOSG Trust Fund Ltd* [1984] A.C. 626 CA; *Polly Peck International plc (No. 4)* [1996] 1 B.C.L.C. 428 at 436–438.

[53] *Commercial Bank of Australia v. O.A. of the Estate of Wilson* [1893] A.C. 181; *Ulster Bank v. Lambe* [1966] N.I. 161 (where B first demanded the difference from D, and then sued D for the whole sum).

[54] See Chap. 11.

[55] See above, Chap. 18.

[56] *Re Fenton* [1931] 1 Ch. 85; Goode, *L.P.C.S.* (2nd ed.), Chap. 7.

in the debtor's bankruptcy for the whole debt even if the limited sum has been paid by the guarantor.[57]

On the other hand, if there is no whole debt clause and the guarantor agrees to be liable simply for a specific sum, the debt is regarded as *divided*, and the guarantee is treated as a guarantee of a separate debt of the debtor. In this case, the guarantor may prove for the debt, provided that he or she has paid the whole of that separate debt (a partial payment of the separate debt does not allow the guarantor to prove,[58] because otherwise he or she would be competing with the bank for the same debt in the insolvency).

(b) Guarantees normally also contain a clause by which the guarantor *contracts* not to compete in the insolvency of the debtor. Bank forms of guarantee normally provide that on the insolvency of the debtor, the bank may prove in the debtor's insolvency[59] without discharging the guarantor's liability. The guarantor will only be liable therefore for the balance after the deduction of payments from the debtor, and his or her right to compete against the bank by proving against it is excluded.[60]

The intention is to increase the bank's share of the assets and to prevent **24–169** the guarantor proving for any independent debt the debtor might owe him or her. Goode suggests[61] that this practice might be improved upon (from the bank's point of view) by providing that the guarantor is obliged, if required by the bank, to prove against the debtor and to hold the proceeds *on trust* for the bank. This means that the total of the claims of the bank and the guarantor is greater than the claim of the bank alone, and the dividend payable on the total will therefore be greater as against other creditors, and will accrue to the bank.[62] Assuming that the guarantee is limited and that the guarantor has made a full payment,[63] there seems to be no reason why a trust of or charge over a dividend in insolvency could not be taken and be effective as suggested, provided the arrangement is not liable to be invalidated as a preference if the guarantor is insolvent.

Payments by a guarantor made after the start of the insolvency order may **24–170** be ignored in the proof,[64] and the bank may claim the whole debt; the guarantor, correspondingly, cannot prove for his or her payment. There is

---

[57] *Re Houlder* [1929] 1 Ch. 205; *Rees, ex p. National Provincial Bank of England* (1881) 17 Ch.D. 98; *Re Sass, ex p. National Provincial Bank of England* [1896] 2 Q.B. 12. Similarly, G cannot set off against a debt owed to D, G's right to indemnity from D: *Re Fenton* [1931] 1 Ch. 85.

[58] *Goodwin v. Gray* (1874) 22 W.R. 312; *Re Sass* [1896] 2 Q.B. 12.

[59] Or may enter into any "compromises, compositions or arrangements" with the debtor.

[60] This may be agreed "to the entire exclusion and surrender of all my rights as surety in competition with B". But note the possible effect of the UCTA 1977 and of the UTCCR 1999; see further above, Chap. 3.

[61] *Legal Problems of Credit and Security*, p. 201.

[62] Unless, perhaps, G were also insolvent and even then, the fact that G holds in trust for the bank would give the bank priority (unless the arrangement amounted to a preference).

[63] So that the rule against double proof does not prevent the bank and the guarantor proving.

[64] *Re Rees* (1881) 17 Ch.D. 98; *Re Sass* [1896] 2 Q.B. 12; *Re Fenton* [1931] 1 Ch. 85.

an exception to this principle, however, where the guarantor is an indorser of a bill of exchange on which the debtor is liable. In this case, any part payment by the guarantor which has been received before the bank has put in its proof must be taken into account in the bank's proof.[65]

The Insolvent Customer: Steps the Bank Should Take

24–171 If the bank becomes aware of the commencement of winding up or the presentation of a petition for bankruptcy, then it ought to take the following steps:

(i) Exercise any rights of set-off, and consider the action it should take with regard to its securities;

(ii) Cease to operate any account for the debtor, for transactions not ratified by the court may be affected as described earlier.[66] The account may, however, be debited for obligations already incurred by the bank on behalf of the customer. Cheques should be returned marked appropriately.

(iii) Joint accounts should also be stopped, even if one party is solvent, to prevent the operation of *Clayton's Case*, and the disposition of any of the assets now belonging to the liquidator or trustee. Cheques should be returned, marked carefully, so as not to damage the credit of any solvent party. The contents of the account are divided between the solvent party and the liquidator or trustee, with the bank interpleading in case of dispute. Unsecured debts may be proved for as against the insolvent party (survivorship does not operate so as to make the remaining partner alone liable) but the bank may also proceed against the other joint party.

(iv) Undischarged bankrupts may operate accounts with the consent of the trustee; for example, their wages may be paid into the account. Such payments will be *after-acquired property*, and the trustee may claim them by notice; unless claimed, they are not part of the bankrupt's estate.[67] The bankrupt is required to tell the trustee of any after-acquired property,[68] but may fail to do so. A bank receiving after-acquired property of a bankrupt is protected, if it acts in good faith and without notice of the bankruptcy,[69] but the protection would not apply to wages innocently received by a bank if those wages are subject to an income payments order, since these form

[65] *Re Blackburne* (1892) 9 Mor. 294; *Re Houlder* [1929] 1 Ch. 205.
[66] See above, paras 24–129 *et seq.* and 24–136 *et seq.*
[67] IA 1986, ss. 307(5) and 310(5).
[68] IA 1986, s. 333.
[69] IA 1986, s. 307(4)(b).

part of the bankrupt's estate. Although there seems no direct requirement to do so, presumably the prudent step for the bank to take on learning that a customer is an undischarged bankrupt is to inform the trustee of payments into the account.

(v) If the payee of a cheque is bankrupt, the chose in action represented by the cheque belongs (or, if after-acquired, may belong) to the trustee. For the sake of its customer, the drawer, a bank should not pay the cheque, since only the trustee can give a good discharge for the debt, and the trustee may say to the customer that he or she should pay again. The bank might also be liable in conversion to the trustee for handling the cheque (although, if the bank is ignorant of the bankruptcy, it is protected by section 60 of the BOEA 1882). The unpaid cheque should be marked "Payee bankrupt".

(vi) If a bankrupt customer has accepted bills payable at the bank, the bank will return the bills unpaid when they are presented.

(vii) If the bank has discounted bills for a customer who is the drawer or indorser of the bills, and the customer becomes bankrupt while the bill is current (not yet payable), the bankrupt's liability is *contingent*, since the acceptor may pay at maturity. The fact that the bill is not yet due does not preclude the creditor from relying on it,[70] and the bank may in any case treat the customer as having repudiated his or her liabilities, and therefore liable for liquidated damages, in which case it may prove immediately on the bankruptcy for the debt. Other parties may, of course, be liable on the bill. The rule against double proof will prevent the bank from claiming more than 100 pence in the pound from the various parties potentially liable.

(viii) If the bank has discounted a bill for the customer and the acceptor of the bill becomes bankrupt, the bank has no immediate remedies against the customer, although it may prove immediately against the acceptor for the full amount of the bill, since at maturity he or she will not be able to pay. It may sue the customer at the maturity of the bill.[71]

[70] *Byles on Bills of Exchange* (26th ed.), p. 454: IA 1986, s. 267(2)(b).
[71] IA 1986, s. 284, Chalmers and Guest, *Bills of Exchange*, p. 267.

Index